Praise for
THE NEW TESTAMENT IN ITS WORLD

Two of today's most prolific evangelical New Testament scholars have now combined their expertise to produce an amazing volume: part introduction and survey, part 'cliff notes' on Wright's four volumes to date in his Christian Origins and the Question of God series, part a sneak preview of what he might say in his remaining two volumes, and part showcase for Bird's always sensible judgments, often nicely alliterated prose, and now and then particularly funny humor. Special features include the book's lavish illustrations, sidebars quoting choice ancient primary sources and hilarious 'emails from the edge' from a confused student to his patient professor who always replies wisely. Overall, the genre, like the quality, is one of a kind.

CRAIG L. BLOMBERG, distinguished professor of New Testament, Denver Seminary

For all who have been anticipating a comprehensive and coherent reading of the entire New Testament from N. T. Wright, the wait is over. Wright and Bird offer their vision for the New Testament, with a lovely interplay of interpretative insights from the world behind the text, the world of the text, and the world in front of the text. Both look and content are energizing and engaging. This magisterial work provides an ideal textbook for courses on the New Testament.

JEANNINE K. BROWN, professor of New Testament, Bethel Seminary, St Paul, Minnesota, USA

Masterful job by Wright and Bird, written with characteristic jauntiness and scholarly rigor. The numerous sidebars add spice to the substantial meal presented in the text. The book's power lies in its thorough historical study combined with its missional voice to the church today.

LYNN H. COHICK, provost/dean, Denver Seminary, Denver, Colorado, USA

This is a distillation of Wright's quarter-century, multi-volume project exploring Christian Origins and the Question of God. Choice nuggets of Wright's most important discussions have been selected and blended with new material by both authors, enhanced with visuals, teaching aids, and online resources. If you want to introduce time-starved seminary students to the New Testament through the eyes of N. T. Wright but can't assign thousands of pages of reading, this is the book you need.

DR J. P. DAVIES, tutor of New Testament and MA course leader, Trinity College, Bristol, England

Those beginning to study the New Testament for the first time can easily become overwhelmed by the sheer volume of what they need to know before they begin. This splendidly clear but wide-ranging introduction is a brilliant way in to serious study of the New Testament and will, deservedly, become the go-to textbook for a large number of readers.

PAULA R. GOODER, Canon Chancellor, St Paul's Cathedral, London

Professors Wright and Bird have essentially given students and scholars alike two books in one: a detailed introduction to the major historical and theological topics of New Testament study, and a primer on each of the New Testament's writings. Their world-class scholarship (wonderfully peppered with images, excerpts from ancient and modern writings, and more) rightly recognizes that the New Testament's aim was—and is—to promote worship, discipleship, and mission.

MICHAEL J. GORMAN, Raymond E. Brown Chair in Biblical Studies and Theology, St Mary's Seminary & University, Baltimore, Maryland, USA

Wright has proven himself a discipline-shaping scholar, Bird a master textbook writer. When you put their minds and skills together, you get an excellent introduction to the New Testament: witty, accurate, accessible, eye-catching. This is a must-have resource for students.

NIJAY K. GUPTA, associate professor of New Testament, Portland Seminary, Portland, Oregon, USA

This is the New Testament introduction of all New Testament introductions! Not only is this a superb New Testament introduction from the keyboards of two of today's most prolific and balanced New Testament scholars, but more advanced students will find here an accessible and mature synthesis of and primer for N. T. Wright's voluminous work.

CRAIG S. KEENER, F. M. and Ada Thompson Professor of Biblical Studies, Asbury Theological Seminary, Wilmore, Kentucky, USA

Wright and Bird have done a great service to the church and the academy with this volume. They introduce readers to the major historical, literary, and theological themes of the New Testament in a way that is highly readable, yet they do not shy away from the difficult questions. They manage to avoid the twin dangers of excessive skepticism and uncritical pietism. It is the epitome of faith seeking understanding, and it will find a welcome home in many colleges and seminary classrooms as well pastors' libraries.

ESAU MCCAULLEY, assistant professor of New Testament, Wheaton College, Wheaton, Illinois, USA

N. T. (Tom) Wright can't write anything that is not interesting and suggestive and even at times provocative. His shelf or two of books is now condensed, reworked, and put in digestible form for even more readers. This is a lifetime of scholarship and a landmark publication by one of the world's leading New Testament scholars. I'm grateful too for the creative contribution Mike Bird makes in pulling all of this into one final heap of fun.

SCOT MCKNIGHT, Julius R. Mantey Chair of New Testament, Northern Seminary, Lisle, Illinois, USA

The big, bold theological interpretation of the New Testament that N. T. Wright has been building, piece by piece, in monographs and commentaries over the years now appears here in an accessible, single-volume New Testament introduction.

DR MATTHEW V. NOVENSON, senior lecturer in New Testament and Christian Origins, University of Edinburgh, Scotland

Tom Wright and Mike Bird give us the opportunity to appreciate the breadth and detail of Wright's vision of the New Testament—one of the most far-reaching of recent times. The format of a New Testament introduction means that we also get to fill in the gaps on New Testament books that have not featured extensively in Wright's major books. We also get to find the answers to many 'So, what would he say about . . . ?' questions. This book will be highly valued by students, scholars, and churches.

PROFESSOR PETER OAKES, Greenwood Senior Lecturer in Theology, School of Arts, Languages and Cultures, University of Manchester, England

With inimitable verve and piquancy, two of this generation's scholarly juggernauts give us a New Testament introduction that unapologetically sets up shop at the all-too-untraveled crossroads of history and theology.

NICHOLAS PERRIN, president, Trinity International University, Trinity Evangelical Divinity School, Deerfield, Illinois, USA

From beginning to end, Tom Wright and Mike Bird relentlessly orient the study of the New Testament to questions of faith, transformation, worship, and mission. Not only does the book assemble Tom's massive scholarship in one volume, but also integrates it with the concern of his ministry as Bishop of Durham, to serve the church. If you are invested in the development of theological students, pastors, and congregations, you should get this book. In fact, no matter what your view, you will find much to benefit you, from discussions of primary texts to practical examples.

ELIZABETH E. SHIVELY, University of St Andrews, Scotland

Interpreting the New Testament is a complex task and Wright and Bird work at it with customary passion and a commitment to clarity and coherence. These qualities make it an ideal starting-point for anyone who wants to understand early Christianity and its canonical texts.

DR SEAN WINTER, Pilgrim Theological College, University of Divinity, Melbourne, Australia

THE NEW TESTAMENT

— IN —

ITS WORLD

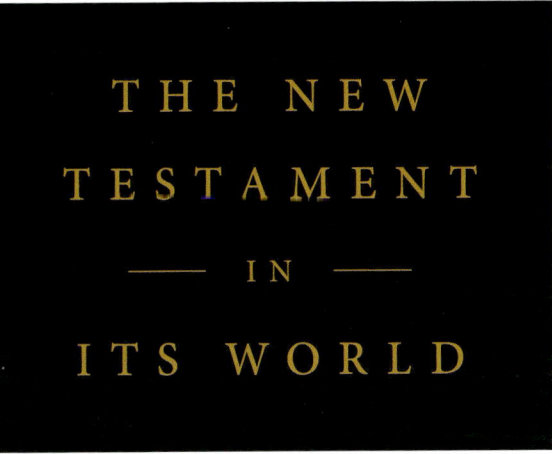

THE NEW TESTAMENT IN ITS WORLD

AN INTRODUCTION TO THE HISTORY,
LITERATURE, AND THEOLOGY
OF THE FIRST CHRISTIANS

N.T. WRIGHT
MICHAEL F. BIRD

The New Testament in Its World
Copyright © N. T. Wright and Michael F. Bird 2019

First published in Great Britain in 2019
Society for Promoting Christian Knowledge

36 Causton Street
London SW1P 4ST
www.spck.org.uk

Published in North America by Zondervan Academic
an imprint of Zondervan, *3900 Sparks Dr. SE, Grand Rapids, Michigan 49546*

ISBN 978-0-310-49930-5 (hardcover)

ISBN 978-0-310-49932-9 (ebook)

All rights reserved. No part of this book may be reproduced or transmitted in any form or by any means, electronic or mechanical, including photocopying, recording, or by any information storage and retrieval system, without permission in writing from the publisher.

SPCK and Zondervan Academic do not necessarily endorse the
individual views contained in their publications.

The author and publishers have made every effort to ensure that the external website and email addresses included in this book are correct and up to date at the time of going to press. The author and publishers are not responsible for the content, quality, or continuing accessibility of the sites.

Unless otherwise stated, quotations from the New Testament are either the authors' own translation or are taken from N. T. Wright's *The New Testament for Everyone* (London: SPCK, 2011; published by HarperOne, San Francisco, as *The Kingdom New Testament*), while those from the Old Testament are either the authors' own translation or are taken from New Revised Standard Version of the Bible, Anglicized Edition, copyright © 1989, 1995 by the Division of Christian Education of the National Council of the Churches of Christ in the USA. Used by permission. All rights reserved.

The authors would like to thank the following publishers for permission to reproduce copyright material:

InterVarsity Press for extracts taken from *The Challenge of Jesus* by N. T. Wright.
Copyright © 2015 by N. T. Wright. Used by permission of InterVarsity Press,
P.O. Box 1400, Downers Grove, IL 60515, USA. www.ivpress.com.

SPCK and Fortress Press for extracts taken from *The New Testament and the People of God, Jesus and the Victory of God, The Resurrection of the Son of God*, and *Paul and the Faithfulness of God* by N. T. Wright. Copyright (c) 1992, 1996, 2003 and 2013 by N. T. Wright. Used by permission of SPCK, London, and Fortress Press, Minneapolis.

British Library Cataloguing-in-Publication Data

A catalogue record for this book is available from the British Library

ISBN 978–0–281–08271–1

eBook ISBN 978–0–281–06870–8

Cover design: Brand Navigation
Cover photo: Ruben Ramirez / Unsplash
Interior design: Kait Lamphere

Printed in China

20 21 22 23 24 25 26 27 28 29 /DSC/ 15 14 13 12 11 10 9 8 7 6 5 4 3

Contents

List of Illustrations 13
Preface 25
Abbreviations 29

Part I
READING THE NEW TESTAMENT

1. Beginning Study of the New Testament 38
    Why the New Testament? 38
    What is the New Testament? 44
    Keeping history, literature, and theology together 47

2. The New Testament as History 50
    Reading the New Testament as a historical document 50

3. The New Testament as Literature 60
    Reading the New Testament as a literary artefact 60
    The author 61
    The text 65
    The reader 70
    Fusing the horizons of author, text, and reader 73

4. The New Testament as Theology 76
    Reading the New Testament as a theological discourse 76
    Discipleship as defining the authoritative story and living it out ... 80

Part II
THE WORLD OF JESUS AND THE EARLY CHURCH

5. The History of the Jews between the Persian and Roman Empires 86
  Introducing the history of New Testament times 86
  The Jews from the Babylonian exile to the Hasmonean dynasty
  (587–63 BC) 87
  The Jews under Roman rule (63 BC–AD 70) 94
  The Jewish world reconstructed (AD 70–135) 103

6. The Jewish Context of Jesus and the Early Church 108
  Jewish life in Palestine 108
  The Jewish sects 118
  Jewish beliefs: one God and one people 137

7. The Greco-Roman Context of the Early Church 142
  Hellenistic culture and Roman empire 142
  The social order 147
  Religion, philosophy, and culture 150
  The Jewish Diaspora 164
  The Septuagint 167

Part III
JESUS AND THE VICTORY OF GOD

8. The Study of the Historical Jesus 172
  Imagining an historical Jesus 172
  Why study the historical Jesus? 173
  The quest for the historical Jesus 176
  Concluding thoughts on the historical Jesus 184

9. The Profile and Praxis of a Prophet 188
  On the road with Jesus 188
  Precursors and prophets: from John the Baptist to Jesus of Nazareth 190
  The campaign begins: Jesus and the kingdom of God 197
  Jesus versus the Temple 208
  A précis on the prophet Jesus 213

10. Who Did Jesus Think He Was? 216
  Who do people say I am? 216
  A prophet, like one of the prophets long ago 218
  Who is this 'son of man'? 220

  The Messiah 226
  Did Jesus think he was God? 231

11. **The Death of the Messiah** 242
  Why did Jesus die? 242
  The charges 245
  Last Supper 251
  Riddles of the cross 256
  Jesus: Messiah and Servant 258
  The victory of God 259

Part IV
THE RESURRECTION OF THE SON OF GOD

12. **The Afterlife in Greek, Roman, and Jewish Thought** 264
  Introducing life after death in antiquity 264
  Greco-roman views of the afterlife 266
  Jewish views of the afterlife 277
  Testimony to the living hope 293

13. **The Story of Easter according to the Apostle Paul** 296
  Jesus, crucified, dead, buried, and risen! 296
  Paul's testimony to the risen Jesus: the son of God in power ... 298
  1 and 2 Thessalonians 298
  Philippians 299
  Ephesians and Colossians 301
  Romans 303
  Interlude 307
  1 Corinthians 308
  Paul: theologian of the risen lord 314

14. **The Story of Easter according to the Evangelists** 316
  The gospels: the lord has risen 316
  The origins of Easter 317
  Mark: fear and trembling 321
  Matthew: earthquakes and angels 324
  Luke: burning hearts and broken bread 326
  John: new day, new tasks 327
  He is risen! 330
  Walking the road to Emmaus in a postmodern world 331

Part V
PAUL AND THE FAITHFULNESS OF GOD

15. The Story of Paul's Life and Ministry.................................. 336
    Paul's significance for the early church 337
    Paul's early life.. 338
    Paul's persecution of the church 341
    Paul's christophany and conversion................................. 344
    Paul and the 'tunnel period' 350
    Paul's missionary career.. 351
    'And so we came to Rome' 361

16. A Primer on Pauline Theology.. 366
    Paul, Philemon, koinōnia, *and the Messiah*...................... 366
    The Pauline trinity: monotheism, election, and eschatology 370
    Rethinking God.. 371
    Rethinking God's people 377
    Reworking God's future 387
    The Pauline legacy 393

17. Galatians... 396
    Introduction 396
    Contextual and critical matters 399
    The argument of Galatians.. 403
    Excursus: recent trends in contemporary Pauline scholarship 413
    Galatians and the big picture 413

18. 1 and 2 Thessalonians 416
    Introduction 416
    Contextual and critical matters 417
    The argument of 1 Thessalonians 422
    The argument of 2 Thessalonians 427
    1 and 2 Thessalonians and the big picture 429

19. Philippians 434
    Introduction 434
    Contextual and critical matters 436
    The argument of Philippians 441
    Philippians and the big picture.. 447

20. Colossians, Philemon, and Ephesians 450
    Introduction 450

  Contextual and critical matters 452
  The argument of Colossians 461
  The argument of the letter to Philemon 465
  The argument of Ephesians 469
  Colossians, Philemon, and Ephesians, and the big picture 471

21. 1 and 2 Corinthians 474
  Introduction 474
  Contextual and critical matters 476
  The argument of 1 Corinthians 485
  The argument of 2 Corinthians 494
  1 and 2 Corinthians and the big picture 499

22. Romans 502
  Introduction 502
  Contextual and critical matters 504
  The argument of Romans 510
  Romans and the big picture 524

23. The Pastoral Epistles 528
  Introduction 528
  Contextual and critical matters 530
  The argument of 1 Timothy 543
  The argument of 2 Timothy 546
  The argument of Titus 548
  The Pastoral Epistles and the big picture 549

Part VI
THE GOSPELS AND THE STORY OF GOD

24. The Gospel according to Mark 554
  Introduction 554
  Contextual and critical matters 557
  Mark's story of Jesus 561
  Mark and the big picture 576

25. The Gospel according to Matthew 578
  Introduction 578
  Contextual and critical matters 581
  Matthew's story of Jesus 589
  Matthew and the big picture 600

26. The Gospel according to Luke and Acts of the Apostles 604
　Introduction 604
　Contextual and critical matters 607
　Luke's story of Jesus 617
　Luke's story of the early church 628
　Luke-Acts and the big picture 644

27. The Gospel according to John 648
　Introduction 648
　Contextual and critical matters 652
　John's story of Jesus 663
　John and the big picture 678

28. The Making of the Gospels 680
　Introduction 680
　The genre of the gospels 681
　The problem of John's gospel 685
　The synoptic problem 686
　The Jesus-tradition 694

Part VII
THE EARLY CHRISTIANS AND THE MISSION OF GOD

29. Introduction to Early Christian Letters 702
　Introduction 702
　The canonical function of the Catholic Epistles 705

30. The Letter to the Hebrews 710
　Introduction 710
　Contextual and critical matters 711
　The argument of Hebrews 715
　Hebrews and the big picture 728

31. Letters by Jesus' Brothers: James and Jude 730
　Introduction 730
　Contextual and critical matters 734
　The argument of James 740
　The argument of Jude 749
　James and Jude in the big picture 754

32. Petrine Letters: 1 and 2 Peter 756
　Introduction 756
　Contextual and critical matters 758

  The argument of 1 Peter 770
  The argument of 2 Peter 777
  1 and 2 Peter in the big picture....................................... 781

33. Johannine Letters: 1, 2, and 3 John 784
  Introduction 784
  Contextual and critical matters 786
  The argument of 1 John... 796
  The argument of 2 John... 803
  The argument of 3 John... 804
  1, 2, and 3 John in the big picture 805

34. Revelation.. 808
  Introduction 808
  Contextual and critical matters 812
  The story of the book of Revelation 829
  Revelation in the big picture 843

Part VIII
THE MAKING OF THE NEW TESTAMENT

35. Introduction to Textual Criticism of the New Testament................ 850
  How we got the New Testament 850
  The goal of textual criticism 852
  The materials used to establish the text of the New Testament 855
  Method in textual criticism.. 856
  Resources for study.. 862

36. The Canonization of the New Testament 866
  How we got the New Testament canon 866
  Conclusion 875

Part IX
LIVING THE STORY OF THE NEW TESTAMENT

37. Bringing It All Together... 878
  Making the New Testament matter for today....................... 878

Bibliography.. 891
Scripture and Other Ancient Literature Index 925
Subject Index 959

List of Illustrations

Plates

The Last Supper, dated to the fifteenth century, National Museum of Russian Art, Kiev	36
Coptic fragment, 2 Cor. 6.5–7 and 2 Pet. 2.4–5 and 7–9	41
Plato, Vatican Museum	45
Aristotle, National Museum of Rome	45
Tacitus, (AD 56–120)	46
Lookout from Masada	48
Tiberian denarius	53
Passover scene, Barcelona Haggadah, dated to the fourteenth century, The British Library	57
Western Wall, Jerusalem Temple Mount	59
Man of Sorrows, fifteenth century, Art Institute of Chicago	70
Minuscule 244, dated to the thirteenth century	74
Icon of Holy Wisdom, dated to the sixteenth century, St George Church, Volodga	78
Jerusalem from the Mount of Olives	81
The calling of the apostles Peter and Andrew by Duccio di Buoninsegna, c. 1308–11, National Gallery of Art, Washington, D.C.	82
Ethiopian icon of the crucifixion	84
Alexander the Great (356–323 BC)	90
Coin featuring Antiochus Epiphanes IV and, on the reverse side, the god Apollo	93
Stone showing dedicatory inscription to Tiberius	101
The triumphal arch of Titus, built in AD 81 to commemorate his conquest of Judea	102
Coin produced under Simeon ben-Kosiba	105

13

First-century Greek inscription honouring Theodotus, leader of a Jerusalem
    synagogue 111
Ancient mikveh located in Qumran 116
The final stronghold of Jewish resistance against the Romans: Masada 123
The Golden Gate, Temple Mount, Jerusalem. 128
The settlement where the Qumran sect are believed to have lived 131
Cave number 4 at Qumran 132
The War Scroll from Qumran (1QM) 134–35
Imperial fora ruins. 145
Coin depicting the goddess Roma on the hills of Rome 146
Bas-relief from the Arch of Marcus Aurelius 152
Remains of the temple of Artemis, Ephesus 154
Reconstruction of the temple of Artemis. 155
Statue of Artemis of the Ephesians 156
A *lararium* depicting two *lares*, honoured as spirits protecting a household . . . 157
The Greek philosopher Socrates depicted in a first-century fresco from Ephesus . . 159
Fresco from a synagogue on the Dura-Europos depicting Jews rescued from
    the Nile 165
The Duke papyrus 740, a fourth-century fragment of Psalm 89. 167
The Mosaic of Jesus, dated 532–7, in the Hagia Sophia, Istanbul 170
Caesarea Philippi 175
Albert Schweitzer. 178
Karl Barth 180
Poster of the musical *Jesus Christ Superstar*. 182
Shoreline of the Sea of Galilee 186–87
Mosaic of Jesus, dated to the fourth century. 189
River Jordan, the traditional site where John performed his baptisms. 192
The Great Isaiah scroll, dated to 100 BC 194–95
Icon of Jesus preaching in the synagogue of Nazareth, from a Vatican manuscript . . 200
Manuscript illumination of the inbreaking of God's reign when Jesus healed
    a demon-possessed boy 202
Mount Beatitude, Capernaum, Israel 205
Temple Mount, South Wall, Jerusalem 207
Bar-Kokhba Revolt coin, *c.* AD 132–35 208
El Greco, *Christ Driving the Money-changers from the Temple*, *c.* 1570,
    Minneapolis Institute of Art. 209
Eastern edge of the Judean wilderness near Qumran 211
Caesarea Philippi 217
Jesus healing the woman with the flow of blood; from the Roman catacombs . . 219
Depiction of the Ancient of Days in Daniel 7, *c.* AD 1091, The British Library . . 223

Mosaic of the healing of the paralytic at Capernaum, Emilia-Romagna 227
Sir Edward John Poynter, *The Visit of the Queen of Sheba to King Solomon*, c. 1890 .. 229
Mosaic of Christ the Pantocrator from Fethiye Camii, Istanbul.............. 232
Fallen stones from the Temple's destruction in AD 70 237
Church of the Holy Sepulchre, Jerusalem 246
Matthias Grünewald, *Crucifixion*, 1515, Isenheim altarpiece 247
The Last Supper, illuminated page, the Book of Hours, Netherlands, dated 1420.. 253
Jaume Huguet, Medieval representation of the Last Supper, dated to the
    fifteenth century, Museu Nacional d'Art de Catalunya, Barcelona....... 255
Dionisius, Russian icon of the crucifixion, c. 1500 257
Titiaian, *Averoldi Polyptych*, c. 1520-2, Santi Nazaro e Celso, Brescia 262
Peter Paul Rubens, *Apotheosis of Hercules*, c. 1637–8, Brussels................ 266
Sculpted relief depicting the apotheosis of Emperor Antoninus Pius and
    his wife Faustina, c. AD 161 271
Volute krater with Hades, Persephone, and Hermes, dated to the fourth
    century BC 286
Antonio Ciseri, *Martyrdom of the Maccabees*, c. 1863, Church of St Felicity,
    Florence... 291
Cave 4, Qumran... 292
Tomb of Herod, Herodium.. 294
Piero della Francesca, *The Resurrection*, c. 1463, Tuscany 297
Theatre at Ephesus... 302
Depiction of the resurrection within an illuminated letter, dated to the
    fifteenth century.. 305
Boris Anrep, mosaic of the conversion of St Paul, dated to the twentieth
    century, St Paul's Chapel, Westminster Cathedral, London............ 310
Replica of right heel bone of crucified person............................. 317
Images from the life of Christ, The Three Maries at the Empty Tomb,
    Psalter of Eleanor of Aquitaine, c. 1185, Dutch National Library........ 318
Resurrection of Jesus, eleventh-century mosaic, Hosios Loukas monastery, Greece.. 322
Duccio di Buoninsegna, *Christ at the Sea of Galilee*, c. 1308–11, Cathedral
    of Siena 328
Plaque depicting the journey to Emmaus and Noli Me Tangere, c. 1115–20,
    The Metropolitan Museum of Art 332
Marco Zoppo, *St Paul*, c. 1470, Ashmolean Museum, Oxford................. 334
John Chrysostom, Leitourgikon, c. 1664, The British Library 337
Ancient road in Tarsus... 338
Synagogue floor mosaic depicting the temple façade and Torah ark,
    Israel Museum... 342
Detail of Paul's conversion, basilica of San Paolo fuori le mura, Rome 345

Coin showing the bust of King Aretas IV, *c.* AD 19–20, Petra 354
Inscription referring to Lucius Gallio, *c.* AD 52, Delphi 357
Onesimus' martyrdom, depicted in the Menologion of Basil II, *c.* AD 1000 . . . 368
Painting of the Trinity, Sant'Antonio Abate, Castelsardo, Sardini. 376
Historiated letter 'A' depicting the generations in the bosom of Abraham,
    dated to the twelfth century 381
3D reproduction of the ark of the covenant 383
Mosaic of Peter and Paul with throne and cross in Baptistery of Arians,
    dated before AD 526, Ravenna 385
Mosaic of Christ with Emperor Constantine and Empress Zoe, dated to the
    eleventh century, Hagia Sophia, Istanbul. 390
Capernaum synagogue, dated to the fourth century AD 392
Roman forum 394–95
Roman cup, dated to the first century AD 401
Foundations of a temple to the emperor Augustus in Pisidian Antioch 402
Icon depicting the embrace of Paul and Peter. 407
Martin Luther. 408
Tomb marker from a Jewish catacomb in Rome, dated to the fourth century . . 410
Roman aqueduct, Pisidian Antioch. 414
The Roman forum in Thessalonica. 419
Mosaic depicting Jesus on his throne from the church of San Vitale, Ravenna,
    c. AD 546. 422
Bust of the Roman emperor Nero 429
Thessalonica forum. 430
Miniature of the second coming, *Benedictional of Æthelwold*, *c.* 963–84,
    The British Library 431
Triptych of the life of Christ, dated to the fourteenth century, Art Institute
    of Chicago 435
Via Egnatia connecting Philippi to the rest of Macedonia and Thrace 436
Prison cell where Paul and Silas are believed to have been imprisoned. 437
Ruins of Roman Philippi. 438
Ancient theatre of Philippi 446
Bas-relief of the Praetorian Guard during the time of Augustus 447
Remains of Roman forum and basilica, Philippi 448–49
A fifth- to sixth-century wall-painting of Paul in a cave in Ephesus. 451
Coin of the goddess Artemis. 453
Ephesian theatre. 455
Huge mound under which the city of Colossae remains buried 457
Ruins of the Laodicean theatre. 462
Terrace houses in ancient Ephesus. 468

Library of Celsus, Ephesus	470
Curetes Street, Ephesus	472–73
Ancient city of Corinth	475
Acrocorinth, the immense feature overlooking the city of Corinth	476
A *peripteros* (small temple with porticoes) located on the eastern side of Corinth	478
First-century inscription excavated in 1929 near the theatre in Corinth	481
Fountain of Peirene, an impressive monument built over a spring	487
The *macellum* (meat market) located next to the temple of Apollo	489
Gulf of Corinth	490
Temple of Apollo, Corinth	491
Statue of the emperor Augustus with a head-covering	493
Urban street in the ancient city of Corinth	496
The *bēma* or judgment seat of Corinth	497
Columns at temple of Apollo	498
The Roman forum, Rome	506
Temple of Vesta, goddess of the hearth	513
Russian fresco of Abraham sacrificing Isaac	516
Fresco of Abraham from Dura Europos, *c.* AD 245	518
Fresco of baptism, dated to the third century, catacombs of San Callisto, Rome	518
Olive tree	521
Coin with bust of Nero	522
$\mathfrak{P}^{46}$	523
Fresco of a woman and man, dated to the first century	525
Colosseum, Rome	526
Road in Ephesus	532
Detail of Saint Thecla, dated to the fifth century, The Nelson-Atkins Museum of Art	534
Depiction of reading at Herculaneum, dated to the first century	535
Stained glass of St Timothy, *c.* 1160, Paris	544
Fresco of St Paul, dated to the sixteenth century	547
Basilica of Agios Titos, Gortyna, Crete	550
The Trinity and the four evangelists from the *Bible historiale* of Charles of France, *c.* AD 1420	552
Mark's gospel, symbolized by a lion	555
Theophanes the Greek, *The Saviour's Transfiguration*, dated to the early fifteenth century	567
Model replica of the Herodian temple from the time of Jesus	569
Crucifixion in an illuminated manuscript, dated to the twelfth century	573
Kursi Church	576
Matthew the Evangelist symbolized by an angel	579

Fourth-century synagogue in Capernaum. 585
Greek-style mosaic of Mary and baby Jesus, Basilica of the Annunciation,
    Nazareth 589
Fresco of the baptism of Jesus 590
Caesarea Phillippi 596
Mount of Beatitudes 602–3
Luke the Evangelist symbolized by an ox. 605
Simon Marmion, *St Luke Painting the Virgin and Child*, c. 1460, Valenciennes . . 609
Title page of the Acts of the Apostles, dated early twelfth century,
    The Walters Art Museum 611
Inside of a replica synagogue in Nazareth Village in Israel 620
Rembrandt, *The Return of the Prodigal Son*, c. 1662–9, Hermitage Museum,
    St Petersburg 623
Herodium. 625
Ivory plaque with scenes from Luke 24.13–35, c. 850–900, The
    Metropolitan Museum of Art. 627
Depiction of Pentecost from High Altar of the Charterhouse of Saint-
    Honoré, The Art Institute of Chicago 629
Caravaggio, *The Conversion of St Paul*, c. 1600, Odescalchi Balbi collection, Rome . . 633
St Peter's Grotto Church, dated to the fourth century, Antioch 636
Detail of Paul, Peter, and Luke in crypt, Rome 644
Aerial view of modern Jerusalem 647
John the evangelist symbolized by an eagle 649
Southern steps into the Temple 650
Emperor Trajan. 655
Mosaic with Polycarp, dated to the second century 658
𝔓^{52}, otherwise known as the John Rylands Papyrus. 661
Stone water jars used for ceremonial washings 666
Steps down to the Pool of Siloam. 670
Clement of Alexandria 671
Ford Madox Brown, *Jesus Washing Peter's Feet*, 1893, Tate Gallery, London . . . 672
Antonio Ciseri, *Ecce Homo*, 1871, Gallery of Modern Art, Florence 674
Nag Hammadi Codex II, folio 32, dated to the fourth century 689
Illustration of Luke and Mark, Codex Washingtonianus, dated to the fifth
    century 698
Icon of the Twelve Apostles. 700
P.Oxy 1229 705
Carlo Crivelli, St Augustine 708
The Arch of Titus commemorating Rome's defeat of Jerusalem and
    destruction of the Temple. 712

Codex Vaticanus, beginning of the epistle to the Hebrews, dated to the fourth-century	716
Abel and Melchizedek offering a sacrifice to God, Basilica di San Vitale, Ravenna	722
Abraham meets Melchizedek, dated to the thirteenth century, St Mark's Basilica, Venice	727
Icon of St James	731
Frère Laurent, *The Sermon on the Mount*, c. 1279	732
Depiction of Jude from illuminated manuscript, dated to the early twelfth century, The Walters Art Museum	737
Gamla synagogue, dated to the first-century	743
Mosaic of the sacrifice of Isaac, dated to the sixth century	744
Fragment of *1 Enoch*	753
Statue of the apostle Peter, Basilica of St John Lateran, Rome	757
3D reconstruction of a Galilean fishing boat	758
Caravaggio, *The Crucifixion of Saint Peter*, c. 1600, Cerasi Chapel, Rome	762
The transfiguration, dated to the late thirteenth century	768
Mosaic of slaves serving at a banquet, dated to the second century, Dougga, Tunisia	773
The crucifixion from a manuscript stored in the Monastery of St Pantaleon, Ethiopia	776
Fresco of the transfiguration, Church of the Transfiguration, Mount Tabor, Galilee	782
Tomb of St John, Ephesus	785
Origen	790
Altar frontal depicting the Trinity, c. 1410–20	797
Remains of the Basilica of St John	802
Christ in majesty flanked by Mary, John the Evangelist, and saints, dated to the twelfth century, Walters Art Museum	806
Remains of the Basilica of St John, Ephesus	807
Icon of John the Evangelist dictating the visions to his scribe, c. 1837	809
Mosaic with John and a disciple	811
Bust of Emperor Vespasian	816
Bust of Emperor Domitian	817
Ancient temple, Laodicea	818
Remains of the temple of Artemis, Sardis	820
The ancient theatre of Pergamum	822
Jaume Huguet, painting of St Michael vanquishing the antichrist, c. 1455–1460, National Art Museum of Catalonia, Barcelona	826
The first resurrection, *The Cloisters Apocalypse*, c. 1330, The Metropolitan Museum of Art	827

The son of man and the seven lampstands, *Bamberger Apocalypse, c.* 1000 831
Silver tetradrachma 837
Bust of Nero... 838
John's vision of Christ in majesty, *The Silos Apocalypse, c.* 1091 843
Terracotta tomb plaque with Christogram and Latin inscription, *c.* 400–800,
    The Metropolitan Museum of Art 845
View of Patmos Island.. 846–47
John 1.1–18 of Codex Sinaiticus 848
Making of papyrus... 857
Uncial 0177 862
Minuscule 321... 864
Plaque with St John the Evangelist, dated to the ninth century,
    The Metropolitan Museum of Art 868
Fresco of banquet scene, Catacomb dei Santi Marcellino e Pietro, dated to
    the fourth century, Rome.. 876
Fresco depicting Abraham's divine visitation, *c.* 1000, St Sophia of Kyiv, Ukraine .. 879
Story of the Bible narrated through mosaics, Cathedral of Monreale, dated
    to the twelfth century, Sicily 883
Sculpture depicting the baptism of Augustine, *c.* 1549, Troyes Cathedral,
    Troyes 887
Jerusalem 888–89

Figures

  1 The role of the 'implied reader' according to narrative criticism......... 66
  2 The role of the 'real reader' according to narrative criticism............. 66
  3 The Augustinian view of Matthean priority 687
  4 The Griesbach hypothesis of Matthean priority 687
  5 The idea of Markan priority 689
  6 The four-source theory for the formation of the synoptic gospels....... 690
  7 The Farrer-Goulder-Goodacre theory of synoptic-gospel formation.... 692
  8 The idea of Matthean posteriority 692
  9 The three-source theory for the formation of the synoptic gospels 693
 10 The historical stages in the production of a modern English Bible...... 852
 11 The text and apparatus of Matthew 24.36 as presented in UBS (5)..... 859

Maps

Route of returning exiles 89
Alexander the Great's empire 91
The Ptolemies and Seleucids in the third century BC...................... 91
Hasmonean kingdom 95

Palestine under Herod the Great 96
The divisions of Herod's kingdom 98
The holy land 109
Roman Empire 143
Galilee 191
Traditional location of the crucifixion 244
Tarsus, in the region of Cilicia 339
Paul's second missionary journey 351
What if Paul had gone east into Bithynia? 353
Political Galatia 398
Ethnic Galatia 398
Thessalonica 417
Achaia and Macedonia 440
Asia Minor in the time of the apostle Paul 452
Ancient city of Corinth 475
Ancient Rome 505
Decapolis and lands beyond the Jordan 558
Galilee 564
Paul's first missionary journey 637
Paul's second missionary journey 639
Paul's third missionary journey 643
An illustration of Herod's Temple 724
Locations of major Jewish Diaspora communities 741
Asia Minor 761
The seven churches 832

Tables

3.1 Classifications of rhetorical criticism 68
7.1 Economic scales for urban contexts in the greco-roman world 147
17.1 Paul's distinction between the spiritual heirs of Sarah and of Hagar 409
17.2 TULIP of the 'Apocalyptic Paul' 412
17.3 TULIP of 'Paul within Judaism' 412
21.1 Social stratification of persons in Corinth according to the
     New Testament 482
25.1 Jewish features unique to the gospel of Matthew 591
27.1 The 'I am' sayings in John's gospel 669
28.1 Earliest copies of the canonical gospels and Acts 681
29.1 Earliest copies of the Catholic Epistles and the apocalypse of John ... 704
30.1 The superlative status of Jesus according to the author of Hebrews 723
31.1 Echoes of the Jesus-tradition in the epistle of James 742

31.2	James and Paul on 'faith' and 'works'	746
32.1	Parallels between 2 Peter and Jude	780
34.1	The reigns of the Roman emperors as a key to dating Revelation	815
34.2	Earliest copies of the book of Revelation	824
36.1	Four early lists of New Testament writings of the second/third centuries	870
36.2	Two canon lists from the fourth century	871
36.3	Books contained in biblical manuscripts of the fourth and fifth centuries	872

Text grids

Alternative ways to read Revelation	841
Ancient and modern Jewish scholars comment on Israel's plight in the first century	140
Critiques of the Pharisees by other Jewish groups	127
Examples of parallel sayings between John and Mark	686
Examples of similarities between John's gospel and letters	788
Examples of the Jesus-tradition in 1 Corinthians	696
Jesus is mocked as a prophet	690
Jesus' 'son of man' language compared with voices from the Old Testament	239
Jesus' words at the Last Supper	252
Texts from the Dead Sea Scrolls	136
The parable of the mustard seed	691

Timelines

Chronology of Roman emperors and prefects	106
Sketch of Pauline chronology	363
Timeline of the Persian and Greek period	87

Boxes/panels

Blasts from the past

Adolf Schlatter on atheistic approaches	77
Albert Schweitzer and the *Quest of the Historical Jesus*	178
Augustine on how the Catholic Epistles balance out Paul	707
Clement of Alexandria on Jesus as the good shepherd	671
Dietrich Bonhoeffer on Christians as the light of the world	206
John Chrysostom on the apostle Paul	337
John Chrysostom on the resurrection	331
Martin Luther on Christian righteousness	408
Martin Luther on the 'righteousness of God'	512
Origen on apostasy	725

Tertullian on the restrainer 428
The correspondence between Pliny and Trajan about Christians 774
Theodore of Mopsuestia on Peter's confession 594

Emails from the edge

Dying and rising gods 275
Ending of Mark's gospel 574
Firstborn 462
Gnosticism? 162
Help with *harpagmos* 444
Josephus? 196
Last Supper date 250
NT history 51
Paul in letters and Acts 347
Rapture theology 425
Salvation in Hebrews 719
Socialism in Acts 630
Sources in Jude 751

Portals and parallels

Ancient prefaces 618
Ancient usages of *gospel* 562
Fallen angels 836
Imperial hymns in Pergamum 833
Irenaeus on Valentinian cosmology 545
Jewish exorcists in first-century Judea 201
Josephus on the 'oracle' that inspired revolution 122
Juvenal and Justin Martyr on the Jews 410
Pliny's letter to Sabinianus 466
Riots at Passover 121
Seneca on the power of words 203
Songs of the Sabbath Sacrifice 460
Suetonius on divorce 488
Tacitus on the Jews 166
The Dead Sea Scrolls on Melchizedek 721
The Enochic son of man 225
The question of circumcision for male converts to Judasim 406
The righteousness of God in Jewish literature 515
Typical greco-roman male sexual attitudes 423
Wisdom dwells on earth 664

Other

Archaeological evidence for the existence of Pontius Pilate	101
Biblical canons of the major ancient Christian churches	168
External evidence for Pauline chronology	355
Israel's post-exilic restoration hopes	88
Judas Maccabaeus rededicates the Temple	93
Luke's unique material	606
Matthew's unique material	583
Ozymandias	55
Paul and slavery	467
Popular prophets in Judea under Roman rule	193
The Christ 'poem'	443
The gospel at work in Philippi	442
The rhetoric of Galatians	404
The story inside the epistle of James	748
The title of the book	830
The warning passages in Hebrews	725
What if Paul had gone east into Bithynia?	353
Where was Golgotha?	243
Women in Christian service and mission	525

Outlines of New Testament books

Outline of Matthew	588	Outline of 1 Timothy	543
Outline of Mark	561	Outline of 2 Timothy	546
Outline of Luke	617	Outline of Titus	548
Outline of John	663	Outline of Philemon	465
Outline of the Acts of the Apostles	628	Outline of Hebrews	715
Outline of Romans	509	Outline of James	740
Outline of 1 Corinthians	486	Outline of 1 Peter	770
Outline of 2 Corinthians	494	Outline of 2 Peter	777
Outline of Galatians	403	Outline of 1 John	796
Outline of Ephesians	469	Outline of 2 John	803
Outline of Philippians	441	Outline of 3 John	804
Outline of Colossians	461	Outline of Jude	749
Outline of 1 Thessalonians	423	Outline of the book of Revelation	829
Outline of 2 Thessalonians	427		

Preface

The eminent British New Testament scholar C. H. Dodd (1884–1973) was once asked if, supposing all written copies of the Greek New Testament were either lost or destroyed, he could reproduce the whole thing from memory. Dodd replied that, having lived with the Greek New Testament for so long, he was confident that he could indeed remember it all. In one account of the same story, the questioner responded with utter amazement: how could someone possibly claim to be able to recall the whole thing, in Greek no less? 'Well,' Dodd is said to have replied, with a comical mixture of humility and coyness, 'it's only a little book.'[1]

The New Testament might only be small, but it is a strange and powerful book. At one level, it tells the history of Jesus and the early church; at another level (and these two go closely together, as we shall see) it is regarded by churches around the world as inspired scripture, normative for the life of faith. For this to become a reality, for the New Testament to come alive, each generation of readers, and especially teachers and preachers, needs help, particularly in the form of thorough, user-friendly, and creative introductions to Jesus, his first followers, and the literature that emerged from that movement. That is what this book is hoping to provide.

The idea for this book came during a conference in 2010. Michael Bird suggested to Philip Law of SPCK that someone ought to work with N. T. Wright and try condensing his massive and still incomplete Christian Origins and the Question of God series into a single volume, thus forming a kind of introduction to the New Testament. Law loved the idea and suggested that Bird himself should be the one to do it. Bird was reluctant at first – preferring to be the progenitor rather than the executor of the idea – but when Wright agreed to the project, Bird signed up enthusiastically.

In the following nine years, Bird's idea would soar and grow in scope and

---

[1] The written source is Dillistone 1977, 221 who refers to this event during Dodd's career in a parenthetical remark, and the oral source is Prof. D. A. Carson.

expression—and not least because Wright kept producing new writings during this time. Both authors also filmed lectures throughout the Holy Land, Greece, and Rome to complement the book, while careful attention and research was given to the book's rich visual and pedagogical features.

Michael Bird was first responsible for working through Wright's substantial corpus of work, selecting key passages, summarizing, and supplementing material. N. T. Wright has been involved at all stages, directing its planning, writing new material, editing, offering manifold suggestions, and affecting the construction of the volume from beginning to end. This New Testament introduction is very much a joint effort.

This book is unique in several ways. First, it is something of an N. T. Wright 'reader' or 'sampler', written up in the genre of an introduction to the New Testament. Several sections of the Christian Origins volumes are directly incorporated, as are various paragraphs from Wright's popular-level books like *Surprised by Hope* and the *New Testament for Everyone* commentaries. The present book thus serves as an introduction not only to the New Testament but also to Wright's corpus; we hope it will function as a gateway to explore his wider academic and popular works.

Second, this volume is a robust and user-friendly introduction to the New Testament, complete with a derivative workbook, online course, video and audio lectures, as well as a church-based video curriculum. A large proportion of the book has been freshly written for this very purpose. What is more, the volume is distinctive in that it aims to introduce the New Testament within the context of the study of early Christianity. Our primary purpose – which we cannot express forcefully enough – is not merely to add knowledge to the things that readers already believe about the New Testament. Rather, we aim to provide the scaffolding for a fully orbed and fully fledged historical description and theological account of Jesus and the early church. We want to cultivate a commitment to a specific account of Christian history, literature, theology, and mission.

Third, the book seeks to avoid some of the standard problems with a 'New Testament introduction'. There is so much to teach, so many debates to explain, so many charts, pictures, and titbits of background a teacher wants to include, that the task might appear endless and the book impossibly cumbersome. We have tried to be reasonably thorough, but in the most precise and pictorial way possible. The chapters that discuss each individual New Testament book proceed by means of a quick thematic introduction. They then discuss critical and contextual matters, provide an outline of the book, offer a miniature commentary, and finish off with some thoughts about application and suggestions for further reading.

In terms of acknowledgments, volumes like this stand on the shoulders of others. While the present volume is clearly based on Wright's work, it would be remiss not to acknowledge the many writings beyond Wright that have deeply shaped the formation and composition of the book as a whole and its several sections. Among these are the erudite works of Richard Hays, Martin Hengel, Morna Hooker, Luke Timothy Johnson, James Dunn, Richard Bauckham, David deSilva, and Ben Witherington. These scholars have proved to be notable modern interpreters to whom we have turned time and again for interpretative decisions on various portions of the New Testament.

Several other people need to be thanked for their assistance in the completion of this project. We are indebted to several scholars who read portions of the text and offered constructive feedback. Among them are David A. deSilva, Patrick Schreiner, Sarah Harris, Brian Rosner, Hefin Jones, Sean du Toit, Stephen Carlson, Michael Holmes, George Guthrie, Joshua Jipp, Brandon Smith, and Nijay Gupta. This book would never have happened without the joint co-operation of SPCK (Philip Law and Alexandra McDonald) and Zondervan Academic (Katya Covrett, Jesse Hillman, Christopher Beetham, T. J. Rathbun, and so many others).

Finally, we pray and hope that this book will benefit university students, seminarians, church people, and interested readers by providing them with an in-depth introduction to the context, message, and significance of the early Christian writings. The New Testament, as C. H. Dodd pointed out, may be small. But in our view it remains the greatest and most important book ever produced.

N. T. Wright and Michael F. Bird

Abbreviations

Stylistic shorthands

c.	*circa*
cf.	confer
ch(s).	chapter(s)
contra	against
cp.	compare
d.	died
ed(s).	editor(s); edited by
edn(s).	edition(s)
e.g.	for example
esp.	especially
et al.	and others
etc.	et cetera
frags.	fragments
i.e.	that is
MSS	manuscripts
n.	(foot/end)note
par.	parallel
repr.	reprinted
rev.	revised
sic	thus (acknowledging an error in original)
tr.	translation/translated by
v(v).	verse(s)
vol(s).	volume(s)

Primary sources

1 Clem.	*1 Clement*
1 En.	*1 Enoch*
1 Macc.	1 Maccabees
1QH	Thanksgiving Hymns
1QM	War Scroll
1QpHab	Pesher Habakkuk
1QS	Rule of the Community
1QSa	Rule of the Community (Appendix a)
2 Apoc. Jas.	*(Second) Apocalypse of James*
2 Bar.	*2 Baruch*
2 Clem.	*2 Clement*
2 Esd.	2 Esdras
2 Macc.	2 Maccabees

29

4 Ez.	*4 Ezra*
4 Macc.	4 Maccabees
4Q176	Consolations
4Q246	Apocryphon of Daniel
4Q405	Songs of the Sabbath Sacrifice
4Q473	The Two Ways
4Q521	Messianic Apocalypse
4Q'Amram	Visions of Amram
4QMMT	Halakhic Letter
11Q13	Melchizedek
Aelian	Aelian (*Hist. Misc.*=*Historical Miscellany*)
Aesch.	Aeschylus (*Eumen.*=*Eumenides*)
Apoc. Mos.	*Apocalypse of Moses*
Apoc. Pet.	*Apocalypse of Peter*
Arist.	Aristotle (*Nic. Eth.*=*Nicomachean Ethics*)
Athanasius	Athanasius (*Ep. Fest.*=*Festal Letters*)
Aug.	Augustine (*Civ. Dei*=*City of God*; *Conf.*=*Confessions*; *Doctr. Chr.*=*Christian Doctrine*; *Fid. Op.*=*Faith and Works*)
Bar.	Baruch
bHag.	Babylonian Talmud, Hagigah
bPesah.	Babylonian Talmud, Pesahim
bSanh.	Babylonian Talmud, Sanhedrin
bShab.	Babylonian Talmud, Shabbat
CD	Cairo Genizah copy of the Damascus Document
Chrys.	John Chrysostom (*Hom. Rom.*=*Homilies on Romans*; *Praef. Hom. Rom.*=*Preface to the Homilies on Romans*)
Cic.	Cicero (*Flac.*=*Pro Flacco*; *Acad.*=*Academicae Quaestiones*)
Clem.	Clement of Alexandria (*Paed.*=*Paedagogus*; *Quis Div.*=*Quis Dives Salvetur*; *Strom.*=*Stromata*)
Did.	*Didache*
Dio Cassius	Dio Cassius (*Hist.*=*Historia Romana*)
Dioscorides	Dioscorides (*Mat. Med.*=*Materia Medica*)
Ep. Apos.	*Epistula Apostolorum* (*Epistle to the Apostles*)
Ep. Arist.	*Epistle of Aristeas*
Ep. Barn.	*Epistle of Barnabas*
Ep. Diog.	*Epistle to Diognetus*
Epiphanius	Epiphanius (*Pan.*=*Panarion*)
Eurip.	Euripides (*Alcest.*=*Alcestis*)
Eus.	Eusebius (*Chron.*=*Chronicle*; *Hist. Ecc.*=*Ecclesiastical History*; *Vit. Const.*=*Life of Constantine*)

Gos. Heb. . . . . *Gospel of the Hebrews*
Gos. Thom. . . *Gospel of Thomas*
Hippolytus . . Hippolytus (*Antichr.=De Antichristo*; *Ref.=Refutation of All Heresies*)
Iamblichus. . . Iamblichus (*Life=Life of Pythagoras*)
Ign. . . . . Ignatius (*Eph.=To the Ephesians*; *Magn.=To the Magnesians*; *Phld.=To the Philadelphians*; *Rom.=To the Romans*; *Smyrn.=To the Smyrneans*; *Trall.=To the Trallians*)
Iren. . . . . Irenaeus (*Adv. Haer.=Adversus Haeresis*)
Jer. . . . . Jerome (*Ep.=Epistle*; *De Vir. Ill.=De Viris Illustribus*)
Jos. . . . . Josephus (*Ant.=Jewish Antiquities*; *Ap.=Against Apion*; *Life=The Life of Josephus*; *War=The Jewish War*)
Jub. . . . . *Jubilees*
Just. . . . . Justin Martyr (*1 Apol.=First Apology*; *Dial.=Dialogue with Trypho*)
Juv . . . . Juvenal (*Sat.=Satires*)
Libanius . . . . . Libanius (*Ep.=Epistle*)
LXX . . . . Septuagint version of the Old Testament
mAboth . . . . . Mishnah, Aboth
Mart. Isa. . . . *Martyrdom of Isaiah*
Mart. Pol. . . . *Martyrdom of Polycarp*
mSanh. . . . . . Mishnah, Sanhedrin
MT . . . . Masoretic Text (of the Hebrew Bible)
Origen . . . . . . Origen (*C. Cels.=Contra Celsum*; *Comm. Jn.=Commentary on John*; *Comm. Matt.=Commentary on Matthew*)
Philo . . . . Philo of Alexandria (*Abr.=De Abrahamo*; *Leg.=Legum Allegoriae*; *(De) Praem.=De Praemiis et Poenis*; *(De) Spec. Leg.=De Specialibus Legibus*; *Heres=Quis Rerum Divinarum Heres Sit*; *Gai.=Legatio ad Gaium*; *Hypoth.=Hypothetica*; *Omn. Prob. Lib.=Quod Omnis Probus Liber Sit*; *Quaest. Gen.=Quaestiones in Genenin*; *Vit. Mos.=De Vita Mosis*; *Sac.=De Sacrificiis Abelis et Caini*; *De Vit. Cont.=De Vita Contemplativa*)
Pliny . . . . Pliny the Elder (*NH=Natural History*)
Pliny . . . . Pliny the Younger (*Ep.=Epistulai*)
Plut. . . . . Plutarch (*Mor.=Moralia*)
Polybius . . . . . Polybius (*Hist.=Histories*)
Polycarp . . . . . Polycarp (*Phil.=To the Philippians*)
Porphyry . . . . Porphyry (*Life=Life of Pythagoras*)
Ps.-Phoc. . . . . . *Pseudo-Phocylides*
Ps. Sol. . . . . . . *Psalms of Solomon*
Sen. . . . . Seneca the Younger (*Ep. Mor.=Moral Epistles*)
Sib. Or. . . . . . . *Sibylline Oracles*

Sir.	Sirach/Ecclesiasticus
Strabo	Strabo (*Geogr.*=*Geographica*)
Suet.	Suetonius (*Claud.*=*Divus Claudius*; *Dom.*=*Domitianus*; *Ner.*=*Nero*; *Tib.*=*Tiberius*; *Vesp.*=*Vespasianus*)
T. Dan	*Testament of Dan*
T. Job	*Testament of Job*
T. Mos.	*Testament of Moses*
Tac.	Tacitus (*Agric.*=*Agricola*; *Ann.*=*Annals*; *Hist.*=*Histories*)
Tert.	Tertullian (*Adv. Marc.*=*Adversus Marcionem*; *Apol.*=*Apology*; *Carn. Chr.*=*De Carni Christi*; *Prae. Haer.*=*De Praescriptione Haereticorum*; *Scorp.*=*Scorpiace*; *Spect.*=*De Spectaculis*)
Tob.	Tobit
Trim. Prot.	*Trimorphic Protennoia*
Wis.	Wisdom
ySanh.	Jerusalem Talmud, Sanhedrin

Secondary sources, etc.

AB	Anchor Bible
ABC	African Bible Commentary
ABD	*Anchor Bible Dictionary*
ABRL	Anchor Bible Reference Library
ACCS	Ancient Christian Commentary on Scripture
ANF	*The Ante-Nicene Fathers*. Edited by A. Roberts, J. Donaldson et al. 10 vols. Buffalo, NY: Christian Literature Publishing Co., 1887.
ANTC	Abingdon New Testament Commentaries
BBC	Blackwell Bible Commentaries
BBR	*Bulletin for Biblical Research*
BECNT	Baker Exegetical Commentary on the New Testament
BETL	Bibliotheca Ephemeridum Theologicarum Lovaniensium
BIS	Biblical Interpretation Series
BNTC	Black's New Testament Commentary
BTC	Belief Theological Commentary
BTNT	Biblical Theology of the New Testament
BZNW	Beihefte zur Zeitschrift für die neutestamentliche Wissenschaft
CBGM	Coherence-Based Genealogical Method
CBR	*Currents in Biblical Research*
CCEL	Christian Classics Ethereal Library
CCSS	Catholic Commentary on Sacred Scripture
CEB	Common English Bible
CITM	Christianity in the Making

ConBNT	Coniectanea Biblica: New Testament Series
ConBOT	Coniectanea Biblica: Old Testament Series
COQG	Christian Origins and the Question of God
CRBS	*Currents in Research: Biblical Studies*
CRINT	Compendia Rerum Iudaicarum ad Novum Testamentum
CSNTM	Centre for the Study of New Testament Manuscripts
ECC	Eerdmans Critical Commentary
ECM	*Editio Critica Maior*
EJT	*European Journal of Theology*
ESV	English Standard Version
Exp. T.	*Expository Times*
FRLANT	Forschungen zur Religion und Literatur des Alten und Neuen Testaments
FS	Festschrift
GH	Gorgias Handbooks
ICC	International Critical Commentary
INTF	Institut für Neutestamentliche Textforschung
IVPNTC	IVP New Testament Commentary
JS	Johannine Studies
JSNT	*Journal for the Study of the New Testament*
JSNTSup	Journal for the Study of the New Testament Supplements
JTI	*Journal of Theological Interpretation*
KJV	King James ['Authorized'] Version
KNT	N. T. Wright, *The Kingdom New Testament*. San Francisco: HarperOne, 2011 [US edn. of *NTE*].
LCL	Loeb Classical Library (various publishers, currently Cambridge, MA and London: Harvard University Press).
LHJS	Library of Historical Jesus Studies
LNTS	Library of New Testament Studies
LPS	Library of Pauline Studies
MSG	Eugene H. Peterson, *The Message*. Colorado Springs, CO: NavPress, 2009.
NA (25)	Nestle-Aland *Novum Testamentum Graece* (25th edn.)
NAC	New American Commentary
NCB	New Century Bible
NCBC	New Cambridge Bible Commentary
NCCS	New Covenant Commentary Series
NIB	*New Interpreter's Bible*. 12 vols. Nashville: Abingdon, 1994–2002.
NIBC	New International Biblical Commentary
NICNT	New International Commentary on the New Testament

NIGTC	New International Greek Testament Commentary
NIV	New International Version
NovTSup	Novum Testamentum Supplements
NRSV	New Revised Standard Version
NSBT	New Studies in Biblical Theology
NT	New Testament
NTC	New Testament in Context
NTE	N. T. Wright, *The New Testament for Everyone*. London: SPCK, 2011 [UK edn. of *KNT*].
NTL	New Testament Library
NTR	New Testament Readings
NTS	*New Testament Studies*
NTT	New Testament Theology
OGIS	*Orientis Graecae Inscriptiones Selectae*. Edited by W. Dittenberger. 2 vols. Leipzig: Hirzel, 1903–5; repr. Hildesheim: Olms, 1960.
OT	Old Testament
OTP	*The Old Testament Pseudepigrapha*. Edited by J. H. Charlesworth. 2 vols. New York: Doubleday, 1983, 1985.
PAST	Pauline Studies
PCNT	Paideia: Commentaries on the New Testament
PNTC	Pillar New Testament Commentary
RSV	Revised Standard Version
SBL	Society of Biblical Literature
SBLGNT	*Society of Biblical Literature Greek New Testament*
SBT	Studies in Biblical Theology
SD	Studies and Documents
SGBC	Story of God Bible Commentary
SNTSMS	Society for New Testament Studies Monograph Series
SP	Sacra Pagina
SRC	Socio-Rhetorical Commentary
THGNT	*The Greek New Testament Produced at Tyndale House*
THNTC	Two Horizons New Testament Commentary
TNTC	Tyndale New Testament Commentaries
TSAJ	Texts and Studies in Ancient Judaism
TTC	Teach the Text Commentary
TynBul	*Tyndale Bulletin*
UBS (5)	United Bible Society *Greek New Testament* (5th edn.)
WBC	Word Biblical Commentary
WUNT	Wissenschaftliche Untersuchungen zum Neuen Testament
ZECNT	Zondervan Exegetical Commentary on the New Testament

Previous works by N. T. Wright: short titles and acronyms (full details in Bibliography)

Climax . . . . . . *The Climax of the Covenant: Christ and the Law in Pauline Theology*, 1991.
DRB . . . . *The Day the Revolution Began*, 2016.
ECL . . . . *Early Christian Letters for Everyone*, 2011.
HGBK . . . . . . *How God Became King*, 2012.
JVG . . . . *Jesus and the Victory of God* (vol. 2 of Christian Origins and the Question of God), 1996.
NTPG . . . . . . *The New Testament and the People of God* (vol. 1 of Christian Origins and the Question of God), 1992.
Paul:
A Biography . . *Paul: A Biography*, 2018.
PFG . . . . *Paul and the Faithfulness of God* (vol. 4 of Christian Origins and the Question of God), 2013.
PP . . . . *Pauline Perspectives: Essays on Paul 1978–2013*, 2013.
PRI . . . . *Paul and His Recent Interpreters*, 2015.
Romans . . . . . 'Romans' in *New Interpreter's Bible*, vol. 10, 2002, pp. 393–770.
RSG . . . . *The Resurrection of the Son of God* (vol. 3 of Christian Origins and the Question of God), 2003.
SC . . . . *Simply Christian*, 2006.
SH . . . . *Surprised by Hope*, 2007.
SJ . . . . *Simply Jesus*, 2011.

The Last Supper, dated to the fifteenth century, Novgorod School, National Museum of Russian Art, Kiev

A. Burkatovski / Fine Art Images

1

READING THE NEW TESTAMENT

The New Testament, we suggest, must be read so as to be understood. It isn't the kind of 'magic' book that simply bypasses the mind. Admittedly, there is a good deal of poetry in the New Testament, and poetry regularly achieves its effects on several different levels; but even then, if we are to avoid mere subjective impressions, the poetry itself must be understood as what it is. All this means that the New Testament must be read within appropriate contexts, both the ancient contexts of its original setting and helpful and supportive contemporary contexts today. It must be 'heard' within an acoustic which will allow its full overtones to stand out. It must be read with as little distortion as possible, and with as much sensitivity as possible to its different levels of meaning. It must be read so that the stories, and the Story, which it tells can be heard *as* stories, not as rambling ways of declaring unstoried 'ideas'. It must be read without the assumption that we already know what it is going to say, and without the arrogance that assumes that 'we'—whichever group that might be—already have ancestral rights over this or that passage, book, or writer. And, for full appropriateness, it must be read in such a way as to set in motion the drama which it suggests.[1]

[1] Based on Wright *NTPG*, 6.

Beginning Study of the New Testament

The New Testament is the very best book that ever was or ever will be known in the world.[1]

CHAPTER AT A GLANCE

This chapter describes how the New Testament consists of history, literature, and theology.

By the end of this chapter you should:

- understand that the New Testament drives us towards worship and mission;
- appreciate the importance of the interrelationship between history, literature, and theology for New Testament studies.

WHY THE NEW TESTAMENT?

Why should anyone spend time studying the contents of the New Testament? Why invest so much time in a relatively small collection of Greek texts? More precisely, exactly what is the New Testament *for* and what does that tell us about *how* we should study it?

I (N. T. Wright, henceforth NTW) own many different kinds of books. I have a lot of history books, and I love to find out more and more not only about what happened in the past but what it was like being there and the ways in which people thought and felt. I want to know what motivated them. I have a good many novels and books of short stories, and though they don't describe things that actually happened they encourage me to think about why people behave the way they do, not least why they get into the messes they do and what might be done about it. I even have quite a few books of plays—Shakespeare of course, but lots of others too: I enjoy the theatre, and if you let your imagination loose you can read the play at home and see it going on in your

---

1   Charles Dickens, *The Life of Our Lord*, cited in Howard 2012, 21.

mind's eye. It would be quite different, of course, if I knew I was going to be acting in a play: I would be reading it not just to learn my lines but to think into the different characters and get a sense of what it would be like to 'be' the person I'd be playing, and how I would relate to the others.

So we could go on, with poetry high on the list as well, and biography too. But there are plenty of quite different books which are really important to me. I have several atlases, partly for when I'm planning travel but also because I'm fascinated by the way different parts of the world relate to one another. Since my work involves different languages, I have several dictionaries which I use quite a lot. I enjoy golf, even though I'm not much good at it; I have quite a few books about the game, and how to play it better. I read these books but don't usually manage to obey them, or not thoroughly. I have a couple of books on car maintenance, a few books about how to make your garden look better, first-aid books for health emergencies, and so on.

Where do we fit the New Testament into all that? For some people, it seems to function at the level of car maintenance or garden tips, or even first-aid: it's a book to turn to when you need to know about a particular issue or problem. ('What does the Bible teach about *x*, *y*, or *z*?') For some, it's like a dictionary: a list of all the things you're supposed to know and believe about the Christian faith, or an atlas, helping you to find your way around the world without getting lost. This is what some people mean when they speak of the Bible being the ultimate 'authority', and so they study it as you might study a dictionary or atlas, or even a car manual.

Now that's not a bad thing. Perhaps it's better to start there than nowhere at all. But the puzzle is that the New Testament really doesn't look like that kind of book. If we assume, as I do, that the reason we have the New Testament the way it is is that this is what God wanted us to have—that this is what, by the strange promptings of the holy spirit, God enabled people like Paul and Luke and John and the others to write—then we should pay more attention to what it might mean that *this* sort of a book—or rather these sorts of books, because of course the New Testament contains many quite different books—is the one we've been given. Only when we do that will we really be living under its 'authority', discovering what that means in practice.

When we rub our eyes and think about this further, we discover that the New Testament includes all those other kinds of books as well: history, short stories which didn't happen but which open up new worlds (I'm thinking of the parables of Jesus in particular), biography, poetry, and much besides. And though none of the New Testament is written in the form of a play to be acted on stage, there is a strong sense in which that is precisely what it is.

Or rather, it's part of a play, the much larger play which consists of the whole Bible. The biblical drama is the heaven-and-earth story, the story of God and the world, of creation and covenant, of creation spoiled and covenant broken and then of covenant renewed and creation restored. The New Testament is the book where

Beginning Study of the New Testament

all this comes in to land, and it lands in the form of an invitation: this can be and should be *your* story, *my* story, the story which makes sense of us, which restores us to sense after the nonsense of our lives, the story which breathes hope into a world of chaos, and love into cold hearts and lives. The New Testament involves history, because it's the true story of Jesus and his first followers. It includes poetry, because there are some vital things you can only say that way. It contains biography, because the key to God's purposes has always been the humans who bear his image, and ultimately the One True Human who perfectly reflects his Image, Jesus himself. And yes, there are some bits which you can use like a dictionary or a car manual or a how-to-play-golf kind of book. But these mean what they mean, and function best as a result, within the larger whole. And when we study the New Testament it's the larger whole that ought to be our primary consideration.

So how do we fit into that larger whole? How do we understand the play, the real-life story of God and the world which reached its ultimate climax in Jesus of Nazareth and which then flows out, in the power of the spirit, to transform the world with his love and justice? How do we find our own parts and learn to play them? How do we let the poetry of the early Christians, whether it's the short and dense poems we find in Paul or the extended fantasy-literature of the book of Revelation, transform our imaginations so we can start to think in new ways about God and the world, about the powers that still threaten darkness and death, and about our role in implementing the victory of Jesus?

One central answer is that we must learn to *study* the New Testament for all it's worth, and that's what this whole book is designed to help us do. Jesus insisted that we should love God with our *minds*, as well as our hearts, our souls, and our strength. Devotion matters, but it needs direction; energy matters, but it needs information. That's why, in the early church, one of the most important tasks was *teaching*. Indeed, the Christian church has led the way for two thousand years in making education in general, and biblical education in particular, available to people of all sorts. A good many of the early Christians were functionally illiterate, and part of the glory of the gospel then and now is that it was and is for *everyone*. There shouldn't be an elite who 'get it' while everybody else is simply going along with the flow. So Jesus' first followers taught people to read so that they could be fully conscious of the part they were to play in the drama. That's why the New Testament was and is for everyone.

By contrast with most of the ancient world, early Christianity was very much a *bookish* culture. We sometimes think of the movement as basically a 'religion'; but a first-century observer, blundering in on a meeting of Christians, would almost certainly have seen them initially as belonging to some kind of educational institution. This is the more remarkable in that education in that world was mostly reserved for the rich, for the elite.

What's more, Jesus' first followers were at the forefront of a new kind of textual technology. From quite early on they used the codex, with sheets stuck together to comprise something like a modern book, rather than the scroll, which couldn't hold nearly so much and which was hard to use if you wanted to look up particular passages. In fact, though the codex had been in use already, the type the early Christians developed was more user-friendly than the earlier models. They really did want everyone to be able to read this vital and life-giving text.

Coptic fragment
2 Cor. 6:5–7 and 2 Pet. 2:4–5 and 7–9, Louvre Museum

This bookish culture, by the way, is why Christianity was a *translating* faith from the beginning. The movement went out very early on from circles where Aramaic was the main language into the larger Greek-speaking world. From there, it quickly moved north-west into Latin-speaking areas, and south and east into regions where Coptic or Ethiopic were dominant. And so on. So those dictionaries remain important too.

But, behind and beyond all that, the reason there's a New Testament at all is because of Jesus himself. Jesus never wrote anything, so far as we know. But what he did and said, and particularly his claim to be launching God's kingdom on earth as in heaven, and his vocation to die a horrible death to defeat the powers of darkness and bring God's new creation into being with his resurrection—all this meant what it meant within its original setting. And that setting was the ancient story of Israel, and the ongoing hopes and longings of the Jews of Jesus' day for God's coming kingdom that would bring that ancient story to its long-awaited conclusion. But, from quite early in the movement, most of Jesus' followers were not from that Jewish world. They needed to be told not only that 'Jesus died for your sins', but also that Jesus was Israel's Messiah and that the meaning of his death was the messianic meaning, to be found in the long story of Israel's scriptures: in other words, as Paul puts it, summarizing the very early 'gospel', that the *Messiah* died for our sins *in accordance with the scriptures*.[2] And to explain what that meant, and how it worked out in practice, four people took it prayerfully upon themselves to tell the story of Jesus in such a way as to bring out its different aspects. Several others, and one person in particular, namely Paul, wrote letters to churches which discussed particular issues but which did so by focusing that same larger story onto whatever needed to be addressed. And one man, out of persecution and prayer and a mind and heart soaked with the scriptures, was granted a breathtaking vision of heaven and earth coming together and Jesus at the middle of it all. Welcome to the New Testament.

So, from very early on, the followers of Jesus discovered that two things were happening. First, when they read these books they were drawn into a life of worship and prayer. The books are self-involving: like plays and poems they say, 'This is what's going on, these are the many dimensions that are drawn together; now come up on stage, learn your lines, and join in.' And the first thing to join in with is worship, the worship rooted in the worship of ancient Israel, not least the Psalms, but now reworked around Jesus and re-energized by his spirit. We can see this going on from many angles, whether it's Thomas saying 'My Lord and my God' (Jn. 20.28) or Paul framing one of his most difficult and painful discussions (Rom. 9—11) like a psalm, with lament at the start, praise at the end, and intercession in the middle. There are, in other words, specific elements of worship. But what really counts is the whole thing: the whole story of the gospels and Acts, the letters as wholes, the book of Revelation as a whole. This is God's story, and we ought to praise him for it and in it; to praise him by reading it, individually and together; to praise him by allowing it to shape our minds and hearts. The whole New Testament invites its readers to praise the God of creation and covenant for renewing the covenant and restoring creation through Jesus, Israel's Messiah and the world's rightful lord.

After all, the phrase 'New Testament' is simply a way of saying 'new covenant'. And a covenant isn't something you study at a distance. It's something you sign on for, or rather, something God calls you to be part of. The whole New Testament is written, not exactly to create the new world and the new-covenant relationship—God has done that in Jesus and is doing it in the spirit—but to tell the story of that new world, that new relationship, in such a way that we, the readers, are drawn into that relationship and that world. It is the world of worship: of lament, yes, of intercession, yes, but always and ultimately of praise. The New Testament exists because God wants to involve real humans, thinking, breathing, loving humans, in the ongoing work and life of the kingdom. If praise is to be directed aright—because there are many false trails, many misunderstandings, which can easily arise—then it is vital that we *study* the New Testament for all it's worth, the history, the maps,

---

2   1 Cor. 15.3.

the dictionary, the gardening manual, the lot. And especially the play. How does God's great drama work, and what part are we called to play in it? You'll only discover that as you study the book on the one hand, and, on the other hand, learn to worship God with your mind as well as your heart.

As we do this, a strange thing happens. Paul says in Colossians 3.10 that the gospel of Jesus will renew us in *knowledge* according to the creator's *image*. When we worship the true God, with that worship shaped by the story of Jesus seen as the fulfilment of Israel's scriptures, we find that we are being made into image-bearers, called to reflect God's love and purposes into the world. The first letter of Peter speaks of us being rescued from sin and death so that we can become 'a royal priesthood' (2.9), an ancient biblical way of summarizing the whole human vocation. We are to reflect the praises of creation back to the creator in worship; that's the 'priestly' bit. We are thereby becoming polished mirrors, set at an angle so as to reflect the powerful and healing love of the creator back into the world. That's the 'royal' bit.

The New Testament is therefore designed—designed, I would say, by the holy spirit!—to be the book which, when we read it, shapes and energizes and directs us not only for worship but also for *mission*. Worship and mission go hand in hand. Reading and studying the New Testament is the vital and non-negotiable means by which both are given their pattern and their power.

The New Testament, in other words, isn't there to tell us simply 'how to get to heaven'. Indeed, to the surprise of many people, that isn't what it's saying at all. That's why some theories about the New Testament and its authority don't work as well as they should. If you try to read it as a 'how-to' book, which sadly is how some people approach it, you may end up frustrated, thinking it would be better if the spirit had given us something more like a car manual or a railway timetable. No: the New Testament is designed to draw us into the story of God's plan, to rescue the world from chaos and idolatry and to launch his new transformative creation. This rescue, and this launch, have happened in Jesus; now, by the spirit, they are to be put into operation through people who are shaped by the biblical vision itself, by the stories of Jesus and his first followers, with ourselves joining in the movement those first followers began. The first Christians found themselves being formed into a community of generous love, bringing healing and hope to the poor and the sick, confronting the bullying powers of the world with a new way of being human. As we get to know the world of the first Christians, and the urgent things that Paul and the others wrote to them, we find ourselves being addressed and our faith built up. We find ourselves called to face suffering and challenges as they did themselves. Above all, we find ourselves called to shine like lights in the world of our own day.

The New Testament, then, is the manual of mission because it is first the manual of worship. We do not worship a distant or remote deity, but the God who made the world and is remaking it. Our mission is not to rescue souls away from the world, but to bring God's rescuing love and glory into every corner of creation. The New Testament tells the story of how, in Jesus, God reclaimed the ultimate saving sovereignty over the world. It tells this story in such a way as to draw us, too, into celebration and gratitude so that we cease to be passive spectators, and become part of that saving purpose in our own right (though always dependent on God's spirit).

This huge purpose and promise is itself vulnerable in the same way that a great work of art is vulnerable. People misunderstand it; they distort it for their own ends, or in the service of other forces and agendas. That happened in the first century, and it's happened ever since. The worship can become stale or self-congratulatory. The mission can become a mere religious veneer on a cultural or personal power-trip. And so on. That is why study, constant study, is vital. Every generation needs to be renewed in knowledge. Every part of the church needs to wake up to the whole larger story of what the New Testament is actually saying. That is why, we believe, a book like the present one is so important.

WHAT IS THE NEW TESTAMENT?

We've just discussed why the New Testament matters. Next, we have to ask: what is the New Testament made of? At one level, the answer is easy. The New Testament is made up of twenty-seven books, including various different genres. It was written by several different authors, and quite possibly edited by others as well. It came into existence in the historical period of the second half of the first century of the present era. It is seen by Christians of all sorts as, in some sense, inspired scripture.

Of course, knowing those facts about the New Testament does not really mean that you actually 'know' it in any meaningful sense. You might know that your mother's eyes are blue, her hair is auburn, she was born in 1965, she likes to drink Earl Grey tea, and she lives with two playful corgis in Newcastle. But telling that to a stranger on the bus will not enable the stranger really to *know* your mother. Really knowing her is far more than listing a lot of facts about her. Similarly, it is one thing to know what the New Testament is in a strictly material sense, but it is quite another to know what the New Testament is really about. Once we ask that question, some people might say it is a 'religious' book; some might say it is 'theological'. Others might want to use words like 'myth'; others again would insist that it is 'divine revelation'. These words can introduce all kinds of muddles. 'Religion', for instance, meant something quite different in the ancient world from what it means today. Many people in the first century might have thought the New Testament was teaching a kind of philosophy; that it was a sort of 'community manual' for a new kind of human life and lifestyle. 'Theology', too, has changed its meaning over time. Certainly the New Testament has some remarkable, even shocking and dramatic, things to say about God, and about God's relationship to the world and particularly to humans. The word 'myth' has so many senses that it's probably no use to us at the moment, though we may come back to it. And anyone who sees the New Testament as 'divine revelation' is bound to face the question: in what sense can these first-century stories, letters, and visions be seen that way?

In fact, the question 'What is the New Testament?' would probably need an expert panel of authorities to answer it properly. Supposing we could use a time machine to go back in history and assemble together several prominent Greeks, Romans, and Jews from antiquity. Supposing we got them to sit around a large table for a group discussion on these questions. Let's make it a serious discussion; we wouldn't snatch just anyone from the streets of Rome or Athens. We would want people with known expertise, related to the fields of ancient history, literature, and discussions of 'the gods' and their relation to the world. We would need people who could reflect meaningfully, discuss vigorously, and debate passionately.

We could put together quite an interesting list of such participants. On the Greek side, we would want Homer, the author of the epic works the *Iliad* and *Odyssey*. We would find the Athenian general-cum-historian Thucydides a marvellous candidate to include. We would want philosophers like Plato, Aristotle, Diogenes, and Plutarch for some intellectual spice. Coming to the Romans, we are again spoiled for choice. We would have to insist on picking Virgil, who was lauded for his Latin poetry and his literary masterpiece the *Aeneid* which provided the mythical story about the founding of Rome and the advent of the Augustan dynasty. Almost as fine a poet, but very different in his worldview, would be the Epicurean Lucretius. From among Roman historians, we would want both Tacitus and Suetonius for their perspectives on the empire and its leaders. Then also Cicero and Seneca, powerful men who shaped the political, literary, and philosophical worlds of their day, and who met their ends by being too close to political power when things turned bad.

Plato, Vatican Museum

Many Jewish representatives would be pressing for a place on our list. The scribe and sage Ben-Sirach would be high on the list for his love of God, Torah, and Wisdom. You would have to include the Alexandrian philosopher Philo, and the historian Josephus; they are in

Aristotle, National Museum of Rome

fact among our best sources for the Jewish world of the first century. The 'Teacher of Righteousness', who founded (or perhaps refounded) the sectarian group at Qumran where the Dead Sea Scrolls were discovered, would have plenty to say. So would Rabbi Akiba, one of the greatest Jewish teachers of all time, known for his monotheistic piety and famous martyrdom in the early second century.

Let us imagine, then, that we could give each member of our colloquy a copy of the New Testament to read and ponder for a few days, and then bring them back together for an evening of energetic discussion on what they think they have been reading about. What would they say?

We can picture Thucydides, Josephus, Tacitus, and Suetonius all being mesmerized by the gospel of Luke and the parallel book we call Acts, with their striking biographical accounts of Jesus and Paul and their scenic historiography of the early church. They would understand the idea of 'history with a purpose'. Josephus in particular would see the point of documents that claimed to be drawing the long history of Israel to a glorious climax—though he would be sceptical about the idea of a crucified and risen Messiah. We can overhear Plato, Philo, and Cicero discussing the meaning of 'equal with God' in Philippians 2.6, and whether a phrase like that could apply to a human being besides the emperor and if so what it might mean, politically as well as theologically. Diogenes might be fascinated with Jesus' command to his disciples to take nothing with them in their missionary travels other than a staff; it would remind him of how the Cynic philosophers used to look (Mk. 6.8–9/Mt. 10.9–10/Lk. 9.3). The 'Teacher of Righteousness' from Qumran might oscillate between delight and rage as he read through the gospel of John, encouraged by the indictment of the Pharisees, but affronted by the depiction of Jesus as the son of God. Homer (who, being reputedly blind, would have had to have someone read to him) might be seen sitting in a corner scratching his head over the book of Revelation, understanding the idea of a 'war in heaven' (Rev. 12.7) from his own writings, but puzzled over the theology and cosmology with which John the Seer has framed his account of heavenly discord. Seneca might well regard Paul's ode to love in 1 Corinthians 13.1–13 as one of the most sublime pieces of rhetoric he'd ever read—but he wouldn't understand what Paul meant when comparing the present and the future worlds.

Tacitus, senator and historian of the Roman Empire, *c.* AD 56–120

The conversations would go on. And if these illustrious figures of antiquity were asked about what kind of book they were reading, what kind of writing it was, or what the thrust of its contents was, I suspect that their answers would be mixed. In the end, however, their conclusions would probably converge around three things: history, literature, and theology. These writings, they would recognize, claim to be based on real people and real events. They employ different styles and genres which have at least partial analogues in the wider worlds of their day. And they all assume the existence and living activity of a creator God, the God of Israel, claiming that this God has now acted decisively and uniquely in the man Jesus. There might be other categories, too: philosophy, politics, and even economics come to mind. 'Religion', to repeat, is too muddled a category to be much use. History, literature, and theology, held together in a new kind of creative tension, are the best starting-points to help us understand what sort of thing the New Testament actually is.

KEEPING HISTORY, LITERATURE, AND THEOLOGY TOGETHER

These three elements comprising history ('the past'), literature ('the text'), and theology ('understanding God and the world') are all sewn together into the fabric of the New Testament. And yet, what we find as whole cloth in the text—a historically situated discourse about God and the world, in various literary forms—can be violently torn asunder by readers who are afraid that too much history, or too much literature, or too much theology might prove that their mighty edifices of scholarship and piety have been built on a foundation of sand. It has been all too easy for some interpreters to highlight one of the trio: history *or* literature *or* theology—and to discard the rest.

Those focused on historical truth as the only real truth would happily sell theology and literature into slavery in the same way that Judah and his brothers sold Joseph to the Ishmaelites. Some, however, care neither for history nor for theology, and simply want to gaze at the literary beauty of the text, blissfully insulated from the torrid debates of historicity and theology, much as David gazed upon Bathsheba while shutting out the realities of the world and his wider responsibilities. Others, unwilling to face the possibility that the truth about a transcendent God might be uniquely unveiled in the accidental facts of history, cling to their theology like the Sadducees holding on to their dogmas, and eject history and literature in much the same way that Paul and Barnabas were ejected from Antioch, Iconium, and Lystra.

Thus, as with any other academic discipline these days, the guild of New Testament studies has more cliques than a Hollywood Oscar party. A-list historians don't want to be seen alongside B-list literary theorists; nobody wants to appear on the cover of *People* magazine standing next to a theologian, not that the theologians

Lookout from Masada

would want to be there anyway. Unfortunately, even when interdisciplinary studies are all the rage, there is a kind of methodological snobbery which remains firmly in place. New Testament scholars can be notoriously dismissive of other sub-disciplines, and tend towards microscopic specialization within their own fields. As Markus Bockmuehl puts it, 'Scholars tend to concern themselves with primary and secondary literature only in their own postage-stamp-sized bailwick.'[3]

It is better, though riskier, to see history, literature, and theology as belonging together. To continue our whimsical biblical parellels, we might liken this to the three friends in Daniel 3 who testified together to God's kingdom in the face of a megalomaniac monarch. The New Testament *is* history *and* literature *and* theology, all at once, and we should not try to reduce it to any one of these at the expense of the others. A close reading and thick description of the New Testament will necessarily involve the messy business of history, the hard work of literary criticism, and the arduous task of theological reflection.

As such, an informed reading of the New Testament, especially for a believing audience, will involve pursuing three main questions. First, the historical one: how did Christianity begin, and why did it take the shape that it did? Second, the literary one: why did the early Jesus-followers write the way they did, and what does this tell us about their worldview? Third, the theological question: what did the early Christians believe about God and the world, and about humans in general and Jesus in particular within that, and what kind of sense might their beliefs make? This volume will not answer all those questions in full. But, as we survey the New Testament writings, the present book offers a first guiding step on how to think about them.

3   Bockmuehl 2006, 35.

Further reading

Blomberg, Craig. 2004. *Making Sense of the New Testament: Three Crucial Questions.* Grand Rapids, MI: Baker.

Bockmuehl, Markus. 2006. *Seeing the Word: Refocusing New Testament Study.* Grand Rapids, MI: Baker.

Moule, C. F. D. 1967. *The Phenomenon of the New Testament.* London: SCM.

Wright, N. T. 1992. *The New Testament and the People of God.* COQG 1; London: SPCK, pp. 1–28.

——. 2011. *Scripture and the Authority of God: How to Read the Bible Today.* New York: HarperOne.

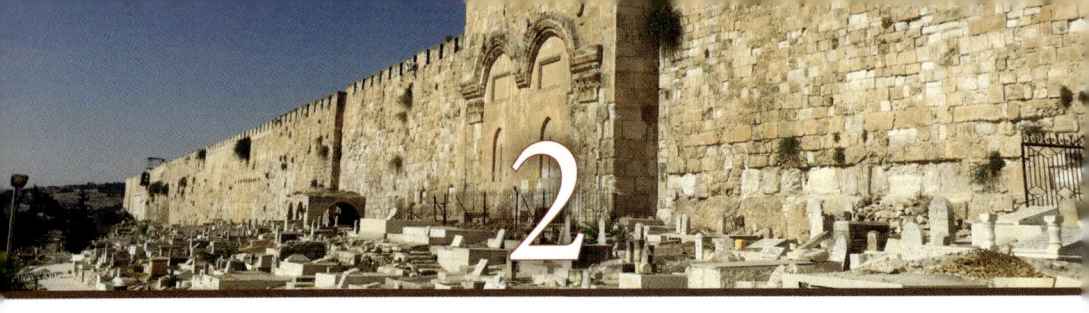

The New Testament as History

The past is a foreign country: they do things differently there.[1]

CHAPTER AT A GLANCE

This chapter explains how the New Testament is a historical source for reconstructing the historical Jesus, for identifying the impression that Jesus made upon his earliest followers, and for mapping the formation of the early church.

By the end of this chapter you should be able to:

- articulate the importance of history for New Testament studies;
- understand the complex problems inherent in trying to excavate history from ancient texts like the New Testament;
- appreciate a critical-realist epistemology as a way of exploring historical questions.

READING THE NEW TESTAMENT AS A HISTORICAL DOCUMENT

Christians have ordinarily claimed that God has decisively revealed himself, not in the realm of existential consciousness, not in the recess of religious feelings, but in the life, death, and resurrection of Jesus of Nazareth. In other words, God has acted within the space-time universe, specifically in the dirt and drama of first-century Palestine, to make good on his covenant promises to Israel by sending his son in the likeness of human flesh. If so, as George Caird used to say, 'Christianity appeals to history, and to history it must go.'[2]

Sadly some will object to this historical enterprise, like a teenager complaining about being made to catalogue the boxes of parental memorabilia in the basement. For many grumblers the historical task seems irrelevant to their own situation: historical events might have provided the foundations for the church, they think, but no-one invests much time inspecting the foundations when there are prayers to pray, sermons to write, the elderly to visit, and services to prepare. Others will complain, not so much about the time-consuming nature of the task, but about the contents they have to pick through.

1 Hartley, 1976 [1953], 7.
2 Caird 1965a, 3.

How can Iron Age texts possibly be relevant in the Internet Age? Whatever people think the texts once 'meant', it is mostly irrelevant to the 'meanings' that we ascribe to them now—or the fresh insights we believe we possess in our own day.

Yet in counter-point to such recalcitrance, the reason why we engage in a study of the history of the New Testament is because of the conviction that Jesus and the apostles constitute the basis for normative Christianity. This 'normativity' emerges from the belief that God has revealed himself in the historical events behind the New Testament, in the writings that make up the New Testament, and in the experiences evoked by the New Testament (see 'Emails from the edge: NT history'). This belief grows out of the ineradicable Christian conviction, held from very early times, that being a Christian means living, believing, and behaving in some sort of continuity with the New Testament (and the Old Testament!). This belief gained additional momentum as a result of the Protestant Reformation, when the principle of *sola scriptura* was articulated, placing the Bible in the position of supreme authority. Reading the New Testament, it has always been felt within Protestantism, is where the Christian begins, and in doing so he or she is equipped, challenged, reinforced, and given a sound basis for belief and life. If that is the case, then study of the New Testament in the context of the early church is a necessary part of Christian discipleship.

EMAILS
from the edge

From: Alan_Daley@aol.com
To: Professor Dana Schuler
Date: Sat, 16 Jan 2016 at 10:02 p.m.
Subject: NT history

Dear Prof.,

I'm a bit confused about the paper you told us to write: 'How Does Knowing Historical Background Help Us to Understand Mark 12.14–17?' I mean, when Jesus says, 'Render to Caesar the things that are Caesar's' (KJV), surely he means Christian folks should simply be honest and pay their taxes. What else is there to understand? Sorry, but I just don't see the point of the question.

Thanks
AD

From:	Professor Dana Schuler
To:	Alan_Daley@aol.com
Date:	Mon, 18 Jan 2016 at 2:25 p.m.
Subject:	Re: NT history

Dear Alan,

Sorry to disappoint you, but this is one passage where knowing some historical background is crucial.

First, remember that the question is actually a trap set for Jesus by the Pharisees and Herodians, not a sincere question about whether Jews (let alone Christians) should be upright tax-payers. How does the trap work? Well, if you read Josephus (*Ant.* 18.23; *Wars* 2.118; 7.410) you'll see that some zealous Galileans had a motto, 'No king but God', and since paying taxes to Caesar meant recognizing him as king, paying taxes was in fact a type of blasphemy or cowardly betrayal of their religion. So when Jesus is asked about paying taxes to Caesar, he's put in a Catch-22. If he says, 'Yes, pay them', Jesus will look like he's compromised and sold out. If he says 'No, don't pay them', then the Herodians can have him arrested on charges of sedition as forbidding the payment of taxes, which was an offence—precisely the claim they fabricated against Jesus at his trial (see Lk. 23.2).

Second, notice Jesus' response: he doesn't try to bluff his way through an answer. Instead, he requests a denarius, and asks, 'Whose image and inscription are on it?' (See attached image.) Now various coins were minted in Palestine, mostly without imperial images, usually with floral designs; only Pontius Pilate printed coins depicting pagan cultic utensils (see Kindler 1973, 37–8, 94–103). But this denarius is probably a Tiberian tribute penny which had on one side an 'image' of Tiberius's bust with an inscription that read, 'Son of the divine Augustus'; then on the other side it said 'High priest', accompanied by a depiction of Tiberius's mother Livia posing as the goddess Roma. The rub is that if Caesar is 'divine', and if this is his image, then it is a violation of the second commandment (see Ex. 20.4; Dt. 5.8). In other words, Jesus is saying, you guys are carrying around pagan money which is an affront to our religion, so give the pagan king back his pagan money.

Third, perhaps there is even more to it. Perhaps Jesus is saying that Caesar should receive taxes because he should get EVERYTHING that he deserves, and he means everything!

> Much like how the father of Judas Maccabaeus could urge his fellow-Judeans to 'Pay back the Gentiles in full'—by which he meant violent retribution (1 Macc. 2.68)! So, far from acquiescing to the view that Jews or Christians should pay taxes, Jesus is being subversive, affirming a critique of pagan power over Israel, and avoiding the trap set for him.
>
> Now do you see the value of historical background knowledge?
>
> The grace be with you
> Prof. Dana Schuler

When it comes to doing history, an emerging problem we have to wrestle with is that since the Enlightenment what counts as 'history' has been very much conditioned by purported 'laws' that have no place for God and (what has come to be called) the 'supernatural'. (In earlier times the 'supernatural' was an extra dimension that enhanced the 'natural' world, not an alternative to it.) Consequently many historians are quite happy to write off 'god' and the description of his actions as the mythic husk that must be peeled away so that the historical kernel behind Christian origins can finally be exposed. As a result, many Christians are somewhat afraid of history, frightened that if we really find out what happened in the first century our faith might collapse. The problem is that without historical enquiry there is no check on Christianity's propensity to remake Jesus, never mind the Christian 'God', in its own image. Equally, much Christianity is afraid of scholarly learning, and insofar as the Enlightenment programme was an anti-dogma venture, Christianity has often responded by retreating into the safe space of a 'confession', a self-reinforcing church circle. But, granted that learning without love is sterile and dry, enthusiasm without learning can easily become blind arrogance. Again, much Christianity has been afraid of reducing a 'supernatural' faith to rationalist categories. But, as I have just suggested, the sharp distinction between the 'supernatural' and the 'rational' *is itself a product of Enlightenment thinking*, and to emphasize the 'supernatural' at the expense of the 'rational' or 'natural' is itself to capitulate to the Enlightenment worldview at a deeper level than if we were merely to endorse, rather than marginalize, a post-Enlightenment rationalist programme. Thankfully there is a better way for us to be proper New Testament historians.

There is no time to offer a full-sized philosophy of historiography, or to provide a detailed map of historical methodology.

Tiberian denarius
Jay King Collection

Others have plotted how that task might be done, and done, moreover, within a supposedly 'open' universe where theism can be part of the wider reality.[3] The rationalistic positivism spawned by 'modernity' supposed that historical truth was accessible simply by laying down your epistemological foundations and setting up your methodological machinery, producing a God's-eye view of history ironically unfettered by the interventions of any god. In contrast, we must remember that there is no 'neutral' or 'objective' history out there to be found. The hope of discovering anything like that was always a figment of the post-Enlightenment imagination. There is no such thing as uninterpreted history nor the possibility of discovering something 'as it really happened' in some neutral sense. Everything in history, including our earliest sources as well as the latest historical analyses thereof, is already enmeshed in an interpretative process. There is no point of view which is nobody's point of view. This does not, of course, mean capitulating to 'postmodernity', with the notion that all knowledge is not only conditioned but also, at the end of the day, artificial. Postmodernists proclaim that no-one sees things as they are, only as they appear to be. Consequently, there is no grand story of history, only local stories that collide, collude, and coalesce. For postmodernists, there is no naked history to be found, only a plethora of historical interpretations to be laid out and compared, with subtextual power-games in the sources waiting to be unmasked, and—in some cases—with drunken celebrations of diversity and *différence* to be held along the French Riviera.

Between the Scylla and Charybdis of 'modernity' and 'postmodernity' is *critical realism*. This is a way of describing the process of 'knowing' that acknowledges the *reality of the thing known, as something other than the knower* (hence 'realism'), while also fully acknowledging that the only access we have to this reality lies along the spiralling path of *appropriate dialogue or conversation between the knower and the thing known* (hence 'critical'). This path leads to critical reflection on the products of our enquiry into 'reality', so that our assertions about 'reality' acknowledge their own provisionality. Knowledge, in other words, although in principle concerning realities independent of the knower, is never itself independent of the knower.[4]

To give an analogy, consider three windows. Modernity liked to think of itself as looking through a transparent window that allowed one to see perfectly through to the other side as long as it was sunny (that is, truth is easily found if you have good

---

[3] See discussion in McKnight 2005, 3–46; Sheppard 2012; Deines, Ocles, and Watts 2013.
[4] For a similar approach see Schnelle 2005, 26–30. Thiselton 2015, 265, provides a concise explanation of critical realism for beginners. For an introduction to the philosophy of critical realism, including its association with philosopher Roy Bhaskar, see Kaldis 2013, 790–1. Very helpful too, though somewhat more advanced, is the collection of essays in López and Potter 2001 about critical realism as an alternative to both positivism and postmodernism. On the relevance of critical realism to New Testament studies, see Meyer 1989 and 1994; Denton 2004, 80–90, 210–25; and Stewart 2008, 77–112; for Christian theology, see Lonergan 1972; Vanhoozer 1998, 299–303; McGrath 2006, 195–244; and A. Wright 2013; for science and theology, see Losch 2009.

sources and good methods). Postmodernity is basically saying that the window is really a mirror and all you see is little more than your own reflection, though you may get lucky if you unconsciously peer through one of the cracks and catch a glimpse of something behind the mirror (that is, truth may be out there, but you'll have a hard time telling it apart from your own reflection). Critical realism says that the mirror has a dark tint caused by the gaps in our knowledge and the shading of our own location, and that part of our own reflection does indeed appear on the window, but we really can see something through it that is not ourselves, nor part of our own making (that is, truth can be seen, but never crisply or perfectly). Modernity exalted itself in claims of incorrigible certainty (and claimed that what you couldn't have certainty about either didn't matter or didn't exist). Postmodernity basked in ambiguity and irony, exposing power-games real and imaginary. Critical realism aims to provide clarity and sobriety to the historical task.

> **OZYMANDIAS**
>
> I met a traveller from an antique land,
> Who said—'Two vast and trunkless legs of stone
> Stand in the desert . . . Near them, on the sand,
> Half sunk a shattered visage lies, whose frown,
> And wrinkled lip, and sneer of cold command,
> Tell that its sculptor well those passions read
> Which yet survive, stamped on these lifeless things,
> The hand that mocked them, and the heart that fed;
> And on the pedestal, these words appear:
> My name is Ozymandias, King of Kings;
> Look on my Works, ye Mighty, and despair!
> Nothing beside remains. Round the decay
> Of that colossal Wreck, boundless and bare
> The lone and level sands stretch far away.'
> *(Percy Bysshe Shelley, 1818)*

The need for critical realism should be clear. Modernity lauded itself, much like the builders of the tower of Babel, for its progressive ascent towards a God's-eye view of the world, stressing the accumulative acquisition of knowledge in the sciences by an academy of so-called disinterested observers. However, it was two European wars, the discovery of non-western ways of thinking, the realization that science rests on paradigms rather than on brute facts, and the 'linguistic turn' (which showed how language shapes ideas) that made people realize that the modernist assertion to have a monopoly on absolute truth was naive at best and arrogant at worst. It was much like the boastful claims of the ancient king 'Ozymandias' described in Percy Shelley's famous poem. In the poem, Ozymandias makes self-adulating boasts about the greatness of his empire, but his kingdom, and indeed his statue, is later found in ruins. The only thing he is then remembered for is not his greatness but his arrogance. Similarly, the modernists' claim to be able to attain indisputable facts has become a shattered visage that memorializes their failure (see box: 'Ozymandias').

Postmodernity then came running through the streets like Nietzsche's madman Zarathustra, shouting that God is dead and truth with him! If so, history is never found, it is written by the victor, and its meaning is imposed by the historian.

Meaning does not exist in texts or in artefacts; it is purely in the eye of the beholder. Works such as Tacitus's *Annals* or Josephus's *War of the Jews* have no inherent meaning, only what we assign to them. Thus, history is more like art than fact; it is aesthetic rather than scientific. If there is no meaning in history or in texts, then the motto might be that 'everything is permissible'. Whether one believes Jesus was a messianic claimant or a Cynic-like philosopher is less about genuine evidence and more about ideological tastes. Understandably, postmodernity became a great way of using the indeterminacy of language and the conditionality of all knowledge to dismantle the permanent structures of human existence and to replace them with a convenient vacuum that was conducive to a particular social project that could deflect any criticism of itself as merely the attempt to reinstate the old modernist regime.[5] Even worse, as José López and Garry Potter argue about postmodernity:

> The alleged loss of hegemonic meanings in the social world were (sic) not so much explained but reproduced in texts through all type[s] (sic) of narrative and rhetorical strategies. This led to a type of writing, and argumentation, which was rich and seductive, dense almost mystical. A type of writing that celebrated ambiguity, and enthroned irony. A type of writing that, at its worst, demanded little in terms of evidence, and argumentative coherence and consistency; the playfulness of language took precedence.[6]

In contrast to this, the critical realist says that there is something in the text to be known, and something in history to be found, even if the knowing and finding is never infallible. The alternative to *absolute* claims is not *anarchic* interpretation but an *adequate* knowledge attained by a critical interaction between the subject and object of study.[7] One can believe in a thing called 'history' without thinking that one has full possession of it. (This discussion can become confusing, because the word 'history' itself is used both for 'things that happened in the past' and for 'things that people write about what happened in the past', and indeed for other things, like the

---

5   For example, the scholars participating in the Postmodern Bible Project are unapologetically explicit in this aim (Aichele 1995, 2–3, 15), seeing themselves as radical: '[B]y sweeping away secure notions of meaning, by radically calling into question the apparently stable foundations of meaning on which traditional interpretation is situated, by raising doubts about the capacity to achieve ultimate clarity about the meaning of a text, postmodern readings lay bare the contingent and constructed character of meaning itself. Moreover, by challenging traditional interpretations that claim universality, completeness, and supremacy over other interpretations, postmodern readings demonstrate that traditional interpretations are themselves enactments of domination or, in simpler terms, power plays.' They claim to be 'certain that the future of biblical criticism hinges squarely on its ability and willingness to make gender, race, ideology, and institutional power substantive concerns—which means a change in its institutional structures, discourses, and practices.'
6   López and Potter 2001, 5.
7   Vanhoozer 1998, 139.

entire sweep of all events past, present, and future, or the scholar's task ['doing history'] in researching all of these.) After all, knowledge, including historical knowledge, is provisional and open to correction. Even the well-tested hypotheses of the hard sciences remain just that: well-tested hypotheses. The relativity of all historical knowledge is no insurmountable barrier to the realism of the past. If so, then the gas chambers of Auschwitz are not a discourse to be interpreted according to one's wishes, nor a text to be deconstructed at one's pleasure; the Holocaust was an event with a context and an after-effect, which is retrievable and intelligible.[8] So, for the critical-realist historian, history is there, independent and accessible, yet it is indescribable apart from the interpretative schemes used to understand it.[9] We may accordingly consider historical hypotheses about the past to be justified and warranted when they exhibit explanatory power to account for all of the known variables or until new data emerges, or new interpretative schemes appear, that force current hypotheses and interpretations to be revised.

Passover scene, Barcelona Haggadah, fourteenth century, The British Library
© British Library Board. All Rights Reserved / Bridgeman Images

But what counts as a justified hypothesis or a warranted belief when it comes to history? One needs a large framework on which to draw, a way of describing the coherence of people and events in their own context. There must always be a leap, made by an imagination that has been attuned sympathetically to the subject-matter, to form a hypothesis, *a story*, that explains the phenomena before us. Stories, after all, are one of the most basic modes of human life and are a characteristic expression of worldview. Human life is constituted by a series of stories, implicit and explicit, that makes sense of experiences, and allows us to describe them in a coherent manner. Consider the story recited at every Passover:

---
8 See Esler 2005, 74–5.
9 Vanhoozer 1998, 322–3.

> My father was a wandering Aramean, and he went down into Egypt with a few people and lived there and became a great nation, powerful and numerous. But the Egyptians ill-treated us and made us suffer, subjecting us to harsh labour. Then we cried out to the Lord, the God of our ancestors, and the Lord heard our voice and saw our misery, toil and oppression. So the Lord brought us out of Egypt with a mighty hand and an outstretched arm, with great terror and with signs and wonders. He brought us to this place and gave us this land, a land flowing with milk and honey . . . [10]

This story is a summation of the events and experiences that define the Jewish people, which speaks to their beliefs, identity, and hopes. As historians, then, we are principally storytellers, trying to get inside the storied lives of ancient peoples—filled with diverse and often competing stories—and constructing our own successful explanatory story to account for theirs.

The relevance of this for our historical enquiry into the New Testament is that we find ourselves describing a certain group of first-century Jews, namely the 'early Christians', who held one particular variant of the first-century Jewish worldview. This strange group was saying in effect, 'The hope which characterizes our worldview has been fulfilled in these events.' And they chose to say this in the most natural and most obviously Jewish way they knew, by telling a *story*—from gospel to apocalypse—encoding in a narrative the sum of their worldview and beliefs. Therefore, a chief task of New Testament study is to construct a hypothesis which explains the story of the first Christians within the storied world of Jews, Greeks, and Romans. This critical-realist theory of story and hypothesis accordingly acknowledges the essentially 'storied' nature of human knowing, thinking, and living, within the larger framework of worldviews. It affirms, in fact, that all knowledge of realities external to oneself takes place within a worldview-framework, within which stories form an essential part. In the end, our task is to construct a hypothesis, a story encompassing the beliefs, aims, identity, praxes, and hopes that constituted the early church's own story, and to show that this hypothesis makes good sense of the evidence and does so in a clear and coherent way, with such simplicity as is appropriate for the dense subject-matter of actual human life.

What does all this mean for the student who wants to wrestle with the New Testament? Several things. (1) Remember that the study of the New Testament as history is not an optional extra. It is a crucial part of any course in 'biblical studies'. (2) You need to be aware of the complexities of what it means to 'do history' (it isn't simply about 'looking up facts in a book'), and critical realism is a way of attempting to acknowledge the possibility of historical retrieval while fully recognizing the

---

10 Dt. 26.5–9.

limitations of the historical enterprise. (3) The past is a very different place. You cannot just jump from Atlanta to Antioch or leap from Rochester to Rome without doing some serious historical, hermeneutical, cultural, and social studies along the way. You will need to roll up your sleeves and be prepared to get your hands dirty.

Further reading

McKnight, Scot. 2005. *Jesus and His Death: Historiography, the Historical Jesus, and Atonement Theory*. Waco, TX: Baylor University Press, pp. 3–46.

Meyer, Ben F. 1989. *Critical Realism and the New Testament*. Allison Park, PA: Pickwick.

Stewart, Robert B. 2008. *The Quest of the Hermeneutical Jesus: The Impact of Hermeneutical Issues on the Jesus Research of John Dominic Crossan and N. T. Wright*. Lanham, MD: University Press of America.

Wright, N. T. 1992. *The New Testament and the People of God*. COQG 1; London: SPCK, pp. 81–120.

Western Wall, Jerusalem Temple Mount

3

The New Testament as Literature

The task of hermeneutics is to clarify this miracle of understanding, which is not a mysterious communion of souls, but sharing in a common meaning.[1]

CHAPTER AT A GLANCE

This chapter describes how the New Testament is a piece of ancient literature which requires a robust understanding of hermeneutics in order to properly understand it.

By the end of this chapter you should be able to:

- understand the significance and limitations of authorial intent for finding meanings;
- grasp the significance and limitations of a text for forming meanings;
- explain the significance and limitations of readers in the process of fostering meanings;
- appreciate the need to fuse the horizons of author, text, and reader in order to construct a robust reading strategy.

READING THE NEW TESTAMENT AS A LITERARY ARTEFACT

The study of early Christianity, especially the theology of the whole movement and of key individuals within it, is conducted by means of the study of literature. (The only exceptions to this rule are the occasional relevant coin, inscription, or other archaeological find. Some parts of ancient history have plenty of such 'material evidence', but the early Jesus-followers, who neither minted coins nor carved inscriptions, didn't leave such things behind them.) The New Testament is literature, not simply a pile of propositional nuggets waiting to be ordered into a systematic theology, nor an inchoate sequence of words designed to activate religious feelings. We must therefore enquire, in general terms at least, what literature does, how it works, and how best to treat it. This conclusion presses particularly upon us at a time when the incoming tide of literary theory has reached the

---

[1] Gadamer 1975, 292.

point on the beach where the theologians have been playing, and, having filled their sandcastle moats with water, is now almost in danger of forcing them to retreat, unless they dig deeper and build more strongly. That is to say, theologians need to take seriously the challenges proposed by literary theorists as to how texts generate and interrelate with beliefs.

A proper place to start is with the idea of 'meaning' itself.[2] What do we mean when we say that biblical texts have meaning? What are we looking for? Where do we find it? Here we enter into the morass of debate about where 'meaning' resides: is it ultimately with the author, or with the text, or with the reader, or some combination of all three?

THE AUTHOR

Once upon a time, the quest for 'meaning' was thought to be coterminous with identifying *authorial intent*. When we know what an author meant—that is, when we uncover his or her intentions and the reactions that he or she was trying to activate in the original readers—then we know what a text 'means', or at least 'meant'. So the author embeds meaning in the text by encoding it in words and symbols which are then decoded by the reader:

author ⟶ text ⟶ reader

There are, however, problems associated with equating meaning with authorial intention. For a start, ancient authors spoke a different language from us. They lived in a vastly different culture; they understood their universe very differently from how we understand ours. Because of the historical differences and cultural chasm between ancient authors and modern readers, we cannot naively assume that a text is an automatic window into an author's mind. Even the most optimistic of readers will struggle to identify the authorial intention behind Mark's cryptic description of the young man who fled naked from the Garden of Gethsemane.[3] It is equally true that interpreters will have to concede that they are really doing guesswork in trying to figure out what Paul meant when he said that 'women will be saved through childbearing'.[4] And that is without even venturing into notoriously obscure passages like Matthew's citation of a prophetic text, which no-one can identify, that asserts that God's servant will be called a 'Nazarene', or the piling of apocalyptic metaphor upon metaphor in John the Seer's vision of a woman clothed with celestial apparel

---

2   See Spinks 2007 for current debates as it relates to theology and meaning.
3   Mk. 14.51–52.
4   1 Tim. 2.15.

being chased by a red dragon.[5] People who claim that they know for certain what the author's intention was in writing these things are simply kidding themselves. The texts are opaque; so interpreters sometimes become befuddled. This simply reinforces what we all instinctively know, namely, that readers, even good readers, are often genuinely perplexed as to what an author was trying to say. So what is the point of identifying 'meaning' with an authorial intention when we cannot guarantee we can identify it with any real confidence? That is why literary critics in the 1940s spoke of the 'Intentional Fallacy', arguing that meaning cannot be tied to authorial intent. This led to the radical literary critics of the 1960s, who, when forming 'meaning', referred to the 'Death of the Author'. The meaning is in the mind of the reader or hearer.

But it gets even worse for those who prize authorial intention. Texts can carry surplus meaning beyond the author's consciousness. Any writing can become more significant as it enters new social, political, and religious spaces. So, what if authors wrote about things that took on a life of their own, long after they were gone? What if people attribute meanings to a text that at one level appears to be based on that text but at another level obviously exceed the author's original intention? For a case in point, consider the fourth Servant Song of Isaiah 52.13—53.12 as an example of literary meaning going beyond authorial intent. The original author (leaving to one side the question of multiple authorship in 'Isaiah' as a whole) may well have envisioned the 'Servant' as a symbolic representation of exiled Israel, projected onto and summed up in the life of the prophet (see especially Isa. 49.1–7). In contrast, early Christian authors seem rather unanimous in identifying the 'Servant' as Jesus and regard this as the proper *scriptural* meaning of the text when seen in the light of the story of Jesus' life, death, and resurrection. (We note at the same time that Paul frequently applied the figure of the 'Servant' to himself, as Jesus' chosen 'apostle to the Gentiles'.[6]) As such, in Luke's narrative Jesus at the Last Supper recites the words 'And he was numbered with the transgressors' from Isaiah 53.12 as a prophetic prediction of his forthcoming Passion.[7] When Peter wanted to explain the atoning nature of Jesus' death, he delved into Isaiah 53.4–6:

> 'He himself bore our sins' in his body on the cross, so that we might die to sins and live for righteousness; 'by his wounds you have been healed.' For 'you were like sheep going astray,' but now you have returned to the Shepherd and Overseer of your souls.[8]

---

[5] Mt. 2.23; Rev. 12.1–17.
[6] Rom. 10.14–16; 15.21; 2 Cor. 6.2; Gal. 1.15–16; 2.2; Phil. 2.16; 1 Thess. 3.5; cf. Acts 13.47. See further Gignilliat 2007; Aernie 2012.
[7] Lk. 22.37.
[8] 1 Pet. 2.24–25.

In both cases, for Luke and Peter, it is crystal clear that Isaiah 53 is, in its truest sense, actually about Jesus, not (or not solely) about an eighth- or fifth-century BC prophet who was called to solidarity with the exiled nation.[9]

This is akin to what is called in patristic exegesis the *sensus plenior* ('fuller sense') of scripture, by which an 'inspired' text actually says more than the author realized at the time. The recognition of such a sense, and the possibilities for allegorical and theological exegesis that it opens up, have at various stages of the church's reading of scripture been ways of allowing for the experience of Christians who affirm that the biblical text 'speaks' to them in ways that the author might not have imagined. Along this line we find Augustine, for whom the truth of scripture was not simply a matter of detecting authorial intention; the author is not directly available for interrogation, and, even if he were, we have no way of knowing whether to believe him. So for Augustine, 'meaning' also derives from the 'inward Truth' arrived at by spiritual study, which hopefully accords with an author's intention but is not bound to it.[10] Let us not forget either that C. S. Lewis, the great Christian apologist and literary critic, said, 'An author doesn't necessarily understand the meaning of his own story better than anyone else.'[11] Theologians have been looking for biblical meaning beyond the cusp of an author's mind for centuries.

One way to get around this seeming disparity between Isaiah's intention and a Christian's theological interpretation is to differentiate between what a text 'meant' (that is, the empirical and descriptive analysis of a text) and what it 'means' (the creative and responsive appropriations of a text).[12] Such an approach is applied to Isaiah 53 by John Goldingay who says:

> Isaiah 53 is not a prophecy of the Messiah but a portrait of how Yahweh's servant-prophet becomes the means of Israel's being put right with God, of Israel's personal renewal, and of the nations' coming to acknowledge Yahweh. But one can see how the chapter came to help people understand Jesus' significance.[13]

This strategy is unobjectionable on one level since it allows us to hold together what an author said and what readers think. However, there are serious drawbacks with it as a complete account of how to conceive biblical interpretation.[14]

First, the two-stage movement from 'meant' to 'means' is a modernist construct. There is an underlying assumption that texts are hermeneutically autonomous,

---

9   See similarly Vanhoozer 1998, 263–5.
10 See Aug. *Conf.* 11.3.5.
11 Lewis 1966, 273.
12 The distinction was best expounded in a dictionary article by Stendahl 1962 and became largely axiomatic for biblical studies.
13 Goldingay 2014, 72.
14 See Adam 1995, 76–86; Gilbertson 2003, 21–31.

so that if you get the history right then the theology and application will look after themselves. The problem is that this reduces the locus of meaning to a 'back-then antiquarianism' in which meaning is reducible to the recovery of a time capsule, rather than regarding 'meaning' as what emerges from the dynamic interplay between author and reader via a text. Privileging authorial intent also makes it difficult, if not near-impossible, to find responsible and faithful ways of allowing the texts to speak beyond their own setting without committing the error of over-interpretation. In contrast, the task of reading texts faithfully should not be constructed as 'authorial intent' versus 'present meanings', but as a hermeneutical enterprise that allows an ancient text to speak to a modern audience without doing injustice to either.[15]

Second, the 'meant' and 'meaning' distinction assumes that texts can be neatly divided into original meaning and later meanings or that it is possible to separate 'fact' from 'value'. Yet there is no escaping value-laden interpretation even by those who are concerned with the 'plain', original, historical, or authorial sense. (This notion itself is puzzling: plenty of people in the first century wrote texts that are anything but 'plain', and the simplistic assumption that the early Christians wrote 'easy' texts which later generations have muddled up is mostly fantasy.) For an interpreter to claim that a faithful reading of a text requires one to insulate the text from anachronistic readings sounds fine, except when one remembers that all interpreters have a tendency to project their own dogmatic agendas and ideological biases onto the text. There is no presuppositionless exegesis. No interpreter can claim to be free from 'theology' (including forms of atheism!) or from 'ideology'. There is no epistemological equivalent of Switzerland, a neutral territory from which one can survey other nations in peace.[16]

Third, early Christian readers did not think of themselves as finding one of many possible meanings of Isaiah 53 beyond what the author originally meant. On the contrary, they insisted that putting Jesus at the front and centre was the true and proper way of reading the Old Testament. That is to say, they did not read their Bible prospectively, moving forward from authorial intent to messianic event. Instead it appears, as Richard Hays has proposed, that they read retrospectively, moving backwards from messianic event to scriptural text. This made excellent sense granted that they believed that Jesus of Nazareth was Israel's long-awaited Messiah, who had drawn Israel's vocation and destiny to its long-intended and much-prayed-for climax. (In other words, this 'reading backwards' was not arbitrary; it went with the basic sense that what had happened in Jesus was the messianic fulfilment of Israel's long story.) In this case, then, the 'meaning' of an early Christian text is the 'product of a catalytic fusion of Israel's Scripture and the story of Jesus. Reading the text this

---
[15] Morgan and Barton 1988, 38.
[16] See Bultmann (1964, 343) who famously said: '*There cannot be any such thing as presuppositionless exegesis . . . Historical understanding always presupposes a relation of the interpreter to the subject matter that is . . . expressed in texts*' (italics original). See further on presuppositions, Thiselton 1992, 44–6.

way doesn't mean rejecting things like authorial intent. It means discovering a mode of divine testimony beyond that which had previously been grasped'.[17]

Taking those conclusions into account—the problems of authorial distance and the failings of a two-stage 'meant-to-means' scheme—we must concede that 'meaning' is not restricted to authorial intent. It is shaped by wider factors like contexts, texts, and communities. If, in reading Isaiah 53, one's context is the canon and creeds of the early church, then readers will naturally identify Jesus in the text so that 'this' (Isaiah's 'Servant') is really 'that' (Jesus)—while again recalling that Paul could cheerfully apply 'servant' texts like Isaiah 49 to his own work. He was, after all, 'a man in the Messiah'.

THE TEXT

If meaning is not exclusively a function of authorial intention, then interpreters have been quick to suggest that the stabilizing force for interpretation resides in the *literary artefact* itself. The concern is not with the formation of the text, identifying its sources and the shape of its editing, but simply with the contours of the text's final form. The task of interpretation, so it goes, is to adopt reading strategies that lay out and explain the storied features and persuasive power of a text, by treating the text as a self-enclosed entity. Several strategies have emerged in recent decades, including narrative criticism and rhetorical criticism. These two methods look at the specific features of a text and the net effect of its devices.[18]

Narrative criticism

Narrative criticism has to do with the analysis of features of a text that indicate *how* the story means. In other words, it traces the perspectives and devices that create meaning for readers.[19] These various perspectives can include those of the 'implied author', 'implied reader', 'narrator', and specific characters. The many devices to be employed include plot, point of view, settings, symbolism, irony, tragedy, repetition of themes, rhetoric, and intertextuality. In a nutshell, a real author writes a text for a real reader, yet within the story there is an implied author (the picture of the author that emerges from the text), who uses a narrator to speak to the narratee in the text by using various literary devices, all in order to influence an implied reader (the picture of the reader that emerges from the text, as opposed to any 'readers' we might reconstruct historically from other data). The objective of

---

17 Hays 2014, xi (and x–xv).
18 On the similarity and complementarity of narrative criticism and rhetorical criticism, see Stamps 1997.
19 Narrative criticism is premised on Chatman's (1978) differentiation between 'story' and 'discourse'. A 'story' is the *what* of a narrative, while discourse is the *how* of a narrative. For a concise introduction to narrative criticism see Malbon 2008 [1992], though helpful too are Powell 1990 and Resseguie 2005. The landmark volume on narrative criticism, applied to the gospel of Mark, remains Rhoads, Dewey, and Michie 1999 [1982], whose achievement is evaluated and celebrated by Iverson and Skinner 2011.

narrative criticism is then to discern how the 'implied reader' would respond to the narrative. The process can be pictorialized (see Figure 1).[20]

FIGURE 1: THE ROLE OF THE 'IMPLIED READER' ACCORDING TO NARRATIVE CRITICISM

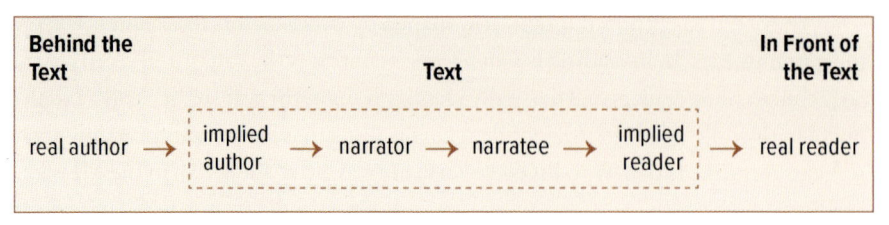

Behind the Text	Text				In Front of the Text
real author →	implied author	→ narrator →	narratee →	implied reader	→ real reader

To give an example, consider the gospel of John. We could tentatively propose that either John, son of Zebedee, or else John the elder is the 'real author'. He writes, not autobiographically, but as the cryptic character known as the 'beloved disciple' (Jn. 13.23; 19.26; 20.2, 7, 20) who is the 'implied author', whose perspective is narrated by a person who provides a testimony to Jesus' true identity as the Logos made flesh (Jn. 1.1–18; 19.25). The narratees are those who have believed this testimony (Jn. 21.25); the 'implied reader' is the Jew or gentile invited to believe that Jesus is the Messiah (Jn. 20.31); and the 'real readers' are persons in Ephesus and beyond who hear the gospel of John. Accordingly, contemporary readers of the gospel of John should strive to identify with the experiences elicited by the implied readers from their encounter with the text, and either 'come to believe' or 'continue to believe' that Jesus is the Messiah. Such a scenario yields the result set out in Figure 2.

FIGURE 2: THE ROLE OF THE 'REAL READER' ACCORDING TO NARRATIVE CRITICISM

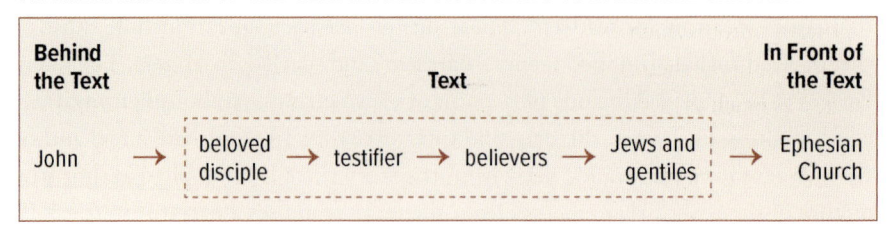

Behind the Text	Text				In Front of the Text
John →	beloved disciple	→ testifier →	believers →	Jews and gentiles	→ Ephesian Church

The advantage of narrative criticism is that the New Testament is filled with stories: miniature stories such as parables, book-sized stories like the gospels and the Acts of the Apostles, and cosmic stories like the Revelation of John. Even when we read essentially didactic books like Romans and Hebrews, it quickly becomes clear that there, too, the ancient Jewish story is being *redrawn around Jesus*, so that the Jewish conceptions of monotheism, the election of God's people, and eschatology

---

20 Malbon 2008, 33 developed from Chatman 1978, 151.

(the promised future for the world) gain new coherence in a new narrative with Jesus at its heart. Narrative criticism also means we can wrestle with a biblical book as a unified whole rather than examine it in piecemeal fashion by engaging in a slavishly atomistic examination of its sources, form, and editing, where we see the trees but miss the forest. What is more, if preachers are mainly storytellers, then learning how to understand the New Testament books as narrative is a great way to prepare preachers to bring the biblical story to the people in their congregation, who may themselves then strive to live out the story in new, spirit-led forms for new circumstances.

Rhetorical criticism

It has long been noted that the New Testament has an affinity with ancient rhetorical practices. On this point one could cite interpreters from church Fathers like Augustine to Reformers like Philip Melanchthon. The recent revival of rhetoric as a facet of New Testament study owes much to Hans Dieter Betz, who attempted to describe Galatians as a type of forensic rhetoric (he saw it, in other words, as modelled on the kind of speech one might make to argue a case in a law court), and George Kennedy, who applied a wider sway of ancient rhetorical conventions to the study of the New Testament.[21] This has spawned a whole industry of rhetorical and socio-rhetorical readings of the New Testament.[22] The primary aim of rhetorical criticism is to classify each New Testament writing against a species of rhetoric such as deliberative (persuading), forensic (defending), or epideictic (praising), and then to identify the rhetorical function of each individual unit of text in order to discern its usage in relation to the original situation of the author and audience (see Table 3.1).[23]

Rhetorical criticism has a number of benefits for New Testament students. If we learn about ancient rhetoric, then we understand something about the literary and cultural world in which the New Testament was written. Rhetoric was always in the air, not just in the rhetorical handbooks in the academies, but in the market-place and theatre as much as in the courts. On top of that, the books of the New Testament are largely attempts at persuasion. The gospel of Mark tries to persuade readers to believe in Jesus as the Messiah not despite the cross but precisely because of it. Romans is composed to persuade the readers in Rome to embrace cross-cultural Jesus-based unity and to support Paul's mission to Spain. Revelation functions to persuade the audience to persevere under times of trial. By grasping the rhetorical texture of the New Testament, we begin to comprehend more fully something of the logical power (*logos*), emotional depth (*pathos*), and exhortatory style (*ethos*) of the biblical authors.

---

[21] Betz 1979; Kennedy 1984.
[22] See the survey of literature on rhetorical criticism in Watson 2006, and the introduction to rhetorical criticism by Classen 2002 [2000] and Witherington 2009.
[23] For good examples of the application of rhetorical studies to the New Testament, see Mitchell 1991 and Malcolm 2013, both in relation to 1 Corinthians.

TABLE 3.1: CLASSIFICATIONS OF RHETORICAL CRITICISM

Types of rhetorical proof	Types of rhetorical discourse	Parts of rhetorical speeches*
Ethos: appeal to moral and intellectual character	Forensic: the attempt to exonerate or indict a person or group	*exordium*: introduction to the subject
Pathos: appeal to emotion	Deliberative: the attempt to persuade or dissuade people regarding a future course of action	*narratio*: setting forth of the facts leading to the matter of discussion
		propositio: statement of the thesis
Logos: appeal to reason	Epideictic: the attempt to bestow praise or blame on something or someone	*probatio*: proofs to prove the thesis
		peroratio: conclusion

*The taxonomy here is a generalized summary of the structure prescribed by rhetorical handbooks; see further Aune 2003, 62–4.

Critique of narrative and rhetorical criticisms

Despite these advantages, a text-centred approach—one relying on a mixture of narrative and rhetorical criticisms—still has inherent failings.

First, on narrative criticism, Rhoads and Michie claimed one should read a text as 'story' rather than 'history'; a text should be read independently of other writings; a text should not be read with cultural assumptions in mind; and a text should not be read with theologies in mind.[24] The problem is that this is exactly how many people want to read the New Testament: as historically referential documents, part of a biblical canon, answering modern questions, and contributing to theological discourse. The insistence on bracketing out the author and reader from the study of a book may help to highlight points that would otherwise be missed, but in the end, by itself, is neither attractive nor helpful. That is simply because the New Testament is a historical document, clearly composed by real authors and designed to affect real readers. The New Testament authors and their readers lived in an extra-textual world, and insofar as this is possible we must try to enter into that world in order to understand the text. (The more we do that, we suggest, the better we are equipped to return to *our* real, extra-textual world shaped by what we have found.) So, while treating a text as a self-enclosed entity might be appropriate for fiction, it seems inappropriate for the genres of the New Testament, including biography, historiography, epistle, and apocalypse, especially when received in a historically

---

24 Rhoads, Dewey, and Michie 1999, 5–6.

situated community that believes that God spoke, and continues to speak, in and through these texts.

In addition, there is no reason to privilege the implied reader over any other reader. If we are concerned with the story 'inside' a text, then we should also be concerned with the effective history of a text in later interpretation, as well as its power to influence contemporary readers. Mark Alan Powell, a narrative critic himself, confesses: 'Ultimately, I believe that a theologically formed, canonical response to Mark's Gospel is preferable to the anticipated response of the Gospel's implied reader.'[25]

Second, concerning rhetorical criticism, its application to New Testament study has met with some resistance.[26] There can be at best only a partial analogy between ancient rhetoric and the New Testament. Rhetoric is primarily meant for speeches rather than for written communication. Irrespective of Luke's presentation of Paul as a master *rhetor*, Paul himself disavows the use of rhetorical verve in his proclamation of the gospel.[27] It does not seem possible to force the gospels and epistles into a rhetorical structure, since both genres cannot be squeezed into the sequence of a rhetorical speech. There are, accordingly, limitations in the comparative study of the rhetorical handbooks and the New Testament. It is better to see the relationship of the New Testament with ancient rhetoric as one of parallel communicative function rather than formal resemblance. In any case, rhetorical criticism is not conducive to an exclusively text-centred method of interpretation, because persuasion can only ever be conceived as the influence of a speaker/author exerted upon a hearer/reader. In other words, one cannot conceive of biblical rhetoric apart from the *rhetorician* and *reader*. Once again, we find ourselves back, not in the text by itself, but in the real world.

Drawing these threads together, it is impossible to insist on an exclusively text-centred mode of biblical interpretation. The attempt to study texts in light of rhetoric, narrative, or even structure[28] will inevitably require reference to entities and phenomena from outside the text. The notion that what the authors had in mind is irrelevant (the 'Intentional Fallacy') or that the perspective of the reader does not

---

[25] Powell 2011, 41–2.
[26] See e.g. Porter 1993a; Kern 1998; Bird 2008a.
[27] 1 Cor. 1.17; 2.1–5, 13; 2 Cor. 11.6; 1 Thess. 2.5. This repeated disavowal sometimes appears deliberately ironic: Paul is using rhetorical skill to say 'I am no rhetorician'.
[28] In the foregoing discussion I have described narrative criticism and rhetorical criticism, but not structural criticism. Structural criticism concerned the application of semiotic theory to biblical texts whereby meaning exists at the level of deeply embedded macro-structures resident in a text (see Patte 1976, 1990; Aichele 1995, 70–83). However, structuralist interpretation faded from the biblical studies scene very quickly in the 1990s. The reasons are easy to understand. Structuralism took a lot of hard work; it involved learning a lot of technical linguistic jargon for what seemed to many to be very little payoff in terms of offering up new and interesting ways of understanding texts (Hurtado 2014, 300–3); also, no-one can preach week by week from deep structures in a text (Wright *NTPG*, 57 n. 23).

matter (the 'Affective Fallacy') fails to stack up with the communicative process that takes place in the flow of reading a text and experiencing its story. While Isaiah 53 is a self-contained story about the Suffering Servant, it derives its literary power from its author (particularly coming where it does as the climax of the great poem we call Isaiah 40—55), and the poignancy of the story connects with readers ancient and modern. If we treat the Suffering Servant as a figure within the communicative process, we might say that by his wounds authors find peace and by his stripes readers are healed.

THE READER

We come now to the role of the reader in interpretation, the range of *reader-centred* approaches to literature, where the locus of meaning is the activity of the reader and his or her community. Much modern study of literature has rejected the idea that we have access to the mind or intention of a writer. All we have is the text itself, seen as an independent entity. What matters now, it seems, is not so much the text *in* itself (discussed in the previous section) as the interaction between reader and text, not of reader and author *via* text.

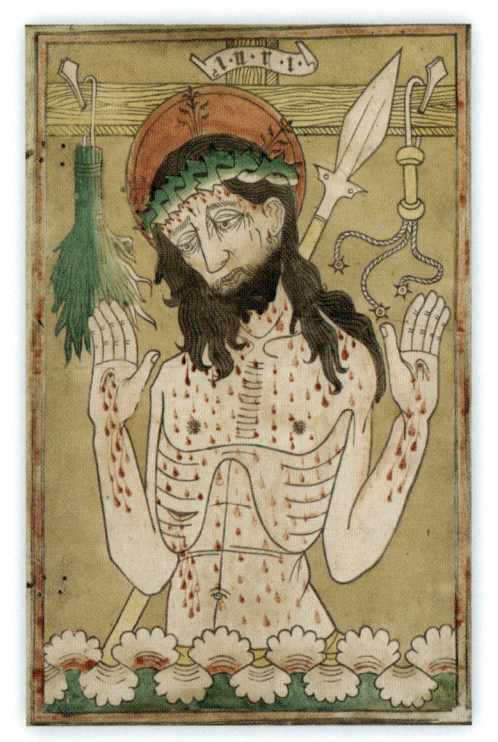

Man of Sorrows, fifteenth century, Art Institute of Chicago
PD-US

The logic seems to be that if the author is distant or dead, if texts themselves elicit a range of possible responses for their readers, then perhaps meaning is not given by an author, not embedded within a text, but created entirely by the reader. There is then a family of interpretative approaches, known broadly as 'reader-response criticism', which allege that meaning is created by the activity of the reader. Such critics dispute the role of the text as containing and constraining meaning; what matters is the readers themselves, not least when seen within their social context.

This opens up new vistas for all sorts of readings like feminist, queer, postcolonial, psychoanalytic, Marxist, and even the eclectic, like an Eco-Evangelical-Estonian reading.[29] The notion that readers bring fresh perspectives that open up

---

29 See introductions by Moore 1989, 71–130; Moore and Sherwood 2011, 101–7; Aichele 1995, 20–69; Fowler 2001 [1991]; with critiques by Porter 1993a and Thiselton 2006, 489–514.

70 Reading the New Testament

a text in new ways should be obvious to anyone who has read the Bible in a multicultural context, where those who read the Bible with Asian, Latin American, or African eyes can point to elements in the text that would not be obvious to most westerners.[30]

Many proponents of reader-response criticism then postulate the irrelevance of the author and inertia of the text for influencing meaning. Dale Martin writes about the myth of textual agency which ascribes objective meaning to a text. Instead Martin contends: 'Texts don't mean. People mean with texts.'[31] In other words, meaning is not *retrieved* from a text but *created* by readers using a text. Martin likes to illustrate this by putting a Bible on a speaker's podium, stepping back, and inviting people to listen to what the Bible 'says' to them. After a few moments of embarrassing silence he likes to say, 'Apparently, the Bible can't talk', by which he means 'Texts don't "say" anything: they must be read.'[32] Martin believes that although authors have intentions, nevertheless the authorial intention is not identical with the meaning of the text. Meaning is not constrained by the author or the text, but by the socialized context of the reader, who is drawn to certain ways of reading and pushed towards particular interpretations, and whose social and cultural prejudices may thereby be exposed to critique.[33]

The idea behind reader-centred literary theories is that the only thing to do with a text is to play with it for oneself: I must see what it does for me, and not ask whether there is another mind out there behind the text. And of course, if that is so, there is not much point discussing the text with someone else. There will be no 'right' or 'wrong' reading; only my reading and your reading. This latter position clearly appeals to many elements in contemporary consciousness. We live in a relativistic and pluralistic age, an age which places self-fulfilment above the integration of self with other selves. The devout predecessor of reader-centred literary theories is that pietistic or devotional reading of the text which insists that what the Bible says to *me, now*, is the be-all and end-all of its meaning; a reading which does not want to know about the intention of the evangelist, the life of the early church, the original meaning of Paul's paragraphs, or even about what Jesus himself was actually like. Alas, there are some strange bedfellows in the world of literary theory.

An effective critique can be mustered against reader-response criticism, especially the more extreme varieties that decry appeal to authors and try to decentralize texts from interpretation. First, on authorial intention, we should not consider

---

30 To give another example, I often ask students what Paul meant when he told Timothy to urge women in his church 'to dress modestly' (1 Tim. 2.9). Male students habitually take the modesty to mean 'don't show too much flesh', whereas female students habitually take it to mean 'don't flaunt too much bling'.
31 Martin 2006, 1.
32 Martin 2006, 5.
33 Martin 2006, 6, 14–15.

an author to be a deceased and disembodied mind, whose spectre readers haplessly try to meet in some sort of literary séance. Yes, texts invoke responses, but those responses are part of the intentionality of the text, which itself is the enacted intentionality of the author.[34] The text orients the reader towards the author by sharing a common language, similar mental processes, a reciprocal desire to communicate and to understand, a capacity for social interaction, and membership of a similar community.[35] Second, on textual (in)determinacy, if texts have no meaning, then they are nothing more than a mirror and an echo chamber: all we see is our own reflection and all we hear is our own voice. Such 'narcissistic hermeneutics stands little chance of expanding one's self-knowledge, or for that matter, of achieving genuine liberation'.[36] However, it seems intuitive that reading is normally a transformative experience, because there really is something 'other' in the text, something other than ourselves, which challenges and changes us as readers.[37] And while texts can be open, carry surplus meaning, and elicit a range of responses, texts can also be closed and invoke predetermined responses, so that texts can place limits on meaning.[38] If that holds true then meaning is more than simply what happens in the mind of the reader.[39]

---

34 Vanhoozer 1998, 201–80 (esp. 252–3).
35 Meyer 1989, 34; Vanhoozer 1998, 387.
36 Vanhoozer 1998, 182.
37 See Vanhoozer 1998, 169–70; Thiselton 1992, 31–5; 2006, 518–20.
38 See Thiselton (1992, 526–9; 2006, 499–500, 623) and Vanhoozer (1998, 151–2), both following Umberto Eco on the difference between 'open' and 'closed' texts.
39 In order to avoid interpretative anarchy, reader-response critics argue that there are limits on textual meaning, but the question is whether that limitation derives from the text itself (so Wolfgang Iser) or in the interpretative community (so Stanley Fish). Martin (2006, 14–16) appeals to the social context and social community of readers as controls which can correct meaning. Yet this merely moves the problem back one step further. On what *basis* does a group correct meaning if not through its texts? What do we do when the social context is the oppressor? Let us give an example. Imagine it is the early 1980s, and you are attending a Bible study in the city of Johannesburg in South Africa with some members of the Dutch Reformed Church who believe that apartheid has biblical support, since the white colonists, like Israel in Canaan, were called to subjugate and segregate the indigenous population in the name of establishing God's reign on earth. On what *basis* do you call that a false reading if there are no real grounds for adjudicating between conflicting interpretations and if texts cannot reform readers from the outside? Whereas Martin protests against readers projecting their unethical prejudices (such as racism, sexism, and homophobia) onto the Bible in order to say that holy writ sanctions their beliefs, what if the prejudice resides at the level of the community itself (see esp. Vanhoozer 1998, 168–74, 317–20; Thiselton 1992, 549–50; 2006, 514, 665–70)? For a case in point, Peter Haas (1988) has argued that the Nazis operated on the basis of an internally consistent ethic that was able to impose itself in western Europe because it presented a compelling matrix of values and ideas for identifying good and evil in continuity with the conventional western system of symbols and ethical convictions (e.g. Darwinism, Christianity, anti-semitism, nationalism, militarism, racism, even Nordic mythology). We may doubt whether self-reflection and self-criticism are an adequate safeguard against such evil ever arising again. Correction must sometimes come from outside the self, and from outside the interpretative community. While texts can be adopted by ideologues for malevolent ends within a community, even so, texts like the Bible can still offer criteria for what is 'true, valid, advantageous, or healthy [l]iving' (Thiselton 2006, 672).

FUSING THE HORIZONS OF AUTHOR, TEXT, AND READER

Whereas some want to find meaning at the horizon of the author, or the text, or the reader, we propose instead that a fully orbed hermeneutical strategy will lead us to affirm that all three components are involved in the communicative process.[40] It appears that authors *intend*, texts *signify*, and readers *understand*; and that 'meaning' occurs in the fusion of all three. Ultimately, 'meaning' is the web of cognitive connections we make with the world behind the text, the world in the text, and the world we inhabit in front of the text. The more connections we make, and the thicker those connections appear to be, the more preferable is a particular meaning ascribed to the text because it explains more of the elements involved in the entire reading experience.

According to Thiselton, interpreters sometimes remain locked into their own horizons, unable to read a text detached from their own time and tradition. However, the distance between interpreter and author is progressively closed by a 'fusion' of horizons, fostered through a responsible reading of the text.[41] The best way to achieve this 'fusion' is, we suggest, by getting into the historical background behind the text, pursuing the authorial intentions embedded inside the text (so far as we can—this is a matter of historical reconstruction, and as such always provisional though nonetheless vital), delving into the story within the text, and prayerfully striving to live out a faithful life in front of the text. Then, by drawing all these into a creative dialogue, we arrive at meanings and significances that can be tested and examined for their explanatory power and life-giving possibility (including ethical responsibility). In which case, as Spinks puts it: 'Meaning is the mediation of God's truth that takes place between authors, readers and the community of God of which they are all a part. It is neither a determined object nor an open-ended idea.'[42]

Given this admittedly long discussion of the New Testament as literature, the task for faithful readers is to engage in a sympathetic and yet inquisitive appropriation of the authors and texts of the New Testament. As a way forward, we suggest a possible hermeneutical model to consummate this fusion of horizons. It is a hermeneutic of *love*.[43] In love, at least in the idea of *agapē* as we find it in the New Testament, the lover affirms the reality and the otherness of the beloved. The lover does not seek to remake the beloved into someone other than who he or she is.

---

[40] A point acknowledged even by conservative commentators like Köstenberger and Patterson 2011, 57–8 and urged similarly by Thiselton 2006, 607–24.
[41] Thiselton 1980, 439–40.
[42] Spinks 2007, 182–3.
[43] Augustine (*Doctr. Chr.* 1.36) said: 'Whoever, then, thinks that he understands the Holy Scriptures, or any part of them, but puts such an interpretation on them as does not tend to build up into this twofold love of God and neighbor, does not yet understand them as he ought.' See similarly on hermeneutics and love, Watson 1994, 265–87; Luz 1994, 91–6; Vanhoozer 1998, 32, 283.

Beginning of the gospel of Luke, minuscule 244 (Gregory-Aland), thirteenth-century New Testament manuscript

At this level, 'love' will mean 'attention', the readiness to let the other *be* the other, the willingness to grow and change oneself in relation to the other.

When we apply this principle to all three components of the reading process, it will be possible to make a number of simultaneous affirmations and denials. First, we need to do justice *both* to the fact that texts do not represent the whole of the author's mind *and* to the fact that they nevertheless do tell us quite a bit about him or her. Second, we need a theory that will do justice *both* to the fact that the author intended certain things *and* that the text may well contain other things—echoes, evocations, structures, and the like—that were not consciously present in the author's mind. Third, we need a theory that will do justice *both* to the fact that the reader is deeply involved in the communicative event *and* to the fact that the text is an entity on its own, not a plastic substance to be moulded to the reader's whim. If that is the case, then we should acknowledge that the author must be resurrected but not deified; that texts genuinely carry meaning like a hard-working mule, yet a text also inspires meaning like an iconic muse; and, while readers have rights, this does not license anarchy. Until we grasp the place of the author, text, and reader in the formation of 'meaning', most of the present battles about reading the New Testament will be dialogues of the deaf, doomed to failure. In sum, this hermeneutic of love is a *lectio catholica semper reformanda* (a reading of and for and in the whole church, but a reading which is always in need of revising and reforming, even as such readings themselves should revise and reform the church). Such a reading seeks to be faithful to what is received, while always open to the possibility of challenge and correction.

Further reading

Thiselton, Anthony C. 2006. *Thiselton on Hermeneutics: Collected Works with New Essays*. Grand Rapids, MI: Eerdmans.

Vanhoozer, Kevin J. 1998. *Is There A Meaning in This Text? The Bible, the Reader, and the Morality of Literary Knowledge*. Grand Rapids, MI: Zondervan.

Wright, Andrew. 2013. *Christianity and Critical Realism: Ambiguity, Truth, and Theological Literacy*. New York: Routledge.

Wright, N. T. 1992. *The New Testament and the People of God*. COQG 1; London: SPCK, pp. 47–80.

4

The New Testament as Theology

[T]o write a New Testament theology is to preside at a conference on faith and order. Around the table sit the authors of the New Testament, and it is the presider's task to engage them in a colloquium about theological matters which they themselves placed on the agenda.[1]

CHAPTER AT A GLANCE

This chapter describes the New Testament as a theological document that contains a message about God.

By the end of this chapter you should be able to:

- understand that the New Testament's authority derives from its theological message from God and about God;
- comprehend that the New Testament's message is a story about God that addresses the wider world;
- grasp how doing New Testament theology involves wrestling with historical questions and exploring the theological texture of its contents;
- identify New Testament theology as part of the script enabling the church to live out its own role in the divine drama.

READING THE NEW TESTAMENT AS A THEOLOGICAL DISCOURSE

The next aspect of the New Testament we must explore is *New Testament theology*. This phrase designates the attempt to read the New Testament from a historical point of view (what theological ideas were the texts articulating in their day?) and, either simultaneously or subsequently, to draw its major theological emphases together into a coherent statement which can then address subsequent generations. In pressing forward with this task several questions emerge. Should one focus on historical description ('this is what Luke thought about God') or discussion of theological content ('this is the biblical view of atonement')? Is Jesus himself, as we glimpse him in the varied accounts of

---

[1] Caird 1994, 19.

the gospels, part of 'New Testament theology', or merely (as Bultmann thought) its presupposition? Should we proceed corpus by corpus, or by tracing theological themes across the canon, or deal with the books in the order in which they were written (supposing we could agree on that)? How are we to find unity when there is so much diversity in the New Testament canon? And should we attempt to find a 'canon within the canon', even if—or perhaps because!—such a thing might artificially elevate one theme and marginalize others?

Ever since J. P. Gabler first conceived of 'biblical theology' as a separate discipline from 'dogmatic theology' in his 1787 address at the University of Altdorf, the nature, scope, and tasks for New Testament theology have been in constant dispute.[2] According to Wayne Meeks, New Testament scholars should 'erase from our vocabulary the terms "biblical theology" and, even more urgently, "New Testament theology"'. Meeks argued strongly that whatever 'contribution these concepts may have made in the conversation since J. P. Gabler, we have come to a time when they can only blinker our understanding'.[3] The objection is not new. It goes back to William Wrede, and has more recently been rehearsed by the Finnish scholar Heikki Räisänen.[4] The idea is that to do a theology of the New Testament will mean subscribing to the authority of these holy books and the institutions that venerate them. Instead, such writers urge, one should pursue a 'theology of early Christianity' and attempt to profile the texture of 'early Christian religion' as a more secular enterprise (see 'Blast from the past: Adolf Schlatter on atheistic approaches').

We could respond by saying that there are very good reasons for pursuing New Testament theology, over and above a detached theological analysis of 'early Christian religion'.

First, if the New Testament is in some sense 'authoritative', as virtually all churches acknowledge, then this 'authority' has been deemed to lie in the *theology*

BLAST FROM THE PAST: ADOLF SCHLATTER ON ATHEISTIC APPROACHES

Adolf Schlatter (1852–1938) was a leading German New Testament scholar in the late nineteenth and first half of the twentieth century. He eschewed the dominating liberal theology of the day and strove to allow the theological vision of the New Testament to speak when many were calling for an atheistic approach to biblical studies. Schlatter (1973, 122) wrote:

> The word with which the New Testament confronts us intends to be believed, and so rules out once for all any sort of neutral treatment. As soon as the historian sets aside or brackets the question of faith, he is making his concern with the New Testament and his presentation of it into a radical and total polemic against it.

---

2 For the text of J. P. Gabler's address see Sandys-Wunsch and Eldredge 1980; for its significance see Stuckenbruck 1999.
3 Meeks 2005, 167–8.
4 See Wrede 1973 and Räisänen 1990 with critical responses by Balla 1997 and Eskola 2013.

that it contains. The caveat we must offer is that the ultimate authority is God, the creator, and since God has revealed himself in Jesus, then Jesus is the one who holds all authority. Jesus did not tell his disciples that all authority is vested in the books that they would write; he insisted that it was vested in his own person.[5] And yet Jesus' authority *operates through* the New Testament message, as it testifies about and on behalf of the risen lord. Knowing that, we must therefore wrestle with what this message is about, how it works, and what its demands might be for followers of Jesus.

Second, the practical context for New Testament theology has been the church's perceived task of addressing itself and the wider world with a message from God. The whole point of Christianity is that it offers a story which is the story of the whole world. It claims to be public truth, not a private self-serving and self-referential cult. The church's job, then, is to know this truth, to live by it, and to make this truth known and put into operation across the globe. New Testament theology fuels the church's mission and preaching, sparking both into action. To put it simply, New Testament theology is necessary to describe what it is about the New Testament that is *authoritative* and to define the *activism* that should characterize the church as a participant in God's plan, namely the intention (as in Eph. 1.10) to sum up in the Messiah all things in heaven and on earth. Or, as Jesus himself put it, the intention that God's kingdom would come and his will be done 'on earth as in heaven'. God has promised to put the world to rights; the early Jesus-followers insisted that this project had been launched in Jesus himself, particularly in the events of his death, resurrection, and ascension; the New Testament, bearing witness to this intention and these events, thereby fuels and energizes the present stage of God's ongoing plan and purpose.

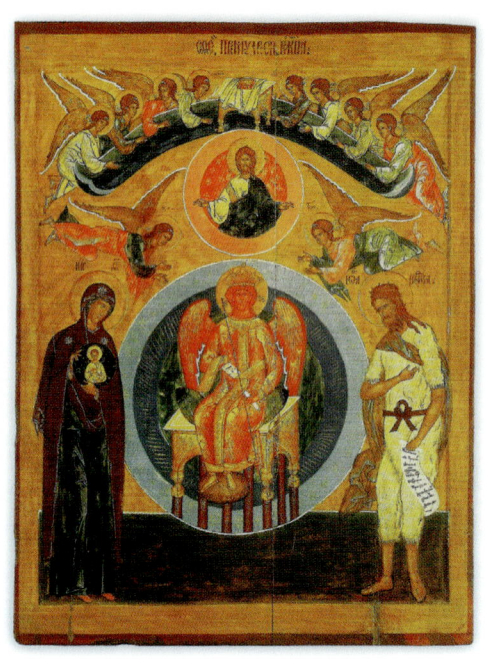

Icon of Holy Wisdom, sixteenth century, St George Church, Vologda
PD-US

---

5   Mt. 28.18. Many will object that this is a false antithesis that plays off Jesus against the Bible, the assumption being that what we know about Jesus we know only in the biblical writings so the biblical writings must be our primary authority. The problem is that this confuses epistemology ('how we know') with authority ('who's in charge'). While a map will be my best guide to get to church on time, when I get there I'll find a vicar rather than the map running the place.

78   Reading the New Testament

A robust approach to study of the New Testament will therefore give sufficient space to its historical context as well as to its theological content.[6] The New Testament is history and theology mixed together—for the very good reason that the faith which the first Jesus-followers inherited from ancient Israel and reshaped around Jesus himself was all about the coming together of heaven and earth. Splitting them apart, as has so often been done, is a sign of our times, more specifically of the Enlightenment's separation of timeless truths from contingent historical realities, whether by sceptics or by their devout opponents. The challenge in studying the New Testament today is to do justice to both, to history and theology alike, disregarding neither and constantly seeking their intended fusion.

The problem of ignoring the historical context of the New Testament is that one can impose other narratives and schemes which become the controlling backdrop for understanding the New Testament's message. If we take seriously the contingent historical nature of the New Testament, its 'back-then-ness', the fact that while it was written *for* us it was not written *to* us, then we will recognize the essential need to situate the New Testament in its social, religious, and historical context. For a case in point, we will struggle to grasp the basic thrust of the incident at Antioch narrated by Paul in Galatians 2.11–14 if we don't have a working knowledge of Jewish social boundaries, food taboos, and debates about fraternizing with gentiles. Discerning the *theological claims* of the text frequently follows from reconstructing the *social context* behind the text. Rather than imposing the structure and questions of later systematic theology (which has often ignored those original contexts), we must allow the text to speak for itself, in its own words, from its own context, on its own terms, so that its theological and missional significance can then be more accurately gauged.

The problem of substituting the study of early Christian religion for New Testament theology, as has been proposed by writers from Wrede to Räisänen, is that it treats the canon as an arbitrary collection of texts, and brackets out as inappropriate any exploration of its theological unity. Yet without the theology we cannot even do the history, since our access to the history is mostly through the New Testament itself, in which the theology is woven tightly with the history all through. Historians of early Christianity must therefore do business with early Christian theology. As Bockmuehl writes about these texts: 'the story they tell is inalienably theological.'[7] The contents of the New Testament are theological—with the theology in question having to do with the revelation in historical action of Israel's God, the creator—and the text assumes that the interests of the readers (implied, ancient, and modern) are also theological to a greater or lesser degree. Wrede himself could not separate

---

6   See Esler 2005 and Bird 2009a.
7   Bockmuehl 2006, 47.

religion from theology in his work on Paul; and the genius of Wrede's successor Rudolf Bultmann (whatever one thinks of the ultimate results) was in his attempt to synthesize the history-of-religions approach with the theological quest to discover meaning for human existence.[8] In fact, when the various biblical writings are read individually, or studied in the context of the biblical canon, or infused into the life of a believing community, they naturally lend themselves to theological formulation, and raise at once the important question of application. It may be fashionable to say that there is no single theology of early Christianity to study, but before too long the early church did opt for what they saw as a single theology, and they called it 'the Holy Scriptures'. In the words of Bockmuehl again:

> At the end of the day, when everything is said and done about the genetic vagaries of the New Testament canon's formation, it remains an equally *historical* phenomenon that the church catholic came to recognize in these twenty-seven books the normative attestation of its apostolic rule of faith.[9]

DISCIPLESHIP AS DEFINING THE AUTHORITATIVE STORY AND LIVING IT OUT

New Testament studies has a two-pronged approach of doing both 'history' (the descriptive part) and 'theology' (the prescriptive part). Our task is accurately to describe the world behind and inside the text, in order to then shape the world—our world—in front of the text. 'History' attempts to trace the stories and beliefs of the early church which formed the backbone of its worldview, while 'theology' subsequently explains the God-dimension of that worldview with all its corollaries. What this means is that the Christian reader of the New Testament is committed to two tasks, mapping 'early Christian history' and then pursuing 'New Testament theology', while remembering that neither of these tasks can be self-sufficient. They are in fact mutually dependent.

To do 'history' without 'theology' will yield only a catalogue of disputable facts and interpretations that can be endlessly analysed and compared, but would not necessarily 'mean' very much today—except, as some sceptics have urged, that Christian origins were strange and pluriform and quite unlike what later generations imagined. This would leave the biblical texts with the same prescriptive force as Egyptian hieroglyphs, that is to say, none. On the other hand, to do 'theology' without 'history' is to set beliefs and ethics adrift from what God has revealed in the mud and mire of human existence. Such an approach would deny the historically referential

---

8   Wrede 1973, 76, 106; Bultmann 1951–5.
9   Bockmuehl 2006, 103.

nature of biblical texts, preferring instead to see the basic stories as myth, touting things that never really 'happened' but somehow remain endearingly 'true' as allegories of human existence. But if we are right, then history and theology need each other. A good cup of coffee does not consist of hot water on the one hand and coffee grounds on the other, the former to be sipped and the latter to be chewed, but a proper fusion of the two together.

To the Christian reader, the beliefs and stories that are unearthed through the study of the New Testament are not mere historical relics. When properly interpreted, and when responsibly appropriated and applied, they carry prescriptive force for what the followers of Jesus believe and the tasks to which they are called. New Testament theology plots the story that answers, as only stories can, the great worldview questions: who we are, where we are, what time it is, what's wrong, what the solution might be, and what we should be doing about it. The church then lives under the 'authority' of the extant story, being required to offer an improvisatory performance of the final act of that story as it leads up to and anticipates the intended conclusion.

How exactly does that notion of 'acts in a story' work? The New Testament can be seen as the *first scene* of the *final act* of God's great narrative. The early Christians saw themselves within a much longer story: the story of (1) creation and (2) fall of humanity, of (3) Israel and ultimately of (4) Jesus himself. Those are the first four acts; the New Testament writers find themselves at the start of the fifth act of God's heaven-and-earth drama, and they sketch here and there how that drama is meant to finish, in the ultimate rejoining and renewal of heaven and earth, the new creation with resurrection itself at its centre.

Jerusalem from the Mount of Olives

The calling of the apostles Peter and Andrew by Duccio di Buoninsegna, dated 1308–11, National Gallery of Art, Washington, D.C.
PD-US

Understanding this and living it out is quite a challenge, as every generation of Christians discovers. But there is no alternative, nor should we seek one. As in a theatre where the actors have to understand 'the story so far' and then improvise their way faithfully towards the intended conclusion, the New Testament calls for a self-involving performance of its text, in which we, the actors, will ourselves be transformed, perhaps painfully. That is because, as Joshua Jipp puts it, New Testament theology is 'inherently self-involving as it summons the reader to believe, confess, obey, and understand the entirety of one's existence—both her or his thinking and willing—in light of the God revealed in the text'.[10] Like an orchestral score or an operatic libretto, the New Testament calls for a self-involving performance of its text characterized by a declaration of its testimony, the imitation of its way, and the transformation of the cast. Theology instructs us in how to use the New Testament

---

10 Jipp 2014, 27.

as the script for the people of God, who perform their role in the gospel-shaped ensemble (that is, the local church) in which God has put them. Theology, in other words, enables us to use the New Testament as the basic script for the mission and life of the people of God—the local church, the global church, and every member within them.[11]

Thus, theological study of the New Testament, within the spirit-driven and prayerful life of the whole church, is meant, ultimately, to enable us to love God with our minds, in order to be constantly stirred up to love him with our heart and soul. That way, our mission—loving God with all our strength, for the benefit of the whole world—will be shaped by the cataclysmic foundational events concerning Jesus. Rooted in history, we are shaped by theology—not least the theological claim that God will put all things right at last—as our lives effect real transformation, in real history, today and tomorrow, and on until God himself, in the ultimate act of creative sovereignty, does for the whole creation what he did for Jesus when he raised him from the dead.

Further reading

Bird, Michael F. 2009. 'New Testament Theology Re-Loaded: Integrating Biblical Theology and Christian Origins.' *TynBul* 60: 265–91.
Caird, G. B., with L. D. Hurst. 1994. *New Testament Theology*. Oxford: Clarendon.
Dunn, James D. G. 2009. *New Testament Theology: An Introduction*. Nashville: Abingdon.
Wright, N. T. 1992. *The New Testament and the People of God*. COQG 1; London: SPCK, pp. 121–44.

---

11 On theology and the metaphor of drama, see further Vanhoozer 2005.

Ethiopian icon of the crucifixion; date and author unknown
Gianni Dagli Orti / Shutterstock

II

THE WORLD OF JESUS AND THE EARLY CHURCH

We have no reason to think that Middle Eastern politics were any less complicated in the first century than in the twentieth. On the contrary, there is every reason to suppose that there were just as many tensions, problems, anomalies and puzzles then as now—just as much reason for some to throw up their hands in despair, for others to grit their teeth and forge ahead, and for others again to try to forget the whole 'situation' in the struggle to survive.[1]

---

[1] Wright *NTPG*, 137.

The History of the Jews between the Persian and Roman Empires

CHAPTER AT A GLANCE

This chapter narrates the history of the Jewish people from the beginning of the Babylonian exile in 587 BC to the suppression of the Bar-Kochba revolt in AD 135.

By the end of this chapter you should be able to:

- appreciate the value of Jewish history as the context for the New Testament;
- identify key persons and events in the hellenistic, Maccabean, and Roman periods;
- understand how Rome governed Palestine through client rulers;
- grasp the significance of the post-AD 70 period for the formation of early Christianity and rabbinic Judaism.

The land of Israel is a small country. You can walk its length, north to south, in a few days, and from its central mountains you can see its lateral boundaries, the sea to the west and the river to the east. But it has had an importance out of all proportion to its size. Empires have fought over it. Every forty-four years out of the last four thousand, on average, an army has marched through it, whether to conquer it, to rescue it from someone else, to use it as a neutral battleground on which to fight a different enemy, or to take advantage of it as the natural route for getting somewhere else to fight there instead. There are many places which, once beautiful, are now battered and mangled with the legacies of war. And yet it has remained a beautiful land, still producing grapes and figs, milk and honey.[1]

INTRODUCING THE HISTORY OF NEW TESTAMENT TIMES

We cannot understand the New Testament unless we make sense of the historical environment in which the

---

1 Wright *NTPG*, 1.

early church was conceived and grew in the first century AD. To understand the origin of Christianity and the meaning of the first believers' 'theology' demands that we get to know the historical setting and the social, cultural, and religious world in which Jesus and the apostles lived. To do that, the following sections will briefly narrate the history of the Jews between the Persian and Roman empires (see box: 'Timeline of the Persian and Greek period'), then describe key features of Jewish life in Palestine and in the Diaspora, and summarize cultural elements of the greco-roman world.

THE JEWS FROM THE BABYLONIAN EXILE TO THE HASMONEAN DYNASTY (587–63 BC)

The story of second-Temple Judaism is one of tension and tragedy. The Babylonians had conquered Judea and destroyed the first Temple in 587 BC and taken a large part of the populace into exile in Babylon. The destruction of the Temple and the removal of the Jews from the land had placed a great question mark against their pre-exilic faith. Had their God forsaken them? Although it seemed like that, the prophets Isaiah and Jeremiah had spoken about a future day when God would bring them back from exile, a time when God would deliver them through a new exodus, with a new king, a new Temple, and the renewal of the covenant, with God himself returning to dwell in the new Temple. Just over fifty years later, this promise came (partly!) true.

TIMELINE OF THE PERSIAN AND GREEK PERIOD

Babylonian period 597–539 BC
- **597**
  Jerusalem taken by Nebuchadnezzar II
- **587**
  Jerusalem destroyed, inhabitants taken into exile in Babylon
- **539**
  Babylon defeated by Persian king Cyrus

Persian–Greek period 538–323 BC
- **538**
  return of exiles from Babylon; rebuilding of Temple begun (completed 516)
- **450s–440s**
  Ezra and Nehemiah in Jerusalem
- **336**
  Alexander the Great rises to power
- **332**
  Alexander conquers Palestine
- **323**
  Alexander dies: his empire divided

Egyptian (Ptolemaic) period 320–200 BC
- Palestine under Ptolemies; administered by high priests in Jerusalem

Syrian (Seleucid) period 200–142 BC
- **200**
  Antiochus III defeats Egyptians
- **175**
  Antiochus IV Epiphanes enthroned
- **167**
  Antiochus IV desecrates Temple: builds altar to Zeus Olympus
- **166**
  Judas Maccabaeus leads revolt
- **164**
  Judas Maccabaeus cleanses Temple
- **164–142**
  running battles with Syria
- **160**
  death of Judas Maccabaeus
- **160–152**
  Jonathan leader of Judean forces
- **142**
  semi-independence from Syria, start of Hasmonean dynasty

The Babylonian army was routed by the Persians in 539 BC, led by their king, Cyrus. The Persians were generous overlords to the Jews. They permitted them to return to their homeland and to rebuild their Temple. But the Persians remained their overlords.

The story of the Judean exiles' return is recounted in the books of Ezra and Nehemiah and in the prophetic books of Haggai, Zechariah, Malachi, and Daniel. This post-exilic period included Ezra's religious reforms and Nehemiah's eventual rebuilding of the Temple and the city wall. But although the Judeans were now back in the land, the full, glorious sweep of prophetic promises about Israel's restoration had not yet materialized (see box: 'Israel's post-exilic restoration hopes'). The twelve tribes had not been regathered, there was no new Davidic king, the rebuilt Temple was a pale comparison with Solomon's original Temple, the glorious divine presence had not yet returned, the nations were not swarming to Zion to worship God, and unrighteousness still abounded. Instead of living under the reign of God, the Jews found themselves living under the power of one pagan kingdom after another. The effects of the exile still lingered; and things were about to get a whole lot worse.

In the fourth century BC, Alexander the Great and his Greek army swept through the old Persian empire and beyond, changing the cultural landscape, and imposing Greek culture wherever they went. Alexander's empire stretched from Greece to India, and Greek language and culture permeated every part of it. After his death in 323 BC, his empire was subsequently divided up among his generals, resulting in a number of regional kingdoms controlling Egypt, Asia Minor, Persia, and Greece. Eventually, in the east, it came down to two major powers, the Seleucids in Syria, to the north of Palestine, and the Ptolemies to the south of Palestine in Egypt. Those two kingdoms constantly vied for control of Palestine as something of a land-bridge between them. The two subsequent overlordships, first by the Egyptian Ptolemies in the third century and then by the Syrian Seleucids in the second century, make the history more complex in terms of military control of Palestine, but do not alter the basic fact that the world was now Greek.

By the time of the first century, in fact, there were three times as many Jews living outside Palestine as in it, and their main language was Greek, not Hebrew. Jesus grew up in Nazareth,

> **ISRAEL'S POST-EXILIC RESTORATION HOPES**
>
> But God will again have mercy on them, and God will bring them back into the land of Israel; and they will rebuild the temple of God, but not like the first one until the period when the times of fulfilment shall come. After this they all will return from their exile and will rebuild Jerusalem in splendour; and in it the temple of God will be rebuilt, just as the prophets of Israel have said concerning it. Then the nations in the whole world will all be converted and worship God in truth . . . All the Israelites who are saved in those days and are truly mindful of God will be gathered together; they will go to Jerusalem and live in safety for ever in the land of Abraham, and it will be given over to them. Those who sincerely love God will rejoice, but those who commit sin and injustice will vanish from all the earth. (Tob. 14.5–7 NRSV)

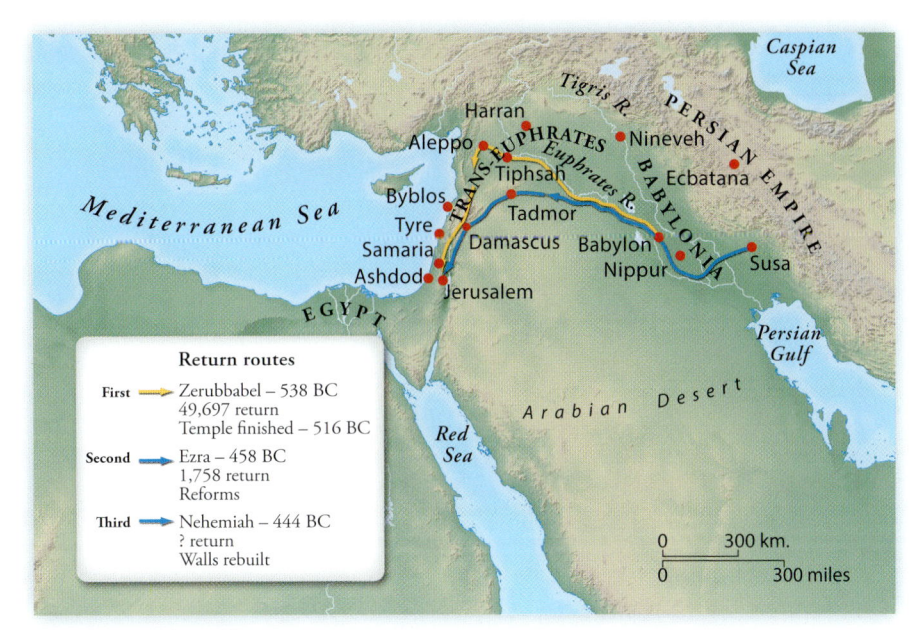

Route of returning exiles

only a few miles from Sepphoris, a Galilean city with Greek influences. Actually, the territory we think of today as 'Israel–Palestine' contained many non-Jewish cities, with significantly different cultures and religious traditions. It is highly likely that Jesus and his first followers would have been able to speak Greek as a second language. If he had wanted to take his disciples to see Euripides' plays performed, he might have only had to walk down the road from Capernaum to Beth Shean. When Paul was kept prisoner in Caesarea Maritima, he would probably have been able to hear, from his prison cell, the shouts of the crowd in the large amphitheatre, or the applause of the audience in the theatre beside the shore. Nearby there was also a temple to Caesar and probably shrines to other pagan gods. Even with the ascent of the Latin-speaking Romans, the east remained linguistically and culturally Greek until the Arab conquests of the seventh and eighth centuries.

This hellenistic setting formed a perpetual cultural and religious threat to the Jews, every bit as powerful as any political danger. The self-understanding of Jews at this time was determined by the pressing question of whether they should attempt to be distinct from this alien culture, and if so, how. Pressure to assimilate was strong in many quarters, especially in places outside Palestine like Egypt and Asia Minor (modern Turkey). Many Jews attempted to assimilate to hellenistic culture in various ways, ranging from token participation in Greek civic life all the way through to apostasy from Judaism.[2]

---

2   See Barclay 1996.

Alexander the Great (356–323 BC) led a Greek coalition that conquered territories including Asia Minor, Egypt, Syria, Persia, and parts of India.
Gianni Marchetti / 123RF.COM

The question of identity was forced upon Palestinian Jews from many angles. But it was under Syrian rule that there occurred the event which became determinative for the self-understanding and aspiration of Jews, and the new focal point of their beliefs, up to the time of Jesus and beyond. The megalomaniac Seleucid ruler Antiochus Epiphanes IV, wanting to use Judea as a buffer state against Egypt, tried to cement his hold on the country, politically and religiously, through a process of forcibly hellenizing it and eliminating the Jewish religion entirely. Antiochus decided to ensure the Jews' loyalty by changing the function and direction of their central religious symbol, the Temple, so that it ceased to make them think independently and turned them in the direction of service to himself. He took over the Temple on 25 December 167 BC, deliberately desecrating it so that the Jews would no longer think of it as the place where they were reaffirmed as a unique people. He established worship of himself there instead.[3]

Very often in the ancient world such moves would have worked quite satisfactorily, at least from the conqueror's point of view. But Antiochus had not reckoned on the tenacity of the Jews. Some of them refused to break the ancestral laws, and died rather than submit, bequeathing a memory of martyrdom-for-Torah that was kept fresh right through our period. Others, having escaped, believed that the covenant God would act in a new way. He would vindicate his own name, his chosen place, his sacred turf, his holy law—and his faithful people, provided they remained faithful to him and to his symbols, no matter what happened to them.

---

3   On this whole episode see 1 Maccabees; Jos. *War* 1.31–40; *Ant.* 12.246–331.

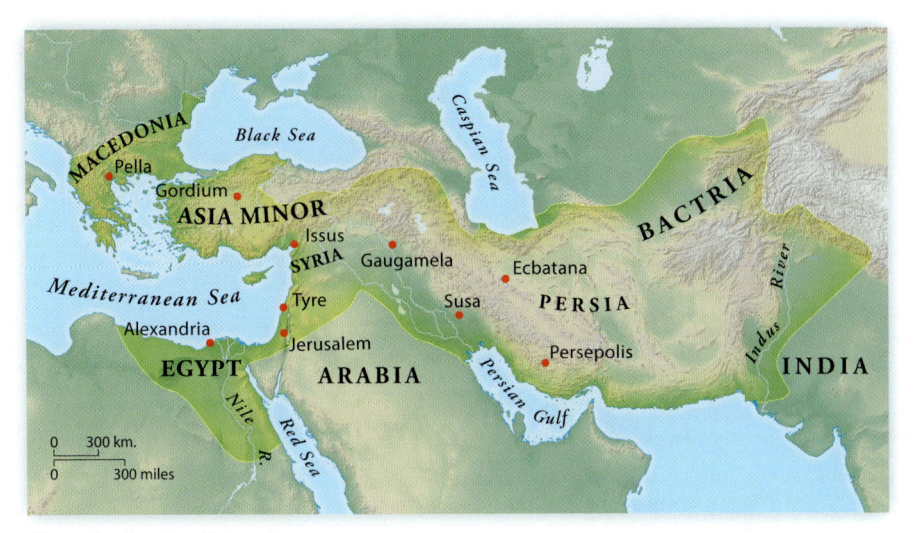

Alexander the Great's empire

The Ptolemies and Seleucids in the third century BC

The History of the Jews between the Persian and Roman Empires 91

HASMONEAN DYNASTY 165–64 BC

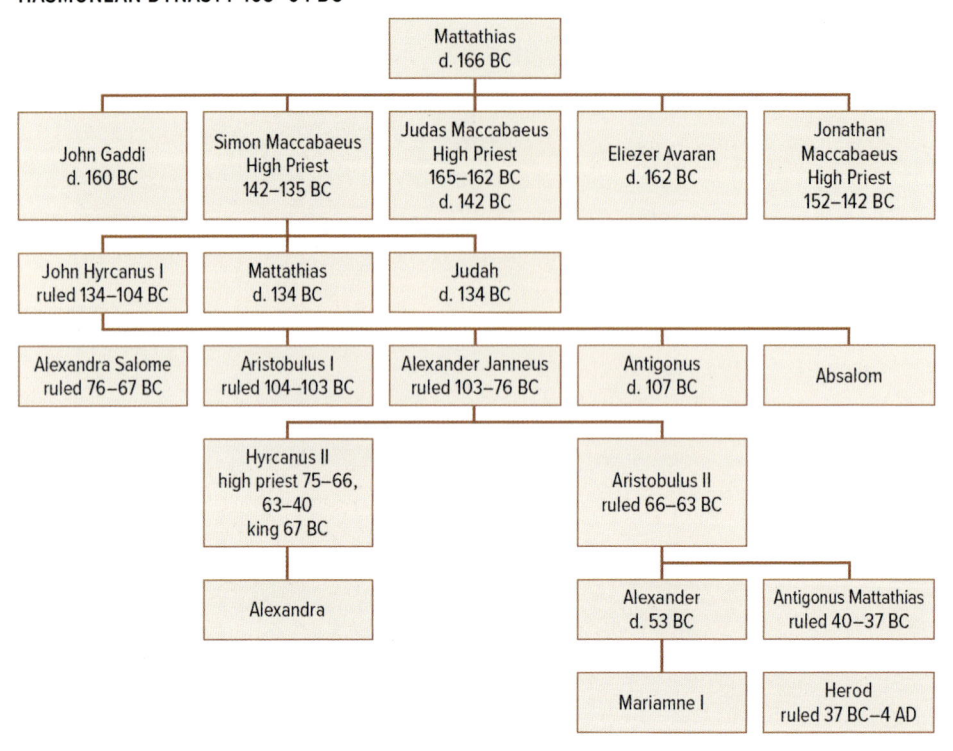

```
                          Mattathias
                          d. 166 BC
   ┌──────────┬──────────────┼──────────────┬──────────────┐
John Gaddi  Simon        Judas          Eliezer Avaran   Jonathan
d. 160 BC   Maccabaeus   Maccabaeus     d. 162 BC        Maccabaeus
            High Priest  High Priest                     High Priest
            142–135 BC   165–162 BC                      152–142 BC
                         d. 142 BC

John Hyrcanus I   Mattathias   Judah
ruled 134–104 BC  d. 134 BC    d. 134 BC

Alexandra Salome  Aristobulus I   Alexander Janneus  Antigonus   Absalom
ruled 76–67 BC    ruled 104–103   ruled 103–76 BC    d. 107 BC

         Hyrcanus II                      Aristobulus II
         high priest 75–66,               ruled 66–63 BC
         63–40
         king 67 BC

         Alexandra                Alexander       Antigonus Mattathias
                                  d. 53 BC        ruled 40–37 BC

                                  Mariamne I      Herod
                                                  ruled 37 BC–4 AD
```

People who believe this sort of thing tend to act with desperate daring. One strand of Jewish self-understanding, belief, and hope coalesced into a single movement. Judas Maccabaeus and his companions accomplished the unthinkable, and organized a protracted insurgency that routed, and eventually wore out, the Seleucid forces. Antiochus IV abandoned the campaign against the Judean rebels, rescinding the ban on traditional Jewish worship, and turned his attention to recovering lost provinces beyond the Euphrates.

Then, three years to the day after the Temple's desecration (25 December 164 BC), Judas cleansed and reconsecrated it (see box: 'Judas Maccabaeus rededicates the Temple'). A new festival (Hanukkah) was added to the Jewish calendar to celebrate the event. The Maccabean revolt became classic and formative in the same way as the exodus and the other great events of Israel's history. It powerfully reinforced the basic Jewish worldview, as you might find it in many passages, for instance Psalm 2: when the tyrants rage, the one who dwells in heaven will laugh them to scorn. YHWH had vindicated his name, his place, his land, his Torah—and his people.

The power vacuum created by the decline of the Seleucid kingdom meant that by 142 BC the Hasmoneans were finally able to achieve complete independence from foreign rule for the Jewish nation for the first time in half a millennium.

92   The World of Jesus and the Early Church

Consolidating their power and wealth, they gradually extended their borders over the surrounding tribal areas of Galilee, Idumea, the Trans-Jordan, and parts of Syria, where they forcibly converted some peoples to Judaism. However, as with most ruling dynasties, internal power struggles and political machinations eventually began to eat away at the kingdom's strength. The Hasmonean dynasty began to crumble under the weight of civil wars, even as it faced external threats from Rome in the west and Parthia in the east.

The ambiguity of the Hasmonean dynasty, in which the heirs of the successful revolutionaries ruled as priest-kings, initially under Syrian auspices but later independently, did not dim the Jews' sense of the victory of their God, but created the same sort of puzzle that was left after the so-called 'return from exile'. A great vindication had occurred, but it now seemed as though there must be yet another one still to come. The great prophecies had not, it seemed, been fulfilled. There had been no blaze of divine glory returning to Jerusalem and transforming the world. By no means were all Jews happy with the new situation. Getting rid of the tyrant and his idolatrous practices was one thing, but was the new Hasmonean regime what God actually wanted? Was it not in its turn heavily compromised with Hellenism, and riding roughshod over the religious sensibilities of the Jewish people—by, for instance, combining the offices of king and high priest? Some opposed it bitterly and set up alternative communities, like the ones at Elephantine in Egypt and at Qumran in the Judean wilderness. Some, like the Hasidim, the forerunners of the Pharisees, stuck it out, but grumbled and tried to reform society from within. Others played the power game to win, a notable example being a certain Idumean called Antipater, the father of Herod the Great. Most Jews—the ones who wrote no literature, led no marches, had no

> **JUDAS MACCABAEUS REDEDICATES THE TEMPLE**
>
> Now Maccabeus and his followers, the Lord leading them on, recovered the temple and the city; they tore down the altars that had been built in the public square by the foreigners, and also destroyed the sacred precincts. They purified the sanctuary, and made another altar of sacrifice; then, striking fire out of flint, they offered sacrifices, after a lapse of two years, and they offered incense and lighted lamps and set out the bread of the Presence. When they had done this, they fell prostrate and implored the Lord that they might never again fall into such misfortunes, but that, if they should ever sin, they might be disciplined by him with forbearance and not be handed over to blasphemous and barbarous nations. (2 Macc. 10.1–4 NRSV)

This coin features a picture of the bust of Antiochus Epiphanes IV and, on the reverse side, the god Apollo enthroned with the inscription 'Antiochus, God Manifest, bearer of victory'.
Classical Numismatic Group, Inc. www.cngcoins.com

voice—struggled to maintain their livelihood and their loyalty, their allegiance to national and cultural symbols, as best they could, always under the social pressures of warring theologies. It was this many-sided response to the ambiguities of the second century BC that created the pluriform Jewish world known by Jesus and Paul.

THE JEWS UNDER ROMAN RULE (63 BC–AD 70)

Roman power had been building for centuries, especially after the defeat of the Carthaginians in the late third century which had left Rome as the unrivalled power in the western Mediterranean. The Romans were soon able to extend their rule eastwards by defeating Philip V of Macedon in 197 BC, and then, the Seleucid king Antiochus III in 189 BC, giving them control of Greece, the Balkans, and Asia Minor. Just over a century later, after defeating the Pontic king Mithridates VI in 66 BC, the great general Pompey would defeat the last vestiges of Syrian power in 64 BC, and then march further south, liberating Greek cities from Syrian and Judean rule, and eventually capturing Jerusalem. Once in Jerusalem, Pompey visited the Temple, as other conquering generals had before—except that Pompey, to the horror of the Jewish people, committed the ultimate sacrilege: he entered the Holy of Holies.

The Romans' arrival in Judea in 63 BC coincided with the confusion of a civil war between rival Hasmonean brothers. Pompey's ability to simply wander into Jerusalem, without anyone putting up much of a struggle, and to then violate the sanctity of the Temple left people with a lot of questions.[4] If God had defeated the tyrant Antiochus Epiphanes when he presumed to desecrate the Temple, how could Pompey walk right in to the Holy of Holies and escape unscathed? From that moment there were bound to be Jews who would identify the Romans as the new great enemy, the Kittim, the power of darkness ranged against the children of light.[5] They were now seen as the archetypal idolaters, and would eventually reap the fruit of their wicked and blasphemous ways. When Pompey died thirty years later, in another campaign and another place, some Jews celebrated this as the downfall that had been coming to him all along.[6] The Romans thus inherited the role, and the odium, of Babylon, of Antiochus, of the whole encroaching hellenistic culture. They managed to make matters still worse by ruling with an insensitive arrogance that constantly bordered on provocation to rebellion.

But no new Judas Maccabaeus arose to lead Israel's faithful heroes in another holy war. Instead, his heirs and successors compromised with the faithless, played the political game, rendered unto Caesar what Caesar thought was due to him, and gave to their God what was left. The Romans, meanwhile, oversaw Palestine from

---

4   Jos. *War* 1.133–54; *Ant.* 14.37–79; Dio Cassius *Hist.* 37.15.2—16.4.
5   The word 'Kittim' is used in e.g. Daniel and Qumran as a generic term for the new pagan enemy, Rome.
6   See *Ps. Sol.* 2.25–31, referring to Pompey's death in 48 BC.

their base in the province of Syria, ruling the country at one remove through the Hasmonean, and then the Herodian, dynasties. The Temple became, *de facto*, the cultic shrine organized by those who had made a somewhat unsteady peace with Rome, while the rigorists, looking on with impotent anger, determined that they at least would be faithful to the covenant God, by keeping his covenant charter to the utmost of their ability. If anyone was to be vindicated when the covenant God finally acted, it would surely be those who had thus demonstrated their unswerving loyalty to him.

Hasmonean kingdom

The History of the Jews between the Persian and Roman Empires

Palestine under Herod the Great

For the next twenty years the Romans controlled Judea through client rulers. Pompey appointed Hyrcanus II as high priest, with the help and backing of Antipater, the wealthy pro-Roman Idumean we met a moment ago. Soon Antipater was appointed as governor of Judea, but after he was poisoned by a rival in 43 BC his two sons ruled in his stead, with Herod the governor of Galilee and Phasael the governor of Judea. Then, in 40 BC, the Parthians invaded and captured Jerusalem and installed Mattathias Antigonus as ruler. Hyrcanus II was exiled, Phasael committed suicide, and Herod managed to flee to Rome. The Roman senate considered the options, declared Herod 'king of the Jews', and sent him back to liberate Jerusalem (in 37 BC) from the Parthian-backed Hasmonean leader with a cohort of Roman troops. Herod eventually became the unrivalled ruler of Judea, Samaria, Galilee, Perea, and Trachontis, earning himself the title 'Herod the Great'. He made every effort to legitimate himself and his successors as genuine kings: he married Mariamne, the granddaughter of Hyrcanus II and thus a Hasmonean princess.

Herod the Great, the most powerful Jewish monarch in the Roman period, ruled from 40 BC until his death in approximately 4 BC. He had been faithful to his patron Mark Antony in the Roman civil war; but, after Octavian's victory over Antony and Cleopatra at the Battle of Actium in 31 BC, Herod swore allegiance to Octavian (later given the honorific 'Augustus') instead. Herod proved to be a loyal client ruler and was duly rewarded. During his reign he amassed great wealth, and engaged in a mammoth programme of building; if you go to the middle east today, you will still see some of the results. His central achievement was to reconstruct and wonderfully adorn the Jerusalem Temple; but he also erected several fortresses, such as Antonia and Masada, established great cities including Sebaste and Caesarea, erected public buildings in cities as far apart as Athens and Antioch, and even built temples for the imperial cult, such as the one at Caesarea Philippi, demonstrating in decisive fashion his loyalty to his Roman overlords.

This last action, coupled with some of Herod's other behaviour, naturally strained relations between him and many of his Jewish subjects. They regarded him as a half-Jew, lax in his commitment to the Jewish way of life. In addition, internal dissensions within his family led him to execute no fewer than three sons and one wife. As a result the jibe about Herod went round that it was safer to be Herod's pig (*hus*) than his son (*huios*). Nevertheless, he did achieve security, relative stability, and even some measure of prosperity for his territories.

HEROD THE GREAT'S FAMILY TREE

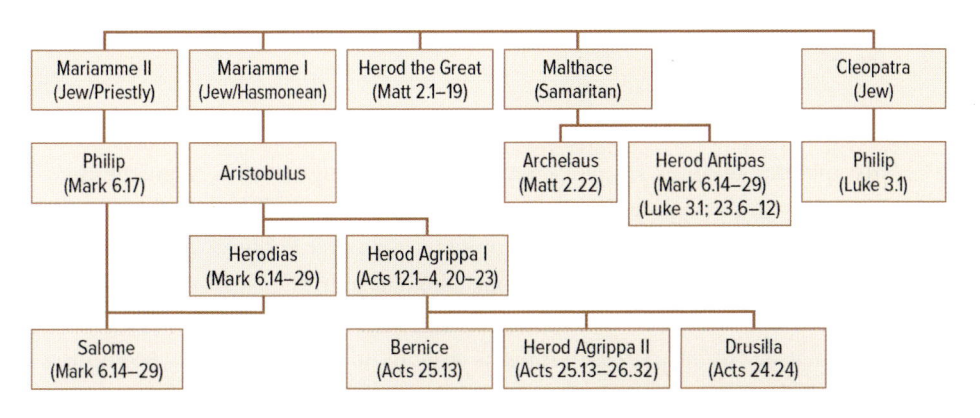

```
┌─────────────┬──────────────┬─────────────────┬──────────────┬────────────┐
│ Mariamme II │ Mariamme I   │ Herod the Great │ Malthace     │ Cleopatra  │
│ (Jew/       │ (Jew/        │ (Matt 2.1–19)   │ (Samaritan)  │ (Jew)      │
│ Priestly)   │ Hasmonean)   │                 │              │            │
└──────┬──────┴──────┬───────┴─────────┬───────┴──────┬───────┴─────┬──────┘
       │             │                 │              │             │
   ┌───┴───┐    ┌────┴─────┐      ┌────┴────┐   ┌─────┴──────┐  ┌───┴────┐
   │Philip │    │Aristo-   │      │Archelaus│   │Herod Antipas│  │Philip  │
   │(Mark  │    │bulus     │      │(Matt    │   │(Mark 6.14–29)│ │(Luke   │
   │6.17)  │    │          │      │2.22)    │   │(Luke 3.1;   │  │3.1)    │
   │       │    │          │      │         │   │23.6–12)     │  │        │
   └───┬───┘    └────┬─────┘      └─────────┘   └─────────────┘  └────────┘
       │             │
       │        ┌────┴─────┬───────────────┐
       │        │Herodias  │Herod Agrippa I│
       │        │(Mark     │(Acts 12.1–4,  │
       │        │6.14–29)  │20–23)         │
       │        └──────────┴───────┬───────┘
       │                           │
   ┌───┴────┐           ┌──────────┼──────────────┬───────────┐
   │Salome  │           │Bernice   │Herod Agrippa │Drusilla   │
   │(Mark   │           │(Acts     │II            │(Acts      │
   │6.14–29)│           │25.13)    │(Acts 25.13–  │24.24)     │
   │        │           │          │26.32)        │           │
   └────────┘           └──────────┴──────────────┴───────────┘
```

The division of Herod's kingdom

Herod bequeathed his kingdom to his three sons, Herod Archelaus, Herod Antipas, and Herod Philip. Despite a power struggle among the sons, Augustus upheld Herod's will, through which Archelaus was made ethnarch over Judea, Samaria, and Idumea; Herod Philip was appointed tetrarch over Batanea, Trachonitis, and Auranitis; and Herod Antipas (the one who had John the Baptist beheaded) was appointed tetrarch over Galilee and Perea. Archelaus's ten-year reign (4 BC–AD 6) was a disaster: he infuriated his subjects with his oppressive measures, prompting a Judean delegation to travel to Rome to get him removed (this is alluded to in Jesus' parable of the wicked nobleman in Luke 19.11–27). Augustus consented; Archelaus was exiled to Gaul; and Judea and Samaria were placed under the supervision of a series of Roman governors. Philip, in the north-east region, ruled in relative peace for some thirty-eight years over a mixed Jewish, Syrian, and Arab territory. He rebuilt the city of Paneas and renamed it Caesarea Philippi in honour of Augustus and himself.

Herod Antipas is the Herodian ruler most mentioned in the New Testament. His chief accomplishments included rebuilding Sepphoris after it revolted upon his father's death, and building a new Galilean capital named Tiberias on the shore of the Sea of Galilee. Antipas also had family issues that proved to be his undoing. He divorced his first wife, Phasaelis, the daughter of King Aretas IV of Nabatea, and then married his niece Herodias, who had previously been married to two of Antipas's half-brothers. This incurred the criticism of the popular Galilean prophet John the Baptist and drew a military reprisal from Aretas, whose victory over Antipas was regarded by many as God's punishment for Antipas's execution of John the Baptist.[7] When Herod Agrippa (Herod Antipas's nephew and Herodias's brother) was made king of Philip's former territory by the new emperor Gaius Caligula in AD 37, Antipas objected; but the result was that he was exiled to Gaul, and Galilee and Perea was bestowed upon Agrippa. Then, after Caligula was assassinated in AD 41, Agrippa supported Claudius's accession; for his loyalty he was rewarded with control of Judea and Samaria as well, which he ruled as king for three years until his death in AD 44. According to Luke, Herod Agrippa had attacked the early church, killing James, son of Zebedee, and imprisoning Peter. It was during a visit to Caesarea at Passover in AD 44 that Agrippa fell ill and died. Luke says that 'an angel of the Lord struck him down, and he was eaten by worms and died'.[8] Agrippa was succeeded by his son Agrippa II; but, because this son was only seventeen years old, control of Judea and Galilee reverted to direct Roman rule.

The Romans did not occupy Judea and Galilee in the same way that the USA occupied Afghanistan. There was no 'surge', with Roman soldiers standing on street corners or patrolling the streets. The Roman governor was based on the coast at Caesarea, with a small military force on the same site; a much larger force of four legions was stationed further north in Syria, under the command of a senior Roman military leader. Nor was Judea overrun with guerilla-style resistance fighters; the Judeans did not 'produce Messiahs by the sackful' as Tim Rice alleged in *Jesus Christ Superstar*.

Even so, the threat of revolution remained in the air during the early years of the new century. Banditry was a constant problem. After the revolt led by Judas the

---

7 Mt. 14.4/Mk. 6.18; Lk. 3.19; Jos. *Ant.* 18.116.
8 Ac. 12.1–5, 23.

Galilean in AD 6, Rome deemed it safer to make Judea a province in its own right, rather than overseeing it from Syria. From then on a succession of 'prefects' and then 'procurators' governed with more or less crass folly. Pontius Pilate was prefect between AD 26 and 32 (see box: 'Archaeological evidence for the existence of Pontius Pilate'), and was described by Philo and Josephus as a person of particular insolence and brutality. The character of Pilate is exemplified by several incidents that took place during the time of his governorship:

1. Pilate tried to bring Roman standards into Jerusalem, but backed down after a mass protest.[9]
2. He used money from the Temple treasury to build an aqueduct, and crushed the resistance that this action provoked.[10]
3. He sent troops to kill some Galileans while they were offering sacrifices in the Temple, presumably because he feared a riot.[11]
4. He captured and condemned to death Barabbas, the leader of a murderous uprising that had taken place in Jerusalem; he then released the man as a gesture of goodwill during the Passover feast.[12]
5. At the same Passover, he faced a quasi-messianic movement, having some association with resistance movements; he crucified its leader along with two ordinary revolutionaries.[13]
6. He provoked public opinion by placing Roman votive shields, albeit without images, in the palace at Jerusalem, which according to Philo annoyed Tiberius almost as much as it did the Jews.[14]
7. Finally, he suppressed with particular brutality a popular (and apparently non-revolutionary) prophetic movement in Samaria. For this he was accused before the Roman legate in Syria, who had him sent back to Rome.[15]

One particularly troublesome incident occurred in Judea in the winter of 39/40: the Syrian minority of Javneh tried to erect an altar to the imperial cult, which the Jewish majority promptly tore down. The incident was reported to the emperor, Gaius Caligula, who was so enraged at the insult to his divine honour that he ordered Publius Petronius, the governor of Syria, to march into Jerusalem with two legions and to erect a huge golden statue of Gaius in the Jewish Temple. The proposal was pointlessly provocative and would certainly have led to open

---

9 Jos. *Ant.* 18.55–9; *War* 2.169–74.
10 Jos. *Ant.* 18.60–2; *War* 2.175–7; Eus. *Hist. Eccl.* 2.6.6–7.
11 Lk. 13.1.
12 Lk. 23.18–25.
13 Matt. 26—27/Mk. 14—15/Lk. 23/Jn. 18—19.
14 Philo *Leg.* 299–306.
15 Jos. *Ant.* 18.85–89.

rebellion. Jewish delegations were sent to Rome to protest, including the philosopher Philo from Alexandria, and Marcus Agrippa I from Judea. Petronius himself urged the emperor to reconsider. Caligula responded by ordering Petronius to commit suicide. Fortunately for Petronius, the news of Caligula's own violent death reached him before the order to commit suicide. During the power vacuum that followed, Agrippa I was in Rome; he was crucial in providing advice to Claudius, the new emperor, and was able to help him become emperor. Claudius rewarded Agrippa for his loyalty, appointing him king over the territory once ruled by his grandfather Herod the Great. Agrippa's brother Herod Chalcis was made ruler of Lebanon.

After the death of Agrippa I, Judea again reverted to direct Roman rule, with a procurator based in Caesarea and under the supervision of the Syrian governor. The situation deteriorated as the procurators overseeing the province between AD 44 and 66 were largely corrupt, incompetent, and brutal. Other factors, too, contributed to the unstable situation: mismanagement by local leaders, socio-economic hardship, increasing banditry, and tension between the Jews and local gentile settlements. During the summer of AD 66, the governor Florus tried to respond to the provocative actions of some Judean youths by marching on Jerusalem with two cohorts to reinforce the small garrison resident there. When the offenders were not delivered up, Florus ordered the soldiers to ransack the market and kill people indiscriminately. He even had some Jewish leaders flogged and crucified. In response, a riot broke out, forcing Florus and his troops to flee back to Caesarea. Herod Agrippa II and his sister Bernice attempted to quell the disturbance and appeal for calm. Yet their efforts proved futile and they were expelled from the city.

> **ARCHAEOLOGICAL EVIDENCE FOR THE EXISTENCE OF PONTIUS PILATE**
>
> A four-line dedicatory inscription was discovered by excavators in Caesarea Maritima in 1961 with these words:
>
> TIBERIEUM
> [PO]NTIUS PILATUS
> [PRAEF]ECTUS IUDA[EA]
> [FECIT D] E [DICAVIT].
>
> It is most likely a building dedication in honour of the emperor Tiberius: 'To Tiberius . . . Pontius Pilate . . . prefect of Judea . . . has made and dedicated.'
>
> *BRBurton / Wikimedia Commons*

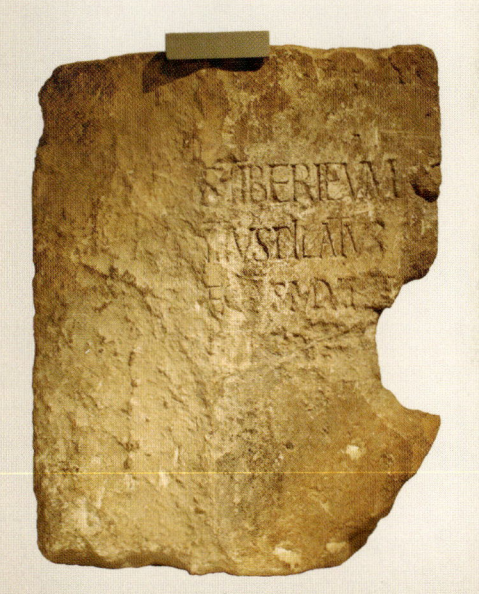

The triumphal arch of Titus, built by the Roman senate in AD 81 to commemorate Titus' conquest of Judea
© 2015 by Zondervan

Soon after, Eleazar, the captain of the Temple and son of the high priest, persuaded a group of rogue priests to cease accepting the sacrifices offered daily on the Roman emperor's behalf. Acceptance of this sacrifice had been the token gesture of Judea's submission to Roman authority in lieu of worshipping Roman gods and participating in the imperial cult. Stopping the imperial sacrifice—refusing, in other words, to pray for Rome—was an open act of defiance, marking the beginning of the war with Rome.

The governor of Syria, Cestius Gallus, made a futile attempt to regain the city, only to be forced back. In the hastily devised retreat his troops suffered heavy casualties. Nero was forced to dispatch a new general, Titus Flavius Vespasianus, to Judea to deal with the crisis. In the meantime, Jerusalem became engulfed in internal power-struggles between various factions. There was a quasi-official revolutionary government, led by Joseph ben-Gurion and Ananus ben-Ananus. There were the Sicarii (Greek *sikarioi*, the 'dagger-men', basically urban terrorists) led by Menahem. John of Gischala formed a different group by allying with some Idumeans. Some priests described themselves as 'zealots'; another faction was led by Simon bar-Giora, who was eventually though briefly seen by some, including the invading Romans, as 'king of the Jews'.

The members of these various factions fought as much among themselves as with the Romans. Mayhem became normative, as Ananus was killed by the zealots,

Menahem and the Sicarii fled to Masada, John of Gischala split from the zealots, and the Idumeans defected and joined Simon bar-Giora. Concurrently Nero committed suicide in AD 68, and after the deaths of the short-lived emperors Galba and Otho in AD 69, the Rhine legions pressed Vitellius's claim for power, while Vespasian's army declared him emperor instead. Vespasian then travelled to Egypt to get the support of the governor and control of the all-important grain supply, before heading to Rome to become emperor after Vitellius had been killed. Vespasian left his son Titus in Judea to continue the siege. Amid the chaos caused by a revolving throne of Roman emperors, there was a three-way tussle in Jerusalem between Simon bar-Giora, who controlled most of the city, John of Gischala, who controlled the outer Temple, and the zealots who were barricaded in the inner Temple.

Titus, aided by the counsel of a Jewish defector named Josephus, initially tried to starve the city. But then, hoping eagerly for a significant victory that would bring glory to the new imperial regime headed by his father, he launched an all-out assault on Jerusalem (AD 70). It worked. The Temple precincts were gradually taken over; the Temple itself was burned; most of the rebels were either killed on the spot or captured and crucified. Simon bar-Giora and many of his followers were taken to Rome in chains. Titus returned to Rome to celebrate a triumphal procession, carrying the vessels of the Temple as booty, with various prisoners including Simon himself, who was ritually executed at the end, signifying the victory of Rome over 'the king of the Jews' and his people. To add to the humiliation, a new tax was imposed on Jews throughout the empire. This *fiscus Judaicus* was paid to the temple of Capitolini Jupiter in Rome. Thus money that would hitherto have been collected from Jews worldwide and sent to support the Jerusalem Temple was paid instead to the Romans and, by implication, to their gods. Jerusalem was put under the control of a praetorian legate, with a colony of veterans established at Emmaus. That was the end of the small Judean state. The period we call 'second-Temple Judaism' came to its close—though that phrase is sometimes made to include the next seventy years as well.

THE JEWISH WORLD RECONSTRUCTED (AD 70–135)

The period after AD 70 was, obviously, of great significance for the future direction of the Jewish world. It has also often been regarded as of great significance for the development of early Christianity. A good many theories about the way in which Christianity developed, particularly about how it came to separate itself from the Jewish world of the synagogue, have hinged on the belief that in the post-destruction period certain events took place which introduced a new factor into the equation. According to rabbinic tradition, a Pharisee named Johanan ben-Zakkai escaped the siege of Jerusalem and surrendered to the Romans. He ingratiated himself to Vespasian by predicting his accession as emperor, and Vespasian in turn permitted

Ben-Zakkai to found a Jewish academy at Javneh, a small town near the coast about fifteen miles south of modern Tel Aviv and about twenty-five miles west of Jerusalem.[16] The new rabbinic movement, shocked and grieving over the loss of Jerusalem and the Temple, allegedly organized itself into a great synod at Javneh and propounded a modification of the twelfth clause within the ancient prayer known as the 'Eighteen Benedictions'; this amendment invoked a curse on heretics in general and Christians in particular, thus making it impossible for Christians to continue worshipping in synagogues, which, according to this theory, many of them had been happily doing until this point. And then, so it goes, the young church, flexing its muscles, responded to polemic with polemic. Sayings, many of them bitterly hostile to Judaism, were put in the mouth of Jesus, even though they reflected the conditions in the 80s and 90s rather than the period of Jesus' own ministry or the first generation of the church. This was the period (according to the theory) when for the first time there was a sense that the Torah and the gospel were incompatible.

What can be said about this theory? There seems little doubt that Ben-Zakkai did indeed establish an academy at Javneh. However, the idea that a legendary 'synod' took place there has become known as 'the "Council of Javneh" Myth'.[17] There is indeed good reason to trace the developing story of worsening Jewish-Christian relations along a line which, beginning very early (already with Paul, starting in the period when, as Saul of Tarsus, he was persecuting the church), sooner or later intersects with the promulgation and popularity of such an anti-heretical 'benediction'.[18] It is probable, though, both that the 'heretics' indicated by the new prayer included many groups of whom the Christians were only one, and that the measures taken against them did not necessarily extend to expulsion as such.

It is more likely, in fact, that the destruction of the Temple created not one single reaction, but a variety of reactions. It is over-simplistic to think that all forms of 'Judaism' were wiped out except a particular type of Pharisaism, which then, transmuting itself into rabbinism, grew and developed in a new way, unhindered by Sadducean pressure on the one hand or revolutionary fervour on the other. We must, rather, envisage a Jewish world which included at least three strands: (1) the anguish apparent in the writings of *4 Ezra* and *2 Baruch*, whose authors lament the fall of the Temple as if their hearts would break; (2) the pragmatism of Johanan ben-Zakkai, calmly recognizing that Hosea 6.6 had long ago spoken of Israel's God as desiring deeds of loving-kindness rather than sacrifice; and (3) the smouldering fire of rebellion, crushed once again by pagan might but seeking nevertheless the way by which to reverse the catastrophe and build the true Temple. There is good reason

---

16 Also spelled 'Jamnia', 'Jabneh', 'Yavneh', etc.
17 See Aune 1991.
18 Among the evidence for early, though not systematized, hostility between the communities, see the letters of Paul, e.g. Gal. 1.13; 4.29; 1 Thess. 2.14–16; and also perhaps 1 Cor. 12.1–3. See Mayo 2006.

to suppose that position (2) was more or less the position of the great sage Hillel, from the Herodian period, while position (3) was the hard-line position taken by his rival Shammai—though simplifying hindsight, and the fact that the relevant texts are all from a much later period, may well be masking many complex diversities. These rivalries, resulting in two 'schools' seen later as 'lenient' and 'strict' in terms of keeping the detail of Torah, may well have originally had to do with political attitudes, Hillel seeking compromise with the ruling pagans and Shammai urging revolt—but, again, this may well be over-simple. (We should note that one of the results of the events of AD 70 was the complete disappearance of the Sadducees, focused as they were on the old Temple hierarchy. In addition, the Romans seem to have destroyed the Essene movement; Qumran was uninhabited thereafter.) To what extent these three main points of view might have overlapped in the post-70 period, and to what extent they stood in continuity with various movements from before the destruction, must remain in question for the moment. What matters is that we recognize the non-monolithic nature of the new situation in the Jewish world following the disaster of AD 70.

We might also include a fourth strand in the Jewish world at this time: (4) the young Christian church, still thinking of itself as the fulfilment of Israel's great story, following Israel's true Messiah, and interpreting the fall of Jerusalem in terms of the divine vindication of Jesus' claims. Since Ignatius of Antioch, writing in the early second century, speaks of Jews attending churches and Christians attending synagogues, it looks as though whatever happened at Javneh did not result in total separation.

What, then, was the significance of the Javneh period for the newly emerging form of Judaism, and for its daughter religion, Christianity? It seems that the period was as much a time of uncertainty for those who lived through it as it has proved for the scholars who have tried to reconstruct it. For Jews, the attempt to re-establish an authentically Jewish way of life in the absence of the Temple produced, as we have seen, a variety of responses ranging from revolutionary determination to the study and debating of Torah. For much of Christianity, which by AD 70 had spread far beyond the borders both of Palestine and of the Jewish communities of the Diaspora, there were pressing questions and issues quite other than that of relationships with the synagogue community. It was a period of transition, when many ambiguities existed side by side; and many people, on both sides

A coin produced under Simeon ben-Kosiba, on one side depicting the Temple with a messianic star above it, and on the other side a lulvav leaf with the inscription 'for the freedom of Jerusalem'.
Classical Numismatic Group, Inc. www.cngcoins.com

> ## CHRONOLOGY OF ROMAN EMPERORS AND PREFECTS*
>
> **27 BC –AD 14 Augustus**
> - 6–9 *Coponius*
> - 9–12 *Marcus Ambivius*
> - 12–15 *Annius Rufus*
>
> **AD 14–37 Tiberius**
> - 15–26 *Valerius Gratus*
> - 18 Caiaphas high priest
> - 26–36 *Pontius Pilate*
> - 30 Crucifixion of Jesus
> - 33/4 Conversion of Saul of Tarsus/Paul the apostle
> - 36 Nabatean king Aretas invades Perea, defeats Antipas
>
> **AD 37–41 Gaius Caligula**
> - 37–41 *Marullus*
> - 37–9 Herod Agrippa becomes king over Philip's (37) and Antipas's (39) territory
> - 40 Crisis over Gaius's attempt to erect a statue of himself in the Temple
>
> **AD 41–54 Claudius**
> - 41 Claudius makes Herod Agrippa king of Judea too
> - 42/3 Agrippa executes James the brother of John, Passover (Ac. 12.2)
> - 44 Death of Herod Agrippa (Ac. 12); Judea reverts to procurators
> - 44–6 *Cuspius Fadus*
> - 44 Famine (Ac. 11.28)
> - 46–8 *Tiberius Alexander*
> - 47 Crucifixion of Jacob and Simon, sons of Judas the Galilean
> - 48–52 *Ventidius Cumanus*
> - 49 Claudius expels Jews from Rome (Ac. 18.2)
> - 50 Paul begins his missionary journeys
> - 50–1 Paul in Corinth during the consulship of Gallio (Ac. 18.12)
> - 52–60 *Antonius Felix*
>
> * Emperors in bold and Roman governors of Judea in italics.

of what was to become the great divide, seemed content to let it be so. We should not forget that early Christianity, claiming the high ground of Israel's heritage, was first and foremost a movement that defined itself in opposition to *paganism*, and only secondarily in opposition to the Jewish movements whose adherents refused to accept Jesus as their Messiah.

This period of transition came to an abrupt and bloody end with the Jewish rebellion against the emperor Hadrian in AD 132–5 (see box: 'Chronology of Roman emperors and prefects'). Hadrian had passed a law forbidding circumcision as a barbaric practice (the Jews were not the only people who practised the custom, but the ban struck them especially due to the centrality of circumcision within their worldview). He had also founded a pagan city, Aelia Capitolina, on the site of ruined Jerusalem, with an altar to Zeus on the site of the Temple itself. These provocations, more serious still than those of the procurators in the 50s and 60s, and comparable to those of Antiochus Epiphanes much earlier, called forth rebellion. Simeon ben-Kosiba began a revolt which quickly roused the whole land. He himself was hailed as Messiah by the great rabbi Akiba, among others, and given the title Bar-Kochba, 'Son of the Star' (referring to the prophecy of Num. 24.17). Not everyone agreed with this designation: some sages contradicted Akiba, perhaps for reasons of speculative chronology, while the Christians resident in the area, recognizing a rival to Jesus, refused to join in the movement and (according to Justin and Eusebius) were subjected to fierce

106   The World of Jesus and the Early Church

persecution. Documents and coins from the period indicate both that Ben-Kosiba and his followers saw the start of the revolt as the beginning of the long-awaited 'age to come', and that he was as concerned with the maintenance of Jewish religious duty as with revolution against Rome. Nearly seventy years had passed since the destruction under Vespasian; perhaps this was the moment when Israel's God would at last liberate his people.

The hope was dashed. Despite inflicting heavy losses on Hadrian's army, the Judeans were massively defeated. Many who survived were sold into slavery in large numbers. Jerusalem became a fully pagan city, with the ban on Jewish customs strictly enforced. Not until the twentieth century could the idea of a self-governing Jewish state in the middle east be spoken of as anything other than the remotest possibility.

Further reading

Bruce, F. F. 1969. *New Testament History*. New York: Doubleday, pp. 1–40.

deSilva, David A. 2010. *Days of Atonement: A Novel of the Maccabean Revolt*. Grand Rapids, MI: Kregel.

Grabbe, Lester L. 1992. *Judaism from Cyrus to Hadrian*. London: SCM.

Rasmussen, Carl. 2010. *Zondervan Atlas of the Bible*. Grand Rapids, MI: Zondervan.

Seeman, Chris, and Adam Kolman Marshak. 2010. 'Jewish History from Alexander to Hadrian.' In *The Eerdmans Dictionary of Early Judaism*. Edited by D. C. Harlow and J. J. Collins. Grand Rapids, MI: Eerdmans, pp. 30–55.

Wright, N. T. 1992. *The New Testament and the People of God*. COQG 1; London: SPCK, pp. 147–66.

(cont.)*

AD 54–68 Nero
- **54** Jews return to Rome after Claudius's death
- **60–2** *Porcius Festus*
- **62** James the Just executed during interregnum (Jos. *Ant.* 20.200)
- **62–5** *Lucceius Albinus*
- **63** Temple finally completed
- **64** Fire of Rome: persecution of Christians
- **65–6** *Gessius Florus*
- **66–70** Judean revolt against Rome

AD 68–9 Galba
- **69** 'Year of four emperors'

AD 69 Otho

AD 69 Vitellius

AD 69–79 Vespasian
- **70** Titus captures Jerusalem
- **post-70** Establishment of a rabbinic academy at Javneh under Johanan ben-Zakkai
- **74** Capture of Masada (last stronghold of rebels)

AD 79–81 Titus

AD 81–96 Domitian

AD 96–8 Nerva

AD 98–117 Trajan
- **110** Pliny governor of Bithynia
- **110–15** Letters of Ignatius of Antioch
- **115–17** Jewish revolts in Egypt, Cyrene, and Cyprus

AD 117–38 Hadrian
- **132** Hadrian's anti-semitic legislation; temple of Jupiter built in Jerusalem
- **133–5** Rebellion of Simeon ben-Kosiba (Bar-Kochba)
- **135** Martyrdom of Rabbi Akiba

* Emperors in bold and Roman governors of Judea in italics.

6

The Jewish Context of Jesus and the Early Church

If Israel were to keep two Sabbaths according to the rules, they would immediately be redeemed.[1]

CHAPTER AT A GLANCE

This chapter describes features of first-century Jewish life in Palestine, including its geography, socio-economic conditions, the various Jewish sects, and key tenets of the Jewish faith.

By the end of this chapter you should be able to:

- describe the geography and socio-economic conditions of Palestine in the first century;
- understand cultural values like kinship and patronage, honour and shame, and purity and impurity;
- identify the main Jewish sects and their distinctive beliefs and behaviours;
- describe features of Jewish monotheism and election, and Jewish hopes for the future.

JEWISH LIFE IN PALESTINE

Geography

The modern state of Israel–Palestine is located at the eastern side of the Mediterranean, at the three-way intersection between Africa, Asia, and Arabia. The biblical boundaries of ancient Israel extended to the mountainous regions of Galilee in the north, east along the River Jordan, south of the Dead Sea along the eastern edge of the Sinai desert to the Gulf of Aqaba, and obviously bounded to the west by the Mediterranean.[2] In the first century, there was no single 'state' in that region with borders in the modern sense. Judea itself was basically Jerusalem and the surrounding country, and there were several other cities in the region without Jewish influence. As we have seen, for administrative purposes the region could be divided different ways (as for instance

---
1 bShab. 118b.
2 See Num. 34.1–15; Jdg. 20.1; Ezek. 37.13–20. Some biblical descriptions extend further to include regions east of the Nile and west of the Euphrates; see Gen. 15.18; Dt. 1.7; 11.24.

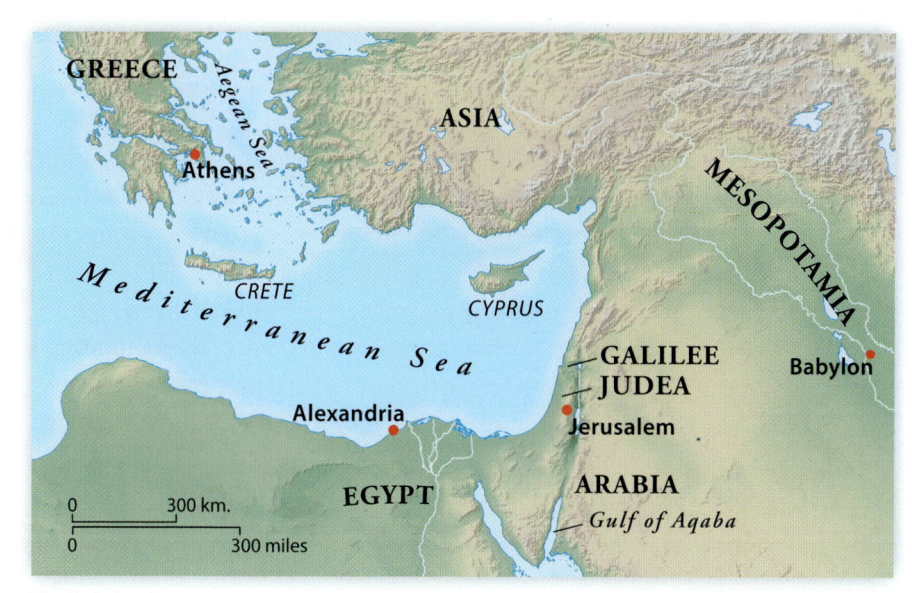

The holy land

between the sons of Herod the Great), rather like central Europe over the last few centuries, where someone living in the same house near Bratislava for fifty years might have found themselves in four or five different 'countries'. The traditional regions of Galilee, Samaria, and Judea were general designations rather than permanently fixed social or geographical entities. This whole area was then surrounded by Idumea to the south-west, Nabatea to the south-east, Perea and the cities of the Decapolis across the Jordan, and the region of Batanea/Gaulantis to the north-east. To the immediate north of Galilee was Coele-Syria. Galilee is called 'Galilee of the Gentiles'[3] not because it was heavily populated with gentiles, but because it was surrounded by gentile regions to the north, east, south, and west.

Granted its small size, Palestine's geography is remarkably varied. The four main features, moving from west to east, are: (1) the coastal plain which runs from Mount Carmel in the north to Gaza in the south; (2) the central mountains, from Galilee in the north to the Negev highlands in the south, rising up as high as three thousand feet above sea level and including Jerusalem, not on the highest hills but certainly quite elevated; (3) the Jordan valley, which dramatically descends to below sea level, containing the River Jordan which, rising in the far north, passes through the Sea of Galilee in the north and flows into the Dead Sea in the south; and (4) the Trans-Jordan, consisting of the plain and then the mountains rising up on the eastern side of the River Jordan.[4]

---

3   Mt. 4.15; 1 Macc. 5.15 NRSV.
4   Rasmussen 2010, 21–8.

Language and literacy

Palestine was a trilingual environment. Aramaic was still the majority language, as it had been the *lingua franca* of the Persian empire. It persisted for centuries, despite Greek and Roman conquests of the region. (It is closely cognate with Syriac, whose ancient form some still use today as a living language.) Hebrew, relating to Aramaic rather as Chaucer's English relates to ours, was found in liturgical settings where scripture was read, but was also spoken by some, and used in writing and inscriptions. Greek, too, was also spoken widely, particularly among merchants and the ruling class. Since Jesus grew up in Nazareth, it is certain that he spoke Aramaic; the transliterated words attributed to him in the New Testament are all in Aramaic (see, for example, Mk. 5.41). It seems he could at least read Hebrew (see Lk. 4.16–20). As we suggested earlier, he will almost certainly have been competent in Greek, maybe conversing in Greek with gentiles like the Syro-Phoenician woman in Mark 7.24–30, or indeed like Pontius Pilate.[5] Those who live in single-language cultures perhaps need reminding that in many parts of the world, then and now, being able to function in three or four languages has been the norm, requiring no great sophistication or high-level education.

When it comes to literacy, the first thing we have to remember is that there are different levels. Saying someone is 'literate', or asking about percentages of 'literate' people in a population, will depend on which level we are talking about. Some people can just about write their own name. Others can also scribble out business contracts, and write short informal letters. Others are capable of reading sustained literary works; others still, of composing them. And there are shades in between. In addition, being functionally multilingual does not always mean having the same degree of literary competency in all the relevant languages. Generally speaking, and working with a 'literacy' somewhere in the middle of the scale just described, ancient literacy levels are estimated to be at around 10–15 per cent, perhaps higher for Jews and Christians, who had a strong book culture with an emphasis on reading sacred texts. However, if we take into account widespread phenomena like inscriptions, graffiti, and so on, there is a good chance that ancient literacy levels might have been even higher still.[6]

Economic life

Palestine, including Galilee and Judea, was an agrarian society.[7] The majority of people lived in rural villages and small towns, rather than in the larger cities like Tiberias and Jerusalem. Agrarian societies generate various socio-economic models of power and privilege, but all of them emphasize the stratification between various tiers.

---

5 See Porter 1993b; Poirier 2007; Fassberg 2012.
6 See studies by Harris 1989 and Hezser 2001 and the bold questioning of the consensus by B. Wright 2015 who thinks literacy rates were considerably higher than many suppose.
7 See Longenecker 2010, 19–35, plus further on the economics of first-century Galilee and Judea, Applebaum 1974; Oakman 1986; Fiensy and Hawkins 2013; Adams 2014, 183–205.

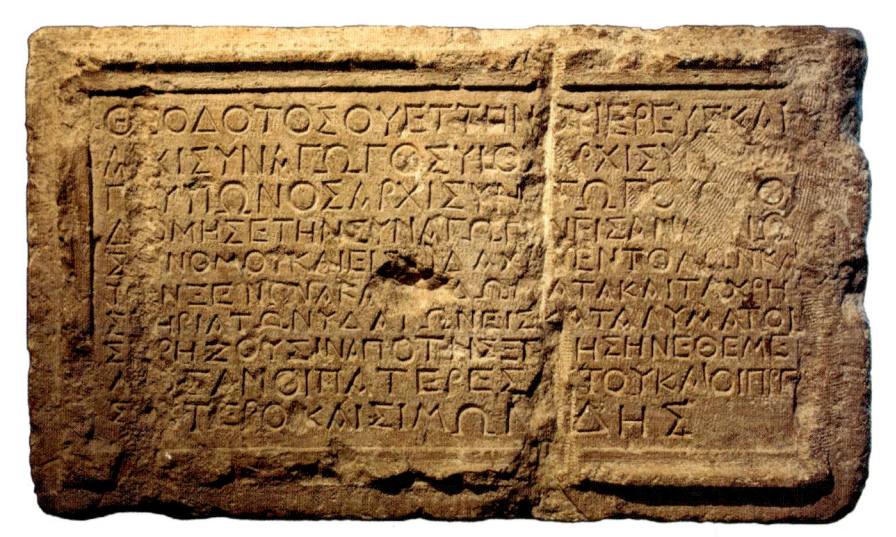

A first-century Greek inscription from a synagogue in Jerusalem honouring Theodotus, the synagogue leader. The inscription is significant because it proves the existence of a building set aside for worship by Greek-speaking Jewish immigrants in first-century Jerusalem (see Ac. 6.9) and it attests the title of *archisynagogos* as 'synagogue leader' (see Lk. 8.49; 13.14; Ac. 13.15; 18.8, 17).
© 2018 by Zondervan

There is, first, a ruling elite, comprising a ruler, his or her immediate family, and a wider body of dependants. Second, there are regional elites: royal officials, large landowners, military leaders, and wealthy merchants.[8] Third, there are municipal elites, those with smaller but stable land holdings, merchants, and some veterans. After this, fourth, there are lower-level retainers like governing officials, scribes, and priests. Then, fifth, there is a professional class of small merchants, shop-owners, fishermen, and skilled artisans like stonemasons or silversmiths. Below this, sixth, there is the peasant class, consisting of subsistence farmers and unskilled labourers. Finally, seventh, there are the destitute: beggars, prostitutes, widows, the disabled and infirm, orphans, and untouchables like lepers.[9] Slaves would be in a different category again, and we moderns need to remind ourselves that in the ancient world anyone could become a slave; all you had to do was to be on the losing side in a battle, or suffer a major business failure. Slavery had nothing to do with ethnic background or skin colour.

People could move up and down this social scale, depending on political stability, famine, disease, population size, and taxation. For the most part it seems that in

---

[8] See e.g. 'Herod gave a banquet for his high officials and military commanders and the leading men of Galilee' (Mk. 6.21).
[9] Mostly following Longenecker 2010, 36–59. Many today find the word 'leper' offensive as a description of someone suffering from one of a number of types of virulent skin diseases. It is difficult to find an appropriate alternative without a lengthy paraphrase each time.

Jesus' world there were constant downward pressures, forcing people towards debt and destitution, and in some cases even towards either banditry or slavery as desperate strategies for survival.

These economic realities are exhibited in various places in the New Testament. The parable of the wicked tenants is a prime example, displaying an economic hierarchy with hired farmers working for an absentee landlord.[10] The radical disparity in fortunes between the rich and the poor is exhibited in the parable of the rich man and Lazarus.[11] The parable of the rich fool portrays a wealthy man trying to store an excess of crops so he can enjoy life even though they will be no good to him in an afterlife.[12] The parable of the ungrateful servant narrates instances where debt could lead to imprisonment.[13] The letter of James describes a setting in Palestine or Syria where wealthy landowners exploited agricultural workers.[14]

Jesus was a 'craftsman' (*tektōn*) living in the rural village of Nazareth.[15] He seems to have largely identified with the peasant class, frequently teaching about the importance of generosity to the poor; he warned severely about the dangers of wealth. Another interesting fact is that Jesus seems to have avoided large urban centres like Sepphoris and Tiberias during his Galilean ministry. This may have been to avoid arrest by Herod Antipas's security forces. It would be wrong, though, to idealize Jesus in modern terms as a kind of proto-Marxist prophet preaching a 'kingdom' to the 'proletariat': his disciples and followers were people on various levels of the economic scale, ranging from prostitutes, to fishermen, to tax-collectors, and upwards to synagogue rulers and the like. Jesus' wider body of supporters and sympathizers could include wealthy women who supported him out of their own means, like Joanna, the wife of Chuza, Herod Antipas's household manager,[16] and even a member of the Sanhedrin named Joseph of Arimathea.[17] Clearly the appeal of Jesus' message transcended economic divisions.

Cultural values

Among the various important social factors in first-century Jewish life are those related to family and kinship, honour and shame, and finally, purity and pollution. Knowing about these reveals various significant dimensions of Jewish life in both Palestine and the wider Diaspora.[18]

---

[10] Mt. 21.32–46/Mk. 12.1–12/20.9–19.
[11] Lk. 16.20–31.
[12] Lk. 12.13–21.
[13] Mt. 18.21–35.
[14] Jas. 2.5–6; 5.1–6.
[15] Mt. 6.3.
[16] Lk. 8.3.
[17] Mt. 27.57/Mk. 15.43/Lk. 23.51; Jn. 19.38.
[18] See deSilva 2000a and Malina 2001.

First, ancient perceptions of family and kinship were markedly different from modern and western conceptions of family, which tend to be much more individualistic. Families were extended household entities, normally comprised of a male head, wife, children, dependants, freedmen, and slaves. The household head, *paterfamilias* or *materfamilias*, was the ultimate source of power and identity for the household, and largely determined the social, economic, and religious activities of the family. His or her political allegiances were those of the family; his or her religion was that of the family.[19] There developed in the greco-roman world particular ethical 'codes' on how to run a household, promoting order, honour, piety, and preparation for life in commerce, agriculture, civil leadership, military achievements, and nurturing a family.[20] Even when children married into other families, their marriage functioned largely for the benefit of their own family in securing an inheritance, dowry, or prestige. If a couple divorced, the woman returned to her father's house until she might be married off again. Families were a means of distributing wealth and property through inheritance and intangibles like honour, the family name, and the family cult. Family members were expected to show solidarity with one another, and to pursue goals that promoted the well-being and reputation of the family as a whole.

While kinship could be created by marriage or birth, kinship could also be created by devotion to a common set of ideals and shared way of life. This type of kinship was 'fictive', not in the sense of 'fake' or pretend, but in the sense of being cultivated apart from biological or marital bonds. For example, Philo praises gentile converts to the Jewish way as those who left behind 'their country, their kinsfolk and their friends for the sake of virtue and religion' by joining a Jewish community and adhering to the Jewish way of life.[21] This corresponds with Jesus' own teaching that his followers would be rewarded for their willingness to leave their own families and follow him:

> 'Truly I tell you,' Jesus replied, 'no one who has left home or brothers or sisters or mother or father or children or fields for me and the gospel will fail to receive a hundred times as much in this present age: homes, brothers, sisters, mothers, children and fields—along with persecutions—and in the age to come eternal life.'[22]

Jesus once rebuffed the efforts of his own family to intervene in his mission, identifying his disciples as his true family, saying: 'Here are my mother and my

---

19 This helps to explain why whole households could be converted to Christianity in NT accounts; see Jn. 5.43; Ac. 16.14–15, 31–34; 18.8; 1 Cor. 1.16; 16.15.
20 See the NT household codes in Eph. 5.21—6.9; Col. 3.18—4.1; 1 Pet. 2.18—3.7.
21 Philo *Spec. Leg.* 1.52.
22 Mk. 10.29–30; see Mt. 19.29.

brothers! Whoever does God's will is my brother and sister and mother.'[23] Paul conceived of his churches as a family, God's family, in which fictive kinship superseded other allegiances. He told the Ephesians: 'Consequently, you are no longer foreigners and strangers, but fellow citizens with God's people and also members of his household.'[24] The family metaphor for the church requires both solidarity and demonstrable affection among believers as Paul instructed the Thessalonians: 'you do love all of God's family throughout Macedonia. Yet we urge you, brothers and sisters, to do so more and more'.[25] Evidently the early church was comprised of people with an ethnically mixed and socially diverse fictive kinship, devoted to Jesus and united by a common concern to love and support one another as a single family.

Second, 'honour' and 'shame' refer to social values that were foundational for Jewish, Greek, and Roman societies. (There are modern equivalents, and any attempt to suggest that the ancient world cared about 'honour and shame' while we do not is blind to contemporary reality.) Honour, then and now, was and is the public affirmation of a person's value by his or her peers. Honour in the ancient world could either be inherited by a noble birth, a product of one's gender or social rank, or acquired through social advancement in public accomplishments and by excelling over others. Shame, in contrast, is the lack or loss of honour due to one's social position or through actions that cause one to lose face (there are, again, plenty of modern equivalents). For males, honour was acquired by showing courage, abilities, and trustworthiness; for women, honour was acquired through modesty, chastity, and the kind of domestic skills praised in the final chapter of the book of Proverbs. In rhetorical discourses, seeking honour and avoiding shame were avenues of appeal in the art of persuasion: in other words, to persuade someone to do something one might point out the honour that would accrue, or the shame if the task was shirked. Also, minority groups like Jews and Christians in the greco-roman world, who did not have much capital in the honour stakes because of their status as outsiders, could claim that God, reason, or nature accorded with their views of honourable belief and practice. All groups also used honour and shame as a way of enforcing their particular values, and urging conformity to a particular ethos.

The gospels emphasize that Jesus is, in the world of his day, 'honourable' by virtue of his prestigious genealogy, his miraculous birth, the sign of his divine sonship at his baptism, and his teachings and prophetic works that received widespread acclaim. A significant feature in the gospels is that Jesus challenges the authority of the Pharisees, scribes, chief priests, and Herodians to speak for God. In each confrontation with such people, Jesus out-performs them in wisdom and ability, and so increases his own honour while shaming his opponents. This is why we are told that

---

23 Mk. 3.34–35/Mt. 12.49–50/Lk. 8.21.
24 Eph. 2.19.
25 1 Thess. 4.10.

the Pharisees, chief priests, scribes, and Herodians plotted to kill him; that is what people do, as the 'honourable' course, if they have been shamed by a social inferior.[26] The evangelists also construct the Passion narrative in such a way as to show that although Jesus died in an utterly shameful manner, namely by the dishonourable method of crucifixion, nonetheless he died in such a way that even a Roman centurion might acknowledge his noble death, calling him a 'son of God' or, according to Luke, 'a righteous man'.[27] The author of Hebrews tries to undo the cultural script that equated crucifixion with shame when he declares that Jesus 'endured the cross, scorning its shame, and sat down at the right hand of the throne of God'.[28] For the author, Jesus' humiliation by the Romans was undone by his exaltation and enthronement with God the father. We also see that the cross, which in the ancient world was considered the lowest point of shame and degradation, was transformed in the thought of the early Jesus-movement, as in the writings of Paul, Peter, and the author of Hebrews, into a central symbol of God's honour, because it reveals the utter love of God and his successful deliverance of his people. Paul and Peter both cite Isaiah 8.16/28.16 that 'the one who believes in him will never be put to shame', whereby God establishes the 'honour' of a movement that the dominating culture regarded as shameful.[29]

'Honour' constituted a vital motivation for behaviour too. Paul instructs the Thessalonians to 'control your own body in a way that is holy and honourable'.[30] He urges the Romans not to compete with one another in the honour–shame game, but instead to, 'Love one another with brotherly affection. Outdo one another in showing honour.'[31] The early Christians thus attempted to renegotiate what 'honour' and 'shame' would actually look like. They exhorted one another towards honourable patterns of behaviour, defined by new codes of holiness and outward-looking love.

Third, ancient cultures exhibit concerns about purity and pollution, which constitute a symbolic code for distinguishing the clean from the contaminated and the sacred from the profane. (Again, we should not suppose that this is irrelevant in modern western society; we all have purity codes of one sort or another, some connected with hygiene, others with implied social practices, and so on.) Purity codes are the attempt to put things in their proper place for their proper time. This is why, in Jewish and Christian writings, you can find references to people and things that are holy, pure, sanctified, unblemished, undefiled, and clean. Generally speaking, impurity and pollution were simply part of life; most people were unclean most

---

[26] See Mk. 3.6; 11.18; 12.12; 14.1.
[27] Mt. 27.54/Mk. 15.39/Lk. 23.47.
[28] Heb. 12.2.
[29] Rom. 9.33; 1 Pet. 2.6.
[30] 1 Thess. 4.4.
[31] Rom. 12.10 ESV.

of the time, and living in common places rather than in holy precincts. Impurity, obviously, was not the same thing as 'sin', though the effects might overlap. In the Jewish world, a person would become impure through sexual intercourse, genital discharge, or childbearing; or by coming into contact with certain foods and liquids, particular animals, or a corpse. However, certain actions, 'sins', would also cause the defilement of persons, their kinship group, and even the land. Before entering into sacred space, a worshipper had to be cleansed both from any regular pollution and from moral blemish. This could be done either through ceremonial washing or by offering a sacrifice through the cultus, or both.

An ancient mikveh located in Qumran and used for ritual washings
Robert Hoetink / Shutterstock

We can easily identify how the practice of purity, and the scruples about pollution, worked out in Jewish and Christian communities. Much of Leviticus pertains to how the Israelites were to 'distinguish between the holy and the common, between the unclean and the clean'.[32] In the cultus of the Temple (and before that, the wilderness tabernacle), 'on this day atonement shall be made for you, to cleanse you; from all your sins you shall be clean before the LORD'.[33] In areas of life where the Torah was silent, the *halakhah* or oral teaching of the Pharisees and rabbis was often vocal with respect to the contagious nature of contaminants like certain

---
32 Lev. 10.10.
33 Lev. 16.30 NRSV.

116   The World of Jesus and the Early Church

liquids, and how to remove the resultant pollution. The Pharisees themselves took seriously the task of Israel to be a 'kingdom of priests', adopting the purity regulations originally intended for the priests and Levites: for them, all of life had to be lived as if one were in the Temple, in the very presence of God. The existence of *miqvaot*, ritual baths, across Judea and Galilee shows how widely the Pharisaic views of ritual cleansing were held and practised.

Several passages in the New Testament indicate how all this worked out. The leper begs Jesus to make him 'clean'; Jesus touches him and then declares that he is indeed now 'clean'. We have to remember that the leper would be socially ostracized from family and community, unable to worship in the Temple because of his contaminated condition. A leper was socially and religiously on the margins. The fact that Jesus touched him shows, first, that Jesus was not worried about being contaminated; rather, his own holiness or power seems to have acted as a contagious force, well able to cleanse the man of his impurity.[34] Second, the relationship between ritual impurity and moral impurity was robustly debated among ancient Jewish groups. The rabbis could distinguish the two without prioritizing one over the other, while those who wrote the Dead Sea Scrolls could conflate the two, so that to be ritually impure was also to be morally impure.[35] It appears that Jesus may have entered this debate in the parable of the Good Samaritan, and in his censure of the table-fellowship practices of the Pharisees.[36] Jesus was not saying that scriptural categories of clean and unclean were silly or irrelevant. He presumably purified himself, like other Jews, before entering the Temple (see Jn. 11.55!). Rather, he was insisting that moral imperatives override ritual imperatives, something with which many other Jews would have concurred.[37] Third, Christian leaders did not abandon the language of purity and pollution. Rather, they adopted the language to describe the saving work of Jesus and the holiness of the Christian assemblies. At the Jerusalem council, Peter testified that the reason why gentile believers did not have to be circumcised and convert to Judaism was because God 'did not discriminate between us [Jews] and them [gentiles], for he purified their hearts by faith'.[38] Paul exhorted the Corinthians to upright living in a pagan city with the words: 'Therefore, since we have these promises, dear friends, let us purify ourselves from everything that contaminates body and spirit, perfecting holiness out of reverence for God.'[39] John the elder wrote that

---

[34] Mt. 8.2–4/Mk. 1.40–45/Lk. 5.12–15. See Blomberg 2005.
[35] See Klawans 2006 and more broadly his other works on purity/impurity in Judaism in Klawans 2000 and 2005.
[36] Lk. 10.29–37; Mt. 15.1–20/Mk. 7.1–23/Lk. 11.38–41.
[37] On this, see Kazen 2002.
[38] Ac. 15.9.
[39] 2 Cor. 7.1.

if we walk in the light, as he is in the light, we have fellowship with one another, and the blood of Jesus, his Son, purifies us from all sin . . . If we confess our sins, he is faithful and just and will forgive us our sins and purify us from all unrighteousness.[40]

Thus, the concepts of purity and pollution continued to be formative for the early Christian understanding both of ultimate salvation and of Christian behaviour.

THE JEWISH SECTS

The demise of the Hasmonean dynasty, and the advent of Roman rule, together spawned several mutually antagonistic Jewish groups, each with their own vision for Israel's future. With a certain over-simplification we can trace easily enough the four options open to Jews in Jesus' day. If you travel around modern Israel, you'll find archaeological remnants of these sects. First, there is the zealot option. The Sicarii took over Herod's old palace-fortress of Masada, near the south-west corner of the Dead Sea, during the Roman–Jewish war. For them, the rule was clear: say your prayers, sharpen your swords, make yourselves holy to fight a holy war, and God will give you a military victory over the hordes of darkness. Second were the Pharisees, the community activists. (The more strict a Pharisee you were, the more likely you might be to sympathize with the zealots; Saul of Tarsus is a good example.) In their earlier days the Pharisees had sometimes been able to ally with the Jewish leaders, but in Jesus' day they held no political position. They were more like a pressure group. Their aim went like this: when ejected from the halls of power, start a grass-roots campaign to get your vision for Israel adopted by the masses, tell everyone to have their own ritual bath if they can, have your bones buried in ossuary boxes waiting for resurrection. If we can be obedient enough, get pure enough, keep Torah most accurately, then maybe the 'son of David' will come. Third, the quietist and ultimately dualist option, taken by the writers of the Dead Sea Scrolls at Qumran: separate yourself from the wicked world, say your prayers, and wait for God to do whatever God is going to do. Fourth, the compromise option taken by the Sadducees: keep the Temple going, offer sacrifices pleasing to God, maintain the peace, get along with your political bosses as well as you can, do as well out of it as you can, and hope that God will somehow validate it all.

Of course, we can take a much deeper look at these sects as well.

Revolutionary movements

The fragile social stability deteriorated when the Romans took over control of Palestine in 63 BC. Economic pressure created a new class of brigands, desperate

---

40 1 Jn. 1.7, 9.

bands of Jews who found no way forward from their poverty except by living outside normal society and sustaining themselves through raids on those who still had property that could be stolen. As we shall see, such brigands were not simply anarchists. A fierce belief in the justice of their cause, and in divine backing for it, sustained them in their desperate lifestyle. By the middle of the first century BC the problem of brigandage had become so acute, helped by the power vacuum while Rome was occupied with civil war and the threat from Parthia, that it was a major achievement to bring it under some sort of control, albeit temporarily. Credit for this was given to Herod the Great, whose rise to power in the 40s BC was marked by his putting down of serious brigandage, notably killing the chief brigand Hezekiah, whose family appears to have continued the struggle in later generations.[41]

A tumultuous sequence of events began in 4 BC. As Herod the Great lay dying, a group of Judean hotheads pulled down the ornamental eagle he had caused to be placed over the Temple gate. They were egged on by two respected teachers of the law with the suspected collusion of the high priest.[42] This incident was punished severely by Herod in one of his last acts. Then, immediately after Herod's death, a fuller revolt took place in Jerusalem at Passover, taking its origin from protests over the treatment of the ringleaders in the previous incident. It was suppressed brutally by Herod's son Archelaus.[43] Archelaus and his brother Antipas then (as we saw earlier) went to Rome to argue their respective right to the succession before the emperor, being followed by a Jewish embassy pleading for autonomy because of the brutality of Archelaus and his father.[44] In the absence of the would-be rulers a new revolt took place, which was crushed by Varus, the Roman general in charge of the province of Syria. Varus left in place an interim procurator, Sabinus, whose actions in turn provoked fresh serious riots during the feast of Pentecost, which he was unable to quell, although in the attempt the Roman soldiers looted the Temple, thus further angering the Jews.[45] These events in Jerusalem were paralleled by a revolt among Herod's veterans in Idumea,[46] and an uprising in Galilee, led by a certain Judas, son of the brigand chief killed by Herod a generation before.[47]

At the same time as these events were going on there were two would-be messianic movements. These involved respectively one Simon, an ex-slave of Herod who was proclaimed king before being killed by the Romans, and a shepherd called Athronges, who gave himself royal airs and organized his followers into brigand

---

41 Jos. *Ant.* 14.158–60, 420–30.
42 Jos. *Ant.* 17.149–66; *War* 1.648–55.
43 Jos. *Ant.* 17.206–18; *War* 2.1–13.
44 Jos. *Ant.* 17.219–49, 299–323; *War* 2.80–100.
45 Jos. *Ant.* 17.250–64; *War* 2.39–50.
46 Jos. *Ant.* 17.269–70; *War* 2.55.
47 Jos. *Ant.* 17.271–2; *War* 1.204; 2.56.

bands before being captured by Archelaus.[48] Varus returned from Syria, settled the Galilean rebellion brutally, relieved Sabinus in Jerusalem, and crucified some two thousand insurgents.[49] Ten years later when Archelaus was deposed in AD 6 another serious incident was occasioned by the imposition of a Roman census, whose implications were not merely economic but, to a Jew, theological: enrolling in Rome's system meant admitting that the land and people were not after all sacred to Israel's God. Judas 'the Galilean' led the revolt which, according to Josephus, was the founding act of the sect that became responsible for the major war two generations later.[50] This flurry of rebellions in the period 4 BC–AD 6 illustrates one main principle of Jewish revolt: the seething unrest which was normally held down tightly by repressive government and brute force could boil over when a power vacuum occurred.

Most of the revolutionary activity during the next sixty years was a response to perceived provocation. Successive 'procurators' acted in a more or less crass and heavy-handed style, which naturally had the effect of inciting Jews towards revolt. We saw earlier a list of several incendiary incidents in the ten years of Pontius Pilate's procuratorship, including the execution of Jesus of Nazareth. Pilate himself was finally removed from his post, precisely because of his antagonistic antics towards the populace.[51] Furthermore, the tinderbox of revolutionary fervour was almost sparked when Caligula tried to place a huge statue of himself in the Temple in Jerusalem, in deliberate contravention of Jewish law and scruples. Caligula ignored the protests, including from his own men on the spot, and only his early death forestalled the blasphemous act and its horrendous possible consequences.[52]

A brief respite from continual provocation occurred during the reign of Herod Agrippa, a grandson of Herod the Great, whom the Romans allowed to rule in place of the procurators from 41 until his early death in 44. His apparent piety, and his care to avoid offending Jewish scruples, held revolutionary tendencies at bay. But with the resumption of procuratorial rule we hear of renewed insurgent movements. The procurator Cuspius Fadus executed a brigand chief named Tholomaeus in the mid-40s, during a larger operation against brigandage in general.[53] Around the same time a leader named Theudas, claiming to be a prophet, led a movement that aroused enough popular support to gain mention in Acts as well as Josephus. It too was put down by the Romans; Theudas was promptly executed.[54] We then hear of the two sons of Judas the Galilean, Jacob and Simon, being crucified under

---

48 Jos. *Ant.* 17.273–7 and 278–84; *War* 2.57–98; 60–5.
49 Jos. *Ant.* 17.286–98; *War* 2.66–79.
50 Jos. *Ant.* 18.4–10, 23–5; cf. *War* 2.118. Ac. 5.37 claims that Judas was executed by the Romans.
51 Jos. *Ant.* 18.85–9.
52 Jos. *Ant.* 18.302–8; *War* 2.203; Philo *Gai.*
53 Jos. *Ant.* 20.5.
54 Jos. *Ant.* 20.97–9; Ac. 5.36.

the procuratorship of Tiberius Alexander (46–8).⁵⁵ We can add into this mix the subsequent revolts under his successor Cumanus (48–52), including a riot at Passover in which perhaps 20,000 Jews were killed (see 'Portals and parallels: riots at Passover'); attacks by brigands on Romans; and further looting of the Temple by Roman troops.⁵⁶ Another purge of bandits took place under the procuratorship of Felix (52–60), who crucified a considerable number of them.⁵⁷

The purge was only short-lived. Josephus says that around this time (the late 50s and early 60s) there arose the group he called Sicarii, the 'dagger-men'.⁵⁸ In addition, groups to whom he refers as 'false prophets' were operating in the Judean desert.⁵⁹ An Egyptian Jew led a mass movement of people who assembled outside Jerusalem on the Mount of Olives, where he promised them that the city walls would fall down and allow them to enter in triumph. His followers, numbering thousands, were cut down by the Romans, while he himself escaped and was not heard of again.⁶⁰ There were also riots over Jewish social status at Caesarea, and plenty of further evidence of brigand activity.⁶¹ Among the first acts of Felix's successor as procurator, Porcius Festus (60–2), was to execute an 'imposter' who had promised his followers 'salvation

---

55 Jos. *Ant.* 20.102.
56 Jos. *Ant.* 20.105–12; *War* 2.224–7; *Ant.* 20.113–17; *War* 2.228–31.
57 Jos. *War* 2.253.
58 Jos. *Ant.* 20.185–7; *War* 2.254; cf. Tac. *Ann.* 12.54.
59 Jos. *War* 2.258–60. See references to the 'imposters and brigands' of *War* 2.264–5.
60 Jos. *War* 2.261–3 (30,000 followers); Ac. 21.38 (4,000 followers).
61 Jos. *Ant.* 20.173–7; *War* 2.266–70.

PORTALS AND PARALLELS: RIOTS AT PASSOVER

Josephus narrates a story of how a riot broke out in Jerusalem during a certain Passover festival while Ventidius Cumanus was procurator of Judea (AD 48–52). It shows just how easy it was to provoke an incident, in this instance when a Roman soldier 'mooned' some Jewish pilgrims and released some obnoxious flatulence.

The usual crowd had assembled at Jerusalem for the feast of unleavened bread, and the Roman cohort had taken up its position on the roof of the portico of the temple; for a body of men in arms invariably mounts guard at the feasts, to prevent disorders arising from such a concourse of people. Thereupon one of the soldiers, raising his robe, stooped in an indecent attitude, so as to turn his backside to the Jews, and made a noise in keeping with his posture. Enraged at the insult, the whole multitude with loud cries called upon [the governor] Cumanus to punish the soldier; some of the more hot-headed young men and seditious persons in the crowd started a fight, and, picking up stones, hurled them at the troops. Cumanus, fearing a general attack upon himself, sent for reinforcements. These troops pouring into the porticoes, the Jews were seized with irresistible panic and turned to fly from the temple and make their escape into the town. But such violence was used as they pressed round the exits that they were trodden under foot and crushed to death by one another; upwards of thirty thousand perished, and the feast was turned into mourning for the whole nation and for every household into lamentation. (Jos. *War* 2.224–7; cp. *Ant.* 20.105–12)

> **PORTALS AND PARALLELS: JOSEPHUS ON THE 'ORACLE' THAT INSPIRED REVOLUTION**
>
> *Josephus describes the broad messianic hopes of Jewish resistance fighters, perhaps based on the book of Daniel, and expresses his own view that the prophecy in fact referred to the accession of Vespasian as Roman emperor.*
>
> But what more than all else incited them to the war was an ambiguous oracle, likewise found in their sacred scriptures, to the effect that at that time one from their country would become ruler of the world. This they understood to mean someone of their own race, and many of their wise men went astray in their interpretation of it. The oracle, however, in reality signified the sovereignty of Vespasian, who was proclaimed Emperor on Jewish soil. (Jos. *War* 6.312–15)

and rest from troubles',[62] and to deal with a strange itinerant Jew called 'Paul' who had been arraigned before Felix on a charge of inciting riots by offending Jewish scruples.[63] Despite further executions of many bandits, wildfire movements of revolt spread faster, fanned by the insensitive actions of Festus's two successors, Lucceius Albinus (62–5) and the notorious Gessius Florus (65–6), who, being unable to control the brigands, actually gave them support and, according to Josephus, shared their plunder.[64]

This brief list of movements of revolt in the years preceding the war of AD 66–70 gives sufficient indication of the mood of the country as a whole (see 'Portals and parallels: Josephus on the "oracle" that inspired revolution'). There is a question, though, as to whether there was a unified and homogeneous revolutionary faction in Galilee and Judea in the first century. Josephus certainly gives that impression when he talks about a 'Fourth Philosophy' founded by Judas the Galilean—which existed, as we have suggested, alongside the Pharisees, Sadducees, and Essenes, and continued through to AD 70.[65] Many scholars have long assumed some kind of 'zealot' party that existed in the first century, to which Jesus' follower 'Simon the Zealot' purportedly belonged (Mt. 10.4/Mk. 3.18/Lk. 6.15; Ac. 1.13). It appears more likely, however, that there were, throughout the first century, many movements which laid claim to the tradition of active 'zeal', a tradition that went back, through the Maccabees (1 Macc. 2), to the cultural memory of Phinehas (Num. 25.11; Ps. 106.30–31) and Elijah (1 Kgs. 19.1–21). Even the Pharisee named 'Saul of Tarsus' could identify himself with this tradition of zeal against a new messianic sect that was perceived to be transgressing against the pillars of Judaism and courting controversy by allowing its members to fraternize with gentiles (see Gal. 1.13–14; Phil. 3.6). Furthermore, a close reading

---

[62] Jos. *Ant.* 20.188.
[63] Ac. 25.1–12.
[64] Jos. *Ant.* 20.252–7; *War* 2.271. This may, of course, be an exaggeration on Josephus's part. But it is not in itself implausible if some at least of the brigands were sufficiently desperate to make temporary alliances with a Roman official in order to prosecute their struggle, which was as much with their richer Jewish neighbours as with Rome.
[65] Jos. *Ant.* 18.9–10, 23–5.

of Josephus shows that most references to the 'zealots' point to one particular group during the war of AD 66–70, associated with John of Gischala, rather than to a pan-Judean movement spanning some decades.[66] The more long-lasting movement is that of the Sicarii, who, as we saw, seem to have sustained some kind of a dynasty from the middle of the first century BC to the fall of Masada. Beginning with the brigand chief Hezekiah, killed by Herod, this movement continued with his son Judas the Galilean, the leader of a revolt after the death of Herod, quite possibly the same person as the leader of the anti-census riots in AD 6. Again as we saw, the sons of Judas the Galilean were crucified under Tiberius Alexander in the mid-40s, and another descendant of Judas, Menahem, became the would-be messianic leader of the Sicarii at Masada during the war of AD 66–70. There is no reason to think that members of this group were regarded by any other as the natural leaders of revolt. But nor is there good reason to drive a sharp ideological wedge between them and any other party or band. These groups, no doubt with considerable social and organizational diversity, shared to some extent a background of socio-economic deprivation, and, most importantly, a common stock of theological symbols and ideas that drove them to armed revolution.

If revolution was in the air throughout this period, how did that fit in with the agendas of the other groups of whose existence we know? The most important of these groups for our purposes is undoubtedly the Pharisees, and we must turn to them now.

The final stronghold of Jewish resistance against the Romans was Herod's mountain fortress of Masada. Josephus (*War* 7.252–406) recounts how the defenders committed suicide rather than surrender to the Romans.
Bill Schlegel / BiblePlaces.com

---

66 Jos. *War* 4.130–61, 208–23.

The Pharisees

Out of all the sects of Judaism there is none more important for the study of the New Testament than the Pharisees.[67] That is for three reasons. First, the Pharisees are depicted in the gospels as Jesus' primary adversaries. Second, the apostle Paul claims to have been once a zealous Pharisee. Third, the Pharisees eventually came to dominate the Jewish world after the capture of Jerusalem in AD 70 and the failure of the Bar-Kochba revolt in 135. There are, however, several problems about the Pharisees, and many intractable debates concerning them.

First, in the Christian tradition, 'Pharisee' has become the most strident and vitriolic term to describe religious hypocrisy and self-righteousness. The result is a caricature of the original Pharisees in which they become nothing more than guardians of an external, ritualistic religion and legalistic merit-seeking. Yet the reality is that Jesus' debates with the Pharisees would be better seen as torrid insider debates between different visions of the same goal: the coming of God's kingdom on earth as in heaven. Jesus was thus in some ways closer to the Pharisaic movement than to any other sect. This is evidenced by the fact that Jesus had Pharisaic sympathizers like Nicodemus; Jesus received and accepted dinner invitations from Pharisees; some Pharisees warned Jesus that Herod Antipas was trying to kill him, and many Pharisees joined the early church.[68]

Second, the aims and ambitions of the Pharisees are much disputed. One strand of scholarship has assumed that the Pharisees were initially a political movement, but when they lost sway at the Hasmonean court, they retreated to promoting a particular vision for Jewish piety and morality among the common people. Others argue that the Pharisees remained politically active, often involved in revolutionary movements, and supported a political change to the status quo. For another matter, why were the Pharisees so concerned with purity? Did they really attempt to replicate the priestly purity codes among themselves, or did they think purity was simply a good thing in and of itself? How influential were the Pharisees? Were they a minority voice? Or did the majority of Jews in Judea and Galilee, as Josephus suggests, look to them for religious instruction (remembering that 'religious' in that world was closely associated with the long-range hopes of Israel)?

Third, the only two Jewish sects who survived the war with Rome were the Christians and Pharisees, which meant that they were now effectively competing to be the voice of the Jewish world in a post-Temple age. Some have accordingly asserted that the disputes between Jesus and the Pharisees in the gospels do not actually reflect incidents during Jesus' career, but reflect conflicts and debates between

---

[67] On the Pharisees, see Wright *NTPG*, 181–203; *PFG*, 179–96; the collection of essays in Neusner and Chilton 2007; and students may wish to consult the concise and helpful introductory article by Cohick (2013a).
[68] Jn. 3.1; Lk. 7.36–50; 11.37–54; 14.1–24; Lk. 13.31–32; Ac. 15.5.

Christians and Pharisees in the post-AD 70 period that have been projected back onto Jesus' lifetime.

Given all those questions, we can affirm three basic theses about the Pharisees to describe their place in Judaism and their fractious relationship with Jesus and the early church.

First, in terms of size and spheres of operation, the Pharisees probably numbered several thousand. There is good evidence from literary sources for their activity outside Judea. There is nothing strange (as some have asserted) about Jesus coming across Pharisees in Galilean villages.[69]

Second, the Pharisees, due to their political marginalization in the Herodian period, became largely concerned with manufacturing the conditions necessary for Israel's eschatological restoration through a strict regime of Torah observance as seen from within their specific tradition. In other words, they were not a separatist religious club. Rather, they were a Jewish renewal movement, seeking to draw Israel towards the conditions that would hasten its restoration before God and its elevation over the surrounding nations. The Pharisaic agenda, then, was to purify Israel by summoning the people to return to the true ancestral traditions; to restore Israel to its independent theocratic status; and to be, as a pressure group, in the vanguard of such a movement through the study and practice of Torah. The Pharisees aimed to demonstrate, in the present time, that they were the ones whom Israel's God would vindicate when, as expected, he acted to rescue his people.

The Pharisees were not an official 'thought police'. Indeed, as Pharisees they held no official post or office (though no doubt some office-holders would also be Pharisees). Even Saul of Tarsus had to get authority from the chief priests for his marauding ventures against the very early church.[70] Nevertheless, what Josephus expressly states, and what Mark implies, is that the Pharisees were highly active in trying to transmit their tradition to the people.[71] Their ardour in this task is documented by Philo who speaks of there being thousands of individuals, 'full of *zeal* for the laws, strictest guardians of the *ancestral traditions*'.[72] Such phrases function in Philo, Josephus, and Paul as regular code for the Pharisees, filled with intense fervour to win the hearts and minds of the people to their programme, and merciless towards those whom they saw as subverting the national customs. Converts to the cause had to be made, even if one had to cross over 'sea and land' to find them.[73] This is because what mattered was not 'religion' but eschatology; not interior morality, but the

---

69 For example, the Jerusalem leadership would not have sent Josephus (allegedly a Pharisee) to take charge of Galilee, and later sent other Pharisees to replace Josephus, if Pharisees held no sway there (see Jos. *Life* 12, 28–30, 191–7).
70 Ac. 9.1–2; 22.4.
71 Jos. *Ant.* 13.288, 296–8; 18.15, 17; *War* 2.162; *Life* 191; Mk. 7.1–15.
72 Philo *Spec. Leg.* 2.253.
73 Mt. 23.15.

coming *apocalypse* of YHWH's kingdom. The Pharisees' programme was filled with zeal for Israel's purity, which is why they had a burning passion for correct instruction in the Torah about tithing, ceremonial washings, agriculture, sabbath and festival observances, vows, and so on, and why some of them at the more extreme wing (perhaps the followers of Shammai rather than Hillel) agitated for the necessity of violence to cleanse the land of defilements, of signs of pagan religion, and even of gentile peoples themselves. The Pharisees, whether those who were filled with anti-Roman zeal or those who were content to try to keep the Torah within the political *status quo*, all agreed that this way *must* be taught to the people *if* Israel was to one day be restored.

Third, this gives us a better chance to understand the Pharisaic concern with purity. The purity codes were not simply 'about' personal cleanliness. As social anthropologists would insist, they were coded symbols for the purity and maintenance of the tribe, the family, or the race. Passage after passage in Jewish writers of the period, and indeed in modern Jewish scholarship, emphasizes that the Jewish laws were not designed as a legalist's ladder up which one might climb to heaven; they were the boundary-markers for a beleaguered people. The agenda of the Pharisees in this period, then, was not simply to do with 'purity' for its own sake, whether their own or that belonging to other people. Instead, all the evidence suggests that at least the majority of the Pharisees, from the Hasmonean and Herodian periods through to the war of AD 66–70, had as their main aim that which purity *symbolized*: the political struggle to maintain Jewish identity and to realize the dream of national liberation. For many Pharisaic leaders, especially the Shammaites, purity had to do with a desire to purify, cleanse, and defend the nation against paganism. It was only later that the lenient Hillelites, who like Gamaliel believed in living and letting live,[74] attained full supremacy after the two disastrous wars of 66–70 and 132–5 had destroyed the morale, and perhaps the very existence, of the stricter Shammaite party.

The clash between Jesus and the Pharisees, therefore, must be seen in terms of two alternative political agendas, generated by the alternative eschatological beliefs of two competing renewal movements (see text grid: 'Critiques of the Pharisees by other Jewish groups'). Jesus was announcing the kingdom in a way that did not reinforce, but rather called into question, the agenda of revolutionary zeal that dominated the horizon of the leading group within Pharisaism.[75] The coming of the kingdom, as Jesus announced it, put before his Pharisaic contemporaries a challenge, an agenda: give up your interpretation of your tradition, which is driving you towards ruin. Embrace instead a very different interpretation of the tradition, one which, though it looks like the way of loss, is in fact the way to true victory, the way of the cross!

---
74 Ac. 5.34–39.
75 On the Pharisees and revolutionary fervour, see Wright *NTPG*, 190–4.

CRITIQUES OF THE PHARISEES BY OTHER JEWISH GROUPS

Damascus Document	*Testament of Moses*	*Gospel of Luke*
For they [i.e. the Pharisees] sought smooth things and preferred illusions; they looked for ways to break the law; they favoured the fine neck. They called the guilty innocent, and the innocent guilty. They overstepped the covenant, violated law; and they conspired to kill the innocent, for all those who lived pure lives they loathed from the bottom of their heart. So they persecuted them violently, and were happy to see the people quarrel. Because of all this, God became very angry with their company. (CD 1.18—2.1; tr. slightly amended from Wise, Abegg, and Cook [2005])	But really they consume the goods of the poor, saying their acts are according to justice while in fact they are simply exterminators, deceitfully seeking to conceal themselves so that they will not be known as completely godless because of their criminal deeds committed all the day long, saying, 'We shall have feasts, even luxurious winings and dinings. Indeed, we shall behave ourselves as princes.' They, with hand and mind, will touch impure things, yet their mouths will speak enormous things, and they will even say, 'Do not touch me, lest you pollute me in the position I occupy'. (*T. Mos.* 7.5–10; tr. J. Priest)	When Jesus had finished speaking, a Pharisee invited him to eat with him; so he went in and reclined at the table. But the Pharisee was surprised when he noticed that Jesus did not first wash before the meal. Then the Lord said to him, 'Now then, you Pharisees clean the outside of the cup and dish, but inside you are full of greed and wickedness. You foolish people! Did not the one who made the outside make the inside also? But now as for what is inside you—be generous to the poor, and everything will be clean for you. Woe to you Pharisees, because you give God a tenth of your mint, rue and all other kinds of garden herbs, but you neglect justice and the love of God. You should have practised the latter without leaving the former undone. Woe to you Pharisees, because you love the most important seats in the synagogues and respectful greetings in the market-places. Woe to you, because you are like unmarked graves, which people walk over without knowing it.' (Lk. 11.37–44)
This text from the Damascus Document, found at Qumran but probably written elsewhere, condemns a Pharisaic leader for leading a congregation into violating the covenant and it castigates the Pharisees as those who 'seek after smooth things' and 'favour the fine neck'.	The *Testament of Moses* is an apocalyptic farewell discourse, written most likely in the first century AD; it here censures the Pharisees for a mixture of self-indulgent affluence, religious hypocrisy, and puritanical piety.	Luke narrates a story where Jesus dines with some Pharisees but then indicts them for focusing on ritual impurity instead of morality and for their love for positions of prestige among the people.

The Jewish Context of Jesus and the Early Church

The Golden Gate on the eastern wall of the Temple Mount, Jerusalem

It was this challenge, we suggest, which generated the heated exchanges between Jesus and the Pharisees and resulted in the plots against Jesus' life. Jesus' clash with the Pharisees came about not because he was an antinomian, or because he believed in 'grace' and 'faith' while they believed in 'justification by works', but because his kingdom-agenda for Israel demanded that Israel leave off its frantic search for national purity and regional hegemony, reinforced as it now was by the ancestral codes, and embrace instead the proper vocation to be the light of the world, the salt of the earth.

The Sadducees, priests, and aristocrats

The great majority of the priests were not aristocrats; nor were they particularly wealthy. They, and the Levites who served as their assistants, were dependent on the tithing practised by the rest of the population. Most of them lived away from Jerusalem, going there in groups, by turn, for the performance of the regular rituals. For the rest of the time, they functioned in a way which has often been ignored: they were the main teachers of the law, the group to whom ordinary Jews turned for judgment and arbitration in the case of disputes or legal problems.[76] It should be no surprise that Jesus tells the cleansed man to 'show himself to the priest'.[77] That would have been normal practice, and it would not involve a journey to Jerusalem; the man would go to the priest residing in the local town or village. The priests were thus the local representatives of mainline 'official' Judaism, as befitted those who had both studied Torah themselves and, from time to time, had the privilege of serving Israel's God in his Temple.

At the top of the priestly tree, so to speak, we find the chief priests themselves. As far as we can

---

[76] See Sanders 1992, ch. 10.
[77] Mk. 1.44/Mt. 8.4/Lk. 5.14.

128   The World of Jesus and the Early Church

tell, they formed in the first century a kind of permanent secretariat, based in Jerusalem, wielding considerable power. They belonged to a small group of families, tight-knit and inbred, who seem on several occasions to have engaged in serious factional disputes among themselves. They formed the heart of the Jewish aristocracy. It was with them, and particularly with the high priest who was chosen from their number, that the Roman governors had to deal in the first instance, holding them responsible for the general conduct of the populace. Not unnaturally, this often put them on delicate if not difficult terms with the various descendants of Herod whom the Romans permitted to use the title 'king'. This priest–king tension goes back to biblical times, as with the clash between King Uzziah and the priest Azariah.[78]

The central symbol of the priestly worldview was obviously the Temple. It represented, no doubt, different things to different priests. To the country priest, living for most of the time in comparative poverty, teaching in his local village and settling local disputes, the regular visit to the Temple, and the chance to take part in its ritual, was the high point of his year, or even of his life. Everything he did away from Jerusalem gained meaning and depth because of the Temple. As we shall see later, it drew together the entire theology and aspiration of Israel. To the Jerusalemite priest, and particularly to the chief priests, the Temple was in principle all of that, but more besides: it was their power base, the economic and political centre of the country. It was because they controlled the Temple that they were who they were. The Temple gave powerful religious legitimation to the status which they had been granted under the Romans and the Herodian monarchs.

The chief priests and the leading aristocrats seem mostly to have belonged to the party we know as the Sadducees. Unfortunately, there is not much more that we know about this party, other than their conservatism, and their apparently perpetual dogfight with the Pharisees. What we can trace in more detail may briefly be described as follows.[79]

First, according to Josephus, the Sadducees believed in free will. Just as I am inclined to think that Josephus's description of the Pharisaic blend of fate and free will is a de-politicized code for their balance between waiting for Israel's God to act and being ready to act on his behalf if necessary, so I am inclined to think that the Sadducean belief in free will has little to do with abstract philosophy and a great deal to do with the politics of power: Israel's God will help those who help themselves.[80] This is a comfortable doctrine for those in power, who maintain themselves there by taking whatever measures seem necessary, just as its mirror image, belief that divine action can only be awaited, not hastened, is a consoling doctrine for those who are out of power and see no hope of regaining it by their own efforts.

---

78 2 Chron. 26.16–21.
79 See Sanders 1992, 332–40.
80 See Jos. *War* 2.164–5; *Ant.* 13.173.

Second, the Sadducees had no time for laws, or scriptures, other than those in the Torah (that is, the Pentateuch, the first five books of Moses). This viewpoint is set over against those who followed 'the traditions of the elders',[81] a pretty clear reference to the Pharisees, who certainly maintained, and applied to themselves at least, a large body of such traditions. Here again we see the Sadducees as an essentially conservative body, unwilling to allow mere innovation. In the political realm, this is again a useful doctrine for those in power to hold if their innovating opponents are engaged, as we have seen at least some of the Pharisees were engaged, in revolutionary activities.

Third, and connected with this, the Sadducees denied the doctrine of the resurrection.[82] The best explanation for the Sadducees' view is that, by the first century, 'resurrection' had long functioned as a symbol and metaphor for the total reconstitution of Israel, the return from Babylon, and the final coming redemption in which God would put everything right—always a worry for those wielding power. Ezekiel 37 spoke of the return in terms of Israel being awakened out of the grave; the Maccabean martyrs, as presented in 2 Maccabees, spoke of their own forthcoming resurrection in the context of claiming that their God would vindicate his people against the tyrant. Although the first-century aristocrats were in one sense the heirs of the Hasmoneans whose vindication 2 Maccabees envisaged, the boot was now on the other foot: resurrection, in its metaphorical sense of the restitution of a theocratic Israel, possibly under a Messiah, would mean the end of their precarious power. If the Sadducees concentrated, for reasons of political necessity, on the affairs of the world, they may have quite genuinely had less concern for doctrines about the afterlife itself. And, since they only believed in Torah, not the subsequent prophetic books where resurrection was taught, they were able to claim scriptural validation and charge their opponents—particularly the Pharisees—with following new-fangled and dangerous innovatory ideas.

The influence of the aristocrats in general and the Sadducees in particular has been controversial, for the same underlying reasons as the question of the influence of the Pharisees. To cut things short, we are inclined to accept Josephus's verdict: in terms of party effectiveness, the Pharisees were far more successful in persuading the mass of people of their views than the Sadducees were. That is, the majority of the people believed in resurrection; the majority of people went on believing that their God would act in history to bring about his promised kingdom; they believed that matters did not lie solely in human hands; and the majority of people were prepared to take at least some of the Pharisaic traditions with at least some seriousness.

What became of the members of the Judean aristocracy? Either they were wiped out in the revolt against Rome (partly by the Romans and partly by other Jewish

---

81 See Jos. *Ant.* 13.297–8, 408; 18.17; Mk. 7.4; Gal. 1.14.
82 Jos. *War* 2.165; *Ant.* 18.16; Mt. 22.23/Mk. 12.18/Lk. 20.27; Ac. 23.8. However, the Sadducees may have believed in some kind of existence in the afterlife as a 'shade' or 'shadow' in Sheol/Hades.

factions), or they assimilated, like Josephus himself, in varying degrees, into the general greco-roman society around them. We hear nothing of them in the period of Javneh. Their worldview, whose central symbol was the Temple, and whose central story concerned an Israel with themselves as its rulers, had been left without trace.

The Essenes

Another Jewish group is named as the Essenes. We know about them from Josephus, Philo, and Pliny. They are not mentioned in the New Testament, though some have speculated that John the Baptist may have had links with them.[83] They appear to have been known for their ascetic way of life, concern for ritual purity, corporate reading of scripture, refusal to own slaves, sharing of property, and communal meals. Some Essenes lived in the south-west quarter of Jerusalem, hence the 'Essene gate' that Josephus mentions, which has been identified by archaeologists as probably adjacent to what is now the protestant cemetery on Mount Zion.[84]

An aerial photo of the Qumran settlement where the sect is believed to have lived.
Duby Tal / Albatross/ Alamy Stock Photo

---

[83] Philo *Omn. Prob. Lib.* 75–91; *Hypoth.* 11.1–8; *De Vit. Cont.* 1; Pliny *NH* 5.15.73; Jos. *Ant.* 13.171–2; 18.18–22; *War* 2.119–61.
[84] Jos. *War* 5.145, and on archaeological discussion see Riesner 1989.

The Essenes lived in other cities (as Josephus says), in Palestinian villages (as Philo says), and out by the shores of the Dead Sea (as Pliny says). They probably emerged in the fragmentation of Jewish social and cultural life during the Hasmonean dynasty. Observing the political corruption of the Hasmonean rulers and rejecting their usurpation of the high priesthood for themselves, the Essenes retreated from mainstream Jewish institutions and life and engaged in a quasi-monastic existence, either in urban centres or—as one group did—out by the north-western shores of the Dead Sea at Qumran.

The majority of scholars identify the Qumran community, from whom we derive the Dead Sea Scrolls, as a marginal splinter group of urban Essenes. However, the origins of the Qumran community and the Scrolls are naturally debated.

Cave number 4, one of ten caves in and around Qumran where some nine hundred scrolls were found during 1947–56.
© 2015 by Zondervan

Some believe that the sect had Sadducean origins and that not all of the Scrolls can be attributed to this group, some being composed elsewhere before they were brought to Qumran. Some archaeologists even deny that a religious centre existed at Qumran in the first century AD.[85] Assuming the majority view for the moment, the community was probably founded by an enigmatic figure known as the 'Teacher of Righteousness', who took issue with the 'wicked priest' (probably one of the Hasmonean leaders) and his re-organization of the Judean Temple-state in which the older high-priestly group were ousted in favour of the new Hasmonean priest-kings.

---

85 For modern scholarship on Qumran and the Scrolls, see surveys in Grossman 2010 and Lim and Collins 2010. For a quick guide for students, see Evans 2010 and Willitts 2010.

The sect separated from other Jews and followed this teacher into the wilderness, where they were trying quite literally to 'prepare the way of the Lord'.[86] The subsequent development of the Qumran sect, including its possible split or change of direction, can probably be traced in relation to the continuing story of the Hasmonean house. At each hypothetical stage, those who wrote the Scrolls saw themselves as the true representatives of Israel's traditions, and the true guardians of its hope, over against the group then in power, the Hasmoneans. The site at Qumran was vacated in the last third of the first century BC (possibly because its residents were favoured by Herod and allowed to come to live in Jerusalem), but it was reinhabited early in the first century AD, and finally taken over and destroyed by the Romans in about AD 68. If it is true that the members of the Qumran community, and/or those who wrote the Scrolls, were part of a wider Essene movement, we have no evidence for the continuation of such a movement after the fall of the Temple.

The Qumranites appear to have had several characteristic beliefs. To begin with, the symbolic world of the group was focused on its own existence as the rightful heir of the Jewish traditions and hopes. The particular form of interpretation used in the biblical commentaries in the Scrolls, usually called *pesher*, focuses attention on the sect as the people whose story and hopes had already been described in scripture. For instance, in the commentary on Habakkuk 1.5, we find:

> This passage refers to the traitors with the Man of the Lie, because they have not obeyed the words of the Teacher of Righteousness from the mouth of God. It also refers to the traitors to the New Covenant, because they did not believe in God's covenant and desecrated His holy name; and finally, it refers to the traitors in the Last Days.[87]

Thus, the Qumranites saw themselves and their struggle as the true subject of scripture's promise about God's deliverance of Israel from the effects of exile and his bringing of Israel into the new covenant. The focal points of the sect's own life, seen as the fulfilment of prophecy and the means whereby the divine purpose would finally be realized, became some of its central symbols.

The council meetings of the community were solemn religious occasions; the mealtimes, sacred festivals. Communal life was governed by strict laws of purity, and the calendar was arranged in such a way as to enable festivals and sabbaths to be kept 'properly', that is, on the correct day. Building on this, and piecing together the ideology of the movement from various hints and statements, we reach the clear conclusion that at least one Jewish group regarded itself not just as the true Israel but

---

[86] Isa. 40.3 cited in 1QS 8.13–16.
[87] 1QpHab 2.1–6 (tr. Wise, Abegg, and Cook [2005]).

as the true Temple.[88] The existing Temple might have been 'cleansed' by the Maccabean revolt, but as far as this group was concerned it was still polluted.[89]

The stories told by members of this group reveal the nature of the worldview they espoused. It was, of course, Israel's story; but, like all retellings of Israel's story in this period, it had a twist to its tail. The scriptures were searched, read, prayed over, studied, copied out with the focus on the present and immediately future moment. Israel's history had entered a bottleneck. The return from exile had not yet really happened. Yet this little group was the advance guard through whom Israel's great day of restoration would come about. Thus the prophecies written before the exile, predicting a future return and restoration, were in fact starting to come true in the history of the group itself. The story of Israel had turned into the story of the Qumranites.[90]

An interesting feature of the Scrolls is their eschatology or hopes for the future. It has long been common to see the Scrolls as representative of 'apocalyptic', and in part this is justified. We should not, however, make the mistake of seeing 'apocalyptic' as marking out a special type of Judaism. The eschatology of the group who produced the Scrolls, while sharing some common features with the views found in other 'apocalyptic' writings, must not be read simply as expecting the literal 'end of

---

88 See e.g. 1QS 8.5–11; 1QH 6.25–9.
89 See e.g. CD 5.6–7.
90 See CD 1.3–11; 3.21–4.4; 7.20–8.2; 4QMMT C 10–17; 1QS 5.5–9.

134 The World of Jesus and the Early Church

The War Scroll from Qumran (1QM), a dramatized liturgy about an end-time battle between the sons of light and the sons of darkness.
© *The Israel Museum, by David Harris / Bridgeman Images*

the world'. The exalted language about a coming great day was intended to refer to the time when Israel's God would act *within* history to redeem his people and re-establish them *as* his people, within his holy land and worshipping in a new Temple (see text grid: 'Texts from the Dead Sea Scrolls'). The hope, however exalted, retained its essentially this-worldly base. When Israel's God acted, he would send the true anointed priest, and the true Davidic king, to be the Messiahs of his people. This belief in *two* Messiahs (here again we see the awkward holding together of royal and priestly categories) may be startling to those accustomed to think of Jews as expecting 'the Messiah' simply, but it is perfectly consistent with the group's firmly held belief in a renewed Temple. It would be quite wrong for a Davidic king, descended from Judah, to preside over the true Temple; only a descendant of Levi, Aaron, and Zadok would do. The royal Messiah would lead the group in their holy war against the enemy, after which Israel's redemption would be complete, and the true Israel would rule in peace and righteousness for ever. Most Jews in our period seem to have believed that their God would act in the future to liberate Israel from its continuing exile. The group whose writings were found at Qumran believed that this God had already begun the process, secretly, in and through them. This belief in the distinction between 'the present age' and 'the age to come' runs through most Jewish literature of this period and on into the later rabbinic age. It does not mark out one special type.

The Jewish Context of Jesus and the Early Church

The sect thus held a form of what later scholarship has called 'inaugurated eschatology'. What would happen in the future would be the dramatic unveiling of what had already been started, just as what had already been started was the fulfilment of prophecies hidden from long ago. At the moment, the rest of Israel would look and look, but never see; the day would come when the righteous would shine like the sun in the kingdom of Israel's God.

TEXTS FROM THE DEAD SEA SCROLLS

1QS 11.10–14	4Q521 2.1–12	4QMMT C 26–32
Surely a man's way is not his own; neither can any person firm his own step. Surely justification is of God; by His power is the way made perfect. All that shall be, He foreknows, all that is, His plans establish; apart from Him is nothing done. As for me, if I stumble, God's loving-kindness forever shall save me. If through sin of the flesh I fall, my justification will be by the righteousness of God which endures for all time. Though my affliction break out, He shall draw my soul back from the Pit, and firm my steps on the way. Through His love He has brought me near; by His loving-kindness shall he provide my justification. By His righteous truth has He justified me; and through His exceeding goodness shall He atone for all my sins. By His righteousness shall He cleanse me of human defilement and the sin of humankind—to the end that I praise God for His righteousness, the Most High for His glory. (Tr. Wise, Abegg, and Cook [2005])	For the heavens and the earth shall listen to His Messiah and all which is in them shall not turn away from the commandments of the holy ones. Strengthen yourselves, O you who seek the Lord, in His service. Will you not find the Lord in this, all those who hope in their heart? For the Lord seeks the pious and calls the righteous by name. Over the humble His spirit hovers, and He renews the faithful in His strength. For He will honor the pious upon the throne of his eternal kingdom, setting prisons free, opening the eyes of the blind, raising up those who are bowed down. And forever I shall hold fast to the hopeful and pious . . . and the Lord shall do glorious things which have not been done, just as He said. For He shall heal the critically wounded, He shall revive the dead, He shall send good news to the afflicted. (Tr. Wise, Abegg, and Cook [2005])	Now we have written to you some of the works of the Law, those which we determined would be beneficial for you and your people, because we have seen that you possess insight and knowledge of the Law. Understand all these things and beseech Him to set your counsel straight and so keep you away from evil thoughts and the counsel of Belial. Then you shall rejoice at the end time when you find the essence of our words to be true. And it will be reckoned to you as righteousness, in that you have done what is right and good before Him, to your own benefit and to that of Israel. (Tr. Wise, Abegg, and Cook [2005])
Compare with Rom. 1.17; 3.21–26.	Compare with Mt. 11.1–6/ Lk. 7.18–23.	Compare with Rom. 3.19–20 and Gal. 2.15—3.10.

The ordinary Jews

Not every Jew living in the Galilean countryside or inhabiting a Judean town necessarily identified with any of the religious parties. Most ordinary Jews were consumed with the daily struggle of human existence: farming, trading, paying taxes, putting food on the table, dealing with family matters like births, marriages, and funerals, and not continually gossiping about the newest teaching and the latest heresy. Yet even without identifying with any particular party, it remains likely that the great majority of Jews cared sufficiently about their God, their scriptures, and their Jewish heritage to take a fair amount of trouble over the observance of scriptural commands. They prayed, they fasted, they went to synagogue, they travelled to Jerusalem for the regular feasts. They did not eat pork or shellfish, they kept the sabbath, they fasted, and they circumcised their male children. Many regarded the Pharisees as respected, though unofficial, teachers, ensuring that some of these basic duties were carried out in a more or less Pharisaic fashion. We may therefore take it that the majority of Jews in Palestine during the Roman period kept more or less faithfully, as far as they were able, to the Jewish way of life. They were not likely to have been deeply reflective theologians. But their symbolic world and their regular praxis give us first-rate insight into the theology to which, however inarticulately, they gave allegiance.

JEWISH BELIEFS: ONE GOD AND ONE PEOPLE

As we have seen, the Jewish world was anything but monolithic in its views, beliefs, and aspirations. If we were to collect together people like Ben-Sirach, Philo, the Teacher of Righteousness, Rabbi Gamaliel, and the apostle Paul and ask them, 'What makes a person a good Jew?', there would be a rather free and frank exchange of ideas. Added to that, we must remember that the Jewish way of life was just that, a way of life; people did not think of it as a 'religion' in the modern sense. It was a totality, comprising ethnic identity, geographical focus, shared history, customs, and traditions. (Indeed, people did not think of it as 'Judaism', which is a relatively modern term. The Greek word *Ioudaismos*, which looks as though it might mean 'Judaism' in our sense, was in fact an active noun, denoting the zealous propagation of the Jewish way of life.)[91] Yet, despite all their diversity, the Jews who practised their ancestral customs would have had several things in common. They shared a commitment to Torah as both story and instruction, even though they disagreed fiercely with one another about what that involved in detail. They recognized the Temple as the intended place of the divine presence, even though nobody in the first century seems to have thought that the full, glorious 'Shekinah' had returned after the exile

---

91 See Paul's remarks in Gal. 1.13–14.

in the way Isaiah had promised.[92] They recognized the importance of the traditional 'land of Israel' as the people's divinely given inheritance, even though it had been many centuries since the boundaries allotted in the book of Joshua had borne any resemblance to actual Jewish presence. They followed the annual calendar of festivals like Yom Kippur and Passover, even though there were disputes between different groups as to how the calendar should be organized.[93] All this is given. However, if we want to get down to the ultimate core of Jewish beliefs, and see what had been sustaining them over several centuries, despite domination by one pagan kingdom after another, it would be this: monotheism and election, or, one God and one people!

The Jews believed in a specific God, of whom there was only one, who had made the whole world and who was active within it even while remaining sovereign over it. They knew this God as YHWH, 'the One Who Is', the Sovereign One. He (they used masculine pronouns for YHWH, though they knew very well that he was beyond gender, and they could often use feminine imagery as well) was not remote or detached. Nor was he simply a generalized sense of a sacred dimension within the world, or for that matter the personification of spiritual forces. Rather, he was the *maker* of all that exists, and he remained powerful and involved within, though by no means reduced to terms of, the creation itself. Classic Jewish monotheism thus came to believe that (1) there was one God, who created heaven and earth, and who remained in close and dynamic relation with his creation; and that (2) this God had called Israel to be his special people. This latter vocation was sometimes explicitly linked with the former belief: YHWH had chosen Israel *for the sake of* the larger world. Election, the choice of Israel, was the focal point of the divine purpose to act within the world to rescue and heal the world, to bring about what some biblical writers speak of as a 'new creation'.

This twin belief in monotheism and election was never simply a pair of abstract propositions arrived at by philosophical enquiry or hypothetical speculation. It was discovered through a particular history, and characteristically expressed through telling and retelling that history in one shape or another. The history was that of Abraham's family going down into Egypt, becoming enslaved, and being dramatically rescued and given their own land. Those who lived through these events explained who they were, and gave shape to their continuing life, by telling the story and dramatically re-enacting it in various festivals. Whatever happened subsequently, whether oppression, suffering, exile, or seeming annihilation, those who belonged to the family of Abraham looked back to the story of the exodus to

---

92 Isa. 40.3–5; 52.7–10.
93 According to James C. Vanderkam (2012, 91): 'The surviving evidence exhibits a richness and diversity in Judaism of the Second Temple era, a diversity so great that some have resorted to the neologism "Judaisms" to express it. Yet, despite the undoubted diversity present in the texts, there are fundamental beliefs and practices that would have been accepted by virtually all Jews during those centuries and that justify retaining the singular noun Judaism.'

rediscover who their God was and to pray that he would do for them once more those great saving acts that had constituted them as his people in the first place.

Part of the story was precisely the discovery of what God's faithfulness and rescuing power would look like in practice. This God would be known as the rescuer, the one who would then accompany his people through the wilderness, leading them in the pillar of cloud and fire, coming to dwell in their midst (or at least, after the 'golden calf' incident, in close proximity to the camp), and giving them his law, his own self-expression of the way of life for his people. The story of the exodus thus included within itself the story of two ways in which the one true God was present and active within the world and Israel: the Shekinah, the glory of God 'tabernacling' within the tent in the wilderness and later within the Temple in Jerusalem; and the Torah, the expressed will of God for Israel, the law of Moses. In addition, a strong strand in the story was the belief that God's own spirit had rested upon and indwelt Moses, enabling him to be the leader of God's people. Some later traditions referred to the strange pillar of cloud and fire in terms of the divine spirit.[94] Thus these three manifestations of YHWH's presence and rescuing love—God's presence, God's law, God's spirit, all seen to great advantage in the rescue-story, the freedom-story, that is, the exodus narrative—mark off the Jews' sense of who their God actually was from the theologies of the surrounding nations.

In many places in Israel's scriptures, and in subsequent post-biblical Jewish writings, these three ways of thinking about God's presence and saving activity, within the world and within Israel, were linked closely with two others: God's Word and God's Wisdom. Both are associated with creation; both are seen as other ways of saying what was said through Shekinah and Torah. Together these five ways form, not indeed a philosophical system, but a controlling narrative. Through retelling and reliving this story in liturgy and festival, in reading, singing, and prayer, Israel was able to rekindle the sense of God's presence. Its people were able to root themselves again in YHWH's rescuing actions in the past; to pray, often in extreme circumstances, for his rescuing help in the present; and, looking to the future, to hope for his final victory, and their own final liberation from all that enslaved them (see text grid: 'Ancient and modern Jewish scholars comment on Israel's plight in the first century').

Into this Jewish picture of the one true God we must now factor two other features characteristic of some Jewish writings in the second-Temple period. First, there was the expectation that YHWH would return to Zion, in power and visible glory, after his abandonment of Jerusalem at the time of the Babylonian exile. Second, there was the tradition of the enthronement of YHWH, and of one who somehow shared that throne. We will return to these themes when discussing Jesus' own self-understanding.

---

94 Isa. 63.11; Hag. 2.5.

> ### ANCIENT AND MODERN JEWISH SCHOLARS COMMENT ON ISRAEL'S PLIGHT IN THE FIRST CENTURY
>
> | Philo | Klausner |
> |---|---|
> | Philo of Alexandria commented in his own day on how Israel was still suffering the effects of exile as the majority of Jews remained dispersed from the land and the nation persisted in a state of slavery, and he looked forward to a day when God would dramatically act to reverse this:

'For even though they dwell in the uttermost parts of the earth, in slavery to those who led them away captive, one signal, as it were, one day will bring liberty to all … When they have gained this unexpected liberty, those who but now were scattered in Greece and the outside world over islands and continents will arise and post from every side with one impulse to the one appointed place, guided in their pilgrimage by a vision and superhuman unseen by others but manifest to them as they come from exile to their home … Everything will suddenly be reversed, God will turn the curses against the enemies of these penitents, the enemies who rejoiced in the misfortunes of the nation and mocked and railed at them …' (Philo *Praem*. 164–9). | Jewish scholar Joseph Klausner, writing in the 1920s, noted that the return of the Babylonian exiles to Judea was a bit of an anti-climax as it did not yield the realization of the prophetic hopes for the restoration of the nation; instead, things seemed to get worse:

'But what was the actual fact? Slavery to foreign governments, wars, tumults and torrents of blood. Instead of all nations being subject to Judah, Judah was subject to the nations. Instead of the "riches of the Gentiles," godless Rome exacted taxes and tribute … Instead of the Gentiles "bowing down with their faces to the ground" and "licking the dust of their feet," comes a petty Roman official with unlimited power over Judea. Instead of Messiah the son of David, comes Herod the Edomite."|
>
> *Klausner 1929, 169–70.

If YHWH were to act afresh, decisively, in history, and if he were to do so through a chosen agent, how might that chosen agent be described? According to some texts from our period, the agent through whom Israel's God acted would be vindicated, exalted, and honoured in a quite unprecedented manner. This is a separate subject in itself, and I must be content with pointing in a general direction with some specific instances.

There is a complex range of Jewish texts from different periods that speculate about the exaltation and heavenly enthronement of a figure who may be either an angel or a human being. These speculations grow from meditation upon, and discussion of, certain key texts such as Ezekiel 1, in which the prophet receives a vision of YHWH's throne-chariot, and Daniel 7, where 'one like a son of man' is presented to 'the Ancient of Days' and shares his throne. Such speculations formed the staple diet of a whole tradition of Jewish mysticism, along with accompanying theological and cosmological enquiry.

How far these speculations were taken is a matter of continuing debate. But the point should be clear: things like this were thinkable; they were not obviously self-contradictory, nor were they necessarily seen as a threat to what second-Temple Jews meant by 'monotheism'. They were attempts to find out what that monotheism would actually mean in practice: how was the one God going to fulfil his promises and purposes for Israel and the world? Thus, out of a much larger and highly complex set of speculations about the action of Israel's God through various mediator-figures, one possible scenario that some second-Temple Jews regarded as at least thinkable was that the earthly and military victory of the coming Messiah over the pagans would be seen in terms of the enthronement-scene from Daniel 7, itself a development of the chariot-vision in Ezekiel 1.

One thing should be clear from this brief survey of first-century Jewish beliefs. At their core is the conviction of the Jewish people that their God was the creator God, not a tribal god or a local deity, but 'God Almighty', the 'maker of heaven and earth'. He had called Israel to be his special possession, the people of his pasture, a kingdom of priests, and a light to the nations. Though the world was ravaged with evil and savaged by dark powers, it would not always remain so. Many Jews cherished, and brought to various expression, the hope that this one true God would deliver Israel through his agents—prophets, priests, and kings—to bring about a new exodus. This would utterly transform Israel's fortunes and future; and, through this transformed Israel, God would one day transform the entire world.

Further reading

Adams, Samuel L. 2014. *Social and Economic Life in Second Temple Judea*. Louisville, KY: Westminster John Knox.

Collins, John C., and Daniel C. Harlow (eds.). 2012. *Early Judaism: A Comprehensive Overview*. Grand Rapids, MI: Eerdmans.

deSilva, David A. 2000. *Honor, Patronage, Kinship and Purity: Unlocking New Testament Culture*. Downers Grove, IL: InterVarsity.

Goodblatt, David. 2006. *Elements of Ancient Jewish Nationalism*. New York: Cambridge University Press.

Green, Joel B., and Lee Martin McDonald (eds.). 2013. *The World of the New Testament: Cultural, Social, and Historical Context*. Grand Rapids, MI: Baker.

Hanson, K. C., and Douglas E. Oakman. 1998. *Palestine in the Time of Jesus: Social Structures and Social Conflicts*. Minneapolis: Fortress.

Rhoads, David. 1976. *Israel in Revolution, 6–74 C.E.: A Political History Based on the Writings of Josephus*. Philadelphia: Fortress.

Sanders, E. P. 1992. *Judaism: Practice and Belief, 63 BCE–66 CE*. London: SCM.

Wright, N. T. 1992. *The New Testament and the People of God*. COQG 1; London: SPCK, pp. 145–338.

——. 2014. *Paul and the Faithfulness of God*. COQG 4; London: SPCK, Part I, pp. 75–196.

The Greco-Roman Context of the Early Church

They [the Romans] ransack the world, and afterwards, when all the land has been laid waste by their pillaging, they scour the sea . . . They plunder, they murder, they rape, in the name of their so-called empire. And where they have made a desert, they call it peace.[1]

CHAPTER AT A GLANCE

This chapter describes features of the greco-roman world, including the dominance of hellenistic culture, Roman political power, and the Jewish Diaspora as the context in which the early church emerged.

By the end of this chapter you should be able to:

- appreciate the importance of Hellenism as a cultural force in the eastern Mediterranean;
- understand the significance of Rome's rise towards becoming the unrivalled military power of the first century;
- identify key features of greco-roman religions and ancient philosophies;
- understand the characteristics and complexities of the Jewish Diaspora.

HELLENISTIC CULTURE AND ROMAN EMPIRE

When we reach the first century, the eastern Mediterranean is culturally Greek, but politically dominated by the Roman empire. The conquests of Alexander the Great had led to a proliferation of Greek language, learning, and civilization. Places like Egypt, the Balkans, Asia Minor, Syria, Palestine, and the Fertile Crescent were all hellenized to varying degrees.[2] This does not mean, of course, that all prior customs and local traditions just vanished. Some Greek culture did displace certain aspects of life, but more often than not, it brought old customs to new expression. Indigenous forms of art, architecture, religion, and language did not die out. They were caught up

---

1   Tac. *Agric.* 30.
2   On the spread of Hellenism, see Ferguson 1993, 13–14.

in the larger, and complex, world of Greek culture. That culture did indeed take over, but the many other local cultures, far from vanishing, blended to create a wealth of hybrid cultural expressions. This ability to fuse cultures together explains why hellenization prevailed, and became as powerful as it did.[3]

The primary instrument of hellenization was language. Greek became the *lingua franca* of the ancient world, and remained dominant for centuries even after the Latin-speaking Romans had gained overall power. Many residents of Rome itself spoke Greek as their first language. The great early work of the church Father Irenaeus, in southern France, was written in his native Greek. Greek was, for the most part, the universal language of trade, government, the military, philosophy, and religion. It is no surprise that the Jewish scriptures, beginning with the Torah or Pentateuch, were translated into Greek, probably as early as the middle of the second century BC. This was the 'Bible' for the Greek-speaking Jews of the Diaspora, and for most early Christians. The widespread usage of Greek enabled trade and cultural interaction on a scale that the Mediterranean world had never experienced before.

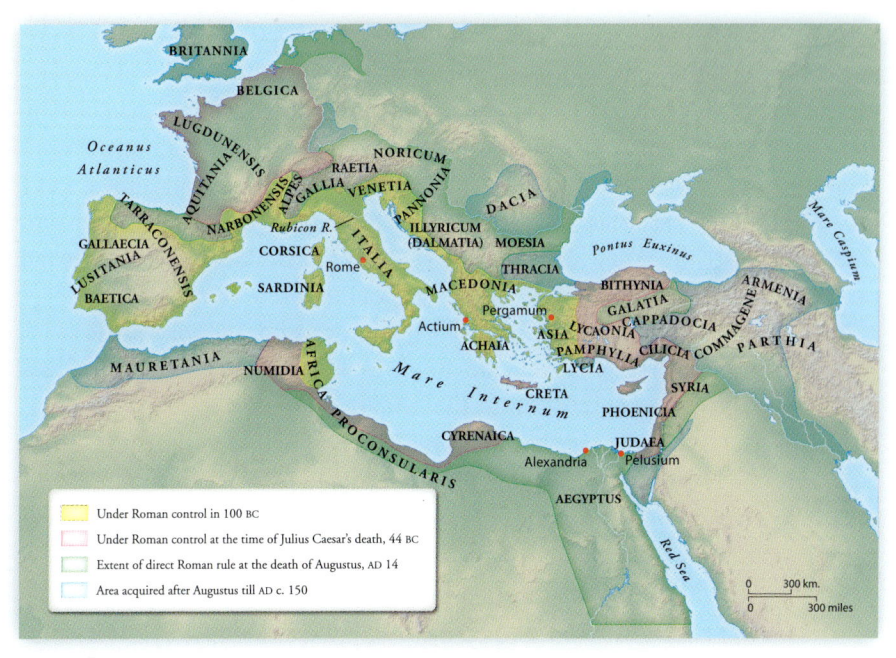

Roman Empire

The second instrument of hellenization was the *polis* or city-state. As the Greeks conquered regions, they established colonies with a Greek way of life. Here the Greek *polis* was the political, economic, educational, religious, and social hub of a

---

3   See introductions to Hellenism in Green 1993 and briefly in Aune 2010.

civilization. Cities were adorned with temples honouring the gods, a *gymnasium* for training young men, schools for instruction in philosophy and rhetoric, an *agora* for traded goods, and amphitheatres and stadiums for arts and sports. The *polis* was the means of forming a cultured urban society.

A third instrument of hellenization was religious syncretism. Local deities could be identified with gods from the Greek pantheon. The Samaritans identified YHWH with Zeus under the Seleucid ruler Antiochus Epiphanes IV in the second century BC, and then with Jupiter (the Roman equivalent of the Greek Zeus) under the Roman emperor Hadrian in the second century AD. The result was partly to universalize local religions by cross-matching deities in one culture with the deities in another culture. On the one hand this led to a proliferation of deities; but, on the other hand, it arguably began a movement towards a kind of monotheism by assimilating the various supposed divine beings to one another. There was even a type of ambiguous monotheism in the cult of the *theos hypsistos* ('most high god') attested in Asia Minor and the Greek cities near the Black Sea.

The Hellenism of the eastern Mediterranean must be distinguished from the culture of the classical Greek period, the time of Sophocles and Socrates. It was now, to speak loosely, more oriental. Greek culture in the time after Alexander was shaped, in the different regions, by Egyptian, Judean, Arabian, Asian, Syrian, and even Iranian influences. Greek influence was also uneven, affecting different regions and the social classes to different degrees. In places like Judea there was a mixture of appropriation and resistance to Hellenism. Nevertheless, Hellenism provided a regnant culture in which Jesus and the early Christians lived their lives and carried out their vocations. We see this throughout the New Testament.

Greece provided the cultural capital of the ancient world, but it was the Romans who spent it in expanding their empire. Rome itself had begun as a city-state, but it had gradually become a transcontinental empire reaching over parts of Europe, Africa, Asia, and the near east. Rome emerged as the dominant force in the Mediterranean after it defeated Carthage in the Second Punic War (218–201 BC). Thereafter, it began to expand its control and power over the various hellenistic city-states in the east, including Macedonia, Illyria, and Asia Minor. By the middle of the first century AD the Romans had also conquered or annexed Syria, Palestine, Egypt, Cyrene, Gaul, Spain, north Africa, and Armenia. Rome thus already had an 'empire' long before it had an 'emperor'; hence the easy confusion between the two meanings of 'empire', the first being the geographical spread of political power and the second being the rule of a single ruler. The transition from the Roman republic to the Roman empire, in the latter sense, began to take place under Julius Caesar (100–44 BC) who, though he was never called 'emperor', paved the way for the idea. After he had crossed the Rubicon and defeated Pompey, he was proclaimed *dictator perpetuus*, 'dictator for life'—which was why a group of staunch republicans killed him (44 BC).

The period after Caesar's assassination saw massive political upheaval as Rome was caught up in a series of civil wars. The first was between forces loyal to Octavian, Caesar's adopted son and heir, and those backing Antony, Caesar's friend, against Caesar's assassins, Brutus and Cassius. This reached its climax in the Battle of Philippi (42 BC) which Octavian and Antony won. They then turned on each other, leading to the victory of Octavian over Antony, and his Egyptian lover Cleopatra, at the naval Battle of Actium in 31 BC. This left Octavian as the undisputed leader of Rome, and gave him the propaganda opportunity to return to Rome and declare that he had brought peace to the world—and that he had restored the 'republic'. Nobody was fooled by this shameless rhetorical move; it was clear that he was now in sole charge. But nobody, after the years of chaos and violence, was going to stand in his way. The senate rewarded Octavian with the honorific name 'Augustus', by which he is now more generally known.

The reign of Augustus (31 BC–AD 14) marked a period of consolidation, reorganization, and renewal throughout the Roman empire. Augustus embarked on an empire-wide policy of fiscal rationalization; he developed a constitutional settlement for Rome; and he centralized his military authority over the various provinces. Writers and artists of the era heralded Augustus's reign as a time of unprecedented peace (from civil war) and security (from the Germanic tribes in the north and the Parthian empire in the east). What was clear was that the old ways of strict republicanism, with elected magistrates changing every year and a complex system of checks and balances to prevent power being concentrated in one person, had gone for ever. As to the geographical extent, it was under Trajan (AD 98–117) that Rome expanded its rule to its largest area, encompassing parts of Britain and Persia.

The Roman empire had grown out of an insatiable hunger for conquest. Rome's military power, famed and feared over a vast area, enabled the capital itself to grow rich with taxes imposed throughout its territories. The lower tiers of society in urban centres swelled with those who were made slaves or else displaced by military conflict. This put considerable pressure on the empire's ability to feed the populace of Rome itself, and the city became dependent on grain levied from Egypt. Life in the empire, including its capital, could be severe for those not part of the

Imperial fora ruins, constructed in Rome between 46 BC and 113 AD

elite classes. Daily life held few securities in employment, food supply, and survival amid narrow streets, crowded apartments, disease and dysentery, and violent crime. All this led to high mortality rates, and a certain degree of social dysfunction, kept in check only by the totalitarian authorities who acted if and when it served their own interests.

The establishment of colonies in places like Corinth and Philippi in Greece and Pisidian Antioch in southern Turkey was intended to deal with the simultaneous problems of overcrowding in Rome and the large number of old soldiers to whom land had been promised. Especially after the civil wars (fought mostly in Greece), Rome had no desire to see hordes of military veterans coming back to the already overcrowded region of central Italy. The colonies thus provided a type of Rome away from Rome, a place to settle troops and cultivate supporters. These colonies became outposts of Roman culture, and a reliable source of labour and soldiers that could be called upon if Rome needed them. This urban context, with a shared language, relative political stability, a melting-pot of peoples, and easy travel and communications, helped both the growth and consolidation of the empire and, as a strange subversive movement within it, the spread of the early church.

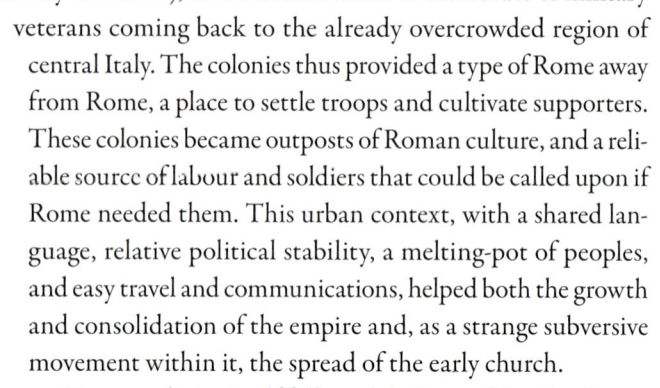

A coin depicting the goddess Roma reclining on the seven hills of Rome
Numismatica Ars Classica NAC AG, Auction 59, lot 658

Roman religion itself followed the lines of the Greek pantheon. The Roman interpretation of Greek religion meant that Zeus was Jupiter; Poseidon, Neptune; Hera, Juno; Athene, Minerva; Aphrodite, Venus. Ares becomes Mars; Artemis, Diana; Demeter, Ceres; Hephaistos, Vulcan; and Dionysos, Bacchus. Heracles changes a couple of letters to become Hercules; Asclepius adds a couple to become Aesculapius. Of the major divinities, only Apollo retains his name unchanged in both cultures. The Capitoline hill was crowned with a temple to the triad of gods comprising Jupiter, Minerva, and Juno. When Augustus dedicated a new temple near his house on the Palatine, he dedicated it to another triad of gods: Apollo, Latona, and Diana. There were other important divinities too. The goddess Roma was the embodiment of the Roman people and state, and was taken to the east as the empire expanded, encouraging conquered subjects to worship the obviously all-powerful divine force that had overwhelmed their local gods. Sometimes this was accepted gratefully: the Roma cult at Smyrna was established in thanksgiving for Roman help against the Syrian king Antiochus III. The emperor Augustus allowed temples for himself to be built in Pergamum in Asia, Nicomedia in Bithynia, and Ancyra in Galatia, but only on condition that temples to Roma be built as well.[4]

Roman 'religion' was largely controlled by the state through a set calendar and the appointment of priests and vestal virgins. It was practised both in public and in the home.

---

4   Tac. *Ann.* 4.37.3.

TABLE 7.1: ECONOMIC SCALES FOR URBAN CONTEXTS IN THE GRECO-ROMAN WORLD

Group	Description	%
Imperial, provincial, and municipal elites	Ruling elites drawn mostly from the senatorial and equestrian classes, plus some decurion families, and retired military officers	3
Moderate surplus wealth	Some merchants, traders, large landowners, some freedmen, some artisans, and military veterans	17
Stable, near subsistence level	Most merchants, traders, artisans, regular wage-earners, large shop-owners, freedmen, some farm families	25
Subsistence level	Small farm families, labourers, artisans, wage-earners, most merchants and traders, small shop-owners	30
Below subsistence level	Some farm families, unattached widows, orphans, beggars, disabled, unskilled day-labourers, prisoners	25

The private 'household gods' in each home were particularly important, with the father of the family acting as priest. These 'household gods' comprised the *lares*, small statues of two young men, and the *penates*, the small cult statues placed at the innermost point of the home, symbolizing the identity of a particular family. Harder to describe, but extremely important, was the *genius* of the father of the household. The *genius* was the deified concept of the person in his true identity or self. It could be represented by a small statue, and was invoked on the occasion of marriage, or of oath-taking. Philosophically speaking, the *genius* was the true, spiritual inner core of a person, or indeed of a place; hence the *genius loci*, the 'spirit of a place', which could also be invoked as a divinity. As such, 'religion' was very much intertwined with social and political life, and indeed one likely meaning of the Latin word *religio* is the 'binding together' of gods and peoples in all aspects of life. Roman religion stressed the importance of its citizens acting with *pietas*, that is, honouring their obligations to the gods, and with *religio* itself, in the sense of maintaining the divine–human link by observing appropriate scruples and rites.

THE SOCIAL ORDER

Social status was usually inherited through family descent and gender, all in an assumed ordered hierarchy. However, social advancement was possible, and many pursued it vigorously, by accumulation of wealth, or by marriage, education, manumission from slavery, and military exploits. All Romans belonged to one of the various social tiers of society: senatorial, equestrian, decurion, plebeian, freedman, and slave (see Table 7.1).[5] Social ranking often determined who would interact with whom, and on what terms. This caused various conundrums for the early church, committed as it was to living in a totally different way.

The senatorial class represented the wealthy nobility of Rome and provided the primary cohort of civil and military administrators. They owned property estimated at one million sesterces. We meet those of the senatorial class in the New Testament with Sergius Paulus, the proconsul of Cyprus, and Gallio, the proconsul of Achaia.[6] The equestrian class (or 'knights' as they are sometimes called in the literature, though one should resist the implications of medieval knights on horseback) was a larger group of less wealthy Roman citizens, normally with an aggregate wealth of around 400,000 sesterces. Governors of Judea such as Pontius Pilate, Marcus Felix, and Porcius Festus were from the equestrian order.[7] Decurions were members of civil councils in provincial cities, leaders of local communities, often acting as magistrates. They normally had a combined wealth of 100,000 sesterces. In the New Testament, Erastus, the city treasurer of Corinth, was probably a decurion; so, too, was Dionysius of Athens, a man who served in the court of the Areopagus.[8] The plebeians represented the general citizenry of Rome, owning little farms, workshops, or small businesses. Finally, there were freedmen, the *libertini*, who were ex-slaves, often remaining in a dependent relationship with their former master, while second-generation freedmen, the *ingenui*, were considered freeborn. Some freedmen, however, rose rapidly because of their innate ability. The emperor Claudius was famous for relying on certain freedmen as his closest advisers and administrators. Perhaps he reckoned there was less chance of them plotting against him than there would have been had he employed more high-born Romans.

Slaves occupied the lowest tier of society in terms of *relative* social status. Slaves were regarded as little more than property, albeit with a soul (at least from a philosophical point of view, though routinely ignored in practice). Slavery was widespread, with slaves comprising up to 30 per cent of the population in some urban areas. One became a slave when captured as a prisoner of war, when kidnapped by slave-traders, or through being sold into slavery by one's family (for instance, when the alternative might be starvation). Indeed, people could sell themselves into slavery to avoid destitution. Or, of course, you could be born the child of slaves, and hence be a slave yourself. Slaves engaged in a wide variety of tasks, including working as farm

---

5 Ferguson 1993, 52–9. For debates over scales of poverty in the greco-roman world, see Longenecker 2010, 36–59 (esp. 45).
6 Ac. 13.7; 18.12.
7 Lk. 3.1; Ac. 24.1–3, 27.
8 Rom. 16.23; Ac. 17.34.

labourers, nurses, midwives, prostitutes, painters, doctors, cooks, and even guardians for children (like the *paidagogos* in Gal. 3.24, the slave charged with keeping the son out of mischief until he reached maturity). The position of a slave in society was contingent upon the position of their master, whether an artisan or perhaps a senator. While slavery often entailed harsh conditions and cruel exploitation, many slaves were managers for wealthy patrons, positions that could be financially lucrative and even socially advantageous. To be a slave in the service of someone great was to be in a position of authority and legitimacy.[9] Freedom from slavery was possible either by payment of a ransom price or else by the master or owner granting release.

If we look at the list of people named in the assemblies of the early church, it is clear that there was social diversity from the very beginning.[10] While the early church contained people from the upper and merchant classes (though not the senatorial class, it seems, in the early decades at least), the largest block of people in the church came from the lower echelons and even from among the slave population.[11] This socio-economic disparity contributed to some of the problems faced by the first churches, such as the congregation in Corinth where the rich (it seems) were unwilling to give up their culture of privilege and patronage, but instead translated it into their behaviour in the church. Paul indicates that some members of the Corinthian assembly were taking others to public courts; because of the cost of litigation this almost certainly means rich members trying to sue poorer ones. In addition, the rich members were beginning their love-feast with a celebration of the Lord's Supper before the poorer members of the house-church had even arrived.[12]

Roman social stratification created other headaches too. For example, Christian noblewomen had a dilemma. There was at times a shortage of Christian men from the upper classes, but Christian noblewomen were not supposed to marry pagan men. If, in order to marry a Christian, they married a social inferior, they would lose their status among the nobility. Bishop Callistus, a third-century bishop of Rome, recognized that mixed marriages with pagans were undesirable for Christian noblewomen, but that it was preferable for them to retain their social status.

> 'Women in the Greco-Roman world had power even if they could not be a general or the emperor. They may have had supreme influence in running the empire or senate if they had power over a man who could make a decree or cast the vote. Livia, Augustus's wife, was a woman reputed to have as much power as her husband due to her influence with him. As [Margaret] MacDonald notes, "the female patron may be best understood as exercising power through the spheres of patronage with its network of clients and obligations".'
>
> **Lynn Cohick**, *Women in the World of the Earliest Christians*, 288.

---

9   Martin 1990, 54–5.
10 See e.g. Rom. 16.1–16.
11 See discussion in Longenecker 2010, 220–58.
12 1 Cor. 6.1–10; 11.17–34.

He therefore gave the church's blessing to Christian women living in concubinage with a socially inferior Christian man, even with a slave, without being legally married.[13] This was the kind of thing that some found necessary if Christians were to negotiate their way within the social structures of the greco-roman world.

RELIGION, PHILOSOPHY, AND CULTURE

God-soaked culture

The problem with trying to understand ancient culture is that we hardly understand our own. Cultures are usually shaped by 'myths' or master narratives which determine identities, values, and aspirations. In the ancient world, mythic master narratives such as Homer's *Iliad* (about the war between Greece and Troy) and Virgil's *Aeneid* (about the founding of Rome after the fall of Troy) were expressed in various media, including coins, poetry, religious rites, statues, inscriptions, architecture, and the like. In our own day many in western culture have lost their roots in older stories (the Bible, Shakespeare, and so on). These days the main 'myths' by which people seem to live consist of a vague belief in 'progress', a number of morality tales about the evils of the last century (for example, the Holocaust; segregation in the American south and South Africa; genocide in Rwanda and elsewhere), the 1960s 'virtues' of personal autonomy and sexual freedom, the post-September 11 fear of militant religion, and the rampant consumerism fostered by the giant multinational technology companies and their new technologies. These myths are expressed in reality TV shows, downloadable apps, blockbuster movies, and the 24-hour news cycle, all of which provide a symbolic world of values and meaning in which we are unconsciously immersed. Various cues activate images from our culture. Saying 'da-dum, da-dum' will evoke, for some at least, movie images of a man-eating shark. Holding out your outstretched arm just above eye-level with fingers extended emulates a Hitler salute from the 1930s and 1940s. Saying 'I am not a crook' casts the mind back to a certain American president of the 1970s. All this is to say that a few musical notes, a small gesture with the hand, or a terse quote can activate memories of cultural scripts that we are all mostly familiar with. Different countries and subcultures have their own local variations.

Obviously the ancient world did not have TV shows, the Internet, or Major League Baseball. But it did have its own literature, theatre, sporting heroes, cultural icons, and political celebrities, all of which were infused with stories and symbols from their mythic past. Presented with any given speech, play, coin, statue, novel, or religious rite, a first-century inhabitant of the greco-roman world would pick up allusions to Hercules, the Trojan War, the founding of Rome by Remus and Romulus (or perhaps by Aeneas), and the deification of Roman emperors. They knew these stories as

---

13 Lampe 2003, 119–22.

well as today's western culture knows the present state of various soap operas, or film franchises such as Star Wars, or the present marital dilemmas of leading celebrities. We cannot begin to understand how ordinary people in the first century thought, imagined, reasoned, believed, prayed, and acted unless we try to get inside their myth-soaked culture. Importantly, this was a culture in which religion was everywhere. Like coffee shops or advertisements for cheap pharmaceuticals in our own culture, it was assumed and taken for granted everywhere. The centre of major cities, including Rome itself, was carefully constructed, with temples of the specific divinities that the rulers regarded as central, so that the whole space constituted a visible parable about the interlocking relationship between the city, its gods, and the emperor.

What the apostle Paul saw in Athens, a city 'full of idols', was typical of towns and cities everywhere in the ancient world, not just as an expression of multiple types of private piety but as the central embodiment and expression of civic, domestic, and personal life. Luke reports that when Paul walked around Athens, he became very distressed at the prevalence of idols in the city; they were everywhere, like weeds. Paul's distress was no small thing. To him, a former Pharisee, it might have felt something like the revulsion of a germophobe being forced to walk through an underground sewer. Importantly, ancient religion was not restricted to temples and academic halls; it was all over the place, in houses, in the market-place, at sporting events, in music and art, and not least in politics. This 'ancient religion' was not set apart from the rest of ancient culture. On the contrary: it was its beating heart, with every part of the body politic related to that heart by active and throbbing blood vessels. If the world was full of gods, the world was therefore also full of religion, full of cult; full of a god-soaked *culture*.

So when someone like Paul arrived in Thessalonica or Ephesus with his message about the one God and his crucified and risen son, he was not offering an alternative way of being 'religious' in the sense of a private hobby, something to do in a few hours at the weekend. He was offering a heart transplant for an entire community and its culture. In cities like Thessalonica, this meant offering a direct challenge to the imperial cult, with its pretentious claim to being the religious and political glue that kept society together. Paul's message implied the eclipse of local rites and cultural identities (as with the goddess Artemis in Ephesus): when people were grasped by the gospel of Jesus they gave up all other worship—but it was that other worship, soaked into every aspect of local culture, that most people regarded as vital for the health and safety of a city, a community, or a household. So it is hardly surprising that Paul's work often produced riots.[14]

All this means that, to understand the New Testament, we need to be able to grasp what ancient religion was and wasn't, and how it differed from our own modern ideas of religion and its boundaries.

---

[14] Ac. 17.1–9; 19.23–40.

Greco-roman religion

A first issue we have to broach is that the ancient world did not have something called 'religion' as we understand it today. If by 'religion' we mean a body of beliefs about 'the supernatural', with various ethical corollaries that can be kept in a separate compartment from secular culture, then clearly there was no such thing as 'religion' in that sense. There wasn't a word for that kind of thing, because it was unknown. The Latin word *religio* could mean 'scruple' in the sense of one's duties to the gods, or the idea (as we said before) of the 'binding together' of gods and humans in a community. In Greek, the main terms we find for religious activity, found also in the New Testament, are 'piety' or 'godliness' (*eusebeia*); 'worship' (*thrēskeia*); and the 'service' associated with it (*latreia*).[15] This language pertains to cult and ritual, not to any complex web of beliefs, worldviews, and practices. The word 'religion' only gradually came to be used in the ancient world in relation to Christianity when it was fashioning a way of separating cult from culture. The idea that there might then be different 'religions' was an innovation of the late sixteenth and early seventeenth centuries. And this sense of a plurality of 'religions' was then exported from the modern west to other parts of the world, causing surprise, for instance, among the sages of India who discovered, thanks to the colonizing British, that they had a 'religion' called 'Hinduism'.[16]

A second issue we have to mention is that the parameters and spheres in which religion exists today are very different from those of the ancient world. We can see this in several ways.[17]

In this bas-relief from the Arch of Marcus Aurelius, the emperor Marcus Aurelius (AD 161–80) and members of the imperial family offer a sacrifice in thanksgiving for victory over the Germanic tribes with the temple of Jupiter on the Capitolium in the background.
Reproduced by permission from Carole Raddato

---

15   See 1 Tim. 3.16; Ac. 26.5; Col. 2.18; Jas. 1.26–27; 3.7–10; Jn. 16.2; Rom. 9.4; 12.2; Phil. 3.3. When Paul comments on the extreme religiosity of the Athenians in Ac. 17.22, the word he uses is *deisidaimonesterous*, 'extremely honouring of the *daimonia*', perhaps broadly corresponding to the Latin *superstitio*.
16   Judge 2008, 407, and on the topic of the modern invention of 'religion' see Nongbri 2013.
17   What follows is mostly drawn from Ehrman 2004, 22–8.

152   The World of Jesus and the Early Church

1. Concern with present life rather than with an afterlife. One of the main attractions of Christianity or even Islam is the promise of life after death in an unending eternity with God. Ancient views on an afterlife were quite diverse. Emperors might, after death, become gods. Some people believed in reincarnation; others denied any future life. Most seemed to think that after death they would join the ranks of those in Hades, in some kind of shadowy and subterranean existence. Men and women pursued the favour of the gods not primarily for what the gods might give them in a future life, but for blessings, boons, help, security, peace, and prosperity in this life here and now.

2. Focus on cultic ritual rather than on doctrinal beliefs. Some ancient authors do, indeed, discuss different views of the gods. Cicero, for instance, wrote a dialogue, *On the Nature of the Gods*, discussing the different views about the gods held by different philosophical schools. But on the whole, greco-roman religion was concerned, not with creedal beliefs about gods, but with cultic acts that demonstrated devotion to the deities. The offering of food to a household spirit, the utterance of prayers before a long journey, the sacrifice of an animal in a temple or at a festival—all this was designed to court the benevolence and benefaction of spirits and gods.

3. No secularism with a separation of religion and state. Secularism, even as we might think of it, is not a monolithic concept. There are diverse expressions of secularism in our world: the secularisms of the USA, Turkey, France, the UK, Australia, and many other countries all take subtly different forms. If, however, one reduces secularism to 'a separation of church and state', then it is safe to say that the ancient world was far from secular. Political leaders wanted peace and security, and 'religion' was one vital way to achieve that. This is why emperors built temples, sponsored religious rites, often attempted to reform religious practices, and sometimes even enforced participation in religious observances by whole cities. The Roman emperor could style himself as the 'high priest' of the empire, but on other occasions as a 'god' to whom worship was owed by his subjects to secure his protection and benefaction. Religious practices were thus part of statecraft. Political authorities took more than a passing interest in religious groups and their rituals.

4. Pluralism but not necessarily tolerance. Worship of a god was never exclusive. There were gods for just about everything: love, poetry, baking, travel, and even bee-keeping. Greco-roman 'religion', both at the public and private level, was usually capable of accommodating various divinities. As groups and individuals migrated around the ancient near east, this resulted in complex, criss-crossing varieties of local 'religions' in any one place, in which, as we have seen, newly arrived gods and goddesses might take the names and attributes of existing local ones. A Greek philosopher named Celsus, himself a pagan monotheist of sorts, wrote a pointed critique of Christianity in the late second century, saying that God can go by various names:

'It makes no difference if one invokes the highest God or Zeus or Adonai or Sabaoth or Amoun, as the Egyptians do, or Papaios as the Scythians do.'[18] From the hellenistic Jews of Egypt, we have a writing called the *Epistle of Aristeas*, which depicts Alexandrian elites as believing that Jews and pagans basically worship the same God, only by a different name:

> These people worship God, the overseer and creator of all, whom all men worship including ourselves, O King, except that we have a different name. Their name for him is Zeus and Jove. The primitive men, consistently with this, demonstrated that the one by whom all live and are created is the master and Lord of all.[19]

However, the ancient pagans were not straightforwardly pluralist in matters of religion. They placed great importance upon accurate performance of time-honoured ritual and the precise wording of prayers. The ostensible reason Socrates was condemned to death included the charge of perverting the youth by introducing foreign divinities into Athens. The reason the Romans banned the rites of Bacchus was as much on the grounds of their novelty, including social novelty, as of their alleged immorality.

Site of the temple of Artemis where the riot in Ephesus occurred. 'The city clerk quietened the crowd and said: "Fellow Ephesians, doesn't all the world know that the city of Ephesus is the guardian of the temple of the great Artemis and of her image, which fell from heaven? Therefore, since these facts are undeniable, you ought to calm down and not do anything rash. You have brought these men here, though they have neither robbed temples nor blasphemed our goddess."' (Ac. 19.35–36 NIV)
Goldika / Shutterstock

---

[18] Origen *C. Cels.* 5.41.
[19] *Ep. Arist.* 16.

In addition, the Jews were expelled from Rome no fewer than three times (c. 139 BC, AD 19, and AD 49), partly on account of the increasing prevalence of observation of their rites in Rome, which supposedly fostered a neglect of the local cult, or else for rioting among themselves over religious disputes. Failure to observe commonplace piety, like attending great festivals or adhering to certain specialized rules such as those concerning the vestal virgins, could result in severe penalties. To give a concrete example, a Roman nobleman named Maecenas purportedly advised the young Octavian (later to become 'Augustus') about his duties regarding religion as a political leader. His advice shows how imperial ideology and religious suppression went hand in hand:

Reconstruction of the temple of Artemis
Serg Zastavkin / Shutterstock

> You should not only worship the divine everywhere and in every way in accordance with our ancestral traditions, but also force all others to honour it. Those who attempt to distort our religion with strange rites you should hate and punish, not only for the sake of the gods ... but also because such people, by bringing in new divinities, persuade many folks to adopt foreign practices, which lead to conspiracies, revolts, and factions, which are entirely unsuitable for monarchy.'[20]

Ancient religion was pluralistic, but not necessarily tolerant.

'Religion' was thus part and parcel of life in the greco-roman *polis*, fully integrated into (what we think of as) the social and political spheres. Certainly, religious *polity* and *practice* would vary from one city to another. Various factors would shape local practice; the particular myths and memories of different towns and regions would come into play. James Rives gives a good summary of religion in the greco-roman *polis*:

> 'Religion' did not exist as a separate area of human activity, but was embedded in the overarching structure of the city; there were no important religious institutions or offices separate from civic institutions and offices. Each city had its own distinctive set of cults, even if most of these were directed at a shared set of deities, and a city's public cults were what defined the distinctive religious identity of its citizens; there was no religious identity separate from political or civic identity. Control of these public cults was in the hands of the local elite,

---

[20] Dio Cassius *Hist.* 52.36.1–2, cited in Rowe 2009, 165.

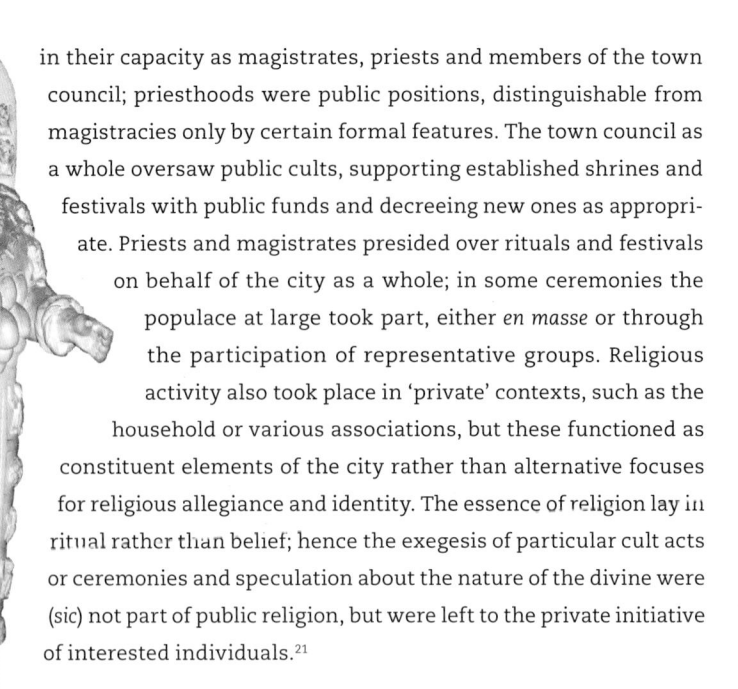

in their capacity as magistrates, priests and members of the town council; priesthoods were public positions, distinguishable from magistracies only by certain formal features. The town council as a whole oversaw public cults, supporting established shrines and festivals with public funds and decreeing new ones as appropriate. Priests and magistrates presided over rituals and festivals on behalf of the city as a whole; in some ceremonies the populace at large took part, either *en masse* or through the participation of representative groups. Religious activity also took place in 'private' contexts, such as the household or various associations, but these functioned as constituent elements of the city rather than alternative focuses for religious allegiance and identity. The essence of religion lay in ritual rather than belief; hence the exegesis of particular cult acts or ceremonies and speculation about the nature of the divine were (sic) not part of public religion, but were left to the private initiative of interested individuals.[21]

Artemis of the Ephesians was the patron deity of Ephesus and widely worshipped in the greco-roman world. She was identified with the Greek goddess Artemis and the Roman goddess Diana, and was worshipped for her fertility blessings. The temple dedicated to her was one of the wonders of the ancient world. The book of Acts records Paul visiting Ephesus and preaching so effectively that it was feared that interest in Artemis would fade. In particular, the silversmiths led by a certain Demetrius were afraid that their trade of making silver shrines of Artemis would be jeopardized (Ac. 19.23–41).

mountainpix / Shutterstock

If we had to distil the substance of ancient 'religion', then, we could say that it pertains to negotiating the relationship between the divine world and the human world through ritual observance. This could be summed up by Cicero as *cultus deorum* ('the cult of the gods') in the sense of the labour of cultivating the divine favour of the gods for human existence. The whole point was to secure the *pax deorum* ('the peace of the gods') whereby harmonious relationship could be maintained between the divinities and mortals in their daily affairs.

In actual practice ancient religion involved a world of temples and sacrifices; patronages and prophecies; shrines and groves; incense and garlands; processions and prayers; music and magic; omens and oracles, even inspecting entrails. It was filled with rituals for keeping the city safe, the home secure, healing the sick, and calming the stormy seas. Priesthoods overlapped with the local aristocracy; the local cult merged with the city, its self-perception and reputation.

---

21 Rives 2010, 269.

Lares were household spirits who protected a household and its occupants. Many Roman families maintained a *lararium*, which was a shrine where the *lares* were honoured. In the photo is a *lararium* depicting two *lares*, each holding a drinking container; in-between them is a *genius/daemon* holding a libation bowl; and a snake (a symbol of agricultural fertility) approaches the altar.
Gianni Dagli Orti / Shutterstock

All this assumed the existence, and the moody unpredictability, of the traditional pantheon of deities, and particularly of the local deity peculiar to any given city. It might include particular cults, 'mysteries' into which one might be 'initiated', thereby gaining a new religious status in the present and the promise of a blissful post-mortem existence.

The differences between all this and the early Christian devotional life are striking. For a start, Christianity had no priesthood and no temple, so to outsiders it would look much more like 'philosophy'. Yet Christianity had some similarities to greco-roman 'religion': Christians, too, could talk about God, about the gods (though they didn't believe in them), about heavenly worlds, spirits, and 'demons' (the latter term covering a range of imprecise supposed beings). Furthermore, Christians exhibited *religio* in the sense of having their own rituals like the Lord's Supper and baptism, cultic acts which bound the members of the community to one another and particularly to the God revealed in and through Jesus. Where pagans consulted sacred books and oracles, the Christians searched the scriptures and prayed for the holy spirit to guide them. Christians, like other groups, had various forms of worship, singing, and prayers, including ecstatic utterance. Knowing all this becomes important when it comes to mapping how Christianity both fits into, and grates against, the religious context of the ancient world, and what Greeks and Romans might have thought when they encountered the little groups of Jesus-believers and their varied life and practice.

Greco-roman philosophy

Another feature of the ancient world for us to consider is that of philosophy. Again, we must resist the anachronism of imposing upon the ancient world our modern idea of philosophy as an abstract academic discipline. Philosophy in antiquity was far more integrated with religion, politics, rhetoric, art, science, and wider culture. It was everyday life as lived, reflected upon, and interpreted in this or that way. Philosophy shaped the intellectual currents of the greco-roman world as it reflected on the meaning and purpose of life, ethics, religion, politics, science, nature, law, public speaking, and even agriculture.

The entire edifice of western philosophy owes its origins to ancient Greece, and to the important trio of Socrates, Plato, and Aristotle. They, building on their predecessors ('the pre-Socratics'), set the questions and agenda for western philosophy ever afterwards.

Socrates (c. 469–399 BC) was regarded as the first great philosopher and the first philosophical martyr as well. To paraphrase Cicero, it was Socrates who brought philosophy down from heaven to earth.[22] In contrast to the pre-Socratics, particularly the Sophists, Socrates did not see philosophy as primarily a discourse about nature, but as a matter of practical living. He emphasized virtue and religious disposition. Socrates established himself as something of a public intellectual in Athens, even an annoying gadfly to his political critics. He lived in a tumultuous time following Athens' disastrous defeat by Sparta after the long-running Peloponnesian War between the two cities and the subsequent identity crisis through which Athens passed. The Socratic method, named after his teaching style, refers to a dialectic form of enquiry that involves asking a series of questions to help a person or group of people determine their beliefs about a topic. Throughout antiquity, Socrates was remembered for personifying the highest ideals of the philosophical vocation: an examined and examining life which embodied the very wisdom that one was teaching.

Socrates' student, Plato (c. 428–348 BC), taught that the world of space, time, and matter was essentially a secondary thing, a world of illusion, by comparison with the ultimate reality, the world of the 'Forms' or 'Ideas', the invisible realities of which this-worldly things were mere space-time copies. True knowledge, for Plato, was therefore knowledge of these 'Forms'. Such knowledge was what the soul desired; and the soul, Plato believed, was immortal. It passed into the body, and departed from it upon death, either into a state of disembodied bliss or into a series

---

[22] Cic. *Acad.* 1.4.15.

of other bodies through reincarnation. Plato established his own school, known as the Academy, in Athens. Over the centuries, the Academy went through several changes. In Cicero's day (the first century BC) it was agnostic, recognizing the difficulty of many of the great questions. By the middle of the first century AD this had given way to what is loosely termed Middle Platonism, seen in the thought of the pagan priest, philosopher, and biographer Plutarch (AD 45–127). (The 'Middle' designation contrasts this period both with earlier versions of Platonism and with the 'neo-Platonism' of Plotinus and others in the third century AD.) This drew eclectically on the thought of other schools, particularly the Stoics, the Peripatetics, and the Pythagoreans. Middle Platonism heavily influenced Philo of Alexandria, Clement of Alexandria, and Origen.[23]

The Greek philosopher Socrates depicted in a first-century fresco from Ephesus
Public Domain

Plato's star pupil was Aristotle, but Aristotle did not become part of the Academy. Aristotle came from northern Greece and returned there after Plato's death to tutor the young Alexander of Macedon, who through his vast conquests would become 'Alexander the Great'. Plato had a flair for the abstract, but Aristotle moved in the opposite direction, towards concrete categorizations of things, distinguishing objects, animals, behaviour, and beliefs. He tackled areas as diverse as biology, virtue, rhetoric, aesthetics, music, and metaphysics, and practically invented the discourse of logic with his three-point syllogisms. Aristotle returned to Athens in 335 BC and established his own school in the Lyceum, just outside Athens. This became known as the Peripatetic school, due to the habit its members cultivated of walking to and fro while discussing a subject.

By the first century, various other philosophical schools besides the Academy and Lyceum joined the scene. Epicurus (*c.* 341–270 BC), who gave his name to Epicureanism, outlined a philosophy that was tantamount to a metaphysical dualism. There were gods, but they were distant and detached deities, uninvolved with the world, supremely happy with themselves, and the best thing a human could do was attempt a similar detachment from the cares of this life. The highest virtue was therefore *ataraxia* ('undisturbedness'), trying to imitate the gods in their happy and carefree state. One of Epicurus's great concerns was to eliminate the fear of death and what lies beyond it. For Epicurus, the body was made up of atoms that dissolved

---

23 Fitzgerald 2013, 143.

at death. There was therefore no surviving 'soul' to migrate either into an afterlife or into an alternative body. Good and evil were aesthetic, rather than absolute: pleasure was good, pain was bad. (Thus the word 'good' comes to mean 'I like this'.) Epicureanism received its greatest expression in the long Latin poem of Lucretius (*c.* 99–55 BC). In the modern period, it has become the implicit underpinning of the western Enlightenment, the multifaceted culture that regards itself as detached from the 'uncivilized' or 'underdeveloped' world all around.

Another significant philosophical school was that of Stoicism, based upon the teachings of Zeno (*c.* 333–264 BC), though subsequently developed by many others, such as Epictetus in the first century AD. Stoicism is a classic form of pantheism, seeing 'divinity' in everything. Zeus and his associates in Greece, and Jupiter and his colleagues in Rome, were all variegated manifestations of the one 'divinity' which permeated all things. World history was based on a number of repeating cycles, at the end of each of which a great cosmic conflagration would purify the world so that its true self would enjoy a time of stillness before history repeated itself again. Stoic philosophers aimed at continual moral enlightenment, with the goal of becoming a genuinely wise and well-formed person, attaining self-mastery and living in accordance with nature.

The thinkers known as the 'Cynics' were not, as the word might suggest today, known for philosophical scepticism. Rather, they prided themselves on pouring scorn on all human pretension. The word 'Cynic', which comes from the Greek *kyōn*, 'dog', was originally a nickname, since the Cynics appeared to bark and yap like dogs at the rich, the respectable, and any who gave themselves airs. Cynicism was a type of uninhibited Stoicism, exulting in its anti-social critique. They saw society as corrupt and worthless, so that the best thing for humans to attempt was a radical re-evaluation of their attitudes to themselves, their property, and their whole lives.[24] This movement goes back to Antisthenes of Athens (*c.* 446–366 BC) and his disciple Diogenes of Sinope (*c.* 412–324 BC). One recent scholar comments that

> Cynics saw themselves as society's watchdogs who, rejecting logic and physics as indispensable components of philosophy, believed that their austere manner of life and simple dress were in accordance with nature, and that their freedom from the conventions and values of aristocratic Greco-Roman society provided a conspicuous model of self-sufficiency that functioned as a shortcut to virtue and happiness.[25]

There are plenty of apparent parallels between certain ideas and themes in the New Testament and the themes, teachings, and ideas found in the greco-roman world.[26]

---

24 See Wright *JVG*, 66–74.
25 Fitzgerald 2013, 145.
26 See Boring, Berger, and Colpe 1995.

In some cases there is direct borrowing (such as when Paul quotes philosophers or poets in Ac. 17 or 1 Cor. 15). Elsewhere there are close analogies, but not necessarily a direct genealogy of ideas. In plenty of places we can see the New Testament authors strongly repudiating standard greco-roman beliefs.

When Jesus himself, and his first followers, engaged with the greco-roman world, we see a mixture of *adaptation* and *confrontation*. Jesus could quote a famous proverb, 'Physician, heal yourself',[27] probably going back to Euripides, to lament how his own home town of Nazareth gave him a frosty reception. Yet he could also censure his disciples for aspiring to the pattern of power and privilege that was prevalent in the gentile world: 'You know that the rulers of the Gentiles lord it over them, and their high officials exercise authority over them. Not so with you.'[28] The very genres of the New Testament, biography (gospels), historiography (Acts), and epistles (Pauline and catholic letters), have all sorts of echoes of greco-roman literary forms, even if their contents have been shaped by the Old Testament and Jewish traditions.

On the whole, the apostle Paul shared the Jewish critique of greco-roman religion and the behaviour-patterns that went with it. His rejection of the central symbols of paganism was sharpened by what he believed about Jesus.[29] Yet Paul lived and breathed the cultural air of the greco-roman world. As a speaker and writer, he exhibited tell-tale signs of rhetorical training, even while claiming not to have preached with rhetorical elegance or proclaimed his message with specious and self-serving reasoning.[30] Furthermore, Paul's thought has often been seen as having affinities with Stoicism, especially in ethical theory,[31] even while he warned of the dangers of 'philosophy'.[32] The gospel of John tells the story of Jesus in thoroughly Jewish and messianic terms, but when John calls Jesus the *logos* ('the Word'),[33] he is not only echoing an important biblical theme (for example Ps. 33.6; Isa. 55.11, and elsewhere) but also borrowing an idea initially developed by the sixth-century BC Greek philosopher Heraclitus, subsequently taken up by Stoic philosophers to describe the rational principle by which the universe came into being and by which all things exist. The Logos, as the personified 'idea', becomes the one through whom the invisible God interacts with the corporeal world. This notion of the Logos was adopted by Jews like Philo of Alexandria, and Christians like the second-century apologist Justin Martyr, employing the philosophical tools of antiquity to explain their beliefs about God. To what extent this development was compatible with John's own intended biblical allusions remains a matter of debate.

---

[27] Lk. 4.23.
[28] Mt. 20.25–26.
[29] See e.g. Rom. 1.18–32; 1 Cor. 8—10; 1 Thess. 4.5.
[30] 1 Cor. 1.17; 2 Cor. 10.10.
[31] See e.g. Rom. 12.3–21.
[32] Col. 2.8.
[33] Jn. 1.1–18.

EMAILS
from the edge

From: Alan_Daley@aol.com
To: Professor Dana Schuler
Date: Wed, 10 Feb 2016 at 8:28 a.m.
Subject: Gnosticism?

Dear Prof.,

I keep coming across references to 'Gnosticism' in some of the textbooks. Am I right in thinking that Gnosticism is mainly about salvation through a secret and special knowledge?

Pax 2 da Max
AD

From: Professor Dana Schuler
To: Alan_Daley@aol.com
Date: Thur, 11 Feb 2016 at 9:25 a.m.
Subject: Re: Gnosticism?

Dear Alan,

On 'Gnosticism', no, that's not quite the full story. The problem is that 'Gnosticism' is quite a slippery and misunderstood term. For a start, the Gnostics did not know that they were Gnostics. It was not their own designation for themselves; it was a designation given to them by others. On top of that, the Gnostics were diverse, so diverse in fact that some scholars wonder if we can even talk about a homogeneous religious system known as Gnosticism. Among the many groups that are identified as Gnostics, yes, there is a big emphasis on esoteric knowledge, especially of weird cosmologies and deities that duplicate and descend to earth. However, a more common feature is 'Demiurgal creationism'. Don't let the term scare you. Demiurgal creationism is basically the belief that the world was created by a wicked Demiurge who made yucky things like matter with all its evil, while Jesus is another god who comes to save us from the Demiurge and his wicked world. In other words, 'Gnosticism'

> separates the god of creation from the God of redemption. The real motivation in Gnosticism is theodicy, explaining why a God who is good would make a world like this, filled with so much evil, suffering, and death. The gnostic answer is that God didn't make this world; it was a lesser and wicked deity who made the world, and the good God comes to save people from the world of bodies and matter. This salvation begins when we apprehend the true knowledge of our primordial origins. The origins of Gnosticism are disputed, but it probably derives from a Jewish interface with Middle Platonism as interpreted through biblical traditions sometime after the second Jewish revolt of AD 132–5 when some Jews began looking to Greek philosophy for a way of making sense of the world. This seems to have been taken up by Christian leaders like Valentinus and Marcion in the second century.
>
> To dig deeper, I recommend these:
>
> Brakke, David. *The Gnostics: Myth, Ritual, and Diversity in Early Christianity.* Cambridge, MA: Harvard University Press, 2011.
> King, Karen L. *What Is Gnosticism?* Cambridge, MA: Belknap, 2005.
> Pagels, Elaine. *The Gnostic Gospels.* New York: Random House, 1979.
> Williams, Michael A. *Rethinking "Gnosticism": An Argument for Dismantling a Dubious Category.* Princeton, NJ: Princeton University Press, 1999.
>
> Yours kindly
> Prof. Dana Schuler

Examples could be multiplied of Christian authors engaging in adaptation of or confrontation with the ethos and ethics of the greco-roman world. But by now the main point should be clear: the New Testament comes to us as a book belonging in the greco-roman world as much as in the Jewish world. To grasp and be grasped by the New Testament, it is important to be immersed as far as possible in its wider culture, greco-roman as well as Jewish. Only so can we avoid anachronism, imagining that the early writers were straightforwardly addressing 'our' concerns. Questions have changed; the words to articulate key ideas have shifted in meaning. By exploring ancient philosophy, culture, politics, religion, and worldview, contemporary readers will be more equipped to see otherwise unimagined depths and dimensions (see 'Emails from the edge: Gnosticism?').

Having a grasp of the wider context of the New Testament, or not having such a grasp, is therefore like the difference between watching a film in black and white on an ordinary screen, and watching the same film in colour on a 3D screen.

The Swiss theologian and text-critic Johann Jakob Wettstein (1693–1754) put it like this: 'If you want to understand the books of the New Testament more clearly and more fully, clothe yourself in the person of those to whom they were first delivered by the apostles for reading.'[34] Serious students of the New Testament should go and do likewise.

THE JEWISH DIASPORA

The ancient historian and geographer Strabo (64 BC–AD 24) once commented about the Jews: 'This people has already made its way into every city, and it is not easy to find any place in the habitable world which has not received this nation and in which it has not made its power felt.'[35] That is because, by the first century, the majority of Jews, up to 80 per cent by some estimates, did not live in Palestine, but in the lands of other nations. In some cities as much as 20 per cent of the population was Jewish. This scattering of the Jews, known as the *diaspora* or 'dispersion', was caused by several factors, such as the Assyrian (721 BC) and Babylonian (597 and 587 BC) conquests through which the people of the northern kingdom of Israel, and then the southern kingdom of Judea, were taken into exile. Many captured Jews were enslaved, and then taken abroad to places like Rome. There were various forced migrations caused by conflict or famine. Many Jews simply chose to relocate to foreign cities due to economic opportunities and family connections. By the first century there were major concentrations of Jews in Alexandria, Syrian Antioch, Rome, Babylon, and elsewhere. And wherever the Jews went, they of course took their scriptures with them. The scriptures functioned as a portable land and Temple: studying Torah, they could come into the divine presence as if they were in the Temple itself. They built synagogues and prayer-houses, wrote their own literature, and tried to live as faithful Jews in a foreign city. So much so that at the Jerusalem council, James could declare: 'For the law of Moses has been preached in every city from the earliest times and is read in the synagogues on every Sabbath.'[36]

On the one hand, the dispersal of the Jewish people was something of a tragedy; hence the lament of the Psalmist: 'By the rivers of Babylon we sat and wept when we remembered Zion . . . How can we sing the songs of the LORD while in a foreign land?'[37] One of the great hopes for Israel's future was for the return of the Jewish exiles and the Jewish Diaspora to Judea, coming to worship God in the Temple, and the gentiles even accompanying them with gifts and offerings.[38]

---

[34] Cited in Sterling 1997, 315.
[35] Jos. *Ant.* 14.115.
[36] Ac. 15.21.
[37] Ps. 137.1, 4.
[38] See e.g. Isa. 43.5; 60.4; 66.20; Zech. 8.7–12; 2 Macc. 1.27–29; Tob. 14.5–7; Bar. 5.5.

A fresco from a synagogue on the Dura-Europos depicting Jewish boys being rescued from the River Nile (c. AD 245–55).
Public Domain

But on the other hand, the dispersion led to a massive diffusion of Jewish culture and religion that left an indelible mark on greco-roman cities. Josephus boasted that:

> The masses have long since shown a keen desire to adopt our religious observances; and there is not one city, Greek or barbarian, nor a single nation, to which our custom of abstaining from work on the seventh day has not spread, and where the fasts and the lighting of lamps and many of our prohibitions in the matter of food are not observed.[39]

Philo claimed that the law of Moses had attracted and influenced 'barbarians, Greeks, dwellers on the mainland and islands . . . nations of the east and the west, of Europe and Asia, of the whole inhabited world from end to end'.[40] And one rabbi was able to say that God 'exiled Israel among the nations for the purpose of making converts'.[41] Greeks and Romans could be attracted to Judaism for a number of reasons, including its oriental origins, its antiquity, its rituals which many considered effective for securing divine favour, the philosophical simplicity of monotheism, and the civic benefits of being a Jew (avoiding military service, an emphasis on ethics, and a well-defined communal identity).[42] Jewish communities often developed

---

[39] Jos. *Ap.* 2.282.
[40] Philo *Vit. Mos.* 2.20.
[41] bPesah. 87b.
[42] Bird 2010a, 83–93.

PORTALS AND PARALLELS: TACITUS ON THE JEWS

Publius Cornelius Tacitus (AD 56–117) was a Roman senator and historian who wrote two major works on the Roman empire in the first century. In the course of his work he issued some strident denunciations of the Jews. His remarks not only underscore the anti-Jewish stance of Roman elites, but also provide something of a window into what Romans thought about the Jews and their practices.

> [T]he other customs of the Jews are base and abominable, and owe their persistence to their depravity. For the worst rascals among other peoples, renouncing their ancestral religions, always kept sending tribute and contributions to Jerusalem, thereby increasing the wealth of the Jews; again, the Jews are extremely loyal toward one another, and always ready to show compassion, but toward every other people they feel only hate and enmity. They sit apart at meals, and they sleep apart, and although as a race, they are prone to lust, they abstain from intercourse with foreign women; yet among themselves nothing is unlawful. They adopted circumcision to distinguish themselves from other peoples by this difference. Those who are converted to their ways follow the same practice, and the earliest lesson they receive is to despise the gods, to disown their country, and to regard their parents, children, and brothers as of little account. However, they take thought to increase their numbers; for they regard it as a crime to kill any late-born child, and they believe that the souls of those who are killed in battle or by the executioner are immortal: hence comes their passion for begetting children, and their scorn of death. (Tac. *Hist.* 5.5)

a following of gentile sympathizers (known as God-fearers) and pagans who made a full conversion to the Jewish way (known as proselytes). Diaspora synagogues provided a crucial stepping-stone as Christianity spread into the greco-roman world; according to Acts and other evidence, many of the first gentiles who embraced the gospel had earlier been involved in this or that Diaspora synagogue.[43]

Life in the Jewish Diaspora was complex. One could be pulled in opposing directions. Officially, of course, Jewish people were supposed to follow customs that would make them separate from non-Jews. They were fiercely critical of gentile immorality and pagan idolatry, and often refused to intermarry with non-Jews. In some instances, this separateness and distinctiveness courted vitriolic counter-denunciations by Roman authors who saw the Jews as polluting the purity of Roman society (see 'Portals and parallels: Tacitus on the Jews'). Anti-Jewish riots took place in cities like Alexandria and Antioch, usually with terrible consequences for the Jewish minority. At the same time, many Jews were content to engage with a city and its people in order to succeed in commerce and civic life. There was, then, a continuum of Jewish interaction with greco-roman culture that included varied degrees of assimilation, acculturation, and accommodation.[44] The Jewish encounter with Hellenism led some Jews, like Tiberius Alexander, the nephew of Philo of Alexandria,[45] and Herod the Great's great-grandchildren,[46]

---

43 See Ac. 13.43, 50; 16.14; 17.4, 17; 18.7.
44 Barclay 1996, 92–102.
45 Jos. *Ant.* 20.100.
46 Jos. *Ant.* 18.141.

to abandon the Jewish way of life altogether. There are inscriptions that speak of Jews offering sacrifices to pagan deities, for instance, giving thanks for a successful sea journey.[47] The question of how to be a faithful Jew in a Greek city was thus a debated and divisive matter among Diaspora Jews themselves. However, many Jews remained faithful to their ancestral way of life while attempting to engage meaningfully with the social fabric of the cities where they lived. Saul of Tarsus, who became the apostle Paul, grew up in Tarsus, one of the great cities of south-eastern Asia Minor (modern Turkey) and a major centre of philosophy. Saul came from a strict Pharisaic family, eager to maintain the ancestral traditions, but he clearly knew a great deal about the wider culture, with its ideas, aspirations, and thought-forms. Even before his experience on the road to Damascus, he had had to work out what it might mean to be loyal to Israel's God, the world's creator, in the wider world that still belonged to God but worshipped idols instead.

THE SEPTUAGINT

The 'Septuagint' is the Greek translation of the Hebrew Bible and several other deutero-canonical writings. According to the legend recounted in the *Epistle of Aristeas*, seventy scholars were commissioned by Ptolemy II of Egypt to translate the Torah into Greek for deposit in the Library of Alexandria. That is how the Septuagint, represented by the Roman numeral 'LXX' for seventy, got its name.

There was, however, no official and authorized Greek version of the Bible called the 'Septuagint' that hellenistic Jews could carry with them when attending the synagogue. What contemporary scholars call the Septuagint can refer to either (1) an eclectic Greek text constructed by carefully weighing up Greek manuscripts containing the Old Testament (typically the *Septuaginta* edited by Robert Hanhart and Alfred Rahlfs); or (2) the assortment of Greek biblical manuscripts themselves, such as codices Vaticanus, Alexandrinus, and Sinaiticus, all of which come from the fourth and fifth centuries AD. What we materially possess is an assortment of Greek texts, usually translating the books

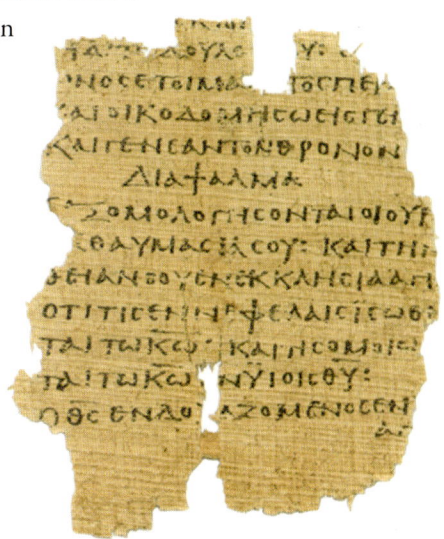

The Duke papyrus 740, a fourth-century fragment of Psalm 89.4–7 in Greek
David M. Rubenstein Rare Book & Manuscript Library, Duke University

---

47 Wilson 2004, 52–65.

BIBLICAL CANONS OF THE MAJOR ANCIENT CHRISTIAN CHURCHES

Books in the Roman Catholic, Greek, and Slavonic Bibles
- Tobit
- Judith
- Additions to Esther
- Wisdom of Solomon
- Sirach
- Baruch
- Letter of Jeremiah
- Additions to Daniel
- 1–2 Maccabees

Books in the Greek and Slavonic Bibles but not in Roman Catholic Bibles
- 1 Esdras
- Prayer of Manasseh
- Psalm 151
- 3 Maccabees

Books in the Slavonic Bible and an appendix in the Vulgate
- 2 Esdras (or *4 Ezra*)

Books in an appendix to the Greek Bible
- 4 Maccabees

Books in the Ethiopian Bible
- *1 Enoch*
- *Jubilees*

contained in the Hebrew Bible, but also including documents that rewrite and expand these Hebrew books (1 Esdras), and other writings that never had a Hebrew original at all (Wisdom of Solomon, 2–4 Maccabees, parts of the Additions of Esther, Judith, and Prayer of Manasseh). Furthermore, there is no agreed list, for either Jews or Christians, as to what books should be recognized as canonical (indeed, the meaning of 'canonical' is itself fluid in the period). Nor was there consensus on an agreed textual form of the collection. In addition, Jewish authors such as Theodotion, Aquila, and Symmachus produced their own distinctive Greek translations of the Hebrew Bible. Aquila and Symmachus may well have composed their translations to counter a perceived Christianization of the Greek Old Testament. All this is to say that 'the Septuagint' refers to a class of ancient Greek translations of the Old Testament and other Jewish books which is not necessarily identical to the critical edition called 'the Septuagint' that one might find in a college library.

The Septuagint is important for several reasons. First, it demonstrates how many Jews tried to embed their religious literature within the hellenistic world. Second, for the early church, the Septuagint was their 'scripture': it is normally the Septuagint that New Testament authors cite when quoting the Old Testament, and the Septuagint became part of the church's biblical canon. It was only in the west, from the fourth century or so, that Jerome's Latin Vulgate supplanted the Septuagint and the Greek New Testament as the preferred Bible of the Roman church (there had been earlier Latin translations but none received the status then given to the Vulgate). Third, in some cases, the assertions of New Testament authors are tied to the particular wording and texture of the Septuagint. This is clearly the case in Paul's argument about Abraham in Romans 4.1–8, where he connects two passages (Gen. 15.6 and Ps. 32.2) through the word *logizomai* which features in the Septuagint of both passages even though there is no verbal connection in the Hebrew. Similarly, at the Jerusalem council, James appealed to Amos 9.11–12 to justify the church accepting gentiles *as* gentiles without becoming converts to Judaism, which is based on the distinctive rendering of the Greek rather than Hebrew form of the text (Ac. 15.15–19). All this reinforces a point made verbally to me (NTW) by the late Bishop Stephen Neill, that one of the most important keys to studying the New Testament is a concordance to the Septuagint. When the early Christians used a Greek term, the meaning they intended is frequently the meaning of that word within the scriptural texts they had in mind.

The term 'Apocrypha' is ordinarily used to describe early Jewish writings included in the Greek Bible (Septuagint) and Latin Bible (Vulgate) but not found in the Hebrew Bible. The word 'apocrypha' means 'hidden, kept secret'. Catholic Bibles assign these books a secondary status as 'deutero-canonical' but nonetheless intersperse the Apocrypha among the Old Testament books, while protestant Bibles usually place them in a section in between the Old and New Testaments or else omit them entirely. The Orthodox churches, however, consider all of the Apocrypha to be canonical and part of the *anagignoskomena* or 'things that are read' for spiritual enrichment and instruction in the liturgy and lectionary. There are distinctive canonical book-lists among the various Orthodox churches. The Armenian, Syriac, Coptic, Georgian, Slavonic, and Ethiopian Orthodox churches all have different canons. The Ethiopian Orthodox Church includes pseudepigraphical books like *1 Enoch* and *Jubilees* in its list of authorized books (see box: 'Biblical canons of the major ancient Christian churches').

Further reading

Aune, David E. 2010. 'The World of Roman Hellenism.' In *The Blackwell Companion to the New Testament*. Edited by D. E. Aune. Malden, MA: Wiley-Blackwell, pp. 15–37.

Barclay, John M. G. 1996. *Jews in the Mediterranean Diaspora: From Alexander to Trajan (323 BCE–117 CE)*. Edinburgh: T&T Clark.

Carter, Warren. 2006. *The Roman Empire and the New Testament: An Essential Guide*. Nashville: Abingdon.

Cohick, Lynn H. 2014. *Women in the World of the Earliest Christians: Illuminating Ancient Ways of Life*. Grand Rapids, MI: Baker.

Green, Peter. 1993. *Alexander to Actium: The Historical Evolution of the Hellenistic Age*. Berkeley, CA: University of California Press.

Gruen, Erich S. 2002. *Diaspora: Jews amidst Greeks and Romans*. Cambridge, MA: Harvard University Press.

Jeffers, James S. 1999. *The Greco-Roman World of the New Testament: Exploring the Background of Early Christianity*. Downers Grove, IL: InterVarsity.

Jobes, Karen H., and Moises Silva. 2000. *Invitation to the Septuagint*. Grand Rapids, MI: Baker.

Perkins, Judith. 2009. *Roman Imperial Identities in the Early Christian Era*. London: Routledge.

Pietersma, Albert, and Benjamin G. Wright. 2007. *A New English Translation of the Septuagint*. Oxford: Oxford University Press.

Sterling, Gregory E. 1997. 'Hellenistic Philosophy and the New Testament.' In *Handbook to Exegesis of the New Testament*. Edited by S. E. Porter. Leiden: Brill, pp. 313–58.

Warrior, Valerie M. 2006. *Roman Religion*. Cambridge: Cambridge University Press.

Wright, N. T. 2014. *Paul and the Faithfulness of God*. COQG 4; London: SPCK, Part I, pp. 197–347.

The Mosaic of Jesus, dated 532–7, in the Hagia Sophia ('Holy Wisdom'), Istanbul, Turkey
Artur Bogacki / Shutterstock

III

JESUS AND THE VICTORY OF GOD

Jesus... took up his own cross. He had come to see it, too, in deeply symbolic terms: symbolic, now, not merely of Roman oppression, but of the way of love and peace which he had commended so vigorously, the way of defeat which he had announced as the way of victory. Unlike his actions in the Temple and the upper room, the cross was a symbol not of praxis but of passivity, not of action but of passion. It was to become the symbol of victory, but not of the victory of Caesar, nor of those who would oppose Caesar with Caesar's methods. It was to become the symbol, because it would be the means, of the victory of God.[1]

---

[1] Wright *JVG*, 610.

The Study of the Historical Jesus

The quest for the historical Jesus, in fact, clearly began soon after Jesus' death and is reflected in the writings of the early church.[1]

CHAPTER AT A GLANCE

This chapter describes the quest for the historical Jesus, including the importance of the quest, the history of the quest, and how the historical Jesus relates to the Christ of faith.

By the end of this chapter you should be able to:

- understand the importance of the quest for the historical Jesus as a theological task;
- describe the history of the quest for the historical Jesus;
- appreciate the place of the study of the historical Jesus in a New Testament theology.

IMAGINING AN HISTORICAL JESUS

Many Christians have a view of Jesus that is more heavenly than historical. They imagine Jesus walking around Palestine while reminiscing about his time with the angels and periodically pining to get away from the muck and mire of his transient earthly life and to return to his heavenly Father's glorious home. In other cases, Jesus' life is little more than the warm-up act to the meaty teaching of the apostle Paul, as if Jesus was a kind of 'John the Baptist' preparing the way for a supposedly Pauline 'gospel of justification'. In fact, one might even go so far as to say that, for many believers, as long as Jesus had a sinless birth from a virgin and underwent a sin-bearing death on the cross, for all it matters he could have lived among the first peoples of northern Canada. In this view, his life was merely the prelude to his death, and his teaching little more than a resource pack for Sunday-school lessons on how to go to heaven or how to be a good Christian. Our churches have settled on reductionistic readings of the gospels whereby the texts

---

[1] Porter 2004, 32.

are used as moralizing vignettes or as extra padding for a theological picture constructed from elsewhere. Jesus' message of the kingdom of God is reduced to private piety, his victory on the cross is turned into comfort for an anxious conscience, and Easter itself is made out to be a happy, escapist ending after a sad, dark tale. Sadly, there is no greater window into the shallowness of the minds of Christians than looking at what they think Jesus was up to during his career in Galilee, Judea, and Jerusalem.

But what if we imagine Jesus' life without the halo, without the cute descriptions of him telling earthly stories with heavenly meanings, and without projecting all the paraphernalia of later Christian tradition onto him? What if Jesus was (among other things) a prophetic figure, acting out a script from Israel's sacred writings, declaring a time of urgent national crisis, announcing that God was becoming king, that Israel's new exodus was at hand, dropping cryptic yet provocative hints about his own identity, engaging in symbolic actions to remind his audience of long-cherished hopes about a new Temple and a new covenant coming true at last? What if he was telling his fellow-Israelites that there was a new way of being Israel—beyond zealous nationalism, without a purity-centred piety, apart from political quietism, and without resorting to monastic escapism—challenging the boundaries about who was in or out with God, showing what covenant righteousness truly meant, and not only believing in but even embodying the long-awaited return of YHWH to Zion? This Jesus would be very different from populist or sentimental caricatures that can be found both within and outside the church. The way to avoid such superficiality is to embark on a fresh encounter with Jesus by a detailed reading (what some would call a 'thick description') of Jesus' life, with all of the sources at our disposal, and in the context of the Jewish people in the greco-roman world.

WHY STUDY THE HISTORICAL JESUS?

The premise for our proposal is that knowing Jesus requires a historical knowledge about Jesus. Without historical study, any picture of Jesus risks becoming ephemeral, malleable to other agendas, or cartoonish. A study about Jesus should be one that does not simply rehearse what the church believed about Jesus, or how Jesus has been interpreted over the centuries, or even why Jesus might be relevant to us now. All those things are good and proper and have their rightful place, but they are insufficient if divorced from a historical engagement with the story of Jesus of Nazareth himself. As we have said before, quoting George Caird, Christianity appeals to history, and to history it must go.[2] It is central to the Christian belief about who the one God really is that he has revealed himself in decisive action within the world of

---

2   See Caird 1965a, 3.

space, time, matter, and events. If this is true, we are compelled to engage in a history of Jesus; in that study we will *begin the journey* to grasp the mode and message of God's definitive revelation of himself. Orthodox Christianity has always held firm to the basic belief that it is by looking at Jesus himself that we discover who God is, so it seems indisputable that we should expect always to be continuing in the quest for Jesus precisely as part of, indeed perhaps as the sharp edge of, our exploration into God himself. Viewed this way, engaging in a historical study of Jesus is a necessary and non-negotiable aspect of Christian discipleship.

This point demands further expansion. First, a primary reason for a historical study of Jesus is that we are made for God: for God's glory, to worship God and reflect his likeness. That is our heart's deepest desire, the source of our deepest vocation. But Christianity has always said, with John 1.18, that nobody has ever seen God, but that Jesus has revealed him. We shall only discover who the true and living God actually is if we take the risk of looking at Jesus himself. That is why the contemporary debates about Jesus are so important; they are inevitably debates about God himself.

Second, studying Jesus should be pursued out of loyalty to scripture. This may seem ironic to some on both sides of the old liberal–conservative divide. Many Jesus-scholars of the last two centuries have largely thrown scripture out of the window, and have reconstructed a Jesus quite different from the one we find in the New Testament. But the proper answer to that approach is not simply to reassert that 'because we believe in the Bible we do not need to ask fresh questions about Jesus'. As with God himself, so with the Bible: our tradition may tell us that the Bible says and means this or that, but that does not excuse us from the challenging task of studying it afresh in the light of the best knowledge we have about its world and context, to see what precisely it means and to weigh up how it all fits together. And this process of rethinking will include the hard and often threatening question of whether some things that our traditions have taken as 'literal' should be seen as 'metaphorical', and perhaps also vice versa—and, if so, which ones.

Third, there is the Christian imperative to truth. Christians, believing in God's good creation, must not be afraid of truth. Of course, that is what many reductionists have said, as with apparent boldness they have whittled down the meaning of the gospel to a few bland platitudes, leaving the sharp and craggy message of Jesus far behind. In contrast, our agenda is to go deeper into the meaning than we have before, and to come back to a restatement of the gospel that grounds the things we have believed about Jesus, about the cross, about the resurrection, about the incarnation itself, more deeply within their original setting. That will always be risky. It means riding out the possibility that we, our churches, or our denominations have professed things about Jesus that were not always quite right, not always expressed as properly as they might have been. But the other side of this is the positive payoff, when the result of searching historically for who Jesus really was might be that the old faith we recited and confessed each week would take on a deeper, more penetrating meaning. Jesus might come alive to us in whole new ways, never before imagined. Our conception of God himself might be transformed, or beautifully enriched.

Fourth, undertaking a study of Jesus is crucial because of the Christian commitment to mission. The question of 'Who is Jesus?' remains very much alive in the public square, and we have to be part of that conversation. The mission of most Christians likely to read this book takes place in a world where Jesus has been a hot topic for several years now. In the USA particularly, Jesus—and the quest for him—has been featured in *Time* magazine, on television shows like *The Bible*, endless documentaries, and elsewhere in the media. Every year or so some publisher comes up with a blockbuster book saying that Jesus was a New Age guru, an Egyptian freemason, a hippie revolutionary, or even that he never existed. Every year or so some scholar or group of scholars comes up with a new book full of imposing footnotes to tell us that Jesus was a peasant Cynic, a wandering wordsmith, or the preacher of liberal values born out of due time.

We may well react to this sort of thing by saying that it is all a waste of time, that we know all we need to know about Jesus, and there is no more to be said. Many devout Christians, taking this line, content themselves with an effortless superiority: we know the truth, those silly liberals have got it all wrong, and we have nothing new to learn. The problem is that the people whom ordinary Christians meet, to whom they must address the gospel, have been told over and over by the media, on the basis of some recent book or other, that the Jesus of the gospels is historically incredible and that Christianity is therefore based on a mistake.

Caesarea Philippi, the location where Jesus asked the disciples, 'Who do people say the Son of Man is?' (Mt. 16.13)

(Even among scholars, including in other related disciplines like Ancient History, one often meets a glib reference to some book or other from twenty or thirty years ago which debunked traditional views of Jesus and which is taken to have settled the matter.) It therefore simply will not do to declare this question out of bounds, to say that the church's teaching will do for us, thank you very much, so we do not need to ask historical questions. One cannot say that to an enquiring person who asks serious questions on a train journey, or to someone who wanders into a church one Sunday and asks what it is all about. If Christianity is not rooted in things that actually happened in first-century Palestine, we might as well be Buddhists, Scientologists, Marxists, or almost anything else. And if Jesus never existed, or if he was quite different from what the gospels and the church's worship affirm him to have been, then we are indeed living in cloud-cuckoo-land. The sceptics can and must be answered. When we try to do that, we will not merely reaffirm the traditions of the church, whether protestant, catholic, evangelical, or whatever. We will be driven to reinterpret them, discovering depths of meaning within them that we had never imagined. In the early history of the church, it was the intellectual effort to answer strange deviant teachings that produced some of the greatest theological works. Perhaps that can and should be happening again, and on this absolutely central issue.

To repeat: the continuing historical quest for Jesus is a necessary part of ongoing Christian discipleship. We doubt very much if in the present age we shall ever get to the point where we know all there is to know and understand about Jesus, who he was, what he said and what he did, and what he meant by it all. But worshipping God, fidelity to scripture, pursuing the truth, and a commitment to mission all drive us towards a historical study of Jesus precisely as something with which faithful Christians ought to engage.[3]

THE QUEST FOR THE HISTORICAL JESUS[4]

Jesus has naturally been a key person of interest to western thought in general and Christian thought in particular. Yet the study of Jesus has been primarily a matter for Christian dogmatics, the business of the church, not part of the content of the humanities. Ancient History courses do not usually study Jesus, though his massive undoubted importance to global culture strongly suggests that they should. In fact, for a long time in European intellectual establishments, Jesus was part of the university curriculum only insofar as theology and philosophy each presupposed the other. That link was broken in the eighteenth century with the advent of new

---

[3] On the theological value of the quest for the historical Jesus, see Bird 2006b.
[4] For a fuller treatment on the various 'quests', see Wright 1992; *JVG*, 3–124; Bird 2004; 2006b.

philosophical movements promoting rationalistic theories of knowledge, which allowed no place for revelation or 'supernatural' intervention that was not empirically verifiable. Thus, in the period known as the 'Enlightenment', beginning in the seventeenth and eighteenth centuries, all knowledge, especially religious knowledge, was questioned. The Christian Bible in particular was scrutinized by new critical methods, and evaluated in the light of a changing of worldview from earlier forms of theism to a mixture of Deism (God as absentee landlord) and atheism (God as absentee). It was inevitable then that the gospels themselves, and the Jesus they hold forth, would be measured against the new rationalist philosophies that were making headway; all in order to test and stretch religious claims made about Jesus by a church that was increasingly regarded, in Europe and America, as stuck in the mud of traditional dogma. A vast range of studies about Jesus appeared during this modernist period, with various phases of research arising, concluding, and transforming themselves into yet further movements.

A useful taxonomy to describe the various periods of modern Jesus research—though by no means rigid and with some overlap—has been the sequence of a First Quest, then a No Quest period, followed up with a New or Second Quest, and then a Third Quest.

The First Quest

In terms of modern historical Jesus works, the first study of Jesus to make a big splash was that written by H. S. Reimarus (1694–1768), entitled *Fragments* and published posthumously. Reimarus presented Jesus as a revolutionary zealot who was duly executed for insurrection. Jesus' disciples stole his body and then touted belief in his resurrection. Several other scholarly portraits of Jesus followed, such as those of David Friedrich Strauss (1835–6), Ernest Renan (1863), William Wrede (1901), and Adolf von Harnack (1908). Despite their manifold diversity, they all agreed that the historical Jesus was unlike the person the gospels make him out to be, not a God-man but God-conscious, spiritual rather than religious, and fitting somewhere between the philosophical poles of the great German thinkers G. W. F. Hegel and Immanuel Kant. The purpose of such studies was basically twofold: (1) to destroy the orthodox view about Jesus, enshrined as it was with religious dogma and belief in the 'supernatural'; and (2) to erect another view of Jesus that would be acceptable to the modern European mind. As such, the 'first' quest for the historical Jesus was an explicitly anti-theological, anti-Christian, and anti-dogmatic intellectual movement, riding the currents of English Deism, and endeavouring to construct a Jesus more palatable to the moral, racial, and philosophical dispositions of the day.

Just when it was thought that the Christ of faith had been deconstructed and displaced by one of these 'historical Jesus' figures, the quest for the historical Jesus was itself soon deconstructed and its motives and errors exposed. It soon became apparent that the many 'Jesuses' that this modern quest had spawned presented little more than artificially constructed figures who were all too conducive to European thought, and had an uncanny resemblance to the liberal Protestants who wrote the relevant books. Albert Schweitzer was one of the first who exposed the quest for the historical Jesus as the attempt to domesticate Jesus to modern sensibilities (see 'Blast from the past: Albert Schweitzer and the *Quest of the Historical Jesus*').

BLAST FROM THE PAST: ALBERT SCHWEITZER AND THE *QUEST OF THE HISTORICAL JESUS*

Albert Schweitzer (1875–1965) was a biblical scholar, philosopher, physician, missionary, and musician. He was born in Kayersberg, Upper Alsace, and in addition to stints in Paris and Berlin he attended the University of Strasbourg, achieving doctorates in both theology (1900) and medicine (1912). Schweitzer was an internationally recognized expert on the music of J. S. Bach, publishing an edition of Bach's works and an important book about Bach's life and musical career. Schweitzer also served for a time as an assistant pastor and taught New Testament in Strasbourg before leaving Europe in 1913 for Africa where he worked with the Paris Mission Society, mainly as a surgeon in Lambarene, Gabon. He wrote major books on the Quest of the Historical Jesus (1906) and the Mysticism of Paul the Apostle (1931), and even on Indian Thought and Its Development (1936). In addition, he supported his medical missionary work financially by performing organ recitals across Europe. Schweitzer was known for his great principle of 'reverence for life' which he believed was found in both scripture and nature. He was strongly opposed to nuclear armament and supported the peace movement. Schweitzer received the Nobel Peace Prize in 1952 and died in Africa over a decade later. Schweitzer's missionary work was largely inspired by his study of Jesus as he believed that one could follow Jesus' example of suffering for the sake of others to bring about a better way of existence for other human beings. His Quest finishes with these notable words, which combine historical enquiry with an invitation to a form of almost mystical discipleship:

> He comes to us as One unknown, without a name, as of old, by the lakeside, He came to those men who knew Him not. He speaks to us the same word: 'Follow thou me!' and sets to us the tasks which He has to fulfil for our time. He commands. And to those who obey Him, whether they be wise or simple, He will reveal Himself in the toils, the conflicts, the sufferings which they shall pass through in His fellowship, and as an ineffable mystery, they shall learn in their own experience who He is.*

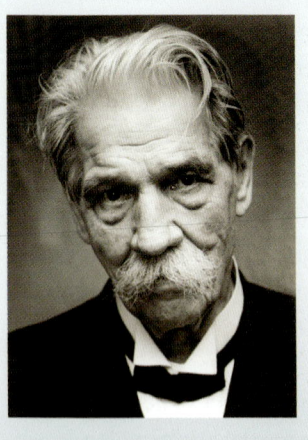

Albert Schweitzer
Tass / UIG / Bridgeman Images

---
* Schweitzer 1945 [1906], 401.

According to Schweitzer, the Jesus of European thought was 'a figure designed by rationalism, endowed with life by liberalism, and clothed by modern theology in an historical garb'.[5] In place of the romantic portraits of Jesus, Schweitzer presented the image of Jesus as an apocalyptic prophet. His Jesus believed that God's kingdom was at the door, and that he could bring about the end of world history, forcing God's intervention through the work of his own public career. But—still according to Schweitzer—when the wheel of history refused to turn in the new direction, Jesus threw himself upon it, was crushed in the process, but succeeded in turning it nonetheless. Schweitzer thus tore down the sentimental portraits of Jesus and, like a revolutionary replacing the monarch's portrait on the schoolroom wall with that of the new leader, put up instead the sharp, indeed shocking, drawing of Jesus the towering prophetic genius, the enigmatic hero figure, totally unlike modern men and women, yet strangely summoning them to follow in the noble path that would bring in the kingdom. Schweitzer's idea of Jesus as announcing 'the end of the world' was, in fact, based not so much on his reading of Jewish texts like *4 Ezra* and *1 Enoch*, as is often supposed, but on his reading *into* that Jewish tradition several 'end-of-the-world' ideas prevalent in German culture at the time, as evidenced by the operas of Wagner and the philosophy of Nietzsche. He was, however, absolutely correct to say that Jesus was speaking of something that was happening, and about to happen, in real history, rather than simply teaching new religious platitudes.

Similarly, George Tyrrell criticized the Jesus of the great liberal theologian Adolf von Harnack: 'The Christ that Harnack sees, looking back through nineteen centuries of Catholic darkness, is only the reflection of a liberal Protestant face, seen at the bottom of a deep well.'[6] As it turned out, the quest for Jesus was a great place to construct a mirror of one's beliefs, but poor history; it was a great way to do autobiography and call it the historical Jesus.[7] Thus the First Quest ended with a bit of a whimper. It did, however, set up (albeit in a distorted form) the questions about Jesus that would dominate discussion for the next century: the formation of the Jesus tradition, history versus theology, preference for the synoptic gospels or John's gospel, the genre of the four gospels, and similar issues.

From no quest to New (Second) Quest

In the aftermath of the failed quest for the historical Jesus, many retreated from a historical pursuit of Jesus. For the two giant figures of twentieth-century Christian scholarship, Rudolf Bultmann and Karl Barth, to go on a historical quest for Jesus

---

5   Schweitzer 1911, 396.
6   Tyrrell 1909, 49.
7   Or as Crossan (1991, xxviii) says, many scholars 'do theology and call it history, do autobiography and call it biography'. Similar is Allison (2009, 24) who wonders if in modern Jesus research, 'Maybe we have unthinkingly reduced biography [of Jesus] to autobiography.'

was to miss the point. For a start, such a quest was methodologically impossible, since the gospel writers were not interested in a Jesus 'according to the flesh', but only in the Christ of faith (a view claiming some spurious support from 2 Cor. 5.16). Moreover, the quest was theologically improper, since it sought to ground faith in historical evidence rather than in trust of God's revelation. What mattered was not the Jesus of history but the Jesus of the church's proclamation. The powerful theological constructs of Barth and Bultmann formed an alliance with the fears of ordinary people as to what might happen to orthodox Christianity if history was scrutinized too closely. In fact, Bultmann went so far as to affirm that '[t]he message of Jesus is a presupposition for the theology of the New Testament rather than a part of that theology itself.'[8] There is of course a sense in which that is true, in that the New Testament was written by Jesus' followers, not by Jesus himself. But they were writing precisely to say that *this* was what was *accomplished*, uniquely, by Jesus, in the totality of his life, death, and resurrection, a totality which included his 'message' since that message was precisely that God was now at last becoming king in the way he had always promised.

Karl Barth
Bill Ingraham / AP / Shutterstock

Not everyone followed Barth and Bultmann. Books about Jesus continued to be written. While most abandoned the entire enterprise of a historical study as such, other pockets of biblical scholarship pressed on with renewed vigour. In Britain, New Testament scholars like F. C. Burkitt, C. H. Dodd, and T. W. Manson all wrote significant works about Jesus' teaching, parables, ethics, and eschatology. On the continent, Joachim Jeremias and Otto Betz went against the grain by continuing to treat the gospels as reliable sources of information. However, those influenced by the Barthian and Bultmannian camps continued to deny that the historical Jesus was part of faith, dogmatics, or even New Testament theology.

Then in 1953, Ernst Käsemann, a former student of Bultmann, presented a lecture at the University of Marburg on 'The Problem of the Historical Jesus'. Käsemann's contention was that Easter-faith did not totally eradicate the continuity between Jesus and the early church. The primitive church never lost its interest in the life-history of Jesus as being properly basic for faith. As long as the one called 'Lord' was also known as the 'crucified one', it was impossible to eradicate history from the Christian message.[9] Käsemann, constantly aware of the dangers of idealism and docetism, insisted that if Jesus was not earthed in history then he might be pulled in any direction, might

---

8 Bultmann 1951–5, 1.3.
9 Käsemann 1964, 15–47.

be made the hero of any theological or political programme. Käsemann was writing in Germany in the aftermath of the Second World War when the memory was still fresh of how Nazi ideologies infiltrated Christian theology and produced an Aryan-compliant Jesus. In any event, Käsemann gave a new impetus to Jesus research, and launched a phase which has subsequently become known as the 'New Quest' or 'Second Quest' for the historical Jesus. Its notable proponents have included James Robinson, Günther Bornkamm, Norman Perrin, Eduard Schweizer, and Edward Schillebeeckx.

The New Questers of the 1960s and 1970s felt a little more confident about constructing a historical Jesus by use of the then standard scholarly tools. Yet they remained sceptical about the majority of material ascribed to Jesus in the gospels, and they did not really extend our understanding of Jesus very far. When you introduce your book on Jesus, as Bornkamm did, with the words 'No one is any longer in the position to write a life of Jesus',[10] you are not exactly setting yourself up to break new ground. New Quest practitioners failed to shake off their crude view of 'apocalypticism' as meaning simply 'the expectation of the end of the world'. (Many Americans reacted strongly to such ideas, associating them with fundamentalist hell-fire preaching.) They were also constrained by the shackles of form and tradition criticism, which were mainly designed to discover facts about the early church from the supposed life-setting behind any given gospel pericope, not Jesus himself, and thus they still put Jesus at arm's length from the gospels.

The reason why the New Quest did not get very far was in fact because its main criterion for assessing the historical veracity of gospel material was to regard as authentic only those sayings or deeds of Jesus that did not resemble anything a Jew or Christian could possibly say or do: Jesus must have been totally different, or at least only if he was could we be sure it was him! That is the so-called criterion of double dissimilarity. Yet such a criterion was a methodological absurdity. It resulted in a Jesus insulated from Judaism and shorn off from his later followers. Despite constructing an apparently more 'historical' portrait of Jesus, the resultant product was a Jesus who often looked far more like a twentieth-century Jewish existential philosopher than a first-century Jewish Messiah.[11]

The New Quest got a temporary revival from the North American Jesus Seminar in the late 1980s, where a band of scholars attempted to reconstruct Jesus by voting on the authenticity or otherwise of materials in the gospels. They posited wider hellenistic and Mediterranean socio-religious currents as the main locus for Jesus' teachings, rather than Judaism or the Old Testament. They also focused on the hypothetical document 'Q' (containing traditions common to Luke and Matthew) and the *Gospel of Thomas* (a second-century esoteric text which some suggested had much earlier

---

10 Bornkamm 1960, 13.
11 Case in point is Vermes 1973, though he very much straddles the New Quest–Third Quest division in some respects.

roots) as their primary sources for reconstructing Jesus' life. Despite the bustling headlines generated by the Jesus Seminar in their reloaded New Quest for Jesus—what was in some ways a neo-Bultmannian movement, though such labels are dangerously generalized—they ended up giving us a Jesus who was still very much made in the image of the historian. Richard Burridge noted that the Jesus Seminar 'produced a Jesus who is not Jewish in his teaching, but more like a Greek wisdom teacher or philosopher, and he's against sexism, imperialism and all the oppressiveness of the Roman empire. In other words, he's a Californian.'[12]

In retrospect, when one looks at both the First and even the Second Quest for the historical Jesus, the results appear to resemble the idea from the opening song of *Jesus Christ Superstar*: that from the earliest days of the movement those who had known Jesus personally saw him as simply 'a man'; they admired him greatly, but there was 'no talk' of his being 'God'. Yet those same followers detected a growing trend to deify him. Following the lyrics of Tim Rice, some scholars claim that they can see clearly down the corridors of history, they can see around the naivety of dogma, they can see beyond the fog of faith, and the Jesus they see is not the Christian one. Jesus is a man, a brilliant man, a religious genius even, a man also worthy of imitation, but he is not the same man as we find in the gospels. For the gospels have so radically reworked the tradition that there remains only but the faintest whisper of the authentic voice of Jesus.

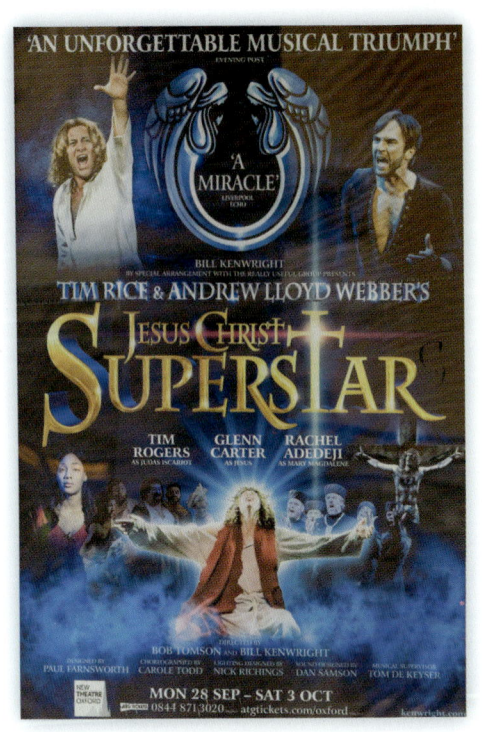

Mim Friday / Alamy Stock Photo

This brings us to the 'Third Quest' for the historical Jesus, which chronologically overlaps somewhat with the Second Quest, but has its own historical trajectory (there are of course few rigid periods in the history of scholarship). The Third Quest for the historical Jesus has antecedents in those many scholars who tried to study Jesus in his Jewish context, going all the way back to the early students of semitic languages. Yet it was Ben F. Meyer and E. P. Sanders, writing in the late 1970s and early 1980s, who really got the ball rolling in their respective works, situating Jesus in terms of first-century Judaism and setting his message within Jewish eschatological hopes, not for

---

12 Burridge and Gould 2004, 32; earlier in Theissen and Merz, 1998, 11; and see other criticisms of the Jesus Seminar in Bird 2006b, 293–7 and Wright *JVG*, 28–82.

the 'end of the world' but for the long-awaited national restoration and renewal. Researchers operating in this Third Quest were far more serious about identifying Jesus within his complex Jewish background, and not artificially partitioning Jesus away from the later church since the early church was, irrespective of how it developed, part of the effective history of the historical Jesus' life and career. John P. Meier, a leading Roman Catholic scholar, lists what he thinks are the gains from the Third Quest:

1. the ecumenical and international dimension to the scholars involved in the research;
2. a re-examination of various texts as reliable sources for the quest;
3. new insights from archaeology, philology, and sociology in the illumination of Jesus and his context;
4. a more accurate picture of the diverse and variegated nature of Palestinian Judaism;
5. clarification of the criteria of historicity which has led to a more balanced appreciation of the historical traditions underlying the gospels;
6. a more positive treatment of the miracle-traditions in the gospels;
7. taking the Jewishness of Jesus with seriousness.[13]

As we stand in the early decades of the twenty-first century, the Third Quest appears to have run out of steam. That is partly due to scholarly dystrophy, an intellectual tiredness from dealing with the subject. Martin Hengel's final volume before his death (*Jesus und das Judentum*) and volume 5 in John Meier's *A Marginal Jew* series will probably mark the end of the Third Quest, since not much more in terms of the Third Quest agendas remains to be prosecuted other than haggling over footnotes. But much has been gleaned from the Third Quest. We have a better methodology, a more Jewish Jesus, a Jesus who is thoroughly eschatological (though the meaning of that term continues to cause difficulty), and a better understanding of how Jesus influenced the praxis, worship, and beliefs of the early church.

However, much like a flowing river, the study of Jesus remains constantly in flux. To give but one example, there are some studies about Jesus that don't fit neatly into the frameworks of the First, Second, or Third Quest. For instance, one could juxtapose three recent books about Jesus and regard them as pre-modern, modern, and postmodern studies respectively. First, Emeritus Pope Benedict XVI's *Jesus of Nazareth* seems pre-modern in the sense that it insists that plotting the life of Jesus is a theological discipline and is pursued out of a faith agenda complete with belief in the supernatural. Second, there is Maurice Casey's work *Jesus of Nazareth*, modernist in the sense that it proposes an independent and 'objective' study of the historical Jesus

---

[13] Meier 1999, 459–87.

while trying to be deliberately disinterested in religious affirmations (apart from occasionally deriding them). Third, on the postmodern side is Bruce Fisk's entertaining and energetic book *The Hitchhiker's Guide to Jesus*, which documents the fictitious story of a college student's study tour through Israel to decide if he believes in Jesus or not.[14]

In every phase of scholarship it has been agreed that Jesus matters. But how to study Jesus, and how to traverse the apparent divide between the Jesus of history and the Christ of faith—and even whether that is the best way of putting the question!—will remain at the heart of the problem in historical Jesus research.

CONCLUDING THOUGHTS ON THE HISTORICAL JESUS

Research into Jesus himself has long been controversial, not least among devout Christians. Several people in the wider Christian world wonder if there is anything new to say about Jesus, and if the attempt to say something fresh is not a denial either of the church's traditional teaching or of the sufficiency of scripture. Beyond that, in terms of method, there are frantic debates as to how to study the historical Jesus, and stern objections as to whether we can separate history and theology in the gospels sufficiently well to do a real historical study at all. Others still complain that historical Jesus scholars use their study to construct a Jesus in their own image. Others again protest that a 'historical Jesus', in the sense of a scholarly reconstruction, becomes essentially a 'fifth gospel', which is then put in deliberate competition to the canonical accounts. Scot McKnight, once a committed Third Quester, confesses how he lost faith in the entire historical Jesus enterprise:

> The scholarly hope that we would discover the original Jesus had crashed against the rugged rocks of reality, and on that day we witnessed the end of a disciplinary era. One by one, most of us had become convinced that no matter how hard we tried, reaching the uninterpreted Jesus was nearly impossible—however fun and rewarding it was and however many insights about the Gospels we discovered along the way. Furthermore, a reconstructed Jesus is just that—one scholar's version of Jesus. It is unlikely to convince anyone other than the scholar, his or her students (who more or less feel obligated to agree), and perhaps a few others.[15]

Despite these concerns, our proposal is that the historical study of Jesus remains crucial to an overall study of early Christianity in general and the gospels in particular. First, any study of the history of Christianity has to do serious business with the history of Jesus of Nazareth. One must pursue the question as to why Christianity

---

[14] See the reviews of all three books in Wright 2012b.
[15] McKnight 2010, 25, contrasted with his earlier works McKnight 1999 and 2005.

began, why it took the shape that it did, why the gospels are what they are, why the first Christians believed and acted as they did, and how all that relates to the first-century figure Jesus of Nazareth. Christianity is, to some extent at least, the effective history of Jesus, the resounding echo of his influence on his closest disciples and upon the movement that consciously identified itself as devoted to him. To outline the history of early Christianity without engaging in a study of the historical Jesus makes about as much sense as plotting the history of modern India without bothering to take into account the life and times of Gandhi. Second, coming to the gospels, the evangelists are themselves fully aware that they are writing about a time prior to their own day. They point us towards the 'back-then-ness' of Jesus. In other words, the evangelists are not writing narrative commentaries on their own post-Easter faith in Jesus, as has often been suggested. They really do intend to write biographical testimonies about the pre-Easter figure of Jesus. The gospels, in fact, are not simply repositories of timeless truth, or treatises on faith, self-authenticity, or even theology; they are actually about Jesus. The historical 'quest', at its heart, need not be in fact an attempt to write a 'fifth' or 'alternative' gospel to the four we have. It can be the attempt to understand what was actually meant, in real first-century historical terms, by the four that we have.

All this is important, because the point of having Jesus at the centre of a religion or a faith is that one has *Jesus*: not a cypher, a strange silhouetted Christ-figure, nor an icon, but the one Jesus the New Testament writers know, the one born in Palestine in the reign of Augustus Caesar and crucified outside Jerusalem in the reign of his successor Tiberius. If we close down that historical referentiality, or simply assume it, without getting our hands dirty in textual and historical excavation, we cease to read the gospels as they were intended, as historically rooted witnesses to Jesus as told by his disciples.

As to how the historical Jesus relates to the entity called 'New Testament theology', that is relatively straightforward. The emerging portrait of the historical Jesus is not a replacement for the Jesus of the gospels, a super-canonical Jesus, or anything equally specious. Instead, a sketch of the historical Jesus is the preliminary narrative that emerges when we interrogate the various sources about Jesus and his context in a kind of group effort. By bringing together Matthew, Mark, Luke, John, Paul, Josephus, the Dead Sea Scrolls, Jesus traditions in 'other' gospels, early manuscripts, Palestinian archaeology, greco-roman history, socio-economic paradigms, and the like, we develop a starting-point from which to begin commenting on Jesus and the early church. What emerges in a study of the historical Jesus should be a kind of opening précis—obviously open to constant revision—about what Jesus said and did, what his aims were, why he died, and who he thought he was. Viewed that way, the study of the historical Jesus is the first step in the recovery of the canonical Jesus, over and against those who would, for a variety of reasons, pull him in any number of directions.[16]

---

16 On reading the gospels both historically and canonically, see Wright *HGBK*, 272–3.

Jesus really did intend to launch the long-promised 'kingdom of God' on earth as in heaven; he really did do and say things which demonstrated in action what this would mean (radically redefining existing expectations as he did so); and he really did believe this would be accomplished through his own death, and that the one he called 'Abba, Father' would vindicate him after his death, raising him from the dead and installing him as the world's rightful lord. The New Testament writers were explaining and promoting this as something which *had now actually happened*. They were not making it up from scratch.

Shoreline of the Sea of Galilee

Further reading

Allison, Dale C. 2009. *The Historical Christ and the Theological Jesus*. Grand Rapids, MI: Eerdmans.

Bond, Helen. 2017. *Jesus, A Very Brief History*. London: SPCK.

Evans, Craig A. (ed.). 2008. *Encyclopedia of the Historical Jesus*. New York: Routledge.

Keener, Craig S. 2009. *The Historical Christ of the Gospels*. Grand Rapids, MI: Eerdmans.

Le Donne, Anthony. 2011. *The Historical Jesus: What Can We Know and How Can We Know It?* Grand Rapids, MI: Eerdmans.

Theissen, Gerd, and Annette Merz. 1998. *The Historical Jesus: A Comprehensive Guide*. Tr. John Bowden; Minneapolis: Fortress.

Witherington, Ben. 1995. *The Jesus Quest: The Third Search for the Jew of Nazareth*. Downers Grove, IL: InterVarsity.

Wright, N. T. 1992. 'Quest for the Historical Jesus.' In *Anchor Bible Dictionary*. Edited by David Noel Freedman. 6 vols.; ABRL; New York: Doubleday, 3.796–802.

——. 1996. *Jesus and the Victory of God*. COQG 2; London: SPCK, pp. 1–126.

9

The Profile and Praxis of a Prophet

CHAPTER AT A GLANCE

This chapter describes the main facets of Jesus' ministry, including the significance of John the Baptist as a precursor, the meaning of the kingdom of God, Jesus' opposition to the Temple, and his overall prophetic pattern of work.

By the end of this chapter you should be able to:

- recognize the importance of Herodian Judea as the political context for Jesus' ministry;
- appreciate the significance of Jewish restoration eschatology for Jesus' message;
- grasp the prophetic dimension of Jesus' career;
- understand the meaning of the kingdom of God in relation to Jesus' teaching, actions, and vision of the future.

[Jesus] believed that Israel was at the cross-roads, that she must choose between two conceptions of her national destiny, and that the time for choice was terrifyingly short. This explains why, in his instructions to his disciples, he speaks of 'towns where they receive you' and 'towns where they do not receive you'. He seems to have expected not individual but mass response. 'It shall be more tolerable for Sodom and Gomorrah in the judgment than for that town.' The disciples were not evangelistic preachers, sent out to save individual souls for some unearthly paradise. They were couriers proclaiming a national emergency and conducting a referendum on a question of national survival.[1]

ON THE ROAD WITH JESUS

It is quite easy to lay out a brief list of things that few will deny about Jesus' life and public activity. He was most likely born in what we now call 4 BC (the calculation of the BC–AD divide took place in the sixth century, based on limited information). He grew up in Galilee, in the town of Nazareth, close to the major city of Sepphoris. He spoke Aramaic, at least some Hebrew, and probably some Greek as well. He emerged as a public figure in

---

[1] Caird 1965a, 9–10.

around AD 28, in the context of the initially similar work of John the Baptist. He summoned people to repent (in other words, to turn back from the ways they were going), and announced the kingdom, or reign, of Israel's God, using parables in particular to do so. He journeyed around the villages of Galilee, announcing his message and enacting it by effecting remarkable cures, including exorcisms, and by sharing in table-fellowship with a socio-culturally wide group. He called a group of close disciples, among whom twelve were given special status. His activities, especially one dramatic action in the Temple, incurred the wrath of some elements in the Jewish world, notably (at least towards the end) of the high-priestly establishment. Partly as a result of this, he was handed over to the Romans and executed in the manner regularly used for insurrectionists. His followers claimed, soon afterwards, that he had been raised from the dead. They carried on his work in a new way, and some of them were persecuted for doing so, both by Jews and by pagans.

People will contest whether 'this' saying or 'that' event actually took place or took place as the evangelists said it did. The explanatory power of any reconstruction of Jesus' life, message, and aims comes down to whether or not it presents a realistic and persuasive narrative about Jesus. That means a narrative that illuminates our available sources, where the Jesus presented makes sense within his Jewish context, and yet is also a believable precursor to some aspects of the life and formation of the early church. Any 'Jesus' who is radically unlike the Jews of Galilee, or disconnected from what his earliest followers believed about him, is highly unlikely to be the genuine Jesus who taught in synagogues in Galilee, healed blind men in Judea, was crucified just outside Jerusalem, and spawned a movement that came to be known as 'the Nazarenes'.

Fourth-century depiction of Jesus, British Museum

In what follows we cannot canvass every event in Jesus' life. Nor can we explore the intentionality behind every saying. Instead, we will try to imagine what it would have been like to be on the road with Jesus. What did Jesus say and do? How does this show us what Jesus was trying to achieve and what he thought his mission was really about? It will soon become clear that Jesus saw himself as announcing and enacting God's rescue plan for Israel. At the heart of his message was the claim that the new exodus, foretold by the prophets, was coming true. He warned Israel that its day of decision had arrived: 'salvation' was to be found not in military revolution against Rome, nor in political quietism in collaboration with Rome, but by the return of YHWH to Zion, a return that Jesus himself embodied. God—the true God, the creator, the God of Abraham, Isaac, and Jacob—was coming back at last, coming to be king. And this was happening in and through Jesus' own work.

The Profile and Praxis of a Prophet

PRECURSORS AND PROPHETS: FROM JOHN THE BAPTIST TO JESUS OF NAZARETH

The first-century Jewish world, with all its pluriformity, had certain dynamics running through it, not least an undercurrent of potential or actual revolution. (We sketched this in an earlier chapter and restate it here as a necessary part of understanding Jesus.) This was not confined to the lowest social classes, but enjoyed the support of at least some Pharisees and, eventually, even some aristocrats. Before Jesus came onto the scene, Palestine had known a number of revolutionary movements that resulted in uprisings in 4 BC and AD 6 and were mercilessly crushed. Concurrently, several prophetic movements were spawned as well, where key figures announced that God was about to do something radical and redemptive for his covenant people (see box: 'Popular prophets in Judea under Roman rule'). Whether it was a revolt by poor unemployed workers in Galilee reacting to a taxation census, or a lonely prophet on the shores of the River Jordan promising that a new conquest was about to occur, they were all interested in the fulfilment of Israel's long-held hopes. The covenant God would act to reconstitute his people, to end their exile, to forgive their sins. When that happened, Israel would no longer be dominated by the pagans. The nation would be free. The means of liberation were, no doubt, open to debate. The goal was not.

John the Baptist came on to the scene some time in the late 20s and quickly became a figure of widespread popularity and political notoriety.[2] He was significant enough that Josephus takes note of him as he does other prophetic figures.[3] We find also that followers of the Baptist continued to revere him after his death and were found as far away as Ephesus.[4] John announced imminent judgment on the nation of Israel, and urged it to repent, warning the Jews that their status as YHWH's covenant people would not be enough by itself to deliver them from the coming disaster. Concurrent with that, he also spoke of a 'Stronger One' who among other things would baptize with the 'Holy Spirit and fire'.[5] The sense of that phrase is not entirely clear, but it may be idiomatic for plunging people into the fiery breath of YHWH, so that the coming one would usher in a divine judgment, a judgment resulting either in a purging of the wicked or in a purification for the prepared.[6] Either way, the Baptist was enacting a coded dramatization of the exodus, hinting strongly that the new exodus, the return from exile, was about to take place.

---

2 See Wright *JVG*, 160–2; Bird 2011a; and more fully Webb 1991 and Taylor 1997.
3 Jos. *Ant.* 18.116–19.
4 Ac. 18.25 and esp. Ac. 19.1–5.
5 Mk. 1.4–8/Mt. 3.1–12/Lk. 3.1–20.
6 See Dunn 2003, 366–9.

Galilee

John's activities and teachings were clearly 'political' as well as 'religious'. This is so not simply because it seems that Herod Antipas was a prime target of his invective (anyone behaving like Herod had lost all right to be 'king of the Jews', so John's announcement of a 'stronger' one who was coming had clear negative implications for Herod and his supporters), but also because anyone collecting people in the Jordan wilderness was symbolically saying: this is the new exodus. Anybody offering water-baptism for the forgiveness of sins was saying: you can have, here and now, what you would normally get through the Temple cult.[7] Anybody inviting those who wished to do so to pass through an initiatory rite of this kind was symbolically saying: here is the true Israel, coming through the waters like Israel through the Red Sea and the Jordan itself: the true Israel that will be vindicated by YHWH. By implication, those who did not join in had forfeited the right to be regarded as the covenant people.

In these ways, completely credibly within the history of first-century Judaism, what John was doing must be seen, and in fact can only be seen, as a prophetic renewal movement within the Jewish world—a renewal, however, that aimed not at

---

[7] See esp. Webb 1991, 203–5.

renewing the existing structures, but at replacing them. Thus, though the synoptic gospels give John's attack on Herod Antipas's marital arrangements as the reason for his arrest, and as we have suggested that makes sense because of the implied critique of Herod as the true Jewish king,[8] it is likely that there were wider reasons as well. As Crossan put it: 'Desert and Jordan, prophet and crowds, were always a volatile mix calling for immediate preventive strikes.'[9]

The River Jordan, the traditional site where John performed his baptisms
iStock.com / Alatom

Jesus clearly regarded John as an important fixed point at the beginning of his own ministry, and those researching Jesus in his historical context can take that as a fixed point as well. There is good reason to think both that John himself did indeed prophesy a coming figure who would complete the work that he had begun, and that Jesus applied this to himself. Though at a later stage John seems, while in prison, to have been puzzled by what Jesus was doing (and more particularly, it appears, by what he was not doing), Jesus continued to regard him as the advance guard for his own work, both as the chronological and theological starting-point for his own ministry, and as in some senses the role model for his own style, the pattern with which he would begin.[10]

---

8   For the attack on Herod's marriage to his brother's wife, see Mk. 1.14; 6.17–18/Mt. 14.3–4; Lk. 3.19–20.
9   Crossan 1991, 235.
10 On John's puzzlement: Mt. 11.2–6/Lk. 7.18–23; Jesus' view of John in relation to himself: Mt. 11.7–19/Lk. 7.24–35; Mk. 9.11–13; *Gos. Thom.* 46, 78; Lk. 16.16; Mk. 11.27–33/Mt. 21.23–27/Lk. 20.1–8; Jesus being seen as John *redivivus*: Mk. 6.14; 8.27–28; 9.11–13/Mt. 17.9–13.

POPULAR PROPHETS IN JUDEA UNDER ROMAN RULE

In the first century AD, several prophetic figures appeared who promised signs of deliverance and that the day of liberation was at hand. They often mobilized groups of peasants and were routinely put down by military confrontation. So much so that Josephus wrote that on the eve of the Jewish uprising against Rome: 'Imposters and demagogues, under the guise of divine inspiration, provoked revolutionary actions and impelled the masses to act like madmen. They led them out into the wilderness so that there God would show them signs of imminent liberation' (Jos. *War* 2.259; see further *Ant.* 20.168).

Year	Bandit/Leader	Activity
36	the Samaritan	led followers to Mount Gerizim (Jos. *Ant.* 18.85–7)
45	Theudas	persuaded followers to accompany him to the Jordan (Jos. *Ant.* 20.97–8; Ac. 5.36)
50–9	the Egyptian	drew followers to the Mount of Olives to witness the fall of Jerusalem (Jos. *Ant.* 20.169–71; *War* 2.261–3; Ac. 21.38)
66	Jesus ben-Ananias	predicted destruction of the Temple (Jos. *War* 6.300–9)
70–9	Jonathan the Refugee	promised followers signs and apparitions in the wilderness (Jos. *War* 7.437–50; *Life* 424–5)

Across the breadth of our sources, Jesus seems to fit into various 'types' of Jewish holy men, including rabbi, sage, healer, exorcist, messiah, and philosopher. Yet if one category stands out, in terms of Jesus' public persona, it is that he is consistently seen as a prophet—by his disciples, by those who witnessed his healings, by Pharisees, by pilgrims entering Jerusalem for Passover, by his Judean opponents, by the early church (which indeed, according to Ac. 3.22, saw Jesus as 'the prophet' of Dt. 18.18–19), and, importantly, by Jesus himself.[11] While the evangelists hint at various typologies that are applied to Jesus, ranging from new Moses to new David, there is characteristic emphasis on Jesus as a prophetic figure.[12] So although Jesus' followers came to regard him as far more than a prophet (and Jesus himself said that about John the Baptist!), they never saw him as less.

It appears that Jesus was modelling his ministry not on any single figure alone,

---

[11] On Jesus identifying himself as a prophet, see Lk. 4.24; Jn. 4.44; Mt. 23.37/Lk. 13.34.
[12] See further Wright *JVG*, 164–5.

The Profile and Praxis of a Prophet

but on a range of prophets from the Old Testament. Like Ezekiel, Jesus predicted that the Temple would be abandoned by the Shekinah, left unprotected to its fate.[13] Like Jeremiah, Jesus constantly ran the risk of being called a traitor to Israel's national aspirations, while claiming all the time that he was nevertheless the true spokesman for the covenant God. This, as we shall see, lies behind a good part of the story of Jesus' action in the Temple, and his subsequent 'trial': Jesus had predicted the destruction of the Temple, and was on trial not least as a false prophet.[14] Jesus replied to earlier critics and questioners with the sign of the prophet Jonah. Jonah was predicting imminent judgment on Nineveh, following his adventure with the fish; Jesus was predicting imminent judgment on Israel, and a similar sign would validate his message too.[15] He was constantly redefining what the coming day would mean for Israel, warning it, like Amos, that it would be a day of darkness, not of light.[16]

Above all, Jesus adopted the style of the prophet Elijah, and consciously seemed to imitate him, particularly in his mixture of healings, mighty deeds, and warnings

---

13 Ezek. 10.1–5, 15–22; 11.22–23; Mt. 23.38/Lk. 13.35.
14 Jer. 7.11; Mt. 21.12–13/Mk. 11.15–19/Lk. 19.45–48; Jn. 2.13–22. For the charge relating to a prophecy of the Temple's destruction: Mt. 26.57–68/Mk. 14.53–62/Lk. 22.54–71; Jn. 2.19; *Gos. Thom.* 71.
15 Mt. 12.38–42/Lk. 11.29–32.
16 Amos 5.18–20.

of judgment. Jesus explained the nature of his ministry by using both Elijah and Elisha as models.[17] It is highly unlikely that the early church, seeing Jesus as the Messiah, and indeed as the embodiment of Israel's God, and hence regarding *John*, not Jesus, as Elijah, created this identification out of nothing. Thus, even if John himself seems to have thought that Jesus might be the new Elijah, Jesus seems to have returned the compliment.[18]

Here we begin to see both parallel and distinction. Jesus' ministry was so like that of Elijah that they could easily be confused. He too was announcing to the faithless people of YHWH that their covenant God would come to them in wrath. But at the same time, he was also acting out a different message, one of celebration and inauguration, which burst the mould of the Elijah-model.

From all of this it should be clear that Jesus regarded his ministry as in continuity with, and bringing to a climax, the work of the great prophets of the Old Testament, culminating in John the Baptist, whose initiative he had used as his launching-pad.

In Luke 4.16–21, Jesus stood up and read Isaiah 61.1–2, indicated here, from a scroll like this. The Great Isaiah Scroll, dated to 100 BC, The Israel Museum.
PD-US

---

17 Lk. 4.25–27.
18 Mt. 3.11–12/Lk. 3.16–17; Jn. 1.21; Mt. 11.2–3/Lk. 7.18–19; Mt. 17.12–13/Mk. 9.13.

The Profile and Praxis of a Prophet   195

EMAILS
from the edge

From: Alan_Daley@aol.com
To: Professor Dana Schuler
Date: Mon, 14 Dec 2014 at 3:01 p.m.
Subject: Josephus?

Dear Prof.,

So the other day I'm sitting on a bus reading my Bible on my tablet and the dude next to me is like, 'The Bible is so fake, it's made up, you can't prove it', and stuff like that. So I talk about proof that Jesus existed from sources like Josephus, and the whole shebang. But then the guy, a Unitarian I think, tells me that the Jesus passage in Josephus was forged and inserted into Josephus's writings to make it look like he knew about Jesus when in fact nobody did. Never heard that view before—what's up with that?

Pax 2 da Max
AD

From: Professor Dana Schuler
To: Alan_Daley@aol.com
Date: Tue, 15 Dec 2014 at 8:22 a.m.
Subject: Re: Josephus?

Dear Alan,

The authenticity of the Jesus passage in Josephus—the *Testimonium Flavianum*—is disputed, but I'm convinced that Josephus did have a Jesus passage even though it was subsequently dressed up a bit. As we have it the passage reads:

> About this time there lived Jesus, a wise man, **if indeed one ought to call him a man.** For he was one who performed surprising deeds and was a teacher of such people as accept the truth gladly. He won over many Jews and many of the Greeks. **He was the Messiah.** And when, upon the accusation of the principal

196 Jesus and the Victory of God

> men among us, Pilate had condemned him to a cross, those who had first come to love him did not cease. **He appeared to them spending a third day restored to life, for the prophets of God had foretold these things and a thousand other marvels about him**. And the tribe of the Christians, so called after him, has still to this day not disappeared. (Jos. *Ant.* 18.63–4)
>
> The bits I've highlighted in bold are the bits which, most probably, were glosses added by a scribe to give Jesus a better spin from Josephus. But in favour of the authenticity of the rest, note: (1) the language here is consistent with Josephus's style elsewhere; (2) there is another mention of Jesus again in *Ant.* 20.200 which presupposes what Josephus first wrote here; and (3) the Arabic and Syriac versions of the text have a slightly less embellished version of the *Testimonium* than the Greek copies and are therefore probably closer to the original wording. So, while it is disputed, I think the *Testimonium* at its core is authentic.
>
> The grace be with you
> Prof. Dana Schuler

Like Elijah or Jeremiah, Jesus was proclaiming a message from the covenant God, and living it out with symbolic actions. He was confronting the people with the folly of their ways, summoning them to a different way, and expecting to take the consequences of doing so. And, like the prophets before him, Jesus was not afraid to take on the establishment. John the Baptist had said it was not enough to be a physical child of Abraham, and had denounced the ruling Herod. Elijah had stood alone against the prophets of Baal and the wickedness of King Ahab. Jeremiah had announced the doom of the Temple and the nation in the face of royalty, priests, and official prophets. Though all had followers, all were politically lonely figures. All were accused of troubling the *status quo*. When people 'saw' Jesus as a prophet, this was the kind of model they had in mind.

THE CAMPAIGN BEGINS: JESUS AND THE KINGDOM OF GOD

One slogan stands out from the revolutionary dreams of some Jewish revolutionary thinkers. The advocates of the Fourth Philosophy, Josephus tells us, were 'zealous' in their attempts to get rid of Rome because they believed that there should be 'no King but God'.[19] All of this, of course, was claiming the fulfilment of an important

---
19 Jos. *Ant.* 18.23; see further Wright *NTPG*, 170–81, 302–7.

theme in Israel's scriptures: that the God who was always king in theory would show himself to be king indeed by the mighty acts of delivering his people.[20] This would be the type of kingdom envisaged in Daniel 2 and 7, a never-ending dominion ruled by the living God.[21]

Thus, 'kingdom of God', historically and theologically considered, was a slogan whose basic meaning was the claim that Israel's God was the world's true Lord, and that Caesar, or indeed Herod, was not. The one God would rule Israel in a whole new way, returning in power and glory to rescue his people, rebuke the wicked, and set up a new rule of justice and peace. 'Kingdom of God' meant that Torah would be fulfilled at last, that the Temple would be rebuilt and the Land cleansed. Israel's God would rule in the way he always intended, through properly appointed persons and means.

What would this mean for the different Jewish groups? For the Pharisees, Essenes, and anyone loosely described as zealots, it would mean a change in the high priesthood. In some writings it also meant a Messiah, though one of the striking features of the period is how comparatively infrequent, and completely unsystematized, expectations of a royal figure seem to be. But however the slogan 'kingdom of God' was interpreted in detail, it clearly implied a new order, fulfilling the prophecies of the Psalms, of Isaiah 40—55, and of Daniel, in which Israel would be vindicated, and then ruled over, by its God—and, by implication, one in which the rest of the world would somehow itself be ruled, whether for blessing or judgment, through Israel.

This kind of hope was not pie-in-the-sky theology. The Jews of Jesus' day, as is well known, had been living under foreign rule for several centuries. The worst thing about that was not the high taxation, the alien laws, the brutality of oppression, and so on, awful though that often was. The worst thing was that the foreigners were pagans. If the people of Israel were truly God's people, why were the pagans ruling over them? If Israel was called to be God's true humanity, surely these foreign nations were like the animals over which Adam and Eve were to rule. Why then were they turning into monsters and threatening to trample on God's defenceless chosen people? This state of affairs had existed ever since the Babylonians had destroyed Jerusalem in 597 BC, carrying the Judeans captive into exile. Thus, though some of them had returned from *geographical* exile, most believed that the *theological* state of exile was still continuing. They were living within a centuries-old drama, still waiting for the turn in the story that would bring them out on top at last.

So, when we find Jesus beginning his public ministry with the words, 'The time has come... the kingdom of God has come near. Repent and believe the good news',[22]

---

20 On God as 'king', see e.g. 1 Sam. 8—10; Isa. 44.6; 52.7; Pss. 89; 98.
21 Dan. 2.44; 6.26.
22 Mk. 1.15.

Jesus was not staking out virgin territory. He was tapping into a long-cherished hope for a new exodus, a new Temple, a reconstitution of the twelve tribes, a renewal of the covenant, a national forgiveness of sins, the release from captivity, an epoch of justice and peace, and an end to foreign rule. In other words, God was now unveiling his age-old plan, bringing his sovereignty to bear on Israel and the world as he had always intended, bringing justice and mercy to all. And he was doing so, apparently, through Jesus. Jesus was declaring that the clock was standing at ten seconds to midnight, that D-Day had arrived, that Israel's God was at last becoming king. He was announcing that God's final campaign had begun, and was already being put into effect. The people had better get ready for it, because it was already beginning.

Throughout his brief public career, Jesus spoke and acted as if God's plan of salvation and justice for Israel and the world was being unveiled through his own presence, his own work, his own fate. For example, in the 'Nazareth Manifesto' we find something like a kind of political declaration about what Jesus and this kingdom stood for and the constellation of hopes that it activated:

> He went to Nazareth, where he had been brought up, and on the Sabbath day he went into the synagogue, as was his custom. He stood up to read, and the scroll of the prophet Isaiah was handed to him. Unrolling it, he found the place where it is written:
>
> 'The Spirit of the Lord is on me, because he has anointed me to proclaim good news to the poor. He has sent me to proclaim freedom for the prisoners and recovery of sight for the blind, to set the oppressed free, to proclaim the year of the Lord's favour.'
>
> Then he rolled up the scroll, gave it back to the attendant and sat down. The eyes of everyone in the synagogue were fastened on him. He began by saying to them, 'Today this scripture is fulfilled in your hearing.'[23]

Here Jesus asserts that the Isaianic signs of deliverance were being manifested as evidenced by the publication of good news for the poor, the release of prisoners from captivity, and the recovery of sight for the blind. Jesus claimed that he was anointed with the spirit—in other words, that he was arriving with the heaven-sent deliverance—and that the end of exile and the start of a new exodus was really happening. God's favour and mercy was at hand, not in the distant future, but in the present moment of his listeners.

The story, of course, was not going to end there. But this was the beginning of the end.

---

[23] Lk. 4.16–21 = Isa. 61.1–2.

All spoke well of him and were amazed at the gracious words that came from his lips. 'Isn't this Joseph's son?' they asked.

Jesus said to them, 'Surely you will quote this proverb to me: "Physician, heal yourself!" And you will tell me, "Do here in your home town what we have heard that you did in Capernaum."'

'Truly I tell you,' he continued, 'no prophet is accepted in his home town. I assure you that there were many widows in Israel in Elijah's time, when the sky was shut for three and a half years and there was a severe famine throughout the land. Yet Elijah was not sent to any of them, but to a widow in Zarephath in the region of Sidon. And there were many in Israel with leprosy in the time of Elisha the prophet, yet not one of them was cleansed—only Naaman the Syrian.'

All the people in the synagogue were furious when they heard this. They got up, drove him out of the town, and took him to the brow of the hill on which the town was built, in order to throw him off the cliff. But he walked right through the crowd and went on his way.[24]

Icon of Jesus preaching in the synagogue of Nazareth; taken from a Vatican manuscript.
Church of St Mamas, Louvaras, Cyprus / Sonia Halliday Photographs / Bridgeman Images

The members of Jesus' audience might well have been on board when he spoke about God's favour, the time of release, the jubilee, and the day of freedom. But he went on to add that it wouldn't work out the way they had expected. In a shocking

---

24 Lk. 4.22–30.

reversal, amounting almost to a slap in the face to his hearers (perhaps even his own family!), Jesus declared that the people who would benefit from this great act of God would not, after all, be the people of Israel as they stood. The people who would benefit would be outsiders, the foreigners, the impure, the outcasts, and those thought to be at the bottom of the pile. Indeed, when all is said and done, pagan widows and gentile cripples might find themselves in a better position than some Israelites, if they made the right kind of response that God expected in his people.

Given the rancorous reaction from the audience, Jesus' 'sermon' went down like a lead balloon. It wasn't just that he appeared to be some local upstart claiming all sorts of wild things about himself. Even worse in their view, he was pouring cold water on many of their cherished beliefs about divine vengeance on foreigners or about God vindicating those who already believed they were automatically his people.

In Jesus' words, the message of forgiveness and jubilee wasn't meant to give everyone a sense of assurance that all would be well because they were, after all, the chosen people. Instead, he was warning them that they might be wrong. John the Baptist had already announced that physical Abrahamic descent was no guarantee of avoiding the coming judgment. Instead, everyone, all Israelites, including the priests, could opt in only by bearing the fruit of repentance.[25] According to Jesus, in God's new reordering of power, insiders became outsiders and outsiders became insiders, invited guests were locked outside and bystanders were jostled into the wedding

---

25 Mt. 3.9/Lk. 3.8.

PORTALS AND PARALLELS: JEWISH EXORCISTS IN FIRST-CENTURY JUDEA

Jesus was not the only exorcist in Palestine; many other Jews attempted to heal people by casting out demons, often with the aid of sacred names and sacred words. According to Matthew and Luke, when accused of casting out demons by the power of Beelzebul (an ancient Philistine deity), Jesus responded, 'If I drive out demons by Beelzebul, by whom do your people drive them out?' (Mt. 12.27/Lk. 11.19). Jesus was of course implying that it is hypocritical to accuse him of being in league with 'the satan' for what he does, when other contemporaries are doing the exact same thing! Josephus records an interesting account of a certain Eleazar who, using the incantations of Solomon and a baaras root, could draw out a demon through a person's nostrils:

> I have seen a certain man from my own country, named Eleazar, releasing people afflicted with demons in the very presence of Vespasian, and his sons, and his generals, and the whole cohort of his soldiers. The manner of healing was like so: he took a ring, one that had a root of the sort mentioned by Solomon, and inserted it into the nostrils of the demoniac, after which he then drew out the demon through his nostrils; and when the person collapsed to the ground he warned the demon not to return into him ever again, making further appeal to Solomon by reciting the incantations that Solomon had composed. (Jos. *Ant.* 8.46–7; tr. M. F. Bird)

The Profile and Praxis of a Prophet

banquet, the first would be last and the last would be first. Israel's God wasn't simply coming to endorse the people's national ambitions, to ratify the status quo, or to give sanction to their prejudices. He was doing what he said he would, but it wouldn't work out the way they had thought. That, repeated over and over again, was the burden of Jesus' song—in parable, in dramatic action, in dark proverbial warnings.

It was one thing to say that the kingdom was beginning, but quite another to prove it. Jesus did not engage in empty sloganeering or drop vague platitudes about God's reign breaking in. To the contrary, he brought about what he talked about. The kingdom's arrival was evidenced by Jesus' exorcisms, performed in the spirit's power (see 'Portals and parallels: Jewish exorcists in first-century Judea').[26] These showed that Jesus was plundering the satan's kingdom;[27] the healing of sick people signalled that a matrix of prophetic expectations was at last being made good.[28] When Jesus told individuals that their sins were forgiven, like a paralytic man or a woman with a tainted reputation, he was not offering pastoral consolation for waves of personal guilt. He was announcing instead a national amnesty for those who repented, declaring on his own authority that they would share in God's liberating work. The contrast with the normal Temple procedure was striking: instead of the priest, or the high priest, declaring that Israel's sins were forgiven, for instance on the Day of Atonement, Jesus spoke as if he had the God-given right to do so. Many sneered at the people Jesus was forgiving, thinking that the boundaries of God's favour stopped with themselves and their colleagues. Jesus pushed back, and insisted that the boundaries were now being drawn in a whole new way.

This brings us of course to a key tenet of Jesus' message: the place of national Israel in God's kingdom. First, Jesus believed, on the basis of the whole narrative of Israel's scriptures, that the creator God had purposed from the beginning to address and deal with the problems within his creation *through Israel*. Israel was not just

Manuscript illumination of the inbreaking of God's reign when Jesus healed a demon-possessed boy, illuminated and illustrated Arabic manuscript of the Gospels, Walters manuscript W.592, fol. 48B, c. 1684, The Walters Art Museum
Public Domain

---
26 Lk. 11.20/Mt. 12.28.
27 Mk. 3.23–27.
28 Lk. 7.22/Mt. 11.4–5.

to be an 'example' of a nation under God; Israel was to be the 'kingdom of priests', the Servant charged with being the light of the world, the means through which the world would be saved. Second, Jesus believed, as did many though not all of his contemporaries, that this vocation would be accomplished through Israel's history reaching a great moment of climax, in which Israel itself would be saved from its enemies, and through which the creator God, the covenant God, would at last bring his love and justice, his mercy and truth, to bear upon the whole world, bringing renewal and healing to all creation. In technical language, what we're talking about here is *election* and *eschatology*: God's choice of Israel to be the means of saving the world; God's bringing of Israel's history to its moment of climax, through which justice and mercy would embrace not only Israel but also the whole world.

Jesus' vision of the kingdom as coming to and through Israel allows us to make sense of a lot of gospel material. For a start, he didn't select twelve disciples as part of his inner circle just because it was convenient to have a dozen or so close followers.[29] The number twelve obviously symbolized the twelve tribes of Israel. However, everyone knew that the Jewish tribal league was long gone. The ten northern tribes had been taken into exile by the Assyrians eight centuries earlier, and the two remaining tribes (Judah and Benjamin, with such Levites as had lived in their midst) had been taken to Babylon in the sixth century. Only a remnant had returned to Judea. In fact, as we saw earlier, 70 per cent of all Jews in Jesus' day lived outside Palestine, in the Jewish Diaspora. A major prophetic hope was that when the age of deliverance dawned, it would be accompanied by a rejoining of the twelve tribes together in a renewed Jewish kingdom.[30] In many prophecies, when Israel returned to God and the exiles returned to the land, the gentiles would accompany them with gifts and offerings to Israel's God.[31] The restored Israel would be a beacon to the nations and comprise the penultimate state before the advent of a new creation.[32] By choosing twelve disciples, heralding the signs of restoration like healings and preaching good news to the poor, Jesus was in effect saying that the restoration of

> **PORTALS AND PARALLELS: SENECA ON THE POWER OF WORDS**
>
> *The Roman politician Seneca made an analogy between words and seeds, similar to Jesus' parable of the sower.*
>
> Words should be scattered like seeds; no matter how small the seed may be, if it has once found favorable ground, it unfolds its strength and from an insignificant thing spread to its greatest growth . . . precepts and seeds have the same quality; they produce much, and yet they are slight things. (Sen. *Ep. Mor.* 38; tr. R. Gummere [LCL])

---

29 Mk. 3.13–16.
30 See e.g. Isa. 34.10; 43.5; 56.8; see discussion in Wright *NTPG*, 299–301; Bird 2006a, 29–38.
31 See e.g. Isa. 2.2–5; 55.5–6; Mic. 4.1–4; Zech. 8.23.
32 See Isa. 60, 65—66.

The Profile and Praxis of a Prophet

Israel had now begun around him and his twelve followers. They were the vanguard for the renewed Israel. That is why Jesus chose twelve, to reign over a renewed nation.[33] This is why (though he envisaged a larger mission at the next stage) he focused his ministry exclusively on Israel,[34] declaring that many would soon be coming from east and west to join in the new moment in God's plan.[35] Yet this news came with a warning too. If Israel's people would not be Israel-for-the-sake-of-the-world, trusting instead in their own power to defeat Rome, then Jesus and his followers would be; and the rest of Israel would face the consequences of its obstinacy. The coming of God's kingdom meant that a transformed Israel would transform the world.

Jesus' teaching about the kingdom frequently took the form of punchy and pointed stories, which (following the gospel-writers themselves) we call 'parables'. Jesus' parables were not simply shrewd stories about human life and motivation. Nor were they simply childish illustrations, earthly stories with heavenly meanings. Again and again they were rooted in Israel's scriptures, in the Jewish narratives that were told and retold officially and unofficially. They were explanations for actions, invitations to new perspectives, and even weapons of political discourse designed to shock as much as to inform. The parables were centred on God, God's people, and God's word. They set forth the pressing challenge: would Israel respond appropriately to the message and the messenger?[36]

Two obvious examples, the parable of the sower (Mk. 4.1–20) and the parable of the prodigal son (Lk. 15.11–32), both illustrate how Jesus retells and even subverts competing understandings of Israel's place in the divine drama. First, the parable of the sower is not simply a wry comment on the way in which many hear the gospel message and fail to respond to it appropriately (see 'Portals and parallels: Seneca on the power of words'). Rather, it rehearses imagery taken from Jeremiah and Isaiah about God again sowing his people in the land after the exile. New plants, new shrubs, will spring up before the people as they return from exile. God will indeed produce the promised great harvest, but it won't work out the way people might have imagined.[37] Second, among the dozens of things people regularly and often rightly say about the 'prodigal son', one thing is missed by most, though it would be blindingly obvious to most first-century Jewish listeners. A story about a scoundrel young son who goes off into a faraway pagan country and is then astonishingly welcomed back home is—of course!—the story of exile and restoration. It was the story Jesus' contemporaries wanted to hear. And Jesus told the story to make the point

---

[33] Lk. 22.30/Mt. 19.29.
[34] Mt. 10.5–6; 15.24.
[35] Lk. 13.28–30/Mt. 8.10–12.
[36] Bockmuehl 2006, 216.
[37] Isa. 40.8; 55.10–11, 13.

that *the return from exile was happening in and through his own work*. The parable was not a general illustration of the timeless truth of God's forgiveness for the sinner, though of course it can be translated into that. It was a sharp-edged, context-specific message about what was happening in Jesus' ministry. More specifically, as Luke insists in his framing of it (Lk. 15.1), it was about what was happening through Jesus' welcome of outcasts, his eating with sinners. It was an explanation of why the party was thoroughly appropriate.

The 'party'—Jesus' apparently scandalous habit of dining with people regarded as 'sinners'—was a central characteristic of Jesus' public career. Wherever he went, there seemed to be a celebration; the accounts of festive meals, at which Jesus welcomed all and sundry, is one of the most securely established features of almost all recent scholarly portraits of his work. This naturally provoked those who had very different visions of what it would look like if God's kingdom were to break in.

Mount Beatitude in Capernaum, close to where Jesus may have taught Galilean crowds
Sopotnicki / Shutterstock

Through his actions, Jesus gained the reputation for being 'a glutton and a drunkard and a friend of tax-collectors and sinners'.[38] How could this Jesus fellow, a clever rabbi, a mighty healer, and even a prophet by all accounts, stoop to the level of keeping company with folk who were morally wretched and ceremonially impure? Wasn't Jesus concerned about his reputation or with his own personal purity,

---

38 Mt. 11.19/Lk. 7.34.

which Israel's worship demanded? Ought not a prophet to be rebuking and admonishing people like these? Jesus' answer was that it wasn't the healthy who needed a physician, but the sick. God had always been in the business of welcoming prodigal children home.[39] Jesus' table-fellowship with outsiders was meant to be a living parable of the open invitation to enter the kingdom of God. It was as if Jesus was handing out the *hors d'oeuvres* of the future messianic banquet, showing in advance who would dine in God's company in the new creation—but he was giving this party-in-advance, it seemed, to the wrong people. The meals spoke powerfully—and offensively to those with different ideas about the coming kingdom—about Jesus' own kingdom-vision. His welcome symbolized God's radical acceptance and forgiveness. Many of his contemporaries would have seen forgiveness and a God-given new start in terms of the Temple and its cult. Jesus was offering it on his own authority, requiring no official interaction with Jerusalem.

Jesus, then, was not simply a great teacher of ethics. He was a prophet, but with his vision of the kingdom a host of ethical corollaries did emerge. He was modelling and articulating a new praxis, a new way of being Israel. He was challenging his contemporaries to a new way of covenantal life, a righteousness better than that of the scribes, a way of forgiveness and prayer, a way of jubilee, which his audience could practise in their own villages, right where they were. The key thing was that the inbreaking kingdom Jesus was announcing created a new world, a new context, and he was challenging his hearers to become the new people that this new context demanded, the citizens of this new world.

This is the context, we suggest, within which we should understand what we call the Sermon on the Mount (Mt. 5—7). The sermon (whether or not it was delivered all at once by Jesus, it certainly represents substantially the challenge he offered to his contemporaries) is not, first and foremost, a private message for individuals to find salvation in Jesus, though of course it includes that in its wider reaches. Nor is it simply a great moral code (though it does of course contain some shining examples of great moral precepts). It makes the sense it does because it depends, all through, on Jesus' kingdom-announcement and on the fact that Jesus himself was, through

---

BLAST FROM THE PAST: DIETRICH BONHOEFFER ON CHRISTIANS AS THE LIGHT OF THE WORLD

Jesus says: 'Let your light so shine before men.' For when all is said and done, it is the light of the call of Jesus Christ which shines here . . . It is in *this* light that the good works of the disciples are meant to be seen. Men are not to see disciples but their good works, says Jesus. And these works are none other than those which the Lord Jesus himself has created in them by calling them to be light of the world under the shadow of the cross.*

---
* Bonhoeffer 1958, 71.

---

39 See Mt. 9.11–12/Mk. 2.16–17/Lk. 5.20–21; Lk. 15.1–2.

this announcement, summoning people to follow him in the new way of life, the kingdom-way. The sermon is a challenge, in particular, to find a way of being Israel over and against competing versions. Those alternative Israel-agendas, a mixture of religion, economics, and politics, were often laced with violent nationalism, rabid exploitation, or puritanical hypocrisy. Jesus' teachings here are not about behaving nicely so that God will reward you with a place in a 'kingdom' called 'heaven'. The sermon is, rather, the agenda for kingdom-people who want to work for the kingdom.

The work of the kingdom is in fact summed up pretty well in the beatitudes. Blessed are the poor, the mourners, the meek, those hungering for justice, the merciful, the pure-hearted, peacemakers, and the persecuted. These people are not only blessed, but more than that, even in their vulnerability and weakness, they are the ones precisely *through whom* Jesus intends blessings to flow to others. These sayings are about the type of people through whom Jesus intends to transform the world. When God wants to change the world, he doesn't launch missiles. Instead, he sends in the meek, the mourners, and the merciful. When God wants to put things to right, he doesn't scramble combat jets; he calls people to love and do justice. Through those kinds of people the blessings of God's reign begin to appear in the world.

Other sayings in the sermon point in much the same direction. 'Do not resist evil'; 'turn the other cheek'; 'go the second mile'; these are not invitations to 'be a doormat for Jesus'. They constitute a warning not to get involved in the ever-present resistance movement. Jesus was urging his hearers to discover the true vocation of Israel—to be the light of the world, the salt of the earth, the city set on a hill that could not be hidden (see 'Blast from the past: Dietrich Bonhoeffer on Christians as the light of the world'). That was what the renewed Israel of the

Temple Mount, South Wall, Jerusalem

new age was supposed to look like. Not the elitist micro-piety of Pharisaic leaders who claimed that their tradition represented the true measure of righteousness; nor the fanatical violence of zealous Judeans who wanted to purge Palestine of gentiles; nor the compromised Jewishness of the Herodians who dressed up hellenistic values in Jewish clothes; nor the members of the equally compromised aristocracy who ran the Temple for their own profit. The 'sermon' was, and still is, a manifesto for those who glimpse the truth of Jesus' kingdom-message and find themselves called to order their lives accordingly.

JESUS VERSUS THE TEMPLE

A climactic and dramatic prophetic action in Jesus' ministry was his 'cleansing' of the Temple. Most contemporary writing about Jesus rightly focuses on the Temple, what Jesus did there and what happened as a result. The Temple in this period was of course the heart and centre of Judaism, the vital symbol around which everything else circled. It was supposed to be where YHWH himself dwelt, or at least had dwelt and would do so again. It was the place of sacrifice, not only the place where sins were forgiven but also the place where the union and fellowship between Israel and its God was endlessly and tirelessly consummated. It was, not least because of these two things, the centre of Israel's national and political life. The chief priests who were in charge of it were also (along with the shaky Herodian dynasty, and under overall Roman supervision) in charge of the whole nation.

Furthermore, the Temple carried all kinds of royal overtones. Planned by David, built by Solomon, restored by Hezekiah and Josiah, its early history was bound up with the great days of Israel's early monarchy. Zerubbabel had been supposed to rebuild it after the exile; his failure is no doubt closely intertwined with his failure to re-establish the monarchy. Judas Maccabaeus and his colleagues cleansed the Temple after the Syrian debacle, and thus founded a dynasty that ran for a hundred years—even though they neither had nor claimed any ancestral connection with David. Herod's rebuilding of the Temple clearly had more than one eye on the legitimation of his kingship within traditional Jewish categories. Menahem and Simon bar-Giora, two of the would-be 'messiahs' during the war against Rome (AD 66–70), presented themselves in public in the Temple before being killed, one by rival Jews, the other by the Romans during Titus's triumph. The last great would-be messiah of the

Bar-Kokhba Revolt coin with inscription within wreath, 'Simon, Prince of Israel,' dated AD 132–35.
Shick Coins / VCoins.com

period, Bar-Kochba, had coins minted (this was itself an act of rebellion) on which the Temple façade was pictured. His own intentions were clear: he was going to rebuild the Temple and establish himself as king. Temple and messiahship went hand in hand.

El Greco's depiction of institutional judgment and disruption in *Christ Driving the Moneychangers from the Temple*, c. 1570, Minneapolis Institute of Art
Public Domain

At the same time, many Jews disapproved of the existing Temple. The Qumranites were strongly opposed to the present ruling elite—that, indeed, was the reason why they existed as a separate group in the first place—and hence to the present Temple, the power base of their rivals. They looked for a time when a new Temple would be built, presumably with their own group running it. The Pharisees had already begun to articulate the view that the blessings one normally got by going to the Temple could be had instead by the study and practice of Torah: 'If two sit together and study Torah, the Divine Presence rests between them.'[40] This early rabbinic saying meant that one could have the Temple-privilege of being in the presence of God anywhere in the world. This theology, designed of course not least for Jews

---
40 mAboth 3.2.

in the Diaspora where regular Temple attendance was out of the question, came into its own after AD 70, and arguably helped the Pharisees' successors, the rabbis, to survive and regroup after that great catastrophe. Thus, though the Pharisees were not themselves opposed to the existing Temple, in their thinking it was already relativized. This was another reason why they scrutinized and criticized Jesus, who was also offering an alternative to the Temple.

Some Jews had a less theological and more socio-economic critique of the existing Temple. Many of the disadvantaged within Judaism saw the Temple as standing for everything that was oppressing them: the rich, corrupt aristocracy and its systematic injustices. A sign of this attitude was the tell-tale actions of the rebels during the war; when they took over the Temple, they did the ancient equivalent of destroying the central computer in a bank: they burned all the records of debt.[41]

Though Jesus' action in the Temple must naturally be seen within this wider context of disaffection, it goes way beyond it into a different dimension.[42] His attitude to the Temple was not 'this institution needs reforming', nor 'the wrong people are running this place', nor yet 'piety can function elsewhere too'. His deepest belief regarding the Temple was *eschatological*: the time had come for God to judge the entire institution. It had come to symbolize the injustice that characterized the society on the inside and on the outside. It appeared to have rejected the vocation to be the light of the world. It was the city set on a hill, but instead of drawing to itself all the peoples of the world it was bent on manning the barricades to keep them out.

All this forms the context for our own question as to what Jesus himself did in the Temple and what he might have meant by it. There is currently a spectrum of opinion on this question, ranging from those who see his action as an attempt to reform or cleanse the system, through to those who see it as an acted parable of destruction. The latter end has arguably been more fruitful in recent discussion. But here there is still a wide divergence of views: if Jesus' action was a sign of judgment, on what grounds, and with what consequent intent? Most likely, we believe, Jesus acted out the Temple's destruction because he envisaged that (in some sense) a new Temple would be built, a new meeting-place for God and his people. Here we touch upon some of the central symbolism of Jesus' work and self-understanding.

Jesus acted and spoke during his Galilean ministry as if he was in some sense called to do and be what the Temple was and did. His offer of forgiveness, with no prior condition of Temple-worship or sacrifice, was the equivalent of someone in our world offering, as a private individual, to issue someone else a passport or a driver's licence. He was undercutting the official system, and claiming by implication to be establishing a new one in its place. In addition, as we have seen, a good deal of Jesus'

---

41 Jos. *War* 2.426–7.
42 Mk. 11.15–18/Mt. 21.12–16/Lk. 19.45–48; Jn. 2.13–25.

warning about impending judgment was focused on the Temple, and the string of public discussions that followed his action, both in John's gospel and in the synoptics, strongly indicates that this was the subtext of the entire episode. Jesus' Temple-action, in other words, was indeed an acted parable of judgment.

When he came to Jerusalem, in fact, the city was not (so to speak) big enough for the two of them together. The central symbol of the national life was under threat, and unless Israel repented it would fall to the pagans. Jesus believed that Israel's God was in the process of judging and redeeming his people, not just as one such incident among many but as the climax of Israel's history. This judgment would take the form of destruction by Rome. It would not be followed by the rebuilding of a new physical Temple. It would be followed by the establishment of the messianic community focused on Jesus himself, a strange new entity that would replace the Temple once and for all.

What, then, about the charge: 'You have made it a cave of brigands' (Mk. 11.17), and indeed the charge that the Temple authorities were making the father's house a market-place (Jn. 2.16)? Does not this indicate that Jesus' primary motive for his attack on the Temple had something to do with economic exploitation? Does it not suggest that he was out to cleanse the Temple, not to symbolize its destruction? Here, as so often, the context of the relevant Old Testament quotation (see Jer. 7.3–15) is all-important. Jeremiah was not advocating a reform of the Temple; he was predicting its destruction. The Greek word *lēstēs*, here translated 'thieves', is in fact the regular word used by Josephus to denote 'brigands' or 'rebels'.

Eastern edge of the Judean wilderness near Qumran

When Josephus refers, as he does twice, to 'caves of *lēstai*',[43] he is talking about the literal caves where the desperate revolutionaries used to hide out.

This suggests that Jesus' underlying charge against the Temple was not that it was guilty of financial sharp practice, though that may have been true as well, and the way it was being treated as a market-place indicated the casual approach to holy things that indicated the mood of many. As in Jeremiah's day, the Temple had become the focal point both for the nationalists in their eagerness for revolt against Rome and for the authorities for whom it was the principal source of income. Even though the people who actually ran it were, as far as the revolutionaries were concerned, part of the problem, the Temple itself was much bigger; it was, they believed, the place where Israel's God had promised to dwell and from which he would defend his people against all comers. How could it then symbolize, as Isaiah had said it should, the desire of Israel's God that it should become the beacon of hope and light for the nations, the city set on a hill that could not be hidden? Jesus saw the present grievous distortion of Israel's vocation symbolized catastrophically in the present attitudes towards the Temple: a symbol that had gone so horribly wrong could only be destroyed. As in one cryptic saying from this scene, the mountain—presumably Mount Zion—would, figuratively speaking, be taken up and cast into the sea (Mt. 21.21).

Why then, specifically, did Jesus banish the traders from the Temple courts? Without the Temple-tax, the daily sacrifices could not be supplied. Without the right money, individual worshippers could not buy pure sacrificial animals. Without animals, sacrifice could not be offered. Without sacrifice, the Temple had—albeit perhaps only for an hour or two—lost its whole *raison d'être*. Jesus' action symbolized his belief that when YHWH returned to Zion he would not after all take up residence in the Temple, legitimating its present functionaries and the nationalist aspirations that clustered around it and them. Rather, as Josephus realized in a similar context, the cessation of sacrifice meant that Israel's God would use Roman troops to execute upon the Temple the fate that its own impurity and its sanctioning of nationalist resistance had brought upon it. The brief disruption that Jesus effected in the Temple's normal business symbolized the destruction that would overtake the whole institution within a generation.

All this explains why, in Luke's account, Jesus came into Jerusalem with great sorrow and floods of tears, knowing that judgment was coming soon. It could perhaps have been averted, but the people were not listening.[44] Somehow Jerusalem had lost its way so drastically; somehow the leaders of the Jewish people had got things so wrong in their collusion with Rome, in their corruption, oppression, and greed;

---

43 Jos. *Ant.* 14.415–16; 15.345–8.
44 Lk. 19.41–44; see Mt. 23.37–39.

somehow the people had got things so wrong in their determination to bring God's victory to the world through military violence and armed rebellion, that the only word to be spoken by Jesus, the last of the prophets, would be the word of judgment: 'Not one stone here will be left on another; every one will be thrown down.'[45] The terrifying warnings are sustained through the Olivet Discourse (Mk. 13; Mt. 24; Lk. 21) which uses end-of-the-world language to demonstrate that with the fall of Jerusalem and with the destruction of the Temple, a world, the socio-political world of first-century Judean life, is coming to an end.

Jesus therefore invoked the language of Daniel—against the very city with which Daniel had been so concerned—to warn that it would be desecrated by the 'abomination of desolation', which would be placed in the Temple.[46] And in that terrible event, Jesus wanted his followers to see the sign of his own vindication. No longer would the Temple in Jerusalem be the place where heaven and earth met. From now on, heaven and earth would meet in and through the person of the 'one like a son of man', who after his suffering would be vindicated, and would be seen 'coming with the clouds of heaven' to be enthroned beside 'the Ancient of Days'.[47] The greatest empires of the world would do their worst, and Israel's representative would be enthroned as their lord, establishing a kingdom that could never be shaken.

The destruction of the Temple would mean God's judgment upon it; it would also be the vindication of Jesus as the prophet who exposed the futility of its function and the corruption of its leadership. Jesus spoke and acted like one who believed that he could replace the Temple because he himself was greater than it. No surprise, then, that Jesus' action in the Temple was the event that turned the members of the Jerusalem aristocracy resolutely against him, and turned their wishes for his death into a calculated effort to orchestrate it.

A PRÉCIS ON THE PROPHET JESUS

How can we hold this complex picture all together? Perhaps like this: Jesus, picking up the mantle after John the Baptist's arrest, acted in the fashion of an Elijah-like prophet with a message drawn from Israel's prophetic tradition as to what God's coming reign would mean for Israel and the Temple. He urged his audience to decide on which side of the ledger they would stand. God's reign meant actualizing the long-cherished hope—end of exile, new exodus, forgiveness of sins, and more—with God making good on his promises and overcoming the dark power of oppressive evil. Jesus' exorcisms and healings were visible demonstrations of the kingdom's saving power, its liberating work, making the jubilee come true. But if the 'Israel'

---

[45] Mk. 13.2/Mt. 24.2/Lk. 19.44; 21.6.
[46] Dan. 9.27; 11.31; 12.11; Mk. 13.14/Mt. 24.15.
[47] Dan. 7.13; Mk. 13.26–27/Mt. 24.30–31/Lk. 21.27–28.

of Jesus' day wanted to share in this blessing, people had to heed the message and get on board. Israel had to repent of its sins, turn from the path that was leading to violent revolution and economic oppression, and adopt its proper covenantal vocation as a kingdom of priests and a light to the nations. Jesus himself embodied that vocation, with the motley group of followers that he had gathered around himself. His parables, the stories of the kingdom, issued a challenge as to what it meant to be Israel, who was in Israel, and who in Israel would enter the kingdom. The parables also explained the joy to be gained, and warned against the perils of rejecting the messenger. Jesus' meals with outsiders and his teaching about Israel's way of life all undermined reigning paradigms about what it meant for God to return as king and inaugurate his new world.

All in all, Jesus was announcing that the long-awaited kingdom of Israel's God was indeed coming to birth, but that it did not look like what had been imagined. The return from exile, the defeat of evil, and the return of YHWH to Zion were all coming about, but not in the way Israel had supposed. The time of restoration was at hand, and people of all sorts were summoned to share and enjoy it; but Israel was warned that its present ways of going about advancing the kingdom were counterproductive, and would result in a great national disaster. Jesus was therefore summoning his hearers to *be* Israel in a new way, to take up their proper roles in the unfolding drama. He assured them that, if they followed him in this way, they would be vindicated when the great day came. In the course of all this, he was launching the decisive battle with the real satanic enemy—a different battle, and a different enemy, from those Israel had envisaged. The conflicts generated by his proclamation were the inevitable outworking of this battle, which would reach its height in events yet to come, events involving both Jesus himself and the Temple, and would drive him into an inevitable confrontation with the Judean leadership.

It may seem a huge step from the historical Jesus of the first century to our own vocation and tasks, whether professional, practical, academic, or whatever. Let us conclude the present chapter by pointing forward to the two ways through which Christians today might make this whole story their own.

First, all that we are and do as followers of Jesus is based upon his one-off unique achievement. It is because he inaugurated the kingdom that we can live out and live for the kingdom. It is because he brought the story of God and Israel, and hence of God and the cosmos, to its designed climax that we can now implement that work today. And we will best develop that Christian vocation if we understand the foundation upon which we are building. If we are to follow Jesus as Messiah and lord we need to know more about the Jesus we are following.

Second, the foundation serves as the model for the building as a whole. Everything we discover about what Jesus did and said within the context of his day must be thought through in terms of what it would look like for the church to do and be this for the world. What Jesus was to Israel, the church must now be for the world. For (as the risen Jesus said to the disciples in the upper room) as the father sent Jesus, so now Jesus sends the church (Jn. 20.21). Just as God's whole style, his chosen way of operating, reflects his generous love, sharing his rule with his human creatures, so too the way in which those humans behave if they are to be agents of Jesus' lordship must reflect the same sense of vulnerable, gentle, but powerful self-giving love. It is because of this that we have had the world changed by people like William Wilberforce the abolitionist and Cicely Saunders the hospice campaigner. If we are to shape our world, and perhaps even to implement the redemption of our world, this is how it is to be done.

Further reading

Bird, Michael F. 2006. *Jesus and the Origins of the Gentile Mission*. LNTS 331; LHJS; London: T&T Clark.
———. 2011. 'John the Baptist.' In *Jesus among Friends and Enemies: A Historical and Literary Introduction to Jesus in the Gospels* . Edited by Chris L. Keith and Larry Hurtado. Grand Rapids, MI: Baker, pp. 60–80.
Crossan, John Dominic. 1991. *The Historical Jesus: The Life of a Mediterranean Jewish Peasant*. San Francisco: Harper.
Dunn, James D. G. 2003. *Jesus Remembered*. CITM 1; Grand Rapids, MI: Eerdmans.
Perkins, Pheme. 1991. *Jesus as Teacher*. Cambridge: Cambridge University Press.
Taylor, Joan E. 1997. *The Immerser: John the Baptist within Second Temple Judaism*. Grand Rapids, MI: Eerdmans.
Webb, Robert L. 1991. *John the Baptizer and Prophet: A Socio-Historical Study*. Eugene, OR: Wipf & Stock.
Wright, N. T. 1996. *Jesus and the Victory of God*. COQG 2; London: SPCK.
———. 2011. *Simply Jesus: Who He Was, What He Did, Why It Matters*. London: SPCK.

10

Who Did Jesus Think He Was?

CHAPTER AT A GLANCE

This chapter explains aspects of Jesus' self-understanding, including his prophetic role, his self-designation as the 'son of man', his messianic consciousness, and his awareness of embodying YHWH's return to Zion.

By the end of this chapter you should be able to:

- recognize complexity in discussing Jesus' own 'christology';
- identify Jesus' description of himself as a prophetic figure;
- grasp the meaning and complexity of the title 'son of man';
- appreciate the messianic role that Jesus believed he was fulfilling;
- understand how Jesus saw himself both as God's 'son' and as also embodying the return of YHWH to Zion.

What would the average Galilean have perceived as Jesus came through the village? What categories would have been available for understanding what was going on? How did Jesus himself regard these basic categories? Only when we have asked these questions is it safe, historically speaking, to work forwards and ask about the other aspects of his mindset, and hence also about his beliefs and his aims.[1]

WHO DO PEOPLE SAY I AM?

The question of 'Who is Jesus?' goes back to the earliest days of Jesus' ministry. When people heard the things that Jesus said, for example how he 'taught them as one who had authority, not as the teachers of the law',[2] and when they witnessed his 'miraculous powers',[3] they were forced to grapple with the question: who is this man?

Modern Christians often face the temptation at this point to short-circuit the question. For many in our world, the question comes down to this: was Jesus, or was he not, 'the son of God' in the sense of being 'divine', 'the second person of the Trinity'? This question comes to us shaped by the scepticism of the eighteenth century

---
1 Wright *JVG*, 147.
2 Mk. 1.22/Mt. 7.29.
3 Mk. 6.2/Mt. 13.54.

between the Aramaic circumlocution and the Danielic theme of Israel's suffering and vindication—as seems clearly to be the case in the gospels—there is no reason why Jesus himself should not have done so as well.

Second, we should certainly interpret the many sayings about the 'coming' of the 'son of man' in terms of the narrative of Daniel 7. We must remind ourselves—against the very common misunderstanding—that Daniel 7 was not about 'the end of the space-time universe'. That is a modern misunderstanding. Nor did the early Christians take it to refer to Jesus' 'second coming'—a belief which they saw well established on other grounds. Read in the context of Daniel 7, the phrase 'one like a son of man' refers to 'the people of the saints of the most high', and invests them, by means of apocalyptic imagery, with the status of being the truly human ones who will be exalted over the 'beasts'. The mysterious 'man', then, is the counterpart to

Depiction of the Ancient of Days in Daniel 7 from the Silos Apocalypse, dated 1091 AD, The British Library
Public Domain

the arrogant 'horn' in Daniel's vision, the final emperor who boasts against God. The 'one like a son of man' is seen to embody God's kingship and reign. He represents the vindication and enthronement of the saints, over against the pagan monsters. Thus the dramatic language and imagery of Daniel 7 constituted in itself a creative reuse of Israel's scriptural and prophetic heritage to address concrete social, political, personal, cultural, and religious issues and institutions, and was open to subsequent re-readings, including those of Jesus and his first followers, for the same purposes. We must never forget, after all, that first-century Jews, reading a passage like Daniel 7, would think of being oppressed, not by mythical monsters, but by real Romans. The content of such an 'apocalyptic' story plays right into the context of Jesus' prophetic ministry. Its language offers itself as the appropriate vehicle for the devastating message he had to announce.

In addition, there is an impressive array of evidence to suggest that the Danielic figure of 'one like a son of man', though not necessarily 'messianic' in its original setting, was in fact read in this way, by some Jews at least, in roughly the time of

Who Did Jesus Think He Was? 223

Jesus.[19] The whole narrative sequence of Daniel (especially Dan. 7), and the ways in which that narrative could be invoked, echoed, or otherwise appropriated among Jesus' near-contemporaries, was adopted as a messianic prophecy that, 'more than anything else, incited the Jews to revolt'.[20] *Fourth Ezra* 11—12 picked up the narrative of Daniel 7 and used it in a fresh, and explicitly messianic, oracle, envisaging the Lion of Judah triumphing over the Eagle of Rome. *Second Baruch* 35—40 did the same, with the 'vine' of Israel opposing the 'cedar' of Rome. The so-called 'parables of Enoch' (*1 En.* 37—71), which used to be thought possibly post-Christian and therefore not relevant, are increasingly now regarded as earlier, and not therefore affected by Christian thought. They reflect a different, but related, messianic development of the Daniel 7 story and picture (see 'Portals and parallels: the Enochic son of man'). These texts do not seem to depend upon one another. They provide good, varied evidence of what appears to be a widespread expression of hope. The setting remains the national hope of Israel: YHWH would vindicate the nation against the pagans, rescuing it like a human figure from among monsters—like, you might say, a solitary but faithful Jew delivered from a den of lions. (We should not forget that Dan. 7 follows at once after Dan. 6!) And at the centre of this picture we find Israel's anointed king.

If we take this understanding of the Danielic son of man, and map it onto Jesus' use of the same designation, what is the result? In the case of the famous passage in Mark 13, it looks like this. Jesus has been asked about the destruction of the Temple. His reply has taken the disciples through the coming scenario: great tribulation, false messiahs arising, themselves hauled before magistrates. They need to know both (1) that Jerusalem is to be destroyed and (2) that they must not stand and fight, but must escape while they can. There will then occur the great cataclysmic event which will be at the same time (1) the final judgment on the city that has now come, with awful paradox, to symbolize rebellion against YHWH; (2) the great deliverance promised in the Prophets; and (3) the vindication of the prophet who had predicted the downfall, and who had claimed to be embodying in himself all that Jerusalem and the Temple had previously stood for.

The only appropriate language for such an event—the only language that could do justice to the rushing together of themes which occurs at this point—is the highly charged metaphor and myth of apocalyptic eschatology. The beasts will make war upon the son of man, upon YHWH's true Israel; the great Babylon will do its worst; and then will come the moment when the tyrant is overthrown and the true Israel is redeemed, publicly vindicated, shown to be the true people of the creator God. In other words, Jesus and his people will be shown to be in the right. Their claim will

---

19 See Wright *NTPG*, 291–7, 312–20.
20 Jos. *War* 6.312–15; see Wright *NTPG*, 312–14.

be proved true. The city that has opposed him (and them) will reap the inevitable result of choosing the way against which he had solemnly warned, the way of confrontation with Rome, of rebellion against the God of mercy and grace. Thus, in the vindication of the son of man, Jesus' people too will be vindicated: his angels, his messengers, will gather in 'his elect' from the whole world, as befits the people of the one creator God. This belongs completely within the framework of the Daniel 7 prophecy. When the 'son of man' is vindicated, all peoples, nations, and language-groups will serve him.

In sum, the phrase 'son of man' is used as a self-designation by Jesus, exploiting the ambiguity of the Aramaic idiom and marrying it to the mysterious figure of Daniel 7.13–14, as a cipher for the eschatological role that he exercises as the divine agent of the kingdom. In this sense, 'son of man' is more of a 'role' than a 'title': the point is that this figure now does two things: he embodies God's own reign, seated at his right hand; and he symbolizes God's people, vindicated after suffering. What is more, when we frame this in the context of Jesus' mission to restore Israel, his eschatological teachings on the kingdom, his comparisons of himself with David and Solomon, his claims to be uniquely anointed with the spirit for his actions, and his symbolic actions themselves, then the vagueness of the designation starts to disappear. What emerges instead is a much more concrete sense, along the lines of a definite messianic claim.[21] How does this then appear?

---

21 Bird 2009b, 97–8.

PORTALS AND PARALLELS: THE ENOCHIC SON OF MAN

The writing commonly referred to as 1 Enoch *is a composite document of five independent works which were written between the third century BC and the first century AD, and pseudonymously attributed to Enoch, the seventh son of Adam (Gen. 5.18–24). One can find mention of a messianic 'son of man' in the Book of Parables or Similitudes (1 En. 37–71), which combine images from the Psalms, Isaiah, and Daniel to describe a heavenly deliverer:*

At that place, I saw the One to whom belongs the time before time. And his head was white like wool and there was with him another individual, whose face was like that of a human being. His countenance was full of grace like that of one among the holy angels. And I asked the one—from among the angels—who was going with me, and who had revealed to me all the secrets regarding the One who was born of human beings, 'Who is this, and from whence is he who is going as the prototype of the Before-Time?' And he answered me and said to me, 'This is the Son of Man, to whom belongs righteousness, and with whom righteousness dwells. And he will open all the hidden storerooms; for the Lord of the Spirits has chosen him and he is destined to be victorious before the Lord of the Spirits in eternal uprightness. This Son of Man whom you have seen is the One who would remove the kings and the mighty ones from their comfortable seats and the strong ones from their thrones. He shall loosen the reins of the strong and crush the teeth of sinners.' (1 En. 46.1–4; tr. E. Isaac [1983–5])

THE MESSIAH

There was no uniform and monolithic 'messianic expectation' shared by all first-century Jews. Scholars used to suggest such a thing, but further research has radically increased the complexity. The only two figures unambiguously spoken of as Messiah between AD 30 and 132 are Jesus of Nazareth and Simon bar-Kochbar (known also as Simeon ben-Kosiba). Yes, other figures emerged from time to time who excited hopes for future deliverance, set themselves up as royal claimants, and echoed biblical traditions in their actions. But few, as far as we know, were explicitly hailed as a Messiah. Simon bar-Giora, as we saw, was taken to Rome in AD 70 as part of Titus's triumph, and there ceremonially killed as 'king of the Jews'. Not many Jews would have endorsed that claim during Simon's brief public appearance, and none, of course, would have echoed it after his death.

Among the Jewish authors and groups who did anticipate a Messiah, there were diverse opinions as to what type of figure he would be.[22] Some envisaged an anointed military leader, who would lead the people in a successful purge of gentiles and sinners.[23] Others imagined a Messiah with transcendent qualities and supernatural powers.[24] The Qumran community envisaged two 'anointed' leaders in the final days: a 'Messiah of Aaron' and a 'Messiah of Israel'.[25] Philo held out a hope for a Hebrew king who would establish a Jewish kingdom and subjugate the nations.[26]

Jewish messianism grew out of earnest reflection on Israel's sacred traditions in the light of the social and political context of the Jewish people in the Persian, Greek, and Roman periods. The shared thread of Jewish messianism in the various tapestries that hung around from time to time was a future hope for a royal and eschatological deliverer to liberate Israel, cleanse or rebuild the Temple (so that Israel's God would at last return in glory), and establish a renewed Jewish kingdom, perhaps thereby bringing justice to the world. In the end we might define the Messiah as 'an agent of God in the end-time who is said somewhere in the literature to be anointed, but who is not necessarily called "messiah" in every passage'.[27]

Did Jesus claim to be the Messiah? Many will suppose that the answer is a blindingly obvious 'Yes, of course!' However, first one must consider the fact that in the gospels Jesus never once uses the title 'Messiah' to describe himself. At the very most, he is called Messiah, king, and 'son of David' by others. By itself such data might suggest that Jesus inspired messianic hopes but did not embrace the title

---

[22] See Bockmuehl and Paget 2007; Fitzmyer 2007; Zetterholm 2007; Collins and Collins 2008; Bird 2009b, 31–62.
[23] See 1QM; *Ps. Sol.* 17–18.
[24] See *1 En.* 37–71; *4 Ez.* 13.
[25] See e.g. 1QS 9.11; CD 12.22–23; 1QSa 2.17–22.
[26] See Philo *Vit. Mos.* 1.290–1; *Praem.* 95–6.
[27] Collins 1995, 11–12.

as the best label for what his ministry was about. The other problem is that the moments in the gospels where Jesus supposedly accepts the messianic designation are thought to bear a striking resemblance to early Christian confessions of Jesus' identity.[28] In other words, some of the gospel accounts look as if the evangelists or their sources might have read their messianic faith back into stories of Jesus' pre-Easter life. Where does this leave us?

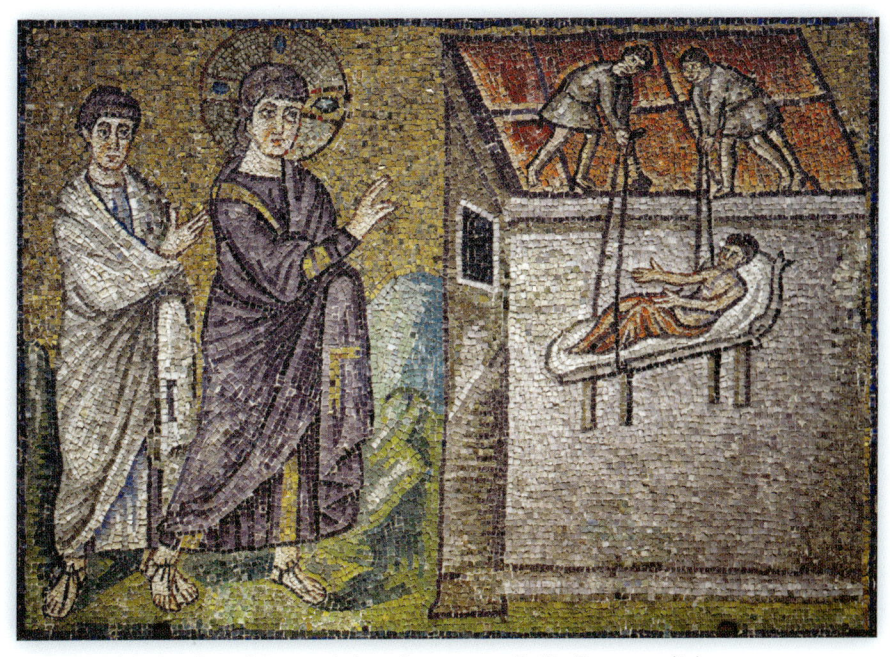

A mosaic of the healing of the paralytic at Capernaum, Emilia-Romagna, Italy
De Agostini Picture Library / A. Dagli Orti / Bridgeman Images

First, a denial that Jesus thought of himself as a messianic leader creates more problems than it solves. We still have the questions of *why* Jesus was crucified as a messianic pretender, *how* the messianic faith of the early church arose in the first place, and *where* the evangelists got the idea to put the story of Jesus into a messianic matrix.

One long-rehearsed explanation is that the early church inferred Jesus' identity as Messiah from his resurrection. If God had raised him, then surely he must be the Messiah. The problem with this is that there is no precedent for deducing messiahship from resurrection. How does 'resurrected' equal 'Messiah'? John the Baptist died a martyr; some even suggested that he had come back to life in Jesus.[29] But no-one thereafter considered the Baptist to be the Messiah. Belief in Jesus' resurrection

---

28 See Mk. 8.29; 14.61–62; Jn. 4.25–26; 18.33–34.
29 Mk. 6.14–16; 8.28.

certainly accentuated messianic beliefs about him,[30] but it did not of itself create the belief in Jesus' messianic identity.

An older explanation, going back to William Wrede, appeals to the so-called 'messianic secret' in the gospel of Mark to explain the origins of messianic faith. One notices in Mark that Jesus is constantly telling his disciples, and people he had healed, things like, 'Don't speak to anyone about this' and 'Tell nothing to anyone.' This is seen rather dramatically in Jesus' response to Peter's confession of him as the Messiah, where Jesus 'warned them not to tell anyone about him'.[31] William Wrede and others, picking up on this, argued that the 'messianic secret' was a literary fiction, without historical basis, to explain why no-one in the early Jerusalem church had known about Jesus claiming to be the Messiah. The answer was that he kept it a deliberate secret from outsiders. The biggest problem with the messianic secret thesis is that what is silenced in the gospel of Mark is not necessarily messianic, like healings and exorcisms (see Mk. 1.44; 7.36), while some material that *is* very messianic is not silenced at all, such as Bartimaeus calling Jesus the 'son of David' (Mk. 10.47–49), Jesus' triumphal entry (Mk. 11.1–10), and his enigmatic remarks about David and his lord (Mk. 12.35–37). Moreover, the injunctions to secrecy regularly fail. Word about Jesus continues to get out, resulting in crowds being drawn to Jesus. Mark has an obvious motif of secrecy and mystery in his gospel, but it does not function as the explanation for the sudden emergence of messianic faith in Jesus. Wrede's theory, growing out of the speculative reconstructions of late nineteenth-century German scholarship, has had a long run for its money, but it is time to set it aside.

Second, there are some good reasons for thinking that Jesus did in fact claim to be a messianic figure. Several lines of evidence can be considered:

1. Isaiah 61, which in its own context concerns an anointed prophetic figure, seems to have played a significant part in Jesus' own vocational understanding. There is an explicit appeal to a spirit-anointed ministry in Luke's Nazareth Manifesto (Lk. 4.18–21) and similar Isaianic echoes in the material common to Luke and Matthew about John the Baptist's question as to whether Jesus really is the 'one who is to come' (Mt. 11.2–6/Lk. 7.18–23). In fact, Jesus' response to John, drawn largely from Isaiah ('Go back and report to John what you hear and see: the blind receive sight, the lame walk, those who have leprosy are cleansed, the deaf hear, the dead are raised, and the good news is proclaimed to the poor'), possesses a striking resemblance to a text from the Dead Sea Scrolls that attributes a similar list of deeds to Israel's Messiah (see 4Q521 2.1–10).

---

30 See Ac. 2.31; 4.10; Rom. 1.2–4; 2 Tim. 2.8.
31 Mk. 8.30.

2. Jesus appears to have envisaged himself as possessing a special role in the future kingdom. Jesus' choice of twelve disciples was symbolic of the restoration of Israel that he believed he was effecting (Mk. 3.13–16). Yet Jesus did not cast himself as one of the Twelve, but rather, as their leader and commander. The Twelve, he said, would sit on twelve thrones judging Israel, and have a kingdom conferred on them in the same way that the Father was conferring his kingly power on Jesus (Mt. 19.28–30/Lk. 22.28–30). It seems that Jesus saw himself as the royal leader-to-be of the restored people of God—a king of a future kingdom.

The Visit of the Queen of Sheba to King Solomon by Sir Edward John Poynter, dated 1890
Public Domain

3. We also have to take into account the prominence of allusions to David and Solomon in Jesus' teaching activities (Mt. 12.42/Lk. 11.31; Mk. 2.23–28; 12.35–37). Solomon and David were both regarded as prophets and allegedly performed exorcisms, which aligns also with the pattern of Jesus' ministry, but obviously their main role was kingly. Jesus appears to have seen himself in a lineage associated with the greatest of royal figures from Israel's ancient past.
4. Jesus' final week was manifestly messianic. We have a messianic action in the triumphal entry that deliberately acts out Zechariah 9 (Mk. 11.1–10) and at the same time mirrors in some ways the triumphal entry of Judas Maccabaeus, which staked an effective claim to royalty (1 Macc. 3.36–59; 2 Macc. 10.1–9). Jesus' action in the Temple, warning of its imminent

destruction, implies that he is claiming royal authority over it (Mk. 11.11–18); elsewhere we are told that he predicted the rebuilding of the Temple, which is a messianic task (Mk. 14.58; Jn. 2.19; cp. 2 Sam. 7.11–14). Jesus engages the scribes on several topics, including the identity of the Messiah as David's Lord (Mk. 12.35–37). At the Last Supper, Jesus appears to think of himself in terms of Zechariah's smitten shepherd, who saves his people from tribulation by his vicarious death (Zech. 13.7; Mk. 14.27). At his trial before Caiaphas, Jesus, having already been interrogated about his intentions in relation to the Temple, is asked point-blank a messianic question, and responds with an oblique but affirmative answer that conflates Psalm 110.1 and Daniel 7.13 (Mk. 14.62).

5. Finally, Jesus was executed on the charge of being a messianic pretender. The 'titulus' nailed above his head (the statement of his 'crime', in Roman practice) mocked him as 'the king of the Jews'. All four gospels highlight this (see Mt. 27.37/Mk. 15.26; Lk. 23.38; Jn. 19.19). This would have been widespread public knowledge; it is difficult to imagine later Christians inventing it, especially in such a shameful context. It is more or less impossible to explain why that charge would have been levelled against Jesus had he never given any indication of royal aspirations. As Dale Allison says, the 'Romans probably crucified Jesus as "king of the Jews" because he did not distance himself from that derisive epithet'.[32]

The messianic faith of the early church did not burst into life from nothing. True, Jesus had not gone around telling people, 'I'm the Messiah.' Still, if you proclaim the kingdom of God in Roman Palestine, declare that the day of national restoration is dawning, compare yourself to David and Solomon, perform what various people considered to be signs of messianic deliverance, enter Jerusalem on a donkey with people shouting 'Hosanna to the son of David', and end up on trial on a messianic charge, being then mocked in death as a Jewish king, it all seems fairly obvious. Jesus deliberately acted out a messianic role. This was why the early church began as a 'kingdom-movement', venerating him as its messianic leader. Of course, none of this would have been taken further had Jesus' first followers not been convinced that he had been raised from the dead. Everybody knew that a crucified Messiah was a failed Messiah. Equally, to repeat what was said above, the resurrection would not have created these stories, with their messianic overtones, out of thin air. The meaning given to the resurrection is only comprehensible historically on the basis of what was known about Jesus prior to his death.

In the theology of Luke, expressed in his version of Jesus' birth and genealogy,

---

[32] Allison 2010, 240.

Jesus is adopted into the Davidic family, and heralded in the nativity story as 'the Messiah, the Lord'.[33] But what kind of 'Lord' did Luke have in mind? How closely can 'Messiah' and 'Lord' be equated in Jesus' own ministry? The royal riddle announced in Mark 12.35–37 indicates that Jesus dealt with the question by provocatively alleging that the Messiah is a son of David but also *more than* a son of David! But how much more? A pre-existent Messiah, or sometimes the pre-existent name of the Messiah, was known in Judaism, but nowhere was the Messiah himself thought to be 'divine' in a sense that would transgress or violate the norms of ancient Jewish monotheism. Even so, in the case of Jesus, what about a Messiah who exercised divine prerogatives, who spoke and acted on God's behalf, who forgave sins, and believed that he was destined to sit co-enthroned with Israel's Lord? How did Jesus' understanding of himself as Israel's Messiah fit with his understanding of Israel's one God?

DID JESUS THINK HE WAS GOD?

When it comes to the question of whether Jesus thought of himself as 'God', there are two options one might take.

On the first side, many Christians are content with some form of the argument advanced by C. S. Lewis in his various writings. According to Lewis, Jesus claimed to be divine. Yet this means that he was either a deliberate crook, a *liar* (which his whole life and particularly his death tells strongly against), or a madman, engaged in the religious ramblings of a *lunatic* (which the rest of his teaching makes very unlikely), or he was telling the truth—he was *Lord* (which we must accept and face up to). The problem is that identifying Jesus as 'Lord' in this way usually ends up with a Jesus who is completely 'heavenly', rather than being the believable Galilean prophet we have seen above. Jesus then appears to cruise around Galilee announcing—to put it in popular language!—'Hi, I'm God. I'm going to die on the cross for your sins soon. But first of all I'm going to teach you how to be a good Christian and how to get to heaven. And after that it would be fitting if you worshipped me as the second member of the Trinity.' This might seem a rather silly way to understand Jesus' identity, but it is a sketch of Jesus that many devout Christians have held, at least by implication.

On the other side, several theologians have said that this talk of Jesus as 'God' is simply nonsense. We know, so many have said, that it is simply absurd to think of God as human or for a person to be divine. The categories are mutually exclusive. No sane person could think of themselves as God incarnate. This line of thought was advanced by (among many others) the American theologian John Knox in the 1950s,

---

33 Lk. 2.11.

and it has been repeated *ad nauseam* in many circles ever since.[34] More particularly, many have been taught, no first-century Jew could think of himself as in any sense 'divine', since Jews were after all monotheists. The idea of a human somehow being divine could only be a later idea, a pagan corruption of the original non-incarnational thinking and teaching of Jesus and indeed of the early church. Appearances to the contrary were dealt with in short order: the 'claims' of Jesus to 'divinity' were, it was said, inventions from the end of the first Christian generation or later, being read back, not least in John's gospel, onto the lips of Jesus.

Of course, to think about Jesus as identifiable with God—whether for or against—presumes a certain set of assumptions about what 'God' even means. Our first move should be to set aside the Enlightenment view of God with its romanticized Deism where a semi-personal God made the world and then permanently retreated into a distant 'heaven'. Instead, we should examine the Jewish account of God and God's relationship to the world. The Jews believed in a specific God, of whom there was only one, who had made the whole world and who was present to it and active within it while remaining sovereign over it and mysteriously other than it. They knew this God (though at some point they stopped saying this name) as YHWH, 'the One Who Is', the Sovereign One. He was not remote or detached. Nor was he simply a generalized sense of a sacred dimension within the world, or for that matter the objectification or personification of forces and drives within the world. Rather, he was the *maker* of all that exists, and remained powerful and involved within, though by no means reduced to terms of, the creation itself. Classic Jewish monotheism thus came to believe that (1) there was one God, who created heaven and earth, and who remained in close and dynamic relation with his creation; and that (2) this God had called Israel to be his special people.

A mosaic of Christ the Pantocrator from Fethiye Camii, Istanbul, Turkey
Pavle Marjanovic / 123RF.COM

---

34 See Knox 1959, 58: 'I, for one, simply cannot imagine a sane human being, of any historical period or culture, entertaining the thoughts about himself which the Gospels, as they stand, often attribute to him.'

In many places in Israel's scriptures and in subsequent post-biblical Jewish writings there were concrete ways of thinking about God's presence and saving activity, within the world and within Israel. We have set these out in a previous chapter: (1) God's glory; (2) God's Torah; (3) God's spirit; (4) God's word; and (5) God's wisdom. These five ways are folded into a *story* in which Israel's God, the creator, was promising to rescue Israel and the world. He would return in person and glory; and, as he took his throne, so he might exalt, to share that throne, 'one like a son of man'. This ancient picture of God, very different from those imagined by much scholarship with its easy references to 'Jewish monotheism', is the proper context for understanding Jesus' own beliefs and aims.

Jesus and the return of YHWH to Zion

The first aspect we need to consider is how YHWH's return to Zion is a major theme of the exilic and post-exilic Old Testament books. It is central to Isaiah, particularly chapters 40—55 and the developing theme, there, of the kingdom of God. Ezekiel, the prophet who declared most emphatically that YHWH had abandoned his people to their fate, envisages him returning to the newly built eschatological Temple. The Psalms celebrate the coming of YHWH to judge the world. Haggai, faced with the puzzling second Temple that failed to live up to expectations, envisages YHWH returning to a yet more glorious house. Zechariah employs exodus imagery—the pillar of cloud and fire—to express the way in which YHWH will return to dwell with and defend his people, and offers an apocalyptic scenario in which YHWH will come with all his holy ones to become king of all the earth, reigning from Jerusalem. Malachi promises that the Lord whom Israel seeks will suddenly come to his Temple, even though his coming will bring judgment as well as salvation.

Most of these writings, clearly, reflect the time *after* the geographical return of some Judean captives from their Babylonian exile. That return, when it came about under Cyrus and his successors, was not accompanied by any manifestations such as those in Exodus 40, Leviticus 9, 1 Kings 8, or even Isaiah 6. Never do we hear that the pillar of cloud and fire that accompanied the Israelites in the wilderness has gloriously led the people back from their exile. At no point do we hear that YHWH has now returned in splendour to Zion. The closest we get is the idea, in Ben-Sirach chapter 24, where 'wisdom' comes, in the form of Torah, to dwell in the Temple. But that optimistic vision, written about 200 BC, had itself been shattered by the events of the subsequent two centuries. In any case, at no point does anyone say that the Temple has once more been filled with the cloud that veils the divine glory. At no point is the rebuilt Temple universally hailed as the true restored shrine spoken of by Ezekiel. No new festival was invented to mark the start of the great new era. Significantly, at no point either was there a final decisive victory over Israel's enemies, or the establishment of a universally welcomed royal dynasty. Temple, victory, and kingship remained intertwined, but the hope they represented remained unfulfilled. It is therefore not surprising that the scriptural tradition that refers unambiguously to YHWH's return to Zion after the exile is maintained in the post-biblical writings. This expectation remained basic to Jewish thought in the time of Jesus.[35]

When Jewish groups spoke about the coming kingdom of God, then, their intended referent was the coming of God as king. This kingdom was 'not primarily a state or place but rather the entire dynamic event of God coming in power to rule his people Israel in the end time'.[36] It meant a divine visitation with the accompanying effects of a new exodus, the forgiveness of Israel's sins, the renewal of the covenant, a new Temple, and God's victory over evil.

One central passage that promised the kingly return of God was Isaiah 40. Verse 3 spoke of 'A voice of one calling: "In the wilderness prepare the way for the LORD; make straight in the desert a highway for our God."' This verse was programmatic for both John the Baptist, out in the Judean wilderness, and the Qumran community on the shores of the Dead Sea. Both were quite literally 'out in the desert', preparing for this future event of God's coming, either by way of prophetic warning to the masses (John the Baptist) or by a separation from the impurity of the masses (Qumran).[37] Later in Isaiah 40 we read more about YHWH's coming reign and YHWH's return to Zion:

> You who bring good news to Zion,
>> go up on a high mountain.
> You who bring good news to Jerusalem,
>> lift up your voice with a shout,
> lift it up, do not be afraid;
>> say to the towns of Judah,
>> 'Here is your God!'
> *See, the Sovereign LORD comes with power,*
>> *and he rules with a mighty arm.*
> See, his reward is with him,
>> and his recompense accompanies him.
> He tends his flock like a shepherd:
>> he gathers the lambs in his arms
> and carries them close to his heart;
>> he gently leads those that have young.[38]

---

[35] On the return from exile and YHWH's return to Zion, see further Wright *NTPG*, 299–301; *JVG*, xvii–xviii, 576–7; *PFG*, 1.139–63.
[36] Meier 1991–2016, 1.452.
[37] Mk. 1.3/Mt. 3.3/Lk. 3.4 and 4Q176 1.4–9; 1QS 8.14; 9.19–20.
[38] Isa. 40.9–11 (italics added).

And, as the great poem reaches its climax, we find the same point reinforced and amplified:

> How beautiful on the mountains
> > are the feet of those who bring good news,
> who proclaim peace,
> > who bring good tidings,
> > who proclaim salvation,
> who say to Zion,
> > 'Your God reigns!'
> Listen! Your watchmen lift up their voices;
> > together they shout for joy.
> *When the* Lord *returns to Zion,*
> > *they will see it with their own eyes.*
> Burst into songs of joy together,
> > you ruins of Jerusalem,
> for the Lord has comforted his people,
> > he has redeemed Jerusalem.
> *The* Lord *will lay bare his holy arm*
> > *in the sight of all the nations,*
> *and all the ends of the earth will see*
> > *the salvation of our God.*[39]

The Isaianic announcement of God's kingship meant that God would bring the exile to an end in a new exodus. He would return to Zion, where he would judge Israel's enemies, then dwell for ever with his people.

This is what Luke has in mind in his portrayal of Jesus approaching Jerusalem. The whole sequence of Luke 19 strongly implies that when Jesus arrives, he is coming not simply as Israel's Messiah, but as Israel's returning God.

First, Jesus' journey through Jericho became the occasion to engage in some scandalous activity seen in his willingness to dine in the house of the much-despised tax-collector named Zacchaeus.[40] As we have seen, reclining with such reprehensible persons was one of the most characteristic parts of Jesus' career.[41] At the end of the story, once Zacchaeus's repentance has become public, Jesus explains why he does such things with the words: 'the Son of Man came to seek and to save the lost.'[42] Jesus does not talk like an ancient prophet, telling wayward sinners to seek out God

---

[39] Isa. 52.7–10 (italics added).
[40] Lk. 19.1–10.
[41] See Mk. 2.15–16; Mt. 11.19/Lk. 7.34; Lk. 15.1.
[42] Lk. 19.10.

Who Did Jesus Think He Was? 235

while he may be found.[43] Instead, he is himself seeking out marginalized Israelites in a manner reminiscent of how God, in his climactic return to Zion, was believed to be coming to regather the lost flock of Israel.[44] The story is full of echoes of YHWH himself coming to seek out and shepherd his people.

Second, Luke follows this story with the 'parable of the talents'.[45] This concerns a nobleman who goes abroad to be granted kingly authority, and then returns to his homeland.[46] This parable has long been read as a prediction of Jesus' second coming. However, Luke's version of the parable is not dealing with what a generation of scholars once thought it was, namely, the sense of anxiety at why Jesus was taking so long to come back, and what might happen when eventually he did. The occasion for the parable is not the problem of the kingdom's postponement; on the contrary, Luke explicitly states that the reason why Jesus uttered the parable was because his audience thought the kingdom was going to appear immediately.[47] Far from extinguishing such hopes, Jesus' parable actually excites them all the more, as we can see by the enthusiasm of his followers in the triumphal entry that follows.[48] On the parable of the talents itself, rather than think of it as a morality tale for the faithful to be ready for the second coming, it is preferable to take the story as Jesus' own retelling of the well-known scriptural narrative about the return of YHWH to Zion. Jesus thereby deliberately evoked the hope that God's saving justice was about to be dramatically revealed—and that this would mean judgment on the unfaithful as well as reward for the persevering.[49]

Third, in Luke's version of the triumphal entry, Jesus approaches Jerusalem weeping with grief over the city. His words sound more like an oracle of woe than an ode of lament: 'They will dash you to the ground, you and the children within your walls. They will not leave one stone on another, because you did not recognise the time of God's coming to you.'[50] Jerusalem faces dire consequences, namely, destruction at the hands of Rome, because the people have not recognized the time of deliverance, or what they should do about it. 'The time of God's coming to you' translates a word sometimes rendered 'visitation', an idea we find elsewhere in Luke and also in the Dead Sea Scrolls, referring to the dramatic arrival of YHWH to sort everything out.[51] Tragically, the great day of YHWH's return has arrived, but it receives at best

---

43 See Amos 5.4; Zeph. 2.3.
44 See Jer. 31.10; Ezek. 34.8–10; Zech. 9.16.
45 Lk. 19.11–27.
46 The Lukan version of the parable in particular looks like a parody about the brief rise to power of Archelaus as the successor to Herod the Great as ruler of Judea. He constitutes an ironic anti-type to Jesus' claim to kingship amid opposition.
47 Lk. 19.11.
48 Lk. 19.37–38.
49 On reading Lk. 19.11–27 this way, see further, Wright *JVG*, 632–9.
50 Lk. 19.44; Mt. 23.39.
51 Lk. 1.68, 78; 7.16; 1QS 3.18; 4.19; CD 7.9; 8.2–3. Cp. Ex. 4.31.

a mixed reception. This will mean that, in God's long-awaited judgment, unrepentant Jerusalem may itself be condemned. Thus Luke presents Jesus, in his final journey to Jerusalem, as intending to enact, symbolize, and personify the climactic hope of YHWH returning to Zion.[52]

Exaltation and enthronement

If YHWH were to act in history, and if he did so through a chosen agent, how might that chosen agent be described? This is the second aspect of first-century Jewish thinking that helps us understand the context of Jesus' symbolic action in the Temple, and the stories and riddles with which he surrounded it. According to some texts from our period, when YHWH acted in history, the agent through whom he acted would be vindicated, exalted, and honoured in a truly unprecedented manner.

There is a complex range of Jewish texts from different periods that speculate about the exaltation and heavenly enthronement of a figure who may be either an angel or a human being. These speculations grow from meditation upon and discussion of certain key texts we have already noted, such as Ezekiel 1, in which the prophet receives a vision of YHWH's throne-chariot, and Daniel 7, where 'one like a son of man' is presented to 'the Ancient of Days' and shares his throne. Such speculations formed the staple diet of a whole tradition of Jewish mysticism and accompanying theological and cosmological enquiry.

Sometimes the texts speak of a mystical journey, of people attempting to attain to the vision of the one true God himself. Sometimes they speak of an angel who has the name of Israel's God dwelling in him. Sometimes they speak of a human being sharing the throne of Israel's God. Several strands of tradition tell the story of Moses in this fashion; some even speak thus of the martyrs or the pious. In one famous story that occurs in various forms and periods the great rabbi Akiba suggests

Fallen stones from the Temple's destruction in AD 70

---

52 Wright *JVG*, 615.

that the 'thrones' spoken of in Daniel 7.9 are 'one for God, one for David'.[53] Akiba, of course, had a candidate in mind: Bar-Kochba, whom he hailed as the Messiah, 'the son of the star'. Other Jewish teachers of the same period seem to have speculated on the possibility of a plurality of 'powers' within 'heaven'.

How far these speculations were taken is a matter of continuing debate. But the point should be clear: this kind of thing was thinkable. Such ideas were not obviously self-contradictory, nor were they regarded as necessarily a threat to what second-Temple Jews understood when they affirmed that God is One. (Our word 'monotheism' is of course a comparatively modern coinage.) They were attempts to find out what that belief actually meant in practice, particularly when dealing with God's involvement with, and reconciling judgment of, his creation and his people. Thus, out of a much larger and highly complex set of speculations about the action of Israel's God through various mediator-figures, one possible scenario that some second-Temple Jews regarded as at least thinkable was that the earthly and military victory of the Messiah over the pagans would be seen in terms of the enthronement-scene from Daniel 7, itself a development of the chariot-vision in Ezekiel 1.

We must tune our modern ears to hear overtones like this when reading Jesus' answer to Caiaphas. The high priest has asked him about the accusations that he had been threatening to destroy the Temple and build another one; as we have seen, this is almost certainly what Jesus' Temple-action implied, and the warnings in Mark 13 and parallels, coupled with the cryptic saying in John 2.19, point in the same direction. Modern ears may fail to pick up the massive significance of this. But a glance at Acts, where the charges against Stephen and then later against Paul have to do with sedition against the Temple, tells its own story.[54] The Temple was the meeting-place of heaven and earth, guaranteeing the security and hope of Israel. What's more, the question of who held authority over the Temple (priest or king?—the high priest, or a coming Messiah?) was a live issue. The exchange is dense, heavy with multiple meanings, and must not be reduced to the flattened-out modern question of whether Jesus was 'claiming to be God'. We must allow the original context to reshape our questions and understanding.

> Again the high priest asked him, 'Are you the Messiah, the Son of the Blessed One?'
> 'I am,' said Jesus. 'And you will see the Son of Man sitting at the right hand of the Mighty One and coming on the clouds of heaven.'
> The high priest tore his clothes. 'Why do we need any more witnesses?' he asked. 'You have heard the blasphemy. What do you think?'
> They all condemned him as worthy of death.[55]

---

53 bHag. 14a; bSanh. 38b.
54 Ac. 6.14; 7.48–53; 21.28; 25.8.
55 Mk. 14.61–64.

JESUS' 'SON OF MAN' LANGUAGE COMPARED WITH VOICES FROM THE OLD TESTAMENT

Jesus at his trial	Daniel and the Psalmist
Again the high priest asked him, 'Are you the Messiah, the Son of the Blessed One?' 'I am,' said Jesus. 'And you will see **the Son of Man** <u>sitting at the right hand</u> of the Mighty One and **coming on the clouds of heaven**.' (Mk. 14.61–62)	In my vision at night I looked, and there before me was one like a **son of man**, **coming with the clouds of heaven**. (Dan. 7.13)
	The Lord says to my lord: '<u>Sit at my right hand</u> until I make your enemies a footstool for your feet.' (Ps. 110.1)

The whole trial-scene in the gospels is, not unnaturally, a morass of textual, historical, and theological issues.[56] Suffice it to say here that one plausible way of reading the exchange goes like this. Rumours have circulated about Jesus' words of warning against the Temple. It is quite plausible that, at his trial, Jesus was asked point blank by the high priest if these rumours were true. Was he really making such seditious statements, apparently attacking God himself by attacking his house? If so, was he claiming to be Messiah? Jesus answers with an affirmative, 'I am.' However, the charge of blasphemy does not come (as some have supposed) from Jesus pronouncing the divine name, the Tetragrammaton 'YHWH', when he says, 'I am.' More probably it comes from the larger context of Temple-subversion, and, in that context, his conflation of Psalm 110.1 and Daniel 7.13. All this implied that with the forthcoming destruction of the Temple Jesus himself would take its place. He was not only claiming *authority over* the Temple, the place where God and his people met. He was claiming that he himself was now that place. He was about to be enthroned alongside the one God. Matthew and Luke both add, to the crucial saying, phrases which mean 'from now on': Jesus' enthronement will happen more or less at once. In Matthew's account of the resurrection, the risen Jesus then declares that it has now happened. Daniel 7.14 has been fulfilled. All authority in heaven and on earth *has already been given to him*.[57]

In his reply to Caiaphas, then, Jesus was clearly identifying himself with the enthroned figure of Daniel 7.13–14 (see text grid: 'Jesus' "son of man" language compared with voices from the Old Testament'). This was and is an astounding

---

56 See Bird 2009b, 136–40.
57 Mt. 26.64; Lk. 22.69; Mt. 28.18. This is how matters were viewed in the very early church, as witnessed e.g. in the apparently creedal statement of Rom. 1.3–5: the resurrection demonstrates that Jesus is enthroned as lord of the world.

claim; we have no example of any other person from the first century saying such a thing. We have to remember that the whole point of Daniel 7 is that when God acted in history to deliver his people, the agent through whom he acted would be vindicated, honoured, enthroned, and exalted in an unprecedented manner.[58] Jesus' claim was not that he was going to sit on his own smaller throne next to God, but rather that he would share the judgment seat of God himself. If Jesus thought that Daniel 7.13–14 was about him, then Jesus was placing himself, as a human being, Israel's representative, within the orbit of divine sovereignty, claiming a place within the divine regency of 'God Almighty'. That is certainly how several early Christian traditions understood the matter.

Jesus as God: postscript

Obviously a lot more could be said for Jesus' self-understanding as 'divine'. We have glanced at his sense of unmediated divine authority, at his implicit understanding that he was in some sense the personal replacement for the Temple.[59] Taking all this together, we could say that Luke seems to have got it right: Jesus' last great journey to Jerusalem was indeed intended to symbolize and embody the long-awaited return of YHWH to Zion. This journey, climaxing in his actions in the Temple and the upper room, and undertaken in full recognition of the likely consequences, was intended to function like Ezekiel lying on his side, or Jeremiah smashing his pot. The prophetic action *embodied* the reality. Jesus was not content to *announce* that YHWH was returning to Zion. He intended to enact, symbolize, and personify that climactic event. And he believed and said in appropriately coded biblical language that he would be vindicated, that he would share the throne of Israel's God.

What might it mean, then, to say that Jesus 'knew' he was God? On the one hand, Jesus knew Israel's God as his own father. He prayed to him, and served him as a faithful son over the course of his life. Yet Jesus also seems to have known that what he was doing was what, in scripture, YHWH had promised to do. In Jesus we see the biblical portrait of YHWH come to life: the creator God who defeats the power of stormy waters, the loving God who rolls up his sleeves to do in person the job that no-one else could do, forgiving sins, renewing the covenant, shepherding the people, defeating the satan, and dwelling in the midst of his people. One could always step back and suggest that all this was a construct of the evangelists or their sources. But historically the convergence of evidence, including in the already rich reflection of Paul, forces us back to a great, hitherto unimagined, historical event and indeed historical person. Jesus, we may say, embodied, and intended to embody, Israel's God. He performed, and intended to perform, the things which YHWH had

---

58 Wright *JVG*, 624.
59 See Wright *JVG*, 629–31; Perrin 2010.

said he would do: 'He will feed his flock like a shepherd, he will gather the lambs in his arms... and gently lead those that are with young.'[60] This is the Old Testament portrait of YHWH, but it fits Jesus like a glove.[61]

If so, Jesus did not 'know' he was God in the same sense that one knows one is hungry or thirsty, or in the sense that he knew he was middle-eastern and Jewish. It was not a mathematical knowledge, like knowing that two and two make four; nor was it straightforwardly observational knowledge, like knowing that there is a bird on the fence outside my room because I can see and hear it. It was more like the knowledge that I am loved by my family; like the knowledge of a musician not only of what the composer intended but of how precisely to perform the piece in exactly that way—a knowledge most securely possessed, of course, when the performer is also the composer. It was, in short, the knowledge that characterizes *vocation*.

If that is the case, then, forget the 'titles' of Jesus, at least for a moment; forget the attempts of some well-meaning Christians to make Jesus of Nazareth conscious of being the second person of the Trinity; forget the arid reductionism that some earnest liberal theologians have produced by way of reaction. Focus, instead, on a young Jewish prophet telling a story about YHWH returning to Zion as judge and redeemer, and then embodying it by riding into the city in tears, symbolizing the Temple's destruction and celebrating the final exodus. We are proposing, as a matter of history, that Jesus of Nazareth was conscious of a vocation: a vocation, given him by the one he knew as 'father', to enact in himself what, in Israel's scriptures, God had promised to accomplish all by himself. He would be the pillar of cloud and fire for the people of the new exodus. He would embody in himself the returning and redeeming action of the covenant God.

Further reading

Bird, Michael F. 2009. *Are You the One Who Is to Come? The Historical Jesus and the Messianic Question*. Grand Rapids, MI: Baker.

———. 2014. 'Did Jesus Think He was God?' In *How God Became Jesus: The Real Origins of Belief in Jesus' Divine Nature—A Response to Bart Ehrman*. Grand Rapids, MI: Zondervan, pp. 45–70.

Perkins, Pheme. 2011. *Understanding Jesus Today*. Cambridge: Cambridge University Press.

Witherington, Ben. 1990. *The Christology of Jesus*. Minneapolis: Fortress.

Wright, N. T. 1996. *Jesus and the Victory of God*. COQG 2; London: SPCK, pp. 477–39, 612–53.

———. 1999. *The Challenge of Jesus: Rediscovering Who Jesus Was and Is*. London: SPCK, pp. 70–93.

---

60 Isa. 40.11 RSV.
61 See now esp. Hays 2017.

11

The Death of the Messiah

CHAPTER AT A GLANCE

This chapter explains Jesus' death as the climax to his ministry, discussing the historical reasons for his arrest and execution, the significance of the 'Last Supper', the Passion predictions, and Jesus' deliberate identification as the Isaianic Servant.

By the end of this chapter you should be able to:

- understand the charges against Jesus at his trial;
- appreciate the meaning that Jesus assigned to his forthcoming death at the 'Last Supper' as a redemptive and covenant-making act;
- grasp how Jesus identified himself with the Suffering Servant of Isaiah;
- understand how Jesus saw his death as part of a divine victory over evil.

Somehow, Jesus's death was seen by Jesus himself, and then by those who told and ultimately wrote his story, as the ultimate means by which God's kingdom was established. The crucifixion was the shocking answer to the prayer that God's kingdom would come on earth as in heaven. It was the ultimate Exodus event through which the tyrant was defeated, God's people were set free and given their fresh vocation, and God's presence was established in their midst in a completely new way for which the Temple itself was just an advance pointer.[1]

WHY DID JESUS DIE?

Crucifixion was a brutal and barbaric form of execution. If you had ever seen a crucifixion (and they were common in places like Judea and Galilee), the experience would have been terrifying. It would leave you with irrepressible memories of naked half-dead men dying a protracted death for days on end, covered in blood and flies, their flesh gnawed at by rats, their members ripped at by wild dogs, their faces pecked by crows, the victims mocked and jeered by sadistic torturers and other bystanders, while relatives nearby, weeping uncontrollably, would be helpless to do anything for them.

If there is one thing we can be certain of about Jesus, it is that he was crucified. However, despite all we know

---

[1] Wright *SJ*, 181–2.

of crucifixion, the evangelists do not treat Jesus' shameful execution as a tragic end to his otherwise fruitful ministry, but as part of his messianic vocation, something Jesus himself deliberately embraced to usher in God's kingdom. This compels the historian, as well as the theologian, to ask: what was Jesus intending? Why and how did his vision of God's coming kingdom on earth as in heaven include his own horrible death?

There are natural starting-points for this investigation. We know of other ancient persons who lived within a century of Jesus and who went to their deaths believing that they died for a particular cause, for some grand purpose. There are the (very different) cases of the Roman aristocrat Seneca (d. AD 65), the Jewish revolutionary Eleazar (d. *c.* AD 73), and the Christian bishop Ignatius (d. *c.* AD 115).[2] But what about Jesus? Did Jesus intend to die in something like the manner he did? If so, why?

Of all the questions regularly asked about Jesus, the question 'Why did Jesus die?' must be among the most frequent. It is certainly the most fascinating, and also among the most frustrating. It has all the ingredients of a classic: dense and complex sources; the confluence of two great cultures (Jewish and Roman) in a single, swirling drama; characters who still leap off the page despite the gap of two millennia; tragedies, and tragic ironies, both small and great; gathering storm-clouds of philosophy and theology; and, at the centre, a towering but enigmatic figure, who, if the sources are to be believed, had the capacity to evoke anger and admiration in full measure.

---

[2] See Wright *JVG*, 106.

WHERE WAS GOLGOTHA?

The gospels report that Jesus was crucified at Golgotha, called 'the place of the skull' (Mt. 27.33/Mk. 15.22/Jn. 19.17). The Church of the Holy Sepulchre is regarded as the traditional site of Jesus' crucifixion and burial, though some have tried to argue for the Garden Tomb as the original location. The scholarly consensus tends to support the traditional site of Golgotha in the vicinity of the Church of the Holy Sepulchre. In one of the most recent studies of the subject, Joan Taylor (1998) has concluded that Jesus was executed just to the south of the present-day church:

> 'Golgotha was an oval-shaped disused quarry located west of the second wall, north of the first wall. It was an area of an old quarry, seeming much like an elongated crater in appearance. Jesus was crucified in the southern part of this area, just outside Gennath Gate, and near to the road going west, but visible also from the road north. He was buried some 200 m (656 ft) away to the north, in a quieter part of Golgotha where there were tombs and gardens. The tombs of this region were emptied when the region was included within the city in AD 41–44, but the garden probably remained. Christians in the city may have visited the site and recalled events there in various ways . . . For those who are interested in the precise location of the proposed site of the crucifixion in today's Old City, the spot . . . is a little to the southwest of where David Street meets Habad Street, but north of St Mark Street. As the Decumanus is plotted with greater certainty, and excavations take place in this area, the localization may become more accurate.'

The Death of the Messiah

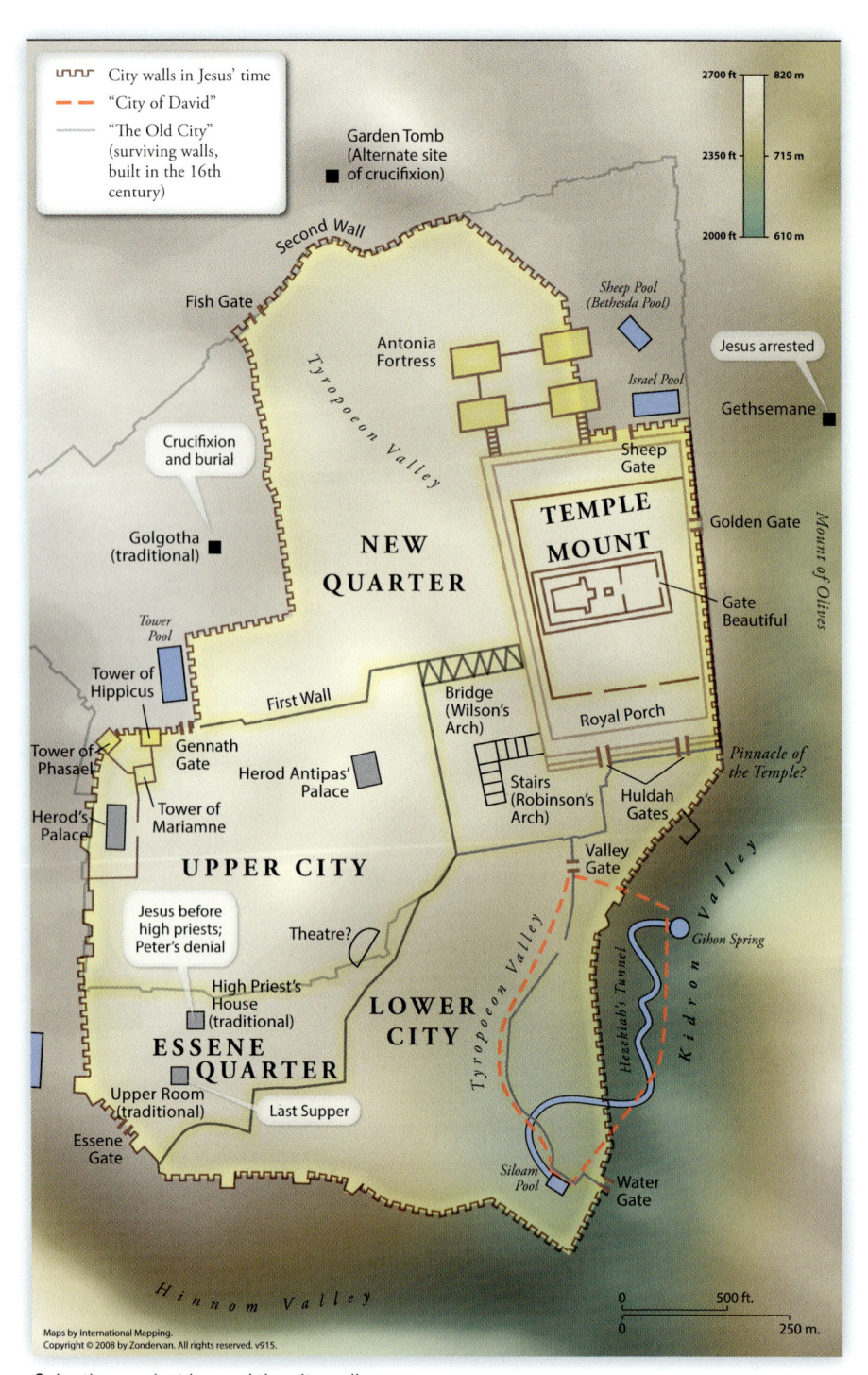

Golgotha was just beyond the city walls.

244　Jesus and the Victory of God

Small wonder that not only historians and theologians, but also artists and musicians, have returned to the subject times without number.

So 'Why did Jesus die?' The question 'why' invites different kinds of answers. Many Christians will naturally opt for a theological answer, following Paul's statement of the gospel in 1 Corinthians 15.3: 'for our sins'. But the New Testament, and especially the four gospels, refuse to get to that answer without also addressing the question historically. Why did the Judean leadership ask the Roman governor to execute Jesus? Why did the governor, Pontius Pilate, agree to their request? And was Jesus then caught in a trap by mistake, or did he—as all the gospels affirm—somehow intend this consequence? How would that relate to, or even (as the texts assert) form the climax of, his public career of launching God's kingdom on earth as in heaven?

THE CHARGES

Crucifixion was a powerful symbol throughout the Roman world. It was not just a means of liquidating undesirables; it did so with maximum degradation and humiliation. It said, loud and clear: we are in charge here; you are our property; we can do what we like with you. It insisted, coldly and brutally, on the absolute sovereignty of Rome, and of Caesar. It told an implicit story, of the uselessness of rebel recalcitrance and the ruthlessness of imperial power. It said in particular: this is what happens to rebel leaders. Crucifixion was a symbolic act with a clear and frightening meaning.[3]

Jesus was executed as a rebel against Rome. This causes an immediate historical problem: Jesus' accusers handed him over, and Pilate duly executed him, on the charge of sedition, but it seems clear that both parties knew he was not really guilty of it, or not in any straightforward sense. People have sometimes tried to argue that Jesus was some kind of a 'zealot', advocating violent revolution, but a close reading of the gospels and a study of the political ethos of the early church shows that the argument will not work.[4] True, Jesus' kingdom-preaching must have been heard by many to carry some sort of revolutionary sense. If YHWH really was becoming king at last, all other rulers, from Caesar downwards, would find their power severely relativized. But Jesus' constant redefinition of the kingdom, in praxis as much as in words, meant that anyone who had observed him closely would have known that he did not fit the same category as rebel leaders like Judas the Galilean before him, or Simon bar-Giora two generations later. How much homework on Jesus had been done by those who served the chief priests and Pilate we cannot be sure, though Roman governors normally had very good networks of spies and informers. The chances are they all knew he posed no normal kind of military or revolutionary threat.

---
3 On crucifixion in the ancient world, see Hengel 1977; Chapman 2010; Samuelsson 2011; Cook 2014.
4 See the latest incarnation of the 'Jesus the zealot' theory in Aslan 2013 and a critique of such theories in Bird 2006d.

Found in the Christian quarter of the Old City is the Church of the Holy Sepulchre, located on the traditional site of Jesus' crucifixion and burial. The Church was built in AD 330 by Constantine, though it has been renovated several times since then. Found inside the church is a rocky outcrop that was part of a landscape outside the original walls of Jerusalem. It has been a pilgrimage site since the fourth century.
dominika zarzycka / Shutterstock

Some scholars, knowing that Pilate was not particularly competent or distinguished at his job, and that his rule was marked by provocation and corruption, have argued that the gospel picture of him as a confused and concerned Roman official, trying feebly to get Jesus off though not ultimately caring much about his fate, is the result of the writers' desire to lay the blame for Jesus' death on his Jewish contemporaries. But if the evangelists *were* trying to make Pilate out to be anything other than weak, vacillating, bullying, and caught between two pressing agendas, neither of which had anything to do with truth or justice, they did a pretty poor job of it. The later Christian adoption of Pilate as a hero, or even a saint, is miles away from his characterization in the gospels: the famous scene of him washing his hands must surely be read, both within history and within Matthean redaction, as merely the high-point of his cynicism. He was the governor; he was responsible for Jesus' death; washing his hands was an empty, contemptuous symbol, pretending he could evade responsibility for something that lay completely within his power. What emerges from the records is not that Pilate wanted to rescue Jesus because he thought he was good, noble, holy, or just, but that Pilate wanted to do the opposite of what the chief priests wanted him to do because he always wanted to do the opposite of what the chief priests wanted him to do. That was his regular and settled way of doing business.[5]

Pilate, then, must have recognized that Jesus was not the ordinary sort of revolutionary leader, a *lēstēs* or 'brigand'. If he was a would-be Messiah, he was a highly unusual one. Pilate must therefore have realized that the Jewish leaders had their own reasons for wanting Jesus executed, and were using the charge of sedition as a convenient excuse. This gave him the opening to do what he would normally be expected to do, which was to refuse their request; he tried this, but failed. He failed, because it was pointed out to him in no uncertain terms that if he did not execute a would-be rebel king he would stand accused, himself, of disloyalty to Caesar.[6] Historically, emotionally, and politically this sequence makes perfect sense. In terms of the Roman authorities, the answer to the question 'Why did Jesus die?' is that Pilate not only put cynical power-games before justice, but also, on this occasion, put naked self-interest before both.

Matthias Grünewald, *Crucifixion*, 1515, Isenheim altarpiece
Public Domain

---

5   As in the matter of the titulus on the cross, see Jn. 19.21–22.
6   See 'If you let this man go, you are no friend of Caesar. Anyone who claims to be a king opposes Caesar' (Jn. 19.12). One only has to read the account of Tiberius's 'reign of terror' in Tacitus (*Ann.* 5—6) to understand Pilate's nervousness.

But why did the Judean leadership, the priestly aristocracy, request that Pilate inflict the death penalty on Jesus in the first place? (As all the sources agree, the Romans did not allow subject peoples the right to use the death penalty.) One immediate answer comes to us from a Jewish tradition preserved in the Babylonian Talmud about Jesus' execution:

> Jesus was hanged on the eve of Passover. The herald went before him for forty days, saying, 'He is going forth to be stoned because he practised sorcery and enticed and led Israel astray. Let everyone knowing anything in his defence come and plead for him.' But nothing was found in his defence, so he was hanged on the eve of Passover.[7]

But in what ways did they think Jesus was 'leading the people astray'? The charge goes back to the times during Jesus' public career when he was accused of being in league with the satan—a charge impossible to imagine being invented by the early church.[8] Such a charge was an obvious way of reacting to powerful and surprising actions (Jesus' miracles) for which there was no other explanation open to people committed to rejecting Jesus' message. Scripture provided a category for such people; they had been warned.[9] But if someone appeared doing signs and wonders but teaching something strange, something which opponents could suspect of compromising Israel's worship, then such a person was 'leading Israel astray' and had to be utterly rejected. The combined impression of Jesus' public actions and teachings, leading eventually to his action in the Temple, will have created in some suspicious minds just this impression. It would not be difficult to present him as someone speaking and acting in opposition to Torah and Temple, and leading others, by word, example, and 'works of power', to do the same. What could he be, in their eyes, if not a false prophet, performing signs and wonders to lead Israel astray?

So we should not reduce the motivation of the Judean leaders simply to the cynical and political. Serious Jewish observers might well have concluded that Jesus was misleading the people in terms of the agendas, and Torah-interpretations, current at the time. Precisely because he would not endorse, but rather opposed, the movement of national resistance, the (Shammaite) majority of Pharisees would find him deeply unsatisfactory. Precisely because he was 'stirring up the people', creating an excitement wherever he went in a highly volatile social and political setting, the chief priests and Sadducees were bound to see him, like his late cousin John, as a troublemaker.

All this clarifies the hearing before Caiaphas still further. The surface text was

---
[7] bSanh. 43a.
[8] e.g. Mt. 12.24.
[9] See Mt. 11.19 with Dt. 21.20; and the whole of Dt. 13.

the framing of a charge which would stick before Pilate, who would not care a fig about someone 'leading Israel astray', but who would care about someone leading a rebel movement against Rome. The subtext, however, was the determination on the part of the court to find Jesus guilty of a crime in Jewish law. Many among the general populace were undoubtedly hoping that Jesus would be the sort of Messiah whom Pilate, if he caught him, would have to execute—the sort who, like Barabbas, would lead a violent revolution in the city.[10] If the Jewish leaders had found Jesus guilty of being a revolutionary Messiah, and had handed him over to Pilate on that charge, they might well have precipitated the riot they were anxious to avoid.[11] But if they were able to claim that he was guilty of a well-known capital crime in Jewish law, they might win the people over. John's account of their anxiety bears all the hallmarks of realism as to what were their likely motivations:

> Then the chief priests and the Pharisees called a meeting of the Sanhedrin. 'What are we accomplishing?' they asked. 'Here is this man performing many signs. If we let him go on like this, everyone will believe in him, and then the Romans will come and take away both our temple and our nation.'[12]

Jesus must be eliminated because he is performing signs; people will be led away after him; the Temple and their national life are at risk.

In terms of the Jewish authorities, then, the question 'Why did Jesus die?' evokes a fivefold answer. He was sent to the Roman governor on a capital charge:

1. because many saw him as 'a false prophet, leading Israel astray';
2. because, as one aspect of this, they saw his Temple-action as a blow against the central symbol not only of national life but also of YHWH's presence with his people and promises for their deliverance;
3. because, though he was clearly not leading a real or organized military revolt, he saw himself as in some sense Messiah, and could thus become a focus of serious revolutionary activity;
4. because, as the pragmatic focus of these three points, they saw him as a dangerous political nuisance, whose actions might well call down the wrath of Rome upon Temple and nation alike;
5. because, at the crucial moment in the hearing, he not only pleaded guilty to the above charges, but also did so in such a way as to place himself, blasphemously, alongside the God of Israel.

---

10 See Lk. 23.19, which reads like a sentence from Josephus: Barabbas had committed *phonos* (murder) during a *stasis* (uprising) in the *polis* (city).
11 See Mt. 26.5/Mk. 14.2; Lk. 22.2; Jn. 11.47–53.
12 Jn. 11.47–48.

EMAILS
from the edge

From: Alan_Daley@aol.com
To: Professor Dana Schuler
Date: Thur, 8 Jan 2015 at 8:23 p.m.
Subject: Last Supper date

Dear Prof.,

Sorry for bothering you over the break. But I'm totally confused about the date of the Last Supper. It looks like Matthew, Mark, and Luke all have Jesus and his crew eating a proper Passover meal at Passover, while John (the crazy cat) has Jesus crucified on the eve of Passover. Can you shed any light on this for me?

Pax 2 da Max
AD

From: Professor Dana Schuler
To: Alan_Daley@aol.com
Date: Fri, 9 Jan 2015 at 9:05 a.m.
Subject: Re: Last Supper date

Dear Alan,

You have a knack for picking some juicy topics to get stuck on. This one in particular is notorious.

If you read the synoptic gospels, they make it clear that this is a Passover meal (see Mt. 26.17/Mk. 14.12/Lk. 22.7), whereas John is equally clear that Jesus died on the Day of Preparation ahead of Passover (see Jn. 13.1; 18.28; 19.14, 31) and John's account finds agreement with the remark in the Babylonian Talmud that Jesus was executed 'on the eve of the Passover' (bSanh. 43a). Various attempts have been made to resolve this problem. Jesus may have been following a rival calendar (perhaps Essene). Or perhaps John has altered the chronology to make the theological point that Jesus is the true Passover lamb, slaughtered at the same time as the lambs

> were being killed in the Temple in preparation for the evening meal (see Jn. 1.29, 36; 19.36). Or the synoptists have turned the meal into a Passover meal in obedience to *their* theology or tradition, etc.
>
> It seems to me virtually certain that the meal in question was *some kind of* Passover meal. Several almost incidental details point this way. It was eaten at night, and in Jerusalem; Jesus and his followers normally returned to Bethany for the night, but Passover meals had to be eaten within the city limits, and after dark. The meal ended with a hymn, presumably the Hallel psalms sung at the end of the Passover meal. At the same time, Jesus might have celebrated what we might call a *quasi*-Passover meal a day ahead of the real thing, especially if he thought he would not live long enough to see Passover. This, of course, would have meant doing without a lamb (since the priests would not be killing them for Passover until the following day); that would be no bar to treating the meal as a proper Passover, since it was after all what happened in the Diaspora (and, of course, what was to happen throughout the Jewish world after AD 70).
>
> The grace be with you
> Prof. Dana Schuler

But what about Jesus himself? Was he simply, as some have suggested, a brash and hotheaded prophet who messed with powers beyond his ken? Could Jesus have been a victim of unfortunate circumstances by doing the wrong thing, in the wrong place, at the wrong time?[13] Did he go to the cross kicking and screaming 'I'm innocent—let me go!' Or did Jesus foresee his own death in Jerusalem, and believe that it was a vital part of God's coming kingdom, the event that would crown his life's work and bring about the end of exile, the launch of a new exodus, the defeat of the satan, the real restoration of Israel, and healing for the nations?

LAST SUPPER

The obvious place to look for insight into what Jesus thought about his forthcoming death is what has come to be called the 'Last Supper'.[14] On the night before his crucifixion, Jesus shared a meal with his closest disciples, a Passover meal of a sort (see 'Emails from the edge: Last Supper date'). This meal was a deliberate double-drama.

---

[13] Vermes 1993, x.
[14] Mk. 14.12–31 and par.; 1 Cor. 11.23–26.

As a Passover meal, it told the story of Jewish history in terms of divine deliverance from tyranny, looking back to the exodus from Egypt and looking on to the new exodus, the still-awaited return from exile. But Jesus' meal fused this great story together with another one: the story of Jesus himself, his own life, and his coming death. It somehow involved him in the God-given drama, not as a spectator, or as one participant among many, but as the central character.

Jesus clearly intended his final meal with his disciples to carry deep significance; if his earlier celebrations with 'tax-collectors and sinners' were signs of the kingdom, how much more this one. When Jesus wanted to fully explain what his forthcoming death was all about, in other words, he didn't give his followers a theory of the atonement.

JESUS' WORDS AT THE LAST SUPPER

Matthew	Mark	Luke	Paul
[26] While they were eating, Jesus took bread, and when he had given thanks, he broke it and gave it to his disciples, saying, **'Take and eat; this is my body.'** [27] Then he took a cup, and when he had given thanks, he gave it to them, saying, **'Drink from it, all of you.** [28] **This is my blood of the covenant, which is poured out for many for the forgiveness of sins.** [29] **I tell you, I will not drink from this fruit of the vine from now on until that day when I drink it new with you in my Father's kingdom.'** (Mt. 26.26–29)	[22] While they were eating, Jesus took bread, and when he had given thanks, he broke it and gave it to his disciples, saying, **'Take it; this is my body.'** [23] Then he took a cup, and when he had given thanks, he gave it to them, and they all drank from it. [24] **'This is my blood of the covenant, which is poured out for many,'** he said to them. [25] **'Truly I tell you, I will not drink again from the fruit of the vine until that day when I drink it new in the kingdom of God.'** (Mk. 14.22–25)	[15] And he said to them, **'I have eagerly desired to eat this Passover with you before I suffer.** [16] **For I tell you, I will not eat it again until it finds fulfilment in the kingdom of God.'** [17] After taking the cup, he gave thanks and said, **'Take this and divide it among you.** [18] **For I tell you I will not drink again from the fruit of the vine until the kingdom of God comes.'** [19] And he took bread, gave thanks and broke it, and gave it to them, saying, **'This is my body given for you; do this in remembrance of me.'** [20] In the same way, after the supper he took the cup, saying, **'This cup is the new covenant in my blood, which is poured out for you.'** (Lk. 22.15–20)	[23] For I received from the Lord what I also passed on to you: the Lord Jesus, on the night he was betrayed, took bread, [24] and when he had given thanks, he broke it and said, **'This is my body, which is for you; do this in remembrance of me.'** [25] In the same way, after supper he took the cup, saying, **'This cup is the new covenant in my blood; do this, whenever you drink it, in remembrance of me.'** [26] For whenever you eat this bread and drink this cup, you proclaim the Lord's death until he comes. (1 Cor. 11.23–26)

252   Jesus and the Victory of God

He didn't give them a sermon, a lecture, or even a set of scriptural texts. He gave them a meal. This meal would interpret and explain not only his death but also his entire vocation.

We should note, first, that this meal, like all Jewish Passover meals, celebrated the exodus, Israel's liberation from slavery in Egypt. To a first-century Jew, it also pointed ahead to the return from exile, the new exodus, the great covenant renewal spoken of by the prophets. The meal symbolized 'forgiveness of sins', YHWH's return to redeem his people, his victory over Pharaohs both literal and metaphorical. It took place 'in accordance with the scriptures', locating itself within the ongoing story of YHWH's strange saving purposes for Israel as those purposes reached their climax. This was the meal, in other words, which said that Israel's God was about to become king. All this is not, actually, controversial. Second, though, and more telling, the meal brought Jesus' own kingdom-movement to its climax. It indicated that the new exodus, and all that it meant, was happening in and through Jesus himself.

The Last Supper, an illuminated page from the Book of Hours, with the Hours of the Virgin, the Short Hours of the Holy Cross, Prayers and Suffrages, Netherlands, dated 1420.
© British Library Board. All Rights Reserved / Bridgeman Images

Jesus' last supper with his disciples was thus full of prophetic symbolism. It was the natural sequel to his previous great prophetic act, the demonstration in the Temple. If Jesus believed that the Temple was corrupt, that it would soon be destroyed by God, and that its sacrificial system was coming to an end, then (as many have seen, including some Jewish scholars) he may well have understood his own commemorative meal as at least pointing to an alternative. If, as we have argued, Jesus had after all seen himself as Messiah, the builder of God's Temple, the focal point of the great divine act of liberation, then the symbols which ordered Israel's life and hope would now focus back upon him. The final meal which he celebrated with his followers was not, in that sense, free-standing. It gained its significance from his own entire life and agenda, and from the events which, he knew, would shortly come to pass. It was Jesus' chosen way of investing those imminent events with the significance he believed they would carry. This—strangely then, and if anything even more strangely now—was how the kingdom would come on earth as in heaven.

The words of Jesus at the supper, the so-called 'words of institution', show that Jesus, in prophetic style, identified the bread with his own body, and the wine with his own blood, and that he spoke about these in language which echoed the context of Passover, sacrifice, and covenant, and applied it to his forthcoming death (see text grid: 'Jesus' words at the Last Supper'). Especially notable are Jesus' words about the cup which identify its content, in obviously symbolic fashion, with his own blood. The four accounts appear to emphasize that Jesus' coming death would effect the renewal of the covenant, that is, the great return from exile for which Israel had longed. The phrase 'the blood of the covenant', which occurs in some form in all the accounts, arguably echoes the story in which Moses established the first covenant with the people at Mount Sinai. It may perhaps also evoke the scene from Zechariah where the covenant is renewed in the context of the messianic victory, which will liberate Israel once and for all from its long exile.[15]

> 'The final saying of Jesus over the cup [Mk. 14.25] echoes words used in the Passover liturgy, where God is blessed as the one who "creates **the fruit of the vine**". It also points forward to the time when Jesus will **drink** wine **new in the Kingdom of God**. The image is that of the messianic banquet, which symbolized the joy that was expected to accompany the new age (see e.g. Isa. 25.6; 2 Baruch 29.5–8; Matt. 8.11; Luke 14.15; Rev. 19.9). Here is yet another tradition about the significance of the cup, and one that may well be the earliest of all.'
>
> Morna Hooker, *The Gospel According to Saint Mark*, 343.

All three synoptic accounts contain a further explanation: Jesus' blood will be shed 'on behalf of the many' (Luke has 'on behalf of you'). To this, Matthew has added 'for the forgiveness of sins'.[16] When situated in its first-century Jewish context, this denotes, not an abstract transaction between human beings and their God, but the very concrete expectation of Israel, namely that the nation would at last be rescued from the 'exile' which had come about because of its sins.[17] Matthew was not suggesting that Jesus' death would accomplish an abstract 'atonement'. He is stressing that it would be the means of rescuing YHWH's people from their exilic plight. These words once more bring the meal's symbolic significance into clear expression.

Luke and Paul both include a command that the meal be repeated, and that this repetition be undertaken as a way of remembering Jesus himself.[18] Such a command again makes explicit what is in any case implicit in the meal's symbolism. If Jesus was about to perform the great messianic action, and if his last meal with his followers would function in relation to that action as Passover functioned in relation

---

15 Ex. 24.6–8; Zech. 9.9–11.
16 Mt. 26.28.
17 On 'forgiveness' and 'return from exile', see Jer. 31.31–34.
18 Lk. 22.19; 1 Cor. 11.24–25.

to the exodus from Egypt, then of course the meal would include the prayer that this messianic action would be successfully accomplished; and of course, as the meal was repeated by Jesus' followers, it would be done not with an eye to YHWH sending the Messiah at last—he had already done that—but with an eye to his remembering the messianic act which Jesus had already accomplished. All this, again, makes sense only once one allows that Jesus really did suppose that he was about to die, and that this was part of the eschatological plan for the fulfilment of YHWH's kingdom-purposes. Jesus' symbolic action deliberately evoked the whole exodus tradition and gave it a new direction. Jesus intended to say, with all the power of symbolic drama and narrative, not only that he was shortly to die but also that his death was to be seen within the context of the larger story of YHWH's redemption of Israel. More specifically, he intended that his death be seen as the central and climactic moment towards which that story had been moving, and for which the events of the exodus were the crucial and determining backdrop; and that those who shared the meal, not only then but subsequently, were the people of the renewed covenant, the people who received 'the forgiveness of sins', that is, the end of exile.

The meal thus gives us an insight, as well, into how Jesus viewed his immediate circle of followers. His disciples, grouped around him, constituted the nucleus of the renewed Israel of the coming age. Part of the point of the meal was that Jesus's followers would now be able to share in its benefits, by sharing, in a new way, in his own life. The gifts of bread and wine, already heavy with symbolic meaning, now acquired a new density: this was how the presence of Jesus was to be known among his followers: sacrifice and presence. This was the new Temple, this strange gathering around a quasi-Passover table. The meal was a way of reminding them that the tyrant had been defeated—the tyrant not being Rome, but the dark power that stood behind the great, cruel empire. God's people were to be liberated, but this 'people' would not now be Israel as it stood, with its corrupt, money-hungry leaders and its mobs bent on violence. It would be the reconstituted Israel for whom the Twelve were now the founding symbol.

Medieval representation of the Last Supper showing the elements of the meal by Jaume Huguet, fifteenth century, Museu Nacional d'Art de Catalunya, Barcelona, Spain.
Heritage Image Partnership Ltd / Alamy Stock Photo

In sum, Jesus knew he was going to die, but he believed he would die as a Passover lamb. He believed that his broken body and his shed blood would bring forgiveness, that his death would turn away God's wrath, and that the whole event, liberating God's people, would usher in the new covenant and the new creation. This is not something which emerges simply out of the Passion story itself. It can be detected in several sayings which Jesus uttered about his approaching death, which make up the other vital pieces of the puzzle as to what Jesus believed as he approached his horrible fate.

RIDDLES OF THE CROSS

What Jesus believed about his fate, and how it related to the arrival of the kingdom of God, becomes evident through several stories, sayings, or what we might even call 'riddles'.

The various 'Passion predictions' should not be dismissed (as many have done) as *ex eventu* prophecies of Jesus' death, projected back into Jesus' life as an apologetic device. The material is too widely attested, and too prevalent across the various traditions, to represent a later Christian invention.[19] Neither are these predictions the melancholic musings of a man with a martyr complex. Rather, they represent the realistic reflection of someone proclaiming God's kingdom, challenging Israel's official (Sadducean) and unofficial (Pharisaic) leaders, attracting crowds, exciting eschatological fervour, imbibing messianic dreams, challenging boundaries about who is 'in', and making a powerful protest in the Temple which appears to be a symbolic foretelling of its downfall. (There are curious modern parallels. The Pakistani minister for minorities, Shahbaz Bhatti, himself a Catholic Christian, never married because he 'knew' that one day he would be killed by Islamic extremists. This belief came true on 2 March 2011, when he was ambushed by militants.) Jesus knew what risks he was taking, what opposition he would face, and how the story was going to end. The difference in his case is that he had already interpreted his forthcoming death in terms of the one-off unique kingdom-bringing event.

Sometimes, then, Jesus made explicit statements about the rejection and death that awaited him in Jerusalem, words which met with confusion, disbelief, and even rebuke by his disciples.[20] At other times, Jesus made cryptic statements about a bridegroom being taken away,[21] about a prophet not dying except in Jerusalem,[22] about a coming time when the disciples would have to fend for themselves in his absence.[23]

---

19 See Wright *JVG*, 574–6, and Bird 2008c.
20 Mk. 8.31–9.1; Mk. 9.12; Mt. 17.22–23/Mk. 9.31/Lk. 9.44; Mt. 20.17–19/Mk. 10.32–34/Lk. 18.31–33.
21 Mt. 9.15/Mk. 2.20/Lk. 5.35.
22 Lk. 13.33.
23 Lk. 17.22; Mt. 24.9–14/Mk. 13.9–13/Lk. 21.12–19.

He would be, he said, like green wood being burnt when all around were dry sticks ready for kindling.[24] He would be like a landowner's son killed by wicked tenants.[25]

The images mount up; they also add up. They carry multiple scriptural resonances. Jesus' death would provide a 'ransom', much like that of Isaiah's 'servant'.[26] He likened himself to a hen that gathers her chicks under her wings to protect them from a barnyard fire, just as YHWH had taken Israel under the shelter of his wings.[27] He would drink from a 'cup', and undergo a 'baptism', both of which spoke scripturally of coming judgment.[28] He would be struck down like the shepherd of Zechariah.[29] All of these sayings, rooted in scripture and found in more or less all strands of tradition, portray Jesus as the one who symbolized Israel's fate in himself, who would suffer death on behalf of others, and who would turn away divine wrath so that Israel could escape the slavery of exile and be launched into the freedom of the 'new exodus'.

The striking thing to note is that these 'riddles' seem markedly different from the atonement theology of the later church. The early church was not reticent

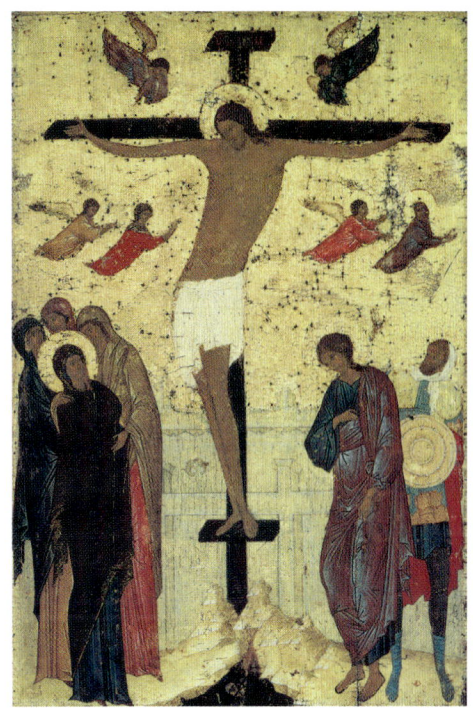

Russian icon of the crucifixion by Dionisius, 1500
PD-US

in speaking about Jesus' death, and in developing a rich, multifaceted interpretation of it as a means of atonement, a source of cleansing, and a path to reconciliation. But the first Christians had no need to use the kind of riddles we have just listed. The cross was public knowledge. It might be a scandal, but it was a nettle that Jesus' followers had grasped, not a strange fact that could be alluded to only with cryptic sayings. These riddles, then, point to what with hindsight we might call a theology of atonement, but not at all in the same way that we find such a thing in the letters

---

[24] Lk. 23.31; see Hos. 10.1–15.
[25] Mt. 21.33–46/Mk. 12.1–12/Lk. 20.9–19.
[26] Mt. 20.28/Mk. 10.45, perhaps alluding to Isa. 53.11–12. See further McKnight 2005, 159–71.
[27] Mt. 23.37–39/Lk. 13.34–35; on YHWH's 'wings' as a shelter see e.g. Dt. 32.11; Pss. 17.8; 36.7; 57.1; 63.7; 91.4; Isa 31.5.
[28] Mk. 10.38–39; on references to baptism/water/flood see e.g. Job 9.31; Pss. 18.16; 32.6; 42.7; 69.14–15; on the cup see e.g. Ps. 75.8; Ezek. 23.31–34; Zech. 12.2.
[29] Mt. 26.31/Mk. 14.27, quoting Zech. 13.7.

The Death of the Messiah

of, say, Paul, Peter, or John, or the writer of Hebrews. All the signs are that they reflect the mind, and cryptic teaching, of Jesus himself.

So how, then, did Jesus understand his death in relation to his entire kingdom-ministry?

JESUS: MESSIAH AND SERVANT

If we bring together what we have learned about the 'last supper' and these various 'riddles' about Jesus' approaching death, then, we are bound to reach the conclusion that Jesus seems to have regarded his own approaching death as being part, indeed the climax, of his vocation. Called to inaugurate God's kingdom, and to do so in and through his own presence, power, teaching, and leading, he saw this work as being accomplished through his own death. This was the point at which the fate he had announced for Israel would become the fate he himself would suffer. He had warned that Israel would be crushed by Rome. Now he went ahead to the cross, which symbolized precisely that outcome.

Jesus saw several scriptural roles and paradigms as spelling out his own vocation: Isaiah's Servant, the smitten shepherd of Zechariah, the righteous one of the Psalms, perhaps even the Maccabean martyrs. These texts contributed to a widespread belief that Israel's present state of suffering was somehow held within the ongoing divine purpose; that in due time this period of woe would come to an end, with divine wrath falling instead on the pagan nations that had oppressed Israel; that the explanation for the present state of affairs had to do with Israel's own sin, for which either the nation itself, or in some cases its righteous representatives, was or were being punished; and that this suffering and punishment would therefore, somehow, hasten the moment when Israel's tribulation would be complete, when it would finally have been purified from its sin so that its exile could be undone at last. There was, in other words, a belief, hammered out not in abstract debate but in and through poverty, exile, torture, and martyrdom, that Israel's sufferings might be, not merely a state *from* which the nation would be redeemed, but paradoxically, under certain circumstances and in certain senses, part of the means *by* which that redemption would be effected. This is the narrative in which Jesus' death should be situated and understood.

Jesus believed that Israel's history had arrived at its focal point. More specifically, he believed that the *exile* had reached its climax. He believed that he was himself the bearer of Israel's destiny at this critical time. He was the Messiah who would take that destiny on himself and draw it to its focal point. He had announced the judgment of YHWH on his recalcitrant people; now, as with the prophets of former days, they were planning to kill him. Jesus had declared that the way to the kingdom was the way of peace, the way of love, the way of the cross. Fighting the battle with the enemy's weapons meant that one had already lost it in principle and would soon lose it, and lose it terribly, in practice. Jesus determined that it was his task and role, his vocation as Israel's representative, to 'lose' the battle on Israel's behalf. This would be the means of Israel's becoming the light, not just of the nation—the Maccabean martyrs seemed only to think of Israel's liberation—but of the whole world. He would thereby do for Israel what Israel could not do for itself. He would fulfil Israel's vocation that it should be the servant-people, the light of the world.

Jesus' shocking combination of scriptural models into a single vocation makes excellent historical sense; that is, it explains at a stroke why he had to die. Jesus, having warned his people of what was to come, went to take it upon himself. His predictions of the destruction of the Temple and the city were matched, stride for stride, by his own vocation. That is part of the mystery of his crucifixion: 'wounded for our transgressions, crushed for our iniquity'.[30] He could not establish the new creation without allowing the poison in the old to have its full effect. He could not launch God's kingdom of justice, truth, and peace unless injustice, lies, and violence had done their worst and, like a hurricane, had blown themselves out, exhausting their force on this one spot. He could not begin the work of healing the world unless he provided the antidote to the infection that would otherwise destroy the project from within. This is how the early work of Jesus' public career, the healings, the celebrations, the forgiveness, the changed hearts, all look forward to this moment. This is what it looks like when Israel's God becomes king. This is what it looks like when Jesus is enthroned as king of the Jews. This is the necessary prelude to the new day in which the kingdom of God will come with power.[31]

THE VICTORY OF GOD

Jesus took his own story seriously—so seriously that, having recommended to his followers a particular way of being Israel-for-the-sake-of-the-world, he made that way thematic for his own sense of vocation, his own belief about how the kingdom would come through his own work and especially in his death. He would turn the other cheek; he would go the second mile; he would take up the cross. He would be the light of the world, the salt of the earth. He would be Israel for the sake of the world. He would be the means of the kingdom's coming, both in that he would embody in himself the renewed Israel and in that he would defeat evil once and for all. But the way in which he would defeat evil would be the way consistent with the deeply subversive nature of his own kingdom-announcement. He would defeat evil by letting it do its worst to him.

---

[30] Isa. 53.5.
[31] Mk. 9.1.

Jesus, then, went to Jerusalem not just to preach, but to die. While there, he deliberately enacted two symbols, which encapsulated his whole work and agenda. The first symbol (the Temple-demonstration) said that the present system was corrupt and recalcitrant. It was ripe for judgment. But Jesus was the Messiah, the one through whom YHWH, the God of all the world, would save Israel and thereby the world. So the second symbol (the Last Supper) said: this is how the true exodus will come about. This is how the exile will end; this is how the new exodus will be launched. This is how sins will be forgiven. This is how, in particular and at the heart of it all, evil (perhaps we should say, Evil with a capital E) will be defeated.

Jesus knew—he must have known—that these actions, and the debates which accompanied them, were very likely to get him put on trial, both as a false prophet leading Israel astray and as a would-be Messiah. Such a trial would inevitably result in his being handed over to the Romans and executed as a failed revolutionary king. This did not, actually, take a great deal of 'supernatural' insight, any more than it took much more than ordinary common sense to predict that, if Israel continued to attempt rebellion against Rome, the Romans would eventually do to it as a nation what they were now going to do to this strange would-be Messiah. But at the heart of Jesus' symbolic actions, and his retelling of Israel's story, there was a great deal more than political pragmatism, revolutionary daring, or the desire for a martyr's glory. There was a deeply theological analysis of Israel, the world, and his own role in relation to both. There was a deep sense of vocation and trust in Israel's God. There was the unshakeable belief—Gethsemane seems nearly to have shaken it, but Jesus seems to have construed that, too, as part of the point, part of the battle—that if he went this route, if he fought this battle, the long night of Israel's exile would be over at last, and the new day for Israel and the world really would dawn once and for all. He himself would be vindicated, and Israel's destiny, to save the world, would thereby be accomplished. Not only would he create a breathing space for his followers and any who would join them, by drawing on to himself for a moment the wrath of Rome and letting them escape. If he was defeating the real enemy, he was doing so on behalf of the whole world. The servant-vocation, to be the light of the world, would come true in him, and thence in the followers who would regroup after his vindication. The death of the shepherd would result in YHWH becoming king of all the earth. The vindication of the 'son of man' would see the once-for-all defeat of evil and the establishment of a worldwide kingdom.

Jesus therefore took up his own cross. He had come to see it, too, in deeply symbolic terms: symbolic, now, not merely of Roman oppression, but of the way of love and peace which he had commended so vigorously, the way of defeat which he had announced as the way of victory. Unlike his actions in the Temple and the upper room, the cross was a symbol not of praxis but of passivity, not of action but of passion. It was to become the symbol of victory, but not the victory of Caesar, nor of those who would oppose Caesar with Caesar's methods. It was to become the symbol, because it would be the means, of the victory of God.

Granted all this, it is worth highlighting how this might shape our own understanding of what it means to follow Jesus. When we speak of 'following Jesus', we are talking about the crucified Messiah. His death was not simply the messy event that enables our sins to be forgiven and which can thereafter conveniently be forgotten. The cross is the surest, truest, and deepest window on the very heart and character of the living and loving God; the more we learn about the cross, in all its historical and theological dimensions, the more we discover about the One in whose image we are made, and hence about our own vocation to be the cross-bearing people, the people in whose lives and service the living God is made known. And when therefore we speak of shaping our world, we do not—we dare not—simply treat the cross as the thing that saves us 'personally', but which can be discarded when we get on with the job. The task of shaping our world is best understood as the redemptive task of bringing the achievement of the cross to bear on the world. In undertaking that task, the methods, as well as the message, must be cross-shaped from start to finish.

Further reading

Bock, Darrell L., and Mitch Glaser. 2012. *The Gospel According to Isaiah 53: Encountering the Suffering Servant in Jewish and Christian Theology*. Grand Rapids, MI: Kregel.
Brown, Raymond E. 1994. *The Death of the Messiah: From Gethsemane to the Grave: A Commentary on the Passion Narratives in the Four Gospels*. 2 vols.; ABRL; New York: Doubleday.
Chapman, David W. 2010. *Ancient Jewish and Christian Perceptions of Crucifixion*. Grand Rapids, MI: Baker.
McKnight, Scot. 2005. *Jesus and His Death: Historiography, the Historical Jesus, and Atonement Theory*. Waco, TX: Baylor University Press.
Pitre, Brant. 2015. *Jesus and the Last Supper*. Grand Rapids, MI: Eerdmans.
Wright, N. T. 1996. *Jesus and the Victory of God*. COQG 2; London: SPCK, pp. 540–611.
——. 1999. *The Challenge of Jesus: Rediscovering Who Jesus Was and Is*. London: SPCK, pp. 52–69.
——. 2011. *Simply Jesus: Who He Was, What He Did, Why It Matters*. London: SPCK, pp. 163–86.
Wright, N. T., and Craig A. Evans. 2008. *Jesus, the Final Days: What Really Happened*. Edited by T. A. Miller. London: SPCK.

The *Averoldi Polyptych* by Titian, dated 1520–2, located in the basilica church of Santi Nazaro e Celso, Brescia, Italy

© *Mondadori Electa / Bridgeman Images*

IV

THE RESURRECTION OF THE SON OF GOD

The widespread belief and practice of the early Christians is only explicable if we assume that they all believed that Jesus was bodily raised, in an Easter event something like the stories the gospels tell; the reason they believed that he was bodily raised is because the tomb was empty and, over a short period thereafter, they encountered Jesus himself, giving every appearance of being bodily alive once more.[1]

---

[1] Wright *RSG*, 710.

The Afterlife in Greek, Roman, and Jewish Thought

CHAPTER AT A GLANCE

This chapter surveys views of the afterlife in Greek, Roman, and Jewish sources as part of the background to the New Testament accounts of Jesus' resurrection.

By the end of this chapter you should be able to:

- understand the diversity of views about the afterlife in antiquity;
- describe beliefs about God, Israel, and the afterlife in the Old Testament and second-Temple Jewish literature;
- appreciate the similarities and differences between the New Testament accounts of Jesus' resurrection and ancient views of the afterlife.

Once a man has died, and the dust has soaked up his blood, there is no resurrection.[1]

While the pyre was burning, it is said that a cloud passed under Hercules and with a peal of thunder wafted him up to heaven.[2]

You accursed wretch, you dismiss us from this present life, but the King of the universe will raise us up to an everlasting renewal of life, because we have died for his laws.[3]

INTRODUCING LIFE AFTER DEATH IN ANTIQUITY

Jesus was crucified; no historian doubts that. But it was not the end of the story: according to early Christian testimony, God raised him from the dead. The God of Israel resurrected Jesus; he did not merely revive him back to mortal existence, but transformed him into a glorious and bodily mode of existence. But what does resurrection mean? How does resurrection fit into Jewish hopes for the future? What did the apostles and

---

1 Aesch. *Eumen.* 647–8.
2 Apollodorus *The Library* 2.7.7.
3 2 Macc. 7.9 NRSV.

evangelists mean when they told stories about Jesus coming back to life? What historical value can we give to their accounts, and how best can we present that case? And what differences might it all make for the way we think about mission, discipleship, and human flourishing? In this chapter we will explore views of the afterlife in greco-roman and Jewish sources as an important prelude to examining the New Testament accounts of Jesus' resurrection.

To begin with, beliefs about death and what lies beyond come in all shapes and sorts and sizes. Even a quick glance at the classic views of the major religious traditions gives the lie to the old idea that all religions are basically the same. There is a world of difference between the Muslim who believes that a Palestinian boy killed by Israeli soldiers goes straight to heaven, and the Hindu for whom the rigorous outworking of karma means that one must return in a different body to pursue the next stage of one's destiny. There is a world of difference between the Orthodox Jew who believes that all the righteous will be raised to new individual bodily life in the resurrection, and the Buddhist who hopes after death to disappear like a drop in the ocean, losing his or her own identity in the great nameless and formless Beyond. And there are of course major variations between different branches or schools of thought in these great religions.

The same sort of diversity existed in antiquity. The three quotes at the start of this chapter illustrate just how diverse were the ancient views of the afterlife. The first, about the permanence of death and the impossibility of resurrection, is drawn from Greek theatre. In Aeschylus's play *Eumenides*, Apollo speaks at the foundation of the Athenian high court, the Areopagus, and declares that death really is the end: 'there is no resurrection.' That is why justice must be done. The second quote is from Apollodorus's account of Hercules' ascent into heaven. There Hercules mounts his own funeral pyre, and, while it is burning, he is assumed into heaven accompanied by a thunderclap. This scheme has obvious affinities with the heavenly assumptions of Enoch and Elijah,[4] and also shaped the Roman tradition that emperors experienced *apotheosis* at death, that is, they were received into heaven and translated into celestial beings, 'divinized', if not, perhaps, fully 'divine' (here opinions differ). Third, we have the martyrdom story from 2 Maccabees about the Jewish youths who defied the Syrian tyrant Antiochus Epiphanes by refusing to abandon their ancestral religion. The story focuses on a mother and her seven sons, who refused to eat the unclean food of the pagans, and were tortured one by one. As they went to their various gruesome deaths, several of them made specific promises to their torturers about their future vindication. One of the sons declared to his tormentors that 'the King of the universe will raise us up to an everlasting renewal of life, because we have died for his laws'. The youth was defiantly saying that his

---

[4] Gen. 5.24; 2 Kgs. 2.11.

loyalty to the covenant would be rewarded and that the torturers' brutality would be punished by the God of justice.

When viewed together, the three accounts are striking for their differences: (1) death is permanent, (2) heroes get translated into heaven without dying, and (3) the faithful who die are returned back to life! There were, then, multiple options about what death was, and how to live beyond it. We will explore these perspectives further by surveying greco-roman and Jewish views of life, death, and the world beyond.

Peter Paul Rubens, *Apotheosis of Hercules*, c. 1637–8, Brussels
Public Domain

GRECO-ROMAN VIEWS OF THE AFTERLIFE

In this section we shall describe the range of options for belief about the dead that were available in the greco-roman world of late antiquity—roughly two or three hundred years either side of the time of Jesus. This explains graphically why the news of Jesus' resurrection appeared sheer foolishness, even though some found that it stirred a strange new hope in their hearts.

Witless shadows in a murky world

The ancient Greek author Homer, whose significance for antiquity is perhaps akin to that of the King James Bible and Shakespeare in our own day, provides a window on ancient views of life after death. In his work, the dead become shades (*skiai*), ghosts (*psychai*), or phantoms (*eidola*). They are certainly not fully human beings. They may sometimes look like them; but the appearance is deceptive, since one cannot grasp them physically. Theirs is a shadowy and wispy existence in an underworld abode, even though they may occasionally appear to the living.

A good example comes from a scene in the *Iliad* where Achilles is confronted with the shade of his recently killed friend, Patroclus. Patroclus has been killed in battle, but remains unburied while Achilles goes off to get revenge for him by killing the Trojan prince Hector. Only then does Achilles return to the task of mourning the now avenged Patroclus. He addresses the corpse as now a resident in Hades, telling him of his vengeance, and he makes preparation for the funeral the next day. That night, however, as he slept:

> There came to him the spirit of hapless Patroclus, in all things like his very self, in stature and fair eyes and in voice, and in like raiment was he clad withal; and he stood above Achilles' head and spake to him, saying: 'Thou sleepest, and hast forgotten me, Achilles. Not in my life wast thou unmindful of me, but now in my death! Bury me with all speed, that I pass within the gates of Hades. Afar do the spirits keep me aloof, the phantoms of men that have done with toils, neither suffer they me to join myself to them beyond the River, but vainly I wander through the wide-gated house of Hades. And give me thy hand, I pitifully entreat thee, for never more again shall I come back from out of Hades, when once ye have given me my due of fire . . . [5]

In response, Achilles tries to embrace his old friend:

> Achilles held out his arms to clasp the spirit, but in vain. It vanished like a wisp of smoke and went gibbering underground. Achilles leapt up in amazement. He beat his hands together and in his desolation cried: 'Ah then, it is true that something of us does survive even in the Halls of Hades, but with no intellect at all, only the ghost and semblance of a man; for all night long the ghost of poor Patroclus (and it looked exactly like him) has been standing at my side, weeping and wailing, and telling me of all the things I ought to do.'[6]

---

[5] Homer, *Iliad* 23.65–76 (tr. Murray [LCL]).
[6] Homer, *Iliad* 23.99–107 (tr. Rieu [2001]).

Achilles then arises from his sleep, and completes the elaborate funeral.

From the context, it seems that Achilles had nurtured doubts as to whether the dead had any existence at all; but now this ghostly vision has settled the matter, though hardly in a pleasing manner. Who is Patroclus now? A ghost or spirit. Where is he? On his way to Hades, but unable to cross the River Styx and find his proper place of rest until the appropriate funeral has been held. What's wrong? Patroclus is no longer properly human, just a gibbering and witless phantom. What's the solution? There is none. He can be helped on his way to Hades, but he will not find a full or enriching existence there, and he will certainly not return. The drama proceeds on its way, but Patroclus is gone for good, and Achilles himself will soon be joining him in gloomy Hades.

So what of the dead according to Homer? They are in Hades, under the eponymous rule of the underworld's god and his dreaded wife. They are sorry both to be where they are and about much that happened in their previous human existence. They are sad at their present subhuman state. In some cases they are tormented, as punishment for particularly heinous crimes. For the most part, Hades holds no comforts, no prospects, but only a profound sense of loss. The inhabitants of Hades remain essentially subhuman and without hope.

Disembodied but otherwise fairly normal

Some cherished the hope that, despite the gloomy Homeric picture, there would after all be elements of normal life. In many ancient cultures it was common to bury the deceased with the kind of household goods that one was accustomed to: furniture, adornments, charms, toiletries, even toys for deceased children. There was still a life, of sorts, beyond the grave, and burial helped to prepare for it.

While that might seem odd, the stories that were told of the dead frequently involved a life similar to the present one—albeit with not much to do, no huntergathering or similar tasks, and hence more time to gossip and mope. Many believed that they would meet old friends again. With the ancient Greek poet Pindar, the Homeric gloom has chinks of light: riding, gaming, gymnastics, and especially drinking-parties feature in writing, painting, and other decorations illustrating the life of the dead. We should not try to reconcile this picture of a fairly normal life with the Homeric one; nobody was looking for consistency in these matters, and though it is possible that the illustrations in question were really designed to evoke memories of the deceased's happier hours, it may well be that, as in our own world, all kinds of contradictory beliefs swirled around cheerfully alongside one another in popular culture. Certainly, though, Socrates envisaged conversing with the famous dead as something to look forward to in the life to come. There is even evidence that people supposed marriage and sexual activity might be possible. We should, however, remind ourselves that most of the written evidence comes from poetry and other writing clearly not intended as literal description. There is little evidence that anyone except very tough-minded philosophers ever took these suggestions so seriously as to face death, their own or that of another, with real composure.[7]

In many cases, despite widespread fear of a gloomy Hades, some practices, pictures, and stories indicated the hope for a continuing life not too different from the present.

Souls released from prison

If Homer functioned as the Old Testament for the hellenistic world—which by the first century included the entire middle east—its New Testament was unquestionably Plato. In contrast to Homer, the Greek philosopher Plato had a very different conception of human existence, its place in the cosmos, and the post-mortem destiny of the individual.

Plato, building on the work of other philosophers like Socrates and Pythagoras, believed that the essence of a human being was a soul, which was non-material. Bodily life was full of delusion and danger; the soul was to be cultivated in the present, both for its own sake and because its future happiness would depend upon such cultivation. The soul, being immortal, existed before the body, and would continue to exist after the body had gone.

The soul would therefore not only continue after bodily death; it would be delighted to do so. If it had known earlier where its real interests lay it would have been longing for this very moment. It would now flourish in a new way, released from its enslaving prison. Its new environment would be just what it ought to have wanted. Popular opinion might lean towards bringing the dead back, if that were possible, but that would be a mistake. Death was frequently defined precisely in terms of the separation of soul and body, seen as something to be desired. The fact that all this sounds quite familiar in our world shows the extent to which modern western culture has been affected by Platonism.

As far as Plato was concerned, then, Hades was not terrifying. It offered a range of pleasing activities—of which philosophical discourse might be among the chief, not surprisingly since attention to such matters was the best way, during the present time, of preparing the soul for its future. The reason people did not return from Hades was that life was so good there. They would of course want to stay, rather than returning to the gloomy and distracting shadows of the world of space, time, and matter.

It is hard to overestimate the importance of Plato for the later and wider world into which there burst the phenomenon we know as Christianity. For the Roman

---

[7] One possible exception is the world of Egypt where the dead were thought of as continuing into a still very complete life.

author Seneca, the immortal human soul had come from beyond this world—from among the stars, in fact—and would make its way back there. Though one might hold that it simply disappeared, it is more likely that it would go to be with the gods. Death was either the end of everything, in which case there was nothing to be alarmed about, or it would be a process of change, in which case, since the change was bound to be for the better, one should be glad. The soul, in fact, was at present kept as a prisoner within the body, which was both a weight and a penance to it. One should not, then, fear death; it would be the birthday of one's eternity.

Platonic thought provided the tectonic plates for much Christian thought well into the middle ages. The second-century Christian apologist, Justin, was an eager Platonist (though he firmly believed in bodily resurrection). The second-century 'heretic' Marcion was well and truly steeped in Platonic ideas, regarding the human body as a 'sack of excrement' unfit for God to incarnate himself in, with the corollary that salvation must mean deliverance of the soul from this body, rather than the body's resurrection.[8] This divergence has continued among Christian teachers to this day.

Becoming a god (or at least a star)

'Oh dear,' the emperor Vespasian is reported to have said on his deathbed, 'I think I'm becoming a god.'[9] He was neither the first nor the last to think such thoughts, though perhaps the only one to put it so memorably. From early Greek writings onwards we find hints that some heroic mortals would not just find their souls going into a state of bliss; they would actually join the Immortals themselves, the gods of the greco-roman pantheon. When it became first possible and then fashionable for Roman emperors to see their predecessors as divine—and for less reserved subjects to accord the same honour to the living emperor—the idea was hardly new. It was, rather, a fresh mutation within a long line of speculation.[10]

In Greek mythology, one could distinguish between gods and heroes, though in some cases the lines were blurred. For instance, Hercules, after his proverbial labours, was admitted not just to the bliss of a righteous Platonic soul, but actually to the company of the gods themselves. Other less well-known heroes were sometimes accorded similar status, among whom we should mention Dionysus, the heavenly twins Castor and Pollux, and the healing god Asclepius. Within the Roman world, similar mythological founding heroes like Aeneas and Romulus may have managed to break the normal taboo against humans becoming divine, though even in these cases things are not straightforward. They may simply have been identified with already existing gods.

---

8   Tert. *Adv. Marc.* 3.10.1.
9   Suet. *Vesp.* 23.
10 See Gradel 2002; Koortbojian 2013.

A sculpted relief depicting the apotheosis of Emperor Antoninus Pius and his wife Faustina, c. AD 161
Alamy Stock Photo

The possibility that a human being could become a god developed from these mythological beginnings through to the divinization of hellenistic rulers, particularly notable in the case of Alexander the Great (356–323 BC). At least as early as 331, Alexander had begun to represent himself as a son of Zeus, and to put himself alongside Hercules, expecting divinization (apotheosis) after his death. Encouraged by the adulation of his Persian and Egyptian subjects, for whom worship of rulers was quite normal, he requested actual worship in Greece and Macedonia.[11] His Greek subjects were not so eager to comply,[12] but after his early death his cult was quickly established and, though imitated by his less well-known successors, outlasted them all, providing both a model and an inspiration for the Roman imperial cult four centuries later.

By the early Christian period similar beliefs were widespread throughout the Roman world. Just as Augustus had his adoptive father Julius Caesar declared a god, so Tiberius did the same for Augustus in his turn. Although living emperors were never officially worshipped as part of the Roman state cult, they were venerated in private cults, family shrines, and various associations in Italy. Temples to

---
11 See Arrian *Anabasis* 3.3.2; 4.10.6–7; 7.29.3; Aelian *Hist. Misc.* 2.19.
12 Alexander's demand that Greece recognize him as a god was met with derisive complicity, with the Spartan Damis laconically stating: 'Since Alexander wants to be a god, let him be a god' (Plut. *Mor.* 219).

the emperor and his family were built across the provinces, and imperial images were revered throughout the empire. This 'divinity' was not merely fictive or political; it was real religious devotion. The emperors, deceased and living, were worshipped because they provided benefaction and benevolence to their subjects. They, in turn, lavished gratefully upon them the highest honours possible, climaxing in divinity and cultic worship. This imperial 'divinity', however, was (in our terms) relative rather than absolute. The emperors were not gods in the same way that Jupiter or Zeus was supposed to be. But this distinction was lost on most people. What mattered was that they were the gods of the Roman state which—so ran the propaganda!—had conferred such blessings on its empire.

The expectation of divinization, and the normal process by which it was accorded, were well established in the early empire. Witnesses were made to swear that they had seen the soul of the late emperor ascending to heaven, a theme made famous by Augustus's interpretation of the comet that appeared at the time of Julius Caesar's death. The system was already sufficiently established to be lampooned by Seneca on the death of Claudius in his famous book about the *Pumpkinification* of Claudius. So useful was the emperor's divinity to the Roman empire and its stability that the practice continued through successive centuries. A detailed description of apotheosis is given by Cassius Dio, himself an eye-witness of the funeral rites of the emperor Pertinax in AD 193.[13] We smile wryly when Bishop Eusebius, with a pious tear in his eye, describes the coin that was struck after the death of his beloved Constantine, representing the emperor as a charioteer, drawn by four horses, being received up into heaven.[14]

Stories on returning to life after death

The section above surveyed greco-roman beliefs about the state of the deceased. Within this world there were several different perspectives about the possibility of the dead crossing back over the chasm into the land of the living.

First, necromancy—communication with the departed—has a long and varied history. Most cultures and most historical periods offer stories of the living establishing contact with the departed, or indeed the departed taking the initiative and appearing unbidden to the living. From Patroclus's appearance to Achilles onwards, ancient literature has plenty of such incidents. Some of the classic encounters between the living and the departed occur in dreams, as with Achilles and Patroclus. Sometimes the dead appear to be summoned back for such visitations by grieving relatives, especially women. Sometimes, in such scenes, the dead have wisdom to offer the living about the realities of which they are now aware; sometimes

---

13 Dio Cassius *Hist.* 75.4.2–5.5.
14 Eus. *Vit. Const.* 4.73.

they come to guide, or to warn, at a particular moment of crisis. Even the Old Testament, where such contact was anathema, furnishes one classic example.[15] These visions and visitations were not, however, cases of people ceasing to be dead and resuming something like normal life. They were precisely about the dead remaining dead, and being encountered as visitors from the world of the dead, without any suggestion that they would then resume the kind of life they had earlier possessed.

There were, however (second), mythic stories of actual returns from the underworld. We have, for instance, Homer's famous tale about Odysseus's visit to Hades. While in Hades he converses with his old friends Agamemnon and Achilles, and even the ghost of Hercules (the 'real' Hercules is feasting with the immortal gods, married to Hebe, the daughter of Zeus and Hera, but even this does not prevent his shade from living in the house of Hades). But soon after, Odysseus has to flee before the goddess Persephone finds out he is there and sets the Gorgon on him.

Another familiar story is the myth of Alcestis. In the legend, Alcestis is the wife of Admetus, king of Pherae (Thessaly), to whom Apollo has been enslaved as a punishment. In return for Admetus's hospitality, Apollo tricks the Fates into granting Admetus the privilege of escaping death on condition that someone else should die in his place. The only volunteer is his beloved wife Alcestis. After her death and burial, she is rescued by Hercules, who fights physically with Death (Thanatos, a character in the play), beats him, and restores Alcestis to Admetus.[16] These stories are fascinating, but they scarcely provide any parallel with resurrection. Odysseus did not die to get to Hades. Alcestis did indeed return from the dead to bodily life (in the legend and in Euripides' play), but she would presumably die again, like Lazarus in John's gospel. In any case, intelligent pagans contemporary with early Christianity knew about such stories, and dismissed them as mythic fictions. A fifth-century Athenian audience would not have regarded such narratives as in any way realistic. A tale in which Apollo and Death appear on stage as speaking characters, and in which Hercules arrives as a guest and displays his extraordinary powers, is hardly good evidence for what ordinary people believed happened in everyday life.

Third, there was one belief, widely held by philosophers, according to which the dead did indeed return to some kind of this-worldly and bodily existence. This was the theory of *metempsychosis*, the transmigration or reincarnation of souls. The classic statement of this is found in Plato, who developed the idea from the work of the sixth-century Pythagoras; but belief in transmigration was also fostered in the Orphic cult, and continued among philosophers and cult practitioners thereafter, though without ever gaining much popular adherence.[17] Plato's basic scheme is reasonably straightforward: after death, the souls of all humans wait for a period,

---
15 See the story of Saul using the 'witch of Endor' to summon the prophet Samuel in 1 Sam. 28.
16 Eurip. *Alcest.* 1144–6.
17 Properly speaking, the theory of transmigration of the soul exists in at least two distinct forms, one

whereupon they are given the choice of what sort of creatures they will become in their next existence (such as a swan, a lion, an eagle, or indeed another human). The souls then proceed through the Plain of Oblivion, drink from the River of Forgetfulness, and so pass into their next existence, unaware of who they have been, or even that they have been anything at all. Since for Plato, as for the Hindu and Buddhist schemes of the same type, return to embodied existence means that the soul is once more entering a kind of prison, the ultimate aim is not simply to choose the right type of existence for one's next life, but to escape the cycle altogether. We are here not far from one version of Hinduism and other doctrines of *karma*.

In any case, from Plato's point of view, to come back into this life at all is clearly to have failed in the soul's ultimate destination. It is to return to jail. By contrast, for believers in resurrection—that is, many Jews and virtually all early Christians— the new embodied life is to be looked forward to and celebrated. It is not part of a cyclic movement, going round and round between life and death (see 'Emails from the edge: dying and rising gods'). As some Jews glimpsed, and as the early Christians emphasized, resurrection life was a matter of going through death and out the other side into a newly embodied life beyond. Transmigration offered a far more interesting prospect for the future life than the gloomy world of Homeric Hades. But Homer's basic rule remained in force. Nobody was allowed to return from Hades and resume the life that he or she had once had.

Conclusion: death as a one-way trip

Clearly there was a diversity of greco-roman perspectives about the afterlife. The dead might have some kind of shadowy existence in Hades. They might experience a positive form of disembodied existence, putting off the prison of the body and living as immortal and disembodied souls. They might even aspire, in some cases, to divinization (though whether Roman emperors, who knew they would be 'divinized' after their death, took this seriously as a personal hope, rather than a political gambit, is open to question). Stories of ghosts and journeys to the underworld were entertaining, but no-one took them seriously as prospects for themselves. The transmigration of the soul was a possibility that some hoped for, while others disdained it as a return to the same mortal drudgery experienced in the previous lifetime.

What everyone knew was that in principle the road to the underworld ran only one way. Throughout the ancient world, from its 'Bible' of Homer and Plato, through its practices (funerals, memorial feasts), its stories (plays, novels, legends), its symbols (graves, amulets, burial-goods), and its grand theories, we can trace a good deal of variety about the road to Hades, and about what one might find upon arrival.

---

holding that the soul passes into another body immediately upon death, the other that the soul waits for a longer or shorter period before entering another body.

EMAILS
from the edge

From: Alan_Daley@aol.com
To: Professor Dana Schuler
Date: Thur, 18 Jan 2015 at 11:11 a.m.
Subject: Dying and rising gods

Dear Prof.,

A friend sent me a weird link on the Internet about dying and rising gods. The basic gist is that Christianity is just a rip-off from oriental myths about dying and rising gods like Adonis. Is this kosher—is there anything to this?

Pax 2 da Max
AD

From: Professor Dana Schuler
To: Alan_Daley@aol.com
Date: Fri, 18 Jan 2015 at 3:55 p.m.
Subject: Re: Dying and rising gods

Dear Alan,

The New Testament's description of Jesus' death and resurrection has prompted comparisons with ancient mystery religions where there were 'dying and rising gods' such as the Egyptian god Osiris and the Phoenician god Adonis. Yet these are hardly good analogies for Christian claims, let alone sources for Christian belief.

First, the cults of dying/rising gods are mistakenly treated as a homogeneous phenomenon, whereas in fact the stories and the cults that venerated these deities were remarkably diverse. Each of these cults and their mythologies needs to be studied individually, rather than being lumped together as if they are all pretty much the same. For example, some gods rise but do not die, while others die but do not rise. So whether they constitute a single category is an open question.

Second, actually determining what the members of these cults believed and when they believed it is not always straightforward. It is more than possible that in many cases they borrowed ideas from Christianity rather than the other way round. The evolution of the Adonis cult is a case in point. It may have begun as the veneration of a young hunter, which then morphed into a myth where Adonis spends part of the yearly cycle in the underworld and the rest on a different plane, and then became a Christian parody of sorts. Tryggve Mettinger writes: 'We must realize that the Adonis cults were exposed to strong competition from the Christian church. Could the notion of the resurrection of Adonis perhaps be a feature "confiscated" from Christianity? To ask that question is to ask whether or not we have reasons to think that Adonis was a dying and rising god already in pre-Christian times' (Mettinger 2001, 136).

Third, there is also a failure to note the seismic differences between these oriental myths about dying and rising gods and the Christian narrative of Jesus' death and resurrection. For a start, the death and resurrection of these oriental gods is repetitive; it is part of the seasonal cycles of nature and is decidedly ahistorical (see J. Z. Smith 1987; M. S. Smith 1998). It is also worth asking in what precise sense these gods actually 'die' and 'rise'. They 'die' in the sense that they descend to the underworld for a time, or they disappear from the agricultural cycle, or else they frame cultural patterns of mourning; but their deaths are not experienced as human events. Likewise, the god's 'resurrection' means another agricultural transition of the seasons, or a divine image's 'appearance' by procession at a particular temple, or it frames ritual traditions of celebration. These events hardly resemble the resurrection traditions expressed in the Jewish texts Ezekiel 37, Daniel 12, and *2 Baruch* 50—51, let alone Christian writings like Luke 24, John 20, or 1 Corinthians 15 (see Frankfurter 2002).

When the Christians spoke of the resurrection of Jesus they did not suppose it was something that happened every year, with the sowing of seed and the harvesting of crops. They could use the image of sowing and harvesting to talk about it; they could celebrate Jesus' death by breaking bread; but to confuse this with the world of the dying and rising gods would be a serious mistake. It is of course quite possible that, when people in the wider world heard what the early Christians were saying, they attempted to fit the strange message into the worldview of cults they already knew. But the evidence suggests that they were more likely to be puzzled, or to mock. When Paul preached in Athens, nobody said, 'Ah, yes, a new version of Adonis and such like! Please tell us more.' More likely, the old assumption remained in force: whatever the gods—or the crops—might do, humans did not rise again from the dead.

> So, yes, there are a few surface similarities between the mystery cults and the story of Jesus' death and resurrection. However, as the example of Adonis demonstrates, drawing a direct correspondence between oriental myths and Jesus' death and resurrection is problematic. That is because (1) the cults defy homogenization, (2) they may have borrowed from Christianity, and (3) the myths are radically different from the story of Jesus' death and resurrection.
>
> Regards
> Prof. Dana Schuler

As with all one-way streets, there is bound to be someone who tries to drive in the opposite direction. One hears of an Alcestis who got out for a while. But the road was generally well policed; Hades, like a lobster pot, was easy to enter and impossible to leave. The apparent exceptions were known to be myths. Nobody expected they would come true.

Whatever the philosophical speculation about the afterlife, in the greco-roman world death was felt as a grievous loss both to the dying and to the bereaved. Rare indeed were those like Socrates and Seneca who could overcome such feelings. Some such people were able to welcome the escape from the prison-house of the body. But if that was seen as a problem—as it obviously was by the vast majority of people, as witnessed by tomb inscriptions and funeral rites throughout the ancient world—there was no solution. Death was all-powerful. One could neither escape it in the first place nor break its power once it had come. The ancient world was thus divided into those who said that resurrection couldn't happen, though they might have wanted it to, and those who said they didn't want it to happen, knowing that it couldn't anyway.

JEWISH VIEWS OF THE AFTERLIFE

In this section, we will explore views of the afterlife in the Old Testament and in a wider sample of post-biblical Jewish literature. Grasping this will not only clarify the context of the resurrection narratives in the gospels, but will also explain what Paul meant when he said (quoting very early tradition) that the Messiah 'was raised on the third day according to the Scriptures'.[18] It will also address the question of why Paul caused such a commotion by telling the Sadducees and Pharisees of the Sanhedrin, 'I stand on trial because of the hope of the resurrection of the dead.'[19]

---
[18] 1 Cor. 15.4.
[19] Ac. 23.6.

What the early Christians said about the resurrection of Jesus was consciously rooted from the start within the second-Temple Jewish worldview, shaped not least by Israel's scriptures. Granted what we have just seen about pagan expectations, this was the only place where the story had any chance of making itself at home. 'Resurrection' was not part of the pagan hope. If the idea belongs anywhere, it is within the Jewish world.

Old Testament

The first thing we have to note is that resurrection makes only rare and late appearances in Israel's scriptures. Hopes for the afterlife were at best on the periphery of the message of the Old Testament as a whole.

One cohort of texts expresses a view, not all that different from that of Homer, that when a person 'slept with his or her ancestors' in death, such a person entered a post-mortem world of next to nothingness:

> Among the dead no one proclaims your name. Who praises you from [the] grave?[20]

> It is not the dead who praise the LORD, those who go down to the place of silence . . . [21]

In these texts, and in others, we find mention of Sheol, the Pit, the grave, and the dark.[22] These almost interchangeable terms denote a place of gloom and despair, a place where one can no longer enjoy life, and where the presence of YHWH himself is withdrawn. As in Homer, there is no suggestion that the dead are happy there; it is a dark and gloomy world. Nothing much happens. It is not another form of real life, an alternative world where things continue as normal.

The most lively biblical scene of continuing activity in Sheol merely confirms this. Isaiah 14 offers a splendid depiction of the king of Babylon arriving in the underworld to join the erstwhile noble shades who are there already. In a passage worthy of Homer, he is grimly informed that things are very different down there:

> The realm of the dead below is all astir
>   to meet you at your coming;
>   it rouses the spirits of the departed to greet you—
>   all those who were leaders in the world;
>   it makes them rise from their thrones—

---

20 Ps. 6.5.
21 Ps. 115.17.
22 See Gen. 3.19; Pss. 30.9; 88.3–10; Isa. 38.10–18; 2 Sam. 14.14; Eccl. 9.5–6, 10; Job 3.13–19.

> all those who were kings over the nations.
> They will all respond,
> > they will say to you,
> 'You also have become weak, as we are;
> > you have become like us.'
> All your pomp has been brought down to the grave,
> > along with the noise of your harps;
> maggots are spread out beneath you
> > and worms cover you.[23]

The dreariness of the fate of the dead reaches tragic lows in the book of Job. Notwithstanding the ambiguous verse, 'after my skin has been destroyed, yet in my flesh I will see God',[24] which, as the marginal notes in English Bibles indicate, is a difficult passage to translate, there remains a pattern of perpetual pessimism about the future. Job laments:

> Remember, O God, that my life is but a breath;
> > my eyes will never see happiness again.
> The eye that now sees me will see me no longer;
> > you will look for me, but I will be no more.
> As a cloud vanishes and is gone,
> > so one who goes down to the grave does not return.
> He will never come to his house again;
> > his place will know him no more.[25]

> But a man dies and is laid low;
> > he breathes his last and is no more.
> As the water of a lake dries up
> > or a riverbed becomes parched and dry,
> so he lies down and does not rise;
> > till the heavens are no more, people will not awake
> > or be roused from their sleep.
> 'If only you would hide me in the grave
> > and conceal me till your anger has passed!
> If only you would set me a time
> > and then remember me!
> If someone dies, will they live again?

---

[23] Isa. 14.9–11.
[24] Job 19.26.
[25] Job 7.7–10.

> All the days of my hard service
> I will wait for my renewal to come.'[26]

While Job knows that 'my redeemer lives'[27] Job is not certain if he himself will live for much longer, or that he will exist in any meaningful post-mortem state.

This of course sounds incredibly glum and fatalistic. However, it is not the whole story of the Old Testament.

We do not have to press deep into the Old Testament before discovering that there is a confident and constant hope in God's love for his people even beyond the veil of death. At the heart of that hope was the knowledge that YHWH, the God of Israel, was the creator of the world; that he would be faithful to the covenant with Israel, and further to that, that his purposes for creation and his special people were love, life, and glory. So, on the one hand, the hope of the biblical writers, which was strong and constant, focused not upon the fate of humans after death, but on the fate of Israel and its promised land. The nation and land of the present world were far more important than what happened to an individual beyond the grave. But on the other hand, the constant love of YHWH was never merely a theological dogma to the ancient Israelites. In many parts of their literature, and supremely the Psalms, we find evidence that they knew this love in vivid personal experience. It gave rise to the suggestion that, despite the widespread denials of such a thing, YHWH's faithfulness would after all be known not only in this life but also in a life beyond the grave.

A cursory reading of Genesis 1—3 suggests that while humanity was not created *with* immortality, they were made *for* immortality, to know God and to enjoy him for ever, to be his priest-kings over creation, and to rule with God over his world. Though death in some form seems to have been present in the world in the natural cycles of the animal and vegetable kingdoms, Death as we now know it, felt as shameful and unnatural, is presented as an alien and tyrannical intrusion into the world, entering through the lie of the 'serpent'. This, the story insists, was not the way it was supposed to be. What is more, if God is the God who gives life and breath to all things, who calls into being that which had no being, then this God of creation must put things right and be the God of a new creation, and make all things new in their time. While Adam's exile from Eden meant death, and death was consignment to nothing, nothingness was God's amphitheatre for staging a new creation. So if death is nothing, it is no match for the God who makes things from nothing. The dead might be asleep; they might be almost nothing at all; but hope lived on within the covenant, in which YHWH had promised to be the God of the living, not of the dead.

---

26 Job 14.10–14.
27 Job 19.25.

The first big hint we get of life as YHWH's purpose for humanity is the very structure of Israel's covenant. Moses held out to the people life and death, blessings and curses, and urged them to choose life—which meant, quite specifically, living in the promised land as opposed to being sent into the disgrace of exile.[28] But already in Deuteronomy there was the promise that even exile would not be final: repentance would bring restoration and the renewal both of the covenant and of human hearts.[29] This explicit link of life with the land, and death with exile, coupled with the promise of restoration on the other side of exile, is one of the forgotten roots of the fully developed hope of ancient Israel. This was the hope that would eventually crystallize into belief about the resurrection of the dead as the ultimate proof of God's faithfulness to Israel. Adam's exile from Eden, and Israel's exile from Canaan, were both experiences of death, simultaneously metaphorical and real; yet there was always hope beyond that, hope for YHWH's covenantal renewal and new creation.

Given the premise of YHWH's assurance of covenant life, and the hope for divine faithfulness, it is unsurprising that there are several texts which appear to offer hope that YHWH will deliver people from Sheol:

> Therefore my heart is glad and my tongue rejoices;
>> my body also will rest secure,
> because you will not abandon me to the realm of the dead,
>> nor will you let your faithful one see decay.
> You make known to me the path of life;
>> you will fill me with joy in your presence,
>> with eternal pleasures at your right hand.[30]

There is legitimate doubt over whether this refers to escaping death or passing through it to a life beyond, but there is no question of the basis of the hope. It is YHWH himself, the one the Psalmist embraces as his sovereign one, his portion and cup, the one who gives him counsel in the secret places of his heart.

Elsewhere the Psalmists hint more clearly at a future where YHWH 'receives' the speaker into glory or else 'ransoms' him from the power of Sheol:

> When my heart was grieved
>> and my spirit embittered,
> I was senseless and ignorant;
>> I was a brute beast before you.

---

[28] Dt. 30.19–20 with 28.1–14, 15–68; 29.14–28.
[29] Dt. 30.1–10.
[30] Ps. 16.9–11; see Pss. 22.29; 104.29–30; Job 33.15–30.

> Yet I am always with you;
>> you hold me by my right hand.
> You guide me with your counsel,
>> and afterwards you will take me into glory.
> Whom have I in heaven but you?
>> And earth has nothing I desire besides you.
> My flesh and my heart may fail,
>> but God is the strength of my heart
>> and my portion for ever.[31]
>
> They are like sheep and are destined to die;
>> death will be their shepherd
>> (but the upright will prevail over them in the morning).
> Their forms will decay in the grave,
>> far from their princely mansions.
> But God will redeem me from the realm of the dead;
>> he will surely take me to himself.[32]

Where we find a glimmer of hope like this, it is based not on anything in the human make-up like an 'immortal soul', but on YHWH and him alone. Indeed, YHWH is the substance of the hope, not merely the ground: he himself is the 'portion', that is, the inheritance, of the righteous, devout Israelite. When this strong faith in YHWH as the creator, the life-giver, the God of ultimate justice, met the apparent contradiction of the injustices and sufferings of life, there was at that point, as we have seen, a chance of fresh belief springing up. Thus, if YHWH was the inheritance of his people, and if his love and faithfulness were as strong as Israel's traditions made out, then there was no ultimate bar to seeing death itself as a beaten foe. That, of course, was what several key texts went on to assert.

The covenantal fixtures of Israel's faith meant that even the virtual 'death' of exile, as experienced by Israel, could only be the dark prelude to a glorious dawn of God's life-giving power. This naturally leads us to Ezekiel 37, the vision of the valley of dry bones, which is arguably the most famous 'resurrection' passage of all. There God promised to open Israel's graves and bring up the dead. This was a highly charged and vivid metaphor of the way in which unclean Israel would be cleansed, exiled Israel restored to the land, and scattered Israel regathered. The Davidic monarchy would be restored, and a new Temple would be built, all by a powerful and covenant-renewing act of new creation.

---

[31] Ps. 73.21–26.
[32] Ps. 49.14–15.

It is in the eighth-century BC prophet Hosea that we find the earliest references to bodily life on the other side of death:

> Come, let us return to the LORD.
> He has torn us to pieces
>   but he will heal us;
> he has injured us
>   but he will bind up our wounds.
> After two days he will revive us;
>   on the third day he will restore us,
>   that we may live in his presence.[33]

In the context of the book, this is a prayer that the prophet regards as inadequate, indicating a failure to repent and a belief that YHWH could easily be bought off. But in later times the prayer was thought to reflect faith in the life-giving, restorative power of YHWH. Another passage from Hosea utilizes similar life-after-death language:

> I will deliver this people from the power of the grave;
>   I will redeem them from death.
> Where, O death, are your plagues?
>   Where, O grave, is your destruction?
> 'I will have no compassion,
>   even though he thrives among his brothers.'[34]

Again, in context, the Hebrew text seems to be denying that YHWH would redeem Israel from Sheol and Death. However, the Septuagint and other ancient versions, and also the apostle Paul, take this in a positive sense.[35] Moreover, it seems that it was taken that way in Isaiah 26, which is arguably influenced by Hosea 13.14. Isaiah there speaks of Israel being dramatically rescued from a national crisis. The pagan nations may have lorded it over Israel for a while, but 'They are now dead, they live no more; their spirits do not rise. You punished them and brought them to ruin; you wiped out all memory of them',[36] whereas God's promise for Israel is:

> But your dead will live, LORD;
>   their bodies will rise—

---

[33] Hos. 6.1–2.
[34] Hos. 13.14–15.
[35] See 1 Cor. 15.55.
[36] Isa. 26.14.

> let those who dwell in the dust
> > wake up and shout for joy—
> > your dew is like the dew of the morning;
> > > the earth will give birth to her dead.[37]

The original Hebrew refers literally to bodily resurrection, and this is certainly how the verse was taken in the Septuagint and at Qumran. It is still possible, of course, that here resurrection was, as with Ezekiel, a metaphor for national restoration. But the wider passage, in which God's renewal of the whole cosmos is in hand, opens the way for us to propose that the reference to resurrection was intended to denote actual concrete events.

The theme of life beyond the grave continues in Isaiah, especially in the fourth Servant Song. After the Servant has suffered, it is said, 'he will see the light of life[38] and be satisfied; by his knowledge my righteous servant will justify many, and he will bear their iniquities.'[39] True, there is no explicit mention of resurrection itself, and only an oblique statement of what will happen to the Servant after his death (Isa. 53.11). But it is clear that the Servant (1) dies and is buried (Isa 53.7–9), and (2) emerges in triumph, however densely this is expressed (Isa. 53.10–12). The text was certainly open to an interpretation of resurrection, and both Jewish and Christian translators and authors took it that way.

Just as Hosea appears to have influenced Isaiah, so too Isaiah probably shaped the way the book of Daniel expressed the future hope of the faithful awakening from dust into glory:

> Multitudes who sleep in the dust of the earth will awake: some to everlasting life, others to shame and everlasting contempt. Those who are wise will shine like the brightness of the heavens, and those who lead many to righteousness, like the stars for ever and ever.[40]

Few now doubt that this always referred to concrete, bodily resurrection, and that is certainly how it was taken by later Jewish writers. The metaphor of 'sleep' for death was already widespread; 'sleeping in the dust of the earth' was a clear biblical way of referring to the dead. It was therefore natural to continue the metaphor by using 'awakening' to denote bodily resurrection—not a different sort of sleep, but its abolition. Thus, what we have here is resurrection, not simply a resuscitation in which the dead will return to life much as they knew it before. This is a new mode

---
37 Isa. 26.19.
38 The LXX and Qumran scrolls read 'light of life', which is absent from the MT.
39 Isa. 53.11.
40 Dan. 12.2–3.

of existence: the wise will be raised to a state of glory in the world for which the best parallel or comparison is the status of stars, moon, and sun within the created order.

This is hardly out of line with the other evidence we have surveyed. The 'wise' are not abandoned to Sheol; that would allow the violent, wicked kingdoms that oppressed the covenant people to get away with it. The 'wise' experience the spirit's regenerating power, much like the dry bones of Ezekiel. They are revived and restored; death holds no lasting ruin for them. The 'wise' come through their suffering and, like the Suffering Servant, see the light of life. They emerge from dust into 'glory', which could mean a literal shining like stars or could mean a position of honour or royalty in the new world. They inherit Isaiah's promise of restoration from exile. The Deuteronomic promise of life, and vindication for covenant faithfulness, comes true in them. These texts all refer, in one way or another, to the common hope of Israel: that YHWH would restore his people's fortunes at last, liberate them from pagan dominion, and resettle them in justice and peace, even if it took a great act of new creation, including resurrection, to accomplish it.

While explicit belief in bodily resurrection is thus rather a late development, it can be seen as growing directly out of the much earlier Israelite emphasis on the goodness of the created order and of embodied life within it. Daniel's unwavering confidence in bodily resurrection is what resulted when the hope of ancient Israel met the radical new challenge of persecution and martyrdom. This is in line with the ways in which Hosea and Isaiah 24—27 met the threat of judgment, and Ezekiel 37 and Isaiah 53 met the fact of exile. So, although the promise of resurrection appears to contradict the evidence we surveyed earlier, in which all hope beyond the grave was ruled out, it forms an equally strong reaffirmation of the hope which ancient Israel did indeed hold: hope for renewal of national life, life in the land as the gift of YHWH the creator God.

The constant factor, throughout the types of belief we have surveyed, is Israel's God himself. The vision of YHWH's creation and covenant; his promises and his faithfulness to them; his purposes for Israel, not least his gift of the land; his power over all opposing forces, including finally death itself; his love for the world, for his human creatures, for Israel in particular, and especially for those who served him and followed in his way; his justice, because of which evil would eventually be condemned and righteousness upheld—this vision of the creator and covenant God underlies the ancient belief in the national and territorial hope, the emerging belief that the relationship with YHWH would be unbreakable even by death, and the eventual belief that YHWH would raise the dead. The biblical language of resurrection ('standing up', 'awakening', and so on), when it emerges, is simple and direct; the belief, though infrequent, is clear. It involves, not a *reconstrual* of life after death (as though 'resurrection' was just a fancy way of saying 'life after death'), but the *reversal of death itself.* 'Resurrection' was not about discovering that Sheol was not such a bad place after all. It was not a way of saying that the dust would learn to be happy as dust. The language of awakening was not a new, exciting way of talking about sleep. It was a way of saying that a time would come when sleepers would sleep no more. Creation itself, celebrated throughout the Hebrew scriptures, would be reaffirmed, remade.

Post-biblical literature

Jews, it used to be said, believed in resurrection, while Greeks believed in immortality. Like most half-truths, this one is as misleading as it is informative, if not more so. If the Old Testament offers a spectrum of belief about life after death, the second-Temple period provides something more like an artist's palette: dozens of options, with different ways of describing similar positions and similar ways of describing different ones. The more texts and tombstones we study, the more views there seem to be. Almost any position one can imagine on the subject appears to have been espoused by some Jews somewhere in the period between the Maccabean crisis and the writing of the Mishnah, from roughly 200 BC to AD 200.

The case against there being any future life at all was maintained distinctively by the Sadducees. They seem to have denied any resurrection, perhaps believing that body and soul would perish together at death. However, since we know about them through their opponents, the Pharisees and their successors the rabbis, it is possible that they did not after all hold such an extreme position. They believed, after all, in the Torah, the first five books, in which there might seem to be some kind of a shadowy post-mortem existence.[41] The document that most closely reflects the Sadducean perspective of the afterlife is the Wisdom of Jesus ben-Sirach, sometimes known as 'Ecclesiasticus':

Hades, Persephone, and Hermes in a palace within the underworld on this volute krater, dated fourth century BC
Public Domain

> Remember that death does not tarry,
>   and the decree of Hades has not been shown to you.
> Do good to friends before you die,
>   and reach out and give to them as much as you can.
> Do not deprive yourself of a day's enjoyment;
>   do not let your share of desired good pass by you.
> Will you not leave the fruit of your labours to another,
>   and what you acquired by toil to be divided by lot?
> Give, and take, and indulge yourself,

---

41 See Mt. 22.23/Mk. 12.18/Lk. 20.27; Ac. 23.7–9; Jos. *War* 2.165; *Ant.* 18.16; mSanh. 10.1.

> because in Hades one cannot look for luxury.
> All living beings become old like a garment,
> > for the decree from of old is, 'You must die!'[42]

The funeral inscription for a Diasporan Jew named Jesus ben-Phameis, from Leontopolis in Egypt, expresses a similarly sombre sentiment:

> Traveller, my name is Jesus, and my father's name is Phameis;
> when descending into Hades I was 60 years of age.
> All of you should weep together for this man, who went at once at the hiding place of ages, to abide there in the dark.
> Will you also bewail me, dear Dositheos, because you are in need of shedding bitter tears upon my tomb?
> When I died I had no offspring, you will be my child instead.
> All of you, therefore, bewail me, Jesus the unhappy man.[43]

The perspectives of Jesus ben-Sirach and Jesus ben-Phameis certainly stand in sharp juxtaposition to the perspective of Jesus of Nazareth, that the generous 'will be repaid at the resurrection of the righteous',[44] or that

> the hour is coming when all who are in their graves will hear his voice [that is, the son of man's] and will come out—those who have done good, to the resurrection of life, and those who have done evil, to the resurrection of condemnation.[45]

Not every Jesus in the Jewish world was necessarily on the same page when it came to the afterlife.

The reason why Jewish aristocrats rejected resurrection might actually have less to do with theology than with sociology. The real problem was that resurrection was from the beginning a revolutionary doctrine. It implied a reordering of power, a radical overhaul of the existing hierarchies of authority. For Daniel 12, resurrection belief went with dogged resistance and martyrdom. For Isaiah and Ezekiel, it was about YHWH restoring the fortunes of his people. It had to do with the coming new age, when the life-giving God would act once more to turn everything upside down—or perhaps, as some might have said, the right way up. It was the sort of belief that encouraged young hotheads to attack Roman symbols placed on the Temple, and that, indeed, led the first-century Jews into the most disastrous war

---

42 Sir. 14.12–17 NRSV; see 17.27–28; 38.21–23.
43 Safrai and Stern 1974–6, 2.1043–4.
44 Lk. 14.14.
45 Jn. 5.28–29 NRSV.

they had experienced.[46] Thus, for those on top of the social pile, whether in Jerusalem or in Corinth, resurrection beliefs might be seen to threaten their established position. People who believe that their God is about to make a new world, and that those who die in loyalty to him will rise again to share gloriously in the rule of that world, are far more likely to lose respect for a wealthy aristocracy than people who think that this life, this world, and this age are the only ones there ever will be.

Moving from pessimism to Platonism, many Jews assimilated to hellenistic culture, and absorbed the belief in the immortality of the soul. The great first-century Jewish exponent of a thoroughgoing hellenistic viewpoint was the Alexandrian philosopher Philo. His subtle and fascinating writings contain much food for thought on this, but it is beyond controversy that he taught the immortality of the soul rather than the resurrection of the dead. Philo is unambiguously dualistic in his thought: for him, the soul is immortal, or more accurately, the soul can be divided into several parts, one of which is immortal. For Philo, release from the prison of the body is God's reward for those who, during their embodied phase, have remained pure from sensual defilement.[47] Those who follow the patriarchs down this road will, after death, become equal to the angels. The immortal soul does not, after all, die, but merely departs. Like Abraham, called to leave his country and go to another one, the soul leaves its present habitation and sets off for the heavenly realms, the 'mother city'.[48]

Josephus was a Judean aristocrat who claimed to belong to the Pharisaic sect. In describing the Jewish world for pagan readers he effectively translated Jewish beliefs into hellenistic categories. He thus describes the Pharisees as holding to something like reincarnation or the immortality of the soul, even though there are strong signs that he knew their beliefs were quite different.[49] Josephus says at one point that one of the reasons he wrote his histories was to demonstrate divine sovereignty over human affairs and to confirm the immortality of the soul—though this, too, may have been a way of trimming his Jewish sails to the Roman wind.[50]

In another work, *Pseudo-Phocylides*, we find a strong confidence in the soul's survival of death:

> For the souls remain unharmed among the deceased.
> For the spirit is a loan of God to mortals, and his image.
> For we have a body out of earth,

---

46 Jos. *War* 1.650; 7.340.
47 See Philo *Abr.* 258; *Leg.* 1.108.
48 Equal to angels (*Sac.* 5); soul departing (*Heres* 276); soul leaving body (*Heres* 68–70); heaven as mother city (*metropolis*) (*Quaest. Gen.* 3.11).
49 Jos. *War* 2.163; *Ant.* 18.14.
50 Jos. *Ant.* 17.354.

and when afterward we are resolved again into earth we are but dust;
and then the air has received our spirit . . .
All alike are corpses, but God rules over the souls.
Hades is our common eternal home and fatherland,
a common place for all, poor and kings.
We humans live not a long time but for a season.
But our soul is immortal and lives ageless forever.[51]

Elsewhere we see a crisp and clear account of resurrection, offering the hope that God will show his faithfulness to his people by raising them to new bodily life.

The second book of Maccabees begins where Daniel left off, with the promise of new bodily life, at some future date, for those who had died horrible deaths out of loyalty to Israel's God and the law. The context is that of pagan persecution. The Syrian tyrant Antiochus Epiphanes, as part of his drive to bring the Jewish world into line with his imperial ambitions, is attempting to make loyal Jews disobey their God-given laws, under pain of torture and death. The narrative describes a Judean mother and her seven sons. The sons refuse to eat unclean food to make them disloyal to Israel's ancestral laws, and one by one they are tortured. Even in the ghastly cruelty that the sons endure, they all defiantly utter their hope in an ultimate vindication by Israel's God:

> You accursed wretch, [said the second brother,] you dismiss us from this present life, but the King of the universe will raise us up to an everlasting renewal of life, because we have died for his laws.[52]

> [The third brother] put out his tongue and courageously stretched forth his hands, and said nobly, 'I got these from Heaven, and because of his laws I disdain them, and from him I hope to get them back again.'[53]

> When he was near death, [the fourth brother] said, 'One cannot but choose to die at the hands of mortals and to cherish the hope God gives of being raised again by him. But for you there will be no resurrection to life!'[54]

> [The mother] encouraged each of them in the language of their ancestors. Filled with a noble spirit, she . . . said to them, 'I do not know how you came into being in my womb. It was not I who gave you life and breath, nor I who set in order the

---

[51] *Ps.-Phoc.* 105–15 (*OTP*). The work is hard to date but is probably from the first centuries BC or AD.
[52] 2 Macc. 7.9; all quotations from 2 Maccabees in this section are taken from NRSV.
[53] 2 Macc. 7.10–11.
[54] 2 Macc. 7.14; note the variation from Dan. 12.2, where the wicked are also raised in order to be judged.

elements within each of you. Therefore the Creator of the world, who shaped the beginning of humankind and devised the origin of all things, will in his mercy give life and breath back to you again, since you now forget yourselves for the sake of his laws.'[55]

[The mother spoke secretly to the youngest son:] 'I beg you, my child, to look at the heaven and the earth and see everything that is in them, and recognize that God did not make them out of things that existed. And in the same way the human race came into being. Do not fear this butcher, but prove worthy of your brothers. Accept death, so that in God's mercy I may get you back again along with your brothers.'[56]

[The youngest son said,] 'You . . . will certainly not escape the hands of God. For we are suffering because of our own sins. And if our living Lord is angry for a little while, to rebuke and discipline us, he will again be reconciled with his own servants . . . For our brothers after enduring a brief suffering have drunk of ever-flowing life, under God's covenant; but you, by the judgement of God, will receive just punishment for your arrogance. I, like my brothers, give up body and life for the laws of our ancestors, appealing to God to show mercy soon to our nation and by trials and plagues to make you confess that he alone is God, and through me and my brothers to bring to an end the wrath of the Almighty that has justly fallen on our whole nation.'[57]

This remarkable chapter draws together the strands we observed in Daniel 12. The martyrs' suffering is seen as redemptive for the nation; there seems to be an element of Isaiah 53 in the final flourish of the youngest brother. Their loyalty will be rewarded, and the torturers' brutality punished, by the God of justice. The new life they will receive, which is seen in very 'bodily' terms, is the gift of the creator God who made them and all the world in the first place. This resurrection is not temporary resuscitation; it is, rather, the overthrow and reversal of death and those who inflicted it. Meanwhile, the claim that their deaths will somehow exhaust the present divine wrath against Israel is vindicated in the following chapter, with the radical reversal of Jewish fortunes and the build-up to the successful Maccabean revolt.

Other Jewish literature, especially the books sometimes designated as 'apocalypses', exhibit a similar hope for bodily vindication and renovation. In the *Similitudes of Enoch* we find visions of the future where '[t]he righteous and elect ones shall rise from the earth and shall cease being of downcast face. They shall wear

---

[55] 2 Macc. 7.21–23.
[56] 2 Macc. 7.28–29.
[57] 2 Macc. 7.31–33, 36–38.

the garments of glory'.⁵⁸ The *Apocalypse of Moses* is clearer.⁵⁹ When Adam dies, God sends the archangel Michael to tell Seth not to attempt to revive him. Oil from the tree of mercy will be given at the end of times, when 'all flesh from Adam up to that great day shall be raised, such as shall be the holy people; then to them shall be given every joy of Paradise and God shall be in their midst.'⁶⁰ Seth will witness Adam's soul making 'its fearful upward journey', but this will not be the end of the matter. God calls to Adam's dead body, and says: 'I told you that you are dust and to dust you shall return. Now I promise to you the resurrection; I shall raise you on the last day in the resurrection with every man of your seed.'⁶¹ Finally, we might consider the *Psalms of Solomon*, most likely from the first century BC, showing strong traces of Pharisaic perspectives. The writer declares that while 'the destruction of the sinner is forever', in contrast, 'those who fear the Lord shall rise up to eternal life, and their life shall be in the Lord's light, and it shall never end'.⁶²

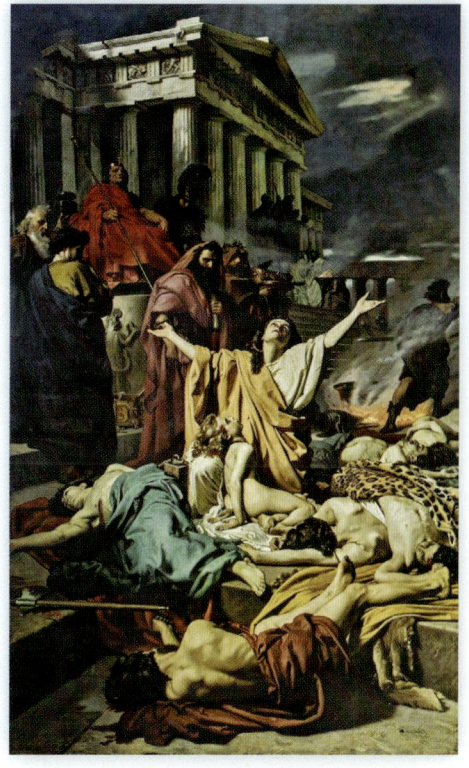

Antonio Ciseri, *Martyrdom of the Maccabees*, 1863, Church of Saint Felicity, Florence, Italy

Resurrection thus belongs clearly within one regular apocalyptic construal of God's intended future. Judgment must fall, because the wicked have been getting away with violence and oppression for far too long. When it does, bringing with it a great change in the entire cosmic order, those who have died, whose souls are resting patiently, will be raised to new life. Many of these apocalypses, as we have seen, allude to Daniel 12 at this point. All of them, in doing so, hold together what we have seen so closely interwoven in the key biblical texts: the hope of Israel for liberation from pagan oppression, and the hope of the righteous individual for a newly embodied, and probably significantly transformed, existence.

---

58 *1 En.* 62.14–15 (*OTP*).
59 This traditional title for the book is misleading; it is a variant on the *Life of Adam and Eve*. The book's date is unknown, but a time between 100 BC and AD 100 is probable.
60 *Apoc. Mos.* 13.3–4 (*OTP*).
61 *Apoc. Mos.* 41.2–3 (*OTP*).
62 *Ps. Sol.* 3.11–12 (*OTP*).

Cave 4, Qumran

Conclusion: death amid covenant hope

Given the preceding survey, it is safe to say that the old assumption that Greeks believed in immortality while Jews believed in resurrection is not merely historically inaccurate; it is conceptually muddled. There was a wide spectrum of belief in the second-Temple Jewish world regarding the fate of the dead. By no means all Jews believed in a coming resurrection. Other views were known and taught, like the general pessimism of the Sadducees and the immortality of the soul as advanced by Philo. Of course, anyone who believes in eventual resurrection is likely also to hold some kind of view about how the person continues to exist between bodily death and bodily resurrection. In the Wisdom of Solomon, this is done by speaking of the 'souls' of the righteous being 'in the hand of God' until the time of their visitation, when they will share God's rule over the new world.[63] A similar view is reflected in Luke's account (Ac. 23.6–10) of Paul before the Jewish council, when the Pharisees, believing in the eventual resurrection but not in Paul's claim that Jesus had already been raised, imagine that perhaps Paul had received a vision of an 'angel' or 'spirit', being two other ways of speaking of the continuing existence of those who would subsequently be raised.[64] Josephus can do his best to hellenize the Jewish beliefs he is describing for his audience, but even he lapses into language that hints at resurrection and cosmic renewal.[65] Views of the afterlife at Qumran are another conundrum. The majority of texts say nothing about the future fate of the dead, and Josephus and Hippolytus give conflicting accounts as to whether the Essenes believed in resurrection.[66] There are some possible intimations of belief in resurrection in the Qumran

[63] See Wright *RSG*, 162–75.
[64] See Wright *RSG*, 132–4.
[65] See Jos. *War* 1.650; 3.374–5; *Ap.* 2.217–18.
[66] Jos. *War* 2.154–8; Hippolytus *Ref.* 9.27.1–3.

hymn-book (1QH),[67] but 4Q521, a messianic apocalypse, appears to go further into a definite statement of belief, stating that the Lord will 'heal the wounded and will make the dead live, he will bring good news to the poor'.[68] Finally, we might consider some minority views such as angelomorphology, the belief that a person translates into an angelic or perhaps celestial being upon death. Here we should be careful. Jesus compared those resurrected with angels, though the point was not that they would *become* angels but that they would be *like* them in this respect, that, being then immortal, they will not need to marry and propagate their species. The slave-girl Rhoda mistook the escaped Peter for his angelic *Doppelgänger*, but again this is likely to be, as with Acts 23, the belief that the recently departed might still exist in some 'angelic' form prior to eventual resurrection.[69] But some evidence does point to a more strictly 'angelic' final hope. The visions of *1 Enoch* declare that the righteous dead are offered a hope like heavenly angels, and the petitioner in the *Prayer of Jacob* requests transformation into an immortal angel.[70]

What we can say with some degree of confidence is that when Jews in this period really did believe in 'resurrection', it had two basic meanings: (1) the restoration of Israel ('resurrection' as metaphor, denoting socio-political events and investing them with the significance that this would be an act of new creation, of covenant renewal); and (2) the reconstitution of dead human bodies into new bodily life ('resurrection' as literal, denoting actual re-embodiment). Importantly, the two go together: resurrection was about the *restoration of Israel* on the one hand and *the newly embodied life of all* YHWH's *people* on the other. This act of re-creation was the great event that would bring the 'present age' to a close and usher in the 'age to come'. All of this was premised on the twin belief in YHWH as both the creator and the God of justice. Without the goodness of creation, divine justice might remake humans in some quite different way. Without justice, the sorrows of the present creation would be unrelieved. Creation and justice go together. The martyrs would be raised; Israel as a whole would be vindicated.

TESTIMONY TO THE LIVING HOPE

This admittedly long survey of greco-roman and Jewish views of the afterlife is a vital backdrop for understanding the New Testament witness to resurrection. It allows us to situate in the story of scripture the words of Jesus that the 'Son of Man ... must be killed and after three days rise again',[71] to note the radical claim of

---

67 1QH 14.29–30, 34–5; 19.10–14.
68 4Q521 2.9–12.
69 Lk. 20.36; Ac. 12.15.
70 *1 En.* 104.4; *Prayer of Jacob* 19.
71 Mk. 8.31; 9.31.

Jesus in John's gospel that 'I am the resurrection and the life',[72] to understand the significance of Paul's terse words that Jesus 'was raised for our justification',[73] and to grasp the meaning of John the Seer's vision of the risen and exalted Jesus as saying, 'I am the Living One; I was dead, and now look, I am alive for ever and ever! And I hold the keys of death and Hades.'[74] When we grasp the background materials, whether about 'Hades' in Homer or about the philosophies of Plato and Philo, we see how the New Testament authors are offering a different narrative about God, God's purposes for this world, the restoration of Israel, and the hope of humanity. 'Resurrection'—the Greek is *anastasis*—always had to do with physical bodies, never with a disembodied 'life after death'. And the only group of people among whom we have clear evidence of this belief in the first century are the Jews.

Tomb of Herod, Herodium

What is more, reading this material reminds us that Jesus and his first followers did indeed enter into discussion with their contemporaries about God's ultimate purposes beyond death, and that these discussions are urgent and relevant for practical life, not just airy-fairy speculations about a fantasy world 'by and by'. (We sometimes talk about 'the afterlife', but since 'resurrection' means a new bodily life *after* a period of being bodily dead we should perhaps call it 'the after-afterlife'.) Whether we think of Jesus putting the Sadducees straight on the subject, or Paul rebuking the

---

72 Jn. 11.25.
73 Rom. 4.25.
74 Rev. 1.18.

Corinthians because some were saying there was no resurrection, the point is not vague speculation about 'the life beyond' (like people today asking whether there will be 'shops in heaven', and so on) but because what we believe about the future tells us something about the God we worship, what that worship should look like, and how the fact that God's new creation has burst into the present time with Jesus' own resurrection can and must energize and shape our work as his people. The church today, too, has to confront our own culture's myths of the afterlife, whether it is a Darwinian determinism which leads to a tragic pessimism, the strange mix of New Age religion and postmodern pop-psychology that fills daytime television, the philosophical nihilism that advocates unbridled hedonism as life's only purpose, the Marxist or materialist vision that says the best we can hope for is an economic utopia, or even the competing eschatologies of Islam and Buddhism. We need to be aware of the fears, hopes, and dreams about death and afterlife that swirl around in our culture, so that we can meaningfully address them with the good news about how God the father 'in his great mercy . . . has given us new birth into a living hope through the resurrection of Jesus Christ from the dead, and into an inheritance that can never perish, spoil or fade'.[75]

Further reading

Bolt, Peter G. 1998. 'Life, Death and the Afterlife in the Greco-Roman World.' In *Life in the Face of Death: The Resurrection Message of the New Testament*. Edited by Richard N. Longenecker. Grand Rapids, MI: Eerdmans, pp. 51–79.

Harrisson, Juliette. 2019. *Imagining the Afterlife in the Ancient World*. New York: Routledge.

Segal, Alan F. 2004. *Life after Death: A History of the Afterlife in the Religions of the West*. New York: Doubleday.

Somov, Alexey. 2017. *Representations of the Afterlife in Luke-Acts*. LNTS 556; London: T&T Clark.

Wright, N. T. 2003. *The Resurrection of the Son of God*. COQG 3; London: SPCK, pp. 32–206.

---

75 1 Pet. 1.3–4.

The Story of Easter according to the Apostle Paul

CHAPTER AT A GLANCE

This chapter looks at the New Testament witness to Jesus' resurrection, majoring on Paul, to show its historical credibility and the theological meaning that was attributed to it.

By the end of this chapter you should be able to:

- describe Paul's testimony about the resurrection of Jesus;
- understand how Paul associates Jesus' resurrection with the future resurrection of believers;
- grasp some of the critical issues about the resurrection such as the resurrection of the body in 1 Corinthians 15;
- identify the importance of resurrection for Paul's theology as a whole.

The historical datum now before us is a widely held, consistently shaped and highly influential belief: that Jesus of Nazareth was bodily raised from the dead. This belief was held by virtually all the early Christians for whom we have evidence. It was at the centre of their characteristic praxis, narrative, symbol and belief; it was the basis of their recognition of Jesus as Messiah and lord, their insistence that the creator God had inaugurated the long-awaited new age, and above all their hope for their own future bodily resurrection. The question we now face is obvious: what caused this belief in the resurrection of Jesus?[1]

JESUS, CRUCIFIED, DEAD, BURIED, AND *RISEN*!

On that fateful Friday afternoon Jesus was dead; his executioners had done their job, and done it with ruthless efficiency. Jesus' body had been given to Joseph of Arimathea, a sympathizer from the Sanhedrin, and hastily buried in a nearby tomb. As for Jesus' disciples, they were afraid and in hiding. As far as Pilate and Herod were probably concerned, that was the end of the matter... but it wasn't. According to early Christian sources,

---

1 Wright *RSG*, 685.

on the third day Jesus' tomb was found empty, and many of his followers claimed that they saw him alive—first a group of women, then his closest disciples including Peter, and even others like his brother James. Indeed, there was a sense of excited bewilderment about what had happened and who had seen him first. Importantly, they didn't claim to have seen Jesus' ghost (though they knew all about such things). Nor did they say they had seen him transformed into an angel, or seen a vision of him resting in the bosom of Abraham, or scooped up to heaven in a chariot of fire. Jesus' followers believed that the God of Israel had raised Jesus from the dead. Jesus had been bodily resurrected. What exactly did they mean by this, and why did they say it?

In this chapter and the next we will conduct a survey (necessarily selective) of the witness to Jesus' resurrection in the writings of Paul and then in the four gospels. We will see that Jesus' bodily resurrection, as a true event in history, is the best explanation for why the early church took the shape and direction that it did, and why its leaders proclaimed the resurrection of Jesus as the fulfilment of Israel's hopes. For the first Christians, belief in Jesus' resurrection and hope for their own future resurrection generated a series of new beliefs and new ways of life that made them stand out in the religious world of antiquity.

Piero della Francesca, *The Resurrection, c.* 1463, Tuscany, Italy
Public Domain

PAUL'S TESTIMONY TO THE RISEN JESUS: THE SON OF GOD IN POWER

Paul is an important witness to Jesus' resurrection, in terms of: (1) the origin of belief in Jesus' resurrection among Jesus' own circle of disciples; (2) Paul's testimony to his own encounter with the risen Jesus; (3) how resurrection, something marginal in Judaism, became central in Christianity; and (4) how 'resurrection' as a metaphor for Israel's socio-political restoration was deployed as a metaphor for participation in the Messiah's life-giving power. In addition, Paul's letters contain early traditions, almost creed-like fragments, that affirm two basic events: Jesus died and rose.[2] Paul expounds this tradition frequently when explaining its pastoral and missional implications and warding off confusions. He is in fact our most important early source for Jesus' resurrection and what it meant to his first followers. Paul was, after all, writing in the 40s and 50s, when (according to most scholars) the four gospels had not yet been produced, though no doubt many traditions about Jesus were circulating. The following survey of Paul's statements on the resurrection can only be brief and selective, but it will highlight the key points.

1 AND 2 THESSALONIANS

Paul's first letter to Thessalonica opens with a grateful summary statement of how the Christians there have come to believe in the true and living God as opposed to the idols of paganism. Then, in a hint of his later exposition, Paul summarizes his gospel message, speaking of the call 'to wait for [God's] Son from heaven, whom he raised from the dead—Jesus, who rescues us from the coming wrath'.[3] Jesus' resurrection; his present location in heaven (God's dimension of present reality, not a 'place' a long way away); his future return; and his deliverance of his people from wrath—all these are commonplace in Paul's developed thinking. Here we see that they were central from early on in his writing, and capable of succinct summary.

Soon after, Paul talks about the believers' future hope:

> Brothers and sisters, we do not want you to be uninformed about those who sleep in death, so that you do not grieve like the rest of mankind, who have no hope. For we believe that Jesus died and rose again, and so we believe that God will bring with Jesus those who have fallen asleep in him . . . For the Lord himself will come down from heaven, with a loud command, with the voice of the archangel and with the trumpet call of God, and the dead in Christ will rise first.[4]

---

2 1 Thess. 4.14; 1 Cor. 15.3–5; 2 Cor. 5.15; Rom. 1.3–4; 4.25; 14.9.
3 1 Thess. 1.10.
4 1 Thess. 4.13–14, 16.

This is a spectacular text, addressing a particular pastoral problem (what happens to those who die before the lord returns?), and exhibiting several of Paul's key beliefs about the resurrection. He clearly indicates that those who have already died will, at some future date, be raised from the dead in the same way that God raised Jesus. Those currently dead will rise up, thereby being 'rescued' or 'saved' rather than being the objects of 'wrath' (see 1 Thess. 1.10; 5.9). The words Paul uses, the nature of his argument, and the underlying story-line, all place him right in the middle of second-Temple Jewish beliefs about resurrection. Whatever beliefs Paul revised following his conversion, resurrection remained constant, with the major innovation being that Jesus himself had been raised in advance of everyone else. This means that we are bound to see resurrection as *bodily*, since there is no indication that what Paul meant by 'rose again' in 1 Thessalonians 4.14 was anything other than what that word would have meant to an ancient pagan or to a reader of the Septuagint. 'Resurrection' meant something bodily, *not* 'ghostly', something the dead did *not* presently enjoy. Resurrection would, in other words, be life *after* 'life after death'.

PHILIPPIANS

Philippians contains some climactic statements about the resurrection. This letter offers a hint, stronger than anywhere else except 2 Corinthians, that Paul was facing the serious possibility of his own imminent death; so we should not be surprised to find here as well some of his clearest statements about the Christian hope beyond death. These are set within a more overtly counter-imperial theology than some of the other letters. Jesus is 'lord' and 'saviour'; by strong implication, easily audible to residents in a Roman colony, Caesar—to whom those words were regularly applied—is not.

Within this letter, confusion has sometimes arisen because in the famous poem of Philippians 2.6–11 Paul speaks, not of Jesus' death and *resurrection*, but of his death and *exaltation*. This should not be taken (as some have suggested) to mean that resurrection and exaltation came to much the same thing. Even though Paul can sometimes mention one and not the other (see Phil. 2.9; Rom. 8.11), it does not follow that he conflated resurrection and exaltation. That is a modern problem, arising from a long-standing disbelief in bodily resurrection and hence a desire to flatten out related themes. As far as Paul is concerned, he knows full well that resurrection and exaltation were differentiated stages in what happened to Jesus after his death (see Rom. 8.34; Eph. 1.20). They carry quite different theological meaning, too, and cannot simply be substituted for each other. And it is the exaltation of Jesus—again, by implicit contrast with Caesar—that comes to the fore in Philippians 2.9–11.

Where we find the resurrection theme in this letter is at the centre of Paul's description of the Christian life and status, in chapter 3. There he speaks of knowing Jesus and participating in his resurrection power. Instead of clinging to his inherited covenantal privileges, like 'circumcision' and Israelite descent, Paul considers these things 'loss' compared to the surpassing worth of knowing Messiah Jesus as his lord. This is in order that

> I may be discovered in him, not having my own covenant status *of righteousness* defined by Torah, but the status *of righteousness* which comes through the Messiah's faithfulness: the covenant status *of righteousness* from God which is given to faith. This means knowing him, knowing the power of his resurrection, and knowing the partnership of his sufferings. It means sharing the form and pattern of his death, so that somehow I may arrive at the final resurrection from the dead.[5]

Out of this dense juxtaposition of almost all Paul's soteriological language and categories—justification, faith, being 'in the Messiah', knowing the Messiah, suffering, and resurrection—we here draw the main point for our current purposes: for Paul, the resurrection is primarily a future event, corresponding to the resurrection of Jesus himself, but its power is already made known in the present life, even in the midst of suffering and death.

Paul continues warning against those who are 'enemies of the Messiah's cross', who are opposed, in other words, to the message set out in Philippians 2.6–8. They are heading, he says, for destruction. Their belly has become their god, and they set their minds on the things of the earth. 'But', he continues, 'our citizenship is in heaven. And we eagerly await a Saviour from there, the Lord Jesus Christ, who, by the power that enables him to bring everything under his control, will transform our lowly bodies so that they will be like his glorious body.'[6] The punchline of Paul's statement—and the heart of our present concern with this passage—is that the body will be *transformed*, not abandoned. This is one of the clearest answers to the question: what did Paul mean by resurrection? Here he means that, in the new world which the creator God will make through the all-encompassing authority of the Messiah, his people will be given renewed bodies. Those who are presently alive, those to whom he is writing, will be transformed. We assume, filling in the gaps from the parallel passages in 1 Thessalonians 4 and 1 Corinthians 15, that those who have died will be raised into bodies that have been similarly renewed and transformed. More specifically, the transformation will be from 'humiliation' to 'glory'.

---

5 Phil. 3.9–11 *NTE/KNT* (italic phrases added).
6 Phil. 3.20–21.

EPHESIANS AND COLOSSIANS

The letters to the Ephesians and Colossians have frequently been seen as non-Pauline by scholars within the modern western academic tradition. Setting that question aside for a later discussion, in terms of 'resurrection' they are completely in line with the other Pauline letters.

Ephesians opens with a paean of praise, telling the story of the sovereign God and of Jesus as an exodus-narrative (Eph. 1.3–14) and as the story of this God's victory in the Messiah over all the powers of the world (Eph. 1.20–23). Paul then tells the story of how humankind has been brought from death to life in the Messiah (Eph. 2.1–10, especially 2.5–6). The present state of those in the Messiah is that they have already been 'raised with the Messiah' and seated with him in the heavenly places. In other words, what is true of the Messiah (in Eph. 1.20–23) is true of those who are 'in him' (according to Eph. 2.5–6). 'Resurrection' here refers, not to the restoration of Israel, but to the restoration of humankind as a whole, effected through the gospel, the 'return' from the exile of sin and death. Without downplaying the future hope of actual resurrection itself, the fact that the church lives in the interval between the Messiah's resurrection and its own ultimate new life means that the metaphorical use of 'resurrection' language can be adapted to denote the concrete Christian living described in Ephesians 2.10: 'we are God's workmanship, created in the Messiah Jesus for good works, which God planned beforehand for us to walk in them.'[7] This metaphorical use—resurrection in the present as the ground of Christian living—is strongly emphasized in Ephesians 5.14, where Paul quotes what appears to be an early Christian song or poem:

> Wake up, you sleeper!
> Rise up from the dead!
> The Messiah will shine on you![8]

The darkness of the present world is contrasted with the light of the creator's new day, a light which Christians, along with the Messiah, must already shine, without in any way implying an over-realized eschatology. Final resurrection remains in the future; but those on their way to it must shine like lights even in the present time (see too Phil. 2.15). As the final chapter of Ephesians makes clear, Christians still have a battle to fight (Eph. 6.10–20). The enemies are not yet finally defeated, but the eschatology that has been inaugurated in the resurrection of Jesus means that victory is assured.

---

[7] Tr. N. T. Wright.
[8] *NTE/KNT*.

Colossians shares this mixture of metaphor and mystery surrounding Jesus' resurrection, and makes it the mode of new life and the ground of future hope. As Paul warms to his theme in the opening chapter, he rejoices in the fact that the creator God has qualified his people to share in the inheritance of the saints in the light, by delivering them from the kingdom of darkness and transferring them into the kingdom of his son, in whom they have redemption, the forgiveness of sins (Col. 1.12–14). Jesus' death and resurrection, in other words, function as the moment of the new exodus, of the 'return' from the long exile of sin and death, of the overthrow of all the powers that enslaved the world. Those who now belong to the Messiah share the benefits of all this. Just as in Ephesians 2, so here those who were estranged from, and hostile to, the one true God have been reconciled by Jesus' death, and must now stand firm on 'the hope of the gospel' which has been announced to every creature under heaven (Col. 1.20–21). This can only mean that, with the resurrection itself, something like a shock wave has gone through the entire cosmos. The new creation has been born, and the old world somehow knows it in its bones. But this new creation must now be implemented in practice.

In the spectacular poem we know as Colossians 1.15–20, Paul places Jesus' resurrection (Col. 1.18) in parallel with the creation of the world (Col. 1.15), seeing it as the ground and origin of what the creator has now accomplished and is now implementing, namely the reconciliation of all things to him. The very shape of the poem insists that Jesus' resurrection, as a one-off event, is an act, not of the *abolition* of the original creation but of its *fulfilment*. The same Messiah and lord is the one through whom all things were made in the first place, the one in whom all things cohere, the one in and through whom all things are now brought into a new relationship with the creator God and with one another.

The result of all this, for basic Christian living, is a new lifestyle in which the divine intention for the human race is at last fulfilled. Notice how, for Paul, baptism is an enacted sign, a ritualized story, of the central gospel message. It depicts the way in which believers die with the Messiah and are raised with him: 'when you

Theatre at Ephesus

were buried with him in baptism, you were also raised with him through faith in the power of the God, who raised him from the dead' (Col. 2.12 NRSV). Those who were 'dead' both in their sins and in their gentile status, excluded from the covenant people, have been 'made alive' with the Messiah, their transgressions being forgiven (Col. 2.13). Therefore, they should 'set [their] minds on things above, not on earthly things' (Col. 3.1–2). This does not, of course, mean that they are to be so heavenly minded as to be of no earthly use, but rather that in their constant choice of actions and the habits of life they produce they are to make their co-resurrection and co-enthronement with the Messiah the intentional lens through which they see their whole life. All this can be summarized as 'putting off the old humanity' and putting on the 'new one', which is 'being renewed in the image of the creator, bringing you into possession of new knowledge' (Col. 3.10 *NTE/KNT*). Sharing Jesus' resurrection in the present, that is to say, means becoming genuinely human.

ROMANS

Paul's letter to the Romans is suffused with resurrection. Squeeze this letter at any point, and resurrection spills out; hold it up to the light, and you can see Easter sparkling all the way through. If Romans had not been hailed as the great epistle of justification by faith, it might easily have come to be known as the chief letter of resurrection.

We begin where Paul begins, with the gospel

> about his son, who was descended from David's seed in terms of flesh, and who was marked out powerfully as God's son in terms of the spirit of holiness by the resurrection of the dead: Jesus, the king, our Lord! Through him we have received grace and apostleship to bring about believing obedience among all the nations for the sake of his name.[9]

The resurrection, in other words, has marked Jesus out as the world's true ruler. Many were descended from David's seed according to the flesh. James the brother of the lord could have made that claim, as could the various blood relatives of Jesus, who were well known in the early church. But only one Davidic descendant had been raised from the dead. This, Paul declares, marks him out as the 'son' of Israel's God: that is, the Messiah. As we saw earlier, this was a new kind of claim in the Jewish world, since nobody to this point had supposed the Messiah would be killed. The resurrection was seen from very early on as *validating the messianic claim that Jesus had already made.*

---

[9] Rom. 1.3–5 *NTE/KNT*.

Moving deeper into Romans, we observe that resurrection forms a significant part of Paul's description of how 'God's righteousness'—that is, God's faithfulness to the covenant with Abraham—has been unveiled in the gospel events concerning Jesus. To this end, Romans 4 expounds Genesis 15, the chapter where the promise was made and the covenant established, and demonstrates that this chapter always envisaged that Abraham and his family would be marked out by faith—not works, not circumcision, not possession of Torah, but by faith in God, who 'gives life to the dead and calls into existence things that do not exist'.[10] This faith is evidenced by the fact that Abraham believed in the divine power to give him a child even when he and his wife Sarah were 'as good as dead' because they were long past childbearing age. Abraham's faith did not waver, confident as he was in God's power; that is why his faith was 'credited to him as righteousness' (Rom. 4.19–22). Part of Paul's purpose here is to reverse the sorry story of human idolatry and corruption in Romans 1. This, he is saying, is how faith in the true God, and in his life-giving power, is the sign that humankind is being restored.

The conception and birth of Isaac is therefore an anticipation of Jesus' resurrection, and Christian faith thus claims its share in the Abrahamic promise of Genesis 15:

> The words 'it was credited to him' were written not for him alone, but also for us, to whom God will credit righteousness—for us who believe in him who raised Jesus our Lord from the dead. He was delivered over to death *for* our sins and was raised to life *for* our justification.[11]

The final pregnant phrases are at first sight obvious in meaning, but become denser and more difficult on closer inspection. That Jesus was crucified for sins is understandable enough.[12] That he was raised for our justification is less so, and needs explanation. Most likely, Jesus was handed over *because of* our sins and was raised *with a view to* our justification.[13] If we view this passage with other key texts like Romans 1.3–4 ('marked out powerfully as God's son . . . by the resurrection of the dead') and 1 Corinthians 15.17 ('if the Messiah wasn't raised, your faith is pointless, and you are still in your sins'),[14] then resurrection is crucial to the meaning of justification and, more widely, salvation itself. Jesus' resurrection was the divine *vindication* of him as Messiah, 'son of God' in that sense, the representative of Israel and thence of the world. The resurrection demonstrates that the cross was not just

---

10   Rom. 4.17 *NTE/KNT*.
11   Rom. 4.23–24.
12   See 1 Thess. 5.10; Gal. 1.4; 1 Cor. 15.3; 2 Cor. 5.14; Rom. 5.8.
13   See Bird 2007, 40–59; Wright *PFG*, 1002–3.
14   *NTE/KNT*.

another messy liquidation of a would-be but misguided Messiah; it was the saving act of God. God's raising of Jesus from the dead was therefore the act in which justification—the vindication of all God's people 'in Christ'—was contained in a nutshell. Romans 4 thus not only shows that for Paul the resurrection of Jesus was a life-giving event, overcoming death itself by the sheer power of the creator God. It was part of the larger story in which the covenant God was demonstrating his faithfulness by vindicating all those who believe in him, as he had promised to Abraham.

Romans 5—8 is perhaps the most majestic set-piece Paul ever wrote. It is carefully structured in sequential arguments, each with its own initial statement, development, and christological climax. Paul brings together the themes of cross, resurrection, grace, glory, kingdom, life, and hope towards an escalating eschatological crescendo.

When Paul speaks in Romans 5.9–10 of being 'reconciled to [God] through the death of his Son', it leads to the exclamation: 'how much more, having been reconciled, shall we be saved through his life!' Clearly this

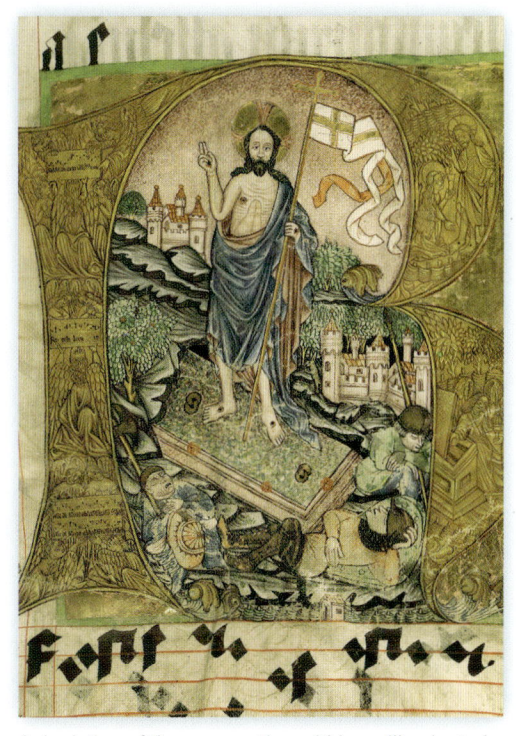

A depiction of the resurrection within an illuminated letter, fifteenth-century Gradual of Friedrich Zollner
Gianni Dagli Orti / Shutterstock

'life' is the resurrection life of the Messiah, the new life that follows his sacrificial death. The next paragraph, Romans 5.12–21, is notoriously dense. But at its epicentre we find a glimmering statement of resurrection: 'So, then, just as, through the trespass of one person, the result was condemnation for all people, even so, through the upright act of one person, the result is justification—life for all people.'[15] Paul splashes his verbal paint onto the canvas in huge dollops, and does not pause to touch it up. We are left to add the smaller details: the 'upright act' appears to be a way of referring to Jesus' obedient death, indicating that it balances and indeed outweighs Adam's trespass, and 'justification—life for all people' appears to refer to the resurrection seen as God's act of vindication, not only of Jesus himself but, proleptically, of all those who are 'in him'. Paul can therefore explain in the next verse that

---

15 Rom. 5.18 *NTE/KNT*.

it is through the 'obedience' of the one man, seeing Jesus' death and resurrection as a single act, that the many are given the status of 'righteous'.

Thereafter, in Romans 6, Paul draws together the future hope of the resurrection of the individual believer culminating in eternal life (Rom. 6.4, 8, 23) in tandem with a metaphorical description of dying and rising with the Messiah already in baptism (Rom. 6.1–11). The pattern continues in Romans 8, where Paul states: 'if the Spirit of him who raised Jesus from the dead is living in you, he who raised [the Messiah] from the dead will also give life to your mortal bodies because of his Spirit who lives in you.'[16] Consequences follow from this. Those who live 'in the Messiah', in the interval between his resurrection and their own, stand on resurrection ground and must therefore continue to resist 'the flesh', the old ways which lead to death, rather than let it reign over them. The climax of the whole section arrives with unequalled poetic beauty and theological flourish in Romans 8.30–39. Can anything now come, Paul asks, between the Messiah's people and final salvation? Each time, Paul answers in terms of what God has already done in the Messiah, emphasizing that Jesus' resurrection is the cornerstone of the Christian hope: 'Who is going to condemn? It is the Messiah, Jesus, who has died, or rather has been raised; who is at God's right hand, and who also prays on our behalf!'[17] The present suffering, persecution, and martyrdom of God's people is as nothing in the light of the love God has poured out through the Messiah. Paul is persuaded that

> neither death nor life, nor angels nor rulers, nor the present, nor the future, nor powers, nor height, nor depth, nor any other creature will be able to separate us from the love of God in *Messiah* Jesus our lord.[18]

The most fundamental reason why Paul is convinced of this is that death itself, heading this list of potential enemies, has been defeated. Not redefined; not understood in a different light, but defeated. That is one of the most central points in the whole of Romans, and it undergirds Paul's belief in both the love and the power of the creator and covenant God.

Romans 9—16, though dealing with very different themes, continues to draw on the same basic gospel message. The careful structure of chapters 9—11 has right at its centre (10.9–11) the central Christian belief and confession that 'Jesus is lord' and that 'God raised him from the dead'. That confession itself is a sign that covenant renewal has taken place; those who exhibit this faith are its true members and beneficiaries—even if, being born gentiles, they have never been part of the ethnic family of Israel (see Rom. 3.27–31; 4.18–22). Later, Paul reminds his gentile

---

[16] Rom. 8.11.
[17] Rom. 8.34 *NTE/KNT*.
[18] Rom. 8.38–39 *NTE/KNT* (amended).

audience that the gospel is for the Jews first and then the gentiles, not for the gentiles instead of the Jews. The destiny of believing gentiles and Israel is indelibly interlocked. So much so that if the Jews' 'rejection brought reconciliation to the world, what will their acceptance be but life from the dead?'[19] Some see here a literal resurrection, so that 'life from the dead' means that the restoration of Jews to membership will come all in a rush on the last day, when they will all be raised to life. Others are persuaded, however, that Paul here intends it metaphorically, thinking of ethnic Jews abandoning their unbelief in the gospel and coming to membership in the polemically redefined 'all Israel' (see Rom. 11.22, 26).[20]

Finally, the risen Christ stands at the centre of Paul's exhortations to unity in Romans 14.1—15.13:

> For this very reason, Christ died and returned to life so that he might be the Lord of both the dead and the living. You, then, why do you judge your brother or sister? Or why do you treat them with contempt? For we will all stand before God's judgment seat.[21]

Paul is clear: at the last judgment, all must give an account of themselves, and the risen lord will 'make to stand', in other words, raise from the dead, not those who have kept to a certain cultural code, but those who have lived as his faithful servants. Combined with Romans 15.12, which quotes Isaiah 11.10, about the root of Jesse who rises to rule over the nations, we have a clear statement that Jesus was raised to reign with unmatched supremacy over God's world.

INTERLUDE

If we can offer an interim report about Paul on Jesus' resurrection, prior to launching into 1 Corinthians 15, we have to say that for Paul, the resurrection of the crucified Jesus of Nazareth is the heart of the gospel. It is the object of faith, the ground of justification, the basis for obedient Christian living, the motivation for unity, and, not least, the challenge to the principalities and powers. Moreover, there can be no question that when Paul speaks of resurrection in

> 'For Paul resurrection is not an isolated axiom but part of a linguistic complex that understands God, humanity's plight, the destiny of God's people, and salvation through faith in Christ in an apocalyptic perspective. Believers are not aliens in a hostile world, but persons in whom the transforming power of the Spirit unleashed by the Messiah's death and resurrection is already at work.'
>
> **Pheme Perkins**, 'Resurrection and Christology: Are They Related?' in *Israel's God and Rebecca's Children*, 75.

---

19 Rom. 11.15.
20 Contrast Wright *Romans*, 682–3 with Bird 2016a, 390–5.
21 Rom. 14.9–10.

all these ways it is the bodily resurrection of Jesus he has in mind. His multiple metaphorical uses of resurrection, in terms of experiencing new life in Christ, highlight rather than diminish the underlying literal meaning. They are in any case consistent developments from within the ancient Jewish picture, where resurrection was used as an image for national restoration and forgiveness as well as referring literally to the new bodily life in store for God's people. But when Paul wants to ground his theological arguments and baptismal metaphors of new life on bedrock, it is to the literal, bodily resurrection that he returns. Something has happened as a result of which the cosmos itself is a different place. And when people are brought into that newness through baptism and faith they, too, become different people.

1 CORINTHIANS

A glance through 1 Corinthians is like a stroll down a busy street. All of human life is there: squabbles and lawsuits, sex and shopping, rich and poor, worship and work, wisdom and folly, politics and religion. But the letter climbs through these upward steps to a summit which is only reached in chapter 15, where Paul responds critically to the news that some of the Corinthians were denying the very possibility of resurrection. They were not saying that the resurrection had already happened, as Hymenaeus and Philetus said in Ephesus.[22] Rather, they were denying a future bodily resurrection, probably on the standard pagan grounds that bodily resurrection was either impossible or undesirable. Paul's response is to argue that what God did for Jesus, resurrection, is both the *model* and the *means* of what he will do for all Jesus' people. If so, resurrection is not a dispensable accessory to Christian faith, but part of its nucleus. It may help to lay out Paul's argument here step by step.

1. The gospel is anchored in the resurrection of Jesus (1 Cor. 15.1–11). Paul emphasizes that the resurrection of Jesus was a real event, and constitutes the foundation story with which a Christian community must not tamper. Paul here quotes what he says is the early tradition that not only he but all other Christian preachers had used: 'The Messiah died for our sins in accordance with the scriptures; he was buried; he was raised on the third day in accordance with the scriptures; and he was seen . . .'

The claim that the Messiah 'died' is uncontroversial enough, but since Paul next says that he was 'buried' and then skips ahead to 'he was raised' without mentioning the empty tomb, some commentators have suggested that perhaps Paul did not know of an 'empty tomb' tradition. However, we should note two responses. First, 'resurrection' in Paul's world meant bodies. To claim 'resurrection' while not caring if there was a body in the tomb would be self-contradictory. The phrase *anastasis ek nekrōn*, 'resurrection from the dead', literally means the 'standing up of dead

---

22 1 Tim. 2.17–18.

corpses'. Second, we should note that Paul doesn't mention, in quoting this early tradition, several other elements of what we know from the gospels to be the story of Jesus' death and resurrection. He here ignores Pilate, Caiaphas, Jerusalem, Judas, and Passover, and their omission can hardly mean either that Paul didn't know about them or that they never existed. The discovery of the empty tomb in the gospel accounts is of course significant, because it was the first thing that alerted Jesus' followers to the fact that something extraordinary had happened, and because 'appearances' of a previously dead person but without an 'empty tomb' would at once have been interpreted as 'visions' or ghostly visitations. The best hypothesis for why 'he was buried' came to be part of this brief tradition is simply that the phrase summarized very succinctly that entire moment in the Easter narratives.

The phrase 'after three days', alluding to Hosea 6.2, is frequently referred to in rabbinic mentions of the resurrection. This does not mean that Paul or anyone else in early Christianity supposed that it was a purely metaphorical statement, a vivid way of saying 'the biblical hope has been fulfilled'. In fact, the mention of any time-lag at all between Jesus' death and his resurrection is a further strong indication of what is meant by the latter: not only was Jesus' resurrection in principle a dateable event for the early Christians, but it was always something that took place, not immediately upon his death, but a short interval thereafter. One hears from time to time people speaking of 'Jesus dying and being raised to heaven', but this is precisely not what Paul is talking about here.

Paul's rehearsal of the tradition of Jesus' resurrection moves forward into the list of witnesses (it isn't clear how much of this list is itself part of that same tradition). Jesus was 'seen', he writes; some have wanted to take the verb *horaō* ('I see') as indicating that the 'seeing' in question was either that of an apparition, without actual bodily form, or else a purely subjective visionary event. The linguistic problem with that suggestion is that the verb can be used to refer to all sorts of visual experiences, ranging from witnessing the appearances of YHWH's glory in the Temple to people just turning up and being seen in an ordinary sense. The list of witnesses, however, gives clear indications that Paul does not suppose Jesus' resurrection to be a metaphorization of his followers' 'experiences', indicating some interior mental event. The list includes prominent disciples like Cephas (that is, Peter; see Lk. 24.34), the 'twelve' (see Mt. 28.16; Lk. 24.36; Jn. 20.19–20; presumably the twelfth in this group is Matthias, as in Ac. 1.15–26), an unknown crowd of some five hundred persons, a familial sceptic in James (see Mk. 3.31–35), a wider group of 'apostles' (perhaps Mary Magdalene, Cleopas, Junia, and Andronicus?), and finally an appearance to the former persecutor Paul himself. Paul did not regard these 'sightings' or 'appearances' as part of normal ongoing Christian experience. This was a complete list ('last of all', he says in relation to his own seeing of Jesus in v. 8). He was aware that the 'seeing' of Jesus that had been granted to him, though belonging in the sequence of the other primitive and non-repeatable 'seeings', was nevertheless peculiar within the sequence. He indicates this peculiarity with the little phrase *hōsperei tō ektrōmati*, which can be translated: 'as to the one born at the wrong time'. When Paul saw Jesus, he (so to speak) only just made it in time. The appearances were more or less at an end, and none had occurred after his own.[23] In sum, as Peter Stuhlmacher comments, 'the great variety in times and places of the appearances makes it difficult to hold all the reports of appearances to be legendary'.[24]

2. If the resurrection did not happen, then the gospel, with all its benefits, is null and void (1 Cor. 15.12–19). Paul responds to the Corinthian denial of resurrection by a series of *reductio ad absurdum* arguments which display the chronic problems that such a denial entails. Those who deny the future resurrection, he insists, are cutting off the branch they are sitting on. Verse 14 takes this at one level: if there is to be no resurrection, the apostles have been talking empty nonsense, and those who believed them have believed empty nonsense. Verse 17 takes this one degree further: their faith is not only 'empty', but 'futile', *mataia*, a waste of time, the crucial point being not just that they are believing rubbish about Jesus and the resurrection but that *the new age in which sins are left behind has not after all been inaugurated*. The foundation-stone of the gospel, mentioned by Paul in 1 Corinthians 15.3–5, has not after all been laid. For Paul, the point of the resurrection is not simply that the creator God has done something remarkable for one solitary individual (as people today sometimes imagine is the supposed thrust of the Easter proclamation), but that, in and through the resurrection, the world is a different place, the power of sin and of the idols has been broken, and a new way of being human has been opened up. That is the only reason there is a 'church' in Corinth in the first place.

3. Jesus' resurrection is the beginning of 'the resurrection of the dead', the final eschatological event (1 Cor. 15.20–28). Paul then spells out his counter-affirmation,

Boris Anrep's mosaic of the conversion of St Paul, twentieth century, St Paul's Chapel, Westminster Cathedral, London
sedmak / 123RF.COM

---

23 See Wright *RSG*, 327–9, 375–98.
24 Stuhlmacher 1993, 49.

beginning with the Messiah's own resurrection and showing how the resurrection of all the Messiah's people follows from it. Here and through much of the chapter he has the entire biblical revelation in mind (as in 'according to the scriptures' in the traditional formula), not least the story of Adam in Genesis 1, 2 and 3—showing that he is indeed dealing with creation and new creation. Death, he says, entered through Adam, and life through the Messiah (vv. 21–22): the future resurrection is guaranteed by Jesus' status as the truly human being, the one who truly reflects the divine image. Jesus is the 'first-fruits' of humanity, now freed from death and ruling over the world, obedient to the father, in the way the creator God had always intended, as envisaged in Psalm 8. Jesus then leads a renewed humanity in triumph over death and establishes God's kingdom. Viewed this way, the human task and the messianic task dovetail together. The whole argument establishes, with rock-solid theology and considerable rhetorical power, the point that the resurrection of Jesus the Messiah is the starting-point and the means whereby the creator, in completing the work of rescuing and renewing the original creation, will raise all the Messiah's people to new bodily life.

4. If the resurrection were not true then the central nerve of Christian living would be cut (1 Cor. 15.29–34). The next paragraph is short: something of an interlude, a brief respite from dense and involved argumentation. Jerky writing; short sentences; swift subject-changes; a quotation from Isaiah and another from pagan poetry. The flavour is both *ad hoc* and *ad hominem*, a quick, improvised, scattergun approach to make sure the listener is still awake. If the dead are not raised, then 'why are people baptized for them?' Paul describes a strange problem here; we can't be sure what precisely he is talking about, but it may be that some had been baptized on behalf of people who had come to faith but died before baptism had taken place. Why, Paul asks, would you do such a thing unless you envisaged a future resurrection life for them? In addition, if the dead are not raised, then what were Paul and his co-workers doing running the gauntlet with 'wild beasts in Ephesus'? Without resurrection, Paul indicates, you might as well embrace some form of Epicureanism: eat, drink, and be merry (as ironically voiced in Isa. 22.13) because tomorrow we die. Even pagan poets such as Menander, quoted here, censure that approach. Carelessness about future bodily resurrection, Paul indicates, will eat away at good present moral habits. Thus, the Corinthians have become senseless, sinful, and ignorant by indulging such false perspectives. Paul accordingly shames them for it. By denying resurrection, some of the Corinthians are undermining what undergirds both their future hope and their moral fibre.

5. The resurrection body is a new and glorious body, of which the risen Jesus' body is the prototype (1 Cor. 15.35–49). Paul now turns to the obvious questions—questions that still come up whenever people face the real challenge of resurrection. What exactly will it involve? How will it happen? What *kind* of body will it be? Paul's answer to the *how* is that the resurrection will transpire by the creator's agency, something that God himself gives: 'God gives it a body' (v. 38). He uses the analogy of sowing seed (it is only an analogy, of course; he is not suggesting that the resurrection body literally grows out of the earlier body like a plant from seed): his point is that there will be both continuity and development. Planting a whole cauliflower will not grow you a cauliflower. Planting a cauliflower seed will not grow you beef. But sowing a cauliflower seed will grow you a cauliflower. Paul is saying that the body is planted in a germinal state of mortality (into death) and comes to life in a whole new state of immortality (in resurrection), even while personhood and bodily identity are retained.

Having established the seed-and-plant principle as a partial analogy for resurrection, Paul begins a different train of thought in verses 39–41. There are different types of 'body' or 'flesh', each with its own dignity and worth. Paul's main purpose here is to establish that there are different kinds of physicality, each of which has its own proper characteristics, whether anthropological, animal, or astral. The idea of different bodies with their diverse 'glories' is then directly applied to resurrection:

> So will it be with the resurrection of the dead. The body that is sown is perishable, it is raised imperishable; it is sown in dishonour, it is raised in glory; it is sown in weakness, it is raised in power; it is sown a natural body, it is raised a spiritual body. If there is a natural body [*sōma psychikon*], there is also a spiritual body [*sōma pneumatikon*].[25]

Paul refers to four contrasts, or more properly, four transitions of the body in resurrection:

1. perishable ⟶ imperishable
2. dishonour ⟶ glory
3. weakness ⟶ power
4. natural ⟶ spiritual

Debate surrounds the last of the contrasts, on how best to translate and understand a *psychikon* body and a *pneumatikon* body. Many translations render these in a very unhelpful way, for instance as 'physical body' and 'spiritual body', which to modern ears sounds as though, whatever the latter body may be, it will not be 'physical' in our sense. But there are two problems here. First, the word *psychikon* certainly doesn't mean 'physical' in our sense; it comes from *psyche*, normally translated

---

[25] 1 Cor. 15.42–44.

'soul', referring to human interiority. So, whatever the contrast Paul is drawing, it can't be the one to which our minds easily jump. Second, Greek adjectives ending with the-*ikos* suffix normally tell you, not what something is *composed of*, but what it is *animated by*. If people had remembered this, a lot of confusion would have been eliminated. Paul is contrasting a body *animated by a soul*, a natural life-force, with a body *animated by the spirit*, God's divinely imparted vitalizing power. The point is that in both cases it is still a 'body', something which in our terms we would call 'physical', even if in the case of the latter body it will be what we might call 'transformed physicality'. The Jerusalem Bible (JB) gives a fairly good translation of verse 44: 'when it is sown it embodies the soul, when it is raised it embodies the spirit. If the soul has its own embodiment, so does the spirit have its own embodiment.' Thus, faced with the question, 'What sort of body will the dead have when they are raised?', Paul answers that they will have a body animated by, enlivened by, the spirit of the one true God, just as Paul stresses in several other passages.[26]

Paul then returns to the Adam–Messiah contrast in verses 45–49, placing the discussions and assertions of the previous twelve verses within a larger narrative, the narrative of creation and new creation, of earth and heaven. As in Romans 5.12–21 and Philippians 3.20–21, the two Adams represent peoples belonging to two different spheres, the earthly/soulish or the heavenly/spiritual. The point is not that the new humanity will exist in a place called 'heaven'. Rather, it will *originate* there, where Jesus himself currently is in his own risen and life-giving body. This new humanity will transform the life of those who are presently located on earth and earthy in character.

6. The resurrection is about the transformation of present corruptible physicality, resulting in the victory of life over death (1 Cor. 15.50–58). Why then does Paul say that 'Flesh and blood can't inherit God's kingdom; decay can't inherit undecaying life' (v. 50 *NTE/KNT*)? Some of Paul's readers have puzzled over this from very early times, imagining that he was taking away with the left hand the solidly physical meaning of 'resurrection' he had just given with the right. That is not the case. For Paul, 'flesh and blood' was a way of referring to ordinary, corruptible, decaying human existence. It did not mean 'physical humanity' in the normal modern sense, but 'the present physical humanity, subject to decay and death'. In any case, Paul's main subject here is the transformation of those who are left alive when the lord returns. They cannot (he says) enter God's final new creation in their present condition. They need to be, not raised (as the dead will be raised), but changed. Thus the dead will receive their new, transformed body through resurrection, while those still alive at the lord's final coming will be transformed in the twinkling of an eye. Both will then possess the same kind of body that Jesus himself has in his resurrection:

---

26 See e.g. Rom. 8.9–11. For background see Job 33.4; Ps. 104.30; Ezek. 36.27; 37.9–10, 14.

an immortal physicality, something hard to imagine in the present world but utterly characteristic of the future one.

Paul then picks up a couple of lines from Isaiah and Hosea and turns them into a taunt-song against Death. The whole chapter has been, not about 'coming to terms with Death', as some people wrongly imagine, but with its defeat, its overthrow. Here, like a warrior triumphing over a fallen enemy, Paul mocks the power that has now become powerless. Victory is assured because the powers that have conspired against God's good creation, the triumvirate of law–sin–death, have been fully dealt with.

The final verse of the chapter ('be firmly fixed, unshakeable, always full to overflowing with the lord's work. In the lord, as you know, the work you're doing will not be worthless'[27]) might seem a bit of an anti-climax after all this glorious vision. It is no such thing. God's promised future does not mean waiting around in idleness for 'life after death'. Paul redirects the Corinthians' gaze to the present time, to the tasks awaiting attention and the call to be resolute in pursuing them. The point is that, despite the discontinuity between the present mode of corruptible physicality and the future world of non-corruptible physicality, there is an underlying continuity between the two, which gives meaning and direction to present Christian living. What you do in the present, in the lord and by the spirit, is not wasted. Paul is echoing the argument of verses 12–19: if the Messiah is not raised, the apostolic preaching and the Corinthians' faith would indeed be 'in vain'. But the Messiah, the lord, was indeed raised; and proclamation, faith, and continuing labour are thereby rescued from 'vanity', from futility. What is done 'in the lord' in the present will last into God's future. That is the severely practical message which emerges from this, the prince of early Christian resurrection discussions.

PAUL: THEOLOGIAN OF THE RISEN LORD

Even from this brief and selective survey we can see that Paul's beliefs about resurrection belong firmly within a Jewish worldview: he believed that Israel's God, being both the creator of the world and the God of justice, had raised Jesus to new bodily life, thereby confirming him as Messiah and lord, and that he would likewise raise from the dead all the Messiah's people. This would be achieved through the spirit, who was already at work in them so that their own work would be genuinely part of the already-begun new creation.

This makes sense, to repeat, within the Jewish world of the day, rather than in any corner of the non-Jewish world.[28] At the same time, Paul believed two things

---

[27] 1 Cor. 15.58 *NTE/KNT* (amended).
[28] Some have suggested that in 2 Corinthians he had shifted his position; but see Wright *RSG*, 361–70.

which are only comprehensible as mutations within the Jewish worldview. First, he believed that 'the resurrection' had, as it were, split into two: the resurrection of the Messiah in the first place, and then, at his 'parousia', the resurrection of all his people. Second, he believed, and articulated in considerable detail, that the resurrection would not only be bodily, but that it would also involve *transformation* into imperishability and immortality.

Furthermore, Paul frequently used the language of resurrection, in a metaphorical way, to denote the concrete, bodily events of Christian living, especially baptism and holiness; and also to denote the renewal of the 'inner human being'. This was a development of the metaphorical use of resurrection-language within Judaism to denote the coming restoration of Israel, the great 'return from exile', the time spoken of in Ezekiel 37 and perhaps other passages. We should be clear that this was not a 'spiritualization' of the idea of resurrection. Nor was it, as has often been suggested, a move away from Paul's now-but-not-yet tension and towards a more fully realized eschatology. It was, rather, a way of bringing to articulation the experience and belief of Jesus' earliest followers: that the Christian life belonged within a historical narrative which began with Jesus' resurrection and ended with the resurrection of all believers, and that the divine spirit who accomplished the first would accomplish the second, and was even now at work to anticipate and guarantee that final event.

Further reading

Dunn, James D. G. 1998. *The Theology of Paul the Apostle*. Edinburgh: T&T Clark, pp. 234–65.
Harris, Murray J. 1998. 'Resurrection and Immortality in the Pauline Corpus.' In *Life in the Face of Death: The Resurrection Message of the New Testament*. Edited by R. N. Longenecker. Grand Rapids, MI: Eerdmans, pp. 147–70.
Wright, N. T. 2003. *The Resurrection of the Son of God*. COQG 3; London: SPCK, pp. 207–398.

14

The Story of Easter according to the Evangelists

CHAPTER AT A GLANCE

This chapter looks at the New Testament witness to Jesus' resurrection from the gospels, to show its historical credibility and the theological meaning that was attributed to it.

By the end of this chapter you should be able to:

- describe the historical origins of belief in Jesus' resurrection;
- understand disputed issues concerning the events and interpretations of the first Easter;
- grasp the significance of Jesus' resurrection as described by each evangelist;
- begin to think through what Jesus' resurrection means for your own context.

The two things which must be regarded as historically secure when we talk about the first Easter are the emptiness of the tomb and the meetings with the risen Jesus. Once we locate the early Christians within the second-Temple Jewish world, and grasp what they believed about their own future hope and about Jesus' own resurrection, these two phenomena are firmly warranted.[1]

THE GOSPELS: THE LORD HAS RISEN

The reader might at this point be wondering why we did not begin with the resurrection narratives in the gospels, rather than starting with Paul. The reason is that Paul's letters pre-date the gospels by between ten and forty years, depending on the uncertain dating of the latter. Paul's letters show us vividly the type of things Christians were saying about Jesus' resurrection within a short time of the events. The gospels were written in a period when the early church, diverse as it was, had already been well shaped by the gospel, particularly by the belief in Jesus' resurrection. Our task now is to survey the Easter stories themselves, noting their distinctive features and assessing their origins and credibility.

1 Wright *RSG*, 686.

THE ORIGINS OF EASTER

Having noted that the four gospels almost certainly reached written form some time after Paul's letters, we should also note that the Easter stories themselves show several signs of reflecting much earlier tradition.

1. The stories lack scriptural embellishment. This is very surprising if they emerged relatively late from within a scripture-reading early community, whose members were making up stories of a bodily resurrection to bolster their beliefs in Jesus. If, as a first-century scripture-reading writer, you started with Paul's theology, or indeed with that of Revelation or Ignatius of Antioch, and tried to turn that theology of resurrection into an artful, just-as-if-it-happened-yesterday sort of narrative, it would be extremely difficult to avoid reference to scripture. As Paul himself says, quoting very early tradition, the first Christians believed that Jesus' resurrection was 'according to scripture',[2] and we can see in 1 Corinthians and elsewhere the kinds of scriptural references he had in mind. Yet the Easter narratives remain scripturally unadorned. They are not littered with quotes of scriptural fulfilment and ancient prophecies come good. This shows decisively that belief in Jesus' resurrection was not generated, as some have suggested, by taking passages like Hosea 6.2 or Daniel 12.2 and building up from them a story about Jesus coming back from the dead. Something else was shaping the narrative: a personal encounter to which witness was borne, a witness which was thereby rooted in history.

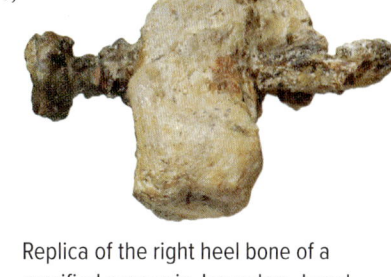

Replica of the right heel bone of a crucified person in Jerusalem, Israel Museum
Todd Bolen / BiblePlaces.com

2. The burial of Jesus, and the discovery of the empty tomb, can be regarded as historically solid. While it is true that many victims of crucifixion were not properly buried, especially during times of war (they were left as carrion for vultures and wild dogs, or dumped in open graves), we know that many victims of crucifixion did indeed receive a proper burial. Roman officials were known to release the bodies of condemned criminals to their families particularly during festivals, as Philo attests.[3] Take the famous example of Yehohanan ben-Hagkol. Yehohanan was a first-century Judean man who died by crucifixion and whose bones were discovered in Jerusalem in 1968 in an ossuary box with his name on it, a nail still lodged in his ankle bone. Roman governors of Judea were probably inclined more often than not to support

---
2 See e.g. Lk. 24.27, 32, 44; Jn. 20.9; 1 Cor. 15.4; Ac. 13.32–37.
3 Philo, *Flacc.* 83.

Jewish burial customs about not leaving victims of execution hanging after sunset lest it cause further commotion (see Dt. 21.22–23).[4]

What is more, given that the tendency of Christian tradition was to implicate and blame the Judean leadership for Jesus' death, it is unlikely that people making up a 'burial story' would have identified Joseph of Arimathea, a member of the Sanhedrin, as the person who buried Jesus. They would have been more likely to have proposed a faithful disciple.[5] In regard to the empty tomb, it is implied in Paul's traditional account in 1 Corinthians 15.3–5 and described in Mark 16.1–8. The clear Palestinian ambience and the distinctly un-Markan language of Mark 16.1–8 indicates a highly primitive tradition. The ending of Mark creates its own problems to which we shall return. For now, it is noteworthy to say that the empty tomb story very probably arose in Jewish-Christian circles. The text refers to devout Jewish practices like keeping the sabbath and respecting the Decalogue's injunction against work on that day (Mk. 16.1–2). Large stones were known to have been used to close tombs in and around Jerusalem (Mk. 16.3–4). Depicting angels as young men reflects Jewish tradition (Mk. 16.5). Mark's story designates Jesus as 'the Nazarene' (16.6). It shows an interest in Galilee (Mk. 16.7). And the language of resurrection is employed to underscore Jesus' vindication (Mk. 16.6). Thus, Mark 16.1–8 expresses the atmosphere and language of the early Jerusalem church.[6] In addition, the earliest Jewish explanation for the empty tomb was that the disciples stole the body, which of course assumes that the tomb was empty and the body was not to be found.[7] Had the tomb not been empty that entire wrinkle in the story would be inexplicable.

Images from the life of Christ, The Three Maries at the Empty Tomb, Psalter of Eleanor of Aquitaine, c. 1185, Dutch National Library

Public Domain

3. The Easter narratives seem to reflect a mixture of eye-witness enthusiasm and strange bewilderment as to what had actually happened. Eye-witness testimony is pasted all over the narratives. The women

---

4   See Evans 2014.
5   Mk. 15.43–47/Mt. 27.57–61/Lk. 23.49–56/Jn. 19.38–42.
6   Allison 2005, 328.
7   Mt. 27.64.

are prominent in all of the gospels: they saw Jesus die, watched his body being laid in the tomb, discovered the tomb empty, and encountered an angel (or two). The evangelists do indeed diverge in some details, like which women were there (Mary Magdalene, Mary the mother of James, Salome, Joanna?), but that is no reason to brush them aside. Richard Bauckham comments:

> The divergences . . . have often been taken as grounds for not taking them seriously as naming eyewitnesses of the events. In fact, the opposite is the case: the divergences, properly understood, demonstrate the scrupulous *care* with which the Gospels present the women as witnesses.[8]

The fact that a woman's testimony was legally worthless in the ancient world means that it would not constitute the surest grounds if one wanted to fabricate a story to win widespread approval. For a case in point, Josephus adds the following gloss to the law of witnesses in Deuteronomy 19.15: 'From women let no evidence be accepted, because of the levity and temerity of their sex.'[9] This is all the more telling in that in the tradition reported by Paul in 1 Corinthians 15 the women have already been airbrushed out: clearly some even in the early days saw their presence as an embarrassment when announcing the gospel to a sceptical audience. Had the gospel stories been invented in the post-Pauline period, then, the likelihood of the women playing such a prominent role would be reduced to nil.

4. *The wide breadth of people who saw Jesus is also telling.* The appearance of Jesus to Simon Peter is significant in the tradition as it is reported by Paul, intimated by Mark, mentioned in passing by Luke, and amplified by John.[10] An appearance to James, which Paul mentions, is interesting too, since Jesus' family had been alarmed by his work. So far as we know, at no point prior to Easter had James been a follower of Jesus; yet he quickly became a key leader in the Jerusalem church.[11] In addition, Jesus is said to have appeared not just to individuals but to groups of disciples, two on the road to Emmaus,[12] the Eleven in an upper room,[13] several on a beach in Galilee,[14] and even up to five hundred all at once.[15] What is more, the Easter narratives are saturated with realistic responses by people experiencing moments of confusion,[16] as well as feelings of fear and joy,[17] while doubt persisted for some even

---

8   Bauckham 2006, 49 (italics original).
9   Jos. *Ant.* 4.219.
10 1 Cor. 15.5; Mk. 16.7; Lk. 24.34; Jn. 21.1–22.
11 See Mk. 3.31–32; 1 Cor. 15.7; Gal. 2.9; *Gos. Heb.* § 5.
12 Lk. 24.13–35.
13 Lk. 24.36–49; Jn. 20.19–30.
14 Jn. 21.1–14.
15 1 Cor. 15.6.
16 Mk. 16.8; Lk. 24.23–24; Jn. 20.2, 9, 13–15.
17 Mk. 16.8; Mt. 28.8; Lk. 24.41, 52.

after the appearances.[18] One gets the impression that the evangelists were really struggling to explain what it was that they and their colleagues had actually seen; they knew full well that the events they were describing were unprecedented to the point of being unbelievable. They have the feel of people saying, 'I didn't understand it at the time, and I'm not sure I do now, but this is more or less how it was.' Looking at the appearances as a whole, the very strong historical probability is that, when Matthew, Luke, and John describe the risen Jesus, they are writing down very early oral tradition, representing three different ways in which the original astonished participants told the stories.

5. *We have to wrestle with the question of why the early Christians said 'Jesus is risen' if all they had intended to describe was a hallucination, a vision, or a vague belief that Jesus had ascended post-mortem into some heavenly, otherworldly realm.* The word 'resurrection' has a specific meaning and it is precisely not any of those things. Resurrection did not mean, 'I have a warm feeling in my heart that our dear friend Yeshua ben-Yoseph is now safely arrived into the bosom of Abraham.' Rather, 'resurrection' means the standing up of a dead corpse, a body coming back to life—a belief that was as precise as it was contested. And yet resurrection was thought to be something that God would do for all of Israel at the end of history, while the disciples claimed that God had done it for Jesus of Nazareth in the middle of history. This meant a radical configuration of God's purposes for Israel and the world, and a radical readjustment of beliefs about God's future, recognizing that a key element of that promised future *had already arrived in the present*. We are wise to infer that what made the early believers recalibrate their views of God and God's plans for the future was their conviction that God really had raised Jesus from the dead.

6. *A further sign that the Easter stories in the four gospels go back to very early, pre-Pauline tradition is the remarkable absence in them of any mention of the Christian future hope.* As we have just noted, thinking through that question was an important part of Paul's work and teaching, and at more or less every other point in the New Testament where Jesus' resurrection is expounded so too is there an exposition of the Christian hope to share in that resurrection. But at no point in the Easter stories in the gospels, or indeed in the opening chapter of Acts, is that even mentioned. Had they been written up in Paul's day or thereafter, that is almost unthinkable.

7. *Another similar point concerns the portrait of Jesus in the stories.* If, as many have suggested, the Easter stories were invented by people who knew their scriptures and the Jewish traditions which developed them, the two models that might have influenced the writing would be Daniel 12, in which the righteous will shine like stars, or Ezekiel 37, where the dead are remade from the bones outwards, with God's breath finally animating them. Later traditions developed these in various ways.

---

18 Mt. 28.17; Lk. 24.11, 41; Jn. 20.24–25.

At no point in the four gospels is Jesus' resurrection described in such fashions. Rather, we have something new, unanticipated: Jesus as a real human being, able to eat and drink, to break bread, to be touched—and at the same time to come and go through locked doors, to appear and disappear, and finally to go into 'heaven', that is, God's dimension of reality, with the promise of return. What could have generated such stories? The simplest answer is the best. Jesus' followers were not expecting any such thing, and had they wanted at a later date to invent stories about a 'resurrection', they would not have done it like this.

8. *It is important to think historically about how the early traditions might have developed.* By themselves, neither the empty tomb alone nor the resurrection appearances alone could have generated belief in Jesus' resurrection.[19] If there had been an empty tomb, but no appearances of Jesus, then the members of the early church might have said that Jesus had been taken into heaven—but they would not have spoken of that as a 'resurrection'. More likely, they would have concluded, like Mary in John's gospel and like the story the soldiers were instructed to tell in Matthew, that someone had removed Jesus' corpse. Equally, if there had been various appearances of Jesus while it was obvious that his body was still in the tomb, then the early believers might have said that Jesus' spirit or his angel had appeared to them in a vision, as they said when they thought Peter had died but heard him knocking on the door.[20] Such post-mortem 'visitations' were well known in the ancient world, as indeed they are in our own day. But nobody would have described such a thing as a 'resurrection'. The belief that Jesus had been bodily raised from the dead emerged *necessarily* from *both* the discovery of the empty tomb *and* the appearances of him alive after his death. The empty tomb and the appearances of a living Jesus, taken together, provide a powerful reason for the emergence of the church's belief in his resurrection.

So when we look broadly at the Easter stories, we find them to be a complex group of narratives, exhibiting a clear Jewish texture, raising various literary and historical questions, pressing a key theological message, while being indelibly lodged in the historical memory of the early Christians as the definitive accounts of what they thought had happened to Jesus.

MARK: FEAR AND TREMBLING

Mark's resurrection narrative, assuming for the moment that the 'longer endings' normally designated Mark 16.8b and 16.9–16 are secondary additions, ends in a peculiar way. The women leave the tomb in fearful confusion: 'Trembling and bewildered, the women went out and fled from the tomb. They said nothing to

---
19 See further Wright *RSG*, 686–96, followed by Allison 2005, 321–6.
20 Ac. 12.15.

anyone, for they were afraid.'[21] If this verse does represent the end of Mark's gospel, as our best textual witnesses indicate, was it Mark's intention to break off right there? Did he really intend his whole gospel, admittedly in rough Greek, to end with the words *ephobounto gar*, 'for they were afraid'? This raises many questions.

Resurrection of Jesus, eleventh-century mosaic, Hosios Loukas monastery, Greece
Basilica di San Marco, Venice, Italy / Cameraphoto Arte Venezia / Bridgeman Images

We note, first, that the longer endings are indeed unlikely to be authentic. The earliest manuscripts of the gospels, the great fourth-century codices Sinaiticus and Vaticanus, conclude with Mark 16.8. They are followed by several later manuscripts. Some of the early Fathers of the church either show no knowledge of the longer ending or show, even while reproducing it, that they know it to be dubious. (Unfortunately, Mark is the least well attested of all the gospels in the manuscript tradition, so we have a smaller pool of manuscripts to draw from.) But the great fifth-century manuscripts, led by Alexandrinus, include the 'longer ending' (Mk. 16.9–20), and most subsequent manuscripts follow this lead. In addition, four manuscripts from the seventh, eighth, and ninth centuries, and some later ones, insert the so-called 'shorter ending', in effect verse 16.8b; and all except one of these then continues with the 'longer ending' as well. A good many of the manuscripts that do contain the

---

21 Mk. 16.8.

longer ending, however, have marks in the margin, such as asterisks and the like, to indicate that the passage is regarded as of doubtful authenticity. In coming to a verdict, the apparently independent omission in the two fourth-century manuscripts, coupled with all the other scattered evidence, makes it highly unlikely that the longer endings are original. Mark 16.9–16 looks suspiciously as if it was derived from elements of the resurrection accounts in the other canonical gospels; it is a kind of early 'resurrection harmony', composed to fill in the gaps in Mark. In which case, 16.9–16 is not a good witness to what Mark actually wrote, but is a good witness to the emergence of a fourfold gospel-collection in the second quarter of the second century, as the longer ending was known to Justin Martyr.

Of course, if Mark 16.8 is not only the extant ending but also the intended ending, what does that mean?

Some have claimed that Mark intended his ending to be deliberately ambiguous, almost parabolic. He was not interested in giving the readers closure; rather, readers had to figure out for themselves what the empty tomb and angelic news meant. Would they run away in fear like the women, or would they have faith and believe that Jesus was truly risen? Mark gives them the options, but not the answer. This all sounds well and good in our supposedly sophisticated reading world. It provides a tantalizing postmodern reading of Mark's strange ending. But it may be a bit too clever to be true.

Others have taken this ending as a sign that the earliest Christians did not know about an empty tomb, and that Mark has conveniently contrived an explanation for the report (recent in his own day) about the empty tomb: 'Well, the women were supposed to tell everyone about the empty tomb, but you know what women are like—they were timid and fearful, and never told anybody.' But there are problems here. To begin with, the fact that the women accompanied Jesus to his crucifixion and burial, and attempted to anoint the body of someone by then regarded as an enemy of the state, highlights their courage rather than their cowardice. In addition, that the women 'said nothing to anyone' does not mean that they failed to inform the disciples of these astonishing events as the angel commanded them, but only that they kept it a secret from outsiders—from people they passed on the way back into the city—for reasons of fear. We need to place the fear and silence in Mark 16.8 within the wider pattern of Mark's gospel where similar injunctions to silence lead to the broadcast of news. For example, when in Galilee, Jesus said to a man who had been healed, 'See that you say nothing to anyone; *but go, show yourself to the priest*.'[22] If we plot Mark 16.8 as part of the familiar Markan pattern of silence to outsiders but dissemination of news to an intended audience, then perhaps we should anticipate something like, 'They said nothing to anyone else, *but went and*

---

22 Mk. 1.44.

told the disciples.'[23] Confirmation for that possibility is that in Mark moments of fear become opportunities for expressing faith and engaging in action.[24] So too for the women at the tomb: despite their fear and bewilderment, we might naturally expect that their next move would be to find their feet and their faith and soon after to run to the disciples to tell them the strange news. That is exactly how Matthew interpreted the Markan episode. Although the women were scared, he says, they were 'filled with joy, and ran to tell his disciples'.[25]

Another option is that Mark 16.8 is not the original ending to the gospel of Mark, but that there was an original longer ending that is now lost. As we have just seen, a more expansive ending, where the women said nothing to anyone but then told the disciples, fits naturally into the Markan secrecy motif and the pattern of fear and faith that Mark has constructed throughout his gospel. Three further observations reinforce this possibility. First, the Markan Passion predictions look forward to Jesus' resurrection as the sequel to his suffering (Mk. 8.31; 9.9) and to a proclamation of the gospel further abroad (Mk. 9.9; 13.10; 14.9). Mark has shown us how the suffering came true; he might be expected to complete the account. Second, the angel's news that 'he has risen' (Mk. 16.6) naturally lends itself to an expectation of appearances of the risen Jesus. Third, Mark 16.7 implies the coming restoration of Simon Peter (analogous to what we find in Jn. 21) and an appearance in Galilee (analogous to what we find in Mt. 28). Mark's gospel, in its extant form, ends on the notes of fear and trembling, but might well have contained additional material about the son of man being raised from the dead and appearing to the disciples, all as further proof of Jesus as the divinely sent prophet who opposed the Jerusalem Temple. That ending, somewhere and somehow, is now lost to us. Many ancient texts—the Dead Sea Scrolls are good examples—lack a beginning and an end. Those are the parts of a scroll which get torn off or rot away. Perhaps that's what happened with Mark.

MATTHEW: EARTHQUAKES AND ANGELS

Matthew goes his own way and poses his own problems. He has two stories which mark him out from the other gospels: sleeping saints walking out of their tombs and a guard of soldiers who get bribed to spread rumours. In the middle of all this, we have a story of the finding of the empty tomb, quite similar to Mark's, though with significant differences. Matthew's narrative then concludes with a final commissioning on a mountain in Galilee.

First, concurrent with the veil of the Temple being torn in two, Matthew notes:

---

23 Bauckham 2002, 289.
24 See Mk. 4.41; 5.15, 33, 36; 9.32; 10.32.
25 Mt. 28.8.

> The earth shook, the rocks split and the tombs broke open. The bodies of many holy people who had died were raised to life. They came out of the tombs after Jesus' resurrection and went into the holy city and appeared to many people.[26]

This is a strange story, not mentioned elsewhere, either in the gospels or outside them. That is part of the problem; another part is that the story is inherently not just shocking and unexpected but also very peculiar: if the dead saints came to life, but did not come out of their tombs until *after* Jesus' resurrection, how did anyone know? One could say that some stories are so odd that they may just have happened. This may be one of them, but in historical terms there is no way of finding out. Alternatively, as Michael Licona suggests, Matthew might here be drawing on some apocalyptic 'special effects', using portents of darkness and resurrections as a dramatic way of saying that a great king has died, or that the 'Day of the Lord' has come.[27] Or perhaps Matthew is blending the present and future together in a kind of eschatological melange, with Matthew previewing the future resurrection and underscoring the life-giving power of Jesus' death.[28]

Second, another story which spills over from Matthew's Passion sequence is the vignette where the Pharisees request that Pilate should place an additional guard at Jesus' tomb to stop the disciples from stealing the body. But then, when the resurrection happens, the guards fold up like a card table, Jesus' body disappears from the tomb, and the chief priests and elders scramble to bribe the soldiers, telling them to spread the rumour that the disciples stole the corpse.[29]

The story, obviously, is part of an apologia for the bodily resurrection of Jesus. It is an attempt by Matthew to ward off any suggestion that the disciples had in fact stolen the body, which must have seemed the most natural explanation for the tomb's being empty. What should be borne in mind is how implausible it is to suppose that the whole story would have been invented in the first place, let alone told and finally written down, unless there was already a rumour going around about a disappeared body, with speculation as to who might be responsible. If nobody had suggested such a thing, it is difficult to imagine the Christians putting the idea into people's heads by making up tales that said they had. It is no surprise, then, that Justin reports that the story was still being told by anti-Christian Jewish apologists in the mid-second century.[30] If the empty tomb itself were simply a late legend, it is unlikely that people would have spread stories about body-stealing in the first place, and doubly unlikely that Christians would have employed the dangerous tactic of

---

[26] Mt. 27.51–53.
[27] Licona 2010, 552.
[28] Bird and Crossley 2008, 69 n. 30.
[29] Mt. 27.62–66; 28.11–15.
[30] Just. *Dial.* 108.

reporting such stories in order to refute them. We remind ourselves again of one thing which the story reinforces: resurrection meant bodies. It did not mean 'spiritual survival' or a new religious experience for friends of the deceased.

Third, Matthew's final scene (Mt. 28.16–20) is highly significant as it condenses so many Matthean themes. The main emphasis of this closing paragraph is upon who Jesus is now revealed to be, the one who has been granted 'all authority in heaven and on earth'—virtually identical in phraseology to the kingdom-clause in the Matthean version of the Lord's Prayer.[31] This, it seems, is how the prayer is being answered; this, in other words, is how the kingdom is coming, how the will of the 'father' is being done. The significance of the resurrection, as far as Matthew is concerned, is that Jesus now holds the role that had been marked out for the Messiah in Psalms 2, 72, and 89, which became concentrated in such imagery-laden figures as the 'son of man' in Daniel 7 (v. 18 echoes Dan. 7.14) and the texts which developed that line of thought. The worldwide commission Jesus gives the disciples depends directly upon his possessing all authority in heaven and on earth, within the 'kingdom' that is now well and truly inaugurated. The only explanation for this messianic authority on the one hand, and this kingdom-fulfilment on the other, is that Jesus has been raised from the dead.

Matthew has written, through and through, a book of Jewish history and theology. His whole thesis is that Israel's God has been at work in Jesus, a point proved climactically and decisively by his resurrection. Matthew believed, every bit as much as did Paul, that Jesus really did rise from the dead, leaving an empty tomb behind him, and that he was now invested with all authority in heaven and on earth.

LUKE: BURNING HEARTS AND BROKEN BREAD

Luke 24 is a small masterpiece, designed as the closing scene for a large-scale work of art. Whether or not, as tradition fancifully suggested, the author of the third gospel was himself a painter, his skill in sketching verbal pictures is unmatched in the New Testament, and his resurrection chapter displays it in full measure.

Luke 24 has three sections and a final conclusion: (1) the story of the empty tomb (Lk. 24.1–12, largely following Mark and Matthew, though with different wording); (2) the journey to Emmaus, and the brief meal upon arrival (Lk. 24.13–35); (3) the appearances of Jesus to the disciples in the upper room (Lk. 34.36–49); and (4) the final description of the ascension, rounding off the gospel as a whole while overlapping with the opening scene in Acts (Lk. 24.50–53; Ac. 1.1–11).

Like the other evangelists, Luke is telling the Easter stories in his own way. He feels himself free to shape them and point up particular lessons, repeated in each section of the chapter. Luke has followed Mark in many ways throughout his gospel,

---

[31] Mt. 6.10; see *Did.* 8.2.

but he cheerfully departs from him here, with no mention of the disciples being told to go to Galilee, and no hint of resurrection appearances anywhere other than in and near Jerusalem. Luke names three women as the early visitors to the tomb: Mary Magdalene, Joanna, and Mary the mother of James; but he also speaks of 'the others with them' (Lk. 24.10). There is no mention of the women seeing Jesus, as they do in Matthew, and as Mary Magdalene does in John. The women fulfil their commission to tell the disciples, but 'their words seemed to them an idle tale, and they did not believe them' (Lk. 24.11). Most noticeably perhaps, among incidental features of the chapter, the entire sequence of resurrection appearances, culminating in the ascension itself, appears to take place on a single day. Luke also has unique material: he refers to a resurrection appearance to Peter (Lk. 24.34), provides particular emphasis on the physicality of Jesus' resurrection body (Lk. 24.38–43), and uses the Emmaus story as the central vehicle by which to convey his message about Easter and its meaning (Lk. 24.13–35).

Across the narrative, Luke highlights two features: the fresh exposition of scripture and the breaking of bread. The hearts of the two on the road to Emmaus are burning within them at the first of these; their eyes are opened at the second (Lk. 24.27, 32, 35). Then, in the upper room, Jesus 'opened their minds to understand the scriptures' (Lk. 24.25). Bring this forward into Acts, and we find two of the four elements in early church life: the apostles' teaching, the fellowship, the breaking of bread, and the prayers (Ac. 2.42). Luke's whole oeuvre is designed, at a large scale, to tell the story of Jesus and the early church in such a way that its position at the climax of Israel's scriptural story can be fully understood and appropriated. Disciples are to understand the scriptures in a whole new way, in the light of the events that have happened to Jesus. They are to make this fresh reading of scripture the source of their inner life of burning zeal (Lk. 24.32) and their framework for understanding who Jesus was and is, who they are in relation to him, and what they must do as a result (Lk. 24.45–48).

JOHN: NEW DAY, NEW TASKS

John's two Easter chapters rank with Romans 8, not to mention the key passages in the Corinthian correspondence, as among the most glorious pieces of writing on the resurrection. John lacks the rigorous logic of Paul's 'Therefore . . .' at the end of a long and gritty argument, and John's Easter narrative is comparatively more dramatic and more laden with deeper symbolism than the synoptic accounts. He provides a breathtaking synthesis of theological testimony, early tradition, apostolic memory, and vibrant metaphor, unmatched elsewhere in the New Testament. John's gospel ends with new-found faith, but it is faith that must now go out into a new world, a risky resurrection-faith facing a new day, and must attempt new tasks without knowing in advance where it will all lead.

Duccio di Buoninsegna, *Christ at the Sea of Galilee, c.* 1308–11, detail from altarpiece, Cathedral of Siena
De Agostini Picture Library / G. Nimatallah / Bridgeman Images

The basic features of John's Easter story are easily laid out. The initial story of the finding of the empty tomb (Jn. 20.1–18) overlaps in content with that of the synoptics, but it is the differences that stand out: Mary Magdalene is mentioned alone among the women, and she meets Jesus (as the women do in Matthew). As in Luke 24.12, Peter runs to the tomb on hearing the news; but in this gospel he is accompanied by the 'beloved disciple', and in a dramatic scene they run together, with the beloved disciple getting to the tomb first.

Next follow two stories set in the evening in the upper room: the first on the same day as the events in the garden; the second a week later. The first (Jn. 20.19–23) seems to correspond, in content though not much in wording, with Luke 24.36–49: Jesus commissions his followers for a mission to the world, and bestows the spirit on them to equip them for the task. The second presents a scene beloved of artists, ancient and modern. Thomas, who was not present on the first evening, acquires his now perpetual nickname by declaring his doubt that the lord has truly risen, and is then confronted by the risen Jesus inviting him to touch and see for himself. Thomas refuses the invitation, blurting out instead the fullest confession of faith anywhere in the whole gospel: 'My lord and my God' (Jn. 20.28). Jesus makes a wry comment, the scene is over, and so too is the book in its original form.

But it is not the end. John 21 provides more appearance-stories, this time set in Galilee. John, just like Matthew, has Jesus appear in both Jerusalem and Galilee, though the appearances are far fuller, and the Galilee appearance is by the lakeshore, not on the mountain. Peter and six others of the disciples go fishing and catch nothing; Jesus, unrecognized, directs operations from the shore, as once before in Luke's gospel, resulting again in a spectacular catch. Coming ashore, they find Jesus already cooking breakfast and inviting them to share it. 'None of the disciples', comments the author, 'dared ask him, "Who are you?" They knew it was the lord' (Jn. 21.12 NTE/KNT [amended]). Jesus then takes Simon Peter for a walk along the shore, and asks him three times if he loves him, corresponding to Peter's triple denial in John 18. Receiving a triple 'Yes' for reply, he commissions Peter to be a kind of under-shepherd, which will require him, too, to face suffering. Then, seeing the beloved disciple following them, they have a brief exchange about him ('Lord, what about this man?') which leads to the open-ended challenge, 'What is that to you? You must follow me!' This leads straight into the ending, which we have already noted.

Some scholars have been quick to treat John's gospel as offering a more or less realized eschatology: 'eternal life' is already present. This is in line with Jesus' claim that 'I am the resurrection and the life' (Jn. 11.25), the raising of Lazarus (Jn. 11), the repeated references to 'eternal life' as a present possession or thereabouts (for example Jn. 3.15–16; 4.14; 6.54; 17.2–3), and the way in which Jesus experiences 'glory' in his Passion (for example Jn. 11.24, 40; 12.16, 23, 28; 13.31–32; 17.1, 4). But the texts themselves are more subtle than the theory warrants. For a start, there is a resilient future perspective in John's gospel that looks ahead to a future day of resurrection and judgment (see Jn. 5.25–29; 6.40; 11.24). To be sure, John can see crucifixion, resurrection, and ascension as a single event. That makes good sense at one level theologically. But he can also differentiate them carefully; and the future horizon is not glibly telescoped into the present. The mere fact that he has written such substantial stories of the resurrection speaks for itself when it comes to the distinction between crucifixion, resurrection, and ascension. Jesus *was* crucified, *has now* been raised, and *will* ascend (20.17).

John's gospel is supremely a gospel of witness, giving its testimony to Jesus' resurrection and the constellation of meaning and mission that it generates. It matters for John that Easter actually happened; it is not just a theological idea or an inner experience of the disciples. Precisely because he is an incarnational theologian, committed to recognizing, and helping others to recognize, the living God in the human flesh of Jesus, it is vital and non-negotiable for John that when Thomas makes his famous confession in John 20.28 he should be looking at the living God in human form, with the eye not simply of faith, but of ordinary human sight, which could be backed up by ordinary human touch—though Thomas, it seems, remained content with sight. Similarly, the 153 fish that Simon Peter dragged up on the shore may well be intended to symbolize something (though interpretations of this have always varied), but the man who cooked breakfast for the disciples was a living person, Jesus, not an allegory of faith. The evangelist reiterates the point by saying that this was the third resurrection appearance of Jesus to the disciples (Jn. 21.11–14). There is, in other words, nothing about John 20—21, seen in the context of the gospel as a whole and particularly of the prologue which it balances so well, to suggest that these stories originated as, or would have been heard by their first hearers as, an allegory or metaphor of spiritual experience. John believes that the Word was made flesh, that he was crucified in this flesh, and that he was bodily raised on the third day.

HE IS RISEN!

The historical verdict before us is this: prevalent and pervasive in the early church was the belief that Jesus of Nazareth had been bodily raised from the dead by the God of Israel. This conviction constituted the axis upon which their prayers, praise, praxis, narrative, symbols, and confession all turned; it was the basis of their recognition of Jesus as Messiah and lord, their insistence that the creator God had inaugurated the long-awaited new age, and above all it provided the pledge for their own hope in Jesus' return, the resurrection of all believers, and God putting all things to right.

Jesus' resurrection is of course more than simply a historical postulate, a random event which we have now demonstrated to be far and away the best explanation for the rise of early Christianity. It also generates a world of meaning.

First, it tells us something about Jesus himself. The resurrection constitutes Jesus as the world's true sovereign, the 'son of God' who claims absolute allegiance from everyone and everything within creation. Jesus is the one in whom the living God, Israel's God, has become personally present in the world, has become one of the human creatures that were made from the beginning in the image of this same God. He is the start of the creator's new world: its pilot project, indeed its pilot.

Second, believing in Jesus' resurrection is not a mere affirmation of a creedal proposition. It is self-involving. It means trusting in God, in *this* God, who raises the dead, who calls for a commitment to discipleship and to the worldwide mission that the resurrection has launched. Resurrection faith calls people to new tasks embodying Jesus' kingdom-praxis, belonging to the renewed covenant-family, and proclaiming Jesus as lord and saviour. For Christians, the road to Emmaus is not just a story. It is a way of life.

Third, resurrection generates a counter-cultural perspective. No wonder the Herods, the Caesars, and the Sadducees of this world, ancient and modern, were and are eager to rule out all possibility of actual resurrection. They are, after all, staking a counter-claim on the real world. It is the real world that the tyrants and bullies (including intellectual and cultural tyrants and bullies) try to rule by force, only to discover that in order to do so they have to quash all rumours of resurrection, rumours that would imply that their greatest weapons, death and deconstruction, are not after all omnipotent (see 'Blast from the past: John Chrysostom on the resurrection'). But it is the real world, in Jewish thinking, that the real God made, and still grieves over. It is the real world that, in the earliest stories of Jesus' resurrection, was decisively and for ever reclaimed by that event, an event which demanded to be understood, not as a bizarre miracle, but as the beginning of the new creation. It is the real world that, however complex this may become, historians are committed to studying. And, however dangerous this may turn out to be, it is the real world in and for which Christians are committed to living and, where necessary, dying. Nothing less is demanded by the God of creation, the God of justice, the God revealed in and as the crucified and risen Jesus of Nazareth.

WALKING THE ROAD TO EMMAUS IN A POSTMODERN WORLD

> **BLAST FROM THE PAST: JOHN CHRYSOSTOM ON THE RESURRECTION**
>
> *John Chrysostom's famous Paschal homily is read every Easter in Orthodox churches. It contains these moving words about the resurrection:*
>
> He has destroyed death by undoing death.
> He has despoiled Hades by descending into Hades.
> He vexed it even as it tasted of His flesh.
> Isaiah foretold this when he cried:
> Hades was filled with bitterness when it met Thee face to face below;
> Filled with bitterness, for it was brought to nothing;
> Filled with bitterness, for it was mocked;
> Filled with bitterness, for it was overthrown;
> Filled with bitterness, for it was put in chains.
> Hades received a body, and encountered God.
> It received earth and confronted heaven.
> O death, where is your sting?
> O hell, where is your victory?

What does all this have to do with Christian mission in a postmodern world? How are you to address this world with the gospel of the risen Jesus? For a start, you cannot just hurl true doctrine at it. Doing that will either crush people or drive them away. Mission and evangelism were never meant to be a matter of throwing doctrine at people's heads. They work in a far more holistic way: by praxis, symbol, and story, pointing beyond the world the way it is to the new world that has been uncomfortably launched within creation by the creator God acting in his son and now by his spirit. We must get used to telling the story of God, Israel, Jesus, and the world as the true metanarrative, the story of healing and self-giving love. We must get used to living as those who have truly died and risen with Christ, so that our self, having been thoroughly deconstructed, can be put back together, not by the agendas that the world presses upon us but by God's spirit.

To drive us towards this goal, we end with a parable, returning once more to the story of the Emmaus road. This parable functions against the background of

Plaque depicting the journey to Emmaus and Noli Me Tangere, ivory, c. 1115–20

The Metropolitan Museum of Art / Gift of J. Pierpont Morgan, 1917

one of the great symbols of secular modernism, Matthew Arnold's poem 'Dover Beach'. There Arnold describes from his late-nineteenth-century perspective the way in which what he calls 'the sea of faith' has emptied; the tide has gone out; all we can hear is the 'melancholy, long, withdrawing roar' of the distant sea, leaving us in the gloom where, all too prophetically, ignorant armies clash by night.

Two serious-minded unbelievers are walking home together, trying to make sense of the contemporary world. The dream of progress and enlightenment has run out of steam. Critical postmodernity has blown the whistle on the world as they knew it. Yet postmodernity has provided no solution for, or even comfort to, the world in its current state, beset as it is with Islamic extremism, with a widening gap of rich and poor, with myths of a secular utopia ('if only we could get religion out of the public sphere!'), and with resurgent cultural imperialism and crooked forms of capitalism.

Our two unbelievers walk along the road to Dover Beach. They are discussing, animatedly, how these things can be. How can the stories by which so many have lived have let us down? How shall we replace our deeply ambiguous cultural symbols? What should we be doing in our world now that every dream of progress is stamped with the word 'Babel'?

Into this conversation comes Jesus, incognito. 'What are you talking about?' he asks. They stand there, looking sad. Then one of them says, 'You must be about the only person in town who doesn't know what a traumatic time the twenty-first century has been. Nietzsche, Freud, Foucault, and Derrida were quite right: life is empty. We thought we'd brought peace to the middle east through war, and we've had nothing but more wars ever since. We had a sexual revolution, and now we have an epidemic of sexual harassment, and more lonely and confused people than ever before. We are so connected with one another through social media that we ignore the people sitting in front of us. We pursued wealth, but we had the global financial crisis and ended up with half the world in crippling debt. We can do what we like, but we've all forgotten why we liked it. Our dreams have gone sour, and we don't even know who "we" are any more. And now even the church has let us down, corrupting its spiritual message with talk of cosmic and political liberation.'

'Foolish ones,' replies Jesus. 'How slow of heart you are to believe all that the creator God has said! Did you never hear that he created the world wisely? And that he has now acted within his world to create a truly human people? And that from within this people he came to live as a truly human person? And that in his own death he dealt with evil once and for all? And that he is even now at work, by his own spirit, to create a new human family in which repentance and forgiveness of sins are the order of the day, and so to challenge and overturn the rule of war, sex, money, and power?' And, beginning with Moses and all the prophets, and now also the evangelists and apostles of the New Testament, he interprets to them in all the scriptures the things concerning himself.

They arrive at Dover Beach. The sea of faith, having retreated with the outgoing tide of modernism, is full again, as the incoming tide of postmodernism proves the truth of Chesterton's dictum that when people stop believing in God they don't believe in *nothing*, they believe in *anything*. On the shore there stands a great hungry crowd—people who had cast their bread on the retreating waters of modernism only to discover that the incoming tide had brought them bricks and centipedes instead. The two travellers wearily begin to get out a small picnic basket, totally inadequate for the task. Jesus gently takes it from them, and within what seems like moments he has gone to and fro on the beach until everyone is fed. Then the eyes of them all are opened, and they realize who he is, and he vanishes from their sight. And the two say to each other, 'Did not our hearts burn within us on the road, as he told us the story of the creator and his world, and his victory over evil?' And they rush back to tell their friends of what happened on the road and how he had been made known in the breaking of the bread.

Actually, that is not a story. It is a play, a real-life drama. And the part of Jesus is to be played by you and me. This is Christian mission in a postmodern world.

Further reading

Allison, Dale C. 2005. *Resurrecting Jesus: The Earliest Christian Tradition and Its Interpreters*. London: T&T Clark.
Bird, Michael F., and James G. Crossley. 2008. *How Did Christianity Begin? A Believer and Non-Believer Examine the Evidence*. London: SPCK, pp. 38–69.
Bryan, Christopher. 2011. *The Resurrection of the Messiah*. Oxford: Oxford University Press.
Evans, Craig A. 2014. 'Getting the Burial Traditions and Evidences Right.' In *How God Became Jesus: The Real Origins of Belief in Jesus' Divine Nature*. Edited by M. F. Bird. Grand Rapids, MI: Zondervan, pp. 71–93.
Lehtipuu, Outi. 2015. *Debates over the Resurrection of the Dead: Constructing Early Christian Identity*. Oxford: Oxford University Press.
Licona, Michael R. 2010. *The Resurrection of Jesus: A New Historiographical Approach*. Downers Grove, IL: InterVarsity.
Perkins, Pheme. 1994. 'The Resurrection of Jesus of Nazareth.' In *Studying the Historical Jesus: Evaluations of the State of Research*. Leiden: Brill, pp. 423–42.
Wright, N. T. 2003. *The Resurrection of the Son of God*. COQG 3; London: SPCK.
———. 2007. *Surprised by Hope*. London: SPCK.

Marco Zoppo, *St Paul*, dated 1470, Ashmolean Museum, Oxford
Public Domain

V

PAUL AND THE FAITHFULNESS OF GOD

If Paul had never been heard of, and his letters had suddenly come to light in a hoard of papyri buried in the sands of Egypt, there are certain questions we would want to ask. Who was the author? Did the same person write all these letters, or only some? In what culture did the author(s) live, and how might that culture help us understand what was being said? When were they written? Were they real letters, or was the literary form simply adopted as a teaching tool? Supposing them to be real letters, who were they addressed to? How would they have been understood? Can we get a sense, from the letters, of the larger world in which author and readers lived? What human motivations can we discern both in the letters themselves and in their circumstances, so far as we can reconstruct them? Historians ask questions like these all the time. Any academic study of Paul, a letter-writer from two thousand years ago, must be grounded in the attempt to answer such questions with all the tools available to us. The aim, all along, is 'exegesis': to get *out* of the text what is there, rather than, as with 'eisegesis', to put into it ideas from somewhere else.[1]

---

1   Wright *PRI*, 3.

15

The Story of Paul's Life and Ministry

CHAPTER AT A GLANCE

This chapter sets out the basic tenets of Paul's apostolic ministry.

By the end of this chapter you should be able to:

- understand the basic contours of Paul's early life, conversion, and missionary work;
- describe the basic chronological sequence of Paul's career, including when his epistles were written;
- develop an appreciation for the complexities of establishing Pauline chronology.

I believe that we need to read Paul with a sense of his own intense conviction that he was exploring a new country—as fertile, beautiful and exhilarating, above all as real and tangible in its working, as any that a sixteenth-century sailor might have run across in his voyages of discovery. Did Paul transform Christianity? Yes, of course. He took a bundle of traditions and practices generated by the mysterious events around and after Jesus' death and struggled, with all the intellectual and imaginative skill he could muster, to see the patterns that held them together. But the more you read him, the more you see how he is labouring to do justice to something that is already there confronting him in these stories and practices—not improvising a new religious system. Sometimes there are still loose ends in his attempts to bring it all together in a consistent pattern; more often he uncovers a set of interconnections so profound that they have set the agenda for centuries of further discussion and elaboration. He is never looking for new religious theories for their own sake; he is always asking what must be true about God, about Jesus, about the human and the non-human world, if the prayer and practice of the early Christians he knew is to make some kind of sense, to them as well as to their baffled and suspicious neighbours.[1]

---

[1] Williams 2015, x–xi.

PAUL'S SIGNIFICANCE FOR THE EARLY CHURCH

Paul stands as a monumental figure in the history of the early church. He was a person of notoriety and controversy from the very beginning, both before and after his conversion, the type of man who could cause riots as much as broker reconciliation between warring parties. Apart from Jesus, no person other than Paul was more *formative* for recasting the Jewish worldview around messianic hopes and establishing kingdom-centred Christian communities in the west. Apart from maybe Peter, no person other than Paul was more influential in *founding* churches across the Roman empire, communities that were distinguished by their devotion to the lord Jesus, and committed to a radically counter-cultural way of life. Apart from maybe Irenaeus, no person other than Paul was more *formidable* when it came to defending the gospel against accommodation and adulteration by dissident groups. Among Paul's legacies are obviously the thirteen letters attributed to him, which make up 24 per cent of the New Testament canon, and constitute a theological centre to the apostolic testimony about Jesus. On top of that, Paul was crucial in the transition of the church from a Jewish sect into a largely gentile religious association—even if that was not exactly what he intended. No wonder that Paul has been called, however exaggeratedly, the 'second' or 'real' founder of Christianity (see 'Blast from the past: John Chrysostom on the apostle Paul'). As we will see, it might be more fitting to see him as the originator, or the first real exponent, of 'Christian theology'.

BLAST FROM THE PAST: JOHN CHRYSOSTOM ON THE APOSTLE PAUL

As I keep hearing the Epistles of the blessed Paul read, and that twice every week, and often three or four times, whenever we are celebrating the memorials of the holy martyrs, gladly do I enjoy the spiritual trumpet, and get roused and warmed with desire at recognizing the voice so dear to me, and seem to fancy him all but present to my sight, and behold him conversing with me. But I grieve and am pained, that all people do not know this man, as much as they ought to know him; but some are so far ignorant of him, as not even to know for certainty the number of his Epistles. And this comes not of incapacity, but of their not wishing to be continually conversing with this blessed man. For it is not through any natural readiness and sharpness of wit that even I am acquainted with as much as I do know, if I do know anything, but owing to a continual cleaving to the man, and an earnest affection towards him. (Chrys. *Praef. Hom. Rom.*)

John Chrysostom, Leitourgikon, dated 1664
© *British Library Board. All Rights Reserved / Bridgeman Images*

The Story of Paul's Life and Ministry

He didn't start the movement. He insisted that, for the movement to flourish, its members needed to learn both what to think and how to think.

Scholars continue to debate what it was that Paul was up to, how he fitted into (or grated against) the Jewish world(s) of his day, what sort of relationship he had with the leaders of the Jerusalem church, what role he had in shaping the early churches, what is the best way to understand his letters, and what have his most lasting contributions been in the realms of intellectual history, ancient culture and religion, and Christian thought. While these are all good questions, a more pressing one for our purposes is to ask: how did Paul become this towering figure? To that end, in this chapter we will examine the basic contours of Paul's biography and apostolic mission, and then in the next chapter we will offer a crash course on the main features of his thought.

PAUL'S EARLY LIFE

Paul the apostle began life as a Diaspora Jew, named Saul of Tarsus. We do not know for sure when Paul was born. In the immediate years after Jesus' death, we hear that he was a 'young man' who minded the coats of a mob as they stoned Stephen to death, and he calls himself an 'old man' when writing to Philemon in the early or middle 50s AD.[2] The terms 'young' and 'old' are of course very imprecise.

Ancient road in Tarsus

---

[2] Ac. 7.58; Philem. 9.

In a world where boys assumed adult responsibilities at puberty, a 'young man' might be in his mid-teens; in a world where most adults died in their fifties one might be 'old' at forty-five. It is impossible to be precise, but Paul was probably born a few years after Jesus, perhaps as late as around AD 10.

Luke informs us that Paul was born in the city of Tarsus, a city to which he returned after his encounter with Jesus on the road to Damascus.[3] Tarsus was the capital of Cilicia in Asia Minor, divided by the River Cydnus, and located south of the strategically vital Cilician Gates, which were the only route through the Taurus mountain range linking Cilicia to Syria. It was an important location for the Romans in their campaigns against the Parthians and Sassanians east of the Euphrates. The city was swept up in Alexander the Great's conquest of the east in the fourth century, and it was annexed for Rome by Pompey in 63 BC. During the reign of the emperor Augustus, when Paul was born, the city grew to a population of about half a million people.

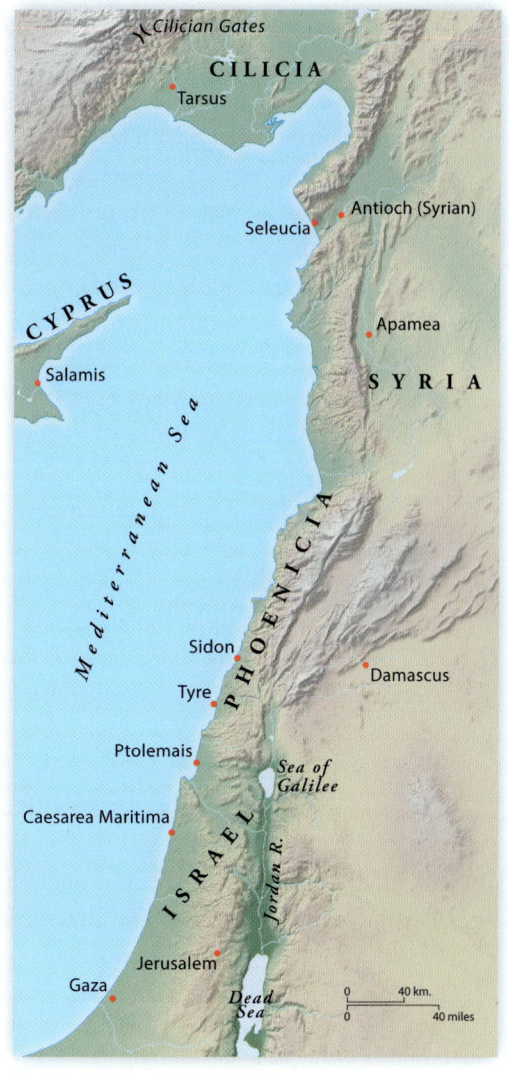

Tarsus, in the region of Cilicia

Strabo reports from the first century that Tarsus surpassed both Athens and Alexandria as a seat of learning, being particularly known for its schools of philosophy and rhetoric, and for its poets.[4] Numerous Jewish families were settled in Cilicia during the Seleucid dynasty in the third century BC.[5] Philo mentions Jewish colonies across Asia Minor, including the regions of Pamphylia, Cilicia, Bithynia, and Pontus.[6] Luke refers to a synagogue of Jewish freedmen in Jerusalem, comprised

---

[3] Ac. 22.3 and 9.30; 11.25; 21.39.
[4] Strabo *Geogr.* 14.5.131.
[5] Jos. *Ant.* 12.119, 147–53.
[6] Philo *Leg.* 281.

The Story of Paul's Life and Ministry

of Greek-speaking Jews from regions including Cilicia, possibly involving those from Tarsus.[7]

Paul's social status is hard to determine. Luke informs us that he was a Roman citizen by birth, though Paul himself never mentions it in his letters.[8] How Paul might have acquired citizenship is impossible to tell. He might have been descended from a Judean who had been captured and enslaved by the Romans at some point, was transported to Syria or Asia, and was subsequently set free and granted citizenship. Paul's grandfather or father may have settled in Tarsus, where there was a significant Jewish community, and Paul grew up learning a craft as a tent-maker or leather-worker.[9] In such an environment, Paul acquired a vivid fluency in Greek. To judge from his letters, he knew a fair amount about both rhetoric and philosophy.[10]

On several occasions Paul underscores his ethnic and religious heritage as a Jew: '[I was] circumcised on the eighth day, a member of the people of Israel, of the tribe of Benjamin, a Hebrew born of Hebrews; as to the law, a Pharisee.'[11] All this indicates that Paul was raised in a devout Jewish family, conscious and proud of his Jewish identity, and committed to the Jewish way of life. Luke records Paul claiming to have been educated in Jewish ancestral customs in Jerusalem; some have disputed this, but it would work very well with Paul's own autobiographical remarks about his training as a Pharisee and his advancement in zealous Jewish activity in his early adulthood.[12]

All in all, Paul was raised in a romanized hellenistic city, in an urban Jewish family, enmeshed in Diaspora Jewish life, probably among the artisan class. Greek was probably his first language, though he knew the Hebrew scriptures intimately, as well as the Septuagint. He was undoubtedly exposed to greco-roman literature, rhetoric, culture, and philosophy in both his city in general and his education in particular. Early on—probably in his teens—he left Tarsus and trained in the Pharisaic tradition in Jerusalem. All the evidence suggests that, in the many ongoing debates about what it meant to be a loyal Jew, he aligned himself with the more politically militant and religiously zealous Shammaite wing.[13]

---

7   Ac. 6.9.
8   Ac. 22.15.
9   Ac. 18.3 (the word in question is *skēnopoios* which seems to be related to the construction and erection of tents). Elsewhere Paul says that he and his colleagues 'worked night and day in order not to be a burden to anyone while we preached the gospel of God to you' (1 Thess. 2.9), 'worked night and day, labouring and toiling so that we would not be a burden to any of you' (2 Thess. 3.8), 'work hard with our own hands' (1 Cor. 4.12), 'work for a living' (1 Cor. 9.6), and among his sources of suffering Paul says that he experiences 'hard work' (2 Cor. 6.5).
10 Paul cites a proverb of Euripides (1 Cor. 15.33), sayings of Epimenides (Tit. 1.12; Ac. 17.28), and the Cilician Stoic philosopher Aratus (Ac. 17.28).
11 Phil. 3.5; see also Gal. 2.15; 2 Cor. 11.22; Rom. 9.3–4; 11.1.
12 Ac. 22.3; 26.4; Phil. 3.5–6; Gal. 1.14.
13 See Wright *PFG*, 85–6.

PAUL'S PERSECUTION OF THE CHURCH

On several occasions Paul refers to his earlier persecution of the church and his efforts to destroy it.[14] So why did this Greek-speaking Diaspora Jew turned Pharisaic neophyte embark on a persecution of the churches in Jerusalem and even as far as Damascus? He does not tell us explicitly, but it is not difficult to work out the reasons.

Examination of the Judean persecutions against the churches provides only fragmentary and ambiguous evidence. Within a few years of Jesus' death the Greek-speaking Jewish Christian Stephen was accused of 'speaking against this holy place and against the law' and saying, 'Jesus of Nazareth will destroy this place and change the customs Moses handed down to us.' For this he was stoned to death by an unruly mob.[15] In addition, James the brother of John was put to death by Herod Agrippa I sometime around AD 41–4, which 'met with approval among the Jews'.[16] Paul, during his mission in Greece in the late 40s or early 50s AD, could commend the Thessalonians for enduring 'the same things those churches suffered from the Jews who killed the Lord Jesus and the prophets and also drove us out'.[17] Finally, we know that, during an interregnum (that is, between Roman governors) around AD 62, the high priest Annas had James the brother of Jesus and some of his friends stoned to death on the charge of being 'breakers of the law'.[18] The members of the Judean church then faced ostracism and persecution from those in their immediate environs, particularly when they refused to join in the revolution against Rome in AD 66.

The most likely reason for the charge against Stephen was because he was rehearsing Jesus' own critique of the Temple, and promoting Jesus' own approach to the Torah. A Judean mob might well regard this as an affront to their own convictions and aspirations: a charge, in other words, of disloyalty to Israel's ancestral customs, a disloyalty that might be disastrous. We should of course recall that other Jewish groups (for instance, the Qumranites) launched strong critiques of the Temple, or at least the way it was being run. Different groups could offer their own particular approach to Torah-observance, as with the Pharisaic schools of Shammai and Hillel, the Essenes, John the Baptist, and so on, without being rounded up and lynched (John the Baptist was killed for other reasons). So Stephen was not put to death on account of anything that we would call 'heresy', over some complicated theological issue, but more out of sectarian rivalry, for promoting Jesus' revolutionary vision of Israel in which the Temple would be judged and elements of Torah set aside in the

---

14 Gal. 1.13, 23; Phil. 3.6; 1 Cor. 15.9; plus Ac. 8.3; 9.1–2; 22.4; 26.10–11.
15 Ac. 6.13–14.
16 Ac. 12.1–3.
17 1 Thess. 2.14–15.
18 Jos. *Ant.* 20.200.

light of the dawning of the kingdom of God. In addition, it is highly unlikely that James was an actual 'lawbreaker', since there is no indication that members of the Jerusalem church had abandoned the Torah. To the contrary, they seem to have been devotedly observant, especially the circle associated with James.[19] It may be that James and his colleagues were put to death for simply being 'other', socio-religious deviants who combined veneration of Jesus with their thoroughly Jewish way of life; or perhaps, especially if the letter of James comes from this James himself, they were outspoken in their critique of the wealthy aristocracy. In addition, James might also have borne the brunt of Jewish opposition to Paul and his co-workers, who in their work in the wider world were (from Jerusalem's point of view) brazenly fraternizing with gentiles and allegedly discouraging Diaspora Jews from observing the Torah.

Synagogue floor mosaic depicting the temple facade and Torah ark, Israel Museum
© 2018 by Zondervan

This was precisely what the members of the delegation from James to Antioch were afraid would happen, which is why they asked Jewish Christians to separate from gentiles in Antioch. Paul's sharp opposition to this request must have been seen as highly dangerous back in Jerusalem; and, in a sense, James's own death later proved the point.[20]

So why did Saul of Tarsus persecute the church? In general, opposition to Jesus-believers may not have involved detailed theological disagreements; it would be

---

19 Ac. 15.19–21; 21.18–25. In addition, the letter of James presents a deep-seated and thoroughly Jewish way of life and devotion which is enriched rather than negated by the infusion of Jesus' teachings.
20 Gal. 2.11–14; 6.12; Ac. 21.20–21.

enough that they were following the Jesus who had been shown up as a troublemaker, 'leading Israel astray'. But those, particularly the Pharisees, whose hopes for the coming kingdom of God were marked by an ever-stricter adherence to Torah, as well as a passionate attachment to the Temple, were bound to see the early Jesus-followers as dangerously disloyal. If that kind of view were to catch on, it could delay or even derail the long-awaited fulfilment of the divine purposes. In addition, of course, their veneration of a crucified man as Messiah and lord was affronting to Jewish scruples, especially if, as seems likely, devotion normally ascribed to YHWH was being given to Jesus. Sociologically, they had become sectarian rivals to existing groups, and potential troublemakers in the eyes of those in the political class. These things were not of course separate from 'religious' concerns. Our distinctions of categories do not apply.

Although it is difficult to nail down the precise contention against Jewish Christians, we are on firmer ground when we enquire after Paul's motivation for his persecution. Paul tells us that he was acting on account of his *zeal*. Paul says that he 'persecuted the church of God' because he was 'extremely zealous for the traditions of my fathers'.[21] This 'zeal' is more than simply hotheaded enthusiasm. It has a particular resonance in Jewish tradition, referring to the violence that might be necessary to preserve Israel's holiness. The most famous zealot of Israel's history was Phinehas, who killed an Israelite and his Midianite mistress in their flagrant disobedience.[22] Elijah is often ranked with Phinehas on account of his slaughter of the prophets of Baal.[23] The Maccabean revolt began when Mattathias 'burned with zeal' and killed a fellow-Judean and a Syrian official for attempting to offer a pagan sacrifice in their village of Modein. Mattathias rallied his sons into the hills with the words, 'Let every one who is zealous for the law and supports the covenant come out with me.'[24] A similar perspective is found in the Qumran scrolls where a hymn says, 'I draw near [to God], I become zealous against all those who practice wickedness and men of deceit.'[25] Philo offers warning to anyone who might transgress Israel's law because: 'There are thousands who have their eyes upon him full of zeal for the laws, strictest guardians of the ancestral institutions, merciless to those who do anything to subvert them.'[26] Several themes, it seems, cluster around 'zeal': holiness, purity, separation, hatred of paganism, violence. This was what drove Saul in his persecution of Jewish Christians.

Given this background, it is not difficult to imagine a young Jew, faced with the sordid power of paganism in the early first century and the shabby compromises of

---

[21] Gal. 1.13–14; see Phil. 3.6; Ac. 22.3–4.
[22] Num. 25.11; see Ps. 106.28–31; Sir. 45.23–24; 1 Macc. 2.26, 54; 4 Macc. 18.12.
[23] 1 Kgs. 18.20–40.
[24] 1 Macc. 2.24, 27 NRSV.
[25] 1QH 6.14 (tr. Wise, Abegg and Cook [2005]).
[26] Philo *Spec. Leg.* 2.253.

many of his countrymen, being fired up by this vision. Cling on to God's faithfulness, stir up your courage, and act! This was what being a Pharisee was all about. This is what the word 'Judaism' meant to the young Saul from Tarsus. The word 'Judaism' (Greek *Ioudaismos*) was not at the time the name for a 'religion'. That again is anachronistic. It referred to the active propagation of the ancestral way of life, and its defence against attack, whether from the outside (as in the case of Mattathias opposing the Syrians) or the inside (as in Saul of Tarsus persecuting Jewish Jesus-believers). Saul, as a faithful young Pharisee, committed to 'Judaism' in this sense, believed it was his duty to stop by whatever means necessary those who perverted Israel's worship and affronted Israel's holiness.

Saul, then, was not just a hothead with a fiery brand of theology. He was a violent zealot of the most extreme kind, believing that God was sponsoring his violence and that he was therefore justified in seeking to destroy anyone who he thought endangered Israel's national purity and hence Israel's future hope. Saul's brand of Pharisaism propelled him into efforts to attack perceived religious deviants with the bloodthirsty righteousness we have seen in the modern world. We might think of a jihadist trying to impose his brand of *sharia* law on a cosmopolitan Turkish city; or perhaps the radical vehemence of a gang of Orthodox Jews, setting fire to a catholic church in Galilee in order to rid the area of filthy *goyim*.

This Saul could have become a distinguished rabbi among the Pharisees. Had he played his cards right he might, like some other Pharisees, have been elevated to the ranks of the Sanhedrin. He certainly had the intelligence and the oratorical abilities to attract followers. Or perhaps he could have been a Pharisaic missionary to non-Jews, as Eleazar was to the Adiabene royal family,[27] or like Philo a leading figure in the protest against Caligula's attempt to instal a statue of himself in the Jerusalem Temple (AD 40).[28] He might even, like his younger contemporary Josephus, have played a significant part in the Judean revolt against Rome (AD 66). We can only imagine. What we do know is that something dramatic and radical happened to Saul of Tarsus in the midst of his persecution of the church. As a result, people would soon be saying of him: 'The man who formerly persecuted us is now preaching the faith he once tried to destroy.'[29]

PAUL'S CHRISTOPHANY AND CONVERSION

Saul's zeal led him to pursue followers of 'the Way' (as the Jesus-movement was sometimes called in the early days) who had fled to Damascus. He was given authority from the chief priests (Pharisees, being a populist pressure-group, had no legal

---

27 Jos. *Ant.* 20.34–50.
28 Philo *Gai.* 188.
29 Gal. 1.23.

standing in themselves) to bring them back by force to Jerusalem.[30] It was on the road to Damascus that Saul experienced a vivid and arresting encounter with the risen lord Jesus that threw his social and theological worlds into a cataclysmic upheaval. Saul met Jesus; that, for him, was the heart of it; and he was never the same again. As a result, he was forced to re-examine his worldview and recalibrate it at the deepest level.

In addition to the three accounts of this incident in Acts, we have Paul's own words referring to the event, including language like seeing the lord, having a light shone in one's heart, the son revealed 'in me', and the rather graphic image of an infant ripped out of its mother's womb. All these are attempts to describe the unexpected and traumatic experience of meeting the person whose followers Saul had been trying to kill.[31]

Luke's accounts are certainly defining points in his narrative—writers do not repeat a story three times unless they really want to stress it—but they are also problematic on some of the details such as what Paul's companions saw and heard and precisely when Paul actually got his commission to go to the gentiles.[32] Luke's underlying aim seems to have been to tell the story in such a way as to align Paul with the prophets and visionaries of Israel's history, and also to place him alongside penitent pagans who turned round and went in a new direction. This serves as both an apologia for Paul's new life and work, a legitimation of him in the eyes of potentially puzzled or hostile readers, and a heightening of the dramatic tension as the story is repeated in a crescendo to accompany Paul's progress, through riots and trials, until his eventual arrival in Rome. Luke, ever the artist, has painted the portrait so as to bring out the features that will speak to his intended audience.

Paul's letters have the benefit of furnishing us with his own first-hand account, but they remain notably terse and remarkably opaque. Scholars have long debated

Detail of Paul's conversion from the Pauline Jubilee doors in the basilica of San Paolo fuori le mura in Rome, Italy
© Fr Lawrence Lew, O.P.

---

30 Ac. 9.1–2. On the Jewish population of Damascus see Jos. *War* 2.559–61; 7. 368; *Life* 27.
31 Ac. 9.1–22; 22.1–21; 26.9–23; 1 Cor. 9.1; 15.8; 2 Cor. 4.6; Gal. 1.15–16.
32 Cp. Ac. 9.7 and 22.9 on what the companions saw and heard. Compare Ac. 9.15; 22.17–21; and 26.16–18 on when Paul got his commission to go to the gentiles.

whether Paul's experience was 'subjective' or 'objective'. Was it 'physical' or 'spiritual'? Was it a tangible person he saw, or merely a vision—or even some interior mental event? What we do know is that Paul doesn't say he saw a ghost, an angel, or a spirit. He claims to have seen the bodily resurrected and glorified Jesus. (To speak of a non-bodily resurrection would be, as we saw in Part IV, a complete oxymoron.)[33]

The effect of this 'revelation' upon Paul was radical and world-changing. He was in the truest sense 'converted', shifting from the Pharisaic brand of Judaism to its messianic cousin in the Jesus-movement. The word 'conversion', though, should not mislead us. Paul did not 'convert' in the sense of abandoning something called 'Judaism' for something called 'Christianity'. Neither of those words, in the modern sense, corresponds to a reality in Paul's world. Saul did, however, experience a 180-degree turn in many of his deeply held convictions about the God he served and how he should serve him; that is, Paul continued to be a loyal servant of the God of Israel, but was now fired with a quite different vision of who that God really was and what he was doing to fulfil his promises.

Paul's description of this moment in Galatians 1.11–17 rings with loud echoes of the call of prophetic figures like Isaiah and Jeremiah from Israel's sacred history.[34] Paul was determined, at the very moment when describing the radically new thing that had happened to him, to anchor that in Israel's ancient traditions, to which, he insisted, he was still absolutely loyal. Paul seems to have seen himself as a prophetic figure, heralding the good news of God's new exodus, and the arrival of the true Davidic deliverer, among Jews and gentiles across the eastern Mediterranean.[35] The biggest change of course was in Paul's evaluation of Jesus himself. Having persecuted Jesus' followers because he regarded them as sectarians, loyal to a false messiah, he now came face to face with living proof that Israel's God had vindicated Jesus against that charge. God had declared, in the resurrection, that Jesus really was 'his son' in a genuine *messianic* sense. The resurrection demonstrated that Jesus was the son of David, the root of Jesse, Israel's Messiah, God's anointed.[36]

If, then, Jesus had been vindicated as Messiah, certain things will have followed at once in Saul's mind. Jesus was to be seen as Israel's true representative: God had done for him, in the middle of history, what loyal Jews had expected God to do for all Israel at the end of history. The great turnaround of the eras had therefore already begun. 'The resurrection' had split into two, with Jesus the Messiah as the first-fruits and the Messiah's people following later at his return. And if Jesus was Messiah, then Paul saw at once that he must also be *the world's true lord*. He was

---

33 Wright *RSG*, 375–98. See ch. 13 above.
34 See Isa. 49.2; Jer. 1.5.
35 See e.g. Aernie 2012.
36 See Rom. 1.3–4; 15.12.

the *kyrios* ('lord' or 'master') at whose name every knee would bow. He was the 'son of man' exalted over the beasts (Dan. 7.13–14, alluded to in 1 Cor. 15), Israel's king rising to rule the nations (Ps. 2.1–12; Isa. 11.1–10). Every step down this road took Saul of Tarsus closer to saying that if Jesus was the *kyrios* now exalted over the world—a deduction, we repeat, from his messiahship—then the biblical texts which spoke in this way were harder and harder to separate from the texts which, when they said *kyrios*, referred to Israel's one God, YHWH himself. Jesus, the Messiah, was *kyrios*. Israel's God had exalted Jesus as the world's true lord; and, with Daniel 7 and Psalm 110 clearly of great significance in the minds of the early Christians, this seemed to mean that the one true God had exalted Jesus to share the divine throne itself. Thus—the move we see perhaps most clearly in Philippians 2.6–11—if Jesus had now been exalted to share the very throne of God, the God who (as Isa. 45.23 declares) will not share his glory with another, then this Jesus must have been from all eternity, somehow or other, 'equal with God'.

Paul's Damascus road experience, while not the only thing shaping his theology, was nonetheless the catalyst and conceptual hub for everything he had to say about Jesus, messiahship, Israel, Torah, justification, gentiles, and hope. Paul did not, as in some caricatures, reject everything about his Jewish way of life. Nor, for that matter, did he keep them all and merely add 'Jesus is Messiah' on the top. Every first-century Jew knew that, if the Messiah was revealed, the true Israel would be defined as those loyal to him.

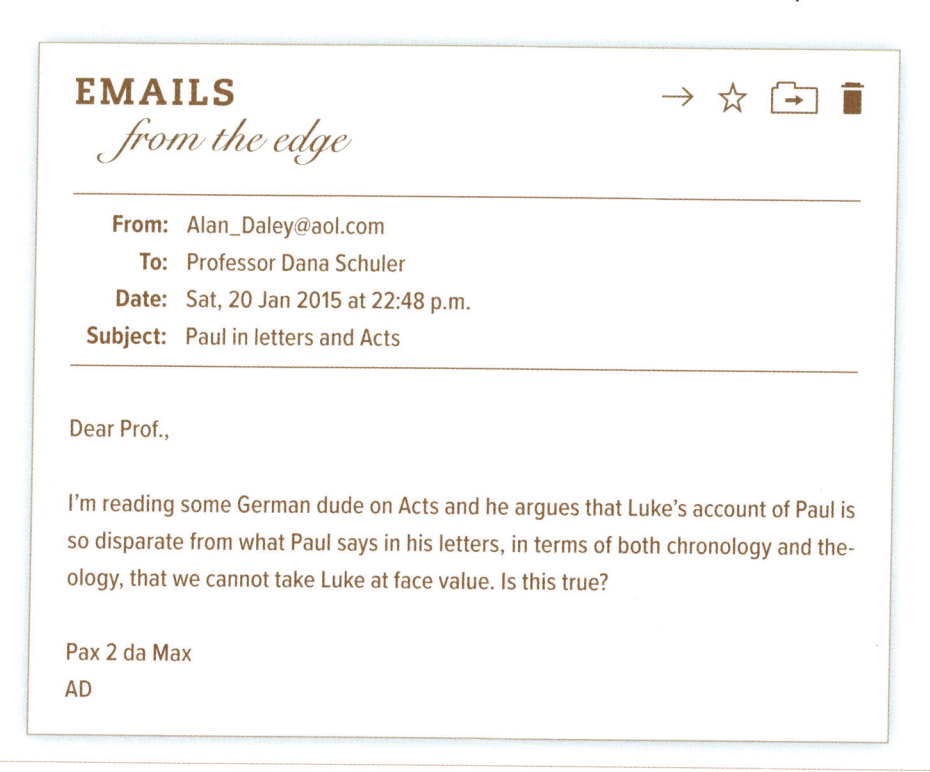

EMAILS
from the edge

From: Alan_Daley@aol.com
To: Professor Dana Schuler
Date: Sat, 20 Jan 2015 at 22:48 p.m.
Subject: Paul in letters and Acts

Dear Prof.,

I'm reading some German dude on Acts and he argues that Luke's account of Paul is so disparate from what Paul says in his letters, in terms of both chronology and theology, that we cannot take Luke at face value. Is this true?

Pax 2 da Max
AD

> **From:** Professor Dana Schuler
> **To:** Alan_Daley@aol.com
> **Date:** Sun, 21 Jan 2015 at 7:34 a.m.
> **Subject:** Re: Paul in letters and Acts
>
> Dear Alan,
>
> The veracity of Luke's representation of Paul has always been something of a quagmire, bound up with an even bigger quagmire of whether Luke is reliable as a historian of the early church. Several problems emerge. For instance, it is alleged to be impossible to reconcile Paul's famine-relief visit in Acts (11.28–30; 12.25) with Paul's claim that 'I was personally unknown to the churches of Judea' (Gal. 1.22) prior to his second Jerusalem visit (Gal. 2.1–10). Some point out the seeming problem of Paul's claim that he is not an eloquent speaker (1 Cor. 2.4; 2 Cor. 11.6) with Luke's presentation of him as a master rhetorician (e.g. Ac. 17.22–31). And why does the Paul of Acts look much more Torah-observant than the Paul of the epistles (contrast Ac. 18.18; 21.21–24 with Rom. 6.14; 14.14)? Luke seems to imply that Paul's most potent adversaries were unbelieving Jews (Ac. 17.5–7, 13; 18.12–14; 20.3; 21.27; 22.30; 23.12; 24.5–9; 25.7–11, 15) whereas in the Pauline letters his main opponents are fellow Jewish Christians (Gal. 2.4–5, 11–14; Phil. 3.2–3; 2 Cor. 11.5, 22). These are engaging questions which draw a range of possible responses.
>
> Luke's depiction of Paul is part of a wider debate about whether Acts is history, theology, fiction, or rhetoric. Some 'conservative' scholars have tended to defend the 'historicity' of Acts, and 'radical' scholars to question it. No surprises so far. But underneath this is a rather different issue. It is precisely part of the implicit worldview of the older liberal protestant ruling paradigm in New Testament studies to suggest that the writing of the four gospels in general, and of Luke in particular, represented a 'failure of nerve' on the part of the early church: the 'parousia' has not arrived on schedule, so let's look back rather than forward! This extended to a highly negative judgment against Luke: at a time when 'salvation history' was seen as just about the most wicked theological mistake one could make, Luke was seen as its primary architect, pushing the early church down the fateful road to 'early Catholicism'. I suspect that this entire way of looking at things rests on some fairly major mistakes (see N. T. Wright, *NTPG*, ch. 13 part 2, ch. 15 part 6). Thus the prejudice against Acts as a historical source is based, in part, on this strange idea that early Christian historiography was a category mistake. The received 'wisdom' suggests a date for Acts in the 80s, 90s, or even later, but there are actually no solid arguments for this, and such dating largely depends on prior

judgments already noted and queried. There were, in other words, theological and ideological reasons why Acts was pushed further away from the events it purports to record and dismissed as a reliable historical account. Now that we see so many things about early Christianity so very differently, it is time to revisit the reasons behind such judgments and submit them in their turn to critical questioning.

Concerning Paul in Acts, Luke's portrait of Paul is often held to be too different from what we find in the letters for them to be the same person. Well, it is of course likely that there will be significant differences between any book about any person and his or her own actual letters (or, today, emails). Compare, for a start, Tacitus's account of Augustus with the great man's own *Res Gestae* (Augustus's funeral inscription listing all the things he accomplished). The Pauline letters include much that Acts doesn't mention, and vice versa, as is only to be expected, granted that both are fairly short and neither is aiming at encyclopedic coverage! Paul tells us in 2 Corinthians of all sorts of escapades, including shipwrecks, which do not feature in Acts; nor does Acts even hint that Paul was a regular and passionate letter-writer, nor does it mention the Collection for the Jerusalem church. While some might suppose that this impugns Luke's historical credentials, things are not so straightforward. The chronological puzzles generated when we try to fit Acts and Paul together are the sort of thing one might expect, granted again the vagaries of first-century writing and the small amount of surviving evidence. Josephus's different accounts of his own activities do not cohere easily, but we do not for that reason assume that one version or the other is straightforwardly fictitious. In addition, the external sources, where we have them, generally tend to prove that Luke knows what he's talking about (e.g. the expulsion of Jews from Rome under Claudius in AD 49, placing Gallio in Corinth in AD 51, and knowledge of sea travel). None of this means, of course, that Acts can be treated naively as though it were a video recording of 'everything that happened'. Have you ever imagined what such a document would look like? All history consists of selection and arrangement . . . But it means that we must hold off from dogmatic negativity and look at the actual evidence afresh.

If you want to delve in further, then I suggest reading these:

Marguerat, Daniel. 2013. *Paul in Acts and Paul in His Letters*. WUNT 310; Tübingen: Mohr Siebeck.
Porter, Stanley E. 2001. *Paul in Acts*. Peabody, MA: Hendrickson.

Regards
Prof. Dana Schuler

And if the *crucified and risen Jesus* was and is Israel's Messiah, then that fate, and its full meaning, would translate into the transformation of what it meant to be Israel. Paul neither rejected nor unthinkingly endorsed the traditions and beliefs he had had when he set off for Damascus. He rethought everything in the light of what had been disclosed to him: that the crucified Jesus, executed as a messianic pretender, had been vindicated by the creator God and thereby marked out as Israel's Messiah, indeed the one appointed to be lord of the world. Paul found himself called to be his special emissary.

PAUL AND THE 'TUNNEL PERIOD'

The period between Paul's conversion in approximately AD 33 and the time when he wrote his first letters—to the Galatians in around AD 48 and to the Thessalonians in around AD 51–2—is often called the 'tunnel period'. It is the segment of Paul's life that is the most obscure to us (see 'Emails from the edge: Paul in letters and Acts'). Different constructions of events and, not least, their chronology are possible; we offer the one that seems to us most likely.

While still based in Damascus, Paul made a visit to Arabia. This was most likely to Mount Sinai, where, like Elijah who had been one of his role models, he went to do business afresh with Israel's God and to discern his own new path. Then, after returning to Damascus, he had to flee because of plots against his life. This takes us to around AD 36.[37]

Paul then visited Jerusalem, where he became acquainted with Peter and James.[38] He then spent a considerable period in Syria and Cilicia, including a solid decade back home in Tarsus, after which he was asked to join the fellowship in Antioch, where he became one of the church's leaders and teachers, acting as an emissary to Jerusalem (along with Barnabas and Titus) after prophetic warnings about an imminent famine.[39] After that he and Barnabas were sent by the church in Antioch as missionaries, travelling through Cyprus and southern Asia (part of the Roman province of Galatia).[40]

Sometime after their return to Antioch two things happened. First, Peter (referred to by Paul as 'Cephas', his Aramaic name) came to Antioch and was happy to join in with the 'open table' policy through which the reality of fellowship in the messianic family was celebrated with believing Jews and believing gentiles eating

---

[37] Gal. 1.17; 2 Cor. 11.32; Ac. 9.23–25.
[38] Gal. 1.18–19; Ac. 9.26–29.
[39] Ac. 11.28–30; Gal. 2.1–10. Debate continues among scholars as to whether the meeting between Paul and the 'pillar apostles' described in Gal. 2.1–10 corresponds to the famine-relief visit in Ac. 11.28–30 or to the Jerusalem council in Ac. 15.1–33. See discussion in Dunn 2009b, 446–50, and Keener 2012–14, 3.2194–202.
[40] Gal. 1.21; Ac. 13–14.

together. But when 'certain men from James' came from Jerusalem, Peter realized what impression this policy would create, and he withdrew—and Paul opposed him to his face.[41] Then, second, news arrived from Galatia that a similar problem had arisen there, taking the form of pressure from Jewish Jesus-believers on the male gentile believers to make them undergo circumcision. There were undoubtedly political dimensions to this problem, to which we shall return. Paul then wrote his letter to the churches in Galatia, highlighting the recent public confrontation with Peter which illustrated the point he needed to make. He then set off with Barnabas for Jerusalem, to hammer out an agreement with the church leaders.[42]

PAUL'S MISSIONARY CAREER

Paul's missionary endeavours, apart from his earlier period with the church in Syrian Antioch, were focused on cities located on either side of the Aegean Sea, in Asia Minor and Greece. Paul's evangelistic and church-planting ministry during the years AD 50–7 constitutes one of the most important periods in the church's history, second only in significance to the mission of Jesus in Palestine during AD 28–30.

Paul's second missionary journey

---

41 Gal. 2.1–10.
42 Ac. 15.

It was during this time that Paul planted gentile-majority churches in several major urban centres, wrote letters to various congregations and individuals, and took up a collection to help the beleaguered Jerusalem church.[43] His evangelistic work in these regions was perhaps the crucial factor in the radical transition of the Jesus-movement from being a minor Jewish sect to becoming a major gentile cultural phenomenon—not just a 'religion'—in the greco-roman world.

After the conference in Jerusalem, Paul and Barnabas had an angry row over whether they should take John Mark on their next journey. He had set off with them on their first trip, but had apparently got cold feet and returned to Jerusalem. He was related to Barnabas, and Barnabas wanted to give him a second chance, but Paul saw him as dangerously unreliable. (How much this dispute reflects the other tensions in the church at this point it is impossible to say, but we may suspect that they were not unrelated.) So, while Barnabas and Mark went off to Cyprus, Paul took Silas as his missionary companion and they journeyed westwards through Syria and Cilicia, encouraging the churches that Paul and Barnabas had established. Paul proceeded northwards to Derbe, Lystra, and Iconium where he met a young man named Timothy, whom he added to their party as another missionary companion.[44] Luke next describes how Paul and his friends went through the Phrygian part of Galatia in the interior of Asia Minor, but the holy spirit prevented them going west into the province of Asia, presumably to Ephesus. Instead they travelled north-west, opposite the region of Mysia, and Paul had intended to go north-east into Bithynia, but Luke says 'The spirit of Jesus did not allow them' (see box: 'What if Paul had gone east into Bithynia?'). So instead, they journeyed to Troas on the central western coast. While in Troas, Paul had a vision of a man from Macedonia pleading with him to visit the region and help them, which is where Paul and his team soon headed.[45]

Luke then tells how Paul and his companions (perhaps including Luke himself, since the 'we'-passages in Acts start at this point)[46] travelled through Neapolis and into Philippi, an important Roman colony on the east–west Via Egnatia. Luke recounts several events, including the conversion of Lydia and her household, Paul's exorcism of a slave-girl, and Paul and Silas's arrest and release.[47] It is clear from Paul's letter to the Philippians that the Philippian church, though experiencing internal rivalries and external persecution,[48] continued to have positive relations with Paul, including sending him financial support.[49]

---

[43] However, as we will see, the authenticity of several of these letters is disputed, and Paul wrote more than the thirteen letters attributed to him in the NT.
[44] Ac. 15.40—16.5.
[45] Ac. 16.6–10.
[46] See ch. 26 below.
[47] Ac. 16.11–40.
[48] Phil. 1.27–30; 2.1–11; 4.2–3.
[49] Phil. 4.10–20.

WHAT IF PAUL HAD GONE EAST INTO BITHYNIA?

The events Luke describes in Acts 16.6–10 are remarkable as they show Paul wanting effectively to do a clockwise loop of Asia Minor (i.e. modern-day Turkey). However, Luke writes that the holy spirit forced Paul to avoid the south-west and the north-east regions and sent him to the north-western coast ready to launch into Greece. This is actually a crucial juncture for Paul's ministry and the history of the church. If Paul had gone north-east into Bithynia, he could have continued the route, travelling eastwards along the northern coast of Asia Minor into Pontus and then south into Cappadocia or Armenia. At this juncture, Paul could either have headed south-west back into Syria or else travelled south-east down to the River Euphrates and on to the many hellenistic cites like Ichnai, Charax Sidou, Charrhae, Dura-Europos, many of which had large Jewish Diaspora communities, perhaps all the way to Babylon, then up the Tigris to Adiabene. Paul had already worked in the east during his time in Arabia, which was Nabatean territory (Gal. 1.17), so there was theoretically nothing to prevent him from returning to the east. If Paul had taken this route, western Christianity might well have ended up being less Pauline, and oriental/Syriac Christianity potentially more Pauline (see Bauckham 2000). However, there are reasons for supposing that as Paul's missionary strategy took shape he became increasingly conscious of the need to announce Jesus as *kyrios* in places where that word was being used increasingly of Caesar.

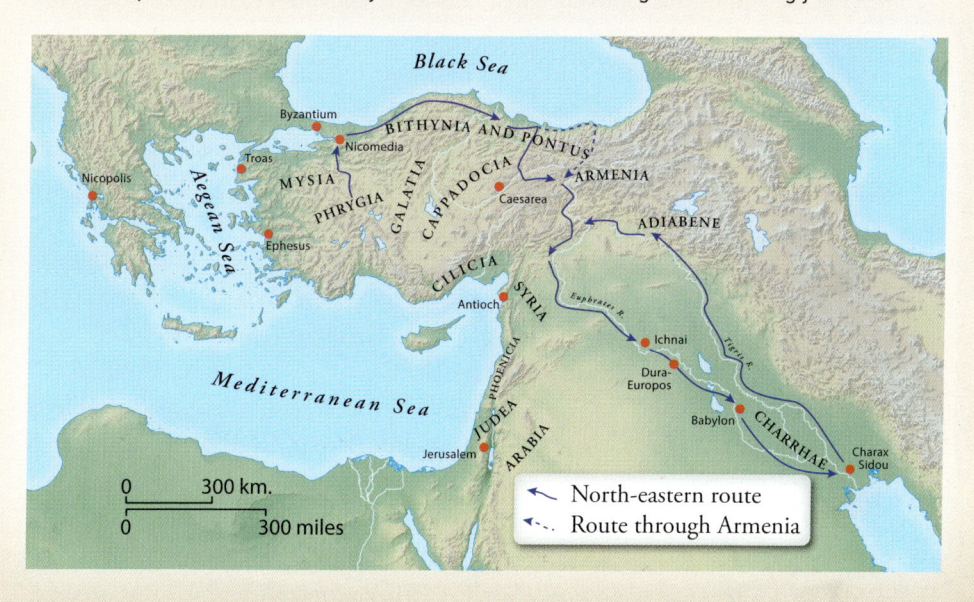

The narrative in Acts presents Paul moving southwards from Philippi through Amphipolis and Apollonia and then arriving in Thessalonica. There Paul followed his convention of preaching in the synagogue, resulting in a small cohort of Jews as well as some gentile God-fearers coming to faith. A church was established in the house of a man named Jason.[50] Paul spent some time in the city, working largely with

[50] Ac. 17.1–7.

gentiles,[51] though his success in gaining adherents resulted in the Jewish community stirring up persecution against the Thessalonian church.[52] Paul was forced to flee to Berea, and when the situation there also soured, he continued south to Athens.[53]

Luke presents Paul's sojourn in Athens as a dramatic moment: the Jewish apostle of Jesus Christ meeting the epicentre of pagan religion and philosophy. Or perhaps we should say, the highest judicial court in the Greek world hearing, to its surprise, of a higher court still, that of the one God of Israel who was going to pass judgment, through the risen Jesus, on the whole world. Paul's speech in the court of the Areopagus, or at least Luke's digest of it, combines several elements. At one level, it is one of the most epic sermons in the history of homiletics, exhibiting as it does gospel proclamation married with missional contextualization. At another, it is a clever exercise in apologetics, using local colour and culture as stepping-stones for the gospel, and engaging by implication with the major philosophies of the time. But underneath both there is a darker strand. The Areopagus was not a debating society. It was a court, designed to try serious cases. Paul was on trial for bringing 'strange new divinities' into the city. The court got more than it bargained for, and Paul was able to leave.[54]

No such trouble greeted Paul at his next port of call, the strategically important city of Corinth. Corinth, located to the south-west of the isthmus that joins northern and southern Greece, was an ideal site for east–west trade. After an earlier sacking, it had been refounded by Julius Caesar in 44 BC as a Roman colony, and had become the epitome of a romanized Greek city. We can accurately date Paul's time in the city after Claudius's edict expelling Jews from Rome (AD 49) and by the proconsulship of Lucius Gallio of Achaia concurrent with Paul's ministry there (AD 51/2) (see box: 'External evidence for Pauline chronology').[55] Paul spent eighteen months in the city, and despite hostility from the Jewish community, it was a time of profitable work. Sadly, the Corinthian churches would also prove to be a constant headache for Paul.

Coin with bust of King Aretas IV, AD 19–20, from Petra
Todd Bolen / BiblePlaces.com

While in Corinth, Paul met a Jewish-Christian couple named Priscilla and Aquila, who had been forced to leave Rome because of the Claudian edict. Paul worked with them in their shared task of tent-making, and also engaged in evangelistic discourse in the Corinthian synagogue.

---

51 1 Thess. 1.9–10; 2.9; Phil. 4.16.
52 Ac. 17.5–15; 1 Thess. 1.6; 2.14–16.
53 Ac. 17.10–15.
54 Ac. 17.16–34.
55 Ac. 18.1–18.

EXTERNAL EVIDENCE FOR PAULINE CHRONOLOGY

Paul in Damascus
King Aretas IV is described as the 'ethnarch' and 'king' of the Nabateans who ruled over Damascus during Paul's escape from the city (2 Cor. 11.32; Ac. 9.23–25). Aretas took control of Damascus in c. AD 36, either after defeating Herod Antipas in battle or when he was granted control over the city by the Roman emperor Gaius Caligula in c. AD 37. Aretas died in around AD 39/40 (Jos. *Ant.* 16.294) and so Paul's flight from Damascus can be dated between AD 36 and 40.

The edict of Claudius
According to Suetonius (*Claud.* 25.4) the emperor Claudius expelled the Jews from Rome on account of a certain 'Chrestus', which is a probable Latinism for 'Christ'. This event is normally dated to the ninth year of Claudius's reign, which is AD 49. Suetonius (*Ner.* 33.1) also records that Nero annulled all decisions by Claudius sometime in AD 54/5. Priscilla and Aquila were expelled from Rome and came to Corinth in AD 49 (Ac. 18.2) and the couple returned to Rome by the time Paul wrote to the Romans in around AD 55/6 (Rom. 16.3).

Gallio as proconsul of Corinth
Paul's ministry in Corinth is described by Luke in Acts 18.1–17, and part of his work there transpired while 'Gallio was proconsul of Achaia' (Ac. 18.12). The tenure of Lucius Gallio, the brother of Seneca, is confirmed by an inscription referring to a letter from the emperor Claudius to the Greek city of Delphi. The inscription is dated to AD 52 and refers to Gallio's successor. Since the proconsuls of senatorial provinces were appointed for a one-year term, it is most probable that Gallio was in office during AD 51/2. Seneca (*Ep.* 104.1) writes in one of his letters that his brother Gallio took ill while in Achaia, which may have cut short his term in office. The result is that Paul can be comfortably dated and located in Corinth during this period of AD 51/2.

Paul was once more expelled from the synagogue, yet appears to have planted various house-churches, based around the families of Titius Justus, the synagogue leaders Crispus and Sosthenes, Chloe, and Stephanus.[56] It was during the time in Athens and Corinth that Paul wrote his two letters to the Thessalonian churches. The first expressed Paul's anxiety that the Thessalonians would remain steadfast in the faith, and it deals with the Thessalonians' anxiety about facing trials ahead of the lord's return. The second letter addresses a concrete matter, with some suggesting that the 'day of the lord' had come already, or else that it was so imminent that Jesus-followers could abandon their occupations and live off the generosity of others. Some also suppose that this was when Paul wrote to the Galatians, though we have good reason to place that letter earlier, during the time in Antioch and before the Jerusalem conference.

The next phase of Paul's work is a roundabout trip: from Corinth to Ephesus to Jerusalem to Antioch, and back again to Ephesus.[57] Luke condenses the whole sequence. He describes briefly how Paul had his hair cut in a manner that suggests

---

[56] Ac. 18.7–8, 17; 1 Cor. 1.1, 11, 16; 16.15–17.
[57] Ac. 18.18—19.1.

a Nazirite vow, and left Corinth via the port city of Cenchreae accompanied by Priscilla and Aquila. Paul then lands in Ephesus but leaves again, after a very brief time of ministry, promising to return. He then proceeds onwards to Caesarea, up to Jerusalem to greet the church (this implies that relations were not as strained as some have imagined), and then north to Antioch. Afterwards, Paul again is on the move, this time returning through the Phrygian part of Galatia and pressing on westwards to Ephesus on the coast. In the meantime, Priscilla and Aquila have encountered an eloquent Greek-speaking Jewish Christian called Apollos, whom they instruct more carefully in the faith before sending him to minister to the churches in Corinth.

Paul spent three years in Ephesus (*c.* AD 52–4), one of the longest sustained periods of his work.[58] Ephesus itself was hugely important, the third largest city of the empire after Rome and Alexandria, central to trade routes by land and sea. The city housed a substantial Jewish minority, and was a significant religious centre containing numerous cults, including the imperial cult and the renowned temple of Artemis. Luke's narrative of Paul's time in Ephesus includes a fast-paced montage of notable events that transpired during this period. These include Paul's ministry to some disciples of John the Baptist about the holy spirit, preaching the kingdom of God in a Jewish synagogue, daily discussions in the lecture hall of Tyrannus, healing the sick, the comical account of the sons of Sceva who tried to imitate Paul's technique in exorcism but ended up being beaten up by a demoniac, the wide-scale rejection of magic by new gentile believers, and of course the anti-Christian riot led by Demetrios the silversmith.[59] Given Luke's account, it is no wonder that Paul could tell the Corinthians that 'a great door for effective work has opened to me, and there are many who oppose me'[60]—though this must be balanced by his account, early in 2 Corinthians, of having suffered so terribly in Ephesus that he despaired, at one point, of life itself.[61]

In addition, it was during this period that Paul's entourage probably established churches in adjacent areas like the Lycus valley among the regional cities of Laodicea, Hierapolis, and Colossae,[62] and perhaps in other nearby Asian cities too like Pergamum, Sardis, Philadelphia, and Thyatira.[63] Such was the growth of churches in this region that Paul could claim to send greetings from the 'churches of Asia'.[64] What is more, if Paul underwent imprisonment in Ephesus, as seems very likely, expressed perhaps metaphorically when speaking of the 'wild beasts' he faced there, and as part of the 'troubles' from the 'many who oppose me' in the 'province of Asia', then it is likely that the captivity letters (namely Philippians, Colossians, Philemon,

---

[58] Ac. 19.10; 20.31.
[59] Ac. 19.1–20.1.
[60] 1 Cor. 16.9.
[61] 2 Cor. 1.8–11.
[62] Col. 1.7–8; 2.1; 4.12–13; Philem. 1–2.
[63] On the spread of churches around this time see Col. 1.5–8.
[64] 1 Cor. 16.19; 2 Cor. 1.8; 2 Tim. 1.15.

and Ephesians) were written in Ephesus (rather than from Rome, as is more usually asserted).[65] The fact that such an Ephesian imprisonment is mentioned neither in Acts nor by Paul himself in his letters is no bar to this very likely hypothesis.

An inscription from Delphi in Greece referring to Lucius Gallio and his time in office in Achaia. The inscription is dated to c. AD 52 and therefore places Gallio and Paul in Corinth c. AD 51. See if you can find the name GALLIO (GALLIŌ).
Todd Bolen / BiblePlaces.com

The matter is clinched, in our view, by the multiple trips made by Onesimus between Colossae and Paul in prison, and by Paul's proposal of a visit to Philemon in the near future.[66] Assuming an Ephesian setting for these letters, it would be relatively easy to receive and return an absconded slave to his master with a letter of reconciliation and to also propose a visit to Philemon soon afterwards. After all, when Paul was under house arrest in Rome, he was still hoping to go westwards on to Spain, not to detour back east towards the middle of Asia Minor to visit Philemon.[67] To place these letters in Ephesus, in the middle of Paul's ministry, before his final visit to Corinth, is easy and natural, and would date all this in the early or middle 50s.

During Paul's stay in Ephesus, he wrote numerous letters to the Corinthians,

---
65 1 Cor. 15.32; 16.9; 2 Cor. 1.5–10; 6.5; 11.23.
66 Col. 4.9; Philem. 10–18, 22.
67 Rom. 15.23–24.

dispatched several colleagues to visit them, and even visited them himself. Many reconstructions of this complex time are possible, of which the following is one of the more likely:[68]

- Paul wrote a first letter based on reports, possibly from Apollos after his initial visit (Ac. 18.27—19.1), of the prevalence of sexual immorality among the Corinthians (1 Cor. 5.9–10).
- Paul then received, probably over an extended period, correspondence from the Corinthians with questions about marriage, food sacrificed to idols, spiritual gifts, the Collection (for Jerusalem), and the prospect of Apollos's return (1 Cor. 7.1, 25; 8.1, 4; 12.1; 16.1, 12), as well as troubling news about the Corinthians from house-church leaders pertaining to factions, incest, lawsuits, women dressing in culturally inappropriate ways, disorder in worship, and denials of the resurrection (1 Cor. 1.11; 5.1; 6.1; 11.18; 15.12; 16.17).
- Paul urged a visit to Corinth by a reluctant Apollos (1 Cor. 16.12).
- Paul wrote 1 Corinthians and sent it from Ephesus (1 Cor. 16.8, 19–20), with Timothy en route as well (1 Cor. 4.17; 16.10).
- Timothy arrived in Corinth and saw that things had deteriorated, and that Paul's instructions had not been heeded; so he returned to Ephesus to communicate the bad news to Paul. On hearing the news of the situation from Timothy, instead of travelling to Corinth via Macedonia as he had planned (1 Cor. 16.5–6; 2 Cor. 1.16), Paul rushed over to Corinth, apparently by direct sea-voyage, and made a 'painful visit', which further strained his relationship with the church (2 Cor. 2.1) as he made stern warnings to the believers there (2 Cor. 12.21; 13.1–2).
- Paul returned to Ephesus, and in his absence was viciously attacked by some ringleader in Corinth. He then wrote a 'letter of tears', delivered by Titus, which grieved the Corinthians further (2 Cor. 2.1–11; 7.8–12).
- Paul intended to meet Titus in Troas while Titus was on his way back from Corinth, but when Titus failed to arrive, Paul travelled to Macedonia (2 Cor. 2.12–13) where he found Titus, who reported how the Corinthians had been reconciled to him through his tearful letter (2 Cor. 7.6–16).
- Titus also informed Paul of the visit by the 'super-apostles' who had disparaged Paul's ministry as inferior to their own (2 Cor. 11.5; 12.11).
- Paul wrote 2 Corinthians from Macedonia, celebrating the Corinthians' reconciliation to him, giving them further instruction about Titus who had the task of finalizing the Collection (2 Cor. 8.6, 16–25; 12.18), and preparing them for his third visit (2 Cor. 12.14; 13.1–2).

---

[68] See similarly Dunn 2009b, 783–5.

Paul's relationship with the Corinthians can be described as tense, incendiary, and frustrating. The Corinthians were a constant headache for Paul, and required continuous attention. Their capacity for internal tumult seems to have persisted well after Paul's time: Clement, the bishop of Rome, had to write to the Corinthians to intervene in an internal dispute at the end of the first century.[69] The Corinthian correspondence is perhaps the best example of how reading Paul's letters is much like reading someone else's mail, enabling you to learn the embarrassing details of a congregation's proclivity for things like fights, factions, and fornication. These letters are also, however, our best insight into Paul's pastoral labours. He never gave up on these problem-child churches, despite the endless exasperation they caused him.

So Paul left Ephesus for Macedonia and Greece, fulfilling his earlier promise to visit Corinth for a third time.[70] While on a three-month stay-over in Corinth, he began planning his journey to Jerusalem to deliver the Collection, and strategizing for his future missionary trip to Spain. Paul seems to have believed that his ministry in the eastern Mediterranean was finished, having completed an arc from Jerusalem to Illyricum. If he was to work further, he needed virgin territory, so that he would not build on someone else's foundations. Spain was his choice—quite possibly because it was one of the main outposts of Caesar's empire.[71] Yet Paul would need a launching-base in the west, equivalent to what Antioch had been for him in the east. Rome was the obvious choice. Paul and his circle had not established churches in Rome, and even though he had many friends there, the Roman churches had emerged independently of him, probably through Jewish-Christian migrants in the 30s and 40s. So he wrote to the churches in Rome the letter that is now universally seen as one of the chief foundation-stones of all subsequent Christian thinking.

Romans was written in or near Corinth in around AD 55/6. Paul had several purposes in mind. He wanted to introduce himself; he wanted to defend his work against miscellaneous rumours; he hoped to address and heal any rifts in the church caused by the sudden return of Jewish-Christian leaders like Priscilla and Aquila after their six-year absence on account of Claudius's edict. The church in Rome, after all, faced the dangers of acculturating to Roman prejudices against foreigners like the Jews, and fracturing along ethnic lines between Jews and gentiles. Paul was hoping that by visiting Rome he might bless the Roman Christians by imparting some gift to them—perhaps a gift of fresh insight into what following Jesus might involve in the days to come—and by preaching the gospel in Rome among them. In return, he hoped they would materially support him in his mission to Spain.[72] In and through it all, Paul wanted them to grasp the full sweep of God's purposes,

---

[69] *1 Clem.*, dated to *c.* AD 90–5.
[70] 2 Cor. 12.14, 21; 13.1–2; Ac. 19.21–22; 20.1–4.
[71] Rom. 15.19–20. See Wright *PFG*, ch. 16.
[72] Rom. 1.8–15; 15.23–33.

from creation to new creation, taking in Abraham, Moses, the law, and above all the dramatic and world-changing gospel events concerning Jesus. Romans sets it all out, in the context of these complex and detailed agendas, in a way that still stretches and challenges thinkers of all sorts.

So Paul, having dictated this great letter, dispatched his benefactor, Phoebe, a deacon in the church in Cenchreae (the eastern port of Corinth), to deliver it to the various churches in Rome and to spearhead his charm-offensive on the believers there.[73] In the end, Paul would indeed make it to Rome. But it would be as a prisoner awaiting trial, rather than as a missionary apostle.

Luke's account of Paul's next journey has him fleeing from Jewish agitators in Greece, travelling through Macedonia, moving on to Troas for a brief stay, and then engaging in a short stopover in Miletus where Paul met with the elders of the Ephesian churches to say his farewells. Paul's subsequent voyage touched several coastal cities, bringing him eventually to the Judean coast at Caesarea where he and his colleagues disembarked and immediately headed for Jerusalem.[74]

Paul was warmly received by the Jerusalem church, though the underlying tensions in Jerusalem appear clearly enough in Luke's account.[75] When Paul was planning this journey, he asked the Roman churches to pray that 'I may be kept safe from the unbelievers in Judea and that the contribution I take to Jerusalem may be favourably received by the Lord's people there'.[76] Strangely, Luke does not mention the Collection, so we are left wondering if it was received or rebuffed. Anyway, Paul's hope of avoiding violent confrontation in Jerusalem proved to be in vain. James convinced Paul to engage in a conciliatory gesture to assuage misgivings about him held by zealous Jewish Christians; this would involve sharing in a purification ritual in the Temple. But the plan backfired because, when Paul and his four companions visited the Jerusalem Temple, a riot broke out. Some Asiatic Jews assumed that Paul had taken one of his gentile companions into the Temple, which would have been a serious offence. Here we return to the underlying suspicion in Jerusalem about the new movement: was it not, as had been suspected even during Jesus' public career, an attempt to replace the Temple itself with something different? Amid the ensuing uproar, Paul was only saved from being beaten to death by the intervention of Roman soldiers. Paul's subsequent speech to the Jews gathered there did not succeed in mollifying them, and he was taken into custody for his own protection.[77]

The next section of Luke's account covers the following three years (c. AD 57–60), during which Paul remained in detention in Caesarea. He endured legal

---

[73] Rom. 16.1–2.
[74] Ac. 20.1–17.
[75] See Gal. 2.11–21; 2 Cor. 11.
[76] Rom. 15.31.
[77] Ac. 21.18—22.30.

proceedings, assassination plots, and manipulation by the governor, who was hoping for a bribe. Paul, no doubt frustrated, finally played the 'citizenship' card, making an official appeal to have his case heard by Caesar himself. Then, after Porcius Festus had become governor, Paul was interviewed by King Herod Agrippa II and his sister Bernice, who concluded—too late to be of any good—that he was indeed innocent, and could have been released had he not appealed to Caesar. Yet the wheels had been set in motion. Paul, the apostle to the gentiles, would now go at last to Rome, the heart of the empire, as a prisoner under guard.[78]

'AND SO WE CAME TO ROME'

Luke's narration of Paul's journey to Rome, accompanied by various friends, is fast-paced and dramatic. It is riddled with theological motifs, rich with ancient nautical information, and bristling with drama and suspense. The voyage took them from Palestine, following the south coast of Turkey, continued around Crete, and then involved a terrifying storm and shipwreck on Malta. Having wintered there, the party continued past Sicily, until finally arriving in Puteoli, where Paul was greeted by fellow-believers. The perilous trip ends with Luke's famous words: 'And so we came to Rome.'[79]

Paul arrived in Rome in around AD 60, where he was warmly welcomed by a party of Roman believers. Luke notes how Paul was permitted to live by himself, with a Roman soldier to guard him, while he awaited an imperial audience. Early in his stay he sought a meeting with local Jewish leaders, where he emphasized (at a time of growing tension between Rome and the Judeans) that he had no intention of accusing the Jewish people. Luke indicates that the leaders of the Jewish community in Rome were happy to judge him on his own merits, without any hostile predisposition. They professed ignorance of Paul, and wanted to hear his account of the messianic sect that everyone was speaking against.[80]

The final episode in Acts then portrays Paul engaged in a local version of what had been his conventional activity: explaining from scripture, to a Jewish audience, what the kingdom of God was about, and trying to persuade his hearers about Jesus. The outcome was once more fairly standard: some believed, but most did not. This occasioned Paul's lament for Jewish unbelief, using Isaiah 6.9–10 (a passage quoted in all four gospels to similar effect) as a key scriptural prediction of Israel's recalcitrance. The result is the same as throughout his work: God's salvation is going to the gentiles.[81] This motif of Jewish rejection and consequent gentile mission is a familiar

---

[78] Ac. 23—26.
[79] Ac. 27.1–28.14.
[80] Ac. 28.15–22.
[81] See Ac. 13.46; 18.6; 28.28.

Lukan theme, but it fits like a glove Paul's own account of the gospel as being 'for the Jew first and then for the Greek'. It also undergirds his argument in Romans 11 about how Israel's rejection of the Messiah was part of God's plan to bring the gentiles to faith and so to rouse Israel to jealousy.[82]

Debate continues as to whether Paul wrote his captivity letters (namely Philemon, Colossians, Ephesians, Philippians) from Rome. (A further debate questions, as we shall see, whether he wrote Colossians and Ephesians at all, or whether they are from a later imitator.) As we suggested above, they are more likely to have been written from Ephesus.

The Pastoral Epistles, however, are in a different category. A majority of scholars has decided that Paul did not write them. These letters are, to be sure, the kind of thing you might expect a leader like Paul to write to junior colleagues, not least (in the case of 2 Timothy) as he approached his own imminent end. There are passages that some have seen as quintessentially Pauline (for example 1 Tim. 2.5–6; 2 Tim. 2.8; Tit. 3.5). But the difference in Greek style has been felt as a problem (though actually there are sharp stylistic differences among the other letters too, not least between the first and second letters to Corinth). Paul's self-presentation has seemed to many to reflect a later generation eulogizing the great apostle. The possibilities here, however, are more complex than the simple either–or of 'authenticity' on the one hand and 'forgery' on the other, as we will explain in chapter 23. For an interim statement, we could say that 2 Timothy probably has the best chance of deriving from Paul, through a secretary, or while written in a different mood. It is quite possible that these letters were put together from short fragments of Paul's correspondence with colleagues, fragments that were terse or torn, and which were then compiled, filled out, and written up by a Pauline disciple like Luke or Timothy as a kind of appendix to a Pauline letter-collection.[83] One thing is clear: the details of travel plans, and notes about Paul's companions, do not fit the narrative of Acts in the way that Paul's other letters do quite easily. That means that if they are genuine they must reflect either some significant journeys that went unrecorded in Acts (which is perfectly possible) or a time, after Paul's probable trip to Spain, in which he undertook a further journey to the east before returning to Rome to face his eventual fate.

The evidence for Paul's last years consists, then, of Acts, possibly the Pastoral Epistles, and some later Christian writings, notably the first letter of Clement. Luke says that Paul spent at least two years under house arrest in Rome; this takes us to AD 62.[84]

---

82 See Rom. 1.16; 15.8–9, which is more fully worked out in Rom. 9—11.
83 2 Tim. 4.9–22 might be the best example of an authentic Pauline fragmentary note embedded within one of the Pastoral Epistles. See Dunn 2009b, 1053–5; Williams 2015, xiii.
84 Ac. 28.30.

SKETCH OF PAULINE CHRONOLOGY

- **c. 4 BC** Birth of Jesus of Nazareth
- **c. AD 5–10** Birth of Saul of Tarsus
- **30** Crucifixion and resurrection of Jesus of Nazareth
- **33** Jesus revealed to Saul on the road to Damascus
- **33–6** Paul in Damascus, Arabia, Damascus again
- **36** Paul's first post-Damascus visit to Jerusalem (Gal. 1.18–24)
- **36–46** Paul in Tarsus; brought to Antioch by Barnabas
- **40** Gaius (Caligula) plans to erect statue in Jerusalem
- **41** Assassination of Caligula; accession of Claudius
- **46/7** 'Famine visit' to Jerusalem (Ac. 11.30; Gal. 2.1–10)
- **47–8** Paul and Barnabas on **first missionary journey: Cyprus and south Galatia**
- **48** Peter in Antioch (Gal. 2.11–21); crisis in Galatia
- **48** GALATIANS
- **48/9** Jerusalem conference (Ac. 15)
- **49** Claudius expels Jews from Rome
- **49** Paul and Silas on **second missionary journey: Greece**
- **50/1** 1 and 2 THESSALONIANS
- **51 (early)—52 (late)** Paul in Corinth
- **52/3** Paul in Jerusalem, Antioch; **third missionary journey: Ephesus**
- **53–6** In Ephesus
- **53** 1 CORINTHIANS
- **53/4** Short, painful visit to Corinth
- **54** Death of Claudius; accession of Nero
- **55** PHILIPPIANS
- **55/6** PHILEMON, COLOSSIANS, EPHESIANS
- **56** Released from prison; **continues journey to Corinth**
- **56** 2 CORINTHIANS
- **57** ROMANS
- **57 From Corinth to Jerusalem**
- **57–9** 'Hearings' and imprisonment in Jerusalem and Caesarea
- **59 (autumn) Voyage to Rome; shipwreck on Malta**
- **60 (early) Arrival in Rome**
- **60–2** House arrest in Rome
- **62–4** Further travels, either to Spain or to the east, or both?
- **After 62** 1 and 2 TIMOTHY and TITUS?
- **64** Fire of Rome; persecution of Christians in Rome
- **64 or later** Death of Paul
- **66–70** Roman–Jewish War
- **68** Death of Nero
- **70** Fall of Jerusalem

If Luke intended to write more, it is impossible to say; he concludes his narrative at this point, probably because the point was not to write a full biography of Paul but to use his story as the story of how the gospel got, in principle, 'to the ends of the earth'.[85]

The Pastoral Epistles—with due caveats on their disputed authenticity—confirm a Roman imprisonment.[86] More disputed, however, is the description of Paul's release from his Roman imprisonment and his subsequent travel across the Adriatic and Aegean, visiting Macedonia and Asia, meeting up with Titus in Nicopolis, and composing 1 Timothy and Titus during this period.[87] However, if we follow this line it appears that matters soon deteriorated, leaving Paul once again awaiting trial in Rome, writing once more to urge Timothy to join him there.[88] By the end, Paul is certain about what awaits him: 'For I am already being poured out like a drink offering, and the time for my departure is near.'[89] He knew his race was just about run.

In other early Christian literature we find evidence that several authors thought that Paul was released from his first Roman imprisonment, that he visited Spain between writing 1 and 2 Timothy, and was thereafter executed by Nero after a second trial in Rome. We have *1 Clement* (*c.* AD 95) which celebrates how Paul was 'a herald in both the east and the west', and that he reached 'the limits of the west', which many have taken to indicate that he made it to Spain.[90] The Muratorian canon (*c.* AD 180) states that Paul travelled as far west as Spain, but one wonders if this is based on inferences drawn from Romans 15.24, 28, rather than being reliant on sound tradition.[91] Eusebius implies a release between Paul's first and second trials in Rome, which could certainly accommodate a trip to Spain, but he never explicitly says this happened.[92] It is quite possible that after such a trip Paul then decided (changing his mind from his earlier plans) on a fresh visit to the east. In the absence of further evidence we simply do not know.

On Paul's death, the earliest reference we have is from *1 Clement* which provides a short summary of Paul's afflictions, and notes that he 'left this world and was taken up to the holy place',[93] without specifying when, where, or how Paul died. Eusebius records that 'Paul was beheaded in Rome itself and Peter likewise was

---

85 Ac. 28.31. See Troftgruben 2010.
86 2 Tim. 1.8, 16–17; 2.9; 4.16–17.
87 1 Tim. 1.3; 2 Tim. 1.15, 18; 4.16; Tit. 3.12; Eus. *Hist. Eccl.* 2.22.1–7.
88 2 Tim. 1.4, 8; 2.9; 4.9, 16–17, 21. Though Koester (2000 [1982], 2.302) thinks that 2 Timothy fictitiously points to Philippi rather than Rome as the place of Paul's death, given the comings and goings of various people mentioned in 2 Tim. 4.
89 2 Tim. 4.6, 18.
90 *1 Clem.* 5.6–7 (tr. M. F. Bird).
91 Muratorian canon § 38–9.
92 Eus. *Hist. Eccl.* 2.22.2.
93 *1 Clem.* 5.7 (tr. M. F. Bird).

crucified under Nero'.[94] Eusebius also notes that the graves of Peter and Paul are traditionally associated with the Vatican and Ostian ways respectively.[95] The death of Paul received hagiographical treatment in writings like the *Acts of Paul* with elaboration on why Nero had Paul 'beheaded according to the law of the Romans'.[96] That Paul died during the Neronian persecutions cannot be proven, but it is completely plausible in the light of Nero's pogrom against Christians in the aftermath of the fire of Rome in AD 64. No competing tradition ever seems to have presented itself as an alternative contender.[97] The most likely conclusion is that Paul was indeed martyred under Nero, in either AD 62 or 64, probably on the charges of sedition (*seditio*) or affronting the divine majesty (*maiestas*) of the emperor and the gods of Rome (see box: 'Sketch of Pauline chronology').[98]

Further reading

Bird, Michael F. 2007. *The Saving Righteousness of God: Studies on Paul, Justification, and the New Perspective.* Milton Keynes: Paternoster.
——. 2008. *A Bird's-Eye View of Paul: The Man, His Mission and His Message.* Nottingham: InterVarsity.
——(ed.). 2012. *Four Views on the Apostle Paul.* Grand Rapids, MI: Zondervan.
——. 2016. *An Anomalous Jew: Paul among Jews, Greeks and Romans.* Grand Rapids, MI: Eerdmans.
Dunn, James D. G. 2009. *Beginning from Jerusalem.* CITM 2; Grand Rapids, MI: Eerdmans.
Gorman, Michael J. 2017. *Apostle of the Crucified Lord: A Theological Introduction to Paul and His Letters.* 2nd edn. Grand Rapids, MI: Eerdmans.
Longenecker, Bruce W., and Todd D. Still. 2014. *Thinking Through Paul: A Survey of His Life, Letters, and Theology.* Grand Rapids, MI: Zondervan.
Meeks, Wayne A., and John T. Fitzgerald. 2007. *The Writings of St. Paul: Annotated Texts: Reception and Criticism.* New York: W. W. Norton.
Riesner, Rainer. 1998. *Paul's Early Period: Chronology, Mission Strategy, Theology.* Grand Rapids, MI: Eerdmans.
Sanders, E. P. 2015. *Paul: The Apostle's Life, Letters, and Thought.* Minneapolis: Fortress.
Schnelle, Udo. 2005. *Apostle Paul: His Life and Theology.* Tr. M. Eugene Boring; Grand Rapids, MI: Baker.
Wright, N. T. 1991. *The Climax of the Covenant: Christ and the Law in Pauline Theology.* Edinburgh: T&T Clark.
——. 2014. *Paul and the Faithfulness of God.* COQG 4; London: SPCK.
——. 2015. *Paul and His Recent Interpreters.* London: SPCK.
——. 2018. *Paul: A Biography.* London: SPCK.

---

94 Eus. *Hist. Eccl.* 2.25.5, 8.
95 Eus. *Hist. Eccl.* 2.25.6–7.
96 *Acts of Paul* 11.3; see Tert. *Scorp.* 15.4; *Prae. Haer.* 36.
97 Tac. *Ann.* 15.44.
98 See Barclay 2015, 13.

16

A Primer on Pauline Theology

CHAPTER AT A GLANCE

This chapter sets out the basic tenets of Paul's theology with a focus on his distinctive contribution to the development of a Christian worldview and a particular way of thinking about God.

By the end of this chapter you should be able to:

- describe Paul's role in the creation of a distinctly Christian task called 'theology';
- understand the major tenets of Paul's thought, centred upon the three points of monotheism, election, and eschatology;
- grasp something of how Paul reworked the Jewish worldview around the Messiah and the spirit.

The reason Paul was 'doing theology' was not that he happened to have the kind of brain that delighted in playing with and rearranging large, complex abstract ideas. He was doing theology because the life of God's people depended on it, depended on his doing it initially for them, then as soon as possible with them, and then on them being able to go on doing it for themselves. All Paul's theology is thus pastoral theology, not in the sense of an unsystematic therapeutic model which concentrates on meeting the felt needs of the 'client', but in the sense that the shepherd needs to feed the flock with clean food and water, and keep a sharp eye out for wolves.[1]

PAUL, PHILEMON, *KOINŌNIA*, AND THE MESSIAH

Paul's letter to Philemon might seem an odd choice for commencing a discussion of Paul's theology, but as we will see it is a helpful place to begin. It showcases the control room behind Paul's theology.

The probable background of the letter takes us to the town of Colossae, a day or two's walk east from Ephesus. Philemon, who has become a Jesus-follower through Paul's ministry (presumably in Ephesus itself),

---

[1] Wright *PFG*, 568–9.

has a slave called Onesimus. Onesimus has absconded—a serious, possibly capital, crime—and has sought out Paul, in prison. We presume that the young man was hoping that Paul would appeal to Philemon on his behalf; there are hints in the letter that he had done something to make Philemon particularly angry, perhaps stealing from him as many absconding slaves did. However, as well as meeting Paul, Onesimus has also come to faith in Jesus, and Paul has come to see him as his own son, begotten through his gospel ministry right there in prison.

When we inspect the substance of Paul's request to Philemon in Philemon 8–22, Paul's request is straightforward and unambiguous. It comes to a head in verse 17: 'So, anyway, if you reckon me a partner in your work, receive him as though he was me' (*NTE/KNT*). The main thing Paul is asking for is that, when Onesimus returns home, Philemon will regard Onesimus as if he were Paul himself: 'if you regard me as a partner [*koinōnos*], then accept him [*proslabou auton*] as if he were me.' That will follow directly from Philemon being prepared to see Onesimus as a brother in Christ (v. 16). It will have the effect, at the very least, in his not condemning Onesimus to any of the usual punishments that might have been expected for a misbehaving slave. Paul, however, wants more than that. He wants Philemon to see Onesimus as a beloved brother. In the interest of partnership/fellowship (*koinōnia*), Philemon should receive (*proslabanō*) Onesimus as a member of the Messiah's people. This is the central thrust of the letter—as it is, indeed, of much of Paul's understanding of what it meant to belong to the Messiah and his family.

Here, as elsewhere, the short letter to Philemon provides an accurate signpost forward to the wider Pauline concerns about the nature of this strange new family, the Messiah-people. Thus, verse 17 not only encapsulates Paul's primary request to Philemon, but maps onto wider themes in Paul's letters. A similar exhortation towards mutual welcome appears in Romans 14 and 15: 'Welcome someone who is weak in faith, but not in order to have disputes . . . because God has welcomed them'; 'Welcome one another, therefore, as the Messiah has welcomed you, to God's glory.'[2] Whatever precise reconstruction we offer of the situation Paul envisages in Rome, the point is clear: at the heart of his work is the yearning and striving for *messianic unity across traditional boundaries*, whether it be the unity of Jew and gentile in the Messiah (the main point of Galatians), the unity of the church under the lordship of the Messiah in a pagan and imperial context (part of the main point of Philippians, coming to memorable expression in Phil. 2.1–4), or, as here in Philemon, the unity of master and slave, expressing again what it means to be *en Christō* ('in Christ'). So Paul tells Philemon: 'So, if you reckon me a *koinōnos*, a partner, *proslabou auton*, welcome him as you would welcome me.'[3] Or, as he puts it in Galatians, 'There is no

---

2 Rom. 14.1, 3; 15.7 *NTE/KNT*.
3 See Philem. 17.

longer Jew or Greek; there is no longer slave or free; there is no "male and female"; you are all one in the Messiah, Jesus.[4] That unity could only be attained, and indeed maintained, through freshly worked theology, rooted in Jesus the Messiah and activated through the spirit.

According to tradition, Onesimus succeeded Timothy as the bishop of Ephesus, and was martyred in Rome during the time of Trajan. Picture from the Byzantine manuscript Menologion of Basil II (c. AD 1000) depicting Onesimus' martyrdom.
Public Domain

It is interesting that Paul does not order Philemon to set Onesimus free. There are good reasons why that would not have been an obvious or even a beneficial move at the time. Within the social world of antiquity, freeing slaves without any idea of what would happen to them next would often mean casting them into destitution. If Paul had simply mounted his apostolic high horse and instructed Philemon to free the young man, Philemon might have responded angrily by giving Onesimus his freedom but declaring that he never wanted to set eyes on him again. That would have meant defeat for Paul—double defeat, indeed, failing to bring about the reconciliation of master and slave and causing a new rift between himself and Philemon. What was needed was not simply manumission but mutuality, not a recalcitrant release but a reconciled relationship. That is why Paul wrote this letter.

Strikingly, Paul does not command Philemon to do anything specifically. He appeals to him to think through the situation from the point of view of 'being in

---

4   Gal. 3.28 *NTE/KNT*.

the Messiah', and to work out for himself what he must do. The prayer at the start of the letter (v. 6) encodes this request: Paul is praying that 'your partnership [with us] in the faith' (*koinōnia tes pisteos sou*) may have its full effect, to 'realize' (both in the sense of understanding and in the sense of 'realizing in practice') the Messiah-shaped unity for which God is at work in his people. Philemon must, in other words, think through and work out what this *koinōnia* means in practice, what it will mean that God is at work in him—and in Onesimus!—to will and to work for his good pleasure.[5] It is out of this *koinōnia* that Philemon's love for the saints and his refreshment for the lord's people has borne fruit; but now, Philemon needs to think how to put that into practice in relation to the new situation with his runaway slave. Paul is teaching Philemon how *to think as a Messiah-shaped kingdom-person*, that is, to allow the fact of the Messiah's cross and resurrection to reshape his reflection not only on what he should do but also on the communitarian context within which he should do it. Paul calls on Philemon, in other words, to *do theology*—to learn, in this new situation, to think and then to act as a Messiah-person, to understand the world in a new way and live accordingly. That is what Paul wanted all Jesus-followers to do.

That is why the story of Philemon and Onesimus is a great launching-pad from which to think about Pauline theology. What we call 'theology', Paul would probably think of in terms of 'having the Messiah's mind'. This meant not only learning fresh truth, but learning to think in a new way: allowing the explosive truths of the Messiah's death and resurrection, the unexpected and shocking fulfilment of the hope of Israel, to reshape the Jewish worldview which itself subverted the multiple pagan worldviews. The Jewish worldview contained within itself the seeds of hope for the world, the news of a creator God who was going to put everything right at last. The messianic events concerning Jesus meant that this global good news had come true—and that the God thereby revealed was now recruiting human beings to be (in the power and under the leading of his spirit) active, intelligent, understanding participants in the project. We begin, then, by assuming that Paul remained a deeply Jewish theologian who had rethought and reworked every aspect of his native theology in the light of the Messiah and the spirit, resulting in his own vocational self-understanding as the apostle to the pagans. The larger greco-roman context is crucial for grasping Paul; that is the world in which Paul's message made its impact; but the impact was the new, Messiah-shaped impact that ancient Israel had been called to make in the world. His Jewish worldview is therefore the proper starting-point for understanding how the great symphony of his thought makes sense. The radical modifications in that worldview caused by the Messiah and the spirit were modifications in *that* worldview, not some other. This has to be

---

5   See similarly Phil. 2.12–13.

emphasized against those who still suppose that, because Paul after Damascus had rejected his earlier zealous Jewish way and embraced 'justification by faith' over against 'works of Torah', we must reject Jewish thought-forms root and branch as clues to his own mature thinking. When we do that, we do not 'start from scratch'. We implicitly adopt other schemes of thought, which then demonstrably pull Paul's theology out of shape.

Jews in Paul's world, and indeed in ours, do not normally 'do theology' in the way that Christians have done. That, to be sure, is part of the 'newness' of Paul's Jesus-shaped viewpoint: it positively requires prayerful, biblically rooted reflection on God, the world, and ourselves. But when Jews ancient and modern do explain what they believe, it all comes down again and again to three things that Paul continued to take for granted, however much they were reshaped around Messiah and spirit. The three categories in question are monotheism, election, and eschatology: one God, one people of God, one future for God's world. The 'reinterpretation' or 'reworking' in which Paul engaged was seen by him, not as a new, quirky, or daring thing to do with ancient traditions, but as the true meaning of those ancient traditions, which had either gone unnoticed or been distorted by more recent readings of Israel's scriptures and the movements of life and culture in which those readings played a key part. Paul's reworking of these three basic theological categories is what we shall briefly explore below as a synopsis of his thought.

THE PAULINE TRINITY: MONOTHEISM, ELECTION, AND ESCHATOLOGY

If there is one God (monotheism), and if this God, living and active in the world (creational and providential monotheism, as opposed, say, to pantheism), has chosen Israel as his covenant people in order thereby to take forward his purposes in the world (election), this must mean that this God intends a future purpose, not yet attained but guaranteed by creation and covenant (eschatology). One could put it more strongly, echoing many Jewish writers from the Psalms and the Prophets to writers of Paul's own time: if there is one God, and if Israel is God's people, something is surely wrong: how is the one God going to fulfil his promises to his people, and indeed to the world? Hence the threefold pattern: one God, one people of God, one future for God's world.[6] In what follows we will see how Paul's rethinking of God, God's people, and the future of God's people, in the light of Messiah and the spirit, emerged out of a dialogue with scripture, how it fashioned the wisdom and weapons for calling out the idolatry of the pagan world, and how it implied the various tasks of the church's mission which he exhorted them towards.

---

6 See Wright *NTPG*, ch. 9.

RETHINKING GOD

There were various 'monotheisms' in the ancient world, just as there are today. 'One God' is not a self-evident or univocal idea. Stoicism was monotheistic, because it was pantheistic: if everything is divine, or if divinity lives within everything, then there is only one divinity. Even within the Jewish world, the conception of God proffered by the Alexandrian philosopher Philo works quite differently from the descriptions of God offered by the (equally monotheistic) Qumran sectarians. In our own time, the nominal Christian west tends to assume a kind of 'moral therapeutic Deism',[7] radically different from the view of God espoused by the Wahhabi sect of Islam. Just as there are many 'gods' and many 'lords', so too are there many 'monotheisms'. It is nevertheless clear that the monotheism reflected in the Pauline letters, itself umbilically linked to the monotheism expressed in the scriptures and the 'one God' language in Jewish second-Temple literature, could be characterized as *creational* and *covenantal* monotheism. The one God of Israel made the world and has remained in dynamic relationship with it; and this one God, in order to further his purposes within and for that world, has entered into covenant with Israel in particular.[8]

This species of monotheism generates a characteristically Jewish view of the problem of evil. Most varieties of Judaism, certainly those varieties from within which early Christian thought emerged, never allowed evil of whatever sort to claim the last word. Evil—moral evil, societal evil, evil within the natural order itself—matters profoundly to God. It distorts and defaces his world and his image-bearing creatures, and contradicts his purposes not only for them but also through them. In Jewish thought, therefore, God would one day not only put the world to rights but somehow deal retrospectively with the horror, violence, degradation, and decay which had so radically infected creation, not least human beings, including Israel. The wolf will in the end lie down with the lamb, and the earth shall be full of the glory of God as the waters cover the sea. Thus, monotheism, election, and eschatology are, at one level, all about the problem of evil. The question of *how* God is involved in the mess and shame of the world at the present time, and more particularly of how he will ultimately deal with it, often remains opaque. Paul believed that God's answer to evil was revealed in the Messiah's death, resurrection, and ascension, and that this answer was being worked out in practice by the divine spirit, not least in shaping and energizing his people to carry forward his purposes.

There are many places where Paul demonstrates a clear and obvious adherence to Jewish-style monotheism, without any particularly striking redefinition.[9] He refers to the oneness of God as a natural baseline for his assertions in Romans 1 and 3,

---

[7] C. Smith 2006.
[8] See Wright *PFG*, 619–33.
[9] See Wright *PFG*, 634–43.

and Galatians 3. He praises the one God, the creator whom much of the world has spurned (Rom. 1). He expounds the resurrection as the ultimate act of new creation by the God who made creation in the first place (Rom. 4; Rom. 8; 1 Cor. 15). He declares, without a shadow of pagan or pantheistic divinizing of creation, that food is good, marriage and sex are good, the created order is good, and that humans ought to enjoy them as what they are—that is, as parts of God's good creation—without worshipping them. When faced with the chance to move towards an ontological dualism, he robustly refuses. That would be the route to a cheap and shallow ethic (the world is a bad place, so stay away from it; human bodies are evil, so never gratify them), and whatever we might say about Paul's exhortations to Christian behaviour they are never cheap or shallow (Paul knows that the world is more complicated than that). Paul remained, then, in principle a Jewish-style monotheist.

But he had also dramatically redrawn this monotheism around Jesus himself.[10] Paul (and it seems others before and alongside him) arrived at this position by a mixture of experience and exegesis, but most of all, by the conviction that the prophetic promise of YHWH's return, and the new exodus associated with it, had transpired in Jesus' person and work. Whereas many scribes and seers pondered what the promises made in the scriptures about YHWH's return to Zion would look like when they finally happened, Jesus' followers believed that in him, and supremely in his death and resurrection, Israel's God had now done what he had long promised. He had returned to be king. He had 'visited' his people and 'redeemed' them. He had come back to dwell in the midst of his people. Jesus had done—in his life, death, resurrection, and ascension—what God had said he and he alone would do. He had inaugurated God's kingdom on earth as in heaven. This explains why *Jesus' first followers, like the apostle Paul, found themselves not only as it were permitted to use God-language for Jesus, but compelled to use Jesus-language for the one God*. We can sum up this redefinition as Paul's 'christological monotheism'.

Perhaps the most famous passage where Paul redefines Israel's 'God', placing Jesus in the middle of the picture, is Philippians 2.6–11. Most scholars recognize that this poem expresses a very early, very Jewish, and very 'high' christology, in which Paul identifies the human being Jesus with one who from all eternity was equal with Israel's 'Lord' (*kyrios*), and who gave fresh expression to what that equality meant by incarnation, humiliating suffering, death, and exaltation. The 'therefore' of verse 9 is crucial: Jesus is now elevated to the position of supreme honour, sharing the glory that the one God will not share with another, *because* he has done what only the one God can do. The logic of the poem forces us to acknowledge that Paul knows perfectly well, in quoting Isaiah 45.23 in the closing verses, just how enormous a claim he is making. In that passage, one of the

---

10 Wright *PFG*, 644–709.

most fiercely monotheistic statements in the Old Testament, YHWH declares that he is God, and there is no other; to YHWH and him alone every knee will bow and every tongue swear. The poem in Philippians 2 has its roots deep in Jewish monotheism, while focusing on Jesus at the centre of the picture of the one God. Or, to put it the other way round, Paul has written (or perhaps quoted) a poem in praise of the humiliation and exaltation of Jesus, both for its own sake and as a model of the mutual submission required in the church—and he has expressed that praise in terms characteristic of ancient Israel's praise of the one true God.

The best word for this theological statement might be 'explosive'. Paul must have known exactly what he was doing. At the centre of his Jewish-style monotheism is a human being who lived, died, and rose in very recent memory. Jesus was not a new god added to a pantheon. He was and is the human being in whom YHWH, Israel's one and only God, has acted within cosmic history, human history, and Israel's history, to do for Israel, humanity, and the world what they could not do for themselves. In Paul's mind, Jesus was to be seen as part of the identity of Israel's God, and vice versa.

> 'As the apostle Paul notes, God takes what humans intend to be the definitive act of disfigurement and dishonour and reclaims it as something uniquely revelatory. Capital punishment. Death. On a cross. The end of a life that reveals the meaning of life. In that case, the cross is the consummate act of divine irony. What the Romans believed to be the cessation of life and meaning, God claims as the marker that defines the possibilities of life for all of us, for all time. The cross, then, becomes the ultimate apocalypse: the revelation of God's intention for humankind. Through struggle and even death, God reveals life.'
>
> Brian Blount, *Invasion of the Dead*, xii.

The same is true in another well-known passage, 1 Corinthians 8.6. Here again the context is all-important. Paul is facing the question of how to live as a Christian within pagan society; more specifically, whether one may or may not eat meat that has been offered to idols. His opening comments on the matter, after an initial remark about knowledge and love, show where he is coming from: we Christians, he says, are Jewish-style monotheists, not pagan polytheists. We know that no idol has any real existence, and that there is 'no God but one'.[11] You could scarcely get clearer than that. Paul is well aware—he could hardly not be, after the places where he had lived and worked—that there were many so-called gods, and many so-called lords, out there on the streets, in temples, in family shrines. But the regular beliefs of pagan polytheism were, for him, decisively challenged by the Jewish claim about the one true God. Who was this one God, and how did Israel most characteristically acknowledge him? He was the God who had revealed himself to Israel's ancestors not least at the time of the exodus, and he was worshipped and acknowledged

---

[11] 1 Cor. 8.4.

supremely in the daily prayer, the *Shema*: Hear, O Israel, YHWH our God, YHWH is one—or, in the Septuagint, *kyrios ho theos hēmōn, kyrios heis estin*.[12]

Within his monotheistic argument, Paul quotes this, the best-known of all Jewish monotheistic formulae, and once again he puts Jesus into the middle of it. For us, he says, there is one God, one lord. More specifically, 'for us there is one God, the father, from whom are all things and we to him, and one lord, Jesus the Messiah, through whom are all things and we through him'. He has quoted the Septuagint formula, glossing *theos* (Greek), that is, *elohim* (Hebrew), with a phrase about the father as the supreme creator and goal of all, and glossing *kyrios*, that is, YHWH, with a phrase about Jesus the Messiah as God's agent in both creation and redemption. Once Jesus is established at the heart of the vision of the one true God, serving and following this God will involve living according to the pattern of *love*. That is why Paul's opening remark in the chapter sets up a contrast between mere 'knowledge' and 'love' itself. This, too, is why he now goes on, in the rest of the chapter, to insist that self-sacrificial love for one's neighbour is the primary consideration when working out how to live within a pagan environment.

The deployment of *kyrios*-language for Jesus in these two texts, taken right out of Isaiah 45.23 and Deuteronomy 6.4, possesses epochal significance. A theological galaxy shifts when Paul writes like this. A small step for the language; a giant leap for the theology! Jesus is not a 'second God': that would abrogate monotheism entirely. He is not a semi-divine intermediate figure. He is the one in whom the identity of Israel's God is revealed, so that one cannot now speak of this God without thinking of Jesus, or of Jesus without thinking of the one God, the creator, Israel's God.

The most shocking thing about all this is of course that Jesus had been *crucified*. There was no chance in Paul's day of quietly forgetting the cross and allowing a fictitious character called 'Jesus', who had never suffered and died, to be apotheosized. For Paul this was not only shocking but ultimately glorious: that, in becoming human to fulfil his own promises, Israel's God, the creator, had chosen to die on a cross. The cross was not, for Paul, a messy business which God had to take care of, as it were, on the side. It was, for him, the fullest possible revelation of both the love and the justice of God, and then, as he announced it to the world, it turned out to be the extraordinary saving power of God, defeating the powers that held people captive in pagan darkness and breaking the long entail of human sin. The cross is the climactic moment in Paul's redefinition of election. It is, for Paul, the ultimate point where the ancient problem of evil, as seen in characteristically Jewish ways, is addressed head on by the one God.

The death of Jesus is not, then, merely bolted on to the outside of Paul's christology. It is the point where the whole thing is going, or, from another angle, the point

---

12 Dt. 6.4.

where it all began. This is why, in the climactic passage Romans 3.21–26, it is the crucifixion of the Messiah that reveals the *dikaiosynē theou*, the faithfulness of God. The covenant God has been faithful to his promise; the creator has been faithful to his creation; the one God has revealed the justice which, like mountains, soars high above the multiple injustices of the world. The cross is the place where Paul sees God's justice fully displayed; his christology, seen as the revision of Jewish-style monotheism, is the context within which we can best understand it.

This leads the eye to one of Paul's remarkable periphrastic statements about God: we believe, he says, in the God 'who raised from the dead Jesus our Lord, who was handed over because of our trespasses and raised because of our justification'.[13] This, at the close of a passage where Paul has been emphasizing the way in which Abraham acknowledged the true God, worshipped him, and recognized his power, by contrast with the pagan world which did none of those things, has enormous force as a further summary redefinition of the true God by means of a reference to Jesus. As every serious reader of Paul has long recognized, though not so many have explored to the full, the cross of Jesus the Messiah stands at the heart of Paul's vision of the one true God.

The second branch of Paul's redefinition of Jewish-style monotheism is closely allied with the first, and concerns the spirit. When Paul articulates the spirit's properties and actions, we find two passages of great power and concentrated theological energy, in which a classically Jewish monotheism is expressed in relation to Jesus and the spirit together.[14]

The first is Galatians 4.1–7. Paul's main aim here is to reinforce his central point in the letter that the Galatian Christians are already complete in Christ and do not need to take upon themselves the yoke of Torah. But as he does this, we can watch him also developing the Jewish monotheistic picture of God in a spectacular new way. This is the full, fresh revelation of the God of Abraham, the God of the exodus: he is now to be known, worshipped, and trusted as the God who sends the son and the God who sends the spirit of the son. Paul knows exactly what he has done here. In the very next passage, ramming home his basic appeal, he speaks of the Galatians having now come 'to know God, *or rather to be known by him*'. This son-sending and spirit-sending God is the one true God, and they have entered into a relationship of mutual knowing with him, with God taking and retaining the initiative. How, then, can they want to go back to the 'weak and beggarly elements', the *stoicheia*, the 'elements of the world', natural parts of and forces within creation that had exercised a strange, malign grip on the pagan world. Paul is here doing something typically Jewish, lining up the God of the exodus against the pagan deities; and he has described the God of the new exodus story as the son-sending and spirit-sending

---

13 Rom. 4.24–25 *NTE/KNT*.
14 See Wright *PFG*, 709–33.

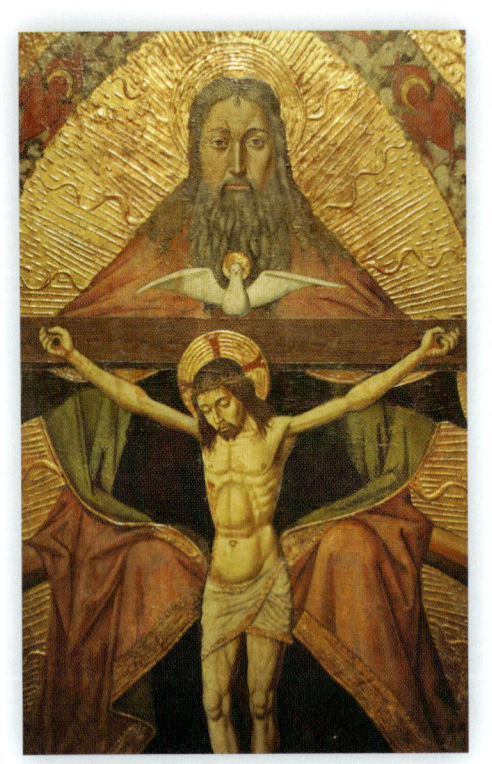

The Trinity depicted by this painting in Sant'Antonio Abate, Castelsardo, Sardini, Italy
imageBROKER / Shutterstock

God. You either have this God, known in this way, or you have paganism. From here on—and Galatians is arguably the earliest Christian document we possess—one might conclude that if the doctrine of the Trinity had not come into existence it would have been necessary to invent it.

This remarkable passage leads the eye naturally to Romans 8, where again Paul draws heavily on the motifs and the language of the exodus. God's people, set free from slavery, must not think of going back to Egypt, but must rely on the presence and leading of God as they press on to their inheritance. Within the original exodus-story, of course, God himself accompanied the people on their journey, so that, despite their rebellion and sin, the divine glory dwelt in the tabernacle just outside the gate of the camp. In Paul's retelling of the story, the spirit takes the place of the divine glory, leading the people to the promised land; and the promised land turns out to be, not 'heaven' (as in much Christian mistelling of the story), but the renewed creation, the cosmos finally liberated from its own slavery, experiencing its own 'exodus'. The spirit then forms the first-fruits, the sign of a larger harvest to come. This is cognate with the idea of the 'guarantee', the *arrabōn*, the initial downpayment that ensures the rest will be paid at its proper time.[15] The redemption of human beings, here as in some other parts of the New Testament, occurs not merely for the sake of the rescued humans, important though that is. It occurs so that, through them and their new life, the one God can bring his wise order and redemption to the rest of the world. This, too, is part of typical Jewish monotheism. Indeed the whole of Romans 8 breathes that very air. What the one God of Israel had done in the exodus narrative, and had promised to do again at the eschaton, Paul sees as being accomplished by the spirit.

In all this, across Galatians 4 and Romans 8, Paul is again working from within the framework of Jewish-style monotheism. He sees the spirit alongside the son as the agents of the one God, doing what Wisdom was to do, doing what Torah wanted

---

15 Rom. 8.24; see 2 Cor. 2.12; 5.5; Eph. 1.14.

to do but could not. This is why, to the puzzlement of so many Pauline readers down the years, Paul himself can speak in strongly positive terms about Torah (it really was God's law, holy and just and good) while insisting that the purposes for which Torah had been given have now been fulfilled, so that Torah itself is no longer necessary in the new messianic family.

Once we start to see this pattern of the son and the spirit together redefining Jewish monotheism, we notice similar things all over the place. For instance, in 1 Corinthians 12.4–6, Paul declares, over against the chaos of pagan-style worship, that when the spirit of the living God is at work there must be genuine unity. But even here, where he wants to stress this unity against the wrong sort of diversity, he says it in three separate ways: there are varieties of gifts, but the same spirit; varieties of service, but the same lord; varieties of working, but it is the same God who accomplishes all in all. The unity in diversity which the church must exhibit in its worship is grounded in and modelled on that unity in diversity which Paul simply names, without further argument or discussion, as spirit, lord, and God.

Paul thus regularly spoke of the spirit in ways which indicate that he regarded the spirit, as he regarded the Messiah, as the glorious manifestation of YHWH himself. This conclusion is not dependent on one or two verbal echoes, but relies on the regular and repeated invocation of the various elements of the foundational exodus-narrative. The spirit is, it seems, the ultimate mode of YHWH's personal and powerful presence with, and even in, his people. The christology of 'divine identity' is thus matched by the pneumatology of 'divine identity', in both cases focused in particular on the Jewish eschatology of the return of YHWH.

RETHINKING GOD'S PEOPLE

This brings us to Paul and God's people, specifically his reworking of Israel's election. When we refer to 'election' here, we are not using the technical sense of the word proper to the theological schemes of either John Calvin or Karl Barth. Rather 'election' here denotes God's choice of Abraham's family, the people historically known as 'Israel' and, in Paul's day, in their smaller post-exilic form, as 'the Jews' or 'the Judeans' (*hoi Ioudaioi*).[16] The word 'election', as applied to Israel, usually carries a further connotation: not simply the divine choice *of* this people, but more specifically the divine choice of this people *for a particular purpose*, to extend YHWH's salvation to the ends of the earth.

---

[16] That word in Greek seems to carry geographical (the inhabitants of 'Judea', the region around Jerusalem) as well as ethnic connotations (members of the tribe of Judah—though 'the Jews' of this period included not only members of the tribe of Judah but also Benjaminites, such as Saul of Tarsus himself, and Levites), and there were of course substantial Jewish communities in a Diaspora stretching from Babylon in the east to Italy, France, and even Spain in the west. See discussion in Bird 2010a, 13–16.

The belief that Israel was the chosen people of the creator God is everywhere apparent in the Old Testament and the second-Temple literature, and indeed in all that we know of the praxis and symbolic world of both ancient Israel and first-century Judaism. The great stories that Israel told year by year were designed to celebrate and reinforce this status, often in the teeth of contrary evidence such as oppression by pagan nations and even corruption within Israel itself. We hardly need rehearse the stories of the patriarchs, the exodus and conquest, the monarchy and its problems, the prophetic tradition of calling Israel back to its God, or the Psalms which simultaneously celebrated Israel's special status and lamented its failure to live up to its calling.[17] Throughout it all was a basic belief: the one creator God had called Israel to be his special people, and, as part of that call, had given Israel the land to live *in* and the Torah to live *by*.

When the people of Israel asked why they had been chosen, the answer came back, from Deuteronomy in particular, that it was purely a matter of God's love.[18] But when Israel asked what purpose God had in mind in doing this, the ultimate answer came back in a variety of ways which were variously embraced, lost sight of, distorted, and re-emphasized down the years. For the writer of Genesis, the call of Abraham was God's answer to the problem of Adam, which had become the problem of Babel. Human rebellion had led to arrogance, pride, and the fracturing of human life. The canonical Old Testament frames the entire story of God's people as the divine answer to the problem of evil: somehow, through this people, God will deal with the problem that has infected his good creation in general and his image-bearing creatures in particular. Israel is to be God's royal nation of holy priests, chosen out of the world but also for the sake of the world.[19] Israel is to be the light of the world: the nations will see in Israel what it means to be truly human, and hence who the true God is.[20] For this purpose, Israel is given Torah, so that the word of the Lord can go out from Zion to the nations.[21] What Adam was in Eden, Israel was to be in Canaan: God's priest, king, and servant before and on behalf of creation. This is why the sectarians at Qumran looked forward to a day when the 'sons of light' would recapture 'the glory of Adam'.[22] It is why Philo believed that the whole point of the exodus was to create a people who would deliver the human race from evil,[23] and the Jewish Sibyl regarded Israel as 'guides of life' to the peoples of the earth.[24]

---

17 See e.g. Gen. 15.1–21; 17.1–22; Ex. 6.1–8; Dt. 9.1–6; 26.5–10; Pss. 79.13; 95.7; 100.3; Isa. 5.1–30; Ezek. 16.1–63; Hos. 2.1–23.
18 Dt. 7.8.
19 Ex. 19.5–6.
20 Isa. 42.6; 49.6.
21 Ps. 9.11; Isa 2.3; 51.4; Mic. 4.2.
22 1QS 4.23; CD 3.20; 1QH 4.15.
23 Philo *Vit. Mos.* 1.149.
24 *Sib. Or.* 3.195.

We could sum up Israel's election this way: 'There is no God but YHWH, and Israel is his prophet.'[25]

The problem was that things had not turned out this way. Israel was not ruling like Adam, but was condemned in Adam, exiled like Adam, and corrupted like the rest of Adam's fallen progeny. Nobody prior to Paul seems to have put it quite like this, but when faced with the disaster of AD 70 the writer of *4 Ezra*, observing the circumstances of Israel's humiliating subjugation to, and desolation by, Rome, complained to God that the world had been made for Israel, but that instead the gentile beasts had trampled down the chosen people. This problem could only have been caused by Adam himself.[26] This illustrates how election was closely bound up with eschatology: because Israel was the one people of the one creator God, this God would soon act to vindicate Israel by liberating it from its enemies with a view to rescuing the nations and renewing all of creation.

Different writers drew the conclusion in different ways. Some documents, like the *Psalms of Solomon*, envisaged a fulfilment of Psalm 2, with Israel under its Messiah smashing the gentiles to pieces with a rod of iron. Others, not least some of the rabbis in the Hillelite tradition, envisaged a redemption which, once it had happened to Israel, would then spread to the nations as well. Both of these represent natural developments of the doctrine of election itself, the point being that because Israel was the chosen people of the one creator God, when God did for Israel what God was going to do for Israel—however that was conceived—then the gentiles would be brought into the picture, whether in judgment or blessing or (somehow) both. One way or another, God's purpose in election, to root evil out of the world and to do so through Israel, would be fulfilled. God's transformation of Israel would mean the transformation of the world.

When Paul reappropriates this kind of train of thought, we see two things operating simultaneously. First, there is a strong affirmation of Israel's election: never for a moment does he doubt that God called Israel and would be faithful to that election. Second, Paul insists that the purposes for which the covenant God had called Israel *had been accomplished through Jesus* precisely as Israel's representative Messiah, and were now being implemented through his people. Here the Jewish view of election is brought into fresh focus, rethought, reimagined, and reworked around Jesus himself, specifically, his death, resurrection, and enthronement.

We need to spell this out in a little more detail. First, while Paul lamented Israel's failure to embrace Jesus as the Messiah, he never questioned Israel's election. This is evident in how he begins his dense and dynamic discourse about the interrelationship between Israel, gentiles, and the Messiah in Romans 9—11: to Israel, he says,

---

[25] From Julius Wellhausen, cited in Bird 2007, 127.
[26] *4 Ez.* 4.30; 6.55–59; 7.11, 46–56; 8.44; 9.13.

belong 'the adoption to sonship... the divine glory, the covenants, the receiving of the law, the temple worship and the promises. Theirs are the patriarchs, and from them is traced the human ancestry of the Messiah'.[27] That itself expands what he had said earlier in the letter, that 'the Jews have been entrusted with the very words of God' and therefore God's solution to the world's problems cannot disregard or bypass Israel.[28] There is an ineradicable link for Paul between one God, one people, and one future for all of creation.

At the same time, Paul also affirms that God's election is more than paternity; it is about promises. It is not reducibly ethnic, but essentially eschatological. Its defining character is not boundaries, but God's bountiful grace. If God can call an undeserving and obstinate nation to be his people, as (according to Israel's own scriptures) he had done for Abraham's family, there is nothing to stop him from doing the same again among the gentiles. This, Paul believes, is just what God has done in the Messiah: God has revealed his glorious mercy to those 'whom he... called, not only from the Jews but also from the Gentiles'.[29] This is why Paul can claim that gentiles are part of God's 'elect' or 'chosen' people,[30] why they can legitimately claim to be the 'circumcision, we who serve God by his Spirit',[31] or 'fellow citizens with God's people and also members of his household'.[32] It is why Messiah-believers from Jews and gentiles alike can together be identified as 'the Israel of God'.[33] This new people, called from among Jews, Greeks, barbarians, and anyone else you can think of, is no longer defined ethnically, but messianically and thus eschatologically. If Jesus is Israel's Messiah (and early Christianity makes no sense whatever without that belief), then any and all who belong to Jesus are the inheritors of the Abrahamic promises. They are part of God's new creation, participating in the Messiah where distinctions of gender, tribe, ethnicity, and social status cease to be badges of privilege and status.[34] (Such distinctions are not erased entirely; men are still men for Paul, women are still women, just as Jews are still Jews and gentiles are still gentiles.) What matters is grace, not race; what marks out this people is not Jewish customs or Roman patrimony but faith working through love, the obedience of faith, and 'keeping the commandments of God'.[35] (Paul must have known that this last phrase was ironic, since for him circumcision, a central command for Jews up to that point, had become irrelevant.) Where faith in Jesus as lord is professed and where the spirit

---

27 Rom. 9.4–5.
28 Rom. 3.2.
29 Rom. 9.24–26, citing Hos. 2.23; 1.10.
30 See e.g. Rom. 8.33; 11.7; 1 Cor. 1.2; 1 Thess. 1.4; Col. 3.12; Eph. 1.11–12.
31 Phil. 3.3.
32 Eph. 2.19.
33 Gal. 6.16.
34 Gal. 3.28; Col 3.11; 1 Cor. 1.18–25; 7.19.
35 1 Cor. 7.19.

performs his life-giving works, these are the signs of God's renewed people.

This focus on Jesus as Israel's Messiah lays the foundation for Paul's interpreters to reject, in a way which sadly has not always been done, the callous supersessionism that imagines that God called the Jews first but that, after they had rejected him, he washed his hands of them and transferred all their blessings and privileges to a gentile-only church that would be a kind of 'replacement Israel'. This horrible caricature of Paul's thought, visible for instance today where writers imagine that Paul embraced a kind of 'apocalyptic' in which all previous sacred stories had been abolished, is just the sort of thing that Paul himself is attacking in Romans 11. His point is not that Israel has been *replaced*, but that Israel has been *renewed* through the promised Messiah and the promised spirit, with gentiles included, in similar prophetic fulfilment. The defining element of election for Paul is not the *supersession* of Israel but the *expansion* of 'Israel' beyond its ethnic and cultural precincts. The problem is that most of ethnic Israel, besides the Jewish-Christian remnant, has not believed in Jesus and so not experienced this renewal. Thus Paul in Romans 11 looks ahead to a time when the Jewish people will be provoked to jealousy by this influx of gentiles into their own heritage and hope, which enables him to hope that those of the Jewish people who presently do not believe in Jesus as Messiah will not 'remain in unbelief' but will ultimately embrace their own messianic deliverer.[36]

The real 'apocalyptic' element in Paul's gospel is that with the coming, and the crucifixion, of Israel's Messiah, 'the old has passed away, and see—the new has come'. New creation has been launched—but Paul, as a good Jew, is no dualist: the new creation is what the old creation was meant to be but, because of idolatry, sin, and corruption, could never be. So too the renewal of the covenant fulfils the

Historiated letter 'A' depicting generations in the bosom of Abraham from the Souvigny Bible (vellum), Ms 1 f.256, twelfth century
© Bibliotheque Municipale, Moulins, France / Bridgeman Images

---

[36] Rom. 11.23 *NTE/KNT*.

ancient promises, albeit in a shocking way. God has acted suddenly, almost horrifyingly, dramatically—as he always said he would. The coming of Israel's Messiah leaves nothing intact, for either Jew or gentile.

The scandal of Paul's gospel, after all, was that the events in which he claimed that Israel's God had been true to what he promised centred on a crucified and risen Messiah. The gentile world was not looking for a Jewish redeemer; the Jewish world was not looking for a crucified redeemer. But with the events concerning Jesus the world had changed, and with it the people of God through whom God was carrying forward his purposes for that world. The solution to ethnic Israel's unbelief, then, is not to insinuate (as some have done) that 'the Jew' is simply an allegory for 'humanity clinging to religion instead of grace'. Nor will it do to say, or to suggest that Paul was saying, that Jesus came to save gentiles while Jews could still carry on under their own covenant, however bemused they might be at what those gentile Christ-believers were claiming for themselves. For Paul, Jesus was Israel's Messiah, and everything else flowed from that. He was saying, unapologetically, that Israel's history and hopes had arrived in the person of Jesus himself, and that it was through him alone and by faith in him alone that God's faithfulness to the covenant was known in practice, with those grasped by this 'good news' then sent out in the power of the spirit to participate in the *missio Dei*.

From all this it should be clear that Paul not only regarded Jesus as Israel's Messiah, the one in whom the promises of the Psalms and Isaiah were fulfilled. He also saw this messianic identity as *incorporative*: God had done for Jesus what many, Paul included, had expected him to do for Israel as a whole, and this seems to have generated a strong and determinative sense for Paul that the 'incorporative' themes in the scriptures (the king representing his people, and so forth) had come true in Jesus. As Israel's Messiah, he had drawn the identity and vocation of God's chosen people onto himself. He was Israel in person. Two things need to be stressed here.

First, the calling and destiny of Israel are brought to fulfilment in the Messiah's death and resurrection. The Messiah has done that for which Israel was chosen in the first place, to bring redemption and renewal and life from the throes of death, to lead peoples from exile to homecoming. Jesus' death, described densely in passages like Romans 3.21–26; 4.25; 8.3; 2 Corinthians 5.21; and Galatians 3.13–14, has provided the means for Israel and the nations to be delivered from evil. Jesus the Messiah has been obedient where Adam was disobedient; Jesus the Messiah has been faithful where Israel failed. His obedience and faithfulness are manifested decisively on the cross, in taking upon himself the condemnation of Adam and all humanity, together with the covenantal curses consequent upon Israel's disobedience. Faced with large-scale human idolatry and sin, God sent him forth as a *hilastērion*, 'mercy seat', the place where the living God met with his people. Faced with Israel's failure to keep the holy law (Rom. 7), God provided his own son to die *peri hamartias* ('as a sin offering') (Rom. 8.3). And in the resurrection, God raised Jesus, declaring him thereby to be Messiah, 'son of God in power', the firstborn of the new creation. Jesus was vindicated; he was, in that sense, justified, declared to be 'in the right'. He had been faithful to God's commission, and that faithfulness becomes the badge, the only identifying mark in fact, for all those who, grasped by the gospel, come to believe in the God who raised him from the dead. This is 'justification by faith'; not that 'faith' is something we 'do' in order to impress God, but that the faith that Jesus is lord and that God raised him from the dead is the one and only sure sign of membership in the people of the faithful Messiah.

3D reproduction of the ark of the covenant with the mercy seat overshadowed by cherubim wings
© 2011 by Zondervan

The Messiah, therefore, has done for the world what Israel was called to do. He has done *in Israel's place* what Israel was called to do but could not, namely to act on behalf of the whole world as the Suffering Servant, the Passover Lamb, and the Righteous One. All those who believe the gospel message of his death and resurrection are now themselves accorded the status of *dikaios*: righteous, forgiven, within the covenant. God's faithfulness is therefore fully and finally unveiled in the cross; God's justice is powerfully and poignantly revealed in the resurrection. God has put the world right in Jesus. He will complete that work through the spirit.

Second, and closely following, is the assertion that believers, by faith and through the agency of the spirit, are incorporated into the Messiah. Paul sees Jesus as the one who has been established as Messiah through his resurrection, drawing Israel's history to its strange but long-awaited resolution, fulfilling the promises made to Abraham, inheriting the nations of the world, winning the battle against all the powers of evil, and constituting in himself the promise-receiving people. The purpose behind this is so that 'in him' everyone might receive those promises, precisely not in themselves but insofar as, being 'in him', they are incorporated into the

True Jew, the one in whom Israel's vocation has been fulfilled. This incorporative meaning is on clear display in passages like Philippians 3.2–11. It is 'in the Messiah', in the Israel-in-person, that Paul finds the identity and resurrection hope he had formerly hoped to find in his identity as a zealous and Torah-observant Jew. The *status* of being 'justified', declared to be 'in the right' and a member of the people of the one God, is recognized by one and only one mark, namely, the faith of the believer which identifies him or her as part of the family of the 'faithful' Messiah. One could make similar points from Paul's remarks on baptism in Romans 6. In baptism, one is literally immersed into the story of the Messiah's death and resurrection. The real-life event of baptism takes the real-life person and etches into his or her personal history the death and resurrection of the Messiah, anticipating the bodily reality of the individual's own future death and ultimate resurrection. What is true of the Messiah now becomes true of the baptized believer.

It is therefore under the heading of 'election', in the sense used here, that we can fill in what was said a moment ago about Paul's famous doctrine of 'justification'. Given the covenantal architecture of Israel's faith, and the sectarian context of first-century Judaism, those who reflected on the state and fate of the Jewish people were faced with two premises and a question: (1) Israel's God will bring about his new world, raising his people from the dead to share in it; (2) clearly this has not yet happened, and clearly not all Jews, with variegated levels of fidelity to the Jewish way of life, are going to share in this new world; therefore, (3) how can one tell *in the present time* who will be among the righteous and resurrected? That is the question to which various first-century doctrines of 'justification' were the answer. Saul of Tarsus, the zealous Pharisee, would have answered this question by stipulating that zealous Torah-observance marked out in advance those who were 'righteous', covenant members, in God's sight.[37] They were the ones about whom one could say in the present time, on the basis of their Torah-observance, that they were already recognizable as those who would be vindicated when God finally acted in power to judge and save. Paul the apostle, however, said that the people marked out in the present as the covenant people who would be saved on the last day were those who had Messiah-faith, whose belief in the God who raised Jesus marked them out as Messiah-people, members of the renewed covenant. How could this be?

Paul believed that a day was to come when God would hold the whole world to account. This judgment would include both condemnation and vindication, for both Jews and pagans. What is more, this would be the fulfilment of the Abrahamic covenant, in which God promised to bless the whole world; the Pentateuch, whose opening narratives display this promise, closes with the urge to Israel to choose life rather than death. Paul saw all this as having come true in the Messiah: he had

---

[37] Phil. 3.5–6; Rom. 9.31; 10.2–3.

forged the way through death into new life beyond, fulfilling in himself the Deuteronomic narrative of exile and restoration and thereby enabling the promises given to Abraham to reach their goal. In other words, Paul believed that what God had said he would do at the end of history, he had done in the middle of history: this 'day' had come in the Messiah's death and resurrection. The verdict of condemnation had been meted out upon the Messiah; the verdict of vindication, righteousness, had been enacted in his resurrection from the dead. Thus, when Paul says that believers have been 'justified by faith', he is saying that they have received in advance the divine verdict of acquittal. They now stand in the proper covenant relationship with God, anticipating their resurrection in the eschaton. They already have a rightful place within God's holy people, anticipating the final revelation of their status within the covenant. This is the *declaration* of a 'righteous' *status*, not the description of a righteous character. The Messiah has been faithful, and vindicated as such, and 'in him' the baptized believers are declared to be God's people. In other words, the Messiah's death constitutes the past event that enables justification to take place, and the Messiah's present incorporative life is the context within which it makes sense for the one God to make the same declaration over people *now* that he made over the Messiah himself in the resurrection. The verdict pronounced over the Messiah's faithfulness is now pronounced over the faith of those who are 'in him'.

Mosaic of Peter and Paul with throne and cross in Baptistery of Arians, Ravenna, built by Theodoric before AD 526
Gianni Dagli Orti / Shutterstock

A Primer on Pauline Theology   385

The Messiah died to sin, once for all; this person is 'in the Messiah'; therefore this person is deemed, reckoned, accounted to have 'died to sin'. Thus *the present declaration 'in the right', rooted in the Messiah's death, is pronounced over all who are 'in the Messiah'.*

We see how this plays out in important passages like Galatians 2.11–21. Paul reports the recent incident in Antioch when Cephas (that is, Peter) lost his nerve and gave in to pressure from a faction of the Jerusalem church, people who insisted that Jewish and gentile believers should eat separately. Paul saw this, not as a failure of table-manners *per se*, but as undermining the truth of the gospel. To prohibit believing Jews and gentiles from sharing table-fellowship, he insists, would be to forget that the Messiah had been crucified, dealing with sins once for all. Jewish separation (which took various forms) was justified because gentiles were 'sinners', idolaters, and impure; but if these gentiles were 'in the Messiah', then all that had been dealt with. The Messiah's death had won the victory over the powers that held the world captive, and now anyone 'in the Messiah' was part of the single new-covenant family. This is what Paul meant when he stressed that nobody could be 'justified' by 'works of Torah', that is, by following the Jewish way of life. Otherwise, why would the Messiah have needed to die? But if the Messiah had died and been raised, then there was no longer a wall (as in the Temple) to keep believing gentiles away from the innermost courts of divine presence. On the contrary, those who tried to build such a wall would be in danger of demonstrating, not that gentiles should be excluded, but that they themselves—Jews trying to fence off gentile access—were 'transgressors', lawbreakers. Thus, if one were to follow Peter and the others in rebuilding the wall separating Jews and gentiles, that would be tantamount to rejecting the grace of God. If Peter and the others had their way, it would mean that covenant status was still defined in terms of Torah, and in terms of Jewish ethnicity; that God had not after all dealt with gentile sin (as well as Jewish sin) on the cross. This is not, as some have supposed, a way of turning 'justification' into 'sociology' rather than 'soteriology', into a matter of social organization rather than salvation from sin. Paul's point is that the social organization of the messianic community—in other words, the visible and practical unity of believing Jews and gentiles—must reflect exactly the belief that God really has dealt with sins on the cross. The doctrine of 'justification by faith', with its life-giving news of forgiveness of sins, came into being as the key doctrine underlying the *unity* of God's renewed people.

This then opens up Paul's teaching about the spirit, again in the context of 'election' in the sense we are meaning. In Israel's prophetic scriptures, a circumcised heart was the sign of a renewed commitment to obey the covenantal precepts governing Israel.[38] Paul suggests that what makes one 'Jewish', a member of the

---

38 Ezek. 36; Jer. 31.

covenant people, is not physical circumcision, but experiencing a circumcision of the heart. This will be a fresh work of the spirit, nothing to do with the 'written code'. This is what he claims has happened to his gentile converts. Their new heart-obedience to the law's requirements meant that 'circumcision', that is, covenant membership, could be imputed to them, even though the males among them were not physically circumcised.[39]

Paul explains the point at length in 2 Corinthians 3, as part of his description of his own apostleship. Importantly, the contrast at the heart of this chapter is not between the Torah itself and the gospel, not between Moses and Jesus, but between those who heard Moses and those who hear and believe the gospel. Torah was given, says Paul, to people with hard hearts and darkened minds. As a result, they were not able to look at the glory of God revealed on Moses' face. But where the spirit of the Lord is, the apostle and the members of his congregation can look one another in the face, can stare at the glory revealed there, and can by this means be transformed from one degree of glory to another. They are therefore the beneficiaries of, the members of, God's renewed covenant; the people who are being renewed by the spirit. In fact, he elsewhere declares to the Corinthians that they are the Temple of the living God, where God dwells by his spirit as he dwelt in the pillar of cloud and fire in the wilderness tabernacle, or in the smoky cloud in Solomon's Temple.[40] This indwelling by the spirit is also the resource and the imperative which calls God's people towards holiness and the renewal of their minds.

REWORKING GOD'S FUTURE

If there is one God, and if this God is the God of Israel, then—granted the present state of the world, and of Israel—this God must act in the future to put things to rights. If he doesn't, then creation and covenant, monotheism and election, are themselves called into question. Eschatology, the question of God's future—both the future that God has in store for the world and, in a sense, God's own future—is up for grabs. For Paul, God's intended purposes for the world, and for his people, had been unveiled embryonically in the present time in Jesus' resurrection. God, he concluded, had had a two-stage plan to put the world to rights: the sending of the Messiah and the giving of the spirit as the first stage (the 'now'), and, in the future, the return of the Messiah and transformation by the spirit (the 'not yet'). That is how Paul has reworked the ancient Jewish eschatology. All the elements are there, but seen in a new light because of the gospel events, backed up by a re-reading of Israel's scriptures. And, if the original hope included the longing for the dark

---

[39] Rom. 2.25–29; Phil. 3.3.
[40] 1 Cor. 3.16; 6.19; 2 Cor. 6.16; Eph. 2.21–22.

powers of the pagan world to be overthrown at last, Paul believed that this, too, had been accomplished in principle through Jesus' death and would be completed at his return.

The other elements of the ancient Jewish hope included the coming of YHWH, the end of exile/a new exodus, agricultural fecundity, building a new Temple, the arrival of a new Davidic king, the return of the dispersed tribes to Judea, peace, the bestowal of God's spirit, gentile submission or conversion, resurrection of the dead, and so forth. What is more, a survey of the wide-ranging evidence for Jewish beliefs in the period (from the Maccabeans and their Pharisaic descendants; John the Baptist; Qumran; Philo; Judean apocalyptic seers; the later rabbis) indicates that these scriptural images for the future could be taken in various ways, fitting in with various different assessments of Israel's problem and various specific aspirations for Israel's future.

When first-century Jews thought of God's future, of a coming 'end' of whatever sort, they saw this *not* simply as a bolt from the blue, descending into an otherwise undifferentiated and irrelevant historical sequence. They saw it precisely as the climax, the denouement, of a story, a plot which had been steadily unfolding both in the mind of God and on the ground in the middle east—even if that denouement, when it came, would come as a shock, from an unexpected angle. Paul knew this story and retold it in a shocking way. The end had already begun in Jesus the Messiah; the end remained to be consummated by Jesus and the spirit. In the Messiah, God's own future had burst into the present. By incorporation in the Messiah, God's people could experience its blessings in the present, and be marked out to enjoy all its fullness in the future.

As we have seen already, Paul believed that what the people of Israel had hoped God would do for them at the end of history, God had already begun to do in the present through the Messiah. That is why Paul can say that the 'end' had already arrived in Jesus; because he was the pre-promised messianic deliverer who had come to Israel and revealed God's saving righteousness (Rom. 1.3–4; 3.21–26; 9.5; 15.8–9). His death ended Israel's exilic curse (Gal. 3.13); he died as a sacrifice for sins (Rom. 3.25; 8.3; 1 Cor. 5.6); he transferred believers from the dominion of darkness to the divine reign (Rom. 5.20–21; Col. 1.13–14); he won the victory over evil (Rom. 8.37; Gal. 1.4; 1 Cor. 15.57; Col. 2.15); his resurrection was the beginning of the general resurrection of the dead (Rom. 1.4; 8.39; 1 Cor. 15.23; Col. 1.18); his heavenly enthronement was the installation of a human being as co-regent of the universe (Rom. 8.34; 14.9; 1 Cor. 15.20–28; Col. 3.1; Eph. 1.20; 2.6). All these are aspects of Israel's hope which Paul saw as fulfilled in the Messiah.

Similarly, the spirit (1 Cor. 2.12; 2 Cor. 11.4) accomplishes further elements of the ancient hope. The spirit takes believers from slavery to sonship (Rom. 8.15; Gal. 4.6–8), turning them into personalized temples of God's presence (1 Cor. 6.19).

The spirit is a downpayment of the good things God still has in store for believers (2 Cor. 1.22; 5.5; Eph. 1.14). For Paul, that which Jewish eschatology looked for in the future, the overthrow of the enslaving evil powers and the establishment of YHWH's reign, had truly been inaugurated in and through the events of Jesus' death, resurrection, and enthronement, and the giving of the spirit.

At the same time, there was yet another component of God's unveiling of salvation still to come. Believers still struggled against sin and fleshly desires; death appeared to continue unabated, a grim tyrant; creation was still groaning; Caesar remained secure on his throne (well, relatively so); idolatry and wickedness continued to prosper; demonic power, even when checked as for a while in Ephesus, was growing like a pugnacious weed. Even Israel, for the most part, had not only rejected the Messiah, but was positively hostile to the messengers of covenant renewal. The Messiah's reign in heaven did not seem to be having much effect on earth. Granted, Paul of all people was used to seeing human lives and human communities transformed by the gospel and making a considerable difference where they were, but that seemed just as likely to stir up hostility as admiration. He therefore looked ahead to a future 'day' when sin and evil would be utterly vanquished, believers completely rescued, God's verdict issued in cross and resurrection finally enacted in the resurrection of the bodies of believers themselves, and God's will completely done on earth as in heaven.[41]

Four elements stand out in which Paul redraws the still-future Jewish eschatology around the Messiah.

First, there is the 'day of the lord' or 'day of the Messiah', a redefinition of the older scriptural 'day of YHWH'. The idea of a coming 'day' when the creator of the world would act in judgment and mercy was an important theme in the Prophets. Paul believed that the accomplishment of Jesus as Messiah, and the gift of the spirit, meant that in one sense the new day had already dawned: 'the day of salvation is here.' But 'the day' could be divided up into the *present* 'day'—the ongoing 'now' of the gospel—in which promises were truly fulfilled, not just anticipated; and the *future* 'day' in which the work would be complete and the creator would be 'all in all'. In places like 1 Corinthians 15.20–28, in which the distinction between these two days is made, 'the end' in verse 24 is described in climactic terms: 'Then the end will come, when he hands over the kingdom to God the Father after he has destroyed all dominion, authority and power.' Importantly this 'day' is particularly related to the scriptural promises of the 'return of YHWH to Zion'.[42] When Paul spoke about the future day of Jesus, he was speaking of the time when, in the person

---

41 See 1 Cor. 1.8; 3.13; 5.5; 15.20–28; 2 Cor. 1.14; 1 Thess. 5.2; 2 Thess. 2.2; Phil. 1.6, 10; 2.16; Rom. 2.5, 16; 13.12; Eph 4.30; 2 Tim. 1.18; 4.8.
42 A point rather explicit in Rom. 11.26 with Paul's citation of Isa. 59.20–21; 27.9 about the deliverer coming from/to 'Zion'.

of his son, Israel's God would come back once and for all, to call the whole world to account and to establish his reign of justice, mercy, and peace.

Second, there is Jesus' return, his royal 'presence' (*parousia*) or 'appearing' (*epiphaneia*). Unlike most of Paul's technical terms, *parousia* has no biblical overtones. It comes, rather, from the classical world, where its simple and basic meaning is 'presence' as opposed to 'absence'. It is often used in association with a royal visitation, as when Caesar might visit a city, or with the manifestation of a divinity to observers, as when Zeus might appear (in disguise, as often as not) in the Greek countryside.

Byzantine mosaic of Christ with Emperor Constantine on the left and Empress Zoe on the right, eleventh century, Hagia Sophia, Istanbul
gezmen / Alamy Stock Photo

By using this language Paul is hinting simultaneously that Jesus will be like a king returning from abroad to reclaim his rightful possession and that he will come to embody and effect God's reign on earth. That is what stands behind Pauline statements like: 'May he strengthen your hearts so that you will be blameless and holy in the presence of our God and Father when our Lord Jesus comes with all his holy ones.'[43] Jesus' *parousia* combines the prophetic hopes for YHWH's return to Zion

---

[43] 1 Thess. 3.13; see 1 Cor. 15.23; 1 Thess. 2.19; 4.15; 5.23; 2 Thess. 2.1, 8.

and the arrival of the royal deliverer. This is the focal point of the final hope for God to rescue his people, not by whisking them up to heaven as in the Platonic view of immortal souls being rescued from hopeless bodies, but by transforming the present creation, including believers still alive at the time, and by raising his people from the dead. As he tells the Philippians, 'We eagerly await a Saviour from there, the Lord Jesus Christ, who, by the power that enables him to bring everything under his control, will transform our lowly bodies so that they will be like his glorious body.'[44]

Third, belonging closely with the coming 'day' of Jesus' *parousia* is the *judgment*. Jesus will bring God's wise justice and order to bear on the whole creation. He will be the one, declares Paul, through whom God will judge the secrets of all hearts. All will 'appear before the judgment seat of Christ, so that each of us may receive what is due us for the things done while in the body, whether good or bad'.[45] Given what Paul believes about Jesus' resurrection and the confirmation of his status as Messiah, it makes sense—good, first-century Jewish sense—to think that Jesus himself would be the one through whom the one God would exercise the judgment that many Jews believed was coming upon the world. The Messiah represented Israel; Israel represented Adam (Abraham's family having been called to be the means of putting Adam's problem to rights); and it was Adam's task to care for creation and to bring it into order. The coming messianic judgment was therefore both the fulfilment of the age-old Jewish hope, the answer to so many prayers in the Psalms and elsewhere, and also the final statement, like that of Daniel to Nebuchadnezzar, that the Lord Most High rules over the kingdoms of mortals. For Paul, there is another twist. Those who belong to the Messiah will themselves share in the work of judging the world, including judging angels. Paul introduces this with a disarming 'don't you know?', but we may suspect that the Corinthians to whom he writes that would be as surprised as we are.[46] His view here depends on a reworking of the Jewish picture of coming judgment, based on Daniel 7 as well as elsewhere, with Jesus both as the embodiment of YHWH and as the inclusive representative of God's people. The task of judgment in Daniel is given to 'the people of the saints of the Most High', and though Paul like other early Christians saw Jesus as occupying this role uniquely, the fluidity of thought between Messiah and people meant that the role could be, and in this case was, easily extended to all those 'in the Messiah'.

Fourth, as part of the 'end', and indeed setting the context for everything else, Paul highlights the promised renewal of all creation through the Messiah. For God's creation to be healed and pacified, it is necessary that the present world, in its state of corruption and decay, should be set free from that 'slavery'. As before, Paul is

---

[44] Phil. 3.20–21.
[45] Rom. 2.16; 2 Cor. 5.10; see also Rom. 14.10; 2 Tim. 4.1.
[46] 1 Cor. 6.3.

thinking in terms of the exodus, here at a cosmic level. Creation will be free to be itself, once God's children are 'glorified', set in proper authority over the world, and able to give it and guarantee it that freedom. This cosmic vision is expressed in Romans 8 through the image of the birth-pangs through which the new world will be born. In 1 Corinthians 15 the same hope is expressed in terms of the great victory over all the forces of evil, up to and including death itself. This cosmic future, we note, is already operative in the Messiah's people themselves, since the new creation is already manifested among those in whom the spirit dwells, a guarantee for the glory and reign still to come.[47] The underlying premise is that 'if the Spirit of him who raised Jesus from the dead is living in you, he who raised Christ from the dead will also give life to your mortal bodies because of his Spirit who lives in you'.[48]

Capernaum synagogue on the shoreline of the Sea of Galilee, dating to the fourth century AD
© 2015 by Zondervan

This is a clue to the old question as to why a good God would create a world that was other than himself. Would that not necessarily mean something less than perfect? Would that not then compromise God's ultimate goodness? No: the creator has made a world that is other than himself, out of sheer generous love. The creation has the capacity, perhaps supremely in human beings, to respond to God's creative power and love in worship and praise. And creation as a whole, as the ancient prophets had seen, has the capacity to be filled with his glory and knowledge, with his breath, his life, his spirit. When that happens, this will not be anything other

---

[47] 2 Cor. 3.18; 5.17; Gal. 6.15.
[48] Rom. 8.11.

than 'the hope of the glory of God', the ancient hope of Israel. That hope, translated and transformed through the Messiah and the spirit, will be fulfilled in and for the entire creation. This will be the ultimate messianic victory: the divine love, poured out in the death of the divine son, will overcome all obstacles and enemies. Indeed, it will enable his people to overcome them, and, as Paul says, 'more than overcome' them.[49]

It should now be clear that Paul's vision of the future is, once again, the radical redrawing of the Jewish expectation. The hope that has been fulfilled has also thereby been reshaped. The 'day of YHWH' in the Old Testament has been transformed into 'the day of the lord [Jesus]' in the New. The return of YHWH is split between the messianic fulfilment of the promises to Israel and the lord's return in glory with his holy ones. The present judgment passed on sin in the Messiah's crucifixion points on to the ultimate judgment that will be passed on the last day. The prophetic hope for prosperity and agricultural fecundity is taken up and intensified so that the whole creation will be set free from its present slavery to decay. Paul seldom says so explicitly, but this is the ancient Jewish hope for 'the kingdom of God', brought into sharp focus through the gospel. This, the ultimate vision of Jewish hope, *has been* fulfilled in Messiah and spirit, and *will be* fulfilled in the same way.

THE PAULINE LEGACY

Paul's theological vision—which he says was rooted in his own literal vision of Jesus—was for the churches of Jews and gentiles to be united together in a common worship of God through Jesus the Messiah and in fellowship with the holy spirit. Paul's career, at least in its mature form, was centred on the unexpected 'revelation' of the kingdom of God through Jesus' death and resurrection, through which he believed that God had renewed the covenant with Israel, throwing it open (as always intended and promised) to all the nations, and launching the new creation from the midst of the old one. The proof that this had happened was the establishment of Messiah-believing communities, made up of Jews and gentiles, a united and holy people of God, reconciled through the Messiah's cross, renewed by the spirit, embodying in their prayers and practices the life of the age to come. This required, of course, a complete recasting of the Jewish worldview, redrawn around Messiah and spirit, radically reorganizing the theological fixtures of God, Torah, Messiah, covenant, and kingdom. It meant a new way of thinking and living: a new type of human being.

To put it simply, Paul believed that Israel's God had, in Jesus' death and

---

49 Rom. 8.37.

resurrection, unveiled his new creation; that Jesus' followers were called to be part of that new creation; and that meant *thinking in a new way*. The content of that thought mattered vitally, but learning to think in the new way mattered above all. For Paul, this vocation and activity (which we might call 'Christian theology') was *load-bearing*: without it, the church would not be, could not be, what it was called to be. Without the constant prayerful and scriptural struggle to understand, in every generation, who God really is, what he's done in Jesus, and what it means for his people, the church easily slips away from its vocation to be united and holy and thereby to be a sign to the world of God's ultimate future. Paul left behind him a network of suffering, struggling, but growing churches. He left a small collection of explosive writings. But his main legacy may well turn out to be the task he articulated, modelled, and urged on his followers: the task of doing Christian theology.

Further reading

Bird, Michael F. 2016. *An Anomalous Jew: Paul among Jews, Greeks and Romans*. Grand Rapids, MI: Eerdmans.
Dunn, James D. G. 1998. *The Theology of Paul the Apostle*. Edinburgh: T&T Clark.
Hooker, Morna D. 1990. *From Adam to Christ: Essays on Paul*. Cambridge: Cambridge University Press.
Matera, Frank J. 2012. *God's Saving Grace: A Pauline Theology*. Grand Rapids, MI: Eerdmans.
Schnelle, Udo. 2005. *Apostle Paul: His Life and Theology*. Tr. M. Eugene Boring; Grand Rapids, MI: Baker.
Schreiner, Thomas R. 2001. *Paul, Apostle of God's Glory in Christ: A Pauline Theology*. Downers Grove, IL: InterVarsity.
Wiles, Virginia. 2000. *Making Sense of Paul: A Basic Introduction to Pauline Theology*. Peabody, MA: Hendrickson.
Wright, N. T. 2005. *Paul: Fresh Perspectives*. London: SPCK.
———. 2014. *Paul and the Faithfulness of God*. COQG 4; London: SPCK.

Roman forum

17

Galatians

I have been crucified with Christ and I no longer live, but Christ lives in me. The life I now live in the body, I live by [the faithfulness of] the Son of God, who loved me and gave himself for me.[1]

CHAPTER AT A GLANCE

This chapter provides a short survey of Paul's letter to the churches in Galatia.

By the end of this chapter you should be able to:

- situate Galatians in Paul's missionary career;
- describe the structure and argument of Galatians;
- identify the main themes and theology of Galatians;
- understand critical issues related to the epistle to the Galatians.

INTRODUCTION

The dense and dramatic argument of Galatians excites and confuses readers. This letter is sometimes perceived as the angry younger sibling of the more composed and reflective letter to Rome. Others have understood Galatians as the point at which Paul says 'Farewell' to his Jewish heritage. Still others use Galatians as the place to work out their own doctrinal debates, with themselves heroically cast as 'Paul' and their own opponents crudely characterized as 'the Galatian intruders'. If we are to avoid making Paul a proto-Marcionite, and if we are going to refuse the temptation to project our own theological disputes into the letter, then we need to read Galatians very carefully, attentive to both its context and content.

In brief, Paul writes this letter to the Galatians after learning that certain agitators or intruders[2] have gained

---

1   Gal. 2.20.
2   Paul's opponents are sometimes called 'judaizers', which is a misnomer because Jews do not 'judaize'. To 'judaize' means 'to try to become Jewish'. Only gentiles can technically 'judaize'. Jews can 'proselytize', that is, urge male gentiles to become proselytes or converts to Judaism by being circumcised; whereas gentiles who follow Jewish customs, particularly by adopting circumcision, are said to judaize. So it is more

a foothold in these churches, urging the male gentile believers to be circumcised. The intruders are effectively trying to bring the Galatians into a closer relationship with the Jewish world in general, and with the Jerusalem church in particular. Paul's animated response is that this not only constitutes a betrayal of the agreement that he reached with the pillar apostles in Jerusalem; it is also a flagrant departure from the truth of the gospel. Paul insists that *you do not have to become physically Jewish in order to belong to the Messiah's family*—and that, if you try to do so, you are denying the crucified and risen Messiah himself. God saves gentiles by making them Messiah-people, not by making them Jews—a paradox, of course, but it is precisely the paradox of the crucified and risen Messiah. It was always God's plan, Paul insists, to have a multi-ethnic family; that is the story scripture tells. That is why the Messiah died and rose. If 'righteousness', that is, the status of being forgiven and possessing a right standing within the covenant, could be gained or validated by means of observing Torah, the Jewish law, then the Messiah died for nothing. If, then, people get circumcised, they are putting themselves under obedience to Torah—but Torah itself, treated this way, offers only the curses of Deuteronomy, ending with exile itself.

So the choice that Paul puts to the Galatian believers is not simply about 'works' versus 'faith'—although this obviously comes into it—but whether or not Jesus is Israel's Messiah, what it means that God's Messiah was crucified, and whether he brings people into the promised new exodus by his own faithfulness, or whether he simply adds to and enhances the old dispensation of Moses. Do the Galatians entrust themselves to the Messiah to give them the status 'righteous', bringing them into the covenant family that God established with Abraham? Or do they wish to labour under the Jewish law as the basis for their standing before God? For Paul this is not a frivolous decision. It is a matter of life and death.

Paul's exhortation to the Galatians could be summarized as follows. By the Messiah's death, believers have been rescued from the evil age. God's new world has dawned, and with it a new community has come into being—but it is the community that God had always promised to create. The curses of Torah have been borne and broken on the cross, with the result that Jews and gentiles can be justified (reckoned 'righteous', within the covenant) by faith, receive adoption into Abraham's renewed family, and fulfil the Torah in a new way, by life in the spirit. If one is 'in the Messiah', then one is in Abraham's family; faith and spirit are the signs of belonging to God's people; and justification and adoption are the benefits of belonging. Therefore, Paul urges, do not submit to circumcision. It effectively brings you into a new form of slavery. Instead, enjoy the freedom of the Messiah and the power of the spirit.

---

accurate to say that the Jewish-Christian teachers/missionaries/intruders are trying to 'proselytize' Paul's gentile converts by urging them to 'judaize'.

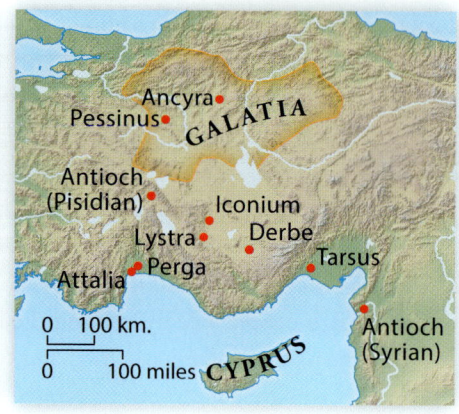

Political Galatia

Ethnic Galatia

To boil this down even further: justification by faith means fellowship by faith; Jesus, not Torah, is the fulcrum of God's saving action; the real way to fulfil Torah is by the spirit, in the law of love.

All these issues were sharpened up by the political situation. The cities of southern Galatia, from Pisidian Antioch eastwards, were a major focus of Roman imperial life and cult, with Antioch itself being a kind of 'new Rome', a proud colony. Civic life, revolving around religious observances, had at its centre the cults related to Rome and the imperial household. Everyone would be expected to show up— except for the Jews, who had official permission to pray 'for' Rome and the emperor rather than praying 'to' them. But now, suddenly, a new group would be staying away from the normal pagan cult, including the Rome-directed ceremonies. Just as the news would travel fast that a group in Thessalonica was absenting itself from normal pagan life (1 Thess. 1.8–9), so word about this new group would get out in the Galatian towns visited by Paul. Local authorities would be alarmed. This might mean trouble from Rome. The members of this new group would claim that they were entitled to the Jewish exemption, since, being followers of Israel's Messiah, they were 'children of Abraham'. The local synagogue authorities, anxious to protect their own status and exemption, would disclaim knowledge of this new group, but they would put pressure on those in the synagogue who had themselves become Jesus-followers. These 'Jewish Christians' would thus find themselves in the middle of a dangerous political and social (as well as theological) struggle, with all kinds of potential consequences. Some of them may have decided that the best thing was to put pressure in turn on the non-Jewish male Jesus-followers to clear up the muddle by getting circumcised, so that everything would look good for the local civic and Roman authorities as well as the synagogue leaders.[3] And, as part of that pressure,

---

3   See Winter 1994; Hardin 2008; Wilson 2007; Wright *PFG*, 1304–5.

398   Paul and the Faithfulness of God

they would be telling the gentile Jesus-believers that the Jerusalem church, an obviously superior body to that wandering teacher Paul, had made all this quite clear . . .

This reading of the situation in Galatia is not an attempt to substitute a 'political' or 'social' understanding for a 'theological' or 'spiritual' one. All these things work together within the Jewish and early Christian world. It is the modern west that has split them apart, and has turned Galatians into a battle of rival theories of 'salvation', detached from the realities of life. Many issues in the letter come into much clearer focus once we see things whole.

CONTEXTUAL AND CRITICAL MATTERS

Northern or southern Galatia?

When it comes to the addressees of the letter, we have to differentiate the interior of Asia Minor, where the ethnic Gauls/Celts settled, and the wider Roman province of Galatia that stretched further south. The Gauls were originally a central European tribe from the Danube basin who spread into Switzerland, southern Germany, northern Italy, France, and Britain. After entering the Balkans and Greece, they crossed the Hellespont into Asia Minor at the invitation of King Nicomedes of Bithynia, who employed them as mercenaries. Eventually they settled in the vicinity of Ancyra, becoming Greek-speaking Gauls, and were absorbed along with Asia Minor into the rest of the Roman empire in 189 BC. In Paul's time, the province of Galatia was located in the interior of Asia Minor, bordered by Cilicia and Pamphylia to the south, Asia to the west, Pontus to the north, and Cappadocia to the east. So, when Paul writes to the Galatians, the question is: did he have in mind political Galatia in the south (Pisidian Antioch, Iconium, Lystra, and Derbe), churches established during his first missionary journey,[4] *or* was he referring to the ethnic Galatians in the north (Ancyra, Pessinus, and Tavium), churches that might perhaps have been established during his second missionary journey?[5] While there are a number of reasons for either option, and a good commentary will spell out the arguments in full, we prefer the south Galatian hypothesis:[6]

1. Paul's travels normally focused on large cities and their neighbouring satellite towns situated along the Mediterranean coast and connected to major Roman roads. Thus it makes sense that Paul would visit cities like Pisidian Antioch and nearby urban centres like Iconium, Lystra, and Derbe along the Via Sebaste.

---
4 Ac. 13.14—14.23.
5 Ac. 16.6; 18.23.
6 See esp. Witherington 1998, 2–8; Dunn 2009b, 666–7, 725; Mitchell 1993, contrasted with e.g. Schnelle 2005, 266–8.

2. The 'churches of Galatia'[7] would be a perfectly sensible designation for the churches of Derbe, Lystra, and Iconium since Paul appears to use Roman provincial terminology to describe geographical areas.[8] The objection that Paul would not call non-ethnic Galatians 'Galatians' fails when we remember: (a) Paul could hardly call them all Phrygians or Lycaonians either; (b) there is inscriptional evidence that the entire region was referred to as 'Galatia'; and (c) even the northern region of Galatia was not inhabited exclusively by ethnic Gauls, but had long since been populated with Syrians, Greeks, Romans, and Jews.
3. Luke's mention of Paul's visit to 'Phrygia and Galatia'[9] need not refer to two separate areas, but might signify the Phrygian part of Galatia, that is, Pisidian Antioch.
4. Christian tombstones in the southern area show evidence from very early times of men named 'Paul'. This is not so in the northern region.

Date

The dating of the letter is even trickier. The main options are that Galatians was sent to:

1. the southern region of Galatia, after Paul's first missionary journey (Ac. 13—14), before the Jerusalem council (Ac. 15), written from Antioch in around AD 48/9; or
2. the southern region of Galatia, after the Jerusalem council (Ac. 15), during an early phase of Paul's Aegean mission (Ac. 18—19), composed perhaps from Corinth in AD 51-2; or
3. the northern part of Galatia, after the Jerusalem council (Ac. 15), during the later phase of Paul's Aegean mission (Ac. 19—20), written from Ephesus or during Paul's later visit to Macedonia in AD 54/5.

On balance we prefer the first of these.

Situation

The question of what precisely had been going on in the Galatian churches is directly related to the questions of destination and dating. We have already sketched a preliminary scenario and now need to amplify it.

The situation behind the letter appears to be that Paul had earlier on won a victory for the principle of male gentiles not needing to be circumcised. This agreement

---

7 Gal. 1.2; 1 Cor. 16.1.
8 See e.g. 'churches of Asia' and 'province of Asia' in Rom. 16.5; 1 Cor. 16.19; 2 Cor. 1.8; 2 Tim. 1.5, plus distinguishing between 'Macedonia' and 'Achaia' within Greece in Rom. 15.26 and 1 Thess. 1.7–8.
9 Ac. 16.6; 18.23.

was hammered out at a Jerusalem meeting, with the pillar apostles (Peter, James, and John) recognizing Paul's ministry and message.[10] But that gain was short-lived when certain people arrived in Antioch from James, and Peter and Barnabas withdrew from table-fellowship with gentiles. Paul saw this as hypocrisy (Peter had earlier been happy to eat with gentile believers, but now was 'play-acting' by pretending to take a different line), and he opposed Peter in person.[11] Shortly afterwards news reached Paul that a group of teachers, perhaps one individual in particular, had been trying to persuade the male gentile believers in the Galatian churches to get circumcised. Their motives were, we may surmise, a rich mixture of (what we call) theology and (what we call) politics.

Theology. They may have been horrified that Jews were sharing fellowship with 'gentile sinners', a practice which might not only pollute the Jews in question but could, by this treasonous behaviour, delay yet further the long-awaited divine act of justice and salvation.

A first-century cup like this would have been used at meals in Roman territories.
British Museum

Politics. The safety of Jewish groups in a Roman territory like southern Asia depended on keeping up good appearances, being good citizens, and exercising responsibly their official exemption from the state cult. If the authorities realized that the new Jesus-movement was claiming the same exemption, but without the normal ethnic rationale, there was no knowing what reprisals might ensue. The important thing, therefore, was to get those puzzling gentile Jesus-believers to come into line. If they wanted to claim the Jewish exemption, they would have to become complete Jews, full proselytes, by getting circumcised (in the case of males) and following the normal distinctive Jewish customs such as the food laws and sabbath observance.[12]

What is more, the intruder(s) will have added, as for that man Paul, we know that he only got his gospel second-hand, while we can appeal to the original apostles in Jerusalem itself. In their mind, Paul was fickle, a 'man-pleaser', who had tried to make conversion easier for gentiles by leaving out the hard bits like circumcision. In any case, he should have known better, since he had been taught the gospel by the Jerusalem church, he had been authorized by the Jerusalem church, he acknowledged their authority on this matter, and he normally preached circumcision anyway.

---

10 Gal. 2.7–10.
11 Gal. 2.11–14.
12 Gal. 5.7–10.

What, then, was really motivating these 'intruders'? First, they may well have genuinely believed that male circumcision was a rite of entry for gentiles, seeing the church as more or less a messianic chapter of ethnic Israel. If Jesus really was Israel's Messiah, he would surely emphasize Israel's Torah even more. Jew and gentile alike, then, would be saved both by faith in the Messiah and by following Torah.[13] This would imply that the ex-pagan Galatians were not fully or truly saved, and the intruders had come to set the Galatians right. (A warning note: the words 'salvation' and 'saved' never occur in Galatians, so it may be that this interpretation should be treated with caution.)

The foundations of a temple to the emperor Augustus in Pisidian Antioch, a city in which Paul preached according to Acts 13
Mark Wilson

Second, the intruders may have been worried that these gentile believers were claiming membership in the family of Israel, despite being uncircumcised, and that this was creating havoc for the reputation of the Jerusalem church. This is altogether more likely. The Jerusalem church was itself under intense pressure from zealous Judeans, who had heard that in Antioch and elsewhere members of the new sect had been sharing table-fellowship with gentiles as if the latter were righteous Jews. This would lower the currency of Israel's election; it would be injurious to the holiness of the covenant people; it would almost certainly delay the coming act of

---

13 Ac. 15.1–5; Gal. 2.15–21; 3.1–12.

divine judgment and salvation. Non-believing zealous Judeans (people such as Saul of Tarsus had been) would do their best to stamp this out, and to engage in violent reprisals against the Jerusalem church if its leaders tolerated it.[14] Such persecution could be averted only if gentile Christians like the Galatians became proper converts to Judaism.

Third, we return to the other 'political' issue: the status of the ex-pagan Christians within the Roman world. It is highly likely that the intruders wanted the Galatians to undergo male circumcision in order to resolve their ambiguous position, as neither pagans nor Jews. We recall how, in ordinary pagan contexts, people who failed to worship the gods would be blamed for any disasters that might strike. Thus, urging the ex-pagan Galatians to get circumcised was necessary to resolve the ambiguous status in which they were not quite Jewish but not proper pagans either. Circumcision would mean that they would enjoy the normal Jewish exemption from local civic cults.[15] Everyone would be happy.

The answer is almost certainly a mix of all the above—and the entire letter shows what Paul thought of it all. He was horrified and angry, both at the rival teachers and at church members giving house-room to such proposals.[16] So he immediately sent a letter to them reminding them of what the gospel was actually all about, warning them of the dangers of falling from grace, and insisting that his own commission came, not from Jerusalem, but from the Messiah, Jesus himself.

It isn't clear whether Paul's opponents in Galatia were Jewish-Christian missionaries from Antioch, as some have suggested, or whether they were local to Galatia. Nor is it clear whether they were actually in close touch with the Jerusalem leaders, or merely appealing to them from a distance. What is clear is that their actions drew forth from Paul a letter of unparalleled theological polemic. Those who prefer their religion or faith to be cool, moderate, a peaceful area away from the rest of real life, should look away now.

THE ARGUMENT OF GALATIANS

(See box: 'Outline of Galatians'.)

OUTLINE OF GALATIANS

1. Greetings and reason for writing (1.1–10)
2. The origin of Paul's gospel (1.11–24)
3. The Jerusalem meeting with Peter, James, and John (2.1–10)
4. The incident at Antioch (2.11–14)
5. Paul's response to Peter's compromise (2.15–21)
6. Paul's defence of the gospel and warning to the Galatians (3.1—5.12)
7. Paul's exhortation to live by the spirit (5.13—6.10)
8. Conclusion and letter closing (6.11–18)

---

[14] Gal. 6.12–13.
[15] Gal. 4.8–10; 6.12.
[16] See esp. Gal. 5.10, 12; 6.12–13. According to Sanders (2015, 475): 'The best way to comprehend Galatians is to read it out aloud, shouting in an angry voice at the appropriate points.'

THE RHETORIC OF GALATIANS

Galatians has been one of the main texts examined in the light of ancient rhetorical conventions. The discussion has centred on what kind of rhetoric Paul employs here: forensic (Paul defends himself and his gospel) or deliberative (Paul tries to persuade the male Galatians not to be circumcised)? Underneath this question is the problem of how to discern a formal rhetorical structure in Paul's argument. Ancient theorists suggested various rhetorical devices that could be used in a speech, including: (1) *exordium* where a speaker begins his or her discourse and tries to make the audience open and well-disposed to the subject; (2) *narratio*, which explains the matter at hand and the circumstances leading up to the discussion; (3) *propositio* as the central thesis to be defended; (4) *probatio*, consisting of the actual arguments in favour of the main thesis; (5) *refutatio* where one refutes an opposing viewpoint or engages potential objections; and (6) *peroratio* as the closing summation. Accordingly there are several proposals for how these devices might provide the building blocks for Paul's argument. H. D. Betz (1979) famously structured Galatians along the following lines:

1. epistolary prescript (1.1–5);
2. *exordium* (1.6–11);
3. *narratio* (1.12–2.14);
4. *propositio* (2.15–21);
5. *probatio* (3.1–4.31);
6. *exhortatio* (5.1–6.10);
7. epistolary postscript with *peroratio* (6.11–18).

It is debatable whether Paul's letters can be structured so woodenly according to rhetorical forms. Paul wrote letters for churches, not speeches for the forum. Paul's letters exhibit at most a functional, rather than formal, rhetoric. That said, it is worth remembering that Paul was certainly trying to persuade his audiences towards certain beliefs and behaviours, and he was undoubtedly immersed in the world of rhetoric and debate. Therefore, he can be expected to have drawn on commonly known rhetorical strategies to make his case. But one cannot use rhetorical patterns developed elsewhere for different purposes as a yardstick to determine his meaning.

See further:
Bird, Michael F. 2008. 'Reassessing a Rhetorical Approach to Paul's Letters.' *Exp. T.* 119.8: 374–9.
Witherington, Ben. 2009. *New Testament Rhetoric: An Introductory Guide to the Art of Persuasion in and of the New Testament*. Eugene, OR: Wipf & Stock.

1. Greetings and reason for writing (1.1–10)

Galatians begins with explosive fervour. Paul bluntly reiterates his apostolic authority as something derived from Jesus and God, not conferred from any human institution (1.1). His subsequent greeting is terse and omits any thanksgiving for the Galatians themselves, emphasizing rather the rescue of believers from the present evil age (1.2–5): Paul is thinking in good Jewish fashion of the 'present age' and the 'age to come', and celebrating the fact that, by Jesus 'giving himself for us', believers have been rescued from the former so that they now belong to the latter. Paul then raises the central issue, namely his bewilderment and anger that the Galatians are abandoning God and turning to a different gospel, giving ear to intruding Jewish-Christian missionaries who are urging the men among them—perhaps with threats—to get circumcised in order to be justified, to be part of God's true family. These intruders, Paul insists, are not perfecting his gospel; they are perverting it. What is more, as Paul had warned them in advance, anyone (even an angel!) who preaches a different gospel should be under God's curse (1.6–9). Paul's point here is that his gospel is the true gospel, in contrast to illicit imitations. Such false preachers are a curse, not a blessing. Paul seems well aware that his rivals have slandered him as a mere 'man-pleaser', presumably because he did not require circumcision. So, he says with a kind of grim irony, reflecting on the heat with which he has written the opening sentences—so, does *that* sound as though I am just trying to please you? No: he is, he insists, a true servant of the Messiah, standing for the truth of the gospel (1.10).

2. The origin of Paul's gospel (1.11–24)

Paul now gets into his stride (see box: 'The rhetoric of Galatians'). His gospel, he says, was not his own invention, nor was it something given to him by the Jerusalem church. Rather, he received it as a revelation from Jesus (1.11–12). Paul then recounts his conversion experience, describing how in his former life as an ultra-zealous Jew he persecuted the church. But then God had revealed his son, literally, 'in me', in order that Paul might preach Jesus among the gentiles (1.13–16a). Paul's response to this revelation was not to consort with anyone from the Jerusalem church. Instead, he went off to Arabia, presumably to Mount Sinai, as Elijah had done when his 'zeal' had ended badly; then, like the prophet, he returned to Damascus (1.16b–17).[17] Throughout this brief autobiographical fragment Paul is careful to echo passages from the Prophets. Anyone suspecting him of being disloyal to Israel's traditions will find that he is consciously and carefully living out his own role within what he sees as the ongoing scriptural narrative.

Paul then describes how he did finally go to Jerusalem, three years after his conversion/call, to meet Cephas (that is, Peter). But while in Jerusalem the only other apostle he saw was James, and no-one else (1.18–19). Paul's emphatic claim not to be lying about this must be because the intruders in Galatia are claiming that, right after his conversion, he had received his message and mandate from the Jerusalem apostles (1.20). Not so, insists Paul: his message came from Jesus himself, and all Jerusalem did was celebrate his work.

Paul, however, did not linger in Judea. He went off, as Acts says, to his native Tarsus in Cilicia. It was after that that Barnabas brought him to Syrian Antioch to help with leading and teaching the exciting young church there (1.21–24; see Ac. 9.23–30; 11.19–26).

---

[17] See Wright *Paul: A Biography*, and 'Paul, Arabia and Elijah' in Wright *PP*, 152–9.

PORTALS AND PARALLELS: THE QUESTION OF CIRCUMCISION FOR MALE CONVERTS TO JUDAISM

The debate about circumcising gentiles was not limited to Christian circles, but was a question faced by all Jews of the Diaspora when dealing with gentile males who wanted to convert to Judaism. Josephus relates a story about King Izates of the Adiabene (situated between the Roman vassal-state Armenia to the north and the Parthian kingdom to the south) in which he describes two Jewish teachers who gave Izates conflicting advice about whether he needed to be circumcised to be fully Jewish:

Now during the time when Izates resided at Charax Spasini, a certain Jewish merchant named Ananias visited the king's wives and taught them to worship God after the manner of the Jewish tradition. It was through their agency that he was brought to the notice of Izates, whom he similarly won over with the co-operation of the women . . . When Izates had learned that his mother was very much pleased with the Jewish religion, he was zealous to convert to it himself; and since he considered that he would not be genuinely a Jew unless he was circumcised, he was ready to act accordingly. When his mother learned of his intention, however, she tried to stop him by telling him that it was a dangerous move. For, she said, he was a king; and if his subjects should discover that he was devoted to rites that were strange and foreign to themselves, it would produce much dissatisfaction, and they would not tolerate the rule of a Jew over them . . . He, in turn, reported her arguments to Ananias . . . The king, could, he [Ananias] said, worship God even without being circumcised if indeed he had fully decided to be a devoted adherent of Judaism, for it was this that counted more than circumcision. He told him, furthermore, that God himself would pardon him if, constrained thus by necessity and by fear of his subjects, he failed to perform this rite. And so, for the time, the king was convinced by his arguments. Afterwards, however, since he had not completely given up his desire, another Jew, named Eleazar, who came from Galilee and who had a reputation for being extremely strict when it came to the ancestral laws, urged him to carry out the rite. For when he came to him to pay his respects and found the law of Moses, he said: 'In your ignorance, O king, you are guilty of the greatest offence against the law and thereby against God. For you ought not merely to read the law but also, and even more, to do what is commanded in it. How long will you continue to be uncircumcised? If you have not yet read the law concerning this matter, read it now, so that you may know what an impiety it is that you commit.' Upon hearing these words, the king postponed the deed no longer. (Jos. *Ant.* 20.34–5, 38–46)

3. The Jerusalem meeting with Peter, James, and John (2.1–10)

Paul now describes his second Jerusalem visit. He had not been summoned; he went in response to a 'revelation', probably the prophetic message about the coming famine (Ac. 11.27–30), not (as many have supposed) to the 'Jerusalem conference' of Acts 15. The question of how gentiles could be included in the new messianic family—substantially the same issue that was haunting Galatia—had come up then, because Paul and Barnabas had taken with them Titus, an uncircumcised gentile believer. Some in Jerusalem wanted to have him circumcised, but Paul had recognized this as a threat to the gospel itself. According to that gospel, as he says in 1.4, the Messiah had won the rescuing victory, through his death, over the powers of the old age, so that gentile believers were already clean, not 'sinners', rescued from the power of the defeated idols. In discussion, the leading Jerusalem apostles were happy with what he was doing, only urging him to 'continue to remember the poor', which Paul readily endorsed (see for example Gal. 6.10).

4. The incident at Antioch (2.11–14)

Paul then refers to the very recent incident when Peter, having arrived in Antioch and taken part in the multi-ethnic church fellowship, withdrew after certain persons had come from James, drawing 'even Barnabas' along with him. This wasn't just a squabble between two ways of interpreting one comparatively trivial point. It involved the very heart of the gospel. Peter was in effect 'compelling gentiles to judaize', saying to male non-Jewish believers, 'If you want to be part of the forgiven, new-covenant family of God, you'll have to get circumcised.' Paul is determined to show how wrong this was (see 'Portals and parallels: the question of circumcision for male converts to Judaism').

Despite the fierce disagreement between Paul and Peter described in Galatians 2.11–14, one of the most common subjects for iconography in Christian art was the embrace of St Paul and St Peter.
Dmitry Kalinovsky / Shutterstock

5. Paul's response to Peter's compromise (2.15–21)

The point, Paul insists, is about *who you are in the Messiah*. Are the true people of God all who belong to the Messiah? Or are the people of God only Jewish Christians (including proselytes, that is, gentiles who have converted to Judaism), with gentile Christians remaining second-class citizens? For Paul, God's true people are summed up in one person: the Messiah. He is the faithful one. He is the true Israelite. That is why a person is not justified 'by works of the law' (keeping Israel's Torah), but by 'the faithfulness of Messiah Jesus'. The only badge of membership in the rescued, forgiven family is the corresponding 'faith'. Believing gentiles are therefore on the same level as believing Jews. Paul himself is the example: 'I through Torah died to Torah.' He has a new identity: the Messiah's own life now mysteriously dwelling in and animating Paul himself. This is the climax of the letter so far. Echoing 1.4, Paul says that 'the son of God . . . loved me and gave himself for me' (v. 20 *NTE/KNT*). To seek identity anywhere other than the crucified and risen Messiah—as Peter, Barnabas, and the Galatian agitators were doing—would be to spurn the incarnate

BLAST FROM THE PAST: MARTIN LUTHER ON CHRISTIAN RIGHTEOUSNESS

Martin Luther, commenting on Galatians 2.20, wrote:

Paul explains what constitutes true Christian righteousness. True Christian righteousness is the righteousness of Christ who lives in us. We must look away from our own person. Christ and my conscience must become one, so that I can see nothing else but Christ crucified and raised from the dead for me. If I keep on looking at myself I am gone. If we lose sight of Christ and begin to consider our past we simply go to pieces. We must turn our eyes to the brazen serpent, Christ crucified, and believe with all our heart that he is our righteousness and our life. For Christ, on whom our eyes are fixed, in whom we live, who lives in us, is Lord over the law, sin, death, and all evil.*

Martin Luther
Public Domain

----
* Luther, *Commentary on Galatians*, 1535 (CCEL edn.).

love-in-action which constitutes the ultimate act of divine grace (see 'Blast from the past: Martin Luther on Christian righteousness'). If covenant membership could be attained, or retained, through Torah, that act would not have been necessary.

6. Paul's defence of the gospel and warning to the Galatians (3.1—5.12)

Paul now advances his main argument, starting with two solid points. God has given the Galatians his spirit, indicating that they are already God's heirs (3.1–5); they are already Abraham's true children on the basis of their faith (3.6–9). The intruders might have countered that Torah was incumbent upon all Abraham's children. Torah itself had set before Israel the options of life and death, with the promise of life for obedience as in Leviticus 18.5. Paul, probing deeper into the story, sees that God's promise to Abraham wasn't simply about the Jews; it was designed for all the nations. But Abraham's family had themselves disobeyed God, and so were suffering Torah's curses (as any first-century Jew could see). What was needed was not more Torah but for the curse of the Torah to be removed.

So, declares Paul, the curses of disobedience spoken of in Deuteronomy 27.26 have been borne by Israel's representative, the Messiah. Jesus, as Israel's Messiah, took the weight of Israel's curse on himself (see Dt. 21.23), not just in some abstract theological sense but literally and historically, when he died on the cross (see Gal. 3.6–14). Escape from covenantal curse, exile, and condemnation has been provided not through Torah but through the Messiah's faithfulness, foreshadowed in Habakkuk 2.4, 'The righteous live by their faith' (NRSV).

TABLE 17.1: PAUL'S DISTINCTION BETWEEN THE SPIRITUAL HEIRS OF SARAH AND OF HAGAR

Sarah's family	Hagar's family
descended from Isaac	descended from Ishmael
children of promise	children of the flesh
free	slave
represent the covenant of the heavenly Zion (implied)	represent the covenant of Sinai
citizens of Jerusalem above (restored future state)	citizens of Jerusalem below (present state of exile)
bereft but now fruitful	in slavery along with all her children
Galatian believers	Jewish-Christian intruders
trusting in God by the spirit	trusting in fleshly identity
persecuted	persecutors
will inherit promises	will be cast out

The way is now clear for the blessing of Abraham to flow out to the nations—in Messiah Jesus (3.14a); and for Jews like Paul himself to receive the spirit, the downpayment for the promised inheritance.

So how do the Abrahamic and Mosaic covenants relate to one another? What was the purpose of Torah in the first place? How does being in the Messiah provide a new identity for believers?

Paul's argument from 3.15 to 3.29 is that God always promised Abraham a single family ('seed'), a promise fulfilled in the Messiah, who represents his people in himself. Torah, by isolating Israel from the nations (a necessary move during the ambiguous period before the Messiah), would have produced a multiplicity of 'families'. To allow this would nullify the Abrahamic promise. When the Messiah comes, the age of 'faith' has arrived, and God's promise to Abraham can be kept through the Messiah-shaped faith, baptism, and single family, with no need any longer for Torah to look after God's people. 'You are all one in the Messiah, Jesus' (3.26–28 *NTE/KNT*). Like Israel in Egypt, the whole world was formerly in captivity, but God sent his son and his spirit, revealing his true nature in redemptive action (4.1–7). Any step back from that is a step into some kind of paganism (4.8–11), idolizing the 'elements of the world', the parts of the old creation upon which the Jew–gentile separation was based (see 'Portals and parallels: Juvenal and Justin Martyr on the Jews').

PORTALS AND PARALLELS: JUVENAL AND JUSTIN MARTYR ON THE JEWS

The Jews were a somewhat recognizable and homogeneous group in antiquity, often despised by Roman elites for their refusal to hellenize or to be fully integrated into Roman culture. It was frequently their separation from non-Jews and their distinctive practices that brought them to the attention of authors, who noted, often with revulsion, their peculiar way of life. Juvenal had nothing nice to say about Romans and Greeks who adopted Jewish customs:

> Some who have had a father who reveres the Sabbath, worship nothing but the clouds, and the divinity of the heavens, and see no difference between eating swine's flesh, from which their father abstained, and that of man; and in time they take to circumcision. Having been wont to flout the laws of Rome, they learn and practice and revere the Jewish law, and all that Moses handed down in his secret tome, forbidding to point out the way to any not worshipping the same rites, and conducting none but the circumcised to the desired foundation. For all which the father was to blame, who gave up every seventh day to idleness, keeping it apart from all the concerns of life. (Juv. *Sat.* 15.96–106)

Justin Martyr, a second-century Christian apologist, records a conversation he had with a Jew named Trypho. Justin reports how Trypho was scandalized as to why Christians claim to believe in God but refuse to follow the Jewish way of life and separate themselves from pagans:

> But this is what we are most at a loss about: that you, professing to be pious, and supposing yourselves better than others, are not in any particular [way] separated from them, and do not alter your mode of living from the nations, in that you observe no festivals or sabbaths, and do not have the rite of circumcision; and further, resting your hopes on a man that was crucified, you yet expect to obtain some good thing from God, while you do not obey His commandments. Have you not read, that soul shall be cut off from his people who shall not have been circumcised on the eighth day? And this has been ordained for strangers and for slaves equally. But you, despising this covenant rashly, reject the consequent duties, and attempt to persuade yourselves that you know God, when, however, you perform none of those things which they do who fear God. If, therefore, you can defend yourself on these points, and make it manifest in what way you hope for anything whatsoever, even though you do not observe the law, this we would very gladly hear from you, and we shall make other similar investigations. (Just. *Dial.* 10)

Fourth-century tomb marker found in a Jewish catacomb in Rome, Israel Museum

---

Paul now changes his topic and tone, away from the metaphors of slavery and subordination, to a personal appeal to the Galatians (4.12—5.1). He will not allow the intruders to drive a wedge between his converts and himself: his appeal is emotional, personal, vivid.

This sets Paul up for an allegorical reading of the story of Abraham's two spouses and two sons (Gen. 16; Gen. 21): Sarah and Hagar, Isaac and Ishmael. Perhaps stealing his opponents' thunder, he likens the Jew–gentile messianic community to Isaac as 'children of promise', and the single-nation family of Torah-keeping Jews to Ishmael, the child of the slave (see Table 17.1).[18] If getting circumcised is to make sense, then the Galatians would have to keep the entire Torah, something the 'intruders', bent on maintaining a good public face, never envisage (5.2–12).

7. Paul's exhortation to live by the spirit (5.13—6.10)

Paul's opponents are implying that there are only two ways to live: the Jewish way, observing Torah, or the gentile (pagan) way, still enslaved to idols. No, says Paul, there is a third way: a double freedom, into which you are released and transformed by the new exodus that God has accomplished in Jesus the Messiah. That results in love, and in the 'fruit of the spirit' as opposed to the 'works of the flesh' (5.13–26). This will give rise to a mutually caring society (6.1–10).

> 'As a community, Christians in the United States must recognize how deeply the history of the idea of race is intertwined with the development of the American church. In the United States, the church is an institution that normalizes the effects of slavery. Further, racially separate churches violate the interdependence that would characterize authentic Pauline Christian communities and would allow both black- and white-born Christians a fuller grasp of the nature of redemption. . . . When Christians suspend the bonds of allegiance to their birth identity even as they preserve the memory of having been Gentiles who were "aliens from the commonwealth of Israel and strangers to the covenants of promise" (Eph. 2.12), they manifest a Christianity that offers hope to a society desperate for racial reconciliation. These Christians demonstrate that they are Paul's intellectual heirs and blood traitors on behalf of the blood of Christ.'
>
> **Love Sechrest**, *A Former Jew*, 229–31.

8. Conclusion and letter closing (6.11–18)

Paul rounds off the letter in his own writing (6.11), contrasting his own 'boast' in the gospel with the intruders' desire to 'boast' (that is, put on a good face in public) in the new outward status for the gentile Messiah-believers. The message of the cross, he says, renders all that irrelevant. Ethnic signs and symbols no longer matter; what matters now is only God's new creation (6.14–15). Paul invokes God's blessing on those who go this way, who comprise the 'Israel of God' (6.16). The letter as a whole shows what this means: 'the household of the faith' (6.10 *NTE/KNT*), 'Circumcision, you see, is nothing; neither is uncircumcision! What matters is new creation. Peace and mercy on everyone who lines up by that standard— yes, on God's Israel' (6.15–16 *NTE/KNT*), and so on.[19] Paul himself bears the gospel marks on his body, the wounds of persecution which point to the suffering of the Messiah (6.17).

---

[18] See on this Dunne 2014.
[19] See discussion in Wright *PFG*, 1142–51.

TABLE 17.2: TULIP OF THE 'APOCALYPTIC PAUL'

Tendency to downplay salvation-historical continuity	The gospel is punctiliar, not linear, and continuity is minimal; it was Paul's opponents who were arguing for continuity with Israel's sacred history by urging gentiles to be circumcised.
Unveiling of salvation in the apocalypse of Jesus Christ	Salvation is revealed exclusively in the Christ-event, his faithfulness, death, and resurrection, which Paul himself experienced in his call to preach the gospel.
Law as agent of oppressive powers	Paul, especially in Galatians, regards the law as part of the evil age that is dominated by hostile powers, from whom Jesus rescues believers.
Invasion of grace as the end of religion	Paul's gospel means the end of all religion, obviously Judaism in particular, but in application this equally applies to moral therapeutic Deism (mainline Protestantism) or boundary-set proselytism (evangelicalism).
***P**istis Christou* as the faithfulness of Christ	The opposite of 'works of the law' is *pistis*, not 'faith' but the 'faithfulness' of Christ.

TABLE 17.3: TULIP OF 'PAUL WITHIN JUDAISM'*

Torah-observant Paul	Paul himself obeyed the Torah and faithfully followed the Jewish life, albeit flexibly at times, depending on his environment.
Under the Jewish covenant	The Jewish people are saved under the aegis of their own covenant. In other words, Jesus is the Messiah for gentiles, not for Jews.
Limited proselytism	Although Paul steadfastly refused to circumcise his male gentile converts, he none the less insisted on a certain degree of Torah-observance by urging his converts to avoid idolatry and sexual immorality.
Identity without essentializing	Jewish identity is complex, and should not be reduced to some kind of fixed 'essence'. Gentile Christians have guest status within 'Israel'; they are not a 'third race', nor part of Israel; nor do they 'replace' Israel.
Polemics as a poor way to map Judaism	Ancient Judaism should not be understood in the light of the polemics within Christian groups, like Paul and his Jewish-Christian opponents, but in terms of its own literature and claims, without imposing Christianized categories and beliefs.

*My thanks to Patrick Schreiner for helping me (MFB) refine this taxonomy.

EXCURSUS: RECENT TRENDS IN CONTEMPORARY PAULINE SCHOLARSHIP

In contemporary scholarship, there are several quite different schools of thought related to the study of Paul. These include the (so-called) 'Apocalyptic Paul' and 'Paul within Judaism' branches of Pauline scholarship.[20] The 'Apocalyptic Paul' approach, associated with scholars like J. Louis Martyn and Douglas Campbell, attempts to plot the main co-ordinates of Paul's theology in terms of an apocalyptic inbreaking of God's saving action in the faithfulness and death of Jesus Christ that is largely discontinuous with Israel's salvation history. Those associated with the 'Paul within Judaism' movement, like Mark Nanos and Paula Fredriksen, are concerned to show that Paul was a Torah-observant Jewish figure who remained completely within first-century Judaism. Both 'schools' are complex and diverse; their claims require lengthy explanation and nuance. However, for the sake of brevity, we may summarize the two schools by using the acronym TULIP (see Tables 17.2 and 17.3).

It should be clear that these two contemporary movements more or less cancel one another out. Better ways are called for.

GALATIANS AND THE BIG PICTURE

Galatians drives us to look at scripture's big picture and to live out the spirit-led life in the ways that Paul instructs. Here we focus on freedom, identity, and ethics.

First, Galatians is a manifesto for Christian freedom. The German biblical scholar Ernst Käsemann wrote a brief, polemical survey of the New Testament called *Jesus Means Freedom*. Despite the author's angry tone, the title sums up Paul's leitmotif: 'For freedom Christ has set us free' (Gal. 5.1 NRSV; see 2 Cor. 3.17). Galatians is fundamentally concerned with breaking the bonds of slavery and setting captives free. This liberation means rescue from the present evil age (Gal. 1.4), redemption from the curse of the law (Gal. 3.13; 4.5), and release from slavery to hostile yet ultimately impotent non-gods (Gal. 4.3–8). Paul constantly echoes and retells the exodus narrative, showing how in the Messiah and by the spirit those who were enslaved to the law's curses or to elemental forces have been liberated. This is a metanarrative like no other. We must therefore guard against any intruder who says, in effect, 'The Messiah is not enough' or that 'the spirit is not all that effective', and that 'to be properly saved . . . righteous . . . complete . . . assured . . . you need x'. Whatever x may be, we are able to invoke Paul's warnings about the dangers of

---

20 On 'apocalyptic' in Paul, see Wright *PRI*, Part II. The rest of that book outlines various other contemporary 'schools'.

preaching a different gospel (Gal. 1.8). They earn Paul's stern and sharp rebukes (2.14; 4.30; 5.12).

Second, although Paul argues ferociously about justification by faith, the key question he is dealing with is, 'Who are God's people and how do you know?' He is, in other words, talking about *identity*. What matters is being a Messiah-person; that is the key to forgiveness, status, and hope. God has launched his new creation in which the old differences, necessary for the time, cease to matter. We have been crucified with Christ (Gal. 2.19–20); we have crucified the flesh (Gal. 5.24); we have been crucified to the world (Gal 6.14). Or, to take a different set of themes, we believe in Christ, we belong to Christ, we are baptized into Christ, and Christ is being formed in us! The most powerful statement our churches can make, amid conflicts of class, tribe, and race, must be made through the actual coming together of believers of all types in a united worshipping family. The single greatest sign that God's kingdom has taken root in a sceptical and suspicious world is that the church, in all of its manifold diversities, comes together, eating at the same table, announcing one lord, one faith, one baptism, and worshipping with one voice. That is the sign that God has been faithful to the promises he made to Abraham and we are all invited, by faith in Christ, to become sons and daughters of Abraham.

Third, Paul's letter is packed with reference to the spirit. We received the spirit by faith, so we should not try to attain perfection through the flesh (Gal. 3.2, 14). The spirit works miracles among the churches by leading people to believe the message of the gospel (Gal. 3.5). The spirit is our adoption to divine sonship (Gal. 4.6).

Roman aqueduct, Pisidian Antioch

The spirit is the source of our future hope (Gal. 5.5) and the mode of our walk before God in the present (Gal. 5.16). Ethics is all about the spirit, because the spirit releases us from the law, the spirit opposes the flesh, and the spirit produces in us a bountiful harvest of mixed fruits (Gal. 5.16–23). Paul would probably put all of this under the heading of 'keeping in step with the spirit' (see Gal. 5.25). Galatians is thus far more than doctrine; it is about how to live a spiritually fruitful life, and the proper resources to do it.

Further reading

Betz, Hans Dieter. 1979. *Galatians: A Commentary on Paul's Letter to the Churches in Galatia*. Hermeneia; Minneapolis: Fortress.
Bird, Michael F. 2009. 'What If Martin Luther Had Read the Dead Sea Scrolls? Historical Particularity and Theological Interpretation in Pauline Theology: Galatians as a Test Case.' *JTI* 3: 107–25.
——. 2016. *An Anomalous Jew: Paul among Jews, Greeks, and Romans*. Grand Rapids, MI: Eerdmans.
Chester, Stephen. 2008. 'When the Old Was New: Reformation Perspectives on Galatians 2:16.' *Exp. T.* 119: 320–9.
——. 2009. 'It Is No Longer I Who Live: Justification by Faith and Participation in Christ in Martin Luther's Exegesis of Galatians.' *NTS* 55: 315–37.
de Boer, Martinus C. 2011. *Galatians: A Commentary*. NTL; Louisville: Westminster John Knox.
Dunn, James D. G. 1993. *The Theology of Paul's Letter to the Galatians*. Cambridge: Cambridge University Press.
Eastman, Susan. 2007. *Recovering Paul's Mother Tongue: Language and Theology in Galatians*. Grand Rapids, MI: Eerdmans.
Elliott, M. W., Scott J. Hafemann, N. T. Wright, and John Frederick (eds.). 2014. *Galatians and Christian Theology: Justification, the Gospel, and Ethics in Paul's Letter*. Grand Rapids, MI: Baker.
Hays, Richard B. 2000. 'The Letter to the Galatians.' In *New Interpreter's Bible*. Edited by L. E. Keck. 12 vols.; Nashville: Abingdon, 11.183–348.
Gaventa, Beverly R. 2003. 'Galatians.' In *Eerdmans Commentary on the Bible*, eds. J. D. G. Dunn and J. W. Rogerson. Grand Rapids, MI: Eerdmans, pp. 1374–84.
Jervis, L. Ann. 2002. *Galatians*. NIBC; Peabody, MA: Hendrickson.
Longenecker, Richard N. 1990. *Galatians*. WBC; Dallas, TX: Word.
Martyn, J. Louis. 1997. *Galatians: A New Translation with Introduction and Commentary*. AB; New York: Doubleday.
Nanos, Mark D. (ed.). 2002. *The Irony of Galatians: Contemporary Issues in Rhetorical and Historical Interpretation*. Grand Rapids, MI: Baker.
Riches, John K. 2008. *Galatians through the Centuries*. Oxford: Blackwell.
Witherington, Ben. 1998. *Grace in Galatia: A Commentary on Paul's Letter to the Galatians*. Grand Rapids, MI: Eerdmans.
Wright, N. T. 2000. 'The Letter to the Galatians.' In *Between Two Horizons: Spanning New Testament Studies and Systematic Theology*. Edited by Joel B. Green and Max Turner. Grand Rapids, MI: Eerdmans, pp. 205–36.
——. 2011. 'Tom Wright Galatians Introduction 2011 St Andrews 1.' Recorded by St John's Nottingham. <https://www.youtube.com/watch?v=IZUDuBu1xvY>. Cited 10 May 2016.

18

1 and 2 Thessalonians

They tell how you turned to God from idols to serve the living and true God, and to wait for his Son from heaven, whom he raised from the dead—Jesus, who rescues us from the coming wrath.[1]

CHAPTER AT A GLANCE

This chapter provides a short survey of Paul's letters to the church in Thessalonica.

By the end of this chapter you should be able to:

- situate 1 and 2 Thessalonians in Paul's missionary career;
- describe the structure and argument of 1 and 2 Thessalonians;
- identify the main themes and theology of 1 and 2 Thessalonians;
- understand critical issues related to 1 and 2 Thessalonians.

INTRODUCTION

The Thessalonian letters, among the earliest of Paul's extant letters, are among the earliest writings of the whole New Testament, probably written within weeks of Paul's first visit to Thessalonica. They reflect confusion in the early church about the 'presence' or 'coming' of Jesus, and what it means for the church in the meantime—perhaps because of things that Paul had stressed in his initial preaching and teaching.[2]

The first problem was *anxiety*: what will happen to believers who have died before the lord's return? The second problem was a heightened sense of *anticipation*: should believers abandon ordinary life and work, relying on Christian generosity in the short time before Jesus came back? Paul addresses these issues—but this doesn't mean that the letters constitute a 'manual' on the 'end times'. The letters are short, sharp, and quick, small flashes of pastoral wisdom and theological teaching. Longenecker and Still offer apt descriptions for these letters by subtitling them as 'Perseverance, Purity,

---

[1] 1 Thess. 1.9–10.
[2] In biblical scholarship, Jesus' return is often called the *parousia*, based on the Greek word for 'presence'.

and Preparedness until the Parousia' (1 Thessalonians) and 'Consolation and Correction for an Afflicted and Confused Church' (2 Thessalonians).[3] Alliteration sometimes assists.

CONTEXTUAL AND CRITICAL MATTERS

Thessalonica

The city of Thessalonica, modern Thessaloniki, was founded in 316 BC by the Macedonian general Cassander, who named it in honour of his wife Thessalonikeia. It is located in the innermost cove of the Thermaic gulf on the north-eastern coast of Greece. The Romans annexed Macedonia in 168 BC; Thessalonica became the capital of the region in 146 BC. In Paul's day, Thessalonica was a free city with tax exemptions. It was predominantly Greek, but with significant numbers of Italians, Thracians, and Jews. The city was in an important location along the Via Egnatia, connecting the Balkans to Asia Minor, facilitating Paul's Macedonian travels. The Jewish community in the city was large enough (unlike the small numbers in Philippi) to support a synagogue building.

Paul and his co-workers left Troas for Macedonia, probably in early AD 50, travelling and working in Philippi. They left Philippi after hostility from the civic authorities, journeying south-west through Amphipolis and Apollonia before arriving in Thessalonica. According to Luke, Paul spent three weeks proclaiming Jesus as the Messiah in the Jewish synagogue (while also working among pagans in his tent-making business); he convinced some Jews, gentile God-fearers, and prominent women about Jesus (or rather, he insisted, it was God's word doing its own work).[4] Paul and the Thessalonian church soon experienced opposition from the Jewish quarter, culminating with an angry mob ransacking the house of Paul's host, Jason.[5] Jason and some other believers were hauled before the city officials;

Thessalonica

---
[3] Longenecker and Still 2014, 62, 75.
[4] Ac. 17.2–4; 1 Thess. 1.9; 2.9.
[5] Ac. 17.5–10; Phil. 4.16; 1 Thess. 1.6 ('in spite of persecution you received the word with joy inspired by the Holy Spirit' [NRSV]); 1 Thess. 2.14–15 ('You suffered from your own people the same things those churches suffered from the Jews who killed the Lord Jesus' [NIV]).

the substance of the complaint against them was that they were harbouring known troublemakers and political subversives:

> These people who have been turning the world upside down have come here also, and Jason has entertained them as guests. They are all acting contrary to the decrees of the emperor, saying that there is another king named Jesus.[6]

In other words, the Messiah-devotees were seen as well-known religiously motivated social deviants opposed to the Roman imperium; they had now brought their brand of counter-imperial messianism to Thessalonica! Paul, Silas, and Timothy fled under cover of night and made their way to Berea where Paul had a brief successful ministry, cut short by some Thessalonian Jews arriving to stir up trouble.[7] Paul then headed further south to Athens. While in Athens he felt 'orphaned' without the Thessalonians, and was anxious to hear how they were holding up, worried that they had been 'unsettled'. He therefore dispatched Timothy to go and find out.[8] Paul then continued to Corinth, where he remained for a time.[9]

It was probably during his extended stay in Corinth in AD 50 that Timothy met up with Paul and reported to Paul that the Thessalonians were doing all right.[10] While this alleviated Paul's concerns somewhat, he remained mindful that although the church had started well (1 Thess. 1.3, 6–9; 2.13), it was still young and vulnerable like a newborn baby (1 Thess. 2.7). The new believers' faith might falter through temptation or distress (1 Thess. 3.3, 5; 5.14); they needed constant encouraging (1 Thess. 2.12; 3.2, 7; 4.18; 5.11, 14; 2 Thess. 2.17) and strengthening (1 Thess. 3.2, 5, 10, 13; 2 Thess. 2.17). So Paul wrote 1 Thessalonians to praise the little struggling church for its perseverance (1 Thess. 1.3, 8; 2.13–16; 3.2–13), assuring the believers there that people who died in faith would not miss out on participating in Christ's return, because the 'dead in Christ will rise first' (1 Thess. 4.13—5.3). He exhorted them to continue in holiness and godliness in a world of darkness (1 Thess. 4.1–12; 5.4–8, 12–22) so that they would be found 'blameless' at the coming of the lord Jesus (1 Thess. 3.13; 5.23).

In addition, Paul dispels any misapprehension that he and his crew were wandering vagabond philosophers out to make a quick profit (1 Thess. 2.1–12). He explains that his failure to visit them again was not because he hadn't wanted to come; 'Satan blocked our way,' he says (2.18). His affection for them is undimmed (1 Thess. 2.17—3.5).

---

6 Ac. 17.6–7 NRSV.
7 Ac. 17.10–14.
8 1 Thess. 2.17; 3.1–3.
9 Ac. 17.15—18.5.
10 1 Thess. 3.6.

The Roman forum in Thessalonica
hdesislava / Shutterstock

Not long after writing 1 Thessalonians, perhaps only weeks or months later, Paul received news that the situation in Thessalonica had deteriorated. First, the persecution had intensified (2 Thess. 1.4–12). Second, a report was circulating that the 'day of the lord' had already arrived, leading to confusion and concern (2 Thess. 2.1–10). Third, the problem of people giving up work to wait for the lord's return had escalated further (2 Thess. 3.6–14). Paul accordingly wrote again, addressing these matters, stressing the importance of remaining steadfast and strong in the face of persecution (2 Thess. 1.4, 11–12; 2.15–17; 3.5). The Thessalonians were to remember what they were taught (2 Thess. 2.5, 15; 3.7, 10), and were to live up to the standard implied by, and inherent in, God's call (2 Thess. 1.5, 11). They were to rejoice, above all, in the hope of sharing in the glory of the lord Jesus (2 Thess. 2.14).

Authorship of 2 Thessalonians

Many have doubted whether Paul himself wrote 2 Thessalonians.[11] The reasons for this include:

1. *Eschatology.* There is a shift from an imminent expectation of Jesus' *parousia* (1 Thessalonians) to a belief that the *parousia* is now more distant and will be preceded by signs performed by an antichrist figure (2 Thessalonians).

---

[11] See esp. discussion in Foster 2012.

2. *Literary features.* It is often claimed that 2 Thessalonians woodenly mimics 1 Thessalonians through near-verbatim replication of the epistolary greeting and benediction, two thanksgiving sections, and double prayers. These similarities, some suggest, indicate a pseudepigrapher studiously copying his source, rather than Paul himself with his usual stylistic flexibility. (The two letters to Corinth show remarkable differences.) In other words, the two letters are so similar as to raise suspicion.
3. *Authorial tone.* The pastoral warmth of 1 Thessalonians recedes as the writer of 2 Thessalonians seems to adopt a more authoritarian persona.
4. *Marks of authenticity.* The warnings about a letter 'supposedly from us' (2 Thess. 2.2) and the large emphasis on the authenticity of Paul's autograph (2 Thess. 3.17) are alleged to signal a pseudonymous author, in the way that a confidence trickster might attempt to win confidence by warning about confidence tricksters.

These arguments can be countered on several grounds:

1. *Eschatology.* A comparison of 2 Thessalonians with the synoptic Olivet Discourses (Mk. 13; Mt. 24—25; Lk. 21) and the revelation of John demonstrates that belief that certain signs will precede the end is fully compatible with an expectation of the imminence of the end (whatever that 'end' might be). Furthermore, Paul himself seems to have oscillated in his expectation of precisely how near the end was: somewhere between imminent (1 Thess. 5.2; 1 Cor. 1.7; 7.29; 15.23, 51–52; Phil. 3.20–21; Rom. 13.11; 16.20) to impending (2 Cor 5.1–10; Gal. 5.5; Col. 3.4), to perhaps being delayed until at least after his own death (Phil. 1.20–25; 2 Tim. 4.6; perhaps 1 Cor. 6.14).
2. *Literary features.* While close literary similarities do exist between the two letters, if 1 and 2 Thessalonians were written close together these similarities are hardly surprising. Foster comments: 'It is not impossible that Paul or his scribe retained a copy or a draft of 1 Thessalonians, or perhaps more plausibly that the two letters were written in a sufficiently close temporal span that key phrases were able to be recalled from memory.'[12] The fact that 1 Corinthians and 2 Corinthians are so very different stylistically is much better explained in terms of the horrific experience Paul had just passed through before the second letter (2 Cor. 1.8–11). In any case, it seems something of a heads-I-win-tails-you-lose argument to say that (for instance) Ephesians and Colossians cannot be by Paul because the style is so different from the other letters, while 2 Thessalonians cannot be by Paul because the style is so similar.

---

[12] Foster 2012, 163.

3. *Authorial tone.* Whether 2 Thessalonians is in fact cold and authoritarian in contrast to the warm and personal 1 Thessalonians should be questioned in the light of Paul's encouraging remarks in 2 Thessalonians (2 Thess. 1.3–5, 11–12; 2.13–17; 3.1–5, 16). But even granting the objection, the Corinthian correspondence shows that Paul can sharply change his tone from joyous, to exasperated, to furious, and back again, within a few paragraphs. If the pastoral circumstances had changed between 1 and 2 Thessalonians, then Paul could have quite reasonably altered his style of persuasion.

4. *Marks of authenticity.* There is no specific warning about a spurious Pauline letter, but a general warning to watch out for any teaching allegedly 'from us' that could take the form of a prophecy, a rumour, or a letter that might lead them astray (2 Thess. 2.2). So, rather than imagining this as a pseudepigrapher warning about pseudepigraphical writings, it looks more like Paul telling the Thessalonians not to believe reports or second-hand claims, purportedly from him and his associates, saying that the 'end' is already here. Also, if the mark of authenticity is the attempt to cover up a forgery by referring to 'the distinguishing mark in all my other letters' (2 Thess. 3.17), one would have to assume that the author is aware of a Pauline letter-collection where he offers his own signature in several other letters (1 Cor. 16.21; Gal. 6.11; Col. 4.18; Philem. 19). But if a pseudepigrapher, who knows the Pauline letter-collection, has appealed to the autograph as Paul's mark of authenticity 'in all my letters', then he has forgotten that in most of Paul's letters there is no signature of authenticity (1 Thessalonians, Romans, 2 Corinthians, Philippians, Ephesians), making it a very odd claim! What is more, dependence on a Pauline letter-collection is all the more unlikely when we remember that the only Pauline letter that 2 Thessalonians appears to presuppose or echo is 1 Thessalonians, which makes sense if these were two of Paul's earliest letters. Finally, another problem is that we struggle to imagine a setting where the claims made in 2 Thessalonians would be relevant and compelling to a non-Thessalonian audience at a later time.

In sum, it is not only plausible, but more probable, that 2 Thessalonians is an authentic Pauline letter.[13]

---

[13] Foster (2012, 169–70): 'The case for the Pauline authorship of 2 Thessalonians appears strong. However, "authorship" must be conceived of as broadly as it is in the case for the seven epistles widely regarded as genuine. Traditional arguments against Pauline authorship appear to have little analytic value.' In addition, in Kenny's stylometric analysis (1986, 86), 2 Thessalonians has more correlation with Paul's style than 1 Thessalonians!

THE ARGUMENT OF 1 THESSALONIANS

(See box: 'Outline of 1 Thessalonians'.)

1. Greetings and gospel thanksgiving (1.1–10)

Paul, thanking God for the Thessalonian Christians, remembers their work produced by faith, their labour prompted by love, and their endurance inspired by hope in the lord Jesus. The gospel has done its work, and they are an example to the whole region, especially in their turning from idols (a dangerously public demonstration of loyalty to the one true God).

2. Paul's recollection of his ministry in Thessalonica (2.1–16)

Paul notes (2.1) that his effective ministry sprang from pure motives (aware no doubt that scoffers could try to tell the new Jesus-followers that he was a charlatan after their money). The ancient world had its fair share of wandering tricksters out for cash. Paul insists—and his readers would know the truth of the claim—that he and his colleagues had conducted their service with the care of a nursing mother, sharing their very selves with the Thessalonians (2.7–8).

Mosaic from the Church of San Vitale, Ravenna, c. AD 546, depicting Jesus on his throne giving a crown to the martyr St Vitalis, while another man, Ecclesius, is depicted presenting a model church to Jesus.
Peter Zamorowski / Shutterstock

Paul's further thanksgiving recognizes the suffering the Thessalonians have been enduring at the hands of their countrymen. This is the same, he says, as Jesus and his first followers experienced from 'the Judeans who killed Jesus', in other words, the Judean leaders complicit in Jesus' crucifixion and the subsequent persecution of the church. This expresses Paul's frustration with those who have tried to obstruct the gentile mission. Paul sees all this as a sign that a time of wrath—perhaps *the* time of wrath—has come upon Judea.[14]

3. Paul's desire to return to Thessalonica (2.17—3.13)

Paul insists once more that he is eager to come back to see the Thessalonian believers, and explains why he had sent Timothy. Now Timothy has returned to Paul in Corinth with good news, and Paul is greatly encouraged.

4. The call to purity and holiness (4.1–12)

Along with abandoning idolatry, one of the most obvious changes for any pagan embracing the gospel was the clear Jewish-style sexual morality, a feature of being 'new creation' people. Paul may have been specifically mindful of the sexual element in the mystery cults like Cabirus, popular in Thessalonica (4.1–3), but the point went wider: followers of Jesus were to be holy, honourable, and self-controlled with their bodies (4.4–6). Instead of mirroring the male-dominated pagan licentiousness (see 'Portals and parallels: typical greco-roman male sexual attitudes'), Paul calls the Thessalonians to a counter-cultural holiness.

OUTLINE OF 1 THESSALONIANS

1. Greetings and gospel thanksgiving (1.1–10)
2. Paul's recollection of his ministry in Thessalonica (2.1–16)
3. Paul's desire to return to Thessalonica (2.17—3.13)
4. The call to purity and holiness (4.1–12)
5. Clarifications about the lord's return (4.13—5.11)
6. Exhortation to the congregation and final greetings (5.12–28)

PORTALS AND PARALLELS: TYPICAL GRECO-ROMAN MALE SEXUAL ATTITUDES

One can find several instances in ancient literature of the sexual behaviours that Paul censures in 1 Thessalonians. In a nutshell, Paul was not a prude with hang-ups about sex, but set forth a Christ-centred alternative to the patriarchal debauchery that characterized greco-roman sexual mores.

Demosthenes, *Against Neaera*: 'We keep mistresses for pleasure, concubines for our day-to-day bodily needs, but we have wives to produce legitimate children and serve as trustworthy guardians of our homes.' (Cited in Bruce, 1982, 87)

Horace, *Sermons* 1.2.116–19: 'If your groin is swelling, and a housemaid or a slave boy is at hand, arousing constant desire, do you prefer to burst with tension? Not me: I enjoy love that is available and easy.' (Cited in Elliott and Reasoner 2011, 252)

---

[14] See events recorded in Jos. *Ant.* 20.1–138.

Paul then commends the Thessalonians for their love for God's family, locally in Thessalonica and throughout all of Macedonia (4.9–10). 'Love' here has to do, not so much with feelings and emotions, but with mutual financial and practical support, living as a real family. Adding to that, he reminds them to lead a quiet life and to mind their own business, avoiding making trouble for themselves. They are to remain engaged in their vocations and trades, not giving up work as some had done—a point to which he returns in 2 Thessalonians 3.6–12. By living this way, they will win the respect of outsiders and require no benefactor to draw them into a social contract of material benefits in exchange for reciprocal loyalty (4.11–12).

5. Clarifications about the lord's return (4.13—5.11)

Paul now comes to his clarifications about the lord's return. He consoles his readers by saying that, although believers should genuinely grieve for the departed, they do not grieve in the same way that everyone else does. The pagan world offered no real hope; pagan grief contrasted sharply with Christian grief.

Paul's explanation of Jesus' return combines scriptural, political, and apocalyptic images, describing Jesus like a king who visits a city and is met by a delegation of people who greet him and then accompany him back into the city itself. Paul is not talking about people being taken away from earth (see 'Emails from the edge: rapture theology'), but is using Daniel's exaltation-imagery ('caught up on the clouds'), in combination with the idea of royal arrival, to say what he says in, for example, Philippians 3.20–21: the lord will return to transform this world and his people along with it. The dead will rise first, and then believers will join them in God's new world (4.16–17). This is a vivid way of saying what we find in 1 Corinthians 15.51–52.

So how soon would it be? Paul echoes Jesus: like a thief in the night (5.1–2). The only sign of his imminent return is—that there will be no sign! The Romans will go on with their imperial propaganda-slogan of 'peace and security', unaware of imminent catastrophe. Like labour-pains, however, the coming ordeal is inescapable (5.3).

In his accompanying exhortation, Paul uses the metaphor of light and darkness to urge the Thessalonians to live appropriately in the light of Jesus' impending return. They are not children of darkness, characterized by depraved nocturnal behaviour. Rather, they are children of the light, who should be prepared, alert, and sober (5.6). And—as though a piece of Ephesians 6.11–18 had fallen out of the sky—they should be equipped like a soldier attired with the triple virtues of faith, love, and hope (1 Thess. 5.8).

> '1 Thess. 5.10 – Christ died, in order that we might live with him; if blessing comes to us, it is because we are in him; if we receive the Spirit, it is because we share his life. . . . It is not, then, a case of Christ and believer changing places, but of the believer sharing in Christ's life. If Christ has been vindicated and raised from the dead, the same must be true of those who are united with him.'
>
> Morna Hooker, *Not Ashamed of the Gospel*, 33.

424 Paul and the Faithfulness of God

What is more, Paul adds that their assurance is not in knowing *when* Jesus will return, but knowing *what* Jesus has in store for them, which is not suffering wrath, but receiving salvation (5.9). The gospel, after all, declares to them that Jesus died and rose; therefore, whether they are dead or alive at his return, they will assuredly live with him (5.10). These are words that should comfort and assure them that they will not miss out on the glory to be revealed (5.11).

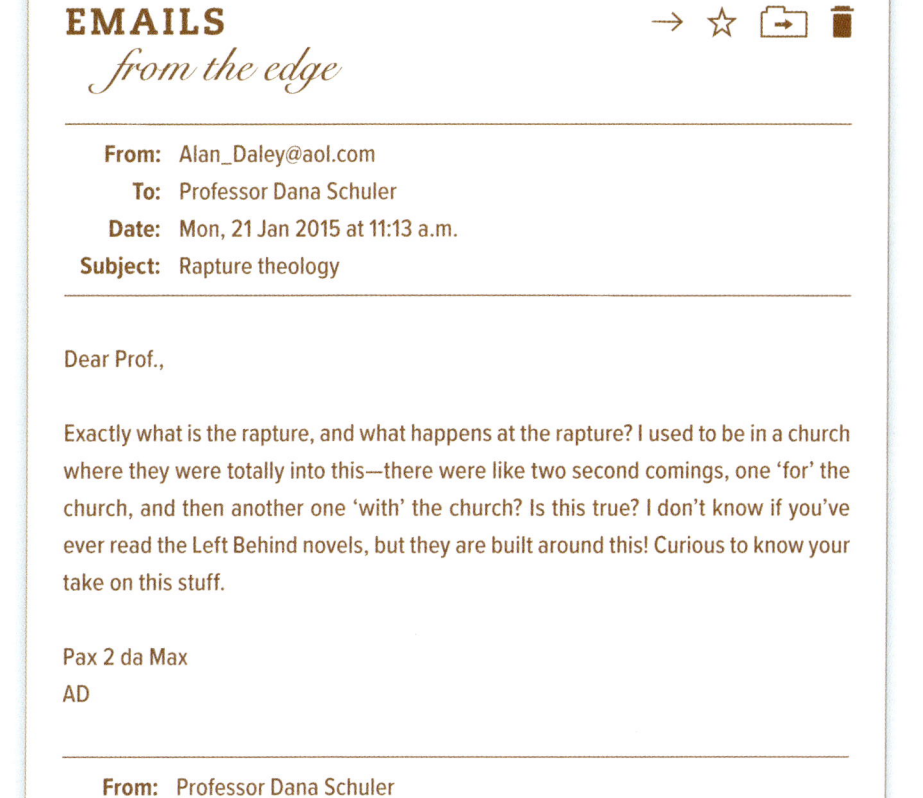

EMAILS
from the edge

From: Alan_Daley@aol.com
To: Professor Dana Schuler
Date: Mon, 21 Jan 2015 at 11:13 a.m.
Subject: Rapture theology

Dear Prof.,

Exactly what is the rapture, and what happens at the rapture? I used to be in a church where they were totally into this—there were like two second comings, one 'for' the church, and then another one 'with' the church? Is this true? I don't know if you've ever read the Left Behind novels, but they are built around this! Curious to know your take on this stuff.

Pax 2 da Max
AD

From: Professor Dana Schuler
To: Alan_Daley@aol.com
Date: Mon, 21 Jan 2015 at 12:01 p.m.
Subject: Re: Rapture theology

Dear Alan,

On what happens at the rapture, let me put it this way: if one day you look out of your window and see people rising up into the air, the natural thing to do is say to yourself, 'Well, I'll be damned!'

More seriously, the New Testament, building on biblical prophecy, envisages a day when the creator God will remake heaven and earth, overcoming its mortality and corruptibility (e.g. Rom. 8.18–27; Rev. 21.1; Isa. 65.17; 66.22). When that happens, Jesus will appear within the resulting new world (e.g. Col. 3.4; 1 Jn. 3.2). Paul's description of Jesus' return in 1 Thessalonians 4 is a brightly coloured version of what he says in two other passages, 1 Corinthians 15.51–54 and Philippians 3.20–21, about how, at Jesus' 'coming' or 'appearing', those who are still alive will be 'changed' or 'transformed' so that their mortal bodies will become incorruptible and immortal. This is all that Paul intends to say in Thessalonians, but here he borrows imagery—from biblical and political sources—to enhance his message. Let me explain.

First, Paul echoes the story of Moses coming down the mountain with the Torah. The trumpet sounds, a loud voice is heard, and after a long wait Moses comes to see what's been going on in his absence.

Second, he echoes Daniel 7, in which 'the saints of the Most High' (that is, the 'one like a son of man') are vindicated over their pagan enemy by being raised up to sit with God in glory. This metaphor, applied to Jesus in the gospels, is now applied to Christians who are suffering persecution.

Third, Paul conjures up images of an emperor visiting a colony or province. The citizens go out to meet him in open country and then escort him into the city. Paul's image of the people 'meeting the lord in the air' should be read with the assumption that the people will immediately turn around and lead the lord back to the newly remade world.

Paul's mixed metaphors of trumpets blowing and the living being snatched into heaven to meet the lord are not to be understood as literal truth as the Left Behind series suggests, but as a vivid and biblically allusive description of the great transformation of the present world of which he speaks elsewhere.

Regards
Prof. Dana Schuler

6. Exhortation to the congregation and final greetings (5.12–28)

1 Thessalonians closes with a dense compilation of exhortations, prayer, and benediction.

THE ARGUMENT OF 2 THESSALONIANS

As we saw earlier, Paul wrote a second letter to the Thessalonians only weeks, or at most perhaps months, after the first one. The reason for writing was now to encourage them in continued persecution, to address concerns that the 'day of the lord' had already happened, and to rebuke persistent idleness (see box: 'Outline of 2 Thessalonians').

1. Greetings and thanksgiving amid trials (1.1–4)

The second letter opens similarly to the first, and Paul immediately launches into thanksgiving for the Thessalonians' perseverance in their faith despite grave adversity (1.3–4).

2. Coming judgment and future glory (1.5–12)

The believers' continued suffering is proof that God's judgment against their adversaries is fully warranted and they themselves are indeed worthy of the kingdom (1.5). Precisely because God is just, he will not allow this situation to continue indefinitely. He will give them relief from their troubles, and pay back those who agitated against them (1.6–7a). This is one of Paul's fullest descriptions of the final condemnation of those who have opposed God, replete with rich biblical imagery. It leads Paul to pray that God would make the faithful worthy of his calling, desiring and performing what is good and faithful (1.11).

3. The turmoil and travail of the lawless one (2.1–12)

Paul then insists that the Thessalonians should not be rattled by any report that the climactic 'day' had already come and that they had missed out on it (2.2). (This means, obviously, that 'the day of the lord' cannot have meant 'the end of the world'.)

> **OUTLINE OF 2 THESSALONIANS**
>
> 1. Greetings and thanksgiving amid trials (1.1–4)
> 2. Coming judgment and future glory (1.5–12)
> 3. The turmoil and travail of the lawless one (2.1–12)
> 4. Exhortation to steadfastness (2.13–17)
> 5. Prayer request (3.1–5)
> 6. Warning against idleness (3.6–15)
> 7. Final greetings and benediction (3.16–18)

> 'Texts such as 2 Thessalonians 2:1–12, however they make us squirm, call us away from a white-bread Christianity, in which neither God nor the gospel has much depth or substance, to a recognition of the presence of evil in the world. They do not answer our questions about why evil exists, and they do not offer a talisman that protects us from its power or its consequences. Nevertheless, they do promise that the day will come when evil will be conquered, conquered by the mere breath of the Lord Jesus.'
>
> Beverly Gaventa, *First and Second Thessalonians*, 120.

> **BLAST FROM THE PAST: TERTULLIAN ON THE RESTRAINER**
>
> The church father Tertullian (c. AD 155–240), a north African lawyer and apologist, one of the first great Latin theologians, identified the 'restrainer' of the Antichrist, which Paul discusses in 2 Thessalonians 2.3–6, as none other than the Roman empire:
>
>> There is also another, even greater, obligation for us to pray for the emperors; yes, even for the continuance of the empire in general and for the Roman interests. We realize that the tremendous force which is hanging over the whole world, and the very end of the world with its threats of dreadful afflictions, is arrested for a time by the continued existence of the Roman Empire. This event we have no desire to experience and, in praying that it may be deferred, we favour the continuance of Rome.
>> (Tert. *Apol.* 32)

They will not be distressed as long as they are not deceived (2.3a). They can know that the day of Jesus' *parousia* has not occurred, because it will only take place after a time of apostasy, and when 'the man of lawlessness is revealed' (2.3b). This figure will 'exalt himself over everything that is called God or is worshipped, so that he sets himself up in God's temple, proclaiming himself to be God' (2.3c–4).

Who did Paul have in mind? What type of person is this 'man of lawlessness'? This 'antichrist' figure is probably built up from various ancient, scriptural, and contemporary figures who set themselves up against God.[15] We think of Antiochus Epiphanes, who desecrated the Temple and is probably the original 'boastful horn' in Daniel's vision;[16] the Roman general Pompey who entered the Holy of Holies in the Jerusalem Temple;[17] and the emperor Caligula who wanted to have his statue put up in the Temple.[18] Later, some Christians would see the emperor Nero as the archetype of the antichrist who was yet to come.[19] The 'man of lawlessness' here is probably Paul's way of referring to this theme, supposing that some new figure would arise to do what Caligula wanted, bringing evil to its height and so precipitating divine judgment. Great evil was afoot, and would come to a head. Paul claims that this should not be news to the Thessalonians; he had taught them as much (2.5). What is perhaps new is that Paul says that 'the restrainer' is holding back the antichrist figure until the time when the restrainer himself is taken out of the way (2.6–7 *NTE/KNT*).

Who then is this 'restrainer', holding back the tide of evil? Suggestions include the holy spirit, the church, the preaching of the gospel, an angel, the Jewish people, God's decree, or even the Roman empire itself (see 'Blast from the past: Tertullian on the restrainer'). But it is hard now to say for sure. Even Augustine wisely admitted,

---

[15] Ezek. 28.2.
[16] Dan. 7.8, 11; 11.31, 36.
[17] *Ps. Sol.* 2, 8, 17.
[18] Jos. *Ant.* 18.261.
[19] Mt. 24.24/Mk. 13.22; 1 Jn. 2.18; 4.3; Rev. 13; 16; 17; 20.

'I frankly confess that I do not know what [Paul] means.'[20] What Paul stresses is that the lawless one will be revealed and defeated, and those who believed the lie will perish (2.8–12). Paul would have his hearers hang on to the fact that God remains sovereign over all, and will one day put all wrongs to rights, bringing all human empires under the rule and judgment of his own saving kingdom.

4. Exhortation to steadfastness (2.13–17)

Paul provides an additional thanksgiving and further encouragement.

5. Prayer request (3.1–5)

Paul asks for prayer for him, his co-workers, and their ongoing labours, confident in God's faithfulness.

6. Warning against idleness (3.6–15)

The tone of the letter abruptly shifts to a warning against idleness. We should not miss the fact that this problem arose, not only because of a mistaken idea about the imminence of the *parousia*, but also because of the correct idea about the church's call to live as 'family'. Such a stunning social experiment was bound to generate teething troubles.

7. Final greetings and benediction (3.16–18)

Second Thessalonians finishes with a prayer for peace (3.16). Paul adds his autograph to authenticate the letter (3.17), and ends with a benediction of grace from the lord Jesus (3.18).

The bust of the Roman emperor Nero whom many Christians saw as a precursor or example of the type of person the antichrist would be.
Public Domain

1 AND 2 THESSALONIANS AND THE BIG PICTURE

Several major themes stand out from the Thessalonian correspondence, inviting multiple applications.

First, the Thessalonian letters call the church to (what we might call) a kingdom-perspective: looking ahead to the end, but recognizing that after Jesus' death and resurrection the kingdom had *already* broken in, shaping the way his followers would live in the present. Amid all the exhortations on sexual behaviour, love, and idleness that Paul makes, nearly every chapter of these letters mentions Jesus' return.[21] The kingdom, the royal rule of God, which began with the death and

---

20 Aug. *Civ. Dei* 20.19.
21 1 Thess. 1.9–10; 2.19; 3.13; 4.13–18; 5.23; 2 Thess. 1.10; 2.14.

resurrection of Jesus (1 Thess. 4.14), would be fully established on the 'day of the lord' (1 Thess. 5.3; 2 Thess. 2.2). This 'hope of glory' for the future means that the church was exhorted in the present to live out the dramatic, world-changing story of how God's purposes for his people would finally triumph over evil.

That is why the church is called to be an exemplary alternative to imperial rule. Believers must not be seduced into an unholy alliance with political masters as a shortcut to power and influence. Instead, they are to put their trust in God and God's purposes, meaning that they will probably, more often than not, resist the dominant culture rather than making common cause with it. Jesus' followers must live according to the code of holiness driven by the vision of new creation under Jesus' lordship. The call of the gospel is not an invitation for people to try 'Jesus' in the way they might try the latest fashionable food or drink. It is more like a fire-fighter dashing around a public square warning people that a wildfire is about to engulf the city, and summoning everybody to take the last bus out of town while they still can—coupled with the image of a brilliant architect putting up a great public new building and inviting all and sundry to come and live in it, assisting with its development.

Thessalonica forum

Of course, in ancient, medieval, and modern times, various teachers and cults have claimed to have worked it all out, knowing precisely when Jesus was going to return—and that the great day was just around the corner! A glance at the Left Behind series of books and movies, websites like the Rapture Index (which tries every day to measure the nearness of Jesus' return), or indeed the plethora of commentaries and charts on the book of Revelation will show what a fanatical end-of-the-world fixation looks like. Paul gives instructions so that the Thessalonians will not be ignorant about the lord's return (see 1 Thess. 4.13; 5.1–4; 2 Thess. 2.1–12), but he doesn't want them to be paralysed with anxiety over it, nor does he want them to speculate or prognosticate on dates. Instead, they are to show by the virtues of love, faith, and hope that they are prepared for the lord's return.

Full-page miniature of the second coming, *Benedictional of Æthelwold*, c. 963–84
© British Library Board. All Rights Reserved / Bridgeman Images

Second, it is often forgotten that these two letters have a remarkable emphasis on holiness, particularly in the area of sexual conduct. Again, we can relate this to the kingdom-theme: God has called the Thessalonians into his kingdom through the gospel, and now they are to live lives worthy of that kingdom (1 Thess. 2.12; 2 Thess. 1.5). In the modern west, sex is arguably the biggest idol. Our consumerist and entertainment culture saturates us with sexual imagery, urging us to worship all things sexual, insisting that we can have and must experience whatever turns us on. We regularly receive the implicit message that celibacy is a fate worse than death, or that God doesn't mind what consenting adults do in private. But this has never been what Christians have believed. Bodies matter; maleness and femaleness matter; they are central parts of God's good creation, not disposable toys. Our bodies are temples, as Paul stresses in the Corinthian letters, and we are to worship God with them, whether in singleness or in marriage. When Paul exhorts the Thessalonians not to live 'in passionate lust like the pagans, who do not know God' (1 Thess. 4.5), he implies that knowing the true God and living in chastity belong together, no doubt because the true God is indeed the creator, whose image is the male-plus-female human life. Our goal, then, should not be gratification on demand, but sanctification through the spirit; placing sex in the context, not of uncontrollable desire, but of discipleship. Paul saw sex as a gift to be enjoyed with a spouse, rather than a craving to be satisfied, no matter with whom. The church is never more counter-cultural than in its refusal to worship the god of sex, which means (among other things) taking especial care of those who may be vulnerable to predators. The church has often failed in its duty of care, and its reputation has rightly suffered as a result. We regularly need Paul's warning: 'That in this matter no one should wrong or take advantage of a brother or sister. The Lord will punish all those who commit such sins, as we told you and warned you before' (1 Thess. 4.6).

A third interesting facet of the Thessalonian letters is the remarkable emphasis on the church as family. As Nijay Gupta comments on these letters: 'The community of Messiah Jesus is more than a club of like-minded religious people. They belong together in the most intimate kind of relationship that can be conceived.'[22] Paul's constant use of the word *adelphoi*, literally 'brothers', calls up in his world the shared working and family life of a close kinship-group. The premise behind much of Paul's exhortation is that if God has created a new Messiah-family in Thessalonica, and if that family is based on and characterized by nothing less than the self-giving love of Jesus himself, then there are certain ways of acting that are necessary, and other ways that are inappropriate (see 1 Thess. 4.9–12). For a start, as a family, it means that each Christian within that church family has the responsibility to look out for the needs of the others, to give comfort, warning, strengthening, and example wherever necessary. It isn't enough to avoid trouble and hope for the best. One must actively pursue what will be good for other Christians, and indeed for everybody. Also, precisely like a tight-knit family, there were certain inappropriate behaviours, like idleness, laziness, being a busybody, and sexual immorality, and where such behaviours occur there are appropriate styles of discipline within that family, ways of making it known to a child or a sibling that a particular kind of behaviour is unacceptable. In our own hyper-individualistic culture, the temptation is to try to opt out of the church family, especially if it means chores, responsibility, and the prospect of discipline. But the Thessalonians didn't have that option. There were only a few of them, and there were no other 'churches' to belong to. They had to deal with the problem head on, just as in a family or a small village. Unless the whole family remained loyal to the gospel, pretty soon they would cease to exist altogether. It would not be an overstatement to say that when the church sees itself as a family, and acts like a family towards its members, it will not only succeed in caring for its own but also flourish in its mission in the world.

---

[22] Gupta 2016, 17.

Further reading

Boring, M. Eugene. 2015. *I and II Thessalonians: A Commentary*. NTL; Louisville, KY: Westminster John Knox.

Byron, John. 2014. *1 and 2 Thessalonians*. SGBC; Grand Rapids, MI: Zondervan.

Donfried, Karl P. 2002. *Paul, Thessalonica, and Early Christianity*. Grand Rapids, MI: Eerdmans.

Fee, Gordon D. 2009. *The First and Second Letters to the Thessalonians*. NICNT; Grand Rapids, MI: Eerdmans.

Foster, Paul. 2012. 'Who Wrote 2 Thessalonians? A Fresh Look at an Old Problem.' *JSNT* 32: 150–75.

Gaventa, Beverly R. 1998. *First and Second Thessalonians*. Interpretation; Louisville, KY: Westminster John Knox.

Gupta, Nijay. 2016. *1 and 2 Thessalonians*. NCCS; Eugene, OR: Cascade.

Harrison, James R. 2002. 'Paul and the Imperial Gospel at Thessaloniki.' *JSNT* 25: 71–96.

Luckensmeyer, David. 2009. *The Eschatology of First Thessalonians*. Göttingen: Vandenhoeck & Ruprecht.

Malherbe, Abraham J. 2000. *The Letters to the Thessalonians: A New Translation with Introduction and Commentary*. AB; New York: Doubleday.

Marshall, I. Howard. 1982. 'Pauline Theology in the Thessalonian Correspondence.' In *Paul and Paulinism: Essays in Honour of C. K. Barrett*. Edited by M. D. Booker and S. G. Wilson. London: SPCK, pp. 173–83.

Paddison, Angus. 2005. *Theological Hermeneutics and 1 Thessalonians*. SNTSMS 133; Cambridge: Cambridge University Press.

Still, Todd D. 2007. 'Interpretive Ambiguities and Scholarly Proclivities in Pauline Studies: A Treatment of Three Texts from 1 Thessalonians 4 as a Test Case.' *CBR* 5: 207–19.

Weima, Jeffrey A. D. 2014. *1–2 Thessalonians*. BECNT; Grand Rapids, MI: Baker.

19

Philippians

Therefore, my dear friends, as you have always obeyed—not only in my presence, but now much more in my absence—continue to work out your salvation with fear and trembling, for it is God who works in you to will and to act in order to fulfil his good purpose.[1]

CHAPTER AT A GLANCE

This chapter provides a short survey of Paul's letter to the churches in Philippi.

By the end of this chapter you should be able to:
- situate Philippians in Paul's missionary career;
- describe the structure and argument of Philippians;
- identify the main themes and theology of Philippians;
- understand critical issues related to the epistle to the Philippians.

INTRODUCTION

Paul's epistle to the Philippians overflows with effervescent joy, sparkling with the delight of family affection. It is encouraging and refreshing, reminding readers of the sheer magnificence of Jesus the Messiah, and of their common joy in him.

The letter was written in prison in—we will argue—Ephesus. While in chains, Paul contemplates the potential end of his life's work, and looks ahead to what might lie in store. It shows Paul as joyful even amid adversity. It is a mature and measured piece of writing. Paul displays heartfelt gratitude to the Philippians, whom he regards as nothing less than his joy and crown. Indeed, this letter goes to show that Paul remained tied with bonds of affection to his churches. He never ceased to be delighted at the joy they gave him.

The letter to the Philippians has been categorized as a letter of friendship, or a family letter, but might more properly be called a letter of fellowship, *koinōnia*.[2]

---

[1] Phil. 2.12–13.
[2] On the theme of 'fellowship' (*koinōnia*, *koinōneō*) in the letter, see Phil. 1.5; 2.1; 3.10; 4.15.

This includes practical support; he thanks the Philippians for their financial aid (prisoners in the ancient world received no food from the local authorities), and for the services of Epaphroditus, while also informing them of his own somewhat difficult situation.[3] Paul, it seems, had entered into financial partnership with the Philippians; this contrasts interestingly with his refusal to accept money from Corinth, a move which may have been prompted by his anxiety lest the Corinthian church would suppose it 'owned' him. For Paul, his arrangement with the Philippians was reciprocal: they supported him materially in his ministry, and they in turn shared the fruits of his labour.[4] At the same time, he warns them against potential intruders, he mediates a dispute between two female leaders, and he exhorts the Philippians to live out the Messiah-story as a counter-imperial colony of heavenly citizens.

The centrepiece of the letter is the famous poem of Philippians 2.6–11, narrating the story of Jesus' incarnation, humiliation, and exaltation. This becomes a paradigm for the Philippians' attitudes and behaviour, as it had been for Paul himself. And, since the poem displays the biblically rooted narrative of the Messiah as an implicit contrast to all human empire (remembering that Philippi was a proud Roman colony), we are not surprised at the many hints throughout of the antithesis between Christ and Caesar—a contrast that was to be displayed in the way the followers of Jesus would 'shine like lights' in the world. At the same time, Philippians as much as any of Paul's letters shows the apostle's knowledge of, and subtle use of, themes from the philosophies of his day. The great poem itself, in its present context, is designed, he says, to teach his readers how to *think* with 'the Messiah's mind'. Learning to think 'in Christ' was central to Paul's vision of Christian life.

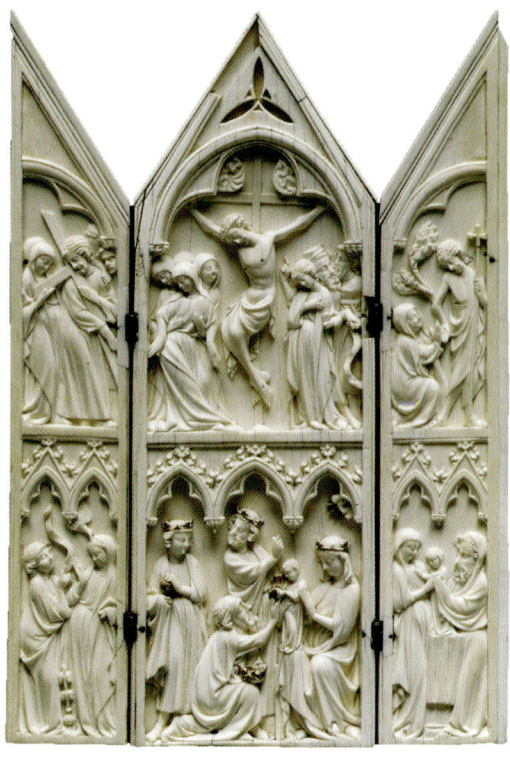

Fourteenth-century triptych of the life of Christ, Art Institute of Chicago
Public Domain

---

3   Phil. 2.25–30; 4.10–20.
4   See esp. Phil. 4.15 and 2 Cor. 8.1–3, and studies by Ascough 2003 and Ogereau 2014.

CONTEXTUAL AND CRITICAL MATTERS

Philippi

The ancient Macedonian city of Philippi is known today by its Greek name Krenides, in the north-east of modern Greece. The town was settled from the nearby island of Thasos in the fourth century BC. Philip II of Macedon, the father of Alexander the Great, aware of silver and gold mines nearby, annexed the region in 356 BC, renaming it 'Philippi' in his own honour. The city was a significant outpost for the border with Thrace to the east. Located as it was on the Via Egnatia, it was an important stop on the land route to the Hellespont and into Asia Minor for those travelling further east.

The city remained important even after the Roman conquest of Macedonia in 168/7 BC. However, in 42 BC the plains of Philippi were the site for one of the most famous and important battles in Roman history, when Mark Antony and Octavian defeated the republican forces of Brutus and Cassius, the assassins of Julius Caesar. The victors settled many of their veterans in Philippi, re-establishing the city as a Roman colony. More Roman veterans settled in the city again after Octavian defeated Mark Antony at the Battle of Actium in 31 BC. Thereafter, Octavian (that is, Augustus) renamed the colony after himself, calling it Colonia Iulia Augusta Philippensis. In Paul's time Philippi had a population of about 10,000, about one tenth of the size of Thessalonica, ninety miles west along the Via Egnatia.[5]

The Via Egnatia connecting Philippi to the rest of Macedonia and Thrace
Todd Bolen / BiblePlaces.com

---

5   See Bockmuehl 1998, 2–10; and further in Verhoef 2013 and Bakirtzis and Koester 2009 [1998].

The prison cell where Paul and Silas are believed to have been imprisoned
www.holylandphotos.org

Philippi was a classic romanized Greek city, complete with a Roman system of government. The colonists enjoyed Italian legal status and certain tax exemptions. Most local first-century inscriptions are in Latin, not Greek. A cohort of praetorians, troops from the emperor's own personal guard, was garrisoned in Philippi.[6] The ruling class were Latin in language, culturally Italian, and politically Roman. However, the outlying areas, and most local labourers, were Macedonian or Thracian, with immigrants coming from as far away as Egypt, Asia Minor, and Judea. Greek language and culture did not disappear; it recovered its ascendancy by the third century AD.

The resident religions reflect the diversity of the city. As many as thirty-five different deities were venerated in Philippi. Prominent among them were the Thracian Horseman, Dionysus, Artemis/Diana, Silvanus, and not least the burgeoning cult of the *divus Augustus*.[7] According to Lukas Borman, one should envisage in Philippi 'a religious identity primarily influenced by Roman religion in which the worship of the princeps and his deified ancestors or predecessors was central besides the traditional Greco-Roman pantheon'.[8]

The Philippian church had the distinction of being the first church in Europe, and the first phase of Paul's mission in Macedonia (that is, northern Greece).

---

6 Verhoef 2013, 8.
7 Verhoef 2013, 10–13.
8 Borman 1995, 63–4, cited in Witherington 2011, 6.

Ruins of Roman Philippi
Karel Gallas / Shutterstock

It marks Paul's move away from cities with a sizable Jewish population, like those in Asia Minor, to cities that were essentially gentile and pagan in both religion and culture. This is where Paul saw a whole new 'beginning of the gospel' (*archē tou euangeliou*).[9] Sometime in AD 49–50, Paul and his co-workers, including Silas and perhaps Luke, left Troas in Asia Minor and arrived at the port town of Neapolis, then taking the twelve-mile walk to Philippi.[10]

Luke reports several events from Paul's initial visit. These include the conversion of Lydia, a gentile God-worshipper; the exorcism of a fortune-telling slave-girl; and the trouble into which this plunged Paul and Silas when the girl's owners saw that their business was ruined.[11] The story is well known: Paul and Silas were beaten and imprisoned without trial; there was an earthquake at midnight (the region was prone to earthquakes, but we should not forget that such things were regularly interpreted as a sign of divine anger); the jailer, about to commit suicide, was instead converted; Paul revealed in the morning that he and Silas were Roman citizens, which must have frightened the magistrates.[12] All this explains Paul's comment not long afterwards: 'We had previously suffered and been treated outrageously in Philippi.'[13]

---

9   Phil. 4.15.
10 Ac. 16.11–12.
11 Ac. 16.16–21.
12 Ac. 16.35–40.
13 1 Thess. 2.2.

Where was Paul when he wrote to the Philippians?

Most commentators have suggested that Philippians was written from Rome, with some favouring Caesarea. We prefer a setting in Ephesus, with a date in the early to mid-50s, for several reasons:[14]

1. We know that Paul spent considerable periods of time in Ephesus.[15] Not only that, but an Ephesian imprisonment is a sound deduction based on Luke's report of Paul's tumultuous time there, his own reference to the 'troubles we experienced in the province of Asia', and his enigmatic remark about how he 'fought wild beasts in Ephesus'. All this could well be a metaphor for how he faced imprisonment and a capital trial in Ephesus.[16]
2. Paul's travel plans cannot be squared with the composition of the captivity letters from Rome. We know from Romans that Paul was hoping to travel to Spain after passing through Rome,[17] yet he told Philemon to prepare a guest-room for him as he hoped to visit him in Colossae.[18] If we place both of these letters in Rome, then it would imply a very strange route, either to travel to Spain in the west via the interior of Asia Minor in the east or vice versa. However, if we locate these two letters in an Ephesian imprisonment, then the incongruity is removed. A trip to Colossae from Ephesus is easily manageable, as is the correspondence between Ephesus and Philippi.
3. Timothy is the co-author of Philippians, yet we have no evidence that Timothy accompanied Paul to Rome. He more likely remained in Ephesus where even the Pastoral Epistles place him.
4. The claim that Paul's reference to 'the praetorium' and the 'saints of the household of Caesar' implies a Roman rather than Ephesian provenance is inaccurate.[19] While it is true that Asia (that is, western Asia Minor) was a senatorial rather than imperial province, it is hardly unexpected that, given the prominence of the city, an imperial residence with imperial administrators and a skeleton garrison would be found in Ephesus.[20]

On the situation reflected in the letter, the Philippians did not present Paul with problems. The church was relatively healthy compared to some of Paul's others.

---

[14] See Koester 1995, 122; Thielman 2003; Watson 2007, 138–9; Reumann 2008, 13–18; Wright 2018, 271–80.
[15] Ac. 18.19–21; 19.1—20.1; 1 Cor. 16.8; 2 Tim. 1.8.
[16] Ac. 19.1–40; 2 Cor. 1.8; 1 Cor. 15.32.
[17] Rom. 15.24, 28.
[18] Philem. 22.
[19] Phil. 1.13; 4.22.
[20] See Reumann (2008, 171–2) who shows that *praitōrion* could designate the military detachment associated with the headquarters of a ruler, as was the case with Herod Agrippa II (Ac. 23.25) and the governor of Syracuse even though it was a senatorial province. There was a *praetorium* in Jerusalem (Jn. 18.28).

The Philippians were undisturbed by the anxieties and idleness that affected the Thessalonians; they did not experience the factionalism and immoralities of the Corinthians. That said, the Philippians were not without their own struggles. They, like the other churches of Macedonia, had undergone persecution and hardship, and were experiencing the same struggles that Paul himself had known.[21]

Achaia and Macedonia

In addition, Paul was worried that Jewish-Christian missionaries, similar perhaps to those who had made trouble in Galatia, either had arrived or might soon arrive on the scene and cause similar problems. Paul refers disparagingly to those who preach Christ out of self-serving motives, and in highly charged vitriolic language he warns of 'those dogs, those evildoers, those mutilators of the flesh'.[22] Their message is to announce the superiority of their inherited privileges as Jews and to urge male gentiles to be circumcised, and they put confidence in the flesh.[23] Scholars have disagreed as to whether Paul thought such persons had already arrived in Philippi, or whether (as we are inclined to think) he was anticipating a problem that might arise in the future.[24] It would make good sense: in a Roman colony, a new group of people, not themselves ethnically Jewish, who claimed the traditional exemption from worshipping the gods, including of course the Roman gods, would pose a threat. Faced with that or other threats, the importance of church unity remained paramount.[25]

The letter includes personal information and exhortations, and expresses Paul's own hopes to be released and to visit Philippi once more.[26] But the principal occasion for the letter is Paul's gratitude for the financial support arriving through Epaphroditus.[27]

---

[21] Phil. 1.27–30.
[22] Phil. 3.2.
[23] Phil. 1.15–18; 3.2—4.1.
[24] On this point contrast Dunn 2009b, 1012–14, with Bockmuehl 1998, 8–10. Hooker 2002 claims that there is no evidence for opponents within the Christian community in Philippi. She contends that the language in Phil. 1.27–30 reflects external threats to the Philippians, while Phil. 3.2 and 3.18–19 indicate only potential threats to the Philippian church. In her view, Paul is reflecting largely his own circumstances which involved personal conflict pertaining to his recent imprisonment.
[25] Phil. 4.2–4, and esp. 2.1–4.
[26] Phil. 1.26; 2.24.
[27] Phil. 4.15–18.

The integrity of Philippians

Does Philippians consist of one letter or two letters—or, indeed, even more—that have been stitched together? Some have claimed that the transition from Philippians 3.1 to 3.2 is too abrupt, as if the end of one letter (3.1) has had a Pauline exhortation (3.2–21) artificially stuck onto it as a secondary attachment. Furthermore, Philippians 4.10–20 has sometimes been seen as an independent thanksgiving letter.[28] There are, however, several problems with such hypotheses. (1) There is a lack of literary precedents for such a practice in the world of ancient letter-collections. (2) If the editors of a Philippian or Pauline letter-collection felt free to unite two or three letters, we might wonder why they did not smooth out the transition. (3) We might also wonder why anyone would compile Pauline letters in this fashion, when the collection was already quite capable of sustaining letters of different length to the same locations, as with Colossians and Philemon. (4) It is not difficult to imagine why Philippians takes the shape that it does, ebbing and flowing between exhortation and what seem to be final remarks, especially if Paul, in prison, was not able to compose the letter straight through, but was delayed or interrupted and took a few days over it.

THE ARGUMENT OF PHILIPPIANS

(See box: 'Outline of Philippians'.)

1. Greetings, thanksgiving, and intercession (1.1–11)

The letter begins with a greeting from Paul and his co-author Timothy, addressed to God's holy people in Philippi with particular mention of the 'overseers' and 'deacons', who were left in charge after Paul departed (1.1) and about

OUTLINE OF PHILIPPIANS

1. Greetings, thanksgiving, and intercession (1.1–11)
2. The advance of the gospel (1.12–26)
3. Exhortations to unity and to the imitation of Christ (1.27—2.18)
4. News about Timothy and Epaphroditus (2.19–30)
5. Warning against Jewish interference (3.1–21)
6. Exhortation to unity, gentleness, and excellence (4.1–9)
7. Paul's thanksgiving for fellowship with the Philippians (4.10–20)
8. Final greetings (4.21–23)

> 'Submission, as portrayed in Philippians, is not the consequence of oppression or coercion. Rather, it is offered freely, and reflects the self-giving character of God in the salvation events (2.6–11). Moreover, as the recipients of that grace, believers are exhorted to demonstrate a similar self-kenotic behaviour/mindset in their mutual relations. Regardless of the context of social order, gender and status, each believer is called to treat the other as a "superior" as Christ submitted to God.'
>
> M. Sydney Park, *Submission within the Godhead and the Church in the Epistle to the Philippians*, 185.

---

28 See e.g. Reumann 2008, 3–13.

THE GOSPEL AT WORK IN PHILIPPI

- I always pray with joy because of your **partnership in the gospel** from the first day until now. (Phil. 1.4–5)
- It is right for me to feel this way about all of you, since I have you in my heart and, whether I am in chains or **defending and confirming the gospel**, all of you share in God's grace with me. (Phil. 1.7)
- Now I want you to know, brothers and sisters, that what has happened to me has actually served to **advance the gospel**. (Phil. 1.12)
- And because of my chains, most of the brothers and sisters have become confident in the Lord and dare all the more to **proclaim the gospel** without fear . . . knowing that I am put here for the **defence of the gospel**. (Phil. 1.14, 16)
- Whatever happens, conduct yourselves in a **manner worthy of the gospel of Christ** . . . striving together as one for **the faith of the gospel**. (Phil. 1.27)
- But you know that Timothy has proved himself, because as a son with his father he has served with me **in the work of the gospel**. (Phil. 2.22)
- Yes, and I ask you, my true companion, help these women since they have contended at my side in **the cause of the gospel**. (Phil. 4.3)
- You Philippians indeed know that in **the early days of the gospel**, when I left Macedonia, no church shared with me in the matter of giving and receiving, except you alone. (Phil. 4.15 NRSV)

---

whom Paul is prayerfully thankful (1.2–3).[29] Paul is thankful because the Philippians are 'partners in the gospel' (see 1.5), 'partners in grace' (1.7 *NTE/KNT*); they are in the gospel business, the grace business, along with Paul, and their gift proves it. Paul goes on to pray for the Philippians, spurred on by his affection for them, that they abound in knowledge, that they would appear as pure and blameless before Christ, and would produce an abundant fruit of righteousness (1.8–11).

2. The advance of the gospel (1.12–26)

Paul's imprisonment, far from hindering the gospel, has served to promote it (1.12). The whole imperial garrison knows that Paul is in chains for his message about a new *kyrios*, a new emperor (1.13). This has given the local church fresh courage to proclaim the word of the gospel (1.14). Paul adds that not everyone preaching about Jesus has the right motives. But he is sanguine: what matters is that the Messiah is being proclaimed (1.15–18b) (see box: 'The gospel at work in Philippi').

Paul's own situation, though, remains uncertain. He may well die in prison; but whatever happens it won't mean that everything's gone wrong. If news of his death suddenly arrives, the Philippians need to know that he was ready for it—though Paul hopes the verdict will go the other way. 'For me to live means the Messiah,' he says. 'To die means to make a profit.' Paul here gives a rare hint of what he thinks happens immediately after a Christian death: 'I would really love to leave all this and be with the *Messiah*' (*NTE/KNT* [amended]). That will not be the end; there is still the resurrection to come. But being with the Messiah will be immediate, vivid, deeply joyful.

---

[29] The persons we know from Philippi are Lydia and her household, the Philippian jailer and his household, Euodia, Syntyche, Clement, and Epaphroditus.

3. Exhortations to unity and to the imitation of Christ (1.27—2.18)

Paul's exhortation here is central to the letter. The Philippians are to stand firm, united in the faith, whatever happens. They will be sharing the sufferings of the Messiah—and of Paul himself.

Paul's previous request for unity among his readers is to be achieved by actively cultivating certain virtues, particularly those connected with learning to think (as we might say) messianically—in other words, thinking as Jesus thought. Their union with him is the ground for such character-development, however counter-intuitive this was in greco-roman culture. And, when he wants to persuade them to imitate the Messiah's own virtues, he offers them a short poem, perhaps the earliest statement we possess of a Christian view of Jesus (see box: 'The Christ "poem"'). Some things can, perhaps, only be said in poetic language; perhaps this is one of them.

The poem provides the foundation for the challenge to self-sacrificing unity (2.1–18) and also, in chapter 3, for self-abnegating discipleship. The poem depicts Jesus' life in three stages: pre-existence (v. 6), incarnation (vv. 7–8), and exaltation (vv. 9–11), each of which has received extensive scholarly treatment. The weight of the poem rests on the decision (of the one who was all along equal with God) to become human, and to travel the road of obedience to the divine saving plan, yes, all the way to the cross. The point is that that decision was not a decision to stop (in some sense) being divine. It was a decision about *what it really meant to be divine* (see 'Emails from the edge: help with *harpagmos*'). His subsequent exaltation demonstrates that on the cross Jesus had done what, in Israel's scriptures, only Israel's God can and will do. Paul has, in effect, rethought Israel's monotheistic tradition and discovered Jesus at its heart, not as an abstract theory but as a human of recent historical memory as well as of present spiritual experience.[30]

The poem then works out the new patterns of thinking and living (2.12–18).

> **THE CHRIST 'POEM'**
>
> [5] This is how you should think among yourselves—with the mind that you have because you belong to the Messiah, Jesus:
>
> [6] Who, though in God's form, did not
> Regard his equality with God
> As something he ought to exploit.
>
> [7] Instead, he emptied himself,
> And received the form of a slave,
> Being born in the likeness of humans.
>
> And then, having human appearance,
> [8] He humbled himself, and became
> Obedient even to death,
>
> Yes, even the death of the cross.
>
> [9] And so God has greatly exalted him,
> And to him in his favour has given
> The name which is over all names:
>
> [10] That now at the name of Jesus
> Every knee within heaven shall bow—
> On earth, too, and under the earth;
>
> [11] And every tongue shall confess
> That Jesus, Messiah, is Lord,
> To the glory of God, the father.
> (Phil. 2.2–11 *NTE/KNT*)

---

30 Isa. 45.23. See Wright *Climax*, 56–97; *PFG* 680–8.

4. News about Timothy and Epaphroditus (2.19–30)

Paul commends two of his co-workers, Timothy and Epaphroditus, and announces their travel plans.

5. Warning against Jewish interference (3.1–21)

The first verse looks like a letter-ending, but instead it precipitates Paul into a sharp warning against possible Jewish proselytizers. He was, as we saw, probably thinking of what had happened in Galatia. Paul assures the faithful that they are already 'the circumcision' (3.3), and that they are to imitate him in discovering the truly Jewish way, following the Messiah through self-renunciation to resurrection.

EMAILS *from the edge*

From: Alan_Daley@aol.com
To: Professor Dana Schuler
Date: Thur, 19 Mar 2015 at 8:26 p.m.
Subject: Help with **harpagmos**

Dear Prof.,

In my campus Bible-study group we are looking at Philippians. We got to chapter 2 and read over the famous hymn about Christ. When we all compared translations on Philippians 2.6, it got really confusing. We noticed some big differences between the translations, for instance, there is:

KJV: 'who, being in the form of God, <u>thought it not robbery</u> to be equal with God';
RSV: 'who, though he was in the form of God, did not count equality with God <u>a thing to be grasped</u>';
NIV: 'who, being in very nature God, did not consider equality with God <u>something to be used to his own advantage</u>'.

I know this has got something to do with the Greek word *harpagmos* (I looked it up in the interlinear you gave me), but I've got no idea why these translations are so different. I have no clue what the good ol' KJV is even saying. Is equality with God something that Jesus refused to snatch after OR is it something he already had but did not use for his own advantage?

---

444   Paul and the Faithfulness of God

Throw this dawg a bone, Prof.

Pax 2 da Max
AD

From: Professor Dana Schuler
To: Alan_Daley@aol.com
Date: Thur, 19 Mar 2015 at 10:19 p.m.
Subject: Re: Help with *harpagmos*

Dear Alan,

You have a talent for finding the most difficult and disputed topics in biblical studies to stumble upon!

To be brief, and somewhat simplistic, the question is whether *harpagmos* means to grasp after something one does not currently have or whether it means to exploit what one already has. If we apply these two options to Philippians 2.6, then: did Jesus refuse to snatch, seize, usurp equality with God? Or did Jesus refuse to use his equality with God as a means to self-promotion?

I'm in favour of the second view because: (1) Jesus was already in the 'form of God', which is parallel to 'equal with God', so *harpagmos* must designate something that he already possessed; and (2) the most thorough surveys and analyses of *harpagmos* have confirmed that, in phrases like this one, it can refer to a verbal idea of exploiting something that one already possesses. As such, Jesus did not, as Alexander the Great might have done, regard his divine status as something to be deployed for his own selfish advantage. In contrast, he condescended to becoming a human being and reduced himself to the position of a slave. The gods, rulers, and politicians of Philippi were characterized by exploiting their positions for their own self-aggrandizement. But Jesus was the exact opposite: he pursued service and shame precisely because he was equal with God. In other words, Paul is saying that the one true God is quite unlike normal ideas of 'divinity'. People would assume then, as they do now, that divinity means great honour; Paul insists, with his eyes on Jesus, that it means self-giving humility and love.

The grace be with you
Prof. Dana Schuler

Paul insists that he hasn't arrived at the glorious goal; true maturity means knowing that you must still keep pressing on forwards towards the goal (3.12–13). He urges the Philippians to follow his example rather than that of his opponents, 'enemies of the cross' (3.18–19). As Messiah-people, his hearers are already citizens of heaven (3.20). This doesn't mean 'so you are looking forward to going back there'; as they would know, being citizens of Rome didn't mean retiring to the mother city one day, but being agents of Roman civilization where they were.

6. Exhortation to unity, gentleness, and excellence (4.1–9)

Paul adds several short exhortations, all part of what it means to 'stand firm in the Lord' (4.1). These focus on a double injunction: his readers should think about anything that is true, noble, right, pure, lovely, admirable, excellent, or praiseworthy (4.8), while at the same time they should live in the way he has himself exemplified (4.9).

7. Paul's thanksgiving for fellowship with the Philippians (4.10–20)

The final paragraph focuses on the letter's underlying purpose: to give thanks for financial support. Everybody gains by it, as the Philippians offer a pleasing sacrifice and Paul is sustained.

8. Final greetings (4.21–23)

The letter ends with greetings, grace, and glory: greetings within the church; the grace of the lord and Messiah, Jesus himself; but, as always, glory to the one true God, the father, for ever and ever.

Ancient theatre of Philippi

PHILIPPIANS AND THE BIG PICTURE

No wonder Philippians is cherished by many, with the majestic heights of its christology, and its call to imitate Jesus, pursue godly virtues, and promote the gospel. Many today find it more immediately relevant to contemporary church life than some other letters. Key themes for focus are fellowship, citizenship, and humility.

Most Christians think of 'fellowship' as a Christian version of 'friendship', which is a start but doesn't go nearly far enough. Fellowship is not simply what you do over coffee after church, but what the church does (for instance) with the missionaries it supports, and with the poor in its own community. Churches are called to 'fellowship in the gospel', entailing giving to and receiving from gospel-workers, local and overseas, to promote the gospel. The fellowship Paul enjoyed with the Philippians continued even while he was in prison, and that has served as a model for the church's work ever since. This has nothing to do with paternalism, and everything to do with genuine partnership, mutual giving and receiving, and a commitment to shared goals won from shared resources. It is such giving that is, Paul says, 'a fragrant offering, an acceptable sacrifice, pleasing to God' (Phil. 4.18). The budgets of all churches must find a place to put something on the altar of sacrificial worship in order to facilitate fellowships in the gospel that are as fruitful in the human realm as they are beautiful in God's eyes.

Second, when Paul says that 'our citizenship is in heaven' (3.20) he is emphasizing that the Messiah, who *reigns in* heaven, and who will one day *return from* heaven, is the object of our hope and loyalty. There was nothing wrong with being a citizen of Rome, just as there is nothing wrong with being a British or even Australian citizen. But when the gospel of Jesus is unveiled it reveals the true empire, the true citizenship, the true lord, and in that light all the pretensions of empire, not least the arrogant and blasphemous claims of the emperor himself, or the propaganda of power-hungry presidents, are exposed as folly. The church's vocation is not to bless the power, policies, and pantheon of civic leaders, but to

Bas-relief of the Praetorian Guard during the time of Augustus
Reproduced by permission from Carole Raddato

Philippians 447

measure them by the standard of Christ, to pursue the things that make for peace and justice, and to proclaim that all will stand before the judgment seat of Christ. The church was never intended to be the religious department of any empire, but always to be building for the true kingdom, setting up an embassy for the one true lord, living lives according to his symbols, his teaching, his story, and no other. If that means suffering, that will mean following the pattern of the Messiah, and confidently expecting his rescue and reward. The church's loyalty cannot be auctioned off to those who promise it political influence; nor can its core convictions be pummelled into submission to fit the reigning zeitgeist. For citizens of heaven, the gospel should be declared, not domesticated.

Third, Paul focuses on humility. This looms large in Philippians 2.1–5, and is the centrepiece of the poem of 2.6–11. Humility was regarded in the ancient world as weakness, the characteristic of inferiors and slaves who had been kicked down to the bottom rungs of society. Pagans usually prized (as most people still do) 'honour' and fame, usually built on the backs of others. But for the Messiah and his people it is different. Paul is more than capable of giving commands. But most of all he wants his readers to absorb the story of Jesus, specifically the story of his humility, death, and exaltation, and to 'work out' what their 'salvation' is therefore going to mean in practice (3.12). He wants them, in other words, to adopt a form of moral reasoning shaped by the story of Jesus as the bedrock of their single-minded unity.

Remains of Roman forum and basilica, Philippi
iStock.com / MikePax

Further reading

Bakirtzis, Charalambos, and Helmut Koester (eds.). 2009 [1998]. *Philippi at the Time of Paul and after His Death*. Eugene, OR: Wipf & Stock.

Bockmuehl, Markus. 1998. *The Epistle to the Philippians*. BNTC; London: A&C Black.

Cohick, Lynn H. 2013. *Philippians*. SGBC; Grand Rapids, MI: Zondervan.

Fee, Gordon D. 1995. *Paul's Letter to the Philippians*. NICNT; Grand Rapids, MI: Eerdmans.

Hellerman, Joseph H. 2005. *Reconstructing Honor in Roman Philippi: Carmen Christi as Cursus Podorum*. SNTSMS 132; Cambridge: Cambridge University Press.

Hooker, Morna D. 2000. 'The Letter to the Philippians.' In *NIB*. Edited by L. E. Keck. Nashville, TN: Abingdon. Volume 11, pp. 469–549.

Marchal, Joseph A. 2015. *The People beside Paul: The Philippian Assembly and History from Below*. Atlanta: SBL.

Müller, Ulrich B. 1999. 'Der Brief aus Ephesus: Zeitliche Plazierung und theologische Einordnung des Philipperbriefes im Rahmen der Paulusbriefe.' In *Das Urchristentum in seiner literarischen Geschichte*. Edited by U. Mell and U. Müller. BZNW 100; Berlin: Walter de Gruyter, pp. 155–71.

Oakes, Peter. 2001. *Philippians: From People to Letter*. SNTSMS 110; Cambridge: Cambridge University Press.

Osiek, Caroline. 2000. *Philippians, Philemon*. ANTC; Nashville, TN: Abingdon.

Reumann, John. 2008. *Philippians: A New Translation with Introduction and Commentary*. AB; New Haven, CT: Yale University Press.

Sanders, E. P. 2015. *Paul: The Apostle's Life, Letters, and Thought*. Minneapolis: Fortress.

Thielman, Frank S. 2003. 'Ephesus and the Literary Setting of Philippians.' In *New Testament Greek and Exegesis*. Edited by A. M. Donaldson and T. B. Sailors. FS Gerald F. Hawthorne; Grand Rapids, MI: Eerdmans, pp. 205–23.

Thurston, Bonnie. 2009. *Philippians and Philemon*. SP; Collegeville, MN: Liturgical.

Verhoef, Eduard. 2013. *Philippi: How Christianity Began in Europe: The Epistle to the Philippians and the Excavations at Philippi*. London: Bloomsbury.

Wright, N. T. 1991. 'Jesus Christ Is Lord: Philippians 2.5–11.' In *The Climax of the Covenant: Christ and the Law in Pauline Theology*. Edinburgh: T&T Clark, pp. 56–98.

20

Colossians, Philemon, and Ephesians

CHAPTER AT A GLANCE

This chapter provides a short survey of Paul's letters to the Asian churches in Colossae and Ephesus, and to Philemon.

By the end of this chapter you should be able to:

- situate the letters to the Colossians, Philemon, and the Ephesians in Paul's missionary career;
- describe the structure and argument of these three Asian letters;
- identify the main themes and theology of these three Asian letters;
- understand critical issues related to the epistles to the Colossians, Philemon, and the Ephesians.

For he has rescued us from the dominion of darkness and brought us into the kingdom of the Son he loves, in whom we have redemption, the forgiveness of sins.[1]

So if you consider me a partner, welcome him as you would welcome me. If he has done you any wrong or owes you anything, charge it to me.[2]

He made known to us the mystery of his will according to his good pleasure, which he purposed in Christ, to be put into effect when the times reach their fulfilment—to bring unity to all things in heaven and on earth under Christ.[3]

INTRODUCTION

Imagine Paul in prison in Ephesus. He is probably malnourished and short of sleep. He may well have suffered horrible illness; he will certainly have been beaten up by guards and perhaps by other prisoners. He feels helpless and alone in the dark and damp, with the smell of rot, excrement, and death all around him.[4]

---

1 Col. 1.13–14.
2 Philem. 17–18.
3 Eph. 1.9–10.
4 On the case for an Ephesian imprisonment as the context for the

450

Picture him then, either scribbling away on a small sheet of papyrus, squinting for lack of light, or else, hearing at last someone whispering through a slot in the door, talking to a visiting colleague and telling him what to put in a letter to one or more of the central Asian churches.

A fifth- to sixth-century wall-painting of Paul in a cave in Ephesus
Todd Bolen / BiblePlaces.com

This is a far darker image than the usual portraits of Paul, sitting peacefully at a desk, quill in hand, with a pensive look on his face like Wordsworth writing about daffodils. What Paul experienced in an Ephesian prison was not serenity, but searing hardship, not soothing tranquillity but brokenness and anxiety. So it is all the more remarkable that it is from this tumultuous period of Paul's career that we get from him, not only the letter to the Philippians, but also the letters to Philemon, the Colossians, and the circular letter we call 'Ephesians'. The church in Colossae, inland from Ephesus, seems to have been founded only recently, with Philemon as one of its local leaders, and a particular problem has caused Paul to write to Philemon as an individual while sending a letter of encouragement, rich with the sense of the Messiah's supremacy over all things, to the new believers there. Ephesians may then have been written shortly afterwards, to be sent to all the churches in the region. These letters all emphasize the universal sovereignty of Jesus and the call for the churches to model, in their own communities, the cosmic reconciliation achieved by God through him.

---

captivity epistles of Philippians, Philemon, Colossians, and Ephesians, see ch. 19 on Philippians; and Wright *Paul: A Biography*.

Asia Minor in the time of the apostle Paul

CONTEXTUAL AND CRITICAL MATTERS

Paul's Ephesian ministry and the origins of the Lycus valley churches

Paul was the first to bring the gospel to Ephesus, though the city later became a hub for other Christian groups, including those associated with the apostle John.[5] Paul's first visit there was brief, lasting only a few weeks.[6] Paul did, however, return to Ephesus, perhaps during the summer of AD 52, and stayed there for the better part of three years.[7] Luke provides brief snapshots from that period: Paul's ministry to some followers of John the Baptist, his initial preaching in a Jewish synagogue, and (after being forced to leave) his daily discussions in the lecture hall of Tyrannus.[8] During this period Paul's co-workers seem to have established churches in the Asian cities of Pergamum, Sardis, Philadelphia, and Thyatira,[9] and in the western interior of Asia Minor in the Lycus valley, in the towns of Laodicea, Hierapolis, and Colossae.[10] It looks as if, during this time, Paul met Philemon and his wife Apphia, gentiles from Colossae, and led them to faith; Philemon was thereafter a 'partner' with

---

5 Iren. *Adv. Haer.* 3.3.4; Eus. *Hist. Eccl.* 3.1; 5.8.4.
6 Ac. 18.19–21.
7 Ac. 19.10; 20.18–21, 31.
8 Ac. 19.1–22.
9 On the spread of churches around this time see Col. 1.5–8 and Paul's reference to greetings from 'the churches in the province of Asia' in 1 Cor. 16.19.
10 Col 1.7–8; 2.1; 4.12–16; Philem. 1–2.

Paul, probably meaning that he contributed financially to Paul's work.[11] A native of the Lycus valley named Epaphras evangelized the cities of Colossae, Laodicea, and Hierapolis, until he joined Paul in Ephesus; he may also have been imprisoned with Paul at the time of these letters.[12] In Epaphras's absence the Colossian church may have been led by Archippus, though meeting in Philemon's house, while the church in Laodicea was led by Nympha and met in her house.[13]

Paul's powerful ministry in Ephesus had three immediate results: a split in the synagogue community, leading to continuing opposition; the burning of magical scrolls by many who, in a strong local tradition, had practised various kinds of sorcery; a decline in the worship of the goddess Artemis. This last caused trouble with the local silversmiths, whose livelihood focused on making and selling Artemis-related idols.[14] Luke's account of the riot that followed is highly compressed and omits any mention of imprisonment, which we infer from 2 Corinthians 1.8–11 and the internal evidence of the letters. Paul clearly had significant friends in the city, including some of the Asiarchs, the local rulers, but also powerful enemies.[15] The murder of the Ephesian proconsul Marcus Junius Silanus in AD 54 by Agrippina, the mother of the new emperor Nero—to remove a potential rival, since Silanus was a great-great-grandson of Augustus—created an interregnum that was less conducive to equitable law and order. This may explain why Paul left.[16]

During this period, then, Paul probably ended up in an Ephesian prison at least once, facing the prospect of a capital trial and perhaps even death.[17] He later praises Priscilla and Aquila who 'risked their necks' for him during this period,[18] and he mentions Aristarchus in one letter, and Epaphras in another, as 'fellow-prisoners'.[19] This evidence points to a complex time with many twists and turns now mostly hidden from us.

Bronze coin, first century, minted in Philadelphia, with a statue of the goddess Artemis; scholars debate whether the baubles around her midsection are breasts, bull testicles, or gift pouches.

Todd Bolen / BiblePlaces.com

---

11 Philem. 1–2, 17.
12 Col. 1.7–8; 4.12–13; Philem. 23.
13 Col. 4.15, 17; Philem. 1–2.
14 Ac. 19.9; 17–20; 24–29, 36; 20.19; 21.27–29.
15 Ac. 19.31; 1 Cor. 16.8–9.
16 On the murder of Silanus, see Tac. *Ann.* 13.1; Dio Cassius *Hist.* 6.16.4–5. In Ac. 19.38 the reference to 'proconsuls' in the plural could be a generalizing plural (Bruce 1980 [1977], 296) or more likely refers to Silanus's three deputies who assumed control in his absence (Riesner 1998, 216–17).
17 Phil. 1.20–26; Ac. 19.38.
18 Rom. 16.4.
19 Col. 4.10; Philem. 23; Ac. 19.29.

It is possible to connect some dots and do some guesswork on how the three Asian letters were composed.[20] First, while in prison, Paul received Onesimus, a slave who had either run away or absconded from Philemon, but who was now contrite and had come to faith in the lord Jesus. Paul wrote to urge Philemon to receive Onesimus back as a fellow-believer, hinting that Philemon might then release Onesimus so he could work with Paul.[21] Second, Paul wanted to warn the churches in the Lycus valley to be on their guard against the varied challenges that might come from the Jewish community, and sent (via Onesimus and Tychicus[22]) a letter which put this warning in a larger, and pastorally encouraging, context.[23] The letter we call 'Ephesians' was probably a circular, a general exhortation to all the Asian churches, based largely on Colossians but broader in content and scope. Some suggest it may have been drafted by Paul's co-workers while Paul himself was incapacitated. This might well be the 'letter from Laodicea' that Paul mentions in Colossians.[24] During this time it is possible that Paul suggested to John Mark that he should make a pastoral visit up the Lycus valley.[25]

After his release, Paul left Ephesus sometime in AD 54/5. We assume from what he says in the letter to Philemon that he will have gone to Colossae, but after that his aim was to get to Corinth, for reasons we shall study later. Rather than sail straight across the Aegean, he decided to go north to Macedonia, and then on to southern Greece to gather up his projected 'collection' before heading to Jerusalem.[26] He may well have left Timothy in Ephesus to wrap things up until they could meet up again in Macedonia.[27] After his final visit to Corinth, Paul then retraced his steps around northern Greece, stopping off at Troas, Assos, Mytilene, Samos, and Miletus, where he addressed the Ephesian elders. But that was the end of his Asian ministry.[28]

---

20 Campbell (2014, 268–9) writes: 'it is not at all unlikely for Paul to have written a cluster of three letters in prison at this time. Unfortunately, it is well attested through human history that incarceration is a fertile space for reflection and literary work, especially by (literate) activists.' While Campbell is probably wrong to suppose that these letters were written *c.* AD 50 during an imprisonment in Apamea (central Asia Minor), he is undoubtedly correct that Philemon, Colossians, and Ephesians (or 'Laodiceans') are 'components in a single extended epistolary event' (Campbell 2014, 319).
21 Philem. 8–21.
22 On Tychicus see Col. 4.7 and Eph. 6.21.
23 See esp. Col. 2.4–23; 4.7–9.
24 Eph. 6.21; Col. 4.7, 16. Note the textual variants in Eph. 1.1 (including the earliest textual witness $\mathfrak{P}^{46}$, from the late second century) which reads: 'To the holy and faithful in Christ Jesus' with no location specified. Marcion, the mid-second-century quasi-gnostic teacher, had his own edition of Paul's letters with our canonical Ephesians addressed 'To the holy and faithful in Christ Jesus in Laodicea'. It is the later majuscules and their correctors, in the fourth and fifth centuries, that include 'to the Ephesians'.
25 Col. 4.10.
26 Ac. 20.1; 2 Cor. 2.12–13; 7.5; 11.9.
27 1 Tim. 1.3 (Timothy left in Macedonia); 2 Cor. 1.1 (Timothy with Paul in Macedonia); Ac. 20.4 (Timothy with Paul on return voyage to Judea).
28 Ac. 20.6–38.

Ephesus

While Pergamum was the capital of Roman Asia, Ephesus was the larger and more prominent of the two cities. Ephesus was lauded by ancient authors as 'the first and greatest metropolis of Asia', the 'light of Asia', and the 'market of Asia'. Strategically located on the sea and land routes, it had vast commercial, cultural, and military importance. The city contained a magnificent amphitheatre, aqueducts, a gymnasium, a stadium, two agoras, impressive gates, and a basilica. In Paul's day it had a population of around 200,000. Only Rome and Alexandria exceeded Ephesus in size and grandeur.[29] Jews were probably a significant minority of the city, but they had a history of mixed relations with the city's officials and Greek populace.[30]

The massive Ephesian theatre which was the site of a huge commotion and protest against Paul by the silversmiths of Ephesus, according to Acts 19
© 2012 by Zondervan

In terms of religious sites, Ephesus had temples to Zeus and Apollos, to the goddess Roma, and to the emperor Augustus. But larger than all, and four times larger than the Athenian Parthenon, the famous temple to Artemis (Roman 'Diana') was situated on the north-eastern edge of the city, one of the wonders of the ancient world, an icon of Ephesus in the same way that London is known by Big Ben and Sydney by its Opera House. Artemis was acclaimed as 'Queen of Heaven' and venerated by adherents as 'Lady' and 'Saviour'. She was associated with protection from

---

[29] See Yamauchi 1980, 79–114 and Koester 1995.
[30] Trebilco 2007, 37–51.

evil spirits, illness, and misfortune.[31] The Artemision was a place of banking, sacrifice, and asylum. Twice a week a procession of devotees took place through the city. The image of the goddess adorned local coins, a month of the year was named after her, games were held in her honour, and she was revered as the divine guardian and benefactor of the city.[32] A measure of the importance of Artemis and her shrine was that a sanctuary dedicated to the emperor Augustus was located *within* its precincts.[33] All this explains what was involved when the silversmiths, aware of their diminishing trade in small models of the shrine, accused Paul of undermining the local culture. 'Great is Ephesian Artemis!', chanted the rioting crowds.[34] This was not simply about what the modern world calls 'religion'.

Colossae and the Lycus valley

Colossae, one of the older cities in the Lycus valley (going back to at least the fifth century BC), was set within south-western Phrygia in the western interior of Asia Minor. Colossae was then, however, dwarfed by the larger cities of Hierapolis and Laodicea, founded during the Seleucid era, each with a population of around 10,000. The three cities are within a day's walk of each other. Colossae, with the surrounding region, was devastated by an earthquake in the early or middle 60s, and, though some civic life may have been reassembled, the city never really recovered.[35] Eventually, at some point during the Byzantine era, the populace abandoned the area, probably moving to the neighbouring town of Chonai.[36] Colossae has never been excavated. Only meagre remains of a necropolis, fragments of columns and architraves, some coins and pottery, and a handful of inscriptions have so far been uncovered.[37] We have to rely on more general information about the Lycus valley to gain a picture of Colossae in the first century.

In 133 BC the last king of Pergamum bequeathed his kingdom to the Romans, who later reorganized it as 'the province of Asia'. The cities of the Lycus valley were then incorporated into the Roman empire. Eventually the network of Roman roads reached the Lycus valley, turning the area into a significant hub in east–west travel. The cults of Zeus and Apollo were prominent in the region; evidence from coins shows the continuance of older Phrygian religions such as the cult of Men Karou.[38]

---

31 Strelan 1996, 69.
32 See Strelan 1996, 24–76 for an overview of the Artemis temple and cult.
33 Yamauchi 1980, 83.
34 Ac. 19.28, 34 *NTE/KNT*.
35 Eusebius dates this in the tenth year of Nero's reign (*Chron.* 210.4), i.e. AD 64; Tacitus reports a major earthquake in Laodicea in the seventh year of Nero, i.e. 61 (*Ann.* 14.27). Strabo (*Geogr.* 12.8.16) wrote that the entire region was known as a centre of repeated catastrophes.
36 Cadwallader 2015 and Cadwallader and Trainor 2011, 151–79.
37 Huttner 2013, 15, but noting the studies and efforts of Cadwallader and Trainor 2011 to organize an archaeological dig of Colossae. On what we can learn from Colossae thus far, see Cadwallader 2015.
38 See Canavan (2012, 22–4) for a brief summary.

The huge mound under which the city of Colossae remains buried, though plans are in place to excavate it by teams from Flinders University (Australia) and Pamukkale University (Turkey).
Clinton E. Arnold

Almost one third of the coins found in first-century Colossae feature Artemis.[39] Colossae's gods were mostly those associated with human needs related to food, health, pleasure, and nature, so that 'Colossae was replete with gods that promised to satisfy such needs'.[40] Huttner believes that the imperial cult was present in the region and that

> we may assume that the emperor was honored not just by the public at large but within the circle of the family: small statues of the emperor were part of the household inventory, and occasionally altars of the emperors as well.

He points to a house in Hierapolis which had two altars erected on its entrance way, one for Apollo and one for the emperor.[41] The region exhibits a fusion of Greek culture and Anatolian traditions as well as those of various migrant populations, including Italians and Jews.[42]

There had been a significant Jewish population in the Lycus valley since the time of the Seleucid empire in the third and second centuries BC.[43] During the Roman period, Laodicea became a collection-point for the payment of the Temple-tax

---

[39] Cadwallader 2015, 56.
[40] Cadwallader 2015, 69.
[41] Huttner 2013, 63.
[42] Huttner 2013, 28, 37.
[43] Huttner 2013, 67–89.

by local Jews; in 62 BC the proconsul of Asia, Lucius Valerius Flaccus, attempted to seize the collection which, according to Cicero, consisted of twenty pounds of gold.[44] In addition, numerous Jewish sarcophagi have been discovered in Hierapolis, indicating a sizeable Jewish presence in the Lycus valley.[45] This resonates with Philo's statement that the Jews dwelt in every city of Asia Minor. Colossae, we rightly assume, was no different.[46]

Authorship of Colossians and Ephesians

Most have accepted that Paul really did write the letter to Philemon. But in the last 150 years or so Ephesians and Colossians have regularly been regarded as non-Pauline or deutero-Pauline. That conclusion was partly based on comparisons of style and language with the undisputed letters, but emerged largely, we suspect, because they do not support the liberal protestant paradigm for reading Paul which dominated the scholarly world for several generations. Quite simply, Ephesians in particular, and Colossians to a considerable extent, seem to have a much stronger and higher view of the church—and, indeed, of Jesus himself—than many scholars have been prepared to allow. The real Paul, such scholars assumed, taught 'justification by faith', and since this was held to be radically incompatible with what was seen as a high view of the church, Paul could not have written letters that offered one.[47] Sadly, despite the fashion of new 'political' and 'sociological' readings of Paul, no-one seems to have noticed that the more rounded view of Paul that has emerged from such studies creates a context into which Ephesians and Colossians fit extremely well, with Paul's vision of Christ as sovereign over 'the powers', and his interest in forming and shaping the early communities rather than merely saving souls. One might suppose that passages like Ephesians 6.12 and Colossians 1.12–14; 2.14–15 would get a green light from 'political' readers of Paul, offering as they do a high christology set over against the powers of the evil age. Or, again, one might suppose that Ephesians 2.11–21 and Colossians 3.11, encouraging ethnic unity in the churches, would be recognized as embodying central Pauline themes which emerge equally powerfully in Galatians and Romans. This has not happened. Instead, we still hear the scholarly mantra that Ephesians and Colossians are on the 'dubious' list, sometimes being cited, astonishingly, as advocating social conformism, with diminished apocalyptic enthusiasm and egalitarian ethos, settling down into a comfortable bourgeois existence of theological bureaucracy and ecclesiastical hierarchy.[48] This position,

---

44 Cic. *Flac.* 28.68.
45 Ameling 2004, 398–440.
46 Philo *Gai.* 245.
47 Campbell (2014, xvii) forthrightly comments, 'I became increasingly offended by the marginalization I was seeing of Pauline letters deemed too Catholic—sometimes simply because they emphasize the church.'
48 The prejudice against Ephesians and Colossians has grown so strong in some circles that it has reached the point where young scholars are warned against using them in the study of Paul lest they be thought

ironically, reflects a modern social conformism—to the 'unwritten rules' of the scholarly guild, and to the modern political liberalism that underlies them.

Arguments from style are clearly important in principle. But they are hard to make in practice. We have a tiny sample of Paul's writing, hardly an adequate database for a serious stylistic analysis such as would support definite conclusions about authorship. Even if an author has an affinity for some words, a few pet interests, and some favourite expressions, variations can emerge based on the contingent situation and topic, not to mention the possible contribution of scribes and secretaries who might have had a hand in composition, especially if the imprisoned Paul was in bad shape.[49] In fact, if it's stylistic differences we want, one might suggest that the most striking are those between 1 and 2 Corinthians. The second letter to Corinth is much jerkier than the first; its sentences are dense and convoluted, bending back on themselves, twisting to and fro with language about God, Jesus Christ, and Paul's ministry. The organization of material is much less crisp. There is a far greater difference between those two Corinthian letters than there is between Galatians and Romans on the one hand and Ephesians and Colossians on the other; yet nobody uses that as an argument against the authenticity of 2 Corinthians.[50] As John A. T. Robinson pointed out from his personal experience a generation ago, a busy church-leader may well write in very different styles for different occasions and audiences. The same person can be working simultaneously on a large academic project, with careful, ponderous sentences, and a short, snappy talk for the Sunday school. More directly to the point, it has recently been argued that Ephesians and Colossians show evidence of an ornamented, almost pompous, 'Asiatic' rhetorical style, which Paul, after many months in the region, could easily have adopted.[51] One speculative suggestion might be that Paul penned the letter to Philemon himself, that he collaborated with Timothy on the letter to the Colossians, and that the circular we call 'Ephesians' was written under Paul's supervision by his co-workers, based largely on Colossians. But it is just as possible that Paul, one of the most energetic and flexible writers of his day or any day, wrote them all himself.[52]

---

unscholarly. This is one of those dogmas that have taken the place, within the western study of the NT, of the older doctrinal tests that used to characterize seminaries: instead of checking out students or indeed would-be professors on the Trinity or the Incarnation, interviewers now enquire cautiously whether they are sound on rejecting Pauline authorship of Ephesians!
[49] See similar reservations by Campbell 2014, 286–92. See Harold Hoehner's essay 'Did Paul Write Galatians?' (2006) where he tried to use stylistic analysis to disprove Paul's authorship of Galatians in order to show the limitations of stylistic analyses.
[50] Kenny (1986, 98) ranks Paul's letters in terms of their demonstrable statistical correlations as Romans, Philippians, 2 Timothy, 2 Corinthians, Galatians, 2 Thessalonians, 1 Thessalonians, Colossians, Ephesians, 1 Timothy, Philemon, 1 Corinthians, and Titus.
[51] Witherington 2007a, 1–6, 17–19.
[52] On authorship of Colossians, see Bird 2009d, 4–9, 15; Dunn 1996, 35–9; Moo 2008, 28–41; Campbell 2014, 260–309. On authorship of Ephesians, see Thielman 2010, 1–5 and Campbell 2014, 309–38.

PORTALS AND PARALLELS: SONGS OF THE SABBATH SACRIFICE

The Songs of the Sabbath Sacrifice is a fragmentary text from Qumran which describes the angels in the heavenly sanctuary singing anthems of divine praise to God. It was perhaps visions of such things that the philosophers in Colossae were urging the believers there to pursue.

The [Cheru]bim fall before Him and bless Him; as they arise, the quiet voice of God [is heard], followed by a tumult of joyous praise. As they unfold their wings, God's q[uiet] voice is heard again. The Cherubim bless the image of the chariot-throne that appears above the firmament, [then] they joyously acclaim the [splend]or of the luminous firmament that spreads beneath His glorious seat. As the wheel-beings advance, holy angels come and go. Between His chariot-throne's glorious [w]heels appears something like an utterly holy spiritual fire. All around are what appear to be streams of fire, resembling electrum, and [sh]ining handiwork comprising wondrous colours embroidered together, pure and glorious. The spirits of the living [go]dlike beings move to and fro perpetually, following the glory of the two [wo]ndrous chariots. A quiet voice of blessing accompanies the tumult of their movement, and they bless the Holy One each time they retrace their steps. When they rise up, they do so wondrously, and when they settle down, they [sta]nd still. The sound of joyous rejoicing falls silent, and the qui[et] blessing of God spreads through all the camps of the divine beings. The sound of prais[es] . . . coming out of each of their divisions on [both] sides, and each of the mustered troops rejoices, one by one in order of rank . . . (4Q405 frags. xxi–xxii, 6–14; tr. Wise, Abegg, and Cook [2005]).

A Colossian heresy?

Did Paul have a specific reason for writing Colossians? Was there, as many have supposed, a particular 'heresy' or 'false teaching' emerging in the town that he needed to nip in the bud? Despite seemingly endless research on this topic, no definite answer has emerged. The letter's second chapter does seem at first sight to be warning against some particular teachings (Col. 2.4, 8, 16–23). It is possible that this is alluded to elsewhere as well (Col. 1.15–20, 22–23; 2.2–3; 3.1–2), though those passages range so widely that it is impossible to be sure. The range of scholarly suggestions about a particular teaching is bewilderingly large (Ebionism, Essenism, Gnosticism, mystery religions, syncretism, or any number of Greek philosophies), indicating the absence of clear signs. The authors of the present book are divided. MFB suggests that the philosophy seems quite specific, and that the use of the indefinite pronouns indicates a group or individual (Col. 2.8, 16, 18). NTW follows Morna Hooker in suggesting that there actually were no 'false teachers' in Colossae, and that Paul merely writes a general admonition to urge the members of the congregation there not to conform to the beliefs and practices of their Jewish and pagan neighbours.[53]

---

53 Hooker 1973; Wright 1986, 23–30, 100–28; see Wright *PFG*, 992–5 and other references there, including Dunn 1996, 23–35; more recently Copenhaver 2018.

If we suppose that Paul was indeed attacking something he refers to as a 'philosophy' (2.8), we might see it in terms of an amalgamation of Jewish thought and practice on the one hand (given the references to the sabbath [Col. 2.16], circumcision [Col. 2.11], and food laws [Col. 2.21]) and pagan ideas on the other (with the references to the 'powers' [Col 1.16; 2.8, 10, 15], the 'worship of angels' [Col. 2.18], asceticism [Col. 2.21–23], festivals [Col. 2.16], and wisdom [Col. 1.9; 2.3, 23; 3.16]). The Lycus valley does seem to have been a melting-pot of various religions, philosophies, and systems of magic, facilitating all kinds of syncretism. Attention has focused particularly, though, on proposals to do with types of Jewish mysticism, perhaps dressed in a garb of hellenistic philosophy and language, appealing to ex-pagan gentile believers.[54] However, once the argument has gone that far, and once we look closely at the ways in which Paul warns against the blandishments of Jewish teaching elsewhere (e.g. Phil. 3.2), it is straightforward to apply Occam's Razor (the principle of not multiplying unnecessary hypotheses) and conclude that it was Paul himself who was dressing Jewish themes in pagan garb, precisely in order to warn against them, as in Galatians or Philippians. The central thrust of Colossians 2, after all, is the affirmation that followers of Jesus are the true monotheists (2.9), that they have already been circumcised (2.11–12), that the Torah can no longer exclude them (2.14–15), and that they ought not to adopt the Jewish food laws (2.10–23). The other details fit well around this. The warnings of 2.8, 16–19 and elsewhere can then be seen as contemptuous references to those who might try, for reasons we would call 'cultural' and 'political' as much as 'religious' or 'theological', to inveigle the new believers into joining the synagogue community. The debate will no doubt continue.

THE ARGUMENT OF COLOSSIANS

(See box: 'Outline of Colossians'.)

> **OUTLINE OF COLOSSIANS**
>
> 1. Greetings, thanksgiving, and prayer (1.1–14)
> 2. The Messiah poem and the gospel (1.15–23)
> 3. Messianic woes, messianic mission, and messianic mystery (1.24—2.5)
> 4. Engaging the empty deceit of Jewish mysticism (2.6–23)
> 5. Christians as transformed and renewed (3.1–17)
> 6. Christian homes in pagan cities (3.18—4.1)
> 7. Prayer request, further instructions, and benediction (4.2–18)

---

[54] See Dunn 1996, 33–5; Witherington 2007a, 165–6; Bird 2009d, 15–26; and esp. I. Smith 2006. Huttner (2013, 131) puts it well: 'The author of Colossians was opposing a competing concept, primarily of Jewish origin, circulating in the guise of a philosophy, reduced to crude angel worship, pointless self-mortification, and pedantic observance of rules.'

The ruins of the Laodicean theatre
© 2012 by Zondervan

EMAILS
from the edge

From: Alan_Daley@aol.com
To: Professor Dana Schuler
Date: Wed, 7 Jan 2015 at 7:57 p.m.
Subject: Firstborn

Dear Prof.,

I have yet another question. You know in Colossians 1.15 and 18 when Jesus is called the 'firstborn', does that mean he is like the first created spiritual being in the universe? 'Cos I have a Jehovah's Witnesses cousin who keeps harping on about this. Is he right?

Pax 2 da Max
AD

From: Professor Dana Schuler
To: Alan_Daley@aol.com
Date: Wed, 7 Jan 2015 at 10:02 p.m.
Subject: Re: Firstborn

Dear Alan,

Some have tried to argue that way, that 'firstborn' means literally first born in order, or first created being. The text was obviously a boon for Arian interpreters who wanted to find scriptural proof for Jesus being a 'lesser divinity' than the father, and thus a 'created being'. But I hardly think the fourth-century christological debates are what Paul has in mind here. First, we should note that 'firstborn' was more of a status than an actual birth-order. God calls Israel his firstborn son in several writings (e.g. Ex. 4.22; Jer. 31.9; *4 Ez.* 6.58) and this description is also applied to the coming king (Ps. 89.27). The 'firstborn' male of a household was ordinarily the appointed heir, even if he was not an actual biological son of the family but was adopted. Second, if Paul had wanted to describe Jesus as a heavenly being, like an angel, whom God made first, he would have done better to use the words *prōtoktistos* ('created first') or *prōtoplastos* ('first made'). Third, I think Paul's main point is that Jesus is the father's delegated authority over both creation (Col. 1.15) and new creation (Col. 1.18). Jesus, in other words, possesses superlative authority over creation and salvation!

Blessings
Prof. Dana Schuler

1. Greetings, thanksgiving, and prayer (1.1–14)

Paul thanks God for the news, from Epaphras, that a community of love has sprung up in Colossae. Clearly the gospel message is bearing fruit among the believers there (1.3–8). This moves him to pray for an increase in knowledge, wisdom, and the corresponding behaviour (1.9–12). When he speaks of God rescuing people from one kingdom and giving them another one (1.13–14), of 'redemption' and 'forgiveness', he is speaking of the 'new exodus' accomplished in the Messiah.

2. The Messiah poem and the gospel (1.15–23)

Colossians 1.15–20 is one of the most remarkable early Christian writings, articulating in the way that only poetry can the symmetry of, and the coherent movement between, creation and new creation, both accomplished in, through, and for

> 'According to the author of Colossians, the house of Nympha offered the perfect space for the performance of this text (4:15–16). Colossians 4:16 calls for a public reading of Paul's letter in the church of Laodicea that in all likelihood met in Nympha's house. Here it is the modern interpreter who encounters irony. We are to imagine patriarchal teaching calling for the subjugation of wives to husbands proclaimed in a spaced ruled by a woman. Nympha's status as a widowed (?), well-to-do woman may have rendered her largely exempt from the impact of the restrictions. Her house and status in the wider community may have offered the church a semblance of protection and respectability – suitable sanctuary for an ethos that relativized the rubrics of household and citizenship within the confines of an invisible spiritual body. We cannot hear her own voice, but in the world of emerging Christianity Nympha herself may have viewed such ethical teaching as obvious and prudent. Or, like many women throughout history who have been confronted with hierarchical authority structures, she may have known that she could work around the rules.'
>
> Margaret MacDonald, 'Can Nympha Rule This House?: The Rhetoric of Domesticity in Colossians,' 115.

the Messiah. Many suppose that Paul is quoting a hymn written by someone else, and that is always possible, though it is equally possible that he wrote it himself, perhaps as a result of his own dark night of the soul.[55] This poem, celebrating the absolute lordship of Jesus over all other authorities, human or otherwise (see 'Emails from the edge: firstborn'), is the foundation of the rest of the letter, not just for verses 21–23 which apply the message to the Colossians in particular. In sum: 'The pre-existent lord of the world has become the human lord of the world, and in so doing has reflected fully, for the eyes of the world to see, the God whose human image he has now come to bear.'[56] And, extraordinarily, Paul declares that this gospel has already been announced to the whole creation (1.23). This can only mean that with Jesus' death and resurrection the old world has been judged and the new world has been born—and that all creation somehow knows it.

3. Messianic woes, messianic mission, and messianic mystery (1.24—2.5)

Paul then announces that he is celebrating his own suffering on behalf of the Colossians, probably reflecting the Jewish belief that salvation would come through a time of intense suffering.[57] He has been working hard for them and longs to see them firmly established (2.1–5).

4. Engaging the empty deceit of Jewish mysticism (2.6–23)

Paul's basic exhortation consists of the reminder that those who belong to Jesus the Messiah are already complete: he is all they need. They should, therefore, watch out for anyone who tries to divert them; particularly for anyone who tries to get

---

55 See Wright *Paul: A Biography*, 289–91.
56 Wright *Climax*, 116.
57 Wright 1986, 89, followed by Bird 2009d, 64–6.

them to join the synagogue community as a kind of surety for belonging to God.[58] Jesus and his victory on the cross is sufficient (2.14–15) to save them and include them in God's family. (See 'Portals and parallels: Songs of the Sabbath Sacrifice'.) They should, therefore, watch out for anyone who tries to divert them; particularly for anyone who tries to get them to join the synagogue community. If they are concerned about living the new moral life, the answer is not to take up Jewish practices but to recognize and capitalize on what is true of them 'in the Messiah': they have already died and been raised and must put that into practice (2.20–23; 3.1–4).

5. Christians as transformed and renewed (3.1–17)

The 'heavenly' life does not mean having one's head in the clouds (3.1–4). It means killing off the vices of sex and speech (3.5–8). For God's new humanity, the old distinctions of race, tribe, gender, and social status do not exist. Nothing lies outside the sphere of the Messiah's sovereign rule (3.5–11). What matters, then, is the life of compassion and love, and the forgiveness which reflects, and the gratitude which responds to, God's own generous love (3.12–17).

6. Christian homes in pagan cities (3.18—4.1)

Paul offers brief guidelines for family life. These early Christian household codes (here and in Ephesians and 1 Peter) are about the ways in which the lordship of Jesus will be manifest in the most obvious social unit. Pagan critics were poised to accuse the Christians of threatening the social order; Paul's resistance to this has nothing to do with 'patriarchy' as normally conceived and everything to do with mutual, humble love.

7. Prayer request, further instructions, and benediction (4.2–18)

The epistle rounds off with final exhortations, a commendation of the ministry of Paul and his co-workers, final greetings, and a blessing.

THE ARGUMENT OF THE LETTER TO PHILEMON

Paul's letter to Philemon has some interesting similarities to that of Pliny to Sabinianus. The most obvious is the standard rhetorical ploy: 'Far be it from me to force

OUTLINE OF PHILEMON

1. Letter opening, greeting, and thanksgiving (1–7)
2. Paul pleads for Onesimus (8–22)
3. Final greetings and benediction (23–25)

---

[58] The rare Greek word *sylagōgeō* ('to take captive') might be a deliberate play on *synagōgē* ('synagogue'), precisely because Paul is worried that a local chapter of hellenistic Jews is dragging the Colossians away from their faith, either into a form of Jewish mysticism and asceticism (MFB) or forcing the men into getting circumcised to avoid the socio-political scandal, as in Galatia (NTW). See Wright 1986, 100–1; *PFG*, 992–5; Bird 2009d, 75.

> ## PORTALS AND PARALLELS: PLINY'S LETTER TO SABINIANUS
>
> The Roman senator and jurist, Pliny the Younger, in around AD 100 wrote to a friend named Sabinianus to intercede for his freedman (that is, a former slave still resident in his household) and to effect a reconciliation between the two. Pliny's letter reflects a social situation, comedy of politeness, and household drama similar to what we find in Paul's letter to Philemon.[*]
>
> To Sabinianus. The freedman of yours with whom you said you were angry has been to me, flung himself at my feet, and clung to me as if I were you. He begged my help with many tears, though he left a good deal unsaid; in short, he convinced me of his genuine penitence.
> I believe he has reformed, because he realizes that he did wrong. You are angry, I know, and I know too that your anger was deserved, but mercy wins most praise when there was just cause for anger. You loved the man once, and I hope you will love again, but it is sufficient for the moment if you allow yourself to be appeased. You can always be angry again if he deserves it, and will have more excuse if you were once placated. Make some concession to his youth, his tears and your own kind heart, and do not torment him or yourself any longer—anger can only be a torment to your gentle self. (Pliny *Ep.* 9.21 [LCL])
>
> ---
> [*] See further Wright *PFG*, 1–22.

your hand—I wouldn't tell you what to do, now, would I?' No, no, of course not, think Sabinianus and Philemon with a wry smile; you merely put me in an impossible position! Friendship, at various levels, is a standard theme right across the world of ancient letter-writing (see 'Portals and parallels: Pliny's letter to Sabinianus').

There is, however, a shocking dissimilarity. Pliny writes as a social superior; Paul writes as a prisoner, which he mentions not as though it decreases his social standing but as though it gives him a higher status. Once we study the two letters side by side, we see that they breathe a different air. There is, after all, a world of difference between saying, 'Now, my good fellow, let me tell you what to do with your stupid freedman and then we'll all be safely back in our proper social positions,' and saying, 'Now, my brother and partner, let me tell you about my newborn child, and let me ask you to think of him, and yourself, and me, as partners and brothers.' Paul is articulating something different: a new way of life, with new patterns of thinking to sustain it.

This letter is basically a challenge to Philemon to think carefully and messianically about how the *koinōnia* ('fellowship') between the lord Jesus, Paul, and himself is to be applied to Onesimus (see box: 'Outline of Philemon'). When Philemon comes to a full practical knowledge of the meaning of this fellowship, that knowledge will work powerfully towards full unity in Christ and result in transformed relationships within the community. Paul's concern for the runaway slave Onesimus reflects his larger concern for *messianic unity across traditional boundaries* in the churches, whether it be the unity of Jew and gentile in the Messiah (the main point of Galatians), the unity of the church under the lordship of the Messiah in a pagan and imperial context (part of the point of Philippians),

PAUL AND SLAVERY

Was Paul pro-slavery?[*] The fact that Paul required slaves to obey their earthly masters has suggested to many that he was complicit with a brutal and oppressive institution.[†] According to ancient definitions, a slave was a person who did not have the right of refusal; nothing more than furniture with a soul. Slaves could come from any ethnic group. Some people sold themselves into slavery in order to avoid destitution. Others were forced into slavery as a result of capture from war, both combatants and civilians. Others again were born into slavery. In major urban centres up to one third of the population were slaves. Many slaves enjoyed good living conditions during their service, even attaining prominence if they were part of a distinguished household. Slaves were frequently emancipated. Yet in the ancient world slaves were susceptible to manifold abuse and exploitation, merciless labour, misery, and hardship. They were often forced into prostitution. Women and children were particularly vulnerable.

As we look at this, several observations need to be mentioned:[‡] (1) Slavery was indelibly part of the social structure, welfare system, and economic activity of the ancient world; no-one seems to have envisaged society operating without the institution of slavery. While the moral treatment of slaves was discussed on a philosophical plane, the fact of slavery was never debated; its necessity was simply assumed. (2) In the absence of a modern democracy and libertarian ethics it would have been impossible to lodge an effective and successful political revolution against slavery. (3) The most effective means of ameliorating a slave's plight was through just and kind treatment by a master, with the hope of manumission at a future point, and the prospect of remaining under the master's patronage as a freedman or freedwoman, which Paul advocates.[§] (4) In one place, Paul urges slaves not to accept the status quo, but to seek their freedom if they can get it.[**] (5) Paul's negative estimation of the practice of slavery comes through when he offers a vice-list that includes all types of immoral behaviours, including the opprobrium of being a 'slave-trader' (Greek *andrapodistēs*).[††] (6) Paul makes statements that in the Messiah 'there is neither Jew nor Gentile, neither slave nor free'; similarly 'there is no Gentile or Jew, circumcised or uncircumcised, barbarian, Scythian, slave or free, but Christ is all, and is in all', and 'we were all baptised by one Spirit so as to form one body—whether Jews or Gentiles, slave or free—and we were all given the one Spirit to drink'.[‡‡] Paul cultivated an ecclesial culture of equality and mutuality where the degradation and humiliation of slavery was eclipsed by a Christian identity. (7) In the epistle to Philemon, Paul urges Philemon to accept Onesimus in a way that radically alters the slave–master relationship. It is their kinship as brothers in the Messiah and co-workers for the kingdom that transcends societal norms and transforms their attitudes and actions towards each other with a decidedly Christian ethic. F. F. Bruce noted that the epistle to Philemon 'brings us into an atmosphere in which the institution of slavery could only wilt and die'.[§§]

In sum, Paul was certainly no William Wilberforce; but without Paul, the ethic that drove William Wilberforce and his friends might not have existed.

---

[*] What follows is largely based on Bird 2009d, 29–30 and Dunn 1996, 306–7. But on the topic more generally, see Byron 2008.
[†] Col. 3.22–24; Eph. 6.5–8; 1 Tim. 6.1–2; Tit. 2.9.
[‡] Dunn 1996, 306–7.
[§] Col. 4.1; Philem. 8–17; Eph. 6.9.
[**] 1 Cor. 7.21.
[††] 1 Tim. 1.9–10.
[‡‡] Gal. 3.28; Col. 3.11; 1 Cor. 12.13; cf. Eph. 6.8.
[§§] Bruce 1980 [1977], 401.

or, as here in Philemon, the unity of master and slave, expressing again what it means to be *en Christō*. 'So,' Paul asks, 'if you reckon me a partner [*koinōnos*], welcome him [*proslabou auton*] as you would welcome me.'[59] That is the main thrust of the letter.

Paul's threefold appeal unfolds in verses 8–22. First, accept Onesimus back; do not punish him, but receive him as if he were me, a reconciled brother in Christ (though still as a slave). Second, please send him back to me as an assistant. Third, perhaps implied, in doing so, you will also give him his freedom. If we are right, Paul is teaching Philemon, and indeed Onesimus, to *think within the biblical narrative*, to see themselves as actors within the ongoing scriptural drama: to allow their erstwhile pagan thought-forms to be transformed by a biblically based renewal of the mind. Here we see one of the most fundamental differences between Pliny and Paul. Pliny's appeal, we remind ourselves, reaffirmed the social dynamics already present. Paul's appeal openly subverted them (see box: 'Paul and slavery').

Terrace houses in ancient Ephesus
© 2012 by Zondervan

We should add that if a young man called Onesimus were indeed to return to Ephesus to work alongside Paul in the mid-50s, it is not entirely impossible that he is the same person referred to sixty years later by Ignatius of Antioch as the bishop of Ephesus in around AD 110. This, however, must remain uncertain, not least since the name was common.[60] If it is the same Onesimus, however, it shows that

---

59 Philem. 6.
60 See Ign. *Eph.* 1.3; 2.1; 6.2. On the frequency of the name, see Fitzmyer 2000, 107.

Paul's vision had taken root in Ephesus, and that the church was indeed a place of reconciliation, fellowship, and mutuality where ecclesial offices were determined by love, devotion, and spiritual and intellectual gifts, not social status or grouping.

THE ARGUMENT OF EPHESIANS

(See box: 'Outline of Ephesians'.)

> **OUTLINE OF EPHESIANS**
>
> 1. Letter opening, acclamation of praise, and thanksgiving (1.1–23)
> 2. Salvation by grace through faith (2.1–10)
> 3. The unity of Jews and gentiles in the renewed Israel (2.11—3.13)
> 4. Paul's prayer for the Ephesians (3.14–21)
> 5. Paul's exhortation to unity and maturity (4.1–16)
> 6. Put off the old and put on the new (4.17—5.20)
> 7. Christian houses in a pagan city (5.21—6.9)
> 8. Withstanding opposition from the powers (6.10–20)
> 9. Letter closing and benediction (6.21–24)

1. Letter opening, acclamation of praise, and thanksgiving (1.1–23)

The earliest manuscripts lack the words 'in Ephesus'.[61] We have argued above that 'Ephesians' was originally a circular letter intended for churches in western Asia Minor, acquiring its name through being part of a collection of letters perhaps based in Ephesus.

After the opening greeting, Paul pours out a majestic hymn of praise, woven through with the exodus-shaped story of what God has done in Jesus the Messiah. God's purpose was 'to bring unity to all things in heaven and on earth under Christ' (1.10), and believers are now folded into that plan. Paul therefore prays that they would understand more fully who they really are 'in the Messiah', and the power with which they are thereby invested.

2. Salvation by grace through faith (2.1–10)

Paul then reminds his Asian readers of their own prior personal history of enmity with God. They were dead in their sinfulness, imprisoned by the trinity of evil (world, flesh, and devil), and courting divine wrath (2.1–3). But God's loving mercy has found them and rescued them 'by grace through faith', placing them within his larger healing and restorative purposes for the world, as living examples of God's artistry (2.4–10).

3. The unity of Jews and gentiles in the renewed Israel (2.11—3.13)

The result is that Jews and gentiles now come together in the Messiah: God has broken down the dividing wall between them (Paul may be thinking of the barrier

---

61 This includes the Chester Beatty Papyrus II ($\mathfrak{P}^{46}$), a papyrus dated to around AD 200, the important fourth-century codices Sinaiticus (ℵ) and Vaticanus (B), plus the second-century heretic Marcion according to Tertullian.

Library of Celsus, Ephesus

in the Temple keeping non-Jews out of the inner courts). Instead, God has established a new Temple where he now dwells by the spirit: the single multi-ethnic messianic family. The united church is not an optional extra to the work of redemption, but is itself part of the reality of gospel, the way in which God is taking forward his plan for the whole cosmos to radiate with his glory (2.11–22). Paul's own role has been to be the specific agent through whom this new work comes about (3.1–13), confronting the powers of the world with the new ecclesial reality (3.10).

4. Paul's prayer for the Ephesians (3.14–21)

Paul therefore prays for the young churches, that they may discover the heart of what it means to be followers of Jesus. It means knowing God as the all-loving, all-powerful father, putting down roots into that love; or, changing the picture, having that love as the rock-solid foundation for every aspect of one's life.

5. Paul's exhortation to unity and maturity (4.1–16)

Ephesians 4—6 emphasizes Paul's great hope for the church: *unity* and *holiness*. The multiple ministries given by the spirit are given to build up the one body, enabling it to withstand distractions and temptations (4.7–16).

6. Put off the old and put on the new (4.17—5.20)

The united church must learn holiness by discovering what it means to have put off the old human nature and put on the new. Old pagan ways are dehumanizing and to be shunned. Renewal must start in the mind and issue in a new style of life (4.17–24). Work, speech, and communal living will all change (4.25–32). Sacrificial love, modelled in the gospel, must be the believers' rule of life (5.1–2). Once they were darkness; now they are light (5.8–10).

7. Christian houses in a pagan city (5.21—6.9)

As in Colossians, only somewhat more fully, Paul now provides instructions on the relationships within Christian households. Mutual submission is the order of the day, a somewhat different ethical basis from today's flattened and puzzling egalitarianism. His idea of male headship is modelled on the Messiah's self-giving love. Giving instructions to children and slaves, thereby treating them as responsible human beings, was itself revolutionary (6.1–9).

8. Withstanding opposition from the powers (6.10–20)

A church that even begins to appropriate all that has been said so far will face satanic opposition, as Paul knew well from experience. The believers must therefore learn to use the spiritual weapons the gospel provides. Paul himself needs prayer in his own continuing ministry.

9. Letter closing and benediction (6.21–24)

Tychicus will deliver not only this circular letter but also updated news of Paul, intending to encourage all the churches. There follows a final benediction.

> 'Through this image [of being one flesh], Paul has introduced reciprocity in marriage. This Christian distinctive, grounded in the charges to the first couple (Gen 2:24), connects to the eschatological vision of Christ and the church as inextricably united. The mystery of God's will (1:9), that Gentiles are coheirs with Jews in Christ, one body (3:3–9), has a further dimension. The marriage of two becoming one develops into a sign of the unity of Christ and the church, effective now and to be fully consummated in the end.'
>
> **Lynn Cohick**, *Ephesians*, 141–2.

COLOSSIANS, PHILEMON, AND EPHESIANS, AND THE BIG PICTURE

Reading Acts 19 alongside 2 Corinthians 1 reveals the triumphs and travails that Paul encountered in the Roman province of Asia in the early 50s. Opposition came from many quarters, not only local Jewish groups but also the social and cultural forces that rallied around the cults of Artemis, Zeus, and the Roman empire. Paul's answer given in Colossians is to think more deeply about the victory and supremacy of Jesus over all other powers, the fulfilment of Israel's scriptures in him, and the vocation of the church to unity and holiness as the sign to the world of the new way of being human. All creation is under Jesus' lordship, and the church must model what that means. That comes into sharp focus in the letter to Philemon, where Paul is revealed, not as an abstract theologian removed from the mess of human relationships, but as a wise and warm-hearted pastor and friend, coming to the aid of the vulnerable, standing in the breach where necessary, and suffering reproach without thought. Paul instructs Philemon out of partnership, not power, and urges him to think through *in the Messiah* what he ought to do and how the principle of the gospel (there is neither slave nor free, and so on) applies to himself and Onesimus. This short letter shows how to do pastoral persuasion in the light of the new creation.

Ephesians sums much of this up, as indeed it may have been intended to do. Paul's clear and celebratory statement of the grace of God in the gospel is anchored in his vision of God's cosmic plan to unite heaven and earth in the Messiah—a plan symbolized by the coming together of Jew and gentile in the church and also of husband and wife in marriage. The powers of darkness will resist this, and Christians will therefore find themselves on the front line of spiritual warfare.

Further reading

Bird, Michael F. 2009. *Colossians and Philemon.* NCCS; Eugene, OR: Cascade.
Byron, John. 2008. *Recent Research on Paul and Slavery.* Sheffield: Sheffield Phoenix.
Cadwallader, Alan H. 2015. *Fragments of Colossae: Sifting through the Traces.* Hindmarsh, SA: ATF.
Cadwallader, Alan H., and Michael Trainor (eds.). 2011. *Colossae in Space and Time: Linking to an Ancient City.* Göttingen: Vandenhoeck & Ruprecht.
Cohick, Lynn H. 2010. *Ephesians.* NCCS; Eugene, OR: Cascade.
Dunn, James D. G. 1996. *The Epistles to the Colossians and to Philemon.* NIGTC; Grand Rapids, MI: Eerdmans.
Fitzmyer, Joseph A. 2000. *The Letter to Philemon: A New Translation with Introduction and Commentary.* AB; New Haven, CT: Yale University Press.
Fowl, Stephen. 2012. *Ephesians: A Commentary.* Louisville, KY: Westminster John Knox.
Gombis, Timothy G. 2010. *The Drama of Ephesians: Participating in the Triumph of God.* Downers Grove, IL: InterVarsity.
Gupta, Nijay. 2013. *Colossians.* Macon, GA: Smyth & Helwys.

Huttner, Ulrich. 2013. *Early Christianity in the Lycus Valley*. Leiden: Brill.
Koester, Helmut (ed.). 1995. *Ephesos: Metropolis of Asia*. Valley Forge, PA: Trinity Press International.
MacDonald, Margaret. 2008. *Colossians and Ephesians*. SP; Collegeville, MN: Liturgical.
McKnight, Scot. 2017. *The Letter to Philemon*. NICNT; Grand Rapids, MI: Eerdmans.
——. 2018. *The Letter to the Colossians*. NICNT; Grand Rapids, MI: Eerdmans.
Moo, Douglas J. 2008. *The Letters to the Colossians and to Philemon*. PNTC; Grand Rapids, MI: Eerdmans.
Murphy-O'Connor, Jerome. 2008. *St. Paul's Ephesus: Texts and Archaeology*. Collegeville, MN: Liturgical.
Osiek, Caroline. 2000. *Philippians, Philemon*. ANTC; Nashville, TN: Abingdon.
Perkins, Pheme. 1997. *Ephesians*. ANTC; Nashville, TN: Abingdon.
Smith, Ian K. 2006. *Heavenly Perspective: A Study of the Apostle Paul's Response to a Jewish Mystical Movement at Colossae*. LNTS 326. London: T&T Clark.
Strelan, Rick. 1996. *Paul, Artemis, and the Ephesians*. BZNW 80; Berlin: De Gruyter.
Thielman, Frank S. 2010. *Ephesians*. BECNT; Grand Rapids, MI: Baker.
Thompson, Marianne M. 2005. *Colossians & Philemon*. THNTC; Grand Rapids, MI: Eerdmans.
Thurston, Bonnie. 2009. *Philippians and Philemon*. SP; Collegeville, MN: Liturgical.
Witherington, Ben. 2007. *The Letters to Philemon, the Colossians, and the Ephesians: A Socio-Rhetorical Commentary on the Captivity Epistles*. SRC; Grand Rapids, MI: Eerdmans.
Wright, N. T. 1986. *The Epistles of Paul to the Colossians and to Philemon*. TNTC; Grand Rapids, MI: Eerdmans.
——. 1991. *The Climax of the Covenant: Christ and the Law in Pauline Theology*. Edinburgh: T&T Clark, pp. 99–119.
Yee, T. L. 2005. *Jews, Gentiles and Ethnic Reconciliation: Paul's Jewish Identity and Ephesians*. SNTSMS 130; Cambridge: Cambridge University Press.

Curetes Street, Ephesus

21

1 and 2 Corinthians

We are therefore Christ's ambassadors, as though God were making his appeal through us. We implore you on Christ's behalf: be reconciled to God. God made him who had no sin to be sin for us, so that in him we might become the righteousness of God.[1]

CHAPTER AT A GLANCE

This chapter provides a short survey of Paul's letters to the churches in Corinth.

By the end of this chapter you should be able to:

- situate the Corinthian letters in Paul's missionary career;
- describe the structure and argument of 1 and 2 Corinthians;
- identify the main themes and theology of 1 and 2 Corinthians;
- understand critical issues related to the Corinthian correspondence.

INTRODUCTION

If there was one church that caused Paul to pull his hair out and made him age before his time, it was probably the 'church of God in Corinth'. Paul spent an initial eighteen months with the believers there, establishing their community. He made at least two further visits to Corinth, the first of which did not go well. He wrote, it seems, four letters to the Corinthians, two of which we have in our New Testament, all of them dealing with problems in the church. Paul's co-workers—Timothy, Titus, and the more independent Apollos—also visited them, often relaying to Paul news of a deteriorating situation.

The problems were numerous: deep divisions, sexual immoralities, suspicions about Paul and his motives, and the visits of people Paul calls 'super-apostles', touting their own credentials and belittling Paul. This church experienced social, spiritual, and sexual problems, pitting members against one another and the congregation against Paul. And yet we see here the heart of Paul.

---

[1] 2 Cor. 5.20–21.

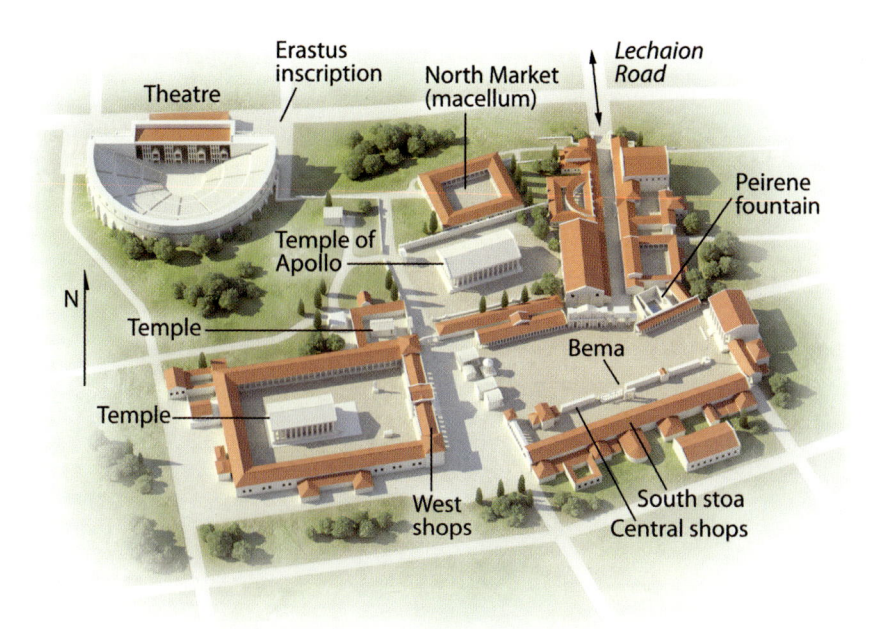

Ancient city of Corinth

Paul saw himself as a kind of father to the Corinthians through the gospel. He constantly affirmed his love for them, even when correction and discipline was necessary. These letters reveal the real Paul, not simply as 'apostle' or 'theologian', but as pastor, caring for his converts with a deep and resilient love.

The Corinthian letters are a prime example of the huge historical and cultural distance between ourselves and the early church. The world of these letters is foreign to us in its geography, language, social relationships, economics, and religious context. Paul deals with many things, including the prizing of rhetorical ability, the love of wisdom, Roman legal proceedings, prostitution practices, ancient views of marriage, celibacy, meat markets, social and ecclesial factions, pagan temples, head coverings, ecstatic utterances, baptisms for the dead, Greek anthropology, and visions of a third heaven. Some of these have semi-parallels in our world, but even there the radically different context changes everything. Paul faced, in addition, the challenge of organizing the collection that he had planned for the Jerusalem church, while simultaneously having to respond to news that certain Jewish Christians had arrived in Corinth and were trying to tarnish his reputation. It takes a continuous effort for us to think our way back into life in Corinth and to grasp just how remarkable was Paul's response to the many different elements of the situation.

Yet the hard work of sowing in the Corinthian fields always leads to new wine. These letters provide endless insight into the challenge of living Christianly in a pagan world. They contain some of the best-known passages in the whole Bible—the description of the foolishness of the cross, the hymn in praise of love, and classic discussions of resurrection and reconciliation. These letters call us to follow Paul as he follows the crucified Messiah. One could sum it up as follows: in 1 Corinthians he urges his readers that, when living in a pagan world, they should see everything through the lens of the cross. In 2 Corinthians, this translates into the unveiling of God's power in the weakness and death of the Messiah and the weakness and suffering of the apostle. The Corinthians, it seems, had asked Paul for his apostolic credentials. He shows them the scars on his back.

The Acrocorinth, the immense feature overlooking the city of Corinth
© 2012 by Zondervan

CONTEXTUAL AND CRITICAL MATTERS

Corinth

Corinth was the capital of the Roman province of Achaia. It sat at the foot of the immense Acrocorinth, a rugged limestone mountain 1,886 feet high that still towers over the city. Corinth had been destroyed by the Romans in 146 BC, but was rebuilt by Julius Caesar in 44 BC and colonized by Roman freedmen from families with connections further east. It grew quickly and soon recaptured its former regional prominence. In Paul's day, Corinth had a population of about 80,000 with a further 20,000 in surrounding villages and settlements.

Part of the reason for Corinth's success was its strategic location on the isthmus between the two halves of Greece: Attica to the north and the Peloponnese to the south. On the east–west axis, Corinth and its outlying villages touched both the

Aegean and Ionian seas with its respective gulfs. Various attempts had been made to dig a canal to enable shipping to sail between the gulfs; none had succeeded in Paul's day (the goal was finally achieved in 1923!), but arrangements could be made to drag certain types of boat overland for the six miles or so between the two bodies of water, enabling pilot and crew to avoid sailing around southern Greece. As early as 602 BC, Periander had proposed digging a canal across the Corinthian isthmus.[2]

Corinth was a greco-roman hybrid. The earlier hellenistic city was now thoroughly romanized, with a Roman administration and architecture. The Roman colonists ruled the roost; native Achaians or immigrants were barred from public office. Until the reign of Hadrian, most inscriptions in Corinth were in Latin rather than Greek (though most graffiti was in Greek, reflecting the culture of the underclass).[3] Various immigrant groups, including Jews, settled in Corinth, as Luke reports and as Philo confirms.[4] Corinth, as a busy port-city, had a transient population with everyone from vagabonds to philosophers (sometimes the same person), merchants and artisans, frequently passing through. Its economy was largely dependent on services offered to travellers. In the words of Ciampa and Rosner, Corinth was 'prosperous, cosmopolitan, and religiously pluralistic, accustomed to visits by impressive, traveling public speakers and obsessed with status, self-promotion, and personal rights'.[5]

Paul arrived in Corinth in around AD 50–1, and spent eighteen months there. During this time he met Aquila, a Jew from Pontus, and his wife Priscilla. They, tent-makers like Paul, had recently come from Rome, after the Jews were seen as riotous and were expelled by Claudius in AD 49.[6] Paul spent some weeks speaking in the synagogue, but eventually was forced to leave, taking with him a mixture of Jews, God-fearers, and a significant number of pagans,[7] and forming a network of house-churches.[8]

After this time, the synagogue leaders tried to bring charges against Paul, hauling him before Gallio, the governor of Achaia. A famous inscription identifies Gallio and helps us to date this incident, placing him in Corinth in AD 51. The *bēma* or 'judgment seat' where Paul was brought is still there today. The Jews complained that Paul was inducing other Jews to practise an unlawful form of worship (perhaps reflecting the way in which, as we see in 1 Corinthians 8.6, Paul was adapting Jewish prayers to include Jesus within them). Gallio was indifferent to the matter,

---

2   Strabo *Geogr.* 8.6.19–20a; See Ciampa and Rosner 2010, 2–3; Murphy-O'Connor 2002.
3   Millis 2010, 23–30.
4   Ac. 18.2–17; Philo *Gai.* 281.
5   Ciampa and Rosner 2010, 3.
6   Ac. 18.1–3; Suet. *Claud.* 25.4. The chances are that the Jewish disturbances were caused by problems over the arrival of the gospel in Rome.
7   See 1 Cor. 12.2: 'when you were pagans'.
8   Ac. 18.4–11; 2 Cor. 1.19.

seeing it as a squabble within the Jewish community, and he refused to render a verdict. He showed no concern even when Sosthenes, the synagogue leader and one of Paul's converts, was beaten in broad daylight.[9] The significance of all this was clear: unlike the situation in Galatia, where tensions continued because the local Jesus-followers were claiming the Jewish exemption from public cult, in Greece a Roman pronouncement had certified that the messianic movement was to be seen as part of the Jewish world.

Paul remained in Corinth for a short time after that. But he soon departed for Ephesus, on the way to Jerusalem and Antioch.[10]

A *peripteros* (a small temple with porticoes) is located on the eastern side of Corinth. A Latin inscription shows that it had been commissioned by Gn. Babbius Philinus, a local ruler of the Roman prefecture of Corinth.
Kim Walton

After Paul left Corinth, the Corinthians were visited by Apollos, a Greek-speaking Jewish Christian and associate of Aquila and Priscilla, and maybe even Peter, passing through Corinth on his way to Rome.[11] These visits, while good for the church in general, seem to have divided the loyalties of the congregation, and generated the beginnings of a personality cult. These problems were compounded by new moral challenges. Paul learned about all this when he arrived back in Ephesus from Syria.[12] He subsequently wrote a letter to Corinth, urging the church

---

9   Ac. 18.12–17.
10 Ac. 18.18–22.
11 Ac. 18.27–28; 1 Cor. 1.12.
12 Ac. 19.1; see 1 Cor. 5.1 ('It is actually reported . . .') and 11.18 ('I hear that . . .').

members not to associate with believers who engaged in blatant sexual immorality.[13] He then wrote the much longer letter we call 1 Corinthians, from Ephesus in around AD 53, and sent it through one of the house-church leaders who had visited him.[14]

He wrote in response to two things. First, he wanted to answer several written questions from the Corinthians about marriage and celibacy, food sacrificed to idols, spiritual gifts, the Collection, and the prospect of Apollos's return.[15] Second, he also wrote in response to disconcerting news from Apollos and several church leaders about factions, incest, lawsuits, women inappropriately dressed, disorder in worship, and particularly (and for Paul crucially) denials of the resurrection.[16]

Things then got worse. Timothy brought news that his instructions had not been heeded. Paul therefore made a second visit to Corinth, probably sailing straight across from Ephesus; he refers to this later as a 'painful visit', since he was clearly rebuffed.[17] He returned to Ephesus, where, as we have seen, the situation deteriorated and ended up with him not only in prison but in seriously bad shape personally and physically. He then may have written what he calls a 'letter of tears' which had a powerful effect on the Corinthian church.[18] After his release from prison, Paul travelled back to Corinth the long way, by land, around northern Greece, anxious through the first half of the journey about what reception he might expect.

Titus, however, came from Corinth to meet Paul in Macedonia, and reported both good news and bad news.[19] On the good side, the Corinthians had dealt with the leading antagonist who was fomenting opposition to Paul; the Corinthians had reaffirmed their affection for their original apostle.[20] On the negative side, Titus also informed Paul of the arrival of the people Paul calls 'super-apostles', who had disparaged Paul's ministry as inferior to their own.[21] It is not clear whether Paul then wrote the whole of 2 Corinthians in Macedonia, or whether he then continued, in a different vein, a letter he had begun either in Ephesus before setting out or at some point on his journey north. The letter celebrates the Corinthians' reconciliation to him, gives instructions for a further visit from Titus to get the collection-money ready, addresses the question of the 'super-apostles' with a brilliant piece of irony, and prepares them for his third visit.

---

13 1 Cor. 5.9–10.
14 1 Cor. 4.17; 16.8, 10, 19–20.
15 1 Cor. 7.1, 25; 8.1, 4; 12.1; 16.1, 12.
16 1 Cor. 1.11; 5.1; 6.1; 11.18; 15.12; 16.17.
17 1 Cor. 16.5–7; 2 Cor. 2.1.
18 2 Cor. 2.1–11; 7.8–12. Scholars debate whether this letter has then been incorporated into what we call '2 Corinthians'.
19 2 Cor. 2.12–13.
20 2 Cor. 7.6–16.
21 2 Cor. 11.5; 12.11.

The Corinthian problem

What was the root of the Corinthian problems? A generation ago, some scholars suggested that the Corinthians had embraced an early form of Gnosticism, but that view is rightly rejected today. More likely, many of the problems were coloured, if not directly caused, by the intense factionalism within the small Corinthian church, reflecting the competitive culture of rivalry and personality politics that was nasty but normal in Corinth. That is why Paul's primary appeal is for unity.[22] Paul then proceeds to attribute slogans to these various parties: 'I follow Paul', 'I follow Apollos', 'I follow Cephas [that is, Peter]', and 'I follow Christ'. These may not have represented precise parties; they may simply indicate a culture of personal loyalties and tensions, generating bickering. Paul's response is to replace the Corinthian obsession with pagan-style 'wisdom' and power with a theology of the cross, exposing human pretensions to greatness and knowledge as mere folly.

Underneath this party spirit lay various theological problems. Some have suggested that Paul's sarcastic remark, 'Already you have all you want! Already you have become rich! You have begun to reign—and that without us!',[23] indicates an over-realized eschatology, in other words, a super-'spiritual' belief that 'the new age' had already fully dawned so that Jesus-believers were now already reigning in the kingdom of God (and could therefore behave how they liked). This might also help to explain the Corinthian denial of a future resurrection (correlated with the error of Hymenaeus and Philetus described in 2 Tim. 2.18).[24] This view, however, may be the wrong way round. Richard Hays has argued persuasively that the problem in Corinth was not too much eschatology, but too little.[25] The Corinthians did not think they had arrived in the kingdom. They were not thinking Jewishly at all, let alone in terms of the Jewish 'two ages' (the present age and the age to come). Rather, they were still mentally living within the pagan world by whose standards they had attained a degree of wisdom superior to—and independent of—Paul himself. This produced a 'boasting' which ignored the judgment that was still to come. In their boasting they were heedless of God's future judgment. Their 'puffed-up' posturing came from putting together their beliefs about themselves as Christians with ideas from pagan philosophy, not least the kind of popular-level Stoicism which taught that all who truly understood the world and themselves were kings. The words 'rich' and 'reigning' had been catchwords of Stoic philosophy since the time of the philosopher Diogenes, who settled in Corinth, and who popularized the aphorism,

---

22 1 Cor. 1.10: 'I appeal to you, brothers and sisters, in the name of our Lord Jesus Christ, that all of you agree with one another in what you say and that there be no divisions among you, but that you be perfectly united in mind and thought.' See too 11.18: 'I hear that when you come together as a church, there are divisions among you, and to some extent I believe it.'
23 1 Cor. 4.8.
24 Thiselton 2000, 40–1, 358.
25 Hays 1997, 70.

'I alone am rich, I alone reign as king.' Jennifer Houston McNeel exposes the sad irony of the situation: 'The Corinthians' problem is not just that they are immature in faith, but that they have misunderstood their own level of maturity.'[26] Against this, Paul urgently wanted to teach them to think of themselves, corporately, individually, and cosmically, in a more thoroughly Jewish fashion, in terms of the great Jewish stories of God, Israel, and the world, all now coming into new focus around the Messiah and the spirit, and all pointing ahead to the future judgment and future resurrection in the light of which—and in this light alone—all present life would make sense.[27]

The social location of the Corinthians

Like most ancient cities, Corinth had a small number of wealthy residents and a large number of poor. This is reflected in Paul's comment: 'Not many of you were wise by human standards; not many were influential; not many were of noble birth.'[28] Scholars used therefore to imagine that the Corinthian believers were drawn from the lower echelons of society, but a new consensus has emerged: the congregation was socially diverse, with some members possessing considerable economic means and holding elevated standing in the city. The stratification of persons in Corinth, based on New Testament sources, is laid out in Table 21.1.[29]

In 1929, excavations in Corinth discovered a first-century inscription on some pavement near the theatre about a certain 'Erastus'. The inscription reads: 'Erastus in return for his ship laid the pavement at his own expense.' This could be the same Erastus, a director of public works, whom Paul mentions in his letter to the Romans (Rom. 16.23).
www.holylandphotos.org

---

26 McNeel 2013, 570.
27 A further point to note is that, unlike the problem in 2 Tim. 2, there is no hint that the Corinthians thought that the resurrection had already happened. Rather, the problem was a normal pagan denial of resurrection altogether. Hence Paul's retort: 'If the dead are not raised . . .' (1 Cor. 15.13, 15, 16, 29, 32).
28 1 Cor. 1.26.
29 See Thiselton 2000, 23–9; Dunn 2009b, 622–37; Longenecker 2010, 220–58.

SOCIAL STRATIFICATION OF PERSONS IN CORINTH ACCORDING TO THE NEW TESTAMENT

Status	Individual(s) mentioned by Paul or Luke	NT source
A director of public works	Erastus	Rom. 16.23
A synagogue leader	Crispus	1 Cor. 1.14; Ac. 18.8
Heads of households	Crispus, Stephanas, Chloe	1 Cor. 1.11, 14, 16; 11.22; 16.15
Those capable of service and benefaction to Paul	Gaius, Titus Justus, Phoebe	1 Cor. 1.14; Ac. 18.17; Rom. 16.1–12
Merchants or artisans	Aquila and Priscilla	1 Cor. 16.19; Rom. 16.3
Labourers and the destitute 'who have nothing'	Unnamed	1 Cor. 11.18–34, esp. 11.22
Slaves	Unnamed	1 Cor. 7.21; 12.13

It would seem that, far from being a socially depressed group, the Corinthians were socially stratified, comprised equally of those living in subsistence and those living in slavery, as well as members of the retainer class, and even some from the social elites.[30]

Who were the 'super-apostles'?

The identity of Paul's opponents in 2 Corinthians, the so-called 'super-apostles', is much debated.[31] Proposals have included Jewish proselytizers, Gnostics, pneumatics (whatever that might be taken to mean), sophists, or a combination thereof.[32] Can we get any clearer? Paul does not engage in the same kind of combative polemics as he did in Galatians and Philippians where, clearly, he was concerned about Jewish-Christian interlopers trying to compel gentile Christians to follow the Torah

---

30 See esp. Judge 1960 and Theissen 2004, 69–120. In counter-point, Justin Meggitt (1998, 179) has offered a corrective to the perception of Paul as a middle-class tradesman, drawing attention to the struggle of survival experienced by the urban poor in greco-roman cities, and argued that Paul and most of his churches were very much on the lower economic tiers of society, probably belonging to the destitute class. In support of that we have to admit that while Erastus was a public administrator (*oikonomos* or *aedile*), this could have been the position of a low-level bureaucrat, or even that of a literate slave. While the current consensus is that the Corinthian church was socially diverse, it remains likely that the majority of members were either slaves or from among the urban poor.
31 2 Cor. 11.5, 13–14; 12.11.
32 See Sumney 2015.

and, in the case of males, to be circumcised. He does not argue about 'works of the law', or 'circumcision', or deploy arguments from Genesis 15.6 and Habakkuk 2.4 about the sufficiency of faith for justification and membership in Abraham's covenant family. The most likely scenario is that some Jewish Christians have arrived in Corinth, boasting of their privileged status as Jews.[33] They claimed to be apostles, servants of Christ, and ministers of righteousness;[34] they carried letters of recommendation;[35] they boasted of their accomplishments in comparison to others;[36] they alleged that Paul was an impostor who was transgressing their apostolic turf;[37] and their criticism of Paul met with misgivings among the Corinthians that Paul lacked eloquence and personal authority.[38] They either claimed to be, or were heralded as, 'super-apostles' who were more than equal to Paul.[39] Most likely, they are not Jewish-Christian proselytizers, but more sophistic and sapiential in their manner of persuasion, that is, they appear to be Greek-speaking Jewish Christians reared in hellenistic rhetoric and wisdom. They began disparaging Paul for his inferiority, for his manual labour, his refusal to accept payment, while boasting of their own superiority.

Paul, in response, claims that these 'super-apostles' peddle the word of God for profit and thereby distort it.[40] They are a satanic deception, preaching a different Jesus and a different gospel, and belonging to a different spirit.[41] While the interlopers might identify as 'servants of righteousness',[42] Paul reasons that they are servants of a deadly and defunct phase of Israel's history, the Sinaitic legislation, with a letter that kills, a ministry of death and condemnation, and a glory that has faded and is inoperable. In contrast, Paul claims that he and his colleagues are servants of a new covenant, which brings life through the spirit, a ministry of righteousness, characterized by a greater and everlasting glory.[43] Unlike the intruders, Paul and his circle do not commend themselves. They proclaim Jesus the Messiah as lord. Their commendation comes from their own character and from the lord himself.[44]

In any case, after all, the Corinthians themselves were Paul's real 'letter of recommendation', the living proof that God's power worked through his gospel

---

[33] 2 Cor. 11.21–23.
[34] 2 Cor. 11.13, 15, 23.
[35] 2 Cor. 3.1.
[36] 2 Cor. 5.12; 10.12; 12.11.
[37] 2 Cor. 6.8; 10.13–16. This may have some echoes of that part of the Galatian problem which focused on the originality or otherwise of Paul's apostolic commission and message.
[38] 2 Cor. 3.1–3; 10.1–11; 12.12; 13.10.
[39] 2 Cor. 11.5, 12; 12.11. The question of whether 'super-apostles' was their own self-designation or Paul's ironic description is hard to decide.
[40] 2 Cor. 2.17; 4.2.
[41] 2 Cor. 11.4, 12–14.
[42] 2 Cor. 11.15.
[43] 2 Cor. 3.1–11.
[44] 2 Cor. 4.5; 10.18.

proclamation.[45] What's more, the interlopers were trying to poison the Corinthians against Paul, and the Corinthians had been lured into putting up with this, being in effect (from Paul's point of view) enslaved, preyed upon, exploited, flattered, and abused.[46] Paul claims that what sets him apart from these interlopers are his apostolic sufferings. His human weakness is the paradoxical location of the apostolic signs of divine power.[47]

The integrity of 2 Corinthians

The integrity of 2 Corinthians has been strenuously debated. The letter, on the surface, appears disjointed both in tone and content, dividing into three sections. In chapters 1—7, Paul explains and defends his apostolic authority; in chapters 8—9, he explains in quite a different tone of voice that he is now coming to receive the Collection which they should have been organizing. In chapters 10—13 he again defends his apostolic authority, this time explicitly against the 'super-apostles'. Even within these sections there appear to be further interruptions. Paul's defence of his travel plans and intentions in 1.1—2.13 and 7.5–16 is interrupted by a defence of his apostolic ministry in 2.14—7.4, which itself is interrupted by miscellaneous admonitions about idolatry (specifically in relation to intermarriage with non-Christians) in 6.14—7.1. Then, in 2 Corinthians 8—9, Paul seems to deal with the Collection twice in succession. And, at the very end, in 2 Corinthians 13, Paul changes quickly from warning the Corinthians of his impending visit (13.1–10) to exhorting them warmly to joy, perfection, unity, and peace (13.11–13). The tone of the letter thus swings wildly from conciliatory to hortatory to polemical. Given this, it is no surprise that 2 Corinthians has been regarded by many as a composite document, spliced together from at least five separate letters:[48]

1. *2 Corinthians 8*—Paul's first attempt to prepare the church in Corinth for the Collection;
2. *2 Corinthians 2.14—7.4 (minus 6.14—7.1)*—Paul's response to questions about his ministry;
3. *2 Corinthians 10.1—13.10*—Paul's 'letter of tears' defending his apostolic credentials;
4. *2 Corinthians 1.1—2.13; 7.5–16; 13.11–13*—Paul's joy in being reconciled to the Corinthians;
5. *2 Corinthians 9*—Paul's later circular to the churches of Achaia about the Collection.

---

[45] 2 Cor. 3.2.
[46] 2 Cor. 11.16–21.
[47] 2 Cor. 4.7–11; 6.4–10; 11.21—12.18; 13.3–4.
[48] See esp. Mitchell 2005.

The theory that several letters were later combined might account for the disparate nature of Paul's argument; but the case is far from certain. None of the early manuscripts give any sign of such a thing. Why would an early collector of Paul's Corinthian letters combine them in this way, rather than leaving them as individual letters? Why would the letters be stuck together in this arbitrary, almost random, way? There is in any case a remarkable thematic unity underneath the disparate segments. Paul's mention of 'some people' who carry letters of recommendation may be an early nudge at the 'super-apostles'.[49] At two different points Paul raises matters of deviant behaviours.[50] Across the letter there are positive and negative instances of boasting.[51] The theme of encouragement runs throughout.[52] The letter provides, in its varied ways, a unified explanation of Paul's apostolic *mission* in general with an accompanying defence of Paul's apostolic *ministry* in particular.[53] As George Guthrie comments:

> Whether he is appealing for sensitivity to his suffering (e.g., 1:8–11), explaining his decisions (1:12–2:4), commending to the Corinthians his mission's authentic embodiment of Christian ministry (2:14–7:4), promoting the collection (chaps. 8–9), or confronting the Corinthians about his opponents (chaps. 10–13), the apostle addresses various aspects of his relationship with the church and their relationship to his mission.[54]

A plausible, though admittedly unprovable, scenario is that Paul wrote 2 Corinthians over some time while in Macedonia, or indeed on the way from Ephesus north to Troas and then across into Greece. He began it by describing the crises he had faced in Asia, the recent horror-story which had scarred him so badly. Then Titus arrived with news of reconciliation but also of new trouble, leading Paul, quite possibly on the road or staying in different places, to elaborate his letter bit by bit, always returning, though from different angles, to the defence of his calling and career. Along the way he made several digressive remarks dealing with different issues, launching near the end into a final ironic tirade, and closing with instructions about his impending visit.[55] There is nothing historically implausible about any of this.

THE ARGUMENT OF 1 CORINTHIANS

(See box: 'Outline of 1 Corinthians'.)

---

49 2 Cor. 2.17; 3.1; 10.11–12.
50 2 Cor. 6.14—7.3; 12.20–21.
51 2 Cor. 1.12–14; 7.14; 9.1–3; 10.8–18; 11.10–30; 12.1–10.
52 2 Cor. 1.3–7; 2.7–8; 5.20; 6.1; 7.4–13; 8.4, 6, 17; 9.5; 10.1; 12.8, 18; 13.11.
53 2 Cor. 3.3–9; 4.1; 5.18–21; 6.3–10; 8.4, 19–20; 9.1–2, 12–13; 11.8, 15, 23.
54 Guthrie 2015, 29.
55 See further on the case for the unity of 2 Corinthians, Dunn 2009b, 834–8, and Schnelle 2005, 237–45.

OUTLINE OF 1 CORINTHIANS

1. Introduction, grace, and thanksgiving (1.1–9)
2. Corinthian factions and the folly of the cross (1.10—3.23)
3. Paul: servant of the Messiah, father in the gospel (4.1–21)
4. Sexual perversity has no place (5.1–13)
5. Lawsuits among believers (6.1–11)
6. The body as temple of the holy spirit (6.12–20)
7. Marriage, divorce, and singleness (7.1–40)
8. Food sacrificed to idols (8.1–13)
9. The apostle Paul's rights and struggle (9.1–27)
10. Living as the people of the new exodus, avoiding idolatry (10.1—11.1)
11. Abuses in worship (11.2–34)
12. Gifts, love, and worship (12.1—14.40)
13. The resurrection of the body (15.1–58)
14. Instructions about the Collection, final exhortations, and letter closing (16.1–24)

1. Introduction, grace, and thanksgiving (1.1–9)

After the opening greetings, Paul thanks God that the Corinthian church has received so many spiritual gifts (1.4–7). These are both the source of problems and the sign of God's continuing work.

2. Corinthian factions and the folly of the cross (1.10—3.23)

Paul appeals for unity in the face of factionalism. Jesus the crucified Messiah is the only focus of the church's identity. All human standards, and the rhetoric that accompanies them, are brought to nothing by the message of the cross, which carries a different kind of power.[56] The cross, after all, was a scandal to Jews (whoever heard of a crucified Messiah?) and folly to pagans (whoever imagined that an executed Jew might be the lord of the world?). But Paul's message does its own work. To those interested in mysteries, Paul offers the cross. To those who like eloquent speech, Paul offers the gospel. For those who want power, Paul invokes the spirit. Christians do possess wisdom, but it is from a different source and of a different nature. The Corinthians, failing to grasp this, remain 'unspiritual' in their factional quarrels (3.1–4).

When it comes to unspiritual behaviour, Paul uses the example of the rivalry between his own apparent devotees and those of Apollos. Both he and Apollos are mere servants, doing their own part in cultivating the kingdom, but it is God who makes things grow (3.5–9). Like a builder, Paul has laid a foundation, namely Jesus the Messiah himself. Anyone who builds on that will be building a new Temple, a place for God to dwell by the spirit, and God's final judgment will test what kind of work has gone into the building—and whether people have been trying to destroy it (3.10–17). So the Corinthians must be careful, not boastful. They should rejoice that a new world belongs to them, because they belong to the Messiah, and the Messiah belongs to God (3.18–23).

---

[56] See Schnelle 2005, 202–3.

Fountain of Peirene, an impressive monument built over a spring in Corinth. It had mythical significance as the place where Bellerophon tamed his Pegasus.
© 2012 by Zondervan

3. Paul: servant of the Messiah, father in the gospel (4.1–21)

Paul urges the Corinthians to think of him as a servant of Christ and a steward of God's mysteries. He is therefore accountable to God alone, not to humans (4.1–7). His apostolic vocation is to model the sufferings of the Messiah. It is by doing that that he has become their 'father', even though he may look a bedraggled wreck (4.8–13). He is not trying to shame them, but to reprimand them for destructive behaviour. If he is their father, they should imitate him; and they should be ready to come into line when he arrives for his forthcoming visit (4.14–21).

4. Sexual perversity has no place (5.1–13)

Paul now addresses an immediate problem within the church: a woman has been co-habiting with her stepson. Paul calls for him to be disciplined, removed from the church, from the sphere in which the Messiah saves, and sent back into the sphere in which the satan's writ runs (5.1–5). The Corinthians seem to think this is something to boast about: look how free we have become, living on a new plane! No, says Paul: being a Christian does not set you apart from previous moral laws (see 'Portals and parallels: Suetonius on divorce'), but rather reinforces an ethic of true creation, which carries and contextualizes the celebratory reaffirmation of marriage. Compromise will lead to ruin (5.9–13).

> **PORTALS AND PARALLELS: SUETONIUS ON DIVORCE**
>
> *The Roman historian Suetonius tells the tale of a Roman nobleman whom Tiberius permitted to divorce his wife on account of her involvement in a sexual relationship with the man's son.*
>
> Married women guilty of adultery, though not prosecuted publicly, he authorised the nearest relations to punish by agreement among themselves, according to ancient custom. He discharged a Roman *equites* from the obligation of an oath he had taken, never to turn away his wife; and allowed him to divorce her, upon her being caught in criminal intercourse with her son-in-law. (Suet. *Tib.* 35)

5. Lawsuits among believers (6.1–11)

Paul then faces a second issue: Christians bringing lawsuits against one another. This almost certainly meant the wealthier members dragging the poorer before a magistrate; it was the rich who could afford lawyers and if necessary bribe the judge. Paul's response is again Jewish-style eschatology: there is a coming judgment, and God's people ('the saints') will be assisting in doing the judging, so that if there are disputes between Christians they ought to be settled internally (6.1–8). God's kingdom, launched in Jesus' resurrection (15.20–28), will finally be complete, but it will not contain those who have given themselves to certain styles of behaviour that tie them to the old world. The Corinthians need to remember that they have been washed, sanctified, and justified in the name of the lord Jesus Christ and in the spirit of God (6.9–11).

6. The body as temple of the holy spirit (6.12–20)

Paul then addresses sexual morality more directly. Against the Corinthian slogans ('I have the right to do anything' and 'Food for the stomach and the stomach for food'), Paul responds that what we do with our bodies is not morally indifferent. The body belongs to the lord and will be raised, so what we do with it matters. Particularly this applies to sex, where intercourse (chemically as well as psychologically, as we now know) binds people together. The Christian's body is itself a temple of the holy spirit, purchased by the Messiah, and must be treated as such (6.19–20).

7. Marriage, divorce, and singleness (7.1–40)

This leads to wider questions of marriage, divorce, and singleness. Paul here offers careful pastoral wisdom in clear-cut cases (marriage is good, and for life, but singleness for men or women is good too—all of which was counter-cultural in Corinth) and sensitive guidance in 'grey areas', including the permission to divorce (and hence presumably remarry) if a non-Christian spouse wishes to leave a Christian. (We remind ourselves that being a Christian in pagan Corinth would mean a total change of lifestyle, including removing idols large and small from the house, and not taking part in the local cults and idolatrous festivities. An unbelieving spouse might well balk at even some of this renunciation.)

Paul was aware, writing the letter, that times were hard. He speaks of 'the present crisis' (7.26, 29) when he is writing; a famine was on the way (as we know historically), perhaps already making life difficult. His judgment was therefore to keep things as they were and not make life harder by big changes of status. What matters is learning to navigate the 'freedom' that is the Christian's birthright and to distinguish it from the licence that is merely a return to paganism.

8. Food sacrificed to idols (8.1–13)

The switch from the cheerful polytheism of the pagan world to the Jewish-style monotheism of the Christians meant all kinds of dilemmas, an obvious one being diet. Most of the meat in the market would first have been offered to an idol, the remains being sold after the worshipper and/or the priests had had their portions. Recent converts might want nothing to do with the whole business. Paul sees, though, that dualism (rejecting the goodness of the present creation) is almost as bad as paganism itself (worshipping elements in the natural world as if they were divine). He therefore lays down the principle to which he returns at the end of chapter 10 (the discussion takes up three chapters, with chapter 9 being a digression on 'freedom'): there is no God but one, and everything created by God is good and to be received with thanksgiving.

Located right next to the temple of Apollo was the *macellum* or meat market. An inscription found at Corinth declares that Quintus Cornelius Secundus, along with his wife, sons, and daughter, built the meat market along with the fish market.
Todd Bolen / BiblePlaces.com

Paul here quotes (8.6) the foundational prayer of monotheistic Jews: 'Hear, O Israel, the Lord our God, the Lord is one'. However, he modifies it, in one of his most stunning theological moves: if 'God' here refers to the father from whom all things come, *'Lord' refers to Jesus the Messiah through whom all things come*. Jesus is *part of the meaning of the one true God*. This leads to an important ethical principle: if the one God is revealed in the crucified Jesus, then one's freedom to eat anything is strictly limited by the conscience of another believer 'for whom the Messiah died' (8.11).

9. The apostle Paul's rights and struggle (9.1–27)

Paul then explains how Christian 'freedom' works in practice, through his own example. He is 'free', yet is called to singleness (9.1–5). He is free to be paid for his apostolic work, yet has chosen not to make use of the right (9.6–18). He is free from obligations, yet tailors his lifestyle to avoid putting stumbling-blocks in the way of his work with different groups (9.19–23). Freedom does not mean licence, but rather the freedom of an athlete in training, eager to win the prize (9.24–27).

10. Living as the people of the new exodus, avoiding idolatry (10.1—11.1)

This brings Paul back to his concerns about idolatry. His overall point is that one may eat whatever one wishes, provided it is in the right attitude and does not cause offence to fellow-believers—and provided one does not enter an idol-temple itself. Ancient temples were not like contemporary churches; they were more like restaurants, pagan altars, brothels, and rentable business-suites, all rolled into one.

Gulf of Corinth from Acrocorinth

In his warning against such places Paul draws (as often) on the exodus story: Israel, though redeemed from Egypt, committed idolatry and incurred judgment. Paul, hinting that baptism and eucharist are a kind of Christian equivalent of the Israelites' crossing of the Red Sea and wilderness feedings, warns that these great blessings did not render them immune to this fate. That is why he insists that one cannot eat and drink from the lord's table and from the table of demons (10.14–22). Though the old gods of ancient paganism are a sham (8.1–6), there are shadowy, sneaky beings he loosely calls 'demons' (the word had much wider application in his world than in ours) who are out to twist and destroy human life. This brings the whole discussion together: the Corinthians must not use their freedom as a licence to indulge themselves, but must avoid the haunt of demons and seek the good of others. Paul, having explained his own approach to 'freedom', asks them to imitate him as he seeks to imitate the example of Christ (10.23—11.1). This is the same point that he makes in building Philippians 3.2–11 on Philippians 2.6–11.

The temple of Apollo in Corinth
© 2012 by Zondervan

11. Abuses in worship (11.2–34)

Paul's praise for the Corinthians in holding to the traditions that he passed on to them is short-lived. He proceeds to chastise them over the matters of head coverings (11.2–6) and practices of the Lord's Supper (11.17–34).

In Paul's day, gender was marked by hair and clothing styles. Paul, having stressed in Galatians 3.28 that there is 'no "male and female" . . . in the Messiah' (*NTE/KNT*), is anxious that some will take this the wrong way, wrongly imagining that equality before the foot of the cross means androgyny, either gender hybridity or else erasing the differences between men and women. In worship it is important for both men and women to be their truly created selves, to honour God by being male and female and not pretending to be something else.

On the Lord's Supper, Paul is appalled to hear of divisions between rich and poor at a meal supposed to be a visible sign of unity and *koinōnia*. This showed contempt for God's assembled people, treating them as a mere convenience. Paul rehearses Jesus' words of institution, reminding them that the meal invokes and commemorates the Jesus who died, was raised, and will return. Dishonouring the Messiah's body, whether in the form of the meal or the form of the church, is courting disaster.

12. Gifts, love, and worship (12.1—14.40)

Paul now responds to questions about worship, beginning with spiritual gifts. He stresses that these are indeed the work of the spirit, given not to divide the church but to build it up in unity: it is the same spirit, the same lord, the same God at work in all. Various Greek and Roman writers had already spoken of communities in terms of a human body, working for the common good; Paul adapts this picture in his belief that if Israel was God's true humanity, the Messiah has taken on that role (see 15.21–22), and those in the Messiah therefore constitute the genuine human race, for which a human body is thus an appropriate metaphor. Diverse gifts and offices are therefore necessary, as diverse limbs and organs are necessary, and any spiritual snobbery is out of place (12.12–31).

Paul then adds one of the most remarkable lyrics in western civilization, rivalling Homer or Shakespeare in its poignant description of love. The point is not simply a reminder about how to behave. It is a link between chapter 12 (many gifts, one body) and chapter 14 (how to avoid chaotic worship): love is the key to both. It is also a reminder, pointing forwards to chapter 15, that what matters is the future world, the 'age to come', *which has already begun in Jesus and the spirit and will be completed in the end*. Love matters because it is the central characteristic of the new world, and we get to practise it in advance (13.1–13).

This then leads to the question of order and intelligibility in worship. Speaking in tongues is fine, but does not have the same edifying power as the prophesying that can strengthen, encourage, and comfort other worshippers. A healthy diet of worship needs far more than ecstatic utterances; it requires didactic content, through prophesying, revelation, a word of knowledge, or a word of instruction (that is, spiritually animated teaching). Paul, not wishing to stifle spiritual vitality, is concerned that worship should be less ecstatic and more didactic. Spiritual gifts should be used in a balanced and orderly fashion.

Still on the subject of order, Paul adds some remarks against women speaking in church. The passage is not found in the same place in all manuscripts, leading some to regard it as an interpolation. Given that Paul expects both men and women to prophesy in church (see 1 Cor. 11.5), he can hardly be barring women from teaching, praying, or prophesying. More likely, he has in mind women who were perhaps annoyingly interruptive, wanting to discuss matters with their husbands across the small room while various activities like singing and tongues were in progress (14.34–35). However lively worship becomes, it must also have a proper order.

> 'The truth is that the Bible doesn't present us with a uniform set of data from which to extrapolate one hard and fast rule, or a rigid protocol for men and women. In fact, we have a set of data that sometimes baffles us but invites us to dig deep and to explore more.'
>
> Lucy Peppiatt, *Unveiling Paul's Women*, 86.

13. The resurrection of the body (1 Cor. 15.1–58)

Paul comes at last to the question lying underneath so much of the letter. The Christian way of life depends at every point on the belief that with Jesus' resurrection God's new world really was born, and that those who belong to the Messiah must live in the present in the light of their own assured future. Denial of the resurrection—an obvious common-sense point, then as now—undermines this entirely: if there is no future life, why bother? Paul's argument builds up slowly, overturning the normal assumptions of cultures ancient and modern by explaining the meaning of Jesus' resurrection and the nature of our own. What God did for Jesus by raising him from the dead is both the model and the means of what he will do for all Jesus' people.

Paul begins with an important (and apparently official) early formulation of the gospel: that the Messiah died for our sins, was buried, and was raised on the third day, all according to the scriptures. He was then seen, by Cephas, the Twelve, five hundred brothers and sisters, James, all the apostles, and last of all Paul. That is the basis of everything else (15.1–11).

Statue of the emperor Augustus with a customary head-covering as a mark of Roman piety.
Kim Walton, taken at the Ancient Corinth Archaeological Museum

If, then, some are denying the resurrection of the dead, they are denying Jesus' resurrection, cutting off the branch on which, as Christians, they are supposed to be sitting (15.12–19). If the dead are not raised, then the Messiah was not raised, so *the old world is still going on uninterrupted and you are still in your sins* (15.17).

The point is (15.20–28) that with the Messiah's resurrection God's new world has been launched, with Jesus as its lord, the defeat of death itself as its ultimate purpose, and a newborn human race as its means. This chapter ranks with Romans 8 as a major statement of Paul's cosmic vision: God, the creator, has rescued his creation from corruption and decay in raising Jesus, and when the gospel work is complete, God will be 'all in all'.

Paul then drops in a short, jerky paragraph (15.29–34): without resurrection, nothing makes sense. No point in being baptized on behalf of the dead;[57] no point in facing persecution; no point in moral life.

---

[57] The two main options for understanding why people were being baptized for the dead are: (1) some people were seeking baptism because a Christian relative or friend had died and they wanted to be sure of being reunited with them in the life to come; or (2) some people who had come to Christian faith in Corinth had died before being baptized, and other Christians had undergone baptisms on their behalf, completing vicariously the unfinished sacramental initiation of the dead. The practice itself seems to have died out quite early.

This brings Paul to the central question: what will the resurrection body actually be? (15.35–49). His answer, building on the foundation of Genesis 1—2, is that believers will bear the image of the man who is from heaven, that is, the 'final Adam', the Messiah.[58] There are different types of bodies, and in particular Paul distinguishes the present body, animated by the ordinary human nature (*sōma psychikon*) and the future body, animated by God's spirit (*sōma pneumatikon*) (15.44). This does not mean that the future body will be 'spiritual' in the sense of 'immaterial'. The adjectives explain not what the body is made of but what is making it alive.

This means that when the dead are raised, any of the Messiah's people still alive will need to be transformed, since the present corruptible body ('flesh and blood') cannot exist as they stand as part of God's new incorruptible world (15.50–58). Death will be defeated; and spirit-led work in the present will be part of God's new world (15.58).

14. Instructions about the Collection, final exhortations, and letter closing (16.1–24)

Paul now gives practical instructions for organizing the collection for Jerusalem (16.1–4). He outlines his plans for a future visit (16.5–9). He has asked Apollos to visit the church, and, despite some reservations, Apollos will do so when the opportunity arises (16.10–12). Paul adds some exhortation towards steadfastness, courage, and love (16.12–14) before commending Stephanas and his household to the Corinthians (16.15–18). After final greetings, Paul closes the letter with the famous Aramaic *Maranatha* ('Come, our lord!') and wishes of grace and love (16.19–24).

THE ARGUMENT OF 2 CORINTHIANS

(See box: 'Outline of 2 Corinthians'.)

1. Letter opening (1.1–11)

After initial greetings from Paul and Timothy (1.1–2), Paul launches into reflections on sufferings in service and consolation from God (1.3–7). Perhaps explaining his earlier remark about hav-

---

OUTLINE OF 2 CORINTHIANS

1. Letter opening (1.1–11)
2. Paul's defence of his ministry (1.12—2.13)
3. Paul and the ministry of the new covenant (2.14—4.6)
4. Paul's ministry as a paradox of power in weakness (4.7—6.10)
5. Paul seeks reciprocal affections and corporate holiness (6.11—7.16)
6. Paul's call to complete the Collection (8.1—9.15)
7. Paul versus the super-apostles (10.1—13.10)
8. Letter closing (13.11–14)

---

58 See similarly Phil. 3.21.

ing fought 'wild beasts in Ephesus',[59] Paul details the intense troubles and near-death travails that he experienced in Asia, from which God delivered him (1.8–11).

2. Paul's defence of his ministry (1.12—2.13)

Paul's primary concern is continued criticism of himself by the Corinthians. They are still measuring him according to 'worldly' or 'fleshly' wisdom. Paul reaffirms his personal integrity in his dealings with them, and hopes that he and the Corinthians will resume their mutual affection and celebration (1.12–14). Having been criticized about making and then changing plans, Paul retorts that he has not vacillated between 'yes' and 'no'; like the gospel itself, his answer is always 'yes'. Paul displays within his ministry the anointing of the spirit, which calls for an 'Amen', not sneering accusations (1.15–22).

Complaints aside, his reluctance to visit was in order to spare his readers further grief. The former letter he wrote, the 'letter of tears', was meant to elicit repentance while reaffirming his love (1.23—2.4). The leader of the anti-Pauline movement has not so much grieved Paul as grieved the Corinthians themselves; the discipline applied is sufficient, and the Corinthians should now forgive him (2.5–11).

Paul returns to the topic of his travel plans, explaining how he came to Macedonia via Troas in search of Titus (2.12–13).

3. Paul and the ministry of the new covenant (2.14—4.6)

Paul now turns to a broader defence of his ministry (2.14—7.16). His first argument (2.14—4.6) contrasts his work, as a 'new-covenant minister', with that of Moses; Moses' hearers were hard-hearted, but by the spirit's work of covenant renewal the Corinthians' hearts have been transformed. Paul therefore does not need 'letters of recommendation', as some had suggested, since the Corinthians themselves are that letter, the living proof that God has authorized his ministry (3.1-5). Paul contrasts the work of Moses with his own, insisting that his new-covenant apostleship produces the 'freedom' which he uses in speaking to them, and which some find offensive in its rhetorical style. Unlike Moses, he has no need to veil the divine glory. Echoing Genesis 1, Paul insists that he does not lose heart, because the God who said 'Let light shine out of darkness' has shone in the hearts of believers, revealing his glory in the face of the crucified and risen Messiah (4.1–6).

4. Paul's ministry as a paradox of power in weakness (4.7—6.10)

The second phase of Paul's defence of his ministry (4.7—6.10) explains the way in which—against the cultural expectations of the Corinthians—his apostleship is modelled on the suffering of the Messiah, because that is how reconciliation happens.

---

[59] 1 Cor. 15.32.

An urban street in the ancient city of Corinth
© 2015 by Zondervan

He has undergone so much (4.7–18) in the knowledge that a new 'tent' (that is, body) has already been prepared for him, with the spirit as its present guarantee (5.1–5). That final hope, including taking responsibility for his work in the last judgment (5.10), is what drives him on: the Messiah's love leaves him no choice (5.14), since what God did in heaping sin on Jesus' innocent head has generated the new world in which the apostolic vocation, echoing the 'servant' promise in Isaiah 49.6, is to be a living embodiment of God's covenant faithfulness (5.11—6.2), bringing about not only covenant renewal but the new creation, of which believers are now part (5.17). He then returns, in a wonderful rhetorical flourish, to his own life and work: suffering everything yet always rejoicing (6.3–10). Apostleship is built on the foundation of the Messiah himself.

5. Paul seeks reciprocal affections and corporate holiness (6.11—7.16)

The third phase of Paul's defence of his apostolic ministry (6.11—7.4) consists of deeply personal pleas, linked with an exhortation to purity. The central section (6.14—7.1) is not, as some have supposed, an interpolation, but a rehearsal of previous themes of disassociating from a corrupt world (6.14—7.1).[60] Paul's multiple scriptural echoes here insist that, in the Messiah, God has fulfilled his many promises, particularly his promises that he would bring his people back from exile. It is now time for God's people to come home, walking in holiness before him. Paul then resumes his personal pleas by pleading his innocence and pursuing a reciprocation of his affection for the Corinthians, speaking frankly to them, but remaining joyous about them (7.2–4).

---

60 deSilva 1993, 57–64.

This is where, perhaps, Paul's dictation of the letter was interrupted by Titus's arrival with positive news. This produces a fresh celebration (7.5–16), picking up from where he broke off at 2.13.

The *bēma* or judgment seat of Corinth upon which Gallio presided when Paul was hauled before him (Ac. 18.12–16). The word *bēma* also occurs in Paul's remark about all believers one day appearing before the 'judgment seat of Christ' (2 Cor. 5.10).
Phoenix Data Systems

6. Paul's call to complete the Collection (8.1—9.15)

Paul's 'Collection' for Jerusalem began with his meeting with the pillar apostles in Jerusalem, where they asked him to 'remember the poor'.[61] He now urges the Corinthians to make good on their promise to contribute (2 Cor. 8—9).[62] The Macedonian churches are ready; he hopes the Corinthians will be as well. The model, after all, is that of the self-giving of Jesus himself (8.8–9). When those with plenty share with those in need, there is equality among churches (8.10–15). Paul commends Titus and an unnamed co-worker whom he sends to receive the Collection (8.16–24).

Paul has, after all, been telling the Macedonian churches that the Corinthians have been ready, and he wants them to live up to his boast (9.1–5). Generosity

---

[61] Gal. 2.7–9.
[62] While it is often supposed that 2 Cor. 8 and 9 are two separate letters, it is noticeable that the theme of Paul's boasting in the Achaians runs across both sections (2 Cor. 8.24; 9.2–3). Note, too, the way the phrase 'Now it is' (*peri men gar*), which begins 2 Cor. 9.1, ordinarily serves to expound or expand something previously said. See deSilva 1993, 45–7.

Seven columns remain standing at the temple of Apollo.

produces its own harvest; God will supply their needs, enriching them so that they can be more generous again (9.6–11). The Collection is a form of thanksgiving to God, leading to praise of God, and evidencing the surpassing grace they have received (9.12–15).

7. Paul versus the super-apostles (10.1—13.10)

Paul now changes his tone again, to answer the charges that the 'super-apostles' have placed against him. He knows that the only boasting that counts, the only commendations that count, are those in the lord (10.12–18). Faced with the charge of being rhetorically feeble, Paul then produces one of his rhetorical masterpieces, precisely in order to say 'I am not a rhetorician'. He pleads with the Corinthians to indulge him in 'foolishness', and proceeds to 'boast' *of all the wrong things*. After preliminary remarks in a bantering tone but with serious intent (11.5–15), he lists, like a senior Roman civil servant, all his civic achievements: the times he's been beaten up, imprisoned, shipwrecked, and so forth, ending it all with his supreme achievement, running away from Damascus when the going got tough (11.16–33). He has prepared the way for this extraordinary piece of rhetoric with his earlier descriptions of suffering (4.7–15; 6.3–10), indicating perhaps that despite the change of tone, the letter has an underlying thematic unity.

This then spills over into Paul's account of his own 'spiritual experiences'—which turns out to be a vague allusion to something that happened a long time ago about which not much can be said except that it left Paul with a 'thorn in the flesh' (12.1–10). The point he learns from it all is that apostolic status does not come from heroic achievements or celestial experiences, but from sharing the weakness of the gospel itself: 'when I am weak, then I am strong' (12.10). That is the spirit in which he is now coming back to see the Corinthians once more, hoping that he will be able to celebrate their life rather than have to deal once more with persistent sin (12.14–21). His desire, after all, is not to tear them down but to build them up (13.1–10).

8. Letter closing (13.11–14)

The letter ends with a plea for maturity, encouragement, unity, and peace—a fitting way to close a letter responding to the travails of a troubled and troublesome congregation.[63] Paul's final words comprise a beautiful Trinitarian benediction, now used worldwide as a standard liturgical formula: 'May the grace of the Lord Jesus Christ, and the love of God, and the fellowship of the Holy Spirit be with you all' (13.11–14).

1 AND 2 CORINTHIANS AND THE BIG PICTURE

Two short reflections on Paul's correspondence with Corinth. First, the biggest lesson may be the importance of creating a Christ-culture in our churches. Christians often simply reflect the values and behaviours in their surrounding culture. As any experienced missionary will confirm, when a tribe or ethnic group becomes Christian, the people rarely get the whole package at once. More often than not, Christianity simply becomes an add-on to their existing worldview. This can result in a confused semi-Christian worldview, or, in the worst cases, syncretism. It can take years or even a generation for their faith to transform what they believe about gender, outcasts, the spirit-world, or how to relate to old tribal enemies. Nor is this a problem for the Global South only; the western world is even worse, often assuming that its culture is in some sense 'Christian' and hence needing no critique, when many aspects of western culture are every bit as 'pagan' as that of Corinth. The Corinthian believers offer a case-study of a church struggling, and frequently failing, to be like Christ rather than like pagan Corinth; hence Paul's repeated theme of imitation.[64] His theological and pastoral exhortations are aimed at creating a different culture, one characterized by the cross, grace, love, and reconciliation. That is our task too.

Second, these letters show that Christian service takes place in a series of strange paradoxes: power in weakness, triumph in tragedy, strength in vulnerability, and death blossoming into life. Paul's most profound summary of Christian ministry is these words:

> We always carry around in our body the death of Jesus, so that the life of Jesus may also be revealed in our body. For we who are alive are always being given

---

[63] Dunn 2009b, 856–7.
[64] 1 Cor. 4.16; 11.1.

over to death for Jesus' sake, so that his life may also be revealed in our mortal body. So then, death is at work in us, but life is at work in you.[65]

A pastor or servant of Christ's body is called to be a personified Passion-story, a walking and talking parable of Jesus' death and resurrection. That is the living proof that God uses death, vulnerability, and weakness to bring about life, hope, and triumph. Christian ministry is about being outwardly battered and bruised but inwardly renewed; this is why we can rejoice with thanksgiving even amid hardship. To the world, such a life smells of death and defeat, but actually it is spreading an aroma that brings life. To the cultural elites, such people often look pathetic and defeated, but in reality they are champions of God's kingdom. To sophistic professors, their message sounds foolish and dishonourable, but in God's eyes they embody his wisdom and righteousness. To the political powers, they are the scum of the earth, but in God's design they are the ones upon whom the end of ages has come, jars of clay concealing the all-surpassing power of God. How can this be, Paul himself asks. Well, he answers: 'All this is from God, who reconciled us to himself through Christ and gave us the ministry of reconciliation.'[66]

Further reading

Adams, Edward, and David G. Horrell. 2004. *Christianity at Corinth: The Quest for the Pauline Church*. Louisville, KY: Westminster John Knox.
Barnett, Paul. 2011. *Paul: A Pastor's Heart in Second Corinthians*. Sydney: Aquila.
Belleville, Linda L. 1996. *2 Corinthians*. IVPNTC; Downers Grove, IL: InterVarsity.
Ciampa, Roy E., and Brian S. Rosner. 2010. *The First Letter to the Corinthians*. PNTC; Grand Rapids, MI: Eerdmans.
Friesen, Steve J., Daniel N. Schowalter, and James C. Walters (eds.). 2010. *Corinth in Context: Comparative Studies on Religion and Society*. Leiden: Brill.
Garland, David. 2003. *1 Corinthians*. BECNT; Grand Rapids, MI: Baker.
Guthrie, George H. 2015. *2 Corinthians*. BECNT; Grand Rapids, MI: Baker.
Hays, Richard B. 1997. *First Corinthians*. Interpretation; Louisville, KY: Westminster John Knox.
Malcolm, Matthew R. 2012. *The World of 1 Corinthians: An Exegetical Source Book of Literary and Visual Backgrounds*. Eugene, OR: Cascade.
Martin, Dale B. 1999. *The Corinthian Body*. New Haven, CT: Yale University Press.
Mitchell, Margaret. 2005. 'Paul's Letters to Corinth: The Interpretive Intertwining of Literary and Historical Reconstruction.' In *Urban Religion in Roman Corinth*. Edited by D. N. Schowalter and J. Friesen. Cambridge, MA: Harvard University Press, pp. 307–38.
Murphy-O'Connor, Jerome. 2002. *St. Paul's Corinth: Texts and Archaeology*. 3rd edn.; Collegeville, MN: Liturgical.
Peppiatt, Lucy. 2018. *Unveiling Paul's Women: Making Sense of 1 Corinthians 11:2–16*. Eugene, OR: Wipf & Stock.

---

[65] 2 Cor. 4.10–12.
[66] 2 Cor. 5.18.

Perkins, Pheme. 2012. *First Corinthians*. PCNT; Grand Rapids, MI: Baker Academic.
Starling, David S. 2014. *Uncorinthian Leadership: Thematic Reflections on 1 Corinthians*. Eugene, OR: Cascade.
Sumney, Jerry. 2015. *Identifying Paul's Opponents: The Question of Method in 2 Corinthians*. London: Bloomsbury.
Thiselton, Anthony C. 2000. *The First Epistle to the Corinthians*. NIGTC; Grand Rapids, MI: Eerdmans.
Witherington, Ben. 2012. *A Week in the Life of Corinth*. Downers Grove, IL: InterVarsity.

22

Romans

I'm not ashamed of the good news; it's God's power, bringing salvation to everyone who believes—to the Jew first, and also, equally, to the Greek. This is because God's covenant justice is unveiled in it, from faithfulness to faithfulness. As it says in the Bible, 'the just shall live by faith'.[1]

CHAPTER AT A GLANCE

This chapter provides a short survey of Paul's letter to the churches in Rome.

By the end of this chapter you should be able to:

- situate the letter to the Romans in Paul's missionary career;
- describe the structure and argument of Romans;
- identify the main themes and theology of Romans;
- understand critical issues related to the epistle to the Romans.

INTRODUCTION

And so we come to Romans! Paul's letter to the church in Rome ranks high, not just in 'religious' literature, but by any standards of culture, intellect, and overall human wisdom. It is about God and the world; about what it means, and what it might mean, to be truly human; about the complex and contested place of Israel in the world, and in the divine purposes; about how to bring together and hold together a whole new way of being human. And it is about all these things because it is about Jesus, Israel's Messiah and the world's true lord; about the holy spirit, at work to bring all creation to new birth and to refashion human lives as an advance sign of, and means towards, that goal. A carefully planned and skilfully polished work of art, Romans ranges from arguments of Aristotelian density to rhetorical pathos that ranks with (and indeed draws on) the poetry of Isaiah. It is theology in the service of mission; biblical exposition (much of Romans is visibly rooted in Israel's scriptures) in the service of the Christian gospel;

---

1 Rom. 1.16–17.

a mixture of hard thinking and prayerful passion. It is not exactly a 'systematic theology', such as people have written in recent centuries, though it offers vast resources for such a project. It is more of an apostolic testament: in telling the Roman church how he understood the gospel, Paul leaves behind almost a formal record of how he had come to understand his own vocation.

No other book of the Bible has so shaped and renewed the church and its thinking. From St Augustine to Martin Luther to John Wesley to Karl Barth, the church has found fresh fuel for faith and fresh energy for mission when it encounters Romans anew. Joseph Fitzmyer did not exaggerate when he said: 'one can almost write the history of Christian theology by surveying the ways in which Romans has been interpreted.'[2]

Romans is the most wide-ranging theological statement of Paul's views, displayed not as a list of topics to be discussed, but as a single, though many-sided, *argument* for a scripturally shaped vision of the church and its mission. Paul soars on scriptural motifs as he explains how God's righteousness (that is, God's creation-restoring justice and covenant faithfulness) is displayed in the gospel message of Jesus' death, resurrection, and universal sovereignty. This gospel, the shocking fulfilment of Israel's long hope for a new exodus, announces reconciliation between God and rebellious human subjects. In doing so, true to the ancient Jewish vision, it challenges head on the self-aggrandizing propaganda of the Roman empire while subverting and redirecting the great philosophical movements of antiquity.

Romans gives us an indication of what the gospel looks like when it takes root in multi-ethnic churches in the tenements of a pagan city. In Paul's mind, justification by faith means fellowship by faith; baptism into the Messiah and reception of the holy spirit provide the necessary resources for moral transformation; and the lordship of Jesus must enable Christians from very different backgrounds to live together as family despite disagreements over inessentials. The long arc of Paul's thought reaches all the way from 'the just shall live by faith' (1.17 *NTE/KNT*), through being 'justified through faith, we have peace with God' (5.1 NIV) and nothing 'will be able to separate us from the love of God' (8.39 NIV), through 'there is no distinction between Jew and Greek, since the same Lord is Lord of all, and is rich towards all who call upon him' (10.12 *NTV/KNT*), all the way to 'Welcome one another, therefore, as the Messiah has welcomed you' (15.7 *NTE/KNT*).

Romans had a particular practical purpose. Paul was eager to make Rome his base for operations in the western Mediterranean—specifically, his projected trip to Spain—as Antioch had been his base in the east. This was a more complex challenge than it sounds, since, as becomes clear, the Roman church consisted of several

---

[2] Fitzmyer 1993, xiii.

house-churches with significantly different viewpoints, and some of these groups might well be suspicious of him, his theology, and his ecclesial practice. So Paul not only nails his colours to the mast on basic issues of the gospel itself, of how that message about Jesus is the ground for justification by faith, of how that in turn is the key to church unity across ethnic boundaries, of how this sustains a new kind of practical holiness, of how God's age-old plan for Israel is thereby paradoxically fulfilled, and of how the new way of being human thus inaugurated must work out in real-life communities. Paul also lays his cards on the table so that the Romans will open their hearts and homes to him, and give him the practical as well as prayerful support he will need for his ongoing mission.

Romans gives us a vision of what Paul thought he was trying to achieve by his apostolic labours. He was not an itinerant philosopher out to make a quick profit. Nor was he selling a kind of messianic faith as a 'Judaism-lite' option for gentiles looking for a new religious path. He was certainly not trying to add one more deity to the already overcrowded pantheon of Roman gods and goddesses. No, Paul believed that it was his vocation, a very Jewish vocation, rooted in Israel's scriptures, to announce that the promises and purposes of Israel's God had been fulfilled, overcoming the dark powers of evil and thus enabling idol-worshipping, sexually immoral, and ritually impure gentiles to come into the transformative 'obedience of faith'. Thus, by fulfilling Israel's scriptures, the 'Gentiles might glorify God for his mercy', while Jews like Paul himself could celebrate the world-changing achievements of Israel's true Messiah.[3]

Romans provides, if we want to look at it like that, a syllabus of topics to expound: God's righteousness, God's love for sinners, God's super-abounding grace, the hope of glory, adoption to sonship, the indwelling spirit, victory through suffering, a foreign people made God's people, love over law, Torah affirmed and Israel saved, and the Messiah fulfilling God's promises to the patriarchs by calling gentiles into the family of Abraham. If Romans was to be summarized and put on a banner at the front of the church, it might read: 'God demonstrates his own love for us: the Messiah died for us while we were still sinners.'[4]

CONTEXTUAL AND CRITICAL MATTERS

Rome

There were Jews living in Rome at least as early as the mid-second century BC, when the Maccabean rulers of Judea, still anxious about their more immediate neighbours, made an alliance with the Romans. There was a further influx of Jews

---

[3] Rom. 1.5; 15.9; 16.26.
[4] Rom. 5.8 *NTE/KNT*.

into Rome as a result of Pompey's conquest of Palestine in 63 BC, with thousands of Jews brought to Rome as slaves, many of whom were later set free, acquiring Roman citizenship and settling in or around the city.[5] Archaeological evidence reveals several synagogues and funeral inscriptions, indicating a vibrant Jewish community in Rome in the first century.[6] The fortunes of the Jews in Rome were positive under Julius Caesar and Augustus, who granted them special rights: freedom from participation in Roman religion, exemption from military service, and respect for their national customs.[7] Relations deteriorated under Tiberius and Caligula with imperial policies towards the Jews being sometimes decidedly hostile. The reign of Claudius was less tumultuous, but not less problematic for Jews in Rome, and Claudius is known to have expelled many of them from the city on account of disputes involving someone called 'Chrestus', a probable Latinism (or simple mistake) for 'Christos'.[8]

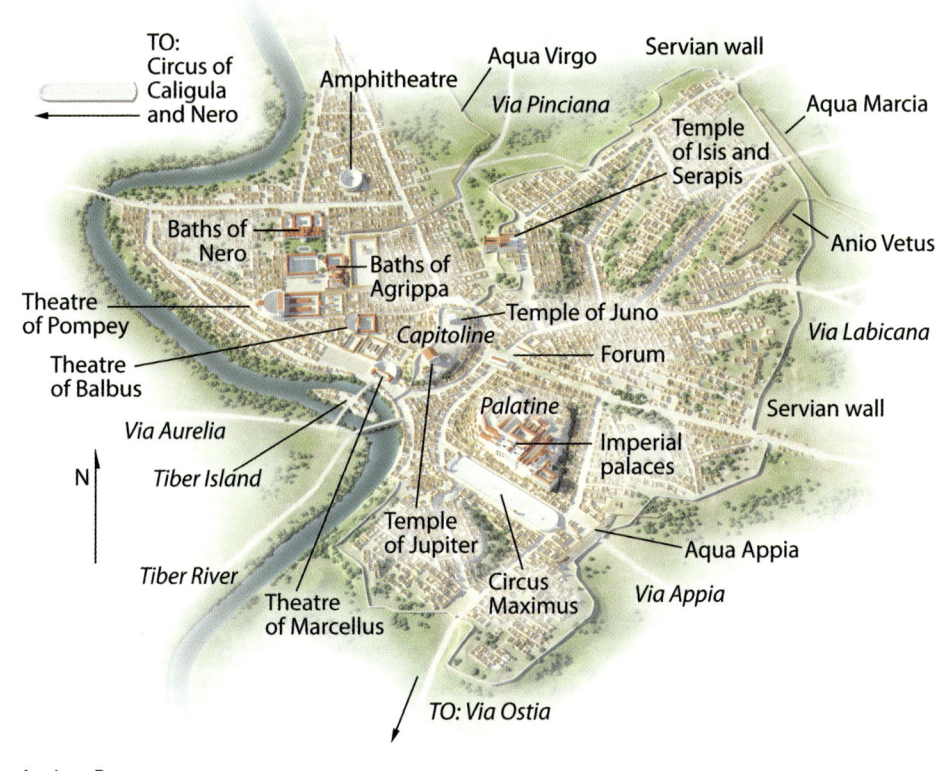

Ancient Rome

---

5 Philo *Gai.* 155.
6 Levine 2011, 105–6.
7 Philo *Gai.* 156–8.
8 Suet. *Claud.* 25.2 and Ac. 18.2.

The Roman forum was the centre of Roman life, containing government buildings, temples, and markets. It was the place for commerce, elections, speeches, and triumphal processions.
pisaphotography / Shutterstock

The church in Rome may well owe its origins, at least in part, to Roman Jews who, visiting Palestine for feasts like Passover or Pentecost, learned about Jesus and then returned to Rome; and also to travelling tradespeople such as Priscilla and Aquila.[9] The role of Peter in the founding of the Roman church, though strongly affirmed in later legends, is impossible to assess with any accuracy.

Paul wrote Romans from Cenchreae, a port-city directly adjacent to Corinth, probably in around AD 56/7. He had just completed an extensive phase of ministry around the eastern Mediterranean, particularly in Greece and western Asia. His plans now were to return to Jerusalem to deliver the collection taken up from the gentile churches, and after that to travel to Rome itself, as he had often longed to do, and then proceed further west to Spain.[10] The three months of respite that Paul spent around Corinth gave him time and opportunity to reflect on his ministry, as well as on the forthcoming journey to Jerusalem and his impending expedition to Spain. He dictated the letter to Tertius (16.22), and entrusted it to Phoebe, his personal benefactor and a deacon in the local church, to deliver it to the Roman congregations. Paul felt himself to be at a point of transition, though it would turn out to be a different kind of transition from what he had expected. He was able to reflect on the past and look ahead to the future.

---

9   Ac. 2.10–11; Rom. 16.3.
10 Ac. 20.2–3; Rom. 1.13; 15.22–29; 16.1.

The purpose of Romans

So why exactly did Paul write this letter? Romans is many times longer than the average first-century letter; Philemon or 3 John would be more typical. It is more like a letter-treatise than a piece of personal correspondence.

From early times many have seen Romans as something like a theological treatise, or a summation of Paul's beliefs. The Muratorian canon (late second century) described the letter as written 'concerning the plan of the Scriptures, showing that their foundation is Christ'. Among the Reformers, Luther regarded Romans as Paul's summary of Christian and evangelical teaching. Similarly, Luther's friend Melanchthon, in his *Loci Communes Theologici*, labelled Romans a 'compendium of Christian doctrine'. More recently, others have identified Romans as a summary of Pauline teaching drawn from his various letters, a theological testament to his life's work, or even a dress rehearsal for his defence of himself in Jerusalem.[11] There is at least a grain of truth in all this. Dunn suggests that

> Paul's primary objective . . . was to think through his gospel in the light of the controversies which it had occasioned and to use the calm of Corinth to set out both his gospel itself and its ramifications in writing with a fullness of exposition which the previous trials and tribulations had made impossible and which would have been impossible to sustain in a single oral presentation.[12]

However, while Romans is undoubtedly the most theologically comprehensive expression of Paul's beliefs, it is unlikely to be a 'theological treatise' as such. (1) It fails to say much about key topics such as the holy spirit, the church, and the second coming. (2) Paul's letters were always situational, and Romans is no different: the beginning and ending of the letter focus on specific details related to Paul's ministry, his travel plans, specific warnings, and so on; and chapters 14 and 15 in particular are clearly directed at the actual situation of Rome itself in a way that would not have been so relevant for many other churches.[13]

Given the situational nature of Romans, two main options have presented themselves for determining the letter's purpose. (1) Was the letter occasioned by circumstances specific to Paul's own situation and ministry? Or (2) was the letter occasioned by the perceived need to address some kind of internal problem in the Roman house-churches?

On the one hand, it is clear that Paul was writing to secure support from the Roman churches for a forthcoming mission to Spain.[14] Accordingly, several scholars

---

11 See several studies in Donfried 1991 and survey in Das 2006.
12 Dunn 2009b, 867.
13 Rom. 1.1–15; 15.14–16.27.
14 Rom. 15.24–28.

have regarded the letter as principally designed to induce the Romans to give material support for Paul's ongoing mission. Luke Timothy Johnson goes so far as to call Romans, in essence, a fundraising letter.[15] The problem, of course, is whether one would write such an elaborate and lengthy letter simply to solicit funds. Granted that, in order to get the support of the Roman churches, Paul would have had to lay out his gospel at length, to show how his vision of God's overall plan worked out in relation both to the Jewish traditions and to the new dynamic of the gospel. But even that would hardly account for the whole letter. The latter half of Romans in particular demands explanation in terms beyond Paul's own situation. It must be addressed to situations and sensitivities in Rome itself.

If that is so, on the other hand, it makes sense to suppose that Paul is indeed writing to address a particular situation of which he has heard through friends like Priscilla and Aquila. Some have supposed that Claudius's expulsion of a substantial number of Jews, including Jewish Christians, from Rome in AD 49 had a significant impact on the shape of Christianity in Rome during that period. The vacuum created by the absence of Jewish Christians would mean that the churches were now almost entirely gentile. Many in Rome were in any case prejudiced against the Jews and would have been happy to see them go; it may be that some gentile Christians in Rome, anticipating Marcion by a century or so, drew the conclusion that despite its originally Jewish foundation this new Jesus-movement was now for gentiles only. (Ironically, this conclusion is matched by some recent scholars who, thinking to defend Paul from anti-Judaism, have suggested that his gospel was aimed only at gentiles since in their view Jews did not need it.)[16] But when Claudius died in AD 54, and Nero became emperor, Claudius's edicts were cancelled. Many Jews, including many Jewish Christians, then returned to Rome.[17] There they may well have discovered that their gentile fellow-believers had not only taken over the house-churches but had implemented policies (on food, for instance) which might make it harder for Jewish Christians to belong or take part. According to this reconstruction, Paul wrote Romans to effect a reconciliation between the 'strong' (that is, gentile believers) and the 'weak' (Jewish-Christian believers).

Much of this is probably correct, but some problems remain. First, Paul never mentions the expulsion and return of Jewish Christians; this might be because it was too obvious to mention, or it might mean that it was not so significant—or it might mean that, as in Romans 14 itself, Paul was trying precisely not to name the underlying issue, lest it stir up existing prejudice, but was wishing to engage first at the level of specifics. Second, we should not automatically assume that the 'strong' were gentile Christians and the 'weak' were Jewish Christians. Paul himself, after

---

15 Johnson 2001a, 6–9.
16 See e.g. Eisenbaum 2010.
17 Ac. 18.2; Rom. 16.3.

all, was a 'Jewish Christian' who considered himself 'strong' in respect to the Jewish food laws.[18] One can easily imagine gentile believers, former God-fearers or proselytes, with a history of Torah-observance, who remained keen to avoid their former idolatry and consequent lifestyle, and would be reluctant to leave the Jewish laws they had come to cherish.

The most likely scenario is that Romans was written for several overlapping and converging reasons. The Roman church may well have been predominantly gentile (see Rom. 1.13; 11.13), but Paul was keen to include the Jewish Christians among his addressees, and refers to his hearers as 'those who know the law' (Rom. 7.1). He is not only planning his trip to Spain; he is also, first, intending to go to Jerusalem with the Collection (Rom. 1.13; 15.24–25). All this implies that he wishes to do two things in particular.

First, he must win the Roman church over to his account of the gospel. This is itself many-sided, rooted in Israel's traditions and promises and yet focused on the crucified and risen Messiah through whom the divine purposes had now spread out into the world. He nuances his account, making it clear both that those 'in the Messiah' are 'not under the law' and that this has nothing to do with what we might call a proto-Marcionite rejection of Israel, the Jewish people, and the God-givenness of Torah itself. Paul wants the Roman believers to exemplify a 'faithful obedience' among the gentiles (Rom. 1.5; 16.26). Since he cannot be there in person to impart a spiritual gift to them, or reap a full harvest by preaching the gospel in Rome just yet, he does the next best thing. He imparts to them

OUTLINE OF ROMANS

1. **Unveiling God's righteousness (1—4)**
   a. Introductions, greetings, and defence of Paul's travel plans (1.1–15)
   b. Thesis statement (1.16–17)
   c. Gentiles and Jews condemned, God's purposes remaining (1.18—3.20)
   d. Covenant fulfilled through faith for faith (3.21—4.25)
2. **From new covenant to new creation (5—8)**
   a. Assurance based on cross and spirit (5.1–11)
   b. Launching the new humanity (5.12–21)
   c. The new exodus: baptism and freedom (6.1–23)
   d. The law and the spirit (7.1—8.11)
   e. Spirit and new creation (8.12–30)
   f. Nothing shall separate us from God's love (8.31–39)
3. **God's faithfulness and Israel's unbelief (9—11)**
   a. Paul's grief (9.1–5)
   b. God's plan in Israel's history (9.6–29)
   c. God's covenant-faithfulness in the gospel (9.30—10.21)
   d. God's abiding faithfulness (11.1–36)
4. **Faithfulness and fellowship in the wider world (12—16)**
   a. The transformed mind and its effects (12.1–21)
   b. Living between the times (13.1–14)
   c. Growing towards unity (14.1—15.12)
   d. Missionary plans and closing greetings (15.13—16.27)

---

18 Rom. 14.14; 15.1.

the blessing of his gospel instruction, hoping that it will strengthen and encourage them (Rom. 1.9–13).

Second, Paul is required to do some preventive pastoral care. Paul knows the dangers that the churches in Rome face. There might be anti-Paulinists arriving in Rome (Rom. 16.17–18). The house-churches might fragment over questions of Torah-observance, exacerbated by the expulsion and return of the Jews. The churches need to navigate the perils of living in a pagan society (Rom. 12—13). Gentile Christians must not imitate the vehement anti-Judaism of Roman cultural elites (Rom. 9—11). The church needs to understand the interlocking nature of Jewish and gentile missions (Rom. 1.16; 10.14–21; 11.13–33; 15.8–9, 27). Those who follow the Messiah will suffer for it (Rom. 8.18–39; 16.20). In sum, Romans is a gospel-based exposition and exhortation; a masterpiece of missionary theology, christological exegesis, pastoral care, and artful rhetoric—all designed to win over the many strands of early Roman Christianity to Paul's gospel, to lend practical support to his mission in Spain and moral support for his immediate visit to Jerusalem, to draw Jewish and gentile Christians in Rome closer together, to strengthen them in their faith despite the perils of Roman culture. All this is woven together into a powerful symphonic form, whose fast pace cannot hide its theological depth and power.

THE ARGUMENT OF ROMANS

Romans, quite unlike any of Paul's other letters, falls into four clear sections: chapters 1—4, 5—8, 9—11, and 12—16 (see box: 'Outline of Romans'). The only debated point is the link between the first two: like Mendelssohn's Violin Concerto, the first two 'movements' are linked, so that some have seen 5.1–11, or even chapter 5 as a whole, as belonging with and summing up chapters 1—4 just as much as they are introducing chapters 5—8. And, to continue the musical analogy, all four movements are linked in numerous ways, with particular themes, words, and scriptural expositions providing a rich, dense texture of interlocking ideas. The older popular belief that Romans 1—4 was concerned with 'justification' and 5—8 with 'sanctification' or perhaps 'salvation', leaving 9—11 as a detached treatise on the Jews and 12—16 as a practical conclusion, has been demonstrated to be too shallow by half. To look no further, the theme of God's righteousness, expounded in chapters 1—4, with its accompanying exposition of the story of Abraham, continues not in chapters 5—8 but in chapters 9—11, with 5—8 therefore functioning both as a triumphant conclusion to one strand of argument in the first section and also as simultaneously heightening the problem to be addressed in 9—11 and providing the tools by which that problem can be addressed. Similar things could be said about the link of all the earlier sections with the fourth: to put it very simply, 'justification by faith' in chapters 3 and 4 must issue in 'fellowship by faith' as in chapters 14 and 15.

This is just to scratch the surface, but such scratches may give an indication of the kind of document we are dealing with.

1. Unveiling God's righteousness (1—4)

The question of 'God's righteousness' resonates through the second-Temple Jewish world. Daniel 9 draws the threads together: why had the exile happened? Because *God was in the right* and Israel had sinned. Why could Israel be sure that God would nevertheless rescue his people? Because, again, he was in the right. The theme goes back to Deuteronomy: God will be faithful to the covenant, but if Israel sins, exile will result, until God renews the hearts of his people and so rescues them at last (Dt. 27—32, a vital passage for Paul, not least in Romans). The problem reached its height for the Jewish people with the destruction of Jerusalem in AD 70. The author of *4 Ezra*, lamenting over this and wrestling with the theological meaning, framed the question in terms of God's righteousness. What did the covenant mean, if all this could happen?

For Paul, the events concerning Jesus raised these questions in a different but equally acute form—and also answered them in an unexpected way, which turned out, so Paul believed, to be what Genesis, Deuteronomy, Isaiah, the Psalms, and many other texts had been indicating all along. The problem of human sin and what was to be done about it, which loomed so large in the sixteenth century in the Protestant Reformation, is extremely important, but for Paul it is framed within the even more important question: what is happening to the creator's plans for his creation, and how is his covenant with Israel (to which he will be faithful) going to address that problem at last? Romans 1—4 is Paul's preliminary answer. It will need the rest of the letter both to be worked through in principle and applied in practice to the particular situations Paul was facing (see above). It was part of his genius to see that the immediate problems he wanted to address demanded, and could be addressed from within, a fresh exposition of what we might even call 'biblical theology', the scriptural narrative of how the creator God had chosen Israel, itself sharing the problem of the human race, to be the means of rescuing humans and the whole creation and thus re-establishing his plan for the cosmos.

> 'What is so disruptive about Paul's understanding of salvation is his challenge to us to hear the gospel in its vastness. The vastness of what God has accomplished is far larger than the word "salvation" usually suggests. Of course, God's action in the gospel speaks to the lives of individuals, to what we often refer to as the "spiritual" life. And, of course, God's action reaches beyond the "spiritual" to include the redemption of our institutions, the reconciliation of ethnic groups, and the confrontation of empires of all sorts. If we think that God's power is restricted to the sphere of the "spiritual," then we have a fairly small notion of God. What we also need to hear is Paul's understanding that the gospel encompasses the cosmos, the whole of creation—all the way out and all the way down in human life.'
>
> Beverly Gaventa, *When in Romans*, 46.

BLAST FROM THE PAST: MARTIN LUTHER ON THE 'RIGHTEOUSNESS OF GOD'

Martin Luther, early in his life as a monk, contemplated with dread the iustitia Dei *('righteousness of God') in Romans 1.17 of his Latin Bible, seeing it as God's righteous judgment of sinners. However, in 1515 Luther happened upon a new way of understanding the phrase, seeing it as the divine righteousness that is given to sinners to acquit them. Luther noted years later:*

> I had greatly longed to understand Paul's Epistle to the Romans, and nothing stood in the way but one expression, 'the justice of God,' because I took it to mean that justice whereby God is just and deals justly in punishing the unjust. My situation was that, although an impeccable monk, I stood before God as a sinner troubled in conscience, and I had no confidence that my merit would assuage him. Therefore I did not love a just and angry God, but rather I hated and murmured against him. Yet I clung to the dear Paul and had a great yearning to know what he meant. Night and day I pondered until I saw the connection between the justice of God and the statement that 'the just will live by his faith.' Then I grasped the truth that the justice of God is that righteousness whereby, through grace and sheer mercy, he justifies us by faith. Thereupon I felt myself to be reborn and to have gone through open doors into paradise. The whole of Scripture took on a new meaning, and whereas before 'the justice of God' had filled me with hate, now it became to me inexpressibly sweet in greater love. This passage of Paul became to me a gateway to heaven.*

* Martin Luther, 'Preface to Latin Writings', in Luther 1955–2016, 34.226–37.

(a) Introductions, greetings, and defence of Paul's travel plans (1.1–15)

The letter opens with Paul's self-identification as a servant of the Messiah and an apostle who was set apart for the gospel of God. Paul here defines 'the gospel' in terms of the scripture-fulfilling events of Israel's Messiah, Jesus, declared publicly in his resurrection to be 'son of God in power' (1.1–4). Paul has received through Jesus the grace of apostleship to bring gentiles to the 'obedience of faith'; the Roman believers are among those who have received this call (1.5–6).

Paul thanks God for the Roman Christians, because news of their faith is being reported all over the world. He has longed to see them, and explains that he had tried many times but had been inhibited. When he does arrive, he hopes to have a harvest among them, just as he has had elsewhere. He is, after all, under obligation to all people, Greeks and barbarians, wise and foolish alike (1.13–15).

(b) Thesis statement (1.16–17)

Romans 1.16–17 functions, in rhetorical terms, as the *propositio*, the central thesis of the letter. Paul is 'not ashamed of the gospel', because 'it's God's power, bringing salvation to everyone who believes—to the Jew first, and also, equally, to the Greek' (*NTE/KNT*). He is referring back to 'the gospel' summarized in the opening verses: the message about Jesus carries divine power. This is so because in that message 'the righteousness of God is revealed' (see 'Blast from the past: Martin Luther on the "righteousness of God"').

The temple of Vesta, the goddess of the hearth, which was served by the vestal virgins.
IR Stone / Shutterstock

In other words, when someone announces that the crucified Jesus has been raised, is Israel's Messiah, and is the world's true lord, that message itself functions to pull aside the curtain and reveal to the watching world that there is a creator God, that he is the God of Israel, and that *he has done what he had always promised* in the covenant with Israel, rescuing the whole creation from chaos and death. 'The righteousness of God' (*dikaiosynē theou*) is not, then, the righteous status which people receive as a gift *from* God (see Rom. 4.11; 5.17; Phil. 3.9). That follows from God's faithful, saving action, but is not what the phrase itself refers to. As in Isaiah and the Psalms, it is God's own in-the-right-ness, his faithfulness to both covenant and creation (see 'Portals and parallels: the righteousness of God in Jewish literature'). Romans is not least a book about God himself; God is mentioned significantly more often in this letter than in any other. The gospel discloses that God has rendered his verdict against evil on Jesus' cross and has enacted his rescue of creation in Jesus' resurrection. Accordingly:

> the death and resurrection of Jesus the Messiah form the initial disclosure of God's righteousness, the major apocalyptic event that burst upon an unsuspecting world and an uncomprehending Israel; now the apocalypse happens again every time the message about Jesus is announced, as God's righteousness is unveiled before another audience.[19]

---

[19] Wright *Romans*, 10.424.

This revelation is 'from faith to faith', a compressed Greek phrase needing to be unpacked further in 3.21—4.25. God's faithfulness is answered by human faith (the Greek for 'faith' and 'faithfulness' is the same). Paul cites Habakkuk 2.4, from a book precisely about the apparent disaster that was befalling Israel, what God was doing about it, and what God's people should be doing in the meantime.

(c) Gentiles and Jews condemned, God's purposes remaining (1.18—3.20)

Gentiles and Jews, Paul explains, are all in the dock before God, guilty with no excuse. God's purposes not only *for* Israel but *through Israel for the world* remain; God will be faithful; but how this can be so when all humans, Israel included, are sinful remains to be seen.

The fundamental charge of 1.18 is that all humans are *ungodly* and *unjust*. In stereotypical Jewish fashion, Paul sees the underlying problem not as 'sin' itself, but as the failure of worship through idolatry, which leads to all evil. Paul echoes Genesis 1—3: God's purposes for humans have been aborted because humans have rebelled, resulting in radical distortions of the creator's purposes (1.18-32). Many moralists, both pagan and Jewish, would heartily agree, but Paul turns the tables on them as well and declares that final judgment is on the way, with the Messiah himself as the appointed judge (2.1-16). In that judgment there will be some who are 'seeking the life of the age to come' by their patience in doing good, but Paul has not yet begun to explain how such people can exist, granted the blanket condemnation of all.

Was not Israel, however, called to be the means of putting the world right (2.17-20)? Yes indeed, but the prophets themselves declared (and virtually all second-Temple Jews would have agreed) that Israel had failed in this vocation, suffering the ongoing 'exile' spoken of in Daniel 9 and referred to by many writers in the period (2.21-24). In fact, if God were to create the sort of people spoken of in Deuteronomy 30 or Jeremiah 4.4; 9.25-26—a new-covenant people whose hearts had been softened so that they were able to 'do the law' in a whole new way—then that would fulfil scripture in a whole new way, even redefining the word 'Jew' in the process (2.15-29). That, however, might seem to call into question God's faithfulness: did he not call Israel for a purpose? What if national Israel lets him down? He will be faithful anyway, replies Paul, without yet explaining how (3.1-8). This then leaves the dilemma, both for all humans as they stand guilty before God, with Torah witnessing against them, and for God himself (3.9-20). How will he then be 'righteous', true to the covenant and thereby to his whole creation?

(d) Covenant fulfilled through faith for faith (3.21—4.25)

God has done what he promised. This is now central. Paul explains what the cross has achieved (3.21-31) in order then to show that God has thereby been faithful to the covenant made with Abraham in Genesis 15. The result is that,

PORTALS AND PARALLELS: THE RIGHTEOUSNESS OF GOD IN JEWISH LITERATURE

Reference to the 'righteousness of God' or 'God's righteousness' has a long history in Jewish tradition, prevalent in the Jewish scriptures and in second-Temple Jewish literature.

- Your righteousness is like the highest mountains, your justice like the great deep. (Ps. 36.6)
- The LORD has made his salvation known and revealed his righteousness to the nations. He has remembered his love and his faithfulness to Israel; all the ends of the earth have seen the salvation of our God. (Ps. 98.2–3)
- Listen to me, my people; hear me, my nation: Instruction will go out from me; my justice will become a light to the nations. My righteousness draws near speedily, my salvation is on the way, and my arm will bring justice to the nations. The islands will look to me and wait in hope for my arm. Lift up your eyes to the heavens, look at the earth beneath; the heavens will vanish like smoke, the earth will wear out like a garment and its inhabitants die like flies. But my salvation will last for ever, my righteousness will never fail. (Isa. 51.4–6)
- Lord, in keeping with all your righteous acts, turn away your anger and your wrath from Jerusalem, your city, your holy hill . . . Give ear, our God, and hear; open your eyes and see the desolation of the city that bears your Name. We do not make requests of you because we are righteous, but because of your great mercy. (Dan. 9.16–18)
- As for me, if I stumble, God's loving-kindness forever shall save me. If through sin of the flesh I fall, my justification will be the righteousness of God which endures for all time . . . By His righteous truth has He justified me; and through His exceeding goodness shall He atone for all my sins. By His righteousness shall He cleanse me of human defilement and the sin of humankind—to the end that I praise God for His righteousness, the Most High for His glory. (1QS 11.12, 14–15; tr. Wise, Abegg, and Cook [2005])
- Then I blessed the Lord of glory and said: 'Blessed be my Lord, the Lord of righteousness, who reigns forever and ever.' (*1 En.* 22.14)
- Depart, therefore, from all unrighteousness, and cleave unto the righteousness of God, and your race will be saved for ever. (*T. Dan* 6.10–11)
- For in this, O Lord, your righteousness and goodness will be declared, when you are merciful to those who have no store of good works. (*4 Ez.* 8.36 NRSV)

as promised there, a single family has come into being, a sin-forgiven family consisting of gentiles and Jews on equal terms, with the only sign of membership being the 'faith' which, believing the gospel, matches the 'faithfulness' with which Israel's Messiah had fulfilled, by himself, the vocation of Israel. The resonances of Isaiah 40—55 which many have heard in this letter, not least in a passage like 4.24–25, and indeed in the theme of 'God's righteousness' itself, provide Paul with a central clue: the Messiah represents Israel, doing for God and thereby for the world what nobody else could do or had done.

In doing so, the Messiah has become the place where the faithfulness of God at last meets the answering faithfulness of the human race. Most ancient cultures saw the divine and human spheres meeting mysteriously and dangerously in sacred space, whether temples or other shrines. Paul, perhaps echoing an earlier formulation, refers to Jesus as the 'mercy seat', the lid placed over the ark of the covenant, the place where and the means by which Israel's God had promised to meet with his people in grace. The tight formula of 3.24–26 brings together what later theology has called 'incarnation' (God himself coming to dwell as a human among humans) and 'atonement' (God providing the means by which human sin, which would otherwise prevent his dwelling with humans, can be blotted out). The blood of the Levitical sacrifices was never a sign of an animal being punished vicariously (Paul believes in Jesus' death as vicarious punishment, as we see in 8.3–4, but this passage is saying something else). It was, rather, the cleansing agent by which all impurity, including sin, would be wiped clean, so that the living God could come in glory to dwell with his people. That is what God has done in Jesus, making it possible for all who believe (who share Messiah-faith) to be declared to be his people indeed. That is the meaning of 3.21–26, one of Paul's many dense and difficult statements of the meaning of the cross.

The immediate result, vital for Paul's whole argument, is that Jews and gentiles alike constitute the renewed family, characterized by nothing other than this Messiah-faith (3.27–31). Paul sees this as the fulfilment of nothing short of Israel's celebrated monotheism: one God, one people (3.29–30). The law is thereby fulfilled—a paradox, since this unveiling of God's righteousness is 'apart from the law', since otherwise only Jews would benefit from it (3.21, 31). This paradox, of God's good law being simultaneously set aside and fulfilled, will recur throughout the letter.

Russian fresco of Abraham sacrificing Isaac
Alamy Stock Photo

The result, in chapter 4, is that all those who believe in 'the God who raised Jesus from the dead' constitute the single family promised by covenant to Abraham. Abraham's own faith in the God who promised to give him this family despite his and Sarah's old age becomes the paradigm for the faith by which the sin-forgiven family is now marked out.

This raises two questions in particular. First, how then does this extraordinary news (that sinners are 'justified' by grace through faith) work out? Second, what then must be said about Abraham's own physical family, the 'Israel' that has failed to respond in faith to the message about its own Messiah? Paul answers these questions in chapters 5—8 and 9—11.

2. From new covenant to new creation (5—8)

Chapters 5—8 present a carefully planned summary of the way in which God's action in the Messiah and the spirit provide 'redemption' for the world. 'Redemption' to ancient Israel often meant the exodus, and these chapters appear to retell that story. Thus chapter 6 echoes the rescue of the slaves, coming through the water of baptism; chapter 7 presents the paradox of the Torah, given by God on Sinai yet apparently serving only to increase the grip of sin; chapter 8 (one of Paul's most glorious passages) expounds the saving work of God through the Messiah's death and resurrection and the gift of the spirit, so that God's redeemed people, like the Israelites in the desert, are being led through trials and tribulations to their final 'inheritance', which turns out to be the entire renewed creation. All this is based on the unbreakable 'love' of God, that covenant love celebrated in scripture and now revealed in personal action in Jesus. Paul underlines this last point by rounding off almost every paragraph of this section with a reference to what God has done either 'through Jesus the Messiah' or 'in Messiah Jesus'.

(a) Assurance based on cross and spirit (5.1–11)

The first paragraph of chapter 5 makes explicit where the argument has now got to. The love of God, displayed in the death of his 'son', guarantees that those who are justified by faith are indeed reconciled to God and will inherit his 'glory'—the divine glory which dwelt in the Temple, and the human glory (see Ps. 8.5) which, as in chapter 8, consists of men and women sharing the Messiah's rule over the new creation. The key factor here (hinted at already in 2.25–29) is the spirit, who will implement the Messiah's achievement in the transformed lives of his people.

(b) Launching the new humanity (5.12–21)

This assurance enables Paul to summarize the entire sweep of saving history. God's call to Abraham was designed to reverse and undo the sin of Adam and its consequences; by fulfilling those promises (Rom. 4) through the Messiah's faithful obedience (there are echoes here of Phil. 2.6–11), God has inaugurated the long-awaited new humanity. Within this narrative, Torah has the necessary but paradoxical role of increasing 'trespass', but this too has a saving purpose, as will be explained in 7.1—8.11. The Adam–Christ typology here could be seen as an extended commentary on 1 Corinthians 15.22 and 15.56: 'For as in Adam all die, so in Christ all will be made alive . . . The sting of death is sin, and the power of sin is the law.' With Genesis 3 in the background, Paul explains not only that Adam's sin brought death, but that the giving of Torah to Israel did not fix the problem, but rather accentuated and focused it. Adam's trespass, however, is then superseded by Jesus' saving obedience.

(c) The new exodus: baptism and freedom (6.1–23)

So where do believers find themselves on this map? Whose jurisdiction are they under? Are they still 'in Adam'? Paul insists that baptism, like the crossing of the Red Sea (compare 1 Cor. 10.1–4), brings them out of the 'old humanity' and into the new, messianic humanity. The slaves have been set free—and, like those in the wilderness generation, have to learn the difficult lessons of living accordingly.

(d) The law and the spirit (7.1—8.11)

Paul then returns to the question of the Torah. Like the civil law binding a woman to a husband, Torah binds Israel—not to God, as might have been supposed, but to the sinful Adamic state. Torah reveals and emphasizes that Israel, the promise-bearing people, are also 'in Adam'. But if 'the old

Fresco of Abraham from Dura Europos, one of the earliest known synagogues, dated *c.* AD 245.
Z. Radovan / www.BibleLandPictures.com

Third-century fresco of baptism from the catacombs of San Callisto, Rome.
Bridgeman Images

man' has died, as in chapter 6, those 'in the Messiah' are free, not from 'the law' as an abstract principle ('moralism', and so forth—though there is truth there too) but from the Torah which, as in Deuteronomy 27—29, insists that the result of covenant disobedience will be exile.

Romans 7.5–6 sums up the sequence of thought: the old state, further expounded in 7.7–25, and the new, expounded in the whole of chapter 8. Paul then describes the arrival of Torah in Israel in terms which echo the 'fall' story in Genesis 3 (7.7–12), and the continuing state of Israel under Torah in terms which end in exile, in Israel being a 'prisoner of war' (see 7.23), seeing how wonderful Torah is but finding that embracing it merely increases the presence and power of sin. No doubt there are many analogies with different moods and moments in Christian moral struggles, but Paul's fundamental point is to explain the work of Messiah and spirit within the larger historical narrative of God's saving purposes.

Paul then clarifies, in far more density of detail than had been possible in 3.21–26 or 5.6–11, how the cross and the spirit achieve God's plan for rescuing humans. Through Torah, sin has been heaped up into one place, namely, Israel itself (as in 5.20), but with a single purpose in view: that 'sin' could finally be condemned in that place, in the person of Israel's representative Messiah (8.3). This is where Paul states most clearly how it is that the Messiah, representing Israel and hence the world, has borne in himself the condemnation of sin: 'there is no condemnation' for his people (8.1), because God has condemned sin in the Messiah's flesh (8.3). But this is no abstract transaction. Because 'sin' has been condemned, the new life of the resurrection, put into operation through the spirit, is now at work to set the Messiah's people free from sin in the present (8.5–8) and free from death itself when they are raised from the dead (8.9–11).

> 'Paul's understanding of interchange is therefore one of interchange *in Christ*. It is achieved, on the one hand, by Christ's solidarity with mankind, on the other, by our solidarity with Christ. The former idea can be conveniently summed up in the non-Pauline term "incarnation"; the latter concerns our incorporation into Christ, and dying and rising with Christ. It is because Christ himself shared in the condition of being "Adam", that man is now offered the possibility of entering a new kind of existence.'
>
> Morna Hooker, *From Adam to Christ*, 27.

(e) Spirit and new creation (8.12–30)

The spirit, then, leads the Messiah's people (8.12–14) to their inheritance, the renewed and reborn creation itself (8.19–23). They share the Messiah's 'sonship', his inheritance, his suffering—though Romans 8 is one of the most joyful chapters in scripture, it is blunt and explicit about the suffering that will accompany the present journey—and his 'glory', which as in Psalm 8.5–8 refers to their sovereignty over the world. In the present this sovereignty is exercised through suffering itself and particularly the prayer which, precisely in its pain and puzzlement, is what happens when the spirit, indwelling the Messiah's people, calls to the father from the place where creation is groaning in labour-pains (8.26–27). Thus the divine purpose is worked out, with humans shaped according to the Messiah-pattern, and God 'glorifying' those whom he 'justified' (8.30).

(f) Nothing shall separate us from God's love (8.31–39)

The final paragraph of the section is a celebration of the unbreakable grasp of divine love. God gave his son; he will give us all things with him. Divine covenant-love, the underlying and driving theme of Deuteronomy, the Psalms, and Isaiah (among Paul's favourite passages, echoed again here), is not wishful thinking. The actual events of the Messiah's death and resurrection guarantee it for all his people.

3. God's faithfulness and Israel's unbelief (9—11)

Romans 9—11 is another extremely careful and balanced piece of writing. It is arguably a 'chiasm', with the different sections balancing one another and drawing the eye and ear to the central statement, which comes in 10.5–13.[20] This is how it appears to work:

```
   9.1–5                                       11.33–36
       9.6–29                              11.1–32
           9.30–33                  10.18–21
               10.1–4    10.14–17
                     10.5–13
                (focused on 10.9)
```

Like some psalms, the section opens with lament and ends with praise, with meditation and petition in between. Also like some psalms, it retells the story of Israel from a particular point of view, bringing into focus the puzzles of Israel's history and holding them within the overall divine promise. The section serves a *theological* purpose: can God really be trusted if he seems to have gone back on his word to his people? It also serves a sharply *practical* purpose, oriented particularly towards the Roman church: gentile Christians must not suppose that God has in fact abandoned the Jewish people, as though from now on the Jesus-movement would be for gentiles only. The whole passage has often been misunderstood by those who have seen the story of Israel simply in terms of advance examples of an abstract salvation and ethical code, for whom Romans could just as well have proceeded from chapter 8 to chapter 12 without this supposed 'excursus'. That merely shows the shocking extent to which many generations of readers ignored what Paul had been saying in

---

20 See Wright *PFG*, 1156–258.

the first eight chapters themselves. A similar problem besets those for whom the passage was a discursive way of addressing abstract theological questions like 'predestination'. These questions are not abstract for Paul. They concern God's purposes for his historical people, focused on the Messiah himself who has brought those purposes to their unexpected goal (10.4).

(a) Paul's grief (9.1–5)

Paul echoes the Israelite traditions of lament, not least that of Moses faced with Israel's rebellion (Ex. 32.32). He lists Israel's historic privileges—privileges which have now been inherited, as he has explained in the previous chapters, by the Messiah and his people.

(b) God's plan in Israel's history (9.6–29)

Paul tells the story of Israel, from Abraham to the exile, in order to make the point that God's word has not failed. On the contrary: Israel was always warned that God's purposes would be carried forward through a smaller and smaller remnant, until the time when this could suddenly open up to include gentiles as well (9.24).

(c) God's covenant-faithfulness in the gospel (9.30—10.21)

Chapters 9—11 focus on Paul's prayer in 10.1 (for Israel to be saved) and the answer to that prayer in 10.13 (all who call upon the name of the Lord will be saved).

Paul uses the olive tree as an analogy.
Ferrell Jenkins / BiblePlaces.com

Israel's covenant-story has come through the predictions of Deuteronomy 27—29 (rebellion and exile) but has now reached Deuteronomy 30 (renewal and restoration), through the Messiah. The reason for the present unbelief of most of Paul's Jewish contemporaries is that, not understanding 'the righteousness of God' (that is, the covenant promises and how they were to be fulfilled, as in 3.21—4.25), they have tried to establish a perpetual covenant-status of their own, whereas God had always planned a worldwide family of salvation which has now come into existence, marked out by the confession 'Jesus is lord' and the heart-belief that God raised him from the dead (10.9).

(d) God's abiding faithfulness (11.1–36)

This leaves Paul in a situation no Jew had faced before: what happens when God fulfils his promises, sending his Messiah to fulfil the ancient promises, and Israel as a whole looks the other way? This is where the incipient Roman anti-Jewish sentiment might kick in: supposing God has changed his mind, so as now to save gentiles only? No, says Paul: there is still a remnant of believing Jews, of which he is an obvious example (11.1–10), and since they are characterized by grace and faith this remnant can always increase (11.11–24). What's more—echoing passages in chapter 5—even the 'trespass' or 'stumble' of the presently unbelieving Jews appears to serve the purpose of gentile salvation; they are, in effect, acting out in a shadowy sense what the Messiah himself has done, being cast away for the sake of the world. But if that is so, God can and will save more and more of them (11.14). Paul exploits the irony he noticed in 9.6: 'Israel' means two different things, and the 'Israel' of promise has now been radically expanded into the 'all Israel' which consists of all believers (11.26). This leads to exalted praise to the majestic if still mysterious God (11.33–36).

4. Faithfulness and fellowship in the wider world (12—16)
(a) The transformed mind and its effects (12.1–21)

If the fundamental problem of the human race was idolatry and consequent wrong behaviour (1.18), Paul will now show that true worship, offering one's whole self to God, leads to genuinely human behaviour. The initial distortion sprang from the darkened *mind* (1.21); so the restoration of humanity will focus on the transformation which comes through the renewed mind, able now to think through and work out the will of God.

This will manifest itself in humble use of one's gifts in the service of the church (12.3–8) and the world (12.9–21—though the two categories overlap). Paul knows that there will be opposition, and urges the church members to bear witness to the victory of the cross by their forgiving spirit and renunciation of revenge (12.14–21).

Nero
Museum Het Valkhof / Wikimedia Commons

(b) Living between the times (13.1–14)

One of the reasons that vigilante vengeance is disallowed (12.19–21) is that it is the God-given role of governing authorities to keep the peace and punish wrongdoing. This belief, part of Israel's scriptural heritage of creational monotheism in which the creator intends humans to look after his world, is not undone by Paul's insistence on the universal sovereignty of Jesus. Governments are still important, and they themselves are answerable to God (compare the remarkable Jn. 19.11). Paul is eager to avoid a repetition of any civil disturbances between Jews and Messiah-believers that led to the expulsion of Jewish Christians under Claudius; he may also be aware of the worsening situation in Judea. Hence the importance of Jesus-followers being good citizens (13.1–7). They must also be good neighbours (13.8–10), since 'love is the fulfilling of the law' (NRSV). All this is set within the *inaugurated eschatology* of the gospel: though the world still seems dark, the day has in fact broken and Jesus' followers must live accordingly (13.11–14; compare 1 Thess. 5.1–11).

(c) Growing towards unity (14.1—15.12)

Paul can now address the complex problems faced by what seems to be a loose and perhaps mutually suspicious network of house-churches. The problems, as we suggested above, are loosely connected to the different traditions and customs of different ethnic groups, particularly the Jewish Christians on the one hand and the gentile Christians on the other; but the connection is only loose, since some Jewish Christians will have followed Paul, himself a Jewish Christian (as he emphasizes in 11.1–10!), in recognizing a new gospel-freedom (1 Cor. 8–10), and some gentile Christians may well have been erstwhile God-fearers who had enjoyed coming under the rule of Torah. But part of the point of Romans 14 is that Paul will not name the problem in those terms, but simply in terms of personal preferences in matters of food, drink, and holy days. It is not up to us to judge, he says; that is the lord's business (see 1 Cor. 4). Nothing is unclean in itself, but if someone behaves with a bad conscience it becomes unclean for him or her (14.14), and anyone putting a fellow-believer in that false position is in danger of undoing the Messiah's redemptive work (14.15). The rule that matters is the messianic principle of

𝔓⁴⁶ is one of the earliest manuscripts containing the epistles of Paul.
Image digitally reproduced with the permission of the Papyrology Collection, Graduate Library, University of Michigan

not pleasing oneself but allowing the needs of others to be paramount (15.1–6), always with the aim of a united fellowship that can worship with one heart and voice (15.6). The mutual welcome and shared worship of Christians from different traditions is the aim, fulfilling the scriptural promises of the gentile ingathering: 15.8–9 forms a short summary of Paul's whole argument, with the Messiah becoming a servant to the circumcised to confirm the patriarchal promises and to bring the gentiles to glorify God for his mercy. In a classic move of Jewish-style conclusion, Paul quotes from Torah (Dt. 32.43), Prophets (Isa. 11.10), and Writings (Pss. 17.50; 117.1) to emphasize that what has happened in the gospel's inclusion of gentiles is what scripture envisaged all along, so that the messianic community would have solid grounds for hope (15.4, 13). This concludes the main theological exposition of the letter with an allusion right back to the messianic gospel announced in 1.3–5.

(d) Missionary plans and closing greetings (15.13—16.27)

Paul explains his plans to go to Jerusalem to deliver the Collection (in connection with which he asks for special prayer), and then to head for Spain—the western limits of the Roman empire—by way of Rome itself. Romans 15.24 may well hint at his hope for financial support. Chapter 16 consists of extended greetings, quite possibly indicating Paul's determination to greet all the different house-churches in Rome (see box: 'Women in Christian service and mission'). He warns against those who cause divisions by deceitful teachings (16.17–20), passes on greetings from his fellow-workers (16.21–23), and ends with a long blessing which, though threatening to collapse grammatically under its own weight, does its best to sum up the entire message of the letter and give all praise to the God now made known in Jesus the Messiah (16.25–27).

ROMANS AND THE BIG PICTURE

Studying Romans could be the occupation of a lifetime. We focus here simply on two themes: gospel and community.

First, the letter is gospel-centred. The noun *euangelion* and the verb *euangelizō* together occur a dozen times in the letter.[21] Paul knows that the Romans have received a true gospel tradition;[22] he wants to fill this out with his own rich gospel insight, emphasizing that gentiles are justified by faith without adopting the Jewish way of life. He offers a concise summary of the gospel (Rom. 1.2–4) and explains how the gospel unveils the 'righteousness of God' (Rom. 1.16–17), including both

---

21 Rom. 1.1, 9, 15–16; 2.16; 10.15–16; 11.28; 15.16, 19–20; 16.25.
22 Rom. 6.17; 15.14; 16.17.

judgment (Rom. 2.16) and justification (Rom. 3.21–26). He displays the gospel as the content of missionary preaching (Rom 1.15; 10.15–16; 15.16, 19–20), and shows how, if the Romans imbibe all this gospel-centred theology, they will be strengthened in their faith (Rom. 16.25). In other words, Paul is doing his best to ensure that the faith, practices, devotion, convictions, and relationships of the Roman Christians are radically shaped by the good news of Jesus, the crucified, risen, and reigning lord. Those who preach and teach the gospel today need to take note; a superficial gospel will produce superficial discipleship. Churches should be 'gospelized' in the same way that magnets are 'magnetized', surgical tools are 'sterilized', and so on. We need to absorb the truth, power, and beauty of the gospel, so that we reflect it outwardly, infect everyone we touch with it, and make gospel proclamation in all its dimensions the church's chief project.[23]

WOMEN IN CHRISTIAN SERVICE AND MISSION

Paul names a number of prominent women in Romans 16.1–6 who are servants and co-workers engaged in Christian service, including:

- Phoebe: deacon, benefactor (vv. 1–2);
- Priscilla: co-worker, church-planter, teacher, fellow-prisoner (vv. 3–5);
- Mary: someone who works hard for others (v. 6);
- Junia: missionary-apostle (v. 7);
- Tryphena, Tryphosa, and Persis: women who work hard in the lord (v. 12);
- the mother of Rufus: modelling mothering care for others (v. 13).

John Chrysostom wrote about Junia: 'O how great is the devotion of this woman that she should be counted worthy of the appellation of apostle!'[*] Origen could infer: 'This passage teaches that there were women ordained in the church's ministry by the apostles' authority . . . Not only that—they ought to be ordained into the ministry, because they helped in many ways and by their good services deserved the praise even of the apostle.'[†]

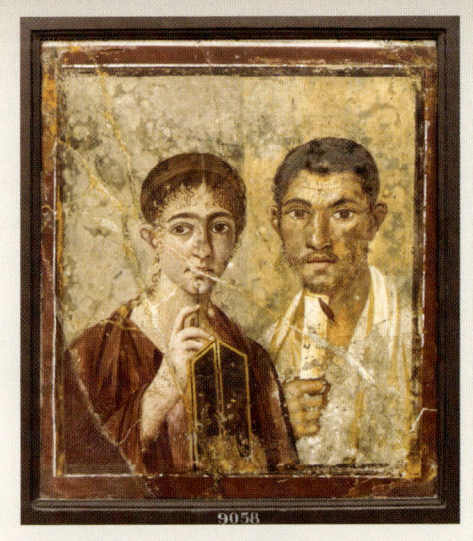

First-century fresco of a woman and man, Neronian era from Pompeii
Public Domain

[*] Chrys. *Hom. Rom.* 31.
[†] Cited in Bray 2005, 355.

---

23 For more on this see Wright *SH*, chs. 13–15.

> 'Paul's colleague, Phoebe, probably carried the letter to Rome and expounded its theology on behalf of Paul, then provided oversight in the preparation of the community for the next phase of Paul's missionary program.'
>
> A. Katherine Grieb,
> *Story of Romans*, xii.

Second, Paul urges an ethnically mixed and potentially fractious network of churches to welcome one another. At the climax of Romans, Paul exhorts the churches to 'Welcome one another, therefore, as the Messiah has welcomed you, to God's glory' (Rom. 15.7 *NTE/KNT*). The church must not mirror the tendency in the wider culture to live in ghettoes. There is to be one church of Messiah Jesus, consisting of Jews, Greeks, Romans, barbarians—anyone and everyone. Just as there is 'no distinction' in sin (Rom. 3.22), so there is 'no distinction' in justification by faith (Rom. 10.12). The same lord is lord of all; Jesus died and rose to be the lord of all; all who call on the name of the lord will be saved. Justification by faith means fellowship by the same faith. To walk the 'Roman road' (as some have called the gospel presentation in this letter) is not only to discover one's sins forgiven by the God of utter love and mercy, but also to learn that this lavish forgiveness was always intended to draw people of all sorts into a single family. Multi-ethnic churches should be the norm, not the exception. This is hard in practice and messy at times, as Paul obviously knew. Paul wrestled with the limits of acceptable diversity (not least in 1 Corinthians), and he is certainly not advocating an 'anything goes' style of unity. Unity and holiness both matter vitally. Either is comparatively easy without the other; the trick is to hold them together. Paul provides the house-churches in Rome with a map of how to get from where they presently are to the shared worship and witness which will glorify God.

Colosseum, Rome

Further reading

Bird, Michael F. 2013. 'Letter to the Romans.' In *All Things to All Cultures: Paul among Jews, Greeks and Romans*. Edited by M. Harding and A. Knobbs. Grand Rapids, MI: Eerdmans, pp. 177–204.

——. 2016. *Romans*. SGBC; Grand Rapids, MI: Zondervan.

Blackwell, Ben, John Goodrich, and Jason Maston (eds.). 2015. *Reading Romans in Context: Paul and Second Temple Judaism*. Grand Rapids, MI: Zondervan.

Bryan, Christopher. 2000. *A Preface to Romans: Notes on the Epistle in Its Literary and Cultural Setting*. Oxford: Oxford University Press.

Das, A. Andrew. 2006. *Solving the Romans Debate*. Minneapolis: Fortress.

Donfried, Karl P. (ed.). 1991. *The Romans Debate*. Rev. edn.; Peabody, MA: Hendrickson.

Dunn, James D. G. 1988. *Romans 1–8, 9–16*. 2 vols.; WBC; Dallas: Word.

——. 2009. *Beginning from Jerusalem*. CITM 2; Grand Rapids, MI: Eerdmans, pp. 863–932.

Gaventa, Beverly. 2016. *When in Romans: An Invitation to Linger with the Gospel According to Paul*. Grand Rapids, MI: Baker.

Grieb, A. Katherine. 2002. *The Story of Romans: A Narrative Defense of God's Righteousness*. Louisville, KY: Westminster John Knox, 2002.

Jewett, Robert K. 2009. *Romans: A Commentary*. Hermeneia; Minneapolis: Fortress.

Keck, Leander E. 2007. *Romans*. ANTC; Nashville: Abingdon.

Keener, Craig S. 2009. *Romans*. NCCS; Eugene, OR: Cascade.

Lampe, Peter. 2003. *From Paul to Valentinus: Christians at Rome in the First Two Centuries*. Minneapolis: Fortress, 1993.

Lancaster, Sarah Heaner. 2015. *Romans*. BTCB; Louisville, KY: Westminster John Knox Press, 2015.

Longenecker, Richard N. 2011. *Introducing Romans: Critical Issues in Paul's Most Famous Letter*. Grand Rapids, MI: Eerdmans.

Mathew, Susan. 2013. *Women in the Greetings of Romans 16.1–16: A Study of Mutuality and Women's Ministry in the Letter to the Romans*. LNTS 471. London: Bloomsbury.

Moo, Douglas J. 1996. *The Epistle to the Romans*. NICNT; Grand Rapids, MI: Eerdmans.

Oakes, Peter. 2009. *Reading Romans in Pompeii: Paul's Letter at Ground Level*. Minneapolis: Fortress.

Reasoner, Mark. 2005. *Romans in Full Circle: A History of Interpretation*. Louisville, KY: Westminster John Knox.

Schreiner, Thomas R. 1998. *Romans*. BECNT; Grand Rapids, MI.

Wright, N. T. 2002. 'The Letter to the Romans.' In *New Interpreter's Bible*. Edited by L. E. Keck. 12 vols.; Nashville: Abingdon, 10.393–770.

——. 2006. *Paul for Everyone: Romans*. London: SPCK.

The Pastoral Epistles

Here is a trustworthy saying that deserves full acceptance: Christ Jesus came into the world to save sinners—of whom I am the worst. But for that very reason I was shown mercy so that in me, the worst of sinners, Christ Jesus might display his immense patience as an example for those who would believe in him and receive eternal life.[1]

CHAPTER AT A GLANCE

This chapter provides a short survey of Paul's letters to Timothy and Titus.

By the end of this chapter you should be able to:

- situate the Pastoral Epistles in the context of Paul's missionary career;
- describe the structure and argument of 1–2 Timothy and Titus;
- identify the main themes and theology of 1–2 Timothy and Titus;
- understand the critical issues related to the Pastoral Epistles.

INTRODUCTION

The collective witness of the New Testament to Paul includes a variety of images: Paul the persecutor, Paul the convert, Paul the evangelist, Paul the pastor, Paul the defender of the gospel, Paul the letter-writer, and Paul the theologian. What we have in 1–2 Timothy and Titus is best described as Paul the mentor. Even though this trio of letters has, since the eighteenth century, gone under the collective title 'The Pastoral Epistles', which is appropriate in its way, they might more fittingly be named 'The Mentoring Epistles', or as Luke Timothy Johnson calls them, 'Letters to Paul's Delegates'.[2] Paul frequently took it upon himself to encourage, strengthen, and rebuke believers when the occasion called for it. In these three letters we see him trying to build up his theological vision in the churches,

1   1 Tim. 1.15–16.
2   In terms of genre, the pastorals are often regarded as letters that embody the literary forms of moral exhortation, mandates, succession, and even a testament. See Johnson 1996; 2001b, 91–7; 2010, 383–4; Towner 2006, 31–6; Wall and Steele 2012, 9–11.

and making his final pleas to his two trusted colleagues Timothy and Titus. We see here both Paul's anxiety for his junior co-workers and his confidence in their ability, combined with warnings for them to heed, a sense of personal warmth towards them, and grave admonitions to guard the gospel. Throughout, as we would expect, Paul continues as ever to celebrate the lordship of Jesus.

Situating the Pastoral Epistles in Paul's career is complex for two reasons. First, it is almost impossible to fit these letters, with their details of personal movements and so on, into the narrative of Acts. Second, the Pauline authenticity of these three epistles has regularly been doubted. Many see them as pseudepigraphical (written in Paul's name but by somebody else). We will look at these questions below. Sufficient for now to say that, historical or imagined, the letters appear to presuppose a scenario in which Paul survives a first imprisonment in Rome and then engages in further travels to the east (despite what he said to the Roman Christians in Rom. 15.23 about having no room in that region any more[3]), writing 1 Timothy and Titus along the way. We then have to imagine that he returned to Rome where he faced a second imprisonment, trial, and probably execution. That imprisonment would be the setting for 2 Timothy.

The Pauline letter-collection as we have it from the earliest manuscripts of the New Testament opens with Romans, the big Pauline manifesto, and ends with the Pastoral Epistles, Paul's testament and *au revoir* to his trusted co-workers. (The even shorter letter to Philemon comes last of all, presumably being seen in the same bracket as a personal rather than ecclesial epistle.) There is a certain genius in this order, starting as it does with Paul's towering theological vision and ending with final instructions to his co-workers. The order constitutes an intra-canonical frame for understanding Paul as theologian and as pastor, both of which are required to grasp the full meaning and significance of his apostolic labours. It is also the case that the ordering reflects for the most part the length of the letters, from Romans as the longest to Philemon as the shortest, but 1 Timothy is actually longer than 2 Thessalonians and similar in length to most of the prison letters. It looks as though the Pauline collection may have been ordered this way to achieve a deliberate effect. The pastoral letters round off Paul's career, passing the baton on to Christians of the next generation, with whom readers are meant to identify. Paul's legacy remains living and active as his apostolic faithfulness and testimony are carried forward. These letters serve, as it were, to inscribe a Pauline 'rule of faith' into the canonical consciousness of the developing church.[4] They could be described as faithful instructions for faithful friends, to keep the household of faith in good order.

---

3 See too Ac. 20.25.
4 On canonical readings of the Pastoral Epistles, see Wall 2004; Childs 2008, 69–75; Wall and Steele 2012, 34–6.

CONTEXTUAL AND CRITICAL MATTERS

Authorship

Who wrote the pastorals? Answers range from pseudepigraphy to authenticity.

1. The Pastoral Epistles are pseudepigraphical and derive from the late first to mid-second century. Several New Testament writings, especially the Pastoral Epistles and 2 Peter, are regarded as 'pseudepigraphical' or 'pseudonymous'. That means that they were falsely or fraudulently attributed to a certain author. The practice of writing under the name of a prestigious earlier figure was common in the ancient world. Examples can be found in greco-roman culture: Galen claimed that large-scale forgery happened when the kings of Alexandria and Pergamum began enlarging their respective libraries. It is well known in the Jewish world, with the so-called *Epistle of Jeremiah*, the *Epistle to Aristeas*, the visions ascribed to Enoch, and so on. In Christian literary culture there are obvious examples, such as the so-called *Gospel of Thomas, 3 Corinthians, Letters of Paul and Seneca, Letters of Jesus to Agbar*, and so on. Was this what happened with the 'pastoral epistles'?

The developing church of the second century was strongly opposed to attributing a book to the wrong person. Bishop Serapion of Antioch rejected the *Gospel of Peter* on the grounds that 'the writings which falsely bear their names [Peter and the other apostles] we reject . . . knowing that such were not handed down to us'.[5] The Christian apologist Tertullian recalled that an Asian presbyter, who had confessed to composing the *Acts of Paul and Thecla* out of 'love of Paul', was duly removed from his church office.[6] The Muratorian canon censures letters forged in Paul's name (the 'epistles to the Laodiceans and Alexandrians'): they were Marcionite compositions that could not be accepted with the authentic letters because 'it is not fitting that gall be mixed with honey'.[7] The church, for the most part, seems to have regarded pseudonymity as a device unsuited to and unworthy of a sacred text.[8]

Several factors need to be remembered here. First, authors knew their ideas might be taken over by others; the ancient world did not have any well-developed notion of 'copyright' or 'intellectual property'. Thus notions of authorial 'ownership', or of plagiarism, as we understand them, did not exist. Second, the idea of authorship must itself be construed flexibly, since authorship can involve more than one person and more than one text. Composing a document can involve secretaries, colleagues, editors, copyists, and collectors. Third, attributing authorship to someone other than the real author does not necessarily entail falsehood. Granted, forgery

---

[5] Eus. *Hist. Eccl.* 6.12.3.
[6] Tert. *On Baptism* 17.4–5.
[7] Muratorian canon § 64–8.
[8] See Baum 2001.

and deception may well be driving pseudepigraphy; Galen, again, knew of works falsely attributed to him, and of others passing off his work as their own. But there might be other motives; for instance, the attempt to propagate afresh the teachings of someone who had founded a school, as with the neo-Pythagoreans who went on attributing writings to Pythagoras even centuries after his death. Some genuinely believed that admiration for a figure could legitimately generate literary impersonation, as with Tertullian's Asian presbyter who wrote the *Acts of Paul*, and the Syrian neo-Platonist Iamblichus who said it was honourable to publish one's own treatise in the name of a venerable teacher. Sometimes people would try to sum up and elaborate upon a particular tradition, putting it all under the name of an appropriate author, as with *1 Enoch*, the *Testament of Solomon*, or *Dionysius the Areopagite*. This might well be a perfectly transparent fiction, with an author composing a document under another's name but with the immediate circle of readers being fully aware of the circumstances while a subsequent audience might not be. Thus, for instance, the fifth-century presbyter Salvia of Marseille wrote *The Four Books of Timothy to the Church*, and when Bishop Salonius of Geneva took him to task for this, Salvia responded that the fictitious ascription to Timothy was transparent.[9] The practice of pseudepigraphy could thus be an assertion of authoritative tradition, not necessarily a statement of literary authorship.[10] Marshall thus proposes that we need an alternative term to pseudepigraphy that does not have negative connotations of falsehood. He suggests 'allonymity' and 'allepigraphy', the act of benignly writing under the name of another.[11]

The Pastoral Epistles have, then, frequently been identified as pseudepigraphy, either as deliberate forgeries or else as pious fictions in which 'Paul' writes to his 'beloved sons' Timothy and Titus. The reasons for this theory are as follows:[12]

  i. *Greek language and style.* The Pastoral Epistles contain a distinctive vocabulary, with 176 words not found anywhere else in the New Testament and 130 words not used in any of the other Pauline letters.[13] Some allege that the Greek vocabulary of the pastorals reflects Christian language of the second century, adopting pagan terminology from the Roman imperial period with the 'epiphany' of Jesus as 'saviour' (*sōtēr*),[14] and 'piety' (*eusebeia*)[15] as a way

---

[9] For a good introduction to pseudepigraphy, see Dunn 1997; 2015, 80–5, and Marshall 1999, 79–84; for further in-depth studies, see Frey 2009; and Porter and Fewster 2013. For key texts, translations, and bibliographies, we strongly recommend Baum 2013.
[10] Meade 1987, 72.
[11] Marshall 1999, 84; see also Dunn 1997, 984.
[12] Largely following Dunn 2015, 86–8.
[13] Harrison 1921, 20–1.
[14] Tit. 2.10, 13; 2 Tim. 1.10.
[15] 1 Tim. 2.2; 3.16; 4.7–8; 5.4; 6.3–6, 11; 2 Tim. 3.5, 12; Tit. 1.1; 2.12.

Paul travelled on roads like this in Ephesus.

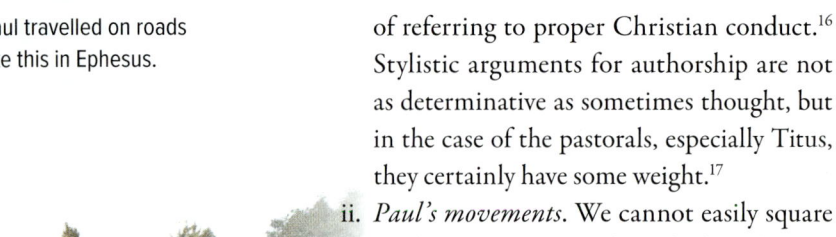

of referring to proper Christian conduct.[16] Stylistic arguments for authorship are not as determinative as sometimes thought, but in the case of the pastorals, especially Titus, they certainly have some weight.[17]

ii. *Paul's movements*. We cannot easily square Paul's movements as described in the Pastoral Epistles with what we know from elsewhere. Second Timothy describes Paul experiencing a first (Roman?) imprisonment, a 'first defence' from which he was purportedly released.[18] But thereafter he seems to be travelling back to Macedonia, Achaia, western Asia, and Crete before finally returning to Rome.[19] Campbell regards this as a 'completely unworkable itinerary' for 'any travelled heading west to Rome by way of Corinth back to Miletus—having just left Ephesus—before turning again and heading westward to Rome'.[20] What is more, Paul himself believed that his work in the northeast quadrant of the Mediterranean was finished, so that his intention had been to head further west to Spain via Rome, not to zigzag across the Adriatic and Aegean seas.[21] Luke's narration of Paul's farewell speech to the Ephesian elders in Miletus is dramatic and poignant because, as far as Luke was aware, this really was the last time the Asian believers would see Paul. Luke may have been writing a decade or more after Paul's death;

---

[16] See e.g. Harrison 1921, 82–3; Koester 2000 [1982], 2.301. Marshall 1999, 78, acknowledges the weight of the argument.
[17] See Mealand 1995; Marshall 1999, 61.
[18] 2 Tim. 4.9–18; Eus. *Hist. Eccl.* 2.22.2.
[19] 1 Tim. 1.3; 2 Tim. 1.18; 4.20–21; Tit. 1.5; 3.12.
[20] Campbell 2014, 372. Even Johnson (2001b, 65–8) is forced to admit that the chronology and geography of the Pastorals are difficult to fit into what we know of the Pauline mission, though ultimately he thinks it is no harder than the problems presented by Galatians, Philemon, and Philippians.
[21] Rom. 15.23–28.

if so, he would presumably have known of another trip to Ephesus had Paul made one.[22]

iii. *Paul's opponents.* The Pastoral Epistles name and oppose various deviant doctrines. These have the character of a Jewish teaching being developed in a gnostic direction, something which fits well into the second century rather than Paul's lifetime. Some even suggest that a family of second-century gnostic beliefs are targeted, in particular the Marcionite heresy.[23] This is all the more plausible since Marcion's *Apostolikon* contained only ten letters of Paul minus the Pastoral Epistles. Hans von Campenhausen goes so far as to attribute the pastorals to Polycarp of Smyrna who composed them in direct opposition to Marcion (d. *c.* AD 155–60).[24] The author might, however, have had no particular deviant teaching in mind, but rather may be generalizing about various teachings that one might find in the post-apostolic period.[25]

iv. *Early Catholicism.* Scholars from the liberal protestant tradition have often suggested that the churches of the late first and early second centuries gradually became less spiritually animated and socially egalitarian, and morphed into hierarchical institutional forms which have come to be labelled as 'early Catholicism'. This is typified by the established offices of overseer/bishop and deacon, and also by the authoritative control of spiritual expression. The pastorals refer to a distinct office of 'elder' (*presbyteros*), equivalent to 'overseer' or 'bishop' (*episkopos*), and the subordinate office of 'deacon' (*diakonos*).[26] Office-holders are appointed in a top-down fashion by the apostles' successors, who have ordained elders/overseers/bishops through the laying

---

[22] Ac. 20.17–28 (esp. vv. 25, 38 about not seeing Paul again). If, of course, we date Acts early, which as we shall see is a minority position, it is possible that Luke might have written it before any subsequent trips.

[23] Campbell (2014, 364–6) contends that 1 Tim. 6.20, with mention of *antithesis* (Marcion wrote a book called *Antitheses* listing alleged contradictions between the OT and the NT) and *pseudōnumou gnōseōs* ('falsely called knowledge', which was Irenaeus's distinctive description for Gnosticism) is not necessarily a smoking gun, but a 'telltale strand of fibre left at the scene of the crime'. Campbell (2014, 390) concludes: 'the Pastorals were written precisely to combat Marcion, along with other perceived Christian deviations, in the second century.' It is certainly interesting that when the Muratorian canon mentions the Pastoral Epistles (63–8) they are immediately contrasted with the pro-Marcionite letters to the Laodiceans and Alexandrians that were forged in Paul's name. The pastorals might have emerged as an orthodox Pauline pseudepigraphy written to counter Marcionite Pauline pseudepigraphy.

[24] Campenhausen 1963, followed by Koester 2000 [1982], 2.308–10, and Pervo 2016, has published a translation of and introduction to the Pastoral Epistles and Polycarp together in one volume. Interestingly, Irenaeus (*Adv. Haer.* 3.3.4) claims that Polycarp visited Rome and confronted Marcion in person. Marshall (1999, 3–5) believes that Polycarp echoed the typical phraseology of the pastorals, not because he too mirrored the language of the second-century church, nor because he wrote them, but most likely because he knew them as part of a Pauline corpus. He thinks it improbable that Polycarp or a colleague wrote the pastorals because: 'The difference in style from the letter of Polycarp is decisive against composition by Polycarp himself, and the closeness in phraseology is insufficient to justify ascribing the P[astoral] E[pistles] to a colleague of his.' See also Johnson 2001b, 86–7, who likewise rejects the thesis of Polycarp's authorship of the pastorals.

[25] Koester 2000 [1982], 2.306.

[26] Elder: 1 Tim. 5.17–19; Tit. 1.5; overseer/bishop: 1 Tim. 3.1–18; Tit. 1.5–9; deacon: 1 Tim. 3.8–13.

on of hands.[27] It is alleged that this has more in common with the letters of Ignatius, centralizing authority in a single bishop, than with the undisputed Pauline letters which see authority residing in the whole congregation, whose grace-given gifts contribute to a strongly egalitarian whole.[28] In particular, the Pauline encouragement for women to prophesy and teach has been eclipsed by a patriarchal vision of leadership.[29]

v. *Orthodox eulogizing of Paul the martyr.* Another feature of the pastorals is that they appear to portray Paul as the ideal convert, as the teacher of true doctrine, and as a martyr. These letters assume an established set of doctrines known as the 'faith'[30] and 'sound teaching',[31] much like later formulations of the 'rule of faith'.[32] Thus the 'Paul' of the pastorals has become not just an itinerant teacher of a messianic sect but a venerated 'true and faithful teacher of the Gentiles'.[33] In addition, 2 Timothy presents Paul approaching his own death with confidence, ready to pass the torch of true teaching to the next generation. This reminds us of the 'testament' genre, and of later martyrological traditions that venerate victims of persecution.[34] It could be argued that the Paul of the pastorals stands somewhere between the Paul of the Acts of the Apostles (especially Ac. 20.17–38) and the Paul of the *Acts of Paul and Thecla* (especially *Acts of Paul* 17). The pastorals then reflect the ongoing reception of Paul's memory as missionary and martyr in the developing church; a memory which will eventually bloom into cultic devotion to Paul the Christian saint.[35]

Detail of Saint Thecla with wild beasts and angels, *c.* fifth century, found in Egypt, The Nelson-Atkins Museum of Art, Kansas City, MO, USA
Wikimedia Commons / R. Higgins, CC-BY-3.0

James Dunn is pessimistic about the possibility of authentic Pauline authorship: 'In the light of all this data it is very difficult to avoid the conclusion that the

---

27 Tit. 1.5; 1 Tim. 4.14; 5.22; 2 Tim. 1.6.
28 See Gal. 3.5, 28–29; Rom. 12.4–8; 15.14; 1 Cor. 12.4–11; 16.3; 2 Cor. 8.13–14. Contrast with Ign. *Phld.* 7.2; *Trall.* 2.2; *Magn.* 6.2; 7.1.
29 Contrast 1 Cor. 11.5 and 14.31 with 1 Tim. 2.11–14 on public speaking.
30 1 Tim. 1.19; 3.9; 4.1, 6; 5.8; 6.10, 12, 21; 2 Tim. 3.8; 4.7; Tit. 1.13; 2.2.
31 1 Tim. 1.10; 4.6, 16; 6.1; 2 Tim. 3.10; 4.3; Tit. 1.9; 2.1, 7, 10.
32 On the Pastoral Letters and the 'rule of faith', see Wall and Steele 2012, 40–3.
33 1 Tim. 2.7.
34 See e.g. 1 Tim. 1.12–16; 2 Tim. 2.1–21; 3.10–14, and comments by Koester 2000 [1982], 303–4; Campbell 2014, 369; and Wall and Steele 2012, 16. Marshall (1999, 79) acknowledges the weight of the point: 'There are some points where the reader may feel that the self-presentation of Paul is more like what other people would have said about him rather than what he himself would have said.'
35 See Aageson 2008; Eastman 2011; White 2014, 142–58; Dunn 2015, 678–82.

Pastorals were not written by Paul and reflect situations which are most probably to be dated to a post-70 context.'[36]

To see the Pastoral Epistles as non-Pauline does not, we should note, necessarily mean dismissing them as fraudulent. Brevard Childs contends that the Pastoral Epistles are unique and cannot be identified with later pseudepigraphical writings attributed to Paul such as *3 Corinthians* or the *Letters of Paul and Seneca*, which are obviously far removed from Paul's words and world. The pastorals may not be directly from Paul, but they still lay claim to the direct voice of Paul himself, even if the Pauline legacy has been extended and transformed to address issues in the post-Pauline era. The Pastoral Epistles, then, could represent a fusion of Pauline tradition and post-Pauline expansion, reflecting fresh developments in the life of the church. If that is so, to label them simply as 'pseudepigraphy' would be inadequate as an account of their origins, contents, and usage.[37]

2. *The Pastoral Epistles were based on Pauline fragments that were redacted and added to a Pauline letter-collection by a follower such as Luke.*[38] While the Pastoral Epistles might appear to be post-Pauline in

First-century depiction of reading, fresco at Herculaneum

style and language, there are also segments that sound authentically Pauline.[39] The description of Paul's approaching death ('For I am already being poured out like a drink offering, and the time for my departure is near. I have fought the good fight, I have finished the race, I have kept the faith. Now there is in store for me the crown of righteousness, which the Lord, the righteous Judge, will award to me on that day—and not only to me, but also to all who have longed for his appearing')[40] does sound like something Paul might well have said.[41] Consequently one may wonder whether the Pastoral Epistles might be made up of fragments of Paul's personal notes, or shorter letters that, expanded into three distinct epistles, have been added to a Pauline letter-collection as a kind of posthumous capstone. A compiler might

---

36 Dunn 2015, 88. Koester (2000 [1982], 2.301) uses even stronger words: 'recent scholarship has accumulated such an overwhelming number of conclusive arguments against the authenticity of the Pastoral Epistles that Pauline authorship can only be maintained on the basis of torturous hypotheses and an amassing of historical improbabilities.'
37 Childs 2008, 70–1.
38 Among other similar options, one might postulate a fragmentary hypothesis without Lukan editing, or Lukan editing without fragmentation.
39 According to Johnson (2001b, 71), the pastorals do not manifest a single and consistent authorial hand; instead 'they appear to alternate sections that are intensely "Pauline" in tone with other sections that are "unPauline"'.
40 2 Tim. 4.6–8.
41 See e.g. Phil. 1.19–26; 2.17–18; 2 Cor. 2.14–17; 4.7–11; 11.23; Rom. 15.23–33 (esp. v. 31).

have known Paul's creedal summaries,[42] his statements about his life and work,[43] his prison experiences,[44] and travel notes from his Asian ministry,[45] all of which might have been combined and embedded within what became the 'Pastoral Epistles'.[46] This 'fragmentary hypothesis' might be strengthened if we consider that the Pastoral Epistles are sometimes alleged to lack a clear structure and overarching coherence, appearing disjointed in places, and containing an almost staccato rhythm. All that would be consistent with them being made up of diverse literary materials such as household codes, creedal fragments, moral exhortation, proverbial statements, liturgical pieces, personal problems, and travel intentions. The pastorals might then be seen as a synthetic combination of pre-existing materials.[47]

One form of the 'fragmentary hypothesis' proposes a connection between Luke and the Pastoral Epistles, such that Luke might have acted as either secretary or redactor.[48] This would explain the biographical references, including Luke's own presence as Paul's sole companion in Rome.[49] It would fit, so it has been said, with the supposed convergences between Luke-Acts and the Pastoral Epistles on such topics as ministry offices, Christian attitudes towards the state, christology, eschatology, and the language of conversion.

This thesis is admittedly speculative. It relies on diverse sources underlying the pastorals; such compositional theories are impossible to prove. The similarities between the Pastoral Epistles and Luke-Acts, which may be partly the effect of the scholarly assumption that both exhibit 'early Catholicism', can be explained in other ways than common authorship. If the pastorals were pseudonymous, the author might well have known Luke's work.[50] Or Luke might have known the pastorals. As frequently in ancient history, we have far too little concrete evidence to make a definite judgment.

3. 1 Timothy and Titus are pseudepigraphical, while 2 Timothy is authentic. One of us (NTW) has proposed elsewhere that '2 Timothy is . . . much more like the "Paul" of the other letters in style, mood and flavour than 1 Timothy'.[51] There are,

---

42 1 Tim. 2.4–6; 3.16; 2 Tim. 2.8.
43 1 Tim. 1.11–16; 2 Tim. 1.3, 11–12, 15–18; 3.10.
44 2 Tim. 4.6–8.
45 2 Tim. 4.9–21.
46 See Harrison 1921, 115–35; Martin 1975–8, 2.302–3, 306; Miller 1997; Marshall 1999, 86; Dunn 2009b, 1053–5; 2015, 89–90; Wall and Steele 2012, 17–22; Williams 2015, xiii. For a historical analogy, the grandson of Jesus ben-Sirach edited and translated his grandfather's wisdom-sayings after Ben-Sirach's death; the same was apparently done by Thessalus, who edited two books of his father Hippocrates.
47 Miller 1997, 17–18. See in contrast Marshall 1999, 13–18, 73; Mounce 2000, cxx–cxxii; and Van Neste 2004.
48 See e.g. Moule 1965; Martin 1975–8, 2.303; Wilson 1979; Mounce 2000, cxxvii–cxxix; Riesner 2006; Westfall 2010; but see critique by Kaestli 1995; Marshall 1999, 87–8; Johnson 2001b, 69, 71–2.
49 See 2 Tim. 3.10–11; 4.11, 13, 20.
50 Some would suggest that 2 Tim. 3.11 is based on Paul's travels in Ac. 13–14.
51 Wright *PFG*, 61, and see Gorman 2017, 613–17 and Longenecker and Still 2014, 289–91 who take a similar line.

in fact, stylistic differences among the pastorals themselves, just as there are among the undisputed letters. Thus treating the three Pastoral Epistles as a distinct group, rather than individually, skews the evidence, failing to account for the style and vocabulary of 2 Timothy being closer to the undisputed letters, while 1 Timothy and Titus, closer to each other in style, are significantly different from both 2 Timothy and the undisputed letters of Paul.[52] Moreover, 2 Timothy is more of a personal encouragement to Timothy, whereas 1 Timothy and Titus appear to be offering somewhat wooden responses to the perceived problems of church order in Ephesus and Crete. This would make 2 Timothy the more personable, and perhaps the more credible, among the pastorals. Whoever first put '1 Timothy' and '2 Timothy' together may have lured us into imagining that they are close companions.

4. Paul wrote the Pastoral Epistles. The case for Pauline authorship of the pastorals involves accepting their self-witness as credible and refuting the counter-arguments.

The problem of the Greek style and language is real. However, there may be mitigating factors.[53] First, non-Pauline words occur most frequently here when dealing with false teachings, and with qualifications for church leaders, neither of which is addressed in the same way in the undisputed Pauline letters.[54] Second, most letters attributed to Paul involve a co-sender or secretary. Yet no-one seems to refer to 'the epistle of Paul and Sosthenes to the Corinthians'; the 'epistles of Paul and Timothy to the Corinthians, Philippians, Colossians and to Philemon'; the 'epistles of Paul, Silvanus, and Timothy to the Thessalonians'; or the 'epistle of Paul—with Tertius's assistance!—to the Romans'. Ephesians, as we saw earlier, is probably a circular letter picking up themes from Colossians. Only Galatians lacks a co-sender or scribe. If the co-senders or scribes shaped in any way the language, contents, structure, and style of these letters, then they cannot be used as a pure or pristine control-sample of Pauline style, able to be contrasted with the pastoral letters.[55] Third, it is notable that whereas the other Pauline letters are addressed to churches—even the epistle to Philemon includes the entire church as co-addressee—the Pastoral Epistles are the only instance of private correspondence written by Paul to individuals. This might

---

52 Whereas Koester (2000 [1982], 2.297) claims that the pastorals 'form a unity in their language, theological, concepts, and intention', Kenny's study suggests otherwise (1986, 100) as he ranks the Pauline letters in terms of their stylistic correlation as follows: Romans, Philippians, 2 Timothy, 2 Corinthians, Galatians, 2 Thessalonians, 1 Thessalonians, Colossians, Ephesians, 1 Timothy, Philemon, 1 Corinthians, and Titus. Kenny (1986, 100) suggests that '2 Timothy, one of the commonly rejected Pastoral Epistles, is as near the centre of the [Pauline] constellation as 2 Corinthians, which belongs to the group most widely accepted as authentic. It is only Titus which is shown as deserving the suspicion cast on the Pastorals.' See further Harrison 1921, 167–75; Prior 1989, 168; Murphy-O'Connor 1991; 1996, 357–62; Marshall 1999, 85–9, 92; Mounce 2000, lx–lxi, lxiii, cxxix; Towner 2006, 23–31.
53 See e.g. Porter 1995; Marshall 1999, 59–66; Mounce 2000, xcix–cxviii; Johnson 2001b, 58–60, 68–72; Towner 2006, 20–5.
54 Marshall 1999, 61; Mounce 2000, cvi–cviii; Johnson 2001b, 69.
55 Prior 1989, 37–45.

provide further reasons for seeing them as different from the letters addressed to whole churches.[56]

The problem of Paul's movements can be resolved fairly easily.[57] It might be the case that, after release from his first Roman captivity, Paul either abandoned or postponed his plans to visit Spain, and instead returned to deal with pressing needs in Greece and western Asia. In due time, Paul would then have dispatched Titus to Crete, leaving Timothy in Ephesus, writing to them both from perhaps Miletus or Macedonia. After two years or so, he somehow returned to Rome, either voluntarily or under arrest, where he was again imprisoned (having either gone to Spain at last, or not), at which point he will have written 2 Timothy from Rome, before finally being executed by Nero.[58]

One should not too quickly assume, in fact, that the pastorals describe a post-Pauline or even post-apostolic period of church life. To begin with, while many like to situate the Pastoral Epistles under the slippery phrase 'early Catholicism', this entity is a chimera. In scholarship 'early Catholicism' is used to designate the ecclesiastical settlement reached between the warring Paulinist and Petrine factions in the early church, describing a hypothetical wing of the church characterized by a waning expectation for the return of Jesus, the eclipse of charismatic energy by emerging hierarchical structures, the influx of hellenistic metaphysics and Stoic ethics, and the solidifying of beliefs into wooden doctrinal forms.[59] As we hinted before, the phrase 'early Catholicism' was invented by liberal Protestants from the nineteenth-century German traditions to describe how Christianity drifted from its supposed original moorings and ended up with the ancient Catholic Church

Altar dedicated to Peter and Paul, Mamertine Prison, Rome

[56] Prior 1989, 50–7.
[57] Murphy-O'Connor (2004, 218–34) provides a virtual novella about Paul's release from a first Roman imprisonment, an 'ill-conceived and ill-prepared' mission in Spain which he abandoned after only one summer (2004, 220), and Paul's subsequent ministry in Illyricum, Macedonia, and Asia, before his final trip to Rome, and his execution there.
[58] See further Wright *Paul: A Biography*, 391–7.
[59] Dunn 1990 [1977], 341–66.

(which was assumed, following Luther, to have largely forgotten the Pauline gospel). We may legitimately doubt whether Clement of Rome, Ignatius of Antioch, Polycarp of Smyrna, or even Luke himself would have recognized themselves and their churches in this caricature.

One could in fact argue that church life as seen in the pastorals fits fairly well into Paul's ministry, and would not require a post-Pauline setting. Paul is often seen as an itinerant leader establishing charismatic communities with only loose, *ad hoc* leadership arrangements, whereas the Pastoral Epistles assume a structured and hierarchical model of community with the muting of charismatic displays and authority. The evidence suggests otherwise. First, the organizational scaffolding erected by Paul in his communities relied on household structures for leadership,[60] or else utilized a scheme of 'elders' and 'deacons' close to that of the pastorals.[61] The pastorals are still a far cry from the mono-episcopacy of Ignatius, or the detailed church order in the *Didascalia* or *Apostolic Constitutions*. Second, religious movements rarely evolve in a neat linear fashion, from charismatic to institutional. Organizational development tends to be constantly in flux, diverse, contingent upon local circumstances, and often adopting fluid models of leadership.[62] Third, 2 Timothy does not deal with church structure at all. The question comes up in 1 Timothy, and to a lesser degree Titus. Even these letters mainly address the character and conduct of leaders, not their institutional power, their transmission of authority, or any form of episcopal legitimacy.[63]

The alleged theological development from Paul to the Pastoral Epistles can likewise be overstated. Although the pastorals do exhibit features that look like post-Pauline confessional terminology (e.g. 'God our Saviour'), nonetheless there is a tight agreement with central Pauline motifs like the centrality of grace,[64] the inclusive scope of salvation,[65] and the transformative power of the gospel.[66] If Paul did not write these, then an imitator has certainly done his or her homework. Also, while the pastorals stress guarding the deposit of sound doctrine ('the faith'),[67] even in the undisputed Paulines we find similar emphases on the word/faith/teaching/instruction that believers have received and are meant to preserve and pass on.[68] The pastorals do not, in fact, envisage the kind of transfer of authority and doctrine that we find in later centuries. They merely emphasize the preservation of the gospel and

---

60 Rom. 16.3–5; 1 Cor. 1.16; 16.15, 19; Col. 4.15; Philem. 2.
61 See e.g. Rom. 16.1; Phil. 1.1; Ac. 14.23.
62 Campbell 2014, 359–60.
63 See Mounce 2000, lxxxvi–lxxxviii; Towner 2006, 50–2.
64 2 Tim. 1.9; Tit. 3.5.
65 1 Tim. 2.3–7; 4.10; 2 Tim. 4.17; Tit. 2.11.
66 1 Tim. 2.10; 5.10, 25; 6.18; 2 Tim. 2.21; 3.17; Tit. 2.14; 3.14.
67 1 Tim. 1.2, 10, 14, 19; 3.9; 4.1, 6; 5.8; 6.1, 3, 12, 21; 2 Tim. 1.13; 3.8, 10; 4.3, 7; Tit. 1.4, 9, 13; 2.1, 10; 3.15.
68 Thus the liberal protestant critique has been maintained by e.g. regarding the mention of a 'tradition' in Rom. 6.17 as a post-Pauline gloss (Bultmann 1947).

the apostolic interpretation of Jesus' death and resurrection, which would be natural enough as Paul approached the end of his life.[69]

One could also argue that Paul's opponents in these letters do bear some resemblance to those we meet in Paul's own career, including Jewish groups with proselytizing agendas.[70] Several of the problems addressed in the pastorals are germane to previous disputes concerning privileged accounts of 'knowledge', abstention from marriage, and erroneous configurations of eschatology.[71] Even the prohibition of women teaching men in 1 Timothy 2.12–15, however we understand it, is not completely out of kilter with Paul's efforts elsewhere to ensure that women did not disrupt the order of worship services.[72]

All of this contributes to the sense that the Pastoral Epistles 'fit well into the period around the death of Paul and the transition to the period in which he was no longer there to lead the congregations which he had planted'.[73]

Date

The Pastoral Epistles were certainly known and circulating by the end of the second century. The question is, how much earlier before that time are they attested?

Sadly for historians, the manuscript evidence is not much help here. The earliest textual witness to a Pauline letter-collection is $\mathfrak{P}^{46}$, a codex ordinarily dated to around AD 200. The papyrus lacks several folios, but includes all or part of Romans, Hebrews(!), 1–2 Corinthians, Ephesians, Galatians, Philippians, Colossians, and 1 Thessalonians. The missing folios towards the end would account for the absence of 2 Thessalonians and Philemon. But was there room for the pastorals? Could they have been squeezed in by compressing the writing style or by adding more folios? Or, if the Pastoral Epistles were not included, was it because they were unknown to the compiler, or because they were intended to be part of another collection of Paul's personal correspondence, perhaps including Philemon? We do not know. $\mathfrak{P}^{46}$ does not help us, then, in establishing an upper limit for the date of the pastorals.[74]

More help here comes from the attestation of the pastorals in sources from the middle and late second century. The Pastoral Epistles were known to Clement of Alexandria, Tertullian, Irenaeus, Athenagoras, Heracleon, Hegesippus, Theophilus, and Justin. The Muratorian canon (*c.* AD 180) reports that the pastorals were regarded as 'sacred' and esteemed as a guide to 'church discipline'.[75]

Another perennial question is whether the Pastoral Epistles were known to

---

[69] Mounce 2000, lxxviii.
[70] 1 Tim. 1.7–9; Tit. 1.10–14; 3.9–11; cf. Ac. 15.1–5; Gal. 2.1–5.12; Rom. 3.21–4.25; Phil. 3.1–11.
[71] 1 Tim. 2.4; 4.3; 6.20; 2 Tim. 2.18, 25; 3.7; Tit. 1.1; cf. 1 Cor. 4.8–13; 7.7–40; 8.1–13; 15.1–58; Col. 1.9–10; 3.10.
[72] 1 Cor. 11.3–16; 14.34–35.
[73] Marshall 1999, 57 and 77; cf. Mounce 2000, lxxxiv–xcix.
[74] See Marshall 1999, 6–7; Johnson 2001b, 17–18; Towner 2006, 6–7.
[75] Muratorian canon § 63–4.

Marcion, who was active in Rome in AD 140–50 or thereabouts. The pastorals formed no part of Marcion's *Apostolikon*, his Pauline letter-collection. Tertullian alleges that Marcion knew the pastorals and simply rejected them, just as he rejected other writings.[76] Alternatively, he might simply not have known them; one might imagine, fancifully, that they were even written in response to him. It is theoretically possible that the Pastoral Epistles were written after Marcion's time, but they are in fact highly unlikely to have been written specifically against Marcion. The false teaching confronted in the pastorals assumes a positive view of the Old Testament law, which is precisely what Marcion denied.[77] If anything, the rejection of 'myths' and 'genealogies' is more likely a swipe against Valentinian teaching, with its cosmology of multiple heavenly emanations, than to Marcion, who lacked such an elaborate cosmology. There are actually good reasons why Marcion would have rejected the pastorals: they rejected asceticism; they affirmed that the law was good and that the Old Testament was inspired, and they echo approvingly the *Shema* of Deuteronomy 6.5.[78] So did Tertullian have reliable information about Marcion's knowledge of Paul's letters, or was he simply drawing polemical inferences from the absence of the pastorals from Marcion's *Apostolikon*?

We do have some evidence for usage of the Pastoral Epistles from Christian writers who preceded Marcion's arrival in Rome. Polycarp, bishop of Smyrna, clearly echoes 1 Timothy 6.7, 10 in his letter to the Philippians (*c*. AD 120).[79]

> 'Is he [Paul] saying that men are natural leaders? It is difficult to prove that men have some special God-given talent for leadership. It is also undeniable that some women have more leadership qualities than some men. Thus it seems likely that Paul is not talking about the ability to lead or about one sex being superior to the other. If this was what he meant, he is contradicting his own words about our equality in Christ (Gal 3:28).'
>
> **Samuel Ngewa**, *1 & 2 Timothy and Titus*, 54.

There is another echo of 1 Timothy 1.3–5 in the letters of Ignatius (*c*. AD 115);[80] some have detected allusions to Titus 3.1 and 1 Timothy 1.17; 2.7 in *1 Clement* (*c*. AD 95).[81] This presses a date back into at least the first quarter of the second century, perhaps even earlier if the reference in *1 Clement* is accepted.

In brief, if the pastorals are authentic, they were composed across the mid-60s, with 1 Timothy and Titus probably written from Miletus or Macedonia after Paul's release from a first Roman imprisonment (and perhaps after a trip to Spain), and 2 Timothy composed in Rome during a second and final Roman imprisonment.

---

76 Tert. *Adv. Marc.* 5.21.
77 See 1 Tim. 1.7–9 and Tit. 3.9, and discussion in Koester 2000 [1982], 2.306 and Marshall 1999, 7 n. 15.
78 1 Tim. 1.8–10; 4.3, 5; 2 Tim. 3.16.
79 Polycarp *Phil.* 4.1; see Holmes 2005, 215–16.
80 Ign. *Eph.* 14.1; 20.1; *Magn.* 8.1; see Foster 2005, 170–2.
81 *1 Clem.* 2.7; 60.4; 61.2; see Marshall 1999, 4 and Towner 2006, 4.

Otherwise, if the pastorals are based on the later collection and redaction of Pauline fragments, then a date in the late first or early second century is plausible. Alternatively, if the pastorals are pseudonymous, then a date as late as the 160s is possible (if the 'allusions' in Polycarp, Ignatius, and Clement are more apparent than real), with the letters written in response to a pool of growing gnostic heresies from Cerinthus to Marcion.

Opponents

On Paul's opponents in the pastorals,[82] one cannot assume that the 'teachers' whom Paul excoriated in Crete (Titus) and Ephesus (1–2 Timothy) were one and the same.[83] Nonetheless there seem to be several homogeneous traits ascribed to the false teachers across all three letters, including deception,[84] promoting controversy,[85] rejecting sound teaching,[86] and engaging in unconscionable behaviour.[87]

By way of summary, the Pastoral Epistles confront deviant theologies, even coining the word *heterodidaskaleō* for 'teach false doctrines',[88] and elsewhere censoring 'demonic teachings'[89] and describing the dangers of a 'diseased craving for disputes and arguments about words'.[90] The false teaching is clearly rooted in Jewish soil and associated with the Torah, including the purity laws, and is associated with 'the circumcision group'.[91] What is more, the deviant teachings are attentive to Jewish 'myths' and 'genealogies',[92] and a rewriting of the creation story.[93] They exhibit a strong asceticism,[94] they possess an over-realized eschatology where the resurrection has already happened (presumably referring to an inward experience),[95] and they rely on something 'falsely called knowledge'.[96] There are perhaps even signs of a docetic christology.[97]

If we put all this together, we might surmise that we are dealing with variant forms of Jewish teaching, heading in the direction of what would later become Gnosticism. We have later evidence of types of Jewish Christianity that, according

---

82 See further Marshall 1999, 40–51; Mounce 2000, lxix–lxxvi; Johnson 2001b, 72–3; Towner 2006, 41–7.
83 On false teaching/teachers, see 1 Tim. 1.3, 7; 2.12; 4.2; 6.1–3; 2 Tim. 2.17; 3.8; 4.3; Tit. 1.11.
84 2 Tim. 3.13; Tit. 1.10.
85 1 Tim. 6.3–5; 2 Tim. 2.14–16, 23; Tit. 1.10; 3.9.
86 1 Tim. 6.5; 2 Tim. 3.8; 4.4; Tit. 1.14, 19.
87 1 Tim. 1.19; 4.2; 2 Tim. 3.1–9; Tit. 1.15–16.
88 1 Tim. 1.3; 6.3 and 2 Tim. 4.3–4; Tit. 1.10–11.
89 1 Tim. 4.1–2 *NTE/KNT*; 2 Tim. 2.26.
90 1 Tim. 6.4 *NTE/KNT*.
91 See 1 Tim. 1.7–9; Tit. 1.10, 15; 3.9; cf. Gal. 2.12; Eph. 2.11; Phil. 3.3.
92 1 Tim. 1.3–4; 4.7; 2 Tim. 4.4; Tit. 1.14; 3.9.
93 1 Tim. 2.11–14.
94 1 Tim. 4.3; Tit. 1.15.
95 2 Tim. 2.17–18. For this, see Wright *RSG*, 267–70.
96 1 Tim. 6.20 and Iren. *Adv. Haer.* 1.23.4; 2.14.7; 3.11.1; 3.12.12.
97 1 Tim. 3.16.

to Hegesippus, evolved into several gnostic sects,[98] including the type which underlies the *Gospel of Thomas*, and transformed further into the heretical teachings of Gnostics like Basilides, Carpocrates, Saturninus, and Cerinthus.[99]

Purpose

The purpose of the pastorals must be explained with respect to the intentions of each letter and their utility as a collection as a whole. The letter to Titus urges Titus to remain in Crete, to continue to instruct the young church, and to assist Zenas and Apollos on their travels. It asks Titus to winter with Paul in Nicopolis. First Timothy is an encouragement to Timothy to remain in Ephesus and to establish the orderliness and orthodoxy of the assembly. Second Timothy, very much Paul's 'testament', asks Timothy to keep the faith, to join him in Rome, and to bring John Mark with him. As a distinct collection, the pastorals constitute the final account of Paul's apostolic labours, an encouragement to hold firmly to the Christian message, and an overall guide to church order and discipline.[100]

> **OUTLINE OF 1 TIMOTHY**
>
> 1. Introductions and greetings (1.1–2)
> 2. Warning of false teachers (1.3–20)
> 3. Persistent prayer and propriety in worship (2.1–15)
> 4. Qualifications for overseers and deacons (3.1–16)
> 5. Refutation of the Ephesian heresy and Timothy's charge (4.1–16)
> 6. Managing the household of God (5.1—6.2a)
> 7. Flee falsehood and fight for the faith (6.2b–21a)
> 8. Letter closing (6.21b)

THE ARGUMENT OF 1 TIMOTHY

(See box: 'Outline of 1 Timothy'.)

1. Introductions and greetings (1.1–2)

Paul's God-given ministry emerges from the dual will of God and the Messiah. He greets Timothy as 'my true son in the faith', with a prayer for 'grace, mercy, and peace'.

2. Warning of false teachers (1.3–20)

Paul reminds Timothy again not to let unhealthy doctrines or esoteric speculations get a foothold in the assembly (see 'Portals and parallels: Irenaeus on Valentinian cosmology'). Strange teachings can lead people astray, not least when the teachers flout Torah itself (1.3–11).

---

[98] Eus. *Hist. Eccl.* 4.22.5.
[99] Irenaeus (*Adv. Haer.* 1.24.6) said about Basilides and his followers: 'They declare that they are no longer Jews, and that they are not yet Christians; and that it is not at all fitting to speak openly of their mysteries, but right to keep them secret by preserving silence.' On the gnostic movements see e.g. Wright *RSG*, 534–51; and Wright *Judas and the Gospel of Jesus*.
[100] The Muratorian canon § 64 says that the pastoral letters are esteemed by the church for 'the regulation of ecclesiastical discipline'.

Paul adds a thanksgiving for his own commission: God has taken the wildest, most violent of blaspheming persecutors, and has transformed him into not only a believer but also a trusted apostle and evangelist (1.12–17).

Paul's charge to Timothy is then that he shouldn't shipwreck his faith like Hymenaeus and Alexander, who left the pattern of sound teaching for some interiorized spirituality of personal awakening. He should hold on tight to two things: faith and a good conscience (1.18–20).

3. Persistent prayer and propriety in worship (2.1–15)

In the interest of peaceful relations with the authorities, Paul tells Timothy that the church should pray for them and for consequent social stability. The church has adopted the stance of the Jews under Rome: to pray, not *to* the authorities, but *for* them. There is, after all, only one saviour and mediator (God and the Messiah) (2.1–7).

Paul next urges men and women to avoid the normal stereotypes in their self-presentation: men must refrain from macho, angry behaviour, and women from endless fixations on jewellery and beauty treatments. Women should be given the leisure to study—a deeply counter-cultural idea; but (perhaps reflecting the all-female cult of Artemis in Ephesus), women should not usurp male leadership in the church. Few passages have so vexed and affronted modern interpreters as this one, partly because of very rare Greek words at the crucial point. Paul is saying that women must have the space and leisure to study and learn in their own way, not in order that they may muscle in and take over the leadership, as in the Artemis-cult, but so that men and women alike can develop whatever gifts of learning, teaching, and leadership God is giving them.

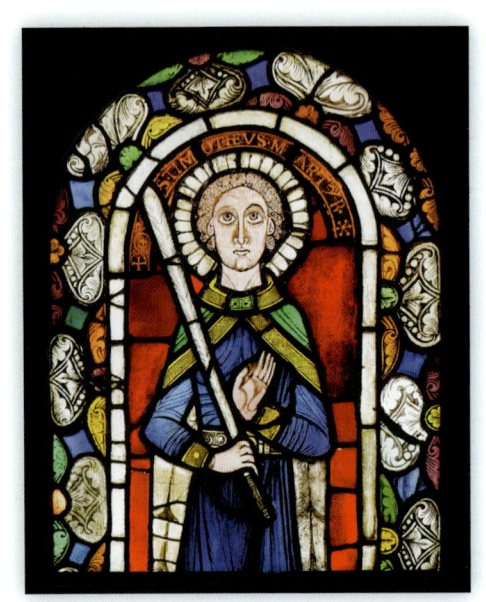

Stained glass of St Timothy, c. 1160, Paris
Selbymay / Wikimedia Commons CC BY-SA 3.0

4. Qualifications for overseers and deacons (3.1–16)

Paul moves on to the subject of church leaders, specifically the qualifications for the roles of overseer and deacon. Individuals holding these posts must be honest, respectable, self-controlled, holding to the faith, and well regarded. In verse 11, the 'women' (possibly women in a deacon's home, a deacon's wife, or perhaps a female deacon like Phoebe in Rom. 16.1) must demonstrate their overall trustworthiness. Paul is hoping to visit Timothy in Ephesus, but in lieu of his presence these instructions will guide Timothy on how the members of the household of God should conduct themselves.

5. Refutation of the Ephesian heresy and Timothy's charge (4.1–16)

Paul then singles out false teaching which has emerged in Ephesus. Deceitful teachers have been urging forms of asceticism, and this must be opposed. Timothy himself, despite his youthfulness, must set an example (4.11–16).

6. Managing the household of God (5.1—6.2a)

Paul then focuses on widows. As in the Thessalonian correspondence, the church clearly faced problems arising out of its determination to live as a single mutually supportive family. So many widows have taken advantage of this that an age restriction is now needed, coupled with other reasonably stringent criteria to decide who really ought to receive the church's financial support. This goes with other practical instructions for the church and for ordinary households.

7. Flee falsehood and fight for the faith (6.2b–21a)

Timothy, transmitting these teachings, must himself flee the love of money and fight the good fight of the faith, keeping these commands until the glorious return of King Jesus (6.11–16). Paul has a word for the wealthy: they should use their wealth to make themselves rich in good deeds, and lay up treasure in the coming age (6.17–18). Paul's final remarks to Timothy are for him to guard what is

PORTALS AND PARALLELS: IRENAEUS ON VALENTINIAN COSMOLOGY

The church Father, Irenaeus, the bishop of Lyon in Gaul in the late second century, wrote an anti-heretical book refuting the beliefs of various Christian sects. Irenaeus composed a mocking critique of the Valentinians, who speculated about a hierarchy and genealogy of heavenly beings, paired to each other, somehow procreating, eventually leading to the being who would make the world. According to Irenaeus, this was completely made up, nonsensical, and utterly absurd. So he offered, with biting sarcasm, his own version of Valentinian cosmology:

> There is a certain *Proarche*, a royal being, surpassing all thought, a power existing before every other substance, and extending into every spatial plane. But along with it there exists another power which I call *Gourd*; and along with this Gourd there exists yet another power which I call *Utter-Emptiness*. This Gourd and this Emptiness, since they are one with each other, they produced a fruit, everywhere visible, eatable, and delicious, which in secret fruit-language is called *Cucumber*. But along with this Cucumber there exists another power of the same essence, which I call *Melon*. These powers, the Gourd, Utter-Emptiness, the Cucumber, and the Melon, they brought forth the rest of the ridiculous assortment of melons so valued by Valentinus. For if it is fitting that language which is normally used for describing the universe can be attributed to some primal Tetrad, and if anyone may make up names at a whim, then who can prevent us from inventing these names, since they are just as credible as anyone else's nonsense, plus they are in widespread usage, and understood by all? (Iren. *Adv. Haer.* 1.11.4; tr. M. F. Bird, based on *ANF*)

entrusted to his care, the church and its gospel, and to turn aside from any debased nonsense that circulates under the name of 'knowledge' (6.19–21a).

8. Letter closing (6.21b)

Paul ends the letter abruptly: 'Grace be with you all.'

OUTLINE OF 2 TIMOTHY

1. Introductions, greetings, and thanksgiving (1.1–5)
2. Paul's exhortation to Timothy to follow his calling (1.6–18)
3. Paul's exhortation to Timothy to remain faithful (2.1–13)
4. Paul's instructions for addressing false teaching (2.14–26)
5. Prophecy, persecutions, and God's presence (3.1—4.8)
6. Paul's request for Timothy to visit him (4.9–18)
7. Final greetings, personal plea, and benediction (4.19–22)

THE ARGUMENT OF 2 TIMOTHY

(See box: 'Outline of 2 Timothy'.)

1. Introductions, greetings, and thanksgiving (1.1–5)

Paul anchors his apostleship in the divine purpose revealed in Messiah Jesus. He greets Timothy as his 'beloved son', for whom he thanks God as he prays towards their next meeting.

2. Paul's exhortation to Timothy to follow his calling (1.6–18)

We are not told what gift Timothy had, but it is likely that it had to do with leading the young church, giving it wise teaching and direction. Paul can tell him to stir up this gift, knowing that God's spirit does not create timidity, but 'power, love, and self-discipline', precisely what Timothy needs. Timothy must therefore not be ashamed. He must, rather, do what Phygelus and Hermogenes failed to do, staying faithful to God, guarding the deposit, and not forsaking Paul when he faces difficulties. Instead, Timothy should be like Onesiphorus, who searched for Paul and came to his assistance both in Rome and in Ephesus. This gives us a further clue as to what Paul was really hinting at earlier when he told Timothy not to be ashamed of him. He wanted him, too, to come and see him, to be with him, to be prepared to be identified with him, however dangerous it might seem (1.15–18).

3. Paul's exhortation to Timothy to remain faithful (2.1–13)

Paul exhorts Timothy to be strong and transmit Paul's teachings to further reliable people. He uses three quick metaphors; in Gorman's words, 'The minister of the gospel must suffer hardships single-mindedly like a soldier, unflinchingly like an athlete, and unceasingly like a farmer.'[101]

---

[101] Gorman 2017, 622–23.

4. Paul's instructions for addressing false teaching (2.14–26)

Timothy himself must not be quarrelsome, or be drawn in to pointless controversies like those with Hymenaeus and Philetus, who are destroying the faith of some by claiming that the resurrection has already happened (2.14–18). The firm foundation of believers is this: we are known by God. Timothy must flee the evil desires of youth; pursue virtue with like-minded people who are pure-hearted; avoid specious arguments; be a teacher, not an agitator; and instruct opponents with gentleness (2.22–26).

5. Prophecy, persecutions, and God's presence (3.1—4.8)

Warning about the likelihood of apostasy, Paul lists the types of behaviours to expect in the last days (3.1–5a), insisting that individuals showing these traits are already present and should be avoided. As the Egyptian magicians 'Jannes and Jambres' opposed Moses (see Ex. 7.11–12), such people will fail; perhaps this alludes to the prevalence of magic in Ephesus (3.5b–9).[102]

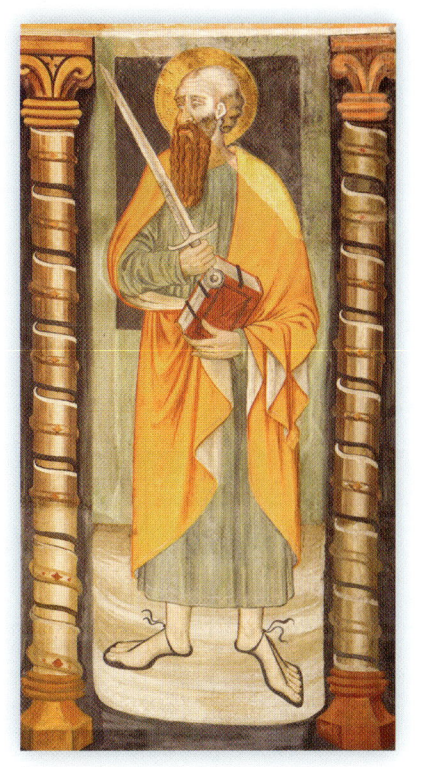

Fresco of St Paul in Chiesa di San Domenico and Capella delle Grazie, sixteenth century
Renata Sedmakova / Shutterstock

Paul, by contrast, urges Timothy to recall 'my teaching, my way of life, my purpose, faith, patience, love, endurance, persecutions, sufferings', and the persecutions he endured in 'Antioch, Iconium and Lystra'.[103] Timothy must hold fast by the God-breathed scripture:

> Every part of Scripture is God-breathed and useful one way or another—showing us truth, exposing our rebellion, correcting our mistakes, training us to live God's way. Through the Word we are put together and shaped up for the tasks God has for us.[104]

Timothy must preach and teach with care and courage (4.1–5). Paul becomes quite emotional as he contemplates his own demise: 'I have fought the good fight,

---

[102] See Ac. 19.17–19.
[103] 2 Tim. 3.10–11.
[104] 2 Tim. 3.16–17 *MSG*.

I have finished the race, I have kept the faith', but trusts firmly in the lord for what lies beyond (4.6–8).

6. Paul's request for Timothy to visit him (4.9–18)

Paul hopes that Timothy will join him in Rome. Others, apart from Luke, have gone their separate ways. He has been saved from one ordeal, but there will be others.

7. Final greetings, personal plea, and benediction (4.19–22)

Paul mixes greetings with an extra appeal: do please come before winter. The Lord and his grace will be with Timothy and his people.

OUTLINE OF TITUS

1. Letter opening (1.1–4)
2. Titus's role to appoint leaders and refute error (1.5–16)
3. The church as a teaching community (2.1–15)
4. Seeking the social good and resisting error (3.1–11)
5. Final instructions and letter closing (3.12–15)

THE ARGUMENT OF TITUS

(See box: 'Outline of Titus'.)

1. Letter opening (1.1–4)

Paul's opening greeting emphasizes the purpose of his apostolic service: to increase the faith, knowledge, and godliness of the elect in the salvation and hope that God has destined them for through the task of proclamation entrusted by God (1.1–3).

We know rather little about Titus. His Greek ancestry had caused trouble when he accompanied Paul to Jerusalem (Gal. 2.1–3). He went on Paul's behalf to Corinth and then met Paul in northern Greece with good news of the Corinthians' new attitude (2 Cor. 2.13; 7.5–16). He was then with Paul on his final journey to Corinth. At some later stage, while in prison, Paul sent him to Dalmatia (2 Tim. 4.10). Paul adds a warm blessing of grace and peace from God the father and the lord Jesus (Tit. 1.4).

2. Titus's role to appoint leaders and refute error (1.5–16)

Paul had commissioned Titus to stay in Crete and put the church in order. This leads to a comment about the requirements for those who serve as elders, not least in the light of opposition and false teaching (1.10–16).

3. The church as a teaching community (2.1–15)

Titus himself must teach sound doctrine, instructing older men to watch their behaviour and to remain sound in faith, love, and endurance. Similarly, older women must have a reverent and wholesome way of life, able to instruct younger women in setting a good example in loving their husbands and caring for their children.

Younger men must cultivate the virtue of self-control, particularly in the light of the tawdry vices of Crete. Titus must set a positive example. Mention of God as 'Saviour' then leads Paul to rejoice in the divine grace that has appeared, offering deliverance to all people. Titus must teach, exhort, reprove, and command (2.11–15).

4. Seeking the social good and resisting error (3.1–11)

Titus must help the church to be subject to ruling authorities and to live at peace with outsiders (Tit. 3.1–2). The salvation given by God's grace must issue in 'good works', the things which show puzzled and possibly hostile onlookers a different way to be human. Again, false teaching must not be allowed to distort all this.

5. Final instructions and letter closing (3.12–15)

Paul closes the letter, as usual, with greetings and travel plans.

THE PASTORAL EPISTLES AND THE BIG PICTURE

It is relatively easy to see what it might take to put the teaching of the Pastoral Epistles into practice. First, they demand that we guard the gospel, and the tradition which embodies it (see 2 Tim. 1.13–14). These letters are gospel-centred through and through. As William Mounce comments:

> At the heart of the P[astoral] E[pistles] is the gospel of Jesus Christ: God has acted in grace and mercy through the death of Christ with an offer of forgiveness, to which people must respond in faith, turning from evil, receiving empowerment through God's Spirit, and looking forward to eternal life . . . In all this, the P[astoral] E[pistles] are fully Pauline.[105]

Paul is anxious that everyone who professes Christian faith should allow the gospel to transform the whole of his or her life, so that the outward signs of the faith express a living reality that comes from the deepest parts of the personality. On top of that, he is also anxious that each Christian, and especially every teacher of the faith, should know how to build up the community in mutual love and support, rather than, by the wrong sort of teaching or behaviour, tearing it apart. We know even today, with the experience of two thousand years of history, how easily things can seem to fall apart. How much more fragile must the little churches have seemed in those early days, existing as tiny communities facing huge problems. An antidote to that is to ensure the integrity of the evangelical and apostolic foundations of any church.

---

[105] Mounce 2000, lxxvi.

The importance of passing on the pattern of teaching and sound doctrine to the next generation reminds us both of an academic paper given at a recent conference. The celebrated contemporary New Testament scholar Richard Hays completed his book *Echoes of Scripture in the Gospels* while undergoing treatment for pancreatic cancer. The book was reviewed by a panel of scholars at the Society of Biblical Literature meeting at San Antonio in 2016. The respondents were positive, but one in particular quibbled at the forceful expression, towards the end of the book, of Richard's view that all the gospel-writers used the Old Testament to identify Jesus with the God of Israel, and his further view that this was absolutely non-negotiable for the life of the church. When pressed as to why he had expressed himself so strongly, Hays began to weep for a moment, right in front of the audience, and his words have remained with us ever since. 'I thought', he explained, 'that these were going to be the last words I was ever going to write.' Happily, prayers were answered positively; the medical profession did its best; and at the time of completing this volume in 2019 Richard Hays is alive and well. As he exemplified, the best legacy to leave at the end of one's life or ministry is a firm grasp of the central truth of the gospel. All Christian teachers should bear in mind the long-term aim of being able to say, at the end: 'I have fought the good fight, I have finished the race, I have kept the faith' (2 Tim. 4.7).

Basilica of Agios Titos, Gortyna, Crete

Second, the pastorals are not woodenly doctrinaire or dogmatic. They abound with an emphasis on doing good deeds and living a life of faith. When I (MFB) first became a Christian, I was discipled by a young pastor of a young church, who took me under his wing and instructed me in the way of Jesus Christ. When it was time for me to leave town, he and his wife gave me a theology textbook with the following words inscribed inside it: 'Watch your life and doctrine closely. Persevere in them, because if you do, you will save both yourself and your hearers (1 Tim. 4.16).' That is advice for all of us if we are to run a good race. It is not enough to have good doctrine; one must be devoted to doing good things (see 1 Tim. 2.10; 5.10, 25; 6.18; 2 Tim. 2.21; 3.17; Tit. 1.8; 3.1, 8, 14). If we follow the example of our best leaders then we will in turn be an example to others (1 Tim. 1.16; 4.12; Tit. 2.7) and be the people whom Jesus redeemed in order 'to purify for himself a people that are his very own, eager to do what is good' (Tit. 2.14).

Third, the pastorals are a robust reminder about the importance of mentoring. Making yourself irreplaceable may be a great way of ensuring job security. But good leaders will always try to make themselves redundant by ensuring that there is someone of character and competence ready to take over. The pastoral letters remind us that we need to identify, train, mentor, and encourage our Timothys and Tituses, and indeed our Phoebes and Priscillas, to pick up the baton and carry forward the mission of the church. There should be no ministry without mentoring successors.

Further reading

Bassler, Jouette M. 1996. *1 Timothy, 2 Timothy, Titus*. ANTC; Nashville, TN: Abingdon.
Besançon Spencer, Aída. 2014. *1 Timothy*. NCCS; Eugene, OR: Cascade.
———. 2014. *2 Timothy and Titus*. NCCS; Eugene, OR: Cascade.
Donfried, Karl P. (ed.). 2008. *1 Timothy Reconsidered*. Leuven: Peeters.
Johnson, Luke Timothy. 2001. *The First and Second Letters to Timothy*. AB; New York: Doubleday.
Marshall, I. Howard, with Philip Towner. 1999. *The Pastoral Epistles*. ICC; Edinburgh: T&T Clark.
Mounce, William. 2000. *Pastoral Epistles*. WBC; Nashville: Thomas Nelson.
Ngewa, Samuel M. 2009. *1 & 2 Timothy and Titus*. ABCS; Grand Rapids, MI: Zondervan.
Pietersen, Lloyd Keith. 2004. *Polemic of the Pastorals: A Sociological Examination of the Development of Pauline Christianity*. London: T&T Clark.
Porter, Stanley E. 1995. 'Pauline Authorship and the Pastoral Epistles: Implications for Canon.' *BBR* 5: 105–23.
Towner, Philip. 2006. *The Letters to Timothy and Titus*. NICNT; Grand Rapids, MI: Eerdmans.
Walker, Peter. 2012. 'Revisiting the Pastoral Epistles—Part I and II.' *EJT* 21: 4–16, 120–32.
Wall, Robert W. 1995. 'Pauline Authorship and the Pastoral Epistles: A Response to S. E. Porter.' *BBR* 5: 125–8.
Wall, Robert W., and Richard B. Steele. 2012. *1 and 2 Timothy and Titus*. THNTC; Grand Rapids, MI: Eerdmans.

The Trinity and the four evangelists from the *Bible historiale* of Charles of France, c. AD 1420, held in Paris

© *British Library Board. All Rights Reserved / Bridgeman Images*

VI

THE GOSPELS AND THE STORY OF GOD

The Gospels were written to invite readers to enter a worldview. In this worldview, there is one God, the creator of the world, who is at work in his world through his chosen people, Israel. With the coming of Israel's Messiah, that long work has reached a moment which is both a climax and a new start. Israel's purpose is accomplished; Israel's long bondage to the pagan world is ended—and all through Jesus. The gospels' major focus on the death and resurrection of Jesus is *not* to be explained as the reading back of 'later Christian theology' into a story whose 'biographical' intent should have kept such reference to a minimum. The evangelists were not downplaying the significance of the life and mission, the aims and achievements, of the one who was thus crucified and raised. They were emphasizing these latter events as the proper and necessary climax of precisely the type of story that was being told. Jesus' kingdom-work was completed on the cross, and publicly vindicated in the resurrection; Calvary and Easter mean what they mean in the light of the kingdom-work that went before. Thus the evangelists' theological and pastoral program has in no way diminished (as some have supposed) their intent to write about Jesus of Nazareth. It actually demands that they do just that.[1]

---

1   Wright *NTPG*, 403.

24

The Gospel according to Mark

Mark, at first blush the easiest of the synoptic Gospels, retreats from the advancing interpreter like a rainbow's end. A simple outline, it seems at first sight: eight chapters to explain who Jesus is, eight to explain that he is going to die. An abrupt beginning and a mysterious end, granted; but a straightforward account in between. But we reckon thus without the literary critics. The abruptness of the opening, and the darkness of the ending, many have said, permeate the whole. Mark is a book of secrets, of veils, of mysteries.[1]

CHAPTER AT A GLANCE

This chapter explains the story, themes, and theology of Mark's gospel.

By the end of this chapter you should be able to:

- understand the origins of Mark's gospel in the context of early Christianity;
- describe the basic features of Mark's story of Jesus;
- grasp the general themes in Mark's gospel.

INTRODUCTION

The gospel of Mark is a densely packed, fast-paced, action-filled narrative about Jesus of Nazareth, his life and teachings, his divine identity and human vulnerability, God's kingdom breaking in through him, and the Judean and Roman opposition mounted against him. It is a story of prophecy and power, resistance and betrayal. The story's climax includes Jesus' violent death by crucifixion and an abrupt and enigmatic ending pointing to his resurrection. While Mark's style of Greek is primitive and even sometimes clumsy, his craft as a storyteller is arguably without peer. Mark more than makes up in power what (by comparison with the other gospels) he lacks in length.

We will have more to say about the genre of Mark and the other gospels later. It suffices here to say that Mark's gospel marries the early church's gospel-preaching with

---

[1] Wright *NTPG*, 390.

the Jesus-tradition, placing them into a literary genre best described, from one viewpoint at least, as a hellenistic biography akin to other biographies of figures like Socrates and Julius Caesar. Mark's gospel is also, however, linked so closely to the story of Israel (which, in scripture, contains other 'biographies' like those of Abraham, Joseph, or Moses) that it is best to see it as an essay in a mixed genre that includes what a first-century audience would have recognized as 'biography' but goes well beyond it.

There are, after all, obvious differences from hellenistic biography, not least in that Mark's gospel is very theocentric. It is, one might say, a God-story; while Jesus is the main protagonist, we must never forget that the scriptural prophecies with which Mark introduces his book are not about the coming

Mark the Evangelist was often symbolized by a lion.
Public Domain

of a Messiah, but about the coming of God himself. The substance of the story, too, is all about God: God's Messiah proclaiming God's kingdom to God's people Israel.[2] Mark, in short, like the other gospels in their different ways (and, we must suppose, like most early Christians), saw the story of Jesus as the culmination of Israel's great story. In addition, Mark, like the others, is writing for the church, intending that what he says will be formative for its mission and life. As the Psalms and prophets regularly insist, when God does for Israel what he has promised to do for Israel, the wider world will be brought in to the drama.

While Mark's gospel is a God-story, and a very Jewish one at that, it demands to be seen in the (admittedly contested) category of 'apocalyptic'.[3] What we mean by this is that Mark highlights the notion of a secret to be penetrated, of a mystery to be explored and grasped by faith. The standard 'apocalypse', after all (we might think of *1 Enoch*, or *4 Ezra*, or the book of Daniel itself), was not a book about 'the end of history', complete with conspiracy theories or—as in some of the wilder interpretations of the book of Revelation!—modern military vehicles described in code as though they were kinds of grasshoppers. Apocalyptic writing did many things, but one central function, using a complex blend of myth and metaphor, was to tell the story of Israel's history, to bring it into the present, and to point forward to the moment when the forces of (this-worldly) evil would be routed and the

---
2 Boring 2014, 3.
3 See esp. Shively 2012 and 2013; on 'apocalyptic' see Wright *NTPG*, 280–338, and *PRI* Part II.

(this-worldly) liberation of Israel would finally take place. Such a book would provide the clue for how to *interpret* history, not to escape from it. Mark, like Elisha at Dothan, intended to draw back the veil for a moment, allowing the heavenly reality to be seen in the midst of the earthly.[4]

Viewed in this light, Mark tells the story of Jesus as the unveiled story of Israel. At key moments in the story—the baptism, the transfiguration, the confession of Peter at Caesarea Philippi, Caiaphas's question at the trial, and the centurion's words at the foot of the cross—the veil is lifted, eyes are opened (at least the eyes of Mark's readers), and, like Elisha's servant, we see the horses and chariots of fire round about the prophet. *Thus Mark's whole telling of the story of Jesus is designed to function as an apocalypse.* The reader is constantly invited by the gospel as a whole to do what the disciples are invited to do in the parable-chapter of Mark 4: to discover the inner secret behind the strange outer story. The secret is this: in the person of Jesus, God has become king, launching the restoration of Israel and the inauguration of the new creation.

This secret was shocking. This was not how Jesus' contemporaries had imagined the prophecies being fulfilled. It was not how Mark's contemporaries expected that a world ruler would emerge.

Mark has, in fact, told the story of Jesus in such a way as to reconfigure the Jewish hope around him: Israel's glorious expectation has been fulfilled paradoxically in the death and resurrection of Israel's Messiah, and the negative side of the fulfilment— the overthrow of Israel's dark enemies—is to be further fulfilled (or, perhaps, has recently been further fulfilled) in the destruction of Jerusalem itself. That is shocking enough. But actually Mark's telling of this story is totally subversive: this whole complex event was actually the coming of the kingdom of Israel's God, the event of which prophets had spoken in golden terms. This event, in terrible paradox, is to be seen as that for which Israel had longed, that for which revolutionaries had fought and martyrs had died. The truth, from Mark's point of view, is so staggering, not least because of what is implied all through, and eventually is stated plainly in the Olivet Discourse (Mk. 13). The coming of the kingdom does not mean the great vindication of Jerusalem, the glorification of the Temple, the real return from exile in terms of Judea living in peace and the gentile forces sent packing. It means, rather, the desolation of Jerusalem, the destruction of the Temple, and the vindication of Jesus and his people. Jerusalem and its hierarchy—the wealthy Sadducean high priesthood, the brooding Herod—have now taken on the roles of Babylon, Edom, and Antiochus Epiphanes in this stark retelling of their story. They are the city whose fall spells the vindication of the true people of Israel's God. The prophecies of rescue from the tyrant have come true in and for Jesus himself, and in and for his people.[5]

---

[4] 2 Kgs. 6.15–19.
[5] See Jer. 51.26 with Mk. 13.2; Isa. 13.10 and 34.4 with Mk. 13.24; Isa. 52.11–12 and Jer. 51.6, 45 with Mk. 13.14–17; Jer. 51.46 with Mk. 13.7–8; Zech. 26 (in context) with Mk. 13.27; and of course Dan. 7.13–14 with Mk. 13.26.

In the end, as Richard Hays comments, the gospel of Mark is 'a mysterious story enveloped in apocalyptic urgency, a story that focuses relentlessly on the cross and ends on a note of hushed, enigmatic hope'.[6] It is a story about how, in the life and death of Jesus, God has become king.

CONTEXTUAL AND CRITICAL MATTERS

Origins of Mark's gospel

The gospel of Mark is strictly anonymous. The author remains unidentified. The only point where some have detected a self-reference is perhaps ironic: a young man in the garden leaves his linen garment and runs away naked.[7] The title *Kata Markon* ('According to Mark') was probably added later when tradition ascribed the book to Mark.[8] Internally, we can infer that the gospel of Mark was written by a Greek-speaking Jewish Christian, deeply familiar with the Old Testament, and clear in his mind that Jesus was indeed 'son of God'. He was perhaps, as very early tradition suggests, basing his work on the preaching of Peter himself; Peter is the first and last disciple mentioned, and many of the stories can easily be seen as reminiscences from Peter himself. Some have detected a theological affinity with Pauline thought, given the emphasis on the cross, redemption, and the gentiles, though this may simply mean that the author was a standard, mainline early Christian.[9] Externally, the early church associated the gospel of Mark with John Mark, a missionary colleague of Paul and Barnabas, who later became Peter's 'interpreter' in Rome.[10] Certainty is impossible, but John Mark is probably the best candidate, not least because his name, as a younger and less well-known early Christian, would not naturally occur to second-century Christians when seeking to name the book. No alternative figure has ever warranted consideration. As to what we know about John Mark, Richard Bauckham gives a good summary:

> John Mark, a member of a Cypriot Jewish family settled in Jerusalem and member of the early Jerusalem church, was then in Antioch, accompanied his cousin Barnabas and Paul on their missionary journey as far as Pamphylia, later accompanied Barnabas to Cyprus, and is finally heard of in Rome . . . where 1 Peter also places him.[11]

---

6   Hays 2014, 17.
7   Mk. 14.52.
8   See Hengel 1985, 74–5; Bird 2014b, 254–60; Dunn 2015, 48–50.
9   See Bauckham 2006, 125; Bird 2011b.
10 On NT references to John Mark, see Ac. 12.11–17, 25; 13.5; 5.36–41; Philem. 24; Col. 4.10; 2 Tim. 4.11; 1 Pet. 5.13. On John Mark as Peter's 'interpreter', see Papias's statement from the 'elder' recorded in Eus. *Hist. Eccl.* 3.39.15 (c. AD 110), and similar statements can be found in the anti-Marcionite prologue (c. AD 160–80), Iren. *Adv. Haer.* 3.1.1–2 (AD 180), Clement of Alexandria (Eus. *Hist. Eccl.* 2.15.1–2; 6.14.5–7) (c. AD 180–200), and implicitly in Justin (*Dial.* 106.3) (AD 150).
11 Bauckham, 1998a, 35; see too Dunn 2015, 50.

Decapolis and lands beyond the Jordan

Date

When it comes to a date for Mark, assuming (see below) that Matthew and Luke used Mark sometime in the late 70s or 80s, most scholars place the date of Mark's composition around AD 65–75. That is rendered all the more plausible by the focus on the destruction of the Temple in Mark 13, where Jesus' prophecy against the Temple is recalled in dramatic fashion probably because it is either an imminent possibility or else a recent memory for the audiences.[12] At the same time, there were major threats to the Judean capital earlier in the century when the emperor Gaius proposed to put up his statue there (AD 39). It is not impossible that Mark 13 reflects that crisis as much as the later one.

---

12 See Hengel 1985, 26–8; Head 2004; Dunn 2015, 52–4.

Place of composition

So where was Mark's gospel written? Some have speculated on Galilee or Alexandria as the right place; but the two primary options have been Rome and Syria.

Rome has been the most popular, given the association of Mark with Peter and Rome (1 Pet. 5.13).[13] Many also appeal to the Latinisms in the text, to the notes which explain that the Greek *lepta* is the equivalent to a Roman *quadrans* (Mk. 12.42) and that the *aulē* ('courtyard') equates to the *praetorium* ('military headquarters') during Jesus' trial (Mk. 15.16).[14] Others see proof of a Roman environment from the anti-Roman posture of Mark, particularly given the parallel language between the Markan story of Jesus and imperial propaganda for the empire and the emperor.[15] Many believe that the stress on enduring persecution reflects the Neronian persecution of Roman Christians in the mid to late 60s (see Mk. 4.13; 8.38; 10.30; 13.9–13). However, the problems with Rome are as follows: (1) many scholars regard 1 Peter as a pseudonymous writing, casting doubt on the connection between Peter and Mark that generated, in the second century, a link which would lend credence to Mark's gospel;[16] (2) the Latinisms could be taken from the military and economic spheres common in any city with significant Roman influence (such as Corinth, Philippi, Pisidian Antioch or Ephesus);[17] (3) an anti-Rome disposition was possible anywhere where Roman power and culture was resented, and need not point to the city itself; and (4) persecution and harassment of Christians in the first century was not limited to Rome.

Others contend that Mark was written in the vicinity of Galilee, Syria, or the Trans-Jordan, perhaps even the Decapolis.[18] The context for understanding Mark would then not be the Neronian persecutions in Rome in the 60s, but the Jewish revolt against Rome (AD 66–70) and its aftermath, when church members fled Judea. The warnings about false messiahs and false prophets (Mk. 13.22) would certainly fit Josephus's description of Judea before and during the revolt.[19] However, while one can imagine a Jewish Christian surviving the Jewish revolt and writing this gospel to encourage fellow-believers in Syria, the Trans-Jordan, and the Decapolis, our sources tell us very little about the churches there at this time.[20] In fact, discerning any provenance in Mark's gospel is notoriously difficult: Mark resonates with Christians wherever they need encouraging in discipleship under duress. That is no doubt one reason why Mark's gospel circulated as widely, and quickly, as it did.

---

13 See Hengel 1985, 1–30; Incigneri 2003; Head 2004; Winn 2008.
14 Hengel 1985, 28–30; Gundry 1993, 1043–5; Incigneri 2003, 100–3.
15 See e.g. Evans 2001, lxxx–xciii; Winn 2008.
16 See e.g. Kok 2015, 159–60.
17 Collins 2007, 100.
18 Theissen 1991, 235–58; Marcus 1992; 2000–9, 1.33–7 (Syria); Roskam 2004 (Galilee); Wardle 2016 (Decapolis); but see critiques of an eastern provenance by Carter 2014 and Incigneri 2014.
19 Jos. *War* 2.433–4, 444, 652; 6.313; 7.29–31.
20 Dunn 2015, 56.

Ultimately, if one accepts John Mark as the author and the link between him, Peter, and Rome, then a setting in Rome in the late 60s may be the most probable option. If not, then the field is open both geographically and chronologically.

Purpose

So why was Mark written? One theory that has had more than its fair share of attention was proposed over a century ago by William Wrede. He argued that the commands to secrecy (for example in Mk. 8.29–31) were invented by the evangelist as a literary fiction to account for the fact that (1) the early church believed Jesus to be the Messiah but (2) nobody could recall him ever claiming to be. The answer was that Jesus himself had kept it secret.[21] Despite its influence, this theory has obvious flaws. What is silenced in the gospel of Mark is not necessarily messianic (like healings and exorcisms [for example Mk. 1.44; 7.36]); and some very 'messianic' material is not silenced at all (like Bartimaeus calling Jesus 'son of David' [Mk. 10.47–49]). Moreover, the injunctions to secrecy fail; word about Jesus is broadcast far and wide, resulting in large crowds being drawn to Jesus. It is much more likely that Mark uses the secrecy motif to accentuate the mystery and power surrounding Jesus himself, with the secret being gradually disclosed as the narrative presses towards its conclusion.[22] Wrede, in fact, seems to have confused 'Messiahship' (and the word 'Christ') with 'divinity', as many still do. His work is an unfortunate period-piece from a time when one influential strand of scholarship took it for granted that Jesus was an 'ordinary man' whom the church subsequently 'divinized'. Wrede, ironically, thus invented a Markan 'messianic secret' to cover up for the lack of evidence for his own position.

Far more general proposals about Mark's purpose have focused on his teaching about who Jesus really was, and about what discipleship really involved. For many scholars, Mark's aim is 'helping the church clarify its understanding of the meaning of the Christ event and discipleship to Jesus in a threatening, confused, and conflicted situation';[23] or 'Mark's aim or message rightly revolve around the two broad areas of christology and discipleship, of who Jesus is and of what it means to follow him'.[24] Such general proposals are hard to fault, but they more likely reflect ways in which Mark would be useful, rather than his overriding purpose.

Far more probable is that Mark's gospel is an *apology* for a crucified Messiah and a *polemic* against the imperial power of Rome.

First, the gospel of Mark spells out that Jesus is the royal son of God, the Messiah, in whom God's kingship is being mysteriously revealed through his kingdom-announcement, his healings, and his exorcisms (overthrowing the dark enslaving

---

21 Wrede 1971.
22 Bird 2009b, 66–70.
23 Boring 2014, 22.
24 France 2002, 23.

powers). But, in contrast to many expectations at the time, Jesus' messianic vocation and inauguration of the kingdom were focused on his suffering and crucifixion. That is where Mark's Jesus holds together Isaiah's 'Suffering Servant' and the mysterious 'one like a son of man' in Daniel, as the hinge on which God's kingdom-plan will turn. Mark's portrait of Jesus is not that of a Galilean prophet who unfortunately got mixed up with powers too strong for him. Rather, Jesus embraced crucifixion as the calling through which Israel's Messiah would redeem and rescue his people. Jesus claimed to speak for God over and against the Pharisees, scribes, high priests, and even the Temple itself; his crucifixion was not an accident, but his own chosen means, on the basis of his strange scripture-shaped vocation, to complete his work of kingdom-inauguration. These observations, which fit well with Mark's narrative all through, suggest that a primary intention of the author was to explain Jesus' crucifixion. Mark wants to lead readers to believe that Jesus is the Messiah—not despite the cross, but precisely because of it.[25]

Second, the gospel of Mark arguably has counter-imperial connotations. The language of 'gospel', 'lord', and 'kingdom of God' presents Jesus as the figure who ushers in a new world-order that will rival, and potentially replace, the Roman empire.[26] Mark's crucifixion scene portrays Jesus' death as a mock-triumph, the antitype to a Roman victory parade (such as the one Titus celebrated in AD 71 when he entered Rome with captives and booty from the overthrow of Jerusalem).[27] The moment Jesus dies, Mark reports that at the scene, 'when the centurion, who stood there in front of Jesus, saw how he died, he said, "Surely this man was the Son of God!"'[28] In deliberate dramatic irony, a Roman centurion addresses Jesus with an honorific designation in regular use for Caesar himself! Evans believes 'the Markan evangelist presents Jesus as the true son of God and in doing so deliberately presents Jesus in opposition to Rome's candidates for a suitable emperor, Saviour, and Lord'.[29]

MARK'S STORY OF JESUS

(See box: 'Outline of Mark'.)

> **OUTLINE OF MARK**
>
> 1. Prologue (1.1–15)
> 2. Galilean ministry (1.16—8.21)
> 3. The revelation of the Messiah in Caesarea Philippi (8.22—9.1)
> 4. Jesus, discipleship, and the way to the cross (9.2—10.52)
> 5. Jesus in Jerusalem (11.1—12.44)
> 6. The Olivet Discourse (13.1—37)
> 7. The Passion of Jesus (14.1—15.39)
> 8. The resurrection (16.1–8 [and 9–20])

---

25 See esp. Gundry 1993, 1022–6; Evans 2001, xciii; deSilva 2004, 218–24; Winn 2008, 28–31; Bird 2012b, 55–6.
26 Evans 2001, lxxi–xciii; Winn 2008.
27 Schmidt 1995.
28 Mk. 15.39.
29 Evans 2001, lxxxix.

PORTALS AND PARALLELS: ANCIENT USAGES OF *GOSPEL*

There are some very good examples of the use of 'good news' or 'gospel' in greco-roman sources, among Diaspora Jews, in the Old Testament, and in second-Temple Jewish literature.

First, from the greco-roman context, the Priene inscription, containing the official calendar of the Asian League (9 BC), mandated that the birthday of the emperor Augustus would mark the beginning of the Asian new year. The decree celebrated the birth of Augustus as a renewal of the natural order and his life as a means of beneficence and benefaction to all the peoples of Roman Asia:

> It seemed good to the Greeks of Asia, in the opinion of the high priest Apollonius of Menophilus Azanitus: 'Since Providence, which has ordered all things and is deeply interested in our life, has set in most perfect order by giving us Augustus, whom she filled with virtue that he might benefit humankind, sending him as a Saviour, both for us and for our descendants, that he might end war and arrange all things, and since he, Caesar, by his appearance (excelled even our anticipations), surpassing all previous benefactors, and not even leaving to posterity any hope of surpassing what he has done, and since the birthday of the god Augustus was the beginning of the *good tidings for the world* that came by reason of him,' which Asia resolved in Smyrna. (*OGIS* 458)

Second, among Diaspora Jews, Josephus refers to the report about General Vespasian's accession to the imperial throne, narrating how:

> . . . every city celebrated the *good news* and offered sacrifices on his behalf. (Jos. *War* 4.618)

Later, Josephus adds:

> On reaching Alexandria Vespasian was greeted by the *good news* from Rome and embassies of congratulation from every quarter of the world now his own . . . the whole empire being now secured and the Roman state saved beyond expectation. (Jos. *War* 4.656–7)

The accession of Vespasian to imperial power was not just a political headline. His accession was celebrated as the socio-political salvation of the Roman empire from the disastrous year of AD 68–9 that had seen three emperors (i.e. Galba, Otho, and Vitellius) all quickly rise and fall in the wake of Nero's suicide.

1. Prologue (1.1–15)

Mark's gospel, as we have it, opens with 'The beginning of the gospel about Jesus the Messiah' (1.1).[30] The word 'gospel' (*euangelion*) was in use in connection with celebrations of the Roman emperor and his achievements. But the term also goes back to Isaiah 40 and 52, where the echoes are of the 'good news' of the end of exile, the 'new exodus', and the return of YHWH himself to rescue his people and to reign over them, and the world, as king (see 'Portals and parallels: ancient uses of *gospel*'). These two ultimately belong together. If the scriptural model means what it says, this 'good news' will involve the God of Israel becoming Lord of all the nations—as is also the case in Daniel 7, a passage of great importance for Mark.

---

[30] Tr. M. F. Bird. Some manuscripts add 'son of God', which would make a good *inclusio* with Mk. 15.39, but the authenticity is doubtful. It is possible that this opening sentence was added later to an early copy that had lost its opening as well as its closing material—as happened to many scrolls.

> *(cont.)*
>
> Third, in the book of Isaiah, the prophet comforts the Babylonian exiles with the words:
>
> > Get you up to a high mountain, O Zion, herald of *good tidings*, lift up your voice with strength, O Jerusalem, herald of *good tidings*; lift it up, do not fear; say to the cities of Judah, 'Here is your God!'*
>
> > This is what the Sovereign LORD says: 'At first my people went down to Egypt to live; lately, Assyria has oppressed them. And now what do I have here?' declares the LORD. 'For my people have been taken away for nothing, and those who rule them mock,' declares the LORD. 'And all day long my name is constantly blasphemed. Therefore my people will know my name; therefore in that day they will know that it is I who foretold it. Yes, it is I.' How beautiful on the mountains are the feet of those who bring *good news*, who proclaim peace, who bring *good tidings*, who proclaim salvation, who say to Zion, 'Your God reigns!'†
>
> Similarly, in the Psalms of Solomon *(c. 40 BC)*, the author echoes Isaianic language in looking for the day when good news is proclaimed, and the exiles finally return to Jerusalem to worship the Lord in peace and prosperity:
>
> > Blow the trumpet in Zion, the signal for the holy ones! Declare in Jerusalem the voice of one bringing good news of God's mercy to Israel in watching over them. Stand on a high place, Jerusalem, and look at your children gathered from the east and the west by the Lord. From the north they come in the joy of their God; from distant islands God has restored them. He levelled the high mountains to the ground for them; the hills fled at their coming. The forests shaded them as they passed by; God made every sweet-smelling tree sprout up for them. So that Israel might come under the watchful care of the glory of their God. (*Ps. Sol.* 11.1–5; tr. M. F. Bird)
>
> ---
>
> * Isa. 40.9. Some translations make Zion/Jerusalem the recipient, rather than the herald, of the 'good tidings', but the content is the same: the rescuing return of YHWH.
> † Isa. 52.4–7.

His portrayal of John the Baptist, the 'voice in the wilderness' preparing the way for the coming 'Lord' about whom Isaiah spoke, sets up the reader to understand the developing scene in scriptural, theological, and also polemically political terms (1.2–3).

Mark provides a short account of John the Baptist's ministry, noting his place in the wilderness, the historical place of covenant renewal (see Hos. 2.14), the masses coming to him, his prophetic attire, and his baptism of repentance for the forgiveness of sins. He testified to a 'coming one', perhaps YHWH himself, who would pour out God's spirit on the people (1.4–8).

Jesus is then baptized by John as an act of solidarity with Israel in this moment of 'new exodus'. The spirit descends on him, and the voice from heaven draws together Psalm 2.7 and Isaiah 42.1. Jesus is anointed for his royal role as the 'servant' who will simultaneously embody Israel and Israel's rescuing God (1.9–11). He then, driven by the spirit, endures a wilderness temptation, from which he returns to launch his public work (1.12–13). The arrest of John signals Jesus' moment: he takes it as his cue to begin announcing that the time has arrived for God to become king. The only appropriate response is the radical change of heart known as 'repentance', corresponding to what Deuteronomy had urged when speaking of the ultimate end of exile (1.14–15; Dt. 30).

2. Galilean ministry (1.16—8.21)

Jesus' public work in Galilee, as described by Mark, is a whirlwind of healings, exorcisms, teaching, and confrontations with local leaders. Jesus calls two sets of brothers to join him as 'fishers of men' (1.16–20 KJV). He astounds the crowds with his unmediated authority, healing a man with an unclean spirit on the sabbath (1.21–28). He heals Simon's mother-in-law, then various others (1.29–34). After retreating to pray, he and his followers take their message on the road throughout Galilee (1.35–39). He heals a man with a virulent skin-disease, who celebrates wildly despite Jesus' injunctions to silence (1.40–45).

Across Mark 2.1—3.6 we find miracle stories that provoke increasingly volatile confrontations with local cultural leaders, perhaps because in apparently deliberately flouting the sabbath commandment Jesus was implicitly declaring that he was inaugurating the 'age to come' (towards which every sabbath was seen as a distant signpost). This implicit claim is reinforced by his claim to forgive sins; is he usurping God's prerogative (2.1–12)? He calls a tax-collector and sits down to celebrate the kingdom with him and other 'sinners', again causing offence for those who cannot imagine that this is what the kingdom will look like. Jesus, however, has come like a doctor to heal the sick (2.13–17). The same puzzle is apparent in the controversy about fasting: the bridegroom is here, so the party cannot stop! What Jesus does is a new thing, a joyous thing, and though a time for mourning will follow, the present is for celebration (2.18–22). A further sabbath controversy (Jesus' disciples plucking grain) is answered with the royal example of David, pointing to the 'son of man' as lord of the sabbath (2.23–28). In the

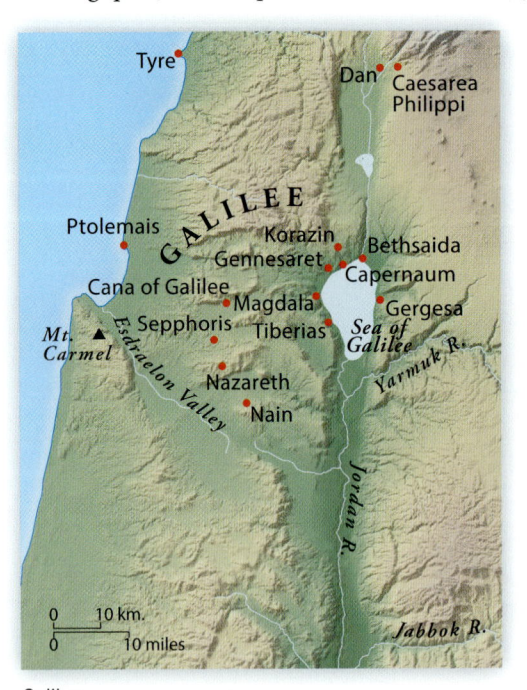

Galilee

final confrontation story, Jesus enters a synagogue and heals a man with a shrivelled hand on the sabbath, shaming the Pharisees in the process, which is why the Pharisees conspire with the Herodians—not their natural allies—to kill Jesus (3.1–6). Throughout this breathless narrative Mark presents Jesus as inaugurating God's long-awaited 'age to come' in and through his own person, with his assumed and effective authority. He is not (as in some grossly anachronistic presentations) teaching a new 'religion' over against something called 'Judaism' with its supposed 'legalism'. He is enacting what, in Mark's presentation, he takes to be a scripturally rooted messianic agenda of planting the seeds of the kingdom, of God's new, healing reign.

Mark then summarizes further work, including exorcisms (3.7–12), leading to the call of the Twelve, obviously symbolic for the reconstituted Israel Jesus was forming around himself. We then encounter what is inelegantly known as a 'Markan sandwich', a larger story with a shorter one inside it. Jesus has returned home to Capernaum; members of his family try to take charge of him, worried that 'He is out of his mind!' But then the scene shifts to the Jerusalem scribes, who have come (as well they might) to check out this dangerous kingdom-prophet. They accuse him of being in league with Beelzebul.[31] Jesus responds by showing the absurdity, as well as the danger, of such an accusation, and with the positive claim that he, Jesus, has plundered the 'strong man' who had held Israel and the world captive. The scene then shifts back to Jesus' family. His mother and brothers are outside looking for him, but Jesus, ignoring them, defines his 'family' as those who do God's will. These two scenes, thus sandwiched together, indicate the enormity of Jesus' explicit as well as implicit claims and the inevitable scandal that would follow (3.20–35).

All this work of 'sowing' the kingdom prepares us for the major discourse in which Mark collects several parables about the kingdom of God (4.1–34). These include the parables of the sower, lamp, bushel basket, growing seed, and mustard seed. In line with prophecy, God is again 'sowing' Israel, restoring its fortunes after exile, but this will not work out the way people expect. The kingdom is a mystery: Mark 4.1–20 has, in itself, the sequence of an 'apocalyptic' vision, with a strange story followed by questions about God's kingdom and, in answer, a step-by-step explanation of the story.[32] The kingdom may indeed have small, inauspicious beginnings, but like a mustard seed it will grow into something great.

Signs of the inbreaking rule—and presence!—of Israel's God now intensify. Jesus and the disciples are caught in a furious squall on the Sea of Galilee in their small boat (4.35–41). The disciples wake Jesus up, and he calms the storm with a word. When the disciples ask, 'Who then is this?', Mark's understanding is clear. As Richard Hays puts it, 'For any reader versed in Israel's Scripture, there can be only one

---

31 Technically, this refers to the Philistine god of Ekron. But the term was used as a nickname for 'the satan'.
32 See e.g. Dan. 2.31–45; 7.1–27; *4 Ez.* 9.38—10.59.

> 'The Gentile [Syro-Phoenician] woman requests a cure outside the context of Jesus' call to Israel; she seems to be asking for a cure which is detached from the inbreaking of God's Kingdom, merely taking advantage of the opportunity provided by the presence of a miracle worker. This is perhaps the reason for Jesus' stern answer; his healings are part of something greater and cannot be torn out of that context. Mark does not interpret the woman's reply as simply a witty retort; by accepting Jesus' terms, she recognizes that salvation belongs to Israel and shows her faith in something more far reaching than a miraculous power to heal the sick. Many of Mark's readers will themselves have been Gentiles. For them, the story will have provided reassurance that Jesus himself responded to the faith of a Gentile and gave her a share in the blessings of the kingdom.'
>
> **Morna Hooker**, *The Gospel According to Saint Mark*, 182.

possible answer: it is the Lord God of Israel who has the power to command wind and sea and to subdue the chaotic forces of nature.'[33] The sense of divine power confronting the forces of chaos continues with the healing, in gentile territory, of a man possessed by a 'legion' of demons. Again Jesus commands silence, and is disobeyed (Mk. 5.1–20).

This leads to a further Markan 'sandwich': the resuscitation of a young girl and the healing of a haemorrhaging woman (5.21–43). The kingdom means renewal and new life, replacing fear with faith. This does not, however, happen in Jesus' home town of Nazareth (6.1–6a).

The third Markan 'sandwich' places the death of John the Baptist within the story of Jesus sending the Twelve on an itinerant mission (6.6b–32). Mark is issuing a warning, indicating the shape of things to come: announcing the kingdom will arouse opposition. Nevertheless, the new exodus is going ahead, with thousands fed in the wilderness (6.33–44), and with Jesus walking on the water, like Israel's God subduing the Red Sea (6.45–52).[34] The work of healing continues unabated (Mk. 6.53–56).

The scene changes in Mark 7.1—8.10, bringing into question the relationship between gentiles and Israel. The complex discussion about the food laws and purity indicates an apparent clash between Torah, as laid down by Moses, and the Pharisaic *halakhah* regulations which appeared to undermine it. The developed purity rules (in this case, handwashing) are hiding the deeper issue: defilement comes from the heart, not from food. Some might read Mark's comment in 7.19b ('In saying this, Jesus declared all foods clean') as an aside meant for gentile readers; others might see it as indicating a new dispensation where, as with Paul, Jew and gentile have entered a new world, sharing a new purity. One can say at least that the Mosaic Torah should always trump the Pharisaic *halakhah*.[35]

Jesus then goes to the region of Tyre, a gentile area to the north-west of Galilee (7.24–30). Initially he rebuffs a woman who was asking him to heal her daughter,

---

33 Hays 2014, 22.
34 See Ps. 77.19; Isa. 43.16; 51.10; Job 9.8, and discussion in Hays 2017, 70–3.
35 See Bird 2008b, 16–23.

but her quick-witted response convinces him otherwise. God's renewing kingdom is advancing into new territory.[36] Back in the Decapolis, Jesus heals a deaf and mute man: another gentile healed on gentile soil (7.31–37). Then, still in gentile territory, Mark records another feeding miracle, perhaps this time indicating that there is enough 'bread' for Jews and gentiles alike (8.1–10). This leads to another clash with the Pharisees, who (despite all that Jesus has done) demand a 'sign' (8.11–21). Jesus seems to regard this request as being itself a sign, to him, that 'this generation' of his contemporaries was determined not to heed his message. On that basis he warns his followers against the Pharisees and Herod.

3. The revelation of the Messiah in Caesarea Philippi (8.22—9.1)

Arriving in Bethsaida, Jesus heals a blind man, unusually taking two attempts: at first, the man sees people but they look like trees; then he sees clearly (8.22–26). This odd little scene, unique to Mark, illustrates what happens next, when Jesus and his disciples head north to Caesarea Philippi and he asks them who people say he is. This is the crucial turning-point in Mark's story. The popular rumour has it that Jesus is a prophet (like the man seeing people dimly as though they were trees), but Peter declares, 'You are the Messiah' (seeing clearly). Once again Jesus commands silence. Then, to his disciples' shock and dismay, he tells them that he must now go to his death. Peter resists this, but Jesus insists. Calling the crowd, he declares that all those who want to follow him must likewise take up their cross. The kingdom of God is indeed coming with power; his own death, rather than denying that victory, will be its instrument. Thus, if the first half of Mark's gospel was about the powerful son of God, the second half will be about the suffering son of man.

4. Jesus, discipleship, and the way to the cross (9.2—10.52)

As though to confirm the story's new direction, Jesus is transfigured in dazzling light (along with Elijah and Moses) before

The Saviour's Transfiguration by Theophanes the Greek, early fifteenth century
Public Domain

---

36 See Bird 2006a, 112–16.

Peter, James, and John on a mountain (9.2–8). A voice comes from heaven, reminding us of the voice at the baptism: 'This is my Son, whom I love. Listen to him!' (9.7) To the puzzled question about Elijah coming before the Messiah, Jesus hints that Elijah had already been and gone: a cryptic reference to John the Baptist (9.9–13).

Coming back down the mountainside, Jesus heals a possessed boy, eliciting a desperate faith from the father (9.14–29). He repeats the prediction of his own suffering (9.30–32). This leads to further teaching on discipleship and the true nature of greatness, to a rebuke when the disciples try to stop someone else casting out demons in Jesus' name, and to warnings about the cost and challenge of following him (9.33–50). Then, with the scene changing to the region of Judea where John had been working, Jesus faces the Pharisees' question about divorce. (This was partly a test of Jesus' stance on the various current interpretations of Dt. 24.1–4, and more particularly a coded political challenge: John had been arrested, and then beheaded, for speaking out against Herod's marital arrangements.) Jesus indicates that now, with the kingdom arriving, what matters is not the temporary permission of Deuteronomy, but the original intention of Genesis: man plus woman for life (10.1–12). Perhaps related to this, he rebukes the disciples for trying to keep children away from him. The openness of children is a window on true faith (10.13–16).

Attention then focuses on Jesus' conversation with a rich young ruler, who wants to know how to be sure of inheriting the 'age to come' (10.17–31). He claims to be Torah-observant, but Jesus wants more: he must sell all, give to the poor, and follow Jesus. *Following Jesus*, in other words, *trumps even Torah*. The incident encapsulates Jesus' teaching about wealth and poverty, but also signals the radical change and challenge of the kingdom. This sets the context for Jesus' third prediction of his Passion (10.32–34) and for James and John, still missing the point, to request positions of power in his coming reign. Mark knows what it will mean to be at Jesus' right and left at his enthronement (see 15.27). The kingdom involves a total redefinition of power itself, and Jesus will embody that in his redemptive death (10.35–45).

Paradoxes continue as blind Bartimaeus calls out to Jesus as 'son of David' and, being healed, follows him 'in the way'—'the way' being a regular early Christian designation of the movement (see 10.46–52). The blind man who sees and follows is Mark's model of true discipleship.

5. Jesus in Jerusalem (11.1—12.44)

Jesus enters Jerusalem in royal fashion, on a commandeered colt, alluding to Zechariah 9.9 but also reminiscent of the Maccabean victory two hundred years earlier (11.1–7).[37] The crowd, echoing Psalm 118.25–26, hopes for a new Davidic kingdom; but Jesus looks around the Temple area and then returns to Bethany,

---

37 2 Macc. 10.1–9.

outside the city (11.8–11). We then have the most dramatic 'Markan sandwich', as Jesus curses an unripe fig tree, pronounces judgment on the Temple, and then finds the fig tree withered away (11.12–25). The Temple has become a haunt of bandits: Jesus was known to promise a new temple (14.58), while the current Temple and its ruling elite will meet destruction when the son of man is vindicated (13.5–37). This prediction will be crucial at Jesus' later hearing (14.55–59). Jesus' action precipitates a challenge: by what authority does he act thus? (11.27–33). For his answer, Jesus points the questioners (and Mark points his readers) to John the Baptist, through whose work Jesus had been marked out as God's son.

A model replica of the Herodian temple from the time of Jesus
Public Domain

Jesus then goes on the offensive with the parable of the wicked tenants, an echo of Isaiah's prophetic warning (5.1–7) about Israel's coming judgment (11.1–12). Citing Psalm 118.22–23 proves the point: the rejected 'stone' and the rejected 'son' are one and the same (in Hebrew 'stone' is *eben* and 'son' is *ben*). Further exchanges follow, first on the question of tribute to Caesar, then on resurrection (12.13–27). Kingdom-talk, and rebellious actions in the Temple, would raise the question of loyalty to Rome and the question of a new world being born: Jesus offers devastating answers on both points. To the standard question 'Which is the greatest command in Torah?', Jesus quotes the *Shema* (Dt. 6.4–5): God is one, and Israel must love God wholeheartedly. He adds a second commandment, from Leviticus 19.18: love your neighbour (12.28–34). But if Jesus thus appears as a loyal Jew, Mark indicates a redefinition from within: David's 'son' is also—according to scripture!—David's 'Lord' (Mk. 12.35–37). Psalm 110, perhaps the most important scriptural text for early Christians, redefines who the Messiah is, and with that who God himself really is. This exalted view of God and the Messiah contrasts with the shabby self-glorifying of the scribes (12.38–40); and this in turn contrasts with the widow who gives to the Temple-treasury all that she has (Mk. 12.41–44).

6. The Olivet Discourse (13.1–37)

Jesus' prophetic denunciation of the Temple reaches a crescendo in the much-misunderstood Olivet Discourse (Mark 13). The chapter is not about the end of the world, except in the important sense that Israel viewed the Temple as the linchpin that held heaven and earth together. 'End-of-world' language was thus appropriate for the forthcoming destruction of the Temple, and that language would have been so understood by both Jesus' hearers and Mark's readers.

Jesus solemnly declares that the huge building would come crashing down (13.2). This will be preceded by portents: messianic pretenders, wars, earthquakes, famine, persecution, rejection by family members, and, remarkably, by the gospel being preached to all nations. Mark's readers would recognize this as a description of their mid-century world (13.1–13). This would be the time when Daniel 9 would be fulfilled: the promised 'end of exile' would come about through a time of trouble in which a 'desolating abomination' would be set up (originally this referred to the Syrian sacrilege of 167 BC[38]). Something like that, only more, is now in view, and when it does come about Jesus' followers must get out and run away (13.14–23). The allusion to Daniel helps us to understand the following passage (Mk. 13.24–32), which is not about the second coming of Jesus, as many suppose it to be, but, as in Daniel 7, the *vindication after suffering* of 'one like a son of man'. Whether or not Matthew interprets it differently (see below), Mark and Luke are both quite clear, as we can see:

1. The whole speech, starting in 13.2, is dominated by the question of when the Temple will be destroyed, not when Jesus will return. (The return of Jesus is clearly taught elsewhere in the New Testament, but not here.)
2. Apocalyptic language is regularly code for socio-political events invested with theological meaning. When those current events involve the Temple, this is only natural. When Mark has Jesus refer to the 'son of man coming in the clouds' and sending 'his angels to gather his elect', this is classic apocalyptic language for Jesus' coming in triumph to God and for the worldwide mission of his disciples.
3. Mark again associates the fig tree with the Temple's fate, only now as a simile: these signs are like the leaves which indicate that summer is almost here. In fact, as in 9.1, 'this generation will not pass away until all these things have happened'. Neither Mark nor any of his early readers worried that this might be unfulfilled (for example by the apparent 'delay' of the 'second coming'). The Temple was indeed destroyed; Jesus was indeed vindicated in resurrection, ascension, and the worldwide mission.

---

[38] See Dan. 9.27; 11.29–32; 12.11; 2 Macc. 6.5; Jos. *Ant.* 12.253.

The emphasis throughout is not on speculative eschatology, but on faithful perseverance (13.33–37).

7. The Passion of Jesus (14.1—15.47)

Mark's narrative now focuses on Jesus' coming crucifixion, in which he is proclaimed, however paradoxically, as Israel's Messiah. The authorities plot (14.1–2); Jesus is anointed by an unnamed woman (14.3–9); Judas conspires with the chief priests (14.10–11). Jesus then, at their Passover meal, warns the disciples that one of them will betray him (14.12–21), and speaks strangely about the bread and the cup, drawing their significance not onto the past events of the first exodus but onto the imminent events of the second, in other words, his own death (14.22–25). As the group heads for Gethsemane, Jesus uses Zechariah 13.7 to issue a dark warning about the shepherd being struck and the sheep scattered, and he warns Peter that he will deny him (14.26–31). Once in the garden, Jesus appears in Mark's portrayal as intensely vulnerable, almost panic-stricken with grief, praying that he might not drink the 'cup'. The disciples cannot stay awake to support him (14.32–42). What Jesus is now doing must be done alone.

Judas arrives with an armed band; after a scuffle, Jesus is arrested. Mark adds the strange note of a young man, wearing nothing but a linen cloth, avoiding capture by fleeing stark naked (14.43–52). How much of that is personal reminiscence, how much allegory, or how much both, we cannot now say.

The hastily convened Sanhedrin attempts to find a legal pretext to have Jesus executed. The original charge focuses on his claim to destroy and rebuild the Temple; that would imply a claim either to royalty or to a new kind of priestly authority, but by itself it would hardly be a capital offence (14.53–59).[39] Finally the high priest, Caiaphas, asks Jesus on oath if he is the Messiah, the son of the Blessed One. (In Mark's Greek the question echoes exactly Peter's confession [8.29], *su ei ho Christos*, the only difference being the implied sneering question mark. This also echoes the voice at the baptism [1.11].) The question of Jesus' identity as 'son of God' (a messianic title from 2 Sam. 7, Ps. 2, and elsewhere) would be implied by the Temple-question, but it would also give the Sanhedrin an accusation of sedition to take to the Roman governor. Caesar was 'son of God'; who then was this? Jesus, however, gives the court yet more (14.62): 'I am . . . And you will see the Son of Man sitting at the right hand of the Mighty One and coming on the clouds of heaven.' This combines Psalm 110.1 with Daniel 7.13, both of which refer to a figure enthroned beside YHWH, an honour most Jews were reluctant to attribute to a mere human being.[40]

---

[39] Mk. 14.58; see Jn. 2.19; Ac. 7.48.
[40] See bSanh. 38b where Rabbi Akiba allegedly said that the plural of 'thrones' in Dan. 7.9 meant one for YHWH and another for David, at which Rabbi Yose accused Akiba of blaspheming the divine glory, since he retorted that one throne is for divine justice and another is for divine mercy.

Jesus' words declare in effect: yes, I am a true prophet; yes, what I said about the Temple will come true; yes, I am the Messiah; *you will see me vindicated*; and my vindication will mean that I share the very throne of Israel's God. At last the masks are off, the secrets are out, the cryptic sayings and parables are left behind. The son of man stands before the official ruler of Israel, declaring that God will prove him in the right—and that God will prove the court, Caiaphas included, to be in the wrong. The high priest now has not only a confession of self-proclaimed Messiahship, but also a charge of blasphemy. Jesus is then mocked and abused, as he had predicted (14.60–65). Peter, meanwhile, likewise fulfils Jesus' prediction, being faithless while Jesus was staying faithful (14.29–31).

Jesus is then taken to the Roman governor, Pontius Pilate, who interrogates him about his kingly pretensions. Pilate, normally obstinate and cynical, knows what the Judean leaders are doing.[41] He gives the crowd a choice between the brigand Barabbas and Jesus, 'king of the Jews'; the chief priests incite the crowd to demand Barabbas. Pilate hands Jesus over to be flogged and crucified (15.1–15).

For Mark's readers, the story of Jesus' death would be dramatically ironic. Mark portrays the event as a triumph, analogous to the celebrations of a returning victorious general.[42] The Praetorian Guard hails Jesus, crowning him with thorns; he is heralded as a 'son of god'. Whether or not Mark's readers knew of Titus's triumph after the capture of Jerusalem, the symbolism would be potent. Schmidt summarizes the parallels between Mark's crucifixion story and a Roman triumph:

> The Praetorians gather early in the morning to proclaim the triumphator. He is dressed in the triumphal garb, and a crown of laurel is placed on his head. The soldiers then shout in acclamation of his Lordship and perform acts of homage to him. They accompany him from their camp through the streets of the city. The sacrificial victim is there in the procession, and alongside walks the official carrying the implement of his coming death. The procession ascends finally to the Place of the (Death's) Head, where the sacrifice is to take place. The triumphator is offered the ceremonial wine. He does not drink it, but it is poured out on the altar at the moment of sacrifice. Then, at the moment of being lifted up before the people, at the moment of the sacrifice, again the triumphator is acclaimed as Lord, and his vice-regents appear with him in confirmation of his glory. Following the lead of the soldiers, the people together with their leaders and the vice-regents themselves join in the acclamation. The epiphany is confirmed in portents by the gods: 'Truly this man is the Son of God!'[43]

---

[41] See Wright *NTPG*, 174, and comments on Pilate's character by Philo (*Leg.* 299–305).
[42] See 2 Cor. 2. 14–15; Col. 2.15.
[43] Schmidt 1995, 16.

At the same time, the historical events themselves were doubtless intended as ironic by Jesus' torturers: 'Call yourself a king? What about this!' As Schmidt comments: 'Mark designs this "anti-triumph" to suggest that the seeming scandal of the cross is actually an exaltation of Christ.'[44] All the threads of Mark's story come together: Jesus announces God's kingdom, and is now placarded, on the cross, as the king. This, Mark is saying, is how the kingdom came: through Jesus' powerful weakness, his redemptive suffering, his scripture-fulfilling self-sacrifice.[45] The bystanders join in the mockery. Everybody knows a crucified Messiah is a failed Messiah. Mark insists, however, that this really is Jesus' royal task and reign. This is the climax of Jesus' kingdom-vocation. This is how the kingdom of God comes in power, defeating all enemies. This is what happens when David's Lord becomes David's son (15.16–32).

The scene moves to its horrible close. Darkness falls at noon; Jesus cries out, echoing Psalm 22.1. He is (Mark wants us to realize) drinking the cup of God's wrath, giving his life as a ransom for many, sharing the sin and suffering that characterized humanity in general and Israel in particular. The dark cloud of evil, Israel's evil, the world's evil, cut him off from the one he called 'Abba' in a way he had never known before. He cries out, not in anger, but in despair and sorrow, as he, the beloved son, enters the judgment of God-forsakenness. With one last cry, he dies (15.33–37). Mark at once reports that the Temple veil was torn in two, indicating that the Temple would indeed be destroyed and Jesus vindicated. The centurion's confession, 'Surely this man was the son of God', is the christological climax to the gospel, echoing once more the voice at the baptism and transfiguration, only now, with increasing irony, on the lips of a pagan soldier. Mark has all along portrayed Jesus as Messiah, the son of God (1.1); this is reaffirmed in God's own voice (1.11; 9.7) and in Jesus' testimony as the beloved son

Crucifixion in an illuminated manuscript from the twelfth century, Italy
Biblioteca Medicea-Laurenziana, Florence, Italy / Alinari Archives, Florence-reproduced with the permission of Ministero per i Beni e le Attività Culturali / Bridgeman Images

---

44 Schmidt 1995, 1.
45 Bird 2012b, 41–3.

(12.6; 13.32). The truth has been blurted out by demons (3.11; 5.7), and now by a centurion (15.39). Mark wants his readers to make the same affirmation, only understanding it in the light of the entire strange story and its multiply subversive aim: the centurion, after all, was used to thinking of Caesar as 'son of God'.

It was female disciples, rather than the Twelve, who remained with Jesus at the end. Then Joseph of Arimathea, a member of the Sanhedrin but a secret Jesus-follower, retrieved Jesus' body and arranged a hasty burial. Despite his shameful death, Jesus was buried with a measure of dignity (15.40–47).

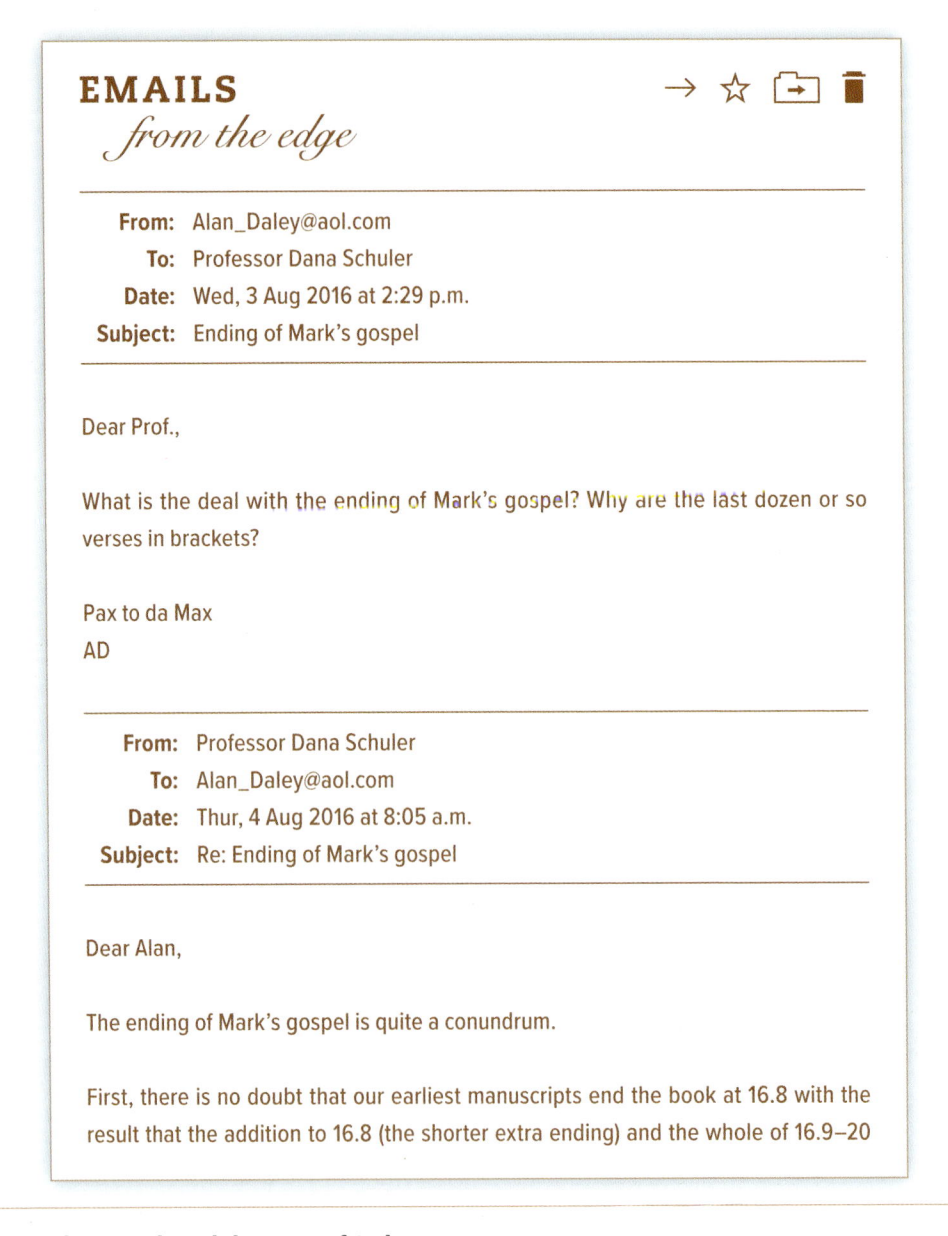

EMAILS
from the edge

From: Alan_Daley@aol.com
To: Professor Dana Schuler
Date: Wed, 3 Aug 2016 at 2:29 p.m.
Subject: Ending of Mark's gospel

Dear Prof.,

What is the deal with the ending of Mark's gospel? Why are the last dozen or so verses in brackets?

Pax to da Max
AD

From: Professor Dana Schuler
To: Alan_Daley@aol.com
Date: Thur, 4 Aug 2016 at 8:05 a.m.
Subject: Re: Ending of Mark's gospel

Dear Alan,

The ending of Mark's gospel is quite a conundrum.

First, there is no doubt that our earliest manuscripts end the book at 16.8 with the result that the addition to 16.8 (the shorter extra ending) and the whole of 16.9–20 (the longer ending) were subsequent scribal creations. The longer ending in 16.9–20 seems to have emerged in the second quarter of the second century, attempting to fill in the gap in Mark's story by pulling in bits from Matthew, John, Luke, and Acts.

Second, the question is whether Mark really did intend to end his gospel in verse 8 or whether the original ending was lost or else unfinished. On the one hand, maybe Mark deliberately wanted to leave his readers in fear and trembling like the women at the empty tomb, and to confront them with the challenge of faith. On the other hand, Mark certainly sets up his readers to expect Jesus' resurrection as well as his crucifixion (see Mk. 8.31; 9.9, 31; 10.34; 14.28; 16.6–7), so perhaps there was a longer ending that is now somehow lost to us. That might be all the more plausible since Mark's gospel, largely neglected in the early church, is the least well attested in terms of manuscript evidence.

Of course, third, if Mark's gospel was originally written on a scroll, then it is quite likely that the end (and perhaps also the start) of the book would have been lost. Have a look at the Dead Sea Scrolls (in the Israel Museum in Jerusalem, if you can get there; online if you can't); most of them lack either the beginning or the ending or both.

See these books if you want to go further:

Black, David Alan (ed.). 2008. *Perspectives on the Ending of Mark's Gospel: Four Views*. Nashville: Broadman & Holman.
Comfort, Philip W. 2015. *A Commentary on the Manuscripts of the New Testament*. Grand Rapids, MI: Kregel, pp. 197–206.
Garland, David E. 2015. *A Theology of Mark's Gospel*. BTNT; Grand Rapids, MI: Zondervan, pp. 535–59.

Kindest regards
Prof. Dana Schuler

8. The resurrection (16.1–8 [and 9–20])

Mark's gospel, at least in its earliest surviving versions, ends with three women arriving at the tomb on the morning after the sabbath to complete the burial process by anointing Jesus' body. They find the stone rolled away, and meet an angel ('a young man dressed in white'). The angel tells them not to be afraid, announces that Jesus has been raised, and instructs them to tell Peter and the others that Jesus will meet them in Galilee. The women disobey: they *are* afraid, and they do *not* tell anyone . . . (see 'Emails from the edge: ending of Mark's gospel').

MARK AND THE BIG PICTURE

Mark's gospel is a narrative epic, full of eschatological intensity and evangelical energy. It is fast-paced and dramatic, captivating as well as challenging. It can leave readers breathless, shaken, and challenged.

First, Mark has an obvious evangelistic utility. The reader cannot escape the haunting question, 'Who is Jesus?' (see Mk. 2.7; 4.41; 6.2; 8.27, 29; 14.60). The titles Mark uses for Jesus (son of God, Messiah, son of Man, son of David, and lord) give part of the answer, but it is the story he tells, of Jesus' kingdom-work and its shocking conclusion, that points to the true answer. Jesus, Mark insists, is Israel's Servant-King, embodying the very presence of Israel's God. He warns of coming judgment, even while throwing open the kingdom-invitation. He himself confronts the reader, both with 'Who do you say I am?' (Mk. 8.29) and 'Come, follow me!' (Mk. 1.17; 2.14; 8.34; 10.21).

Kursi Church, traditional site for the miracle of the swine (Mk. 5.1–20)

Second, Mark is equally concerned with discipleship. Mark's story allows us to see a new vision of God's people: defined by the kingdom, transformed by the life of new creation, crossing ethnic and social boundaries, having compassion for the poor and destitute, holding a faith that can move mountains, enduring under persecution, persistent in prayer. Central to all this is (1) self-renunciation, taking up one's own cross (Mk. 8.34), and (2) pursuing the upside-down greatness of humble service, as demonstrated by Jesus himself (Mk. 10.43). Mark is a book to confront outsiders with the reality of Jesus. It is also a book to challenge believers who are 'committed' only as far as their own convenience allows, urging them to embrace the way of self-giving love as the Jesus-shaped pattern of true life.

Further reading

Beavis, Mary Ann. 2011. *Mark*. PCNT; Grand Rapids, MI: Baker.
Bird, Michael F. 2012. *Jesus Is the Christ: The Messianic Testimony of the Gospels*. Downers Grove, IL: InterVarsity, pp. 32–56.
Boring, M. Eugene. 2014. *Mark: A Commentary*. NTL; Louisville, KY: Westminster John Knox.
Collins, Adela Y. 1992. *The Beginning of the Gospel: Probings of Mark in Context*. Minneapolis, MN: Augsburg Fortress.
———. 2007. *Mark: A Commentary*. Hermeneia; Minneapolis: Fortress.
Evans, Craig A. 2001. *Mark 8:27–16:20*. WBC; Nashville: Thomas Nelson.
France R. T. 2002. *The Gospel of Mark: A Commentary on the Greek Text*. NIGTC; Grand Rapids, MI: Eerdmans.
Garland, David. 2015. *A Theology of Mark's Gospel*. Grand Rapids, MI: Zondervan.
Gundry, Robert H. 1993. *Mark: A Commentary on His Apology for the Cross*. Grand Rapids, MI: Eerdmans.
Hays, Richard B. 2014. *Reading Backwards: Figural Christology and the Fourfold Gospel Witness*. Waco, TX: Baylor University Press, pp. 15–103.
Hengel, Martin. 1985. *Studies in the Gospel of Mark*. London: SCM.
Hooker, Morna D. 1991. *The Gospel According to Saint Mark*. BNTC; London: A&C Black.
Kok, Michael. 2015. *Gospel on the Margins: The Reception of Mark in the Second Century*. Minneapolis: Fortress.
Marcus, Joel. 2000–9. *Mark: A New Translation with Introduction and Commentary*. 2 vols.; AB; New Haven, CT: Yale University Press.
Rhoads, David, Joanna Dewey, and Donald Michie. 1999 [1982]. *Mark as Story: An Introduction to the Narrative of a Gospel*. 2nd edn.; Minneapolis: Fortress.
Shively, Elizabeth E. 2012. *Apocalyptic Imagination in the Gospel of Mark: The Literary and Theological Role of Mark 3:22–30*. Berlin: De Gruyter.
Stamper, Meda A. A. 2014. *Embodying Mark: Fresh Ways to Read, Pray and Live the Gospel*. London: SPCK.
Tan, Kim Huat. *Mark*. NCCS. Eugene, OR: Cascade, 2015.

The Gospel according to Matthew

'Every scribe who has been trained for the kingdom of heaven is like the master of a household who brings out of his treasure what is new and what is old' (Mt 13.52). These words, concluding the collection of parables that falls midway through Matthew's Gospel, have often been seen as a kind of signature, a hint that in this book we have exactly that: things new and things old, a treasure-house of scribal lore. But how is this treasure laid out? What sort of a book has 'Matthew' written? What sort of story does he tell? What is its narrative structure, its plot?[1]

CHAPTER AT A GLANCE

This chapter explores the story, themes, and theology of Matthew's gospel.

By the end of this chapter you should be able to:

- understand the origins of Matthew's gospel in the context of early Christianity;
- describe the basic features of Matthew's story of Jesus;
- grasp the general themes that appear in Matthew's gospel.

INTRODUCTION

The gospel of Matthew was the early church's favourite book. It was the most quoted, most copied, most read, and the most preached Christian book of the early centuries.

This immense popularity can easily be accounted for. First, Matthew served then, as it can still serve, as a great instruction manual on the person of Jesus and the nature of discipleship. Matthew presents Jesus as a new Moses and the long-awaited Davidic deliverer. His Jesus embodies God's presence, ushers in the kingdom of heaven on earth, and by his death brings the forgiveness of sins. The five major discourses in Matthew's gospel function as something of a manifesto for the church, outlining its vocation, its mission, its way of

---

1 Wright *NTPG*, 384.

life, and its hopes. The discourses define the way of 'righteousness' that should characterize kingdom-people. It is above all a teaching book about how to be a follower of Jesus. According to Edouard Massaux: 'Until the end of the second century, the first gospel remained the gospel par excellence. People looked to Mt. for teaching which conditioned Christian behavior so that the Gospel of Mt. became the norm for Christian life.'[2]

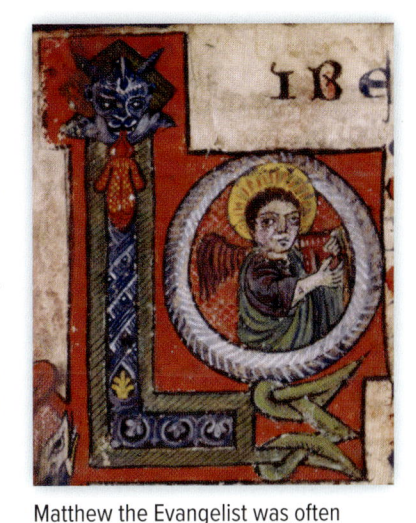

Second, Matthew enabled the church to hold on to its Jewish heritage even while looking ahead to a gentile future. Matthew was written at a precarious time; that, of course, could mean any time from Easter onwards, but many suppose that a likely setting for Matthew is in the period AD 80–100, when those Jewish Jesus-followers who survived the catastrophe of AD 70 in Judea found themselves marginalized or even expelled by local Jewish communities. They were at the same time witnessing an influx of gentile converts into churches in the eastern part of the empire. We have to remember that for much of early Christianity, certainly during Paul's work in the 40s and 50s and certainly reflected in Matthew, one of the main presenting issues was the abrasive relationship between following Jesus and the culture and expectations of the Jewish world.

Matthew the Evangelist was often symbolized by an angel.
The New York Public Library Digital Collections

The questions faced were difficult, even paradoxical. How does a Messiah-believer lay claim to Israelite ancestry, when this particular 'Messiah' and his followers have been rejected by most Jews? Or else, what kind of people are we when our God is Israel's God, the Messiah and his apostles were Jewish, but most of our members are now gentiles? This is where Matthew comes into his element. Matthew sees the identity of the Christian community as authorized by the Jewish scriptures, which find their fulfilment in Jesus the Messiah, and in this fulfilment gentiles come to the God of Israel through Jesus, Israel's Messiah. In other words, in Matthew's gospel, christology, story, and social identity are all interwoven to demonstrate that the church, comprised of Messiah-believers whether Jewish or non-Jewish, are not deviant apostates, but are legitimate heirs of Israel's heritage and stand at the centre of God's saving purposes.[3]

Matthew thus provides a theological and ethnographic map for locating Christian identity at the intersection of Jewish heritage and faith in Jesus. Jewish

---

2 Massaux 1990–3, 3.187.
3 deSilva 2004, 246.

Christians do not have to jettison their Jewishness; gentile Jesus-believers do not have to 'judaize' to belong to Jesus' church. Though (to say it again) all those issues were on the table when Paul was writing Galatians, Corinthians, and Romans, the tensions were increased even more once the Romans had destroyed Jerusalem.

Martin Hengel was right, then, to see Matthew as trying to bind together the Jewish past and the gentile future:

> By virtue of the Jewish-scribal origin of its author and its composition in geographical proximity to Jewish Palestine the First Gospel was really something like a connecting link between—earlier—Jewish Christianity and the church which had become Gentile Christian.[4]

So we are dealing with a Christian writing which attempts to build a bridge between the old and the new by bringing forth treasures old and new (Mt. 13.52), preserving both the old wineskins and the new wine (Mt. 9.17), narrating the story of prophecy and fulfilment (Mt. 1.22; 2.15, 17, 23; 4.14; 8.17; 12.17; 13.14; 21.4–5; 26.56; 27.9), marrying together law and gospel (Mt. 5.17–20), seeing Israel as renewed into the church of Jesus Christ (Mt. 2.6; 10.5–6; 15.24; 16.18–19; 18.19–20; 19.28; 28.19–20), emphasizing Israel's priority (Mt. 10.5–6; 15.24) alongside gentile inclusion (Mt. 1.5; 2.1–12; 8.5–13; 12.18, 21; 15.21–28; 22.1–10; 24.14; 27.54; 28.19–20). The gospel of Matthew is the Jewish story of Jesus for what is becoming an increasingly gentile church.

One could make a case for seeing an overall plot for Matthew's gospel in terms of the programmatic statement in Matthew 1.21, where the angel tells Joseph: 'You are to name him Jesus, for he will save his people from their sins' (NRSV). The gospel can be understood as the story of how this is accomplished, through the paradoxical sub-plots whereby Jesus is successfully opposed by the Jewish leaders on the one hand, and unsuccessfully supported by the disciples on the other.[5] This is a kind of comedy-through-tragedy: the sub-plots look as though they will prevent the hero from accomplishing his mission, but in fact they precipitate him into the real—and ultimately successful—battle, which was all along not against the Jewish leaders but against the satan.

Powell points out that this story, as far as Matthew is concerned, is part of a larger story: the gospel ends with a beginning, as the disciples are sent out to preach to the whole world.[6] But this is not all. The very sentence which is found to be thematic for the main plot—the prediction that Jesus 'will save his people from their sins'—presupposes a previous story as well. It assumes that the gospel story comes

---

4   Hengel 2000, 75.
5   Powell 1992.
6   Powell 1992, 203–4.

towards the end of a larger and longer narrative, in which 'his people' fall victim to 'their sins'. And it does not take much imagination, much reading in Matthew, or much knowledge of the Jewish background, to see what story that is. For most modern western readers, the sentence will sound individualistic (I have committed sins; Jesus will save me from them and their effects). No first-century Jew would have heard it like that—though Jews of that era would have wanted to include that meaning within the much larger one which would be the obvious reference for them. The basic plot of Matthew's gospel is that when God fulfils his promise to Abraham by sending the Davidic Messiah, he will rescue his people from their present exile, the sorry state which resulted from their sins. When this happens, it will be like a new exodus, a new covenant.

To get into the right mood for reading Matthew, imagine yourself on a working holiday in a messianic kibbutz. You have to leave your comfortable urban world, rising early to work in Matthew's exegetical fields of narratives and parables, sowing righteousness to harvest wisdom, and building a house on the rock of Jesus' words, all the while trying to see the surrounding landscape through the eyes of a first-century Jew. Then, in the evening, you relax with your friends over a supper of bread and wine while sitting in the presence of the one who is 'God with us' and our 'only teacher' (Mt. 1.23; 23.10).[7]

CONTEXTUAL AND CRITICAL MATTERS

Origins of Matthew

This gospel is sometimes called 'the first gospel', because of its place in the emerging canon of scripture. Many earlier readers reckoned it was also the first to be written; but not many today would agree. The early church ascribed the book to 'Matthew', identifying him as the tax-collector whom Jesus called to follow him, and who was later appointed one of the twelve apostles.[8] But the book itself is strictly anonymous. Nothing substantial in it identifies the author as Matthew the Galilean tax-collector. In addition, one might wonder why Matthew would rely on the gospel of Mark as a major source for his book, as most suppose,[9] since Matthew was an eye-witness but Mark most likely was not. (That is one of several reasons for the 'minority' position that still holds to Matthean priority.) Perhaps a disciple of Matthew took Matthew's teachings and combined them with the basic outline and content of Mark's gospel—though of course guesses like that prove nothing. If Matthew was then associated with one or more of these non-Markan sources, it would have been natural to name the gospel after him.

---

[7] Tr. M. F. Bird.
[8] Mt. 9.9; 10.3; Ac. 1.13. Mark identifies the tax-collector as 'Levi' in Mk. 2.14.
[9] See ch. 28 below on the 'synoptic problem'.

When we enquire after external evidence for the origins of Matthew's gospel, we find Eusebius (fourth century) reporting Papias (early second century) as saying, allegedly from John the elder, 'Concerning Matthew these other things were said, "Therefore, Matthew set in order the sayings [of the Lord] in the Hebrew language [Greek *Ebraidi dialektō*], and each interpreted them as best as they could."'[10] Papias is thus a very early witness to the idea that Matthew himself stands behind this gospel, but it isn't clear what exactly he means. He could mean the following. (1) Matthew originally wrote his gospel in Hebrew or Aramaic, which was then translated into Greek by others. But this is unlikely since Matthew's gospel, despite its Jewish ambience, does not appear to be based on an underlying Aramaic text. As it stands, it is a Greek composition. (2) Matthew collected a list of Jesus' sayings (*logia*), often identified as the sayings source called 'Q', which were later incorporated into the gospels of Matthew and Luke. But Papias uses *logia* to title his own commentary on Jesus' life and teachings and also to describe the narratives and sayings in the gospel of Mark; so *logia*, a word with quite a wide reference, cannot be taken as a technical description for a collection of sayings. (3) Matthew wrote according to Jewish style and forms, creating a sort of template which the other evangelists followed. That would solve a lot of problems, but we cannot be sure that it is what Papias meant. The probability is that Papias believed that (a) Matthew wrote his gospel as the first-ever gospel, and that (b) he wrote it in Aramaic—but these are points that most scholars now normally reject. Papias was certainly early, but it may be that he was reflecting informed guesswork in the early church rather than accurate memory.

So what can we say about the sources of Matthew's gospel? He incorporates 90 per cent of Mark's gospel, usually in an abridged form—assuming 'Markan priority', which will be discussed below.[11] What Matthew thought of Mark's work is a good question: some think Matthew was revising it, others that he was aiming to replace it. One likely answer was given a century ago by F. C. Burkitt: 'Matthew is a *fresh edition* of Mark, revised, rearranged, and enriched with new material.'[12] Matthew basically follows Mark's outline, but makes subtle changes. He tones down the 'secrecy' motif; he plays down the dullness of the disciples; he stresses prophetic fulfilment, intensifies eschatological hopes, and edits episodes that might offend certain readers, not least anxious 'Jewish Christians'. Above all, Matthew supplements Mark's story with extra unique material (usually referred to as 'M'; see box: 'Matthew's unique material') and some materials shared with Luke, these last being possibly derived from the common source that scholars have called 'Q', or else explicable in terms of Luke's use of Matthew.[13]

---

10 Eus. *Hist. Eccl.* 3.39.16 (plus 3.24.6; 5.8.2; 5.10.3; 6.25.4); see similarly Iren. *Adv. Haer.* 3.1.1.
11 See ch. 28 below.
12 Cited in Stanton 1993, 51–2.
13 Again, see ch. 28 below.

MATTHEW'S UNIQUE MATERIAL

Matthew seems to have received traditions about Jesus from many sources, including, most now think, some taken from Mark and some shared with Luke. Matthew has edited, arranged, and supplemented these, including unique material (sometimes called 'M' for 'Special Matthew'). This includes:[*]

genealogy of Jesus	1.2–17	miracle of the coins in the fish's mouth	17.24–27
birth of Jesus	1.18–25	disciplining one who sins	18.15–20
visit of the Magi	2.1–12	Peter's question about forgiveness	18.21–22
fulfilment of the Torah	5.17–20	parable of the unforgiving servant	18.23–25
teaching on anger	5.21–24	parable of the vineyard labourers	20.1–16
teaching on adultery	5.27–29	parable of the two sons	21.28–32
teaching on divorce	5.31	prohibition of titles	23.2–5, 7–12
teaching on oaths	5.33–37	woes against the Pharisees	18.15–22
prohibition of revenge	5.38–39	parable of the ten bridesmaids	25.1–13
love for enemies	5.43	the nations gathered before the son of man	25.31–46
instructions on piety	6.1–19	the suicide of Judas	27.3–10
saying on pearls before swine	7.6	Pilate washes his hands	27.24–25
prediction of persecution	10.21–23	resurrection of dead saints	27.52–53
offer to find rest	11.28–30	guards at the tomb	27.62–66
parables of the weeds, pearl, net, and treasure	13.24–30, 36–52	report of the guards	28.11–15
Peter walks on water	14.28–31	the Great Commission	28.16–20
Jesus appoints Peter as the rock	16.17–19		

[*]See further Brooks 1987 and more briefly Jones 2011, 18–46.

Date

If Matthew used Mark, as normally assumed, that might help with dating—the caveat being that the dating of Mark, too, is disputed. In any case, many assume that Mark was written in around AD 70, so that Matthew, notionally dependent on Mark, would have to have been written sometime later, though how much later is open to debate. An upper limit for the composition of Matthew is around AD 117, since Ignatius of Antioch cited Matthew's account of Jesus' baptism in one of his letters. In addition, the *Didache* ('Teaching of the Twelve Apostles') seems to have absorbed distinctly Matthean features, and though this too is disputed, the *Didache* is normally associated with Syria around AD 100–20 or even earlier.[14] So, most likely, Matthew can be dated between AD 70 and 100.

Matthew and Jewish sectarianism

Matthew became popular, we may surmise, partly because the book offers a historical tradition about Jesus in a form that was easy to use in worship and instruction by churches in any location. But many, looking more closely, have discerned that the Matthean traditions have been interpreted through the lens of particular sectarian debates between Jewish Christians and Pharisees in the post-70 social context. One plausible suggestion is that Matthew was written in a Greek-speaking urban centre in Syro-Palestine, among a network of churches that included Jews and gentiles, in proximity to a sizable Jewish community influenced by Pharisaic/rabbinic leaders. Such Jewish groups would retain their horrified resentment of the Roman destruction of Jerusalem and the surrounding countryside. This description would fit many places and times, but one possible guess would be Syrian Antioch[15] in the 80s of the first century.[16]

We have to remember that the Pharisees and Jewish Christians were the only Jewish sects that survived the Roman subjugation of Judea and the sacking of Jerusalem. On the eve of the siege of Jerusalem, the Jerusalem church is said to have fled to the Trans-Jordan.[17] Many Jewish Christians probably settled thereafter in

---

14 Ign. *Smyrn.* 1.1 = Mt. 3.15; *Did.* 6.2 = Mt. 5.48 and 11.29–30; *Did.* 8.1 = Mt. 6.16–18; *Did.* 8.2 = Mt. 6.5, 9–13; *Did.* 9.5 = Mt. 7.6; *Did.* 11.7 = Mt. 12.31; *Did.* 13.1–2 = Mt. 10.10. See discussion on Matthew and *Didache* in Garrow 2004.
15 It is interesting that Mk. 3.8 states, 'When they heard all he was doing, many people came to him from Judea, Jerusalem, Idumea, and the regions across the Jordan and around Tyre and Sidon', while the Matthean parallel in Mt. 4.24–25 says, 'News about him spread *all over Syria*, and people brought to him all who were ill with various diseases, those suffering severe pain, the demon-possessed, those having seizures, and the paralysed; and he healed them. Large crowds from Galilee, the Decapolis, Jerusalem, Judea and the region across the Jordan followed him.' Perhaps Matthew added 'Syria' because it was relevant to his immediate audience. We should remember, however, that the geographical terms were more fluid then than we would suppose today.
16 See e.g. Davies and Allison 1988–97, 1.9, 143–7; Keener 2009c, 42.
17 Eus. *Hist. Eccl.* 3.5.3.

places like Antioch, where other believers had already migrated as a result of earlier persecutions.[18] Later Jewish legend suggests that, after the Jewish revolt and the destruction of Jerusalem, Johanan ben-Zakkai established a new Pharisaic/rabbinic academy in the coastal town of Jamnia (Yavneh), west of Jerusalem. The new academy gradually came to exert authority over Jews living in Palestine, and at some point purportedly issued a new version of the 'Eighteen Benedictions', including a curse on heretics in general and Christians in particular. Many have supposed that Matthew reflects the socio-religious situation that would then arise, in which a Pharisaic group like that at Jamnia was trying to reconstruct and consolidate a Jewish way of life from which its central symbol, the Temple, had been removed. It would be natural for such a group, living in the period when agonized books like *4 Ezra* were written, to be casting about for explanations of the disaster. Some would undoubtedly blame the strange sect that had followed Jesus into disruptive new paths, and their spotlight would fall on Jewish Christians in particular.[19]

A fourth-century synagogue in Capernaum, though probably built on the foundations of a first-century synagogue
Bill Schlegel / BiblePlaces.com

We have to be cautious here. The academy at Jamnia was only one of the emerging Jewish centres. It had no immediate capacity to dictate policy to other Jewish communities. There is no evidence for a widespread purge of Jewish Christians—or, indeed, for the promulgation in that period of a 'benediction' designed to exclude

---
18 See Ac. 11.19–21.
19 See Davies and Allison 1988–97, 1.133–8.

Jesus-followers, who would be unable to call down a curse on themselves.[20] That said, we have reason to suspect that the pre-70 opposition to Jewish Christianity[21] was intensified in the post-70 period. Jewish Christians were flogged in synagogues, as we know already from Paul.[22] Many, reading between the lines of Matthew and John, have supposed that Christians were being driven out of synagogues,[23] though that historical proposal is in danger of circularity. There was certainly internecine rivalry between Jews and Christians in Asia Minor,[24] and at a later point Christians were indeed cursed as part of synagogal prayers.[25] Both groups—the Pharisaic/rabbinic leadership and the Jewish Christians—were trying to reconfigure their beliefs and communities without the Temple; the Jewish Christians were known to be associated with an increasing number of gentile Christ-believers; the Pharisees were in the germinal stages of transforming the debris of the second-Temple Jewish world into what would become 'rabbinic Judaism'. Clashes were inevitable. Our problem is that all of this is very difficult to date.

The conflict between the two groups is reflected in numerous passages in Matthew, though once again there is a danger of circularity. Some of the regular arguments appear to grow from an unwillingness to ascribe any great tension to the time, or the teaching, of Jesus himself. (The problem with that, of course, is that it becomes much harder to explain why Jesus incurred opposition, death threats, and finally crucifixion.) But, whatever we make of it, we find in Matthew (1) an emphasis on the Jewish rejection of Jesus;[26] (2) a ferocious denunciation of the Pharisees;[27] (3) a defence against the kinds of criticisms that Jews were making against Jewish Christians;[28] and (4) an alternative vision for Israel, based on the fulfilment in Jesus of the hope of Israel. Matthew can be read as explaining that the destruction of the Temple was warranted by the priestly opposition to Jesus. He stresses that Torah was to be fulfilled by Jesus' love ethic, rather than the Pharisaic *halakhah*. He tells how God, through Jesus, has included gentiles in the kingdom. Matthew has written an apology for what might be called 'messianic Judaism' as the proper heir of the older Jewish way. The fact that most of this could equally well be said of Paul should make us wary of concluding that it must all be taking place after AD 70; but the case can still be made that that is the more likely time for the book to be written.

So did Matthew himself, his initial audience, or his implied readers think of

---

20 Wright *NTPG*, 161–6.
21 See 1 Thess. 2.14–15; 2 Cor. 11.23; Rom. 15.31; Ac. 7.54–60; 11.19; 12.1–2; 21.26—22.30; Jos. *Ant.* 20.200.
22 Mk. 13.9; Mt. 10.17; 23.24; 2 Cor. 11.24.
23 Mt. 23.24; Jn. 9.22; 12.42; 16.2.
24 Rev. 2.9; 3.9.
25 Just. *Dial.* 16.4; 96.2; 137.2.
26 Mt. 8.11–12; 11.16–24; 12.38–45; 22.8; 21.33–46; 22.7–8; 27.25.
27 Mt. 5.20; 12.24–39; 23.1–39.
28 Mt. 5.17–20; 27.63–66; 28.12–15.

themselves as still in some way part of the social fabric of Judaism centred on the synagogue? Or have they been expelled, and forced now to live and worship elsewhere?[29] We should note that in geographical terms there was no 'Jewish state' as such: Judea and Galilee did not function like that. But was Matthew's church effectively a sect within Judaism, engaging in intra-factional polemics, or have Matthew and his church been ejected, so that they are now defining themselves over against some kind of Jewish world? 'Judaism' itself was not, of course, a rigidly fixed entity with well-defined dogmas and policed social boundaries. Indeed, as we have seen, the word 'Judaism' itself referred at this time not to a 'religion' but to the activity of zealous propagation of Jewish allegiance and symbolic life. In addition, leaving 'Judaism' was not like leaving a Baptist church for a Presbyterian one. To be excluded from the Jewish world meant a painful break in the network of family, religious, social, and commercial relationships. It frequently entailed a form of social death with all the shame and shunning that went along with that.[30]

To complicate matters, however—and perhaps to undermine this sketch altogether—we know that Christians and Jews, while becoming in some ways distinct from one another, still retained a certain family resemblance, and remained in close social proximity, with many people moving to and fro between the two groups and trying to belong to both. This is evidenced by Ignatius of Antioch's complaint against those Christians who fraternized with Jews or who followed Jewish customs; something people would not have worried about had the two communities been isolated from one another.[31] This situation continued for many generations, with Chrysostom in the fourth century facing similar problems to those of Ignatius.[32] So the Christian 'break with Judaism'—the so-called 'parting of the ways'—was never final or complete, at least not until the fourth century.[33]

Has this really helped us to locate Matthew? Perhaps, though the question is probably more complicated than is often made out. Matthew is most likely written in, and for, an environment where Jewish Christians and their gentile converts wanted to remain in some sense part of Jewish communities, but where there was mounting pressure for them to be expelled. Perhaps that had already begun to happen. But this generalized conclusion does not help with dating as much as has sometimes been thought. The Pauline parallel suggests that much of this might have been true already in the 30s, 40s, and 50s; the fall of Jerusalem suggests that it might have become more acute in the 70s or 80s. Ancient historians often have to conclude that we do not know.

---

29 See Keener 2009c, 45–51; Stanton 1993, 146–68; Evans and Carlston 2014.
30 Davies and Allison 1988–97, 3.695.
31 Ign. *Magn.* 8.1; 10.3; *Phld.* 6.1.
32 See Chrysostom's at times cringingly derisive homilies *Against the Jews* compared with his more sanguine comments on the Jews in his *Hom. Rom.* 16–19.
33 See e.g. Dunn 2006 as well as Becker and Reed 2007.

OUTLINE OF MATTHEW[*]

The most obvious structural feature of Matthew's gospel is the five discourses, which many have seen as deliberately evoking the five books of Moses. The first (chs. 5, 6, and 7) and the fifth (chs. 23, 24, 25) are the longest, and may reflect the 'blessings and curses' of Deuteronomy. The central one (ch. 13) consists of the parables, which sketch out Jesus' radical vision of God's kingdom. The second (ch. 10) offers instructions for the apostles, while the fourth (ch. 18) offers instructions for the church. Matthew marks out these blocks of teaching with a concluding formula: 'When Jesus had finished these sayings', or something similar, ending with 'When Jesus had finished *all* these sayings' (26.1 NTE/KNT). This seems to be one of Matthew's own clearly intended structural markers.[†]

1. Infancy narrative (1.1—2.23)
2. Beginning of Jesus' ministry (3.1—7.29)
   Narrative: 3.1—4.25
   Discourse 1 (Sermon on the Mount): 5.1—7.27
   Concluding formula: 7.28–29
3. Revelation of Jesus' authority (8.1—11.1)
   Narrative: 8.1—9.35
   Discourse 2 (missionary): 9.36—10.42
   Concluding formula: 11.1
4. Jesus' ministry causes division (11.2—13.53)
   Narrative: 11.2—12.50
   Discourse 3 (parables): 13.1–52
   Concluding formula: 13.53
5. Jesus and his disciples (13.54—19.2)
   Narrative: 13.54—17.27
   Discourse 4 (rule of the community): 18.1–35
   Concluding formula: 19.1–2
6. Jesus, judgment, and Jerusalem (19.3—26.2)
   Narrative: 19.3—22.46
   Discourse 5 (rejection of Pharisees/Olivet Discourse): 23.1—25.46
   Concluding formula: 26.1–2
7. Passion, resurrection, and Great Commission (26.3—28.20)

----

[*] deSilva 2004, 239; see further discussion in Davies and Allison 1988–97, 3.58–72.
[†] See Wright *NTPG* on Matthew.

Purpose

So why did Matthew write his book? Clearly, to draw out the manifold ways in which the story of Jesus of Nazareth brought the long and prophecy-laden story of Israel to its God-ordained goal. This would mean simultaneously offering a manifesto for Jewish believers to retain their allegiance to their ancestral scriptures and controlling narrative, and outlining the way in which they should also embrace the new world in which Jesus had been revealed as Israel's Messiah and as the Emmanuel, the living embodiment of Israel's God. This would also mean effectively offering an *apology*, before the watching Jewish world, for following Jesus, presenting this as the fulfilment of Israel's heritage, the true form of loyalty to Israel's ancestral calling and hopes. Most Jewish groups, after all, were struggling with this kind of question at the time. The Dead Sea Scrolls advance an agenda like that; Bar-Kochba would claim in the 130s that his group was the true fulfilment of Israel's purposes; the rabbis who compiled the Mishnah were saying 'this is what true allegiance to the Torah should look like'. Matthew would fit right into this picture, as (once more) would Paul.

Finally, Matthew is quite clearly offering a *manual* for discipleship, for a church living as a minority group in a hostile majority culture.

MATTHEW'S STORY OF JESUS

(See box: 'Outline of Matthew'.)

1. Infancy narrative (1.1—2.23)

Matthew's opening, so apparently boring to a modern western reader, would be electrifying for a first-century Jew. He traces Jesus' genealogy in three stages: Abraham to David, David to the exile, and the exile to Jesus—with fourteen generations in each. In other words, there have been six 'sevens' so far . . . and now comes the goal, the perfection, the seventh seven, the aim of it all. The genealogy summarizes Israel's history, climaxing in Jesus.[34]

Abraham of course is the start; Jesus' Davidic descent is stressed by Matthew even more than by the other evangelists; but what about the exile? As we've seen earlier (see chapter 5), many Jews of the second-Temple period regarded themselves as, in a sense, still in exile, still suffering the result of Israel's 'sins', languishing under pagan powers. The long story of Abraham's people, Matthew is saying, will come to fulfilment with a new David who will rescue his people from their exile, that is, 'save his people from their sins'.

A Greek-style mosaic of Mary and baby Jesus from the Basilica of the Annunciation in Nazareth
Public Domain

The Matthean birth story describes how a Galilean virgin named Mary, though pledged to Joseph, became pregnant 'through the holy spirit'. Joseph was planning to set aside the marriage privately, on suspicion of infidelity, until an angel of the Lord appeared to him in a dream and told him that 'what is conceived in her is from the holy spirit'. Matthew adds an editorial remark that Jesus' birth fulfils the words of Isaiah 7.14 about the virgin bearing a child who is to be called 'Immanuel', which means 'God with us' (1.18–23). This is the more interesting in that we know of no pre-Christian readers of Isaiah who took the passage in this way. It seems far more likely that the story of Jesus' extraordinary conception generated a search for relevant texts rather than (as has often been suggested) the other way round.

---

34 See Hood 2011.

Jesus is born in Bethlehem. Matthew follows this with the story of the visit of the Magi from the east (2.1–12), the flight of the holy family from Judea to Egypt in order to escape Herod's Pharaoh-esque attempt to kill the child (2.13–18), and their return to Nazareth after Herod's death (2.19–23). Matthew peppers this story with Old Testament citations that identify Jesus as either rehearsing a biblical pattern or else fulfilling prophetic promises for Israel's deliverance.[35] The narrative exhibits several points of contact with exodus and exile traditions where Jesus' infancy recapitulates a *new exodus* and the *end of exile*, marking him out further as the true representative of Israel (Mt. 2.13–18) (see Table 25.1).[36]

2. Beginning of Jesus' ministry (3.1—7.29)

John the Baptist now appears on the scene as the Isaianic 'voice' crying in the wilderness, preparing the way of the Lord by preaching repentance and administering baptism. The Baptist's message was that judgment was imminent. No-one would escape it by claiming Abrahamic descent, so they had better produce fruit in keeping with repentance, with that 'turning back to the Lord' spoken of in Deuteronomy.[37] Someone was about to arrive—a 'Coming One'—who would usher in a time of purification. His 'baptism' would be one of spirit and fire.

Fresco of the baptism of Jesus in Baptistery, Parma, Italy
Renata Sedmakova / Shutterstock

---

35 Isa. 7.14 = Mt. 1.23; Mic. 5.2 = Mt. 2.6; Hos. 11.1 = Mt. 2.15; Jer. 31.15 = Mt. 2.18; Isa. 11.1 (?) = Mt. 2.23.
36 See Bird 2010b.
37 Dt. 4.30; 30.2; see e.g. 1 Sam. 7.3; Isa. 55.7; Jer. 4.1; Hos. 6.1; Joel 2.12.

TABLE 25.1: JEWISH FEATURES UNIQUE TO THE GOSPEL OF MATTHEW[*]

Source	Subject
Mt. 1—2	Jesus presented as a new Moses
Mt. 1.1; 9.27; 12.23; 15.22; 21.9, 15; 22.42	Emphasis on Jesus as the 'son of David'
Mt. 2.4; 3.7 etc.	Increased focus on Pharisees
Mt. 3.2; 4.17; 5.3, 10, 19, 20, etc.	Matthew prefers 'kingdom of heaven' over 'kingdom of God' with 'heaven' functioning as a circumlocution for 'God'
Mt. 4.5; 27.53.	Jerusalem is described as the 'holy city'
Mt. 5.32	The condition 'except for sexual immorality' reflects Shammaite teaching on the grounds for divorce
Mt. 5.47; 6.7	Righteous behaviour contrasted with what the 'pagans' or 'gentiles' do
Mt. 6.2–18	Contrast of synagogue behaviour with Christian behaviour
Mt. 9.13; 12.7	Contest with Jewish leaders over the meaning of Hos. 6.6, 'I desire mercy, not sacrifice', in the post-Temple era
Mt. 10.5; 15.24	Jesus' ministry restricted to 'the house of Israel'
Mt. 13.52	Matthew's ideal disciple, and perhaps an explanation of what he thought he was doing, is: 'Therefore every teacher of the law who has become a disciple in the kingdom of heaven is like the owner of a house who brings out of his storeroom new treasures as well as old.'
Mt. 15.17	Omits Mark's parenthetical remark 'In saying this, Jesus declared all foods clean' from Mk. 7.19
Mt. 15.22	Changes Mark's 'Syro-Phoenician woman' (a Roman designation to distinguish such people from Libyo-Phoenicians) to 'Canaanite woman'
Mt. 16.17–18; 18.18	Language of 'binding' and 'loosing' reflects Jewish background
Mt. 23.3	Enjoins obedience to those who sit in Moses' seat
Mt. 23.5	Mention of Jewish dress including 'phylacteries' and 'tassels'
Mt. 23.7–8	The honorific nature of the title 'Rabbi'
Mt. 23.40	Disciples should pray that the flight from Jerusalem is not on a sabbath

[*]Following Davies and Allison 1988–97, 1.26–7 with further additions.

> 'Preaching the beatitudes should follow their contours as blessings of the kingdom now arriving in Jesus. And as God has come in Jesus to make all wrong things right and all upside-down things right side up, reversals are happening. The most destitute are beginning to receive and will receive blessing. And although these are announcements of eschatological blessing, an ethical invitation flows from them. As we who are followers of Jesus participate in this way of life and the kingdom values of justice, mercy, and faithfulness, we will also participate in the blessings of the kingdom that Jesus announces.'
>
> Jeannine Brown, *Matthew*, 56.

In other words, he would plunge the people into the fiery breath of God; they would be either purified or purged by the experience (3.1–12).

Jesus then presents himself for baptism, leaving John somewhat embarrassed. 'I need to be baptized by you,' he says, 'and do you come to me?' Jesus replies that it must be done to 'fulfil all righteousness'; meaning apparently that Jesus' humble submission to baptism symbolizes his vocation, the task to which he has been appointed by God the father. When Jesus is then baptized, the holy spirit descends on him like a dove, and a voice from heaven, quoting Psalm 2.7, announces God's pleasure with the divine son (3.13–17).

Jesus is then led by the spirit into the wilderness to be tested by the devil (4.1–11). The temptations focus on the radical distortion and perversion of the vocation to which Jesus had pledged his loyalty in baptism and which had just been confirmed by the voice from above: is he *really* God's son? If so, should he 'prove' it by a self-serving use of his miraculous powers? Each time, Jesus resists the devil by quoting Deuteronomy.[38] As throughout the stories of his birth and baptism, the temptation narrative thus portrays Jesus as the true Israelite. In the words of Terence Donaldson:

> Matthew, therefore, presents Jesus as one who in his experience recapitulates the story of Israel. Like Israel of old, Jesus has been called by God out of Egypt to a life of humble obedience; like Israel, this calling was put to the test in the wilderness. The hope of the story is that, unlike Israel, Jesus will remain faithful where Israel was disobedient.[39]

Matthew then offers a snapshot of Jesus' ministry in Galilee, seeing Jesus' work in the traditional tribal areas of Zebulun and Naphtali as the fulfilment of Isaiah 9.1–2, with the great light shining on the people as Jesus announces the inbreaking kingdom and summons people to repent (4.12–17). He then calls two fishermen, Simon Peter and his brother Andrew, to follow him and 'fish for people' (4.18–22). The narrative rounds off with a description of Jesus' public ministry, attracting crowds from Jewish and gentile regions (4.23–25).

---

38 Dt. 8.3; 6.16; 6.13.
39 Donaldson 2005, 116.

The first discourse, the Sermon on the Mount (chs. 5—7), features Jesus on a mountain, like a new Moses, giving the people a new Torah (5.1–2). Jesus teaches a series of beatitudes (5.3–12), calls disciples to be salt and light (5.3–16), and then clarifies that his teaching fulfils rather than nullifies the Torah (5.17–20). Thereafter comes a series of antitheses, marked by the formula 'You have heard that it was said . . . but I tell you', which mostly intensify Torah commands, closing with an exhortation to imitate the perfection of God the father (5.21–48). This is followed by a call for traditional Jewish piety (almsgiving, prayer, and fasting) but without pretentiousness or hypocrisy (6.1–18). What matters above all is God's kingdom (6.19–34). The 'golden rule'—treating others the way one wants to be treated—is seen as the fulfilment of the law and the prophets (7.1–12, echoing 5.17). The discourse ends with a variation of the Jewish 'two-ways' sketch of ethical teaching,[40] offering a series of contrasts: wide and narrow gates, wolves and sheep, fruitless and fruitful trees, mere profession versus actual devotion, and the foolish and wise builders (7.13–27). What strikes the crowds about all this is not just the particular teachings, but the authority with which Jesus delivers them (7.28–29).

3. Revelation of Jesus' authority (8.1—11.1)

That note of authority continues in the next section, with stories of dramatic healings that lead to further teaching on the kingdom (for instance, its extension to the gentiles) and discipleship. Matthew links the healings to the Isaianic prophecies about the Servant who 'took up our infirmities and bore our diseases' (Mt. 8.17 = Isa. 53.4). The challenge of discipleship is encapsulated in the story of the boat caught in the storm (8.23–27). Jesus' offer of forgiveness, and his fraternizing with tax-collectors and 'sinners', produces strong opposition (9.1–13), and Jesus insists that the new life he is bringing cannot be constrained by the old practices such as fasting (9.14–17). More healings follow in chapter 9, leading Matthew to portray Jesus as the Davidic shepherd-king of Israel, who looks upon the crowds with compassion, like sheep without a shepherd, and whose harvest is in urgent need of workers (9.36–38).

Jesus then appoints the Twelve as 'apostles', with authority to cast out impure spirits, to heal the sick, and preach the kingdom of heaven (10.1–4). This leads in to the gospel's second great discourse (10.5–42), containing instructions for the Twelve in their urgent and dangerous itinerant ministry. For the moment, this is confined to 'the lost sheep of the house of Israel' (10.6); Jesus has already predicted the ingathering of gentiles (8.11), but this will not happen until after the climactic events in Jerusalem (28.19). The apostles must not be afraid, but must remember that the response they get is the equivalent of a response to Jesus himself.

---

[40] See Dt. 30.1–20 (esp. v. 15); Sir. 15.17; 4Q473; *1 En.* 91.3–4, 18–19; 94.1–5; taken up by Christians in *Did.* 1—5 and *Ep. Barn.* 18—20.

4. Jesus' ministry causes division (11.2—13.53)

All this raises for Matthew's readers, as for Jesus' contemporaries, the question of whether Jesus really is Israel's Messiah. Even John the Baptist, now in prison, sends messengers to ask Jesus if he really is the 'one to come', namely, the Messiah. Matthew stresses that Jesus really was the Messiah. But Jesus was operating off a different script, a different way of understanding Israel's story. He wasn't thinking of himself in terms of Elijah calling down fire from heaven. He was thinking of passages like Isaiah 35, the great prophecies of what would happen when Israel was not so much judged and condemned, as restored after judgment. A time when the exile would be over, the blind and the lame would be healed, and God's people would be set free at last. Jesus' remarks about John indicate that he saw his imprisoned cousin as the coming 'Elijah'; and Elijah, in Malachi 4, prepares the way not simply for the Messiah but for the arrival of Israel's God in person. John therefore marks the termination of the epoch of the law and the prophets (11.2–15). This leads Jesus to denounce the towns that had not responded to his proclamation (11.20–24). The message, it seems, is hidden from the learned and revealed to babes, since only the father knows the son and only the son knows the father. Recognizing this enables those who are weary and perplexed to find 'rest' in Jesus. He has brought the great sabbath, the time of true refreshment, the genuine anticipation of God's final kingdom. The rabbis offered 'the yoke of Torah'; Jesus offered a different 'yoke', which, growing out of his mercy and love, was easy to bear (11.25–30).

Conflict, however, continues, not least over things Jesus did on the sabbath. His many healings, particularly exorcisms, prompt his opponents to charge that he is in league with the devil, and Jesus denounces such talk as blasphemy against God's spirit (12.22–32). If the Pharisees

> **BLAST FROM THE PAST: THEODORE OF MOPSUESTIA ON PETER'S CONFESSION**
>
> *Theodore of Mopsuestia (c. AD 350–428) was the bishop of Mopsuestia in Cilicia in the late fourth and early fifth century and was a popular teacher in the eastern churches. His account of Peter's confession in Matthew 16.16–18 sounds like a proto-protestant interpretation by identifying the 'rock' principally as Peter's confession and only secondarily as Peter himself. Theodore wrote:*
>
> This is not the property of Peter alone, but it came about on behalf of every human being. Having said that his confession is a rock, [Jesus] stated that upon this rock I will build my church. This means he will build his church upon this same confession and faith. For this reason, addressing the one who first confessed him with the title, on account of his confession he applied to him this authority, too, as something that would become his, speaking of the common and special good of the church as pertaining to him alone.'
>
> *This seems, in fact, to have been the dominant interpretation of this passage right up to the Roman Catholic 'counter-Reformation' in the second half of the sixteenth century.*†
>
> ---
> * Cited in Simonetti 2002, 45–6.
> † Meyer 2014, 89.

want a 'sign', he will give them the sign of Jonah, 'three days and three nights in the heart of the earth', a reference to his coming Passion and resurrection. He compares the current generation to a man who has been exorcized, but the demon has returned and repossessed him. By analogy, the Jews of this generation have tried to sort out their 'house' with all types of military schemes, apocalyptic dreams, pious practices, and sectarian gatherings, but it's always in vain. The demons return, and people end up worse off than they were before (12.43–45). Even Jesus' own relatives don't understand what's going on (12.46–50).

Then comes the third major discourse of Matthew's gospel, a series of parables about the kingdom of heaven (and we remind ourselves that 'kingdom of heaven' in Matthew, as with its equivalent 'kingdom of God' in the other gospels, does not refer to 'heaven' as the final post-mortem destination of God's people but to the arrival of God's sovereign, saving, 'heavenly' rule on earth itself—as in the prayer which Jesus taught). The first series of parables (soils, weeds, mustard seeds, and yeast) explains the nature of the kingdom to the crowds, yet they are unable to penetrate the mystery, making them like the recalcitrant generation of Isaiah's day (13.1–43). The second series of parables (hidden treasure, expensive pearl, net) focuses on the astonishing and all-surpassing value of the kingdom and the consequent joy of belonging to it. Matthew's own comment may be autobiographical: the ideal believer is a scribe who, having learned the mystery of God's reign, brings the old and the new together with wisdom (13.51–52).[41]

5. Jesus and his disciples (13.54—19.2)

The polarizing nature of Jesus' ministry is expressed through a series of vivid episodes. These include the rejection of Jesus in Nazareth, his home town (13.54–58), Herod's suggestion that Jesus was John the Baptist risen from the dead, leading to the morbid side-story of how Herod had the Baptist put to death (14.1–13), followed by the feeding of the five thousand (14.14–21). Jesus then stills a storm on the Sea of Galilee (Peter having tried and failed to walk on the water), inducing awe and worship (14.22–33). When he and the disciples land in Gennesaret, the people recognize Jesus and bring out their sick for him to heal them (14.34–36).

The scene changes abruptly to another confrontation, this time over purity traditions (15.1–20). Jesus then withdraws northwards, outside the land, where his normal principle of working only with Jewish people is overridden by the witty persistence of a mother on behalf of her daughter (15.21–28). Returning to Galilee, Jesus once again heals many sick people, and once again feeds a large crowd (15.29–39).

Matthew switches back to the opposition with a strange coalition of Pharisees and Sadducees demanding a sign from Jesus, no doubt hoping to bring a charge

---

41 Meyer 2014, 88.

Caesarea Philippi

against him that he was a false prophet, using signs and wonders to lead Israel astray. But Jesus once again will only offer them the 'sign of Jonah' (16.1–4; see 12.39), warning the disciples about the Pharisees' teaching, which like yeast would work its way into their minds (16.5–12).

All this prepares for Matthew's version of the scene at Caesarea Philippi, where Jesus elicits from Peter the confession 'You are the Messiah, the Son of the living God' (16.16). Jesus responds by assuring Peter that he can only say this because God has shown it to him, and that he will have a crucial role in the establishment of the kingdom (see 'Blast from the past: Theodore of Mopsuestia on Peter's confession').[42] Jesus is building, not a physical city, but a community of allegiance (16.13–20).

As soon as Peter has recognized him as Messiah, Jesus insists that his vocation, precisely as Messiah, is to go to Jerusalem, not to conquer like a military general, but to be rejected, killed, and raised up on the third day. Peter tries to talk him out of this; but, echoing chapter 4, Jesus rejects Peter's protest as a satanic temptation. Following him will mean denying oneself, taking up one's cross, and accompanying him to crucifixion! (16.21–28). The glory of the coming kingdom is then previewed in the 'transfiguration', where Jesus appears in splendorous array with Moses and Elijah (17.1–13). This leads to further healings, further predictions of Jesus' forthcoming 'Passion', and a strange little story about paying a tax with a coin found in a fish's mouth (17.14–27).

If there is a common theme in Matthew 14—17, it might be the mission of Jesus to bring Israel to its appointed eschatological goal of national restoration (especially 16.18; 17.11–13) while Israel's leaders conspicuously reject Jesus' claims and his message (especially 16.1–4). If Jesus is to reconstitute Israel around himself, renew the covenant community, and rebuild

---

[42] Mt. 16.17–19.

596   The Gospels and the Story of God

the nation on messianic foundations, then he must also outline the manner of intramural life that characterizes this community. How are the children of the king to live together? This is the point of the fourth discourse (18.1–35), which functions, much like the Rule of the Community (1QS) did for the Qumran sectarians, to define the ethos and discipline of the believing community, focused here on humility and reconciliation—with warnings about the severe danger of not forgiving one another.

6. Jesus, judgment, and Jerusalem (19.3—26.2)

As Jesus makes his way towards Jerusalem, Matthew emphasizes the cost of discipleship: the stringent discipline of marriage, the challenge to childlike humility and trust, and the summons to a rich young man to sell all, give to the poor, and follow Jesus (19.1–30). This leads to the parable of the workers in the vineyard: all who obey God's call are on an equal footing (20.1–16). But, after another 'Passion prediction' (20.17–19), the mother of James and John requests positions of power in the coming kingdom. Jesus responds with two Isaianic images about drinking the cup of God's wrath (Isa. 51.17, 22) and giving his life as a ransom for others (Isa. 53.10–12). For Jesus, power is about service, and service is about sacrifice (20.20–28). Jesus' public ministry in Galilee and Judea ends, in the healing of two blind men, with another reference to Jesus as the Davidic shepherd-king who has power to heal his people (20.29–34).

Jesus then stages a strange kind of 'royal' entry into Jerusalem, evoking Zechariah 9.9 by riding on a donkey while the crowds hail him as 'Son of David' and the 'prophet from Nazareth' (21.1–11). Jesus goes straight to the Temple courtyard where he enacts a prophetic protest against its failure to embody God's purposes. Matthew adds another Davidic touch, but this time ironically: Jesus heals the blind and the lame, the ones David had excluded (21.12–17; see 2 Sam. 5.8). Jesus' denunciation of the Temple is then acted out with the cursing of the fig tree.

This introduces stories of conflict and debate, all focused on the significance of Jesus' Temple-action and his larger kingdom-vision. These include the question of Jesus' authority (21.23–27), the parable of the two sons (21.28–32), the parable of the wicked tenants (21.33–46), the parable of the wedding banquet (22.1–14), the question of paying taxes to Caesar (22.15–22), the question of the resurrection of the dead (22.23–33), the question

> 'From the beginning of [Matthew's] narrative, it is not meant to be a militant victory of the Davidic messiah; rather, it is meant to be the arrival of the compassionate eschatological Shepherd who has come for the harassed and down-trodden sheep without a shepherd. After Jesus' entry into Jerusalem, the shepherd image is pushed forward to the climax of the story of the Son of David as the king of the Jews. Jesus as the representative of the shepherds of Israel in the past is to be smitten (26:31), and his healing ministry reaches its climax when the smitten shepherd himself is resurrected with the saints (27:51–53). Finally, the Davidic-Shepherd is appointed with all authority in view of the extended reign over the nations (28:16–20).'
>
> Young Chae, *Jesus as the Eschatological Davidic Shepherd*, 326.

of which is the greatest commandment (22.34–40), and Jesus' counter-question about the Davidic sonship of the Messiah (22.41–46). The net effect of these stories is that the boundaries of the kingdom do not correspond to the patronage, approval, or penchants of either the priestly ruling class or the populist Pharisees. God's mercy is scandalous in its scope, not puritanical in its parameters. To embrace this means joy; to oppose it means judgment. That is why, in Jesus' kingdom, outsiders are insiders and vice versa; the first will be last and vice versa; service is greatness and vice versa. Matthew stresses—all in the context of the build-up to Jesus' crucifixion—that what counts is faith and fruit, not power, purity, or prosperity.

This brings us to the fifth and largest discourse of Matthew's gospel, with chapters 23, 24, and 25 corresponding to and balancing out the 'sermon on the mount' of chapters 5, 6, and 7. This final discourse is really two speeches back to back: first, the denunciation of the Pharisees (Mt. 23), and then the Olivet Discourse (Mt. 24—25). The first of these, echoing the 'woes' of Deuteronomy 27 and 28 (as opposed to the 'blessings' of Dt. 28.1–14, echoed in the 'beatitudes' in Mt. 5), denounces the Pharisees for hypocrisy, the externality of their religion, their pretentiousness, and their predatory behaviour. We remind ourselves that Jesus was himself closer to the Pharisees than to any of the other Jewish sects because of his belief in God's coming kingdom and the resurrection; many Pharisees joined the Jesus-movement.[43] If we believe the rabbinic writings, not all Pharisees were hypocrites; Matthew's account must be situated in the light of the intra-Jewish conflicts of his time which tended towards invective, angry polemic, and hyperbole.

Matthew's version of the Olivet Discourse largely follows Mark, but adds certain materials like that pertaining to the 'days of Noah', the parables of the ten virgins and the 'talents', and the scenario of the nations gathered for judgment, like sheep and goats, before the 'son of man'. Mark and Luke seem to insist that the Olivet Discourse is fulfilled in the events of AD 70. It is possible that Matthew, in his more extended version, is seeing the devastation of Jerusalem and the destruction of the Temple as an eschatological dress-rehearsal for a yet-to-come fulfilment involving the kind of ultimate final judgment we find in Paul, Hebrews, and Revelation.

7. Passion, resurrection, and Great Commission (26.3—28.20)

Matthew's narrative now accelerates towards the crucifixion. Jesus warns his followers of what is about to happen; for Matthew this focuses on Jesus as 'son of man', the one who will suffer and be vindicated (26.2). The chief priests and elders conspire to arrest Jesus and kill him. Meanwhile, Jesus is anointed at Bethany by an anonymous woman with perfume from an alabaster jar, after which Judas offers to betray Jesus to the chief priests for silver (26.3–16).

Jesus then celebrates the Passover meal with the disciples, a meal that memorialized

---

43 See Jn. 3.1; Ac. 15.5; 23.6; 26.5; Phil. 3.5.

how the people of Israel came out of Egypt, through the Red Sea, leaving behind their slavery and going on to freedom in the promised land. Jesus draws the meaning of the whole meal and all it represented onto himself, identifying the bread and the wine with his body (about to be broken in death) and his blood (about to be spilt on the cross), and inviting his followers to share it and find in it the gift of forgiveness of sins, of new life, of God's kingdom (26.17–30).

Jesus then takes his disciples to the Mount of Olives, where he warns them that he will be betrayed and they will be scattered, until he rejoins them in Galilee. Peter promises not to desert Jesus, but will in fact deny him three times that very night. Jesus is then overwhelmed with sorrow as to what awaits him, and with Peter, James, and John close by (but sleepy with exhaustion) prays urgently and in agony that he might be spared the coming trial. Eventually Judas arrives with a cohort of armed guards, and after a brief melee, they arrest Jesus. The disciples, as predicted, desert him (26.31–56).

Jesus is brought before the Sanhedrin for trial; Peter follows secretly. The trial focuses on Jesus' predictions of the Temple's destruction and rebuilding. Is Jesus claiming authority over the Temple—either messianic authority or actually divine authority? Caiaphas sharpens the question: is Jesus 'the Messiah, the son of God?' Jesus replies obliquely yet affirmatively, 'You have said so . . . and I say to all of you: *from now on* you will see the Son of Man sitting at the right hand of the Mighty One and coming on the clouds of heaven.' These apparently blasphemous words—Jesus sharing God's throne?—give Caiaphas the warrant for a death sentence. The council goes into a frenzy of physical violence against Jesus. Peter, meanwhile, has been recognized as a follower of Jesus, and three times he denies knowing Jesus, before finally bursting into tears and rushing out (26.57–75).

Early next morning Jesus is brought before the governor, Pontius Pilate. After mentioning the fate of Judas, Matthew leads quickly to the choice Pilate gives the crowd: Jesus or Barabbas? (He inserts into this the tale of Pilate's wife having nightmares about Jesus.) Pilate hedges his bets: he is innocent, and places the blame on those in the crowd, who respond in a phrase ('His blood be on us and our children') which has done untold damage in the church's attitude to the Jewish people but which Matthew certainly sees simply in terms of the fall of Jerusalem in AD 70. Pilate then releases Barabbas and has Jesus flogged and handed over to be crucified (27.11–26).

Matthew follows Mark in the account of the crucifixion, with minor changes and additions. The soldiers mock Jesus as king (27.27–31), Simon of Cyrene is made to carry Jesus' cross (27.32–33), Jesus refuses the offer of wine mixed with gall (27.34); he is crucified beside two bandits, with the soldiers casting lots for his clothes and onlookers hurling insults (27.35–44). Just before Jesus dies, the land is shrouded in darkness. Jesus calls out in prayer the words of Psalm 22.1; when he dies, the curtain of the Temple is torn in two.

Matthew then adds a strange and disturbing scene. 'The tombs broke open,' he writes. 'The bodies of many holy people who had died were raised to life. They came out of the tombs after Jesus' resurrection and went into the holy city and appeared to many people.'[44] In our judgment it is unlikely that Matthew intended this to be a 'literal' description. He is probably blending together the present and the future, underscoring the life-giving power of Jesus' death.[45] The centurion in charge of operations is terrified. 'Surely,' he blurts out, 'this man was the son of God' (27.45–54).

Some of Jesus' female followers (Mary Magdalene, Mary the mother of James and Joseph, and the mother of the Zebedee brothers) look on as Joseph of Arimathea buries Jesus' body in a tomb newly cut in the rock. The chief priests and Pharisees, worried about the body being stolen, persuade Pilate to seal the tomb and post a guard (27.55–66).

Matthew's resurrection-narrative follows Mark's up to a point, but with significant differences. When the two Marys arrive at the tomb, there is an earthquake, an angel rolls back the stone then sits on it, and the Roman guards become catatonic in fear; the angel tells the women not to be afraid and to let the disciples know that they will see Jesus alive in Galilee. The women scurry away; but unlike in Mark's account they were 'afraid yet filled with joy, and ran to tell his disciples'. On the way, the risen Jesus greets them, and, says Matthew, they 'clasped his feet and worshipped him'. Jesus tells them not to be afraid, and that the disciples will see him in Galilee (28.1–10).

Matthew describes the guards reporting to the priests what had happened, and the priests instructing them to say that the disciples had stolen the body while they were sleeping. This, says Matthew, is the story circulated among Jews to his day (28.11–15).

The eleven disciples then go to Galilee where they meet Jesus on a mountain. A great deal in Matthew happens on mountains: the temptations; the Sermon on the Mount; the transfiguration; the final discourse on the Mount of Olives; and now this parting scene. Jesus commissions the disciples to go, teach, make disciples, and baptize, all on the basis of two claims that sum up Matthew's whole gospel: all authority in heaven and earth is given to him; and Jesus' presence will always remain with them (28.16–20). In other words, Emmanuel, God-with-us, means Jesus-always-with-us. Or, as James Dunn puts it: 'For Matthew, Jesus was not simply Son of God, son of David, Messiah, Son of Man, Moses, prophet. He embodied God's presence and universal authority in a way that no other servant of God had done before.'[46]

MATTHEW AND THE BIG PICTURE

Reading Matthew's gospel from beginning to end can induce a kind of joyful exhaustion. It is like following Jesus through a marathon maze of Jewish history, sectarian

---

44 Mt. 27.52–53.
45 Bird and Crossley 2008, 69 n. 30.
46 Dunn 2015, 257–8.

tensions, and dense discipleship, all leading to a shockingly dramatic climax. Matthew's story is jolting, convicting, heartening, and above all demanding—if Jesus' followers take it seriously. With that in mind, there may be two main things to take away.

First, listen to Jesus as *teacher*, indeed, our one and only teacher (Mt. 23.10). His words are a rock (Mt. 7.24–25), enduring into the ages (Mt. 24.35). He possesses all authority in heaven and earth (Mt. 28.18), and everything he said must be obeyed (Mt. 28.20). Of course, Jesus' words as we find them in the gospels are unlikely to be verbatim quotations. Jesus almost certainly spoke Aramaic, not Greek, and the process of translation has included summarizing, interpreting, and applying what Jesus said. Some Bibles print Jesus' words in red, which, while naturally drawing attention to them, ought not to make us think those words more inspired or authoritative than the rest of the scriptures. Nonetheless, any serious follower of Jesus will be interested not simply in doctrines about Jesus but in the actual teaching of Jesus. The truth is that following Jesus requires effort because Jesus, as A. E. Harvey observed, issued 'strenuous commands' to his followers.[47] Yes, Jesus relaxes some purity regulations for gentile believers. But he intensifies the moral vision of the Torah: forget adultery, don't even look at another person lustfully, forgive a brother or sister who sins against you, no matter how often, be perfect as your heavenly father is perfect, turn the other cheek rather than slap an assailant back, and so forth. This is not take-it-or-leave-it advice. These are not 'guidelines' or 'recommendations'. These are not lofty ideals to try to aim for (while everybody knows we won't live up to them and shouldn't worry too much). This really is how kingdom-people are meant to live. This is the divine perfection we are meant to pursue. This—particularly Jesus' strong words about caring for the poor—is what will separate the sheep from the goats. For some, it may be helpful to memorize the words of Jesus, and ask frequently in prayer how far one is measuring up to them. We all need to cultivate a spirituality of increasing obedience, not out of legalistic pretentiousness, not out of a servile fear of God, but from a trust in the one whose yoke is easy and whose burden is light. Discipleship means, quite simply, learning to obey Jesus' teachings and following where he has led.

Second, it would be negligent to talk about Matthew's gospel without mentioning the Great Commission. It was John Stott who said at the 1966 World Congress on Evangelism in Berlin that

> In the last resort, we engage in evangelism today not because we want to or because we choose to or because we like to, but because we have been told to 'go,' to 'preach,' to 'make disciples,' and that is enough for us.[48]

---

[47] Harvey 1990.
[48] Stott 1967, 37.

The church's unfinished task is to keep going out into the world to proclaim the good news of Jesus Christ to all people. Yes, we are to help the poor, speak up for the oppressed, visit those in prison, defend the defenceless, but all that is at best only part of the task. We are also to declare to people, locally and globally, that God has come to us in Jesus, Israel's Messiah, to offer us the forgiveness of sins. Jesus sends us into the street corners, the slums, the sweatshops, the schools, the suburbs, to invite people to take the yoke of Jesus upon them, to discover that our master is good, and that his love endures for ever. When Jesus says 'Go!' we should not ask 'Why?' but 'Where, my lord?'

Further reading

Balch, David (ed.). 1991. *Social History of the Matthean Community*. Minneapolis: Fortress.
Brown, Jeannine K. 2015. *Matthew*. TTC; Grand Rapids, MI: Baker.
Chae, Young S. 2006. *Jesus as the Eschatological Davidic Shepherd: Studies in the Old Testament, Second Temple Judaism, and in the Gospel of Matthew*. Tübingen: Mohr Siebeck.
Davies, W. D., and Dale C. Allison. 1988–97. *A Critical and Exegetical Commentary on the Gospel According to Saint Matthew*. 3 vols.; ICC; Edinburgh: T&T Clark.

The Mount of Beatitudes where Jesus is believed to have delivered the Sermon on the Mount
Bill Schlegel / BiblePlaces.com

Evans, Craig A. 2012. *Matthew*. NCBC; Cambridge: Cambridge University Press.
Evans, Craig A., and Charles E. Carlston. 2014. *From Synagogue to Ecclesia: Matthew's Community at the Crossroads*. WUNT 33; Tübingen: Mohr Siebeck.
Foster, Paul. 2004. *Community, Law and Mission in Matthew's Gospel*. WUNT 2.177; Tübingen: Mohr Siebeck.
Hagner, D. A. 2004. 'Matthew: Christian Judaism or Jewish Christianity?' In *The Face of New Testament Studies*. Edited by S. McKnight and G. Osborne. Grand Rapids, MI: Baker, pp. 263–82.
Keener, Craig A. 2009. *The Gospel of Matthew: A Socio-Rhetorical Commentary*. 2 vols.; Grand Rapids, MI: Eerdmans.
McKnight, Scot. 2013. *Sermon on the Mount*. SGBC; Grand Rapids, MI: Zondervan.
Meyer, Ben F. 2014. *Five Speeches that Changed the World*. Eugene, OR: Wipf & Stock.
Nolland, John. 2005. *The Gospel of Matthew: A Commentary on the Greek Text*. NIGTC; Grand Rapids, MI; Eerdmans.
Stanton, Graham. 1993. *A New Gospel for a New People: Studies in Matthew*. Louisville, KY: Westminster John Knox.

26

The Gospel according to Luke and Acts of the Apostles

> Luke, as a historian, inhabited the worlds of both Judaism and Hellenism. As a theologian, he remained firmly Jewish while claiming to address the world of paganism. Like all well-taught Jews, he believed that one could understand paganism from the perspective of creational monotheism, as one who knows what a sphere is can understand what a circle is; and that, if one was called by the creator god to a task vis-à-vis the pagan world, one could accomplish that task by subverting the world's story with the true Jewish one. That, I suggest, is precisely what Luke has done.[1]

CHAPTER AT A GLANCE

This chapter explains the story, themes, and theology of Luke-Acts.

By the end of this chapter you should be able to:

- understand the origins of Luke-Acts in the context of early Christianity;
- describe the basic features of Luke's story of Jesus and the beginning of the church;
- grasp the main themes that appear across Luke-Acts.

INTRODUCTION

The gospel of Luke, and the Acts of the Apostles, are regularly seen as a double work from a single author. For that reason people today regularly refer to them together, as 'Luke-Acts'. This two-volume work has enormous significance in the New Testament and within early Christianity as a whole. First, it is the largest sub-corpus of the New Testament. Luke-Acts makes up a massive 28 per cent of the New Testament. Paul's letters comprise only 24 per cent; the Johannine corpus covers a mere 20 per cent—and that's assuming the authenticity of the authorship of all the writings attributed to Paul and John, which is disputed. Second, Luke is both an evangelist (in the sense of

1 Wright *NTPG*, 384.

'a gospel-writer') and the first church historian. He has his own unique depiction of Jesus as the 'Lord's Messiah' and he narrates the beginnings of the church with emphasis on the ministries of Peter and Paul. In fact, Luke's two-volume work is something of a New Testament in miniature, telling the story of Jesus and the apostles in one continuous narrative.[2] Third, Luke is the literary artist of the New Testament. He writes in very elegant and well-polished Greek. The scope of his work is truly epic, telling a story that begins in Nazareth and Jerusalem and ends in Rome. His narrative contains an exciting mix of tragedy, comedy, and drama.[3] Fourth, Luke-Acts contains some highly distinctive elements (see box: 'Luke's unique materials'). What stands out is Luke's depiction of Jesus as the saviour and the prophetic Messiah; his emphasis on the holy spirit; the beginnings of the church; female disciples; prayer; the poor; wealth and riches; and—not least—the mission of the church. It is Luke who gives us some of the most memorable moments in the New Testament: Mary's *Magnificat* (Lk. 1.46–55), Jesus' sermon in Nazareth (Lk. 4.16–31), the parable of the prodigal son (Lk. 15.11–32), the two disciples on the road to Emmaus (Lk. 24.13–35), the ascension (Lk. 24.50–53; Ac. 1.9–11), the day of Pentecost (Ac. 2.1–47), and the Jerusalem council (Ac. 15.1–31). Luke-Acts takes centre stage among early Christian writings.

Luke the Evangelist was often symbolized by an ox. The Metropolitan Museum of Art. Public Domain

If Luke-Acts has one central theme, it might be 'salvation'—though that word has become such a Christian cliché that saying this may carry less weight than it ought.[4] Luke-Acts is the story of the 'Saviour',[5] the story of 'those who are being saved',[6] and traces how salvation extends from Israel to the ends of the earth.[7] This salvation is multi-faceted. It includes deliverance from disaster, healing from physical afflictions, the removal of shame, status reversal, forgiveness of sins, and justification, as well as receiving life, peace, mercy, and grace. All this is accessed through faith and repentance, and is principally appropriated by following Jesus in 'the way'.[8]

---

2   Barrett 1996.
3   A good example of Luke's flair for the dramatic is his account of Paul's shipwreck on the coast of Malta in Ac. 28.39–44.
4   Marshall 1988, 77–102 (esp. 92); Bovon 2006, 1–85; Dunn 2009b, 288–9.
5   Lk. 1.69; 2.11; Ac. 5.31; 13.23.
6   Ac. 2.47.
7   Lk. 1.77; 2.30; 3.6; Ac. 13.26, 47; 16.17; 28.28.
8   See Bock 2012, 227–78; González 2015, 61–75.

LUKE'S UNIQUE MATERIAL

Luke has received various traditions about Jesus from his many sources (see Lk. 1.1–2). In the materials that he has inherited from Mark, and in the double tradition that he shares with Matthew, we can detect something of Luke's own editorial hand in his various abridgments, re-wordings, omissions, and glosses. Elsewhere Luke has his own body of unique content, stories, and sayings found only in his gospel, which are either Luke's own creation or else derive from sources peculiar to Luke. This unique Lukan material is usually called 'L' for 'Special Luke'. It includes:[*]

preaching of John the Baptist	3.10–14	healing of a man with oedema	14.1–5
Elijah's miracles for gentiles	4.25–27	parable of choice places at a banquet	14.8–10, 12–14
Jesus raises the widow of Nain's son	7.11–15	counting the cost of following Jesus	14.28–32
the sinful woman forgiven	7.36–47	parable of the lost sheep	15.4–6
parable of the good Samaritan	10.30–37	parable of the lost coin	15.8–9
conflict between Mary and Martha	10.39–42	parable of the prodigal son	15.11–32
parable of the persistent friend	11.5–8	parable of the dishonest manager	16.1–8
parable of the rich fool	12.16–20	parable of the rich man and Lazarus	16.19–31
parable of the doorkeeper	12.35–38	teachings on sin, faith, and duty	17.7–10
warning to repent or perish	13.1–5	healing of ten Samaritan lepers	17.12–18
parable of the barren fig tree	13.6–9	parable of the unjust judge	18.2–8
healing of a crippled woman	13.10–17	parable of the Pharisee and tax-collector	18.10–14
warning about Herod	13.31–32	story of Zacchaeus	19.1–10

[*] See further Paffenroth 1997 and more briefly Jones 2011, 47–90.

Luke has not (as some have imagined) replaced an older 'apocalyptic' hope for Jesus' imminent return with a theory of the progress of Christian 'salvation history' (*Heilsgeschichte*). Rather than marking off history into periods to explain its continuities, Luke is more interested in explaining how God's purpose and plan for salvation works itself out *from* Israel *through* Jesus *into* the church and *out* to the world.

For a microcosm of the whole sweep of Luke-Acts, we might consider Jesus' sermon in Nazareth and the story of Zacchaeus from Luke 19. The spirit-anointed Messiah brings salvation to Israel; if the Jewish people reject it, the outcasts, the poor, the tax-collectors, and the gentiles will receive it.[9]

I (MFB) have often imagined Luke as a cross between the Anglo-Irish literary critic and Christian apologist C. S. Lewis and the Scottish archaeologist and biblical scholar William M. Ramsay. Luke writes in stylish prose, contends for faith in Jesus, defends Paul, and interprets Israel's scriptures through a messianic grid, all while being immersed in the history and culture of the Roman empire. There are many questions we might wish to ask him. Exactly which sources did he use in his composition? (He tells us up front that he has compared things that other people have written.) How might he explain some of the apparent discrepancies between the Paul he describes in Acts and the Paul of the actual letters? What would he say about the continuing Jewish people who have not recognized Jesus as Messiah? Is he biased—either against them or for them? Or is that the wrong question? Are the sermons by the apostles in Acts a reliable account of their preaching, or did he just make them up? What might he say to those who have called him an 'early Catholic'? Is there more to be said about women in the church? Was the early church really a proto-socialist movement? What was an average worship service actually like? And so on.

We may suspect, however, that Luke would deflect such questions. He might be more interested in giving us a fresh sermon, explaining once more how 'God has raised this Jesus to life, and we are all witnesses of it'; *and* 'salvation is found in no one else, for there is no other name under heaven given to mankind by which we must be saved.'[10]

CONTEXTUAL AND CRITICAL MATTERS

Origins of Luke-Acts

Tradition has identified the author of the third gospel and the Acts of the Apostles as Paul's travelling companion Luke, a physician, who was with Paul on many of his missionary journeys and also during Paul's imprisonments in Ephesus

---

9   Lk. 4.16–30; 19.1–10.
10 Ac. 2.32; 4.12.

and Rome.[11] Sources in the late second century (including Irenaeus, the Muratorian canon, and the anti-Marcionite prologues) ascribe authorship to this Luke.[12] The title 'The Gospel according to Luke' (*Euangelion kata Lukan*) is first attested in $\mathfrak{P}^{75}$ which is our earliest copy of the third gospel and is normally dated to around AD 175–225. The titles for all the canonical gospels, while not part of the original compositions, are probably based on local knowledge of the origins of each gospel and were added to distinguish them from one another when they began to circulate together in the late first or early second century.[13] Thus, by the end of the second century, the idea of Lukan authorship of Luke and Acts seems to have been unanimously held and without alternative.

Internal evidence for Luke's authorship meshes with the tradition, but is far from decisive. The author is obviously a Christian, a well-educated Greek-speaker, acquainted with Diaspora Judaism, well-versed in the Septuagint, intimately familiar with life and travel in the eastern Mediterranean, and quite possibly a gentile (though that is less certain).[14] The books are dedicated to 'Theophilus', whose name means 'friend of God', which could be symbolic for everyone who seeks such friendship. Yet it is more likely that Theophilus is actually Luke's patron, sponsoring his literary enterprise, or maybe even a disciple of Luke to whom the teacher writes.[15] There is not very much in the gospel (as opposed to Acts) to identify the author as a travelling companion of Paul. Contrary to common conception, the presence of medical terminology and vivid descriptions of illnesses do not require that the author was a medical professional; he was merely familiar with the medical terminology of antiquity, just as other classical authors were.[16] More telling is the close link between the Lukan account of the Last Supper and Paul's rehearsal of Jesus' words of institution.[17] But even then the similarity can be explained on the basis of two authors sharing a common tradition, without needing to postulate direct dependence of Luke on Paul (or vice versa).

---

11 Philem. 1.24; Col. 4.14; 2 Tim. 4.11.
12 Iren. *Adv. Haer.* 3.1.1; 3.11.8; 3.13.3; 3.14.1; Muratorian canon § 2–8, 34–9; for the anti-Marcionite prologues, see Koester 1990, 335.
13 See Hengel 2000, 116–27; Bauckham 2006, 300–5; Bird 2014b, 254–60.
14 According to the anti-Marcionite prologues (Koester 1990, 335): 'Luke is a Syrian of Antioch, a Syrian by race, a physician by profession. He had become a disciple of the apostles and later followed Paul until his [i.e. Paul's] martyrdom, having served the Lord continuously, unmarried, without children; filled with the Holy Spirit he died at the age of eighty-four years in Boeotia.' The association of Luke with Syria appears also in Eusebius (*Hist. Eccl.* 3.4.6–8) and Jerome (*De Vir. Ill.* 7). This influenced Fitzmyer (1981–5, 1.41–7) who supposed that Luke was a semitic gentile, a native of Syria. Others think that the author was a Jewish Christian (e.g. Sterling 1999, 217), and Strelan (2008) claims he was a Jewish priest. The majority of scholars favour a gentile author, perhaps even a God-fearer (e.g. Keener 2012–14, 1.405).
15 According to Alexander (1993, 73–5, 133, 188), 'Theophilus' was a common name among Diaspora Jews and there is meagre evidence for dedications to fictitious recipients. On Theophilus as Luke's student, see Strelan 2008, 36, 106–10.
16 See Keener 2012–14, 1.414–22. So too Alexander 1993.
17 Lk. 22.14–20; 1 Cor. 11.23–27.

A more promising line of enquiry can be found in Acts. During Paul's second missionary journey, the author abruptly starts using the first-person plural, 'us' and 'we', starting when Paul and his friends are in Troas. This feature is then repeated, ending with Paul's dramatic voyage and shipwreck.[18] These sections are usually referred to as the 'we'-passages. At first glance they appear to indicate that the author of Acts accompanied Paul during this phase of his missionary travels.[19] This would correspond to Paul's noting of Luke's presence in some of his letters.

Simon Marmion's *St Luke Painting the Virgin and Child*, c. 1460, Valenciennes, France. According to tradition, Luke was the first to paint Mary and Jesus. But note the difference in how they look and how Luke paints them. According to Bockmuehl (2006, 18): 'Marmion draws out the exquisite and excruciating dilemma of the religious artist. Before Luke are a mother and child who, in the disarmingly unremarkable humanity of their demeanor, appear at one level like a thousand others, as if arbitrarily invited in from the street to sit for the artist on this particular fine spring morning. And yet Luke's piercing eye perceives the deeper reality of what is barely hinted at in the faint haloes of his models: his gaze and brush reveal the truth that this is none other than the Mother of the divine word made flesh.'

© *British Library Board. All Rights Reserved / Bridgeman Images*

---

18 Ac. 16.10–17; 20.5–15; 21.1–18; 27.1—28.16.
19 See e.g. Bruce 1988, 7–8; Hengel 1980, 66–7; Keener 2012–14, 1.406–22.

Alternatively, some have proposed that the 'we'-passages come, not from the author himself, but from his sources; or else that they are simply a literary device, without direct links to the author's own participation in the relevant events.[20] However, the most natural reading of the 'we'-passages is still to see them as reflecting the autobiographical recollection of a Pauline colleague who can be identified as the writer.[21]

Some scholars have objected to authorship by a Pauline colleague such as Luke on several grounds.[22] First, there is no direct attribution of authorship, no claim that the author was an eye-witness to any of the events recounted in either the gospel or Acts (agreeing with the family of hypotheses which see the 'we'-passages as not being first-person accounts by the author). Second, postulating Luke's authorship relies on information derived from 2 Timothy and Colossians to anchor the association of Luke and Paul, yet the authenticity of those two letters, especially 2 Timothy, has been heavily disputed. Third, many have posited a chronological distance—up to seventy or more years!—and a theological breach between the author of Acts and Paul. Perhaps, people have suggested, the author is dependent on a Pauline letter-collection as his primary source for Paul, rather than on first-hand knowledge of the apostle himself. It is also sometimes alleged that the author departs from Paul on matters of christology, the spirit, and the Jewish law. Many claim that he even misrepresents Paul's sermons, putting in Paul's mouth ideas which are closer to the other sermons in Acts rather than being distinctively Pauline. Those who specially highlight Pauline motifs like the cross of Jesus and justification by faith note their apparent absence in Acts (for instance, people sometimes contrast Ac. 17.22–32 with Rom. 1.18–24 on God's self-revelation in nature, and play off the Pauline sermons in Acts with the sort of preaching described in 1 Cor. 1.18—2.5). Fourth, it is often suggested that when Irenaeus ascribed the authorship of Luke and Acts to Luke himself he was motivated by apologetics; that is, Irenaeus was eager to legitimize the apostolicity of 'orthodox' literature over against the literature of 'heterodox' Christians like Marcion and the Gnostics, who were claiming that their own

---

20 See e.g. Barrett 1998, 2.xxix (Luke used a travel diary); Porter 2001, 42–6 (Luke incorporated an independent source with first-person testimony); Haenchen 1965 and Wedderburn 2002 (Luke used a source and inserted 'we' to indicate that eye-witness testimony undergirded it); Robbins 1978 (Luke adopts the sea-voyage genre which was often written in the style of the first person); Bovon 2002–13, 1.8 (Luke tries to substantiate the credibility of his story and to make it more vivid); Campbell 2007 (the 'we' character is the narrative replacement for Barnabas who testifies to Paul's chosenness for his apostolic mission).
21 According to Sean Adams (2013a, 142): 'To date, I have not seen an ancient author use "we" to indicate a source of which he did not consider or present himself to be a member.' Dunn (2015, 58) complains, 'In some cases it almost appears to be regarded as a test of critical integrity, a proof of critical virility, to find an explanation for these passages which can provide a believable alternative to the most obvious solution (that the narrator was personally involved in the episodes related). In fact, none of the alternatives has proved so credible as the most obvious solution. And the most probable solution remains that the author of Acts was indeed personally involved in the "we/us" episodes, and so provides an eye-witness and near third-hand authority for most of at least the second half of Acts.'
22 See Dicken 2011, 11–17.

writings went back to secret, early, genuine apostolic traditions.

Those are all reasonable objections, but they are hardly conclusive. First, the 'we'-passages still suggest authorial eye-witness involvement as the simplest option. Second, even if we discount 2 Timothy and Colossians as evidence of a connection between Paul and Luke, we still have the mention of Luke in Philemon 24. Third, although Luke may well be familiar with some of the Pauline letters, that is precisely what one would expect of a co-worker who was involved in Paul's missionary and literary endeavours. Familiarity with some or all of Paul's writings is not necessarily a sign of composition in a post-Pauline period; the anti-Lukan theories sometimes seem to want it both ways, with the author of Acts both too suspiciously familiar with Paul and too suspiciously different in theology.

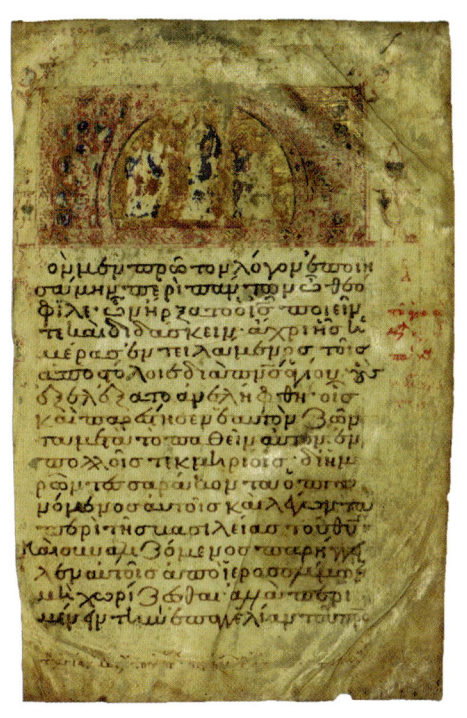

Title page of the Acts of the Apostles, Walters Manuscript W.533, fol. 1r, dated early twelfth century, The Walters Art Museum, Baltimore

In addition, Luke is by any showing an independent follower of Paul, not afraid to go his own way, summarizing and interpreting Paul through the lens of his own literary and theological goals. At the same time, scholars such as Steve Walton have identified clear affinities between Paul's farewell address to the Ephesian elders (Ac. 20.18–35) and his exhortations in 1 Thessalonians. Again, Stanley Porter has shown that Luke and Paul are quite close on topics such as use of the Old Testament, christology, Jesus' resurrection, and the Lord's Supper.[23] Fourth, if one wanted to ascribe authorship to an apostolic figure or apostolic companion to legitimize the apostolicity of Luke-Acts (in other words, if we were thinking our way into the motivation of Irenaeus or others in the second century), a peripheral character like Luke would not necessarily be an obvious choice when candidates such as Timothy, Titus, Silas, or Barnabas would have been available. The second-century attribution of authorship to Luke was unanimous, but only for the reason that the tradition was regarded as credible and perhaps even primitive.

Thus, though a clear reference to Luke as the author of both works is not found before the second half of the second century, there was then no opposition to the

---

23 Walton 2000; Porter 2011.

claim. The theory meshes well with the credible view that Acts was written by one of Paul's travelling companions. In sum, attributing the authorship of Luke-Acts to Luke the physician remains the most viable hypothesis. The only alternative is to plead ignorance and uncertainty.

Date

Most scholars today would insist that Luke-Acts is to be dated after AD 70.[24] First, Luke is dependent upon Mark's gospel, and Mark is normally dated sometime around AD 70. Second, a post-70 dating corresponds with the view that Luke 19 and 21 seem to regard the destruction of the Jerusalem Temple as a past event that has now ushered in the 'times of the Gentiles'.[25] Some suppose that a pre-70 date is possible, because Luke would have recorded the deaths of Paul and perhaps Peter if he knew about them. Without the result of Paul's forthcoming trial before the emperor, Acts has appeared to many as truncated—though there could be many reasons for the author stopping where he does. The omission of the apostles' martyrdoms is normally seen as meaning either that Luke's audience already knew what fate had befallen Paul and Peter, or else—and more likely—that his purpose was not to write Paul's biography but to show the spread of Christianity from Jerusalem to Rome, which by Acts 28 he had already done.[26]

So: if the two books are to be dated after AD 70, how far after 70 should we go? An upper limit is certainly the 180s. The Muratorian canon and Irenaeus both mention Luke and Acts by name. Plus allusions to Luke-Acts can be found in Justin Martyr, the longer ending of Mark, and the apostolic Fathers, datable to the early to mid-second century.[27] Some, such as Richard Pervo, date Acts to AD 110–20 on the grounds that the author allegedly used both Paul's letters and Josephus, and Acts is sometimes thought to portray a more institutionalized form of Christianity such as had not developed until the second century. This is a very uncertain line of argument.[28] But if we are dealing with a Pauline travel companion as the author, and if it is post-70, then one should probably favour a date between AD 80 and 90.[29]

Unity of Luke-Acts

Should Luke and Acts then be understood as a single narrative and theological unity, or should they be seen as independent of each other? Lukan authorship of

---

[24] See survey in Keener 2012–14, 1.383–401.
[25] Lk. 19.43–44; 21.8–24. Some have pointed out, however, that the 'prophecies' in those passages do not correspond to the very detailed account, in Josephus, of what actually happened as the Romans closed in, thus reopening the possibility that these were genuine reminiscences of scripture-based prophecies by Jesus himself.
[26] So too Bruce 1988, 10–12, and Keener 2012–14, 1.384.
[27] Gregory 2003.
[28] Pervo 2006; 2009, 5, but see the responses of Gregory 2016 and Keener 2012–14, 1.395–400.
[29] See e.g. Fitzmyer 1981–5, 1.53–7; Bruce 1988, 6–13.

both works has largely been affirmed across church history and in modern scholarship, but treating these two books as a literary unity with a coherent theology is a relatively recent phenomenon, starting with Henry Cadbury's monograph of 1927 which first introduced the phrase 'Luke-Acts' into scholarly parlance.[30] While the unity of Luke-Acts is now axiomatic in contemporary scholarship, Mikael Parsons and Richard Pervo wonder if the hyphen in 'Luke-Acts' should perhaps be loosened.[31] There are some factors to consider.[32]

From early times, the gospel of Luke and the Acts of the Apostles circulated in distinctive collections and were mostly studied in isolation from one another. There are indeed two third-century manuscripts ($\mathfrak{P}^{45}$ and $\mathfrak{P}^{53}$) which place Acts alongside the four gospels, but more often than not Acts is located by itself in other manuscripts of similar date (for example $\mathfrak{P}^8$, $\mathfrak{P}^{29}$, $\mathfrak{P}^{38}$, $\mathfrak{P}^{48}$, $\mathfrak{P}^{91}$). In most of the later manuscripts Acts was situated either before the Pauline or Catholic Epistles ($\mathfrak{P}^{74}$, 020, 025, 048, 81, 0166, 307, 945, 1175, 1409, 1739). Only Irenaeus and the Muratorian canon in antiquity tried to relate the gospel of Luke and book of Acts as a combined literary project.[33] The universal canonical order is Matthew, Mark, Luke, John, and then Acts—and this, of course, implies a deliberate partition between Luke and Acts.[34] The two books were not commented on together, nor was any 'theology' of Luke-Acts written, prior to the twentieth century. In addition, Luke and Acts are often said to contain different genres (biography and historiography), different plots (the career of Jesus and the beginnings of the church), different methods of christology (the gospel is narrative whereas Acts is largely titular in its depiction of Jesus), and each book can stand alone without requiring knowledge of the other (hence the need for two accounts of the ascension, first in Lk. 24 and then in Ac. 1).

However, scholars are for the most part convinced of the overall narrative unity of Luke-Acts and that these two works were intended to be read together.[35] First, the evidence garnered from the prologues in Luke 1.1–4 and Acts 1.1–2 signifies that we have two parts of the one work. Second, the gospel of Luke is constructed specifically to prepare the way for Acts by omitting materials from Mark (like those about gentile inclusion) which are set out in Acts, while also foreshadowing several themes that will be developed later, such as the holy spirit, discipleship, the scope of salvation, and Jewish hostility to the gospel. Third, it is hard to go past the observation that there are deliberate parallels developed between Jesus, Peter, and Paul in

---

30 Cadbury 1927.
31 Parsons and Pervo 1993.
32 For the state of the debate on the unity of Luke-Acts, see Gregory and Rowe 2010.
33 Muratorian canon § 2–8, 34–9; Iren. *Adv. Haer.* 3.1.1; 3.14.1; see Gregory 2003.
34 The majuscule D (Codex Bezae) takes the order Matthew, John, Luke, Mark, the last few verses of 3 John, and then Acts.
35 See essays in Verheyden 1999 and the approach of Tannehill 1986–90 which highlights the repetition of themes across Luke-Acts. For briefer defences of unity see Keener 2012–14, 1.550–74 and Bock 2012, 55–61.

terms of proclamation and miracles performed. Fourth, at the macro-level, Luke-Acts is united in its depiction of the single purpose of God. As Joel Green puts it:

> Luke's agenda is not to write the story of Jesus, followed by the story of the early church ... Rather, his design is to write the story of the continuation and fulfillment of God's project—a story that embraces both the work of Jesus and of the followers of Jesus after his ascension. From start to finish, Luke–Acts brings to the fore one narrative aim, the one aim of God.[36]

Given that evidence, the consensus is strong and virtually certain: Luke-Acts must be seen as both a literary and theological unity.

Genre

Luke calls his story of Jesus and the early church a 'narrative account' (*diēgēsis*).[37] That, however, is a broad, bland description. What precise genre is Luke-Acts? Do Luke and Acts constitute the same genre, or do they comprise two separate genres?

Regarding the gospel of Luke, two things are clear. First, Luke has composed a very Jewish narrative, a continuation of Israel's prophetic history where Jesus is seen as the 'true David'. According to Luke, Jesus' life, death, resurrection, and the sending of the divine spirit are the end-product of the long story that began with King David and the divine promises made to him (see 2 Sam. 7.12–16). Luke tells the story of Jesus *as* the fulfilment, the completion, of the story of David and his kingdom—and, more broadly, the fulfilment of all the scriptures (for example 24.25, 44–45). Second, Luke's gospel is written up in the mode of a hellenistic biography, a story that focuses on a central protagonist, showing portents of greatness in his youth, commending his teaching, acclaiming his virtue, and protesting his innocence against detractors. Luke has, in effect, blended these two genres of Jewish prophetic narrative and hellenistic biography together, so as to stake the controversial claim that through Jesus the restoration of the Davidic kingdom has taken place and the good news of this established kingdom confronts and impinges on the gentile world. Luke artistically narrates the story of Jesus *as* a Jewish story, indeed as *the* Jewish story, and he has told it in such a way as to say to his non-Jewish greco-roman audience: here, in the life of this one man, is the Jewish message of salvation that you pagans need.

The genre of Acts is a little more complicated.[38] To begin with, Acts is preceded by the gospel of Luke, a biography. Does that make Acts a biography too? Certainly not. Some genres of greco-roman literature can utilize biographical components without becoming actual biographies. In addition, we should not forget the generic

---

36 Green 1995, 47.
37 Lk. 1.1–4.
38 See survey in Phillips 2006; Adams 2012; 2013b, 5–22.

and intertextual connections between Acts and Israelite sacred history, rendering the book effectively an extension of biblical history.[39] Acts can, in fact, be likened to many different genres, and these genres can overlap in style and mode of expression.

Various suggestions for the genre of Acts have thus been proposed. Perhaps it is a novel, or a piece of pious historical fiction (just like the much later *Acts of Andrew* or the *Acts of Peter*). Or maybe it should be seen as an epic, a grand foundation-story of the emergence of the church, akin to Homer's *Odyssey* (think of Paul's journeys!) or Virgil's *Aeneid*. Or maybe it is a biography of Jesus' two main successors, Peter and Paul, reminiscent of Diogenes Laertius's *Lives of Eminent Philosophers* or Plutarch's *Parallel Lives*. Perhaps it is really a 'history' with a capital H, a carefully investigated yet rhetorically charged account of the emergence of the Christian movement (Luke is careful to say where the word 'Christian' originated[40]) from its founder (Jesus) to his main followers (the apostles). Taking all this into account, we suggest that Acts is best seen as a composite genre, combining the theography of the Old Testament with the sort of apologetic historiography one finds in Josephus, resulting in a historical work containing significant elements of biography and intended to defend a movement, its founder, and its key leaders against prejudice and accusations from both Jews and pagans.[41]

Purpose

Luke's motives for writing his two-volume work were clearly complex. Among the many scholarly proposals are: to catechize gentile converts; to chronicle the church's mission; to defend Paul at his trial; to attempt a synthesis of Jewish and Pauline Christianities, resulting in an 'early Catholicism'; to account for the delay of Jesus' return by periodizing history into 'salvation history'; to commend Christians to pagan onlookers as a strange but peaceful sect while indicting the Jews as incendiary rabble-rousers; to legitimate Christians as God's people; to respond to criticism of Paul from the Jewish Diaspora and from Jewish-Christian groups; to justify the division between Christianity and Judaism; to refute, albeit indirectly, the heresies of Docetism and Gnosticism; to exonerate Jesus while giving an account of the church as the ideal *collegium*; or, more simply and perhaps naively, to explain how Christianity spread from Jerusalem to Rome.[42]

Most would at least agree that Luke was writing with a measure of apologetic intent.[43] He is defending something, something about the early Christians, something about their distinctive claims and beliefs, and something about Paul in particular. That said, it is quite true that if one started off simply wanting to address an

---

39 Rosner 1994.
40 Ac. 11.26.
41 On the parity of ancient biography and historiography, see Burridge 2011. See too J. Andrew Cowan on Luke, Josephus, and Dionysius of Halicarnassus (2019).
42 See surveys in Maddox 1982; Strauss 2011; Keener 2012–14, 1.435–58.
43 See e.g. Bruce 1988, 8–13 and Sterling 1992.

apologia for early Christianity to the Roman authorities, one would not necessarily produce a work like Luke-Acts, since so much would seem extraneous. There are, to be fair, enormous differences between Luke-Acts on the one hand and second-century Christian apologists like Aristides and Justin on the other hand.[44] In addition, we should note that most apologetic literature is meant for internal consumption, written for insiders, affirming the beliefs and group-identity that is at stake.[45] However, even if we take those caveats seriously, a clear picture still emerges, one in which Luke-Acts is intelligible as an apologetic narrative about Christian identity.

It is worth remembering that Luke was writing in a context where the Jewish people had for a long time been put in a special category by the Romans. As far as the Romans were concerned, the Jews were anti-social atheists. But they were not persecuted by Rome simply for being Jews; they had been granted the status of a permitted religion. Luke's massive two-volume work can be read as claiming, among many other things, that this status ought now to belong to the Christians. They are the ones who have inherited the Jewish promises of salvation; they are the ones to whom accrues the status proper to a religion of great antiquity.[46] They, time and again, are shown to be in the right, to be innocent, even when magistrates have pronounced them guilty: from Jesus on the cross, to the apostles before the Sanhedrin, to Paul (in Philippi, then before Agrippa and Festus, or, later, on the voyage to Rome), the Christians are declared to be innocent of the charges of sedition or subversion that are laid against them.[47]

Thus, while Luke-Acts has several utilities, didactic, polemical, and evangelistic, it is principally an apologetic work. Luke's gospel extols and exonerates Jesus, while Acts presents Paul as a divinely chosen agent, a faithful herald of Jesus Christ, warmly received by Jewish Christian leaders like James, slandered and menaced by Jews, and treated unfairly by Roman officials. In Luke's narration, the church is radical but harmless, the proper heirs of Judaism's religious heritage. Luke engages in a form of ethnic reasoning that legitimates the multi-ethnic churches as God's new-covenant people. In the end, Christians retain what pagans respected about Judaism (antiquity, homogeneity, monotheism, and ethics), while jettisoning what pagans found unattractive about Judaism (ethnically based social separation and strange customs). There is more to Acts than this, but not less.

---

44 Barrett (1961, 63) famously snarled: '[Acts] was not addressed to the Emperor, with the intention of proving the political harmlessness of Christianity in general and Paul in particular . . . No Roman official would ever have filtered out so much of what to him would be theological and ecclesiastical rubbish in order to reach so tiny a grain of relevant apology.'
45 See White (1995, 259): 'most apologetic literature was really addressed to insiders who were looking toward that margin with the larger society as the arena of acculturation and self-definition'; and Marguerat (2002, 30): 'Luke's apologetic is addressed to "insiders" of the movement and a circle which gravitates around it.'
46 Aune 1987, 136–8.
47 Lk. 23.47; Ac. 5.33–39; 16.35–39; 26.32; 27.3, 43.

LUKE'S STORY OF JESUS

(See box: 'Outline of Luke'.)

> **OUTLINE OF LUKE**
>
> 1. Prologue (1.1–4)
> 2. Precursor and the saviour (1.5—2.52)
> 3. Preparation for Jesus' ministry (3.1—4.13)
> 4. Jesus' Galilean ministry (4.14—9.50)
> 5. Jesus' journey to Jerusalem (9.51—19.48)
> 6. Explaining Jesus' Temple-action (20.1—21.38)
> 7. The Passion of Jesus (22.1—23.56)
> 8. The resurrection and ascension of Jesus (24.1–53)

1. Prologue (1.1–4)

Luke's prologue stresses both the historical accuracy of his investigation and the theological content of his book, focused as it is on the 'word' that has been 'fulfilled' in the community to which both Luke (the author) and Theophilus (the dedicatee) belong (see 'Portals and parallels: ancient prefaces').

2. Precursor and the saviour (1.5—2.52)

Luke's infancy narrative concentrates on the intertwining destinies of John the Baptist and Jesus. He crafts his story around the hope for Israel's restoration, the outpouring of eschatological joy that accompanies the appearance of both figures, and the identification of Jesus as the promised Davidic saviour. The stories of their births are joined to three hymns of praise in the form of Mary's *Magnificat*, Zechariah's *Benedictus*, and Simeon's *Nunc Dimittis*. The journey of Mary and Joseph to Bethlehem comes about because of a census during the reign of Augustus, with Joseph probably returning to register his claim on ancestral lands. The holy family is presented as faithful and devout, illustrated by Jesus' parents in their undertaking of the rites of purification after childbirth and presenting Jesus in the Temple. After returning to Nazareth, the family makes a regular pilgrimage to Jerusalem for Passover where Jesus' greatness is foreshadowed by his teaching in the Temple as a child and astounding the audience. Luke rounds off Jesus' infancy with the report that Jesus grew in wisdom and divine favour.

3. Preparation for Jesus' ministry (3.1—4.13)

Luke introduces John the Baptist as the prophetic forerunner to Jesus. He fulfils the words of Isaiah 40.3–5 by warning that ethnic heritage (descent from Abraham) will not save people from the coming judgment. Rather—in line with the warnings and promises in Deuteronomy and elsewhere—the people must repent, bear fruit, and ready themselves for the coming deliverer who will baptize with the holy spirit and fire (Lk. 3.1–20).

Jesus is then baptized by John; Luke adds the detail that the holy spirit descended on Jesus in 'bodily form like a dove' (3.21–22). Luke then offers a genealogy of Jesus which traces his ancestry back to Adam—and thence to God!—rather than simply to Abraham as Matthew does (3.21–38). There follows Luke's version of the temptation story (4.1–13).

PORTALS AND PARALLELS: ANCIENT PREFACES

An interesting exercise is to compare the prologue of Luke's gospel and Acts with the prologues of other works from antiquity (histories, technical manuals, and fictitious works) and to note the similarities and differences between them. In the table below are a number of prologues from other works which bear variegated levels of similarity to the prologues of Luke 1.1–4 and Acts 1.1–2.

Author and document	Text
Polybius (202–120 BC) *Histories* A historical work about Rome and the Roman conquest of Carthage	In my **former book** I explained the causes of the second war between Rome and Carthage; and described Hannibal's invasion of Italy, and the engagements which took place between them up to the battle of Cannae, on the banks of the Aufidus. I shall now take up the history of Greece during the same period, ending at the same date, and commencing from the 140th Olympiad. But I shall first recall to the recollection of my readers what I stated in my second book on the subject of the Greeks, and especially of the Achaeans; for the league of the latter has made extraordinary progress up to our own age and the generation immediately preceding. (*Hist.* 4.1)
Dioscorides (c. AD 40–90) *Materia Medica* An ancient handbook on medicines	Although **many reports have been made**, not only in the past, but also recently, about the production, effects, and testing of medicines, I nevertheless intended to **instruct** you, **dear Areios**, about them: the decision to **undertake** such a thing is neither needless nor injudicious, for some of my predecessors have not completed their works, and others have written most things down from hearsay. (*Mat. Med.* 1.1)

4. Jesus' Galilean ministry (4.14—9.50)

Luke recounts the Galilean phase of Jesus' ministry with a general snapshot of Jesus as empowered by the spirit and teaching in various synagogues to wide acclaim (4.14–15).

Jesus enters his home village of Nazareth and delivers a sermon in the synagogue, quoting Isaiah 61.1–2 and declaring its immediate fulfilment. The passage from Isaiah 61 is unambiguously Davidic, and explicitly messianic: YHWH's spirit has anointed the messenger to bring good tidings to the poor. Despite their initial enthusiasm, Jesus' hearers become alarmed and then angry, probably because Jesus is speaking, not about Israel's vengeance on its enemies as they might have expected, but about God's welcome to outsiders. He comments on their smug indignation by quoting the proverb about a prophet being rejected in his own home town, and backs up his main point by citing the biblical stories of two foreigners, the widow of

(cont.)

Author and document	Text
Josephus (c. AD 37–100) *Against Apion* A response by Josephus to those who criticize his work *Antiquities of the Jew* and slander his character	I suppose that my books of the Antiquity of the Jews, **most excellent Epaphroditus**, have made it evident to those who peruse them, that our Jewish nation is of very great antiquity, and had a distinct subsistence of its own originally; as also, I have therein declared how we came to inhabit this country wherein we now live. Those Antiquities contain the history of five thousand years, and are taken out of our sacred books, but are translated by me into the Greek tongue. However, since I observe a considerable number of people giving ear to the reproaches that are laid against us by those who bear ill-will to us, and will not believe what I have written concerning the antiquity of our nation, while they take it for a plain sign that our nation is of a late date, because they are not so much as vouchsafed a bare mention by the most famous historiographers among the Grecians **I therefore have thought myself under an obligation to write somewhat briefly about these subjects**, in order to convict those that reproach us of spite and voluntary falsehood, and to correct the ignorance of others, **and withal to instruct all those who are desirous of knowing the truth** of what great antiquity we really are. As for the **witnesses whom I shall produce for the proof of what I say**, they shall be such as are esteemed to be of the greatest reputation for truth, and the most skillful in the knowledge of all antiquity by the Greeks themselves. I will also show, that those who have written so reproachfully and falsely about us are to be convicted by what they have written themselves to the contrary. I shall also endeavor to give an account of the reasons why it has so happened, that there have not been a great number of Greeks who have made mention of our nation in their histories. I will, however, bring those Grecians to light who have not omitted such our history, for the sake of those that either do not know them, or pretend not to know them already. (*Ap.* 1.1–4)

Zarephath and Naaman the Syrian.[48] Luke 4.16–30 offers a programmatic description of Jesus' ministry, introducing the various motifs of Luke-Acts: spirit, mission, christology, Israel's rejection of Jesus, and God's acceptance of outcasts.[49]

Jesus' ministry continues in Capernaum where he performs exorcisms and healings that demonstrate his power and authority (4.31–44). Thereafter Jesus gathers disciples, performs healings, arouses opposition over sabbath observance, and generally displays his remarkable authority (4.31—6.16).

This opens up the way for Luke's second major presentation of Jesus' teaching: a 'sermon' on a 'level place', corresponding in some ways to Matthew's 'sermon on the mount' (6.17–49). This address, opening with balanced 'blessings' and 'woes' (again,

---
[48] 1 Kgs. 17.1–24; 2 Kgs. 5.1–14.
[49] Green 1997, 207.

like Deuteronomy), urges the way of love, of non-retaliation, of the transformed heart, and of taking Jesus' words as the foundation for a new way of life. Jesus then returns to Capernaum where, impressed by the faith of a Roman centurion, he heals the man's slave (7.1–10). This is followed by the raising of a dead man, a widow's son in Nain (7.11–17), at which the crowds declare that God has 'visited' his people—an echo of Zechariah's song in 1.68 and 1.78, and an anticipation of the fateful moment when Jesus arrived in Jerusalem (19.44), all of them echoing what the Israelites had said on hearing the news of the forthcoming exodus (Ex. 4.31). To the consternation of onlookers Jesus then praises a sinful woman who sneaks in to a dinner-party in a Pharisee's house in order to anoint him (7.36–50). In between these stories is Luke's account of John the Baptist's delegation, questioning whether Jesus really is 'the one who was to come'; Jesus describes his own activity in terms which echo Isaiah, then stressing that John really was the advance messenger for the 'coming one'—in other words, that Jesus himself is indeed the one who was to come, which in Malachi 3.1 was of course Israel's God himself (7.18–35). Finally, Jesus continues his itinerant travels, proclaiming the gospel of the kingdom of God, accompanied by the Twelve and by female followers who financially supported him (8.1–3).

The inside of a replica synagogue in Nazareth Village in Israel
© 2015 by Zondervan

This brings us to Luke's presentation of some of the parables found in Mark 4 and Matthew 13, starting with 'the sower and the seed'. The kingdom of God is indeed arriving, but it is mysterious as well as powerful. It will encounter opposition, but will take root in receptive hearts (8.4–15). The kingdom is like light: it radiates, and does not retreat (8.16–18), even from opposition by family members (8.19–21).

Further indications of Jesus' identity and power are seen in the stilling of the storm, echoing God's power over the sea (8.22–25). He is confessed as the 'son of the Most High God' by a demoniac in the Decapolis (8.26–39); he raises a girl from the dead and heals a woman with constant bleeding (8.40–56). He grants his disciples the power and authority to duplicate his miraculous deeds (9.1–9), and feeds the five thousand (9.10–17). All this leads up to Peter's confession that Jesus is 'God's Messiah' (9.18–20), at which Jesus at once speaks of his forthcoming death and resurrection (9.21–27). This double message—Jesus' secret messianic identity and his coming death—is dramatically emphasized in the transfiguration (9.28–36), pointing to Jesus' coming 'glory' (9.32) but stressing that Jesus' vocation was to 'his departure' (the Greek word is *exodos*) 'which he would accomplish in Jerusalem' (9.31): in other words, Jesus' death will be the new, true, 'exodus', consequent upon Israel's God 'visiting' his people at last. Immediately afterwards comes another challenge in the form of a demon-possessed boy whom the disciples couldn't cure. Jesus, however, succeeds, and the crowds are 'amazed at the greatness of God' (9.37–45). Luke's account of Jesus' public work in Galilee then closes with a second prediction of Jesus' death, followed absurdly by the disciples arguing about who would be the greatest in the kingdom. Jesus corrects them by stating that kingdom-greatness is defined by humility (9.46–50).

> 'Jesus is making a bold claim that the salvation hoped for by generations of Israelites has arrived and he is the Spirit-anointed agent through whom all forms of oppression will be lifted.'
>
> Diane Chen, *Luke*, 62.

5. Jesus' journey to Jerusalem (9.51—19.48)

Once Jesus' intention to go to Jerusalem is disclosed, opposition to him increases and is intertwined with instruction to the disciples. The Samaritan rejection of him (9.52–56) is juxtaposed with a passage on the cost of discipleship (9.57–62). Jesus then sends out seventy-two disciples, warning them to expect a mixture of triumph and rejection (10.1–24). Faced with a challenge from a lawyer ('Who is my neighbour?') Jesus undermines the normal ethnic divisions by telling a parable with a Samaritan as the hero (10.25–37). In a similar reversal, he commends Mary of Bethany for choosing 'what is better' by listening to his teaching along with his other disciples rather than doing domestic work (10.38–42), and he instructs his followers that they should pray shamelessly and expect to receive good things from their father in heaven (11.1–13).

Jesus' kingdom-work once again arouses controversy. Pharisees attribute his powerful deeds to the prince of demons, and demand more 'proof' of his authority; Jesus responds by denouncing them and warning against hypocrisy and its consequences (11.14—12.12). He adds a further warning against storing up riches instead of being rich towards God (12.13–21), and extends that by urging his followers to trust in God's provision, freeing them up for generosity (12.22–34). God's future is coming, heavy with warning and promise, and it is vital to be ready, to interpret the present time and take appropriate action (12.35–59). The warnings are highlighted by current events, Pilate's massacre of Galilean pilgrims and the collapse of the tower of Siloam, from which Jesus draws the conclusion that unless the people repent there will be far more yet who are cut down by Roman swords or crushed by falling stonework. God's people are like a fig tree which, after several years of patient gardening, remains fruitless and can only be cut down (13.1–9). God's kingdom, though, is making its way, with further healings to celebrate God's new day (13.10–17), coming like a small seed producing a great plant or the yeast that transformed a whole loaf (13.18–21). The door to the kingdom, however, remains narrow, and it is the outsiders, those despised, who will have entry (13.22–30).

The Pharisees warn Jesus of Herod Antipas's intention to seize him, but Jesus replies that nothing will deter him from his destiny in Jerusalem. Jerusalem is where all prophets die, and while Jesus longs to gather the city under his wings like a hen gathering her chicks to protect them, he knows that rejection awaits him when he gets there (13.31–35). This saying is remarkable both for Jesus' obvious self-identification as a prophet (as more than a prophet, to be sure, but not less) and for the implicit understanding of Jesus' forthcoming death. Judgment is coming upon Israel, and Jesus, like the hen protecting the chicks, is determined to take its full weight upon himself.

The confrontation with the Pharisees is amplified in the following chapters. Jesus challenges their sabbath-interpretation and their pride; he warns that the way to the kingdom is costly; and, in perhaps the best known of all parable-chapters, he speaks of a lost sheep, a lost coin, and the 'prodigal son' in order to explain that his own regular kingdom-celebrations with all the 'wrong' people are a clear reflection of the celebration which the angels are having when people repent (14.1—15.32).

The critique of the Pharisees continues with the parable of the shrewd manager, which challenges the disciples on how to prioritize their use of wealth for the sake of the kingdom. Instead of hoarding money and land, Jesus' advice was to use it, as far as one could, to make friends. A crisis was coming, in which alternative homes would be needed. The Pharisees were attempting to divide their loyalties between God and money, but this cannot be done (16.1–15). The law and the prophets remain as pointers to God's eventual purpose, with the prohibition on divorce as an example of their continuing validity (16.16–18). But those who will not hear the law and the prophets will not be convinced, according to the parable of the rich man and Lazarus, even if someone were to rise from the dead (16.19–31). As with the 'prodigal son' (15.24, 32), 'resurrection' is happening already through Jesus' work in welcoming penitent sinners, but the Pharisees are determined not to see it.

As Jesus journeys towards Jerusalem, the next two chapters collect together various scenarios and sayings which highlight the importance of faith, obedience, and trustful hope (17.1—18.30). Jesus adds a further warning of his coming death and resurrection, which once again the disciples fail to grasp (18.31–34). This brings us to Jericho, where a blind man, hailing him as 'son of David', is healed and commended for his faith (18.35–43). In Jericho itself Jesus invites himself to dinner with a chief tax-collector named Zacchaeus, who then epitomizes the repentant rich man, the exact opposite of the rich young ruler in 18.18–25: he gives half of his possessions to the poor, and promises to repay fourfold anyone he has wronged. His story summarizes the fact that 'the son of man came to seek and to save the lost' (19.1–10 *NTE/KNT* [adapted]).

Rembrandt, *The Return of the Prodigal Son*, c. 1662–9, Hermitage Museum, St Petersburg
Public Domain

As Jesus and his entourage approach Jerusalem itself, some of the party clearly think that God's kingdom is about to appear—meaning, it seems, that Jesus will sweep all before him as the new Davidic king, free Israel from the Roman oppression, and set up a new regime of justice and peace—which might well involve, as the Maccabean revolt had involved, a cleansing of the Temple so that Israel's God could return to dwell there in glory. In response to this expectation, Jesus tells the parable of the ten pounds, given by a nobleman to three servants to trade with until his return (19.11–27). Some have seen this as a way of saying that the kingdom was *not* going to appear immediately, since Jesus himself was going to go away like the nobleman, leaving his followers with tasks to do until his return. This is not how Luke understands it.[50] The idea of a king going away and returning, with servants either obedient or disobedient in his absence, would be heard in Jesus' day as a story about Israel's God himself, leaving the Temple at the time of the exile but promising to return at last (as in Isaiah, Zechariah, and Malachi), with Israel represented by the servants who might, or might not, be trustworthy in his absence. This is Luke's point: *Jesus is embodying the return of* YHWH *to Zion*. The disobedient servant in the parable corresponds directly to the impenitent Jerusalem which must now hear the word of judgment 'because you did not recognize the time of your visitation from God' (19.44), another echo of 1.68; 7.16; and

---

50 See Wright *JVG*, 632–9.

> 'For every Zacchaeus who is found, there are many scribes and Pharisees who do not even acknowledge their lostness. No rupture of the divine-human relationship is so irreparable that the call to repentance and offer of forgiveness are withdrawn, yet it takes both gracious divine initiative and humble human response for reconciliation to occur.'
>
> Diane Chen, *Luke*, 252.

similar passages.[51] The point is rammed home both by Jesus' royal entry into the city (19.29–40), his stark warnings in 19.41–44, and his symbolic 'cleansing' of the Temple (19.45–48), clearly to be seen as an acted parable of the destruction he had just foretold. His action is a solemn prophetic warning, echoing those of Jeremiah and others, that if the Temple becomes a hide-out for brigands, literally or metaphorically, it will come under God's judgment. The chief priests and scribes are instantly incensed and plan to kill him. Such a plot proves what Luke has been saying: this is how it 'must' be. This is how God's plan of salvation must be accomplished.

6. Explaining Jesus' Temple-action (20.1—21.38)

The next two chapters collect together, mostly following Mark, a succession of sharp discussions with what amounts to a who's who of important people in Jerusalem: priests, scribes, Herodians, Pharisees, and Sadducees. The key questions are all related: what did Jesus' Temple-action mean? Where did he get the authority to do such a thing? Is he really claiming to be bringing in the 'age to come'—and, if so, what does that imply about paying taxes to Rome and indeed about the 'resurrection' itself? Does he think he is Israel's Messiah, and if so, what does he mean by it? (At that point Jesus takes the initiative with his own exposition of Ps. 110 in 20.41–44.) These discussions occupy chapter 20; then, in 21, after the little scene of the widow putting two tiny coins into the treasury, Jesus addresses the disciples' question about the coming destruction of the Temple. This focuses on a coded 'apocalyptic' warning about how the prophecy of Daniel 7 (the vindication of the 'son of man') would be accomplished. Jesus is casting the Temple and its present hierarchy in the role of the 'monsters' or 'beasts' from Daniel: when they are overthrown, that will be the sign, that he, 'the son of man', has indeed been vindicated by God. In the meantime his followers must not be deceived by the terrible events that will come. They are to hold fast and pray for strength to persevere (21.34–36). Luke does, of course, believe in the 'second coming' of Jesus (see Ac. 1.11), but this passage is not about that. It is about the vindication of Jesus, and the rescue of his people from the system that has oppressed them (21.5–38).

7. The Passion of Jesus (22.1—23.56)

The narrative quickly accelerates with the report of Judas's plot to betray Jesus (22.1–6), followed by the Last Supper with the disciples, where Jesus describes

---

51 See too e.g. Jer. 6.15; Wis. 3.7; Sir. 2.14.

how he will become the new Passover lamb: he will die to establish the new covenant by the shedding of his blood (22.7–38). Jesus then retreats to the Mount of Olives to pray (22.39–46), and is arrested (22.47–53). The description of Peter's denial (22.54–62) is matched with the scene of cruel mocking (22.63–65). When Jesus says (reported only by Luke) 'this is your hour, and the power of darkness' (22.53 NRSV), we sense his utter aloneness in the face of the destructive force of evil.

The council of elders, chief priests, and scribes gathers for an impromptu trial, whose outcome is predictably predetermined. They want a capital charge against Jesus, and Jesus responds to their questioning by stating that 'from now on, the Son of Man will be seated at the right hand of the mighty God', which seems sufficient from their point of view to deliver him to Pilate (22.66–71). The charge is threefold: subverting the nation, opposing the payment of taxes, and claiming to be a king (23.1–2). Pilate declares Jesus innocent, but, learning that he is a Galilean, refers him to Herod Antipas, who treats him cynically and sends him back. (This double meeting of Jesus with Herod and with Caesar's representative foreshadows the confrontations in Acts. There, Jesus is first heralded as king of the Jews, ending with the death of (a different) Herod (Ac. 1—12), and is then announced as 'another king' (Ac. 17.7), that is, a rival to Caesar, with the gospel finally reaching Rome itself (Ac. 13—28). By this time the mob has gathered and demands Jesus' death. Barabbas, a murderous brigand, is released, and Jesus dies in his place (23.25). This sense of the innocent dying the death of the guilty is enhanced by Jesus' cryptic comments to the lamenting women (23.26–31) and the insistence of one of the two men crucified alongside him that Jesus really was guiltless (22.39–43)—with Jesus' astonishing response that 'today you will be with me in paradise'. (That 'paradise', we should note, is not 'heaven' as in popular

Herodium

Christian parlance, but the idyllic part of Hades, the place where the dead wait for final resurrection. Jesus will not be there for long.)

At the heart of Luke's picture of the cross is the mocking of Jesus as king of the Jews, which draws into a single stark sketch the meaning expressed by the various characters and the small incidents elsewhere in the narrative. Jesus has stood on its head the meaning of kingship, the meaning of the kingdom itself. He has celebrated with the wrong people, offered peace and hope to the wrong people, and warned the wrong people of God's coming judgment. Now he is hailed as king at last, but in mockery. Here comes his royal cupbearer, only it's a Roman soldier offering him the sour wine that poor people drank. Here is his royal placard, announcing his kingship to the world, but it is in fact the criminal charge that explains his cruel death. Unlike traditional martyrs, who died with a curse against their torturers, Jesus prays for their forgiveness. Like a king on his way to enthronement, Jesus promises a place of honour and bliss to one who requests it (23.32–43).

Jesus' death is accompanied by the portent of darkness and the tearing of the curtain in the Temple. Jesus expires, not with a whimper, but as a faithful prophet committing his life to God. A nearby centurion sees how Jesus dies, praises God, and then—unlike in Matthew and Mark where he declares him to be 'Son of God'—he says, 'Surely this was a righteous man.' Luke says it again: Jesus was innocent, dying the death of the guilty (23.44–49). After this, Jesus is buried by Joseph of Arimathea. Some of Jesus' female followers are there too, seeing the place where Jesus was buried (23.45–56).

8. The resurrection and ascension of Jesus (24.1–53)

When the women return to the tomb to complete the burial process, they discover the stone rolled away. An angel in shining clothes announces that Jesus has been raised, and urges them to remember his predictions about rising from the dead (24.1–8). The women tell this to the eleven disciples who regard it as a bit of folly (grief-stricken women with crazy mutterings), though Peter rushes to the tomb, finds it empty except for the linen, and is himself confused (24.9–12).

Luke next introduces the two travellers, Cleopas and an unnamed companion, on the road to the nearby village of Emmaus. As they are discussing the recent tragic events, they are joined by a stranger, the risen Jesus, whom they do not recognize.[52] The scene is quietly comical: Jesus pretends not to know about recent events, and the two travellers explain about the Jesus they have followed, who they had hoped would 'redeem Israel'. Then the narrative takes a dramatic twist as the stranger responds: 'How foolish you are, and how slow to believe all that the prophets have spoken! Did not the Messiah have to suffer these things and then enter his glory?' To which Luke

---

[52] On the risen Jesus not being immediately recognized, see Mt. 28.17 and Jn. 20.14; 21.4, 12.

adds: 'And beginning with Moses and all the Prophets, he explained to them what was said in all the Scriptures concerning himself' (24.13–27).[53]

When they reach Emmaus, Jesus seems to be going further, but the two ask him to join them, it being already late. At table, Jesus breaks bread, gives thanks, and gives it to them—evoking, no doubt, several earlier bread-breakings, climaxing in the Last Supper itself. 'Their eyes', says Luke, 'were opened, and they recognised him.'[54] He disappears, and the two rush back to Jerusalem to tell the Eleven what had happened, only to be informed that Jesus has already appeared to Simon Peter (24.28–35).

Ivory plaque with scenes from Luke 24.13–35, *c.* 850–900, made in northern France, Metropolitan Museum of Art, New York
Public Domain

Jesus then appears to all of them with a greeting of peace. To reassure them that he is not a ghost, and perhaps to assure Luke's readers that Jesus' resurrection body was no incorporeal phantasm, Jesus invites them to touch him, and then eats some grilled fish. He explains that his suffering and rising were the focal point of God's messianic purpose, as written in the scriptures. Now that this has happened—exactly in line, once more, with scriptural prophecy—the message must go out to the nations. The disciples are the key witnesses; they must remain in Jerusalem until they are clothed with heavenly power for this task (24.36–49).

Luke closes by describing the ascension (24.50–53); unlike in Acts, where he speaks of forty days of Jesus appearing to the disciples, in the gospel account he makes it seem as though everything happens on the same day. Jesus leads his

---
[53] Lk. 24.25–27.
[54] Lk. 24.31.

followers out to Bethany, blesses them, and is taken up into heaven. The Jerusalem Temple had always been seen as the place where heaven and earth were joined; Luke's description of the ascension assumes that now it is Jesus himself who joins heaven and earth in one (though the Temple remains for a while, and the disciples worship in it for the moment). Thus the first instalment of Luke's *diēgēsis* about Jesus ends with Jesus having fulfilled God's plan, as announced in the scriptures, for the Messiah to suffer and enter his glory. The ancient and millennia-long story has reached its goal; the new story is about to begin.

> **OUTLINE OF THE ACTS OF THE APOSTLES**
>
> 1. Prologue and recapitulation (1.1–2)
> 2. The story of the Jerusalem church (1.3—8.1a)
> 3. The gospel spreads to Samaria, Ethiopia, and Syria (8.1b—9.31)
> 4. Persecution of the church and Peter's gentile breakthrough (9.32—12.25)
> 5. The mission of the Antiochene church (13.1—15.35)
> 6. Paul's Asian and Aegean mission (15.36—21.16)
> 7. Paul's arrest in Jerusalem and imprisonment (21.17—26.32)
> 8. Paul testifies to the gospel in Rome (27.1—28.31)

LUKE'S STORY OF THE EARLY CHURCH

(See box: 'Outline of the Acts of the Apostles'.)

1. Prologue and recapitulation (1.1–2)

Luke's narrative continues in the Acts of the Apostles. He refers back to his gospel as the story of 'all that Jesus began to do and to teach' (1.1); the story he now tells is of what Jesus *continued* to do and to teach, through the presence and power of the holy spirit operating in the apostles (1.2).

2. The story of the Jerusalem church (1.3—8.1a)

Luke tells how the risen Jesus spent time with his disciples, teaching them, and readying them to receive the holy spirit, before describing the ascension more fully than he had done in the gospel (1.2–11). Verse 8 of chapter 1 functions as a 'virtual table of contents' for Luke's second volume:[55] the story moves outwards, beginning in Jerusalem, spreading into Judea, then into the contested territory of Samaria, and then onwards into the wider world, ending up with Paul in Rome announcing God as king and Jesus as lord 'openly and unhindered' under the nose of Caesar himself. It is easy to be disappointed when reaching the end of Acts, because when Paul gets to Rome the reader naturally wants to know 'what happened next?' But the hero of Luke's story is not Paul, but the Jesus-gospel itself. All roads in Luke's world led not only *to* Rome but also *from* Rome. Once the gospel has taken root there, it will spread to the rest of the world.

---

[55] Bruce 1988, 36–7.

The first task of the disciples was to elect a replacement for Judas, and Matthias was chosen by lot (1.1–26). Then, on the day of Pentecost, while the disciples were gathered together, the spirit descended upon them, clothing them with power as Jesus promised, and enabling them to speak in foreign languages about the wonders of God. As heaven and earth were joined in the person of the ascended Jesus, so now the breath of heaven comes to earth, constituting Jesus' followers as the new Temple, the people in whom the powerful divine presence truly dwells. The cacophony of praise in distant tongues amazes the many visitors to Jerusalem who heard their own language being spoken with, it seems, a Galilean accent. Their explanation is that the disciples must be drunk (2.1–13).

Peter then stood up, giving one of the most pivotal speeches of the entire book of Acts. He explained that the sudden dramatic multi-lingual speech was not drunken revelry, but the fulfilment of prophecy! Peter's sermon is built around the biblical quotations of Joel 2.28–32 and Psalms 16.8–11; 132.11; 110.1. He explained how the outpouring of the spirit proved that the 'last days' had arrived, with Jesus himself dispensing the spirit to his followers. All this had happened through God's foreknowledge and plan, evidenced in God's raising Jesus from the dead

Depiction of Pentecost and the tongues of fire on a panel from the High Altar of the Charterhouse of Saint-Honoré, Thuison-les-Abbeville, The Art Institute of Chicago

and exalting him to the position of world sovereignty at his right hand, making Jesus both 'lord' and 'Messiah'. Peter then urged the crowd to repent and be baptized in the name of Jesus for the forgiveness of sins, with the promise that they would themselves receive the holy spirit (2.14–41). All this makes the sense it makes within the larger Jewish expectation of covenant renewal, focused on actual personal renewal.

Luke recounts the aftermath with an idealized portrait of the church. He describes the first believers as being devoted to the apostles' teaching and committed to fellowship and prayer, performing many miracles, selling their possessions and giving to those in need, worshipping in the Temple and in private homes, enjoying the favour of the locals, and growing daily in number. To our eyes, the church looks charismatic, sacramental, and evangelical all at once (2.42–47).

The next major episode has Peter and John healing a crippled beggar, and Peter then explaining that the healing power came from the glorified Jesus. He was the 'prophet' predicted by Moses, prophesied by Samuel, the one in whom God's promise to Abraham to bless Israel and the nations would be fulfilled (3.1–26).[56] The stress is both on the radical new thing that was happening and on the fact that this was what had been promised all along.

The authorities arrest Peter and John, beginning the story of persecution. Peter explains that the power of Jesus was responsible for the healing, and when the members of the Sanhedrin try to tell the two men not to speak of Jesus any more they naturally enough refuse: they must obey God rather than human authorities (4.1–22). They return to the other disciples and, invoking Psalm 2, pray that as God has exalted Jesus over Herod and Pilate—representing Israel and the nations—so now he will give them continuing boldness to speak the word, with powerful results. As a result, Luke says that they were filled with the holy spirit and spoke the word of the gospel with great boldness (4.23–31).

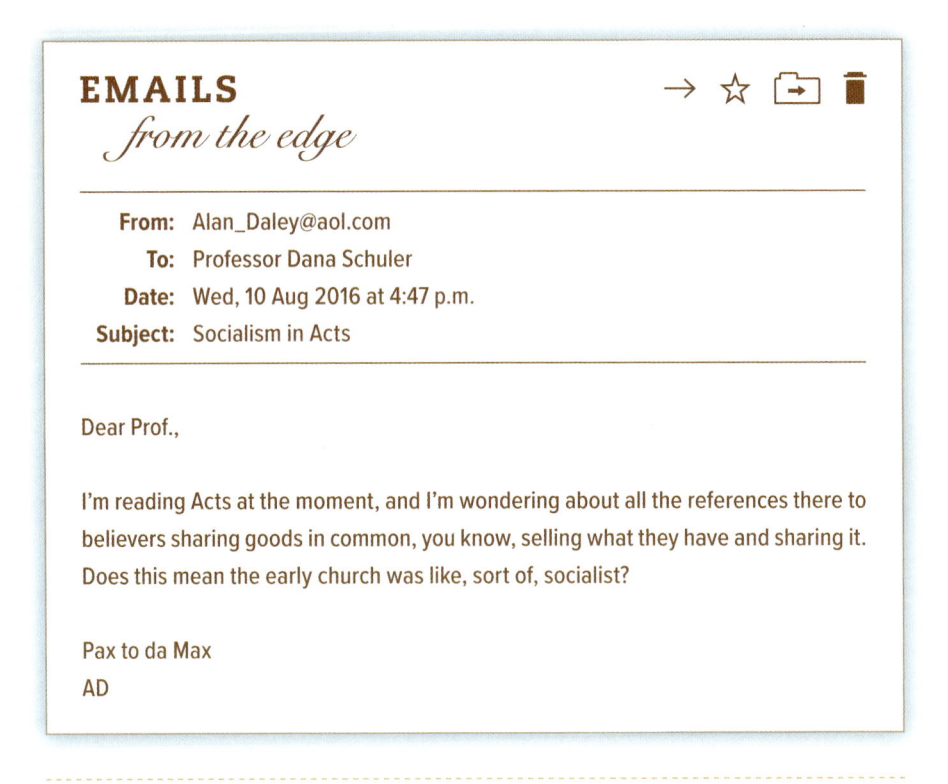

EMAILS
from the edge

From: Alan_Daley@aol.com
To: Professor Dana Schuler
Date: Wed, 10 Aug 2016 at 4:47 p.m.
Subject: Socialism in Acts

Dear Prof.,

I'm reading Acts at the moment, and I'm wondering about all the references there to believers sharing goods in common, you know, selling what they have and sharing it. Does this mean the early church was like, sort of, socialist?

Pax to da Max
AD

---

[56] Dt. 18.15–19; 2 Sam. 7.12–16; Gen. 22.18; 26.4.

From: Professor Dana Schuler
To: Alan_Daley@aol.com
Date: Wed, 10 Aug 2016 at 9:22 p.m.
Subject: Re: Socialism in Acts

Dear Alan,

Yes, I'm aware of the famous passages in Acts 2.44–45 and 4.32–35 about the believers selling property and depositing the proceeds in a general fund, and people touting the first Christians as proto-socialists. On the one hand, this has some traction since the Lukan Jesus always sides with the 'poor' and frequently condemns the rich (e.g. Lk. 16.19–31 on the rich man and Lazarus). Plus Luke describes how in the church there was 'no needy person among them' (Ac. 4.34), which itself looks back to the law of Moses which commanded that the covenant community be one where there were no persons in need (Dt. 15.4); it even resonates with the sentiments of Roman authors like Seneca, who idealized a past when 'you could not find a single pauper' (*Ep. Mor.* 90.38). It helps as well to remember that another Jewish sect, the Essenes, appear to have pooled wealth and possessions (CD 14.13; Philo *Omn. Prob. Lib.*, 76–7, 85–7; *Hypoth.* 11.4–13; Jos. *Ant.* 18.20–2; *War* 2.122–7), as did the Greek philosopher Pythagoras who founded a school at Croton that practised communal ownership of property (Iamblichus *Life* 6.29–30; Porphyry *Life* 20). The Jewish tradition was strong on giving alms to the poor (Dt. 15.11; Sir. 3.30; 7.10; Mt. 6.1–4), just as the Greek philosophical tradition took it as settled that 'for friends all things are held in common' (Arist. *Nic. Eth.* 9.8.2). Given this context, it makes sense that the early church, thinking of itself as the vanguard of a renewed Israel and as the ideal *collegium*, believed that it was called to a particular form of covenanted communal justice where wealth was shared and no-one was left to cope alone (see also Gal. 2.10; 2 Cor. 8.13–15; Jas. 1.26—2.7). What is more, this sort of thing was necessary if the church, made up mainly of Galileans, was to sustain itself in Jerusalem, as it would need economic support for its leaders and care for the vulnerable in its ranks.

As to whether this is 'socialism', well, technically no, it isn't. I don't think Peter or John were interested in getting the state to regulate the means of production when it came to the amount of olives, wheat, and grapes that was harvested; with the state also controlling the distribution of these goods by selling them at a fixed price at specified times of the year. In addition there is no indication that disciples were expected to give up all private property. The donation of goods was voluntary (see Ac. 5.4;

> 11.29) and it seems that people kept some property; otherwise, they would have had nowhere to live and nowhere to meet (see Ac. 2.46; 12.12–13)! Certainly, while Paul takes it for granted that his communities will look out for the poor in their midst he also assumes that the believers will still own their own houses, not least the larger ones where the church would gather (1 Corinthians is the best source for all this).
>
> See further:
>
> Hays, Christopher. 2010. *Luke's Wealth Ethics: A Study in Their Coherence and Character*. WUNT 2.275; Tübingen: Mohr Siebeck.
> Johnson, Luke Timothy. 2011. *Sharing Possessions: What Faith Demands*. 2nd edn.; Grand Rapids, MI: Eerdmans.
> Longenecker, Bruce W. 2010. *Remember the Poor: Paul, Poverty and the Greco-Roman World*. Grand Rapids, MI: Eerdmans.
> Walton, Steve. 2008. 'Primitive Communism in Acts? Does Acts Present the Community of Goods (2:44–45; 4:32–35) as Mistaken?' *Evangelical Quarterly* 80: 99–111.
>
> Kindest regards
> Prof. Dana Schuler

Luke again mentions the property-sharing practice of the first disciples (see 'Emails from the edge: socialism in Acts'), with Joseph-called-Barnabas noted for his particular generosity (4.32–37). Those who try to cheat the system for their own advantage are confronted and judged for their duplicity (5.1–11).

We watch as Luke depicts the church in transition from its early mode as a renewal movement into a persecuted sect. The apostles continue performing many signs and miracles among the people, particularly healings; people are in awe of them but frightened to join them (5.12–16). The persecution steps up as the jealous high priests arrest and imprison the apostles. Yet an angel of the Lord sets them free and sends them to preach in the Temple courts. After some head-scratching and searching by the authorities—where are those men we locked up?—the apostles are found and dragged once more before the Sanhedrin where they are reprimanded for disobeying orders to cease preaching. Peter and the others reply once more that they must obey God, not humans, since their task is to witness to the exalted Jesus as the one who grants repentance and forgiveness to Israel (5.17–32).

A Pharisee named Gamaliel then dissuades the Sanhedrin from reacting with violence. Crazy movements, he says, come and go; but if this one really is from

God one should not be found opposing it. The disciples thus escape with a flogging, which unsurprisingly has no effect on their continuing gospel-announcement (5.33–42).

External trouble gives way to internal: a complaint arises that the Aramaic-speaking widows are being cared for while the Greek-speaking widows are neglected. (This speaks volumes for the fact that the first Christians were living as *family*, with mutual responsibilities, especially for the needy.) The Twelve delegate the distribution of food to seven 'deacons' (that is, 'servants'), so that they can continue to focus their energies on the ministry of prayer and the word (6.1–7). Little is said about how the leaders spent most of their waking hours, but this hint suggests that prayerful study and teaching of the scriptures was central to their new lives.

Attention turns to Stephen, one of the Seven, who, though appointed to an administrative task, seems to have turned into a powerful speaker and teacher as well. He arouses the indignation of fellow hellenistic Jews who are offended by his teaching about Torah and Temple—probably emulating Jesus' own teaching on these topics—with the consequence that Stephen is seized by a mob and brought before the Sanhedrin. His speech before the council gives a synopsis of Israel's history and has three foci: God's faithfulness to his promises; God's mobile presence, meaning that he is not limited to either Israel or the Temple;[57] and Israel's repeated acts of disobedience. This enrages the council, and Stephen is rushed out of the city and stoned to death, but not before he shouts out that he can see Jesus standing at God's right hand—perhaps to intercede, or perhaps to welcome him into his presence. Unlike all pre-Christian martyrs, Stephen copies Jesus by dying with a prayer for his killers (7.60). Luke comments that a young man named Saul was there, approving of the stoning (6.8—8.1a).

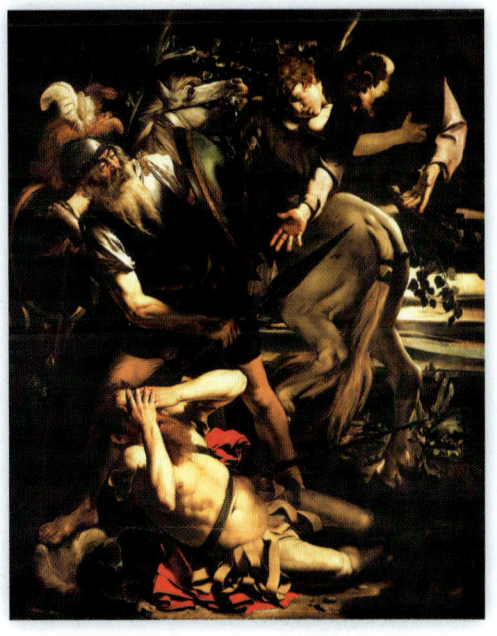

Caravaggio, *The Conversion of St Paul*, c. 1600, Odescalchi Balbi collection, Rome
Public Domain

---

57 Stephen says that the Most High does not live in houses 'made by human hands [*cheiropoiētos*]' (Ac. 7.48), which in the scriptures was a way of describing idols (see Pss. 115.4; 135.15; Ac. 19.26).

3. The gospel spreads to Samaria, Ethiopia, and Syria (8.1b—9.31)

Stephen's death marks the beginning of wide-scale persecution of the believers, with everyone except the apostles—who decided to remain and tough it out—scattered across Judea and Samaria. We then read that Saul tried to crush the church, going from house to house, dragging people off into prison (8.1b–3).

Philip, one of the seven Greek-speaking 'deacons', fled to a city of Samaria to take the gospel there. He encountered a sorcerer known as Simon Magus, who believed and was baptized.[58] Peter and John visited Samaria, laying hands on the Samaritan believers so that they would receive the holy spirit. When Simon Magus asked to buy, as it were, the Samaritan franchise on this ability to bestow the holy spirit on people, he was sternly scolded by Peter for having such a thought and for the bitterness of heart it demonstrates (8.4–25).

Philip was then instructed by an angel to go south, where he came upon an Ethiopian eunuch in his chariot, heading home after worshipping in Jerusalem. He was reading Isaiah 53.7–8; the line about 'who can speak of his descendants' might be of particular interest to a eunuch. Beginning with this passage—which became, unsurprisingly, one of the early Christians' favourite texts about Jesus—Philip explained the gospel of Jesus, and, when the man professed faith, baptized him in some nearby water. The Ethiopian presumably took the gospel message home to Ethiopia; Philip, meanwhile, was transported to the Palestinian coastal town of Azotus, where he began preaching in the adjacent areas until he settled in Caesarea (8.26–40).

In the meantime, Saul continued his ruthless campaign against the church, pursuing believers as far as Damascus in Syria. However, while on the way to Damascus, Saul experienced a vision of the risen lord, and heard the now famous words, 'I am Jesus whom you are persecuting.'[59] Saul was of course persecuting Jesus' followers, but Jesus was identifying them with himself. Blinded, Saul was led into Damascus. There, a Jesus-follower named Ananias had a vision, instructing him to find Saul and pray for his sight to be restored. Ananias was naturally frightened, but the lord assured him that he had plans for Saul and all would be well. Ananias carried out the commission: Saul's sight was restored, he received the spirit, and was baptized (9.1–19a).

Saul at once began a powerful ministry, explaining to the Jews in Damascus that Jesus was the Messiah. Forced to flee for his own safety, he went to Jerusalem, where the believers were understandably wary of his story. Barnabas, however, protected him and introduced him to the other Jesus-followers. There too, however, Saul's powerful speaking was too hot to handle, and the believers sent him off home to Tarsus in Cilicia (9.19b–30). Luke rounds off this section of the book by describing

---

58 In church history, Simon Magus was regarded as the progenitor of Gnosticism.
59 Ac. 9.5.

the churches in Judea, Galilee, and Samaria as enjoying peace, being encouraged by the spirit, and growing in number (9.31).

4. Persecution of the church and Peter's gentile breakthrough (9.32—12.25)

The scene then changes and we pick up Peter's story. Peter visited the towns of Lydda and Joppa, down by the coast, and replicated the miracles of Jesus by healing a paralytic and raising a dead woman back to life (9.32–43). While he was lodging with Simon the tanner in Joppa, a God-fearing centurion in Caesarea named Cornelius had a vision of an angel who told him to send for Peter; Peter, meanwhile, had a vision of a large sheet filled with unclean animals for him to eat. Peter refused: he had kept the food regulations all his life. But the voice in the vision told him not to call anything impure if God had made it clean.[60] Right away Cornelius's messengers arrived, and Peter went with them, explaining on arrival how he was obeying a vision and being taught that God has no favourites.[61] As he then began to tell Cornelius and his friends about Jesus, the holy spirit came on all who heard the message and they began to praise God in tongues, just like the first apostles on the day of Pentecost. Peter therefore ordered that they be baptized (not, we note, circumcised—though that question would come up later): God had given them the same gift as the early believers[62] (10.1–48). Peter's dramatic action—crossing the line of ethnic division and eating with gentiles—came in for criticism from the Christians in Jerusalem. He explained the whole story; Luke, repeating it in its essentials, clearly regards it as of high significance (11.1–18).

The scene then switches again, this time to Antioch, where believers from Cyprus and Cyrene began preaching the gospel to gentiles, resulting in a mixed church of Jews and gentiles. Barnabas, sent from Jerusalem to see what was going on, saw the gracious hand of God at work, and went to Tarsus to find Saul to get him to come and help with teaching and leading the lively and diverse young church. It was in Antioch, Luke says, that the disciples were first called 'Christians', meaning 'partisans of the Messiah', or a 'messianic sect'. In response to a prophecy of a coming famine, the Antiochene church, through Barnabas and Saul, sent aid to the Judean churches (11.19–30).

The first half of Acts concludes with dramatic scenes concerning Herod Agrippa I, who had James the son of Zebedee put to death and Peter arrested. Persistent prayer for Peter was rewarded with a miraculous jail-break (12.1–19). The vindication of the church is highlighted by what happened next, as Herod makes an arrogant speech to the people of Tyre and Sidon, pretending himself to be divine, and is

---

60 Ac. 10.15.
61 Ac. 10.28, 34.
62 Ac. 10.47.

struck down with a deadly illness. This incident, reported also by Josephus, is seen by Luke as a clear sign: the gospel of King Jesus is going ahead, and other would-be kings of the Jews are put in their place (12.20–25). This paves the way for the next phase: now it is time for the gospel to go out 'into all the world'—in other words, into the larger territory of Caesar.

5. The mission of the Antiochene church (13.1—15.35)

Luke has thus described how the gospel went from Jerusalem and Judea through Samaria, including dramatic moments like the conversion of Paul, and Peter's 'gentile breakthrough'. He now begins the story of the wider mission, focusing particularly on Paul. As the church at Antioch was worshipping, the spirit gave instructions for Saul and Barnabas to be commissioned to a new work (13.1–3).

St Peter's Grotto Church is a fourth-century church in Syrian Antioch. Tradition says Peter preached and taught here from AD 47–54.
David Padfield / BiblePlaces.com

The first step for Saul and Barnabas—and for John Mark, Barnabas's nephew, who was to assist them—was to sail to Cyprus, Barnabas's original home. There they confronted a Jewish sorcerer, known as Elymas or 'Bar-Jesus', and secured the conversion of the proconsul, Sergius Paulus. This is the point where, according to Luke, Saul becomes known as 'Paul', the name he is given in the narrative from then on (13.4–12).

The second phase was a period of proclamation in central south Asia Minor, notably, Pamphylia and southern Galatia. John Mark left their company in Perga, returning to

Jerusalem, while Paul and Barnabas headed north to Pisidian Antioch. There, in the synagogue, Paul delivered his first major sermon with an opening synopsis of Israelite history, a narration of Jesus' death and resurrection, an announcement of the fulfilment of prophecy, and an appeal for belief and the offer of forgiveness. This begins a common pattern in Acts. Paul wins a few converts among Jews, proselytes, and God-fearers, but hostility manifests itself from the local Jewish community. In the face of such opposition, stirring up civic leaders, Paul and Barnabas retort that they will now 'turn to the gentiles', as they are forcibly expelled from the region (13.13–52).

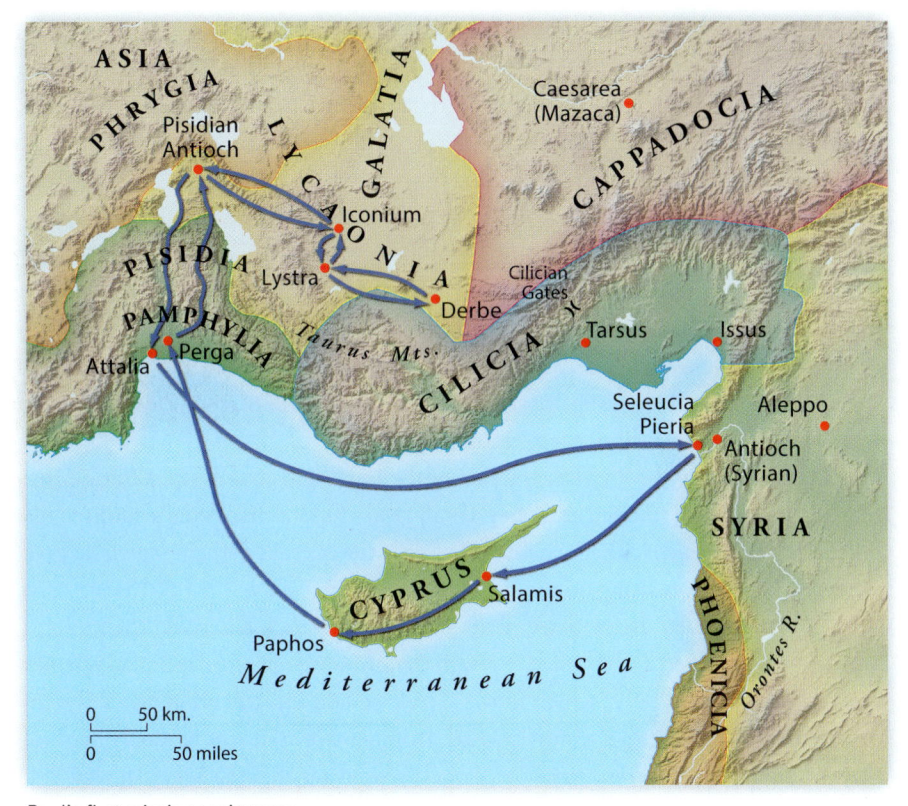

Paul's first missionary journey

The pattern was repeated in other southern Galatian cities. In Iconium, Paul and Barnabas preached in the local synagogue, a number of Jews and gentiles believed, then some unbelieving Jews stirred up the local authorities, so Paul and Barnabas fled. In Lystra, Paul healed a lame man, with the result that Barnabas was hailed as Zeus and Paul as Hermes, causing a local priest to try to offer sacrifices to them. Mortified by this idolatrous identification with pagan gods, Paul spoke urgently about the need to turn from idolatry and begin worshipping the one true God who shows his providence and common grace to all human beings.

The Gospel according to Luke and Acts of the Apostles

The mood of the crowd changed drastically, and Paul was stoned and left for dead, though in fact he was able to revive and move on to nearby Derbe, where he and Barnabas won a number of disciples (14.1–21a).

The third phase was the journey back to Syrian Antioch. Paul and Barnabas retraced their steps, encouraged the disciples in Lystra, Iconium, and Pisidian Antioch, appointed elders to lead them, then headed south into the Pamphylian cities of Perga and Attalia. From Attalia they sailed back to Syrian Antioch, reporting what God had done, particularly that he had 'opened a door of faith to the Gentiles'.[63] It was among the gentiles, Luke is stressing, rather than the Jews, that fertile soil for the gospel was being discovered (14.21b–28).

The influx of gentiles in the Antiochene church created controversy and conflict within the broader church. A faction of Jerusalem believers, former Pharisees, took it upon themselves to visit Antioch and to teach the gentile believers there that they had to obey Torah in order to be saved, meaning that males had to be circumcised. In their mind, the coming of the Messiah did not alter the mainline Jewish framework: the usual rites of passage through which gentiles could enter Israel through proselytism remained intact. Paul and Barnabas disputed the teaching of the intruders, contending that one did not have to become physically Jewish in order to belong to the Messiah's people. The Antiochene church dispatched Paul and Barnabas to Jerusalem to consult with the apostles and elders, to make sure that everyone was singing off the same sheet of gospel music (15.1–4).

At the gathering the Pharisaic faction of the Jerusalem church stuck to its guns: gentiles must be circumcised and obey Torah (15.1–5). But first Peter recounted his missionary experience with Cornelius: God gave the gentiles the same spirit he gave to Jewish believers, making no distinction. What mattered was the purification of the heart, effected by divine grace. Paul and Barnabas then described the miraculous signs that God had performed through them among the gentiles. Finally, James expounded Amos 9.11–12, which in the Greek version indicates that gentiles were destined to participate in a restored Israel. In other words, it was precisely because God had fulfilled his covenant with Israel in sending Jesus as Messiah that the covenant-family was now thrown open to all, without distinction. The only burden to be placed on gentiles was the commitment to avoid idolatry, which could be spelled out in terms of converts avoiding idol-food, sexual immorality, and consuming blood from the meat of strangled animals (15.6–21). The apostles and elders of the Jerusalem church sent a letter censuring the views of the intruders, and adding only those instructions for gentile believers. This decision, not unnaturally, caused great rejoicing among the believers in Antioch (15.22–35).

---

63 Ac. 14.27.

6. Paul's Asian and Aegean mission (15.36—21.16)

Paul and Barnabas next intended to visit the churches they had founded, not least to deliver the apostolic decree. But they quarrelled over John Mark, who had deserted them during their first missionary journey: Barnabas wanted to take him with them again, but Paul refused. As a result, Barnabas and John Mark went to Cyprus, while Paul took Silas and went to Syria and Cilicia. Thus began Paul's second missionary journey (15.36–41).

Travelling through southern Galatia, Paul added Timothy to his team, and then passed through the Phrygian part of Galatia in central west Asia Minor. The spirit led them away from the provinces of Asia (south-west) and prevented them going into Bithynia (north-east). In the coastal city of Troas, Paul had a vision of a Macedonian man calling him to come over and help. At once, Paul and his companions crossed the Aegean Sea and landed in Macedonia, and the gospel of Jesus landed for the first time on European soil (16.1–10).

That brought Paul and Silas to Philippi, a Roman colony. Luke reports a flurry of activity: a woman named Lydia was converted, Paul caused a riot by exorcising a slave-girl fortune-teller, and he and Silas were beaten up and thrown into prison, whereupon, following an earthquake, he led his Philippian jailer to faith.

Paul's second missionary journey

The charge against Paul, such as it was, had been that he 'advocated customs unlawful for us Romans to accept or practice'.[64] When Paul pointed out that he was a Roman citizen, the authorities were embarrassed, and he left a free man (16.11–40).

The travellers next arrived in the Macedonian city of Thessalonica. Paul preached in the synagogue, with the usual effect of winning a few Jews and God-fearers to the faith, but the local Jewish community then stirred up a mob against him. This time the complaint was that: 'These men who have caused trouble all over the world have now come here . . . They are all defying Caesar's decrees, saying that there is another king, one called Jesus.'[65] This time Paul and Silas were able to escape under cover of night (17.1–9). Paul got a more receptive audience in Berea; but Jews from Thessalonica followed him to arouse opposition, and so Paul was hurried away south to Athens, leaving Silas and Timothy behind (17.10–15).

Paul, distressed at how much Athens was infested with idols, spoke in the synagogue and market-place, and was taken off to the Areopagus, the highest court there—not, then, for a philosophical debate, but on the dangerous charge of bringing foreign divinities into the city. Paul, starting by mentioning an altar he had seen dedicated to an 'unknown god', delivered one of his most memorable speeches, discoursing about God's invisibility and providence, the call to repent of idolatry, and concluding with God's appointment of Jesus to judge the world as witnessed by his resurrection. This speech was not so much translating the gospel into pagan language, as declaring the Jewish message of the one God, and its new Christian twist about Jesus as the risen lord and coming judge, into the ancient pagan philosophical context which Paul knew very well could not contain it. He was, in effect, offering a new way to talk about God and the world, a way focused on this Jesus.[66] In the end, Paul gained a few converts, including Dionysius and Damaris, and then headed off to Corinth (17.16–34).

In Corinth, Paul stayed with two other Jewish Christians, Priscilla and Aquila, who had recently been expelled from Rome by Claudius's anti-Jewish edict. In the synagogue, Paul persuaded many Jews and gentiles about Jesus, until he was opposed and attacked. Reunited with Silas and Timothy, Paul turned to the gentiles, basing himself in the house of Titius Justus, next door to the synagogue. He taught there for eighteen months. The Jewish community then brought charges against Paul—that he was advocating illegal worship, which perhaps reflects Paul's practice of adapting Jewish prayers so as to include Jesus—but the proconsul Gallio refused to arbitrate on what he saw as an internal Jewish religious matter. This created breathing space for the Christians. Paul was able to stay on in Corinth for some time (18.1–17).

---

64 Ac. 16.21.
65 Ac. 17.6–7.
66 Rowe 2009, 40.

Paul then returned to Syria. He had his head shaved as part of a vow (one of many things in Acts we wish Luke had explained a bit more). He took Priscilla and Aquila with him to Ephesus and left them there, promising to return. He then travelled via Caesarea to Syrian Antioch, though it seems he did not stay long, because soon afterwards he went off again to visit some of the churches in southern Galatia and Phrygia to strengthen the disciples, finally returning to Ephesus. In the meantime, Priscilla and Aquila met Apollos, instructed him further in the faith, and then sent him to Corinth to help the struggling church there (18.18–28).

Back in Ephesus, Paul instructed some disciples of John the Baptist who did not know about the holy spirit. He spent some time preaching the kingdom of God in a synagogue, but then formed his own school based in the hall of Tyrannus, where he taught for two years. Luke reports that God performed extraordinary miracles of healing through Paul there—including a comical vignette about a Jewish family: the seven sons of a chief priest tried imitating Paul and using Jesus' name in exorcisms, only to be brutally beaten up by a demoniac. Luke also states that the word of God spread in Asia and the name of the lord Jesus was held in high esteem, so much so, that many of those who believed burned their magical scrolls (19.1–20).

Paul intended to head back to Jerusalem, but first wanted to visit the churches of Macedonia and Achaia. However, before he departed, a riot broke out, led by the Ephesian silversmiths whose livelihoods had suffered due to the growth of Christian faith in Asia. The town clerk intervened to stop the riot from getting worse. The scene is a further example of how Paul's ministry created serious divisions in the cities where he worked; Luke can hardly draw a veil over such a well-known fact, but as ever he tries to make out that Paul was not to blame (19.21–41).

> 'In Acts 9, 22, 26 Luke describes the encounter between Paul and the Risen Lord that changed Paul from a persecutor of "the Way" into one of its most ardent proclaimers. Luke tells the story in a different manner each time, depending on the demands on the context.... In short, Luke tells the story of Paul's conversion in three different ways, each of which he has adapted very carefully to its narrative context. What Luke has is *one story*, or one tradition, which he has employed in different ways.'
>
> **Beverly Gaventa**, *From Darkness to Light*, 90.

Paul visited Macedonia (northern Greece, including Philippi and Thessalonica) and Achaia (southern Greece, focused on Corinth) as intended, picking up some disciples along the way to accompany him on his return journey, which, as we know from Paul's letters, had as a main object the delivery of money collected from gentile churches to help the struggling Jerusalem community. Paul travelled from Macedonia via Troas to Miletus, with adventures in the first town and a significant farewell address in the second, before going on to the eastern Mediterranean and eventually arriving in Jerusalem, undeterred by warning prophecies (20.1—21.16).

7. Paul's arrest in Jerusalem and imprisonment (21.17—26.32)

Luke's narrative now picks up speed and a sense of threat. James requests that Paul underwrite a vow for four men, to show that, contrary to reputation, he is himself a loyal Jew (21.17–26). The plan backfires: Paul is recognized and a riot begins, from which Paul is rescued by the Roman tribune. Protected by soldiers, he tries to address the crowd, but at the mention of his being sent to the gentiles the Jews riot again. He is saved from the normal Roman practice of torturing suspects by revealing his Roman citizenship. The tribune decides that Paul needs to appear before the Sanhedrin (22.22–30). Paul puts the cat among the pigeons by declaring that the main question is the resurrection of the dead, which (as he knew it would) divides the Sadducees and the Pharisees, and no decision is reached. A plot against Paul's life is discovered and the Roman tribune has Paul sent under guard to Caesarea where he has various hearings with the successive governors, Felix and Festus, and finally before Herod Agrippa. Luke takes the opportunity to write up Paul's defence, summing up his career and challenging his hearers with the gospel message, leading to the strong conclusion that Paul had done nothing wrong and could have been released had he not appealed to Caesar (23.1—26.32). Paul's speech sums up Luke's perspective: the Jesus-movement is the true fulfilment of Israel's scriptures, now blossoming out into a worldwide movement.

8. Paul testifies to the gospel in Rome (27.1—28.31)

The reader of Acts has known ever since 1.8 that the gospel must go to the ends of the earth, and it has become increasingly apparent that Luke intends to fulfil the early promise by having Paul arrive in Rome.[67] However, just as the magicians of Samaria, Cyprus, and Ephesus opposed the gospel as it set off on the different stages of its journey, so now the dark power itself, the mysterious depths that lent themselves so readily to the apocalyptic musings of Jewish mythology, will oppose the gospel (in the person of its archetypal representative) as it arrives on Caesar's doorstep. In other words, Paul will not get to Rome without going through fire and water, the first as metaphor, the second as fact. And so the apostle and his companions began their journey to Italy by boat, under Roman military guard. Luke seems to have been fully aware that in placing the story of the voyage, the storm, the shipwreck, and the remarkable rescue where he does, he is bringing his narrative to a climax, with the shipwreck taking the place in Acts that corresponds to the place of Jesus' crucifixion in the gospel. He cannot have been unaware, as well, that in writing a passage like this he was awakening, in some readers' minds at least, memories of great Greek literature, Homer's *Odyssey* in particular.

---

[67] See Lk. 21.12; Ac. 1.8; 9.15; 23.11.

Paul's third missionary journey

The voyage and its twists, turns, and eventual disaster is dramatically described, with Paul taking quite a leading role (being of course a very experienced traveller) in offering advice to those in charge. Having been shipwrecked on Malta, the party stays there through the winter, while Paul is engaged in a healing ministry. Finally the spring comes, sailing is again possible, and the party arrives in Rome, where Paul is allowed to live in his own lodgings with a soldier guarding him (27.1—28.16).

At this point the normal reader wants to know what happened when Paul appeared before Caesar, but Luke does not tell us. Perhaps he wanted to avoid at all costs allowing Paul's death to be in any way parallel to that of Jesus in the gospel. Perhaps, as some have thought, Acts was actually written early as a document for use in Paul's defence at trial. Or perhaps Luke is simply determined, as we hinted before, to tell the story, not of Paul, but of the gospel itself. It is particularly important for him to stress—whenever he was writing—that though tensions between Rome and the Jewish communities there and in Palestine were mounting, Paul was not trying to accuse his fellow-Jews of anything. He was simply convinced that Jesus really was and is Israel's Messiah. The fact that this creates a problem when some Jewish people do not recognize him as such does not undermine the scripturally supported claim (28.17–29). Luke's point is that the promise of chapter 1 has been fulfilled.

The Gospel according to Luke and Acts of the Apostles

Detail of Paul, Peter, and Luke in a crypt below Santa Maria in via Lata, Rome. Built in the first century and reconstructed in the third century, this is the possible location for Paul's house arrest. © 2015 by Zondervan

The one God of Israel is proclaimed as king, and Jesus, Israel's Messiah, is proclaimed as the one 'lord', 'with all boldness and without hindrance' (28.31). Luke gives us the impression that, irrespective of what happened to Paul, the word of God was going to continue to spread, multiply, and flourish, in Rome and from Rome, just as it had done elsewhere.[68] Luke has crafted Acts 28 not as a definitive ending, but more rightly as the end of a beginning.[69] He expects his readers, equipped now with the narrative of Jesus and his first followers, to pick up the story and take it forward from there, living a kind of 'Acts 29' in whatever ways are appropriate. As one writer has put it: 'Acts is not so much about community or the beginnings of a community. It is about, well, acts. About making a move through the Holy Spirit and seeing what comes next.'[70]

LUKE-ACTS AND THE BIG PICTURE

Luke-Acts is partly a manual for discipleship and partly a blueprint for operating a church. Luke gives plenty of guidance on how to be followers in the way of Jesus Christ in a world full of social upheaval and economic inequalities, amid secular suspicion of religion, and living under the shadow of various empires in the east and west. Here are a few take-away points.

---

[68] Ac. 2.41; 4.4; 6.7; 8.4, 14; 10.36; 11.1, 19; 12.24; 13.49; 19.10, 20.
[69] Troftgruben 2010, 179–83.
[70] Brown 2016, 86.

First, the Lukan Jesus is clearly on the side of the poor. Importantly, 'the poor' are not just the economically disadvantaged; the phrase includes those of low status, like those with virulent skin-diseases (rendering them 'untouchable' in society), tax-collectors, and prostitutes. The poor, in other words, are both financially challenged and socially marginalized.[71] What Jesus promises them is reversal: reversal of status (from shame to honour), reversal of religious position (from outsider to insider), and reversal of fortunes (from need to abundance). Luke sees the church called to embody a life of jubilee, not some idolatrous theology of prosperity: debts are cancelled, sins are forgiven, people are released from the conditions which create economic inequality, and the broken are restored to wholeness. That is why our churches must remain active not only in their assistance to the poor through charities but also in their advocacy for the poor in lobbying governments, and continue to be compassionate in assisting outcasts such as refugees, and helping with the rehabilitation of criminals. The church's business is the holistic salvation of people—body, mind, heart, and soul—to the ends of the earth.

Second, if Luke had his way, we'd all be 'Pentecostal' in some form or another. Darrell Bock wishes that Luke 3.16 was just as well known as John 3.16![72] In Luke 3.16, Jesus is the spirit-anointed and spirit-dispensing Messiah, who comes to drench his people in the holy spirit, to plunge them into the fiery and holy breath of God, bestowing God's kingly power and kingdom-presence upon them. Prophets like Ezekiel and Joel looked forward to a day when YHWH would pour out his spirit in a new and unexpected way; Peter's Pentecost sermon announces that the day has come at last, and that it has happened to the followers of Jesus. What is more, the spirit turns the family of Jesus-followers into a strange kind of new Temple. Many Jews longed for a new event in which the divine glory would fill Israel's Temple once more, as for instance in Exodus 40 or 1 Kings 8. The wind and fire of Pentecost answers to this expectation, indicating that now the Temple is a community, not a building. The church, as the spirit-filled Temple of God, goes into the world with this fresh wind and fire, living out its vocation to be a light to the nations, burning ever more brightly.

Third, Luke draws attention to the oneness of the church. Luke is fond of the word *homothymadon*, referring to the 'single-minded purpose' of the early church.[73] That did not indicate a bland uniformity or a total absence of disagreement. There were clear grumblings over the Greek-speaking widows being neglected (Ac. 6) and against Peter for fraternizing with gentiles (Ac. 11). There was nearly a split over the issue of whether male gentiles had to be circumcised (Ac. 15), and a personal rift between Paul and Barnabas (Ac. 15.36–39). Luke does not whitewash the early

---

71 See Green 1994.
72 Bock 2010, 12–14 (esp. 14).
73 Ac. 1.14; 2.46; 4.24; 5.12; 8.6; 15.25.

church's internal struggles. But on the whole, Luke presents the church as unified in its quest to remain faithful to Jesus as lord, in its devotion to God's purposes, and with a developed habit of mutual concern. As churches today face secular indifference in the west, and horrifying persecution in the east, we need a united front more than ever. I can't help but think that Paul's words to the centurion about stopping some of the sailors from abandoning the ship in the midst of the storm might ring true also for us: 'Unless these men stay with the ship, you cannot be saved.'[74] Whatever problems the church is facing today, we need to stick together, and we can only be saved together. (Of course, along with unity goes the imperative to holiness; unity is easy if you don't care about holiness. The church in Acts cared passionately about both.) It is easy to go off and do your own thing, pursue what is right in your own eyes, fill a church with clones of yourself, prize your independence, without any concern for the wider body of Christ. No bishop or bureaucracy to bother you. But that is not the church in Acts. The church is called to messianic mutuality, tangible and visible expressions of partnership, taking an interest in one another's affairs, laced with accountability and encouragement. Luke calls Christians and their churches to be *homothymadon*, united in one mind, in the one mission, and in service to one lord, Jesus.

Otherwise, for a final thought, it is hard to better J. A. Bengel:

> The victory of the Word of God, Paul at Rome, the culmination of the gospel, the conclusion of Acts . . . It began at Jerusalem: it finishes at Rome; Here, O church, you have your pattern. It is your duty to preserve it and to guard it.[75]

Further reading

Adams, Sean A., and Michael Pahl (eds.). 2012. *Issues in Luke-Acts: Selected Essays*. Piscataway, NJ: Gorgias.
Barrett, C. K. 1994–8. *The Acts of the Apostles*. 2 vols.; ICC; Edinburgh: T&T Clark.
Bock, Darrell. L. 1994–6. *Luke*. 2 vols.; BECNT; Grand Rapids, MI: Baker.
———. 2007. *Acts*. BECNT; Grand Rapids, MI: Baker.
———. 2012. *A Theology of Luke and Acts: God's Promised Program, Realized for All Nations*. BTNT; Grand Rapids, MI: Zondervan.
Chen, Diane G. 2017. *Luke*. NCCS; Eugene, OR: Cascade.
Dunn, James D. G. 2016 [1996]. *The Acts of the Apostles*. Grand Rapids, MI: Eerdmans.
Fitzmyer, Joseph A. 1981–5. *The Gospel According to Luke: Introduction, Translation, and Notes*. 2 vols.; AB; Garden City, NY: Doubleday.
———. 1998. *The Acts of the Apostles: A New Translation with Introduction and Commentary*. AB; Garden City, NY: Doubleday.
Gaventa, Beverly R. 2003. *Acts*. ANTC; Nashville, TN: Abingdon.

---

[74] Ac. 27.31.
[75] Cited in Marshall 1988, 221–2.

Green, Joel B. 1997. *The Gospel of Luke*. NICNT; Grand Rapids, MI: Eerdmans.
Gregory, Andrew. 2003. *The Reception of Luke and Acts in the Period before Irenaeus: Looking for Luke in the Second Century*. WUNT 2.169; Tübingen: Mohr Siebeck.
Johnson, Luke Timothy. 1991. *The Gospel of Luke*. SP; Collegeville, MN: Liturgical.
——. 1992. *The Acts of the Apostles*. SP; Collegeville, MN: Liturgical.
Keener, Craig A. 2012–14. *Acts: An Exegetical Commentary*. 4 vols.; Grand Rapids, MI: Baker.
Levine, Amy-Jill, and Ben Witherington. 2018. *The Gospel of Luke*. NCBC; Cambridge: Cambridge University Press.
Longenecker, Bruce W. 2016. *The Lost Letters of Pergamum: A Story from the New Testament World*. Grand Rapids, MI: Baker.
Marshall, I. Howard. 1978. *The Gospel of Luke*. NIGTC; Grand Rapids, MI: Eerdmans.
——. 1980. *The Acts of the Apostles*. TNTC; Grand Rapids, MI: Eerdmans.
——. 1988. *Luke—Historian and Theologian*. 3rd edn.; Guernsey: Paternoster.
Parsons, Mikael. 2008. *Acts*. Paideia; Grand Rapids, MI: Baker.
——. 2015. *Luke*. Paideia; Grand Rapids, MI: Baker.
Ringe, Sharon H. 1995. *Luke*. WBC; Louisville, KY: Westminster John Knox.
Rowe, C. Kavin. 2009. *World Upside Down: Reading Acts in the Graeco-Roman Age*. Oxford: Oxford University Press.
Tannehill, Robert. 1986–90. *The Narrative Unity of Luke-Acts: A Literary Interpretation*. 2 vols.; Minneapolis: Fortress.

Aerial view of modern Jerusalem, looking over the Damascus Gate toward the golden Dome of the Rock

The Gospel according to John

The deeds and words of Jesus are the deeds and words of God; if this be not true the book is blasphemous.[1]

CHAPTER AT A GLANCE

This chapter explains the story, themes, and theology of John's gospel.

By the end of this chapter you should be able to:

- understand the origins of John's gospel in the context of early Christianity;
- describe the basic features of John's story of Jesus;
- grasp the general themes in John's gospel.

INTRODUCTION

John stands out from the rest of the New Testament. With Paul we are in the seminar room: arguing things out, looking up references, taking notes, and then being pushed out into the world to preach the gospel to the nations. Matthew takes us into the synagogue, where the people of God are learning to recognize Jesus as their king, their Emmanuel. Mark writes a short tract, challenging his readers with the very idea of a crucified king and turning it into a handbook on discipleship for followers of the servant-king. Luke addresses the educated Greek world of his day and paints a big picture of God's purposes through Israel's Messiah for the whole world.

John, by contrast, takes us up the mountain, and says quietly: 'Look—from here, on a clear day, you can see for ever.' *We beheld his glory, glory as of the father's only son.* John does not include the story of Jesus' transfiguration, as the other evangelists do. But there is a sense in which John's whole story is about the transfiguration. He invites us to be still and know; to look again into the

---

[1] Barrett 1978 [1956], 156.

human face of Jesus of Nazareth, until the awesome knowledge comes over us, wave upon terrifying wave, that we are looking into the human face of the living God.

Part of the point, then, is that John is teaching us to discern the presence of God in the mess and muddle of historical reality. No apologies, then, for plunging into the questions the book inevitably raises. John's gospel is in some ways remarkably like the three synoptic gospels, yet in other ways it is very unlike them. Why? What account can we give of this?[2]

The similarities are clear. John and the synoptics share a comparable genre; they rely on a common intertext, the scriptures of Israel, as they narrate the same story: a Jewish prophet sent by God to Israel, one who teaches throughout Galilee and Judea, who performs miraculous deeds, attracts many followers and calls them to trust him, is referred to as 'son of God', 'son of man', and 'Messiah', engages in polemics against the Pharisees, incurs the rage of the Judean priestly leadership, is crucified by the Roman authorities, and then is raised by God from the dead and seen alive by his disciples. It is, of course, substantially the same story.

John the Evangelist was often symbolized by an eagle.
Public Domain

But then there are the stark differences. How long was Jesus' public career, and where was it located? John has his dramatic Temple-action near the beginning; the synoptics put it near the end.[3] But then John has Jesus going to Jerusalem frequently; for Mark there is only the one visit. Was the Last Supper a Passover meal, as in the synoptics, or held on the night before, as John seems to suggest? There are also theological differences: the Johannine Jesus appears more forthright and explicit about his divine status than the Jesus of the synoptics, and the Johannine Jesus talks more about 'eternal life' than the 'kingdom of God' (though there is overlap on both).[4] The Johannine Jesus uses discourses rather than parables (though some may be 'buried'—parables woven into discourses like the image of the 'apprentice son' in John 5.19–23). The Johannine Jesus performs no exorcisms. We do not see Jesus baptized, nor are we told about his words of institution at the Last Supper. In the synoptics, the high priests seek to kill Jesus because of jealousy, but in John's gospel

---

2 See Bird 2013c. For a well-rounded account of the mutual interdependence of John and the synoptics, see Bauckham 2015, 185–201.
3 A problem the early church was well aware of; see Tert. *Adv. Marc.* 4.2; Eus. *Hist. Eccl.* 3.24.11–13.
4 E.g. Mk. 10.17 ('eternal life'); Jn. 3.3, 5 ('kingdom of God').

it is because he raised Lazarus from the dead. That incident, indeed, is one of many things found in John but not elsewhere. Others include the 'I am' sayings, the dialogues with Nicodemus and with the Samaritan woman, the turning of water into wine, Jesus' washing of the disciples' feet, the teaching about the holy spirit as the 'Comforter', and so on. John is clearly making a distinctive, unique contribution.

Why should this be so? What did John think he was doing?

First, John was writing a new Genesis. His whole book, opening with the words 'In the beginning', which echo Genesis 1.1, is about how the world's creator has come at last to remake his world. John 20 is about Jesus' resurrection, but every sentence breathes the life of 'the first day of the week', the start of new creation. And if John hints that his prologue is heralding a new version of Genesis 1, then the equivalent of the climax of that great chapter, the creation of humans in the divine image, is precisely when the Word becomes flesh. John 1.14 corresponds to Genesis 1.26–28: the one through whom the world was made now becomes the one through whom the world is rescued and remade. This theme runs throughout the gospel, reaching its own climax in John 19.5 when Pilate declares 'Here's the man!'

Second, John was also writing a new Exodus. Moses led the people out of Egypt and gave them the Torah, to prepare them for God coming in person to dwell with them (in the tabernacle) and to lead them to their inheritance. Now 'the Word became flesh and [literally translated] "tabernacled in our midst"' (Jn. 1.14). Jesus is the place where the one God has come to dwell among us and to reveal his true glory. The whole gospel resonates with this temple-theme, reaching a climax in the 'Farewell Discourses' (Jn. 13—17) when Jesus' followers, too, become temple-people by the promise that God's own spirit will come to dwell in them.

Southern steps into the Temple

Third, as a result, John was also writing about Pentecost. John bears witness to what he remembers, but his memory of Jesus is augmented and animated by the holy spirit, the *paraclete*, who will 'teach you all things and will remind you of everything I have said to you' (Jn. 14.26). John, it seems, sees himself as part of a Jewish movement that has experienced the fulfilment of Israel's hopes in Israel's Messiah, and as someone who has received the gift of YHWH's own spirit from this Messiah. John is providing an *epitome* of Jesus' life, written by one who has *experienced* the streams of living water promised by Jesus to his followers, with the story *expounded* in the co-ordinates of Israel's scripture. This is no bland *bios*, with the sayings of a famous teacher strung together in a loose narrative framework. John has written a theologically creative and spiritually rich fusion of personal memory and Pentecostal faith, suffused with scriptural motifs that together make the point: *this is the fulfilment of Israel's hope*, which means that *this is therefore the way creation itself is renewed*, and, crowning it all, *this is what it looked like when Israel's God, the creator, came in person to do what only he could do*. John thus artistically blends together the life of Jesus with the love of God revealed in Jesus. He offers historical testimony married to the spirit of truth, allowing the scriptural voice to serve as the background harmony to the living voice of the spirit. The Johannine gospel yields a creative blend of memory, mystery, and midrash.[5] The Johannine Jesus is what Jesus looks like viewed through the lens of the spirit, the *paraclete*. While John 20.22 has been nicknamed the 'Johannine Pentecost', in a sense the entire book is a Johannine Pentecost. The spirit uses Israel's scriptures and John's testimony to reveal who Jesus was and is— and who he is calling his followers to be, and what he is commissioning them to do.

The gospel of John sets out several vital biblical themes. There is rich teaching about God as father and his love for his world. There are clear warnings about the evil and darkness that have invaded God's world, and about the tragic unbelief of so many Judeans in the face of divine witnesses. John has more to say about the spirit than all the other gospels put together, generating a strong theme about discipleship, which stems from faith in God and issues in love for others, and about the God-breathed mission to the wider world. John's Jesus regularly refers to salvation in terms of 'eternal life'—presumably, as elsewhere in the New Testament, 'the life of the age to come', not a Platonic dream beyond space, time, and matter.

But the heart of John's thematic world is christology. John constructs a christological cascade, presenting Jesus as the father's supreme agent, the heaven-sent

---

[5] See also Thatcher (2007, 173–4) who describes John's unique portrait of Jesus this way: 'John's Christology, his image of Jesus, emerges at the intersection of three currents: the recall of things that the historical Jesus presumably did and said; a post-resurrection understanding of Jesus' ultimate destiny; and a messianic interpretation of the Hebrew Bible, not only specific passages but the entire text taken as a whole. The interplay of memory, faith, and Scripture may therefore be viewed as John's christological formulae, the generative matrix through which he developed statements about Jesus' messianic identity.'

son, the pre-existent Word who is enfleshed with full humanity. Jesus feels human fatigue; he weeps human tears; he really was and is a Galilean rabbi, a prophet—and Israel's Messiah. As the son of man, Jesus is the nexus between heaven and earth, the object of divine worship. His crucifixion radiates God's glory, the glory of utter self-giving love.[6] At climactic moments Jesus is said to be 'equal with God', the 'I am' associated with the divine name, and even confessed as 'my Lord and my God'.[7] He is differentiated from the father, and yet is one with the father, even though he is neither the father in a human mode, nor a second god in addition to the father. Ernst Käsemann famously believed that John's figure of Jesus was 'God striding across the earth', but this is a radical misunderstanding. John well understands the dialectic tension between Jesus as *vere homo et vere deus* (truly man and truly God).[8] In John's account, the one true God of Israel is revealed in the fully and genuinely human Jesus of Nazareth. What is more, *that is part of the theological point*, not a mere concession within an otherwise 'divine-only' view of Jesus. Humans were made in God's image. When Pilate says 'Behold the man', he is voicing what John wants to say every bit as much as when he writes 'King of the Jews' above Jesus' head—or as when John's Caiaphas declares that it is expedient for one man to die for the people.[9]

CONTEXTUAL AND CRITICAL MATTERS

Origins of John

As with the other canonical gospels, John's gospel makes no mention of its own author. However, a central character in the second half of the gospel is the 'disciple whom Jesus loved', usually referred to in modern times as the 'beloved disciple'. This figure was reclining beside Jesus in the upper room; he was, it seems, with Peter in the high priest's hall; he was with Jesus' mother at the foot of the cross; he runs with Peter to investigate the empty tomb; he was among those to whom the risen Jesus appeared by the Sea of Galilee.[10] He is portrayed as being, literally and metaphorically, one step ahead of Peter, almost as if there might have been a friendly rivalry between them.[11] Although the beloved disciple is not explicitly mentioned prior to Jesus' final meal with his disciples in Jerusalem, this does not mean that he had no part in Jesus' ministry before that point. It might well be that he was the unnamed one of the two disciples of John the Baptist—the named one being Andrew—to whom the Baptist spoke about Jesus and who both then began to follow Jesus.[12]

---

6   Jn. 1.51; 3.13; 9.35–38; 12.23; 13.1–2, 31.
7   Jn. 5.18; 8.58; 10.32; 20.28.
8   Käsemann 1968, 73; Hengel 1989, 99.
9   Jn. 19.5, 19; 11.49–53.
10 Jn. 13.23–25; 18.15–18; 19.26–27, 35; 20.1–8; 21.7, 20–23, 24.
11 See Jn. 18.15–16; 20.1–8; 21.7, 20–22.
12 Jn. 1.35–40.

It is, after all, very unlikely that someone could be called 'the disciple Jesus loved' if he had not already been intimately involved with Jesus.[13] (Thomas is introduced into the story only at Jn. 11.16, yet it is clear that he was an associate long before that.[14]) So the beloved disciple comes to special prominence towards the end; and, in the epilogue in chapter 21, we hear of a rumour that he would not die before the Lord returned. This rumour is quashed. The last lines of the book seem to be written by someone else, an editor who insists that the beloved disciple was the real author, and to be trusted as such.[15] But who was the beloved disciple himself?

Some scholars regard the 'beloved disciple' as a purely literary invention, an ideal disciple, a symbolic character.[16] That seems unlikely, granted the controversy about his forthcoming death and Jesus' reported remark that whether he lives or dies is none of Peter's business.[17] The beloved disciple is more likely a historical figure, a Judean follower of Jesus, a community founder, whose eye-witness testimony and personal authority undergird and vouch for the fourth gospel's veracity.[18] But this only presses the question once more: who was he?

According to tradition, the beloved disciple was John the son of Zebedee, brother of James, one of the senior apostles among the Twelve.[19] Many early Christians believed that he wrote the gospel of John and the three letters of John, and that he received the revelation of Jesus Christ on the island of Patmos, where he composed the book of Revelation.[20] Thus the title 'According to John' was attached to the gospel at least from the end of the second century, if not earlier. It is found in the manuscripts $\mathfrak{P}^{66}$ and $\mathfrak{P}^{75}$, which are usually dated around AD 200. In the late second century, the Muratorian canon states that 'The fourth of the Gospels is that of John, one of the disciples.'[21] Around the same time, Irenaeus wrote that 'John, the disciple of the Lord, who also had leaned upon his breast, did himself publish a Gospel during his residence in Ephesus in Asia.'[22] Irenaeus traces this view back to

---

13 Bauckham 2006, 402.
14 Keener 2003, 1.84.
15 Jn. 21.20–24.
16 See e.g. Lincoln 2005, 22–4 and discussion in Charlesworth 1995, 134–8. For a response, see Bauckham 2006, 393–401; 2007, 73–91.
17 Jn. 21.23.
18 Jn. 1.14; 19.35; 21.24.
19 Mk. 1.19–20; 3.17; 5.37; 9.2, 38–40; 10.35–45; 13.3; 14.33; Lk. 9.52–55; Ac. 1.13; 3–4, 8; Gal. 2.9; *Ep. Apos.* 2.
20 See *Ep. Apos.* 2; Hippolytus *Antichr.*, 36; Clem. *Quis Div.* 42; Eus. *Hist. Eccl.* 3.23.1; 3.24.5, 11; 5.24.16. See also Irenaeus's references to 'John' as the author of the gospel (*Adv. Haer.* 2.22.5; 3.1.1; 3.16.5), the letters (*Adv. Haer.* 3.16.5, 8; 1.16.3), and the apocalypse (*Adv. Haer.* 1.26.3; 4.12.2; 4.17.6; 4.18.6; 4.20.11; 4.21.3), but see more below on Irenaeus! Some anti-Montanist writers attributed John's gospel to the Gnostic Cerinthus (Epiphanius *Pan.* 51.3.1–6). But even early Valentinian writers like Ptolemy and Heracleon attributed it to John the lord's disciple and apostle (Iren. *Adv. Haer.* 1.8.5; Origen *Comm. Jn.* 6.2). And though Eusebius attributed the book of Revelation to a different John (*Hist. Eccl.* 3.39.6), Justin is very early in postulating the apostle John as the author (*Dial.* 81.4).
21 Muratorian canon § 9.
22 Iren. *Adv. Haer.* 3.1.1.

a group of Asian elders, probably including Papias of Hierapolis (d. *c.* AD 130) and Polycarp of Smyrna (d. *c.* AD 155), who had conversed with John before his death after a long old age, probably during the reign of Trajan (AD 98–117).[23] According to Irenaeus, Papias had been a 'hearer of John';[24] according to Philip of Side, Papias was a 'disciple of John the theologian'.[25] Irenaeus says that Polycarp 'was not only instructed by apostles, and conversed with many who had seen Christ, but was also taught by apostles in Asia, [and was] appointed bishop of the church in Smyrna'.[26] Thus, the testimony of Irenaeus, written quite possibly well within a century of the publication of the fourth gospel, is linked directly through Polycarp and Papias to John, 'the disciple of the Lord', as the author of this gospel.[27]

Within the New Testament, there is a consistent and distinctive Johannine ring to certain materials attributed to the apostle John. In Acts, Peter and John, replying to the Sanhedrin, say that they 'cannot help speaking about what *we have seen and heard*'.[28] The wording here is characteristically Johannine, not Lukan. The first letter of John declares, 'We proclaim to you what *we have seen and heard*, so that you also may have fellowship with us.' The John of Revelation announces, 'I, John, am the one who *heard and saw* these things.'[29] We are not then surprised to find the Muratorian canon combining a hagiographic tale about John writing his gospel with a citation of 1 John 1.1, 4, concluding, 'Thus he professes himself not only an eyewitness and hearer but also a writer of all the miracles of our Lord in order.'[30] All this points in the same direction: to the apostle John, the son of Zebedee.[31]

Evidence within the gospel itself points the same way. The beloved disciple is normally paired with Peter,[32] perhaps reflecting their later collegiality.[33] In the epilogue to the gospel, five disciples are named as meeting the risen Jesus by the Sea of Galilee: 'Simon Peter, Thomas (also known as Didymus), Nathanael from Cana in Galilee, the sons of Zebedee, and two other disciples'.[34] If the beloved disciple was one of these disciples, as John 21.20–23 indicates, then he was either one of the sons of Zebedee or one of the two other unnamed members of the party.

---

23 Iren. *Adv. Haer.* 2.22.5; 3.3.4; 5.30.1; 5.33.3.
24 Iren. *Adv. Haer.* 5.33.4.
25 Philip of Side, *Church History*, extant only from excerpts in Codex Baroccianus 142, cited in Holmes 2007, 743.
26 Iren. *Adv. Haer.* 3.3.4; Eus. *Hist. Eccl.* 5.20.5–6.
27 Dunn 2015, 75.
28 Ac. 4.20.
29 1 Jn. 1.3; see Jn. 3.32; Rev. 22.8.
30 Muratorian canon § 9–33.
31 Anderson 1997, 274–7.
32 See Jn. 13.24–25; 18.15–16; 20.1–8; 21.7, 20–22.
33 Gal. 2.9; Lk. 22.8; Ac. 3—8; 8.14–25.
34 Jn. 21.2.

James Dunn draws this conclusion:

> [T]he internal testimony of the Gospel itself, the implication of the inscription, and the claim of Irenaeus to be [part of] a reliable chain of witness, together make a strong case for the tradition that the Gospel of John should be attributed to John, son of Zebedee, who is probably referred to in the Gospel itself as the beloved disciple.[35]

The case, however, is not quite as clear-cut as this would make it seem. First, we should not automatically assume that the same 'John' wrote the gospel, the letters, and Revelation. Despite sharing some features, they have notable differences in genre, vocabulary, and even theological framing. They may after all go back to two if not three different authors. The name 'John' was common, and there may have been more than one in the early church. We might be faced with several different people: John the son of Zebedee, John the evangelist (author/redactor of the gospel), John the elder (author of the letters), and John of Patmos (author of Revelation).

Second, nobody (except in gnostic circles) identified John the son of Zebedee as the author of the fourth gospel prior to the end of the second century. Earlier authors (including Ignatius, Papias, Polycarp, and Justin in their surviving works) are all silent on the question.[36] Papias in particular complicates the picture by referring to two Johns among the 'Lord's disciples': 'John' the son of Zebedee and the 'elder John'.[37] The evidence from the Muratorian canon and Irenaeus add yet more complexity, as we will presently see.

Emperor Trajan

---

[35] Dunn 2015, 76. See also Carson 1991, 68–81; Morris 1995, 4–25; Blomberg 2001, 22–41; Keener 2003, 1.114–15.
[36] However, Hill (2004, 385–94) believes that Eusebius's report that the apostle John wrote the fourth gospel is derived from Papias (*Hist. Eccl.* 3.24.5–13). See, in response, Bauckham 2006, 433–7.
[37] Papias § 3.3–4 (Eus. *Hist. Eccl.* 3.39.3–4).

Third, the refrain about what 'we have seen and heard' is not necessarily the literary signature of the apostle John.[38] Similar things are said in pseudo-apostolic works like the *Epistula Apostolorum*.[39] This language is an authorizing device, not an authorial sign.

Fourth, while John the son of Zebedee was among the seven disciples to whom Jesus appeared in John 21, there were two other anonymous disciples there as well. The beloved disciple could just as easily have been one of them.

Fifth, if the beloved disciple was John the son of Zebedee, it is strange that the fourth gospel gives so little information about Jesus' Galilean ministry (including no reference to the calling of the sons of Zebedee),[40] and so little focus on the Twelve. It isn't clear how a Galilean fisherman like John the son of Zebedee could gain access to the high priest's courtyard when Peter, by himself, could not.[41] Perhaps the beloved disciple was a Judean disciple, quite well connected socially, who was not around during the Galilean phase of Jesus' ministry. This would imply that, like Nathanael, Nicodemus, and the family at Bethany, he was not one of the Twelve. (One of the points to note is that, despite the medieval paintings, there may well have been considerably more than twelve disciples at the Last Supper: the 'beloved disciple' could be a younger, Jerusalem-based follower who had become close to Jesus while not one of the Twelve.)

Other options have been suggested. James Charlesworth has advanced a creative argument that Thomas was the beloved disciple.[42] Others have flirted with the suggestion of Lazarus.[43] (Lazarus is described as 'the one you love'; this might account for why some people thought that the beloved disciple would remain alive until Jesus returned, because the lord had raised him from the dead.)[44] None of these suggestions has gained much support.

A more compelling alternative to John the son of Zebedee is another John, 'John the elder'.[45]

This hypothesis rests on Papias's statement about preferring oral testimony over written records when accessing Jesus' teachings. He mentions two distinct Johns:

> I will not hesitate to set down for you, along with my interpretations, everything I have carefully learned then from the elders and carefully remembered, guaranteeing

---

[38] Jn. 3.32; Ac. 4.19–20; 1 Jn. 1.3.
[39] *Ep. Apos.* 2: 'We do write according as we have seen and heard and touched him, after that he was risen from the dead: and how that he revealed unto us things mighty and wonderful and true.'
[40] Mt. 4.21–22/Mk. 1.19–20; Lk. 5.10.
[41] Jn. 18.15–16.
[42] Charlesworth 1995, esp. 225–437.
[43] See discussion in Morris 1995, 6 n. 14; Charlesworth 1995, 185–93; Witherington 1995b, 14; deSilva 2004, 393.
[44] Jn. 11.3; 21.23.
[45] Largely following Hengel 1989 and Bauckham 2006, 412–33.

their truth. For unlike most people I did not enjoy those who have a great deal to say, but those who teach the truth. Nor did I enjoy those who recall someone else's commandments, but those who remember the commandments given by the Lord to the faith and proceeding from the truth itself. And if by chance someone who had been a follower of the elders should come my way, I inquired about the words of the elders—what <u>Andrew or Peter</u> *said*, or <u>Philip or Thomas or James or John or Matthew</u> or any other of the Lord's disciples, and whatever <u>Aristion and the elder John</u>, the Lord's disciples, *were saying*. For I did not think that information from books would profit me as much as information from a living and abiding voice.[46]

Papias here distinguishes 'James [and] John', the sons of Zebedee, from the 'elder John'. He (Papias) designates all the persons he mentions as 'elders' and the 'Lord's disciples', but he separates members of the Twelve (Andrew, Peter, Philip, Thomas, James, John, and Matthew) from two others (Aristion and the elder John). The difference Papias highlighted was between what the former (members of the Twelve) *had said in the past* (*eipen*—aorist tense form) and what the duo 'were saying' (*legousin*—present tense form). The aorist tense did not automatically refer to a past event. The 'historical present' could also refer to the past; so this distinction is not a strong base for a theory. However, the impression from the context is that Papias was remembering a time when he could have heard about Jesus' words from followers of the lord's disciples, so that, after the deaths of the Twelve who had originally 'said' things, others (namely Aristion and the elder John) were still *saying* them. Thus there seems to have been another 'John' in play: a disciple, though not one of the Twelve, someone who could have written, and perhaps did write, a gospel. The list of disciples named by Papias looks similar, in other respects, to the lists in John 1.35–51 and John 21.2. It is a tantalizing prospect—and perhaps a bridge too far for any certain argument—that the elder John and Aristion might have been the two anonymous disciples referred to in John 21.2.

Papias's identification of the 'elder John' can also be correlated with the self-designation of the author in the second and third Johannine letters.[47] Assuming a close connection between the gospel of John and the letters of John, the clearest self-identification of the author is not as an 'apostle', but as an 'elder', and a 'witness' to the events of Jesus' life. While Papias and Eusebius both designate the 'elder John' to distinguish him from John the son of Zebedee,[48] the title may well have emerged as an honorific reference to his venerable age and longevity. He himself might have adopted it as a self-designation when writing his letters.[49]

---

[46] Papias § 3.3–4 (Eus. *Hist. Eccl.* 3.39.3–4) (tr. M. Holmes [2007]; italics and underlining added).
[47] 2 Jn. 1; 3 Jn. 1.
[48] Papias § 3.3–4 (Eus. *Hist. Eccl.* 3.39.4); § 3.14 (Eus. *Hist. Eccl.* 3.39.14).
[49] Bauckham 2006, 420–3.

Furthermore, when Irenaeus (and Polycarp upon whom Irenaeus appears to rely) refers to 'John', one of the 'Lord's disciples', as the author of the gospel, we do not necessarily need to assume that this would be John the son of Zebedee. John the son of Zebedee could indeed be called a 'disciple' and an 'apostle' interchangeably, and the author of John's gospel was frequently reckoned to be one of the twelve disciples. However, while Irenaeus calls John both 'the Lord's disciple' and an 'apostle',[50] he may mean by 'apostle' not 'one of the Twelve', but 'one of those who wrote down apostolic teaching' (similar to his reference to the apostles Peter, John, Matthew, and Paul in *Adv. Haer.* 3.21.3). Irenaeus's 'John' is distinguished as a prominent custodian of the apostolic tradition, whom Polycarp knew well. Nothing Irenaeus says about John as an 'apostle' compels us to think of John the son of Zebedee; nothing rules out the possibility that he is referring to a different John, perhaps indeed someone like John the elder.[51]

It is interesting (as with Sherlock Holmes's dog that didn't bark in the night) that sometimes John the evangelist is compared with the apostles but is not himself called an apostle. The Muratorian canon attributes the fourth gospel to John, 'one of the disciples', who is co-ordinated with his 'fellow disciples and bishops', and distinguished from Andrew, 'one of the apostles' who urged him to write.[52] This John would therefore have been a disciple of Jesus, but not a member of the Twelve. Bauckham considers this account to be an embroidered version dependent upon Papias, who distinguished John from the Twelve and claimed that his gospel was certified by local elders.[53] In addition, when Bishop Polycrates of Ephesus wrote to Bishop Victor of Rome in the late second century, he referred to 'Philip, one of the twelve apostles', who died in Hierapolis, and 'John, who was a witness and a teacher, who reclined at the side of the

Mosaic with Polycarp, second-century bishop of Smyrna
Public Domain

---

50 Iren. *Adv. Haer.* 1.9.2, 3; 2.22.5; 3.3.4; 3.5.1; 3.11.9; 3.21.3; Eus. *Hist. Eccl.* 5.24.16.
51 As to how the (mis-)identification of John the son of Zebedee with John the elder as author of the fourth gospel happened, Hengel (1989, 8) proposes that it took place first among gnosticizing Christians, while Bauckham (2006, 424–5; cf. Hengel 1989, 21, 31) conjectures that Eusebius deliberately suppressed Papias's testimony that John the elder wrote the fourth gospel, because he wanted to attribute the book of Revelation—a book he regarded as non-canonical—to a non-apostolic figure like John the elder. Perhaps, in addition, Eusebius also rejected Papias's solution to the differences between the order of the gospels (Papias had said that John wrote to fill in the gaps in the synoptics).
52 Muratorian canon § 10–14.
53 Bauckham 2006, 425–33.

Lord', and died in Ephesus.[54] This John, regarded by Polycrates as the most significant teacher in Asia, was identified as the beloved disciple. But he was not labelled an apostle.[55]

To identify John the elder with the beloved disciple makes sense of a lot of evidence. The gospel points us to someone who, though not one of the Twelve, claimed nonetheless to have been an eye-witness during Jesus' public career,[56] having formerly perhaps been a follower of John the Baptist,[57] perhaps even (like the Baptist himself) part of a priestly family, familiar with the high priest,[58] and being closely involved with Jesus' final days in Jerusalem.[59] Jesus requested that he look after his mother,[60] and together with Peter he discovered the empty tomb.[61] The author of the gospel is clearly familiar with the topography of Judea and Jerusalem,[62] and he has an intimate knowledge of Jewish customs and festivals.[63] The external and internal evidence dovetail nicely: the 'John' behind the gospel, we cautiously conclude, was probably John the elder, a Judean disciple of Jesus, not one of the Twelve.[64]

Most scholars have supposed that the fourth gospel reached its present form through several stages of composition and editing.[65] Chapter 21 looks very much like a secondary epilogue after an original 'conclusion' (Jn. 20.31), with a final

---

[54] Eus. *Hist. Eccl.* 5.24.2–3.
[55] Hengel 1989, 7; Bauckham 2006, 438–45.
[56] Jn. 1.14; 19.35; 21.24.
[57] Jn. 1.35–40. Andrew is one of the disciples to whom the Baptist witnesses, and an association between John and Andrew is also made in the Muratorian canon § 9, 14.
[58] Jn. 18.15–16. In a letter written by Bishop Polycrates of Ephesus (c. AD 189–98), John is also described as a 'priest wearing the high-priestly head-dress' (Eus. *Hist. Eccl.* 5.24.2). This could be no more than a way of expressing the priestly texture of the gospel of John, or else it might rehearse the memory of John's priestly lineage.
[59] Jn. 13.23–26.
[60] Jn. 19.26–27.
[61] Jn. 20.1–10; 21.7.
[62] See references to the village of Ephraim (Jn. 11.54), various Jerusalem sites like the pool at Bethesda near the sheep gate (Jn. 5.2), the treasury (Jn. 8.20), the pool of Siloam (Jn. 9.7), Solomon's Portico (Jn. 10.23), Caiaphas's house and the *praetorium* (Jn. 18.28). See Bauckham 2007, 95–100.
[63] This includes knowledge of the water used for purification rites (Jn. 2.6) and of rituals associated with the Feast of Tabernacles (Jn. 7.37–39) and Hanukkah (Jn. 10.22); he also frequently mentions Passover (Jn. 2.13, 23; 4.45; 6.4; 11.55; 12.1; 13.1; 18.28, 39; 19.14) and is aware of sectarian differences with Samaritans (Jn. 4.9, 22–23). See Keener 2003, 1.172–5.
[64] Not everyone is convinced. Morris, for example (1995, 21), claims: 'The trouble is that, for all its popularity in some circles, there is little evidence for the existence of John the Elder.'
[65] Brown (1966–70, 1.xxxiv–xxxix) envisages a process including: (1) the existence of a body of traditional material independent of the synoptic tradition about the words and works of Jesus, (2) developed over decades of preaching in the Johannine community, (3) then set out into a consecutive and cohesive gospel by a dominant theologian (4) which was edited by an anonymous evangelist, and then (5) given a final reworking by a subsequent redactor. Also, von Wahlde (2010, 1.50–5) postulates a gradual process of development and dissemination: (1) a first edition about the life, death, and resurrection of Jesus (AD 55–65); (2) a second edition which redacted the gospel in the light of conflict with official Judaism (AD 60–5); (3) an internal crisis within the community, leading to the composition of the Johannine letters (AD 65–70); (4) the death of the 'elder' (AD 80–90); and (5) a third edition which enshrined the elder's testimony as the beloved disciple and addressed new issues in the community (AD 90–5).

editorial comment (Jn. 21.24–25).[66] But there may have been much more editing and rearranging, too, though the frequently observed signs of awkward connections and dislocations could equally well be the result of an untidy original being left as it was. The best guess is that, while the 'beloved disciple', probably John the elder, is identified as the author and authority behind the gospel, the text as we have it comes through the work of one or more others. Some see the final editor as the 'evangelist', the one who selected, arranged, and supplemented the oral and written testimony of the beloved disciple himself.[67]

Date

The most decisive evidence for dating John's gospel is the John Rylands Papyrus 457, otherwise known as $\mathfrak{P}^{52}$. This is an Egyptian papyrus fragment containing the text of John 18.33–36, which is datable somewhere between AD 125 and 175. The gospel seems to have been used occasionally by Justin Martyr and the author of the *Epistle to Diognetus*, both writing in around AD 150–60.[68] Gnostic authors cited the gospel, and alluded to it, perhaps as early as AD 135.[69] Polycarp and Papias both quote from 1 John, indicating familiarity with Johannine writings in the early second century.[70] Ignatius of Antioch may have alluded to John's gospel in the second decade of the second century.[71] At the lower limit, many have put the gospel around or after AD 70, since John 21.18–19 appears to allude to Peter's martyrdom, which probably took place under Nero in the mid-60s. It used to be suggested that the book reflected sectarian debates between Jews and Christians in the post-Temple era, though it is now recognized that we know a lot less about the 'Synod of Jamnia' than used to be thought, and in fact the strongest evidence for sharp controversy between Jesus' followers and unbelieving Jews is from Paul's day.[72] If, as many suppose, John was dependent on the synoptic tradition, that might push us to a later date, but only if we could be more certain than we are about the dating of the

---

[66] See Hengel 1989, 94–6, 102–8; Keener 2003, 1.105–15; and esp. Baum 2012. For a recent argument about the authenticity and integrity of Jn. 21, see Porter 2015, 225–45.
[67] See e.g. Witherington 1995b, 18; 2006, 394–6. According to Bauckham (2006, 416 n. 9), an older generation of British scholarship thought that John the son of Zebedee was the beloved disciple, while John the elder was the author or evangelist responsible for writing the gospel. For an argument identifying John the son of Zebedee, the beloved disciple, and the evangelist, as the same person, see Carson 1991, 75–81.
[68] *Ep. Diog.* 6.3; 7.5; 11.2–5; Just. *1 Apol.* 61.4; *Dial.* 88.7; Justin's Logos christology is inexplicable without knowledge of Jn. 1.1–14, e.g. *Dial.* 61.1; *1 Apol.* 46.1–3, and Justin's disciple Tatian wrote a gospel harmony that made the fourth gospel the primary template for its chronology.
[69] See Hippolytus *Ref.* 7.22.4; 7.27 (Basilides); Iren. *Adv. Haer.* 1.8.5 (Ptolemy); 3.11.7 (Valentinians); Origen *Comm. Jn.* 6.2–3 (Heracleon); allusions and echoes in Valentinian writings such as the *Gospel of Truth*, *Gospel of Philip*, *Epistle of Reginos* (see Hengel 1989, 9, 146–7).
[70] Polycarp *Phil.* 7.1; Eus. *Hist. Eccl.* 3.39.17.
[71] Ign. *Rom.* 7.2; *Phld.* 7.1.
[72] For the older view, see Martyn 2009 [1968] for the older view of scholarship on the significance of Jamnia, and discussion in *NTPG* 161–3.

synoptics themselves. There is no strong evidence against the traditional date near the end of the century, either towards the end of Domitian's reign (AD 81–96) or at the beginning of Trajan's (AD 98–117).[73] But that double negative indicates the continuing uncertainty on the topic. Some have continued to argue that a much earlier date is possible and even preferable.[74]

Place of writing

So where was the gospel written? Early and unanimous tradition suggests Ephesus.[75] This might look more plausible if the references to being 'put out of the synagogue' were thought to reflect the abrasive experience that Christians sometimes had with the Jews of western Asia, though our evidence for first-century Christian–Jewish relations in most places is so thin that such judgments can never be very strong.[76] Belief in Jesus as the Messiah is treated as contentious in both the Johannine gospel and letters, but again the same could be said of Paul's work.[77] The letters of Ignatius may help, in that they, addressed to churches in western Asia, face the problem of Docetism (the belief that Jesus was not truly human, but only 'seemed' to be), and the Johannine letters face similar challenges—though again Docetism was popular in other places too.[78] If not Ephesus, then Egypt would be the next best option, since the gospel of John became very popular there among gnostic and proto-orthodox authors. All this simply shows how elusive the answer remains. Scholarship has swung wildly from hypotheses about a gnostic or Manichean context for the gospel (based upon John's supposed 'dualism' of light and darkness, and so on) to equally speculative suggestions about a possible Jewish context evidenced in the Qumran scrolls.

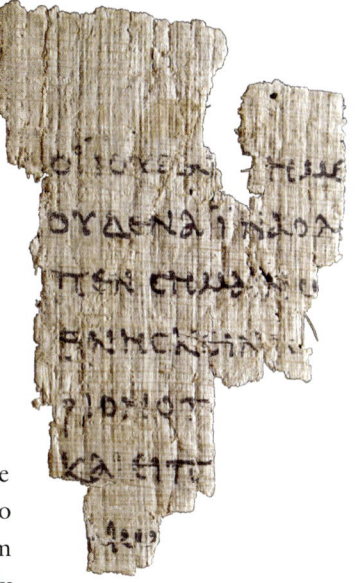

$\mathfrak{P}^{52}$, otherwise known as the John Rylands Papyrus, with the words of John 18.33–36; normally dated to AD 125–75
Reproduced by courtesy of the University librarian and director, The John Rylands University Library, The University of Manchester

But the contrasts of light and darkness, of flesh and spirit, and above all of life and death are not things that most people learn from books and recondite traditions. They are part of being human. The fourth gospel is obviously deeply familiar

---

73 Iren. *Adv. Haer.* 2.22.5; 3.3.4; Eus. *Hist. Eccl.* 3.23.1. Hengel (1989, 3) saw the upper limit as AD 110.
74 See Robinson 1976, 307, arguing for around AD 65.
75 Iren. *Adv. Haer.* 3.1.1; 3.3.4; Polycrates' letter to Victor (Eus. *Hist. Eccl.* 5.24.2–3); Clem. *Quis Div.* 42; *Acts of John* 18—19.
76 Jn. 9.22; 12.42; Rev. 2.9; 3; Ac. 6.9; 21.27–29; 24.19; Ign. *Phld.* 6.1; 8.2—9.2; *Magn.* 8.1–2.
77 Jn. 4.25–29; 7.25–31, 41–42; 9.22; 10.24; 20.31; 1 Jn. 2.22; 4.2; 5.2; 2 Jn. 7.
78 1 Jn. 4.2; 2 Jn. 7; Ign. *Trall.* 10.1; *Eph.* 7.2; *Smyrn.* 2.1; 3.1–3; 4.2; 5.2; 7.1; 12.2.

with a Judean environment and with Israel's scriptures. But it is written in the language and idiom of Diaspora Jews who knew their way around the intellectual currents of the hellenistic world. It has distant affinities with the Jewish worlds both of Qumran and of Philo of Alexandria.[79] But saying that is merely to say that it is a fairly typical product of the complex Jewish world of its time. Judgments about John's date, place, and cultural context must be made in the light of exegesis, not the other way round.

Purpose

Several purposes have been proposed for John's gospel. These include supplementing or superseding the synoptic gospels, arguing for the superiority of Jesus over John the Baptist, confronting the heresies of Docetism and Gnosticism, reinforcing group identity after the Johannine community was expelled from Jewish synagogues, and trying to evangelize Diaspora Jews. All these have some plausibility, but the book as we have it seems to far transcend such specific intentions. It is an altogether bigger thing.

On the surface, John's gospel gives us a clear purpose-statement at the end of the resurrection narrative: 'But these are written that you may believe that Jesus is the Messiah, the Son of God, and that by believing you may have life in his name.'[80] The words 'that you may believe' should perhaps say: 'that you may *come to believe*'; there is a difference of one letter in the Greek, and both readings are strongly attested in the manuscripts. So is the gospel designed to evoke faith or to confirm faith? The obvious answer is, both.[81] This is such a wide statement of purpose that all kinds of contexts might be suitable. John's story seeks to prove that Jesus has legitimate messianic credentials, while also staking the claim that he is the unique divine agent with an unprecedented unity with the father; making him both a fitting object of faith and a worthy recipient of worship. Nor are the stories of Jesus in this book simply 'illustrations' of an abstract point; the 'faith' to be elicited is that the Word became *flesh*, specifically the human flesh of this unique human being, doing these unique things.

This christology generates an ecclesiology, as John seeks to reinforce a particular form of group identity that construes Messiah-believers as God's children, the true worshippers, those of the light, his sheep, who have vexatiously been labelled as schismatics or apostates by their fellow-Jews. This explains why, in the course of the narrative, Jesus' messianic identity is so disputed, and why, the more clearly Jesus is

---

79 See Keener 2003, 1.172–232 for a general description of the Jewish background to John; Bauckham 2007, 125–36 on comparing John and Qumran; and Borgen 2014, 43–66, 79–99 on John and Philo/hellenistic Judaism.
80 Jn. 20.31.
81 Bird 2012b, 135–7.

identified with God, the more ferocious the opposition against him becomes. Consequently, for John's implied audience, the more hostile their rejection by the synagogue or 'the world', the surer they can be of their election, of their chosen-ness by God. Again, we note that much of this could be said about Paul's work; or about the context of 1 Peter; or about Matthew. All we are really saying is that all these works, and John's gospel among them, are central to and typical of the turbulent world of the first-century church.

John's gospel, then, is a masterpiece of evangelistic proclamation and intra-Jewish apologetics, deeply rooted in Israel's scriptures, witnessing to Jesus' identity as the divine Messiah and claiming that his followers, gentile as well as Jewish, were the legitimate heirs of Israel's heritage and promises. This accounts for the evangelist's emphasis on showing that Jesus is Israel's Messiah,[82] in whom God's presence is enfleshed and who bridges the heaven–earth divide,[83] who embodies God's grace, glory, and truth,[84] whose actions fulfil the words of scripture,[85] and who brings the fullness of God's gift of life to those who believe.[86] Along the way, the author clarifies Jesus' relationship to Israel's patriarchs,[87] to its various rituals, institutions, and festivals,[88] and to the Mosaic law.[89] M. M. Thompson infers from all this that the 'consistency and intensity of this line of argument may suggest that the Gospel serves to exhort, encourage, and persuade readers for whom the symbols and reality of Scripture and Judaism exerted a powerful pull'.[90] Perhaps we should add that if there were any readers for whom Israel's scriptures did *not* exert such a pull, the fourth gospel was designed to put them straight. John, no less than Paul, insists that the gospel of Jesus is to be understood 'according to the scriptures'.

JOHN'S STORY OF JESUS

(See box: 'Outline of John'.)

1. Prologue (1.1–18)

The prologue functions like an overture to an opera. It tells the story from creation to new creation; from covenant to new covenant. It introduces the

> **OUTLINE OF JOHN**
>
> 1. Prologue (1.1–18)
> 2. The book of signs (1.19—12.50)
> 3. The book of glory (13.1—20.31)
> 4. Epilogue (21.1–25)

---

[82] Jn. 1.41; 4.25–29; 7.25–31, 41–42; 9.22; 10.24; 11.27; 12.34, 42; 17.3; 20.31.
[83] Jn. 1.14, 51.
[84] Jn. 1.14, 17; 14.6, 13; 17.5, 24.
[85] Jn. 12.38; 13.18; 15.25; 17.12; 19.24, 28, 36.
[86] Jn. 1.4; 2.10; 3.15–16, 36; 4.14; 5.21–40; 6.26–71; 10.10–17, 28; 11.25; 15.13; 17.2–3; 20.31.
[87] Jn. 4.12; 6.32; 8.53–54.
[88] Jn. 2.1–11, 19–22; 4.21–24; 6.32–41; 7.37–39; 10.36.
[89] Jn. 1.17; 5.39–40, 45–47; 7.19–23.
[90] Thompson 2015, 19.

main motifs in the drama that are about to unfold: Jesus is God's light and life, the supreme manifestation of divine glory, grace, and truth, evoking also the divine Word and its human witnesses. John draws together the story of creation ('In the beginning') and Israel's election ('he came to his own'), with Israel's Temple as the location of the divine presence ('glory' and 'dwelling among us'), and Israel's covenant charter

PORTALS AND PARALLELS: WISDOM DWELLS ON EARTH

Jewish authors could picture Wisdom, the personified word of YHWH, looking to dwell among the people but struggling to find a place, until she took up residence in Israel (see Prov. 8.22–31; Wis. 8.4; 9.9). According to Sirach, the figure of Wisdom comes to dwell permanently among humans, specifically in the Temple at Jerusalem, depositing the divine word and divine glory in Israel's midst. However, in 1 Enoch, *the picture is darker: Wisdom had been trying to find somewhere to live, but finding none, she went back home. In her absence Iniquity went out and found somewhere to dwell, and turned what should have been Wisdom's home into a den of iniquity. Consequently, there is now no hope for the world, or Israel, or individual humans. John's development of this same theme is of a different order altogether. He agrees with Sirach that the divine Wisdom does indeed find a home. He recognizes, and takes on board, the tragedy that lies behind* 1 Enoch 42: *the world did not know the* logos, *its creator, and even 'his own people did not receive him'. But this did not make him return home, having abandoned the world to 'iniquity'. The light shines in the darkness, and the darkness did not overcome it. The* logos *has come, as mainstream Judaism fully expected, not to judge the world but to redeem it. But instead of Shekinah and Torah, the Jerusalem Temple and the covenant code, as the places where Wisdom/*logos *dwells and reveals the divine glory, John says that the* logos *became flesh, became a human being, became Jesus of Nazareth.*

Sirach 24.1–12
Wisdom praises herself, and tells of her glory in the midst of her people. In the assembly of the Most High she opens her mouth, and in the presence of his hosts she tells of her glory: 'I came forth from the mouth of the Most High, and covered the earth like a mist. I dwelt in the highest heavens, and my throne was in a pillar of cloud. Alone I compassed the vault of heaven and traversed the depths of the abyss. Over waves of the sea, over all the earth, and over every people and nation I have held sway. Among all these I sought a resting-place; in whose territory should I abide? Then the Creator of all things gave me a command, and my Creator chose the place for my tent. He said, "Make your dwelling in Jacob, and in Israel receive your inheritance." Before the ages, in the beginning, he created me, and for all the ages I shall not cease to be. In the holy tent I ministered before him, and so I was established in Zion. Thus in the beloved city he gave me a resting-place, and in Jerusalem was my domain. I took root in an honored people, in the portion of the Lord, his heritage.' (NRSV)

1 Enoch 42.1–3
Wisdom could not find a place in which she could dwell; but a place was found (for her) in the heavens. Then Wisdom went out to dwell with the children of the people, but she found no dwelling place. (So) Wisdom returned to her place and she settled permanently among the angels. Then Iniquity went out of her rooms, and found whom she did not expect. And she dwelt with them, like rain in a desert, like dew on a thirsty land. (*OTP*)

('law given through Moses'). The back story is that God called Israel to be the means of rescuing the world, so that he might one day rescue the world *by becoming Israel in the person of its representative Messiah*. Thus, in the prologue, God's promise to dwell with his people and to rescue them from the darkness takes place through the sending of the divine Word into the world, into the human flesh of the true Image; and when the Word is received, it begets new children. The tragedy is that the Word has been resisted by Israel ('he came to his own, and his own did not receive him'). But God's new Temple has been built in the person of Jesus and through the work of the spirit. As in Revelation's picture of the new Jerusalem (21.3), the dwelling of God is with humans. John has often been misread as though it was telling humans how to leave the present world and get to heaven. In reality, it is explaining how heaven itself, in the person of its Lord, came to dwell among us; how the one through whom all things were made came to rescue and renew that created world.

So John describes the coming of the Word into the world, bringing with it life and light (1.1–4). John the Baptist witnessed to the light (1.6–8), the light which evoked the twofold response of either unbelief or belief (1.9–13). Finally, the Word entered human existence as the 'only begotten son' of God the father (1.14–18). This gives the reader the signal that the 'son of God' in the rest of the narrative, while being a recognizable designation for the Messiah, was now also to be understood in terms of the eternal Word through whom all things were made.

The climax, then, is obviously verse 14: 'the Word became flesh'. Much like Wisdom in traditions associated with that concept (see 'Portals and parallels: Wisdom dwells on earth'), the pre-existent Word 'tabernacled' or 'pitched his tent' in the very creation that he helped bring into existence. The startling implication is that all prior forms of divine presence were either transitory or preparatory: the Word-made-flesh is a unique mode of divine disclosure, the climactic manifestation of God's covenant favour (grace) and of divine testimony (truth).[91] The story the prologue tells is thus the story of the whole gospel in miniature. This is the story of Jesus *told as* the true and redeeming story of Israel, *told as* the true and redeeming story of the creator and the cosmos.

2. The book of signs (1.19—12.50)

The first main section of the gospel is sometimes referred to as 'the book of signs' because of the sequence of 'signs' which John himself flags up as he introduces the first two (2.11; 4.54). John seems, with these, to be hinting at a longer sequence, which most assume will mean seven, but opinions differ as to which incidents in the subsequent narrative should be seen as the remaining five. There is a lot to be said for seeing the raising of Lazarus (11.1–45) as the seventh, which might suggest that

---

[91] Morris 1995, 92.

the third is the healing of the crippled man (5.2–16), the fourth the feeding of the five thousand (6.1–15), the fifth the walking on water (6.16–21), and the sixth the healing of the man born blind (9.1–7). On balance, however, we prefer the perhaps bolder move of seeing Jesus' crucifixion itself as the seventh sign, with the raising of Lazarus as the sixth, omitting the walking on water which, though obviously significant in various ways, does not stand out in the same way in John's narrative. The point of the 'signs', as John says at 2.11, is that they reveal Jesus' glory and elicit faith. For John, this is supremely true of the crucifixion.

The 'signs', however, are thereby doing the job which John assigns first and foremost to John the Baptist, namely, pointing to Jesus and starting to explain his significance. John, already mentioned in the prologue, is brought on stage at once in 1.19, claiming to be neither the Messiah nor the new Elijah (Mal. 4.6), nor yet the coming 'prophet' (Dt. 18.15), but simply the 'voice' of Isaiah 40.1–8; in other words, the one who prepares the way for God himself to return in glory (1.19–28).

John declares that Jesus is the 'Lamb of God who takes away the sin of the world',[92] combining the images of the Passover lamb and Isaiah's 'suffering servant'.[93] John, having seen the spirit descend on Jesus, testifies that he is the 'son of God', signifying both Jesus' messianic identity and his unique filial relationship with Israel's God—and perhaps that these two things were always designed to merge into one (1.29–34). This leads two of John's disciples (Andrew and Simon) to follow Jesus, with Jesus renaming Simon as 'Cephas', the Aramaic word for 'rock', corresponding to the Greek *petros*. When Jesus then calls more disciples, including Philip and Nathanael, he promises the latter that he will see heaven opened, and 'the angels of God ascending and descending on the Son of Man'.[94] This heaven-and-earth commerce, echoing Jacob's ladder in Genesis 28.10–17, is a Temple-idea, picking up from 1.14 and looking ahead to 2.21 and beyond: where Jesus is, there the living God is 'tabernacling' with his people (1.35–51).

The Jews used stone jars because they were believed to be unable to contract impurities, and the water was used for ceremonial washing of hands and utensils.
© 2018 by Zondervan

---

92 Jn. 1.29.
93 Ex. 12.1–11; Isa. 53.4–12.
94 Jn. 1.51.

At a wedding in Cana, Jesus performs his first 'sign' (*sēmeion*), turning water into wine at his mother's request. The story resonates with the promises of divine generosity and plenty in the messianic age.[95] Other overtones abound: the six jars used for Jewish ceremonial washing are transformed into wine-flagons, and the master of ceremonies comments that the best wine has only now appeared. All this points to Jesus' renewal and transformation of the Jewish world, revealing Jesus' glory and evoking the disciples' faith (2.1–11).

The next scene reaches the same conclusion by a startlingly different route. In Jerusalem for Passover (the first of three Passovers in this gospel), Jesus drives out money-changers, traders, and animals from the Temple courtyards—the famous scene which in the synoptic gospels comes towards the end of the story. Jesus' explanation is stark: the Temple is to be destroyed and rebuilt (2.19). This saying reappears in various forms in Jesus' trial in the synoptics;[96] John insists that it refers primarily to Jesus' own death and resurrection, the 'Temple' being his own body (as we were already learning from 1.14 and elsewhere). Herod the Great had begun to rebuild the Temple, as a way of claiming royal status. Now, forty-six years later, one of his sons was completing it. Jesus, however, is the royal reality to which the Temple itself points. His death and resurrection will be the ultimate Passover.

John's story then broadens out into three extended scenes in which, in contrast again to the synoptics, Jesus engages in complex conversations: in chapter 3, with Nicodemus; in chapter 4, with a Samaritan woman; and, in chapter 5, with a crippled man, and then with bystanders who observe his healing.

Nicodemus, coming at night, is told about the new birth that Jesus is offering. The Jewish world knew the importance of being born into Abraham's family; Jesus is claiming that a new kind of 'birth' is now both necessary and, by the spirit, possible. It will be achieved through the 'lifting up' of the 'son of man' (3.14)—combining the echo of 1.51 with an allusion to the 'exaltation' of 'one like a son of man' in Daniel 7.13, and pointing thereby to a major theme of the gospel. This will unveil the greatest Johannine theme of all, the breathtaking scope of God's love (3.16). There is no break in the text to indicate that John, rather than Jesus, is speaking in 3.13–21; this is typical of the gospel as a whole, and many interpretations are possible. The same is true of the meditation (3.31–36) that follows the little scene about John the Baptist and his disciples (3.22–30), emphasizing again that John must not be mistaken for the Messiah himself. Only in Jesus is there found the 'life' of God's new age (3.36).

The personal challenge to Nicodemus, framing so many theological themes, is echoed in the very different personal challenge to the Samaritan woman.

---

[95] Lincoln 2005, 125.
[96] Mk. 14.58; 15.29.

Despite centuries of deep mutual suspicion between Jews and Samaritans, and despite the alarm-bells that would ring at a man being alone with an unattended woman, Jesus asks the woman for a drink from Jacob's well (4.1–42). Another Johannine theme is thereby introduced: water, the water of life promised here and in 7.37–38. In a teasing dialogue, Jesus questions her about her husband, then revealing that he knows about her sad and chequered past. She changes the subject—right into what we now know to be a central Johannine theme: Jews worship in Jerusalem, Samaritans on Mount Gerizim, but Jesus is doing something new that will upstage both. His prophetic knowledge convinces her that he is the long-awaited Messiah, and she eagerly tells her fellow-Samaritans that he is the 'Saviour of the world'.[97] Jesus then travels north again to Galilee, healing the son of a royal official by a word from a distance (4.43–54).

If chapter 3 emphasized the new birth (over against ordinary Abrahamic descent), and chapter 4 the new worship (over against the Jerusalem Temple), chapter 5 emphasizes the new age itself, the reality towards which the weekly sabbaths had long pointed. (Many Jewish teachers then and now have seen the sabbath as the anticipation of the age to come.) Jesus heals a paralysed man, instructing him to pick up his mat and walk; but the Judeans object, because it is the sabbath. Jesus' response, developed in another extended discourse, implies that the age to come is already here, the age to which Moses pointed but which he could not deliver, the age which would issue in resurrection itself (5.25–26).

The longest discourse so far accompanies the next 'sign': the feeding of the five thousand, echoing the wilderness feeding of Israel after the exodus. This stirs up the possibility that the crowd might try to make Jesus king in the wrong way (6.15), and he retreats up the mountain while the disciples set sail across the lake. The storm that follows sets the scene for Jesus' YHWH-like powers, striding over the sea and bringing them safe to shore. The crowds are confused, but Jesus insists that they should look beyond his provision of ordinary bread to the reality which he embodies in himself. The language is stark: they must eat Jesus' flesh and drink his blood![98] This would sound preposterous, even to those who might hear the echo of 2 Samuel 23.17. Most would now say that John intends us to hear echoes of the eucharist (6.32–59). It is indeed a 'hard saying' but, as Peter insists, Jesus has the words of 'eternal life', the life of the age to come which is already breaking in.[99]

John has now firmly linked Jesus' work with Passover; he now has Jesus also fulfilling the Feast of Tabernacles. This agricultural festival involved the lighting of lamps and processions, ending with the pouring out of water and wine in the Temple, commemorating the divine provision of water in the wilderness. Jesus' presence

---

[97] Jn. 4.42.
[98] Jn. 6.53–54.
[99] Jn. 6.68.

and teaching confuse the crowds and the authorities, but he declares (echoing Isa. 55.1) that thirsty people should come and drink—from him. As before (4.10–15), he is offering living water, like the water flowing from the Temple in Ezekiel's vision (47.1–12; also Zech. 14.8). John interprets this in a stark phrase: the spirit wasn't available yet (literally 'there was not yet spirit') because Jesus was not yet 'glorified'. In other words, Jesus' ultimate 'glorification' on the cross would effect the necessary purification of human beings so that the living divine presence could dwell within them—and, what's more, flow through them to the world around.

At this point the narrative flow is sharply broken by the story of 'the woman caught in adultery'—or, better perhaps, the men caught in hypocrisy (Jn. 7.53—8.11). The earliest manuscripts omit the passage, and some later ones place it at different points in John and even in Luke. This doesn't mean it didn't happen; it might be that the story was thought so radical that some early scribes left it out. Its present placing has the effect that John 8 starts with Jesus protecting a woman from being stoned and ends with Jesus himself having to escape stoning. It focuses on the powerful mercy which triumphs over the negative judgment of the law, as resurrection-life triumphs over death—without slackening the moral demand ('from now on don't sin again', 8.11 *NTE/KNT*), while highlighting Jesus' condemnation of those who presumed to judge but were themselves just as sinful (8.9).

We should then read John 8.12–59 as a continuation of the previous conflict between Jesus and the Judean leaders at the Feast of Tabernacles. This section is bracketed by two great 'I am' statements ('I am the light of the world' and 'before Abraham was born, I am') (see Table 27.1). This section contains further disclosures by Jesus of his sent-ness from the father; the polemic both ways ratchets up in intensity.

TABLE 27.1: THE 'I AM' SAYINGS IN JOHN'S GOSPEL

I am the bread of life	6.35, 41, 48
I am the light of the world	8.12; 9.5
I am the sheep gate	10.7, 9
I am the good shepherd	10.11, 14
I am the resurrection and the life	11.25
I am the way, the truth, and the life	14.6
I am the true vine	15.1
Absolute 'I am' statements	4.26; 6.20; 8.24, 28, 58; 13.19; 18.5–8

Steps down to the Pool of Siloam
Public Domain

The Pharisees, dismissing and condemning Jesus, are in fact accusing the father who sent him, proving despite themselves that they are indeed walking in darkness. This is one of the sharpest depictions in the gospel of the fact that 'he came to what was his own, and his own people did not accept him' (1.11 *NTE/KNT*). God the father is seeking Jesus' honour, and will vindicate him, proving that he is in fact the fulfilment of the divine promise to Abraham himself.

Having already claimed to be 'the light of the world', Jesus then puts this into dramatic effect by healing a man born blind (9.1–41). Again this happened on the sabbath, generating further controversy between the Pharisees and the newly sighted man, and also his parents, who were drawn into the discussion. The man sticks to his story, and is thrown out of the synagogue for his pains. But this, like so much in John, is ironic: if Jesus is the light of the world (see 8.12; 9.5), then it is his opponents who are outside in the dark.

People often think of what follows, with Jesus' claim to be the 'good shepherd', as almost a pastoral interlude: a placid scene with Jesus surrounded by calm sheep. In fact the statement was as dangerous a claim as Jesus could have made. 'Shepherd' was a regular image for 'king', and when Jesus declares that all his predecessors were thieves and robbers he presumably indicates at least the Hasmonean dynasty (alluded to from the fact that this takes place at Hanukkah, commemorating the rededication of the Temple in 184 BC) and, more specifically, the House of Herod. Jesus' kingship will be radically different, characterized by his self-giving death. That is how he will not only rescue Israel but also 'other sheep' from further afield—a hint of the coming gentile mission (see 'Blast from the past: Clement of Alexandria on Jesus as the good shepherd').[100]

As the claim to kingship and a worldwide rescuing rule becomes more explicit, so too does Jesus' statement about his own identity: 'I and the Father are one' (10.30). He is the true Temple, the place where God and his people meet as one. Perhaps we should put it the other way: in the light of John's gospel, we ought to say that the Temple itself gained its meaning, in advance as it were, from God's intention to come in person as the heaven-and-earth person, the incarnate son.

---

[100] Jn. 10.16.

John's account of Jesus' public career reaches its dramatic climax in the raising of Lazarus from the dead (11.1–55). Jesus sees Lazarus's serious sickness as the opportunity for God to be glorified, and appears deliberately to delay going to help until it is, in human terms, too late. Lazarus has been dead for four days; his grieving sisters Martha and Mary meet Jesus with a mixture of lament and complaint. Martha recognizes that Lazarus *will* rise again in the final resurrection, but the point of John's whole story is that Jesus is bringing the promised future into the present: 'I am the resurrection and the life.' This leads Martha to confess that Jesus himself is 'the Messiah, the Son of God',[101] which is what the evangelist regards as the true faith (20.31). Jesus' strange delay is then explained: he has prayed that God would bring Lazarus back to life, and when the tomb is opened—despite Martha's protests that the flesh would already be rotting—he knows his prayer has been heard. John is looking forward, and is suggesting that Jesus too is looking forward, to Easter itself.

The Jewish leaders then worry that Jesus' deeds will create a tumult which will force the Romans to eradicate their local leadership and perhaps even the nation itself. Caiaphas, the high priest, utters a statement dripping with Johannine irony: it is better for one man to die than for the whole nation to perish. Yes, says John: as high priest, he prophesied that Jesus would die for God's people and also for the dispersed children of God—Diaspora Jews, certainly, but, in John's terms, the whole of humanity. This two-level scene—the politicians anxiously plotting a judicial murder, and John interpreting it as a divine prophecy—brings John's slow build-up on

> **BLAST FROM THE PAST: CLEMENT OF ALEXANDRIA ON JESUS AS THE GOOD SHEPHERD**
>
> *Clement of Alexandria (c. AD 150–215) was a well-educated convert to Christianity, thoroughly steeped in Greek philosophy, who eventually became a leading theologian in the catechetical school of Alexandria. Commenting on John 10, he said:*
>
> In our sickness we need a Saviour, in our wanderings a guide, in our blindness someone to show us the light, in our thirst the fountain of living water that quenches forever the thirst of those who drink from it. We dead people need life, we sheep need a shepherd, we children need a teacher, the whole world needs Jesus! (Clem. *Paed.* 1.9.83)
>
> Clement of Alexandria

---

[101] Jn. 11.25–27.

The Gospel according to John

the meaning of Jesus' death towards its climax. From the very beginning he has told us that Jesus is the lamb of God (1.29, 36). Jesus has spoken of his own death and resurrection in terms of the destruction and rebuilding of the Temple (2.19–21). He has declared that the son of man is to be 'lifted up', so that anyone who believes in him can have eternal life (3.14–15). He has spoken of giving his own flesh for the life of the world (6.51), and of the shepherd giving his life for the sheep (10.15–18). At the same time, we have seen the build-up of hostility towards Jesus, especially among the Judean leaders. Several times they have wanted to arrest him; sometimes, even, to stone him. Now the whole picture comes together. Jesus' sense of vocation, on the one hand, meets the leaders' political calculation on the other.

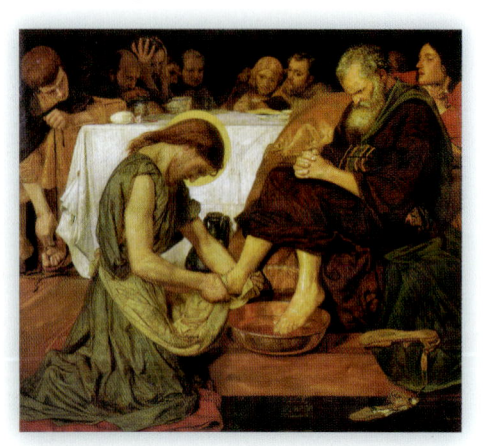

Ford Madox Brown's painting of *Jesus Washing Peter's Feet*, 1893, Tate Gallery, London
Public Domain

Jesus returns to Bethany, and then to Jerusalem, for his ultimate Passover. Mary anoints him with expensive perfume, revealing (at least in John's mind) her own perception of his coming fate. Judas objects; this, too, anticipates what is to come (12.1–11, looking ahead to Judas's betrayal in chs. 13, 18). Jesus enters Jerusalem with pilgrims celebrating his apparently royal arrival. But time is short: the 'hour' is at hand (another Johannine theme reaching its climax), and at last the 'son of man' is to be glorified. Only through this will the dark powers that have ruled the world be overthrown; only so, then, will the Greeks who come looking for Jesus be drawn to him (12.20–34). Jesus describes his forthcoming death as a kernel of wheat falling to the ground and dying, but reaping a great harvest. As Carson comments: 'Like the seed whose death is the germination of life for a great crop, so Jesus' death generates a plentiful harvest. The seed is thereby vindicated; the Son is thereby glorified.'[102] For the moment, though, the battle between darkness and light continues, with Jesus' hearers challenged to embrace the latter and spurn the former (12.35–50).

3. The book of glory (13.1—20.31)

The second half of the book opens with a solemn statement: having loved his own in the world, Jesus now loved them 'right through to the end' (13.1 *NTE/KNT*). There was nothing that love could do for them that he did not do. The most immediate outworking of this is that, after supper (John, unlike the synoptics,

---

[102] Carson 1991, 438.

does not describe the meal itself), Jesus does the slave's job of washing the disciples' feet. Like so much in the gospel, this action carries its own meaning—the example of humble service—and also resonates with the larger theme. John's description of the scene in verses 3–5 is almost as theologically explicit as Philippians 2.6–8:

> Jesus knew that the father had given everything into his hands, and that he had come from God and was going to God. So he got up from the supper-table, took off his clothes, and wrapped a towel around himself. Then he poured water into a bowl and began to wash the disciples' feet . . .[103]

Jesus would 'cleanse' his followers by his coming death, thereby bequeathing them the sign of recognition for all his followers: humble, suffering love. The scene is the more poignant in that Judas is heading off into the night to betray Jesus (13.30), and Peter, though he does not realize it, is about to deny him (13.18–38). The power of darkness is closing in, but Jesus is meeting it with love, and even joy. Chapter 13 thus introduces both the continuing scene in the upper room and, with that, the story of the trial and crucifixion that follows.

John 14—16 is, in fact, Jesus's farewell address to his disciples, similar in genre and function to other 'testament' speeches in Jewish literature.[104] The whole thing, as we would expect from John, has the flavour of the Temple, where the one God comes to dwell with his people: the discourse is all about (1) the way in which the father is acting in Jesus and (2) the way in which the spirit (the *paraclete* or 'advocate') will indwell the disciples to bind them into that same divine-human fellowship. Jesus is to 'go away' and 'return', but they

> 'God is the Father who is the source of life. Jesus, the Son of the Father, confers God's life but, even more, is God's life-giving Word embodied in the flesh for the life of the world. The Spirit of God is the power of life and the agency through which life is received. To a large extent, then, John sketches the identity of God through what God does and, even more specifically, primarily through the various ways in which God gives life through the Son and the Spirit.'
>
> Marianne Meye Thompson, *The God of the Gospel of John*, 229.

are the branches in the vine (an obvious Israel-image). That is the framework for the disciples' own joyful new life, including the life of prayer. They eventually understand enough to say: 'we believe that you came from God.'[105]

This then sets the scene for Jesus' so-called 'high-priestly' prayer in chapter 17. With 'the world' (creation organizing itself in rebellion against its creator) closing in and threatening, Jesus comes to the father with his people on his heart, praying for their protection, their sanctification, and above all for their unity (17.1–26).

---

103 Jn. 13.3–5 *NTE/KNT*.
104 See e.g. Gen. 49; Josh. 23—24; 1 Chron. 28—29; Ac. 20.18—35; *2 Bar.* 31—34.
105 Jn. 16.30 NRSV.

Antonio Ciseri, *Ecce Homo*, 1871, Gallery of Modern Art, Florence, Italy
Public Domain

The mood changes as Jesus and the disciples depart for the Kidron valley, where Jesus knows Judas will lead the soldiers to arrest him. John's Jesus retains the initiative throughout, telling them 'I am'—apparently, the divine name!—when the troops say who it is they are looking for. As Lincoln states:

> The ultimate powerlessness of the massed representatives of this world's powers—the Roman forces, the Jewish guards and the disciple turned betrayer—is revealed, as they have to retreat and prostrate themselves in the presence of the unique divine agent who is one with God.[106]

Jesus is taken to Annas, the former high priest and father-in-law of the current high priest. In case we don't see the point, John reminds us what Caiaphas had said back in 11.49–50: it is good for one man to die for the people (18.1–14).

Thanks to 'another disciple' (regularly supposed to be 'the beloved disciple'), Peter is able to gain entrance to the high priest's courtyard, though he is soon recognized as one of Jesus' disciples. John skips briefly over the proceedings before the

---

[106] Lincoln 2005, 445.

Jewish authorities, and brings Jesus face to face with the Roman governor, Pontius Pilate. He and Jesus then argue about kingdom, truth, and power, where Jesus, acknowledging that he is claiming some kind of kingship, insists that his kingdom is not the sort that grows in this world. His kingdom is certainly *for* this world, but it isn't *from* it. It comes from somewhere else—in other words, from above, from heaven, from God (18.36). The crowd, shouting down Pilate's protestations, demands that Barabbas be released and Jesus crucified (18.28–40); Barabbas, says John laconically, was a brigand (18.40). The Judeans have opted for the normal kind of kingship. Jesus, going to his death, will embody the true version.

Pilate has Jesus flogged and mocked, presenting him to the crowd with the pregnant words 'Here's the man'—with John, looking back to the prologue, seeing Jesus as the truly human one, the ultimate image of the creator (19.5). The people continue to push Pilate into a corner: if he lets Jesus go, he is no friend of Caesar.[107] Pilate hands Jesus over to be crucified (19.1–16a).

John's crucifixion scene is noticeably different from the accounts in the synoptics. No Simon of Cyrene; no mockery from bystanders; no cry of abandonment; no midday darkness; no tearing of the Temple curtain; no centurion's acclamation. Many details, however, remain: the crucifixion itself, soldiers casting lots for Jesus' clothes, Jesus offered wine vinegar. John adds further points: the dispute between Pilate and the Judean leaders over the trilingual title on the cross; the scriptural citations (Pss. 22.18; 69.21; Ex. 12.46/Num. 9.12; Zech. 12.10); the presence of Mary wife of Clopas; the exchange between Jesus and his mother; the breaking of the legs of the brigands on either side; the Roman soldier's spear-thrust into Jesus' torso, and the resultant outflowing of water and blood, showing that Jesus was already thoroughly dead. Jesus' final word in John, *tetelestai*, 'it's all done' or 'it's finished', echoes the creation story itself: God 'finished' his work on the sixth day, and rested on the seventh. The incarnate son of God does the same.

The beloved disciple adds his own testimony: 'The man who saw it has given testimony, and his testimony is true. He knows that he tells the truth, and he testifies so that you also may believe.'[108] Scripture has been fulfilled. Jesus has completed the father's plan. The true Passover has taken place, and the lamb of God has borne the sins of the world (19.16b–37). Jesus is buried by Joseph of Arimathea, a secret disciple, and Nicodemus, who had earlier visited Jesus by night (19.38–42).

Mary Magdalene is not mentioned in John's gospel until she appears, with the other Marys, at the foot of the cross. Early on the first day of the week she discovers the empty tomb and runs to tell Simon Peter and the beloved disciple, who themselves run to see what has happened. The latter 'saw and believed', but neither fully

---

[107] Jn. 19.12.
[108] Jn. 19.35.

understood what it meant. Mary was then the first to see the risen Jesus, and became 'the apostle to the apostles', the first to be instructed to tell others that he had risen and was going to the father (20.1–18).

John begins the resurrection story with 'On the first day of the week', and he repeats that now in verse 19, his account of what happened that evening. For John, Jesus' resurrection is the start of God's new creation, now that the anti-creation powers of darkness have done their worst and been overthrown. Jesus then commissions the disciples for their global mission, rooted in his own and energized by his spirit. The disciples become new-Temple people, those in whom the living God comes to dwell.[109] That is why they will now pronounce God's forgiveness—and also, worryingly, God's 'retaining' of impenitent sins. They must warn the world that sin is a serious, deadly disease, and that to remain in it will bring death.

> 'The model and ground of the church's mission is what Jesus did and spoke in the world. The purpose of Jesus' appearance to his disciples is not only to show himself alive, but to send them into the world to continue the work of building up his community by witnessing to the truth (18:37), by delivering the world from eternal destruction (3:16–17), and by giving divine life in abundance (10:10). Jesus' community is sent to bring "other sheep" into his sheep-fold (10:16) so that unity and love may be communicated to the world (13:34–35; 17:21). There is no difference between God sending his Son and the Son sending his newly founded community into the world.'
>
> Jey Kanagaraj, *John*, 199.

All this comes into special focus in the story of Thomas. Thomas was the dour, dogged disciple, who suggested they might as well go with Jesus, if only to die with him (11.16), who complained that Jesus hadn't made things anything like clear enough (14.5), and who just happened to be somewhere else on the first Easter day. He sees the others excited, elated, unable to contain their joy. But he's not convinced. Finally, though, he sees Jesus for himself, making the memorable confession, 'My Lord and my God!'[110] Thomas's personal story illustrates the true faith that embraces the gospel testimony to Jesus (20.24–29).

John is working towards his conclusion. Jesus, he says, did many other signs which are not written here; but these are written to enable you to believe (or perhaps to continue to believe—there is uncertainty whether this is 'first-time faith' or not) that 'the Messiah, the son of God, is Jesus'. Most translations put that the other way round; but this follows the Greek syntax, and corresponds closely to the end of chapter 1 where Philip tells Nathanael that 'we have found the one Moses and the prophets wrote about—and it's Jesus of Nazareth'. It isn't so much that they are starting with Jesus and finding something to say about him. They are starting with the hope of Israel (see 4.22) and seeing that hope fulfilled *and radically transformed*

---

[109] Jn. 20.21–22. On resolving the conflicting chronology between Jn. 20 and Ac. 2 about the disciples receiving the spirit, see discussion in Carson 1991, 649–55.
[110] Jn. 20.28.

through him and his death and resurrection. Bringing these things together—Israel's Messiahship as the embodiment of Israel's returning God, and all this predicated of Jesus himself—constitutes the faith which is the sure sign that the believer already possesses 'life' (20.31).

4. Epilogue (21.1–25)

It looks as if the book should finish at 20.31, but it does not. Someone, whether the original author or a close friend, has added a final powerful, poignant scene. Some of Jesus' followers are fishing in the Sea of Galilee. A stranger on the shore enquires as to their progress, and tells them to cast their net on the right side of the vessel. They do so, and take in a huge haul of fish—a scene reminding them of their original calling (see Lk. 5). They come to shore; Jesus is cooking breakfast. 'None of the disciples dared ask him, "Who are you?"', says John, since they knew it was Jesus himself. That sentence remains profoundly strange: you don't ask someone 'Who are you?' when you've been with them for three years. The risen Jesus was somehow different—which is well explained by Paul in Romans 6: Jesus had gone through death and out the other side. He was no longer 'mortal'. Still human, still bodily; but with a body that belonged to the new creation, even though it was standing there, confusingly, in the midst of the old.

Jesus then confronts Peter—it seems that they walked away from the others—by asking him three times, 'Simon son of John, do you truly love me?' Jesus uses the word *agapaō*, the word he reserves for the ultimate depth of self-giving love. Peter responds with *phileō*, the word of friendship: it looks as though Peter can't bring himself (after what had happened) to affirm the full, dangerous love which Jesus himself had embodied. But on the third time Jesus switches, and uses Peter's word: Simon, son of John, *are you my friend?* Peter is upset at this, John says, but to each answer Jesus responds with fresh commissioning: feed my lambs, look after my sheep, feed my sheep. Somehow, it seems, the fresh word of commission carries within itself the assurance of forgiveness that Peter so craved. And it comes with a warning: Peter, too, will bear witness by his own death. He must not worry about what others will be doing. He must heed Jesus' words, 'Follow me' (21.15–19).

In particular—and this is most likely why this final chapter was added—he is not to worry about the 'beloved disciple' himself. It may well be that the chapter was drafted after the beloved disciple himself had died, when some in the church, having misunderstood Jesus' words ('If it's my intention that he should remain here until I come, what's that got to do with you?'), worried that Jesus should have returned by now. That was never the point (21.20–23). The final editor adds a note verifying that the beloved disciple was the real author, and 'we know that his evidence is true'. He also adds, touchingly, that Jesus did many other things, and that the world itself would be incapable of containing the books that would be written if they were all set down. The claim is not simply about shelf-space in the great libraries. The accomplishments of Jesus were, and remain, so explosive, bringing to birth the age to come within the present age, that the world in its present state would not be able to contain the vast revelation that would result.

JOHN AND THE BIG PICTURE

We could spend a day, a night, or a lifetime plumbing the theological insights, historical details, and spiritual depth of John's gospel. For those who are already committed to living within the story John is telling, a few things present themselves for consideration.

The gospel of John is the big book of *faith*. It is about believing, not just because of remarkable signs, but because one accepts the verdict of the witnesses: God sent Jesus, Jesus is God's son, the son has returned to the father, and the father sends the spirit of the son. This gospel calls us to faith: a rich, deep faith, an energetic faith, a faith that abides in Jesus the Messiah, a faith that can survive denials and doubts, a faith that can overcome the world because Jesus has already overcome it for us. This believing constitutes a special kind of knowledge: a spiritual knowing, knowing the truth, knowing a person who is the embodiment of truth, and enjoying the freedom that this truth brings.

One cannot ignore the clear christological core of the gospel of John. This is not a book about a generalized spirituality or religious outlook on life. It is about Jesus himself from first to last. The book is written by a disciple whose passion for Jesus is intoxicating. The Jesus of the fourth gospel is to be believed, trusted, obeyed, and worshipped. Why? Because he has the words of eternal life. He laid down his life for his friends. He is the good shepherd, the lamb of God, the true vine. He is the door between our world and the new creation. Jesus is not merely one option on a religious smorgasbord. He is unique, unprecedented, cosmically singular. He is not *a way* up the mountain; he *made* the mountain in the first place! He is the way, the truth, and the life. The way for all people, Jews, Samaritans, Greeks, and whosoever will believe in him. John bids us believe the exclusive claims of the all-inclusive saviour.

To that we must add that, like all the New Testament stories, this story isn't only about Jesus. It's about us as well. Jesus is lifted up to draw us all to himself, and to enable us to be for the world what he was for Israel. The prologue says that 'To all who received him, who believed in his name, he gave the right to become the children of God' (Jn. 1.12). Or, again: in John 7.38 Jesus says, 'Whoever believes in me, as Scripture has said, rivers of living water will flow from within them.' There is the creation-image once again (Gen. 2.10–14), and also the Temple-image (Ezek. 47.1–12); only now, the rivers of living water that flow out of the new-creation Temple of God come, not just from Jesus, but from all those who believe in him, who follow him, who become in their turn the channels through which his healing love can flow to the world. Therefore the risen Jesus says, in John 20.21, 'As the Father has sent me, so I send you' (NRSV). And he breathes on the disciples, as God breathed upon Adam and Eve in the beginning, and gives them his own spirit, his own breath of life.

The whole amazing story of Jesus, with all its multiple levels, is thus given to be our story as we follow him. This is John's ultimate vision of the nature of Christian discipleship. At the end of John 21, after Jesus' strange and beautiful conversation with Peter, he issues that haunting summons: don't think about the person standing next to you; your call is simply to follow me (21.22). Because of the cross, Jesus offers us, here and now, his own sonship; his own spirit; his own mission to the world. The love which he incarnated, by which we are saved, is to become the love which fills us beyond capacity and flows out to heal the world; so that *the Word may become flesh* once more, *and dwell* (not just among us, but) *within us*. Having beheld his glory, *we must then reveal his glory, glory as of the beloved children of the father, full of grace and truth*.

Further reading

Akala, Adesola Joan. 2015. *The Son-Father Relationship and Christological Symbolism in the Fourth Gospel*. LNTS 505; London: T&T Clark.

Bauckham, Richard. 2007. *The Testimony of the Beloved Disciple: Narrative, History, and Theology in the Gospel of John*. Grand Rapids, MI: Baker.

——. 2015. *Gospel of Glory: Major Themes in Johannine Theology*. Grand Rapids, MI: Baker.

Carson, D. A. 1991. *The Gospel According to John*. PNTC; Grand Rapids, MI: Eerdmans.

Estes, Douglas, and Ruth Sheridan (eds.). 2016. *How John Works: Storytelling in the Fourth Gospel*. Atlanta: SBL.

Hengel, Martin. 1989. *The Johannine Question*. London: SCM.

Hill, Charles. 2004. *The Johannine Corpus in the Early Church*. Oxford: Oxford University Press.

Kanagaraj, Jey J. 2013. *John*. NCCS. Eugene, OR: Cascade.

Keener, Craig S. 2003. *The Gospel of John: A Commentary*. 2 vols.; Peabody, MA: Hendrickson.

Koester, Craig R. 2008. *The Word of Life: A Theology of John's Gospel*. Grand Rapids, MI: Eerdmans.

Köstenberger, Andreas. 2009. *A Theology of John's Gospel and Letters*. Grand Rapids, MI: Zondervan.

Lieu, Judith, and Martinus C. de Boer (eds.). 2018. *The Oxford Handbook of Johannine Studies*. Oxford: Oxford University Press.

Lincoln, Andrew T. 2005. *The Gospel According to Saint John*. BNTC; London: Continuum.

Morris, Leon. 1995. *The Gospel According to John*. Rev. edn.; NICNT; Grand Rapids, MI: Eerdmans.

Porter, Stanley E., and Hughson T. Ong (eds.). 2016. *The Origin of John's Gospel*. JS 2; Leiden: Brill.

Thompson, Marianne M. 2015. *John: A Commentary*. NTL; Louisville, KY: Westminster John Knox.

28

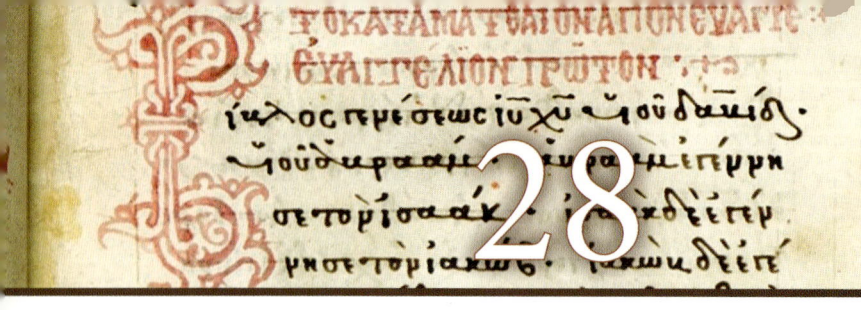

The Making of the Gospels

New Testament scholars have long supposed that between the death of Jesus and the writing of the Gospels, Jesus' words and deeds were handed down by word of mouth in something called 'oral tradition.' This has never meant denying a role for written documents as well; hypothetical texts such as Q, miracle-story collections and sayings collections have long been proposed. The point is rather that the word-of-mouth transmission of Jesus-material is assumed to have played a major role in the formative stages of the Jesus tradition, and that this 'oral tradition' can be invoked as a full or partial explanation of why the evangelists were able to use the material they did.[1]

CHAPTER AT A GLANCE

This chapter explains the origins and genre of the gospels.

By the end of this chapter you should be able to:

- identify the genre of the gospels as a form of ancient biography mixed with the scriptural story of Israel;
- grasp the complexities of John's relationship to the synoptics;
- describe the synoptic problem and its various solutions;
- understand the nature of the Jesus-tradition from which the gospels were composed.

INTRODUCTION

It might seem odd to wait until now, after examining the gospels in depth, to reflect on what type of literature they are and how they were put together. The reason is twofold. First, we actually possess the four gospels; we do not possess, in any straightforward sense, any of the sources which the writers may have used (see Table 28.1). Second, it is better to proceed from the known (the gospels) to the unknown (their sources, and how they may have been used) than vice versa. Of course, this process is always a spiral: from the basic data to a hypothesis, checking back to the data, refining the hypothesis, and so on. But as an introductory exercise it makes sense to move

---

1 Eve 2013, xiii.

from the texts we have to possible theories about what they really are and how they came to be. Underneath all this is the perennially fascinating question: why did four early Christians decide to write books like this?

TABLE 28.1: EARLIEST COPIES OF THE CANONICAL GOSPELS AND ACTS*

Book	Siglum	Manuscript name	Date	Contents
Matthew	$\mathfrak{P}^{104}$	P.Oxy 4404	2nd century	21.34–37, 43, 45
Mark	$\mathfrak{P}^{137}$	P.Oxy 83.5345	c. AD 150–250	1.7–9, 16–18
Luke	$\mathfrak{P}^{75}$	P.Bodmer XIV + XV	3rd century	3.18–22; 3.33—4.2; 4.34—5.10; 5.37—6.4; 6.10—7.32, 35–39, 41–43; 7.46—9.2; 9.4—17.15; 17.19—18.18; 22.4—24.53
John	$\mathfrak{P}^{52}$	John Rylands 457	c. AD 125–75	18.31–33, 37–38
Acts	$\mathfrak{P}^{29}$	P.Oxy 1597	3rd century	26.7–8, 20

* Hill and Kruger 2012.

THE GENRE OF THE GOSPELS

Suppose you were the person in charge of the great library in ancient Alexandria and you were given, in around AD 100, a single codex containing the four gospels. Where would you put it? What section of the library would you think might be its appropriate home? Would it belong with tragedies, comedies, biographies, histories, letters, scientific texts, or prophecies? What type of writing, in other words, would a gospel appear to be within the ancient world itself? To what genre might it belong?

Such questions matter, because genre, actual or implied, determines how a text will function. Still thinking of librarians, if I get an email from the head librarian at my university telling me that my borrowing limit has been reached, and instructing me to click on a link to extend my allowance, I might be tempted to obey. But if I suddenly realize that this may be a clever scam from someone wanting to infect my computer, I will delete the message as quickly as I can. It's a matter of recognizing the genre: genuine administrative message, or dangerous spoof?

Genre affects the way a text functions in the lives of readers, in the life of the church, and in wider society.[2] David thought he had understood Nathan's story about a rich man, a poor man, and a little lamb, until Nathan revealed that the story was a parable—aimed at David himself.[3] Genre, to be technical, is a set of conventions, or recognizable textual features, that carry clues to the author's intention, while also activating the expectations of readers and hearers as to how a text is supposed to be understood. Actors who play villains on television are sometimes attacked in the street by people who, caught up in the drama, forget that its genre is precisely drama, not reportage. Genre is the 'rhetorical eco-system'[4] that provides the conventions and contexts for how an author uses a text to communicate to readers.

Several proposals have been advanced about the genre of the gospels.[5] Some have likened them to works of 'aretalogy', a type of biography about a 'divine man' (*theios anēr*) who does miraculous deeds and dies a heroic death. They have also been compared to ancient tragedies, novels, and epics of various kinds. Common for a long time in the twentieth century was the view that the gospels were a distinctive type of Christian literature that combined Old Testament narrative with Christian proclamation about Jesus. Equally common was the view, espoused by the highly influential Rudolf Bultmann, that the gospels could not be 'biography' because the early Christians were not concerned about 'knowing the Messiah according to the flesh'.[6]

However, 'biography'—of some sort—has been making a come-back. Many have now agreed that the most persuasive generic label for the gospels is that they represent a form of greco-roman biography (Greek *bios*; Latin *vita*).[7] One of the first descriptions of the gospels comes from Justin Martyr, who in the mid-second century called them the 'memoirs of the apostles', aligning them by implication with biographical works such as Xenophon's *Memoirs of Socrates*.[8] The gospels are similar to greco-roman biography in several material respects. They are written in continuous prose; they present the stylized career of a public leader; they provide a chronological framework of his birth, deeds, death, and legacy; they contain vignettes highlighting his character and achievements; they have a good deal to say about the manner of his death; and they extol their central figure for his virtues while defending him from accusation. The gospels thus resemble the biographical 'Lives' of great philosophers and statesmen (we think of Plutarch and many others), especially the books written, as many were, with specific apologetic and/or didactic intent.

At the same time, the gospels are significantly different from greco-roman biographies. The world they describe, the air they breathe, is Jewish. Israel's scriptures, too,

---

2   Collins 2007, 17.
3   2 Sam. 12.1–15.
4   Bawarshi 2003, ch. 1.
5   See Diehl 2010; Bird 2014b, 222–40.
6   See 2 Cor. 5.16. Few would now suppose that this Pauline saying should be taken in this way.
7   See esp. Burridge 2004 [1992]; 2013; Bird 2014b, 235–40.
8   See e.g. Just. *Dial.* 100.4; 101.3; 102.5; 103.6, 8; 104.1; 105.1; 106.1, 3; 107.1; *1 Apol.* 66.3; 67.3.

have significant biographical elements, as witness the stories of Abraham, Jacob, Joseph, Samson, Saul, David, and many others. Post-biblical Jewish literature can sometimes focus on a particular life, as with the book of Tobit, or Philo's *Life of Moses*. The fact that most of these stories are embedded within the larger narrative of Israel's chequered story, poised between God and the nations, makes the point, because the gospels share that characteristic: in very different ways, each of them takes care to present the story of Jesus, not as that of a man appearing out of nowhere, a 'once upon a time' figure teaching interesting novelties, but as the one to whom Israel's scriptures had been pointing all along. The gospels rehearse scriptural themes and literary patterns; they echo scriptural promises; but, above all, they claim—controversially of course, within the Jewish world—that if Israel's scriptures were telling a great story in search of an ending, *this was the ending to which that story had always pointed*. They could thus be said to display the fulfilment of Israel's hopes in the form of, or under the guise of, the story of a human life. Some might say they were, in this respect, fulfilling the implicit promise of Genesis 1.26 (the creation of humans to reflect the divine purpose into the world). Some might say that this was the point John, in particular, was making quite explicitly ('Behold the man!' said Pilate).[9]

None of this tells against the identification of the gospels as (in some sense) greco-roman biography. Not only was the biographical form flexible, capable of diverse expression. Part of the point of Jewish eschatology was that when Israel's God fulfilled his purposes for his people this would address the wider world: using the form of a *bios* to tell the story of Jesus-as-Israel's-fulfilment makes exactly this point.[10]

For both worlds, it matters that these things happened in real space and time. Jesus, like some other teachers, could tell 'parables' whose genre makes it pointless to ask 'But did it actually happen?' The gospels *contain* such things, but the gospels *as a whole* are not like that. The evangelistic proclamation of the early church was not, after all, that through Jesus and his death people could find a new detached spirituality, or a new hope of post-mortem salvation. It was that, through the events concerning Jesus, the creator God had become king on earth as in heaven. The questions of meaning and genre are importantly intertwined. Corporate memory and the transmission of teaching played their part (see below), and the four evangelists pulled it all together in their different ways.

These reflections about genre carry implications concerning the intended audiences. For much of the twentieth century it was thought that the gospels were community documents, in the sense that, though they ostensibly narrated a story about Jesus, this was merely the overlay beneath which one could discern the history and

---

[9] Jn. 19.5 KJV.
[10] Wright *NTPG*, 418; Pennington 2012, 35.

preoccupations of a particular community. The gospels were thus seen as two-tiered dramas, containing a cache of community traditions about the remembered Jesus while also displaying and addressing various conflicts in the Matthean, Markan, Lukan, and Johannine communities. This makes Matthew, in effect, a Jesus-story through which we see the trials and travails of the Matthean community within (perhaps) Syrian Judaism. Mark would be a Jesus-story reflecting persecution, quite possibly in Rome. Luke—for whom the 'community' hypothesis has always been weakest—would be a Jesus-story written, amid the struggles of Luke's church, to stake out an identity between Jewish and greco-roman social groupings. John would (so some have thought) be a Jesus-story reflecting the expulsion of the Johannine community from the synagogues in Ephesus or elsewhere. In this kind of theory, the gospel writers were using the story of Jesus to write *about* and *for* these intramural events that shaped their (hypothetical) communities.[11]

There are two problems with this kind of community hypothesis. First, although there is no question that the gospels are told from the vantage point of particular individual and corporate experiences—as all books inevitably are—that does not entail that they are primarily *about* the communities in question, always assuming such communities even existed. Once we realize how the evangelists are using Israel's scriptures, it becomes clear that they do indeed intend to refer to Jesus himself, not simply to use an arm-waving reference to a fictitious character by that name as a cryptic code through which to address their own concerns.[12]

Second, it is equally unlikely that the gospels were directed principally towards such isolated and introspective communities. The four gospels might indeed have been intended in the first instance to be read by a local cluster of churches, but it is far more probable that they were intended to circulate widely throughout the networks of Christian assemblies that were spreading across the eastern Mediterranean. The mobility of Christians in the Roman empire, especially among its leaders, meant that authors would have known, hoped, and expected that their works would be read by people in a wide geographical spread of Christian groups. The early church did not comprise isolated enclaves of believers; it comprised 'a network of communities with constant, close communication among themselves'.[13] The greco-roman *bios* genre was ideally suited to giving such a story widespread dissemination.[14] The four gospels, then, were most likely not written for a single community, but for as many as would read them.[15]

---

11 See studies in Klink 2010b.
12 Smith (2015, 212–13) writes: 'At their core, the gospels are about a person (Jesus); their focus is not on the author of the text, nor on the audience that exists somewhere behind or underneath the texts. The gospels are about Jesus, and not explicitly about first-century Christian communities.' See too Wright *NTPG*, ch. 14; Hays 2017.
13 Bauckham 1998a, 30.
14 Bauckham 1998a, 26–30; Smith 2015, 208, 212.
15 See Bauckham 1998a; Hengel 2000, 106–15; Bird 2006e; Klink 2010a; 2010b; Smith 2015.

THE PROBLEM OF JOHN'S GOSPEL

In the previous chapter we explored at length the authorship of the fourth gospel and concluded that the book was most likely written by John the elder, though John son of Zebedee remains an alternative candidate. Our question now concerns the sources behind John's gospel, and the relationship of John to the synoptic gospels.

The fourth gospel claims the 'beloved disciple' as its authority, and implies that he had access to Judean traditions about Jesus, which he had woven into his narrative, including some of them to be seen as special 'signs'. This testimony remains largely independent of, and unparalleled within, the synoptic gospels.

But the fourth gospel is not completely independent. John shares the same biographical genre as the synoptics, and (not surprisingly) uses the same basic plot of Jesus' public career, starting with John the Baptist and ending with the Passion and resurrection. Various sayings in John have parallels in the synoptics (see below). In addition, some blocks of material in John exhibit a mixture of sameness to and difference from the synoptics, a good example being the stories of the multiplication of loaves and fishes.[16] At some points John appears to presuppose knowledge of the synoptic story-line, for instance when the evangelist makes the parenthetical remark that certain things happened 'before John was put in prison', though John's imprisonment is not mentioned elsewhere. When introducing Mary and Martha, the evangelist adds that 'Mary . . . was the same one who poured perfume on the Lord and wiped his feet with her hair'. Since the synoptics do not name Mary in this connection, John is filling a gap.[17] It is particularly noteworthy that John has several similarities with Luke. Only they refer to Mary and Martha of Bethany. Only they mention the former high priest Annas; only they refer to the satan entering Judas Iscariot.[18]

There are also, however, significant parallels between John and Mark (see text grid: 'Examples of parallel sayings between John and Mark').

How are we to explain the similarities between John and the synoptic gospels?[19] Perhaps John and the synoptics accessed the same pool of oral tradition, or drew on similar sources. The different traditions may perhaps have influenced one another at some stage (which is to say that we know very little about the pre-literary stages of such material). Perhaps John had read Mark, or at least heard it read. Once we move away from an older idea of the evangelists simply trying to 'include everything they knew', all sorts of options open up. John certainly appears to presuppose, for himself and his audience, elements of the synoptic tradition, but his independence is marked and obvious.[20]

---

16 Jn. 6.1–15; Mk. 6.30–44/8.1–13.
17 Jn. 3.23–24; 11.1–2. See further Bauckham 1998a.
18 Jn. 11.1–12.8/Lk. 10.38–42; Jn. 18.13, 24/Lk. 3.2; Ac. 4.6; Jn. 13.2, 27/Lk. 22.3.
19 See Bird 2013c; 2014b, 194–212.
20 Bird 2014b, 211–12.

EXAMPLES OF PARALLEL SAYINGS BETWEEN JOHN AND MARK[*]

Jesus answered them, 'Destroy this temple, and in three days I will raise it up.' (Jn. 2.19)	'We heard him say, "I will destroy this temple that is made with hands, and in three days I will build another, not made with hands."' (Mk. 14.58)
When the two days were over, he went from that place to Galilee (for Jesus himself had testified that a prophet has no honour in the prophet's own country). (Jn. 4.43–44)	Then Jesus said to them, 'Prophets are not without honour, except in their home town, and among their own kin, and in their own house.' (Mk. 6.4)
'Those who love their life lose it, and those who hate their life in this world will keep it for eternal life.' (Jn. 12.25)	He called the crowd with his disciples, and said to them, 'If any want to become my followers, let them deny themselves and take up their cross and follow me. For those who want to save their life will lose it, and those who lose their life for my sake, and for the sake of the gospel, will save it.' (Mk. 8.34–35)

* All biblical quotations in this text grid are taken from NRSV.

THE SYNOPTIC PROBLEM

Matthew, Mark, and Luke are known as the 'synoptic' gospels because they can be viewed 'synoptically', displayed in columns to indicate their parallels and differences. Despite their many individual features, they offer overall a generally homogeneous account of Jesus's public ministry, Passion, and resurrection. Their close similarities and verbal parallels can hardly be coincidental, and together they generate the famous 'synoptic problem': what account can we give of their mutual relationship? Did they borrow from one another, or from similar sources (now lost), or what? Large swaths of Mark are paralleled in Luke, so that around half of Luke's (much longer) gospel is 'Markan' material, while Matthew replicates 90 per cent of Mark, though likewise containing a good deal of non-Markan material. The material in which all three overlap is known as the 'triple tradition', which contains many passages with quite similar wording. Some material is shared by Matthew and Luke but not found in Mark (the 'double tradition'). Material special to Luke and Matthew is often called 'L' or 'M' respectively.[21] So what account can we give of how this complex textual situation came about?[22]

---

21 See chs. 25 and 26.
22 See Bird 2014b, 125–54.

We must assume that a great many traditions about Jesus circulated orally in the early church, presumably in both Aramaic and Greek. It is very unlikely that the three synoptic evangelists just happened, by accident as it were, to tell the same story in the same order, summarizing it in the same way, using very similar wording throughout,[23] inserting Old Testament quotations in the same places,[24] and even making near-identical editorial asides.[25] We should take it for granted that continuing oral tradition affected the shape and content of the gospels, but the evidence points strongly to some kind of literary dependency as well: in other words, some kind of borrowing or copying has taken place. Luke, after all, tells us in his prologue that he knew of other oral and written sources.[26] This already suggests that if our other surviving sources, in this case particularly Mark, make sense as possible sources for Luke, we should perhaps start the investigation there. But how can we proceed? All sorts of theories have been suggested, and we must review them briefly. All we can do here is to summarize; the only way a student can really understand the problem in detail is to work carefully through a synopsis, preferably in Greek.

During the early, medieval, and Reformation periods, it was assumed that Matthew wrote first, composing a comprehensive gospel, which was subsequently supplemented by Luke and summarized by Mark (opinions differed as to whether Luke or Mark wrote last). There are two main versions of the theory of 'Matthean priority': the Augustinian view and the Griesbach hypothesis (see figures 3 and 4).

These theories have their modern advocates.[27] The biggest problem they face is the apparently overwhelming counter-argument for the priority of Mark. This theory has been the bedrock of much modern research on the synoptics: that Mark wrote first and was used by both Matthew and Luke.

The normal arguments for the priority of Mark are as follows:

1. *Content absorption.* Mark is not only the shortest gospel; it also has the least amount of unique material.[28]

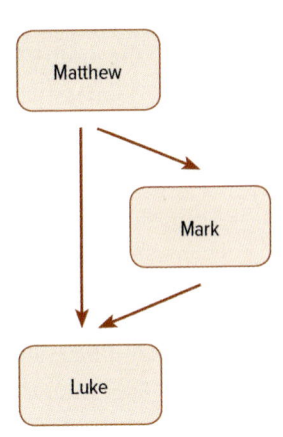

Figure 3: Augustinian view

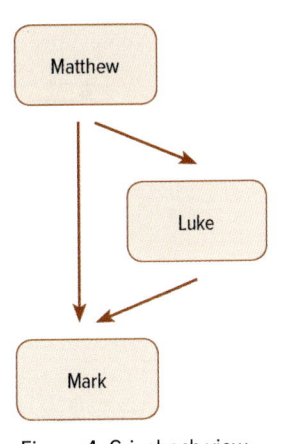

Figure 4: Griesbach view

---

23 See e.g. the calling of Levi in Mk. 2.13–15/Mt. 9.9–10/Lk. 5.27–32.
24 See e.g. Mk. 1.2/Lk. 3.4.
25 See e.g. Mk. 13.14/Mt. 24.15–16.
26 Lk. 1.1.
27 See e.g. Farmer 1976.
28 Only Mk. 7.33–36; 8.22–36; and 14.51–52 are unique to Mark.

Most of its contents appear (albeit often with somewhat different wording) in Matthew, and to a lesser degree in Luke. What is more, when we study the 'triple tradition' closely we find that Mark is normally the common denominator or shared middle term: Matthew and Luke are usually in closer agreement with Mark than they are with one another. It has often been pointed out that, if Mark was writing after either Matthew or Luke, and using them as a source, it is remarkable how much significant material he left out. At this point we see, peeping out from behind an apparently rational argument, a flagrant unargued assumption, namely that we know ahead of time that the motive for writing a gospel was to 'tell as much of the story as possible'. As many have pointed out, as soon as we start to investigate the evangelists' motivations in detail, we find all sorts of other possible motives, which might suggest other possibilities. Why, people have asked, would Mark leave out Matthew's 'sermon on the mount', if he had it in front of him? One possible answer might be: 'Because Mark was writing a fast-paced, subversive evangelistic tract, and a long discourse like that serves a quite different purpose.' However, if Mark is anything other than the first gospel, then it is a strange summary of Luke or Matthew, leaving out so much of what looks to us like 'significant' material.

2. *Order.* Mark's gospel appears to provide the chronological scaffolding which Matthew and Luke then use. When either Matthew or Luke departs from Mark's order, the other usually maintains it. Thus, Mark's ordering appears to be more original.

3. *Redaction.* Mark's rough Greek is improved by Matthew and Luke, and they enhance his overall portrait of Jesus. For example, concerning the holy spirit sending Jesus into the wilderness after his baptism, Mark 1.12 uses the word *ekballō*, which means 'expel' or 'drive', the same word for what Jesus does to demons in an exorcism. Matthew and Luke change it to the Greek words *agō* and *anagō* respectively, which is a far less convulsive description for the spirit's 'leading' of Jesus.[29] There are many other parallel 'improvements', such as when Matthew enlarges Peter's confession at Caesarea Philippi from Mark's 'You are the Messiah' to 'You are the Messiah, the Son of the living God', while Luke has 'You are the Messiah of God'.[30]

On the whole, the order, content, and development of the synoptic tradition makes a lot more sense on the presumption of Markan priority, with Matthew and Luke both dependent on Mark (see Figure 5). We should note, however, that if both

---

[29] Mt. 4.1; Lk. 4.1.
[30] Mk. 8.29/Mt. 16.16/Lk. 9.20.

Matthew and Luke have used Mark, they have done so in quite different ways. Luke (on this theory) employs Mark in large sections, interspersed with other sections of his own special material. Matthew—again on this theory—has woven Markan material into his book in a much more complex fashion.

What then about the 'double tradition', the places where Matthew and Luke overlap in their non-Markan material? How do we account for this? Fifty years ago most gospel students were taught that the answer had been found, and could be used as a fixed point; the theory in question continues to be regarded by many as unquestionable. Life has, however, become much more complicated and confusing in recent discussion.

The proposal in question is that Matthew and Luke had access to Mark and also to another source; this was called 'Q', reflecting the German word *Quelle*, 'source'. This source, Q, was assumed to be a document, consisting mostly of sayings of Jesus, together with some short stories, and perhaps, in some bold theories, even an infancy narrative about Jesus. Advocates of Q have, however, always disagreed as to its precise contents and genre, though the most plausible versions focus on sayings of Jesus (many collections of sayings from famous teachers were known in antiquity, and among the later Jesus-traditions one famous collection, the so-called *Gospel of Thomas*, has been proposed as a parallel).[31] Thus one standard 'solution' to the 'synoptic problem' has been the combination of Markan priority with the use by Luke and Matthew of Q, adding their own special material (L and M). This yields what has been known as the 'four-source' theory (see Figure 6).

One of the problems in postulating the existence of Q is the way it has generated so

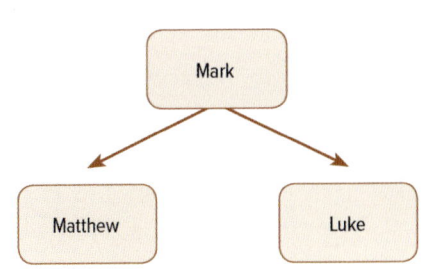

Figure 5: Markan priority

Ending of the Apocryphon of John and beginning of the Gospel of Thomas, folio 32, Nag Hammadi Codex II, *c.* fourth century
PD-US

---

31 As used, for example, in Crossan 1991 and 2008.

The Making of the Gospels

many complex and unprovable speculative secondary hypotheses. Some scholars have claimed to excavate different layers of redaction in Q, detecting entities named Q^1, Q^2, and Q^3 respectively, then mapping the contours of a hypothetical and developing 'Q community'. Some have seen 'early Q', and supposedly early versions of the so-called *Gospel of Thomas*, as the earliest layer of the Jesus-tradition: this can be used to paint Jesus as some kind of first-century peasant Cynic philosopher, screening out the supposedly later layers of tradition which transformed Jesus into an apocalyptic Jewish prophet (which was precisely the kind of 'Jesus' that strand of scholarship was trying to eliminate, on the supposition that apocalyptic prophecy was second cousin to modern fundamentalism).[32] There is nothing whatever wrong with speculation; all hypotheses, scientific as well as literary, start out life with people soaking themselves in the data and speculating as to how to explain it. But when one hypothetical construction is mounted on top of another—and when, as actually with most theories of synoptic origins, theological and even political motivations start to show up and even seem to be driving the new theory—we are right to hold back.[33]

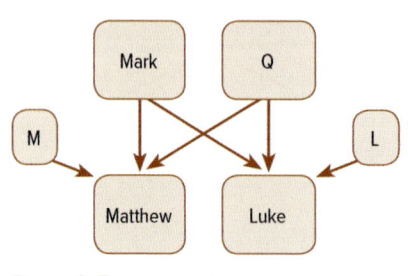

Figure 6: Four-source theory

A quite different approach has been to propose eliminating 'Q' altogether, and all its paraphernalia, by suggesting simply that Luke used Matthew or vice versa. All you have to do is to suppose that Matthew and/or Luke were not simply *collectors* trying to patch together as much 'Jesus material' as they could, but *theologians and editors* with their own ideas about what they wanted to say.

JESUS IS MOCKED AS A PROPHET

Mark 14.65 (NRSV adapted)	*Matthew 26.67–68 (NRSV)*	*Luke 22.64 (NRSV)*
Some began to spit on him, to *blindfold* his <u>face</u>, and to strike him, saying to him, '**Prophesy!**' The guards also took him over and beat him.	Then they spat in his <u>face</u> and struck him; and some slapped him, saying, '**Prophesy to us, you Messiah! Who is it that struck you?**'	they also *blindfolded* him and kept asking him, '**Prophesy! Who is it that struck you?**'

---

32 See Crossan 1991 with response by Wright *JVG*, 44–74.
33 Meier (1991–2016, 2.178) believes that researchers of the gospels should daily recite the following mantra: '*Q is a hypothetical document whose exact extension, wording, originating community, strata, and stages of redaction cannot be known.*'

Once we grant the likelihood of motivations other than merely assembling data—and, as we have seen, recent studies of the gospels have explored their theological and practical motivations and editorial activities at great length—then the old theories suddenly look shaky. This larger outflanking point can then note something that has always haunted 'Q' theorists and 'four-source' views in particular: there are times *even in the triple tradition* when Matthew and Luke agree *against Mark*, which on the normal view seems very unlikely, except by occasional coincidence. These so-called 'minor agreements' in the triple tradition have even led to the head-scratching possibility of an *overlap of Mark and Q*. Granted that the very definition of 'Q' is 'material in Matthew and Luke but not in Mark', such an overlap has the same ontological status as a square circle. Consider the parallel scriptures laid out in the text grid 'Jesus is mocked as a prophet'. The triple agreements are in bold brown; Mark–Matthew agreements are underlined; Luke–Matthew agreements are in bold black; Luke–Mark agreements are in italics.

THE PARABLE OF THE MUSTARD SEED

Mark 4.30–32 (NRSV)	*Matthew 13.31–32 (NRSV)*	*Luke 13.18–19 (NRSV)*
30 *He also said*, 'With what can we compare the **kingdom** of God, or *what* parable will we use for *it*? 31 It is like a **mustard seed**, which, when sown upon the ground, is the smallest of all the seeds on earth; 32 yet when it is sown it grows up and becomes the greatest of all shrubs, and puts forth large branches, so that **the birds of the air** can make nests in its shade.'	31 He put before them another parable: 'The **kingdom** of heaven **is like** a **mustard seed** that **someone took** and sowed in his field; 32 it is the smallest of all the seeds, but when it has grown it is the greatest of shrubs and becomes a **tree**, so that **the birds of the air** come and make nests **in its branches**.'	18 *He said* therefore, '**What is the kingdom** of God **like**? And to *what* should I compare *it*? 19 It is like a **mustard seed** that **someone took** and sowed in the garden; it grew and became a **tree**, and **the birds of the air made** nests **in its branches**.'

If Matthew and Luke both independently follow Mark in the Passion narrative, and if (as is commonly thought) Q had no Passion narrative, then why do Matthew and Luke both contain the mocking question from Jesus' tormentors, 'Who is it that struck you?' Maybe some early scribe, knowing either Matthew or Luke, added the words in one of them . . . or, just maybe, Luke knew Matthew, or vice versa. But if we grant that as a possibility, and if we recognize each of the evangelists as creative and theologically motivated writers rather than mere collectors, life becomes much more complex and interesting—and might not include Q.

Consider the passage set out in the text grid 'The parable of the mustard seed'. Mark is often the middle term between Luke and Matthew, but here things are different. The triple agreements are in bold brown; Mark–Matthew agreements are underlined; Mark–Luke agreements are in italics; Luke–Matthew agreements are in bold black. Some four-source theorists would argue that Matthew has conflated Mark and Q. Another possibility, though, is that Luke has conflated and condensed Mark and Matthew.

Evidence like this has enabled several scholars to maintain Markan priority and to eliminate Q by postulating that Luke used Matthew. This was advocated by the mid-twentieth-century Anglican scholar Austin Farrer, and bears his name—in the 'Farrer' hypothesis (though also associated with Michael Goulder and Mark Goodacre in more recent time). In this Farrer(-Goulder-Goodacre) hypothesis, Luke is the *final* term, the point where other traditions are drawn together (a view otherwise known as 'Lukan posteriority').[34] Luke, in this theory, has absorbed Matthew's non-Markan material, using Mark's outline and fleshing it out with his own versions of Matthean material and his own individual contributions. This approach has become more popular in recent years, though many still see some version of the four-source hypothesis as the norm.

There are of course problems with eliminating Q. Not everything is solved overnight. Some have proposed reversing Farrer's central move and suggesting that Matthew used Luke, thus creating the theory of 'Matthean posteriority' (see figures 7 and 8). Evidence for this might be found, for instance, in Matthew's version of the double tradition, which is more expansive and perhaps 'developed' than the Lukan equivalent. (This, like all such moves, again disguises an easy but perhaps fallacious assumption. How do we know that the tradition 'developed' into longer forms? Might not Luke, faced with Matthew's wordy and biblically allusive text, have sometimes edited it into a punchier form?) Some have suggested that it is more likely that Matthew gathered up Lukan materials into his five major discourses than that Luke

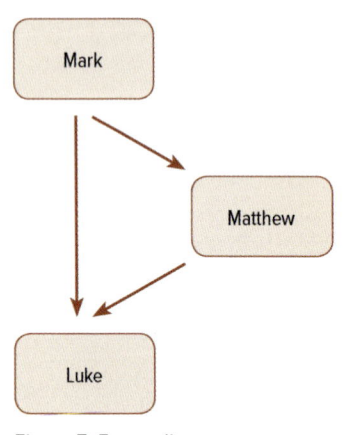

Figure 7: Farrer diagram

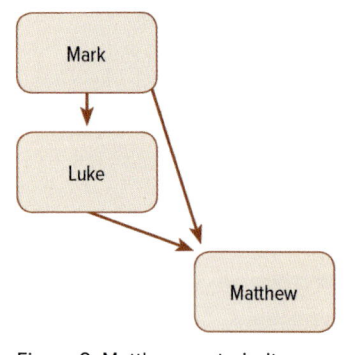

Figure 8: Matthew posteriority diagram

---

34 See e.g. Farrer 1985 [1955]; Goodacre and Perrin 2004; Goodacre 2016.

scattered Matthew's neatly arranged material across his gospel.[35] But, either way, there would be no more Q.

A mediating view is possible. Perhaps we should combine Markan priority, some sort of a 'Q-lite'—including a variety of oral and written sources—and Luke's use of Matthew. This produces the 'three-source theory'.[36] This view allows for much more first-century flexibility, which seems inherently likely granted that neither the evangelists nor their communities were teams of scholars sitting at desks carefully working over documents. As Morna Hooker pointed out a generation ago, just as people have imagined Jesus in their own image, they have done the same with the evangelists.[37] Once we recognize the complex and confused pre-print world of the first century, and the multiple motivations of storytellers, writers, and editors, such fluidity seems only appropriate. The centre of gravity in this hypothesis is the recognition that we cannot explain the double tradition, especially the various sayings of Jesus, purely by Luke's use of Matthew or vice versa. When Luke and Matthew overlap, they are still significantly different, and such differences are more easily explained by their having additional sources, not just by Luke's editing of Matthew (see Figure 9).

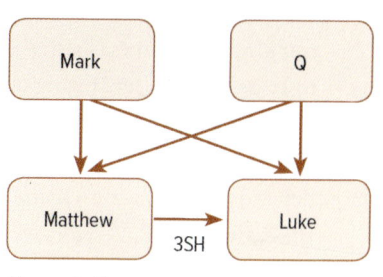

Figure 9: Three-source theory

At the end of the day, we simply do not know for certain how the synoptic gospels were put together. A literary relationship between the synoptics seems clear. Markan priority is still probably the best bet. Luke tells us he has used sources; if we suppose that Mark was one of those sources, all sorts of things make sense. But after that it gets murky. Things might be far more complicated than we can ever know. Oral tradition was a lively but untrackable factor; people did not stop telling stories about Jesus, and there were plenty of people around with their own memories, their own favourite versions of this or that incident or saying. As for written documents themselves, it is quite possible that one or more of the evangelists produced two or more editions of their books. We can see from later manuscripts that scribes, copying one gospel, would sometimes allow well-known phrases from a different one to creep in. What is more, it is highly likely that there were other 'Jesus traditions' and texts that some early Christians knew. The gospel of John is the obvious candidate, but then we have those 'other gospels', the so-called *Gospel of Thomas* and various sayings of Jesus found outside the canonical gospels.[38] Where did they come from?

---

[35] Hengel 2000, 68–73; MacEwen 2015.
[36] Sanders and Davies 1989, 117; Bird 2014b, 154–87, where it is also called the 'Holtzmann-Gundry hypothesis'.
[37] Hooker 1975.
[38] See e.g. Ac. 20.35; Just. *Dial.* 47; P.Oxy 840; 1224.

How did they shape the development of the tradition as a whole? The synoptic problem is, and will remain, a problem.

Should we care? Does it matter? The reason people in the nineteenth and early twentieth centuries spent decades working on Q and similar theories, often at a microscopic level, was not simply out of love for crossword puzzles. Up to the present, many who have laboured in this field have done so in the conviction that by tracking the sources further and further back they might be getting closer and closer to Jesus himself, separating out genuinely early material from supposedly later additions. The trouble with that, of course, is not simply that knowing which might be early and which might be later is much harder than people used to think, and depends in any case on some kind of implicit theory as to what sort of community the early Christians really were. It is that, as with all ancient history, the occurrence of a story in only one source does not, of itself, make it historically less likely. Legends and myths are sometimes witnessed by multiple sources but that doesn't make them historically true; in all history, particularly ancient history, a single source can often be right. But in any case, in the confused state of gospels-scholarship over the last two generations, a quite different motivation has emerged: no longer the 'quest for the historical Jesus' but the 'quest for the kerygmatic church' (that is, the early church and its message). That is where Q studies, and related activities, have been focused more recently: on the possibility that the 'Q community' might be retrievable, a group of wandering radicals living a counter-cultural lifestyle, justifying and maintaining their group identity by telling 'Jesus-stories'.

The trouble with all this, fascinating though it is, is actually that we know more about Jesus himself, on the one hand, and about the four gospels themselves, on the other, than we do about the traditions, oral and written, that we may suppose to have existed, in however confused a fashion, in between them.

THE JESUS-TRADITION

Ever since the beginning of (so-called) historical-critical study of the gospels there has been interest in the various sources, both written and oral, that must be supposed to underlie the gospels. This material is usually referred to as 'the Jesus tradition'.[39] Where did all that material about Jesus come from? Why did it take the shape that it did? Was it transmitted reliably?

It is highly likely that in some cases, perhaps many, the sources now embodied in the gospels go back directly to eye-witnesses. Luke says as much in the prologue to his gospel (Lk. 1.2). Early tradition suggests that Peter was the principal source behind Mark's gospel, and good sense can be made of this. Likewise it is possible to suppose

---

[39] See Le Donne 2009; 2011; Eve 2013; Eddy 2013; Bird 2014b, 21–124.

that the tax-collector Levi really does stand behind Matthew's gospel, and that Luke the physician, Paul's companion, knew several disciples and supporters of Jesus from the Jerusalem and Antiochene churches. The 'beloved disciple' who stands behind John's gospel may be a shadowy figure, but that doesn't mean that he didn't exist, or that he was not, after all, giving faithful testimony.[40] In addition, there may well have been early written sources—collections of Jesus' sayings, and of accounts of his miracles and Passion—of which the evangelists were able to make use. In any event, it is reasonable to assume that the Jesus-tradition—comprising traditions transmitted both from Jesus and about Jesus—was carried in people's memories and transmitted orally. The early church, both in Palestine and the eastern Mediterranean, was part of a vivid oral culture. We whose culture has depended on print for half a millennium, and on electronic media for half a century, may find it difficult to imagine this fact, but people with neither print nor electronic toys were well able to use their minds, their memories, and their communal traditions of storytelling to good effect. The New Testament is the literary product of the largely oral phenomenon of preaching, teaching, storytelling, rhetorical persuasion, praying, prophesying, worship, debating, and catechetical instruction. Even when things were written down, for instance in the form of letters, these were normally meant, not for private consumption, but for public reading.[41]

We can see good examples of how Jesus' own words were recalled in the early church simply by looking at 1 Corinthians. Paul here explicitly refers to Jesus' prohibition on divorce and remarriage; he alludes to Jesus' teaching about workers deserving their wages; he rehearses Jesus' words of institution at the Passover meal he shared with his disciples the night before he died (see text grid: 'Examples of the Jesus-tradition in 1 Corinthians'). This is as good evidence as any that Jesus' words were remembered, transmitted, and regarded as authoritative. However, Paul, as we have seen, was concerned not simply to spoon-feed his hearers with 'correct answers', or even 'words of Jesus', addressed to current problems. He wanted them to learn to think for themselves from the first principles of Jesus' completed kingdom-work, focused on his cross, resurrection, and ascension. His churches, out in the wider gentile world, faced neither the same crisis that Jesus' hearers were facing (the imminent judgment on recalcitrant Israel) nor the same practical context. Jesus' hearers were not worried about whether or not to eat meat offered to idols, or whether or not male gentile converts should be circumcised. It was never going to be a matter, then, of simply quoting Jesus-sayings to a gentile audience. The Jesus-*events* remained basic, supplemented with some sayings on occasion. (The letter of James likewise alludes to several Jesus-sayings.) And the larger narratives of the gospels, when they appeared, were therefore written not out of mere antiquarian interest ('by the way, this is what he was really like').

---
[40] See esp. Bauckham 2006.
[41] On public reading of Paul's correspondence, see 1 Thess. 5.27 and Col. 4.16, plus reference to the 'public reading of Scripture' in 1 Tim. 4.13.

EXAMPLES OF THE JESUS-TRADITION IN 1 CORINTHIANS

Divorce	¹⁰ To the married I give this command (not I, but the Lord): a wife must not separate from her husband. ¹¹ But if she does, she must remain unmarried or else be reconciled to her husband. And a husband must not divorce his wife. ¹² To the rest I say this (I, not the Lord): if any brother has a wife who is not a believer and she is willing to live with him, he must not divorce her. (1 Cor. 7.10–12)	² Some Pharisees came and tested him by asking, 'Is it lawful for a man to divorce his wife?' ³ 'What did Moses command you?' he replied. ⁴ They said, 'Moses permitted a man to write a certificate of divorce and send her away.' ⁵ 'It was because your hearts were hard that Moses wrote you this law,' Jesus replied. ⁶ 'But at the beginning of creation God "made them male and female". ⁷ "For this reason a man will leave his father and mother and be united to his wife, ⁸ and the two will become one flesh." So they are no longer two, but one flesh. ⁹ Therefore what God has joined together, let no one separate.' ¹⁰ When they were in the house again, the disciples asked Jesus about this. ¹¹ He answered, 'Anyone who divorces his wife and marries another woman commits adultery against her. ¹² And if she divorces her husband and marries another man, she commits adultery.' (Mk. 10.2–11)
Remuneration	In the same way, the Lord has commanded that those who preach the gospel should receive their living from the gospel. (1 Cor. 9.14)	'Stay there, eating and drinking whatever they give you, for the worker deserves his wages. Do not move around from house to house.' (Lk 10.7)
Lord's Supper	²³ For I received from the Lord what I also passed on to you: the Lord Jesus, on the night he was betrayed, took bread, ²⁴ and when he had given thanks, he broke it and said, 'This is my body, which is for you; do this in remembrance of me.' ²⁵ In the same way, after supper he took the cup, saying, 'This cup is the new covenant in my blood; do this, whenever you drink it, in remembrance of me.' (1 Cor. 11.23–25)	¹⁷ After taking the cup, he gave thanks and said, 'Take this and divide it among you. ¹⁸ For I tell you I will not drink again from the fruit of the vine until the kingdom of God comes.' ¹⁹ And he took bread, gave thanks and broke it, and gave it to them, saying, 'This is my body given for you; do this in remembrance of me.' ²⁰ In the same way, after the supper he took the cup, saying, 'This cup is the new covenant in my blood, which is poured out for you.' (Lk. 22.17–20)

They were the story of how Israel's great narrative had reached its goal and how God's kingdom had been inaugurated, though of course not yet consummated, on earth as in heaven. That was the story into which Paul's hearers had to think their way.

So, if Jesus-traditions were carried by what we loosely call 'oral tradition', what precise model of such a thing might we be talking about? The older 'form critics', like Rudolf Bultmann, supposed that the Jesus-tradition was transmitted in a fluid and flexible manner, being subject to unsupervised alteration. It became contaminated (Bultmann supposed) with prophetic utterances spoken in the name of Jesus though not by him personally, so that it would now be hard to tell which bits of which sayings went back to Jesus himself. The tradition, in this theory, was susceptible to large-scale invention to meet community needs (such as on topics like fasting), or in relation to the arguments that developed with the Pharisees after AD 70. All this assumes, however, a virtual disinterest in Jesus himself, and what he did and said. It ignores or rules out personal authorities like eye-witnesses and teachers, who could have regulated the transmission of the Jesus-tradition. There are no sayings attributed to Jesus dealing with topics like circumcision and speaking in tongues, which one might expect if sayings had been invented and ascribed to Jesus in order to solve the community conflicts we know to have been pressing in the early church. In the comparative samples of the Jesus-tradition we have from places like 1 Corinthians, we have good indicators that the Jesus-tradition as expressed in the gospels was carefully passed on.

On the other end of the spectrum from Bultmann, the Scandinavian school, with scholars like Harald Riesenfeld, Birger Gerhardsson, Rainer Riesner, and Samuel Byrskog, have appealed to a rabbinic model of memorization. In that Jewish culture, pupils memorized and transmitted the sayings of their teachers. The advantage of this view is that memorization was indeed a vital part of greco-roman and especially Jewish education.[42] It resonates with the language of 'handing over' and 'receiving' traditions in early Christian literature.[43] According to Gerd Theissen: 'Despite reservations concerning a direct transfer of rabbinic techniques of transmission to early Christianity, we must recognize that we have here a historical analogy to the process of tradition in Christianity's earliest phase.'[44] However, some misgivings are appropriate. Jesus did not set up a rabbinic school. The early church was indeed a 'teaching' community, but it did not function as a rabbinic academy. If Jesus' words were

---

42 According to the author of 2 Maccabees, the story of the Maccabean revolt was composed with the stated purpose that: 'we have aimed to please those who wish to read, to make it easy for those who are inclined to memorize, and to profit all readers' (2 Macc. 2.25 NRSV).
43 See e.g. Lk. 1.2; 1 Thess. 4.1–2; 1 Cor. 11.2, 23; 15.3–5; Phil. 4.9; Rom. 6.17; *Did.* 4.13. The post-sixteenth-century anxiety of many Protestants about 'tradition' has led to many ignoring or downplaying this theme, which as these Pauline references attest is early and plentiful, not a sign of a later or degenerate 'early Catholicism'.
44 Theissen 1991, 3 n. 3.

Illustration of Luke and Mark from the last page of Codex Washingtonianus, fifth century
PD-US

memorized strictly, it is not clear why we find a certain elasticity in the tradition, or how John's gospel came to be so different from the synoptics. If even the Lord's Prayer, and the words of institution at the Last Supper, appear in our sources with interestingly different Greek wording, then something other than a word-by-word rabbinic method is being used. If Jesus' words were learned, repeated, and transmitted, that process was initially taking place on the road with Jesus in his travels, and then in the developing tradition which migrated around the social networks of first-century Judean and Galilean villages. This would not be controlled or supervised, though that would not mean it was random or wild.

Other models of oral tradition could be considered. Biblical scholars have examined different paradigms of orality, based on sociological and anthropological studies. The interface between textuality and orality needs to be factored in to the picture. In addition, once we study the ways in which texts were orally performed and aurally received ('performance criticism'), yet more insights may emerge.

But the most significant trend in study of the Jesus-tradition in more recent scholarship has been situating it in terms of 'social-memory theory'. We do not, of course, have direct access to Jesus. He wrote no book; photography was not invented. What we have is 'the remembered Jesus', carried in the memories of the early disciples—complicated by the ongoing sense of Jesus' personal presence in the power of the spirit, which distinguishes how the early Christians thought about such things from the remembered traditions of, say, figures like Socrates.[45] Social memory theory explores the psychology and sociology of memory in order to understand how the past is both retrieved and refracted by the act of remembering.[46] All retrieval of memory involves a continuous negotiation between a memorialized past and the contingencies of the present. This accounts for both stability and variance in the rehearsal of the Jesus-tradition. Remembrance of Jesus' words was a significant facet

---

45 Dunn 2003, 130–1; Le Donne 2009, 76; Eve 2013, 108–34.
46 For the term 'refracted', we are indebted to Le Donne 2009, 50–2.

of the early church as it recalled the words, work, and witness of its lord.[47] But this remembrance was not simply out of nostalgia for a past 'golden moment'. It was vital to the current life of the church, facing new challenges. And, to say it again—and this is the point where Bultmann's theories took off into the stratosphere—it combined with the ongoing sense, through the spirit, of Jesus himself as a living presence.

The gospels, then, are not like what we might now have if someone had been able to follow Jesus around Judea and Galilee, filming him with a smartphone. Rather, the gospels are more like a documentary-drama, the recollection and refraction of a significant past, a past only available through the corporate memory of Jesus as it was transmitted in the early church. There was undoubtedly some memorization of the Jesus-tradition. Jesus' words, and many stories from his public career, were told and retold to undergird and direct the life of the church and to guide it in its struggles. The point was that *the kingdom had arrived on earth as in heaven*, that *this was how it had happened*, and in particular that *this was the reality in which Jesus' followers were now living*. The challenge of living out that new reality was to be met, not simply by the memory of a few helpful stories or examples, but by living within that repeatedly told story and finding it as both historical foundation and present scene-setting. In that ongoing work, eye-witnesses and teachers, as Luke indicates, were available to correct erroneous accounts of the tradition. The theological framing was of course that of the post-Easter and post-Pentecost communities. But the point of Easter and Pentecost was that the kingdom-movement initiated in Jesus' public career was now launched into its new, dynamic phase, celebrating and putting into effect Jesus' dramatic victory over the enslaving powers of darkness. All this, put together into a rich and complex series of documents, provides for the church to this day a fusion of authenticity and artistry, fact and faith, history and hermeneutics, rehearsal and reinterpretation. The remembered melody modulates into new keys, to fit new moments, or to encourage new singers to join in. But the tune remains the same.

Further reading

Bird, Michael F. 2014. *The Gospel of the Lord: How the Early Church Wrote the Story of Jesus*. Grand Rapids, MI: Eerdmans.
Burridge, Richard. 2004. *What Are the Gospels? A Comparison with Graeco-Roman Biography*. 2nd edn.; Grand Rapids, MI: Eerdmans.
Diehl, Judith A. 2010. 'What Is a "Gospel"? Recent Studies in Gospel Genre.' *CBR* 20: 1–26.
Dunn, James D. G. 2013. *The Oral Gospel Tradition*. Grand Rapids, MI: Eerdmans.
Eve, Eric. 2013. *Behind the Gospels: Understanding Oral Tradition*. London: SPCK.
Goodacre, Mark. 2007. *The Synoptic Problem: A Way through the Maze*. London: T&T Clark.
Le Donne, Anthony. 2009. *The Historiographical Jesus: Memory, Typology, and the Son of David*. Waco, TX: Baylor University Press.
Perkins, Pheme. 2007. *Introduction to the Synoptic Gospels*. Grand Rapids, MI: Eerdmans.

---

[47] See e.g. Jn. 2.22; Lk. 24.6–8; Ac. 11.16–17; 20.35, *1 Clem.* 13.1–2; 46.7–8.

Icon of the Twelve Apostles
Public Domain

VII

THE EARLY CHRISTIANS AND THE MISSION OF GOD

The 'early Christian letters' are sharp and to the point. They are full of clear practical advice for Christians taking their early steps in the faith and needing to know where the problems were going to come and what resources they could find to cope with them. But they also breathe the fresh air of delight in a new-found faith, hope and life. They are full of wonder at the fact of Jesus himself, at what he'd done in giving his life to rescue people, at what he had revealed about who God himself is. They are realistic in facing the dangers a Christian community will meet in the world around: the world will try to squash the church into its own ways of life and to stifle the rumour that the living God might be on the loose. They are equally realistic in highlighting difficulties which may arise within the community itself. They draw richly on the ancient scriptures of Israel to help give the young Christians that all-important sense of depth in discovering who they really are within God's love and purposes. They range widely across issues of everything from politics to private life. They are a vital resource for every church and every Christian.[1]

---

[1] Wright *ECL*, x–xi.

29

Introduction to Early Christian Letters

The unity of the message of the General Epistles originates in the common experience of the men who were said to have written them, namely, James, Peter, John, Jude, and their close associates. They knew each other personally; they preached, evangelized, and supervised the churches during the same decades; and they had all experienced firsthand, or by one degree of separation, the resurrection of Jesus, whom they believed to be the embodiment of Israel's living God. That historical starting-point provides the soundest foundation for seeking a unified New Testament theology and the most reasonable context in which to read and understand these books.[1]

CHAPTER AT A GLANCE

This chapter provides an overview of the Catholic Epistles.

By the end of this chapter you should be able to:

- identify the contents of the Catholic Epistles;
- understand how the Catholic Epistles function as a distinct canonical collection within the New Testament.

INTRODUCTION

The New Testament can be divided up into three main sections. First, there is the *evangelium*, the four canonical gospels. Second, there is the *Paulinium*, the thirteen letters attributed to Paul, plus the epistle to the Hebrews (which sounded sufficiently Pauline to justify placing it there). Third, there is the *apostolos*, which normally includes the Acts of the Apostles and the Catholic Epistles, with the apocalypse of John often following after.

While these groupings make sense, we might want to tinker with them. First, although the Acts of the

---

[1] See Jobes 2011, 18; though Jobes may be over-optimistic in identifying the authors.

Apostles was normally grouped with the Catholic Epistles (in the manuscripts known as $\mathfrak{P}^{74}$, 0166, 307, 945, 1409), it is not unknown for it to be joined to the four gospels ($\mathfrak{P}^{45}$, $\mathfrak{P}^{53}$), especially since Luke-Acts comprises a narrative and theological unity. Second, despite the best efforts that went into imagining Paul as the author of Hebrews, it is not in fact Pauline, though it has some interesting similarities to his writing; so we think it best to place Hebrews among the Catholic Epistles. Third, while one might be inclined to create a distinctive Johannine corpus comprised of the gospel of John, the letters of John, and the apocalypse of John, we nevertheless think it best to keep these Johannine writings where they are, in order to ensure a more even distribution of the Johannine witness across the New Testament. On top of that, while the apocalypse does not belong within the Catholic Epistles, its apocalyptic texture and prophetic message should not disguise the fact that it has the features of an encyclical epistle, composed to instruct and assure several congregations.[2] Thus the apocalypse of John is a natural sequel to the Catholic Epistles. It forms a fitting end to the Christian Bible, with its vision of creation redeemed, renewed, and restored to its original purpose of worshipping God, and of the redeemed community summing up creation's worship and reigning with God and the 'lamb' in the new heaven-and-earth reality. In our presentation, then, the Catholic Epistles include Hebrews, James and Jude, 1–2 Peter, and 1–3 John, with the apocalypse of John artificially attached to round off the New Testament canon.

In the ancient world, letter-writing was largely a substitute for personal presence. The Greek sophist Libanius wrote, 'Now, it would be sweeter to be able to see each other, but neither is the second-best choice trivial, namely to send and to receive a letter', and 'When you look at my letter, think that you are looking at me.'[3] There was a wide variety of ancient letters. The New Testament epistles mirror this variety. We can loosely suggest the following: a protreptic discourse in letter form (Romans), circular letters (Ephesians, 1 John), Diaspora letters (James, 1 Peter), a letter of commendation (Philemon; 3 John), a letter of rebuke (Galatians), a paraenetic letter (2 Peter), a letter of warning (Jude), and letters of friendship (Philippians; 2 John). Christian letters are also similar to the general form of hellenistic letters with a greeting, thanksgiving, main body, and benediction. Yet, while some New Testament letters are of a comparable length to the mundane letters of family life and commerce (especially Philemon, 2 John, 3 John, and Jude), the New Testament letters are often much longer than most standard letters, conveying sermon-like content (for example Hebrews, James, 1 John), comprising theological treatises (for example Romans, Ephesians), or representing lengthy responses to complicated

---

2   Rev. 1.4; 2.1–3.22.
3   Libanius *Ep.* 37.1; 245.9.

social situations (for example 1–2 Corinthians). It seems clear that a significant number of early Christians were highly literary and quite bookish. This was partly inherited from Judaism, which had its own culture of sacred texts and other valued texts that led on from them. But it was also driven by frequent communications and exchanges between various Christian assemblies across the Roman empire. This propensity to share opinions and concerns is evident in the apostolic decree noted in Acts 15, in the Pauline correspondence, in the letters to seven churches in Revelation 2—3, and in somewhat later examples such as the letter of Clement of Rome to the Corinthians, the letters of Ignatius, and the flurry of letters associated with the Quartodeciman controversy in the late second century. Christians wrote letters to one another precisely because they were conscious of being a worldwide movement, one that crossed geographical and ethnic boundaries. They felt to some degree invested in, and even responsible for, other believers.[4] The Catholic Epistles are part of this literary and social phenomenon, with letters composed to assemblies both near and far, to help sort out existing problems and to encourage fellow-pilgrims in their life of faith.

TABLE 29.1: EARLIEST COPIES OF THE CATHOLIC EPISTLES AND THE APOCALYPSE OF JOHN*

Book	Siglum	Manuscript name	Date	Contents
Hebrews	𝔓46	P.Chester Beatty II	c. AD 200	1.1—9.16; 9.18—10.20, 22–30; 10.32—13.25
James	𝔓20 𝔓23	AM 4117 P.Oxy. 1171 P.Oxy 1229	3rd century 3rd century	2.19—3.9 1.10—12, 15–18
Jude	𝔓72	Bodmer VII-VII	3rd/4th century	complete
1 Peter	𝔓72	Bodmer VII-VII	3rd/4th century	complete
2 Peter	𝔓72	Bodmer VII-VII	3rd/4th century	complete
1 John	𝔓9	P.Oxy 402	3rd century	4.11—12, 14–16
2 John	B	Vaticanus	4th century	complete
3 John	B	Vaticanus	4th century	complete
Revelation	𝔓98	P.IFAO II 31	c. AD 200	1.13–20

* Hill and Kruger 2012.

---

4 See Rom. 1.8; 1 Cor. 1.2; Col 1.6.

In some surviving early manuscripts (see Table 29.1), the Catholic Epistles are usually headed with the designation 'epistles' or 'catholic epistles' with a further mention of James, Peter, John, and Jude as the authors.[5] The Catholic Epistles are 'catholic' (Greek *katholikē*, meaning 'according to the whole [world]', coming into Latin as the loan-word *catholicus*) in the sense of being applicable to the universal church, that is, the church 'catholic'.[6] Strictly speaking, the Catholic Epistles are not general or encyclical letters; they are written to specific addressees, such as Jewish Christians in a rural setting (Jas. 2.1–7; 5.16), marginalized Christians in Asia Minor (1 Pet. 1.1), or specific leaders

P.Oxy X 1229, excerpt, James 1.15–18
Courtesy of The Spurlock Museum, University of Illinois at Urbana-Champaign

in Asian house-churches (2 Jn. 1; 3 Jn. 1). While Hebrews, 1 John, 2 Peter, and Jude are without explicit addressees, they are occasioned by a specific situation discernible in each letter. That said, these letters do exhibit a valuable blend of pastoral assurance and moral exhortation that transcends their original audiences. In particular, the sermonic and paraenetic character of Hebrews, James, 1 Peter, and 1 John certainly makes them conducive to a wide and 'catholic' readership.

THE CANONICAL FUNCTION OF THE CATHOLIC EPISTLES

There is a certain intra-canonical logic to the Catholic Epistles. For a start, the epistle to the Hebrews makes a good transition from the Pauline letters to the Catholic Epistles proper. Hebrews is a 'word of exhortation',[7] one that is influenced by Pauline themes, perhaps even stemming from the Pauline circle, yet the argument and imagery proceeds in a direction that is quite unlike anything Paul himself ever wrote. Hebrews is thus an effective bridge between the Pauline and catholic collections. When the New Testament is seen as a whole, it reminds readers that the two letter-collections are interdependent.[8] James is something of a rehearsal of Jesus' teachings, particularly about caring for the poor; the letter lays out a clear

---

5 Trobisch 2000, 39.
6 Anxiety about the word 'catholic' has led some Protestants to refer to these letters as 'the General Epistles'.
7 Heb. 13.22.
8 Wall 2002, 371.

and practical mode of discipleship. James is an important warning against reducing Christian faith to the cerebral and creedal realms: faith without works is dead. Jude affirms the confessional and the practical. The letter insists on the importance of contending for a common and holy faith, warning against licentiousness and urging readers to keep themselves in God's love. The two Petrine letters describe the church as a redeemed and royal people, which must live up to the high vocation required by its election and calling. Although Jesus' followers face harassment and persecution, they know that Christ has died for them, he has left them an example, and in the fullness of God's time he will return to complete the work of new creation. The Johannine letters are principally about the continued witness to the Word and the legacy of love in the churches. According to John the elder (if he is indeed the author), following Jesus means walking in the light, loving one another, and spurning the world and its antichrists. Love confronts error with the light of truth.

Another function of the Catholic Epistles is to present a comprehensive witness to Jesus and an exhortation to discipleship beyond that which was expressed in the Pauline corpus. These letters stem from the Jerusalem 'pillars' of James (the brother of Jesus), Peter, and John (see Gal. 2.9) and another relative of Jesus (Judah, normally known by his anglicized version 'Jude'). The Catholic Epistles remind us, then, that Paul is not, so to speak, the only apostolic show on tour. Although Paul was very careful to marry the assurance of the gospel with the necessity of moral transformation (see for example Rom. 6.1–23; 8.1–11; Gal. 5.6; Eph. 2.10), he himself was quite aware that he was open to the accusation of fostering antinomianism or inadvertently promoting a kind of lukewarm easy-believism (Rom. 3.8; 6.1–2). Paul's teaching, it is clear, could be distorted, and taken in the direction of cheap discipleship (as Jas. 2.14–26 warns). Or his legacy could be twisted (as was done by Marcion) so as to deny the validity of Israel's scriptures and their vision of the creator God. The Catholic Epistles thus rule out certain misconstruals of Paul's message, even as they inhibit any veneration of Paul at the expense of the wider apostolic witness (see 'Blast from the past: Augustine on how the Catholic Epistles balance out Paul').[9] At the same time, the Catholic Epistles are a testimony to Paul's stature, since Hebrews arguably shows Pauline influence, 1 Peter is at least congruent with Paul's theology, and 2 Peter 3.15–16 treats Paul's letters themselves as 'scripture'. Viewed this way, the Catholic Epistles prove that Paul is not alone in his evangelistic mission and ecclesial endeavours. He is at home among the pillar apostles.

The Catholic Epistles are also characteristic of a particular species of apostolic exhortation. Most of Paul's letters were written to relatively young congregations, ones that either he had planted himself, or his co-workers and wider circle of supporters had recently cultivated. However, the Catholic Epistles appear to have been

---

9 See esp. Nienhuis 2011.

written to established churches facing duress, perhaps even to second-generation believers in the midst of external hardship and internal division. Among the addressees of the Catholic Epistles are some, it seems, who may be waning in their enthusiasm for a future eschaton, becoming lax in their moral discipline, driven into doubt by in-house rivalries, tempted perhaps by persecution to give up meeting together, or possibly even contemplating giving up altogether. The Catholic Epistles, then, address a particular set of circumstances, including social dislocation (Hebrews), poverty (James), cultural alienation (1 Peter), external hostility combined with internal schism (1–3 John), as well as intrusive disruption (2 Peter, Jude).[10] The audiences are typically marginal: they are the 'poor' (Jas. 2.5), the 'pilgrim' (Heb. 11.8–13), 'foreigners and exiles' (1 Pet. 1.1; 2.11), and the varyingly assailed 'children of God' (1 Jn. 3.1–2, 10; 4.4; 5.2, 19). The Catholic Epistles impress upon such people both theological instruction and moral exhortation, aimed at specific pastoral and practical ends.[11] In each case, the aim is endurance, fellowship, and transformation. The respective authors urge their readers to keep their faith in Christ, to keep walking in the footsteps of Christ, and to keep the fires of hope alight. As such, a consistent theme is for believers to continue in their pilgrimage towards the consummation of all things in Christ.

> **BLAST FROM THE PAST: AUGUSTINE ON HOW THE CATHOLIC EPISTLES BALANCE OUT PAUL**
>
> *In the fifth century, Bishop Augustine of Hippo wrote a work about the correct relationship between faith and works. He declared at one point:*
>
> Even in the days of the Apostles certain somewhat obscure statements of the Apostle Paul were misunderstood, and some thought he was saying this: 'Let us do evil that good may come from it' [Rom. 3.8] because he said: 'Now the law intervened that the offense might abound. But where the offense has bounded, grace has abounded yet more' [Rom. 5.20] . . . Since this problem is by no means new and had already risen at the time of the Apostles, other apostolic letters of Peter, John, James and Jude are deliberately aimed against the argument I have been refuting and firmly uphold the doctrine that faith does not avail without good works. (Aug. *Fid. Op.* 21, cited in Nienhuis 2007, 2)

As a literary collection, the Catholic Epistles function much like the Book of the Twelve Minor Prophets in the Old Testament: a diverse and distinct witness to God. Although each of the Catholic Epistles has its own context, content, and unique features, some common themes emerge:

1. the Old Testament authorizes the church's kerygma and validates the church as God's royal and holy people;

---

10 Wall 2002, 377.
11 Wall 2002, 371.

2. suffering is the crucible that tests and refines authentic faith;
3. genuine faith is characterized by perseverance, love, obedience, and transformation;
4. believers are called to keep the teaching of Jesus and follow the example of Jesus;
5. Jesus' death cleanses believers from the contamination of sin;
6. Jesus' resurrection brings believers into a living hope;
7. Jesus' ascension marks him out as the lord of the universe;
8. elders should shepherd the church with gentleness and compassion;
9. the church must be vigilant against allowing licentiousness to gain a foothold;
10. the church should guard against inadequate accounts of Christ's person and work;
11. the church should be characterized by holiness and hospitality;
12. the church should face Christ's return with confidence in receiving its reward of eternal life.

In sum, the Catholic Epistles are focused on bringing adolescent congregations to maturity in Christ. They aim to equip these congregations with a deep and enduring faith, as robust as it is contagious, in a hostile and volatile environment.

Further reading

Hockey, Katherine M., Madison N. Pierce, and Francis Watson (eds.). 2017. *Muted Voices of the New Testament: Readings in the Catholic Epistles and Hebrews*. LNTS 587; London: T&T Clark.

Jobes, Karen H. 2011. *Letters to the Church: A Survey of Hebrews and the General Epistles*. Grand Rapids, MI: Zondervan.

Carlo Crivelli, St Augustine, 1487/8
National Museum of Western Art

Lockett, Darian. 2017. *Letters from Pillar Apostles: The Formation of the Catholic Epistles as a Canonical Collection.* Eugene, OR: Pickwick.

Niebuhr, Karl-Wilhelm, and Robert Wall (eds.). 2009. *The Catholic Epistles and Apostolic Tradition: A New Perspective on James to Jude.* Waco, TX: Baylor University Press.

Nienhuis, David. 2007. *Not by Paul Alone: The Formation of the Catholic Epistle Collection and the Christian Canon.* Waco, TX: Baylor University Press.

Nienhuis, David, and Robert Wall (eds.). 2013. *Reading the Epistles of James, Peter, John and Jude as Scripture.* Grand Rapids, MI: Eerdmans.

Wright, N. T. 2011. *Early Christian Letters for Everyone: James, Peter, John, and Judah.* London: SPCK.

30

The Letter to the Hebrews

In many ways and by many means God spoke in ancient times to our ancestors in the prophets; but at the end of these days he spoke to us in a son.[1]

CHAPTER AT A GLANCE

This chapter provides an overview of the letter to the Hebrews.

By the end of this chapter you should be able to:
- grasp the provenance and purpose of Hebrews;
- describe the structure and argument of Hebrews;
- understand the themes and theology of Hebrews.

INTRODUCTION

Hebrews is, to us at least, a strange and difficult book. To the casual reader today, it seems to ramble on about things that are not exactly burning topics of discussion over breakfast or bitterly debated on Christian blog sites. It begins with a complex discussion of angels and what God did not say to them; continues with a brief treatment of Psalm 95 and what 'rest' really means; moves on to discuss a man named Melchizedek whom Abraham once met but who remains unknown to most people today; goes on to talk about the furniture in the wilderness tabernacle; and ends with an exhortation to 'go outside the camp'. None of this is the kind of thing that comes up routinely in conversation, even among practising Christians.

What's more, Hebrews has a different feel and texture when we place it alongside the gospels and Paul's letters. Many in the ancient church thought that Paul wrote Hebrews; but, as the more perceptive realized

---

1 Heb. 1.1–2.

even then, this doesn't quite hold up. Entering the world of Hebrews after a close study of Paul is like listening to Monteverdi after listening to Bach. We are in the same world, but the colour is different; or in musical terms, the notes are similar, but they are being played on different instruments.

Perhaps the most difficult thing for us is the emphasis, in this letter, on animal sacrifice. For today's readers this is likely to feel completely foreign. Most of us are quite happy to purchase our meat from supermarkets, conveniently packaged and wrapped, with no thought of how it got there. Unless you've lived on a farm or worked in an abattoir, you probably haven't watched animals being killed. We tend, as well, to associate 'sacrifice' with archaic and apparently bloodthirsty rituals of ancient peoples; or we sanitize the word by using it as a colourful and vaguely religious metaphor for 'giving up' something significant, like money or career. In Hebrews, however, 'sacrifice' constitutes one of the key images for the meaning of Jesus' death. Even those who read their Bibles carefully may still find the ancient Israelite cults strange and incomprehensible, and struggle to apply them in any but the vaguest terms to the understanding of Jesus' death and what it means.

At the same time, however, Hebrews clearly belongs closely with the New Testament message as a whole. The letter is telling the same basic story as the evangelists, Paul, Peter, and John the Seer. World history, focused on Israel's story, has led up to a dramatic point, namely the overthrow of the powers of darkness and the call of the nations to worship the one true God. The Old Testament provided the scaffolding, and now God has built the new Jerusalem, forming a multi-ethnic Abrahamic family and putting the world right at last. Hebrews insists that the scaffolding is now eclipsed by the actual building, the fulfilment of the scriptural hopes in Jesus, the son. All the emblems of Israel's call, and all the instruments of Israel's vocation—Temple, law covenant, priesthood, cultus, Mount Zion—are there; but now they have come to a new fulfilment in the Messiah and his people. We could perhaps look at Hebrews as, in a sense, a Christian introduction to the Old Testament. The letter points out that Israel's scriptures were always looking ahead to something yet to come: a new covenant, a new type of priesthood, a new altar, a better sacrifice, a city to which the present Jerusalem would only be an advance signpost. We could summarize Hebrews this way: the scriptures had always pointed ahead to something new and better, and it has now arrived in Jesus.

CONTEXTUAL AND CRITICAL MATTERS

Authorship

The authorship of Hebrews has always been a conundrum. Many in the early eastern church assumed that it was written by Paul. This is why the earliest copy of Hebrews that has come down to us is found in $\mathfrak{P}^{46}$ (*c.* AD 175–225), an early Pauline letter-collection, which places Hebrews in between Romans and 1 Corinthians. Pantaenus, the founder of the catechetical school in Alexandria, regarded the epistle as Pauline, with Paul omitting his name because the lord Jesus was the apostle to the Jews and Paul was apostle to the gentiles. Clement of Alexandria (AD 150–215) attributed Hebrews to Paul, suggesting that it had been written initially in Hebrew for Hebrews, and then translated by Luke into Greek. Origen (AD 185–253) leaned towards Pauline authorship, but acknowledged the lack of certainty and famously opined: 'But who wrote the epistle, in truth only God knows.'[2]

The Arch of Titus commemorates the Roman general's defeat of Jerusalem and the destruction of the Temple. The candelabra or seven-branched candlestick was a well-known symbol of Jewish life in the ancient world.
Matt Ragen / Shutterstock

In the western church, Pauline authorship was largely rejected until the fourth century. For example, Hebrews is absent from the Muratorian canon in the late second or early third century, and is not attributed to Paul by either Irenaeus or Hippolytus. In the fourth century, Hilary of Poitiers affirmed the Pauline authorship of Hebrews, ensuring its canonical status and making it available for use in the Arian debates.[3] The change in the west came with Jerome and Augustine, who followed the eastern

---

2 Eus. *Hist. Eccl.* 6.14.2–4, 13; 6.25.12, 14.
3 Hilary *Trinity* 4.11.

view, and assumed that because Hebrews was canonical, it must have been written by an apostle, namely, Paul. Jerome acknowledged the doubts held about its Pauline authorship, and professed that the question of the actual author was not in the end all that important because the book is 'honoured daily by being read in the churches'.[4]

The medieval church continued to regard Paul as the author, as is still the case in the King James translation. Aquinas followed Clement of Alexandria in supposing that Hebrews was penned by Luke, operating as Paul's secretary.[5] Since the Reformation, however, Pauline authorship has been mostly rejected. Alternative proposals, from ancient to modern times, have included Barnabas (Tertullian), Clement of Rome (Calvin), Apollos (Luther), and Priscilla (Adolf von Harnack). There are, however, significant differences in vocabulary, style, and rhetorical texture, as well as what seem to many an unPauline theological emphasis on the Temple and priesthood. Elsewhere Paul always identifies himself in either the greeting or ending of his letters. It would be very odd for Paul to describe himself as someone who heard the gospel not from the lord but from 'those who heard him'.[6] All this makes Pauline authorship grossly improbable. The author does, however, know Paul's travelling companion Timothy (Heb. 13.23); and there are several overlaps with Paul in themes such as Jesus' sonship and sacrificial death, and the use of particular scriptural texts like Psalms 8 and 110 and Habakkuk 2.[7] Perhaps the most we can say is that the author was probably a well-educated second-generation Greek-speaking Jewish Christian, thoroughly versed in the Septuagint, familiar with Greek philosophy, and at home both in Roman rhetorical techniques and Jewish interpretative traditions.

Date

If the authorship remains uncertain, so does the date. It might be as early as AD 50; it might be as late as AD 95. The main factors here are the following. (1) It appears that *1 Clement* (c. AD 96) alludes to several passages from Hebrews.[8] (2) Timothy, referred to at 13.23, joined Paul in his missionary journeys in around AD 49.[9] (3) In particular, the arguments about the superiority of Jesus' atoning death over the atonement purportedly attributed to the animal sacrifices performed in the Jewish cult might lead one to expect a reference to the Temple's destruction in AD 70. Strictly speaking, the author's arguments about the tabernacle and Levitical priesthood could work within either a pre- or post-70 context (see Heb. 5.1–4; 7.20, 23, 27, 28; 8.3, 4, 13; 9.6, 13; 10.11).[10] However, after declaring that the annual sacrificial

---

4 Jer. *Ep.* 129.3.
5 On Luke and Hebrews in modern scholarship, see Allen 2010; Pitts and Walker 2010.
6 Contrast Heb. 2.3 with Gal. 1.11–12.
7 See Witherington 1991.
8 *1 Clem.* 36.1–5 = Heb 1.1–14; 2.17–18; 4.14–16.
9 Cf. Ac. 16.1–3.
10 Koester 2001a, 69. In addition, appeals made to the use of verbs in the present tense to describe the

offerings are ineffective, the writer adds, 'Otherwise, would they not have ceased being offered, since the worshippers, cleansed once for all, would no longer have any consciousness of sin?' (Heb. 10.2 NRSV). The question demands an affirmative answer, implying that these annual sacrifices have *not* stopped. This would favour a date before AD 70.[11] (4) The letter's implied audience has been suffering persecution but not yet martyrdom (Heb. 10.32–34; 12.4). That would fit with persecutions experienced by Christians in Rome in the late 40s during the reign of Claudius, and might indicate the riots in Rome (and the subsequent expulsion of Jews, mentioned also in Acts) referred to by Suetonius as 'instigated by Chrestus'.[12] Tacitus mentions that, even before Nero's pogrom, the Christians were 'hated' by the Roman people.[13] It is possible that Hebrews looks back to this period when referring to earlier struggles and suffering (Heb. 10.32) and urges its readers to remember those still in prison (Heb. 13.3). But this would provide only a very loose indication of the letter's date.

Genre

Hebrews is a homily in letter form (Heb. 13.22), written by a Christian leader from somewhere in Italy (Heb. 13.24) to Jewish Christians in Rome, quite possibly on the eve of the Neronian persecutions in the early 60s. The author urges the members of his (or her) audience to remain steadfast in their loyalty to Jesus as Messiah, son of God and true high priest, and not to look for security to the symbols of their Jewish identity. They must continue in faith despite opposition from wider society (Heb. 11.26; 13.13) and must hold on tightly to their confession, because the one who announced the message to them is faithful (Heb. 10.23).

Purpose

The letter to the Hebrews seems designed to persuade Jewish Christians not to go back to the forms of Jewish life that did not acknowledge Jesus as Messiah. Many will have felt pressure to do so, particularly under threat of persecution. The Jewish world, enjoying official Roman recognition, represented a much safer social and legal option than belonging to an unpopular sect. This explains the exhortations to endurance (see Heb. 2.1–4; 3.12–14; 10.39; 12.3–11) and the recollection of earlier harassment (Heb. 10.32–39).

Levitical priesthood *do not* require that the Levitical sacrifices are still in present operation at the time of the author (Heb. 7.27–28; 8.3–5; 9.6–7, 25; 10.1–3, 8; 13.10–11). This is because the present tense form can be used to describe past, ongoing, undefined (gnomic), or timeless action, and the temporal situation of the verb is determined by context, not by tense form (Porter 1994, 29–33).

11 Of course, *Ep. Diog.* 3.4–5, written about a century after the destruction of the Jerusalem Temple, critiques the Jerusalem sacrificial cultus as if it were still in operation or still thought to be theoretically valid. Thus, critique of the Jewish cultus alone is not a determinative factor for dating.
12 Suet. *Claud.* 25.1–5; Ac. 18.2. See the discussion in *NTPG* 354–5.
13 Tac. *Ann.* 15.44.

THE ARGUMENT OF HEBREWS

(See box: 'Outline of Hebrews'.)

1. Prologue about God's son (1.1–4)

The letter launches straight into one of the most sublime early Christian statements of who Jesus was and is. He is the 'son', who shares in the shining reflection of God's glory; he is the precise expression of God's own being. Jesus is the heir of all things, the divine agent of creation, the reflection of God's glory, the very imprint of God's being, the sustainer of all things, the redeemer who is enthroned next to God. He has a name greater than the angels. Whatever else the letter is about, it clearly emphasizes (what we might call) the *ultimacy* of Jesus. He is the *prophet* through whom God declared his final word. He is the *priest* who accomplished a perfect work of purification. He is the *king* who sits enthroned beside the majesty of God.[14]

> **OUTLINE OF HEBREWS**
>
> 1. Prologue about God's son (1.1–4)
> 2. Jesus is greater than the angels (1.5—2.9)
> 3. Jesus the great high priest (2.10—6.20)
> 4. Jesus' priesthood and the new covenant (7.1—10.18)
> 5. A call to faithfulness and endurance (10.19—12.29)
> 6. Living righteously for the city of God (13.1–21)
> 7. Final greetings (13.22–25)

> '"You are my Son; today I have begotten you" is not just a claim about Jesus reaching an exalted status. It is a declaration of his eternal relationship with the Father that is always in effect.'
>
> **Madison Pierce**, 'Hebrews 1 and the Son Begotten "Today",' in *Retrieving Eternal Generation*, 131.

2. Jesus is greater than the angels (1.5—2.9)

The christological claim is demonstrated by comparing 'the son' and the angels, to whom the son is superior. Psalm 2.7 and 2 Samuel 7.14 imply that the sonship of Jesus is unique and is much greater than the sonship of the angels. Psalm 97.7 indicates that the angels must worship the son; the son must then be far greater. Psalm 104.4 stresses that angels are ministers of God, not embodiments of him. In contrast, Psalm 45.6–7 applies the title 'God' to Israel's king, and this has become a reality in the Messiah. Psalm 102.25–27 refers to the son's role in creation, both of the old heaven and earth and of the new heaven and earth. Unlike the created order, then, and also unlike the angels, the son is not subject to change or dissolution. Psalm 110.1 gives to the son the privilege, never afforded to an angel, of sharing God's throne. In short, the angels are subjects of God, servants of those who inherit salvation. In other words, the angels are inferior both to the son and also to those whom the son saves, namely those who belong to the church (1.6–14).

---

[14] Bruce 1990, 50.

The front page of the epistle to the Hebrews according to Codex Vaticanus, a fourth-century manuscript of the New Testament
Art Collection 3 / Alamy Stock Photo

This emphasis on the son's superiority to angels was not simply a way of showing how great he was and is, or to warn the readers against worshipping angels. The point—standing as an introduction to the whole letter—is that for many Jews one of the things that guaranteed the ultimacy of the law of Moses itself was that it had been given through angels.[15] The author does not challenge this belief, but insists that in Israel's scriptures themselves the constant reference to the coming son of God as superior to angels indicates that all along, in Israel's traditions themselves, the law of Moses, angel-given though it was, was never intended as God's final word. Thus the readers must not ignore this new and decisive rescuing revelation (2.1–4).

---

15 See Dt. 33.2 (LXX); Ac. 7.38, 53; Gal. 3.19.

The comparison with angels now takes on a new twist with a reflection on Psalm 8 (2.5–9). God did not place the world under the control of angels; God always intended to crown *humans* as vice-regents of creation. Psalm 8 looks back to the human vocation as in Genesis 1 and 2. The key phrase is 'son of man' in Psalm 8.4, quoted in 2.6: this can simply mean 'human beings', but through the connection with Daniel 7 it was easy to see Jesus himself as the 'one like a son of man', in whom God's ultimate purposes have been decisively launched. Jesus as Messiah represents Israel; Israel was designed to represent the whole world; thus Jesus represents humanity as a whole. Hebrews thus stresses God's placing of everything under the Messiah's feet, as already indicated through Psalm 110.1 in Hebrews 1.13.[16] All this speaks both of the *future* role of Jesus in God's new creation and of his *present* position as lord. Because he *represents his people* as the true human being, he can also *substitute for them* by tasting death in their stead. As Messiah, he won the victory, dealing a death-blow to death itself.[17]

3. Jesus the great high priest (2.10—6.20)

Jesus is qualified by God to be the pioneer of salvation through what he suffered (2.10–18). United with his brothers and sisters, he has brought a 'cleansing' for sins (as already in 1.3) and made 'atonement' for sins (2.17). Psalm 22.22 and Isaiah 8.17–18 explain: Jesus became one with his people, sharing an existence of flesh and blood, and overcoming the fear that enslaved them and the power of death that the devil held over them (2.14–15). He does this, obviously, not for angels but for his people—Abraham's extended family. Jesus thus becomes 'a merciful and trustworthy high priest in God's presence, to make atonement for the sins of the people' (2.16–17). This is the first mention of Jesus' priesthood, a theme that will dominate the centre of the letter, and it introduces the pastoral theme: because the high priest was tempted like us, he can help us in our temptations (2.18; 4.15).

This brings us to the point of this whole Jesus-greater-than-the-angels argument (3.1–6). Jesus is *superior to Moses*; Moses was great, God's true servant, but Jesus is incomparably greater.

This leads to the next major warning (3.7—4.13), which comes in the form of an exegesis of Psalm 95. The psalm warns against copying the Israelites of the wilderness generation, who rebelled and were not allowed to enter the promised land (3.7–12). The writer's point is subtle: the psalm speaks to David's generation about still 'not entering' the coming 'rest', which must mean that the psalm was envisaging a 'rest' for which the entry into the land was just a foretaste. Scripture itself therefore points to a fulfilment out beyond what Moses had been promising.

---

[16] See the similar combination in 1 Cor. 15.23–28, again echoing Genesis.
[17] Heb. 2.5–9, 14; see again 1 Cor. 15.23–28.

The readers are then to see themselves as like that generation, on a pilgrimage towards God's promised future, and they must not make the same mistake. The challenge then focuses on the word 'Today': God had acted definitively in Jesus the Messiah, so the longed-for new day had come. There was therefore still a 'rest' to enter—or, as it might be, a 'rest' to forfeit (3.12–13). There will be a new kind of land, a new sort of city, a new creation, which will be brought to full reality after the present heaven and earth have been 'shaken' (12.25–28). This will be the 'rest' which mirrors God's own 'rest' on the seventh day of creation (Gen. 2.3). This is the 'Today' to which Israel's scriptures had always pointed. The readers of the letter must therefore get rid of continuing unbelief (3.14–19) and press on to the goal, reckoning with the danger of disobedience and the inherent power of God's word (4.1–13).

All these themes are then focused on Jesus as the great high priest. Here, too, the underlying point is the same: that scripture itself points ahead to a new dispensation when the present system will give way to that for which it was meant all along as a foretaste. (Here and throughout, we should avoid any suggestion that the Old Testament and its 'religion' or 'theology' was somehow 'bad' and that the Christian dispensation is somehow a 'replacement'. The author is stressing that Israel's scriptures always looked ahead and saw the key elements of Israel's life as forward-looking signposts, recognizing that when you arrive at your destination you don't need the signposts any more, not because they were bad but because they have done their job.)

Anyway, the point here is that Jesus, having died and been raised from the dead, was then exalted in the ascension to the very throne of the father in order that he might continue to implement the work he had accomplished on earth; and that the role he is thereby taking is that of the true high priest. This priest was and still is one of us. He can sympathize with our weaknesses, having been tested and tried just like us, yet without sinning. In Jesus we have a champion over death and a victor over sin, who enables us to approach the throne of God with confidence to receive the grace and mercy that we need (4.14–16).

Jesus, however, is no ordinary priest. The Levitical priests were selected from the people to bring gifts and sacrifices to God for the forgiveness of sins. They had a pastoral role in looking after the people and sympathizing with them. But the priests were themselves weak and sinful, and so had to offer sacrifices for the people's sins and also for their own. Jesus, however, can sympathize, but not because he is a sinner. He belongs to a different order of priesthood, itself explicitly foretold in scripture, and can thereby do all that Levitical priests can do, only better (5.1–3).

The author explains, using the same type of argument about Psalm 110 that had been used about Psalm 95: *scripture itself points beyond itself.* Here the messianic psalms 2 and 110 join together the royal and priestly roles of the coming Messiah, but with the priesthood not that of Aaron's descendants but 'according to Melchizedek'.

EMAILS
from the edge

→ ☆ 📁 🗑

From: Alan_Daley@aol.com
To: Professor Dana Schuler
Date: Mon, 12 Dec 2016 at 4:08 p.m.
Subject: Salvation in Hebrews

Dear Prof.,

My pastor preached a sermon on Hebrews 6 a few weeks back where he said that you could lose your salvation. Is this true?

Thanks
AD

From: Professor Dana Schuler
To: Alan_Daley@aol.com
Date: Mon, 12 Dec 2016 at 4:22 p.m.
Subject: Re: Salvation in Hebrews

Dear Alan,

This is a tricky one. Many theologians and traditions argue that salvation is something that can be lost or forfeited. However, I would point out that in Hebrews salvation is essentially future! See Hebrews 1.4; 2.3; 5.9; 6.9; and 9.28. You cannot lose what you do not fully have! But I tend to think that these warnings, terrifying and serious as they are, are addressed to those on the fringes of the community, who taste the good things of the Lord but have never fully closed the deal in terms of complete conversion. This explains why the author still expects the audience to persevere (see Heb. 6.9 and 10.39). I think the main point is that members of the Christian community as a whole should make sure that it does not become a place where God's grace can be received in vain by anyone (see Heb. 12.15).

The grace be with you
Prof. Dana Schuler

(This will be fully explained in Heb. 7.) Again, the author stresses Jesus' own human experience, wrestling in agony with his vocation while remaining obedient to his father's will (5.7–8). His perfection as the 'son' meant that his death became a source of eternal salvation for those who obey him. He has thus become a priest in this new Melchizedekian order (5.9–10).

In a short digression, the author complains about his readers' lack of spiritual maturity and their unwillingness to learn. They are still in infancy when they should be in the adulthood of their faith (5.11–14). They know the basics and need to move on (6.1–3). There is, he stresses, no returning to the faith once someone has known its power and enlightenment and then firmly renounced it. That would be 'crucifying God's son all over again' and 'holding him up to contempt' (6.4–6 *NTE/KNT*). Land gets watered, ready to grow crops; but if all it produces is thorns and thistles the farmer will turn it into a bonfire (6.7–8). The author seems confident that his present hearers will not be like that (6.9–12; see 10.39). He seems to be thinking of people who have belonged to the church, who have taken part in its common life, but who then decide for one reason or other that it isn't for them, and join the chorus of malicious contempt for the faith. Such persons, he says, enter a point of no return (see 'Emails from the edge: salvation in Hebrews').

Hebrews then makes its way back to Melchizedek, who features in the story of Abraham, by referring back to God's sure and certain promises to Abraham himself (Gen. 22.17). We, the heirs of those promises, may be encouraged by the fact that Jesus has himself guaranteed them by entering into the inner sanctuary of God's presence on our behalf (6.17–20). He is there for us like an 'anchor': if we are firmly fastened to him, we are already secure. He is, after all, the promised priest 'after the order of Melchizedek' (6.19–20). With this, we have rejoined the argument that broke off at 5.10.

4. Jesus' priesthood and the new covenant (7.1—10.18)

The author then explains. Once again the underlying argument is that Israel's scriptures themselves indicate that they are pointing ahead to something beyond themselves. In this case, they point to a priesthood which is both more ancient and more long-lasting than the Aaronic line. Psalm 110.4 indicates that the coming Davidic king will be a priest in the order of Melchizedek, thus solving at a stroke a puzzle over which other Jews of the period puzzled: could a coming Messiah be *both* a priest *and* a king? The writer is drawing on Genesis 14.18–20, the account of how Melchizedek blessed Abraham, and Abraham in turn gave Melchizedek a tenth of the plunder from his conquest of the pagan kings. Hebrews explores Melchizedek a bit further: his name means 'king of righteousness'; he was also 'king of Salem' (that is, pre-Israelite Jerusalem), which means 'king of peace'; he was a 'priest of God Most High' (Gen. 14.18), and his priesthood did not depend on genealogy

(7.3) (see 'Portals and parallels: the Dead Sea Scrolls on Melchizedek'). In all these respects he looks forward to the Messiah, whose priesthood is thus superior to that of the house of Levi. There are, then, scriptural grounds for seeing Jesus as superior to the ongoing line of Jewish priests (7.11–19). It isn't that the old dispensation was bad. It was pointing forwards. The new dispensation is *even better* than what went before. Jesus is a priest *for ever*, not only for the span of an earthly life; so he is always there to intercede for his people (7.20–25).

A priest like this is obviously different. He is set apart from sinners, holy and blameless, so he can intercede for them. He does not offer one sacrifice after another; instead he offered himself as an atonement for sins, once and for all. The law appointed human priests with inherent weakness, but the oath appointed the son who has been made perfect for ever (7.26–28).

The author sums up the argument thus far and points to the crucial result (8.1–6): a change in priesthood means a change in *covenant*—and, once again, this is predicted in scripture itself. It turns out that the tabernacle in the wilderness (to which the author refers throughout, rather than the Jerusalem Temple which may in his day have been regarded as corrupt beyond repair) is a copy of the true tabernacle, the dwelling of God in heaven; and that is where Jesus has gone to exercise his perpetual priesthood (8.1–6). The Levitical priests, then, offer sacrifices according to the law, in a sanctuary that is a copy or shadow of the heavenly one. By entering heaven Jesus has a superior ministry, acting as the mediator of the long-promised 'better covenant' established on 'better promises'. 'Better' is, indeed, a major theme of Hebrews, particularly the present section (see Table 30.1).

This time the key passage that points beyond Israel's scriptures to a new kind of fulfilment is Jeremiah 31.31–34, which the writer quotes at length. The prophet

> **PORTALS AND PARALLELS: THE DEAD SEA SCROLLS ON MELCHIZEDEK**
>
> *One of the scrolls from Qumran depicts the year of jubilee with a melange of scriptural texts that includes the forgiveness of sins and judgment of God's enemies. The key agent of deliverance at this moment is Melchizedek, a relatively minor and enigmatic biblical figure mentioned only in Genesis 14 and Psalm 110, but one who is transformed into an exalted divine being who makes atonement for the sins of the Sons of Light, brings divine vengeance, and defeats Belial (the satan).*
>
> And this thing will [occur] in the first week of the Jubilee and that follows the nine Jubilees. And the Day of Atonement is the e[nd of the] tenth [Ju]bilee, when all the Sons of [Light] and the men of the lot of Mel[chi]zedek will be atoned for. [And] a statute concerns them [to prov]ide them with their rewards. For this is the moment of the Year of grace for Melchizedek. [And h]e will, by his strength, judge the holy ones of God, executing judgment as it is written concerning him in the Songs of David, who said ELOHIM *has taken his place in the divine council, in the midst of the gods he holds judgment*. (11Q13 6–10; tr. G. Vermes [1995])

explains the nature of this new covenant: (1) it will include a reunited Israel; (2) it will endure because the people will remain steadfast; (3) God will write his law in their minds and hearts; (4) they will know God in a new depth of spiritual intimacy; and (5) God will be merciful to the people and remember their sins no more. This new covenant will render the old one obsolete (8.7–13).

Abel and Melchizedek offering a sacrifice to God, Basilica di San Vitale, Ravenna, Italy; sixth century
ribeiroantonio / Shutterstock

The comparison of the earthly and heavenly sanctuaries continues with due emphasis on the fact that the priestly ministry in the inner and outer rooms of the sanctuary could not provide what Jesus Christ does: true atonement (9.1–10). How all this relates to the new covenant is then explained. First, the fact that there was no free and unhindered access to God implies that the holy spirit was showing that the way into the most holy place had not been disclosed while the old tabernacle was still operational. Second, the gifts and offerings are really a 'picture' or 'parable', unable to cleanse the conscience, merely a matter of external appearances until the new order of things is put into proper effect (9.8–10). The point is that God has all along had a master plan for how the world would be put to right. The sacrificial system was a step towards that end, but it was not the final goal.

In a further contrast, the death of Jesus Christ provided a permanent and complete atonement for sin because he entered the heavenly sanctuary with the offering of his own blood, which secures eternal redemption (9.12). The author is leading readers to the heart of the deep mystery which Jesus' death involves.

As the representative human being (Heb. 2) and the appointed high priest (Heb. 7), Jesus can provide what the old order of sacrifices could only point to: redemption and cleansing. He offered this not in an earthly abode, but in heaven, the tabernacle 'not made with hands', which is to say, 'not of the present creation' (9.11–14 *NTE/KNT*). Note also the Trinitarian thrust in the 'blood of the Messiah', offered to 'God', and 'through the eternal spirit'. Rather than ending up trapped in 'dead works', we are free to serve 'the living God' (9.14 *NTE/KNT*).

The whole point of the sacrificial system was never, after all, about animals being killed by way of vicarious punishment. That notion has crept in to Christian understandings of 'sacrifice' by an illegitimate transfer of ideas from Paul's law-court imagery. The point was not to punish people's sins so that they could enter God's presence, but to cleanse every trace of sin and death from the people and the sanctuary so that God could come to dwell with them. The sacrificial blood acted as the cleansing, purifying agent so that the stain of death, and the sin which leads to it, would not compel God to absent himself. In the same way, the point here is not to enable people to come into God's presence (though from our point of view that appears part of it) but to enable the living God to dwell in us and with us.

All this is vital as the author returns to the topic of 'covenant', explaining what is 'new' about the 'new covenant' (9.15–28). Jesus' death makes him the 'mediator of a new covenant' bringing a 'promised inheritance of the age to come': in him, earth and heaven are finally joined together as he, in his fully human body, enters the heavenly sanctuary on our behalf. Having done this 'once for all' (one of the great emphases of Hebrews), he makes it valid for all time. When he reappears it will not be, like the high priest on the Day of Atonement, to sort out continuing problems among the people, but to save those who are eagerly awaiting him (9.28).

Hebrews then backs up this argument with another scriptural passage. Psalm 40.6–8 indicates that God's ultimate intention was never a continuing round of sacrifices, but the listening and willing human heart to which they pointed (10.1–10). That is the way in which all the arguments are drawn together, with Psalm 110 and Jeremiah 31 all witnessing to the single covenant-renewing and sin-forgiving act of the Messiah (10.11–18).

TABLE 30.1: THE SUPERLATIVE STATUS OF JESUS ACCORDING TO THE AUTHOR OF HEBREWS

Jesus is a better . . .	
high priest	Heb. 4.15
hope	Heb. 7.19
covenant	Heb. 7.22
promise	Heb. 8.6
sacrifice	Heb. 9.23
possession	Heb. 10.34
country	Heb. 11.16
resurrection	Heb. 11.35
word	Heb. 12.24

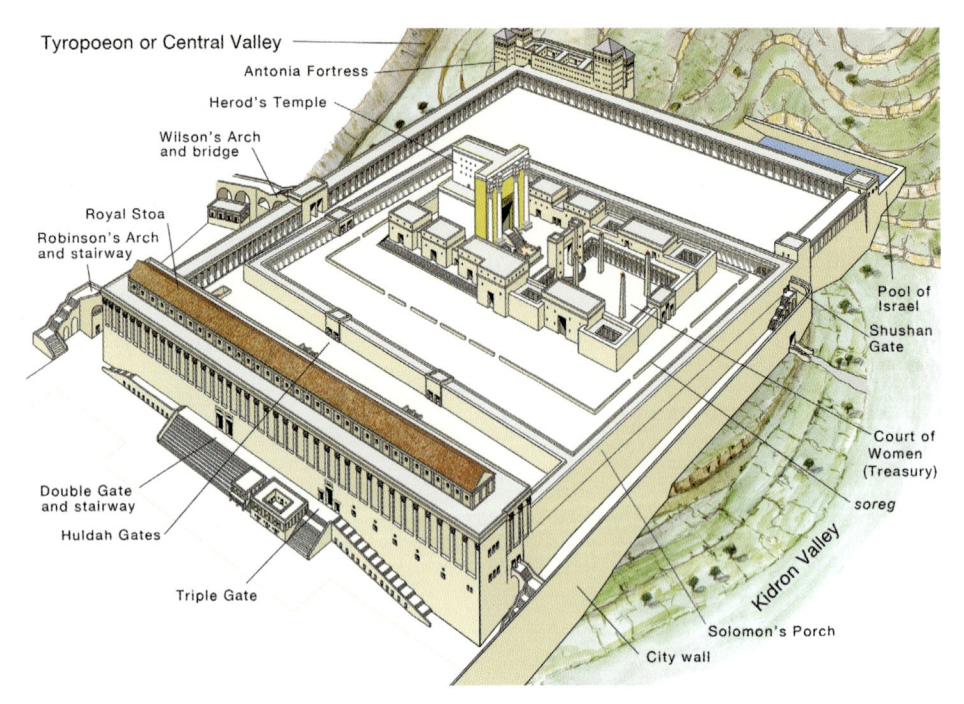

An illustration of Herod's Temple
A reconstruction by Dr. Leen Ritmeyer

5. A call to faithfulness and endurance (10.19—12.29)

The writer turns from expounding the new covenant to exhorting his readers to worship and perseverance. The privileges of the new covenant are listed and celebrated. Confidence in the Messiah, confession of faith, celebration in worship, and continual meeting together—all these flow from the work of Jesus as the great high priest.

Celebration, though, gives way to admonition, with the fourth major warning-passage in the letter (see box: 'The warning passages in Hebrews'). To spurn this new covenant—to turn away deliberately from what has now been done by the Messiah—means that there is no further sacrifice for sin. Rather, what remains is the prospect of judgment and a consuming fire for those who oppose God (10.26–29). Faced with the temptation for Jewish Jesus-followers to retreat into the (supposed) security of the Jewish community that has rejected the gospel, the author warns that to have come close to genuine and lasting Christian faith and worship, and then to reject it, can only mean condemnation (see 'Blast from the past: Origen on apostasy'). Once again, however, he turns back to encouragement: surely, he says, this is not true of you (10.30–39).

The greatest encouragement comes from knowing that one stands in a long line of people who have faced similar challenges and met the test. Many ancient Jewish writers told the story of Israel by highlighting specific moments and individuals and locating their own hearers at the end of the narrative.[18] The early Christians often did this with Jesus himself as the climax, and his followers were then incorporated into the renewed story that would follow—as, for instance, with the genealogies in Matthew 1 or Luke 3 or the speech of Stephen in Acts 7.[19] Hebrews 11 fits into this pattern, with the highlighted theme this time being the 'faith' which marked out one person after another, a faith that was focused on reaching out in hope for God's future. Faith here is, then, an assurance in hope and a conviction about things not yet seen (11.1); this might seem to be questioned when the first example is about the world being made by God's word (11.3), but the point here too is God's sovereign ability to create new things not yet seen.

There then follows a list of witnesses to authentic faith, from Abel and Noah, through Abraham and Sarah, to the other patriarchs and Moses, to monarchs, prophets and martyrs (Heb. 11.4–38). All of them were looking and waiting for the ultimate promised reality for which the 'promised land' was just a foretaste: the 'better resurrection' (11.35) that would mean not simply a return to present existence but a going forward, like the Messiah himself, into the new heaven-and-earth reality of an utterly transformed new creation (12.1–3). All these heroes and heroines of faith were out of tune with the rest of the world, pointing ahead to the fact that the God who had

> **THE WARNING PASSAGES IN HEBREWS**
>
> - Hebrews 2.1–4
> - Hebrews 3.7–4.13
> - Hebrews 5.11–6.12
> - Hebrews 10.19–39
> - Hebrews 12.14–29

> **BLAST FROM THE PAST: ORIGEN ON APOSTASY**
>
> *The Alexandrian theologian Origen (c. AD 184–253) made this comment on John 11:*
>
> Now we ought to be aware that there are some Lazaruses even now who, after having become friends of Jesus, have become sick and died. As dead persons they have remained in the tomb and the land of the dead with the dead ... Consider the one who has fallen away from Christ and returned to the Gentiles' life after he has received knowledge of the Truth. He has been enlightened and tasted the heavenly gift and become a partaker of the Holy Spirit ... yet now is in hades with the shades and the dead and to be in the land of the dead or the tombs. Whenever, therefore, on behalf of such persons, Jesus comes to his tomb and, standing outside it, prays and is heard, he asks that there be power in his voice and words, and he cries out with a loud voice to summon him who was his friend to the things outside the life of the Gentiles and their tomb and cave. (Origen *Comm. Jn.* 28.54–6, cited in Heen and Krey 2005, 87)

---

18 Obvious examples include Sir. 44—50 and 1 Macc. 2.
19 See Wright *PFG*, 114–39.

made the world was intending to remake it. God has promised something 'better for us', declares the writer, so that believers both ancient and contemporary would reach perfection together (11.39–40). In this light, the members of his audience are invited to see themselves as part of the list of wonderful witnesses to God's promises, and as people who stand even closer than they to the city of God.

The final example of faith and perseverance is the human being Jesus of Nazareth himself, whose personal struggles have already been described in terms every bit as vivid as anything in the four gospels (2.14–18; 4.14—5.10). All the other models of faith are like crowds cheering us on as we run a race, but Jesus himself stands at the finishing line (12.1–3). We must leave behind the sin that weighs us down, so that like Jesus we may not give up but finish the course. The community may be thankful that they have not yet suffered martyrdom (12.4); but they are not excused from hardship, which can function as divine discipline (12.4–11) to prevent us—here is the exhortation again—from giving up the struggle, as Esau unfortunately did (scripture can provide examples of the wrong approach as well as the right one) (12.12–17).

The final great contrast in a letter of contrasts (Moses and Jesus, Levitical priesthood and Melchizedek, old and new covenant, and so on) is the contrast between Sinai, where the law was given, and the heavenly Jerusalem, the ultimate city of God in which Jesus-believers are already citizens. This is the city that cannot be shaken (12.27), and to reflect on it is to have one's resolve stiffened and one's heart warmed for gratitude and worship (12.28).

6. Living righteously for the city of God (13.1–21)

Several concluding exhortations follow, starting with the theme of love. Practising hospitality and remembering those in prison are vital components in the life of a church undergoing persecution (13.1–3). Next come sex and money: marriage must be honoured, while freedom from money-love will lead to contentment (13.4–5). Trusting God is the key (13.5–6). The community's leaders are setting an example to follow, but ultimately all things come back to Jesus the Messiah, the same yesterday, today, and for ever (an allusion to the overall theme of the letter as it joins together Israel's past, the church's present, and the new Jerusalem). All this leads to further encouragements to continue in the faith, rather than going back into the apparent security of the Jewish community that has resisted the message of Jesus (13.9–16). The letter draws to a close with a call to respect those in leadership and a prayer-request for the author and his co-workers; but these open out into a remarkable benediction, invoking God as 'the God of peace', the one who 'led up from the dead our Lord Jesus, the great shepherd of the sheep, through the blood of the eternal covenant', an obvious reference back to the central themes of the letter. It is God himself who will 'make you complete in every good work so that you may do his will', and who will 'perform, in you, whatever will be pleasing in his sight, through Jesus the Messiah' (13.20–21 *NTE/KNT*). As with the rest of the letter, this blessing looks from the dangerous present to the perfect future, a future guaranteed by God's action in Jesus once for all and by God's continued action in his people now.

7. Final greetings (13.22–25)

The letter closes with instructions about Timothy and a final greeting (13.22–25). The author reminds his audience to take his 'word of exhortation' seriously, brief though it is! Timothy, he tells them, has been released; from where, and after what process, we are frustratingly ignorant. But if Timothy comes to visit the readers, it will obviously be a good opportunity for everyone to catch up. The writer then extends greetings, from himself and from 'those from Italy'—another frustrating reference to people about whom we can only guess. There is no guesswork involved, however, in understanding the final words: 'Grace be with you all' (13.25). The whole letter has been about the powerful grace of the one God, grace in the preparatory covenant with Abraham, Moses, and Israel, grace now triumphant in Jesus and his death, resurrection, and ascension, and grace powerfully active in the community of the faithful to lead them to 'the city of the living God' (12.22).

Abraham meets Melchizedek, thirteenth century, St Mark's Basilica, Venice
PD-US

HEBREWS AND THE BIG PICTURE

The letter to the Hebrews contributes three principal things to the tapestry of Christian thought: christology, hermeneutics, and atonement.

First, Hebrews is a rich and powerfully laden exhortation to faithfulness that is so effective because it forces us to set our sights on Jesus, the one who leads us into the presence of God through his once-for-all-time sacrifice. At the heart of the theology of Hebrews is its christology. At the head of the letter we learn that Jesus the son of God is superior to the angels. There were some in the early church who thought Jesus was just a sort of special angel; no, says the writer, he is in a different order altogether. But it is important not to get the wrong idea from this. Jesus is also totally and truly human, *and he still is*. Jesus is 'our man in heaven'. The one who lived our life and died our death has now been exalted and glorified precisely as a human being. God has put a human being at the helm of the universe (Heb. 1—2). Hebrews is, as much as any other book in the New Testament, the great exponent of 'the ascension', in which Jesus completes his sacrifice not on the cross but, as though in a single action, when he presents his blood in the heavenly sanctuary, thus clearing the way for the heaven-and-earth new reality in which God himself will dwell with his people for ever. Thereafter, Old Testament images abound as they are applied to Jesus by the author. Jesus is the true Joshua, who leads the people of God into the promised land (Heb. 3—4). Jesus is the true high priest—from the order of Melchizedek, not that of Levi or Aaron—who unites the messianic and priestly offices in his own person. Jesus is not a transient priest; rather, he remains a priest for ever. Jesus offers the new, ultimate sacrifice in his body; he is the mediator of the new covenant (Heb. 5—8). The great cloud of witnesses cheers us on as we run the race of faith and follow after Jesus, the pioneer and perfecter of our faith (Heb. 11—12). Then, at the very end of the letter, the writer insists explicitly that Jesus Christ is the same yesterday, today, and for ever. He is the great shepherd of the sheep, the one brought back from the dead (Heb. 13).

Second, Hebrews is immensely important for hermeneutics, as it shows us a new way of reading the Old Testament. The point, of course, is that the Old Testament is an unfinished story, with several strands explicitly looking on to a further reality which the early Christians believed had now arrived. Like an incomplete motorway under construction, the Old Testament points ahead to its final destination, but without actually having enough bitumen to take you there. More particularly, the scriptures point to a great day of salvation, of dealing with sin, which they do not themselves offer, and an extraordinary heaven-and-earth new reality which is only glimpsed in faith. This great act has now been accomplished in Jesus, and the new reality is now revealed in him. Readers of Israel's scriptures, then, should follow this

Jesus to find where their book was leading all along. The letter to the Hebrews gives us a thoroughly 'christotelic' way of reading the Jewish scriptures.[20]

A final feature of Hebrews, third, is that the letter emphasizes the sacrificial death of Jesus as God's deal-making act to reconcile the human race. The sacrifices of the Old Testament were designed to highlight the seriousness of sin and the holiness of God, within the action of purifying the sanctuary from the corruption, sin, and death of the people so that God could dwell in their midst. For the author of Hebrews, the Old Testament sacrifices made one outwardly clean, but not inwardly clean (Heb. 9.13). Neither did they really effect a change in circumstances, as it is impossible for the blood of goats and bulls to take away sin (Heb. 10.4). But the Old Testament points to God as the one who provides the sacrifice. Jesus is the one true sacrifice towards which all others pointed. Jesus' own blood brought 'a redemption that lasts for ever', which can 'cleanse our conscience from dead works to serve the living God' (Heb. 9.12–13).

Further reading

Bateman, Herbert W. (ed.). 2006. *Four Views on the Warning Passages in Hebrews*. Grand Rapids, MI: Kregel.
Bauckham, Richard, Daniel Driver, Trevor Hart, and Nathan MacDonald (eds.). 2008. *A Cloud of Witnesses: The Theology of Hebrews in Its Ancient Contexts*. LNTS 387; London: T&T Clark.
——. 2009. *The Epistle to the Hebrews and Christian Theology*. Grand Rapids, MI: Eerdmans.
Bruce, F. F. 1990. *The Epistle to the Hebrews*. Rev. edn.; NICNT; Grand Rapids, MI: Eerdmans.
deSilva, David A. 2000. *Perseverance in Gratitude: A Socio-Rhetorical Commentary on the Epistle to the Hebrews*. Grand Rapids, MI: Eerdmans.
Healy, Mary. 2016. *Hebrews*. CCSS; Grand Rapids, MI: Baker.
Johnson, Luke Timothy. 2006. *Hebrews: A Commentary*. Louisville, KY: Westminster John Knox.
Lincoln, Andrew. 2006. *Hebrews: A Guide*. London: T&T Clark.
Mason, Eric F., and B. Kevin McCruden (eds.). 2011. *Reading the Epistle to the Hebrews: A Resource for Students*. Atlanta: SBL.
Peeler, Amy. 2014. *You Are My Son: The Family of God in the Epistles to the Hebrews*. LNTS 486; London: T&T Clark.
Westfall, Cynthia Long. 2005. *A Discourse Analysis of the Letter to the Hebrews: The Relationship Between Form and Meaning*. LNTS 297; London: T&T Clark.

---

20 On 'christotelic', see Enns 2005, 154–6.

31

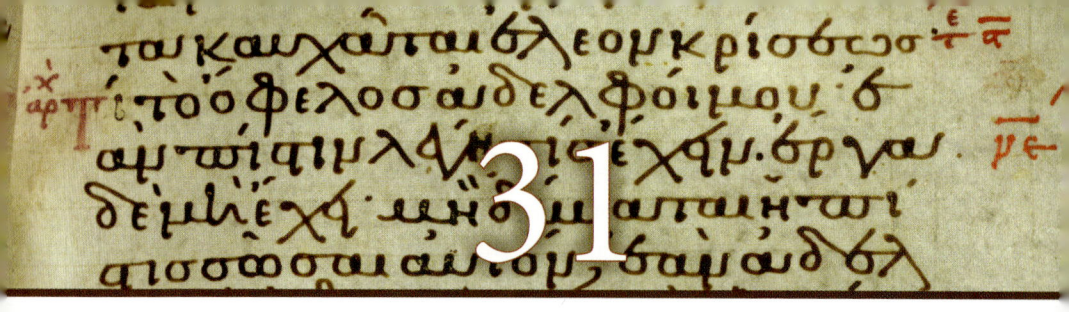

Letters by Jesus' Brothers: James and Jude

Religion that God our Father accepts as pure and faultless is this: to look after orphans and widows in their distress and to keep oneself from being polluted by the world.[1]

Dear friends, although I was very eager to write to you about the salvation we share, I felt compelled to write and urge you to contend for the faith that was once for all entrusted to God's holy people.[2]

CHAPTER AT A GLANCE

This chapter provides an overview of the letters of James and Jude.

By the end of this chapter you should be able to:

- understand issues of authorship and date related to the letters of James and Jude;
- describe the structure and argument in the letters of James and Jude;
- understand the themes and theology in the letters of James and Jude.

INTRODUCTION

The Catholic Epistles, in their traditional western order, begin with the epistle of James and end with the epistle of Jude.[3] Thus, the Catholic Epistles are usually bookended by letters attributed to Jesus' two brothers; though tradition and scholarship debates whether they were stepbrothers, half-brothers, first cousins, or even full brothers.[4] Anyway, it is these

---

[1] Jas. 1.27.
[2] Jude 3.
[3] It is noteworthy that the Council of Laodicea (c. AD 360), Athanasius's *Festal Letter* of AD 367, and Codex Vaticanus arrange the New Testament canon in the order of gospels, Acts, the Catholic Epistles, Pauline epistles, Revelation. One advantage here is that this order ensures that the New Testament is not regarded as consisting of Jesus, Paul, and a few other friends. See Bauckham 1999, 115; Painter 2002, 34.
[4] On how Jesus is related to his 'brothers', see Bauckham 1990, 19–32; more briefly, deSilva 2012, 31–4.

two 'brothers of the Lord', James and Jude, who teach the members of the church how to show their family resemblance to Jesus. 'James' is a regular modern version of 'Jacob'; 'Jude' is an English version of the Hebrew 'Judah' or the Greek 'Judas'. The two names, alluding to the patriarchs, were obviously popular in the first century.

James and Jude are first mentioned as Jesus' brothers when members of the synagogue in Nazareth disparaged Jesus as a local upstart trying to make a name for himself.[5] Jesus' mother and brothers initially had grave misgivings about his public ministry and even tried to seize him.[6] Yet Jesus, after his resurrection, appeared specifically to James.[7] He soon (particularly after Peter had disappeared on his travels) became the leading figure in the Jerusalem church,[8] right until his martyrdom in AD

Icon of St James
Public Domain

62 when he was stoned to death at the behest of the high priest during an interregnum between Roman governors.[9] James was venerated in Christian memory as the first bishop of Jerusalem, a martyr, the brother of the lord. He was acclaimed by both proto-orthodox and gnostic circles as 'James the Just'.[10]

While James remained in Jerusalem, the other brothers of Jesus (Joseph, Jude/Judas, and Simon) seem to have travelled with their wives in missionary work around Syro-Palestine. This is the clear implication of something Paul says in 1 Corinthians.[11] In addition, after James was executed, he was succeeded as bishop in Jerusalem by his cousin, Symeon, the son of Clopas.[12] Eusebius also relates a story from

---

5 Mk. 6.3/Mt. 13.55.
6 Mk. 3.21, 31–25.
7 1 Cor. 15.7; *Gos. Heb.* § 5.
8 Ac. 12.17; 15.13–21; 21.18–25; Gal. 1.19; 2.9, 12.
9 Jos. *Ant.* 20.200–3; Eus. *Hist. Eccl.* 2.1.5; 2.23.1–23; *2 Apoc. Jas.* 61–2.
10 In the *Gos. Thom.* § 14, we find mention of 'James the Just, for whose sake heaven and earth came into being'. According to Eusebius (*Hist. Eccl.* 2.1.2–5) James was 'called the brother of the Lord' and 'this same James, to whom the men of old had also given the surname of Just for his excellence of virtue, is narrated to have been the first elected to the throne of the bishopric of the church in Jerusalem'.
11 1 Cor. 9.5; also Eusebius (*Hist. Eccl.* 1.7.14) reports from Julius Africanus that relatives of Jesus from the villages of Nazareth and Kokhaba 'travelled around the rest of the land'. Bauckham (1990, 68) thinks that it was the presence of Jewish Christian missionaries from Galilee in the Trans-Jordan, like Jesus' family, which was the reason why the Jerusalem church fled to Pella on the eve of the Roman invasion of Judea.
12 Eus. *Hist. Eccl.* 3.11.1; 4.22.4.

an earlier writer, Hegesippus, about the emperor Domitian trying to eliminate any would-be claimants to the throne of David, and having the grandsons of Jude/Judas brought before him as, supposedly, members of a royal house (and hence potentially subversive). They showed him their hands, hard from their work as impoverished labourers. The kingdom they were awaiting, they said, was heavenly and angelic, still to come in the future. Domitian released them and stopped his policy of banishing Christians.[13] The relatives of Jesus were, then, active in the early church from the very beginning and throughout the first Christian century.

Turning to the letter of James itself, we note an apparent absence of detailed christology, and indeed little mention of any actual 'gospel'. Some have therefore regarded it as sub-Christian, perhaps even to be seen as an old synagogue-sermon into which two references to Jesus have been added at a later stage.[14] Martin Luther, famously, dismissed James for containing nothing evangelical, teaching nothing about Jesus; he even declared that it is not an apostolic letter but an epistle of straw.[15] Yet such a claim is demonstrably false. James is indeed Jewish in ambience, theocentric in worldview, heavily reliant on Jewish wisdom-traditions, and immersed in Torah, but it has all kinds of Christian elements.[16]

To begin with, if James is an epistle of straw, then the Sermon on the Mount is a sermon of straw, since James echoes much of Jesus' teaching in the sermon.[17] The paraenetic sections are far from commonplace. They are, in fact, christologically shaped exhortations derived principally from Jesus-traditions.[18] The author is also 'kerygmatic', rooted in the proclamation of the good news, insisting that God 'chose to give us birth through the word of truth, that we might be a kind of firstfruits of all

Frère Laurent, *The Sermon on the Mount*, from La Somme le Roi, 1279
Kharbine-Tapabor / Shutterstock

---

13 Eus. *Hist. Eccl.* 3.19.1—3.20.7; 3.32.3–6. How much the description of the coming kingdom here owes to Eusebius rather than to the two men in question remains imponderable.
14 Jas. 1.1; 2.1.
15 Dunn 2009b, 1123 n. 86.
16 Johnson 1995, 49.
17 Baird 1992, 1.136.
18 McKnight 2011, 40, 44.

he created'.[19] He urges readers to accept the 'implanted word that has the power to save your souls'.[20] The references to the 'Lord's coming', to the 'Judge [who] is standing at the door', and to the 'name of the Lord' invoked for anointing the sick could all be indicating Israel's God, but they work even better as implied references to Jesus. In addition, the letter refers to 'elders of the church [*ekklēsia*]'.[21] James is not christocentric after the manner of the gospels, Paul's letters, and Hebrews. Neither, for that matter, is 2 John or 3 John. But the letter of James is demonstrably Christian, serving as a moral map to sketch out the way of wisdom for the church.

The letter of James reminds us that what we now call 'Judaism' and 'Christianity' are not two polarized ends of a socio-religious spectrum. They never were. Even in the first century Jews who believed that Jesus was Messiah, and Jews who did not, constituted overlapping social groups with obvious claims to a common religious heritage. 'Indeed,' Matt Jackson-McCabe argues, 'one might now say that the Letter of James is Jewish precisely because of, not in spite of, its veneration of Jesus.'[22]

The short letter of 'Judah' or 'Jude' is attributed to the 'brother of James' (Jude 1), so, by implication, the brother or half-brother of Jesus as well. Jude warns against false teachers who have surreptitiously entered the audience's assembly. He urges the readers to work hard to defend the faith as originally given (Jude 3–4). He is trying to persuade his readers not to be influenced by the intruders' teaching and example, but rather to commit themselves to a model of faith and praxis that will bring them into line with the original apostolic teaching and pattern of discipleship. He therefore denounces the character, motivation, and practices of the intruders.[23] Once that is done, and the warnings have been duly noted, one should always return to the basic Christian activity, which is the glad celebration and praise of the God who has saved us through Jesus the Messiah (Jude 24–25).

The letter of Jude—which has been much neglected in Protestantism—is an important witness to the reception of Jewish traditions in the early church and a significant source for Christian theology in the last third of the first century (though dating a document like this is inevitably difficult).[24] It shows the struggle the churches faced with hellenistic culture, the emergence of a recognizable 'faith', the propensity for intra-church sectarianism, and modes of piety and devotion, as well as attesting to a vibrant tradition of scriptural interpretation.

The authors of these two epistles, James and Jude, share a common commitment to describe Jesus, their brother, as God's long-awaited agent of deliverance. Jesus had

---

[19] Jas. 1.18.
[20] Jas. 1.21 NRSV. On 'new birth', see 1 Pet. 1.2 and Jn. 3.3–7; on the 'word of truth', see Jn. 17.17; Eph. 1.13; 2 Tim. 2.15; on the power of the 'word' to save, see 1 Cor. 15.2; Rom. 10.8–11, 17.
[21] Jas. 5.7–8, 9, 14.
[22] Jackson-McCabe 2010, 783.
[23] deSilva 2012, 57.
[24] Frey 2015, 2.

taught the way of God in wisdom and righteousness, and now exercises lordship over God's gathered people. He will come again to put all things right.[25]

CONTEXTUAL AND CRITICAL MATTERS

The origins of James

There were several people called James (that is, Jacob) in the early church; but the predominant view of church history has been to identify the author of the 'letter of James' as the lord's actual brother.[26] Many scholars reject Jacobean authorship of this letter, preferring instead to see it as late, even from the second century, and pseudepigraphical.[27]

Consider the evidence. The letter is written in good Greek. It uses the Greek translation of the Jewish scriptures. It employs greco-roman rhetorical features such as the diatribe. One might not expect this from a rural Galilean artisan. The many parallels to other New Testament writings might indicate a dependence on Matthew and 1 Peter; it may perhaps be responding to Paul's letters, or at least to an antinomian understanding of them. In addition, there is no explicit mention of the epistle of James until Origen's references in the third century.[28] James could, then, be one of the latest writings of the New Testament. If so, it is no wonder that Eusebius says that few ancient authors cited it; Eusebius himself counted it among the 'disputed writings' (*antilegomena*) that struggled to gain acceptance into the canon.[29]

On the other hand, Jacobean authorship should not be too quickly dismissed.[30] For a start, there are none of the features in the letter that often appear in pseudonymous apostolic literature (such as fictionalized embellishments that identify the

---

25 deSilva 2012, 258.
26 James the brother of Jesus, the son of Mary (Mk. 6.3/Mt. 13.5; Gal. 1.19; 2.9, 12; Ac. 12.17; 15.13; 21.18; Jude 1); James the father of Judas (Lk. 6.16; Ac. 1.13); James the younger, the son of Mary (Mk. 15.40/Mt. 27.56; Mk. 16.1; Lk. 24.10); James the son of Alphaeus (Mk. 3.18/Mt. 10.3/Lk. 6.15; Ac. 1.13); James the son of Zebedee and brother of John (Mk. 1.19; Mk. 3.17/Lk. 6.14; Ac. 1.13).
27 See e.g. Allison 2013. Martin Luther's preface to James and Jude claimed that 'some Jew wrote it who probably learned about Christian people but never encountered any' and 'he cites the sayings of St. Peter' (see Allison 2013, 34 n. 196, 67 n. 353). J. A. T. Robinson (1976, 118 n. 1) cites the somewhat flippant comment of Kirsopp Lake that, in terms of its teaching, the letter might be dated anywhere from the second century BC to the eighteenth century AD.
28 A point conceded by Johnson 1995, 126 and exploited by Nienhuis 2011; see further Allison 2013, 13–18.
29 Eus. *Hist. Eccl.* 2.23.25; 3.25.3.
30 On the authenticity of the epistle of James, see e.g. Johnson 1995, 118–23; 2004, 105–17; Bauckham 1999, 23–5; and deSilva 2012, 45–54. Dunn (2009b, 1128) thinks 'it is . . . likely that the teaching contained in the letter was teaching which James was known to have given and which had been remembered, and perhaps early on partially transcribed for wider circulation'. Davids (2014, 41) regards it as a posthumous collection of James's teaching: 'the best explanation of the data is that the letter of James was written shortly after the death of James, the brother of Jesus, making use of sermons and sayings stemming from James (and/or Jesus).' Jerome (*De Vir. Ill.* 2) had earlier said that the epistle was 'published under his [i.e. James's] name by another'.

734   The Early Christians and the Mission of God

author, lengthy digressions about church order, and lurid descriptions of an eschatological dénouement). More positively, the author is intimately acquainted with Judean life and Jewish tradition.[31] His writing style is full of semitisms.[32] He presents a substantial number of Jesus' sayings in a way that implies access to oral tradition rather than literary dependence on a gospel.[33] Like other first-century Christian writers, James believes that Jesus will return soon (though, to be fair, so does Tertullian at the end of the second century).[34]

The letter of James shows a striking affinity with some Jewish writings of the second-Temple period. In its genre and contents it resembles *2 Baruch* 78—87. Its stress on the perseverance of Job is echoed, not in the book of Job itself, but in the *Testament of Job*. James's account of the 'binding of Isaac' is similar to that in *Jubilees*. James replicates Palestinian sources by stressing how Elijah prayed that it would not rain for three and a half years—something not mentioned in 1 Kings.[35] All this puts James much closer to the world of first-century Palestinian Judaism than to Christian writings of the second century.

When it comes to the passage about justification by faith or works, which some have seen as a response to a distortion of Pauline teaching, we might comment that this is exactly what one might expect from a mediating figure like James who affirmed Paul's gospel (Gal. 2.9–10), who accepted gentile believers without male circumcision but asked them to respect Jewish scruples by avoiding idolatry and immorality (Ac. 15.13–21), and who warned Paul that he needed to repudiate rumours that he encouraged Jews to abandon Torah (Ac. 21.20–25). Viewed in this way, it is fair to say that 'James puts us in touch with first-generation Christianity'.[36]

So can we credit the brother of Jesus with good Greek? There is no reason why not. Many adult males in the region would be functionally bilingual. The Jerusalem church included Greek-speaking Jews from the start. Alternatively, maybe the letter was written in Aramaic and translated into Greek by a secretary.[37]

In the end, there are some good arguments both for and against authenticity. McKnight is correct, though, that the evidence marginally favours authenticity.[38]

---

[31] See Jas. 1.6, 11; 2.2, 19; 3.4, 6, 11–12; 5.7, 11, 17–18.
[32] Allison 2013, 86–7.
[33] According to Davids (2014, 42): 'There is no New Testament work outside of the Gospels that is so deeply influenced by the teaching of Jesus as James.' On the Jesus-tradition in James, see esp. Johnson, 1995, 57, 119–20 and McKnight 2011, 36–7, yet disputed by Allison 2013, 59–62 who identifies instead dependency on the gospel of Matthew.
[34] Jas. 5.8; see 1 Thess. 4.13–18; Rom. 13.11–12; Rev. 1.3; 22.10. See Tert. *Spect.*; and the discussions in *NTPG* 462–4 and e.g. Daley 2010 [1991].
[35] Compare Jas. 5.11 with *T. Job* 1–27; Jas. 2.21–23 with *Jub.* 17–18; Jas. 5.17 with 1 Kgs. 17–18; Lk. 4.25; 2 Esd. 7.109.
[36] Dunn 2009b, 1122.
[37] Josephus (*Ap.* 1.50), though he was familiar with Greek, still used secretaries to polish his Greek.
[38] McKnight 2011, 37.

Date of James

There is no explicit mention of James prior to the works of Origen, but possible allusions to James are found in *1 Clement* (c. AD 96) and probably in the *Shepherd of Hermas* (c. AD 140).[39] If the epistle of James was indeed written by James, the brother of Jesus, then it would obviously have been written by AD 62 (the date of his death) even if it was subsequently translated or edited into Greek. The polemic about faith and works fits with a date during Paul's lifetime, which would render a date of about 45–60 reasonable.

Genre and purpose of James

James shows many similarities to the kind of greco-roman ethical discourse we find in Epictetus. But it also has some analogies to the 'wisdom' tradition we see in Ben-Sirach, and it has points of contact, too, with Jewish sapiential works such as the *Sentences of the Syriac Menander* and *Pseudo-Phocylides*. However, in terms of genre, James is best generalized as a paraenetic encyclical letter, offering exhortations on life and conduct.[40] More precisely, it is a Diaspora letter, like those written from Judean leaders to Jews living outside of Palestine, to instruct on matters of cultic observance, to communicate halakhic decisions, and to assure God's people of divine deliverance.[41] The epistle of James, then, was written to urge Jewish Christians outside Palestine, perhaps in Syria and Asia Minor in particular, to maintain and keep the highest standards of Jewish moral teaching and to demonstrate that following Jesus embodied the righteousness and wisdom of God. This would enable them to offer a powerful witness to their fellow Diaspora Jews.

The origins of Jude

The epistle of Jude is a letter of exhortation, partly urging its readers to hold to a common faith, but also warning about certain libertine or antinomian intruders who have entered into their assembly.[42] Jude's epistle is a Jewish Christian writing, saturated with citations and allusions to Jewish literature (both scriptural and not). It shows signs of what is sometimes called an 'apocalyptic' worldview, slippery though that term is. It is 'sectarian' in the sense of trying to preserve the doctrinal homogeneity and ethical integrity of the group to whom it is addressed as they face intruders.

The letter is attributed in the opening verse to 'Jude [Greek *Ioudas*],[43] a slave of Jesus Christ, a brother of James'. This 'Jude' (or 'Judas') is explicitly identified

---

39 See discussion in Johnson 1995, 72–9 which is contested by Allison 2013, 17, 20–4, 96.
40 Bauckham 1999, 13.
41 On Jewish Diaspora letters, see Jer. 29.1–23; Ac. 15.23–29; 2 Macc. 1.–10a; 1.10b–2.18; *2 Bar.* 78–87; ySanh. 1.2. See further on James as a Diaspora letter, Bauckham 1999, 19–28; Doering 2012, 452–63; Allison 2013, 73–6.
42 Jude 3–4.
43 The other people called Judas in the New Testament are Judas Iscariot, the disciple who betrayed Jesus

as the brother of James, most likely the lord's brother, making Jude, too, part of Jesus' family.[44] The language of the letter, as with James, is quite good Greek; again, some might say it was too good for a rural Galilean, but we should not underestimate the hellenistic penetration of Galilee or the Greek facility of the early Christians. The author appears to know the Jewish scriptures in a form closer to the Hebrew than to the Septuagint, but this simply means that, like many at the time, the author shows signs of a genuinely bilingual Greek–Aramaic Jewish world.[45] In addition, although Jude was among the contested writings of the New Testament canon because of its use of apocryphal sources like *1 Enoch*, nobody in the early centuries questioned Jude's actual authorship of the letter, a matter on which it is hard to pronounce since, apart from this letter itself, we know next to nothing about the historical Jude.[46] The letter could be pseudepigraphical,[47] but it could just as well be authentic. Certainty (as on many matters of ancient history) is impossible, but there is nothing in the letter which rules out the ascription of authorship to a brother of Jesus named Jude.[48]

Depiction of Jude from illuminated manuscript, Walters Manuscript W.533, fol. 129r, dated early twelfth century, The Walters Art Museum, Baltimore. *Public Domain*

Opponents in Jude

The intruders whom Jude vilifies (in the harshest rhetoric he can muster!) have been variously identified. Some have seen them as followers of Paul (who might be suspected of moral deviance); others, as early gnostic Christians. Jude labels them as 'ungodly people' who 'pervert' divine grace into a licence for debauchery, and 'deny Jesus Christ'.[49] They are denounced for a sexual immorality that imitates Sodom and Gomorrah. The intruders probably laid claim to pneumatic inspiration, leading the writer to dismiss them as 'dreamers'.[50] They denied or slandered angels

---

(e.g. Mt. 10.4); Judas the son of James (Lk. 6.16; Ac. 1.13; cf. Jn. 14.22); Judas of Damascus, who provided lodgings for Saul (Ac. 9.11); and Judas called Barsabbas, a prophet in the Jerusalem church (Ac. 15.22, 27, 32).
44 Mk. 6.3/Mt. 13.55. The Syrian tradition tended to equate 'Judas' with 'Thomas', a tradition known to Eusebius (*Hist. Eccl.* 1.13.10).
45 Bauckham 1983, 7.
46 Eus. *Hist. Eccl.* 3.25.2; Jer. *De Vir. Ill.* 4.
47 See e.g. Frey 2015, 20–6.
48 Bauckham 1983, 15–16; 1990, 177–8; McKnight 2003a, 1529; Green 2008, 1–9; deSilva 2012, 45–54.
49 Jude 4.
50 See Jude 8.

and celestial powers.[51] Jude describes their teaching as fruitless and futile.[52] They contaminate those around them, perhaps by turning community 'love feasts'[53] into Greek-style symposia or bawdy drinking-parties.[54] They are rapacious and greedy, self-absorbed and self-serving, taking advantage of people.[55] They are driven by evil and godless 'desires',[56] quick to complain and criticize.[57] No wonder their presence is divisive. Jude assesses them as 'worldly' and says that they 'do not have the Spirit'.[58] He lines them up beside various scriptural models of rebellion, immorality, and wickedness, including Cain, the angels who rebelled against God and departed from heaven, the Israelites who grumbled in the wilderness, the citizens of Sodom and Gomorrah, Balaam, and Korah.[59] Jude does not mince his words about what awaits such people. They are destined, he says, for 'destruction', 'condemnation', 'eternal fire', 'the blackest darkness', and 'judgment'.[60] His image of these intruders is of persons who have transgressed boundaries, indicating not only arrogance but a denial of Christ and God, and serious moral deviance.[61]

Are such remarks merely rhetorical tropes about wickedness in general, or is Jude writing about specific persons, and if so who? If the intruders are real, they may be a cross between the itinerant pseudo-apostles and false prophets mentioned in the *Didache* and the antinomian Carpocratians described by Clement of Alexandria:

> Now concerning the apostles and prophets, deal with them as follows in accordance with the rule of the gospel. Let every apostle who comes to you be welcomed as if he were the Lord. But he is not to stay for more than one day, unless there is need, in which case, he may stay another. But if he stays three days, he is a false prophet. And when the apostle leaves, he is to take nothing except bread until he finds his next night's lodging. But if he asks for money, he is a false prophet.[62]

> These are the doctrines of our noble Carpocratians. They say that these people and some other zealots for the same vicious practices gather for dinner (I could never call their congregation a Christian love-feast), men and women together,

---

51 Jude 8–10.
52 Jude 12.
53 Jude 8, 12.
54 Green 2008, 12–14.
55 Jude 11–12, 16.
56 Jude 16, 18.
57 Jude 16.
58 Jude 19.
59 Jude 5–7, 11.
60 See Jude 4, 5, 6, 7, 13, 15.
61 Frey 2015, 35.
62 *Did.* 11.3–6 (tr. M. Holmes [2007]).

and after they have stuffed themselves ('The Cyprian goddess is there when you are full,' they say), they knock over the lamps, put out the light that would expose their fornicating 'righteousness,' and couple as they will with any woman they fancy. So in this love-feast they practice commonality. Then by daylight they demand any woman they want in obedience—it would be wrong to say the Law of God—to the law of Carpocrates. I guess this sort of legislation Carpocrates must have established for the copulation of dogs, pigs, and goats.[63]

We simply do not know who these wicked persons are, but can well understand Jude's disgust at antinomian behaviour.

Date and purpose of Jude

The epistle of Jude was incorporated almost in its entirety into 2 Peter 2. We shall presently see that 2 Peter may well date to the second century. Clement of Alexandria wrote a commentary on Jude (*c.* AD 180–200), and Jude is mentioned in the Muratorian canon (*c.* AD 180). Before then it is hard to be sure whether anyone refers to it, though it is possible that there are echoes of Jude's doxology in the *Martyrdom of Polycarp*.[64]

Those who argue for a late date for Jude do so on several grounds. First, the idea of a 'common faith' as a fixed body of belief is thought to belong to a time in the second century when statements of faith become formalized.[65] However, 'the faith', as a type of formulae or set of confessional claims, is known even prior to AD 70 in Paul's undisputed letters.[66] Second, the mention of 'what the apostles of our Lord Jesus Christ foretold' is also said to place the epistle in at least the late first century or thereafter.[67] That might be the case, but what is being referred to is the apostles' missionary activity, not the apostles themselves.[68] Paul himself could refer to apostles in the plural, and discuss their respective activities;[69] and the author of Hebrews could urge his readers to remember their leaders who taught them the word of God.[70]

In sum, Jude is a letter of exhortation, written to a specific audience in a particular situation. The questions of where and to whom it was written remain a matter of educated guesses. We could imagine an appropriate context, with Jude writing

---

63 Clem. *Strom.* 3.2.10 (tr. J. Ferguson [1974]). According to Clement (*Strom.* 3.2.11), 'Jude was speaking prophetically of these and similar sects in his letter.'
64 *Mart. Pol.* 20.2 and Jude 25.
65 Jude 3.
66 1 Cor. 16.13; 2 Cor. 13.5; Gal. 1.23; Phil. 1.25, 27; Philem. 6. See also Heb. 4.14 on a confession *presumably* of faith and 1 Pet. 5.9 for faith as both trust and theological commitment.
67 Jude 17.
68 Bauckham 1983, 13; deSilva 2012, 52.
69 Rom. 16.7; 1 Cor. 4.9; 9.5; 12.28; Gal. 1.17, 19. See too Eph. 2.20 (though some would of course consider that as evidence for a late date for Ephesians).
70 Heb. 13.7; see too Rev. 3.3.

> **OUTLINE OF JAMES**
>
> 1. Opening greeting (1.1)
> 2. Word, wisdom, and piety (1.2–27)
> 3. Warnings against favouritism (2.1–13)
> 4. Exhortation on faith and deeds (2.14–26)
> 5. Exhortation on the ethics of speech (3.1–12)
> 6. Exhortation on enmity and friendship (3.13–4.10)
> 7. Warnings against arrogance (4.11–17)
> 8. Warnings against wealth (5.1–6)
> 9. Exhortation on endurance (5.7–11)
> 10. Life in community (5.12–20)

to Jewish Christian assemblies, any time from the 50s to 90s AD, in Syro-Palestine, the Trans-Jordan, or perhaps Egypt.[71] The letter is an energetic exposition of one facet of early Christian teaching.

THE ARGUMENT OF JAMES

(See box: 'Outline of James'.)

1. Opening greeting (1.1)

The author describes himself as 'James'. He does not expressly identify himself as the brother of the lord, but instead as 'a servant of God and of the Lord Jesus Christ'. This omission is no false modesty. The church was not dynastically organized. A familial relationship with Jesus would not in itself constitute grounds for authority.[72]

The addressees are 'the twelve tribes scattered among the nations', which could mean that the letter was written to Diaspora Jews. That might indicate that we should see the letter as a commendation of Jewish Christianity to non-Jesus-believing Jews; that in turn might explain why explicitly Christian traits appear subtle or subdued. James's purpose could be to clarify a Christian Judaism to non-Christ-believing Jews while simultaneously edifying Jewish Christians.[73] However, the language of 'dispersion' and 'exiles' can just as well describe Christian assemblies, as 1 Peter demonstrates.[74] So, more likely, the mention of the twelve tribes 'evoked the hope of the regathering of all the tribes in the land of Israel by God in the messianic age'.[75]

---

[71] To complicate things, Jude the man is more likely to have been an authority in Palestine. The author cites Palestinian literature like *1 Enoch*, he prefers the Hebrew OT to the Septuagint, he uses Palestinian midrashic exegesis of the OT, and the mention of James is because James was a respected figure in the Judean churches. But, if written to a Palestinian audience, why not write in Aramaic? Unless it was written to a hellenized urban centre like Tiberias, Tyre, Sidon, Pella, Caesarea, or the Decapolis? Alternatively, the epistle of Jude became popular in Egypt as attested by Clement of Alexandria, writing the first commentary on the letter, and the earliest extant manuscripts of Jude come from Egypt ($\mathfrak{P}^{72}$ and $\mathfrak{P}^{78}$). Or else, Jude could have been opposing the type of Gnosticism that arose in Syria, all the more possible given the Syrian tradition of conflating Judas and Didymus Judas Thomas. But then again the epistle of Jude was not accepted in the Syrian church until the sixth-century edition of the Philoxenus. See discussion in Green 2008, 9–16.
[72] Bauckham 1990, 125–30; 1999, 17.
[73] Allison 2013, 34–50.
[74] 1 Pet. 1.1, 17; 2.11.
[75] Bauckham 1999, 15.

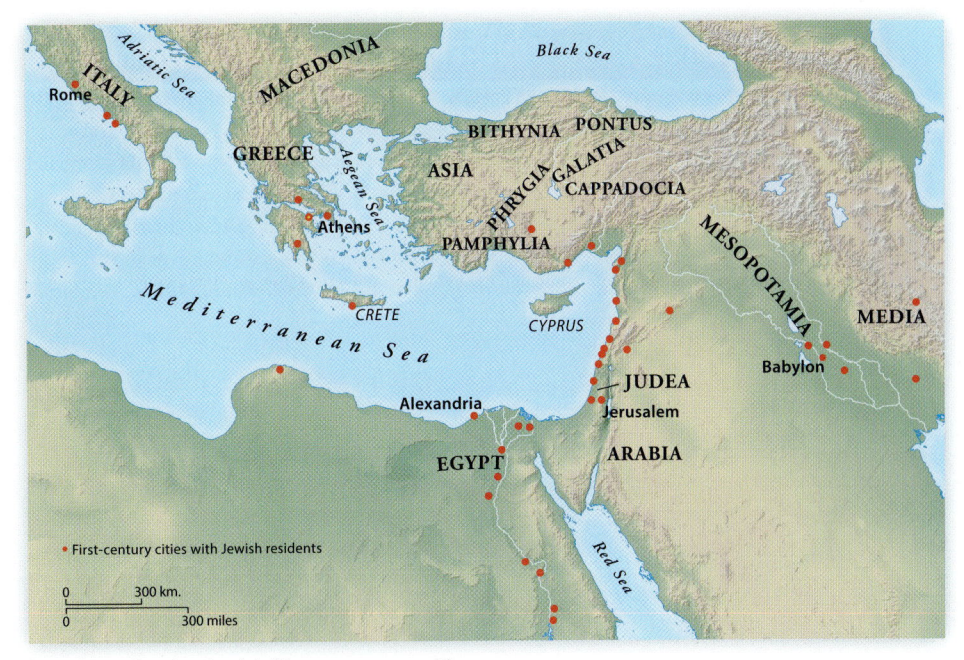

Locations of major Jewish Diaspora communities

2. Word, wisdom, and piety (1.2–27)

The first chapter of the letter sketches approximately a dozen subjects which are then explored in 2.1—5.18.[76] This includes joy in the midst of trials (because it produces endurance) (1.2–4); trials should evoke prayer for wisdom rather than doubt or double-mindedness (1.5–8). The poor should 'boast' in their exaltation, and the rich in their humiliation, because God will reverse it all (1.9–11). A person who has persevered under adversity and loves the lord will receive the 'crown of life'; some fail to do so because they are enticed away by their own desires, which conceive sin and thence death (1.12–15). The audience should remember that God the father is good and constant, not capricious (1.16–17). God's goodness is shown in his bringing believers to 'birth' by the 'word of truth', that is, the proclamation of the gospel, resulting in the messianic community being the 'firstfruits', the start of a new creation (1.18). Human anger does not produce the righteous behaviour God requires (1.19–20). Jesus-followers should get rid of impurity and malevolence, and cling instead to the 'implanted word' which alone can cultivate true righteousness and deliver from judgment (1.21 NRSV). All these topics receive fuller treatment later on.

James's main emphasis then emerges: Jesus-followers should not just hear the 'word' but should do it (1.22–25). The 'word' in question is 'the perfect law that

---

[76] Johnson 1995, 14–15; Bauckham 1999, 69–72; esp. Allison 2013, 69.

TABLE 31.1: ECHOES OF THE JESUS-TRADITION IN THE EPISTLE OF JAMES*

Subject	James	Gospels
Joy in the midst of trials	Jas. 1.2	Mt. 5.10–12/Lk. 6.22–23
The importance of perfection	Jas. 1.4	Mt. 5.48
God's generosity	Jas. 1.5	Mt. 7.7–9/Lk. 11.9–11
Faith and doubt	Jas. 1.6	Mt. 21.21
One who perseveres will be saved	Jas. 1.12	Mt. 10.22; 24.13
The danger of anger	Jas. 1.20	Mt. 5.22
The importance of doing/obeying the word	Jas. 1.22–25	Mt. 7.24–27/Lk. 6.46–49
Blessed are the poor	Jas. 2.5	Mt. 5.3, 5/Lk. 6.20
Love-command	Jas. 2.8	Mk. 12.38–44/Mt. 22.39–40
Keeping the whole law	Jas. 2.10	Mt. 5.19
Do not murder	Jas. 2.11; 5.6	Mt. 5.21–30
The importance of mercy	Jas. 2.13	Mt. 5.7
Friendship with God	Jas. 2.23	Mt. 6.24/Lk. 16.13
Blessed are the peacemakers	Jas. 3.18	Mt. 5.9
Blessed are the pure in heart	Jas. 4.8	Mt. 5.8
God exalts the humble	Jas. 4.10	Mt. 23.12/Lk. 14.11; 18.14
Refusal to judge others	Jas. 4.11–12	Mt. 7.1–5/Lk. 6.37–38, 41–42
Rich must weep and mourn	Jas. 5.1	Lk. 6.24–25
Against hoarding of riches	Jas. 5.2–3	Mt. 6.19–21/Lk. 12.33–34
The dangers of riches	Jas. 5.4–6	Mt. 6.24–25/Lk. 16.13
Coming of the lord who is at the door	Jas. 5.8–9	Mt. 24.33
Patience of the prophets in suffering	Jas. 5.10	Mt. 5.12/Lk. 6.23
Avoid taking oaths	Jas. 5.12	Mt. 5.33–37
Restoring a straying brother or sister	Jas. 5.19–20	Mt. 18.15; Lk. 17.3

* See discussion in Johnson 1995, 55–7; Bauckham 1999, 93–11; McKnight 2011, 25–7.

gives freedom', cognate with his reference elsewhere to the 'royal law found in Scripture', 'the whole law', and the 'law that gives freedom'.[77] This 'law' denotes the love-command of Leviticus 19.18 and the Decalogue, indicating that for James the 'law' is concerned with right relations between people rather than with negotiating divine favour through ritual observance.[78] Highlighting the moral fibre of the Torah and sidelining its cultic or ritual aspects is hardly irregular for a Jewish author. Arguably, Philo, Josephus, Pseudo-Phocylides, and Jesus himself do much the same (see Table 31.1).

First-century synagogue at Gamla, located in the north-east hills of the Sea of Galilee
Great Siberia Studio / Shutterstock

The section ends with two aphorisms on true 'religion' (Greek *thrēskeia*), including the necessity of keeping a tight rein on one's speech (1.26) and of care for the vulnerable, especially widows and orphans. This kind of moral behaviour keeps one free from pollution and makes one pure and blameless (1.27).

3. Warnings against favouritism (2.1–13)

James writes against 'favouritism' in the church as inconsistent with allegiance to 'our glorious Lord Jesus Christ' (2.1). He gives the example of an assembly (Greek *synagōgē*; literally, 'synagogue') where a rich man is given preferential treatment but poorer members are treated with disdain. However normal this was in the ancient world, it is an affront to God, discriminating against those whom God has chosen, and depriving those who will inherit the kingdom (2.2–6a). James adds that it is after all the rich who exploit his readers and use the courts to oppress them, and who also slander the name of God and/or Jesus to whom they belong (2.6b–7); this presumably refers to members of the Jewish aristocracy who were doing their best

---

77 Jas. 1.25; 2.8, 10, 12.
78 Jas. 2.8, 11. A similar combination of the Decalogue and Lev. 19 is found in *The Sentences of Pseudo-Phocylides*; see Johnson, 1995, 30–2.

to stamp out the new movement. A church that discriminates is failing in the law of neighbour-love, thereby becoming a community of Torah-breakers.[79] They should, however, act with full respect to the Torah, especially the Decalogue,[80] knowing that they will be judged for breaking a single command. There is judgment without mercy for those who discriminate without mercy (2.8–13).

4. Exhortation on faith and deeds (2.14–26)

This section, with the contention that 'faith without deeds is dead' and using the stories of Abraham and Rahab to show that 'a person is considered righteous by what they do and not by faith alone', has often been regarded as James's denunciation of Paul's doctrine of justification by faith.[81] This apparent intra-canonical tension between James and Paul has led to an allergic reaction to James in some quarters. Protestants in particular have clung to the doctrine of *sola fide*, justification 'by faith alone', based on their reading of Paul—though the only place where the words 'faith alone' occur in the New Testament is James 2.24, where James explicitly denies that faith alone justifies. This is of course why Luther, who added the word 'alone' to Romans 3.28, was so opposed to the letter—and why many counter-Reformation catholic apologists appealed frequently to James.[82]

Mosaic of the sacrifice of Isaac, dated to the sixth century, Beth Alpha synagogue, Beit She'an, Israel
PD-US

---

79 Ironically, according to Josephus (*Ant.* 20.200), James and his colleagues were accused of being 'law-breakers' (*paranomeō*).
80 Ex. 20.13–14/Dt. 5.17–18.
81 Jas. 2.24, 26.
82 See Johnson 1995, 140–43.

It helps if we remember that sixteenth- and seventeenth-century debates about whether justification is by the imputation of merit or by the infusion of charity is simply not what either James or Paul were talking about. In addition, the Jacobean account of justification does not necessarily render the protestant doctrine of *sola fide* exegetically invalid; it only requires that the doctrine involve careful articulation in order to avoid accusations of promoting ethical laxity.[83] With those caveats in mind, it is possible, once we put James and Paul in context, to bring them together on justification.

For a start, James is not attacking Paul, and Paul would probably be receptive to James's concerns. James appears to be offering, almost as an aside, a clarifying response to Pauline teaching, not composing an anti-Pauline tract.[84] At no point does James demand that converting gentiles undergo circumcision and adopt Torah, nor does he insist that Jewish Christians should refrain from table-fellowship with gentile Christians. Those were the sharp edges of Paul's teaching (see Gal. 2.11–14; 5.12; 6.12–14; Phil. 3.2–3). According to Acts, while James affirmed Paul's ministry and message, he had concerns about those who were taking Paul's teaching in a possibly antinomian direction (see Ac. 21.20–21). What James offers here is not so much a denunciation as a qualification. As in Paul himself (Rom. 2.1–16; 2 Cor. 5.10), final justification is never independent of moral transformation. Paul knew perfectly well that his teaching on God justifying ungodly-gentile-sinners by faith apart from works of Torah was incurring accusations of promoting ethical laxity, and he actively rebutted such ideas (see Rom. 3.8; 6.1–2). We can imagine Paul reading James 2.14–24 and responding by quoting from Romans 6 and Galatians 5.

Furthermore, the apparent discrepancy between James and Paul dissipates when we observe what they are each arguing for and against. They are using the same language, but they have different referents in mind, and they address different concerns (see Table 31.2).

Paul is against those who demand that gentiles become Jewish proselytes as a condition of being followers of Jesus. James is against those who teach salvation by mere assent without actually following the words of Jesus. James and Paul can be brought together when we remember that James's statement that 'faith without deeds is dead' can be correlated with Paul's remark that 'the only thing that counts is faith working through love'.[85] In addition, James's reference to the 'word of truth' and the 'implanted word, which can save you' is very similar to Paul's 'message of truth, the gospel of your salvation' and his statement about how faith comes from 'hearing the message and the message is the word of Christ'.[86]

---

83 See Reasoner 2005, 25; Vanhoozer 2016, 71–107.
84 Despite the persistence of efforts to read James as an anti-Pauline writing (e.g. Hengel 1987), Johnson (1995, 111) rightly points out that it is unfair to take 12 of James's 108 verses as the key to its purpose and aims. The letter is far more than a repudiation of, or even a qualification to, Pauline teaching.
85 Jas. 2.26; Gal. 5.6.
86 See Jas. 1.18, 21; Eph. 1.13; Rom. 10.17.

TABLE 31.2: JAMES AND PAUL ON 'FAITH' AND 'WORKS'

Subject	Paul	James
Faith	Trust in God's redeeming action in Jesus and allegiance to Jesus as Messiah and lord. Such faith justifies.	Mere assent to the existence of one God (Jewish 'monotheism'), which does not lead to upright conduct. Such faith does not justify.
Works	Connected with the Jewish way of life codified in the Torah, a kind of 'doing' that leads to 'boasting' in ethnicity and effort. Such works do not save.	Loving expression of faith in action. Such works are required for justification.

These two towering apostles agree on this: the word of truth brings salvation and transformation.

That said, James and Paul do materially disagree on the significance of Genesis 15.6. Paul employs the passage to prove that Abraham was justified prior to his circumcision; James opts for a standard Jewish approach that read Abraham's willingness to sacrifice Isaac (Gen. 22) as the reason he had righteousness credited to him proleptically in Genesis 15.6.[87] Different readings of the same text merely show that Paul and James are part of the richly diverse traditions of Jewish scripture-reading.

5. Exhortation on the ethics of speech (3.1–12)

James then warns teachers that they expose themselves to a potentially severer sentence at the final judgment (3.1). It is hard to be perfect in speech (3.2). Several illustrations make the point (a horse's bridle, a ship's rudder, a small fire) to stress the need to exercise discipline and control over speech. Taming animals is easy, but taming the tongue is harder. The tongue can bless but also curse, but a spring ought not to produce both fresh and salt water. As Jesus had taught, the words we use indicate the inner character (3.3–12).

6. Exhortation on enmity and friendship (3.13—4.10)

James 3.13—4.10 is best seen as a single section, stressing that friendship with God requires peace in the church and enmity with the world. Wisdom and its fruits are contrasted with selfish, envious behaviour (3.13–17). Genuine God-given wisdom will tend towards peace (3.18). Conflicts derive from one's own warring desires

---

87 See Gal. 3.6–18 and Rom. 4.1–25 versus Jas. 2.21–23 and 1 Macc. 2.52.

746 The Early Christians and the Mission of God

which turn into actions, and such self-indulgent motives generate inappropriate and unfruitful prayers (4.1–3). People showing these traits, says James (echoing scripture), are spiritual adulterers. If they were friends of God, they would necessarily be enemies of the world and its wicked ways. 'Adulterers' though some may be, there is still grace, because as Proverbs 3.34 says, 'God opposes the proud but gives grace to the humble' (NRSV). If the readers seek God's wisdom, make peace, spurn evil desires, pursue friendship with God, and align themselves with the poor, then they will come into God's favour (4.4–6).

The section proceeds by means of rapid-fire aphorisms, urging the readers to submit to God, resist the devil, draw near to God, purify their hearts, grieve for sins, and humble themselves before God. Genuine repentance can yield a genuinely renewed relationship with God (4.7–10).

7. Warnings against arrogance (4.11–17)

James next warns about the dangers of arrogance in terms of relationships and presuming upon divine favour. Those who judge others risk sitting in judgment on God's law, since there is only one Lawgiver and Judge, able to save and destroy (4.11–12). He then urges that, since all human life is transitory, one should plan with God's purposes in mind. Like all sins of omission, failing to recognize God's sovereign will in governing human affairs is sin (4.13–17).

8. Warnings against wealth (5.1–6)

James now issues words of condemnation and lament for rich farmers. They should weep and mourn: their rich possessions will either rust or rot. Their surplus wealth is indicative of greed, since they have cheated their day-labourers. God hears the cries of their victims and stands against them. One explanation of this—particularly verse 6 where the rich have condemned and killed 'the righteous one' (NRSV)—is that James has in mind the rich Jerusalem elite responsible for handing Jesus over to his death.

> 'Both Deuteronomy and James reveal God as acting in solidarity with the poor and the helpless, and it is because of this that Christians ought also to humble themselves before God and act in solidarity with the poor, whether they are poor themselves or not. Indeed, James would argue that each person has the choice between the self-chosen humility of acting in accordance with God's character or of the divinely inflicted humiliation given to those who live for their own pleasures.'
>
> Mariam Kamell, 'The Economics of Humility,' 174–5.

9. Exhortation on endurance (5.7–11)

James now repeats his exhortation about patience and perseverance ahead of the lord's *parousia* (that is, 'coming'). As farmers wait for the harvest, and as the prophets persevered amid suffering, so the church must wait for the lord, and do so without grumbling (5.9).[88] So too with Job who (according to the *Testament of Job*) persevered through personal tragedy and whose later blessings were attributed to his enduring faithfulness. The ultimate resource for perseverance is not, however, personal impetus, but the fact that 'the Lord is full of compassion and mercy' (5.10–11).

10. Life in community (5.12–20)

The final section of the letter covers a variety of topics, all related to the ethos and welfare of the community as a whole. James rehearses Jesus' injunction against swearing oaths (Jas. 5.12), adding the aphorism that in times of suffering one should pray, while in times of happiness one should sing psalms of praise (5.13).

Unlike other letters, rather than express a desire that the audience enjoy good health and blessings, James offers instead a mandate on what to do in the case of illness. Sick individuals should summon the elders to pray for them and anoint them with oil in the name of the lord (Jesus). If the sickness is related to sin—as it might or might not be—it can be forgiven. Consequently, members of the community must confess their sins to one another and pray for healing in their bodies and souls. Viewed this way, the person praying stands with one foot in the place of trouble, sickness, and sin, and with the other foot in the place of healing, forgiveness, and hope. Prayer brings the latter to bear on the former (5.15a–16a).

The underlying premise is that prayers offered by a righteous person are effective. This time he gives the example of Elijah, who in post-biblical tradition was a man of faithful and effective prayer (5.16b–18).

Some scholars regard James 5.19–20 as stating the purpose of the letter, while others see it as a further example of somewhat randomly arranged aphorisms (see box: 'The story inside the epistle

---

> **THE STORY INSIDE THE EPISTLE OF JAMES**
>
> While James might seem to provide little more than an *ad hoc* series of ethical aphorisms with some theological filling, there is an implicit story in the letter. Robert Wall detects an underlying Jacobean narrative which takes the following form: (1) God is the only true God, immutable and just, the heavenly father, who has created human beings in his likeness, who gives generously, who makes promises, who gave Israel the law, who has elected the poor, and will judge the world (Jas. 1.5, 17, 27; 2.5, 19; 3.9; 4.11–12; 5.9). (2) God sends 'the word of truth' into the world to save God's people from sin and death, to bring his people to new birth and participation in the new creation, and to make them friends of God (Jas. 1.17–18, 21; 2.23; 5.19–20). (3) When this word is properly implanted—received by faith-and-deeds—believers are able to perform the perfect law of freedom, persevere under trial, and resist the devil (Jas. 1.3, 4, 12, 23, 25; 2.5, 8–12, 20; 4.7; 5.11). (4) The community's hope is expressed in terms of receiving the crown of life and inheriting the kingdom, promises to be fulfilled at the lord's 'coming' (Jas. 1.12; 2.5; 5.7–8).*
>
> ---
> * Wall 1997, 27–34.

---

[88] Davids 2014, 67.

of James').[89] Either way, for a writing concerned with practical and pastoral matters, inside a Jewish community which was itself nested within greco-roman culture, James 5.19–20 is a very apt conclusion. In brief, James calls for the community to seek the restoration of those who stray from the truth. To lead stragglers back to the truth saves their lives from death and covers over the sins caused by their estrangement from the truth. Perhaps these verses are an encoded exhortation about the role of Jewish Christians within Diaspora Jewish communities, suggesting that their task might be to convert/restore (Greek *epistrephō*) their fellow-Jews to the 'word of truth' when their leaders, including members of the Jerusalem aristocracy, sadly 'deny the truth'.[90]

THE ARGUMENT OF JUDE

(See box: 'Outline of Jude'.)

> **OUTLINE OF JUDE**
> 1. Opening greeting (1–2)
> 2. Purpose of the letter (3–4)
> 3. God's judgment against the wicked (5–19)
> 4. Exhortation to perseverance (20–23)
> 5. Concluding doxology (24–25)

1. Opening greeting (1–2)

The letter opening introduces the author as Jude (or more properly 'Judah'), a brother of James, and therefore, like James, a brother of Jesus. Yet Jude's authority rests not on familial bonds, but on his role as a slave of Jesus Christ. He addresses his audience as called, loved, and kept; descriptions often applied to Israel in Isaiah and now applied to the church as the eschatological people of God.[91] Bauckham comments:

> They are those whom God has called into his kingdom, who are embraced by God's love, and whom God is keeping safe through the dangers of their life in this world until Jesus Christ at his Parousia claims them for his own.[92]

This leads to an affectionate greeting, wishing the hearers an abundance of 'mercy, peace and love'.

2. Purpose of the letter (3–4)

Jude declares that his initial intention was to write to the believers to encourage them in a 'salvation we share'. Yet he has deliberately departed from that aim, to compose instead an exhortation for his readers to strive, like an athlete, for the 'faith that was once for all entrusted to God's holy people'. This 'faith' is not the stale dogma of a so-called 'early Catholicism'. Rather, it is the apostolic testimony to God's saving

---

[89] Contrast McKnight 2011, 452 with Davids 2014, 70.
[90] Jas. 1.18; 3.14.
[91] See e.g. Isa. 41.8–9; 43.1–4; 48.1–12.
[92] Bauckham 1983, 26.

action in Jesus Christ and its immediate implications. By referring to this apostolic 'faith' as being given 'once for all', Jude underscores its implicit christological foundation: what God did in Jesus the Messiah he did once and for all, with neither the need nor the possibility of the achievement being repeated or added to. The 'faith' in question is thus permanent, effective, and rooted in the primary work of the spirit.[93]

Intruders, however, have arrived, and their character must be exposed to view. (1) They are 'godless' or 'impious'. (2) Their condemnation is prefigured in Israel's scriptures—Jude will in fact expound this point at length in verses 5–16. (3) They pervert God's grace into licence for sin. (4) They deny the moral implications of the gospel, thereby effectively denying the authority of Jesus himself.[94]

3. God's judgment against the wicked (5–19)

Jude's first move by way of response is to use scriptural examples to remind his readers that God does judge and condemn those who presume to rebel against his way. Jude recounts how the 'Lord'[95] delivered his people from Egypt in the exodus, but later destroyed those of the wilderness generation who did not believe (Jude 5; Num. 14). The angels, also called 'the Watchers', who rebelled against God and descended from heaven to earth in order to marry human wives and corrupt humanity, are now bound under the earth until the time of judgment.[96] The men of Sodom and Gomorrah, inflamed with lust for the 'unnatural flesh' (*NTE/KNT*) of the angelic visitors, were destroyed by 'a scene of sulphurous devastation' which 'provided ever-present evidence of the reality of divine judgment' (Jude 7; Gen. 19.4–11).[97]

The intruders, says Jude, are emboldened by dreams or visions to do similar things by defiling their bodies through sexual sin, by rejecting the lord's authority, and by slandering celestial or angelic beings. The slander of angels is a curious charge, referring perhaps to the cursing of evil angels in spells for healing, or denigrating angels as the givers of the law to Moses (Jude 8).[98] Jude counters with a story taken from the lost ending of the *Testament of Moses*, where the archangel Michael was embroiled in a dispute with the devil over Moses' body. Yet, rather than slander the devil for his accusation, Michael appealed to the Lord's judgment to settle the matter (Jude 9).[99] It is ironic, Jude adds, that those who claim to have heavenly dreams or visions seem to understand so little of the heavenly world. Far from being spiritual, they are 'irrational animals' who are destined to be 'destroyed' (Jude 10).

---

93 McKnight 2003b, 1530.
94 Painter and deSilva 2012, 196.
95 A few manuscripts read 'Jesus' at this point (MSS A and B), which would be a tantalizing indication of his pre-existence in Israel's covenant-history, much like 1 Cor. 10.4 where Paul says that the spiritual rock that the Israelites drank from in the wilderness was Christ.
96 Jude 6; Gen. 6.1–4 with influence from *1 En.* 6–19.
97 Bauckham 1983, 54.
98 *Jub.* 1.27–29; Ac. 7.38, 53; Gal. 3.19; Heb. 2.2.
99 See Bauckham 1983, 60–2.

EMAILS
from the edge

From: Alan_Daley@aol.com
To: Professor Dana Schuler
Date: Tues, 13 Dec 2016 at 1:12 p.m.
Subject: Sources in Jude

Dear Prof.,

I was reading through the letter of Jude the other day and I noticed that it quotes two Jewish texts that are not in the Old Testament. Something called *1 Enoch* and the *Testament of Moses*. Are these texts the real deal? Are they supposed to be in the Bible as well?

Pax 2 da Max
AD

From: Professor Dana Schuler
To: Alan_Daley@aol.com
Date: Tues, 13 Dec 2016 at 1:42 p.m.
Subject: Re: Sources in Jude

Dear Alan,

Yes, this is a curious case indeed, it raises questions about inspiration, sources, and canonicity.

In verse 9, Jude quotes the lost ending of a document known to us as the *Testament of Moses*, probably a Palestinian writing of the first century AD, now extant only in Latin (though the document may have been revised and gone under the name the *Assumption of Moses*). In this text, Jewish mythology about a contest between the satan and the angel of the Lord (see *Jub.* 17—18, 48 and 4Q'Amram) is interwoven with a story about what happened to Moses' body after he died. There, the satan most likely argued with Michael that Moses, a murderer, was not entitled to an honourable burial, and Michael responded with a rebuke taken from the wording of

> Zechariah 3.2. See discussion in Richard Bauckham's *Jude, 2 Peter* commentary (1983, 65–76).
>
> In verses 14–15, Jude quotes *1 Enoch*, a composite document made up of five major books, compiled over a period from roughly 200 BC to AD 300 (but scholars dispute the dating of *1 En.* 37—71 in particular). Jude quotes *1 Enoch* 1.9, taken from the Book of Watchers (*1 En.* 1—36), concerning how God will come in judgment to destroy the wicked. For a good summary, see David deSilva's *Jewish Teachers* book (2012, 101–40).
>
> Tertullian (*On the Apparel of Women* 1.3) accepted *1 Enoch* based on Jude's usage, and Clement of Alexandria (*Comments on the Epistle of Jude*) thought the same for both *1 Enoch* and the *Testament of Moses*. To this day, the Ethiopic Orthodox Church regards *1 Enoch* as part of its canon of sacred literature.
>
> In my mind, Jude cited these two texts because he believed they were in some sense true, perhaps historically true, since he talks about Enoch prophesying, or maybe he believed they were true in the sense of stating two valid principles: it is wrong to slander celestial/angelic beings (*Testament of Moses*) and God with his angels will indeed judge the wicked (*1 Enoch*). Jude clearly accepted the *Testament of Moses* and *1 Enoch* as useful for the argument he was making and he cited them because his audience probably knew them and regarded them highly. Now Jude might consider these texts to be illustrative rather than authoritative, in much the same way as a preacher might use a sermon illustration from the Left Behind novels. Alternatively, we have to bear in mind that there was no fixed 'canon' yet, either for Jews or Christians, just a body of sacred texts that commanded assent in many quarters. Jude may well have regarded these texts as on par with scripture!
>
> The grace be with you
> Prof. Dana Schuler

This leads Jude into a compressed catalogue of scriptural villains of whom these false teachers remind him: Cain the murderer, Balaam the false prophet, Korah the leader of a rebellion against Moses. Rebellion, in fact, is near the heart of their problem. The intruders are overthrowing or ignoring the proper structures of authority, and the result is moral chaos and pollution—even at their love-feast. These people are dangerous, like hidden reefs. They are selfish, like shepherds who only tend to their own needs. Their futility is signalled by a further bewildering mix of metaphors: waterless clouds, fruitless trees, splashing waves, and wandering stars. These all have in common the fact that they appear to promise something but don't deliver it: no rain from the clouds, no fruit from the trees, no safe passage on the stormy sea, no regular movement of stars across the sky. The intruders appear to offer a way of life which is 'different' and liberating; but the only thing they achieve is shame, darkness, and chaos (Jude 11–13).

A further indictment of the intruders is made with a citation from *1 Enoch* (see 'Emails from the edge: sources in Jude'), which in its opening chapter refers to God coming in judgment with his angels—whom the intruders have slandered—to destroy the godless. The intruders, though relying on the generosity of the church, are characterized by bickering complaints, and evil impulses. They engage in a mixture of self-adulation and sycophancy to gain their way into people's confidence. Jude is clear: they will be judged (Jude 14–16).

1 Enoch fragment
Courtesy of The Leon Levy Dead Sea Scrolls Digital Library; Israel Antiquities Authority, photo: Shai Halevi

Jude rounds off his warning about the intruders by an appeal to apostolic prophecy about the rise of mockers, apostates, and deviants in the last days. He urges his audience to 'remember' how the apostles had previously instructed the church that, 'In the last times there will be scoffers who will follow their own ungodly desires' (Jude 18). This arguably refers to a pattern of teaching about a time of cosmic catastrophe, political upheaval, apostasy, and rampant immorality that would come upon the world prior to the end of all things.[100] The intruders—further described as divisive, 'natural' or 'earthly', and without the spirit—are the first-fruits of a coming age of rebellion and wickedness (Jude 17–19).

4. Exhortation to perseverance (Jude 20–23)

Jude turns his attention to his readers themselves. They must build themselves up in the most holy faith, retaining the apostolic gospel upon which the church is founded. They must hold to the moral implications of the gospel, so that the church can grow into the eschatological temple. They must keep 'praying in the Holy Spirit', revealing the true charismatic nature of the church by their prayer life. They must remain within God's love, vigilant against moral or confessional deviancy. They must continue to set their hope on Jesus the Messiah, and the ultimate revelation of his mercy at his return (Jude 20–21).[101]

---
[100] See Mt. 7.15; 24.4–14; Ac. 20.29–31; 2 Thess. 2.1–12; 1 Tim. 4.1–5; 2 Tim. 3.1–9; 1 Jn. 2.18; 4.1–3; 2 Pet. 3.3–4.
[101] Bauckham 1983, 117.

Jude has three final commands for his audience. First, those driven into doubt need mercy. Second, those seduced by the intruders need rescuing. Third, the intruders themselves need 'mercy, mixed with fear'. They must be urged to repent and warned of judgment.

5. Concluding doxology (Jude 24–25)

The letter closes with one of the most remarkable doxologies of the entire New Testament. This may be traditional liturgical material, forming a prayer that God in his love and mercy will preserve his people from error and receive them into his glorious presence. The worship is binitarian in form, *to God* and *through Jesus Christ our lord*, and commends God as the God who saves, and who from eternity past to eternity future, is worthy to receive acclamations of 'glory, majesty, power and authority' (Jude 24–25).

JAMES AND JUDE IN THE BIG PICTURE

James and Jude have much to contribute to anyone who is serious about being a Christian. James confronts half-hearted discipleship; Jude fiercely denounces false teachers. Together they stress faithfulness: both putting 'faith' into action and contending for 'the faith'.

For James, faith is living and active, not a passive collection of ideas to be believed. The faithful receive God's word and do it, in line with biblical examples.[102] For too long James has been regarded as an epistle of straw by those who had a strawman view of true discipleship. We are certainly not 'saved by works', but James's point is that neither are we saved without them. God's implanted word brings us to faith, and that faith works itself out in love, mercy, and true worship. If your faith has no verbs, no imperatives, no discipline, no denial, no mercy, and no struggle, then you are probably doing it wrong.

What then about Jude? Clement of Alexandria showed the value of using Jude to confront the false teaching and blatant wickedness that infiltrated the church in his day. Much of what Jude refers to may initially sound strange to our ears. Yet if we pause and reflect, as Gene Green notes,

> 'Jude has instructed his audience that God's power is exhibited in the created order and that God's judgment has been effective from the earliest times. God's condemnation of the wicked and the false teachers who are disrupting Jude's church was decreed in ancient times (v. 4). When it occurs at the judgment, those who have reviled and blasphemed God will discover that they should have honoured and praised God. This conclusion also brings the rhetorical agenda of the letter to its close. Jude invites his readers to picture themselves standing with Christ in the heavenly court. Of course, they would desire to be unstained and holy in such a setting. God's eternal power and majesty makes it clear that he can bring the faithful to that glorious destiny.'
>
> **Pheme Perkins**, *First and Second Peter, James, and Jude*, 156–7.

---

[102] Johnson 2010, 453 (following Jas. 2.23–25; 5.11, 17–18).

the themes that emerge from that ancient milieu are surprisingly familiar and linger with us today as the church seeks to live out its faith in a postmodern world, which has lost all sense of absolutes and embraces hedonism in the extreme.[103]

Parts of the Christian church today seem ideationally vacuous, with little or no confessional content to their faith. They tend also to be places where manifold forms of immorality are permitted and even celebrated. In such a context, we are to contend for the faith without being contentious over tertiary matters. In such an environment, we are to embrace and embody the moral implications of the gospel. In such a time, we are to rescue those who are blown about by false teaching and who get flustered with doubts over what they should actually believe. To keep ourselves in God's love we must keep the faith, and keep ourselves from being seduced by bad characters masquerading as teachers.

Further reading

Allison, Dale C. 2013. *James*. ICC: London: T&T Clark.
Bauckham, Richard J. 1983. *Jude, 2 Peter*. WBC; Waco, TX: Word.
——. 1990. *Jude and the Relatives of Jesus in the Early Church*. London: T&T Clark.
——. 1999. *James*. NTR; London: Routledge.
Blomberg, Craig L., and Mariam J. Kamell. 2008. *James*. ZECNT; Grand Rapids, MI: Zondervan.
Davids, Peter H. 2014. *A Theology of James, Peter, and Jude*. BTNT; Grand Rapids, MI: Zondervan.
Green, Gene L. 2008. *Jude and 2 Peter*. BECNT; Grand Rapids, MI: Baker.
Johnson, Luke Timothy. 1995. *The Letter of James: A New Translation with Introduction and Commentary*. AB; New York: Doubleday.
——. 2004. *Brother of Jesus, Friend of God: Studies in the Letter of James*. Grand Rapids, MI: Eerdmans.
Mbuvi, Andrew M. 2015. *Jude and 2 Peter*. NCCS; Eugene, OR: Cascade.
McKnight, Scot. 2011. *The Letter of James*. NICNT; Grand Rapids, MI: Eerdmans.
Painter, John, and David A. deSilva. 2012. *James and Jude*. Paideia; Grand Rapids, MI: Baker.
Penner, T. C. 1999. 'The Epistle of James in Current Research.' *CRBS* 7: 257–308.
Perkins, Pheme. 1995. *First and Second Peter, James, and Jude*. Interpretation; Louisville, KY: Westminster John Knox.
Reese, Ruth Anne. 2000. *Writing Jude: The Reader, the Text, and the Author in Constructs of Power and Desire*. BIS 51; Leiden: Brill.
——. 2007. *2 Peter and Jude*. THNTC; Grand Rapids, MI: Eerdmans.
Wall, Robert W. 1997. *Community of the Wise: The Letter of James*. NTC; Valley Forge, PA: Trinity Press International.
Webb, Robert L., and Peter H. Davids (eds.). 2008. *Reading Jude with New Eyes: Methodological Reassessments of the Letter of Jude*. LNTS; London: T&T Clark.
Webb, Robert L., and John S. Kloppenborg (eds.) 2007. *Reading James with New Eyes: Methodological Reassessments of the Letter of James*. LNTS; London: T&T Clark.
Wright, N. T. 2011. *Early Christian Letters for Everyone: James, Peter, John, and Judah*. London: SPCK, pp. 3–44, 193–206.

---

103 Green 2008, 25–26.

32

Petrine Letters: 1 and 2 Peter

For you know that it was not with perishable things such as silver or gold that you were redeemed from the empty way of life handed down to you from your ancestors, but with the precious blood of Christ, a lamb without blemish or defect. He was chosen before the creation of the world, but was revealed in these last times for your sake.[1]

His divine power has given us everything we need for a godly life through our knowledge of him who called us by his own glory and goodness. Through these he has given us his very great and precious promises, so that through them you may participate in the divine nature, having escaped the corruption in the world caused by evil desires.[2]

CHAPTER AT A GLANCE

This chapter provides an overview of the letters of 1 Peter and 2 Peter.

By the end of this chapter you should be able to:

- understand issues of authorship and purpose related to the Petrine letters;
- describe the structure and argument in the Petrine letters;
- understand the themes and theology in the Petrine letters.

INTRODUCTION

Simon bar-Jonah was one of the front rank of leaders in the early church. Jesus nicknamed him 'rock' (Aramaic *Kêpā*; Greek transliteration *Cēphas*; Greek translation *Petros*), from which we get the name 'Peter'.[3] Simon Peter was a fisherman from Bethsaida whom Jesus called to be his follower and fellow-worker.[4] Not only was he one of the Twelve; he, along

---

1 1 Pet. 1.18–20.
2 2 Pet. 1.3–4.
3 Jn. 1.42; Mt. 16.17–18.
4 Mk. 1.16–18/Mt. 4.18–20; Lk. 5.1–11; Jn. 1.40–42, 44.

with the brothers James and John, was part of Jesus' inner circle.⁵ It was Peter who made the dramatic pronouncement that Jesus was the Messiah.⁶ It was also Peter, notoriously, who denied Jesus in the high priest's hall.⁷ However, he became a key witness to Jesus' resurrection, not least through a personal meeting with the risen Jesus in which he was restored to his position of leadership.⁸

The early chapters of Acts display Peter as a key leader in the early church, working in Judea and Samaria. Luke links him with the early stages of the gentile 'breakthrough'.⁹ At the Jerusalem council, Peter became an advocate for gentile inclusion without male circumcision as practised in Antioch—despite his temporary lapse in Antioch itself.¹⁰ Herod planned to kill Peter, but he had a miraculous escape and left Jerusalem.¹¹ According to tradition, Peter eventually journeyed to Rome, perhaps travelling via Corinth. The Roman churches were probably founded by Jewish Christians very early on, and Peter gravitated towards them as a possible mission-field. It was during the late 50s or early 60s that Peter probably wrote 1 Peter from Rome (that is, 'Babylon') to churches in Asia Minor.¹² Tradition, once more, has it that Peter was martyred during Nero's pogrom against Christians.¹³ It may have been shortly after that that John Mark wrote a gospel based largely on Petrine reminiscences.¹⁴

Statue of the apostle Peter in the Basilica of St John Lateran in Rome
Omi Studio / Shutterstock

Peter is remembered in Christian tradition as a fisherman who became a fisher of men and women, an apostle, a martyr, saint, and even the first pope. His memory

---

5 See e.g. Mk. 5.37; 9.2, 14; 14.33.
6 Mk. 8.29/Mt. 16.16/Lk. 9.20.
7 Mk. 14.66–72/Mt. 26.69–75/Lk. 22.54–62/Jn. 18.25–27.
8 Lk. 24.34; 1 Cor. 15.5; Jn. 21.15–19.
9 Ac. 10.1—11.18.
10 Ac. 15.7–11; Gal. 2.11–15. See above on Galatians.
11 Ac. 12.1–17.
12 1 Pet. 5.13.
13 Eus. *Hist. Eccl.* 2.25.5; 3.1.2; 3.30.2.
14 Eus. *Hist. Eccl.* 3.39.15.

is woven into the gospels, Acts, and the two epistles bearing his name, as well as into various apocryphal writings like the *Gospel of Peter*, the *Preaching of Peter*, the *Acts of Peter*, and the *Apocalypse of Peter*. An entire Petrine hagiography developed around his legacy.[15] In the end, Peter can be lauded for his role as a successful organizer of the early churches, a mission strategist to Jews and gentiles, and a bridge-builder among factional divides.[16]

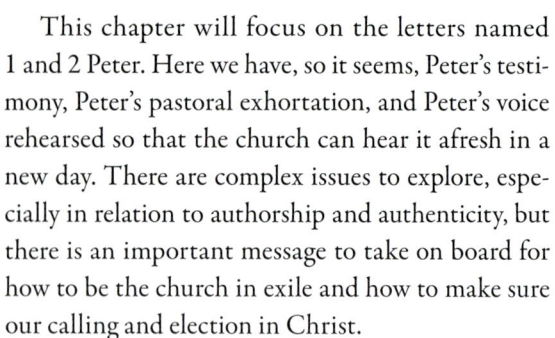

This chapter will focus on the letters named 1 and 2 Peter. Here we have, so it seems, Peter's testimony, Peter's pastoral exhortation, and Peter's voice rehearsed so that the church can hear it afresh in a new day. There are complex issues to explore, especially in relation to authorship and authenticity, but there is an important message to take on board for how to be the church in exile and how to make sure our calling and election in Christ.

3D reconstruction of a Galilean fishing boat from the first century
© 2013 by Zondervan

CONTEXTUAL AND CRITICAL MATTERS

Origins of 1 Peter

The opening verse of 1 Peter declares the author to be 'Peter, an apostle of Jesus the Messiah'.[17] Petrine authorship has regularly been questioned on various grounds: the epistle is written in good Greek, quoting the Septuagint and not the Hebrew scriptures, and employing conventions of greco-roman rhetoric. Many suppose these unlikely if the author was indeed an unschooled Galilean fisherman.[18] There are, in addition, said to be signs of influence from Pauline and deutero-Pauline writings.[19] Many suppose the life-setting of the epistle to reflect a later period when Christians had spread into northern Asia Minor and believers were undergoing persecution like that under Domitian (AD 81–96) or Trajan (AD 98–117). Some have seen this letter not as the literary production of an early founder of the church, but as a post-70 pseudepigraphical writing which was attempting to universalize Peter's memory and turn him into a generic apostle with Pauline traits. At most, say some, the letter is the

---

15 On the history, memory, and hagiography of Peter, see Hengel 2006; Bockmuehl 2012; Dunn 2015, 724–54; Bond and Hurtado 2015.
16 Hengel 2006, 89–97; Dunn 1990 [1977], 385.
17 1 Pet. 1.1 *NTE/KNT*.
18 Ac. 4.13.
19 Among the alleged signs of Paulinism are: the language of 'revelation' (1 Pet. 1.7, 13; 4.13), 'in Christ' (1 Pet. 3.16; 5.10, 14), and 'grace-gifts' (1 Pet. 4.10); the focus on Jesus' substitutionary death (1 Pet. 2.21–24); the mention of 'die to sins and live for righteousness', which mirrors Pauline ethics (1 Pet. 2.24); the call for submission to governors, which sounds like Rom. 13.1–7 (1 Pet. 2.13–14, 17); and the household code (1 Pet. 3.1–7). See Achtemeier 1996, 15–19; Elliott 2000, 22–3, 37–40; and Davids 2014, 110–12.

758 The Early Christians and the Mission of God

product of a 'Petrine school' that attempted to offer a 'fitting tribute to the quality, character, and content of what Peter was remembered as teaching and preaching'.[20]

The problem is that Peter's memory is found all over the early church—in the gospels, Acts, Paul's letters, the apostolic Fathers, then later in pseudepigraphical and apocryphal literature—but always second-hand or from a subsequent generation. Peter's direct voice is never found in the sources, unless 1 Peter itself is an exception; so we have no control document against which to measure the present one.[21] There could well be Petrine influence in Mark; we have 'Petrine' speeches in Acts; but these obviously reflect the redaction and editing of their respective authors.[22] Any attempt to recover a 'historical Peter' is prone to the difficulties inherent in our sparse sources and their layers of interpretation.

However, we should not too quickly assume that 1 Peter is pseudepigraphical. To begin with, we should not underestimate Peter's facility in Greek. He grew up in Bethsaida, a Greek-speaking territory with a gentile majority. He spent a considerable amount of time in the Jewish Diaspora.[23] In any case, as we have observed elsewhere, Greek was at least the second language of most males right across the old imperial lands of Alexander the Great. For Peter to be able to write good Greek is no more remarkable than for someone brought up speaking Arabic in the Gulf States to be able to write good English. In any case, while the Greek style of 1 Peter is proficient, it is hardly highbrow. Some have suggested that the syntax exhibits signs of bilingual influence from a person whose first language was semitic rather than Greek.[24] Moreover, if Silvanus acted as Peter's scribe or secretary (as well as carrying the letter), then maybe he could have edited or refined Peter's expression.[25] There are too many variables here to be on secure ground.

Furthermore, the supposed Pauline traits in 1 Peter may indicate that much of Paul's language and emphases were not unique to him, but were shared with others in the early church. In fact, in musical terms, 1 Peter is hardly a Pauline cover, but more like a collection that incorporates several theological, intertextual, and ethical motifs that were current in various wings of the Christian church.[26] The letter displays signs of the Jesus-tradition,[27] as well as a residue of traditional

---
20 Dunn 2009b, 1157.
21 Horrell (2002, 46) notes: 'If 1 Peter were authentic, then it would of course constitute a unique piece of evidence for precisely such a "Petrine" formulation of Christian theology.'
22 Dunn (2009b, 1147) reckons: 'the more "authenticity" is attributed to the Petrine speeches in Acts, the weaker (not stronger) the case for Petrine authorship of 1 Peter'. In contrast, see Elliott 2000, 25–7 who lists the affinities between 1 Peter and the Petrine speeches in Acts.
23 See Bockmuehl 2012, 166–76.
24 Jobes 2005, 7–8, 325–38; 2011, 278. Achtemeier (1996, 2) concedes: 'The quality of its Greek ought nevertheless not [to] be exaggerated.'
25 1 Pet. 5.12.
26 Elliott 2000, 20–41 (esp. 27–8); Horrell 2002.
27 See e.g. 1 Pet. 1.4 = Mt. 25.34; 1 Pet. 2.12 = Mt. 5.11–12; 1 Pet. 3.14 = Mt. 5.10; see Elliott 2000, 24–5; Dunn 2009b, 1154.

materials.[28] There are even plot similarities between 1 Peter, James, and Hebrews.[29] As for the life-setting of 1 Peter, nothing here requires a post-70 date. The persecutions appear to consist mostly of social ostracism, not imperial suppression or official persecution. The readers seem to be facing the same kind of localized and periodic harassment that we see described in Acts, Paul's letters, and Hebrews.

In the end, we surmise that Petrine authorship cannot be proven but remains entirely plausible. If so, we do not have to treat 1 Peter as a petrified tradition looking for apostolic legitimation by artificially borrowing a famous name. We are free to hear in the letter the authentic testimony of Peter himself.

Date of 1 Peter

Irenaeus made explicit citations of 1 Peter in the 180s AD.[30] Polycarp echoed 1 Peter in his letter to the Philippians dated perhaps around 120 to 140 AD.[31] Even earlier, Papias's testimony to 1 Peter (as recorded by Eusebius) may date as early as 110, though it might be a bit later.[32] Some would even suggest influence from 1 Peter on *1 Clement*, which would take us into the 90s, but this is less certain.[33] If 1 Peter is pseudepigraphical, then a date around AD 80–110 is most likely. However, if the letter derives from the historical Peter himself, as we are proposing, then any time from the late 50s to the early 60s AD would do. The letter would then be written in the vicinity of Rome (referred to in the letter as 'Babylon') on the eve of Nero's persecution.

Audience of 1 Peter

The letter is addressed to churches in Pontus, Galatia, Cappadocia, Asia, and Bithynia, which together encompass parts of western, northern, and central Asia Minor (modern-day Turkey). We know a little (through Paul and Acts) of how Christianity came to the Roman province of Asia and the region of southern Galatia, but we do not know when the other regions mentioned first heard the gospel.[34] Perhaps Jewish pilgrims visiting Jerusalem for the Pentecost of Acts 2 joined the Jesus-movement and took their new faith back to Asia Minor.[35] We also know that the emperor Claudius (AD 41–54) established Roman colonies in all five of the

---

28 See Achtemeier 1996, 21–3; Elliott 2000, 30–7; Dunn 2009b, 1154–7.
29 See e.g. 1 Pet. 1.1 = Jas. 1.1; 1 Pet. 1.6–8 = Jas. 1.2–4; 1 Pet. 4.8 = Jas. 5.20; 1 Pet. 5.5–9 = Jas. 4.6–10; 1 Pet. 1.2; 2.11 = Heb. 11.13; 1 Pet. 2.25 = Heb. 13.20; 1 Pet. 3.18 = Heb. 9.28; see further Johnson 1995, 54–5; Elliott 2000, 23–4.
30 See e.g. Iren. *Adv. Haer.* 4.9.2; 4.16.5; 5.7.2 (see further in Dunn 2015, 744 n. 82).
31 Polycarp *Phil.* 1.3 = 1 Pet. 1.8, 12; *Phil.* 2.1–2 = 1 Pet. 1.13–14; *Phil.* 5.3 = 1 Pet. 2.11, 3.14; *Phil.* 8.1 = 1 Pet. 2.21–24; *Phil.* 10.2 = 1 Pet. 2.12–13. Polycarp's citation of 1 Peter is noted by Eus. *Hist. Eccl.* 4.14.9.
32 Eus. *Hist. Eccl.* 3.39.16.
33 Contrast Achtemeier 1996, 45–6, and Elliott 2000, 138–40, on this point.
34 See Ac. 16.7 where Paul is forbidden to visit those other regions.
35 Ac. 2.9–11. Luke tells us that Aquila, husband of Priscilla, was a 'native of Pontus' (Ac. 18.2).

regions mentioned in 1 Peter 1.1. It is quite possible that Jewish émigrés from Rome were settled there, or perhaps fled there after Claudius's expulsion of Jewish Christians in AD 49.[36]

Are the intended readers Jewish or gentile or both? In favour of a Jewish audience is the description of the believers (reminiscent of Jas. 1.1) as 'foreigners' and 'exiles', making it sound as though they were part of the Jewish Diaspora.[37] It might then make

Asia Minor

sense to detect further signs of their Jewish identity in the scriptural designations of the audience as 'Sarah's children',[38] God's 'elect',[39] people called to the covenantal vocation of holiness.[40] The motifs of election and holiness climax with the designation of the audience as 'a chosen people, a royal priesthood, a holy nation, God's special possession'.[41] The audience is also explicitly contrasted with the 'Gentiles'.[42] If Peter was the apostle to the 'circumcision', then this is exactly who we would expect his letter to be addressed to.[43] Readers from Eusebius to Calvin have agreed: 1 Peter is addressed to a Jewish audience.[44]

Others, however, have thought a gentile (or at least mixed) audience is intended.[45] They point out remarks about the 'evil desires' the readers had during a time of 'ignorance', how they have left the 'empty way of life handed down to you from your ancestors', mentioning a time when 'you were not a people', who were called 'out of darkness', who had been 'like sheep going astray,' and how they formerly 'spent enough time in the past doing what pagans choose to do.' All this would better describe a gentile audience.[46] It is true that such language reminds us of fairly

---

36 See Jobes 2005, 28–41.
37 See e.g. Elliott 2000, 95–7; Jobes 2005, 23–7; Witherington 2007b, 22–39; Dunn 2009b, 1158–60, with 1 Pet. 1.1, 17; 2.10. Elliott (2000, 101–2) takes 'exiles' literally, believing that the audience comprised both 'resident aliens living in these provinces for a greater period of time and visiting strangers briefly passing through. This group of persons, as we may envision it, encountered missionaries of the messianic movement and was attracted to this new community as a way of attaining a haven of acceptance, security, and belonging in an alien and often hostile environment.'
38 1 Pet. 3.6.
39 1 Pet. 1.1, 2, 4, 9; similar to e.g. Ps. 104.6, 23; Isa. 65.9, 23; Tob. 8.15.
40 1 Pet. 1.15–16; Lev. 11.44–45; 19.2.
41 1 Pet. 2.9; Ex. 19.6.
42 1 Pet. 2.12; 4.3 NRSV.
43 Gal. 2.9.
44 Eus. *Hist. Eccl.* 3.4.2.
45 See e.g. Achtemeier 1996, 51; deSilva 2004, 842–3; Johnson 2010, 426, 432; Davids 2014, 102–6.
46 1 Pet. 1.14, 18; 2.9–10, 25; 4.3.

Petrine Letters: 1 and 2 Peter   761

typical intra-Jewish prophetic rebukes, treating Israelites as if they were pagans. But, equally, we should remember that Paul sees gentile converts as having been grafted into the renewed people of Israel, and can address them in language very similar to that of the ostensibly 'Jewish' designations noted above.[47] Perhaps it is best to remain agnostic on this question.

Genre and purpose of 1 Peter

In terms of genre, 1 Peter is much like James: it is a Diaspora letter with a mixture of exhortation and consolation.[48] It was written to exhort Christians in Asia Minor to maintain their faith in the midst of social scorn, shaming, slander, and stigma. They do not appear to be facing organized persecution, sponsored officially by this or that city-state. Their adversaries are more likely local groups who have come to regard Christians as dangerous social deviants and are pressuring them, verbally and perhaps physically, to return to the normal web of socio-religious relationships and cultural and religious practices that characterized the city and/or province.[49] We remind ourselves once more that in the ancient world those who abstained from worshipping the local gods were suspected of wishing trouble upon their city or region. Peter encourages the believers to hold fast, stressing the divine verdict about their identity: they may be disparaged by their neighbours, but in God's eyes they are precious, royal, and holy.[50] They enjoy the promises given in Israel's sacred history. They have experienced a new birth, purification, and redemption. They look forward to a future salvation with an imperishable inheritance.[51] Peter further urges his readers to give outsiders no reason for malice;[52] they should rest in

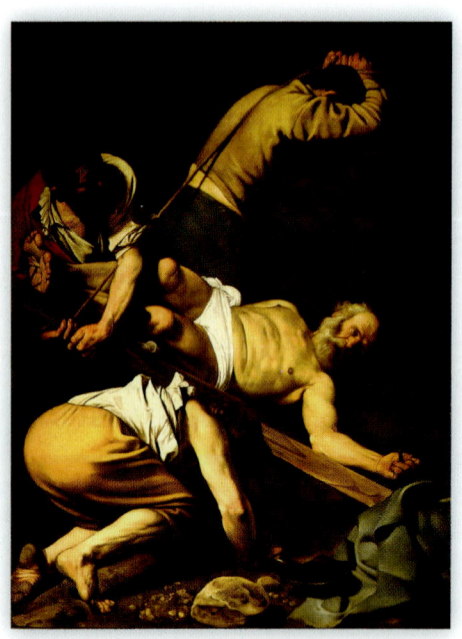

Caravaggio's *The Crucifixion of Saint Peter*, dated 1600, Cerasi Chapel, Rome
PD-US

---

47 See e.g. Rom. 2.25–29; 9.22–26; 1 Cor. 10.1; Gal. 6.16; and the whole argument about incorporation into Abraham's family in Rom. 4 and Gal. 3.1—4.31.
48 See Elliott 2000, 12; Jobes 2005, 54–5; Doering 2012, 434–52.
49 1 Pet. 1.6; 2.12, 19; 3.16; 4.12–16.
50 1 Pet. 2.4–12.
51 1 Pet. 1.4–5, 7–12, 18–19, 22–23.
52 1 Pet. 1.1; 2.1, 11–20; 3.1–17; 4.1–5, 12–19.

their baptized identity as 'Christians'.[53] Jesus died for them, leaving them an example:[54] the letter's emphatic christology, supported by carefully crafted citations of and allusions to the Old Testament, underlies the entire appeal. One may legitimately regard the letter as a kind of christological exposition of Isaiah, Psalms, and Proverbs, applying scripture to a Christian audience facing severe hardships.[55]

Origins of 2 Peter

Did Peter write 2 Peter? The authenticity of the second Petrine letter is one of the most disputed in New Testament studies. The reasons for doubting authenticity are as follows:

1. The reference to Paul's letters being on par with the 'other scriptures' presupposes the collection and acceptance of Paul's letters as authoritative scripture, while the comment that 'ignorant and unstable people' distort them implies a contest over Paul's literary legacy between proto-orthodox and 'heretical' groups—both of which might be thought to take us forward into the mid-second century at the earliest.[56]
2. The second chapter of 2 Peter incorporates a large section of the epistle of Jude; this might be thought odd if Peter, the apostle, was the author.[57]
3. The writer seems to draw on the gospel of Matthew concerning the transfiguration and the gospel of John regarding Peter's martyrdom.[58]
4. The author calls himself *Symeōn* rather than *Simōn*; which might be a deliberate allusion to James's recognition of the validity of Peter's testimony at the apostolic council of Acts 15, which is the only other place in the NT where Peter is called *Symeōn*.[59]
5. The style of Greek and mode of argument in 2 Peter is markedly different from that in 1 Peter. Notwithstanding some spasmodic replication of wording and themes from 1 Peter into 2 Peter,[60] stark literary differences remain.[61] The rhetorical style of 1 Peter is elegant and measured, but the style of 2 Peter has been labelled, somewhat colloquially, as 'Asiatic Greek on steroids'.[62] First Peter is

---

[53] 1 Pet. 3.21.
[54] 1 Pet. 1.18–19; 2.21–24; 3.18; 4.1.
[55] See Elliott 2000, 12–17.
[56] 2 Pet. 3.16. On Pauline terminology in 2 Peter, see Neyrey 1993, 133–4.
[57] On the priority of Jude, see Bauckham 1983, 141–3; Wasserman 2006, 73–98; Grünstäudl 2013, 14–20; Frey 2015, 154–62.
[58] 2 Pet. 1.17–18 = Mt. 17.5–6; 2 Pet. 1.14 = Jn. 21.18–19.
[59] 2 Pet. 1.1; Ac. 15.14.
[60] See Kruger 1999, 656–60; Neyrey 1993, 134–5; Jobes 2011, 378–9.
[61] Jerome (*De Vir. Ill.* 1) said: 'He [Peter] wrote two epistles which are called catholic, the second of which, on account of its difference from the first in style, is considered by many not to be by him.'
[62] Witherington 2007b, 264 n. 18.

full of scriptural language, while 2 Peter is filled with greco-roman words for deification ('become divine'), moral discourse (talk of self-mastery and virtue), and even pagan terms like 'Tartarus' (the underworld).[63] Second Peter includes fifty-seven *hapax legomena* (words not found elsewhere in the New Testament). And, as for the tone of voice, '2 Peter is bellicose as 1 Peter is irenic'.[64]

6. The language and theology of 2 Peter more closely resembles Christian vocabulary and phrasing in the second century than the first century.
7. Second Peter is not explicitly mentioned by anyone until Origen[65] in the third century; the first manuscript to contain it is $\mathfrak{P}^{72}$, dated to the third to fourth century.[66]
8. Eusebius indicates that many in the ancient church doubted the authorship and antiquity of 2 Peter.[67]

Some think that 2 Peter could still have been written by Peter, using a secretary. Others suppose that it was composed in the late first century (perhaps in the 80s) in a Petrine circle in Rome, aiming to honour Peter's apostolic legacy. Others again have suggested that the letter is not only pseudepigraphical but was written as late as the end of the second century, perhaps in Asia Minor. Postulating the apostle Peter as the author of this letter feels to us like pushing a big rock up a steep hill; the indications of post-Petrine authorship appear overwhelming.[68] It seems to be a pastiche of so many parts of the New Testament—mentioning Paul's letters, echoing episodes from Matthew and John, incorporating the polemical sections of Jude, and making deliberate connections back to 1 Peter.

This does not mean that 2 Peter is a 'forgery'. It is more probable that 2 Peter is what Richard Bauckham calls a 'transparent fiction', whereby an author might use

---

63 See 2 Pet. 1.4–6; 2.4.
64 Johnson 2010, 439.
65 Eus. *Hist. Eccl.* 6.25.8.
66 Frey (2015, 144) comments: 'The result is relatively clear: while Jude is fairly well-attested and known by 200 AD, there are no reliable testimonies of the reception of 2 Peter in the entire second century' (tr. M. F. Bird).
67 Eusebius (*Hist. Eccl.* 3.3.1) said that 'the so-called second epistle [of Peter] we have not received as canonical, but nevertheless it has appeared useful to many, and has been studied with other Scriptures'. Elsewhere (*Hist. Eccl.* 3.25.3) he lists 2 Peter among the 'disputed writings' (*antilegomena*) and records how Origen regarded it as 'doubtful' (*Hist. Eccl.* 6.25.8).
68 Among 'evangelical' scholars who regard 2 Peter as not written by Peter, see Bauckham 1983, 158–62; McKnight 2003a, 1504; Marshall 2004, 670; deSilva 2004, 876–8; Witherington 2007b, 260–72; Davids 2014, 195. However, a courageous minority do try to argue for Petrine authorship; see e.g. Kruger 1999; Schreiner 2003, 255–76; Green 2008, 139–44; and van Houwelingen 2010, while Gilmour 2001 and Mbuvi 2015 remain agnostic. Jobes (2011, 364) comments: 'Even the most conservative doctrine of Scripture does not presume to prescribe what genres the Holy Spirit may or may not have chosen when inspiring Scripture, and so the pseudonymity of 2 Peter cannot be ruled out without due consideration.' We do well to remember that God's inspiration includes his divine influence on the cognitive–linguistic horizon of authors, but also extends to the holy spirit's 'hallowing creaturely processes', like pseudepigraphy as well as the collection and canonization of ancient texts as the church's scripture (Webster 2003, 17).

the device of pseudepigraphy, inherent in the 'testament' genre (as in the largely Jewish *Testaments of the Twelve Patriarchs*), in order to be a faithful tradent of apostolic tradition. Eventually, however, the later gentile church did not recognize or accept the conventions of Jewish literature, and appealed to apostolic *authorship* rather than apostolic *content* to justify 2 Peter's inclusion in the canon at a time when other late (and often heretical) books were being excluded.[69] One way of looking at it may be to suggest that 2 Peter functions within the canon as a kind of capstone, a final drawing together of the different parts of the church's witness, imagining what Peter might say if he were to address his 'testament' to the churches of the author's own day.[70]

Date of 2 Peter

So when might this letter have been written? It is conspicuous by its absence from second-century writings.[71] It is not mentioned in the Muratorian canon (though, for that matter, the same is true of 1 Peter, James, and Hebrews), and, while Clement of Alexandria mentions Jude, he does not seem to know of 2 Peter. The general verdict is that there are no certain allusions to 2 Peter in any of the apostolic Fathers or among the apologists of the second century.[72] If we cannot detect 2 Peter in the second century, how can we date it to the first century?

Richard Bauckham has suggested that 2 Peter was written from Rome sometime around AD 80–90, though he leaves open the possibility of a date in the second century. He bases his argument on the letter's composition after Peter's death; its similarity to other Roman writings from the period, including the *Shepherd of Hermas* and *1–2 Clement*; and the dependency of the *Apocalypse of Peter* (c. AD 110–40) on 2 Peter. In addition, if the mention in 2 Peter 3.4 of 'ancestors' who died does not refer to the parents of the scoffers but to the first Christian generation, then this would plausibly suggest a setting among second-generation Christians towards the end of the first century. Bauckham contends that 2 Peter can be situated within the context of the Roman church's pastoral concern for sister-churches during the late first century (much like how *1 Clement* functioned in the 90s by trying to intercede in a dispute within the Corinthian assembly).[73]

Bauckham's suggestion is plausible, though we might contest his dating of the *Shepherd of Hermas* and *2 Clement*; most would see them as second-century texts.

---

69 Bauckham 1983, 134, 161–2. Schreiner 2003, 274 believes that Bauckham's conclusion is consistent with a view of biblical inspiration even though he himself disagrees that 2 Peter is a testament.
70 See similarly Trobisch 2000, 95.
71 Some think that patristic references to a thousand years being like a day to the Lord is based on 2 Pet. 3.8, but it is just as well from Ps. 90.4 (*Ep. Barn.* 15.4; Iren. *Adv. Haer.* 5.23.2). A better possibility, but no more than that, is that Justin (*Dial.* 82.1) alludes to 2 Pet. 2.1 by contrasting false prophets and false teachers. Others have pointed to 2 Pet. 3.4 being echoed in the Clementine letters (*1 Clem.* 23.3; *2 Clem.* 11.2), but this could be nothing more than different authors responding to the same problem of the delay in Christ's return.
72 Contrast Picirilli 1988.
73 Bauckham 1983, 157–59; 1998b, 290–303.

However, a bigger problem for Bauckham's dating might be Wolfgang Grünstäudl's recent study, arguing that it is 2 Peter that is dependent on the *Apocalypse of Peter*, not the other way round.[74] Grünstäudl argues as follows. (1) Second Peter 1.16–18 is a conflation of the transfiguration account in Matthew 17.1–8 and the *Apocalypse of Peter* 15–17, since 2 Peter differs from the Matthean version in those places where 2 Peter and the *Apocalypse of Peter* specifically agree. (2) Symeōn Peter's recollection of the lord foretelling his martyrdom in 2 Peter 1.14 might reflect influence from John 21.18–19, but it might also reflect the martyrdom-tradition in *2 Apocalypse of Peter* 14 (a Greek fragment). (3) The description of the cosmic conflagration in 2 Peter 3.10 is arguably a summary of *Apocalypse of Peter* 4–6. (4) If the *Apocalypse of Peter* borrowed from 2 Peter, it is curious that it has not utilized any of the apocalyptic materials drawn from Jude, especially when the *Apocalypse of Peter* shows an interest in matters relating to angels, the wicked, and the final judgment. Grünstäudl concludes: 'Taking all of these observations together, a clear verdict emerges for the view of the literary dependence of 2 Peter on the *Apocalypse of Peter* which accounts for the difficulties pertaining to the textual-tradition.'[75] If that is indeed the case, and if we date the *Apocalypse of Peter* to AD 120–140, then a date of AD 150–200 would be probable for 2 Peter. Many other views, of course, continue to be championed, and it is unlikely that any consensus will emerge in the foreseeable future.

Opponents in 2 Peter

Many have proposed that the false teachers and false prophets in 2 Peter 2–3 represent a precise group inside the church addressed in the letter.[76] Proposals have included Gnostics and Epicureans as key suspects (though the radical differences between those two shows how tenuous all such proposals must be). The epistle of Jude provides the primary scaffolding upon which the author builds his indictment of these teachers and proscribes their theology and behaviour. Like Jude, Symeōn Peter regards the opponents as debauched, deniers of Jesus, disavowing celestial entities, and destined for destruction. What is distinctive from Jude is that 2 Peter identifies the opponents thus: (1) they are teachers with a circle of followers who are eager to recruit more adherents;[77] (2) they promote 'heresies' (Greek *haireseis*);[78]

---

[74] Grünstäudl 2013, 97–144 (see esp. 141–4 for a summary). I thank Prof. Jörg Frey for pointing me (MFB) to this work and providing me with a summary of Grünstäudl's thesis in his paper, 'A New View on Second Peter: Its Eschatology and Ethics: Explaining the "Canonical" Epistle from the "Non-canonical" *Apocalypse of Peter*', presented at St Andrews University in 2016. See also Frey 2015, 170–3.
[75] Grünstäudl 2013, 142 (tr. M. F. Bird).
[76] See the useful survey in Green 2008, 150–9 who points out that the widespread view that the opponents were Epicureans (a view championed by Neyrey [1993, 122–8]) is not tenable.
[77] 2 Pet. 2.1–3, 14, 18.
[78] 2 Pet. 2.1.

(3) they deny the return of Jesus;[79] (4) they are apostates who claim to have escaped corruption through knowledge of the lord Jesus;[80] and (5) they are contentious about Paul.[81]

It may be easier to suggest that there were no precise opponents, because 2 Peter was written to no precise church. It was written to counter a wide range of competing philosophical positions, heresies, and deviant practices that emerged, confusingly and sometimes seductively, within the religious milieu of the time. This could include Epicurean critiques of Christian sexual ethics, Cynic encomia about freedom, Platonic rejoinders to Christian eschatology, Christians looking through a hellenistic rather than an apocalyptic lens, Marcionite or Valentinian cells with their radical re-readings of Paul, and miscellaneous tirades by former adherents of the Christian movement. Second Peter responds to an eclectic set of rivals, renouncements, and ripostes to Christian belief.

Audience of 2 Peter

The letter begins by stating that it is addressed to those who 'have received a faith as precious as ours', which indicates a fairly wide, we might even say 'catholic', audience.[82] Later, however, the author says that this is 'my second letter to you', implying that it is written to the same audience as 1 Peter, namely Jewish (or Jewish and gentile) Christians scattered among 'Pontus, Galatia, Cappadocia, Asia and Bithynia'.[83] To complicate matters further, the author also refers to things that 'our dear brother Paul also wrote to you',[84] implying that the audience had previously received correspondence from the apostle Paul. Therefore, the implied audience of 2 Peter would include both the recipients of 1 Peter and the Pauline assemblies in Asia Minor.

Yet there are difficulties in the way of imagining 2 Peter being written to the same audience as 1 Peter. The clear Jewish atmosphere of 1 Peter has been swapped for a texture in 2 Peter that is more at home in the greco-roman world and plays well for a gentile audience. First Peter deals with the problem of persecution, while 2 Peter focuses on heresy.[85] In addition, Paul never wrote (so far as we know) to communities in the northern region of Asia Minor—though the later we date 2 Peter, the more chance there is that a collection of Paul's letters might already have been

---

79 2 Pet. 3.3–4.
80 2 Pet. 2.20–23.
81 2 Pet. 3.16.
82 2 Pet. 1.1.
83 2 Pet. 3.1; 1 Pet. 1.1.
84 2 Pet. 3.15.
85 Admittedly, this argument is not cast-iron; circumstances can change, and the style of discourse can change with them, as the radical difference between 1 Corinthians and 2 Corinthians shows well enough.

circulating. Consequently, the references to a previous Petrine letter and to Paul's letters is probably meant simply to show that author and readers share the same literary inheritance from the two towering apostles, Peter and Paul, as the foundation for their common faith.

It seems more likely, then, that 2 Peter is an encyclical letter, meant to be read widely as a general exhortation to its readers in their many and diverse circumstances. That said, given that 2 Peter is first mentioned by Origen, and Jude by Clement of Alexandria, both in Egypt, one might wonder whether 2 Peter may have emerged in Alexandria, being intended initially for that area, before circulating more widely.[86] But, as with so many issues in the ancient world, these are guesses and cautious probes rather than certain 'results'.

Genre and purpose of 2 Peter

Second Peter resembles the genre of a 'testament': a deathbed exhortation by a revered figure of sacred history, who recounts incidents from the past and makes warnings about the future, often weaving together ethical paraenesis and apocalyptic discourse.[87] Jacob's speech to his sons in Genesis 49 provided the impetus and template for this genre. Examples of testaments include the *Testament of Job*, *Testament of Moses*, *Testament of Abraham*, and *Testaments of the Twelve Patriarchs*. Several of these 'testaments' can be found within larger works such as the Epistle of Enoch in *1 Enoch*, the Epistle of Baruch in *2 Baruch*, Paul's farewell speech to the Ephesian elders at Miletus in the book of Acts, and in *Jubilees*.[88] Second Peter is analogous to this genre, since the author, 'Symeōn Peter',

The transfiguration, illumination from Byzantine gospel book, late thirteenth century
PD-US

---

86 See Grünstäudl 2013; Frey 2015, 187–9.
87 See Bauckham 1983, 131–5; deSilva 2004, 877–8; Johnson 2010, 443–4; Jobes 2011, 356. For an introduction to the testament genre see Kugler 2010. Matthews (2011) points out that 2 Peter lacks several features common to testaments: no deathbed scene, no gathering of followers, no record of death or burial, and no use of third-person narrative.
88 *1 En.* 91–104; *2 Bar.* 78–87; Ac. 20.18–35; *Jub.* 20–22, 36.

recollects key events from his past, mentioning particularly his witnessing the transfiguration. He knows that his death is impending; he will soon 'put his body aside', and then after his 'departure' false teachers are destined to infiltrate the assemblies. When that happens, the audience must recall his instruction, the words of the prophets, and the commands of the lord and saviour given through 'your apostles'.[89] The ethical exhortations which bracket the letter seem designed to prepare the audience for a future without him,[90] though Symeōn promises to guide them even from his post-mortem state.[91] Towards the end we also find a mixture of eschatological forecast and exhortation to readiness, both of which are typical of 'testaments'.[92] Second Peter, however, is also a letter; the document appears to marry the two genres.[93] It is therefore perhaps best described as an *encyclical epistolary testament*; that is, it is Peter's 'testament', framed as a letter, and intended for wide circulation.

The purpose of 2 Peter is stated in 2 Peter 2–3. There the author writes against a general tide of philosophies and heresies that have either infiltrated the church or might draw people away from the church (or from a proper 'apostolic' church). Hence his admonition: 'be on your guard so that you may not be carried away by the error of the lawless and fall from your secure position.'[94]

Second Peter can also be regarded as an affirmation of Paul for the churches in the second century; churches that looked to Peter as the pre-eminent apostle needed to know that Paul was part of the same team. At a time when 'ignorant and unstable people' (2 Pet. 3.16) were distorting Paul's letters (individuals such as Marcion and Valentinus), when groups like the Ebionites had rejected Paul, and some like Justin basically ignored Paul, the author makes an important reclamation of Paul as one of the primary apostolic witnesses for the orthodox faith. Dunn is right to observe:

> Here 2 Peter can be heard as the voice of the great church trying to retain Paul as one of its spokesmen and to prevent Paul from being taken over by a more radical gnosticizing tendency; the significance of such high praise of *Paul* being attributed to *Peter* should not be missed. If 2 Peter can be given some credit for retaining Paul's own radicalism within the spectrum of orthodoxy (as Christian 'scripture'), then the debt which Christianity owes to 2 Peter was probably sufficient to secure 2 Peter's place within the NT canon.[95]

---

89 2 Pet. 1.12–18; 2.1–3; 3.2–4.
90 2 Pet. 1.3–11; 3.14–18.
91 2 Pet. 1.15.
92 2 Pet. 3.4–15.
93 In a way analogous to *1 En.* 91—104 and *2 Bar.* 78—87 which are also letters with the characteristics of a testament.
94 2 Pet. 3.17.
95 Dunn 2015, 730 (italics original).

> **OUTLINE OF 1 PETER**
>
> 1. Letter opening (1.1–2)
> 2. God's salvation in Jesus Christ (1.3–2.10)
> 3. God's people among the gentiles (2.11—4.11)
> 4. Exhortation to endure suffering (4.12–5.11)
> 5. Letter closing (5.12–14)

THE ARGUMENT OF 1 PETER

(See box: 'Outline of 1 Peter'.)

1. Letter opening (1.1–2)

The letter begins with Peter identifying himself as an 'apostle of Jesus Christ' and addressing his letter to God's 'elect exiles' scattered among the provinces of 'Pontus, Galatia, Cappadocia, Asia and Bithynia'. We detect here a clear consciousness of the church as a 'renewed Israel'. According to Johnson:

> This should not be construed as evidence for a later form of Christianity that was distanced both chronologically and theologically from its Jewish beginnings. Rather, it reveals what was inherent in early Christianity from the start: God was forming a new people through Christ and all those who believe—both Jew and Gentile—are God's 'chosen.'[96]

The readers' chosen nature is elaborated further as indebted to God's foreknowledge, operative through the sanctifying work of the spirit. Their calling is to be obedient to Jesus, who has cleansed them with his blood sprinkled for them like a sacrificial offering.

2. God's salvation in Jesus Christ (1.3—2.10)

Peter launches into an encomium of praise to God the father and the lord Jesus Christ because divine mercy has resulted in new birth into a living hope. According to Miroslav Volf: 'The new birth is neither a conversion to our authentic inner self nor a migration of the soul into a heavenly realm, but a translation of a person into the house of God erected in the midst of the world.'[97] Believers experience new life through Jesus' resurrection and have received an inheritance that cannot spoil because it is kept safe in 'heaven', God's space, not in order that believers may then 'go to heaven' to experience it but in order that in due time it will be revealed, transformatively, on the earth. Knowing this, the audience can rejoice in the midst of trials, knowing that faith is their divinely empowered shield, tested and proved through adversity. Peter praises his readers' faith: although they have not seen Jesus in person, they believe in him, they love him, and they are filled with joy about him.

---

[96] Johnson 2010, 432.
[97] Volf 1994, 19.

The result of such faith is the salvation promised by the prophets, who pointed ahead to the Messiah's sufferings and glory even though they never quite knew when or how this event would transpire (1.3–12).

Peter addresses the letter's recipients with a series of ethical exhortations that follow on from the value of their faith and the certainty of their hope. They should be ready, literally, to 'gird up the loins of your mind' and 'be fully sober'. Negatively, they must resist the evil desires that characterized them when they lived in ignorance. Positively, they are to be holy in all they do because the one who called them is himself holy (1 Pet. 1.13–16).

We could easily regard 1 Peter 1.17–21 as a synopsis of New Testament teaching:

> God as Father, as impartial judge, redemption through the blood of Christ, Christ as sacrificial lamb, Christ as preexistent, Christians living in the last days, resurrection and exaltation of Christ by God, God as the one in whom Christians place their trust and hope.[98]

The members of the audience, though 'foreigners' (Greek *paroikia*), must live in reverent fear, as is fitting for those for whom Christ died a redemptive and sacrificial death. They must trust in God through him, and wait for the fulfilment of their hope when he is revealed.

Attention shifts to the responsibility of the community members towards one another. They have been purified by obeying the word of truth. This leads to a moral renewal, where they can exhibit heartfelt and sincere love for one another. The source of their new birth is the living and enduring word of God, which contrasts with the transitory and fleeting nature of human life (1.22–25). According to Achtemeier:

> The contrast between what is transitory and what is permanent . . . would be highly appropriate for a beleaguered community of Christians facing what gave every appearance of being the permanent, even eternal, power and glory of the Roman Empire. In such a situation, the announcement that the glitter, pomp, and power of the Roman culture was as grass when compared to God's eternal word spoken in Jesus Christ, available through the gospel preached to and accepted by the Christians of Asia Minor, would give them courage to hold fast to the latter while rejecting the former.[99]

Peter urges his readers to rid themselves of the many vices that interfere with their capacity to love one another. Since they are new babes, they need pure milk,

---

[98] Achtemeier 1996, 123.
[99] Achtemeier 1996, 142.

God's holy word, which nourishes them into salvation. They have tasted this salvation and therefore know that the 'Lord is good' (2.1–3).

The topic shifts, somewhat abruptly, to Christ as the living stone, rejected by people, but precious to God. The same imagery is applied to the church as a corporate entity being built into a spiritual house, a temple, with sacrifices and offerings acceptable to God. Peter then quotes Isaiah 28.16, Psalm 118.22, and Isaiah 8.14 in quick succession to stress that Christ is the chosen 'stone', and that believers in him will never be ashamed, while those who rejected him and disobey him stumble and fall away from God. Again, as for Christ so for believers, they are God's chosen and special people, a fact bolstered with a cascade of intertextual imagery from the Old Testament.[100] The key idea is that the church is elect and precious to God because Christ is elect and precious to God. However, if the elect and precious Christ was rejected by human beings, then it should come as no surprise that the community constituted by him would similarly be rejected.[101]

3. God's people among the gentiles (2.11—4.11)

Peter now turns to a lengthy central section focusing on the exemplary way of life which believers must display in a hostile context. Rooted in a rich christological exposition, this is intended to highlight just how different the Christian way of life is from the surrounding culture while also mitigating any animosity that their social nonconformity might invoke. Peter, by calling his readers 'foreigners and exiles', reminds them of the social displacement they have already experienced. Their continuing response should be to abstain from sinful desires and to live lives filled with good deeds so that the gentiles might glorify God on the day of his visitation (2.11–12).

Peter adds that believers must be subject to governing authorities, even those as ungodly as the Roman emperor. Political leaders are sent by God to maintain order in society and so must be respected. Serving the true God by living a peaceful, wise, visibly good life is, in the end, far more revolutionary than simply overthrowing one corrupt regime and replacing it with another. Although Christians' ultimate allegiance is to God and to the church family, they are no less obligated to show proper regard for everyone else (2.13–17).

In the ancient world, slavery was assumed in the same way that we assume the use of cars or electricity. Many of the early Christians were themselves slaves, vulnerable to all kinds of ill-treatment. Peter calls on slaves to submit to their masters, whether kind or harsh. If they suffer, it should not be because they deserved it. The unjust suffering of Christ himself is the obvious example. He was sinless, and did not repay evil for evil, but simply entrusted himself to the one who judges justly.

---

100 Ex. 19.5–6; 23.22; Isa. 43.20–21; Mal. 3.17; Hos. 1.6, 9; 2.23.
101 Achtemeier 1996, 152–3.

Mosaic of slaves serving at a banquet, found in Dougga, Tunisia, dated second century
Gianni Dagli Orti / Shutterstock

Then, with a dense series of allusions to Isaiah 53, Peter adds that Christ bore in his body the sins of others. The crucifixion was an atoning death that has brought healing. This is one of the clearest statements in the whole New Testament of the fact that Jesus, the Messiah, took upon himself the punishment that his people deserved. Jobes correctly notes how 'Peter uses Isaiah's words to explain that suffering unjustly because of faithfulness to Christ is actually evidence that, like the Messiah, they have been chosen of God' (2.18–25).[102]

Some cultural norms, it appears, are to be resisted; others are to be adopted, if modified. The latter is the case in Peter's presentation of the classic greco-roman household codes, in which wives were expected to submit to their husbands—in this case, Peter stresses, to the unbelieving husbands who might thereby be won over to the faith. At the same time, in a radical break with normal culture, husbands are to respect their wives, particularly given their physical vulnerability, and to regard them as co-heirs of God's grace (3.1–7).

The instructions given to slaves, wives, and husbands are then applied to the entire church *vis-à-vis* wider society. The believers' attitudes and posture should be characterized by harmony, sympathy, love, and humility. They should not allow the hostility of the wider culture to provoke them to retaliation.

---

[102] Jobes 2005, 200.

BLAST FROM THE PAST: THE CORRESPONDENCE BETWEEN PLINY AND TRAJAN ABOUT CHRISTIANS

Pliny the Younger was the Roman governor of Bithynia between AD 111 and 113. He wrote to the emperor Trajan about what to do with those who had been discovered to be Christians or had been denounced as Christians yet protested their innocence. In this correspondence we get both Pliny's letter and Trajan's reply. Its relevance to 1 Peter is clear as it shows how, in north-west Asia Minor, Christians were known and despised, and mere profession of Christianity was a capital offence.

Pliny to the emperor Trajan

It is my practice, my lord, to refer to you all matters concerning which I am in doubt. For who can better give guidance to my hesitation or inform my ignorance? I have never participated in trials of Christians. I therefore do not know what offences it is the practice to punish or investigate, and to what extent. And I have been not a little hesitant as to whether there should be any distinction on account of age or no difference between the very young and the more mature; whether pardon is to be granted for repentance, or, if a man has once been a Christian, it does him no good to have ceased to be one; whether the name itself, even without offenses, or only the offenses associated with the name are to be punished.

Meanwhile, in the case of those who were denounced to me as Christians, I have observed the following procedure: I interrogated these as to whether they were Christians; those who confessed I interrogated a second and a third time, threatening them with punishment; those who persisted I ordered executed. For I had no doubt that, whatever the nature of their creed, stubbornness and inflexible obstinacy surely deserve to be punished. There were others possessed of the same folly; but because they were Roman citizens, I signed an order for them to be transferred to Rome.

Soon accusations spread, as usually happens, because of the proceedings going on, and several incidents occurred. An anonymous document was published containing the names of many persons. Those who denied that they were or had been Christians, when they invoked the gods in words dictated by me, offered prayer with incense and wine to your image, which I had ordered to be brought for this purpose together with statues of the gods, and moreover cursed Christ—none of which those who are really Christians, it is said, can be forced to do—these I thought should be discharged. Others named by the informer declared that they were Christians, but then denied it, asserting that they had been but had ceased to be, some three

---

They must not repay evil for evil, but instead repay evil with blessings. Responding to hostility with kindness is the only way a vulnerable minority can survive in an adversarial context, and—as Psalm 34.12–17 proves—such behaviour is filled with God's promise of blessing (3.8–12).

Peter adds an important element: Christians need to be ready to offer a public defence for the hope they possess. Yet, as always, the medium is the message: the defence must be made with gentleness, respect, and a clear conscience. People must be won over not just with arguments but with example (3.13–17).

All this is again rooted in the events of Jesus' death and resurrection. Jesus, as Messiah, died a substitutionary and atoning death, 'the righteous for the unrighteous', to bring people to God. But at this point Peter introduces one of

(cont.)

years before, others many years, some as much as twenty-five years. They all worshipped your image and the statues of the gods, and cursed Christ.

They asserted, however, that the sum and substance of their fault or error had been that they were accustomed to meet on a fixed day before dawn and sing responsively a hymn to Christ as to a god, and to bind themselves by oath, not to some crime, but not to commit fraud, theft, or adultery, not to falsify their trust, nor to refuse to return a trust when called upon to do so. When this was over, it was their custom to depart and to assemble again to partake of food—but ordinary and innocent food. Even this, they affirmed, they had ceased to do after my edict by which, in accordance with your instructions, I had forbidden political associations. Accordingly, I judged it all the more necessary to find out what the truth was by torturing two female slaves who were called deaconesses. But I discovered nothing else but depraved, excessive superstition.

I therefore postponed the investigation and hastened to consult you. For the matter seemed to me to warrant consulting you, especially because of the number involved. For many persons of every age, every rank, and also of both sexes are and will be endangered. For the contagion of this superstition has spread not only to the cities but also to the villages and farms. But it seems possible to check and cure it. It is certainly quite clear that the temples, which had been almost deserted, have begun to be frequented, that the established religious rites, long neglected, are being resumed, and that from everywhere sacrificial animals are coming, for which until now very few purchasers could be found. Hence it is easy to imagine what a multitude of people can be reformed if an opportunity for repentance is afforded.

Trajan to Pliny

You observed proper procedure, my dear Pliny, in sifting the cases of those who had been denounced to you as Christians. For it is not possible to lay down any general rule to serve as a kind of fixed standard. They are not to be sought out; if they are denounced and proved guilty, they are to be punished, with this reservation, that whoever denies that he is a Christian and really proves it—that is, by worshipping our gods—even though he was under suspicion in the past, shall obtain pardon through repentance. But anonymously posted accusations ought to have no place in any prosecution. For this is both a dangerous kind of precedent and out of keeping with the spirit of our age. (Pliny *Ep.* 10.96–7)

---

the most perplexing christological descriptions in the entire New Testament: 'After being made alive, he went and made proclamation to the imprisoned spirits—to those who were disobedient long ago when God waited patiently in the days of Noah while the ark was being built.'[103] This has been understood in various different ways. It could conceivably refer to: (1) the preaching of the pre-existent Christ, through Noah, to those bound in sin, urging them to repent; (2) the offer of salvation to the 'imprisoned spirits' who were alive in Noah's day, but who then resided in Hades; (3) the risen Jesus announcing his triumph to the imprisoned wicked angels of Noah's time, telling them of the judgment still

---

103 1 Pet. 3.19–20.

to come.[104] The third option is in fact the most likely. It corresponds with a well-known motif in which rebellious angels were held in subterranean subjugation ahead of a final judgment, which would in turn foreshadow the judgment of all human powers who opposed God and God's people. Pierce rightly concludes that Peter 'offers comfort to a marginalized community: because of the victorious resurrection of Christ, all forces of evil, both human and cosmic, are now under the lordship of Christ'.[105]

All this is woven together with the allusion to Noah. His building of the ark, to rescue his family, points forward to baptism, and baptism is less about washing people clean and more about 'the appeal to God of a good conscience'. The final proof of all this is that the Messiah has ascended to heaven, where he is seated at the father's right hand, with angels, authorities, and powers in subjection to him (3.18–22).

This sets the context for a renewed exhortation to those facing suffering. Again the sufferings of the Messiah serve as example. Peter is encouraging those who have to face downright hostility because of their following of the Messiah, and because they refuse to go along with the wild and dehumanizing behaviour of those around them. All this, he says, will be sorted at the final judgment (4.1–6).

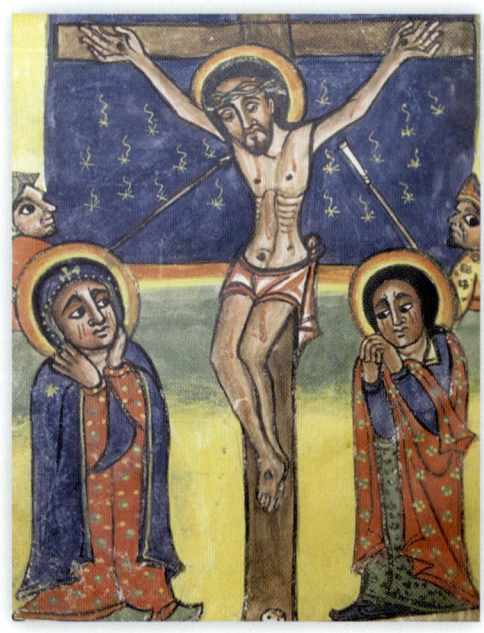

We next encounter some general ethical instructions. Peter premises his appeal with a sense of eschatological urgency: 'The end of all things is near.' This requires sobriety of mind and prayerfulness. During times of adversity, followers of Jesus need to show love and hospitality, and to exercise their grace-gifts for the ultimate end of God's glory through Jesus the Messiah (4.7–11).

The crucifixion from a manuscript stored in the Monastery of St Pantaleon in Ethiopia
age fotostock / Wojtek Buss

4. Exhortation to endure suffering (4.12—5.11)

Peter now recapitulates earlier themes: persecution, Christ's suffering, doing good, and God's glory. His readers are not to be surprised at the 'fiery ordeal'

---

104 See survey in Pierce 2011, 2–20.
105 Pierce 2011, 237–8.

that has fallen upon them—possibly a reference to the start of Nero's persecution, or, more likely, a localized persecution in Asia Minor. They are sharing in the Messiah's own sufferings. If they are insulted, then God will bless them. If they suffer, it should not be for criminal behaviour, but as 'Christians' (see 'Blast from the past: the correspondence between Pliny and Trajan about Christians'). Peter uses the name *Christianoi*, which probably meant 'partisans of the Messiah' or 'sectarian messianist', a term quite possibly coined by pagan authorities to distinguish Messiah-followers from Jews who did not believe Jesus to be Messiah.[106] Judgment, and a sharp judgment at that, will begin with God's household (4.12–19).

Elders of the church receive special instructions on how they are to lead the congregations during times of hardship, with the emphasis on ethos, not organization. The elders must be shepherds, operating selflessly. They are responsible to the Messiah, the chief shepherd. Younger members of the community must heed the elder's leadership and clothe themselves with humility, trusting God for everything (5.1–7).

All this is the more important because there is a diabolical enemy, like a roaring lion, hungry for prey. The believers must stand firm and trust God to bring them through their trials (5.8–11).

5. Letter closing (5.12–14)

The letter ends with Peter commending Silvanus (that is, Silas), probably the letter-carrier. Urging the believers to stand fast in God's true grace, he sends them greetings (from 'Babylon', presumably code for 'Rome')[107] and wishes them peace (5.12–14).

THE ARGUMENT OF 2 PETER

(See box: 'Outline of 2 Peter'.)

1. Opening greeting (1.1–2)

The opening of the letter is quite involved. The author writes in the name of 'Symeōn Peter', further identified as a 'slave and apostle of Jesus the Messiah'.

> **OUTLINE OF 2 PETER**
>
> 1. Opening greeting (1.1–2)
> 2. Exhortation to confirm one's calling and election (1.3–11)
> 3. Exhortation to remember apostolic instruction (1.12–15)
> 4. Validation of the apostolic message: eye-witnesses and prophecy (1.16–21)
> 5. Warning of false teachers and false prophets (2.1–22)
> 6. Explanation for the delay of the day of the lord (3.1–13)
> 7. Exhortation to perseverance and preparation (3.14–18)

---

[106] Ac. 11.26.
[107] *4 Ez.* 3.1–3, 28–31; *2 Bar.* 10.1–3; 11.1; 67.7; *Sib. Or.* 5.143, 159–60; Rev. 14.8; 16.19; 17.5; 18.2, 10, 21. Some suppose that referring to Rome as 'Babylon' requires a date post AD 70 after the destruction of the Jerusalem Temple by Rome. However, even before AD 70, Jewish authors, like those at Qumran, could equate Rome with 'the Kittim of Asshur' which meant Assyria (1QM 19.10). The equation of Rome with Babylon was not a concealed code-name for Rome as the Temple-destroyer, but more likely a qualification of Rome as ultimately responsible for the persecution and dispersion of God's people (so Doering 2012, 445).

The letter's recipients are designated, not by name, but by the salvific benefits they have received: they are those who, 'through the righteousness of our God and Saviour Jesus Christ' have received a 'faith as precious as ours'. Here 'righteousness' is not Christ's obedience or saving work, but his moral rectitude. Jesus is seen as the divine patron, acting justly, to grant faith to his clients (1.1–2).[108]

2. Exhortation to confirm one's calling and election (1.3–11)

'Symeōn Peter' opens the body of the letter with a rather grand paragraph, sketching out the gift of God in the gospel and urging his hearers to make it their own in their moral character.[109] First, he expounds God's rescuing power which enables believers to escape corruption and, remarkably, 'participate in the divine nature' (1.3–4). This does not mean 'becoming a god', but it does indicate 'transformative participation in the kenotic, cruciform character of God through Spirit-enabled conformity to the incarnate, crucified, and resurrection/glorified Christ'.[110]

Second, Peter provides a chain-link of virtues, creating a cascade of faith, goodness, knowledge, self-control, perseverance, godliness, mutual affection, and love, which has the impact of preventing believers from becoming fruitless and useless (1.5–9). As Richard Bauckham stresses, 'the ethical fruits of Christian faith are objectively necessary for the attainment of final salvation' (1.10–11).[111]

3. Exhortation to remember apostolic instruction (1.12–15)

The primary purpose of the letter now emerges: to refresh the audience's memory of Peter's testimony to the 'truth' before Peter puts aside the 'tent of this body'. Peter has made it clear that he will soon depart (referring perhaps to John 21.18–19, though there is nothing there about the timing of Peter's demise). Peter's insistence that he will 'make every effort to see that after my departure you will always be able to remember these things'

> 'While the primary purpose is to refute the accusation of Jesus' story as *mythos*, it is not difficult to envision in this declaration also a response to the Caesars' claim to be sons of God. While Caesars pronounced themselves (or were pronounced by others – e.g., Roman Senate) to be divine (*divus*), Jesus' status was announced, not by humans, but by a heavenly voice of God, in an unmistakable public display of divine majesty. . . . The divine pronouncement gives an independent confirmation of Jesus' status in public, and before witnesses, of his elevated position. Second Peter wants to make it clear the Christian God actually speaks on *personal* volition, making a public display that is an unmistakable evidence of divine authority and power. This God needs no spokespersons and is able to communicate directly without intermediaries.'
>
> Andrew Mbuvi, *Jude and 2 Peter*, 95.

---

108 Neyrey 1993, 149.
109 McKnight 2003a, 1505, describes this as an *exordium* with homiletical qualities.
110 Gorman 2009, 5, 7, 162.
111 Bauckham 1983, 190.

could point ahead to a future writing, a third Petrine letter, or perhaps to the forthcoming gospel of Mark as a deposit of Petrine memories about Jesus.

4. Validation of the apostolic message: eye-witnesses and prophecy (1.16–21)

The author now underscores the reliability of the apostolic testimony. The stories of Jesus, especially here the transfiguration, were neither 'crafty myths' (CEB) nor 'cleverly devised stories' (NIV), but were derived from eye-witnesses, those who saw Jesus' majestic glory for themselves and heard the divine voice authenticating him (1.16–18). From this perspective, the apostles could look back on the entire world of biblical prophecy and see in retrospect that it all made sense. Among the great prophecies was that of the 'star' that would arise in Jacob, which was widely regarded as a prophecy of the Messiah.[112] What Symeōn Peter is saying, then, is that the stories of Jesus, reaching something of a climax in the extraordinary glory of the transfiguration, mean that one can now read the entire ancient Jewish scriptures knowing the end from the beginning, and can see with God-given hindsight how everything came rushing together at the point where the Messiah himself emerged. The revelation of God's glory in him brings the two great promises of the letter together: becoming partakers of the divine nature and awaiting Jesus' *parousia* (1.19–21).

5. Warning of false teachers and false prophets (2.1–22)

A characteristic feature of ancient 'testaments' was the warning of deceivers and deviants to come. Symeōn Peter cautions that, just as there were false prophets in Israel, so too there will be false teachers in the churches. Such people deserve the punishment they will receive (2.1–3).

The content of 2 Peter 2.4–10a closely parallels Jude 6–10 (see Table 32.1). But, instead of focusing on the final condemnation of the wicked as Jude does, the emphasis here is on God's capacity to save the righteous.[113] God did not spare rebellious angels, the ancient world of Noah, or the cities of Sodom and Gomorrah; neither will he spare those who indulge the corrupt desire of the flesh and despise authority. The indictment of the intruding teachers continues with reference to their arrogance, blasphemy of angelic beings, and brazen carousing, acting as if they will never be held to account (2.10b–13). The writer draws on scripture and a vivid range of metaphors and similes to portray the false teachers as apostates, worse off than non-believers. They have returned to the wickedness and perversity from whence they came. So Peter fittingly cites two proverbs: 'A dog returns to its vomit' and 'A sow that is washed returns to her wallowing in the mud' (2.14–22)![114]

---

[112] Num. 24.17.
[113] McKnight 2003a, 1507.
[114] Prov. 26.11 and the *Story of Ahiqar* 8.15.

TABLE 32.1: PARALLELS BETWEEN 2 PETER AND JUDE

2 Peter	Jude	Subject
2.1–3	4	The false teachers will face judgment.
2.4	6	God will judge rebellious angels.
2.6	7	God has judged Sodom and Gomorrah.
2.10	8	The false teachers defile the body and despise authority.
2.11–12	9–10	The false teachers are irrational animals who blaspheme what they do not understand.
2.15	11	The false teachers follow the way of Balaam and seek reward.
2.13, 17	12–13	The false teachers share meals with acute irreverence, are 'waterless' sources, and will be kept in darkness.
2.18	16	The false teachers are driven by desire.

6. Explanation for the delay of the day of the lord (3.1–13)

The third chapter turns to a specific and difficult topic: the 'scoffers' who question whether Jesus will, after all, come back. History has continued much as before, and the first Christian generation has passed away with no change in the world's affairs, so perhaps there will be no return of Jesus, no justice for the elect, no final goal for the world (3.3–4).

Peter responds in two ways. First, the scoffers seem to agree that God made the earth and formed it out of water, but they forget that God also used water as an instrument of judgment as in the great flood. The God of creation is also a God of judgment; when God judges the world again it will not be with water but with fire (3.5–7). Second, one should remember God's forbearance and patience. God operates on his own eschatological schedule: a thousand years is like a single day to him (Ps. 90.4). The apparent delay in the lord Jesus' return is due to God's patience, not wanting any to perish and so leaving time for people to repent. But, as promised elsewhere in the New Testament, the 'day of the lord' will come like a thief in the night.[115] It will issue in some sort of cosmic conflagration, but this will not be a matter of creation being 'burned up', as some manuscripts put it, but more properly 'laid bare'. Peter is not saying that the present world of space, time, and matter is going to be destroyed. That is more like the view of ancient Stoicism. What will happen, as many early Christian teachers said, is that some sort of 'fire', literal

---

115 See e.g. Mt. 24.43; 1 Thess. 5.2; Rev. 3.3.

or metaphorical, will come upon the whole earth, not to destroy the world, but to test everything out, and to purify it by burning up whatever does not meet the test (3.8–10).[116] Given all this, what should believers do now? Live godly lives in preparation for the new heavens and new earth, where righteousness dwells (3.11–13).

7. Exhortation to perseverance and preparation (3.14–18)

All this constitutes a call to patience and holiness, corresponding to God's own patience and utter holiness.[117] This, as the writer says, is a regular feature of Paul's letters (3.14–15). It is easy to pervert what Paul says, and believers must avoid that danger (3.15–16). What matters is their growth in grace and the knowledge of the lord and saviour (3.16–17).

Finally, Peter offers a benediction, unusually centred on Jesus alone: 'to him be glory both now and in the day when God's new age dawns' (3.18 *NTE/KNT*).

> 'As an urban pastor, I'm frequently confronted with the reality of violence. Every summer there are shootings and stabbings near my office as well as near the homes of my church members. It is not a theoretical issue or the story of people "over there". Young people in the United States die regularly through violence. . . . Large numbers of our young people have resorted to violence to settle disputes. I don't think they learned this behaviour on their own. We have to help them find ways to settle disputes without violence. And for all of us, even when we are confronted with injustice, we must learn to distinguish personal retaliation from thoughtful protest.'
>
> **Dennis Edwards**, *1 Peter*, 122–3.

1 AND 2 PETER IN THE BIG PICTURE

The Petrine tradition as we have it in these two letters contains a rich mixture of theology, exhortations, ethics, and assurances. Central to all this we find exile, election, effort, and eschatology.

First Peter is unique for its theme of the church as a community of exiles, strangers, and aliens (1 Pet. 1.1, 17; 2.11). This in one sense applies biblical exilic imagery, and the realities of Diaspora life, to church members who have experienced marginalization and hostility in their own social context. However, the Petrine account of exile is thoroughly christocentric. As Miroslav Volf points out:

> The root of Christian self-understanding as aliens and sojourners lies not so much in the story of Abraham and Sarah and the nation of Israel as it does in the destiny of Jesus Christ, his mission and rejection which ultimately brought him to the cross.[118]

---

116 Compare the similar, though not identical, train of thought in 1 Cor. 3.12–15.
117 See Eph. 1.4; 5.27; Col. 1.22; 1 Thess. 3.13; 5.23; Jude 24.
118 Volf 1994, 17.

When Christians experience the same alienation and rejection that Jesus did, they prove themselves to be his followers. The adversarial context faced by the Asian churches forced Peter to think about how the church could be visibly Christian in ways that would ensure its growth and survival. This required a flexible approach to local culture and society: there were areas where one could fit in with the culture, and areas where that would be decidedly inappropriate. So, 'in a sense', argues deSilva, '1 Peter really sets the agenda for the next two centuries of Christianity as Christians continue to struggle to demonstrate that their way of life is virtuous and worthy of imitation, not persecution'.[119]

What does this have to do with us? Well, as most have known for a long time, 'Christendom' is over (if it ever really existed as people imagine). Western societies today are largely post-Christian, though this means different things in different contexts. If we dare generalize about the western churches, the Baby Boomers (the generation represented by NTW) respected the church but became detached from it, Gen-Xers (represented by MFB) saw the church as irrelevant and ignored it, while millennials (our children and grandchildren) have been either perplexed or offended as to why the church continues to exist. The church, then, is in a new phase of exile, somewhere between estranged from, and despised by, culture-makers. Yet Peter does not call the church to pout, plead victimization, and weaponize its grievances through political action. Peter calls on the church to be encouraged, to be strong, to follow Christ's example, and to resist pagan culture. Beyond that, the church must demonstrate an attractive way of life, give no cause for retaliation, show respect to those in authority, and, where appropriate, bring the faith into expression within existing cultural forms. The mission of the church today, then, requires the tasks of resistance, apologetics, and contextualization.

One overlooked theme in 2 Peter is that of election and moral effort (see 2 Pet. 1.10). The author presents election not as a contentious matter of debate—whether election is based on predestination or

Fresco of the transfiguration in the Church of the Transfiguration, Mount Tabor, Galilee, Israel
Anastazzo / Shutterstock

---

119 deSilva 2004, 844.

foreknowledge—but as something to be tested out and validated by one's pattern of life. Symeōn Peter urges readers to 'make their calling and election sure', to signal that they really do belong to the elect, by producing the virtues that should properly characterize God's people (see 2 Pet. 1.5–9). If one is cultivating godliness, it is impossible to fall away or be fruitless. The believers are destined to be there at the end of history and need to consider what type of people they want to be found to be on the last day (2 Pet. 3.11). Given the future eschatological judgment, election is a responsibility to 'make every effort to be found spotless, blameless and at peace with him' (2 Pet. 3.14). In the end, moral effort does not make one elect; rather, it demonstrates that one is elect.

First Peter and 2 Peter converge on eschatology. They both witness to the new thing that God has done in the Messiah, bringing about a 'new birth' (1 Pet. 1.3) and leading to a 'new heaven and new earth' (2 Pet. 3.13). The church lives between these two realities, trying to appropriate the power and meaning of the new life that God has infused into it by the spirit, while also looking ahead and preparing for the new creation yet to come. What sustains us during that time is hope (1 Pet. 1.3, 13, 21; 3.15) and remembering the apostolic gospel (2 Pet. 1.12, 15; 3.1). Irrespective of what 'fiery ordeal' has come upon us (1 Pet. 4.12), we must continue to 'grow in the grace and knowledge of our Lord and Saviour Jesus Christ' (2 Pet. 3.18) until the day when God is ready to 'judge the living and the dead' (1 Pet. 4.5). Then, and only then, will our exile be over, and our election be finally confirmed.

Further reading

Achtemeier, Paul J. 1996. *1 Peter*. Hermeneia; Minneapolis: Fortress.
Bauckham, Richard J. 1983. *Jude, 2 Peter*. WBC; Waco, TX: Word.
Bockmuehl, Markus. 2012. *Simon Peter in Scripture and Memory: The New Testament Apostle in the Early Church*. Grand Rapids, MI: Baker.
Davids, Peter H. 2014. *A Theology of James, Peter, and Jude*. BTNT; Grand Rapids, MI: Zondervan.
Edwards, Dennis R. 2017. *1 Peter*. SGBC; Grand Rapids, MI: Zondervan.
Green, Gene L. 2008. *Jude and 2 Peter*. BECNT; Grand Rapids, MI: Baker.
Horrell, David G. 2002. 'The Product of a Petrine Circle? A Reassessment of the Origin and Character of 1 Peter.' *JSNT* 86: 29–60.
Jobes, Karen H. 2005. *1 Peter*. BECNT; Grand Rapids, MI: Baker.
Martin, Troy W., and Eric F. Mason (eds.). 2014. *Reading 1–2 Peter and Jude: A Resource for Students*. Atlanta: SBL.
Mbuvi, Andrew M. 2015. *Jude and 2 Peter*. NCCS; Eugene, OR: Cascade.
Neyrey, Jerome H. 1993. *2 Peter, Jude*. AB; New York: Doubleday.
Perkins, Pheme. 1995. *First and Second Peter, James, and Jude*. Interpretation; Louisville, KY: Westminster John Knox.
Reese, Ruth Anne. 2007. *2 Peter and Jude*. THNTC; Grand Rapids, MI: Eerdmans.
Witherington, Ben. 2007. *Letters and Homilies for Hellenized Christians, vol. 2: A Socio-Rhetorical Commentary on 1–2 Peter*. Downers Grove, IL: InterVarsity.
Wright, N. T. 2011. *Early Christian Letters for Everyone: James, Peter, John, and Judah*. London: SPCK, pp. 47–125.

Johannine Letters: 1, 2, and 3 John

> *My dear children, I write this to you so that you will not sin. But if anybody does sin, we have an advocate with the Father—Jesus Christ, the Righteous One. He is the atoning sacrifice for our sins, and not only for ours but also for the sins of the whole world.*[1]

CHAPTER AT A GLANCE

This chapter provides an overview of the Johannine letters.

By the end of this chapter you should be able to:

- understand issues of authorship and purpose related to the Johannine letters;
- describe the structure and argument in the Johannine letters;
- understand the themes and theology in the Johannine letters.

INTRODUCTION

The three short letters of John are most probably by the same author as the gospel of John. They definitely seem to have emerged from the same community, or cluster of churches, that was involved in the production of the fourth gospel. This trio of letters offer a wonderful account of 'truth' and 'love', as well as drawing together the atonement, the holy spirit, and the church as a community made up of children of God, and all within a meditative style, quite different from the other letters in the New Testament, reflecting from many angles on the outpoured love of God in Jesus the Messiah.

It is all the more poignant, then, that these letters seem to have been written under adverse circumstances. The network of Christians associated with the author has experienced painful division with the local Jewish community over Jesus' messiahship.[2] A further division

---

1 1 Jn. 2.1–2.
2 By referring to a Johannine 'network' we do not mean a 'school' understood as a clique of authors, nor a catechetical setting, nor an

had broken out, it seems, over whether Jesus really had appeared in the flesh, with some separatists denying this and subsequently departing.[3] We also glimpse intra-church rivalries, exemplified by a certain Diotrephes who does not recognize John's authority. Yet, in the end, these letters are a reminder that the best response to heresy and haughtiness is the practice of love.

The tomb of St John in Ephesus
Public Domain

The first letter moves in widening circles around the main theme of the love of God, revealed in Jesus and his death and needing to be worked out in and through the life of the community. Those who belong to Jesus have a new identity which will be fully revealed when Jesus appears, committing them in the present to a life of purity as well as love. Many will try to deceive the church, even from among their own number, either denying that Jesus is the Messiah, or denying that he came in the flesh. The sign of true belonging, however, is a resolute turning from sin, embodying

---

isolated and introspective 'community' insulated from other expressions of the church. Rather, we envisage a collection of house-churches scattered across a region, probably Asia Minor, with varying degrees of association with John the elder (Gaius and Diotrephes are two ends of that spectrum), and which had various degrees of interaction with other expressions of Christianity associated with Pauline churches, Greek-speaking Jewish Christians, and Judean churches. See further Strecker 1996, xxxv–xlii; Bauckham 1998a; Painter 2002, 53–60; Klink 2010a.
[3] 1 Jn. 2.19; 4.2; 2 Jn. 7.

the self-sacrificial love of Jesus for others. The letter binds together a rich faith in Jesus with a robust call to the love which will make that faith known in the world.

The short second letter continues the same theme as the first, addressed by 'the Elder' to a particular church, seen as 'the Chosen Lady'. The author is part of a sister church, whose members he refers to as 'the children of your Chosen Sister'.[4] The letter, with its warning of 'deceivers', provides a quick glimpse of an early church in which different teachers are moving to and fro from place to place, so that local communities need to know who is to be trusted. The gold standard remains the coming of Jesus the Messiah in the flesh: from early days in the church this extraordinary truth, celebrated in the dramatic opening of John's gospel ('the Word became flesh', Jn. 1.14), was under attack. The central thesis of the letter is that anyone who abides in 'the teaching'—the true teaching of the father and the son—is part of the fellowship of 'truth and love'.

The third Johannine letter is about hospitality. As the church spread, with groups of a dozen or two believers in a town or village, and with increasing hostility from the surrounding culture, it was vital that Jesus-followers travelling from place to place as teachers, or on other business, should be able to trust one another. This letter, to 'beloved Gaius', an otherwise unknown Christian, congratulates him on the hospitality that he has offered to 'family members', that is, fellow-Christians, who have subsequently given glad testimony to the welcome they had received. Unfortunately, however, not everyone is behaving in such a generous spirit. The writer warns against one Diotrephes, who is spreading false rumours about the elder himself, and is refusing to welcome genuine fellow-believers and expelling, from his community, other Jesus-followers who want to do so. The writer denounces him: he is simply trying to boost his own prestige. At the same time, Demetrius is well attested; perhaps he was the carrier of this third letter. Anyway, this letter, like the others in the group, offers a small vignette on the challenges of living as a Jesus-follower in troubled times.

In reading the Johannine letters, one cannot help but notice the strong pastoral language, and the warmth of the author. On the one hand, these letters offer necessary warnings against false teaching, but on the other hand they are deeply reassuring to those who do believe. The Johannine letters urge their readers to know the love of God in truth and full assurance.

CONTEXTUAL AND CRITICAL MATTERS

Origins of the Johannine letters

The authorship of the Johannine letters, like that of the fourth gospel, is variously contested. First John is strictly anonymous, but 2 and 3 John are written by someone who calls himself 'the elder'. There are enough similarities in language,

---

[4] 2 Jn. 1, 13 *NTE/KNT*.

theology, and texture for us to posit a very close relationship between the Johannine gospel and epistles, with the likelihood being that the same person wrote them all.[5] So it is very likely that either John the son of Zebedee or perhaps (and more likely) John the elder is the author of these three letters.[6] They belong together: the problem of schism which prompted 1 John is summarized in 2 John, while 2 John and 3 John share the same designated author, letter form, and subject of mission-related hospitality.[7] The letters were probably composed some time after the gospel of John, though this cannot easily be demonstrated (see text grid: 'Examples of similarities between John's gospel and letters'). It may well be that the letters reflect a time when some are contesting the legacy of the Johannine gospel in the churches of Asia.[8]

First John was probably a circular letter, rooted in the author's preaching. It was sent, we may suppose, to a number of churches in Asia Minor. Second and 3 John, by contrast, have specific audiences of 'the elect lady and her children'[9] (2 John) and 'Gaius' (3 John). A plausible scenario is that 1 John is a circular pastoral letter, reinforcing christological boundaries against the teaching of the secessionists. Second John was a covering letter to a specific but unknown church, where the elder writes on behalf of the 'children of your elect sister' to the 'elect lady' (probably metaphors for two sister-churches), urging them to watch out for, and to refuse hospitality to, certain deceivers and anti-Christs who were teaching Docetism (the belief that Jesus only *seemed* to have a physical body). Third John is a personal letter from the elder to Gaius, probably a leader and ally in the church that received the other two letters. The writer is warning Gaius about Diotrephes and the threat he poses.

---

[5] See above, on the authorship of the fourth gospel. Eusebius (*Hist. Eccl.* 7.25.21) commented: 'In a word, it is obvious that those who observe their character throughout will see at a glance that the Gospel and Epistle have one and the same complexion.' Bauckham (2006, 371) notes how the gospel of John and the Johannine epistles 'share characteristic linguistic usages, whether these belong to the "idiolect" of one author or to the "socioelect" of a school of Johannine writers'. According to George Parsenios (2014, 9), '1–3 John share with the Gospel of John not only a common vocabulary and basic syntactical structures but also larger structuring devices. To borrow a musical analogy, the texts not only use the same individual notes but also combine those notes into similar harmonies. The commonalities are both broad and deep.' Some, such as Strecker (1996, xl, 9 n. 8) and Lieu (2008, 17–18), see a dependence on Johannine tradition shared with the evangelist rather than a dependence upon the gospel of John. However, the tables and analysis formulated by Painter (2002, 22, 58–74) make the case for literary dependence on the gospel of John almost certain (though Painter denies that the evangelist who wrote the gospel is the author of 1 John). Particularly telling are the similar prologues (Jn. 1.1–18; 1 Jn. 1.1–4) and purpose statements (Jn. 20.30–31; 1 Jn. 5.13).
[6] Papias and Eusebius differentiate John the son of Zebedee from John the elder (Eus. *Hist. Eccl.* 3.39.3–6), and Jerome (*De Vir. Ill.* 9.5) splits the difference by positing the apostle John as the author of 1 John, and John the elder as the author of 2 and 3 John.
[7] Painter (2002, 52) observes: '1 John stands closer to 2 John than 3 John, and 2 John is closer to 3 John than 1 John. Thus 2 John is the link connecting 1 and 3 John.'
[8] Alternatively, some think it possible that it was the christological incongruity and error of a certain faction in the Johannine network that prompted the writing of the gospel of John in order to provide an authoritative and apostolic narrative to limit or even silence interpretations of Jesus that were headed in what we would today call a docetic direction. What we can say, as Jobes (2011, 409) does, is: 'Clearly the teaching of the fourth gospel stands behind 1 John, even if the gospel was not in final written form before 1 John was written.'
[9] 2 Jn. 1 NRSV.

EXAMPLES OF SIMILARITIES BETWEEN JOHN'S GOSPEL AND LETTERS

Gospel of John	1 John	2 John	3 John
In the beginning was the Word, and the Word was with God, and the Word was God . . . The Word became flesh and made his dwelling among us. We have seen his glory, the glory of the one and only Son . . . (Jn. 1.1, 14)	That which was from the beginning, which we have heard, which we have seen with our eyes, which we have looked at and our hands have touched—this we proclaim concerning the Word of life. (1 Jn. 1.1)		
But whoever lives by the truth comes into the light . . . (Jn. 3.21)	If we claim to have fellowship with him and yet walk in the darkness, we lie and do not live out the truth. But if we walk in the light, as he is in the light, we have fellowship with one another, and the blood of Jesus, his Son, purifies us from all sin. (1 Jn. 1.6–7)	It has given me great joy to find some of your children walking in the truth . . . (2 Jn. 4)	It gave me great joy when some believers came and testified about your faithfulness to the truth, telling how you continue to walk in it. (3 Jn. 3)
Very truly I tell you, whoever hears my word and believes him who sent me has eternal life and will not be judged but has crossed over from death to life. (Jn. 5.24)	We know that we have passed from death to life, because we love each other. Anyone who does not love remains in death. (1 Jn. 3.14)		

Date

Our earliest manuscript of the Johannine letters is 𝔓[9], dated to the third century. First John was well known in the second century; there is less good early evidence for 2 John, and very limited evidence for 3 John. The first person to mention all three Johannine epistles is Origen in the third century.[10] First John, along with 1 Peter, was among the undisputed texts of the catholic letters, while 2 John and 3 John were noted as 'disputed writings'.[11] Around the 180s, 1 and 2 John are

---

10 Eus. *Hist. Eccl.* 6.25.10.
11 Eus. *Hist. Eccl.* 3.25.2–3; 6.25.10.

(cont.)

Gospel of John	1 John	2 John	3 John
If you remain in me and my words remain in you, ask whatever you wish, and it will be done for you. (Jn. 15.7)	See that what you have heard from the beginning remains in you. If it does, you also will remain in the Son and in the Father. (1 Jn. 2.24)	Anyone who runs ahead and does not continue in the teaching of Christ does not have God; whoever continues in the teaching has both the Father and the Son. (2 Jn. 9)	
My command is this: love each other as I have loved you. (Jn. 15.12)	And this is his command: to believe in the name of his Son, Jesus Christ, and to love one another as he commanded us. (1 Jn. 3.23)	I am not writing you a new command but one we have had from the beginning. I ask that we love one another. (2 Jn. 5)	
	Dear children, this is the last hour; and as you have heard that the antichrist is coming, even now many antichrists have come. (1 Jn. 2.18)	Many deceivers, who do not acknowledge Jesus Christ as coming in the flesh, have gone out into the world. Any such person is the deceiver and the antichrist. (2 Jn. 7)	
But these are written that you may believe that Jesus is the Messiah, the Son of God, and that by believing you may have life in his name. (Jn. 20.31)	I write these things to you who believe in the name of the Son of God so that you may know that you have eternal life. (1 Jn. 5.13)		

mentioned in the Muratorian canon; Irenaeus cited both letters in the same period.[12] Around the mid-second century we have attestation by Justin Martyr and the *Epistle to Diognetus* for 1 John.[13] A good case can be made for Polycarp quoting from 1 and 2 John in his letter to the Philippians dated around 140.[14] According to Eusebius, Papias, writing somewhere between AD 110 and 130, made use of 1 John.[15] Taking all this evidence together, we can date the Johannine epistles at the latest in

---

12 Muratorian canon, § 68; Iren. *Adv. Haer.* 3.16.5, 8. See esp. Painter 2002, 41–3.
13 Just. *Dial.* 123.9 = 1 Jn. 3.1–2; *Ep. Diog.* 10.2–3 = 1 Jn. 4.9, 19; *Ep. Diog.* 11.4 = 1 Jn. 1.1; 2.7, 13–14.
14 Polycarp *Phil.* 7.1 = 1 Jn. 4.2–3/2 Jn. 7. See Hill 2004, 418–19.
15 Eus. *Hist. Eccl.* 3.39.16.

the last two decades of the first century. They might, however, quite easily be earlier; we just do not know.

The secessionists

Unlike in the fourth gospel there is no polemic against 'the Judeans' (Greek *hoi Ioudaioi*), but critical remarks are levelled against a group of secessionists, former members of the community who had left (see 1 Jn. 2.19). This group had attempted to move their part of the church in a trajectory towards a denial of Jesus' messianic identity on the one hand and of his genuine humanity on the other—thus conflicting with two of the central claims of John's gospel, that Jesus is the Word made flesh, and that Jesus is the Messiah, the son of God.[16] One possible scenario is that the secessionists regarded Jesus as a 'revealer' of esoteric truths, rather than the messianic agent of Israel's renewal. Thus they jettisoned messianism as the relic of an inferior or repugnant prior dispensation.[17] Concurrently, their denial that Jesus came in the flesh probably reflected a hellenistic influence which would be antipathetic towards physical matter and strongly in favour of divine immutability and/or impassibility. In this view, a truly divine being could neither become genuinely human nor suffer in a physical body (see below on 'Docetism 101').[18] This might have emerged from a Jewish view that denied the possibility of either incarnation or deification,[19] combined with a desire to safeguard Jesus' divine nature by rescuing him from the crucifixion, so that he only 'appeared' to suffer. That view (which might have paved the way for a more gnostic interpretation of Jesus' person) was combated later on by Ignatius of Antioch.[20] Anyway, after failing to win support for their recasting of christology, the rival teachers had left the Johannine network of churches. The writer points out that their lack of love goes exactly with their view of Jesus: the incarnate love of God is meant to work through into fresh incarnations of that love in the community. As Parsenios points out, 'Their anemic Christology diminishes the profundity of the incarnation, and their act of separating themselves

---

[16] Jn. 1.14, 18; 20.31.
[17] 1 Jn. 2.22; 5.1; 2 Jn. 9.
[18] 1 Jn. 4.2–3; 2 Jn. 7; perhaps reflected also in Jn. 6.54–58.
[19] According to Philo (*Gai.* 118): 'It would be easier to change God into a man than a man into God' (tr. M. F. Bird).
[20] Ign. *Trall.* 10.1; *Smyrn.* 2.1; 3.1–3; 4.2; 5.2; 7.1; 12.2. *Eph.* 7.2; Polycarp *Phil.* 7.1.

from the broader community diminishes the love expressed through the concord of the community.'[21]

A significant motif employed across these letters is the repetition of the phrase 'from the beginning'. The letter is addressed to those who know the Johannine tradition *from the beginning*, including its eye-witnesses' testimony to the 'Word of life', the community's acknowledgement of the 'truth', and the practice of the love-commandment.[22] The secessionists have not remained faithful, it seems, to the original proclamation upon which the Johannine churches were founded.[23] They are accused of being 'liars' and 'deceivers'; they 'walk in darkness'; they 'hate' the brothers and sisters of the community; they are 'false prophets'. Perhaps they even claim to be without sin. They are 'trying to lead you astray', and they receive the radical label of 'antichrists'.[24] In response, John the elder reminds his readers that they are led into truth by the spirit of truth.[25] They have indeed been born of God,[26] and know God.[27] He calls the churches to hold fast to the confession of Jesus as the son of God, to the teaching of the Messiah, the example of the Messiah, and to abide in the Messiah.[28]

Can we speak, already at this early date, of 'proto-orthodoxy' and 'heresy' in relation to these letters? It does seem appropriate, given John the elder's exhortation to 'confess' a particular faith (Greek *homologeō*) over and against the denial of the secessionists (Greek *arneomai*).[29] Yet it would be wrong to regard the Johannine epistles as simply polemical tracts. The focus is not so much on the secessionists as on those who remain and abide in the truth. The author regards the recent division not as the occasion for vitriolic denunciation, but primarily as an opportunity to renew the community's identity through a remembrance of the basic elements of the community's own faith.[30]

Excursus: Docetism 101

'Docetism' comes from the Greek word *dokeō*, which means 'to seem', 'to appear'. The belief in question was that Jesus only 'seemed' or 'appeared' to be genuinely and embodiedly human, but that in reality he was an incorporeal being projecting an outward appearance. Our modern culture finds it hard to imagine why such a belief might be attractive, but in the ancient world it was a compelling option for those

---

21 Parsenios 2014, 24; see similarly Hengel 1989, 72–3.
22 1 Jn. 1.1–3; 2.7, 13–14, 24; 3.11; 2 Jn. 5–6.
23 Dunn 2015, 775–6.
24 1 Jn. 1.10; 2.4, 9, 11, 18, 22, 26; 3.15; 4.1, 3, 20; 2 Jn. 7.
25 1 Jn. 2.20, 27; 3.24; 4.13; reflecting Jn. 15.26–27.
26 1 Jn. 2.29; 3.9; 4.7; 5.1, 4, 18; see Jn. 3.3–5.
27 1 Jn. 2.3–5, 14; 3.6, 24; 4.6–8, 13; 5.20.
28 1 Jn. 2.6; 4.9, 13, 15, 17; 5.5, 9–13, 20; 2 Jn. 9.
29 1 Jn. 2.22–23; 4.2–3, 14–15; 2 Jn. 7. See Johnson 2010, 496.
30 Johnson 2010, 501–2.

with a particular view of God, namely, that God was uninvolved in change, suffering, or (particularly) shame.[31]

The idea that Jesus was merely a phantasm, not truly physical, was held by a certain Saturninus. He held that Jesus was 'without birth, without body, and without figure, but was, by supposition, a visible man'.[32] Similarly, in a gnostic document called *Trimorphic Protennoia*, 'Jesus' says: 'I revealed myself to them in their tents as Word, and I revealed myself in the likeness of their shape.'[33] This makes Jesus a shape-shifter who could morph into human-like appearance but without being actually human. Such a view might claim support from Paul's statement that God sent Jesus 'in the likeness of sinful flesh' (Greek *en homoiōmati sarkos hamartias*), though careful study of Paul's whole sentence would make it clear that he was not at all denying Jesus' genuine humanness. Such wording, however, was claimed by some as supporting a form of Docetism.[34]

Some others accepted that Jesus did have a physical body, but claimed that 'the Christ' (here meaning his 'divine' self, not, as in its original meaning, his 'messianic' identity) departed from Jesus prior to the crucifixion. Another way to a similar conclusion was to claim that Jesus changed his form at the last minute, and that some other person was crucified in his place, thus safeguarding Jesus's divinity from suffering. If, after all, divinity is impassible, then the divine Christ did not suffer, so the father must have rescued the heavenly Christ before he was crucified.

Such a belief is not without precedent. The Roman poet Ovid suggested that, just before the murder of Julius Caesar, the goddess Vesta 'snatched him away and left a naked semblance; what died by the steel was Caesar's shadow'. The real Julius Caesar 'was raised to the heavens', to the halls of Jupiter.[35] Another way of saying this is to suggest that the gods were so impressed with Julius Caesar that they took his soul up to heaven, leaving only the vestiges of his shadowy self to be assassinated. One can see how this sort of view might be applied to Jesus by any who believed that he could not really have suffered the shameful death of the cross.

This docetic perspective plays out in different ways among 'heretical' accounts of the crucifixion. A notorious figure known as Cerinthus, an Egyptian who came to Ephesus and was regarded as the gnostic opponent of John the apostle,[36] is said to have taught that Jesus was not conceived virginally, but was born of the union of Mary and Joseph; that 'the Christ' (again, note that the word has moved away from its Jewish messianic meaning) descended upon Jesus in the form of a dove at his

---

[31] For a good introduction, see Wilhite 2015, 61–85.
[32] Iren. *Adv. Haer.* 1.24.2.
[33] *Trim. Prot.* 47.14–16 (tr. J. D. Turner [1984]).
[34] Rom. 8.3.
[35] Ovid *Fasti* 3.701–2.
[36] See Iren. *Adv. Haer.* 3.3.4; 3.11.1.

baptism, but later 'the Christ' departed from Jesus, and that then 'Jesus suffered and rose again, while Christ remained impassible, inasmuch as he was a spiritual being'.[37] Similarly, a certain Basilides had a 'trading places' theory of the atonement. He is alleged to have taught that Simon of Cyrene was transformed into Jesus while Jesus transformed into Simon. According to Irenaeus, Basilides believed that

> He appeared, then, on earth as a man, to the nations of these powers, and wrought miracles. Wherefore he did not himself suffer death, but Simon, a certain man of Cyrene, being compelled, bore the cross in his stead; so that this latter being transfigured by him, that he might be thought to be Jesus, was crucified, through ignorance and error, while Jesus himself received the form of Simon, and, standing by, laughed at them. For since he was an incorporeal power, and the Nous (mind) of the unborn father, he transfigured himself as he pleased, and thus ascended to him who had sent him, deriding them, inasmuch as he could not be laid hold of, and was invisible to all. Those, then, who know these things have been freed from the principalities who formed the world; so that it is not incumbent on us to confess him who was crucified, but him who came in the form of a man, and was thought to be crucified, and was called Jesus, and was sent by the father, that by this dispensation he might destroy the works of the makers of the world.[38]

The same perspective is given a fuller description in the *Second Treatise of the Great Seth*, a gnostic document originating in the second century:

> For my death, which they think happened, happened to them in their error and blindness, since they nailed their man unto their death. For their Ennoias did not see me, for they were deaf and blind. But in doing these things, they condemn themselves. Yes, they saw me; they punished me. It was another, their father, who drank the gall and the vinegar; it was not I. They struck me with the reed; it was another, Simon, who bore the cross on his shoulder. It was another upon whom they placed the crown of thorns. But I was rejoicing in the height over all the wealth of the archons and the offspring of their error, of their empty glory. And I was laughing at their ignorance. And I subjected all their powers. For as I came downward, no one saw me. For I was altering my shapes, changing from form to form.[39]

Also, and (to our minds) stranger still, we find the Coptic *Apocalypse of Peter*, a third-century gnostic document. This work describes a vision of Peter, in which the

---

37 Iren. *Adv. Haer.* 1.26.1.
38 Iren. *Adv. Haer.* 1.24.4.
39 *Second Treatise of the Great Seth* 55.30—56.25 (tr. J. A. Gibbons and R. A. Bullard [1990]).

'Saviour' led Peter on a tour of the crucifixion scene featuring the 'living Jesus' laughing at the spectacle, while some other person, the 'son of their glory', was substituted for him and subjected to shame. (Note how exactly this reverses a major emphasis of the early gospel: someone else suffering shame and death in the place of Jesus!) The body on the cross was merely a demon-ridden shell, made by Elohim (the Old Testament God), while the living Jesus transcended the body and escaped pain and dishonour:

> When he had said those things, I saw him seemingly being seized by them. And I said 'What do I see, O Lord? That it is you yourself whom they take, and that you are grasping me? Or who is this one, glad and laughing on the tree? And is it another one whose feet and hands they are striking?'
>
> The Saviour said to me, 'He whom you saw on the tree, glad and laughing, this is the living Jesus. But this one into whose hands and feet they drive the nails is his fleshly part, which is the substitute being put to shame, the one who came into being in his likeness. But look at him and me.'
>
> But I, when I had looked, said 'Lord, no one is looking at you. Let us flee this place.'
>
> But he said to me, 'I have told you, "Leave the blind alone!" And you, see how they do not know what they are saying. For the son of their glory instead of my servant, they have put to shame.'
>
> And I saw someone about to approach us resembling him, even him who was laughing on the tree. And he was filled with a Holy Spirit, and he is the Saviour. And there was a great, ineffable light around them, and the multitude of ineffable and invisible angels blessing them. And when I looked at him, the one who gives praise was revealed.
>
> And he said to me, 'Be strong, for you are the one to whom these mysteries have been given, to know them through revelation, that he whom they crucified is the first-born, and the home of demons, and the stony vessel in which they dwell, of Elohim, of the cross, which is under the Law. But he who stands near him is the living Saviour, the first in him, whom they seized and released, who stands joyfully looking at those who did him violence, while they are divided among themselves. Therefore he laughs at their lack of perception, knowing that they are born blind. So then the one susceptible to suffering shall come, since the body is the substitute. But what they released was my incorporeal body. But I am the intellectual Spirit filled with radiant light.'[40]

Even the Islamic tradition is docetic in its description of the cross, denying that Allah would allow Jesus to be killed or crucified. Jesus, seen in Islam as a great prophet, only appeared to die; in fact, Allah took Jesus up into heaven:

---

40 *Apoc. Pet.* 81.3—83.10 (tr. J. Brashler and R. A. Bullard [1990]).

And because of their saying: We slew the Messiah, Jesus son of Mary, Allah's messenger—they slew him not nor crucified him, but it appeared so unto them; and lo! those who disagree concerning it are in doubt thereof; they have no knowledge thereof save pursuit of a conjecture; they slew him not for certain. But Allah took him up unto Himself. Allah was ever Mighty, Wise.[41]

Varieties of Docetism were prevalent on the edge of, and sometimes infiltrating right into, the early Christian communities. That is clear from the many denunciations, ranging from those of John the elder in Asia, to Ignatius of Antioch in Syria, and Tertullian in north Africa. The latter wrote:

Surely he is anti-Christ who denies that Christ has come in the flesh. By declaring that his flesh is simply and absolutely true, and taken in the plain sense of its own nature, the scripture aims a blow at all who make distinctions in it.[42]

Genre and purpose

As for genre and purpose, the Johannine epistles (much like the Pastoral Epistles) should not be lumped together. All three letters may have been sent together as part of one package, as we have suggested, but each of the three has an individual element:

- 1 John is an encyclical homily written to a network of churches with whom 'the elder' is in communion. The purpose is to assure his readers of God's love for them and to urge them to continue to walk in that love towards God and one another. The polemics against the secessionists are ancillary to the wider design, which is the pastoral exhortation to hold fast the testimony to the Word of life, to rest in the security of God's love, and to embrace the identity of God's children.
- 2 John is probably a covering letter for 1 John, written to a specific church, urging the recipients to continue walking in truth and love, and warning that the recently departed secessionists may attempt to encroach upon their assembly.
- 3 John has three purposes. It is a letter of friendship to consolidate the support of Gaius; a letter of commendation of Demetrius; and a warning against the inhospitality and insubordination of Diotrephes.

---

41 Qur'an, sura 4.157–8.
42 Tert. *Carn. Chr.* 24.

> **OUTLINE OF 1 JOHN**
>
> 1. Prologue (1.1–4)
> 2. The message of atonement (1.5—2.2)
> 3. Knowledge of God and love for others (2.3–11)
> 4. Exhortation to endurance (2.12–17)
> 5. Denunciation of the secessionists (2.18–27)
> 6. God's love for his children (2.28–3.10)
> 7. Communal love and confidence in Christ (3.11–24)
> 8. Test the spirits (4.1–6)
> 9. Love, new birth, and victory (4.7–5.5)
> 10. The community's confession of faith (5.6–12)
> 11. The community's assurance in the faith (5.13–21)

THE ARGUMENT OF 1 JOHN

(See box: 'Outline of 1 John'.)

1. Prologue (1.1–4)

First John opens by rehearsing themes from the gospel's prologue. John talks about what 'we' (a source for authoritative testimony differentiated from the community that receives and accepts that testimony) have heard, seen, and touched about the 'Word of life'.[43] In the opening sequence 'verbs of sensory experience pile up—hearing, seeing, touching—emphasizing a physical reality that grounds what the author is about to write'.[44] John testifies and proclaims 'life' and 'eternal life' coming from the 'Father' to 'us'. Jesus was the life-in-person of God's coming age, both the life of God himself and the gift of life from God to the world. What is more, the 'fellowship' between the father and son has now been extended to all who know, trust, and love Jesus. John considers it joy to write this to his audience.

2. The message of atonement (1.5—2.2)

John expounds the message by offering the first divine predicate: 'God is light' and 'in him there is no darkness at all'. This leads to certain tests for having fellowship with God based on five conditional clauses. If we have fellowship with him, we should not walk in darkness. If we walk in the light, we have fellowship together and Jesus' blood purifies us from sin. If we claim to be without sin, we are self-deceived. If we confess our sins, God is faithful and forgiving. If we claim to not have sinned, we make God a liar. John is warding off the teaching of the secessionists, who claim to be without sin and thus have no need for Jesus' blood to be shed for their purification (1.5–10).

John is writing, he says, so that 'you will not sin', yet he comforts his readers by adding, 'But if anybody does sin, we have an advocate with the Father—Jesus Christ, the Righteous One.' He goes on: 'He is the atoning sacrifice for our sins, and not only for ours but also for the sins of the whole world.' Whenever we date the letter, that last

---

[43] Bauckham 2006, 373–5, stating also, 'The prologue to the letter is quite evidently designed to state emphatically the author's authority to address his readers on the basis of his having heard and seen the reality of which he speaks' (375).
[44] Jobes 2011, 399.

phrase might perhaps suggest that John is writing within a largely Jewish-Christian context, and reminding his readers that what the Messiah achieved was for the whole world (see for example Jn. 11.50–52). John has thus far spoken of the defiling and destructive power of sin, for which the answer is the purifying power of Jesus' death. The blood that flowed from Jesus' body as he hung on the cross was somehow, strangely, the very lifeblood of God himself, poured out to deal with sins in a universal way that, much like John 3.16, encompasses the entire world (2.1–2).

3. Knowledge of God and love for others (2.3–11)

A second test of fellowship with God is whether one truly knows God. A person who disobeys Jesus' 'commandments' does not know him. In contrast, those who keep his word, who live as Jesus lived—such people know God, they know that they abide in Christ, and the love of God is fulfilled or made perfect in them (2.3–6).

Altar frontal depicting the Trinity between St Sebald and Archangel Michael, *c.* 1410–20
Germanisches Nationalmuseum, Nuremberg, Germany / Bridgeman Images

John hastens to add that this is not a new commandment, but an old one. If people love their brothers and sisters, they are in the light, but if they hate their brothers or sisters they walk in darkness. All other commandments are the outflowing of this love, the love which has been newly revealed in Jesus, the love which God now intends should be revealed in and through all those who follow Jesus (2.7–11).

4. Exhortation to endurance (2.12–17)

John interrupts the flow of his exhortation with some words of assurance. The first set addresses children who have had their sins forgiven, fathers who know him from the beginning, and young men who have overcome the evil one. The second set addresses children who know 'the Father', fathers who know the one who was from the beginning, and young men who are strong and have the word of God dwelling in them. These are not prosaic pastoral utterances. They are strong and evocative reminders to members of a community traumatized by schism: they remain a family of faith (2.12–14). The opposite of love for the household of faith, after all, is love for the world. While 'the world' is for John the object of God's saving love, it remains a force of darkness and a source of illicit desire. The world and its seductions are ephemeral, but the one who does God's will already possesses the life of the age to come (2.15–17).

5. Denunciation of the secessionists (2.18–27)

John states that it is the 'last hour', which seems to approximate to the 'last day' we find mentioned also in John's gospel.[45] The proof for this claim is that strange and dangerous new things are happening: 'the Antichrist' is coming, akin to Paul's 'man of lawlessness' and John the Seer's 'beast'.[46] In fact, says John, 'even now many antichrists have come'. These strange figures are not the notorious representatives of über-rebellion and ultra-wickedness that are yet to come. Rather, they stand in opposition to the community's testimony about Jesus as *the* Messiah. They embrace the archetypal lie, denying that Jesus is the Messiah. This is not simply an intra-Jewish squabble about titles, but amounts to a denial of the father and the son. The Jewish myth of a boastful figure who opposes God (see Dan. 7.8, 11, 20–21; 9.26) has been reworked around the schism that affected the community. The antichrists left the community, taking their lie with them; and it is this leaving and disbelieving that proves that they never really belonged to the community in the first place (2.18–23).

The secessionists may deny the Messiah, the 'Anointed One', but John's audience have the 'anointing' from the holy one, and they know the truth. If they abide in the truth that was 'from the beginning', they will abide in close fellowship with the son and the father. To abide in the truth means to possess the life of the age to come, already in the present; to be led astray from the truth means to lose that life.

> 'In the ancient world, the gods were parochial and had geographically limited jurisdictions. In the mountains, one sought the favour of the mountain gods; on the sea, of the sea gods. Ancient warfare was waged in the belief that the gods of the opposing nations were fighting as well, and the outcome would be determined by whose god was the strongest. Against that kind of pagan mentality, John asserts that the efficacy of Jesus Christ's sacrifice is valid everywhere, for people everywhere, that is "the whole world". The Christian gospel knows no geographic, racial, ethnic, national, or cultural boundaries.'
>
> Karen Jobes, *1, 2, & 3 John*, 80.

6. God's love for his children (2.28—3.10)

This leads to two criteria for remaining in the truth and being children of the father. First, those who do righteousness are born of him, belong to him, and abide in him (1 Jn. 2.28–29). Second, those who purify themselves are the children of God. The Jesus-followers are called 'children of

---

45 Jn. 6.39–40, 44, 54; 11.24; 12.48. See Painter 2002, 210–11.
46 See 1 Jn. 4.3; 2 Jn. 7; 2 Thess. 2.3, 7–8; Rev. 13; 17.

God', yet still await the full revelation of their identity and status at the return of Jesus. The mark of this hope is purifying oneself to be like Jesus, who is pure (3.1–3).

The alternative is of course sin, which in the broadest sense is breaking God's law, living in dissonance with the sinless Jesus (3.4–5). There is a delicate balance here. John has already criticized the secessionists for claiming to be without sin and hence without the need for Jesus to atone for sin (1.8, 10). However, John appears to be saying here that those who are children of God 'do not continue in sin'. John clearly knows that Christians do sometimes sin and need restoration (see 1.6—2.2). What he seems to have in mind is not temporary moral lapses or character struggles, but sin as a mixture of the settled habit and drift of life. The devil, he says, is sinful; those who are like him are characterized by continuous sinning. In contrast, those who are born of God abide in Christ, and habitually do what is righteous. The children of God prove their familial identity by doing what is right and by loving their brothers and sisters.

7. Communal love and confidence in Christ (3.11–24)

What distinguishes the children of God from the children of the devil is choosing love over hatred. The message has always been 'love one another' (see Jn. 13.34). The opposite is hatred, and the most supreme manifestation of hatred is murder, as with Cain's murder of Abel. The most supreme example of love, of course, is Jesus 'who laid down his life for us' (see Jn. 15.12); it befits disciples to lay down their lives for one other. As a less dramatic and more practical example, perhaps, believers should seek to meet one another's physical needs and provisions where they are lacking. The children of God love others, not with warm intentions, but 'with actions and in truth' (3.11–18).

The various tests and criteria that John makes about abiding in Christ and being a child of God might be unsettling to some of his audience. John balances the imperatives with words of assurance designed to engender confidence that the believers really do belong to God. First, if their hearts do not condemn them, if their hearts are not over-weighed with guilt, then God—who knows the heart—will not condemn them either. Second, if they believe in God's son, and if they keep the command to love others, they are clearly dwelling in God, and God in them. Third, the spirit who effects the mutual indwelling and guidance into the truth provides added assurance (3.19–24).

8. Test the spirits (4.1–6)

Mention of the spirit's work leads John to warn against being too ready to believe any and every spiritual manifestation. There are lying spirits as well as the holy spirit. God's spirit is easily recognizable through the confession that Jesus Christ did indeed come in the flesh. Here again John is probably refuting a form of Docetism (see 'Excursus: Docetism 101', above), either one that denied Jesus any true physical body, or one that suggested that the divine 'Christ' came upon the man 'Jesus' at his baptism, but departed before the crucifixion (4.1–3). Christology thus forms the yardstick for discerning the spirit of truth (4.4–6).

9. Love, new birth, and victory (4.7—5.5)

All this brings John back to one of his favourite themes, namely love. Twice he declares that 'God is love' (4.8, 16), as is proved by the father sending the son to die for sinners. Love, then, is the ultimate test for being born of God and knowing God (4.7–12). Jesus is the proof of God's love for the 'world' and for 'us'. As Painter puts it:

> Abiding in love, abiding in God who is love, is dependent on the recognition of Jesus as the revelation of the being and character of love, of God. Consequently abiding in love is dependent on the christological confession of faith.[47]

Christian faith grows out of this confession about God's love and how the one true God has revealed himself through the son as love incarnate. Accordingly, love incarnate must be the badge worn by the members of the community, the sign not only of who they are but of who their God is (4.12–16a).

The language of abiding is married, again, with assurance. 'God is love,' John repeats, and those who love abide in God and God in turn abides in them. This love is 'made complete' (NIV) or 'perfected' (CEB; NRSV) by all who abide in love, knowing themselves to be loved by God, and in turn loving one another. The result is assurance rather than anxiety, since faith casts out fear. Love is completed wherever Jesus' example is emulated, so that nothing perturbs his people as they look ahead to 'the day of judgment'. If God revealed himself in the world by turning his love into flesh and blood, we should realize that, when we do the same, we are completing God's love. That should increase our assurance (4.16b–18).

John stresses again the *priority* of divine love: 'We love because God first loved us.' God's love reflects in our own love back towards God and then rebounds to others since 'anyone who loves God must also love their brother and sister'. This brings us back full circle to 1 John 3.11–12: hatred is incompatible with love. Thus John weaves together the love-command, the completing of love, and the christological confession: it all forms a single story (4.19–21).

Believing in Jesus as Messiah therefore entails loving all of God's children (perhaps, again, a point to be stressed to any Jewish Jesus-followers who might be nervous about accepting gentile believers as full family-members). The secessionists claim to love God, but do not love all the brothers and sisters in the Johannine churches, which must mean that they are not truly born of God, nor do they truly

---

47 Painter 2002, 280.

love God. Keeping God's command to love the brothers and sisters is not onerous, but it is an obstacle for the schismatics, proving once more that they do not know God (5.1–3). John further claims that everyone born of God triumphs over the world. The victory comes from the confession of faith, and the victory even is 'our faith', allegiance to the Messiah in a world riddled with the evil one, anti-Christs, and deceivers (5.4–5).

10. The community's confession of faith (5.6–12)

John unpacks the community's christological confession through the symbolically laden language of 'water and blood'. The 'water' is probably a reference to Jesus' baptism, while the 'blood' probably refers to Jesus' death.[48] Jesus did not come by 'water only', a possible refutation of the teaching of the secessionists, who accepted that the Christ and/or Logos descended on Jesus at his baptism, but who denied that Jesus' flesh was crucified or his blood was shed on the cross. At the same time, the water and blood that flowed from Jesus' side after the thrust of the Roman spear (Jn. 19.34) were the sure sign that he was really dead; the crucifixion was not a sham. Added to that is the spirit's testimony to Jesus, since the spirit tells the truth about Jesus.[49] Thus all three together—water (baptism), blood (atonement), and spirit (interior testimony)—testify to the truth that the crucified Jesus is the Messiah, the son of God.[50] Those who make this confession have the testimony abiding within them, while those who deny this confession are liars. To accept the testimony about the son is to believe in the son, and there is life, the life of the age to come, in the son, and it is freely available for all who believe in him.

11. The community's assurance in the faith (5.13–21)

In drawing to a close, John states his real purpose in writing: 'I am writing these things to you so that you may know that you, who believe in the name of the son of God, do indeed have the life of the age to come.'[51] The language and intent reminds us of John 20.31. The son of God came to the world (see 4.9) to impart this new life; John wants his readers to know that they really do possess it. The recent schism and departure of the secessionists has created division and confusion; John is writing to bring unity to the network of churches, clarity to the believers' confession, and

---

[48] See 1 Jn. 1.7.
[49] Jn. 15.26.
[50] A longer version of 1 Jn. 5.7–8 is called the 'Johannine Comma'. It is not found in any Greek manuscript prior to AD 1400, but it found its way into popular usage via Erasmus's Greek New Testament, and eventually was adopted into the text of the KJV: 'For there are three that bear record in heaven, the Father, the Word, and the Holy Ghost: and these three are one. And there are three that bear witness in earth, the Spirit, and the water, and the blood: and these three agree in one.' All the signs are that this was the work of a pious medieval scribe who saw an opportunity to insert an explicit Trinitarian confession into the text—which of course was and is already robustly Trinitarian on its own terms.
[51] 1 Jn. 5.13 NTE/KNT.

confidence in their position before God. Such is their confidence that, as children of God, they can be assured that God always hears their requests and petitions (5.13–15).

John returns to the topic of sin. This might seem odd, but it is a further implication of the schism. He counsels those who mentor other believers to pray for those who sin or waver in their faith, but not to pray for those whose sin is of a type that leads 'to death'. That presumably refers to those who, by leaving the community, have separated themselves irreversibly from the life that is found in the son. Those born of God are kept safe by God so that they will not abide in sin nor be harmed by the evil one (5.16–18).

The secessionists, however, have tragically returned to the world of sin, the abode of the evil one. Yet the author and his audience 'know' who they are (children of God), who Jesus is (the son of God), and what he has given them (knowledge of the truth). Because of the unique relation between the father and the son, to abide in the father is to also abide in the son. To be in the true God is to truly have, already, the life of the age to come (5.19–20).

The letter ends on a note that, though it may be unexpected to modern readers, made a lot of sense to the first hearers: 'Children, guard yourselves against idols' (5.21). An idol is anything that, though not itself divine, invites worship and service as if it were. The whole letter is about wrong views of Jesus, which are ultimately wrong views of God, and about the behaviour which, as always, follows from worshipping that which is not the true God.

Remains of the Basilica of St John, built in the sixth century by Justinian over what is believed to be the burial site of John
Gelia / Shutterstock

THE ARGUMENT OF 2 JOHN

(See box: 'Outline of 2 John'.)

> **OUTLINE OF 2 JOHN**
>
> 1. Greeting (1–3)
> 2. Exhortation to remain in the truth and resist deceivers (4–8)
> 3. Hold to the teaching and turn away false teachers (9–11)
> 4. Letter closing (12–13)

1. Greeting (1–3)

The author identifies himself as 'the elder', both a description of his age, and an honorific title for a venerated bearer of apostolic tradition.[52] The letter is addressed to the 'elect lady and her children' (NRSV), which, in the light of verse 13, probably designates a sister church. We have no idea which churches these were. One may have been in Ephesus, and another in a city nearby or far away. They could even be two churches within the same large city; Ephesus was populous enough to feature several house-churches. Immediately the themes of love and truth are introduced, with the elder affirming his true love for the hearers. This love is shared by all who know the truth, a truth that abides in 'us' for ever.

2. Exhortation to remain in the truth and resist deceivers (4–8)

The elder commends the sister church for walking in the truth. He denounces the Docetists who deny that Jesus came in the flesh and asks that such persons be denied hospitality. He delights in the church's true confession, and its following of the love-command, a central element of their shared tradition (though one spurned by the deceivers and secessionists). Many 'deceivers' and 'anti-Christs', the persons mentioned in 1 John (see 1 Jn. 2.18–22; 4.3), who deny that Jesus came in the flesh (see 1 Jn. 4.2), have left the elder's own church, gone out into the world, and may try to slip into the sister church's sphere. The elder urges his readers to 'watch out' lest they be seduced by this false teaching and risk losing the reward that they have all worked for. God's love in the flesh, in Jesus, is the source and framework for God's love coming to all Jesus' people. Anything that waters down this truth is not to be tolerated.

3. Hold to the teaching and turn away false teachers (9–11)

The deceivers with their docetic beliefs might have thought that they were progressive or even perceptive in their christology. But the elder declares that they have abandoned the Jesus-tradition, the messianic faith. Only those who continue in the authentic teaching have an authentic relationship with the father and the son. The sister church must then turn away any itinerant teacher or wandering prophet who does not possess this authentic apostolic teaching.

---

[52] See 1 Pet. 5.1; Philem. 9.

> **OUTLINE OF 3 JOHN**
>
> 1. Greeting (1–4)
> 2. Commendation of Gaius for showing hospitality (5–8)
> 3. Denunciation of Diotrephes (9–12)
> 4. Letter closing (13–14)

4. Letter closing (12–13)

The elder has more to say, but wants to do so in person, with the joy of true meeting, not in writing. He and his own congregation, 'the children of your elect sister' (NRSV), send greetings.

THE ARGUMENT OF 3 JOHN

(See box: 'Outline of 3 John'.)

1. Greeting (1–4)

As in 2 John, the author identifies himself as 'the elder'. This time, however, the addressee is an individual, a certain 'Gaius', most likely a leader in a nearby church. The elder affirms his love for Gaius 'in the truth'. The elder then describes his 'joy' at hearing from 'some believers', presumably travelling missionaries or delegates, that Gaius is faithful to the truth and continues to walk in it. As with 2 John 4, the elder is joyful to hear that 'my children are walking in the truth'. 'Walking in the truth' means behaving with an integrity that both reflects and embodies the truth of the Johannine tradition. This involves not just correct doctrine and proper outward behaviour, but love for God and love for one's fellow-believers, something proven by Gaius's hospitality.

2. Commendation of Gaius for showing hospitality (5–8)

The elder had sent some family members to Gaius, and he commends Gaius for his faithfulness in welcoming them. They were 'strangers' to him, but he received them with enthusiasm and affection. The elder now requests that Gaius should send these people on their way with the honour befitting them, which means providing them with the material and moral support needed to complete the rest of their journey. These people are, after all, sent out for the sake of 'the Name', presumably of Jesus;[53] they are travelling missionaries of the gospel. They receive no help from the 'pagans', so they need assistance and are worthy of it.

3. Denunciation of Diotrephes (9–12)

The elder turns his attention now to Diotrephes, who, unlike Gaius, refused to welcome the travelling missionaries sent from the elder's church. Gaius and Diotrephes are probably not members of the same church, but leaders of two churches not far from one another. The elder had written to Diotrephes, presumably asking him and his church to welcome the travelling missionaries, yet Diotrephes had refused,

---

[53] See e.g. Mk. 9.37, 41; 13.13; Ac. 3.16; 4.18; 9.15–16, 27–28.

and had even threatened to expel from his church anyone who did welcome the missionaries.

We cannot tell whether Diotrephes's actions were linked with the secessionists described in 1 and 2 John. That is possible, but it seems somewhat unlikely, since the elder seems to have expected Diotrephes to comply in welcoming the missionaries. The elder infers from this that Diotrephes's actions are driven by his love of being 'first'; he complains that Diotrephes is 'spreading malicious nonsense about us'. This is likely to represent a clash of ecclesiastical authority rather than of theological dogma. The real offence of Diotrephes is not his snub to the elder, but its implications for the shared testimony and common mission in the Johannine network. As Lieu points out: 'Authority lies not in individuals' status or calling but in the shared giving and receiving of witness.'[54] It is principally on this point that Diotrephes was in error (3 Jn. 9–10). The elder follows this up with an ethical aphorism: 'Do not imitate what is evil but what is good. Anyone who does what is good is from God. Anyone who does what is evil has not seen God.' This is the basis both for his denunciation of Diotrephes and for his commendation of Gaius. Diotrephes has chosen to do evil, and this proves his inability to see Jesus, while Gaius, if he continues to do good, will show that he is genuinely of God.[55] On the back of that, the elder commends Demetrius, the letter-carrier, as one who has a good reputation. If Gaius receives Demetrius then he is also receiving the elder who sent him.

4. Letter closing (13–14)

The letter ends much like 2 John, wishing to say more, but not wanting to say it with papyrus and ink, hoping instead to say it one day face to face. The elder extends greetings from his friends, and asks in turn that Gaius pass on greetings to their mutual friends.

1, 2, AND 3 JOHN IN THE BIG PICTURE

The epistles of John are obviously a product of their own context and environment, and yet they have a timeless quality about them. The message of these letters is apt for any congregation at almost any time in its existence. We constantly need to be reminded of the key points, and in particular the interlocking nature of obedience–truth–love,[56] rooted in the identity of the children of God.

These letters commend doctrinal truth, truth to be believed, confessed, and upheld (see 1 Jn. 4.6; 5.13; 2 Jn. 2). Married to that we find the language of obeying and walking in the truth as a way of life (see 1 Jn. 1.6–7; 2.5; 2 Jn. 4, 6; 3 Jn. 3–4).

---

54 Lieu 2008, 9.
55 Parsenios 2014, 161.
56 Yarbrough 2008, 25–6.

'But', as Yarbrough observes, 'correct behaviour, even combined with high orthodoxy, can be overrated. Who has not encountered the doctrinaire, morally scrupulous, but hate-filled self-confessed follower of Jesus?'[57] That is why we need love, since love is the mark of authentic disciples (see 1 Jn. 3.10–18; 4.7–21).

Also prominent in the Johannine letters is the dealing with sin. Modern western culture holds a strong belief in moral autonomy, with belief and behaviour being measured exclusively by their perceived therapeutic effect (or lack thereof). This makes it difficult to talk today about the concept of sin, or to hear what John the elder has to say (see 1 Jn. 1.7–10; 2.1–2; 3.4–9; 5.16–18). His approach is paradoxical, admitting that sin continues to be a struggle for any believer (1 Jn. 1.7–9; 2.1) while also saying that those born of God do not habitually sin (1 Jn. 3.5, 9). The solution to this is not (starting from 1 Jn. 5.16–17) to differentiate between venial sin (sins of a lesser degree) and mortal sins (sins leading to death). Rather, we have to remember that John's letters are characterized by a thorough duality, an overlap of the light and darkness of continuing reality in a world where the age to come has already been launched—and believers already share in its life—while the old age of sin and death continues on its horrid way.[58] That is why followers of Jesus continue to confess their sins and receive the promised forgiveness. The elder urges believers to apply their faith at this point: to believe that Jesus has indeed made atonement for them, and then to live lives in which they are no longer under the irresistible compulsion to sin.

Christ in majesty flanked by Mary, John the Evangelist, and saints, twelfth century
Walters Art Museum

The main feature of John the elder's ecclesiology is that believers are 'children of God'. This motif has obvious connections with John's gospel (see Jn. 1.12–13; 11.52). The filial relationship with God is evidence of the lavish love that God has displayed towards them by making them his children (see 1 Jn. 3.1). Being a child of God is a prestigious and privileged status, but also a vocation. The children of God stand in opposition to 'the world'. Although God sent his son to be saviour of the world (1 Jn. 4.9, 14), the children must not love the

---

57 Yarbrough 2008, 25.
58 Lieu 2008, 22 speaks of 'apocalyptic' in this connection; but the word is too many-sided to be particularly helpful here, as is the complex idea of 'dualism'.

world, but must resist it (see 1 Jn. 2.15–16), repelling its hatred (1 Jn. 3.1, 13) with love for God and love for one other (1 Jn. 3.10–11; 5.1–2). They must live like Jesus the Messiah (1 Jn. 3.16; 4.17), knowing that he has overcome the world in them and for them (1 Jn. 4.4; 5.4–5). The church is to be seen as a community of God's warrior children, engaged in a struggle against the 'world', armed with love and the example of Jesus. Faith is what makes them children of God; faith is, simultaneously, their victory against the world.

Further reading

Hill, Charles. 2004. *The Johannine Corpus in the Early Church*. Oxford: Oxford University Press.
Jensen, Matthew D. 2014. *Affirming the Resurrection of the Incarnate Christ: A Reading of 1 John*. SNTSMS 153; Cambridge: Cambridge University Press.
Jobes, Karen H. 2014. *1, 2, and 3 John*. ZECNT; Grand Rapids, MI: Zondervan.
Kruse, Colin G. 2000. *The Letters of John*. PNTC; Grand Rapids, MI: Eerdmans.
Lieu, Judith M. 2008. *I, II, and III John: A Commentary*. NTL; Louisville, KY: Westminster John Knox.
Painter, John. 2002. *1, 2, and 3 John*. SP; Collegeville, MN: Liturgical.
Parsenios, George L. 2014. *First, Second, and Third John*. Paideia; Grand Rapids, MI: Baker.
Streett, Daniel R. 2011. *'They Went Out from Us': The Identity of the Opponents in First John*. BZNW 177; Berlin: De Gruyter.
Thompson, Marianne M. 1992a. *1–3 John*. IVPNTC; Downers Grove, IL: InterVarsity.
——. 1992b. 'Intercession in the Johannine Community: 1 John 5:16 in the Context of the Gospel and Epistles of John.' In *Worship, Theology and Ministry in the Early Church*. Edited by M. J. Wilkins and T. Paige. JSNTSup 87; Sheffield: Sheffield Academic Press, pp. 225–45.
Wright, N. T. 2011. *Early Christian Letters for Everyone: James, Peter, John, and Judah*. London: SPCK, pp. 129–90.
Yarbrough, Robert W. 2008. *1–3 John*. BECNT; Grand Rapids, MI: Baker.

Remains of the Basilica of St John, Ephesus

34

Revelation

To the seven churches in the province of Asia: Grace and peace to you from him who is, and who was, and who is to come, and from the seven spirits before his throne, and from Jesus Christ, who is the faithful witness, the firstborn from the dead, and the ruler of the kings of the earth. To him who loves us and has freed us from our sins by his blood, and has made us to be a kingdom and priests to serve his God and Father—to him be glory and power for ever and ever! Amen.[1]

CHAPTER AT A GLANCE

This chapter provides an overview of the book of Revelation.

By the end of this chapter you should be able to:

- understand issues of authorship, genre, and purpose related to the book of Revelation;
- describe the structure and argument of the book of Revelation;
- understand the themes and theology of the book of Revelation.

INTRODUCTION

Revelation is a strange book, nearly as strange as some of its readers. People have found in Revelation a dramatic account of the cosmic struggle of the church against the satan, a powerful consolation that God will one day end all suffering, a timetable for the end times, a mirror of the tyrants and turmoil of their own day, or—in many cases—a montage of pictures that they simply do not understand. The book is popular in the way that some music is popular: we don't understand it but it's an exciting set of tunes! Yet the book is as majestic as it is mysterious and magnetic. According to Richard Bauckham, one of the finest recent scholars in this area, 'Revelation is a book of profound theology, intense prophetic insight and dazzling literary accomplishment.' Despite its many eccentric and esoteric interpreters, it has 'inspired the martyrs, nourished the imagination of visionary artists

---

1   Rev. 1.4–6.

and hymn-writers, resourced prophetic critiques of oppression and corruption in state and church, and sustained hope and resistance in the most hopeless situations'. So much so that 'Revelation can be seen to be not only one of the finest literary works in the New Testament, but also one of the greatest theological achievements of early Christianity'.[2] We might not fully understand Revelation—who does?—but nobody can afford to ignore it.

In terms of content, the book is John's account of the 'revelation of Jesus Christ' which he received on the island of Patmos (setting aside for the moment the question of which 'John' we are talking about). So far, so good; but it is the particular way that John narrates his revelation that causes readers excitement and consternation. To begin with, the genre of 'revelation' itself is eclectic, combining features of letter-writing on the one hand and prophecy on the other, while ultimately resembling an 'apocalypse', a particular species of Jewish literature in which the Jewish vision of heaven and earth coming together is turned into literary artistry. Interpretation is thus challenging, because apocalyptic language and imagery is foreign to most people today; the book is in any case filled with dense allusions to biblical types and prophecies, and unless the reader is familiar with them the experience will be like watching the movie *Shrek* without knowing the nursery rhymes and fairy tales that it parodies.[3] The book also uses deliberately coded language about the Roman empire. John piles one metaphor on top of another in order to describe his visions and draw out their significance. Indeed, readers have always struggled to say what in the book is literary art and what is transcription of the author's visions. Perhaps the author himself could not have answered that question.

It is certainly fair to say that John struggles to find language, categories, or word-pictures to explain fully what he has seen and heard. We should sympathize with him. His task of explaining his vision of the risen Jesus, heavenly worship,

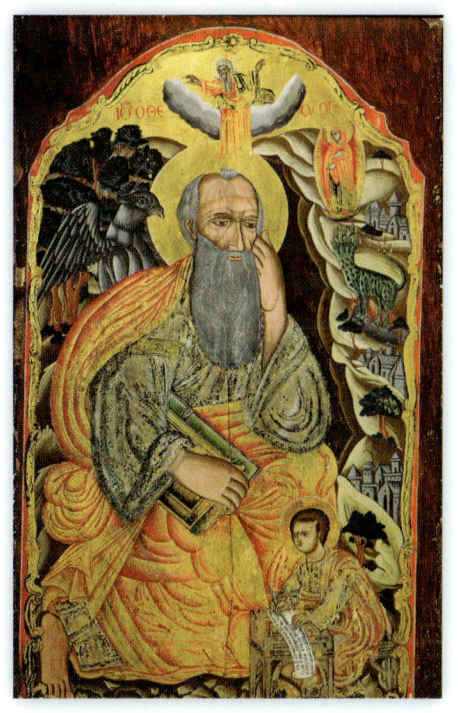

Icon of John the Evangelist dictating the visions to his scribe, c. 1837
Alfredo Dagli Orti / Shutterstock

---

[2] Bauckham 2001, 1287; 1993a, 22. Contrast this with Bultmann (1951–5, 2.175) who called Revelation 'weakly Christianised Judaism'.
[3] Bull 2017.

the ongoing war against the dragon, the fall of the Roman empire, and the ultimate consummation of the creator's purposes for the world, could be likened to our coming across a primitive tribe, deep in the highlands of Papua New Guinea, people living in stone-age conditions, who have never had contact with western civilization—and then trying to explain the Internet to them. Where would you begin?[4] The author of Revelation has seen and heard things which probably put him in that position in relation to people of his own day; how much more in relation to us.

The other complicating factor is that John's vision assumes a deep connection between heaven and earth. George Caird provides a memorable analogy. Imagine, he says, a military headquarters. Flags are clustered together on a map, and then an official gets up to move the flags around. The flags signify either current manoeuvres on the battlefield or else proposed positions for the various units to be deployed. Caird comments:

> The strange and complex symbols of John's vision are, like the flags in this parable, the pictorial counterpart of earthly realities; and these symbols too may be either determinative or descriptive. John sees some things happening in heaven because God has determined that equivalent events should shortly happen on earth, but other heavenly events take place . . . because earthly events have made them possible.[5]

John is trying to explain, in the light of the current crisis, what is going on with God's purposes in heaven, and how all that corresponds to his audience's earthly plight. For John, as in much Jewish thought (with the Temple as its anchor), heaven is not something spatially and temporally removed from earth. Rather, heaven is that dimension of God's reality and plan which shapes and impacts events on earth. Heaven and earth are two aspects of the one stage in which God's drama to put the world to rights is being played out. In view of all that, John's vision provides us with a dramaturgical commentary on the current crisis. Revelation is partly previewing what is to come and partly clarifying how the tragic events that are occurring make sense within the wider narrative of ultimate divine triumph.

The point is that John is witness to an 'unveiling'. He has been granted a glimpse of God's glory, of the divine strategy and plan for the world. He has seen things which, though normally invisible, are radically shaping the world around us. We are given to understand that there is considerably more going on than meets the eye: tyrannical power is neither absolute nor everlasting. God's purposes for his people and the

---
4 I owe this illustration to Carson 2014, 175–6.
5 Caird 1965b, 61.

world will not be thwarted. John is trying to explain, in fact, how the divine purpose is working itself out to bring about a marriage between heaven and earth, and how, at the centre of it all, is Jesus himself, the 'lamb' who was slain, the king who will return to conquer all his adversaries, so that God will in the end dwell fully and finally with his people. John's pastoral purpose is as much to exhort his hearers to endurance as to assure them of God's ultimate victory over their adversaries. He therefore provides a God's-eye view of the plight of the Asian churches, and explains how Jesus' people are destined to reign with him in the new creation. Along the way there are exhortations and prophecies, warnings and judgments, triumphs mixed with tears, old adversaries and a new world. For all the (to us) vagueness of John's vision, and the vagaries of his language, the book of Revelation gives its audience confidence and hope that 'the lamb' has triumphed, and will yet triumph, over the evils of the world.

John describes how his vision was granted him while he was in exile on the small Aegean island of Patmos. His vision, of Jesus himself, was blinding and glorious (Rev. 1.12–20), commissioning 'John' to write to the 'seven churches' in the province of Asia (what is now western Turkey): Ephesus, Smyrna, Pergamum, Thyatira, Sardis, Philadelphia, and Laodicea. These specific 'letters', with relevant local colour and specific warnings and challenges, form the foundation in Revelation 2—3 for a kind of second introduction in Revelation 4—5, where John sees the heavenly throne-room, with all creation worshipping the true God and celebrating the victory of the 'lamb' over the dark powers that have held back the creator's intentions for the world.

Mosaic with John and a disciple marking the place, according to tradition, where John saw the visions on the island of Patmos.
iStock.com / johncopland

Now, it seems, humans who are rescued from their sin and its consequences are to take their place as 'a kingdom and priests to our God', and 'will reign on the earth' (Rev. 1.6; 5.10; 20.6 *NTE/KNT*). The implementation of this victory is unfolded in a sequence of overlapping visions, through the trouble and suffering that will follow, particularly at the hands of the 'monsters'—a reference, in Revelation 13, to the emperor and his local officials—who will rage against the lamb's followers but will be overthrown in the final outworking of his victory over 'Babylon', the oppressive imperial power and the demonic powers which sustain it. Then the true 'city of God', the 'new Jerusalem', will appear (Rev. 21—22).

The book of Revelation has always appealed to artists: here, above all, the reader needs a disciplined imagination as well as a praying heart and a reasoning mind. Like a great piece of music that will only yield its secrets to the mature and sensitive player, the New Testament is designed not just to offer information about God, Jesus, the world, and ourselves, but also to urge us, by inviting us to penetrate its innermost core, to become the kind of people for whom, and indeed through whom, it will at last all make sense. That challenge applies to every book in the New Testament, but perhaps to Revelation even more than the others.

CONTEXTUAL AND CRITICAL MATTERS

Origins of the book of Revelation

Jewish apocalypses are usually pseudonymous: the author writes under the assumed name of an ancient figure like Adam, Enoch, Abraham, Moses, Baruch, or Ezra. Some Christian apocalypses used a similar literary form, writing under the name of ancient authors (such as the books known as the *Ascension of Isaiah*, the *Apocalypse of Peter*, and so on). The purpose of pseudonymity was to claim authority from a religious figure from antiquity, and to present contemporary events as prophecy come to fulfilment. The book of Revelation shares a great deal with this kind of literature, but it is not anonymous: the author announces himself as 'John', and further describes himself as a 'brother' (that is, a fellow-Christian),[6] a 'servant' (meaning a Christian leader),[7] a 'prophet' (that is, a speaker inspired by the spirit),[8] and in effect a 'seer' (someone who receives visions).[9] The author never claims to be an apostle or eye-witness to Jesus' ministry, which sets this book apart from, for instance, the claim of the 'John' who wrote the gospel and epistles.[10] There are many signs that the author was a Palestinian Jew now removed to the Greek

---

6 Rev. 1.9; 19.10.
7 Rev. 1.1; 19.10; 22.9.
8 Rev. 22.9 and elsewhere; he was 'in the Spirit' according to Rev. 1.10; 17.3; 21.10.
9 Rev. 1.1; 22.8, and repetition of 'I saw . . .' e.g. Rev. 1.12, 17; 5.1–2, 6; 6.9; 7.1–2; 8.2; 9.1.
10 Jn. 1.14; 21.24; 1 Jn. 1.1–3.

islands: the apocalyptic genre; his immersion in the Old Testament; his own awareness of a prophetic call; the influence of the Septuagint on his Greek. Many Jewish refugees joined the growing Diaspora after the debacle of AD 70. Perhaps he was one of them.[11]

Or perhaps not... Which 'John', after all, are we talking about? John the son of Zebedee, the apostle; or John the elder, who wrote the epistles; the author of the gospel, if he was different from both of the above; or a different John, to be called 'John the Seer' or 'John the Divine'? Early tradition, beginning with Justin Martyr, regarded the apostle John, the son of Zebedee, as the author of the gospel, epistles, and Revelation.[12] Many have pointed to the theological and terminological similarities between the gospel of John and the revelation of John as proof that the apostle John is the author of both works (though we have argued in chapter 27 that it was John the elder rather than John the son of Zebedee who wrote the gospel of John). The gospel and Revelation appear to share the idea of Jesus as the Word, the 'lamb', and 'son of man' (though the Greek words used for 'word' and 'lamb' are different in each work). Both speak of salvation in terms of the 'living water'; both align the gospel message with the 'manna' in the wilderness; both frame their narratives with motifs belonging to the exodus story; both emphasize the theme of 'witness'. Thus John's gospel and epistles do share with the apocalypse of John a certain family resemblance.[13]

Others, however, retort that the apocalyptic eschatology of Revelation is radically different from the realized eschatology of the gospel of John. This contrast, however, is overdrawn. The gospel of John retains a strong future eschatology;[14] and Revelation understands the victory of the lamb as having already taken place, now to be implemented. Indeed, the notion of time itself becomes more complex in Revelation than it might appear at first glance, with future events like resurrection somehow also realized in the present.[15] What is more, 1 John, with its mixture of realized eschatology—expressed in terms of 'life' and 'victory'—and an intense hope for Jesus' *parousia*, can be seen as a middle point between the gospel of John and Revelation.[16]

When all is said and done, however, it may be the contrasts between the gospel and Revelation which stand out more starkly. There are striking differences in language, grammar, and mode of discourse. The Greek of John's gospel is simple yet

---

11 Aune 1997–8, 1.1; deSilva 2004, 894; Dunn 2015, 107.
12 Just. *Dial.* 81.4; Irenaeus (*Adv. Haer.* 3.11.1, 8; 4.20.11) attributed Revelation to the 'Lord's disciple' who also wrote the gospel and epistles (*Adv. Haer.* 1.16.3; 3.1.1; 3.11.1; 3.16.5, 8); Muratorian canon § 9, 57–8, 71; Tert. *Adv. Marc.* 3.14.3; 3.24.4; Hippolytus *Antichr.* 36–42.
13 See e.g. Morris 1987, 27–35 and esp. Frey 1993.
14 See e.g. Jn. 5.29; 6.39–40, 44, 54; 14.3.
15 See e.g. Rev. 20.4.
16 See on 'life', 1 Jn. 3.14; 5.4–5, 12; and see on 'victory', 1 Jn. 2.17–18, 28; 3.2; 4.17.

sublime. The Greek of Revelation falls within 'the range of possible registers of Greek usage of the 1st century';[17] nonetheless it evidences Septuagintalisms (that is, the author imitates Greek translations of the Old Testament), it is full of solecisms (irregular grammar, especially when alluding to scripture), and is prolix, using more words than required, especially when compared with the often economical and elegant Greek of the gospel. All this may, some have suggested, be intending to make the text sound more 'biblical'.[18] Added to this are differences in texture and intent. The gospel of John is about how God's kingdom and God's life are revealed in the person of Jesus: his person is visible and tangible, and meets people in the here and now. In Revelation there is such a mixture of light and darkness, revelation and mystery, that one is quickly confused as to events that may transpire in the near or distant future, or perhaps are happening already.

Many in early Christian circles had doubts about whether the apostle John wrote Revelation. Marcion was among the first to reject his candidacy.[19] Others of a more proto-orthodox persuasion in the early church, including Dionysius of Alexandria (d. AD 264), rejected the apostle John's authorship, partly due to the book's millenarianism, and partly due to its different style of expression and unique theological profile compared to the Johannine gospel and letters.[20] Eusebius developed Papias's mention of two people called 'John' active in Asia, and postulated the apostle John as the author of the gospel and John the elder as the author of Revelation.[21] Some in the second century, the so-called Alogoi of Asia Minor and a Roman presbyter named Gaius, both driven by anti-Montanist impulses, went so far as to claim that Revelation was in fact written by the heretic Cerinthus under John's name.[22]

In the end, we may allow that John's gospel, epistles, and Revelation all come from the same circle, but that different authors are responsible for them.[23] Neither John the son of Zebedee nor John the elder is the 'John' of Revelation. To distinguish him, we will call him 'John the Seer'.

Date and provenance

Irenaeus, at the end of the second century, reckoned that Revelation was to be dated towards the final years of the reign of the emperor Domitian (AD 81–96).[24] Domitian was remembered as a megalomaniac, consumed with the promulgation

---

[17] Porter 1989, 603.
[18] Beale 1999, 100–3.
[19] Tert. *Adv. Marc.* 4.5.
[20] Eus. *Hist. Eccl.* 7.25.
[21] Eus. *Hist. Eccl.* 3.39.4–6; 7.25.16–17.
[22] Epiphanius *Pan.* 51.1.3–6; 51.32.2–33.3; Eus. *Hist. Eccl.* 3.28.1–5; 7.25.2.
[23] Contra Koester (2014, 80–1) and Aune (1997–8, 1.lv–lvi) who thinks that different authors associated with the fourth gospel, Johannnine epistles, and Revelation, have developed biblical and early Christian traditions independently of each other.
[24] Iren. *Adv. Haer.* 5.30.3.

of his own divine status, demanding to be addressed as 'lord and god'.[25] He was thought to have unleashed a brutal persecution against Christians, and many from early times have supposed that it was his malevolent figure that could be seen looming up in the darker passages of Revelation.

While this dating might be correct, there are two points to consider. First, most persecutions of Christians were local rather than empire-wide. More often than not, they were spasmodic rather than a matter of ongoing imperial policy. Second, while Domitian was autocratic, often ruthless with enemies, and had little patience with the Roman senate, the portrayal of him as a despotic tyrant owes more to the propaganda of subsequent regimes and writers than it does to actual fact. Domitian's legacy was trashed precisely to make subsequent emperors look all the more benevolent. We therefore need to take the historical accounts of Domitian's megalomania and malevolence with a pinch of salt.[26] So if Domitian was not the cruel tyrant later writers made him out to be, and if Christian persecution in Asia was localized rather than part of an imperial policy, we are under far less compulsion to choose a date in the 80s or 90s.

Complicating matters, the reference in chapter 17 to the seven kings, of whom 'five have fallen, one is still there, and the other has not yet arrived', has invited speculation on a date, despite the fact that the text is notoriously opaque as to which emperor is the sixth one who is currently reigning.[27] It depends on which emperor starts the list (see Table 34.1). If we start with Julius Caesar (not that he was technically 'emperor', but he was clearly a major figurehead), that yields Nero as the sixth. If we begin with Augustus, it makes Galba sixth. Or, if we begin with Galba, then Domitian would be sixth. Or perhaps this is the wrong way of reading the text. The number 'seven', after all, signifies totality and perfection.

TABLE 34.1: THE REIGNS OF THE ROMAN EMPERORS AS A KEY TO DATING REVELATION

Emperor	Dates of reign
Julius Caesar	49–44 BC
Augustus	31 BC—AD 14
Tiberius	AD 14–37
Gaius Caligula	AD 37–41
Claudius	AD 41–54
Nero	AD 54–68
Galba	AD 68–9
Otho	AD 69
Vitellius	AD 69
Vespasian	AD 69–79
Titus	AD 79–81
Domitian	AD 81–96
Nerva	AD 96–8
Trajan	AD 98–117
Hadrian	AD 117–38

---

25 Suet. *Dom.* 13.2; see Rev. 4.11.
26 Thompson 1990, 15–17, 97, 101–9, but see criticism of Thompson in Beale 1999, 9–12 and Witherington 2003, 5–6. The portrayal of Domitian in director Richard Mertes's *The Apocalypse* (2002), starring Richard Harris as 'John', is a good example of the depiction of Domitian as the megalomaniacal tyrant.
27 Rev. 17.10.

The 'seven kings' correspond to the 'seven hills' of Rome; together they make a polyvalent portrayal of Roman power and the dominion of the beast. In other words, seven literal emperors may not even be in the author's mind.

There is an attraction in starting with Julius Caesar and making Nero the featured 'sixth'. That would put Revelation in the late 60s, around the time of or after Nero's pogrom against the Christians in Rome, perhaps after Nero's suicide, during the year of the four emperors in AD 68/9, with the chaos of Roman civil war and the ongoing siege of Jerusalem producing a vision of global nightmare. Others, however, would place the composition of the book much later, during the reigns of Trajan (98–117)[28] or even Hadrian (117–38).[29] No agreement is in sight.[30]

However, one suggestion worthy of consideration is that of Martin Hengel. He proposed that Revelation was an earlier work, the nucleus of which was written over an extended period after the Neronian persecution, the Judean revolt against Rome, the Temple's destruction, the murder of Nero, and the subsequent Roman civil war which led to the Flavian dynasty (Vespasian onwards). The book might then have been substantially reworked, during the reign of Trajan, by a pupil of John the elder who depicted his teacher as having received the 'revelation' in question.[31] An upper limit for the final version of the book would then be AD 130, since Papias, a millennialist, seems according to Eusebius to have been influenced by Revelation.[32]

This is highly ingenious, and there is no reason to rule it out. Still, the traditional datings, during the reigns of either Nero or Domitian, are not unlikely. There is in fact little proof that Christians suffered empire-wide persecution under Domitian, but he does seem to have zealously promoted the imperial cult, thereby sustaining enthusiasm for the Flavian

Bust of Emperor Vespasian, reigned AD 69–79
© Sailko / Wikimedia Commons CC BY 3.0

---

28 John was thought to have lived into the reign of Trajan; see Iren. *Adv. Haer.* 2.22.5; 3.3.4 and Eus. *Hist. Eccl.* 3.23.2–4.
29 See survey in Witulski 2007, 14–52.
30 The problem with an early dating is that Revelation assumes the development and wide circulation of the *Nero redivivus* myth whereby Nero would return from the east with an army to fight against the Roman empire; see Rev. 17.8, 11, 14 and *Sib. Or.* 3.63–74; 4.119–24, 137–9; 5.361–5; *Mart. Isa.* 4.2–8. Persons claiming to be Nero appeared in AD 69 (Tac. *Hist.* 2.8), again in AD 80 (Dio Cassius *Hist.* 66.19.3), and yet again in AD 88 (Suet. *Ner.* 57.2).
31 Hengel 1989, 51, 81. See similarly Aune 1997–8, 1.lviii, cxxi. Koester (2014, 70) wisely warns here: 'Although it is possible that Revelation was written over a period of time, the attempts to reconstruct the stages of writing and editing are not compelling.'
32 Eus. *Hist. Eccl.* 3.39.12.

regime, in the Asian cities of Ephesus and Pergamum. The book seems to indicate that some Christians had already suffered martyrdom;[33] that they were being pressured to participate in the imperial cult;[34] and that a threat of further large-scale persecution was never far away.[35] That would make sense, given that Pliny's letter to Trajan, written some twenty years after Domitian, refers to Christians who had apostatized under persecution some twenty years earlier.[36]

Eusebius and his sources were later to regard Domitian as a new Nero: he executed and exiled many members of the nobility, confiscated their property, and stirred up persecution against the church.[37] That view might well have been coloured by the attempts of subsequent emperors and their court apologists to discredit Domitian. But it coheres with some of the odd incidents that are recorded. We hear about Domitian executing the nobleman Flavius Clemens and banishing his wife Flavia Domitilla on the charge of 'atheism', and for 'drifting into Jewish ways'. Atheism was a common charge arrayed against Christians, and 'Jewish ways' might have included Christians too.[38] One need not accept the jaundiced tradition of Domitian's slide into a reign of anti-Christian terror to believe that Christians, especially those who were socially prominent, were facing duress to engage in the imperial cult at the initiative of provincial authorities who were keen to ingratiate themselves with the imperial regime. So, most likely, Domitian was worse than his predecessors and immediate successors, but not as bad as later Roman writers made him out to be. He did not have a settled and violent anti-Christian policy even if some of his Asian supporters did.[39] Consequently, as Dunn puts it, 'The likelihood remains . . . that the Apocalypse reflects the pressures building up from the local provincial elite for citizens and residents to express their loyalty to Rome by participating in the imperial cult during the reign of Domitian.'[40] We note at the same time that it would not take much to swing the argument back to say similar things about Nero.

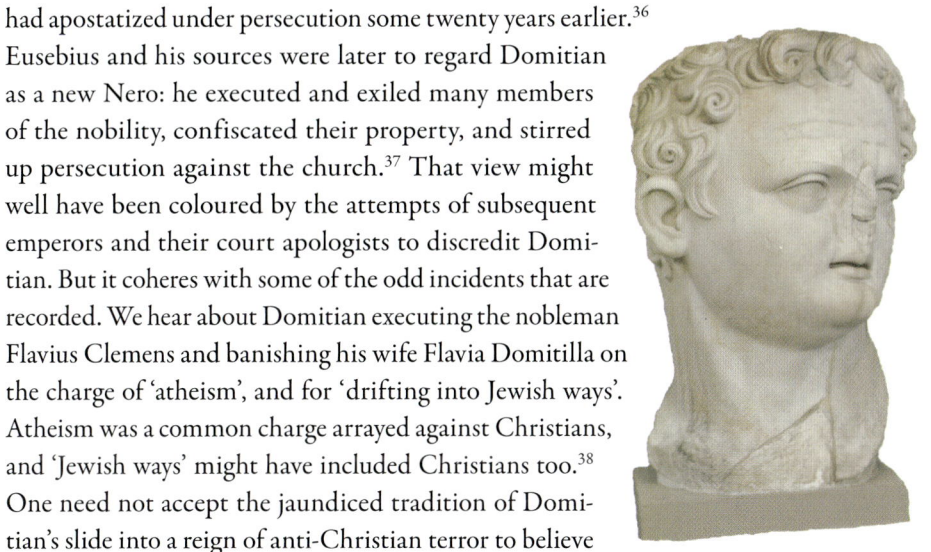

Bust of Emperor Domitian, reigned AD 81–96
© William D. Mounce

---

[33] Rev. 2.13.
[34] Rev. 13.4–8, 15–16; 14.9–11; 15.2; 16.2; 19.20; 20.4.
[35] Rev. 2.3, 10, 13, 19; 6.9–11. See Thompson 1990, 16–17.
[36] Pliny *Ep.* 10.96–7.
[37] Eus. *Hist. Eccl.* 3.17; 3.20.9–10.
[38] Dio Cassius *Hist.* 67.14; Eus. *Hist. Eccl.* 3.18.5.
[39] Beale 1999, 12.
[40] Dunn 2015, 110. Also, as deSilva (2009, 52) points out: 'Domitian's attitude toward his own divinity is less relevant than the enthusiasm of the local elites in Asia Minor to demonstrate their loyalty and make bids for the attention and favour of the imperial house—by means of offering cult to the Flavian household.'

John claims to have had his vision on Patmos, one of the Sporades islands in the Aegean Sea, some thirty-seven miles south-west of Miletus off the west Asian coast. According to tradition, he was banished to Patmos during the reign of Domitian, but returned when Domitian died and his decrees were annulled.[41] The problem is that so far as we know Patmos was a military garrison, not a penal colony.[42] A plausible scenario is that John had been something of a nuisance in Asia, and had been sentenced to exile by a local governor. Then, after experiencing his visions on Patmos (not necessarily the first visions he had ever received), he returned to Ephesus to meditate upon them, share them, and write about them to the churches of Asia Minor.[43]

The setting of the seven churches addressed in the book is remarkably diverse.[44] Contrary to popular opinion, not all of them were experiencing persecution. Many churches faced a quite different challenge: that of affluence and the temptation to compromise with an idolatrous and oppressive system. The churches of Ephesus, Sardis, and Laodicea were showing signs of spiritual lethargy.[45] The church of Pergamum had a martyr in Antipas.[46] Thyatira and Philadelphia were commended for their endurance in the face of opposition;[47] the church of Smyrna was going to face persecution;[48] Philadelphia was promised that though there was a trial coming, it would escape.[49] The churches of Smyrna and Philadelphia were encountering religious rivalry and slander from

Ancient temple, Laodicea

---

[41] Eus. *Hist. Eccl.* 3.18.1; 3.20.8–9; 3.23.1, 6.
[42] Thompson 1990, 143.
[43] See Bauckham 1993a, 3–4, and deSilva 2004, 890.
[44] See Bauckham 1993a, 15–17; Koester 2001b, 54–69; deSilva 2009, 29–63.
[45] Rev. 2.4–5; 3.1–3, 15–18.
[46] Rev. 2.13. Longenecker (2016) bases his stirring and informative fictional work on this character; well worth reading!
[47] Rev. 2.19; 3.8–10.
[48] Rev. 2.10.
[49] Rev. 3.10.

local synagogues.[50] The Christians in Pergamum and Thyatira were chastised for eating food sacrificed to idols and engaging in sexual immorality, the hallmarks of assimilating socially to the local pagan culture.[51] There were different economic conditions since the Smyrneans were poor whereas the Laodiceans were rich.[52] The Ephesian church was commended for resisting false apostles and the Nicolaitans,[53] while Pergamum and Thyatira were rebuked for tolerating false teachers, including the Nicolaitans and a certain 'Jezebel'.[54] Consequently, some churches needed encouragement while others needed stern rebuke. There is no sign of a universal problem afflicting them all.

Another important factor in assessing the setting of the book is the extent to which onlookers could see just how expansive and dominant Roman political, military, and economic power had become. Roman power was celebrated in public media like coins and inscriptions, and was venerated through the imperial cult and the famous temple to Mars Ultor ('the avenger') in Rome itself. Babylon the Great became for the early church a symbol of Rome, seen as both a luxuriating whore and the seat of Mediterranean military power. John offers a voice from elsewhere, from among the 'others' who lived on the margins of the empire, with the boot of Roman power on their throat. Rome's prosperity and glory was the cause of their poverty and shame; Roman 'justice' was often perceived as its opposite. As one subdued chieftain was alleged to have said about the Romans: 'To violence, rape, and plunder, they give the name "empire"; they create desolation and call it "peace".'[55] John's apocalypse is a theologically loaded critique of Rome's vaunted greatness and goodness, its self-styled blessedness and benevolence. The book decries Rome's actual pretentiousness and brutality, offering an alternative perspective on how Rome looks from below. David deSilva puts it elegantly:

> John raises his voice alongside those of other protesters like the authors of 4 Ezra and 2 Baruch. John was not a solitary, raving lunatic. The asylum was full of people who just couldn't 'see things' in line with the official picture. The multiplicity of voices calling out against Rome's injustices at the close of the first century, of which John's voice was one, help us to see that Jews and Christians in Asia Minor were not only concerned about local affairs, internecine strife, or throwing stones at the church or synagogue across the way. The 'system,' together with all its local manifestations, was also a major problem. Uniting the

---

50 Rev. 2.9; 3.9; see Witherington 2003, 98–100; deSilva 2009, 55–8.
51 Rev. 2.14, 20. Some have seen this as a jibe at the position of Paul as in 1 Cor. 8–10.
52 Rev. 2.9; 3.17.
53 Rev. 2.2, 6.
54 Rev. 2.14–16, 20–23.
55 Tac. *Agric.* 30 (tr. M. F. Bird).

practice of exerting control and maintaining peace through violent suppression of dissent, the promotion of an economy arranged for the great benefit of the few, and the prominent use of religious language and ritual to claim sacral legitimation for these arrangements—uniting these is both the genius of Rome and the heap of her sins for which John excoriates her.[56]

The 'religious' dimension of the empire is very significant for understanding the book of Revelation.[57] Temples to the goddess Roma and to the emperor and his family, along with shrines, coinage, and images celebrating the emperor's status and divinity, had saturated Asia Minor since the time of Augustus. Serving as a priest in the imperial cult was much coveted and sought after, bestowing a special relationship to imperial power. The emperor offered benefactions in the form of stability, security, peace, and prosperity, and the highest mode of reciprocation by cities who enjoyed his favour was divine worship, with worship graded according to the benefactions given. By the end of the first century, all seven cities that John mentions had cultic sites for imperial devotion. Six (all except Thyatira) possessed imperial temples; five (all except Philadelphia and Laodicea) had imperial altars with a priesthood.[58]

Remains of the temple of Artemis, Sardis
© *William D. Mounce*

[56] deSilva 2009, 48.
[57] On 'religion' in the first-century Roman world, and the sharp differences between what 'religion' meant then and what it means now, see e.g. Wright *PFG*, ch. 4.
[58] deSilva 2009, 41.

Participation in rites and rituals, whether at the dinner of a trade guild, during public games, or before a family shrine featuring the emperor's image, was the moment to demonstrate one's loyalty and gratitude towards the imperial family. This is why John singles out Pergamum as the place where 'Satan has his throne',[59] since Pergamum was among the first to receive the title 'temple warden' of the imperial cult. It had a temple to the goddess Roma and to the Augusti, along with an immense altar to Zeus on top of a nearby mountain. Yet John urges his readers to flee from Babylon the Great, to refuse to worship the beast, and to reject the seduction of prosperity enmeshed in blasphemy. According to John, it was not Rome's *dios* (Zeus/Jupiter) but Israel's *theos* (God) who was in charge of history; it was not the *sebastos* (venerable emperor) but the *christos* (Messiah) who was the agent of salvation; and it was not the Roman people, but the church, that was destined to reign over the earth.

Genre

The book of Revelation is an eclectic mixture of epistle, prophecy, and apocalypse. First, the book is bracketed with an epistolary framework and contains several prophetic oracles couched as letters.[60] Second, Revelation is umbilically connected to biblical prophecy in both form and content, and explicitly presents itself as 'prophecy' (see further below).[61] Third, above all, the book is an *apocalypse* since it is titled as the 'apocalypse of Jesus Christ' and exemplifies several devices and themes associated with the slippery category of 'apocalyptic'.[62] The book of Revelation is, then, a lengthy circular letter, substantively a prophetic apocalypse, that was intended for dissemination among the Asian churches.[63]

Before we go any further, we have to pause and consider what we might mean by the contested term 'apocalyptic', paying attention to its cognate areas of revelatory experiences, worldview, sociology, and literary expression.[64]

First, central to 'apocalyptic' is the report of *revelatory experiences* like visions or dreams. We refer here to someone, the 'seer', who experiences a revelation of things not usually perceptible—sometimes seeing, sometimes hearing, sometimes both. We know about this because seers often write down what they remember having seen and heard, which they interpret as an 'unveiling' of the true nature, the God's-eye perspective perhaps, of present reality and/or events yet to come. This kind of

---

[59] Rev. 2.13.
[60] Rev. 1.4–5; 22.21; Rev. 2.1–3.22. See Koester 2014, 109–12.
[61] Rev. 1.3; 22.6–7. See Boring 1974; Aune 1983, 274–88; 1997–8, 1.lxxv–lxxvi; Koester 2014, 107–9.
[62] Rev. 1.1. The major differences between Revelation and Jewish apocalypses are: (1) Revelation is not pseudonymous; (2) Revelation is prolific in the extent of visual imagery employed and is meagre when it comes to the interpretation of the imagery itself (Bauckham 1993a, 9–12).
[63] Bauckham 1993a, 2; 2001, 1288.
[64] See Aune 1987, 227–31; Thompson 1990, 23–4; Collins 2016, 14–26 for a similar breakdown. On 'apocalyptic' in recent Pauline scholarship, see Wright *PRI*, Part II.

experience presupposes that reality is more complex and multi-dimensional than it normally appears, and that, in particular, the sphere of normal human experience is not after all separated from the sphere of the angels and their creator by a great gulf, but rather 'heaven' and 'earth' in fact overlap and interlock in a variety of ways.

Second, this leads us to what some have supposed to be a particular *apocalyptic worldview*, the theological map of reality that is disclosed through an unveiling of otherwise concealed mysteries. Here we have to be careful, because the literary genre, and the experience which may or may not lie behind it, should not itself be mistaken for a 'worldview'. 'Apocalyptic' texts regularly display a number of binary configurations (present and future, heaven and earth, light and darkness, good and evil).

The ancient theatre of Pergamum
kathmanduphotog / Shutterstock

These are, however, common to most Jewish writings across a long period, including the writings of the rabbis, who set their faces firmly against the dangerous and revolutionary tendencies of 'apocalyptic'. The idea that 'apocalyptic' was 'dualist' goes back to a fear, on the part of some nineteenth-century scholars, of the revolutionary tendencies of the literature when contrasted with what they saw as the smoother lines of 'prophecy'. Writings we label 'apocalypses' do not in fact necessarily display a crude dualism between the earthly and the heavenly, much less the material versus the spiritual. They presuppose, as do the Hebrew scriptures as a whole, the belief that heaven and earth overlap, with the Temple as the obvious locus where that overlap becomes reality. Just like the 'historical' and 'prophetic' books of the Old Testament, 'apocalyptic' writings stress—though in a different literary mode—that there is an ongoing struggle on several planes, and a hidden divine plan to resolve that struggle. The message of the seers, varyingly described, pertains to how the earth's inhabitants have gone their own way, and their rulers have abused their power. Heaven's answer to that is not to pull up the drawbridge and provide backstairs access for those who can escape, but to reassert the claims of the God of heaven and earth on his whole two-sided creation. This always involves conflict with the powers that have usurped his rule on earth, whether pagan or Jewish. We should note that all of this might be said of books such as Deuteronomy, 1 and 2 Kings, Isaiah 40—55, and many other prophets. In other words, 'apocalyptic' writing highlights what in other Jewish writing is often only implicit: the narrative of a struggle between earthly and heavenly agents, culminating in God's reversal of the suffering of his people and retribution meted out on the wicked.

Third, when Jewish groups throughout the period were faced with a crisis, such as a major threat from pagan powers, their understanding of this crisis and their yearning for their God to act to undo the problem could and sometimes did lead to what some have perhaps misleadingly called *apocalypticism*. This purported *apocalypticism* is an entire mood or mode in which a group organizes itself socially, culturally, narratively, and religiously around the perceived crisis, believing that it is playing a central part in the situation and looking for a divine resolution. (Again, we note that this would well describe the underlying view of the book of Esther, which is about as 'un-apocalyptic' in other respects as one can imagine.) Some groups that acquire the modern label 'apocalyptic' claimed a privileged perspective on world affairs, often by revelation or inspiration, on the true nature of the opposition, and on the final resolution of the group's plight. At least one third of the Psalms exhibit signs of this, though they are not often referred to in discussions of 'apocalyptic'. What we moderns have called 'apocalypticism', then, appears to be a heightened version of a phenomenon known much more widely in the Hebrew scriptures, in second-Temple Jewish life, and indeed among early Christians: a situation of trauma, alienation, persecution, or disempowerment is interpreted within a 'theological' perspective, from which emerges the hope for resolution and rescue, and a word of encouragement and perhaps a call to action for the faithful—in the Christian context, for the Messiah himself to implement on earth the victory already won, and for his people to take courage and stand firm.[65] The writing we call 'apocalyptic' is then designed to encode at least a tacit protest, through narratives freighted with intertextuality and metaphor, against the threatening powers. Such writing, like many other writings in Jewish and early Christian circles, is earthed in, and designed to strengthen, a community which hopes for the subversion of the current order and its replacement with a new divinely sanctioned one.

---

65 Becker and Jöris 2016.

Fourth, an 'apocalypse' is therefore the specific literary expression, in the mode of 'revelation', of this much larger worldview. An apocalypse, according to one definition, is

> a genre of revelatory literature with a narrative framework, in which a revelation is mediated by an otherworldly being to a human recipient, disclosing a transcendent reality which is both temporal, insofar as it envisages eschatological salvation, and spatial, insofar as it involves another supernatural world . . . intended to interpret present, earthly circumstances in light of the supernatural world of the future, and to influence both the understanding and the behaviour of the audience by means of divine authority.[66]

The genre we call 'apocalypse' frequently contains extended symbolic reviews of world history (such as the statue with its four metals in Dan. 2) and/or the description of otherworldly journeys. The result is the narration of a God's-eye view of history, the present, and the future, also offering 'a transcendent, usually eschatological perspective on human experiences and values'.[67] Again, we note that the same could be said of a good many biblical and sub-biblical books not usually thought of as 'apocalypses'.

EARLIEST COPIES OF THE BOOK OF REVELATION

Siglum	Manuscript name	Date	Contents
$\mathfrak{P}^{98}$	P.IFAO II 31	2nd century	1.13–20
$\mathfrak{P}^{18}$	P.Oxy. VIII 1079	3rd century	1.4–7
$\mathfrak{P}^{47}$	P.Beatty III	3rd century	9.10—17.2
$\mathfrak{P}^{115}$	P.Oxy LXVI 4499	3rd/4th century	2.1–3, 13–15, 27–29; 3.10–12; 5.8–9; 6.4–6; 8.3–5
$\mathfrak{P}^{24}$	P.Oxy X 1230	4th century	5.5–8; 6.5–8
ℵ	Codex Sinaiticus	4th century	complete
A	Codex Alexandrinus	5th century	complete

---

66 J. J. Collins 1979, 9; 2016, 5; A. Y. Collins 1986, 7. See also Aune (1997–8, 1.lxxxii) who focuses on a mixture of form, content, and function. See too especially Rowland 1982.
67 Aune 1997–8, 1.lxxxii.

Given all this, we note that John the Seer has not written an 'apocalypse' after the manner of, say, *4 Ezra*. He writes in his own name, without employing pseudonymity. The way he makes fresh use of the ancient prophets is quite different from the authors of contemporary Jewish apocalypses such as *4 Ezra*, *2 Baruch*, *3 Baruch*, *2 Enoch*, and the *Apocalypse of Abraham*. He does occasionally report conversations between himself and an angelic interpreter, but never do we have that step-by-step interpretation of visions which, beginning with Daniel 7, became the stock-in-trade of later writers. He oscillates, as Daniel does, between fairly literal description (as in Rev. 18) and reported visions which, if uninterpreted, would remain dense and impenetrable (as in Rev. 13—20). The book may be titled the 'apocalypse of Jesus Christ' (Rev. 1.1),[68] but it is also described as 'prophecy' (Rev. 1.3; 10.11; 22.7, 10, 18–19) that takes place 'in the Spirit' (Rev. 1.10; 4.2; 17.3). The writer classes himself among the 'prophets' (Rev. 22.9), and his testimony is 'the Spirit of prophecy' (Rev. 19.10). Thus, while John has written an apocalypse, clearly analogous to other Jewish apocalypses in terms of literary devices and theological assumptions (replete with vision reports, numerology, cosmic phenomena, angelic visitations, cataclysmic judgments, and multi-layered symbolism),[69] his book is more properly understood as prophecy, written up in 'apocalyptic' mode.[70]

Interpretation and purpose

The history of the interpretation of the book of Revelation reveals something of the open nature of the book. It has generated a constellation of interpretative strategies and elicited a wide range of meanings.[71] From Hippolytus's *Christ and Anti-Christ* to the Left Behind novels, many have seen it as offering a timetable, a road map towards the 'end times'. From as early as the second century there has been a steady stream of 'millennialist' interpreters who saw the book as prophesying a concrete 'new world' very like the present one, only with evil, sin, and death banished. This kind of approach was taken by Papias, Cerinthus, Justin Martyr, and Tertullian. The first actual commentary on Revelation, that of Victorinus in the third century, was also millennial (in other words, believing that Jesus would reign on earth for a thousand years). On the other hand, there have always been interpreters who have understood the book to be figurative, symbolic, and thus inviting allegorical interpretation.

---

68 Tr. M. F. Bird.
69 See Bauckham 1993b, 38–91; Aune 1997–8, 1.lxxxii–xc; Collins 2016, 338–50.
70 Aune (1997–8, 1.lxxxix–xc) calls Revelation a 'prophetic apocalypse' and Beale (1999, 38) says: 'John combines an epistolary form together with the apocalyptic-prophetic style.' Note also the observation of J. J. Collins (2015, 6–7): 'To say that a text is an apocalypse is not to exclude the possibility that it may be simultaneously something else; or to put it another way, the fact that a text can be profitably grouped with apocalypses does not exclude the possibility that it may be also profitably grouped with other texts for different purposes.'
71 See Koester 2014, 27–65; Kovacs and Rowland 2004.

Jaume Huguet's painting of St Michael vanquishing the antichrist reveals scriptural imagination of the fifteenth century, c. 1455–1460, National Art Museum of Catalonia, Barcelona.
PD-US

Debates about its interpretation go back to at least third-century Egypt, where Nepos argued for a 'Jewish' and 'literal' interpretation, while in response Dionysius commended what he thought was a deeper and more considered allegorical appropriation.[72] Others again—one thinks here of John Calvin, who wrote commentaries on all the books of the New Testament *except* Revelation—are honest enough to confess to being straightforwardly confounded as to what the book is about. To look at it positively, the multiple ways the book has been received and interpreted around the world proves just how rich and powerful the text is, and how many ways it can resonate with readers in diverse cultural contexts.[73]

Four major approaches to the interpretation of the book of Revelation have emerged down the years.[74]

First, there are *preterist* perspectives. These look for a specific fulfilment of the prophecies of the book in actual events that have now already happened, with some fixing on the events leading up to the fall of Jerusalem in AD 70 and others supposing that fulfilment came in the fourth-century collapse of the pagan Roman empire and its Christianization under Constantine. This view certainly appears to make Revelation relevant to the immediate circumstances of its early readers, but it appears to make it much less relevant to subsequent generations, including our own. And, as many have noted, even Constantine's Christian empire does not look exactly like the new heavens and new earth promised in Revelation 21—22.

Second, there are *historicist* approaches.[75] By this scholars have meant that Revelation was predicting the entire course of subsequent world history, including things

---

72 Eus. *Hist. Eccl.* 3.24–5.
73 See Rhoads 2005.
74 See Beale 1999, 44–9; deSilva 2009, 2–6.
75 The words 'historicist' and 'historicism' are used in many different ways, but this is how the view here described is often labelled.

826 The Early Christians and the Mission of God

like the rise of the Goths, the Arabs, the Mongols, the medieval papacy, Napoleon, Hitler, and the Soviet Union. This has the opposite problem to the preterist interpretation: instead of the book being relevant to early readers but to nobody else, these readings make it sporadically relevant from time to time in subsequent history while making it hard to see what its first readers were supposed to think of it. Such readings have proved a happy hunting-ground for various small groups who have managed to interpret this or that passage in specific reference to their own localized situation.

Third, there are *futurist* perspectives. This is like the 'historicist' reading, with Revelation predicting long-range future events, except that the 'history' in question only begins in what, for us, is the 'modern' period. Revelation is thus seen as primarily predicting distant future events, usually transpiring in the twentieth or twenty-first century, such as the rise of the European Union, the establishment of the modern state of Israel, the United Nations, and the World Council of Churches, and the emergence of Saddam Hussein, or even Al Qaeda and ISIS. Interpreters of this type usually understand the letters to the seven churches in Revelation 2—3 allegorically, as temptations faced by the church in every age, and then treat the visions of Revelation 6—19 as a literal and linear series of events, complete with the 'rapture', the 'tribulation', and the 'millennium' that is to take place on the eve of the world's end. The problem here is that interpreters fail to grasp the rhetorical and symbolic nature of apocalyptic discourse, and frequently display a highly parochial and provincial interpretative strategy, supposing that world history is all about themselves.

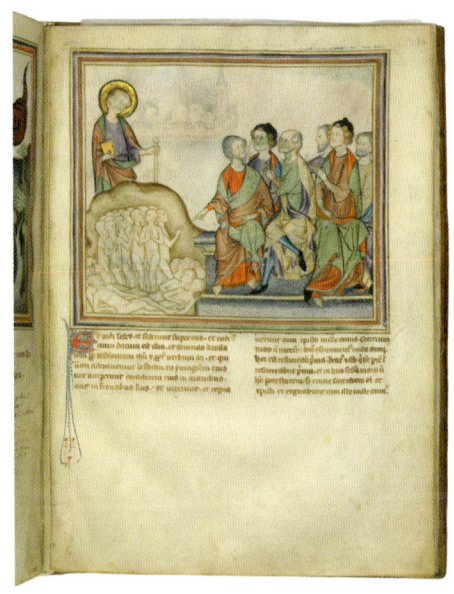

Vivid depiction of the first resurrection from the French illuminated book, *The Cloisters Apocalypse*, f. 34 r., c. 1330, Metropolitan Museum of Art, New York
Public Domain

Fourth, there are *idealist* interpretations.[76] These regard Revelation as a multi-layered symbolic portrayal of the conflict taking place between the kingdom of God and the kingdoms of this world in the time between the victory of Jesus on the cross and his final return. This generalized account leaves room for various

---

[76] Again, the word 'idealist' carries a great many possible connotations, but is used here simply as a convenient label for the view described.

kinds of allegorical and symbolic understandings of the theological, spiritual, and political realities of the whole period. What can be lost with this approach, however, is the sense of imminence. John insists that he is talking about things that will happen 'soon'.

The best course seems to be an eclectic approach to the interpretation of Revelation. We must insist that the book would have been highly relevant to its first readers (who lived in a culture where this kind of book was much better known than it has been in the modern period). There were specific challenges and Revelation was written to meet them; we should not regard the problems facing the seven churches, or the letters addressed to them, as other than specific words to specific situations (though of course with multiple subsequent resonances). At the same time the book clearly envisages an eventual triumph over all the powers of evil including death itself, which, as with Romans 8 or 1 Corinthians 15, has clearly not happened yet. The preterist and the futurist views thus both have something going for them, but not everything. At the same time, as with biblical prophecy more generally, the rich symbolic language invites multiple 'applications' and 'interpretations' as the various systems of pagan power behave in characteristic ways and the church is faced with the challenge both of understanding what is happening and acting appropriately. One should, in fact, read Revelation with a robust biblical-theological perspective in mind, ready to engage simultaneously with the concrete historical life of the church in first-century Asia Minor and with the challenges posed for God's people by the worldviews, and world events, of our own day.

John the Seer's apocalypse is designed to be highly affective, not just by stirring the emotions, but in challenging and reshaping the audience's imagination. The book is designed to inspire its readers to reaffirm their allegiance to God and his Messiah, and in that light to praise the faithful, shame the wicked, and steel the resolve of the churches to resist the monstrous and idolatrous Roman power. John intends to call out lukewarm faith and acculturation, and above all to urge his hearers to persevere in the faith despite suffering. It is those who 'overcome' who will receive the crown of life. To achieve this end, Revelation uses vivid imagery to describe a cosmic conflict, layered with symbolism, dripping with biblical allusions, and replete with local knowledge. A. D. Callahan writes:

> The auditors who came together to hear the Apocalypse were summoned to a transformative experience. Those first ancient auditors of the Apocalypse came together not merely to be informed, but to be transformed, to undergo a collective change in consciousness, an aspiration that makes modern individual and group reading practices trivial by comparison, with the possible exception of the reading of wills. Reading the Apocalypse aloud, and hearing the Apocalypse read aloud, was effectual: through exhortations and exclamations, threat and

thunder, the reading of the Apocalypse moved its hearers, affected them; the text *did* something to them.[77]

The author is not trying to console his audience with the truth that all is well in heaven and one day all will be blissful on earth. Rather, he is calling them to believe and behave in the light of the triumph of the 'lamb' and the coming redemptive judgment of God. He reassures readers, but also calls them to repent if they have compromised with false teaching or consorted with the beast and its agents. John's descriptions of his own visions are designed to recast the church's vision of God and the world by seeing them in the light of the 'divine actions above, within, and beneath the surface of history's tapestry'.[78]

THE STORY OF THE BOOK OF REVELATION

(See box: 'Outline of the book of Revelation'.)

1. Prologue (1.1–3)

The first line designates the book as 'the revelation of Jesus Christ' (see box: 'The title of the book'). The word *apocalypsis* means the *unveiling* of a hitherto unknown transcendent reality. Jesus is both the author and content of this unveiling, which pertains to events which 'must soon take place'. The order of the transmission of the revelation depicted here runs:

God ⟶ Jesus Christ ⟶ angel ⟶ John ⟶ servants of God

As a prophet-servant of God, John had a vision; he now provides a 'testimony' to what he saw, which is no less than 'the word of God' and the 'testimony of Jesus'.

> **OUTLINE OF THE BOOK OF REVELATION**[*]
>
> 1. Prologue (1.1–3)
> 2. Opening greetings, doxology, and oracle (1.4–8)
> 3. John's vision of the son of man (1.9–20)
> 4. Letters to the seven churches (2.1—3.22)
> 5. John's visions of the heavenly thrones (4.1—5.14)
> 6. The seven seals (6.1—8.5)
> 7. The seven trumpets (8.6—11.19)
> 8. The dragon, the beast, and the church (12.1—15.4)
> 9. The seven bowls (15.5—16.21)
> 10. Babylon the whore (17.1—19.10)
> 11. The open heaven and the new Jerusalem (19.11—21.8)
> 12. The bride of the lamb (21.9—22.9)
> 13. Epilogue (22.10–21)
>
> ---
>
> * There is considerable debate over the structure of the book of Revelation, particularly pertaining to the organization of the cycles of visions in Rev. 6—19. Debate focuses on whether the various visions, with their seals, trumpets, and bowls, are meant to be taken in a linear and successive fashion, or whether there is a series of recapitulations and rehearsals. Are there any interludes or overlaps? See discussion in Bauckham 1993b, 1–37; Aune 1997–8, 1.xc–cv; Beale 1999, 108–51.

---

77 Callahan 1995, 460 (italics original).
78 Witherington 2003, 15.

> ### THE TITLE OF THE BOOK
>
> In most early manuscripts, the title of the book is simply 'Revelation of John' (*Apokalypsis Iōannou*), but in later witnesses there are manifold varieties of, and expansions to, the title. The longest and most descriptive title comes from a manuscript housed at Mount Athos, numbered 1775, which reads: 'The Revelation of the all-glorious Evangelist, bosom-friend [of Jesus], virgin, beloved to Christ, John the theologian, son of Salome and Zebedee, but adopted son of Mary the Mother of God, and Son of Thunder.'*
>
> ---
>
> * Metzger 1994, 729.

Added to that is a benediction, the first of several, indicating that John expects the readers and auditors of this prophecy to be blessed if they adhere to its message (evidently it was to be read out in corporate worship). They must do so because 'the time is near': many of the events displayed here will soon come to pass.

2. Opening greetings, doxology, and oracle (1.4–8)

John, writing this 'letter', designates himself as the author and greets the 'seven churches of the province of Asia' (as in chapters 2 and 3). The greeting comes from the triune God himself: throughout the book Jesus the Messiah is the mediator of divine testimony, pre-eminent in the new creation, and supreme over the kings who conspire against God's reign (1.4–5a). John refers to the spirit dramatically in terms of *seven* spirits, reflecting the number of perfection. God's gospel of love has rescued people from sin, to make them 'priests' and 'kings' (see Ex. 19.5; Rev. 5.10; 20.6). The church, like the 'son of man' and his people in Daniel 7.14, 27, are destined to hold dominion in a transformed world-order. Christ is the Passover lamb whose love and sacrifice brings about a new exodus and a reordering of power in heaven and earth where the church has a royal and priestly vocation (1.5b–6).[79] John adds two prophetic oracles, rooted in scripture, highlighting respectively the vindication of Jesus and the overall sovereignty of God (1.7–8).

3. John's vision of the son of man (1.9–20)

John's opening vision, constituting his prophetic commission, came to him when in a spirit-given ecstasy on the lord's day.[80] A loud voice told him to write an account of what he saw and send it to the seven churches (1.9–11). When he 'turned to see the voice', he saw the glorified Christ, whom he describes in language drawn from Daniel 7.9, 13 and 10.5–6: 'one like a son of man' standing among 'seven golden lampstands', recalling the seven-branched lampstand in the Temple.[81] The figure is majestic, both royal and divine, and John falls at his feet; but Jesus tells him not to be afraid, and commissions him as his messenger. The words 'Do not be afraid, I am the first and the last' echo Isaiah's strongly monotheistic vision of

---

[79] Bauckham 2001, 1290.
[80] On the visions experienced by Christian leaders, see Ac. 10.10; 16.9; 2 Cor. 12.2–3.
[81] See Ex. 25.31–40; Zech. 4.2.

God (see e.g. Isa. 41.10–14; 43.1; 44.6; 48.12) and the identification of God as 'Alpha and Omega' in Revelation itself (see Rev. 1.8). Christ therefore 'shares in the power, the rule, the glory, and the being of the one true God'.[82]

4. Letters to the seven churches (2.1—3.22)

The letters to the seven churches are prophetic oracles of paraenesis (advice, counsel), praise, and rebuke. They follow the general pattern of: (1) a command to write to 'the angel' of a given church (that is, its angelic representative); (2) a pronouncement formula, 'Thus says' (Greek *tade legei*, sometimes rendered 'These are the words of'), combined with a self-description by Christ,

The son of man and the seven lampstands from *Bamberger Apocalypse*, c. 1000
Public Domain

drawn mostly from imagery already given in Revelation 1.16–20; (3) a statement of something Christ knows about the church, generating particular exhortations, commendations, and/or accusations, all in the light of Christ's *parousia*;[83] (4) a command to heed what the spirit is saying to the churches; and (5) a promise of deliverance, made to 'the one who overcomes'. Most of the letters draw on local circumstances peculiar to each region, though the connections are not always certain.[84]

The letter to the Ephesians (2.1–7) commends the church for endurance and the non-tolerance of wicked and deceitful persons. But Christ rebukes them for forsaking their first love.

The Smyrneans (2.8–11) are characterized by social poverty, perhaps because they refused to partake in commerce tainted with idolatry; but they are spiritually rich. They are involved in sectarian tensions with local Jewish groups, who 'denounce' the church to the local authorities for not worshipping the local gods or the emperor. By calling them a 'synagogue of Satan', John indicates that these Jewish leaders have become 'accusers', siding with Roman idolatry against the Messiah's people.[85] This will lead to suffering, but the Smyrnean Christians must remain faithful.

---

[82] Koester 2001b, 54.
[83] Bauckham 2001, 1291.
[84] See Hemer 1986; Thompson 1990, 95–167.
[85] Bauckham 2001, 1291.

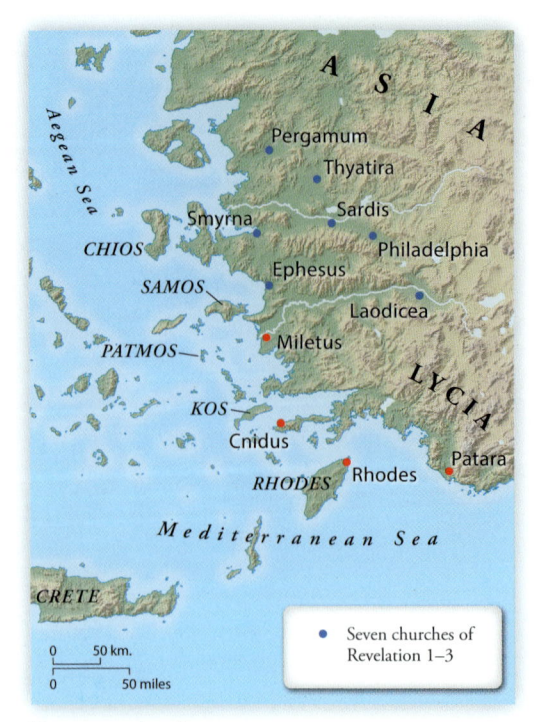

The seven churches

Jesus addresses the Pergamum church (2.12–17) from his position as the one bearing a 'sharp, double-edged sword', symbolizing his role as judge. The church has remained true, right there where the satan is enthroned (referring to the Altar of Zeus and the imperial cult). But there is false teaching and immoral practice in the church, and its members must repent. Paul had permitted believers to eat idol-food, as long as it did not offend a fellow-believer and was not consumed in a pagan temple.[86] John (perhaps following the apostolic letter of Acts 15.20, 29) took a harder line, forbidding the consumption of any meat associated with pagan sacrifices, and regarding it as a form of spiritual adultery. Whereas some, the 'Jezebel' of Thyatira and the 'Nicolaitans' of Pergamum, were attempting to secure the participation of Christians in social and economic life (see 'Portals and parallels: imperial hymns in Pergamum'), for John, true faithfulness requires the churches to adopt a separatist disposition.[87] If the believers in Pergamum avoid idol-food, they will be given 'hidden manna' and a 'white stone' with a new name written on it, that is, nourishment and protection.

The church in Thyatira (2.18–29) is praised for many virtues, but scolded for tolerating immorality, represented by the figure of 'Jezebel'.[88] As Stuckenbruck observes: 'For John the influence of Jezebel within the Christian community is the microcosm of a *porneia* that is taking place on a grander scale in the Roman Empire.'[89] Those who resist such idolatry, a spiritual and political form of *porneia*, are promised a share in the Messiah's worldwide rule, as in Psalm 2.

The church in Sardis (3.1–6) has a history of good deeds, but is in spiritual torpor. The believers there need to wake up and change their 'dirty clothes' for clean ones. The lord is coming like a thief in the night and they must be ready.[90] The book of life will contain the names of those who 'conquer'.[91]

---

86 1 Cor. 8.4–13; 10.14–33; Rom. 14.6, 21.
87 Stuckenbruck 2003, 1542.
88 1 Kgs. 16.21; 2 Kgs. 9.22.
89 Stuckenbruck 2003, 1542.
90 See Mt. 24.42–44; Lk. 12.39–40; 1 Thess. 5.2; 2 Pet. 3.10; Rev. 16.15.
91 Rev. 3.5; 13.8; 17.8; 20.12, 15; 21.27.

The letter to the church in Philadelphia (3.7–13) stresses Jesus' messianic authority as the one who holds the all-powerful 'key of David'.[92] The Philadelphians are faithful yet weakened through opposition from a local synagogue. Jesus offers them a door into his presence, reversal of status from marginalization to vindication, and defence in the coming trial.

The Laodicean letter (3.14–22) is perhaps the most famous of all. Laodicea was a prosperous church, yet riches had corrupted the believers. Whereas the nearby cities of Hierapolis and Colossae were known for hot springs and cold fresh water respectively, the Laodicean water, half way between, was known for its tepid temperature. The Laodiceans are like that: spiritually lukewarm. Jesus is nauseated by them. He is knocking on their door, offering them close mealtime fellowship. If they accept the offer and overcome, they will share his throne, just as Jesus shares the father's throne. The reference to thrones points ahead to the dramatic visions which now follow.

5. John's visions of the heavenly thrones (4.1—5.14)

John is now granted access into the divine throne-room in heaven itself. He is not, as some have supposed, looking into the ultimate future; contrast this vision with that in chapters 21 and 22. Rather, he is glimpsing what is going on in God's presence throughout the present time. God is on the throne, surrounded by twenty-four elders, seven spirits of God, and four living creatures (4.1–8a). They are perpetually worshipping the one on the throne: the creatures praise the holy God, and the elders give the reason: *because* he created all things (4.8b–11). Whatever is happening with God's people on earth, this praise continues perpetually. The apparent tension emerges in chapter 5: God's purposes cannot go forward, because there is no human being to act on God's behalf to rescue the human race and so get the project of creation itself back on track. The 'lion of Judah', however, who is also the

---

> **PORTALS AND PARALLELS: IMPERIAL HYMNS IN PERGAMUM**
>
> *The cities of Asia would celebrate and worship the imperial family in a number of ways, often with festivals, featuring singing, feasting, and merriment. Those who did not turn up to sing, cheer, eat, and make merry would have been noticeable by their absence, and would eventually have aroused suspicions about their loyalty and devotion to the local deities and the imperial regime. One inscription from Pergamum reads:*
>
>> Since one should each year make clear display of one's piety and of all holy, fitting intentions towards the imperial house, the choir of all Asia, gathering at Pergamum on the most holy birthday of Sebastos Tiberius Caesar god, performs a task that contributes greatly to the glory of Sebastos in hymning the imperial house and performing sacrifices to the Sebastan gods and conducting festivals and feasts . . .*
>
> * Cited in Price 1984, 105.

---

92 Taken from Isa. 22.22–23.

'lamb of God', has won the victory over the dark powers. A new song emerges from the assembled company, whose ranks then vastly swell: blessing, honour, glory, and power belong to the one on the throne, and the lamb. Jesus, the lion-lamb, Israel's Messiah, the true man, shares the worship which belongs uniquely and exclusively to the one creator God.[93]

6. The seven seals (6.1—8.5)

The scroll has seven seals which the 'lamb' must now undo. The first four release four riders, bringing judgment in the shape of conquest, deadly warfare, famine, and multifarious forms of death (6.1–8). Breaking the fifth seal brings forth cries from the martyrs, longing for vindication in the form of divine retribution. The sixth seal, when broken, unleashes portents of destruction, from which people try to hide. The warning is clear: God will avenge his people (6.9–17).

Before the seventh seal comes an interlude, hinting at an explanation for why God's judgments have been held back. God's servants must first be protected from disaster and are presented as a kind of messianic army. The number of 144,000 from the twelve tribes is symbolic for the church as the continuing expression of Israel (7.1–8). They are joined by a vast uncountable throng, consisting of all the martyrs now promised the healing and consoling divine presence (7.9–17).

Then at last the seventh seal is broken. After a time of silence (a sign of God's presence),[94] seven angels are given trumpets to blow to unleash judgments. At the same time, another angel, at the altar in the heavenly temple, is dispersing incense, symbolizing the prayers of God's people and God's startling purposes (8.1–5).

7. The seven trumpets (8.6—11.19)

In Jewish tradition trumpet blasts often mean impending judgment.[95] Here the trumpet blasts unleash various portents and manifestations of divine judgment. John has in mind the exodus, preceded by the 'plagues' on the Egyptians (Ex. 7—12): he sees the Passover-like rescue of God's people preceded by similar judgment against the world's inhabitants. This parallel, and other features, indicates that though John describes the events in a linear sequence, they are to be seen as concurrent and overlapping judgments (8.6–12).

The next three trumpets are distinguished from the first four as 'woes'. They signal an attack not just on people's habitations but on the people themselves. John the Seer describes seeing a falling star, a destroying angel, who opens the Abyss, a vat of

---

[93] Bauckham (2001, 1293) says: 'This heavenly worship before the throne is an unequivocal indication of the inclusion of Christ in the identity of the one God who, for Jewish and Christian faith, is alone entitled to worship.'
[94] See Hab. 2.20; Zech. 2.13.
[95] See Ex. 19.16–19; Amos 3.6; Zeph. 1.15–16.

834 The Early Christians and the Mission of God

supernatural evil. From the Abyss rises toxic smoke and an army, described as locusts (see again Ex. 10.1–6). The angel's name is given as 'Apollyon', the destroyer (8.13—9.12). The sixth trumpet brings further plagues of destruction, unleashing an army of 200 million cavalry troops from the River Euphrates. This image plays on the Roman fear of a massive Parthian invasion from the east; the description of the army as exuding fire, smoke, and sulphur indicates its demonic origin. The onslaught is another opportunity to repent from various practices—murder, magic, perversion, and theft—which all follow from not worshipping the true God (9.13–21).

Just as there was an interlude between the sixth and the seventh seal, so now there is another interlude between the sixth and the seventh trumpets. First, John receives a renewed commission (10.1–11). Second, in the scroll he is given, there is a metaphorically charged account of the church as witness to the Roman empire and its preservation despite its hostility. John is told to measure the temple and altar of God (here symbolizing the church), even while gentiles trample its outer court and the holy city (11.1–2). Just as Ezekiel's measuring of his visionary temple was a way of marking out God's intended dwelling-place (Ezek. 40—42; see Zech. 2.1–5), so John's marking out of this human temple signals that God intends to come and dwell with his people, as indeed in the climactic chapter 21. The two witnesses who prophesy about this (11.3–14) are perhaps an echo of Moses and Aaron, confronting Pharaoh, as well as of Zechariah 4.11–14. Their invincible testimony, suffering, and vindication mirror the whole narrative of Revelation. As Bauckham comments:

> This is the heart of the revelation contained in the scroll, the heart of Revelation's message: that the church redeemed from all nations is called to suffering witness which, by virtue of its participation in Jesus' sacrificial witness, can bring the nations to repentance of idolatry and conversion to the true God. In this way—as Jesus' witness is extended universally in the life and death, as well as the preaching, of the church—God's kingdom can come to the nations as salvation, rather than judgement [11.1–14].[96]

The seventh trumpet, blown at last (11.15), leads to praise and thanksgiving in heaven: the division between God's kingdom and worldly kingdoms has been dissolved. God's rule and wrath have pacified the angry nations, judgment has begun, and the heavenly temple is open to view, however dangerously (11.15–19).

8. The dragon, the beast, and the church (12.1—15.4)

If the first half of the book (broadly speaking) is focused on the seven trumpets, a similar role is given in the second half to the seven 'plagues' (once again, echoing

---

[96] Bauckham 2001, 1296.

PORTALS AND PARALLELS: FALLEN ANGELS

Several Jewish sources interpret and expound Genesis 6.1–4 by narrating how angels left their heavenly abode to take human women as wives and to have children with them.[*] *It is these evil angels who are often regarded as the progenitors of evil in the world. One document that takes this approach is* 1 Enoch, *which, in its* Book of Watchers *(1 En. 1—36), has the following account:*

> In those days, when the children of man had multiplied, it happened that there were born unto them handsome and beautiful daughters. And the angels, the children of heaven, saw them and desired them; and they said to one another, 'Come, let us choose wives for ourselves from among the daughters of man and beget us children.' And Semyaz, being their leader, said unto them, 'I fear that perhaps you will not consent that this deed should be done, and I alone will become (responsible) for this great sin.' But they all responded to him, 'Let us all swear an oath and bind everyone among us by a curse not to abandon this suggestion but to do the deed.' Then they all swore together and bound one another by (the curse). And they were altogether two hundred; and they descended into 'Ardos, which is the summit of Hermon. (1 En. 6.1–6 [OTP])

---

[*] See Stuckenbruck 2017, 1–34.

---

the original exodus). Between these is a bridging narrative, central to the book, which provides a rhetorically charged depiction of the insidious and demonic power of Rome as it threatens the church.

The first phase in that sequence is a symbolic nativity scene (12.1–6). This evokes Jewish traditions about Leviathan and fallen angels, as well as the mythic tale of how Apollo killed a python for stalking his mother while she was pregnant with him. The episode features the people of Israel and/or the messianic community, described as a woman who is about to give birth to the messianic son who will rule over the nations. Opposing the woman is a seven-headed red dragon, the satan, who conspires to destroy the child the moment he is born. However, the child is snatched away to God's throne while the woman is taken to a deserted place to be cared for.

A war then rages in heaven between the archangel Michael with his angels against the dragon and his angels (12.7–18). The dragon and his minions are expelled to the earth where they will lead the whole world astray (see 'Portals and parallels: fallen angels'). The heavenly community celebrates the victory (12.10) which must then be worked out in the suffering and endurance of the church.

The dragon was left on the shore of the sea—the sea symbolizing the untamed power of chaos and evil (12.18). John then describes (13.1–10) a beast coming out of the sea; it is in fact a kind of super-beast, combining the features from Daniel's four monsters.[97] The beast—obviously Rome and its empire—is given authority by the satan, and is revered and worshipped by the whole world. Like Daniel's fourth beast, this one utters blasphemies, and makes war on the saints; its apparently fatal wound, now healed, is reminiscent of what many thought happened to Nero. There is

---

[97] Stuckenbruck 2003, 1555.

then a second beast, 'from the land', also called the 'false prophet'; this seems to be the local priesthoods of the imperial cult, the civic elites who enforce Rome's will. If the first beast is a parody of Christ (died and returned to life), then the second beast is a parody of the spirit-led prophetic witness of the church (leading worship, doing miracles).[98] The mark of the beast, which people need in order to buy and sell things, is again a parody of God's sealing the foreheads of faithful believers.[99] The number of the beast is '666',[100] and the number is the calculation (by the letter–number method called 'gematria') either of the Greek word for 'beast' when transliterated into Hebrew, or of the name 'Nero Caesar' written in Hebrew (13.11–18).[101]

John then depicts the redeemed saints, again described as an army of 144,000 (see 7.4–12), ready to do battle against the beast, emphasizing their purity and moral fitness. The holy army is accompanied by three angels who warn the people of the earth to repent of worshipping the beast. The beast will face formidable judgment, while those who die resisting are promised a blessed rest (14.1–13). The nations thus stand on the crest of either salvation (symbolized by a harvest) or judgment (symbolized by a wine press). The angels gather together a harvest of the faithful and inflict a punitive pressing of the wicked (14.14–20).

Silver tetradrachma minted in Asia Minor during reign of Domitian, with image of the emperor
Todd Bolen / BiblePlaces.com

This brings John to the seven plagues, the final elements of God's wrath. The judgment on the 'Egypt' of the world is balanced by the new 'victory song', corresponding to the song of Moses and Miriam in Exodus 15 (15.1–4).[102]

9. The seven bowls (15.5—16.21)

The third and final cycle of seven judgments is now expressed in the form of seven bowls of wrath, again largely echoing the plagues in Egypt.[103] The judgments are partly punitive and partly aimed at driving people to repentance,[104] and to

---

98 Bauckham 2001, 1298.
99 Rev. 7.3; 14.1.
100 In some manuscripts, the number of the beast is '616'.
101 On '666', see Koester (2014, 538–40, 597–9) who sides with most in seeing Nero as the referent, and Beale (1999, 718–25) who sees the number as symbolizing how the beast and its followers fall short of the 777 that would symbolize God's perfect creative purposes for humanity. This would mean that the symbolism could be regularly reapplied to tyrants in every age.
102 Ex. 15.1–17; Dt. 32.4; Pss. 86.9; 98.2; 111.2–3; Jer. 10.7.
103 Ex. 7–10 and see earlier Rev. 8.12—9.12.
104 Rev. 9.20–21; 16.9, 11.

worship the God who is just and true;[105] but their effect is to make people curse God.[106] The catastrophes then become more complete and even climactic.

The first four bowls are poured out on the various spheres of creation: land, sea, waterways, and heavens. These directly affect the worshippers of the beast. The fifth bowl attacks the very throne of the beast, plunging his kingdom into darkness (15.5—16.9). The sixth bowl, only indirectly a form of judgment, dries up the River Euphrates, so that armies from the east (namely Parthia, Arabia, and India) can easily manoeuvre to join the beast and defeat the returning Jesus at 'Armageddon'. The dragon, beast, and false prophet are thus allied with the eastern armies, and unleash a trio of evil spirits to deceive and direct the kings of the world (16.12–16). The seventh bowl, completing the judgment, falls massively on 'Babylon the Great'.

10. Babylon the whore (17.1—19.10)

The fall of Babylon (that is, Rome) is now narrated at length. This is where John the Seer comes closest to the normal 'apocalyptic' genre in which an angel interprets visions. Babylon is pictured as a woman—a whore, in fact—who rides on the beast: Rome's economic power depends on its military power. She is like a rich courtesan who exploits her clients and enriches herself, just as Rome does with its own client-kingdoms. The vision causes John great anxiety, and the angel explains the nature of the beast. The beast is both a parody of God (who was, and is, and is to come), since the beast 'once was, now is not, and yet will come'.[107] This appears to be based on the legend that Nero would return from the east with the Parthian armies to wreak vengeance on Rome. Nero belongs to the seven previous emperors mentioned in Revelation 17.10, but he is also—truly or typologically—the eighth still to come, the climax to all their evil. John the Seer thus splices together the propaganda of Roman invincibility and the fear of an eventual eastern conqueror. In the end, the beast with its client kings will make war against the lamb; Rome and its allies will persecute the church; but they will be defeated by the Messiah because of his superior might as 'Lord of lords and King of kings' (17.7–18).

Babylon's demise is heralded by an angel coming down from heaven. The declarations of destruction are modelled on prophetic

Nero
Gordon Franz

---

105 Stuckenbruck 2003, 1559.
106 Rev. 16.9, 11, 21.
107 See Rev. 1.4, 8; 4.8.

denunciations of Babylon and Tyre.[108] John portrays Rome as the epitome of evil empires and, like them, as subject to divine judgment. Accordingly: 'OT Babylon prefigures Rome's political supremacy and oppression, but OT Tyre prefigures Rome's economic power and oppression.'[109] The nations and kings of the earth have committed adultery with a city that is demonic and defiled (18.1–4).

A voice from heaven, echoing the instruction to God's people to leave Babylon in Isaiah 52.11–12, exhorts God's people to get out of 'Babylon' lest they share in its sins and the coming torture, grief, death, mourning, famine, and fire that will result. This is John's way of warning Christians to avoid not only Rome's idolatry but also spiritual idolatry by not embedding oneself in Rome's oppressive, exploitive, and idolatrous system of economic power. The fall of Babylon is grievous to the kings of the earth, the merchants, and the sea captains who had enriched themselves through Babylon's luxury and opulence. The church can rejoice because Babylon has been judged for the way it mistreated the saints, apostles, and prophets (18.5–20).

An angel now throws a boulder into the sea (the place of chaos) as a symbol for the downfall of Babylon. The daily life of Babylon, its labour, love, and leisure, is coming to an end. The seer here provides the most formidable indictment of Roman power anywhere in ancient literature, exposing the repressive and self-serving nature of Rome's socio-economic system, the cruelty of its military power, and the falsehood of its propaganda about its own eternal invincibility. Rome had subjugated and suppressed nations and different groups, from Jews to Druids. It will be judged for 'all who have been slaughtered on the earth' (18.21–24).

The fall of Babylon occasions a multitude of voices in heaven to sing 'hallelujah' to God for his salvation, for condemning Babylon and avenging the blood of his servants. A further voice celebrates the arrival of God's sovereign rule and the wedding supper of the lamb (19.1–8). At this point, John—strangely—mistakes the angel speaking to him for God himself and begins to worship him but is duly rebuked. Only God can be worshipped (19.9–10).

11. The open heaven and the new Jerusalem (19.11—21.8)

John's vision takes us from Babylon to the new Jerusalem via Christ's *parousia* and the final judgment. This section could be aptly named, as it is by Stuckenbruck, 'The End of Evil'.[110] John sees 'heaven standing open' and he narrates Christ's return in terms of a divine warrior leading a heavenly army—probably the 'saints' as in Revelation 7.1–17; 14.1–5; 17.14—to make war on the nations who were seduced by the beast (19.11–16). An angel summons the faithful for a feast where kings and

---

108 See against Babylon (Isa. 13.1—14.23; 21.1–10; 47.1–15; Jer. 25.12–38; 50.1–46) and against Tyre (Isa. 23; Ezek. 26—28).
109 Bauckham 2001, 1301.
110 Stuckenbruck 2003, 1565.

> 'This portrait of God imposing eternal suffering seems as un-Christlike a punishment as imaginable. Yet John is dealing with the twin concepts of justice and mercy/grace. For him, one cannot exist without the other. For the evil that has been perpetrated, there needs to be justice, and he conceives of it in its most undiluted form as eternal suffering in the lake of fire and sulfur (brimstone). It is important to remember, however, that this is a figurative and not a literal "lake". What John is describing is not real, physical torture but the kind of continuous, perpetual spiritual torment that he imagines must occur when a being is separated forever from the presence of God.... He was trying to think of an image that would have "teeth" for them, an image that would shock persons who were accommodating to the draconian lordship demands of Rome into resisting them and testifying in word and deed to the lordship of God and the Lamb instead. He wanted them to fear being forever separated from the presence of God. His most forceful metaphorical attempt at conveying what that separation would feel like is the lake of fire and sulfur (brimstone). A twenty-first-century effort should focus on the language of separation from God's presence and look for a contemporary metaphor appropriate to that separation, one that does not include the image of physical torture, whether eternal or otherwise.'
>
> Brian Blount, *Revelation*, 371–2.

generals are the main course, a graphic if stomach-churning image for the defeat and subjugation of their foes. The actual battle scenes are not described. But the beast, the false prophet, and the kings are soundly defeated, with the first two being thrown into a 'fiery lake of burning sulphur', an obvious cipher for a punishment from which there will be no return (19.17–21). The point is that when God has finally dealt with evil it will have no chance to return, to spoil the renewed world he is now making.

Excursus: Revelation 20.1–10 and the millennium

Revelation 20 narrates the binding of the satan for a thousand years. During that time, resurrected martyrs will be reigning with Christ (20.1–6). The satan will then be released for a short while, ahead of his final defeat and destruction (20.7–10). All will be judged according to deeds (20.11–15). This passage has generated much discussion: is the millennium in Revelation 20.4–5 literal or figurative?[111] The case for a literal reading, and the case for reading this passage as a recapitulation of themes in the book, can be laid out in grid form (see text grid: 'Alternative ways to read Revelation').[112]

John goes on to describe the arrival of the new heavens and new earth, which takes the form of the new Jerusalem descending from heaven, described as a bride on her wedding day. Its arrival signals that God is truly, fully, and finally dwelling with his people. Just as the story of the original exodus ended with the construction of the tabernacle and the divine glory coming to dwell in it, so this new exodus finishes not with humans going up to heaven but with the God of heaven coming to earth.

---

[111] Contrast Witherington 2003, 239–52, and Beale 1999, 995–1021. Recommended also is Marshall 2000.
[112] See further Bird 2013d, 274–300.

ALTERNATIVE WAYS TO READ REVELATION

Literal reading	*Recapitulation reading*
(1) The sequence of Christ's return (Rev. 19.10–15), a preliminary judgment (Rev. 19.16–21), millennium (Rev. 20.1–6), final judgment (Rev. 20.7–15), and new heavens and new earth (Rev. 21.1—22.17), makes sense as a linear and literal reading. Such a reading is known as a 'chiliasm'.	(1) The defeat of God's enemies in Revelation 19.11–21 looks and sounds rather conclusive.
(2) The reference to a millennium belongs with other Jewish apocalypses that envision an earthly reign by a messianic figure in an interim kingdom ahead of a final consummation (*1 En.* 91.12–16; 93.12–17; *4 Ez.* 7.26–44; 12.31–4; *2 Bar.* 29.3–30.1; 40.1–4; 72.2–74.3; *Sib. Or.* 3.635–701).	(2) Revelation 20.1–10 is a *recapitulation* of an overall narrative featuring persecution and vindication and an *anticipation* of the new heavens and new earth. The proof is that (a) the narrative focuses exclusively on the martyrs and so rehearses earlier episodes where the martyrs enter into God's presence after a harrowing of opposition from Satan and the beast (see Rev. 7.14–17; 11.7–11; 12.1–17); and (b) the description of the heavenly city in Rev. 21.9—22.5 could easily describe something like this thousand years of reigning with Christ.
(3) It is problematic to take the first resurrection as spiritual (i.e. regeneration) and the second resurrection as literal (i.e. raised to immortal bodily life) since those who participate in this first resurrection, who reign in the millennium, do not participate in the resurrection of the rest at the end of the millennium.	(3) John's numbers are typically symbolic and we should expect the same here. We are cued to this by the mention of 'thrones', which echoes Daniel 7.9, and describes not a thousand-year reign on earth, but the heavenly reality where the martyred saints are already reigning with Christ. In other words, Revelation 21.4–6 is a narrativization of Ephesians 2.6/Colossians 3.1 about being seated with Christ as it applies to martyrs.
(4) Many of the early church Fathers, such as Papias, Melito of Sardis, Justin Martyr, Irenaeus, Tertullian, and others, were chiliasts. It was not really until after Constantine that amillennialism became popular; the church, now operating under the sponsorship of the empire, no longer looked forward to its overthrow.	(4) It is likely that John is adapting Jewish traditions pertaining to a temporary quarantining of evil and expectations of a messianic reign ahead of the final judgment and deploying them as a symbol for the vindication of the martyrs which Christ's return entails.

This will signal the end of suffering, and the old order of sin and death passing away. The abolition of 'the first heaven and the first earth' (21.1) does not mean that God will destroy the present space-time world and create a new one from scratch; the 'oldness' of the first heaven and earth consists precisely in their corruption, their subjection to decay and death (see Rom. 8.18–30). God now speaks directly from his throne, declaring that all things are made new (21.1–8).

12. The bride of the lamb (21.9—22.9)

One of the angels then shows John 'the bride, the wife of the Lamb' (21.9). We realize that the picture of the great whore, Babylon, was always a parody of the true 'city of God', just as the tower of Babel (Babylon) had been an arrogant human attempt to create a single worldwide community by human power alone when God's plan was to call Abraham and promise him that worldwide family by sheer grace. Thus, now, 'carried away in the Spirit', John beholds a great mountain with the new Jerusalem coming down out of heaven from God. The city is built around a series of twelves (that is, twelve gates, angels, foundations), symbolizing both the Israelite tribes and the apostles. The angel measures the city in front of John, and it turns out—as we might have guessed from the parallel towards the end of Ezekiel—that the whole new world is a vast temple, just as Genesis 1 was a 'temple', a heaven–earth construction with an 'image' at its heart. The city, at the heart of the new creation, is a giant cube, like the Holy of Holies in the original tabernacle and Temple. That is why, of course, the city has no temple: the Jerusalem Temple was always an advance signpost to God's new creation, just as the sun, the source of light and heat in the original creation, is no longer needed when the true light and life is visibly present in the form of the Lord God Almighty and the lamb. The city is both universal and accessible. The nations walk in its light, the gates are never shut, and the glory of the nations is brought into it. The city has nothing impure or shameful, but is filled with those whose names are written in the lamb's book of life (21.9–27).

The angel shows John a river of water of life—echoing the rivers flowing from Eden in Genesis 2—that flows from the throne of God and the lamb into the middle of the city. Abnormal water-flows were a feature in prophetic visions of Jerusalem's re-creation.[113] On each side of the river stands 'the tree of life', with supernatural fecundity; its leaves are for 'the healing of the nations'. All this results in the reversal of creation's curse; the luminous divine presence; the redeemed seeing the very face of God; and their active reign over God's new world (22.1–5).

John's interaction with the angel in Revelation 22.6–9 is similar to that in Revelation 19.9–10, where the concluding message about the destruction of one city (Babylon) has its sequel with a concluding message about the descent of the

---

113 Ezek. 47.1; Zech. 14.8.

heavenly city (New Jerusalem). The angel tells John that the visions he has received are 'trustworthy and true' and pertain to things 'that must soon take place'. John is once more tempted to worship the angel, and once more rebuked. Only God is to be worshipped (22.6–9).

13. Epilogue (22.10–21)

The epilogue draws together various diverse materials and motifs. First (and unlike Dan. 12.4) John is instructed not to seal up the words of prophecy, because the time is near, and its message must get out. There is still time for repentance, but those unwilling to hear will be hardened into their habits of wrong-doing (22.10–11). Jesus himself assures John that he is coming soon, and that he (like God himself earlier on) is 'Alpha and Omega' (1.8; 21.6; 22.12–13). The city's inhabitants will be pure; nothing impure can enter it (22.14–15). Jesus again assures John that the messages he has been given really are from him, the Davidic deliverer (22.16). The universal invitation then follows: as in Isaiah 55, all who are thirsty are to come to the living water, and the spirit and the bride—the church, inspired and indwelt by God's own spirit—pray 'Come' to the risen Jesus.[114]

John's vision of Christ in majesty, *The Silos Apocalypse*, Spain, 1091
© British Library Board. All Rights Reserved / Bridgeman Images

John then warns auditors and scribes not to add or take away anything from this book, lest plagues be added to them, or God take away their share in the tree of life and holy city (22.18–19). Jesus provides a final word of testimony: 'Yes, I am coming soon.' This has been repeated right across the final section (22.7, 12, 20), and John replies with the words 'Come, Lord Jesus', reflecting an early Aramaic prayer, *Maranatha*.[115] This leads to a final benediction (22.21).

REVELATION IN THE BIG PICTURE

The book of Revelation is hard to understand today. It is even harder to apply with exegetical understanding, theological acumen, and pastoral sensibility. The Geneva

---

114   Bauckham 2001, 1306.
115   See 1 Cor. 16.22; *Did.* 10.6.

Bible offers good advice for interpreters of this book: 'Read diligently; judge soberly and call earnestly to God for the true understanding hereof.' That's a good saying, well worth remembering. We can turn it into practical advice as follows.

First, remember that the book of Revelation is not a timetable for 'the end'. It is time to leave behind a tradition of preaching and teaching Revelation, still popular in some quarters, that involves conspiracy theories, obscure charts, and novels that are simply a kind of apocalyptic soap opera. There is something far more satisfying, stimulating, and edifying to offer our churches and their worshippers. John is holding out a new way of looking at reality, opening our imaginations to a divine perspective on past, present, and future. As Richard Bauckham says, Revelation is not an esoteric and encoded forecast of historical events, but a theocentric vision of the coming of God's universal kingdom. We appropriate this vision for our twenty-first-century context by remembering that there are many Babylons and beasts, and we need to resist them all. In fact,

> to resist idolatry in the world by faithful witness to the truth, the church must continuously purify its own perception of truth by the vision of the utterly Holy One, the sovereign Creator, who shares his throne with the slaughtered Lamb.[116]

That, as they say, will preach—though it will be demanding for preacher and hearers alike.

Second, John's apocalypse has powerful implications for configuring our own social and political engagement with the world. According to John, the church's task is to live as a prophetic witness to Jesus, summoning people to believe and follow him, speaking truth to power, and declaring the judgments of God against all wickedness. Not everyone likes to hear this kind of message. Some want us to believe that the state—particularly a modern democratic state—is now absolute. It is, for many, the bastion of our humanity, and all our lives should be oriented towards its workings and worship. There is nothing wrong with being a noble and active citizen, seeking the good of one's fellow-citizens and the wider world. Yet John calls us to resist and denounce as idolatrous any veneration of the state as god-like, any investing of all our hopes in its political vision, any praise to its leaders that would border on deification. The book of Revelation is, after all, subversive literature for a people with a message and mode of community that threatens the edifices of all the empires around us, be they pagan, plutocracies, politburos, or progressive regimes bent on eradicating religion. There is a reason why the Chinese communist government has banned the preaching of Revelation in the state-sanctioned Three-Self churches. The kingdom of God will one day dethrone and condemn the kingdoms of this world, including that regime.

---

[116] Bauckham 1993a, 162–3.

However, let us add an important qualification. Jesus Christ's kingdom is not destined to replace one malevolent empire with another, to supplant earthly Rome with a heavenly Rome, to install a Christianized Caesar or a Caesarized Christ. Constantinian 'Christendom' was not entirely bad, especially if the alternative was a cruel, heartless paganism. However, the Constantinization of the church, where religious authority was infused with political power, does seem to have been one of the most devastating things ever to happen to European Christianity. The church must hold on to its prophetic vocation to the establishment, not aspire to sink that vocation within an establishment that will muzzle or silence its voice. Accordingly, the church's task is not to bless or broker the empires of the world. Our task is to be faithful to the empire of Jesus, the kingdom of God. We are to consider our churches as the advance guard of that kingdom, and to do our best to prepare for the day when what Revelation says has already happened will become fully and finally true, and the kingdoms of this world will become the kingdom of our God and his Messiah.

Terracotta tomb plaque with Christogram and Latin inscription, *c.* 400–800
The Metropolitan Museum of Art

Third, the book of Revelation is obviously a warning to the churches about complacency and compromise, as well as an exhortation to endurance and to keep to the testimony of Jesus in a hostile environment. However, we should not forget how important the theme of God's glory is for the entire book, seen clearly in the throne scenes of Revelation 4—5, where we get a snapshot of the heavenly praise and a reminder as to why the 'lamb' is worthy of our worship. John's apocalypse has at its epicentre 'the glory due to God because he has accomplished full salvation and final judgment'.[117] That is why John's apocalypse is in a sense a commentary on his opening prayer:

> To him who loves us and has freed us from our sins by his blood, and has made us to be a kingdom and priests to serve his God and Father—to him be glory and power for ever and ever! Amen.[118]

---
117 Beale 1999, 171–2.
118 Rev. 1.5b–6.

There is the famous story of two Moravian missionaries who went to the Caribbean to share the gospel with African slaves on the plantations. Because it was illegal for white people to preach Christianity to the slaves—the European slave-owners evidently did not want their holdings corrupted with notions of 'redemption' or with the dangerous notion that 'in Christ there is neither slave nor free'—the two Moravians sold themselves into slavery so that they could preach to the slaves. The final words of the Moravian duo to their families as their ship headed out across the waters was, 'May the Lamb who was slain receive the reward of His suffering.' John the Seer would have understood, and applauded.

Further reading

Allen, Garrick V., Ian Paul, and Simon P. Woodman (eds.). 2015. *The Book of Revelation: Currents in British Research on the Apocalypse*. WUNT 2.411; Tübingen: Mohr Siebeck.

Bauckham, Richard. 1993. *The Climax of Prophecy: Studies in the Book of Revelation*. Edinburgh: T&T Clark.

———. 1993. *The Theology of the Book of Revelation*. NTT; Cambridge: Cambridge University Press.

———. 2001. 'Revelation.' In *The Oxford Bible Commentary*. Edited by J. Barton and J. Muddiman. Oxford: Oxford University Press, pp. 1287–1306.

Beale, Greg A. 1999. *The Book of Revelation*. NIGTC; Grand Rapids, MI: Eerdmans.

Blount, Brian K. 2009. *Revelation: A Commentary*. NTL; Louisville, KY: Westminster John Knox.

View of Patmos Island from the Monastery of Saint John
© Marlaine / Bigstock

Caird, George B. 1965. *A Commentary on the Revelation of St John the Divine*. London: A&C Black.
Collins, Adela Y. (ed.). 2017. *New Perspectives on the Book of Revelation*. BETL; Leuven: Peeters.
deSilva, David A. 2009. *Seeing Things John's Way: The Rhetoric of the Book of Revelation*. Louisville, KY: Westminster John Knox.
——. 2013. *Unholy Allegiances: Heeding Revelation's Warning*. Peabody, MA: Hendrickson.
Fee, Gordon D. 2011. *Revelation*. NCCS; Eugene, OR: Cascade.
Gorman, Michael. 2011. *Reading Revelation Responsibly: Uncivil Worship and Witness: Following the Lamb into the New Creation*. Eugene, OR: Cascade.
Koester, Craig R. 2001. *Revelation and the End of All Things*. Grand Rapids, MI: Eerdmans.
——. 2014. *Revelation: A New Translation with Introduction and Commentary*. AB; New Haven, CT: Yale University Press.
Morton, Russell S. 2014. *Recent Research on Revelation*. Sheffield: Sheffield Phoenix.
Rhoads, David (ed.). 2005. *From Every People and Nation: The Book of Revelation in Intercultural Perspective*. Minneapolis: Fortress.
Rowland, Christopher. 1982. *The Open Heaven: A Study of Apocalyptic in Judaism and Early Christianity*. London: SPCK.
Stuckenbruck, Loren T. 2003. 'Revelation.' In *Eerdmans Commentary on the Bible*. Edited by J. D. G. Dunn and J. W. Rogerson. Grand Rapids, MI: Eerdmans, pp. 1535–72.
Witherington, Ben. 2003. *Revelation*. NCBC; Cambridge: Cambridge University Press.
Wright, N. T. 2011. *Revelation for Everyone*. London: SPCK.
——. 2012. 'Revelation and Christian Hope: Political Implications of the Revelation of John.' In *Revelation and the Politics of Apocalyptic Interpretation*. Edited by R. B. Hays and S. Alkier. Waco, TX: Baylor University Press, pp. 105–24.

John 1.1–18, Codex Sinaiticus
© British Library Board. All Rights Reserved / Bridgeman Images

VIII

THE MAKING OF THE NEW TESTAMENT

Many early Christians were functionally illiterate, at least at the time of their conversion. Part of the glory of the gospel, however, is that it's for *everyone*, that there shouldn't be an elite who 'get it' while everybody else is simply going with the flow. So the leaders and teachers in the early church taught people to read, so that they could become thinking, reflective, contributing actors in the drama. The New Testament is indeed for everyone—which is why the first followers of Jesus were keen to translate the message into different languages, even if sometimes (as in Acts 2) the holy spirit found ways to bypass even that process.

In fact, in contrast with most cultures and religions in the ancient world (except perhaps Judaism), early Christianity was very much a *bookish* culture. Though we do indeed sometimes think of the movement as a 'religion', a first-century observer, blundering in to a meeting of Christians, would almost certainly have seen it first and foremost as some kind of educational institution, a kind of philosophical school in which prayer and worship happened to be central but didn't displace the sense of eager learning. This is the more remarkable in that education in that world was mostly reserved for the rich, for the elite.

What's more, the Christians were at the forefront of a new kind of book: the codex, with sheets stuck together something like a modern book. This quickly came to displace the scroll, which couldn't hold nearly as much, and which was hard to use, particularly to find different passages. The Christians in fact developed a kind of codex that was more user-friendly than previous types. They really did want everyone to be able to read these vital, life-giving early writings. Our task now, as we pull together the threads of this whole project, is to look at how that book was made (textual criticism), and how that book came to be seen as an authoritative collection (the canonization of the New Testament).

35

Introduction to Textual Criticism of the New Testament

There is nothing like the Greek New Testament to rejuvenate the world, which came out of the Dark Ages with the Greek New Testament in its hand. Erasmus wrote in the Preface to his Greek Testament about his own thrill of delight: 'These holy pages will summon up the living image of His mind. They will give you Christ Himself, talking, healing, dying, rising, the whole Christ in a word; they will give Him to you in an intimacy so close that He would be less visible to you if He stood before your eyes.' The Greek New Testament is the New Testament. All else is translations.[1]

CHAPTER AT A GLANCE

This chapter provides a brief overview of textual criticism of the New Testament.

By the end of this chapter you should be able to:

- grasp the basic features of textual criticism of the New Testament;
- understand why New Testament scholars might prefer some textual readings over others.

HOW WE GOT THE NEW TESTAMENT

In the ancient world, without the benefit of modern printing and computers, books were published by lone copyists, or sometimes by teams of scribes copying them out word by word. If you've ever copied out anything from a poem to a page of history, from a shopping list to a chapter from a textbook, you'll have noticed how easy it is for mistakes to creep in. The eye jumps to and fro, often leaping from a word at one point in a sentence to the same word later in the sentence and leaving out the bit in the middle, or perhaps going from the end of one line back to the start of the same line by mistake and so copying it out twice, and so on. Sometimes, if we know a similar poem already, we may instinctively

---

1 A. T. Robertson, cited in Porter 2013, 11.

adjust the one we're copying out so it's more like the one we know. Sometimes we may be startled by what the writer says or the way he or she says it, and try to smooth things out a bit. All of these things and many other similar problems were bound to creep in as the early Christians copied and recopied the New Testament. We have thousands of manuscripts of the New Testament, either as a whole or more often in parts. Actually there are far more early manuscripts of the New Testament than of any other books from the ancient world, including the works of Julius Caesar, Plato, Homer, or Virgil. Some of the greatest classical texts exist today only in one or two medieval copies, but for the New Testament there is so much early evidence it hurts. And it's no surprise that in many of those manuscripts there are slight, or even larger, variations. These variations have been studied intensively in the last two hundred years, as more and more manuscripts have come to light, and a whole careful science has been built up which we call 'textual criticism'. This scientific analysis of variations in the manuscripts is designed to get us back as close as we can, line after line and book after book, to what the original authors wrote. The good news is that the evidence for the New Testament as a whole is massively strong, and we can be quite sure that, despite lots of small-scale variations here and there, we are reading substantially what the writers intended us to read. But it's always worth checking things out in any given passage. Even when we are looking at something a later scribe has added or omitted by accident, what we are seeing is a slice of early-church history, a faithful and perhaps tired worker doing his or her laborious best to get the message through, so the next generation, too, can be drawn into worship and energized for mission.

Let us, then, look at this whole subject a little more closely. If you are reading this book, then you probably own a Bible, or at least have a Bible app on some electronic device. As we all know if we stop to think about it, the Bible did not fall out of the sky, accompanied by a chorus of angels, landing in your lap with its pristine leather-bound cover, with the words of Jesus in red, complete with introduction, charts, tables, cross-references, and study notes. Clearly that isn't how the Bible arrived.

No: your Bible came from a publisher. That publisher printed a particular English translation. That translation was based on the work of a translation committee (or perhaps a single translator) who worked with the New Testament in Greek and the Old Testament in Hebrew (and, for a few short passages, Aramaic), using what are called 'critical editions'. The word 'critical' here doesn't mean that the editors were criticizing what the Bible says. It refers to the way in which editors have studied the early manuscripts, noting the key places where they differ, and using scholarly historical judgment to figure out what was probably the original text.

Many critical editions of the Greek and Hebrew texts have been made since the Renaissance, based on the study of various manuscripts. (Prior to the Renaissance, the eastern churches used an early version of the Greek Bible and the western churches used the Latin Vulgate.) These manuscripts have been gradually discovered, collected, compiled, and compared ever since the start of the Christian movement, but more particularly over the last five hundred years. The manuscripts are housed in museums, libraries, institutes, and private collections all over the world. There are photos, microfilms, and digital copies of them, stored in places like the Institute for New Testament Textual Research in Münster, Germany (INTF), the Centre for the Study of New Testament Manuscripts in Dallas, Texas (CSNTM), and great libraries like the British Library, the Bodleian Library in Oxford, and the Vatican Library in Rome. Those manuscripts, some dating from as late as the middle ages, some as early as the second century, were copied by scribes based on even earlier manuscripts. Somewhere along the line these go back to a text whose original recipients decided to make it available (see Figure 10). This text itself is based on an original autograph composed by an author—though quite possibly written down by somebody else, as in the case of Paul whose letters were dictated to a scribe (see for example Rom. 16.22).

FIGURE 10: THE HISTORICAL STAGES IN THE PRODUCTION OF A MODERN ENGLISH BIBLE

English translation ⟶ translation committee ⟶ critical editions ⟶ manuscript collections ⟶ manuscripts ⟶ earlier manuscripts ⟶ authors

'Textual criticism' is therefore a kind of science, collecting data and trying to sort it out and explain it. This work includes the study of these ancient manuscripts, analysing their contents, provenance, and copyists, noting the similarities and differences between them (including different styles of handwriting), tracing the interrelationship between manuscripts, and identifying distinctive features in a manuscript, all with a view to establishing a 'critical text' that reflects, as best we can, the original autographs, or at least the earliest ascertainable form of the text. This chapter, therefore, includes a brief overview of textual criticism, and explains how the Greek New Testament text is compiled into critical editions from the various materials available.

THE GOAL OF TEXTUAL CRITICISM

Strange as it may sound, there is actually some debate as to what textual criticism should really be aiming at. The older view, that the point was to establish what the original author wrote, is challenged by some who regard that as difficult or even impossible, and perhaps not even desirable. Other tasks and possibilities are sometimes advocated.

For instance, David Trobisch considers one of the fundamental aims of textual criticism to be establishing what he calls the 'first edition of the New Testament'. According to Trobisch, the New Testament, at least in the form that achieved 'canonical' status (see chapter 36 below), is not the result of a centuries-long and complicated collection process. He suggests that the New Testament canon goes back to a specific edition made in the second century, a compilation and redaction of the various texts into a single volume at a specific moment, at a specific place, by a specific group of editors. The goal of textual criticism, he says, is then to identify that first edition and explain how it was formed. Because the early Christians permitted a certain amount of fluidity in their transmission and translation of the text, what matters would not be exact wording, but the ways the texts were brought together, and the distinctive features used by those who edited that first edition.[2] Thus Trobisch suggests that: 'Modern textual criticism should strive to produce an edition of the Greek text that closely represents the *editio princeps* of the Canonical Edition.'[3]

David Parker is another who argues that textual criticism means far more than recovering an original autograph. Parker regards the wealth of textual variations among the manuscripts as proof that Christians treated them as *living texts* that could be expanded, reworded, or reduced in order to bring out the true meaning. If so, there is no getting back to an original text, and the best we can do is to reconstruct, as best we can, the earliest collected editions of the text from the period AD 200–300. However, unlike Trobisch, Parker is not interested in recovering a single edition. He is primarily concerned with the living process of textual transmission, the historical and theological forces that shaped textual transmission, and the impact that textual variations had upon the theology of the churches. For Parker, textual variations are an exercise in interpretation, and are thus meaningful and significant in their own right as a way of thinking into the minds of the early Christians. This means investigating the theological tendencies and scribal habits of different manuscripts, and learning by this means more about the copyists and their churches.[4]

The traditional aim of textual criticism, however, has been to establish by study of the ancient manuscripts the precise words of the New Testament authors as they wrote them. Just as classical scholars have attempted to establish the original texts of Plato or Virgil, so too do New Testament text critics pursue an original text given by authors.[5] The stand-off between these two views reflects the wider theological debates of the last few centuries: does 'authority' lie in the Bible itself, or in the Bible *as mediated by and understood within* the Christian tradition? Some of those who stress the impossibility of reconstructing the 'original version' do so in order to cast doubt on whether 'biblical authority' is a coherent concept; others, to show that whatever authority we ascribe to the Bible has in fact always been mediated through the ongoing life of the church.

---

2   This would include, for instance, the title of 'new covenant' that the editors gave to the edition itself, the titles ascribed to individual books, the order of books, the use of *nomina sacra* (shorthand forms for divine names), and other signs of their editorial activity.
3   Trobisch 2000, 102–3.
4   Parker 2006; 2007.
5   See Porter 2013, 12–36.

The problem with pursuing an 'autograph', an 'original version', is of course that we simply do not have such a manuscript. We only have copies, of copies, of copies. We should celebrate the fact that there are over five thousand Greek manuscripts attesting the text of the New Testament, plus over ten thousand manuscripts in Latin and other ancient languages; this is light years ahead of the evidence for *any* of the other great texts by authors from the ancient world, including Homer, Plato, and Julius Caesar, whose works survive in a very small number of mostly medieval manuscripts. It is, however, frustrating that these thousands of manuscripts contain hundreds and thousands of variants. No two manuscripts are the same. As anyone who has ever copied a complex document will know, accidental changes creep in. As anyone who has ever transcribed a politically or ideologically sensitive text will know, it is tempting to introduce deliberate changes ('surely he can't have meant *that* . . . we'd better put it right'). As with many classical sources, there are some passages where none of the existing manuscripts seems to make sense, and scholars have used cautious conjecture as to what the original reading might have been. After all, while some of our manuscripts are close in time to the originals (for example 𝔓[52], which can be dated to *c.* AD 125–50), most manuscripts are some centuries or even a millennium removed from the autographs. All sorts of things may have been subtly changed—though one should quickly add that the vast bulk of the New Testament text remains constant, with most of the variations being irrelevant to the overall meaning.

To complicate matters, it is quite possible that authors or their associates may themselves have revised their works and created both an *original* first edition and then an *original* corrected edition. Some people think this happened with the book of Acts, and even with the collection of Paul's letters. The question of an 'original text' would then look different: which original text? Some have concluded, therefore, that retrieving an original text, an autograph even, is impossibly ambitious. They argue that the goal of textual criticism should be more modest and realistic. Some would prefer to pursue an archetype, a hypothetical intermediate text, upon which a subsequent family of manuscripts depended, but which is itself materially and chronologically removed from an original text. Alternatively, others think we should be working towards establishing the *Ausgangstext*, the 'initial text', as the *earliest attainable* form(s) of the text. Such a text would arguably be prior to an archetypical text behind a family of manuscripts, but posterior to an original text. It is not necessarily an autograph, but rather the textual form that was utilized—by an author or his or her readers—for further dissemination. To define that further: 'The initial text is a hypothetical, reconstructed text, as it presumably existed, according to the hypothesis, before the beginning of its copying.'[6]

---

[6] Mink 2004, 25.

Pursuing an 'initial text', though, does not mean that the quest for an absolute original has been abandoned.[7] The discussion of variants, and even of 'living texts', assumes an earlier text that was composed and then altered. The effort to reconstruct the 'initial text' can thus remain oriented towards recovering an original text, even if we have to concede that a one-to-one correspondence between them is never certain. We may therefore still aim for the reconstruction of an 'initial text' that conforms as closely as we can establish to an original version. We have, after all, no evidence in the textual transmission to suggest that there was ever a drastic interruption between the initial text of scholarly reconstruction and its underlying authorial text. It was only with early 'critics' like Marcion that major surgery was applied to the texts, and such attempts were disowned by the developing church.

THE MATERIALS USED TO ESTABLISH THE TEXT OF THE NEW TESTAMENT

Textual critics use various materials in studying the text of the New Testament:

1. *Papyri*. The earliest copies of the New Testament were written on papyrus sheets, either scrolls or small codices. The number of papyri attesting to the New Testament has markedly increased in the last hundred years, due to discoveries made in Egypt. These include $\mathfrak{P}^{52}$ (the earliest fragment of John's gospel), $\mathfrak{P}^{45}$ (containing portions of the four gospels and Acts), and $\mathfrak{P}^{46}$ (the earliest copy of most of Paul's letters, minus Philemon and the pastorals, but with Hebrews). These are usually dated to the second or third century.
2. *Majuscules*. The majuscules are named after their script, which employs capital letters with no spaces between words. This tradition persisted from the fourth to the eleventh centuries. The major fourth- and fifth-century codices (Vaticanus, Sinaiticus, Alexandrinus, Ephraemi, and Bezae) are classified as majuscules, sometimes called 'uncials'.
3. *Minuscules*. The minuscules are written on parchment or paper in the minuscule script, that is, lower case with word spacing to make reading easier. Minuscules were introduced in the ninth century. Most medieval manuscripts have this form.
4. *Versions*. The 'versions' refer to the different languages into which the New Testament was translated. This includes Latin, Syriac, Coptic, Armenian, Georgian, Ethiopic, Arabic, Slavonic, Gothic, and more. In some languages there are various translations, with their own textual features. In Latin there is the Old Latin and Jerome's Vulgate; in Syriac there is the Old Syriac, the

---

[7] Strutwolf 2011; Holmes 2012.

Peshitta, the Philoxenian, and Harklean translations; the Coptic is extant in several dialects, of which the most prominent are the Sahidic and Bohairic.

5. *Patristic quotations.* The church Fathers often cite and discuss passages from the New Testament. 'Indeed,' says Metzger, one of the great textual critics of the twentieth century, 'so extensive are these citations that if all other sources for our knowledge of the text of the New Testament were destroyed, they would be sufficient alone for the reconstruction of practically the entire New Testament.'[8] Patristic authors can sometimes cite texts quite loosely, as if from memory, but in their commentaries they tend to be tighter and tidier in their attention to the wording.

6. *Lectionaries.* Church writings that contain a sequence of yearly readings for use in the liturgy are called lectionaries. Some two thousand lectionaries are extant, mostly in minuscule script, dated to after the tenth century, though a few are in majuscule script and date as early as the fifth century (for example *l*1043).

METHOD IN TEXTUAL CRITICISM

Establishing the relationship between manuscripts

If one studies something like, say, the Greek text of Galatians or Jude,[9] it is not enough to know the text and its variants. That is because, as Stephen Carlson notes,

> The history of individual textual variation is not the history of the text. A text is more than its individual readings. It is a *pattern* of readings, in a specific sequence and embodied in a single witness, and it is this pattern of readings that may tell us whether the readers of the text were consistent or scatter-brained in their attitude to Christology, apologetics, Judaism, and women. A text is a pattern of readings, so the history of the text ought to be concerned with the history of those patterns of readings, not disembodied variants.[10]

In other words, it is one thing to be able to read and recognize the variants one finds in the apparatus of a modern Greek New Testament, like NA (28) or UBS (5), but it is situating the overall pattern of readings within a wider manuscript tradition that truly brings perspicuity and plausibility to the readings that are preferred. Or, to put it more simply, the individual variants only truly have significance when understood as part of a wider analysis of the relationships between manuscripts.

The transmission of the text was, of course, a process that took place in history,

---

8   Metzger and Ehrman 2005, 126.
9   See Wasserman 2006 on Jude, and Carlson 2015 on Galatians.
10 Carlson 2015, 6–7 (italics original).

in the complex (and mostly, to us, opaque) early history of the church. Such access as we have to this process is gained through study of the surviving manuscripts which, across a millennium or more, attest the copying, corruption, and correction of a sequence of words that make up the New Testament text. In order to create an edition of the Greek New Testament, therefore, one must adjudicate upon the many readings in these manuscripts. This requires postulating what was before and what was after, what was original and what is derivative within the manuscript tradition as a whole. In other words, textual criticism requires mapping the genealogy of the textual tradition. There are, of course, several ways of undertaking such a task.[11]

First, one could start with a base-text, like Codex Vaticanus, and correct it against other witnesses, using the Vulgate or other Greek minuscules, or by one's own conjectures as to what was more probably the original text. Of course, if the base-text was not particularly close to the original to begin with (how would we know?), then we cannot be sure if we are actually moving towards the original text.

Second, other researchers have tried to arrive at an original text by appealing to a 'majority' text. This involves accepting the most frequently attested variants among the extant witnesses. This approach assumes that the various Greek manuscripts are independent of each other, and all equally reflect an original text. This has a pleasantly democratic feel to it, with every manuscript getting a vote on every contested reading, but as with democracy itself the majority is not always right. It is only by a succession of massive historical accidents that we have the manuscripts we have. It is in any case far more likely that the manuscripts are interrelated at some level, that is, the manuscripts and their ancestors were copied from one another. Witnesses need, then, to be weighed rather than just counted. In the end, the 'majority' text method does not establish a genealogical relationship between manuscripts. Rather, it imposes one.

Making of papyrus

Third, there is the stemmatic model, which attempts to establish a family tree of manuscript relationships and thereby work back towards a hypothetical original. Usually this is done through tracing the emergence of erroneous readings in the

---

11 Here I'm (MFB) largely following the summaries of Parker 2008, 159–81, and Carlson 2015, 18–42.

texts by looking at where they were introduced and where they were copied. Yet it can become problematic when the level of contamination is so great that we cannot establish precisely where the errors were introduced; and it becomes all the more complicated if some identical alterations were made independently, or if a branch in a tree of witnesses suddenly switches back to an earlier textual form.

As a result, fourth, many critics now accept the need for a more eclectic method, employing both external attestation (that is, weighing manuscript variants) and internal evidence (examining an author's style and thought) to reconstruct and repair a textual archetype. The operating assumption here is that a reading is more likely to be original if it accounts for all the competing variants with respect to both internal and external evidence.[12] The eclectic model has often been used in relation to the idea of text-types, which are identifiable families of manuscripts whose relative sameness and interrelationship can be safely established. Three main text-types have been postulated: the Alexandrian, the western, and the Byzantine groups. Proponents of text-types are usually right about which text-types are earlier and later, and generally right about what type a manuscript belongs to, but the precise relationships within the types, and between the types, remain opaque. What is more, we are often dealing with small numbers of manuscripts in these types, and their relevance is not equal across the entire New Testament. They are more relevant to the gospels and Pauline letters than to the Catholic Epistles, and are negligible in relation to the book of Revelation.

Fifth, the Coherence Based Genealogical Method (CBGM) is a new computerized method developed by Gerd Mink of the Institute for New Testament Textual Research in Münster, Germany (for which the acronym INTF reflects the German name). Unlike the stemmatic model, this method makes no attempt at strict identification of links between manuscripts. Rather, it pursues the relationship between manuscripts at the place of variation, to generate various sub-stemmata which indicate a textual flow. Once a cohort of sub-stemmata have been made, the database can be interrogated, and inferences about relationships between witnesses can be drawn up. Unlike the text-type model, texts are not grouped geographically, nor by a loose family resemblance, but by a thoroughgoing genealogical analysis in which the traditional types generally break down. The advantage of the CBGM is that it takes into account all the variants in all the manuscripts and demonstrates coherent relations between texts. The objective of the CBGM is to plot textual flows between manuscripts through variations, and to clarify the initial text as the basis for a new critical edition of the New Testament called the *Editio Critica Maior* (*ECM*) (see Figure 11).[13]

---

[12] Holmes 2013 [1995], 771–3.
[13] See Wasserman 2015; Gurry 2016; Wasserman and Gurry 2017.

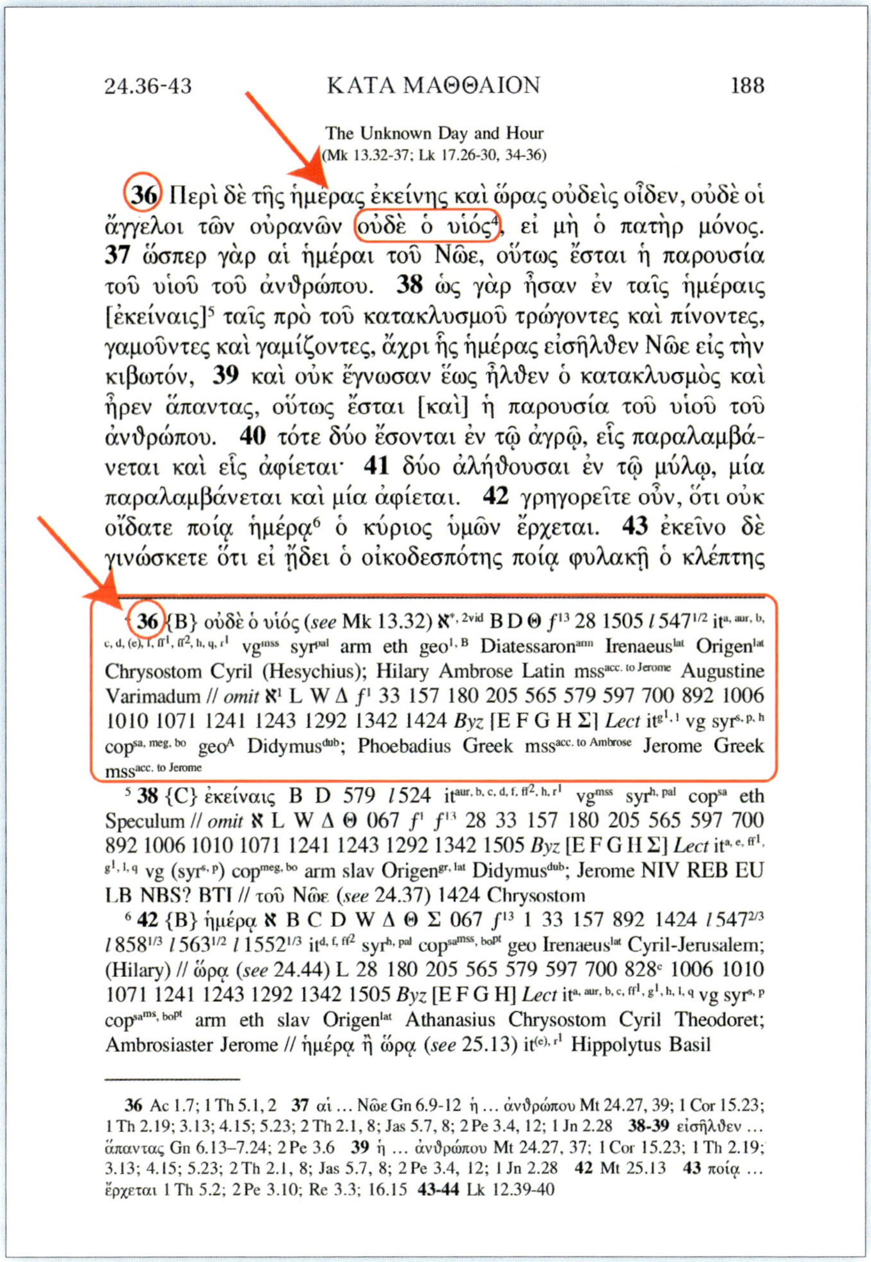

24.36-43 ΚΑΤΑ ΜΑΘΘΑΙΟΝ 188

The Unknown Day and Hour
(Mk 13.32-37; Lk 17.26-30, 34-36)

36 Περὶ δὲ τῆς ἡμέρας ἐκείνης καὶ ὥρας οὐδεὶς οἶδεν, οὐδὲ οἱ ἄγγελοι τῶν οὐρανῶν οὐδὲ ὁ υἱός⁴, εἰ μὴ ὁ πατὴρ μόνος. **37** ὥσπερ γὰρ αἱ ἡμέραι τοῦ Νῶε, οὕτως ἔσται ἡ παρουσία τοῦ υἱοῦ τοῦ ἀνθρώπου. **38** ὡς γὰρ ἦσαν ἐν ταῖς ἡμέραις [ἐκείναις]⁵ ταῖς πρὸ τοῦ κατακλυσμοῦ τρώγοντες καὶ πίνοντες, γαμοῦντες καὶ γαμίζοντες, ἄχρι ἧς ἡμέρας εἰσῆλθεν Νῶε εἰς τὴν κιβωτόν, **39** καὶ οὐκ ἔγνωσαν ἕως ἦλθεν ὁ κατακλυσμὸς καὶ ἦρεν ἅπαντας, οὕτως ἔσται [καὶ] ἡ παρουσία τοῦ υἱοῦ τοῦ ἀνθρώπου. **40** τότε δύο ἔσονται ἐν τῷ ἀγρῷ, εἷς παραλαμβάνεται καὶ εἷς ἀφίεται· **41** δύο ἀλήθουσαι ἐν τῷ μύλῳ, μία παραλαμβάνεται καὶ μία ἀφίεται. **42** γρηγορεῖτε οὖν, ὅτι οὐκ οἴδατε ποίᾳ ἡμέρᾳ⁶ ὁ κύριος ὑμῶν ἔρχεται. **43** ἐκεῖνο δὲ γινώσκετε ὅτι εἰ ᾔδει ὁ οἰκοδεσπότης ποίᾳ φυλακῇ ὁ κλέπτης

⁴ **36** {B} οὐδὲ ὁ υἱός (see Mk 13.32) ℵ*, 2vid B D Θ f¹³ 28 1505 l547¹/² itᵃ, ᵃᵘʳ, ᵇ, ᶜ, ᵈ, ⁽ᵉ⁾, ᶠ, ff¹, ff², ʰ, q, r¹ vgᵐˢˢ syrᵖᵃˡ arm eth geoˡ, ᴮ Diatessaronᵃⁿⁿ Irenaeusˡᵃᵗ Origenˡᵃᵗ Chrysostom Cyril (Hesychius); Hilary Ambrose Latin mssᵃᶜᶜ· ᵗᵒ ᴶᵉʳᵒᵐᵉ Augustine Varimadum // omit ℵ¹ L W Δ f¹ 33 157 180 205 565 579 597 700 892 1006 1010 1071 1241 1243 1292 1342 1424 Byz [E F G H Σ] Lect itᵍ¹·¹ vg syrˢ, ᵖ, ʰ copˢᵃ, ᵐᵉᵍ, ᵇᵒ geoᴬ Didymusᵈᵘᵇ; Phoebadius Greek mssᵃᶜᶜ· ᵗᵒ ᴬᵐᵇʳᵒˢᵉ Jerome Greek mssᵃᶜᶜ· ᵗᵒ ᴶᵉʳᵒᵐᵉ

⁵ **38** {C} ἐκείναις B D 579 l524 itᵃᵘʳ, ᵇ, ᶜ, ᵈ, ᶠ, ff², ʰ, r¹ vgᵐˢˢ syrʰ, ᵖᵃˡ copˢᵃ eth Speculum // omit ℵ L W Δ Θ 067 f¹ f¹³ 28 33 157 180 205 565 597 700 892 1006 1010 1071 1241 1243 1292 1342 1424 1505 Byz [E F G H Σ] Lect itᵃ, ᵉ, ff¹, ᵍ¹, ˡ, q vg (syrˢ, ᵖ) copᵐᵉᵍ, ᵇᵒ arm slav Origenᵍʳ, ˡᵃᵗ Didymusᵈᵘᵇ; Jerome NIV REB EU LB NBS? BTI // τοῦ Νῶε (see 24.37) 1424 Chrysostom

⁶ **42** {B} ἡμέρᾳ ℵ B C D W Δ Θ Σ 067 f¹ 33 157 892 1424 l547²/³ l858¹/³ l563¹/² l1552¹/³ itᵈ, ᶠ, ff² syrʰ, ᵖᵃˡ copˢᵃᵐˢˢ, ᵇᵒᵖᵗ geo Irenaeusˡᵃᵗ Cyril-Jerusalem; (Hilary) // ὥρᾳ (see 24.44) L 28 180 205 565 579 700 828ᶜ 1006 1010 1071 1241 1243 1292 1342 1505 Byz [E F G H] Lect itᵃ, ᵃᵘʳ, ᵇ, ᶜ, ff¹, ᵍ¹, ʰ, ˡ, q vg syrˢ, ᵖ copˢᵃᵐˢ, ᵇᵒᵖᵗ arm eth slav Origenˡᵃᵗ Athanasius Chrysostom Cyril Theodoret; Ambrosiaster Jerome // ἡμέρᾳ ἢ ὥρᾳ (see 25.13) it⁽ᵉ⁾, r¹ Hippolytus Basil

---

36 Ac 1.7; 1 Th 5.1, 2   **37** αἱ … Νῶε Gn 6.9-12 ἡ … ἀνθρώπου Mt 24.27, 39; 1 Cor 15.23; 1 Th 2.19; 3.13; 4.15; 5.23; 2 Th 2.1, 8; Jas 5.7, 8; 2 Pe 3.4, 12; 1 Jn 2.28   **38-39** εἰσῆλθεν … ἅπαντας Gn 6.13–7.24; 2 Pe 3.6   **39** ἡ … ἀνθρώπου Mt 24.27, 37; 1 Cor 15.23; 1 Th 2.19; 3.13; 4.15; 5.23; 2 Th 2.1, 8; Jas 5.7, 8; 2 Pe 3.4, 12; 1 Jn 2.28   **42** Mt 25.13   **43** ποίᾳ … ἔρχεται 1 Th 5.2; 2 Pe 3.10; Re 3.3; 16.15   **43-44** Lk 12.39-40

Figure 11: Matthew 24.3 from UBS (5)

The problem of textual variants

The problem of textual variants has long been noted, both by Christian authors and by critics of Christianity. Origen reports that the second-century pagan philosopher Celsus observed how

Some believers, as though from a drinking bout, go so far as to oppose themselves and alter the original text of the Gospels three or four or several times over, and they change its character to enable them to deny difficulties in the face of criticism.[14]

Origen himself, when commenting on a passage in Matthew, opined that

There are many other (differences of this kind) so that many copies of the Gospel of Matthew do not harmonize with each other. The same thing (is true) also with the other Gospels . . . For it is clear that there has been much alteration of these writings, whether due to the same carelessness of certain scribes, or due to boldness on the part of some who intentionally alter them, such as those who insert (something) or remove the proper reading in order to support their own beliefs.[15]

It is indeed undeniable that the text of the New Testament has been altered in individual manuscripts, either by accident or deliberately. However, the mass of variations should not make us sceptical about recovering a very close approximation of the original text. The quest is not futile. Nor does this imply that the text was fluid and unstable, and has been corrupted beyond all recovery. It is easy to be startled by the mass of small and largely irrelevant changes and ignore the fact that the textual tradition exhibits a pattern of general cohesion, albeit characterized by local contamination. The sheer volume of material evidence with its variations is certainly a problem, but it is a good problem to have, since, to repeat, no other writing from antiquity is attested in anything like such a voluminous way.[16] The number of passages which are textually indeterminable, with D readings for 'uncertain' in the UBS (5), is in fact relatively small. No piece of Christian doctrine hinges on any of these variants.

Martin Heide has actually calculated the stability of the New Testament as ranging from 89 to 98 per cent. That overall stability, measured from early papyri through to Byzantine minuscules, averages out at 92.6 per cent.[17] As Michael Holmes points out, we have here macro-level stability (that is, a remarkable textual sameness in terms of episodic content, narrative structure, and arrangement) and micro-level fluidity (that is, variations normally restricted to the level of words, phrases, and verses, rather than to whole paragraphs or pages).[18] The task for text critics, and indeed for students learning to read the Greek New Testament, is how to adjudicate between the many textual variants that appear in the apparatus of modern editions.

---

[14] Origen *C. Cels.* 2.27 (tr. H. Chadwick [LCL]).
[15] Origen *Comm. Matt.* 15.14, cited from Dungan 1999, 72.
[16] At last count, the textual evidence according to the INTF included 124 papyri, 280 majuscules, 2,808 minuscules, and 2,343 lectionaries.
[17] Heide 2011.
[18] Holmes 2012.

Criteria for assessing variants

Alterations can be introduced for all sorts of reasons. A scribe can simply misread a text by skipping a word or a whole line, or simply misspell a word. Or the scribe might mis*hear* a text read: people often suspect that this happened with Romans 5.1, where the two readings 'we have' (*echomen*) and 'let us have' (*echōmen*) have a subtle change of vowel sound that changes the form of the verb. Or the scribe might be trying to correct the text, as may have happened with the words 'nor the son' in Mathew 24.36, omitted perhaps because it seemed to tell against Jesus' omniscient divinity (see figure 11); or indeed to harmonize it, as with the way some tried to make Luke's version of the Lord's Prayer conform to Matthew's. To isolate these variations and to uncover the earliest text, scholars ordinarily employ a number of criteria. There are various ways of summarizing and expressing these, but the following are the main features.

External evidence

1. *Date of witnesses*. Preference is generally given to earlier witnesses, usually the papyri, though often the major majuscules.
2. *Geographical distribution of witnesses*. This is a form of multiple attestation, which in theory is a valid way of providing substantiation for a reading by appealing to diversified sources. It works best when appealing to versions which are at least linguistically separated from one another. However, this criterion assumes that the manuscripts compared are to some degree independent, something about which we can never be certain. Its value is diminished when we consider that most of our manuscripts are geographically clustered, the papyri being mostly from Egypt, and most Latin texts coming from western Europe.
3. *Genealogical coherence*. A reading is preferred if it has coherence with textual witnesses whose ancestor was the initial text; whereas a reading has poor 'coherence' if it is only found among texts that are distantly related to an initial text.[19]

Internal evidence

1. *The more difficult reading is to be preferred*. For example, it is more likely that a scribe omitted 'nor the son' from Matthew 24.36 than added it, since it was potentially embarrassing to the theological proclivities of some copyists.
2. *The shorter reading is to be preferred*. Notwithstanding spelling errors and occasional scribal efforts to avoid superfluity, it is thought more likely that a scribe would expand a text rather than reduce it.

---

[19] Carlson 2015, 43.

3. *Contextual considerations.* Text critics determine preferred readings based on the style and vocabulary of an author, the literary context of a passage, the assumed priority of the gospel of Mark, privileging readings which do not look like harmonizations or improvements, and imagining possible influence by a Christian community on the transmission of the passage.
4. *Explanatory power.* A reading is preferred if it explains and accounts for not only the passage in question but also the other variants.

To give an example of how all this plays out, we return to Matthew 24.36: 'But about that day or hour no one knows, not even the angels in heaven, nor the Son, but only the Father.' The words 'nor the Son' are lacking in the majority of the Greek witnesses of Matthew. Even so, the phrase is found in the major majuscules (ℵ B D Θ) (external attestation). As we have already suggested, the words were probably omitted because of the doctrinal difficulty they present; this is more probable than that they were added by assimilating the passage to Mark 13.32 which contains the same wording (internal evidence).[20]

RESOURCES FOR STUDY

The following list of resources is by no means exhaustive. But, in addition to the recommended reading list at the end of the chapter, these recommendations are designed to point towards resources that are useful for either understanding or engaging in textual criticism.

Editions

Students should familiarize themselves with several critical editions of the Greek New Testament.

Luke 1.59–73, uncial 0177 (Gregory-Aland), tenth-century New Testament manuscript

---

[20] Metzger 1994, 51–2.

1. *ECM*. The *Editio Critica Maior* is a massive critical edition of the Greek New Testament, currently being produced by the Münster Institute for New Testament Textual Research in partnership with associated organizations. It provides the most thorough apparatus available, detailing every listable variant, often with only one primary line of text per page and the myriad of variants listed underneath. To date, only the Catholic Epistles and book of Acts have been completed by the Institute; work continues on the gospel of John, through the International Greek New Testament Project in Birmingham, England. The overall project is expected to be completed by 2030. The *ECM* provided the basis for the Catholic Epistles in the NA (28) and UBS (5).
2. NA (28). The 28th edition of Nestle-Aland *Novum Testamentum Graece* is the preferred scholarly edition of the Greek New Testament. The apparatus is designed to help readers engage in the practice of textual criticism by giving them both positive evidence for a text and negative evidence against it. The NA (28) also notes the Eusebian canons (an early system for identifying gospel parallels) and Kephalaia (chapter divisions used in most manuscripts), New Testament cross-references, and many useful appendices about manuscripts, minor variants, and citations/allusions of the Old Testament in the New.
3. UBS (5). The UBS (5) is the 5th edition of the United Bible Society's *The Greek New Testament*. It is meant primarily for seminarians, pastors, and Bible translators. It uses the same base-text as the NA (28), but it has a simpler apparatus than the NA (28), and focuses only on variants that have an impact on translation. (This tells its own story: the vast majority of textual variants would never show up in a translation.) As such, it does not list as many variants as the NA (28), but, when it does give variants, it gives a more detailed list, especially with citations in the church Fathers. The UBS (5) also provides information about how different modern translations divide up paragraphs.
4. *SBLGNT*. The *Society of Biblical Literature Greek New Testament* is a critical edition of the Greek New Testament compiled by Michael Holmes, and published by SBL and the Faithlife Corporation in 2010. The apparatus does not list manuscripts; it simply notes differences between several editions of the Greek New Testament. Unlike the NA and UBS texts, which were influenced by the scholarly tradition going back to the great nineteenth-century critics Westcott and Hort, the *SBLGNT* reflects the influence of G. Zuntz, and differs from the NA and UBS text in about 540 places. It also has a generous 'end-use agreement', and can be used royalty-free in non-commercial and many commercial situations.

5. *THGNT. The Greek New Testament Produced at Tyndale House* emanates, as its name suggests, from Tyndale House, a biblical research centre in Cambridge, England. It is edited by Dirk Jongkind and Peter Williams. It offers its own re-evaluation of the standard text based on recent papyri discoveries from the last century and studies of scribal habits. Its apparatus is limited, and includes only (a) variants that are genuine contenders for inclusion in the main text; (b) variants of exegetical importance; and (c) variants illustrating scribal habits.

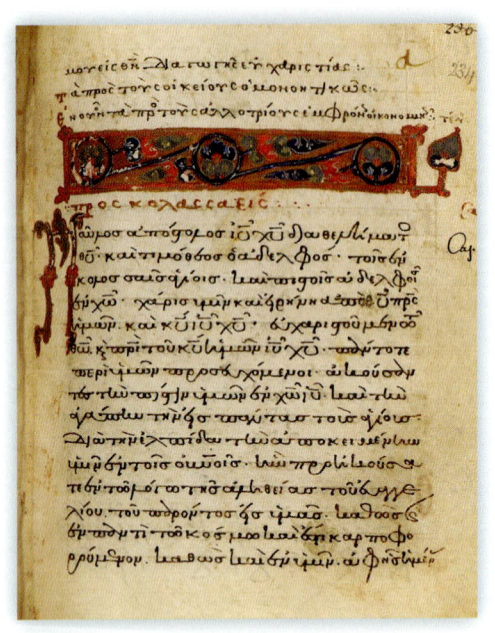

Commentaries on the textual variants

Given that most students and pastors are not textual critics, working away in some academic institution, it is not only important to learn how to read an apparatus and decide between variants for oneself; one will also usually need to consult commentaries that explain why some readings are preferable to others. Among the most useful ones are:

Comfort, Philip W. 2015. *A Commentary on the Manuscripts of the New Testament*. Grand Rapids, MI: Kregel.

Metzger, Bruce M. 1994. *A Textual Commentary on the Greek New Testament*. 3rd edn.; Stuttgart: German Bible Society.

Beginning of Colossians, minuscule 321 (Gregory-Aland), twelfth-century New Testament manuscript
PD-US

Online resources

- The fifth-century majuscule Codex Sinaiticus is fully digitized, available online, and searchable: <www.codexsinaiticus.org>.
- Sites where students can research individual manuscripts and look at actual photos of the texts are provided by the New Testament Virtual Manuscript Room of the Münster INTF (<ntvmr.uni-muenster.de/home>) and by the Centre for the Study of New Testament Manuscripts based at Dallas Theological Seminary (<www.csntm.org>).
- A useful site for keeping up on new studies pertaining to biblical manuscripts, new editions, and textual criticism is the Evangelical Textual Criticism blog, run by a team of scholars from all over the world (<evangelicaltextualcriticism.blogspot.com.au>).

Further reading

Carlson, Stephen C. 2015. *The Text of Galatians and Its History*. WUNT 385; Tübingen: Mohr Siebeck, pp. 1–43.

Comfort, Philip W. 2015. *A Commentary on the Manuscripts of the New Testament*. Grand Rapids, MI: Kregel.

Hill, Charles E., and Michael J. Kruger (eds.). 2012. *The Early Text of the New Testament*. Oxford: Oxford University Press.

Holmes, M. W. 2001. 'Textual Criticism.' In *Interpreting the New Testament: Essays on Methods and Issues*. Edited by D. A. Black and D. S. Dockery. Nashville: Broadman & Holman, pp. 46–73.

———. 2013 [1995]. 'Reasoned Eclecticism in New Testament Textual Criticism.' In *The Text of the New Testament in Contemporary Research: Essays on the Status Quaestionis*. Edited by B. D. Ehrman and M. W. Holmes. 2nd edn.; Leiden: Brill, pp. 771–802.

Metzger, Bruce M., and Bart D. Ehrman. 2005. *The Text of the New Testament: Its Transmission, Corruption, and Restoration*. New York: Oxford University Press.

Parker, David C. 2008. *An Introduction to the New Testament Manuscripts and Their Texts*. Cambridge: Cambridge University Press.

Porter, Stanley E. 2013. *How We Got the New Testament: Text, Transmission, Translation*. Grand Rapids, MI: Baker.

Schnabel, Eckhard J. 2004. 'Textual Criticism: Recent Developments.' In *The Face of New Testament Studies: A Survey of Recent Research*. Edited by S. McKnight and G. R. Osborne. Grand Rapids, MI: Baker, pp. 59–75.

Wasserman, Tommy, and Peter Gurry. 2017. *A New Approach to Textual Criticism: An Introduction to the Coherence-Based Genealogical Method*. Atlanta: SBL.

36

The Canonization of the New Testament

The one who believes the divine Scriptures has an incontrovertible standard for his judgment and obtains as an irrefutable demonstration the voice of God that the Scriptures have given to us.[1]

CHAPTER AT A GLANCE

This chapter provides a brief overview of the canonization of the New Testament.

By the end of this chapter you should be able to:
- understand how the New Testament came to be recognized as a collection of twenty-seven books;
- comprehend why some books were included and others were rejected.

HOW WE GOT THE NEW TESTAMENT CANON

The Bible itself nowhere tells us which books should be in the Bible. So who decided? This is the question of the formation of the Christian 'canon' ('canon' derives from the Greek word *kanōn* for 'rule' or 'measure'). This question is different when it comes to the Old Testament, and for this book we shall focus exclusively on the New.[2]

We first have to debunk two erroneous views of how the New Testament canon took shape.

First, in popular (secular) imagination, the creation of the Bible was undertaken at the behest of the emperor Constantine, in the fourth century, or else by a gaggle of bishops who tried to impose their own narrow brand of Christianity on a previously pluralistic church by restricting the list of sanctioned writings. The Bible as we know it, according to this view, was created to

---

[1] Clem. *Strom.* 2.9.6.
[2] On the OT canon, see Beckwith 2008.

buttress an unholy alliance of imperial and ecclesiastical power by composing and then compiling books that sanctioned a particular version of religious and civil order. Adherents to such a view include those of a post-religious generation and even Ivy League professors; but this theory has more to do with Dan Brown's novel *The Da Vinci Code* than with serious history. (It also reflects, with amusing anachronism, the American suspicion of 'Constantinian Christianity' as supposedly stretching from the fourth century to the eighteenth when George III sent bishops to Massachusetts, invoking the modern ideal of political and religious freedom.)

At the opposite end of the scale, second, there are many who, taught to 'believe the Bible', treat the New Testament canon as a self-evident and self-authorizing collection. For them, it would only be a slight caricature to say that the church Fathers, like early versions of Indiana Jones, went searching for 'scriptures', finding hidden scrolls in ancient catacombs or sneaking into imperial palaces to steal confiscated copies of the gospels. Then, equipped with some kind of magic device for telling which documents were 'inspired', they added their freshly discovered texts to their collection of what became 'Holy Scriptures'.[3]

The New Testament canon, however, was neither artificially invented by authorities nor discovered by Bible-questing adventurers. The church did not create the word of God; rather, the church itself is a *creatura verbum Dei*, 'a creature of the word of God'. Jesus himself, the incarnate Word, and the apostolic word of the gospel, are what call, gather, encourage, admonish, and sustain the church. However, the church—with all its discussions, debates, and decisions—was the instrument by which the inspired word of apostolic testimony was put into its canonical location, to be seen as an authoritative collection of sacred texts. In other words, 'canonization' is a shorthand way of referring to God's sanctifying work in the ecclesiastical processes that led to the compilation and promulgation of the New Testament canon. Admittedly, there remains to this day a multiplicity of biblical canons. Catholics, Protestants, Greek Orthodox, and Oriental Orthodox Christians have interestingly different collections. This, however, affects the Old Testament rather than the New. There is firm consensus about the main constituent parts of the New Testament canon that are shared by all forms of Christianity across the globe.

Long before the church's ratification of the canon and the crises that crystallized that process, there was a gradual and steady growth of the literary collection that became the New Testament. Indeed, the basic contents of the New Testament seem to have been well established in the second half of the second century.

---

3 Inspiration was not so much a criterion for inclusion in the canon as a corollary (McDonald 2007 [1995], 416–17). The early church could call many non-canonical and apocryphal books inspired and even refer to ecclesial offices and church councils as inspired (see Allert 2007, 60–5, 185–8). Inspiration would, then, never be a satisfactory criterion for canonicity. Other grounds were required to accept a book as normative and authoritative.

Plaque with St John the Evangelist, ninth century
The Metropolitan Museum of Art

The early phases of that process are mostly lost to us. Who first put the four gospels together? Who collected the Pauline letters? Who decided to put Hebrews with the Pauline texts, granted that Paul is not named in it? When did the Johannine letters first circulate outside Asia Minor? We do not know the answer to any of these questions. But we can get some glimpses into what happened. Luke Timothy Johnson says we are best not to imagine a 'late, arbitrary, or artificial imposition' imposed, top-down, by episcopal hierarchy. It was, he says, more of a 'natural and organic development' of the church's own witness to Jesus Christ and his gospel.[4]

The apostolic and post-apostolic church venerated Israel's scriptures (usually in their Greek translation), the sayings and story of Jesus (whether in oral tradition, located in various written gospels and Jesus books, or even isolated sayings found here and there), and apostolic instructions (especially the epistles of Paul, Peter, and John). When fused together, these three elements created a narrative that told a story about God, creation, Israel, the Messiah, his church, and the coming consummation. It formed a mosaic of shared beliefs and ethics. It stipulated a recognizable set of church offices and practices. Thus, prior to any 'biblical canon', there was already in existence a 'canon' or 'rule of faith' that told a *story*, a historical account stretching from creation to *eschaton*, following the story of Israel and seeing Jesus as the climax of that story and the driver of its ultimate fulfilment. This summed up the inherited way of establishing the contents and coherence of basic Christian beliefs.[5] These beliefs simultaneously derived from what was known as 'scripture' and, in circular fashion, became the basis for classifying what counted as 'canon'.[6]

---

4   Johnson 2010, 526–7.
5   Iren. *Adv. Haer.* 1.10.1–3; 3.4.1–2.
6   The terms 'scripture' and 'canon' are not synonymous. Prior to the fourth century, writings which would

Many people in the early church, being originally illiterate and/or operating in languages other than Greek, received this 'scripture' in many ways: corporate readings, sermons, catechesis, creeds, apologetic debates, in-house disputations, liturgies, and pastoral care.[7] Thus scripture, its text and interpretation, remained important to church members, even if they were uneducated. Christianity became a movement—more than just a 'religion' in either their sense or ours—in which texts played a key role. Churches in turn generated their own distinctive book-culture, with specific media, pedagogies, copying practices, abbreviations, reading aids, reading communities, commentaries, and a promiscuous sharing of books.[8] The early church, as a self-conscious network spread across the Mediterranean basin, immersed in its textuality and oral expressions, and facing internal debates as to the meaning of its own faith, was driven to establish the limits of the sacred texts which in turn authorized its faith and practices.

It was thus amid the literary and theological culture of the nascent post-apostolic church that Christian books began to be collected, copied, shared, and used in worship. Very quickly, probably post-70 but prior to AD 110 during the time of Ignatius and Papias, certain literary clusters emerged. By the first quarter of the second century a fourfold gospel (*Tetraevangelium*) and a Pauline letter-collection (*Paulinium*) were widely circulated and regarded as authoritative for determining faith and practice. Likewise, 1 Peter and 1 John also seem to have had widespread usage and acceptance in many places by the time of Polycarp and Irenaeus several decades later.

By the end of the second century, there was a need for an authoritative list of sacred books for Christian usage. Other, somewhat less well-known, Christian writings were circulating, including Acts, James, 2–3 John, Jude, and Revelation, as well as *1 Clement*, *Apocalypse of Peter*, and the *Shepherd of Hermas*. Their status, and fitness for use in worship, needed to be resolved. A further impulse towards making lists of accepted books was created by heterodox Christian groups who composed their own literature (for example the Valentinians) or else issued their own truncated editions of Christian writings (Marcion and his followers). There was also a growing awareness that several writings ascribed to apostolic figures, like the so-called *Gospel of Peter* or *Gospel of Thomas*, might not necessarily be authentic. It became more urgent to assess and weigh the many writings in circulation; left to themselves, they might well have produced (as some of today's apologists would like them to have produced) very different forms of the Christian movement.

---

later be regarded as canonical, and others which would later be classified as disputed or apocryphal, were designated as 'scripture'. So it is more accurate to say that 'scripture' refers to a religious text that is regarded as truthful or useful, while 'canon' refers to an authorized collection of scriptural texts. Viewed this way, while all canons are scripture, not all scripture is canonical, at least not before the fourth century. See Allert 2007, 44–7.

7   Markschies 2015, 273.
8   See Hurtado 2006; B. Wright 2017.

The 'Muratorian canon' and the 'anti-Marcionite prologues' were probably composed towards the end of this period, the aim being to list books that were accepted by the churches, to offer commentary on their apostolic origins, and to identify books that were rejected. Thereafter, in the succeeding centuries, several lists of authorized books were put forward (see tables 36.1, 36.2, and 36.3).

TABLE 36.1: FOUR EARLY LISTS OF NEW TESTAMENT WRITINGS OF THE SECOND/THIRD CENTURIES

Irenaeus (c. AD 130–202)[*]	*Clement of Alexandria* (c. AD 150–215)[†]	*Origen* (c. AD 184–254)[‡]	*Muratorian canon* (c. AD 200)[§]
Matthew	Jude	Matthew	[Matthew]—implied
Mark	*Epistle of Barnabas*	Mark	[Mark]—implied
Luke	*Apocalypse of Peter*	Luke	Luke
John	Hebrews	John	John
Revelation	Acts	1 Peter	John's epistles
1 John	Paul	2 Peter—	Acts
1 Peter	Matthew	acknowledged	Paul's epistles:
Shepherd of Hermas	Luke	but doubted	1–2 Corinthians
Wisdom of Solomon	Mark	Revelation	Galatians
Paul	John	1 John	Romans
		2–3 John—	Ephesians
		acknowledged	Philippians
		but doubted	Colossians
		Hebrews	1–2 Thessalonians
		Paul	Philemon
			Titus
			1–2 Timothy
			Jude
			1–3 John (again)
			Wisdom of Solomon
			Revelation
			Apocalypse of Peter
			Marcionite epistles—rejected:
			Laodiceans
			Alexandrians

[*] Eus. *Hist. Eccl.* 5.8.2–8.
[†] Eus. *Hist. Eccl.* 6.14.1–7.
[‡] Eus. *Hist. Eccl.* 6.25.3–14.
[§] Metzger 1987, 305–7.

TABLE 36.2: TWO CANON LISTS FROM THE FOURTH CENTURY

Eusebius (c. AD 320–30)*	Athanasius (Festal Letter of AD 367)†
Recognized books (Greek *homolegomena*): 'holy tetrad of the Gospels' Acts Paul's epistles 1 John 1 Peter Revelation **Disputed books (Greek *antilegomena*):** James Jude 2 Peter 2–3 John **Spurious books (Greek *notha*):** *Acts of Paul* *Shepherd of Hermas* *Apocalypse of Peter* *Epistle of Barnabas* *Didache* Revelation *Gospel According to the Hebrews* **Heretical books (Greek *hairetikōn*):** *Gospel of Peter* *Gospel of Thomas* *Gospel of Matthias* *Acts of Andrew* *Acts of John*	Matthew Mark Luke John Acts James 1–2 Peter 1–3 John Jude Fourteen epistles of Paul (including Hebrews) Revelation

* Eus. *Hist. Eccl.* 3.25.1–7.
† Athanasius *Ep. Fest.* 39.

There were thus various concurrent and paradoxical impulses within the literary culture of the developing church.

On the one hand there was openness to a variety of Christian writings to be used in worship and read for edification. Serapion, the bishop of Antioch (c. AD 191–211), initially allowed a congregation at Rhossus to read the *Gospel of Peter* in public; he forbade it later, when it created division and was deemed to be conducive to a docetic christology (in which Jesus only 'seemed' to be human, but was not really).[9]

---

9 Eus. *Hist. Eccl.* 6.12.3–6.

TABLE 36.3: BOOKS CONTAINED IN BIBLICAL MANUSCRIPTS OF THE FOURTH AND FIFTH CENTURIES*

Codex Vaticanus	Codex Sinaiticus	Codex Alexandrinus
Matthew	Matthew	Matthew
Mark	Mark	Mark
Luke	Luke	Luke
John	John	John
Acts	Romans	Acts
James	1–2 Corinthians	James
1–2 Peter	Galatians	1–2 Peter
1–3 John	Ephesians	1–3 John
Jude	Philippians	Jude
Romans	Colossians	Romans
1–2 Corinthians	1–2 Thessalonians	1–2 Corinthians
Galatians	Hebrews	Galatians
Ephesians	1–2 Timothy	Ephesians
Philippians	Titus	Philippians
Colossians	Philemon	Colossians
1–2 Thessalonians	Acts	1–2 Thessalonians
Hebrews	James	Hebrews
Omitted due to missing folios:	1–2 Peter	1–2 Timothy
1–2 Timothy	1–3 John	Titus
Titus	Jude	Philemon
Philemon	Revelation	Revelation
Revelation	*Epistle of Barnabas*	*1–2 Clement*
	Shepherd of Hermas	*Psalms of Solomon*

* Cited from McDonald 2007, 451.

We also find, in this period, proto-orthodox authors quite happy to cite other gospels, and sayings attributed to Jesus in various sources, not polemically, but as anecdotal evidence about some point of interpretation or to clarify a saying or event in Jesus' life. Clement of Alexandria and Origen are cases in point, combing through any and every book about Jesus they could find, affirming truth wherever they found it. What is more, in roughly the third century, the period between Irenaeus and Athanasius, there was a fluctuating penumbra of books that remained in contest for canonization, not just 2–3 John, 2 Peter, Jude, James, Hebrews, and Revelation, but also the *Gospel of the Hebrews, Gospel of the Egyptians, Acts of Paul, Acts of Peter, 3 Corinthians, Letter to the Laodiceans, Apocalypse of Peter, Shepherd of Hermas, Didache, 1 Clement, 2 Clement,* and *Letter of Barnabas*—all of which were regarded by some people, at some times, as 'scripture'.[10] Several of these books were even included as quasi-appendices in several manuscripts (see Table 36.3). The early church had more than two categories of writings. It was never a matter of seeing everything as *either* 'inspired' *or* 'heretical'. Christian teachers recognized that there was a larger body of works that were, at least, para-canonical, useful to be read alongside the authorized body of normative Christian texts. When the church produced lists of books, the point was not so much to ban everything else, but to identify the central core of works that were to be seen as 'true, genuine, and recognized'.[11]

We do, however, detect a tendency to narrow the list of approved writings in order to define Christian faith in a restrictive sense. (Some will hear that sentence in a strongly negative sense, indicating a harsh or judgmental stance. That would only apply if we knew in advance, as some would prefer, that Christian faith was so loose and generalized a phenomenon that it could incorporate an infinite range of views without damaging itself or changing into something else.) Early apologists like Irenaeus and Tertullian warned against heretical or forged writings composed by deviant groups. Marcion tried to reduce Christianity to a sort of putative Paulinism, viewed through a gnostic and anti-Jewish lens, recognizing only Paul's letters (and then only a truncated version of them) with a redacted version of Luke. (Marcion also wrote his *Antitheses* to justify excluding the Old Testament; Marcionites wrote their own book of psalms to complement their literary corpus.) In many places, doubts were raised about the authorship of 2 Peter and the book of Revelation. The Syriac-speaking church did not officially recognize the catholic letters and Revelation until the fifth century.[12]

It is generally thought that the church employed several criteria to determine the approved register of sacred books. Four stand out:

1. *Apostolicity*. A text was more likely to be accepted if it was attributed to an apostle or to one of the apostle's associates, and if it actually looked like an apostolic document as opposed to a forgery.[13] The church was constantly aware of the need to get back to Jesus and the apostles; they were not simply empty ciphers for conveying abstract truth.[14]
2. *Orthodoxy*. Texts were accepted if they comported with the apostolic proclamation which crystallized into the rule of faith. In the same way that the Christian gospel was said to comport with the Jewish scriptures,[15]

---

[10] Holmes 2008, 419.
[11] Eus. *Hist. Eccl.* 3.25.6.
[12] The catholic letters were in the Philoxenian and Harklean versions, but the Peshitta only included James, 1 Peter, and 1 John. See Nienhuis 2011, 79–81.
[13] Iren. *Adv. Haer.* 3.3.3; 3.4.1; Eus. *Hist. Eccl.* 3.25.6.
[14] See *1 Clem.* 42.1–2; Ign. *Magn.* 13.1–2; Iren. *Adv. Haer.* 3.2.2; 3.3.1–4; 3.4.1; 3.5.1.
[15] See Lk. 24.27; Jn. 2.22; Ac. 13.32–33; Rom. 1.2; 1 Cor. 15.3–4; 2 Cor. 1.20.

so too did collections of sacred texts have to correspond to the gospel of the churches.[16]
3. *Antiquity*. Writings close to the time of Jesus and the apostles, even if not strictly by apostles themselves, were still candidates for acceptance. It was for this reason that many popular writings were rejected as obviously post-apostolic; this applies to *1 Clement*, the *Didache*, and the *Shepherd of Hermas*.
4. *Catholicity*. Writings were accepted if they were recognized by a wide geographical distribution of churches.[17] Some centres may have had local affinities for some writings (such as *1 Clement* and the *Shepherd* in Rome); some harboured suspicions about other books (such as *2 Peter* in Alexandria); but what shaped the eventual canonical collection was the overall consensus of east and west. Thus, while many writings were regarded as in some loose sense 'scripture', only those books which were traceable to the apostles, which offered access to Jesus and contained apostolic proclamation, and which were widely venerated, became accepted as 'canonical'.

Thus it was that the contested context of Christian theology in the second and third centuries saw the emergence of what became the canon of the New Testament. In this period, Christian beliefs and their literary expression developed and diversified. There was a perceived need to maintain strong continuity with the past, to develop models of coherence between Christian liturgical and literary traditions, and to contextualize faith in the presenting philosophical environment. All these factors, seen of course as part of the vocation of the church to bear faithful witness to its lord, generated the strong sense of a certain normative core of books, even if the outside limits of that collection were still up for negotiation for some centuries to come.

That observation is reinforced by Christoph Markschies, who examines Christian institutions in relation to canon, and identifies a shared core of texts between free teachers (such as Justin and Valentinus), monarchial bishops (such as Irenaeus), and people using scriptures in worship services and in teaching, as well as in public and private libraries.[18] Consequently, the New Testament canon did not emerge either as a self-evident collection of inspired texts that any genuine Christian would automatically recognize or as a top-down imposition through an imperially enforced episcopal edict. Rather, the New Testament canon was the consensus that the church arrived at by a complex, many-sided process of discernment and definition.

---

16 Iren. *Adv. Haer.* 3.1–5.
17 Aug. *Doctr. Chr.* 2.8.12.
18 Markschies 2015, 297–8.

CONCLUSION

The New Testament canon was shaped and developed, in the first three centuries, because the leaders of the early church were determined to keep alive, and present afresh, the news that in Jesus the one true God was setting up his kingdom on earth as in heaven. The development and ultimate authorization of the New Testament canon, the list of the twenty-seven books we know today, came because the early church was determined to be loyal to Jesus himself. That meant that it had to make available to the next generations the books through which the God of creation and covenant, of new covenant and new creation, would be worshipped, and his will would be done in mission and service, on earth as in heaven. Some suspicions remained, some decisions were still debated, but there was strong central consensus among the churches of east and west that the 27 books of our New Testament constituted the true testimony of the apostles to God, Jesus, and the holy spirit, expressing the faith of the new-covenant people and shaping and directing their mission.

Further reading

Allert, Craig A. 2007. *A High View of Scripture: The Authority of the Bible and the Formation of the New Testament Canon*. Grand Rapids, MI: Baker.

Holmes, Michael W. 2008. 'Biblical Canon.' In *The Oxford Handbook of Early Christian Studies*. Edited by S. Ashbrook Harvey and D. G. Hunter. Oxford: Oxford University Press, pp. 406–26.

Kruger, Michael J. 2012. *Canon Revisited: Establishing the Origins and Authority of the New Testament Book*. Wheaton, IL: Crossway.

Markschies, Christoph. 2015. *Christian Theology and Its Institutions in the Early Roman Empire: Prolegomena to a History of Early Christian Theology*. Tr. W. Coppins; Waco, TX: Baylor University Press.

McDonald, Lee Martin. 2007 [1995]. *The Biblical Canon: Its Origin, Transmission, and Authority*. 3rd edn.; Peabody, MA: Hendrickson.

Metzger, Bruce M. 2009. *The Canon of the New Testament: Its Origin, Development, and Significance*. Oxford: Clarendon.

Fresco of banquet scene, Catacombe dei Santi Marcellino e Pietro, Rome, Italy, dated fourth century
De Agostini Picture Library / Bridgeman Images

IX

LIVING THE STORY OF THE NEW TESTAMENT

The New Testament's appeal to people for a new way of relating to one another, a way of kindness, a way that accepts the fact of anger but refuses to allow it to dictate the terms of engagement, is based four-square on the achievement of Jesus. His death has accomplished our forgiveness; very well, we must then pass that on to one another. We must become, must be known as, the people who don't hold grudges, who don't sulk. We must be the people who know how to say 'Sorry', and who know what to do when other people say it to us. It is remarkable, once more, how difficult this still seems, considering how much time the Christian church has had to think about it and how much energy has been spent on expounding the New Testament where it is all so clear. Perhaps it is because we have tried, if at all, to do it as though it were just a matter of obeying an artificial command—and then, finding it difficult, have stopped trying because nobody else seems to be very good at it either. Perhaps it might be different if we reminded ourselves frequently that we are preparing for life in God's new world, and that the death and resurrection of Jesus, which by baptism constitute our own new identity, offer us both the motivation and the energy to try again in a new way.[1]

This reflection offers one sharp-edged example of the wider challenge facing all those who read the New Testament with the intention of allowing it to shape their life and work.

---

[1] Wright *SC*, 196.

37

Bringing It All Together

In much popular modern Christian thought we have made a three-layered mistake. We have Platonized our eschatology (substituting 'souls going to heaven' for the promised new creation) and have therefore moralized our anthropology (substituting a qualifying examination of moral performance for the biblical notion of the human vocation), with the result that we have paganized our soteriology, our understanding of 'salvation' (substituting the idea of 'God killing Jesus to satisfy his wrath' for the genuinely biblical notions of atonement, victory, and reconciliation).[1]

CHAPTER AT A GLANCE

This chapter provides some suggestions as to how the New Testament matters for believers today.

By the end of this chapter you should be able to understand how the New Testament relates to developing a:
- storied theology;
- worldview;
- mission;
- way of Christian living;
- hope.

MAKING THE NEW TESTAMENT MATTER FOR TODAY

In the course of this introduction we have explored the setting, origin, purpose, and meaning of the New Testament documents. However, it would be irresponsible for a biblical teacher not to offer some thoughts—however fleeting—on why the New Testament matters. In other words, after all the historical labours and theological reflections, we must now ask, 'So what?' or 'How does any of this matter?' Several implications come to mind.

Storied theology

The New Testament, of course, holds out a faith to confess. It makes alarmingly specific claims about God, Jesus, and the holy spirit. It provides clear and bracing teaching about how to live. But none of this should

---

1   Amended from Wright *DRB*, 147.

obscure the fact that the truth of which the New Testament speaks is always deeply personal: indeed, it is a person, Jesus, Israel's Messiah and the world's lord, the one in whom God's truth is incarnated and his purpose accomplished. Biblical truth is not, in the last analysis, simply a series of propositions to be put in their logical order. It is a story, a story that climaxes in Israel's Messiah, Jesus, and finds its ultimate resolution in the final new creation. Unless we know that story, and know how the New Testament authors are rehearsing it and retelling it, we will never quite grasp what the early Christians were wanting to say.

Fresco depicts Abraham's divine visitation from Genesis 18.2, *c.* 1000, St Sophia of Kyiv, Ukraine

It helps to remember that the New Testament's use of the Old Testament was never about random proof-texting. Some Old Testament citations and allusions in the New Testament may indeed feel wooden or even laboured to us, but for the most part the early Christians saw themselves as aligning the stories of creation, Israel, exile, and the hope for a new exodus with the story of the church's gospel. For example, the place of Abraham in the argument of Romans 4 and Galatians 3 is not, as some assume, an example of 'proof from scripture', an ancient instance of someone who was 'justified by faith'. No: Abraham belongs within the larger story, the story of Israel, so that Abraham is the starting-point of the divine rescue-operation, the Messiah is its dramatic and unexpected conclusion, and the believing community is the world-wide people charged with putting it all into practice, led by the spirit. Some have tried to resist the idea of a grand biblical narrative, supposing that it reduces grace to the mere outworking of an immanent historical 'progress'. This is a pernicious distortion, combining elements of Reformational protests against 'works' (and hence against 'history'—that strange connection would take too long to unpack just now) with elements of early twentieth-century protests against Hegelian and similar progress-schemes. When we grasp the thought-world, and particularly the narrative world, of second-Temple Jews such as Paul, Peter and John, and even of Luke who was probably a gentile, we see how, for them, the good news of Jesus the Messiah, crucified and risen, made the sense it did within that world. Their allusions to Adam, Abraham, and Israel were not random 'proofs' to which they were appealing. Rather, they knew they were tapping into a single linear story—albeit with a shocking and subversive twist in the middle—in which various sub-stories were intimately interlocked.

For instance, for some second-Temple readers of Genesis, Abraham was seen as the divine answer to Adam, or rather the start of the divine answer to Adam, requiring the full answer in the later achievement of the Messiah. In addition, there is a close connection between Abraham and the house of David, as is clear in many texts. Psalm 2 comes immediately to mind, so vital for Paul and other early Christians: the Abrahamic promises of inheritance are globalized so that the true 'David', the 'son of God', will now inherit the whole world. This fits exactly with the evangelists' and Paul's sense that Isaiah 40—55 has now come true in Jesus and is now coming true through the spirit-led church. The work of the 'servant' has accomplished the divine purpose to end Israel's long exile and restore creation itself.

The trouble for us here is that most western exegetes until recently have ignored four themes which were obvious to many in the first century but quite opaque to many later ones. We start with three interlocking ones and then return to the fourth.

First, the principle just mentioned: God's purpose through Abraham was to rescue the human race. Second, the point of rescuing the human race was that God always purposed to work within creation *through his image-bearers*, so that saving humans from sin and death was not simply for their own benefit but so that, through renewed humans, God would rescue creation itself. Third, the New Testament authors invoke again and again the biblical prophecies which spoke of God's frustrated judgment on the people of Israel, resulting in exile—not just the exile in Babylon itself, but the much longer exile, spoken of in Daniel 9, in which most Jews of Paul's day believed they were still living. The exiles, still enslaved under foreign overlords, longed for the much-promised new exodus. Not only Paul, but most of the New Testament writers, insist in their various ways, not least through scriptural allusion and echo, that this is what has happened in the events concerning Jesus. (The reason they can all be so sure of this is not least because Jesus himself chose Passover as the moment to do what had to be done.) The different stories all fit together: the exile of Israel is the long outworking of the exile of Adam and Eve from the Garden, and the new exodus is therefore the rescue of Israel—in the person of the Messiah as he defeats the powers of darkness and is raised from the dead—and with that the rescue of the human race as a whole.

Doing biblical theology, therefore, is not just a matter of knowing the facts about the faith and organizing them through the correct system. (There is certainly a place for different kinds of 'systematic theology', so long as it is umbilically connected to a proper narrative and biblical theology.) Christian theology is about knowing the story, its plot, the characters, the protagonist, the villains, the struggle, and the resolution. And then—most of all—knowing the church's place, and one's own place, within that story, the ongoing act of the divine drama. Doing biblical theology means learning your lines, playing your part, and discovering a new way not only of viewing the world but of acting within the world.

Worldview

Christian theology is *storied theology*. It tells the grand narrative about God and God's relationship with the world, from creation to new creation, with Jesus in the middle. (You can see that in the great Creeds, which are not simply a list of 'things to believe' but, in embryo, tell this same story.) *The narrative concerns a creator and his creation; humans made in this creator's image and called to perform certain tasks; the rebellion of humans and the dissonance of creation at every level; and particularly about the creator's acting, through Israel and climactically through Jesus, to rescue his creation from its ensuing plight. The story continues with the creator acting by his own Spirit within the world, to bring it towards the restoration and new flourishing which is his intended goal.* A great deal of Christian theology consists of the attempt to tell this story as clearly as possible, and to allow it to subvert other ways of telling the story of the world, including those which offer themselves as would-be Christian tellings but which, upon close examination, fall short in some way or other.

On top of that, this story also constitutes a *worldview*, a way of understanding the realities and relationships in the world as we perceive them. Worldviews are the basic stuff of human existence, the lens through which the world is seen (a 'worldview' is not what you look *at* but what you look *through*). It generates a blueprint for how one should live in the world, and above all the sense of identity and place which enables human beings to be what they are. To ignore worldviews, either our own or those of the culture we are studying, would result in extraordinary shallowness. 'Worldviews' provide the answers, normally unstated and implicit but all the more powerful for that reason, to questions that begin with 'Who?' 'Where?' and 'What?' 'How?' and 'When?' Beliefs and actions emerge from the underlying combination of stories, symbols, praxes, and questions that make up the 'worldview'.

Christian theology offers answers to the five basic questions that make up a worldview:

1. *Who are we?* We are humans, made in the image of the creator. We have vocational responsibilities that come with this status. We are not fundamentally determined by race, gender, social class, or geographical location; nor are we simply pawns in a determinist game.

2. *Where are we?* We are in a good and beautiful, though transient world, the creation of the God in whose image we are made. We are not in an alien and hostile world (as the Gnostic imagines); nor in a cosmos to which we owe allegiance as to a divine being (as the pantheist would suggest); nor in a random and ultimately meaningless universe (as suggested by Epicureanism, both ancient and modern).

3. *What is wrong?* Humanity has rebelled against the creator. This rebellion reflects a cosmic dislocation between the creator and the creation, and the world is consequently out of tune with its created intention. A Christian worldview rejects dualisms that associate evil with createdness or physicality; equally it rejects monisms that analyse evil simply in terms of some humans not being fully in tune with their environment. Its analysis of evil is more subtle and far-reaching. It likewise rejects as the whole truth all partial analyses, such as those of Marx or Freud, which elevate half-truths to the status of the whole truth.

4. *How is this to be put right?* The creator has acted, is acting, and will act within his creation to deal with the weight of evil set up by human rebellion, and to bring his world to the end for which it was made, namely that it should resonate fully with his own presence and glory. This action, of course, is focused upon Jesus and the spirit of the creator. We reject, that is, solutions to the human plight which only address one part of the problem.

5. *What time is it?* From ancient Israel to second-Temple Jews and on into early Christianity there was always a sense of 'where we are in the story'. From the Christian point of view, we are living in the time of fulfilment, the time when God's kingdom has already been decisively launched on earth as in heaven through the work of Jesus himself, and yet before all things, including death itself, are subjugated to his reign. This is the 'fifth act' of the cosmic five-act play that began with creation, continued with human rebellion, saw the call of Abraham and his family, and then saw this bear ultimate fruit in Jesus. The spirit-led church is called to live the genuinely human life, anticipating in the present the life of the 'age to come', freed from the power of evil, which has been launched through Jesus' death and resurrection.

This Christian worldview gives rise to a particular type of praxis, a particular mode of being-in-the-world (a point beautifully made in *Ep. Diog.* 6.1 where it is said that 'what the soul is in the body, this is what the Christians are in the world',[2] namely a means of life, preservation, healing, and love diffused across the world). Actually, this might be better expressed, in the Christian case, as being-*for*-the-world, since in the fundamental Christian worldview humans in general are part of the creator's designed means of looking after his world, and Christians in particular

---

2 Tr. R. Brannan (2018).

are part of his means of bringing healing to the world. As with all other worldviews, of course, its adherents are not noticeably successful in attaining a complete correlation between their statements about their own being-in-the-world and their actual practice; in other words, we too mess it up on a regular basis. This is in no way fatal to the theory. It merely means that Christians, like everybody else, are often muddled, mistaken, foolish and wayward, and are probably trying to ride at least one other horse at the same time as the Christian one. But in principle the Christian worldview supplies its adherents with a sense of direction, namely, the vocation to work in whatever way may be appropriate for the glory of the creator and the healing of his world, anticipating in the present the final fulfilment.

Story of the Bible narrated through mosaics in the Cathedral of Monreale, c. twelfth century, Sicily
cristian ghisla / Shutterstock

A Christian worldview thus generates *basic beliefs* about God, Jesus, the atonement, resurrection, spirit, the future, and so forth. We might see this set of beliefs as 'Simple Christianity', those elements of the Christian faith that transcend culture (though they include the call to be culture-makers and culture-transformers). They constitute a kind of portable story which Christians take with them wherever they go, from Tasmania to Tripoli. And from these *basic beliefs* there emerge what we may call *consequent beliefs*, beliefs that vary more widely based on context and environment, as Christians in all places have to navigate and negotiate how to live faithfully in their unique situation. Christians living in Lebanon, after all, face different challenges to those living in London, England, or Lynchburg, Virginia. Christianity will always have certain local variations and global diversity as the body of Christ discerns what it means to be faithful in many places and spaces. Part of the urgent task facing global Christianity in our own day is to figure out what is basic (and therefore unalterable) and what is consequent (and therefore open for debate). The second century, picking up directly from the New Testament itself, insisted that redemption meant God's reaffirmation of the goodness of the original creation. The third and fourth centuries, again echoing the New Testament, insisted that Jesus was and is to be identified as embodying in human form the one God of Israel. The fourth and fifth centuries, reflecting a further biblical strand, insisted that Christian life, work and witness was and is itself the work of the same living God in the person of his spirit. And so on. Being Christian involves an ever-deeper commitment to these basic beliefs and a fresh application of them to ever-changing circumstances and ideas.

The New Testament thus provides the basis for a theology and a worldview in which we can explain and enact, under the guidance of the Spirit, several things universal to human experience: justice, spirituality, relationships, beauty, freedom, truth, and power. A Christian worldview tells us what those things mean, what to do with them, how to enjoy them, and how not to abuse them. A Christian worldview, focused on such topics, will enable us to engage in authentic worship, enact the Christian vocation, and promote the flourishing of humans, individually and together.

Mission

The mission of the church—or, more properly, the mission of God through the church, the ongoing tasks for which the living God 'sends' and equips the church—can only be properly understood in the light of a fully biblical eschatology. This means firmly embracing the biblical vision of new creation, of new heavens and new earth, inaugurated when Jesus announced God's kingdom and rose from the dead after defeating the powers of darkness, and to be consummated when he returns in glory to make all things new. The mission of the church *derives from* that inauguration, energised by the same spirit by whose power Jesus was raised, and *points forward to* that consummation, anticipating it, demonstrating its life-transforming reality even in the present time, and calling men, women, and children to share in the new life, communal and personal, which is already a reality and which will be fully revealed at the last. In that fully orbed and eschatologically oriented mission, the church's task is to proclaim the lord Jesus, to summon people to follow him with faithful allegiance, to nurture believers so that they become holy disciples, and to do mercy and justice in every context and setting. We are not trying to 'build the kingdom' on earth—as if we could be arrogant enough to think such a thing—but we are building *for* the kingdom on earth. God will establish the kingdom, implementing Jesus' death and resurrection, in his own way and time; but part of believing in the holy spirit is believing that the life, work, and prayer of the church in the present is *part of that kingdom-establishing operation*, so that what the church does in the present time, through evangelism and discipleship, by pursuing justice, and through our ministries of mercy, constitutes a multiplex and genuine anticipation of the state of things to come. We are, as it were, borrowing from God's future, planting seeds of hope, raising the flag of the yet-to-be-consummated kingdom.

The different vocations within the body of Christ are all part of this eschatological project. The church, in its fascinatingly varied life, is to be the advance guard of what is still to come (see especially Eph. 4.1–16).

This holistic vision of new creation, and all that follows from it, may be startling to many people. There are plenty of Christians for whom 'eschatology', if they use the word at all, regularly focuses on 'going to heaven when you die' on the one hand, or, on the other hand, a 'second coming' in which Jesus will snatch his people away from the wreck of the present world and take them to 'heaven' at last. This western vision, deeply rooted (albeit with variations) in the middle ages, gives rise to a sense of 'mission' simply in terms of 'saving souls for heaven', despite the fact that the Bible nowhere speaks of the future in those terms. Instead of thinking of mission in terms of 'How can I find a merciful God?' we might find that Milton's epics, of 'Paradise Lost' and 'Paradise Regained', offer far more promising horizons for plotting the direction for mission. Yes, at one level, we are tasked with rescuing individuals, seeing them set free from the sin that has entangled them, transferring them from the dominion of darkness and shepherding them into the kingdom of the son of divine love (Col. 1.13–14), bringing people through their own personal 'exodus' from the clutches of the Adamic triangle of sin–law–death into an inheritance filled with an abundance of grace. All that is vital as a regular focus of Christian work. But—if we take the panoramic view—our mission is far more cosmic. We are called, as Ernst Käsemann liked to put it, to participate in what God is doing, repossessing the world for himself—always with the caveat, from Karl Barth, that one never learns 'what God is doing' simply by observing things in the world, but only through the gospel itself. In the phrase I (NTW) have preferred, God has promised to put the world to rights; he has accomplished this in principle in Jesus; and he now calls humans, by the gospel and in the power of the spirit, to participate in his putting-right project for the world. Mission, then, is what we do within the death-throes of a corrupted and evil-ridden world and by the creation-renewing power of the gospel. The holy spirit, in the New Testament, is the 'downpayment' of what is still to come. Jesus' followers are called to reflect the love, peace, and joy that will characterize the new creation.

The cultural, political, and personal challenges that arise from this missional hermeneutic—particularly related to the *unity* and the *holiness* of the church, and the readiness to be counter-cultural even if it means suffering—is where the challenge really bites. Our view of the church (*ecclesiology*) derives from, and must be shaped by, the call to *mission*; but we must remember that mission itself derives from *eschatology*. In Jesus' cross and resurrection God defeated the powers that have enslaved the world, and launched the new creation. Without this perspective, 'mission' collapses into trying to persuade people that they really want a new religious experience, or that they really want to go to heaven when they die (and that we have the secret ticket). Mission in the New Testament is about colonizing earth with the life of heaven, so that one day, whenever the Lord wills, the old earth will be healed and renewed, God's renewed people will reign with Jesus over his new world, peace and life will subdue hostility and death, and God will be all in all.

A way of Christian living

Christian living means dying with Christ and rising again. That is part of the meaning of baptism, the starting-point of the Christian pilgrimage. The model of pilgrimage, indeed, is helpful, since baptism awakens echoes of the children of Israel coming out of Egypt and going off to the land of promise. The whole world is now God's holy land, and God will reclaim it and renew it as the ultimate goal of all our wanderings.

Our pilgrimage begins with the death and resurrection of Jesus, and has for its goal the renewal of the presently corrupt creation. The route through the wilderness, the path of our pilgrimage, will therefore involve two things in particular: renunciation on the one hand and rediscovery on the other.

Renunciation. The world in its present state is out of tune with God's ultimate intention, and there will be a great many things, some of them deeply woven into our imagination and personality, to which the only Christian response will be 'No'. Jesus told his followers that if they wanted to come after him they would have to deny themselves and take up their cross. The only way to find yourself, he said, is to lose yourself (a strikingly different agenda from today's finding-out-who-I-really-am philosophies). From the very beginning, writers like Paul and John recognized that this is not just difficult, but actually impossible. You can't do it by some kind of Herculean moral effort. The only way is by drawing strength from beyond ourselves, the strength of God's spirit, on the basis of our sharing of Jesus' death and resurrection in baptism.

Rediscovery. New creation is not a denial of our humanness, but its reaffirmation. There will be a great many things, some of them deeply counter-intuitive and initially perplexing, to which the proper Christian response is 'Yes'. The resurrection of Jesus enables us to see how living as a Christian is neither a matter of discovering the inner truth of the way the world currently is, nor a matter of learning a way of life that is in tune with a totally different world and thus completely out of tune with the present one. It is a matter of glimpsing that in God's new creation, of which Jesus' resurrection is the start, all that was good in the original creation is reaffirmed. All that has corrupted and defaced it—including many things which are woven so tightly into the fabric of the world as we know it that we can't imagine being without them—will be done away. Learning to live as a Christian is learning to live as a renewed human being, anticipating the eventual new creation, with a world which is still longing and groaning for that final redemption.

The problem is, of course, that it is often unclear what we are to renounce and what we are to rediscover. How can we say 'No' to things which seem so much part of life that to reject them appears to us as the rejection of part of God's good creation? How can we say 'Yes' to things which many Christians have seen not as good and right but as dangerous and deluded? How can we avoid dualism on the one hand and paganism on the other? Somehow we have to work out which styles of life and behaviour belong with the corrupting evil which must be rejected if new creation is to emerge, and which styles of life and behaviour belong with the new creation which must be embraced, struggled for, and celebrated.

This takes nerves of steel, and a careful searching after wisdom. We are to be informed by the life, teaching, death, and resurrection of Jesus; by the leading of the spirit; by the wisdom we find in scripture; by the fact of our baptism and all that it means; by the sense of God's presence and guidance through prayer; and by the fellowship of other Christians, both our contemporaries and those of other ages whose lives and writings we should use as wise guides. Listing all these in that fashion makes them sound as if they are separate sources of teaching, but in reality it isn't like that. They work together in a hundred different ways. Part of the art of being a Christian is learning to be sensitive to all of them, and to weigh what we think we are hearing from one quarter alongside what is being said in another.

Sculpture depicting the baptism of Augustine, dated 1549, Troyes Cathedral, Troyes, France
Public Domain

Only when we have set all that out quite clearly can we ever speak of 'rules'. There *are* rules, of course. The New Testament has plenty of them. Always give alms in secret. Never go to law against a fellow-Christian. Never take private vengeance. Be kind. Always show hospitality. Give away money cheerfully. Don't be anxious. Don't judge another Christian over a matter of conscience. Always forgive. And so on. And the worrying thing about that randomly selected list is that most Christians ignore most of them most of the time. It isn't so much that we lack clear rules; we lack, I fear, the teaching that will draw attention to what is in fact there in our primary documents, not least in the teaching of Jesus himself.

The rules are to be understood, not as arbitrary laws thought up by a distant God to stop us having fun (or to set us some ethical hoops to jump through as a kind of moral examination), but as the signposts to a way of life in which heaven and earth overlap, in which God's future breaks into the present, in which we discover what genuine humanness looks and feels like in practice.

When we start to glimpse that, we find that we are listening to the voice of Jesus, calling us to follow him into God's new world, the world in which the hints, signposts, and echoes of the present world turn into the reality of the next one. All that we do here comes down to this: to prepare for, and to enter into, that already-inaugurated new creation, the world which will at the last fulfil all our hopes.

Hope

The purpose of scripture, Paul says in Romans 15.4, is so that 'we might have hope'. He was speaking, of course, of Israel's scriptures, but with hindsight the same applies to the early Christian writings. If that is so, then a prominent purpose of New Testament study ought to be to explain and illuminate the substance of that hope. In fact, we could even say that the mission of the church is to share and reflect the future hope as the New Testament presents it.

Hope is, in fact, the foundation for the daily workings of a church. Faithful Christian ministry will often take Jesus' followers to places where hope is in short supply: places where a sense of hopelessness hangs over a community, where the effects of global financial chaos are still in effect, where there is unemployment and family breakdown, where refugees feel alienated and despised in their adopted homes, where racial injustice is regarded as a kind of ugly normality that we have to put up with, and xenophobia is part of normal political rhetoric. We are called to work with, and for, people who are one illness away from financial ruin, or who fear for their children's safety when walking down the street; people who find that cultural elites mock and attack them because they do not signal 'progressive virtues'; communities where politics means partisan policies on the one hand and acute apathy on the other; a world in which, while all this is going on, the rich keep getting richer and the poor keep getting poorer. To such places, and the sad people who live in them, as well as to those who find themselves battered by circumstances beyond their control, the message of Jesus and his death and resurrection comes as good news from a far country, news of surprising hope.

The church, in the power of the spirit, must signal in its life and teaching that there is more to being human than mere survival, more than hedonism and power, more than ambition and entertainment. Life, we must insist, does have purpose; there is comfort for those weighed down by moral injury; narcissism is not the true 'normal'; there is something more powerful than economics and bombs. There really is a different way to be human, and it has been decisively launched with Jesus. There is a new world, and it has already begun, and it works by healing and forgiveness and new starts and fresh energy. The world will probably raise its cynical eyebrows: can these things really be true? Yes, answers the church; and they come about as people worship the God in whose image they are made, as they follow the Lord who bore their sins and rose from the dead, as they are indwelt by his spirit and thereby given new life, a new way of life, a new zest for life. It is often pointed out that some of the places most lacking in hope are not the industrial wastelands or the bleak landscapes shorn of beauty, but the places where there is too much money, too much high culture, too much of everything except faith, hope, and love. This is the good news—of justice, redemption, truth, beauty, and above all Jesus—that the church is called upon to live and to speak, to bring into reality, in each place and each generation.

The church, because it is the family that believes in the new creation, a belief constantly reinforced by the New Testament, should stand out in every city, town, and village as the place where hope bursts forth. Not just hope that something better lies in 'the hereafter'; rather, a belief that God's new world has been sown, like seeds in a field, and that it is already bearing surprising fruit. The life of the new world has already been unleashed in the present time, and what we do as a result of that life, that spirit-given direction and energy, is already in itself part of the new world that God is making. Where this hope takes root, the story told by the whole New Testament comes to life again and again: through Jesus, and by his spirit, the new world has been born. All that we do in the present, in working for justice and beauty, in searching for truth in every sphere of life, above all in speaking cheerfully and wisely of Jesus, is rooted in the scriptures, both of Israel and of the early church, and is designed to produce hope. When that hope is present, it will thus reinforce, for communities and individuals of every sort, the message which the New Testament proclaims on every page.

View of Jerusalem from the Mount of Olives

Bibliography

Aageson, James W. 2008. *Paul, the Pastoral Epistles, and the Early Church*. LPS; Peabody, MA: Hendrickson.

Achtemeier, Paul J. 1996. *1 Peter*. Hermeneia; Minneapolis: Fortress.

Adam, A. K. M. 1995. *Making Sense of New Testament Theology: Modern Problems and Prospects*. Macon, GA: Mercer University Press.

Adams, Edward, and David G. Horrell (eds.). 2004. *Christianity at Corinth: The Quest for the Pauline Church*. Louisville, KY: Westminster John Knox.

Adams, Samuel L. 2014. *Social and Economic Life in Second Temple Judea*. Louisville, KY: Westminster John Knox.

Adams, Sean A. 2012. 'The Genre of Luke and Acts: The State of the Question.' In *Issues in Luke-Acts: Selected Essays*. Edited by S. A. Adams and M. Pahl. Piscataway, NJ: Gorgias, pp. 97–120.

———. 2013a. 'The Relationships of Paul and Luke: Luke, Paul's Letters, and the "We" Passages of Acts.' In *Paul and His Social Relations*. Edited by S. E. Porter and C. Land. PAST 7; Leiden: Brill, pp. 125–42.

———. 2013b. *The Genre of Acts and Collected Biography*. SNTSMS 156; Cambridge: Cambridge University Press.

Adams, Sean A., and Michael Pahl (eds.). 2012. *Issues in Luke-Acts: Selected Essays*. Piscataway, NJ: Gorgias.

Aernie, Jeffrey W. 2012. *Is Paul Also among the Prophets? An Examination of the Relationship between Paul and the Old Testament Prophetic Tradition in 2 Corinthians*. LNTS 467; London: T&T Clark.

Aichele, George, et al. 1995. *The Postmodern Bible: The Bible and Culture Collective*. New Haven, CT: Yale University Press.

Akala, Adesola Joan. 2015. *The Son-Father Relationship and Christological Symbolism in the Fourth Gospel*. LNTS 505; London: T&T Clark.

Alexander, Loveday. 1993. *The Preface to Luke's Gospel: Literary Convention and Social Context in Luke 1.1–4 and Acts 1.1*. SNTSMS 78; Cambridge: Cambridge University Press.

Allen, David L. 2010. *Lukan Authorship of Hebrews*. Nashville: Broadman & Holman.

Allen, Garrick V., Ian Paul, and Simon P. Woodman (eds.). 2015. *The Book of Revelation: Currents in British Research on the Apocalypse*. WUNT 2.411; Tübingen: Mohr Siebeck.

Allert, Craig A. 2007. *A High View of Scripture: The Authority of the Bible and the Formation of the New Testament Canon*. Grand Rapids, MI: Baker.

Allison, Dale C. 2005. *Resurrecting Jesus: The Earliest Christian Tradition and Its Interpreters.* London: T&T Clark.
——. 2009. *The Historical Christ and the Theological Jesus.* Grand Rapids, MI: Eerdmans.
——. 2010. *Constructing Jesus: Memory, Imagination, and History.* Grand Rapids, MI: Baker.
——. 2013. *James.* ICC; London: T&T Clark.
Ameling, Walter (ed.). 2004. *Inscriptiones Judaicae Orientis, vol. 2: Kleinasien.* TSAJ 99; Tübingen: Mohr Siebeck.
Anderson, Paul N. 1997. *The Christology of the Fourth Gospel.* Valley Forge, PA; Trinity Press International.
Applebaum, Shimon. 1974. 'Economic Life in Palestine.' In *The Jewish People in the First Century: Historical Geography, Political History, Social, Cultural and Religious Life and Institutions.* Edited by S. Safrai and M. Stern. CRINT 1; Assen: Van Gorcum, 2.631–700.
Ascough, Richard S. 2003. *Paul's Macedonian Associations: The Social Context of Philippians and 1 Thessalonians.* WUNT 2.161; Tübingen: Mohr Siebeck.
Aslan, Reza. 2013. *Zealot: The Life and Times of Jesus of Nazareth.* New York: Random House.
Aune, David E. 1983. *Prophecy in Early Christianity and the Ancient Mediterranean World.* Grand Rapids, MI: Eerdmans.
——. 1987. *The New Testament in Its Literary Environment.* Philadelphia: Westminster.
——. 1991. 'On the Origins of the "Council of Javneh" Myth.' *Journal of Biblical Literature* 110: 491–3.
——. 1997–8. *Revelation.* 3 vols.; WBC; Dallas: Word.
——. 2003. *The Westminster Dictionary of New Testament and Early Christian Literature and Rhetoric.* Louisville, KY: Westminster John Knox.
——. 2010. 'The World of Roman Hellenism.' In *The Blackwell Companion to the New Testament.* Edited by D. E. Aune. Malden, MA: Wiley-Blackwell, pp. 15–37.
Baird, William. 1992. *History of New Testament Research, vol. 1: From Deism to Tübingen.* Minneapolis: Fortress.
Bakirtzis, Charalambos, and Helmut Koester (eds.). 2009 [1998]. *Philippi at the Time of Paul and after His Death.* Eugene, OR: Wipf & Stock.
Balch, David (ed.). 1991. *Social History of the Matthean Community.* Minneapolis: Fortress.
Balla, Peter. 1997. *Challenges to New Testament Theology: An Attempt to Justify the Enterprise.* WUNT 2.95; Tübingen: Mohr Siebeck.
Barclay, John M. G. 1996. *Jews in the Mediterranean Diaspora: From Alexander to Trajan (323 BCE–117 CE).* Edinburgh: T&T Clark.
——. 2015. 'The Last Years of Paul: What Are the Issues?' In *The Last Years of Paul: Essays from the Tarragona Conference, June 2013.* Edited by A. P. I. Tàrrech, J. M. G. Barclay, and J. Frey. WUNT 352; Tübingen: Mohr Siebeck, pp. 1–14.
Barnett, Paul. 2011. *Paul: A Pastor's Heart in Second Corinthians.* Sydney: Aquila.
Barrett, C. K. 1961. *Luke the Historian in Recent Study.* London: Epworth.
——. 1978 [1956]. *The Gospel According to St John: An Introduction with Commentary and Notes on the Greek Text.* 2nd edn.; London: SPCK.
——. 1994–8. *The Acts of the Apostles.* 2 vols.; ICC; Edinburgh: T&T Clark.
——. 1996. 'The First New Testament?' *Novum Testamentum* 38: 94–104.
Bassler, Jouette M. 1996. *1 Timothy, 2 Timothy, Titus.* ANTC; Nashville, TN: Abingdon.
Bateman, Herbert W. (ed.). 2006. *Four Views on the Warning Passages in Hebrews.* Grand Rapids, MI: Kregel.
Bauckham, Richard J. 1983. *Jude, 2 Peter.* WBC; Waco, TX: Word.

———. 1990. *Jude and the Relatives of Jesus in the Early Church*. London: T&T Clark.
———. 1993a. *The Theology of the Book of Revelation*. NTT; Cambridge: Cambridge University Press.
———. 1993b. *The Climax of Prophecy: Studies in the Book of Revelation*. Edinburgh: T&T Clark.
———. 1998a. 'For Whom Were the Gospels Written?' In *The Gospels for All Christians: Rethinking the Gospel Audiences*. Edited by R. Bauckham. Grand Rapids, MI: Eerdmans, pp. 9–48.
———. 1998b. '2 Peter and the Apocalypse of Peter.' In *The Fate of the Dead: Studies in Jewish and Christian Apocalypses*. NovTSup 93; Leiden: Brill, pp. 290–303.
———. 1999. *James*. NTR; London: Routledge.
———. 2000. 'What If Paul Had Travelled East Rather Than West?' *Biblical Interpretation* 8: 171–84.
———. 2001. 'Revelation.' In *The Oxford Bible Commentary*. Edited by J. Barton and J. Muddiman. Oxford: Oxford University Press, pp. 1287–1306.
———. 2002. *Gospel Women: Studies in the Named Women in the Gospels*. Grand Rapids, MI: Eerdmans.
———. 2006. *Jesus and the Eyewitnesses: The Gospels as Eyewitness Testimony*. Grand Rapids, MI: Eerdmans.
———. 2007. *The Testimony of the Beloved Disciple: Narrative, History, and Theology in the Gospel of John*. Grand Rapids, MI: Baker.
———. 2015. *Gospel of Glory: Major Themes in Johannine Theology*. Grand Rapids, MI: Baker.
Bauckham, Richard, Daniel Driver, Trevor Hart, and Nathan MacDonald (eds.). 2008. *A Cloud of Witnesses: The Theology of Hebrews in Its Ancient Contexts*. LNTS 387; London: T&T Clark.
———. 2009. *The Epistle to the Hebrews and Christian Theology*. Grand Rapids, MI: Eerdmans.
Baum, Armin D. 2001. *Pseudepigraphie und literarische Fälschung im frühen Christentum*. WUNT 2.138; Tübingen: Mohr Siebeck.
———. 2012. 'The Original Epilogue (John 20:30–31), the Secondary Appendix (21:1–23), and the Editorial Epilogues (21:24–25) of John's Gospel.' In *Earliest Christian History*. Edited by M. F. Bird and J. Maston. WUNT 2.320; Tübingen: Mohr Siebeck, pp. 227–70.
———. 2013. 'Authorship and Pseudepigraphy in Early Christian Literature: A Translation of the Most Important Source Texts and an Annotated Bibliography.' In *Paul and Pseudepigraphy*. Edited by S. E. Porter and G. P. Fewster. Leiden: Brill, pp. 11–64.
Bawarshi, Anis S. 2003. *Genre and the Invention of the Writer: Reconsidering the Place of Invention in Composition*. Logan, UT: Utah State University Press.
Beale, Greg K. 1999. *The Book of Revelation*. NIGTC; Grand Rapids, MI: Eerdmans.
Beavis, Mary Ann. 2011. *Mark*. PCNT; Grand Rapids, MI: Baker.
Becker, Adam H., and Annette Yoshiko Reed (eds.). 2007. *The Ways that Never Parted: Jews and Christians in Late Antiquity and the Early Middle Ages*. Minneapolis: Fortress.
Becker, Patrick, and Steffen Jöris. 2016. 'Toward a Scientific Designation: *Apocalypticism* in Biblical and Modern Studies—A Comparative Approach.' *Horizons in Biblical Theology* 38: 22–44.
Beckwith, Roger. 2008. *The Old Testament Canon of the New Testament Church and Its Background in Early Judaism*. Eugene, OR: Wipf & Stock.
Belleville, Linda L. 1996. *2 Corinthians*. IVPNTC; Downers Grove, IL: InterVarsity.
Besançon Spencer, Aída. 2014. *1 Timothy*. NCCS; Eugene, OR: Cascade.
———. 2014. *2 Timothy and Titus*. NCCS; Eugene, OR: Cascade.
Betz, Hans Dieter. 1979. *Galatians: A Commentary on Paul's Letter to the Churches in Galatia*. Hermeneia; Minneapolis: Fortress.

Bird, Michael F. 2004. 'Should Evangelicals Participate in the "Third Quest for the Historical Jesus"?' *Themelios* 29: 6–7.

———. 2006a. *Jesus and the Origins of the Gentile Mission*. LNTS 331; LHJS; London: T&T Clark.

———. 2006b. 'The Peril of Modernizing Jesus and the Crisis of Not Contemporizing the Christ.' *Evangelical Quarterly* 78.4: 291–312.

———. 2006c. 'Is There Really a "Third Quest" for the Historical Jesus?' *Scottish Bulletin of Evangelical Theology* 24.2: 195–219.

———. 2006d. 'Jesus and the Revolutionaries: Did Jesus Call Israel to Repent of Nationalistic Ambitions?' *Colloquium: Australian and New Zealand Theological Review* 38.2: 127–39.

———. 2006e. 'Bauckham's *The Gospel for All Christians* Revisited.' *European Journal of Theology* 15: 5–13.

———. 2007. *The Saving Righteousness of God: Studies on Paul, Justification, and the New Perspective*. Milton Keynes: Paternoster.

———. 2008a. 'Reassessing a Rhetorical Approach to Paul's Letters.' *Expository Times* 119.8: 374–9.

———. 2008b. 'Jesus the Law-Breaker.' In *Who Do My Opponents Say that I Am? An Investigation of the Accusations against Jesus*. Edited by Joseph B. Modica and Scot McKnight. LHJS; London: T&T Clark, pp. 3–26.

———. 2008c. 'Passion Predictions.' In *Encyclopedia of the Historical Jesus*. Edited by Craig A. Evans. New York: Routledge, pp. 442–6.

———. 2008d. *A Bird's-Eye View of Paul: The Man, His Mission and His Message*. Nottingham: InterVarsity.

———. 2009a. 'New Testament Theology Re-Loaded: Integrating Biblical Theology and Christian Origins.' *Tyndale Bulletin* 60: 265–91.

———. 2009b. *Are You the One Who Is to Come? The Historical Jesus and the Messianic Question*. Grand Rapids, MI: Baker.

———. 2009c. 'What If Martin Luther Had Read the Dead Sea Scrolls? Historical Particularity and Theological Interpretation in Pauline Theology: Galatians as a Test Case.' *Journal of Theological Interpretation* 3: 107–25.

———. 2009d. *Colossians and Philemon*. NCCS; Eugene, OR: Cascade.

———. 2010a. *Crossing Over Sea and Land: Jewish Missionary Activity in the Second Temple Period*. Peabody, MA: Hendrickson.

———. 2010b. 'Birth of Jesus.' In *Encyclopedia of the Historical Jesus*. Edited by Craig A. Evans. New York: Routledge, pp. 71–4.

———. 2011a. 'John the Baptist.' In *Jesus among Friends and Enemies*. Edited by Chris L. Keith and Larry Hurtado. Grand Rapids, MI: Baker, pp. 60–80.

———. 2011b. 'Mark: Interpreter of Peter and Disciple of Paul.' In *Paul and the Gospels: Christologies, Conflicts, and Convergences*. Edited by M. F. Bird and J. Willitts. LNTS 411; London: T&T Clark, pp. 30–61.

——— (ed.). 2012a. *Four Views on the Apostle Paul*. Grand Rapids, MI: Zondervan.

———. 2012b. *Jesus Is the Christ: The Messianic Testimony of the Gospels*. Downers Grove, IL: InterVarsity.

———. 2013a. 'Josephus and the New Testament.' In *The Background of the New Testament: An Examination of the Context of Early Christianity*. Edited by Joel B. Green and Lee Martin McDonald. Grand Rapids, MI: Baker, pp. 398–404.

———. 2013b. 'Letter to the Romans.' In *All Things to All Cultures: Paul among Jews, Greeks and Romans*. Edited by M. Harding and A. Knobbs. Grand Rapids, MI: Eerdmans, pp. 177–204.

——. 2013c. 'Synoptics and John.' In *Dictionary of Paul and His Letters*. Edited by J. B. Green, J. K. Brown, and N. Perrin. 2nd edn.; Downers Grove, IL: InterVarsity, pp. 920–4.

——. 2013d. *Evangelical Theology: A Biblical and Systematic Introduction*. Grand Rapids, MI: Zondervan.

——. 2014a. 'Did Jesus Think He was God?' In *How God Became Jesus: The Real Origins of Belief in Jesus' Divine Nature—A Response to Bart Ehrman*. Grand Rapids, MI: Zondervan, pp. 45–70.

——. 2014b. *The Gospel of the Lord: How the Early Church Wrote the Story of Jesus*. Grand Rapids, MI: Eerdmans.

——. 2016a. *Romans*. SGBC; Grand Rapids, MI: Zondervan.

——. 2016b. *An Anomalous Jew: Paul among Jews, Greeks and Romans*. Grand Rapids, MI: Eerdmans.

Bird, Michael F., and James G. Crossley. 2008. *How Did Christianity Begin? A Believer and Non-Believer Examine the Evidence*. London: SPCK.

Black, David Alan (ed.). 2008. *Perspectives on the Ending of Mark's Gospel: Four Views*. Nashville: Broadman & Holman.

Blackwell, Ben, John Goodrich, and Jason Maston (eds.). 2015. *Reading Romans in Context: Paul and Second Temple Judaism*. Grand Rapids, MI: Zondervan.

Blomberg, Craig. 2001. *The Historical Reliability of John's Gospel: Issues and Commentary*. Leicester: InterVarsity.

——. 2004. *Making Sense of the New Testament: Three Crucial Questions*. Grand Rapids, MI: Baker.

——. 2005. *Contagious Holiness: Jesus' Meals with Sinners*. NSBT 19; Downers Grove, IL: InterVarsity.

Blomberg, Craig L., and Mariam J. Kamell. 2008. *James*. ZECNT; Grand Rapids, MI: Zondervan.

Blount, Brian K. 2009. *Revelation: A Commentary*. NTL; Louisville, KY: Westminster John Knox.

——. 2014. *Invasion of the Dead: Preaching Resurrection*. Louisville, KY: Westminster John Knox.

Bock, Darrell L. 1994–6. *Luke*. 2 vols.; BECNT; Grand Rapids, MI: Baker.

——. 2007. *Acts*. BECNT; Grand Rapids, MI: Baker.

——. 2010. *Recovering the Real Lost Gospel: Reclaiming the Gospel as Good News*. Nashville: Broadman & Holman.

——. 2012. *A Theology of Luke and Acts: God's Promised Program, Realized for All Nations*. BTNT; Grand Rapids, MI: Zondervan.

——. 2013. 'Son of Man.' In *Dictionary of Jesus and the Gospels*. Edited by J. B. Green, J. K. Brown, and N. Perrin. 2nd edn.; Downers Grove, IL: InterVarsity, pp. 894–900.

Bock, Darrell L., and Mitch Glaser. 2012. *The Gospel According to Isaiah 53: Encountering the Suffering Servant in Jewish and Christian Theology*. Grand Rapids, MI: Kregel.

Bockmuehl, Markus. 1998. *The Epistle to the Philippians*. BNTC; London: A&C Black.

——. 2001. '1 Thessalonians 2:14–16 and the Church in Jerusalem.' *Tyndale Bulletin* 52: 1–31.

——. 2006. *Seeing the Word: Refocusing New Testament Study*. Grand Rapids, MI: Baker.

——. 2012. *Simon Peter in Scripture and Memory: The New Testament Apostle in the Early Church*. Grand Rapids, MI: Baker.

Bockmuehl, Markus, and James Carleton Paget (eds.). 2007. *Redemption and Resistance: The Messianic Hopes of Jews and Christians in Antiquity*. London: T&T Clark.

Bolt, Peter G. 1998. 'Life, Death and the Afterlife in the Greco-Roman World.' In *Life in the Face of Death: The Resurrection Message of the New Testament*. Edited by Richard N. Longenecker. Grand Rapids, MI: Eerdmans, pp. 51–79.

Bond, Helen K., and Larry W. Hurtado (eds.). 2015. *Peter in Early Christianity*. Grand Rapids, MI: Eerdmans.

Bonhoeffer, Dietrich. 1958. *The Cost of Discipleship*. Tr. R. H. Fuller; New York: Macmillan.

Borgen, Peder. 2014. *The Gospel of John: More Light from Philo, Paul and Archaeology*. NovTSup 154; Leiden: Brill.

Boring, M. Eugene. 1974. 'The Apocalypse as Christian Prophecy.' In *SBL Seminar Papers, 1974*. Edited by G. W. MacRae. 2 vols.; Missoula, MT: Scholars, 2.43–62.

——. 2014. *Mark: A Commentary*. NTL; Louisville, KY: Westminster John Knox.

——. 2015. *I and II Thessalonians: A Commentary*. NTL; Louisville, KY: Westminster John Knox.

Boring, M. Eugene, Klaus Berger, and Carsten Colpe. 1995. *Hellenistic Commentary on the New Testament*. Nashville: Abingdon.

Bormann, Lukas. 1995. *Philippi: Stadt und Christengemeinde zur Zeit des Paulus*. NovTSup 78; Leiden: Brill.

Bornkamm, Günther. 1960. *Jesus of Nazareth*. Tr. I. Mcluskey, F. Mcluskey, and J. Robinson; New York: Harper & Row.

Bovon, François. 2002–13. *Luke*. 3 vols.; Hermeneia; Minneapolis: Fortress.

——. 2006. *Luke the Theologian: Fifty-Five Years of Research (1950–2005)*. Waco, TX: Baylor University Press.

Brannan, Rick. 2018. *The Apostolic Fathers: A New Translation*. Bellingham, WA: Lexham.

Brashler, James, and Roger A. Bullard. 1990. 'Apocalypse of Peter.' In *The Nag Hammadi Library in English*. Edited by James M. Robinson. San Francisco: HarperSanFrancisco, pp. 372–8.

Bray, Gerald (ed.). 2005. *Romans*. ACCS; Downers Grove, IL: InterVarsity.

Brooks, Stephenson H. 1987. *Matthew's Community: The Evidence of His Special Sayings Material*. JSNTSup 16; Sheffield: Sheffield Academic Press.

Brown, Jeannine K. 2015. *Matthew*. TTC; Grand Rapids, MI: Baker.

Brown, Kris. 2016. 'How Acts Means.' *Horizons in Biblical Theology* 38: 74–87.

Brown, Raymond E. 1966–70. *The Gospel According to John*. 2 vols.; AB; Garden City, NY: Doubleday.

——. 1994. *The Death of the Messiah: From Gethsemane to the Grave: A Commentary on the Passion Narratives in the Four Gospels*. 2 vols.; ABRL; New York: Doubleday.

Bruce, F. F. 1969. *New Testament History*. New York: Doubleday.

——. 1980 [1977]. *Paul: Apostle of the Free Spirit*. Rev. edn.; Carlisle: Paternoster.

——. 1982. *1 and 2 Thessalonians*. WBC; Waco, TX: Word.

——. 1988. *The Book of the Acts*. Rev. edn.; NICNT; Grand Rapids, MI: Eerdmans.

——. 1990. *The Epistle to the Hebrews*. Rev. edn.; NICNT; Grand Rapids, MI: Eerdmans.

Bryan, Christopher. 2000. *A Preface to Romans: Notes in the Epistle in Its Literary and Cultural Setting*. Oxford: Oxford University Press.

——. 2011. *The Resurrection of the Messiah*. Oxford: Oxford University Press.

Bull, Mike. 2017. 'Rescuing Revelation: Part 1.' *Theopolis Institute*. 5 October 2017. <https://theopolisinstitute.com/rescuing-revelation-part-1/>. Cited 6 October 2017.

Bultmann, Rudolf. 1947. 'Glossen im Römerbrief.' *Theologische Literaturzeitung* 72: 193–8.

——. 1951–5. *Theology of the New Testament*. 2 vols.; London: SCM.

——. 1964. 'Is Exegesis without Presuppositions Possible?' In *Existence and Faith*. London: Collins, pp. 342–52.

Burridge, Richard A. 2004 [1992]. *What Are the Gospels? A Comparison with Graeco-Roman Biography*. 2nd edn.; Grand Rapids, MI: Eerdmans.

———. 2011. 'The Genre of Acts—Revisited.' In *Reading Acts Today*. Edited by S. Walton, T. E. Phillips, L. K. Pietersen, and F. S. Spencer. LNTS 427; London: T&T Clark, pp. 3–28.

———. 2013. 'Gospel: Genre.' In *Dictionary of Jesus and the Gospels*. Edited by J. B. Green, J. K. Brown, and N. Perrin. Downers Grove, IL: InterVarsity, pp. 335–42.

Burridge, Richard A., and Graham Gould. 2004. *Jesus Now and Then*. London: SPCK.

Byron, John. 2008. *Recent Research on Paul and Slavery*. Sheffield: Sheffield Phoenix.

———. 2014. *1 and 2 Thessalonians*. SGBC; Grand Rapids, MI: Zondervan.

Cadbury, Henry. 1927. *The Making of Luke-Acts*. London: Macmillan.

Cadwallader, Alan H. 2015. *Fragments of Colossae: Sifting through the Traces*. Hindmarsh, SA: ATF.

Cadwallader, Alan H., and Michael Trainor (eds.). 2011. *Colossae in Space and Time: Linking to an Ancient City*. Göttingen: Vandenhoeck & Ruprecht.

Caird, G. B. 1965a. *Jesus and the Jewish Nation*. Ethel M. Wood Lecture; London: Athlone.

———. 1965b. *A Commentary on the Revelation of St John the Divine*. London: A&C Black.

Caird, G. B., with L. D. Hurst. 1994. *New Testament Theology*. Oxford: Clarendon.

Callahan, A. D. 1995. 'Language of the Apocalypse.' *Harvard Theological Review* 88: 453–70.

Campbell, Constantine R. 2008. *Basics of Verbal Aspect in Biblical Greek*. Grand Rapids, MI: Zondervan.

Campbell, Douglas A. 2014. *Framing Paul: An Epistolary Biography*. Grand Rapids, MI: Eerdmans.

Campbell, William S. 2007. *The 'We' Passages in the Acts of the Apostles: The Narrator as Narrative Character*. Atlanta: SBL.

Campenhausen, Hans von. 1963. 'Polykarp von Smyrna und die Pastoralbriefe.' In *Aus der Frühzeit des Christentum*. Tübingen: Mohr Siebeck, pp. 197–252.

Canavan, Rosemary. 2012. *Clothing the Body of Christ at Colossae: A Visual Reconstruction of Identity*. WUNT 2.334; Tübingen: Mohr Siebeck.

Carlson, Stephen C. 2015. *The Text of Galatians and Its History*. WUNT 385; Tübingen: Mohr Siebeck.

Carson, D. A. 1991. *The Gospel According to John*. PNTC; Grand Rapids, MI: Eerdmans.

———. 2014. 'Home at Last: The Spectacular God at the Center.' In *Here Is Our God: God's Revelation of Himself in Scripture*. Wheaton, IL: Crossway, pp. 173–205.

Carter, Warren. 2006. *The Roman Empire and the New Testament: An Essential Guide*. Nashville: Abingdon.

———. 2014. 'Mark and Syria? An Assessment.' *Expository Times* 125: 531–7.

Casey, Maurice. 2010. *Jesus of Nazareth: An Independent Historian's Account of His Life and Teachings*. New York: T&T Clark.

Chae, Young S. 2006. *Jesus as the Eschatological Davidic Shepherd: Studies in the Old Testament, Second Temple Judaism, and in the Gospel of Matthew*. Tübingen: Mohr Siebeck.

Chapman, David W. 2010. *Ancient Jewish and Christian Perceptions of Crucifixion*. Grand Rapids, MI: Baker.

Charlesworth, James H. 1995. *The Beloved Disciple: Whose Witness Validates the Gospel of John?* Harrisburg, PA: Trinity Press International.

Chatman, Seymour. 1978. *Story and Discourse: Narrative Structure in Fiction and Film*. Ithaca, NY: Cornell University Press.

Chen, Diane G. 2017. *Luke*. NCCS; Eugene, OR: Cascade.

Chester, Stephen. 2008. 'When the Old Was New: Reformation Perspectives on Galatians 2:16.' *Expository Times* 119: 320–9.

——. 2009. 'It Is No Longer I Who Live: Justification by Faith and Participation in Christ in Martin Luther's Exegesis of Galatians.' *New Testament Studies* 55: 315–37.
Childs, Brevard S. 2008. *The Church's Guide for Reading Paul: The Canonical Shaping of the Pauline Corpus*. Grand Rapids, MI: Eerdmans, pp. 69–75.
Ciampa, Roy E., and Brian S. Rosner. 2010. *The First Letter to the Corinthians*. PNTC; Grand Rapids, MI: Eerdmans.
Classen, Carl Joachim. 2002 [2000]. *Rhetorical Criticism of the New Testament*. Leiden: Brill.
Cohen, Getzel M. 2013. *The Hellenistic Settlements in the East from Armenia and Mesopotamia to Bactria and India*. Berkeley, CA: University of California Press.
Cohick, Lynn. 2010. *Ephesians*. NCCS; Eugene, OR: Cascade.
——. 2013a. 'Pharisees.' In *Dictionary of Jesus and the Gospels*. Edited by J. B. Green, J. K. Brown, and N. Perrin. 2nd edn.; Downers Grove, IL: InterVarsity, pp. 673–9.
——. 2013b. *Philippians*. SGBC; Grand Rapids, MI: Zondervan.
——. 2014. *Women in the World of the Earliest Christians: Illuminating Ancient Ways of Life*. Grand Rapids, MI: Baker.
Collins, Adela Y. 1986. 'Introduction: Early Christian Apocalypticism.' *Semeia* 36: 1–11.
——. 1992. *The Beginning of the Gospel: Probings of Mark in Context*. Minneapolis, MN: Augsburg Fortress.
——. 2007. *Mark: A Commentary*. Hermeneia; Minneapolis: Fortress.
——(ed.). 2017. *New Perspectives on the Book of Revelation*. BETL; Leuven: Peeters.
Collins, Adela Y., and John J. Collins. 2008. *King and Messiah as Son of God: Divine, Human, and Angelic Messianic Figures in Biblical and Related Literature*. Grand Rapids, MI: Eerdmans.
Collins, John J. 1979. 'Introduction: Towards the Morphology of a Genre.' *Semeia* 14: 1–20.
——. 1995. *The Sceptre and the Star: The Messiahs of the Dead Sea Scrolls and Other Ancient Literature*. ABRL; New York: Doubleday.
——. 2015. *Apocalypse, Prophecy, and Pseudepigraphy: On Jewish Apocalyptic Literature*. Grand Rapids, MI: Eerdmans.
——. 2016. *The Apocalyptic Imagination: An Introduction to Jewish Apocalyptic Literature*. 3rd edn.; Grand Rapids, MI: Eerdmans.
Collins, John J., and Daniel C. Harlow (eds.). 2012. *Early Judaism: A Comprehensive Overview*. Grand Rapids, MI: Eerdmans.
Comfort, Philip W. 2015. *A Commentary on the Manuscripts of the New Testament*. Grand Rapids, MI: Kregel.
Cook, John Granger. 2014. *Crucifixion in the Mediterranean World*. WUNT 327; Tübingen: Mohr Siebeck.
Copenhaver, Adam. 2018. *Reconstructing the Historical Background of Paul's Rhetoric in the Letter to the Colossians*. LNTS 585; London: T&T Clark.
Cowan, J. Andrew. 2019. *The Writings of Luke and the Jewish Roots of the Christian Way: An Examination of the Aims of the First Christian Historian in the Light of Ancient Politics, Ethnography, and Historiography*. LNTS 599; London: T&T Clark.
Crossan, John Dominic. 1991. *The Historical Jesus: The Life of a Mediterranean Jewish Peasant*. San Francisco: Harper.
——. 2008. *The Essential Jesus: Original Sayings and Earliest Images*. Eugene, OR: Wipf & Stock.
Daley, B. E. 2010 [1991]. *The Hope of the Early Church: A Handbook of Patristic Eschatology*. Grand Rapids, MI: Baker.
Das, A. Andrew. 2006. *Solving the Romans Debate*. Minneapolis: Fortress, 2006.
Davids, Peter H. 2006. *The Letters of 2 Peter and Jude*. PNTC; Grand Rapids, MI: Eerdmans.

———. 2014. *A Theology of James, Peter, and Jude*. BTNT; Grand Rapids, MI: Zondervan.

Davies, W. D., and Dale C. Allison. 1988–97. *A Critical and Exegetical Commentary on the Gospel According to Saint Matthew*. 3 vols.; ICC; Edinburgh: T&T Clark.

de Boer, Martinus C. 2011. *Galatians: A Commentary*. NTL; Louisville, KY: Westminster John Knox.

Deines, Roland, Christoph Ocles, and Peter Watts (eds.). 2013. *Acts of God in History: Studies towards Recovering a Theological Historiography*. WUNT 317; Tübingen: Mohr Siebeck.

Denton, Donald L. 2004. *Historiography and Hermeneutics in Jesus Studies: An Examination of the Works of John Dominic Crossan and Ben F. Meyer*. JSNTSup 262; London: T&T Clark.

deSilva, David A. 1993. 'Measuring Penultimate against Ultimate Reality: An Investigation of the Integrity and Argumentation of 2 Corinthians.' *Journal for the Study of the New Testament* 52: 41–70.

———. 2000a. *Honor, Patronage, Kinship and Purity: Unlocking New Testament Culture*. Downers Grove, IL: InterVarsity.

———. 2000b. *Perseverance in Gratitude: A Socio-Rhetorical Commentary on the Epistle to the Hebrews*. Grand Rapids, MI: Eerdmans.

———. 2004. *An Introduction to the New Testament: Context, Methods and Ministry Formation*. Downers Grove, IL: InterVarsity.

———. 2009. *Seeing Things John's Way: The Rhetoric of the Book of Revelation*. Louisville, KY: Westminster John Knox.

———. 2010. *Days of Atonement: A Novel of the Maccabean Revolt*. Grand Rapids, MI: Kregel.

———. 2012. *The Jewish Teachers of Jesus, James, and Jude: What Earliest Christianity Learned from the Apocrypha and Pseudepigrapha*. Oxford: Oxford University Press.

———. 2013. *Unholy Allegiances: Heeding Revelation's Warning*. Peabody, MA: Hendrickson.

Dicken, Frank. 2011. 'The Author and Date of Luke-Acts: Exploring the Options.' In *Issues in Luke-Acts: Selected Essays*. Edited by S. A. Adams and M. Pahl. GH 26; Piscataway, NJ: Gorgias, pp. 7–26.

Diehl, Judith A. 2010. 'What Is a "Gospel"? Recent Studies in Gospel Genre.' *Currents in Biblical Research* 20: 1–26.

Dillistone, F. W. 1977. *C. H. Dodd: Interpreter of the New Testament*. London: Hodder & Stoughton.

Doering, Lutz. 2012. *Ancient Jewish Letters and the Beginnings of Christian Epistolography*. Tübingen: Mohr Siebeck.

Donaldson, Terence L. 2005. 'The Vindicated Son: A Narrative Approach to Matthean Christology.' In *Contours of Christology in the New Testament*. Edited by Richard N. Longenecker. Grand Rapids, MI: Eerdmans, pp. 100–21.

Donfried, Karl P. (ed.). 1991. *The Romans Debate*. Rev. edn.; Peabody, MA: Hendrickson.

———. 1997. 'The Imperial Cults of Thessalonica and Political Conflict in 1 Thessalonians.' In *Paul and Empire: Religion and Power in Roman Imperial Society*. Edited by R. A. Horsley. Harrisburg, PA: Trinity Press International, pp. 215–23.

———. 2002. *Paul, Thessalonica, and Early Christianity*. Grand Rapids, MI: Eerdmans.

———(ed.). 2008. *1 Timothy Reconsidered*. Leuven: Peeters.

Dungan, David L. 1999. *A History of the Synoptic Problem: The Canon, the Text, the Composition, and the Interpretation of the Gospels*. New York: Doubleday.

Dunn, James D. G. 1988. *Romans 1–8, 9–16*. 2 vols.; WBC; Dallas: Word.

———. 1990 [1977]. *Unity and Diversity in the New Testament: An Inquiry into the Character of Earliest Christianity*. 2nd edn.; London: SCM.

———. 1993. *The Theology of Paul's Letter to the Galatians*. Cambridge: Cambridge University Press.
———. 1996. *The Epistles to the Colossians and to Philemon*. NIGTC; Grand Rapids, MI: Eerdmans.
———. 1997. 'Pseudepigraphy.' In *Dictionary of the Later New Testament and Its Documents*. Edited by P. Davids and R. Martin. Downers Grove, IL: InterVarsity, pp. 977–84.
———. 1998. *The Theology of Paul the Apostle*. Edinburgh: T&T Clark.
———. 2003. *Jesus Remembered*. CITM 1; Grand Rapids, MI: Eerdmans.
———. 2006. *The Parting of the Ways: Between Christianity and Judaism and Their Significance for the Character of Christianity*. 2nd edn.; London: SCM.
———. 2009a. *New Testament Theology: An Introduction*. Nashville: Abingdon.
———. 2009b. *Beginning from Jerusalem*. CITM 2; Grand Rapids, MI: Eerdmans.
———. 2013. *The Oral Gospel Tradition*. Grand Rapids, MI: Eerdmans.
———. 2015. *Neither Jew Nor Greek: A Contested Identity*. CITM 3; Grand Rapids, MI: Eerdmans.
———. 2016 [1996]. *The Acts of the Apostles*. Grand Rapids, MI: Eerdmans.
Dunne, John Anthony. 2014. 'Cast Out the Aggressive Agitators (Gl 4:29–30): Suffering, Identity, and the Ethics of Expulsion in Paul's Mission to the Galatians.' In *Sensitivity to Outsiders: Exploring the Dynamic Relationship between Mission and Ethics in the New Testament and Early Christianity*. Edited by J. Kok, T. Nicklas, D. T. Roth, and C. M. Hays. WUNT 2.364; Tübingen: Mohr Siebeck, pp. 246–69.
Eastman, David L. 2011. *Paul the Martyr: The Cult of the Apostle Paul in the Latin West*. Leiden: Brill.
Eastman, Susan. 2007. *Recovering Paul's Mother Tongue: Language and Theology in Galatians*. Grand Rapids, MI: Eerdmans.
Eddy, Paul R. 2013. 'Orality and Oral Transmission.' In *Dictionary of Jesus and the Gospels*. Edited by J. B. Green, J. K. Brown, and N. Perrin. 2nd edn.; Downers Grove, IL: InterVarsity, pp. 641–50.
Edwards, Dennis R. 2017. *1 Peter*. SGBC; Grand Rapids, MI: Zondervan.
Ehrman, Bart D. 2004. *A Brief Introduction to the New Testament*. Oxford: Oxford University Press.
Eisenbaum, Pamela. 2010. *Paul Was Not a Christian: The Original Message of a Misunderstood Apostle*. New York: HarperCollins.
Elliott, John H. 2000. *1 Peter*. AB; New York: Doubleday.
Elliott, M. W., Scott J. Hafemann, N. T. Wright, and John Frederick (eds.). 2014. *Galatians and Christian Theology: Justification, the Gospel, and Ethics in Paul's Letter*. Grand Rapids, MI: Baker.
Elliott, Neil, and Mark Reasoner. 2011. *Documents and Images for the Study of Paul*. Minneapolis: Fortress.
Enns, Peter. 2005. *Inspiration and Incarnation: Evangelicals and the Problem of the Old Testament*. Grand Rapids, MI: Baker.
Eskola, Timmo. 2013. *Beyond Biblical Theology: Sacralized Culturalism in Heikki Räisänen's Hermeneutics*. Leiden: Brill.
Esler, Philip F. 2005. *New Testament Theology: Communion and Community*. Minneapolis: Fortress.
Estes, Douglas, and Ruth Sheridan (eds.). 2016. *How John Works: Storytelling in the Fourth Gospel*. Atlanta: SBL.
Evans, Craig A. 2001. *Mark 8:27–16:20*. WBC; Nashville: Thomas Nelson.
———(ed.). 2008. *Encyclopedia of the Historical Jesus*. New York: Routledge.

———. 2010. *Holman Quick Source Guide to the Dead Sea Scrolls*. Nashville: Broadman & Holman.
———. 2012. *Matthew*. NCBC; Cambridge: Cambridge University Press.
———. 2014. 'Getting the Burial Traditions and Evidences Right.' In *How God Became Jesus: The Real Origins of Belief in Jesus' Divine Nature*. Edited by M. F. Bird. Grand Rapids, MI: Zondervan, pp. 71–93.
Evans, Craig A., and Charles E. Carlston. 2014. *From Synagogue to Ecclesia: Matthew's Community at the Crossroads*. WUNT 33; Tübingen: Mohr Siebeck.
Eve, Eric. 2013. *Behind the Gospels: Understanding the Oral Tradition*. London: SPCK.
Farmer, William R. 1976. *The Synoptic Problem: A Critical Analysis*. Dillsboro, NC: Western North Carolina Press.
Farrer, Austin M. 1985 [1955]. 'On Dispensing with Q.' In *The Two-Source Hypothesis: A Critical Appraisal*. Edited by A. J. Bellizoni. Macon, GA: Mercer University Press, pp. 321–56.
Fassberg, Steven E. 2012. 'Which Semitic Language Did Jesus and Other Contemporary Jews Speak?' *Catholic Biblical Quarterly* 74: 263–80.
Fee, Gordon D. 1995. *Paul's Letter to the Philippians*. NICNT; Grand Rapids, MI: Eerdmans.
———. 2007. *Pauline Christology: An Exegetical-Theological Study*. Peabody, MA: Hendrickson.
———. 2009. *The First and Second Letters to the Thessalonians*. NICNT; Grand Rapids, MI: Eerdmans.
———. 2011. *Revelation*. NCCS; Eugene, OR: Cascade.
Ferguson, Everett. 1993. *Backgrounds of Early Christianity*. 2nd edn.; Grand Rapids, MI: Eerdmans.
Ferguson, John. 1974. *Clement of Alexandria*. New York: Twayne.
Fiensy, David A., and Ralph K. Hawkins (eds.). 2013. *The Galilean Economy in the Time of Jesus*. Atlanta: SBL.
Fisk, Bruce N. 2011. *A Hitchhiker's Guide to Jesus: Reading the Gospels on the Ground*. Grand Rapids, MI: Baker.
Fitzgerald, John T. 2013. 'Greco-Roman Philosophical Schools.' In *The World of the New Testament: Cultural, Social, and Historical Contexts*. Edited by J. G. Green and L. M. McDonald. Grand Rapids, MI: Baker, pp. 135–48.
Fitzmyer, Joseph A. 1981-5. *The Gospel According to Luke: Introduction, Translation, and Notes*. 2 vols.; AB; Garden City, NY: Doubleday.
———. 1993. *Romans: A New Translation with Introduction and Commentary*. AB; New Haven, CT: Yale University Press.
———. 1998. *The Acts of the Apostles: A New Translation with Introduction and Commentary*. AB; Garden City, NY: Doubleday.
———. 2000. *The Letter to Philemon: A New Translation with Introduction and Commentary*. AB; New York: Doubleday.
———. 2007. *The One Who Is to Come*. Grand Rapids, MI: Eerdmans.
Foster, Paul. 2004. *Community, Law and Mission in Matthew's Gospel*. WUNT 2.177; Tübingen: Mohr Siebeck.
———. 2005. 'The Epistles of Ignatius of Antioch and the Writings that Later Formed the New Testament.' In *The Reception of the New Testament in the Apostolic Fathers*. Edited by A. F. Gregory and C. M. Tuckett. Oxford: Oxford University Press, pp. 159–86.
———. 2012. 'Who Wrote 2 Thessalonians? A Fresh Look at an Old Problem.' *Journal for the Study of the New Testament* 32: 150–75.
Fowl, Stephen. 2012. *Ephesians: A Commentary*. Louisville, KY: Westminster John Knox.
Fowler, Robert M. 2001 [1991]. *Let the Reader Understand: Reader-Response Criticism and the Gospel of Mark*. Harrisburg, PA: Trinity Press International.

France, R. T. 2002. *The Gospel of Mark: A Commentary on the Greek Text*. NIGTC; Grand Rapids, MI: Eerdmans.

Frankfurter, David. 2002. 'Review of Tryggve N. D. Mettinger, *The Riddle of Resurrection*.' In *Bryn Mawr Classical Review*. <http://ccat.sas.upenn.edu/bmcr/2002/2002-09-07.html>. Cited 5 March 2007.

Frey, Jörg. 1993. 'Erwägungen zum Verhältnis der Johannesapokalypse zu den übrigen Schriften des Corpus Johanneum.' In *Die johanneische Frage: Ein Lösungsversuch*. Edited by M. Hengel. Tübingen: Mohr Siebeck, pp. 326–49.

——(ed.). 2009. *Pseudepigraphie und Verfasserfiktion in frühchristlichen Briefen*. WUNT 246; Tübingen: Mohr Siebeck.

——. 2015. *Der Brief des Judas und der zweite Brief des Petrus*. Leipzig: Evangelische Verlagsanstalt.

Friesen, Steve J., Daniel N. Schowalter, and James C. Walters (eds.). 2010. *Corinth in Context: Comparative Studies on Religion and Society*. Leiden: Brill.

Gadamer, Hans-Georg. 1975. *Truth and Method*. London: Seabury.

Garland, David E. 2003. *1 Corinthians*. BECNT; Grand Rapids, MI: Baker.

——. 2015. *A Theology of Mark's Gospel*. BTNT. Grand Rapids, MI: Zondervan.

Garrow, Alan J. P. 2004. *The Gospel of Matthew's Dependence on the Didache*. LNTS 254; London: Bloomsbury.

Gaventa, Beverly R. 1986. *From Darkness to Light: Aspects of Conversion in the New Testament*. Philadelphia: Fortress.

——. 1998. *First and Second Thessalonians*. Interpretation; Louisville, KY: Westminster John Knox.

——. 2003a. *Acts*. ANTC; Nashville, TN: Abingdon.

——. 2003b. 'Galatians.' In *Eerdmans Commentary on the Bible*. Edited by J. D. G. Dunn and J. W. Rogerson. Grand Rapids, MI: Eerdmans, pp. 1374–84.

——. 2016. *When in Romans: An Invitation to Linger with the Gospel According to Paul*. Grand Rapids, MI: Baker.

Gaventa, Beverly R., and Richard B. Hays (eds.). 2008. *Seeking the Identity of Jesus: A Pilgrimage*. Grand Rapids, MI: Eerdmans.

Gibbons, Joseph A., and Roger A. Bullard. 1990. 'The Second Treatise of the Great Seth.' In *The Nag Hammadi Library in English*. Edited by James M. Robinson. San Francisco: HarperSanFrancisco, pp. 362–71.

Gignilliat, Mark S. 2007. *Paul and Isaiah's Servants: Paul's Theological Reading of Isaiah 40–66 in 2 Corinthians 5:14–6:10*. LNTS; London: T&T Clark.

Gilbertson, Michael. 2003. *God and History in the Book of Revelation: New Testament Studies in Dialogue with Pannenberg and Moltmann*. SNTSMS 124; Cambridge: Cambridge University Press.

Gilmour, Michael J. 2001. 'Reflections on the Authorship of 2 Peter.' *Evangelical Quarterly* 73: 291–303.

Goldingay, John. 2014. *The Theology of the Book of Isaiah*. Downers Grove, IL: InterVarsity.

Gombis, Timothy G. 2010. *The Drama of Ephesians: Participating in the Triumph of God*. Downers Grove, IL: InterVarsity.

González, Justo L. 2015. *The Story Luke Tells: Luke's Unique Witness to the Gospel*. Grand Rapids, MI: Eerdmans.

Goodacre, Mark. 2007. *The Synoptic Problem: A Way through the Maze*. London: T&T Clark.

——. 2016. 'The Farrer Hypothesis.' In *The Synoptic Problem: Four Views*. Edited by S. E. Porter and B. R. Dyer. Grand Rapids, MI: Baker, pp. 47–66.

Goodacre, Mark, and Nicholas Perrin (eds). 2004. In *Questioning Q: A Multi-Dimensional Critique*. Downers Grove, IL: InterVarsity.

Goodblatt, David. 2006. *Elements of Ancient Jewish Nationalism*. New York: Cambridge University Press.

Gorman, Michael J. 2017. *Apostle of the Crucified Lord: A Theological Introduction to Paul and His Letters*. 2nd edn. Grand Rapids, MI: Eerdmans.

——. 2009. *Inhabiting the Cruciform God: Kenosis, Justification, and Theosis in Paul's Narrative Soteriology*. Grand Rapids, MI: Eerdmans.

——. 2011. *Reading Revelation Responsibly: Uncivil Worship and Witness: Following the Lamb into the New Creation*. Eugene, OR: Cascade.

Grabbe, Lester L. 1992. *Judaism from Cyrus to Hadrian*. London: SCM.

Gradel, Ittai. 2002. *Emperor Worship and Roman Religion*. Oxford: Clarendon.

Green, Gene L. 2008. *Jude and 2 Peter*. BECNT; Grand Rapids, MI: Baker.

Green, Joel B. 1994. 'Good News to Whom? Jesus and the "Poor" in the Gospel of Luke.' In *Jesus of Nazareth: Lord and Christ: Essays on the Historical Jesus and New Testament Christology*. Edited by J. B. Green and M. Turner. Grand Rapids, MI: Eerdmans, pp. 59–74.

——. 1995. *The Theology of Luke*. NTT; Cambridge: Cambridge University Press.

——. 1997. *The Gospel of Luke*. NICNT; Grand Rapids, MI: Eerdmans.

Green, Joel B., and Lee Martin McDonald (eds.). 2013. *The World of the New Testament: Cultural, Social, and Historical Context*. Grand Rapids, MI: Baker.

Green, Peter. 1993. *Alexander to Actium: The Historical Evolution of the Hellenistic Age*. Berkeley, CA: University of California Press.

Gregory, Andrew. 2003. *The Reception of Luke and Acts in the Period before Irenaeus: Looking for Luke in the Second Century*. WUNT 2.169; Tübingen: Mohr Siebeck.

——. 2016. 'Acts and Christian Beginnings: A Review Essay.' *Journal for the Study of the New Testament* 39: 97–115.

Gregory, Andrew, and C. Kavin Rowe (eds.). 2010. *Rethinking the Unity and Reception of Luke and Acts*. Columbia, SC: University of South Carolina Press.

Grieb, A. Katherine. *The Story of Romans: A Narrative Defense of God's Righteousness*. Louisville, KY: Westminster John Knox, 2002.

Grossman, Maxine (ed.). 2010. *Rediscovering the Dead Sea Scrolls: An Assessment of Old and New Approaches and Methods*. Grand Rapids, MI: Eerdmans.

Gruen, Erich S. 2002. *Diaspora: Jews amidst Greeks and Romans*. Cambridge, MA: Harvard University Press.

Grünstäudl, Wolfgang. 2013. *Petrus Alexandrinus: Studien zum historischen und theologischen Ort des zweiten Petrusbriefes*. WUNT 2.354; Tübingen: Mohr Siebeck.

Gundry, Robert H. 1993. *Mark: A Commentary on His Apology for the Cross*. Grand Rapids, MI: Eerdmans.

Gupta, Nijay. 2013. *Colossians*. Macon, GA: Smyth & Helwys.

——. 2016. *1 and 2 Thessalonians*. NCCS; Eugene, OR: Cascade.

Gurry, Peter J. 2016. 'How Your Greek NT Is Changing: A Simple Introduction to the Coherence-Based Genealogical Method (CBGM).' *Journal for the Evangelical Theological Society* 59: 675–89.

Guthrie, George H. 2015. *2 Corinthians*. BECNT; Grand Rapids, MI: Baker.

Haas, Peter. 1988. *Morality After Auschwitz: The Radical Challenge of the Nazi Ethic*. Philadelphia: Fortress.

Haenchen, Ernst. 1965. '"We" in Acts and the Itinerary.' *Journal for Theology and the Church* 1: 65–99.

Hagner, D. A. 2004. 'Matthew: Christian Judaism or Jewish Christianity?' In *The Face of New Testament Studies*. Edited by S. McKnight and G. Osborne. Grand Rapids, MI: Baker, pp. 263–82.

Hanson, K. C., and Douglas E. Oakman. 1998. *Palestine in the Time of Jesus: Social Structures and Social Conflicts*. Minneapolis: Fortress.

Hardin, Justin K. 2008. *Galatians and the Imperial Cult: A Critical Analysis of the First-Century Social Context of Paul's Letter*. WUNT 2.237; Tübingen: Mohr Siebeck.

Harris, Murray J. 1998. 'Resurrection and Immortality in the Pauline Corpus.' In *Life in the Face of Death: The Resurrection Message of the New Testament*. Edited by R. N. Longenecker. Grand Rapids, MI: Eerdmans, pp. 147–70.

Harris, William V. 1989. *Ancient Literacy*. Cambridge, MA: Harvard University Press.

Harrison, James R. 2002. 'Paul and the Imperial Gospel at Thessaloniki.' *Journal for the Study of the New Testament* 25: 71–96.

Harrison, P. N. 1921. *The Problem of the Pastoral Epistles*. Oxford: Oxford University Press.

Harrisson, Juliette. 2019. *Imagining the Afterlife in the Ancient World*. New York: Routledge.

Hartley, L. P. 1976 [1953]. *The Go-Between*. Harmondsworth: Penguin.

Harvey, A. E. 1990. *Strenuous Commands: The Ethic of Jesus*. London: SCM.

Hays, Christopher. 2010. *Luke's Wealth Ethics: A Study in Their Coherence and Character*. WUNT 2.275; Tübingen: Mohr Siebeck.

Hays, Richard B. 1997. *First Corinthians*. Interpretation; Louisville, KY: Westminster John Knox.

——. 2000. 'The Letter to the Galatians.' In *New Interpreter's Bible*. Edited by L. E. Keck. 12 vols.; Nashville: Abingdon, 11.183–348.

——. 2014. *Reading Backwards: Figural Christology and the Fourfold Gospel Witness*. Waco, TX: Baylor University Press.

——. 2017. *Echoes of Scripture in the Gospels*. Waco, TX: Baylor University Press.

Head, Ivan. 2004. 'Mark as a Roman Document from the Year 69: Testing Martin Hengel's Thesis.' *Journal of Religious History* 28: 240–59.

Healy, Mary. 2016. *Hebrews*. CCSS; Grand Rapids, MI: Baker.

Heen, Erik M., and Philip D. W. Krey (eds.). 2005. *Hebrews*. ACCS; Downers Grove, IL: InterVarsity.

Heide, K. Martin. 2011. 'Assessing the Stability of the Transmitted Texts of the New Testament and the *Shepherd of Hermas*.' In *The Reliability of the New Testament: Bart D. Ehrman and Daniel B. Wallace in Dialogue*. Edited by R. B. Stewart. Minneapolis: Fortress, pp. 125–59.

Hellerman, Joseph H. 2005. *Reconstructing Honor in Roman Philippi: Carmen Christi as Cursus Podorum*. SNTSMS 132; Cambridge: Cambridge University Press.

Hemer, Colin. 1986. *The Letters to the Seven Churches in Their Local Setting*. Grand Rapids, MI: Eerdmans.

Hengel, Martin. 1977. *Crucifixion in the Ancient World and the Folly of the Message of the Cross*. Philadelphia: Fortress.

——. 1980. *Acts and the History of Earliest Christianity*. Philadelphia: Fortress.

——. 1985. *Studies in the Gospel of Mark*. London: SCM.

——. 1987. 'Der Jakobusbrief als antipaulinische Polemik.' In *Tradition and Interpretation in the New Testament: Essays in Honor of E. Earle Ellis*. Edited by G. F. Hawthorne and O. Betz. Grand Rapids, MI: Eerdmans, pp. 248–78.

——. 1989. *The Johannine Question*. London: SCM.

——. 2000. *The Four Gospels and the One Gospel of Jesus Christ: An Investigation into the Collection and Origin of the Canonical Gospels*. London: SCM.

——. 2006. *Saint Peter: The Underestimated Apostle*. Grand Rapids, MI: Eerdmans.
Hengel, Martin, and Anna Maria Schwemer. 2007. *Jesu und das Judentum*. Tübingen: Mohr Siebeck.
Hezser, Catherine. 2001. *Jewish Literacy in Roman Palestine*. TSAJ; Tübingen: Mohr Siebeck.
Hill, Charles. 2004. *The Johannine Corpus in the Early Church*. Oxford: Oxford University Press.
Hill, Charles E., and Michael J. Kruger (eds.). 2012. *The Early Text of the New Testament*. Oxford: Oxford University Press.
Hockey, Katherine M., Madison N. Pierce, and Francis Watson (eds.). 2017. *Muted Voices of the New Testament: Readings in the Catholic Epistles and Hebrews*. LNTS 587; London: T&T Clark.
Hoehner, Harold. 2006. 'Did Paul Write Galatians?' In *History and Exegesis*. Edited by S.-W. Son. FS E. E. Ellis; London: T&T Clark, pp. 150–69.
Holmes, Michael W. 2001. 'Textual Criticism.' In *Interpreting the New Testament: Essays on Methods and Issues*. Edited by D. A. Black and D. S. Dockery. Nashville: Broadman & Holman, pp. 46–73.
——. 2005. 'Polycarp's *Letter to the Philippians* and the Writings that Later Formed the New Testament.' In *The Reception of the New Testament in the Apostolic Fathers*. Edited by A. F. Gregory and C. M. Tuckett. Oxford: Oxford University Press, pp. 187–227.
——. 2007. *The Apostolic Fathers: Greek Texts and English Translations*. 3rd edn.; Grand Rapids, MI: Baker.
——. 2008. 'Biblical Canon.' In *The Oxford Handbook of Early Christian Studies*. Edited by S. Ashbrook Harvey and D. G. Hunter. Oxford: Oxford University Press, pp. 406–26.
——. 2012. 'From "Original Text" to "Initial Text": The Traditional Goal of New Testament Textual Criticism in Contemporary Discussion.' In *The Text of the New Testament in Contemporary Research: Essays on the Status Quaestionis*. Edited by B. D. Ehrman and M. W. Holmes. 2nd edn.; Leiden: Brill, pp. 637–88.
——. 2013 [1995]. 'Reasoned Eclecticism in New Testament Textual Criticism.' In *The Text of the New Testament in Contemporary Research: Essays on the Status Quaestionis*. Edited by B. D. Ehrman and M. W. Holmes. 2nd edn.; Leiden: Brill, pp. 771–802.
Hood, Jason B. 2011. *The Messiah, His Brothers, and the Nations (Matthew 1.1–17)*. LNTS 441; London: T&T Clark.
——. 2013. *Imitating God in Christ: Recapturing a Biblical Pattern*. Downers Grove, IL: InterVarsity.
Hooker, Morna D. 1973. 'Were There False Teachers in Colossae?' In *Christ and the Spirit in the New Testament*. Edited by B. Lindars and S. S. Smalley. Cambridge: Cambridge University Press, pp. 315–31.
——. 1975. 'In His Own Image?' In *What about the New Testament? Essays in Honour of Christopher Evans*. Edited by M. D. Hooker and C. Hickling. London: SCM, pp. 28–44.
——. 1990. *From Adam to Christ: Essays on Paul*. Cambridge: Cambridge University Press.
——. 1991. *The Gospel According to Saint Mark*. BNTC; London: A&C Black.
——. 1994. *Not Ashamed of the Gospel: New Testament Interpretations of the Death of Christ*. Carlisle, UK: Paternoster.
——. 2000. 'The Letter to the Philippians.' In *NIB*. Edited by L. E. Keck. Nashville, TN: Abingdon. Volume 11, pp. 469–549.
——. 2002. 'Philippians: Phantom Opponents and the Real Source of the Conflict.' In *Fair Play: Diversity and Conflict in Early Christianity*. Edited by I. Dunderberg, C. Tuckett, and K. Syreeni. NovTSup 103; Leiden: Brill, pp. 377–95.

Horrell, David G. 2002. 'The Product of a Petrine Circle? A Reassessment of the Origin and Character of 1 Peter.' *Journal for the Study of the New Testament* 86: 29–60.

Howard, Mackenzie. 2012. *A Charles Dickens Devotional*. Nashville: Thomas Nelson.

Hurtado, Larry. 2003. *Lord Jesus Christ: Devotion to Jesus in Earliest Christianity*. Grand Rapids, MI: Eerdmans. ——. 2006. *The Earliest Christian Artifacts: Manuscripts and Christian Origins*. Grand Rapids, MI: Eerdmans.

——. 2014. 'Fashions, Fallacies and Future Prospects in New Testament Studies.' *Journal for the Study of the New Testament* 36.4: 299–324.

Huttner, Ulrich. 2013. *Early Christianity in the Lycus Valley*. Leiden: Brill.

Incigneri, Brian J. 2003. *The Gospel to the Romans: The Setting and Rhetoric of Mark's Gospel*. Leiden: Brill.

——. 2014. 'Local Colour in Mark's Gospel.' *Australian Biblical Review* 62: 58–78.

Isaac, E. 1983–5. '1 (Ethiopic Apocalypse of) Enoch.' In *Old Testament Pseudepigrapha*. Edited by J. H. Charlesworth. 2 vols.; New York: Doubleday, 1.5–89.

Iverson, Kelly R., and Christopher W. Skinner (eds.). 2011. *Mark as Story: Retrospect and Prospect*. Atlanta: SBL.

Jackson-McCabe, Matt. 2010. 'James, Epistle of.' In *The Eerdmans Dictionary of Early Judaism*. Edited by J. J. Collins and D. C. Harlow. Grand Rapids, MI: Eerdmans, pp. 782–4.

Jeffers, James S. 1999. *The Greco-Roman World of the New Testament: Exploring the Background of Early Christianity*. Downers Grove, IL: InterVarsity.

Jensen, Matthew D. 2014. *Affirming the Resurrection of the Incarnate Christ: A Reading of 1 John*. SNTSMS 153; Cambridge: Cambridge University Press.

Jervis, L. Ann. 2002. *Galatians*. NIBC; Peabody, MA: Hendrickson.

Jewett, Robert K. 2009. *Romans: A Commentary*. Hermeneia; Minneapolis: Fortress.

Jipp, Joshua W. 2014. 'The Beginnings of a Theology of Luke-Acts: Divine Activity and Human Response.' *Journal of Theological Interpretation* 8: 23–44.

Jobes, Karen H. 2005. *1 Peter*. BECNT; Grand Rapids, MI: Baker.

——. 2011. *Letters to the Church: A Survey of Hebrews and the General Epistles*. Grand Rapids, MI: Zondervan.

——. 2014. *1, 2, and 3 John*. ZECNT; Grand Rapids, MI: Zondervan.

Jobes, Karen H., and Moises Silva. 2000. *Invitation to the Septuagint*. Grand Rapids, MI: Baker.

Johnson, Luke Timothy. 1991. *The Gospel of Luke*. SP; Collegeville, MN: Liturgical.

——. 1992. *The Acts of the Apostles*. SP; Collegeville, MN: Liturgical.

——. 1995. *The Letter of James: A New Translation with Introduction and Commentary*. AB; New York: Doubleday.

——. 1996. *Letters to Paul's Delegates: 1 Timothy, 2 Timothy, Titus*. Valley Forge, PA: Trinity Press International.

——. 2001a. *Reading Romans: A Literary and Theological Commentary*. Macon, GA: Smyth & Helwys.

——. 2001b. *The First and Second Letters to Timothy*. AB; New York: Doubleday.

——. 2004. *Brother of Jesus, Friend of God: Studies in the Letter of James*. Grand Rapids, MI: Eerdmans.

——. 2006. *Hebrews: A Commentary*. NTL; Louisville, KY: Westminster John Knox.

——. 2010. *The Writings of the New Testament: An Interpretation*. 3rd edn.; Minneapolis: Fortress.

——. 2011. *Sharing Possessions: What Faith Demands*. 2nd edn.; Grand Rapids, MI: Eerdmans.

Jones, Brice C. 2011. *Matthean and Lukan Special Material: A Brief Introduction with Texts in Greek and English*. Eugene, OR: Wipf & Stock.

Judge, E. A. 1960. *The Social Pattern of the Christian Groups in the First Century: Some Prolegomena to the Study of New Testament Ideas of Social Obligation.* London: Tyndale.

———. 2008. *The First Christians in the Roman World: Augustan and New Testament Essays.* Edited by J. R. Harrison; Tübingen: Mohr Siebeck.

Kaestli, Jean-Daniel. 1995. 'Luke-Acts and the Pastoral Epistles: The Thesis of a Common Authorship.' In *Luke's Literary Achievement: Collected Essays.* Edited by C. Tuckett. JSNTSup 116; Sheffield: Sheffield Academic Press, pp. 110–26.

Kaldis, Byron. 2013. *Encyclopedia of Philosophy and the Social Sciences.* Los Angeles: Sage Reference.

Kamell, Mariam. 2009. 'The Economics of Humility: The Rich and Humble in James.' In *Engaging Economics: New Testament Scenarios and Early Christian Reception.* Edited by Bruce W. Longenecker and Kelly D. Liebengood. Grand Rapids, MI: Eerdmans, pp. 174–75.

Kanagaraj, Jey J. 2013. *John.* NCCS. Eugene, OR: Cascade.

Käsemann, Ernst. 1964. 'The Problem of the Historical Jesus.' In *Essays on New Testament Themes.* Tr. W. J. Montague; London: SCM, pp. 15–47.

———. 1968. *The Testament of Jesus: A Study of the Gospel of John in Light of Chapter 17.* Philadelphia: Fortress.

Kazen, Thomas. 2002. *Jesus and Purity Halakhah: Was Jesus Indifferent to Impurity?* ConBNT 38; Stockholm: Almqvist & Wiksell.

Keck, Leander E. 2007. *Romans.* ANTC; Nashville: Abingdon.

Keener, Craig S. 2003. *The Gospel of John: A Commentary.* 2 vols.; Peabody, MA: Hendrickson.

———. 2009a. *The Historical Christ of the Gospels.* Grand Rapids, MI: Eerdmans.

———. 2009b. *Romans.* NCCS; Eugene, OR: Cascade.

———. 2009c. *The Gospel of Matthew: A Socio-Rhetorical Commentary.* Grand Rapids, MI: Eerdmans.

———. 2012–14. *Acts: An Exegetical Commentary.* 4 vols.; Grand Rapids, MI: Baker.

Kennedy, George A. 1984. *New Testament Interpretation through Rhetorical Criticism.* Chapel Hill, NC: University of North Carolina Press.

Kenny, Anthony. 1986. *A Stylometric Study of the New Testament.* Oxford: Clarendon.

Kern, Philip. 1998. *Rhetoric and Galatians: Assessing an Approach to Paul's Epistles.* SNTSMS 101; Cambridge: Cambridge University Press.

Kindler, Arie. 1973. *Coins of the Land of Israel.* Jerusalem: Keter.

Klausner, Joseph. 1929. *Jesus of Nazareth: His Life, Times, and Teachings.* Tr. Herbert Danby; London: Allen & Unwin.

Klawans, Jonathan. 2000. *Impurity and Sin in Ancient Judaism.* Oxford: Oxford University Press.

———. 2005. *Purity, Sacrifice, and the Temple: Symbolism and Supersessionism in the Study of Ancient Judaism.* Oxford: Oxford University Press.

———. 2006. 'Moral and Ritual Purity.' In *The Historical Jesus in Context.* Edited by A. J. Levine, D. C. Allison, and J. D. Crossan. Princeton, NJ: Princeton University Press, pp. 266–84.

Klink, Edward W. 2010a. *The Sheep of the Fold: The Audience and Origin of the Gospel of John.* SNTSMS 141. Cambridge: Cambridge University Press.

———(ed.). 2010b. *The Audience of the Gospels: The Origin and Function of the Gospels in Early Christianity.* LNTS 353; London: T&T Clark.

Knox, John. 1959. *The Death of Christ: The Cross in New Testament History and Faith.* Nashville: Abingdon.

Koester, Craig R. 2001a. *Hebrews: A New Translation with Introduction and Commentary.* AB; New York: Doubleday.

———. 2001b. *Revelation and the End of All Things.* Grand Rapids, MI: Eerdmans.

——. 2008. *The Word of Life: A Theology of John's Gospel*. Grand Rapids, MI: Eerdmans.

——. 2014. *Revelation: A New Translation with Introduction and Commentary*. AB; New Haven, CT: Yale University Press.

Koester, Helmut. 1990. *Ancient Christian Gospels*. London: SCM.

——. 1995. *Ephesos: Metropolis of Asia*. Valley Forge, PA: Trinity Press International.

——. 2000 [1982]. *History and Literature of Early Christianity*. 2 vols.; 2nd edn.; New York: De Gruyter.

Kok, Michael. 2015. *Gospel on the Margins: The Reception of Mark in the Second Century*. Minneapolis: Fortress.

Koortbojian, Michael. 2013. *The Divinization of Caesar and Augustus: Precedents, Consequences, Implications*. Cambridge: Cambridge University Press.

Köstenberger, Andreas. 2009. *A Theology of John's Gospel and Letters*. Grand Rapids, MI: Zondervan.

Köstenberger, Andreas, and Richard D. Patterson. 2011. *Invitation to Biblical Interpretation: Exploring the Hermeneutical Triad of History, Literature, and Theology*. Grand Rapids, MI: Kregel.

Kovacs, Judith L., and Christopher Rowland. 2004. *Revelation: The Apocalypse of Jesus Christ*. BBC. Malden, MA: Blackwell.

Kruger, Michael J. 1999. 'The Authenticity of 2 Peter.' *Journal of the Evangelical Theological Society* 42: 654–71.

——. 2012. *Canon Revisited: Establishing the Origins and Authority of the New Testament Book*. Wheaton, IL: Crossway.

Kruse, Colin G. 2000. *The Letters of John*. PNTC; Grand Rapids, MI: Eerdmans.

Kugler, Robert. 2010. 'Testaments.' In *The Eerdmans Dictionary of Early Judaism*. Edited by D. C. Harlow and J. J. Collins. Grand Rapids, MI: Eerdmans, pp. 1295–7.

Lampe, Peter. 2003. *From Paul to Valentinus: Christians at Rome in the First Two Centuries*. Tr. M. Steinhauser. Edited by M. D. Johnson. Minneapolis: Fortress.

Lancaster, Sarah Heaner. 2015. *Romans*. BTCB; Louisville, KY: Westminster John Knox Press.

Le Donne, Anthony. 2009. *The Historiographical Jesus: Memory, Typology, and the Son of David*. Waco, TX: Baylor University Press.

——. 2011. *The Historical Jesus: What Can We Know and How We Can Know It?* Grand Rapids, MI: Eerdmans.

Lehtipuu, Outi. 2015. *Debates over the Resurrection of the Dead: Constructing Early Christian Identity*. Oxford: Oxford University Press.

Levine, Amy-Jill, and Ben Witherington. 2018. *The Gospel of Luke*. NCBC; Cambridge: Cambridge University Press.

Levine, Lee I. 2011. *The Ancient Synagogue: The First Thousand Years*. New Haven, CT: Yale University Press.

Lewis, W. H. (ed.). 1966. *The Letters of C. S. Lewis*. New York: Harcourt, Brace & World.

Licona, Michael R. 2010. *The Resurrection of Jesus: A New Historiographical Approach*. Downers Grove, IL: InterVarsity.

Lieu, Judith M. 2008. *I, II, and III John: A Commentary*. NTL; Louisville, KY: Westminster John Knox.

Lieu, Judith, and Martinus C. de Boer (eds.). 2018. *The Oxford Handbook of Johannine Studies*. Oxford: Oxford University Press.

Lim, Timothy H., and John J. Collins (eds.). 2010. *The Oxford Handbook to the Dead Sea Scrolls*. Oxford: Oxford University Press.

Lincoln, Andrew T. 2005. *The Gospel According to Saint John*. BNTC; London: Continuum.
——. 2006. *Hebrews: A Guide*. London: T&T Clark.
Lockett, Darian. 2017. *Letters from Pillar Apostles: The Formation of the Catholic Epistles as a Canonical Collection*. Eugene, OR: Pickwick.
Lonergan, Bernard. 1972. *Method in Theology*. New York: Herder & Herder.
Longenecker, Bruce W. 2010. *Remember the Poor: Paul, Poverty, and the Greco-Roman World*. Grand Rapids, MI: Eerdmans.
——. 2016. *The Lost Letters of Pergamum: A Story from the New Testament World*. Grand Rapids, MI: Baker.
Longenecker, Bruce W., and Todd D. Still. 2014. *Thinking Through Paul: A Survey of His Life, Letters, and Theology*. Grand Rapids, MI: Zondervan.
Longenecker, Richard N. 1990. *Galatians*. WBC; Dallas: Word.
——. 2011. *Introducing Romans: Critical Issues in Paul's Most Famous Letter*. Grand Rapids, MI: Eerdmans.
López, José, and Garry Potter (eds.). 2001. *After Postmodernism: An Introduction to Critical Realism*. London: Athlone.
Losch, Andreas. 2009. 'On the Origins of Critical Realism.' *Theology and Science* 7: 85–106.
Luckensmeyer, David. 2009. *The Eschatology of First Thessalonians*. Göttingen: Vandenhoeck & Ruprecht.
Luther, Martin. 1955–2016. *Luther's Works*. Edited by J. Pelikan et al. 78 vols.; Saint Louis: Concordia.
Luz, Ulrich. 1994. *Matthew in History: Interpretation, Influence and Effect*. Minneapolis: Fortress.
——. 2001–7. *Matthew: A Commentary*. 3 vols.; Minneapolis: Augsburg.
MacDonald, Margaret Y. 2005. 'Can Nympha Rule This House?: The Rhetoric of Domesticity in Colossians'. In *Rhetoric and Reality in Early Christianities*. Edited by Willi Braun. Studies in Christianity and Judaism 16; Waterloo, ONT: Wilfrid Laurier University Press, pp. 99–120.
MacEwen, Robert K. 2015. *Matthean Posteriority: An Exploration of Matthew's Use of Mark and Luke as a Solution to the Synoptic Problem*. LNTS 501; London: T&T Clark.
Maddox, Robert. 1982. *The Purpose of Luke-Acts*. Edinburgh: T&T Clark.
Malbon, Elizabeth Struthers. 2008 [1992]. 'Narrative Criticism: How Does the Story Mean?' In *Mark and Method: New Approaches in Biblical Studies*. Edited by J. C. Anderson and S. D. Moore. 2nd edn.; Minneapolis: Fortress, pp. 29–57.
Malcolm, Matthew R. 2012. *The World of 1 Corinthians: An Exegetical Source Book of Literary and Visual Backgrounds*. Eugene, OR: Cascade.
——. 2013. *Paul and the Rhetoric of Reversal in 1 Corinthians: The Impact of Paul's Gospel on His Macro-Rhetoric*. SNTSMS 155; Cambridge: Cambridge University Press.
Malherbe, Abraham J. 2000. *The Letters to the Thessalonians: A New Translation with Introduction and Commentary*. AB; New York: Doubleday.
Malina, Bruce J. 2001. *The New Testament World: Insights from Cultural Anthropology*. 3rd edn.; Louisville, KY: Westminster John Knox.
Marchal, Joseph A. 2015. *The People beside Paul: The Philippians Assembly and History from Below*. Atlanta: SBL.
Marcus, Joel. 1992. 'The Jewish War and the Sitz im Leben of Mark.' *Journal of Biblical Literature* 111: 441–462.
——. 2000–9. *Mark: A New Translation with Introduction and Commentary*. 2 vols.; AB; New Haven, CT: Yale University Press.

Marguerat, Daniel. 2002. *The First Christian Historian: Writing the 'Acts of the Apostles'.* SNTSMS 121; Cambridge: Cambridge University Press.

——. 2013. *Paul in Acts and Paul in His Letters.* WUNT 310; Tübingen: Mohr Siebeck.

Markschies, Christoph. 2015. *Christian Theology and Its Institutions in the Early Roman Empire: Prolegomena to a History of Early Christian Theology.* Tr. W. Coppins; Waco, TX: Baylor University Press.

Marshall, I. Howard. 1978. *The Gospel of Luke.* NIGTC; Grand Rapids, MI: Eerdmans.

——. 1980. *The Acts of the Apostles.* TNTC; Grand Rapids, MI: Eerdmans.

——. 1982. 'Pauline Theology in the Thessalonian Correspondence.' In *Paul and Paulinism: Essays in Honour of C. K. Barrett.* Edited by M. D. Booker and S. G. Wilson. London: SPCK, pp. 173–83.

——. 1988. *Luke—Historian and Theologian.* 3rd edn.; Guernsey: Paternoster.

——. 2000. 'The Christian Millennium.' *Evangelical Quarterly* 72: 217–35.

——. 2004. *New Testament Theology: Many Witnesses, One Gospel.* Downers Grove, IL: InterVarsity.

Marshall, I. Howard, with Philip Towner. 1999. *The Pastoral Epistles.* ICC; Edinburgh: T&T Clark.

Martin, Dale B. 1999. *The Corinthian Body.* New Haven, CT: Yale University Press.

——. 2006. *Sex and the Single Savior: Gender and Sexuality in Biblical Interpretation.* Louisville, KY: Westminster John Knox.

Martin, Ralph B. 1975–8. *New Testament Foundations: A Guide for Christian Students.* 2 vols.; Grand Rapids, MI: Eerdmans.

Martin, Troy W., and Eric F. Mason (eds.). 2014. *Reading 1–2 Peter and Jude: A Resource for Students.* Atlanta: SBL.

Martyn, J. Louis. 1997. *Galatians: A New Translation with Introduction and Commentary.* AB; New York: Doubleday.

——. 2009 [1968]. *History and Theology in the Fourth Gospel.* Louisville, KY: Westminster John Knox.

Mason, Eric F., and B. Kevin McCruden (eds.). 2011. *Reading the Epistle to the Hebrews: A Resource for Students.* Atlanta: SBL.

Massaux, Edouard. 1990–3. *The Influence of the Gospel of Saint Matthew on Christian Literature before Saint Irenaeus.* Macon, GA: Mercer University Press.

Massey, Preston T. 2014. 'Cicero, the Pastoral Epistles, and the Issue of Pseudonymity.' *Restoration Quarterly* 56: 65–84.

Matera, Frank J. 2012. *God's Saving Grace: A Pauline Theology.* Grand Rapids, MI: Eerdmans.

Mathew, Susan. 2013. *Women in the Greetings of Romans 16.1–16: A Study of Mutuality and Women's Ministry in the Letter to the Romans.* LNTS 471; London: Bloomsbury.

Matthews, Mark D. 2011. 'The Genre of 2 Peter: A Comparison with Early Jewish and Christian Testaments.' *Bulletin for Biblical Research* 21: 55–68.

Mayo, Philip L. 2006. 'The Role of the *Birkath Haminim* in Early Jewish-Christian Relations: Reexamination of the Evidence.' *Bulletin for Biblical Research* 16: 325–44.

Mbuvi, Andrew M. 2015. *Jude and 2 Peter.* NCCS; Eugene, OR: Cascade.

MacDonald, Margaret. 2008. *Colossians and Ephesians.* SP; Collegeville, MN: Liturgical.

McDonald, Lee Martin. 2007 [1995]. *The Biblical Canon: Its Origin, Transmission, and Authority.* 3rd edn.; Peabody, MA: Hendrickson.

McDonough, Sean M. 2007. *Christ as Creator: Origins of a New Testament Doctrine.* Oxford: Oxford University Press.

McGrath, Alister E. 2006. *A Scientific Theology, vol. 2: Reality*. London: T&T Clark.
McKnight, Scot. 1999. *A New Vision for Israel: The Teachings of Jesus in National Context*. Grand Rapids, MI: Eerdmans.
———. 2003a. '2 Peter.' In *Eerdmans Commentary on the Bible*. Edited by J. D. G. Dunn and J. W. Rogerson. Grand Rapids, MI: Eerdmans, pp. 1504–11.
———. 2003b. 'Jude.' In *Eerdmans Commentary on the Bible*. Edited by J. D. G. Dunn and J. W. Rogerson. Grand Rapids, MI: Eerdmans, pp. 1529–34.
———. 2005. *Jesus and His Death: Historiography, the Historical Jesus, and Atonement Theory*. Waco, TX: Baylor University Press.
———. 2010. 'The Jesus We'll Never Know.' *Christianity Today* (April): 22–6.
———. 2011. *The Letter of James*. NICNT; Grand Rapids, MI: Eerdmans.
———. 2013. *Sermon on the Mount*. SGBC; Grand Rapids, MI: Zondervan.
———. 2017. *The Letter to Philemon*. NICNT; Grand Rapids, MI: Eerdmans.
———. 2018. *The Letter to the Colossians*. NICNT; Grand Rapids, MI: Eerdmans.
McNeel, Jennifer H. 2013. 'Feeding with Milk: Paul's Nursing Metaphors in Context.' *Review & Expositor* 110: 561–75.
Meade, David G. 1987. *Pseudonymity and Canon: An Investigation into Authorship and Authority in Jewish and Earliest Christian Literature*. Grand Rapids, MI: Eerdmans.
Mealand, David L. 1995. 'The Extent of the Pauline Corpus: A Multivariate Approach.' *Journal for the Study of the New Testament* 59: 61–92.
Meeks, Wayne A. 2005. 'Why Study the New Testament?' *New Testament Studies* 51: 155–70.
Meeks, Wayne A., and John T. Fitzgerald. 2007. *The Writings of St. Paul: Annotated Texts: Reception and Criticism*. New York: W. W. Norton.
Meggitt, Justin. 1998. *Paul, Poverty and Survival*. Edinburgh: T&T Clark.
Meier, John P. 1991–2016. *A Marginal Jew: Rethinking the Historical Jesus*. 5 vols.; ABRL; New Haven, CT: Yale University Press.
———. 1999. 'The Present State of the "Third Quest" for the Historical Jesus: Loss and Gain.' *Biblica* 80: 459–87.
Mettinger, Tryggve N. D. 2001. *The Riddle of Resurrection: 'Dying and Rising Gods' in the Ancient Near East*. ConBOT 50; Stockholm: Almqvist & Wiksell.
Metzger, Bruce M. 1987. *The Canon of the New Testament*. Oxford: Clarendon.
———. 1994. *A Textual Commentary on the Greek New Testament*. 3rd edn.; Stuttgart: German Bible Society.
———. 2009. *The Canon of the New Testament: Its Origin, Development, and Significance*. Oxford: Clarendon.
Metzger, Bruce M., and Bart D. Ehrman. 2005. *The Text of the New Testament: Its Transmission, Corruption, and Restoration*. New York: Oxford University Press.
Meyer, Ben F. 1979. *The Aims of Jesus*. London: SCM.
———. 1989. *Critical Realism and the New Testament*. Allison Park, PA: Pickwick.
———. 1994. *Reality and Illusion in New Testament Scholarship: A Primer in Critical Realist Hermeneutics*. Collegeville, MN: Liturgical.
———. 2014. *Five Speeches that Changed the World*. Eugene, OR: Wipf & Stock.
Miller, James D. 1997. *The Pastoral Letters as Composite Documents*. SNTSMS 93; Cambridge: Cambridge University Press.
Millis, Benjamin W. 2010. 'The Social and Ethnic Origins of the Colonists in Early Roman Corinth.' In *Corinth in Context: Comparative Studies on Religion and Society*. Edited by S. J. Friesen, D. N. Schowalter, and J. C. Walters. Leiden: Brill, pp. 13–35.

Mink, Gerd. 2004. 'Problems of a Highly Contaminated Tradition: The New Testament: Stemmata of Variants as a Source of a Genealogy for Witnesses.' In *Studies in Stemmatology II*. Edited by P. van Reenen, A. den Hollander, and M. van Mulken; Amsterdam: John Benjamins, pp. 13–85.

Mitchell, M. Margaret. 1991. *Paul and the Rhetoric of Reconciliation: An Exegetical Investigation of the Language and Composition of 1 Corinthians*. Louisville, KY: Westminster John Knox.

——. 2005. 'Paul's Letters to Corinth: The Interpretive Intertwining of Literary and Historical Reconstruction.' In *Urban Religion in Roman Corinth*. Edited by D. N. Schowalter and J. Friesen. Cambridge, MA: Harvard University Press, pp. 307–38.

Mitchell, Stephen. 1993. *Anatolia: Land, Men, and Gods in Asia Minor*. Oxford: Clarendon.

Moo, Douglas J. 1996. *The Epistle to the Romans*. NICNT; Grand Rapids, MI: Eerdmans.

——. 2008. *The Letters to the Colossians and to Philemon*. PNTC; Grand Rapids, MI: Eerdmans.

Moore, Stephen D. 1989. *Literary Criticism and the Gospels: The Theoretical Challenge*. New Haven, CT: Yale University Press.

Moore, Stephen D., and Yvonne Sherwood. 2011. *The Invention of the Biblical Scholar: A Critical Manifesto*. Minneapolis: Fortress.

Morgan, Robert, and John Barton. 1988. *Biblical Interpretation*. Oxford: Oxford University Press.

Morris, Leon. 1987. *Revelation: An Introduction and Commentary*. 2nd edn.; TNTC; Leicester: InterVarsity.

——. 1995. *The Gospel According to John*. Rev. edn.; NICNT; Grand Rapids, MI: Eerdmans.

Morton, Russell S. 2014. *Recent Research on Revelation*. Sheffield: Sheffield Phoenix.

Moule, C. F. D. 1965. 'The Problem of the Pastoral Epistles: A Reappraisal.' *Bulletin of the John Rylands Library* 47: 430–52.

——. 1967. *The Phenomenon of the New Testament*. London: SCM.

Mounce, William. 2000. *Pastoral Epistles*. WBC; Nashville: Thomas Nelson.

Müller, Ulrich B. 1999. 'Der Brief aus Ephesus: Zeitliche Plazierung und theologische Einordnung des Philipperbriefes im Rahmen der Paulusbriefe.' In *Das Urchristentum in seiner literarischen Geschichte*. Edited by U. Mell and U. Müller. BZNW 100; Berlin: Walter de Gruyter, pp. 155–71.

Murphy-O'Connor, Jerome. 1991. '2 Timothy Contrasted with 1 Timothy and Titus.' *Revue Biblique* 98: 403–18.

——. 1996. *Paul: A Critical Life*. Oxford: Oxford University Press.

——. 2002. *St. Paul's Corinth: Texts and Archaeology*. 3rd edn.; Collegeville, MN: Liturgical.

——. 2004. *Paul: His Story*. Oxford: Oxford University Press.

——. 2008. *St. Paul's Ephesus: Texts and Archaeology*. Collegeville, MN: Liturgical.

Mbuvi, Andrew M. 2015. *Jude and 2 Peter*. NCCS; Eugene, OR: Cascade.

Nanos, Mark D. (ed.). 2002. *The Irony of Galatians: Contemporary Issues in Rhetorical and Historical Interpretation*. Grand Rapids, MI: Baker.

Nanos, Mark D., and Magnus Zetterholm (eds.). 2015. *Paul within Judaism: Restoring the First-Century Context to the Apostle*. Minneapolis: Fortress.

Neusner, Jacob, and Bruce D. Chilton (eds.). 2007. *In Quest of the Historical Pharisees*. Waco, TX: Baylor University Press.

Neyrey, Jerome H. 1993. *2 Peter, Jude*. AB; New York: Doubleday.

Ngewa, Samuel M. 2009. *1 & 2 Timothy and Titus*. ABCS; Grand Rapids, MI: Zondervan.

Niebuhr, Karl-Wilhelm, and Robert Wall (eds.). 2009. *The Catholic Epistles and Apostolic Tradition: A New Perspective on James to Jude*. Waco, TX: Baylor University Press.

Nienhuis, David. 2007. *Not by Paul Alone: The Formation of the Catholic Epistle Collection and the Christian Canon*. Waco, TX: Baylor University Press.

Nienhuis, David, and Robert Wall (eds.). 2013. *Reading the Epistles of James, Peter, John and Jude as Scripture*. Grand Rapids, MI: Eerdmans.

Nolland, John. 2005. *The Gospel of Matthew: A Commentary on the Greek Text*. NIGTC; Grand Rapids, MI; Eerdmans.

Nongbri, Brent. 2013. *Before Religion: A History of a Modern Concept*. New Haven, CT: Yale University Press.

Oakes, Peter. 2001. *Philippians: From People to Letter*. SNTSMS 110; Cambridge: Cambridge University Press.

——. 2009. *Reading Romans in Pompeii: Paul's Letter at Ground Level*. Minneapolis: Fortress.

Oakman, Douglas E. 1986. *Jesus and the Economic Questions of His Day*. Lewiston, NY: Mellen.

Ogereau, Julien M. 2014. *Paul's Koinonia with the Philippians: A Socio-Historical Investigation of a Pauline Economic Partnership*. WUNT 2.377; Tübingen: Mohr Siebeck.

Osiek, Caroline. 2000. *Philippians, Philemon*. ANTC; Nashville, TN: Abingdon.

Paddison, Angus. 2005. *Theological Hermeneutics and 1 Thessalonians*. SNTSMS 133; Cambridge: Cambridge University Press.

Paffenroth, Kim. 1997. *The Story of Jesus According to L*. JSNTSup 147; Sheffield: Sheffield Academic Press.

Painter, John. 2002. *1, 2, and 3 John*. SP; Collegeville, MN: Liturgical.

Painter, John, and David A. deSilva. 2012. *James and Jude*. Paideia; Grand Rapids, MI: Baker.

Park, M. Sydney. 2007. *Submission within the Godhead and the Church in the Epistle to the Philippians: An Exegetical and Theological Examination of the Concept of Submission in Philippians 2 and 3*. LNTS 361; London: T&T Clark.

Parker, David C. 2006. *The Living Text of the Gospels*. Cambridge: Cambridge University Press.

——. 2007. 'Textual Criticism and Theology.' *Expository Times* 118: 583–9.

——. 2008. *An Introduction to the New Testament Manuscripts and Their Texts*. Cambridge: Cambridge University Press.

Parsenios, George L. 2014. *First, Second, and Third John*. Paideia; Grand Rapids, MI: Baker.

Parsons, Mikael. 2008. *Acts*. Paideia; Grand Rapids, MI: Baker.

——. 2015. *Luke*. Paideia; Grand Rapids, MI: Baker.

Parsons, Mikael C., and R. I. Pervo. 1993. *Rethinking the Unity of Luke and Acts*. Minneapolis: Fortress.

Patte, Daniel. 1976. *What Is Structural Exegesis?* Philadelphia: Fortress.

——. 1990. *Structural Exegesis for New Testament Critics*. Minneapolis: Fortress.

Peeler, Amy. 2014. *You Are My Son: The Family of God in the Epistles to the Hebrews*. LNTS 486; London: T&T Clark.

Penner, T. C. 1999. 'The Epistle of James in Current Research.' *Currents in Research: Biblical Studies* 7: 257–308.

Pennington, Jonathan. 2012. *Reading the Gospels Wisely: A Narrative and Theological Introduction*. Grand Rapids, MI: Baker.

Peppiatt, Lucy. 2018. *Unveiling Paul's Women: Making Sense of 1 Corinthians 11:2–16*. Eugene, OR: Wipf & Stock.

Perkins, Judith. 2009. *Roman Imperial Identities in the Early Christian Era*. London: Routledge.

Perkins, Pheme. 1991. *Jesus as Teacher*. Cambridge: Cambridge University Press.

——. 1994. 'The Resurrection of Jesus of Nazareth.' In *Studying the Historical Jesus: Evaluations of the State of Research*. Leiden: Brill, pp. 423–42.

——. 1995. *First and Second Peter, James, and Jude*. Interpretation; Louisville, KY: Westminster John Knox.

——. 1997. *Ephesians*. ANTC; Nashville, TN: Abingdon.

——. 2007. *Introduction to the Synoptic Gospels*. Grand Rapids, MI: Eerdmans.

——. 2007. 'Resurrection and Christology: Are They Related?' In *Israel's God and Rebecca's Children: Christology and Community in Early Judaism and Christianity*. Edited by D. B. Capes, A. D. DeConick, H. K. Bond, and T. Miller. Waco, TX: Baylor University Press, pp. 67–75.

——. 2011. *Understanding Jesus Today*. Cambridge: Cambridge University Press.

——. 2012. *First Corinthians*. PCNT; Grand Rapids, MI: Baker Academic.

Perrin, Nicholas. 2010. *Jesus the Temple*. Grand Rapids, MI: Baker.

Pervo, Richard I. 2006. *Dating Acts: Between the Evangelists and the Apologists*. Santa Rosa, CA: Polebridge.

——. 2009. *Acts*. Hermeneia; Minneapolis: Fortress.

——. 2016. *The Pastorals and Polycarp: Titus, 1–2 Timothy, and Polycarp to the Philippians*. Salem, MA: Polebridge.

Phillips, Thomas E. 2006. 'The Genre of Acts: Moving towards a Consensus.' *Currents in Biblical Research* 4: 365–96.

Picirilli, Robert E. 1988. 'Allusions to 2 Peter in the Apostolic Fathers.' *Journal for the Study of the New Testament* 33: 57–83.

Pierce, Chad T. 2011. *Spirits and the Proclamation of Christ*. WUNT 2.305; Tübingen: Mohr Siebeck.

Pierce, Madison N. 2017. 'Hebrews 1 and the Son Begotten "Today".' In *Retrieving Eternal Generation*. Edited by S. Swain and F. Sanders. Grand Rapids, MI: Zondervan, pp. 117–31.

Pietersen, Lloyd Keith. 2004. *Polemic of the Pastorals: A Sociological Examination of the Development of Pauline Christianity*. London: T&T Clark.

Pietersma, Albert, and Benjamin G. Wright. 2007. *A New English Translation of the Septuagint*. Oxford: Oxford University Press.

Pitre, Brant. 2015. *Jesus and the Last Supper*. Grand Rapids, MI: Eerdmans.

Pitts, Andrew W., and Joshua F. Walker. 2010. 'The Authorship of Hebrews: A Further Development in the Luke–Paul Relationship.' In *Paul and His Social Relations*. Edited by S. E. Porter. PAST 7; Leiden: Brill, pp. 143–84.

Poirier, John C. 2007. 'The Linguistic Situation in Jewish Palestine in Late Antiquity.' *Journal of Greco-Roman Christianity and Judaism* 4: 55–134.

Porter, Stanley E. 1989. 'The Language of the Apocalypse in Recent Discussion.' *New Testament Studies* 35: 582–603.

——. 1990. 'Why Hasn't Reader-Response Criticism Caught on in New Testament Studies?' *Journal of Literature and Theology* 4: 278–92.

——. 1993a. 'The Theoretical Justification for Application of Rhetorical Categories to Pauline Epistolary Literature.' In *Rhetoric and the New Testament: Essays from the 1992 Heidelberg Conference*. Edited by S. E. Porter and T. H. Olbricht. JSNTSup 90; Sheffield: Sheffield Academic Press, pp. 100–22.

——. 1993b. 'Did Jesus Ever Teach in Greek?' *Tyndale Bulletin* 44: 199–235.

——. 1994. *Idioms of the Greek New Testament*. Sheffield: Sheffield Academic Press.

——. 1995. 'Pauline Authorship and the Pastoral Epistles: Implications for Canon.' *Bulletin for Biblical Research* 5: 105–23.

——. 2001. *Paul in Acts*. Peabody, MA: Hendrickson.

——. 2004. 'Reading the Gospels and the Quest for the Historical Jesus.' In *Reading the Gospels Today*. Edited by S. E. Porter. Grand Rapids, MI: Eerdmans, pp. 31–55.
——. 2011. 'Luke: Companion or Disciple of Paul?' In *Paul and the Gospels: Christologies, Conflicts, and Convergences*. Edited by M. F. Bird and J. Willitts. LNTS 411; London: T&T Clark, pp. 146–68.
——. 2013. *How We Got the New Testament: Text, Transmission, Translation*. Grand Rapids, MI: Baker.
——. 2015. *John, His Gospel, and Jesus: In Pursuit of the Johannine Voice*. Grand Rapids, MI: Eerdmans.
Porter, Stanley E., and Gregory P. Fewster (eds.). 2013. *Paul and Pseudepigraphy*. PAST 8; Leiden: Brill.
Porter, Stanley E., and Hughson T. Ong (eds.). 2016. *The Origin of John's Gospel*. JS 2; Leiden: Brill.
Powell, Mark Allan. 1990. *What Is Narrative Criticism?* Minneapolis: Fortress.
——. 1992. 'The Plot and Subplots of Matthew's Gospel.' *New Testament Studies* 38: 187–204.
——. 2011. 'Narrative Criticism: The Emergence of a Prominent Reading Strategy.' In *Mark as Story: Retrospect and Prospect*. Edited by K. R. Iverson and C. W. Skinner. Atlanta: SBL, pp. 19–43.
Price, S. R. F. 1984. *Rituals and Power: The Roman Imperial Cult in Asia Minor*. Cambridge: Cambridge University Press.
Priest, J. 1983–5. 'Testament of Moses.' In *Old Testament Pseudepigrapha*. Edited by J. H. Charlesworth. 2 vols.; New York: Doubleday, 1.919–34.
Prior, Michael. 1989. *Paul the Letter Writer and the Second Letter to Timothy*. JSNTSup 23; Sheffield: JSOT Press.
Räisänen, Heikki. 1990. *Beyond New Testament Theology: Story and Program*. London: SCM.
Rasmussen, Carl. 2010. *Zondervan Atlas of the Bible*. Grand Rapids, MI: Zondervan.
Ratzinger, Joseph (Pope Benedict XVI). 2007–12. *Jesus of Nazareth*. 3 vols.; New York: Doubleday.
Reasoner, Mark. 2005. *Romans in Full Circle: A History of Interpretation*. Louisville, KY: Westminster John Knox.
Reese, Ruth Anne. 2000. *Writing Jude: The Reader, the Text, and the Author in Constructs of Power and Desire*. BIS 51; Leiden: Brill.
——. 2007. *2 Peter and Jude*. THNTC; Grand Rapids, MI: Eerdmans.
Resseguie, James L. 2005. *Narrative Criticism of the New Testament: An Introduction*. Grand Rapids, MI: Baker.
Reumann, John. 2008. *Philippians: A New Translation with Introduction and Commentary*. AB; New Haven, CT: Yale University Press.
Rhoads, David. 1976. *Israel in Revolution, 6–74 C.E.: A Political History Based on the Writings of Josephus*. Philadelphia: Fortress.
——. 2005. *From Every People and Nation: The Book of Revelation in Intercultural Perspective*. Minneapolis: Fortress.
Rhoads, David, Joanna Dewey, and Donald Michie. 1999 [1982]. *Mark as Story: An Introduction to the Narrative of a Gospel*. 2nd edn.; Minneapolis: Fortress.
Riches, John K. 2008. *Galatians through the Centuries*. Oxford: Blackwell.
Riesner, Rainer. 1989. 'Josephus' "Gate of the Essenes" in Modern Discussion.' *Zeitschrift des deutschen Palästina-Vereins* 105: 105–9.
——. 1998. *Paul's Early Period: Chronology, Mission Strategy, Theology*. Grand Rapids, MI: Eerdmans.

———. 2006. 'Once More: Luke-Acts and the Pastoral Epistles.' In *History and Exegesis*. Edited by S.-W. Son. FS E. E. Ellis; London: T&T Clark, pp. 239–58.
Rieu, E. V. (tr.). 2001. *Homer, the Iliad*. London: York Press.
Ringe, Sharon H. 1995. *Luke*. WBC; Louisville, KY: Westminster John Knox.
Rives, James B. 2010. 'Graeco-Roman Religion in the Roman Empire: Old Assumptions and New Approaches.' *Currents in Biblical Research* 8: 240–9.
Robbins, Vernon K. 1978. 'By Land and by Sea: The We-Passages and Ancient Sea Voyages.' In *Perspectives on Luke-Acts*. Edited by C. H. Talbert. Edinburgh: T&T Clark., pp. 215–42.
Robinson, J. A. T. 1976. *Redating the New Testament*. London: SCM.
Rodriguez, Raphael. 2014. *Oral Tradition and the New Testament: A Guide for the Perplexed*. London: T&T Clark.
Roskam, H. N. 2004. *The Purpose of the Gospel of Mark in Its Historical and Social Context*. NovTSup 114; Leiden: Brill.
Rosner, Brian R. 1994. 'Acts and Biblical History.' In *The Book of Acts in Its Ancient Literary Setting*. Edited by B. W. Winter and A. D. Clarke. 6 vols.; Grand Rapids, MI: Eerdmans, 1.65–82.
Rowe, C. Kavin. 2009. *World Upside Down: Reading Acts in the Graeco-Roman Age*. Oxford: Oxford University Press.
Safrai, S., and M. Stern (eds.). 1974–6. *The Jewish People in the First Century: Historical Geography, Political History, Social, Cultural and Religious Life and Institutions*. 2 vols.; CRINT 1; Assen: Van Gorcum.
Samuelsson, Gunnar. 2011. *Crucifixion in Antiquity: An Inquiry into the Background and Significance of the New Testament Terminology of Crucifixion*. WUNT 2.310; Tübingen: Mohr Siebeck.
Sanders, E. P. 1985. *Jesus and Judaism*. Philadelphia: Fortress.
———. 1992. *Judaism: Practice and Belief, 63 BCE–66 CE*. London: SCM.
———. 2015. *Paul: The Apostle's Life, Letters, and Thought*. Minneapolis: Fortress.
Sanders, E. P., and Margaret Davies. 1989. *Studying the Synoptic Gospels*. London: SCM.
Sandys-Wunsch, John, and Laurence Eldredge. 1980. 'J. P. Gabler and the Distinction between Biblical and Dogmatic Theology: Translation, Commentary, and Discussion of His Originality.' *Scottish Journal of Theology* 33: 133–58.
Schlatter, Adolf. 1973. 'The Nature of New Testament Theology.' In *The Nature of New Testament Theology: The Contribution of William Wrede and Adolf Schlatter*. Edited by Robert Morgan. SBT 25; London: SCM.
Schmidt, T. E. 1995. 'Mark 15.16–32: The Crucifixion Narrative and the Roman Triumphal Procession.' *New Testament Studies* 41: 1–18.
Schnabel, Eckhard J. 2004. 'Textual Criticism: Recent Developments.' In *The Face of New Testament Studies: A Survey of Recent Research*. Edited by S. McKnight and G. R. Osborne. Grand Rapids, MI: Baker, pp. 59–75.
Schnelle, Udo. 2005. *Apostle Paul: His Life and Theology*. Tr. M. Eugene Boring; Grand Rapids, MI: Baker.
Schreiner, Thomas R. 1998. *Romans*. BECNT; Grand Rapids, MI.
———. 2001. *Paul, Apostle of God's Glory in Christ: A Pauline Theology*. Downers Grove, IL: InterVarsity.
———. 2003. *1, 2 Peter, Jude*. NAC; Nashville: Broadman & Holman.
Schweitzer, Albert. 1911. *The Quest of the Historical Jesus*. London: A&C Black.
———. 1945 [1906]. *The Quest of the Historical Jesus: A Critical Study of Its Progress from Reimarus to Wrede*. London: Adam & Charles Black.

Sechrest, Love L. 2009. *A Former Jew: Paul and the Dialectics of Race*. LNTS 410; London: T&T Clark.

Seeman, Chris, and Adam Kolman Marshak. 2010. 'Jewish History from Alexander to Hadrian.' In *The Eerdmans Dictionary of Early Judaism*. Edited by D. C. Harlow and J. J. Collins. Grand Rapids, MI: Eerdmans, pp. 30–69.

Segal, Alan F. 2004. *Life after Death: A History of the Afterlife in the Religions of the West*. New York: Doubleday.

Sheppard, Beth. 2012. *The Craft of the New Testament and the Study of the New Testament*. Atlanta: SBL.

Shively, Elizabeth E. 2012. *Apocalyptic Imagination in the Gospel of Mark: The Literary and Theological Role of Mark 3:22–30*. BZNW 189; Berlin: De Gruyter.

———. 2013. 'Apocalyptic Imagination in the Gospel of Mark: The Literary and Theological Role of Mark 3:22–30.' *Bulletin for Biblical Research* 23: 429–31.

Simonetti, Manlio. 2002. *Matthew 14–28*. ACCS; Downers Grove, IL: InterVarsity.

Smith, Christian. 2006. 'Is Moral Therapeutic Deism the New Religion of American Youth? Implications for the Challenges of Religious Socialization and Reproduction.' In *Passing on the Faith: Transforming Traditions for the Next Generation of Jews, Christians, and Muslims*. Edited by J. L. Heft. New York: Fordham University Press, pp. 55–74.

Smith, Ian K. 2006. *Heavenly Perspective: A Study of the Apostle Paul's Response to a Jewish Mystical Movement at Colossae*. LNTS 326; London: T&T Clark.

Smith, Jonathan Z. 1987. 'Dying and Rising Gods.' In *Encyclopedia of Religion*. Edited by M. Eliade. 16 vols.; New York: Macmillan, 4.521–7.

Smith, Justin Marc. 2015. *Why Bios? On the Relationship between Gospel Genre and Implied Audience*. LNTS 518; London: T&T Clark.

Smith, Mark S. 1998. 'The Death of Dying and Rising Gods in the Biblical World.' *Scandinavian Journal of the Old Testament* 12: 257–313.

Somov, Alexey. 2017. *Representations of the Afterlife in Luke-Acts*. LNTS 556; London: T&T Clark.

Spinks, C. Christopher. 2007. *The Bible and the Crisis of Meaning: Debates on the Theological Interpretation of Scripture*. London: T&T Clark.

Stamper, Meda A. A. 2014. *Embodying Mark: Fresh Ways to Read, Pray and Live the Gospel*. London: SPCK.

Stamps, Dennis L. 1997. 'Rhetorical and Narratological Criticism.' In *A Handbook to the Exegesis of the New Testament*. Edited by S. E. Porter. Leiden: Brill, pp. 219–39.

Stanton, Graham. 1993. *A New Gospel for a New People: Studies in Matthew*. Louisville, KY: Westminster John Knox.

Starling, David S. 2014. *Uncorinthian Leadership: Thematic Reflections on 1 Corinthians*. Eugene, OR: Cascade.

Stendahl, Krister. 1962. 'Biblical Theology, Contemporary.' In *Interpreter's Dictionary of the Bible*. Nashville: Abingdon, pp. 418–32.

Sterling, Gregory E. 1992. *Historiography and Self-Definition: Josephos, Luke-Acts and Apologetic Historiography*. NovTSup 64; Leiden: Brill.

———. 1997. 'Hellenistic Philosophy and the New Testament.' In *Handbook to Exegesis of the New Testament*. Edited by S. E. Porter. Leiden: Brill, pp. 313–58.

———. 1999. '"Opening the Scriptures": The Legitimation of the Jewish Diaspora and the Early Christian Mission.' In *Jesus and the Heritage of Israel: Luke's Narrative Claim upon Israel's Legacy*. Edited by D. P. Moessner. Harrisburg, PA: Trinity Press International, pp. 199–225.

Stern, Menahem. 1974–84. *Greek and Latin Authors on Jews and Judaism*. 2 vols.; Jerusalem: Israel Academy of Sciences and Humanities.

Stewart, Robert B. 2008. *The Quest of the Hermeneutical Jesus: The Impact of Hermeneutical Issues on the Jesus Research of John Dominic Crossan and N. T. Wright*. Lanham, MD: University Press of America.

Still, Todd D. 2007. 'Interpretive Ambiguities and Scholarly Proclivities in Pauline Studies: A Treatment of Three Texts from 1 Thessalonians 4 as a Test Case.' *Currents in Biblical Research* 5: 207–19.

Stott, John. 1967. 'The Great Commission.' In *One Race, One Gospel, One Task*. Edited by C. F. Henry and W. S. Mooneyham. 2 vols.; Minneapolis: World Wide Publications, pp. 37–56.

Strauss, Mark L. 2011. 'The Purpose of Luke-Acts: Reaching a Consensus.' In *New Testament Theology in Light of the Church's Mission*. Edited by J. C. Laansma, G. Osborne, and R. Van Neste. Eugene, OR: Cascade, pp. 135–50.

Strecker, George. 1996. *The Johannine Epistles*. Hermeneia; Minneapolis: Fortress.

Streett, Daniel R. 2011. *'They Went Out from Us': The Identity of the Opponents in First John*. BZNW 177; Berlin: De Gruyter.

Strelan, Rick. 1996. *Paul, Artemis, and the Ephesians*. BZNW 80; Berlin: De Gruyter.

——. 2008. *Luke the Priest: The Authority of the Author of the Third Gospel*. Aldershot: Ashgate.

Strutwolf, Holger. 2011. 'Original Text and Textual History.' In *The Textual History of the Greek New Testament*. Atlanta: SBL, pp. 23–41.

Stuckenbruck, Loren. 1999. 'Johann Gabler and the Delineation of Biblical Theology.' *Scottish Journal of Theology* 52: 139–57.

——. 2003. 'Revelation.' In *Eerdmans Commentary on the Bible*. Edited by J. D. G. Dunn and J. W. Rogerson. Grand Rapids, MI: Eerdmans, pp. 1535–72.

——. 2017. *The Myth of Rebellious Angels: Studies in Second Temple Judaism and New Testament Texts*. Grand Rapids, MI: Eerdmans.

Stuhlmacher, Peter. 1993. 'The Resurrection of Jesus and the Resurrection of the Dead.' *Ex Auditu* 9: 45–56.

Sumney, Jerry. 2015. *Identifying Paul's Opponents: The Question of Method in 2 Corinthians*. London: Bloomsbury.

Tan, Kim Huat. *Mark*. NCCS. Eugene, OR: Cascade, 2015.

Tannehill, Robert E. 1986–90. *The Narrative Unity of Luke-Acts: A Literary Interpretation*. 2 vols.; Minneapolis: Fortress.

Taylor, Joan E. 1997. *The Immerser: John the Baptist within Second Temple Judaism*. Grand Rapids, MI: Eerdmans.

——. 1998. 'Golgotha: A Reconsideration of the Evidence for the Sites of Jesus' Crucifixion and Burial.' *New Testament Studies* 44: 180–203.

Thatcher, Tom. 2007. 'Remembering Jesus: John's Negative Christology.' In *The Messiah in the Old and New Testaments*. Edited by S. E. Porter. Grand Rapids, MI: Eerdmans, pp. 165–89.

Theissen, Gerd. 1991. *The Gospels in Context: Social and Political History in the Synoptic Tradition*. Tr. Linda M. Maloney; Minneapolis: Fortress.

——. 2004. 'Social Stratification in the Corinthian Community: A Contribution to the Sociology of Early Hellenistic Christianity.' In *The Social Setting of Pauline Christianity*. Eugene, OR: Wipf & Stock, pp. 69–120.

Theissen, Gerd, and Annette Merz. 1998. *The Historical Jesus: A Comprehensive Guide*. Tr. John Bowden; Minneapolis: Fortress.

Thielman, Frank S. 2003. 'Ephesus and the Literary Setting of Philippians.' In *New Testament Greek and Exegesis*. Edited by A. M. Donaldson and T. B. Sailors. FS G. F. Hawthorne; Grand Rapids, MI: Eerdmans, pp. 205–23.

———. 2010. *Ephesians*. BECNT; Grand Rapids, MI: Baker.
Thiselton, Anthony C. 1980. *The Two Horizons: New Testament Hermeneutics and Philosophical Description with Special Reference to Heidegger, Bultmann, Gadamer and Wittgenstein*. Grand Rapids, MI: Eerdmans.
———. 1992. *New Horizons in Hermeneutics: The Theory and Practice of Transforming Biblical Reading*. London: HarperCollins.
———. 2000. *The First Epistle to the Corinthians*. NIGTC; Grand Rapids, MI: Eerdmans.
———. 2006. *Thiselton on Hermeneutics: Collected Works with New Essays*. Grand Rapids, MI: Eerdmans.
———. 2015. *The Thiselton Companion to Christian Theology*. Grand Rapids, MI: Eerdmans.
Thompson, Leonard L. 1990. *The Book of Revelation: Empire and Apocalypse*. Oxford: Oxford University Press.
Thompson, Marianne M. 1992a. *1–3 John*. IVPNTC; Downers Grove, IL: InterVarsity.
———. 1992b. 'Intercession in the Johannine Community: 1 John 5:16 in the Context of the Gospel and Epistles of John.' In *Worship, Theology and Ministry in the Early Church*. Edited by M. J. Wilkins and T. Paige. JSNTSup 87; Sheffield: Sheffield Academic Press, pp. 225–45.
———. 2001. *The God of the Gospel of John*. Grand Rapids, MI: Eerdmans.
———. 2005. *Colossians & Philemon*. THNTC; Grand Rapids, MI: Eerdmans.
———. 2015. *John: A Commentary*. NTL; Louisville, KY: Westminster John Knox.
Thurston, Bonnie. 2009. *Philippians and Philemon*. SP; Collegeville, MN: Liturgical.
Towner, Philip. 2006. *The Letters to Timothy and Titus*. NICNT; Grand Rapids, MI: Eerdmans.
Trebilco, Paul R. 2007. *The Early Christians in Ephesus from Paul to Ignatius*. Grand Rapids, MI: Eerdmans.
Trobisch, David. 2000. *The First Edition of the New Testament*. Oxford: Oxford University Press.
Troftgruben, Troy M. 2010. *A Conclusion Unhindered: A Study of the Ending of Acts within Its Literary Environment*. WUNT 2.280; Tübingen: Mohr Siebeck.
Turner, John D. 1984. 'Trimorphic Protennoia.' In *The Nag Hammadi Library in English*. Edited by James M. Robinson. Leiden: Brill, pp. 461–70.
Tyrrell, George. 1909. *Christianity at the Crossroads*. London: Longman Green.
van Houwelingen, P. H. R. 2010. 'The Authenticity of 2 Peter: Problems and Possible Solutions.' *European Journal of Theology* 19: 119–29.
Van Neste, Ray. 2004. *Cohesion and Structure in the Pastoral Epistles*. JSNTSup 280; London: T&T Clark.
VanderKam, James C. 2012. 'Judaism in the Land of Israel.' In *Early Judaism: A Comprehensive Overview*. Edited by J. J. Collins and D. C. Harlow. Grand Rapids, MI: Eerdmans, pp. 70–94.
Vanhoozer, Kevin J. 1998. *Is There A Meaning in This Text? The Bible, The Reader, and the Morality of Literary Knowledge*. Grand Rapids, MI: Zondervan.
———. 2005. *The Drama of Doctrine: A Canonical-Linguistic Approach to Christian Theology*. Louisville, KY: Westminster John Knox.
———. 2016. *Biblical Authority after Babel: Retrieving the Solas in the Spirit of Mere Protestant Christianity*. Grand Rapids, MI: Brazos.
Verheyden, J. 1999. *The Unity of Luke-Acts*. BETL 142; Leuven: Leuven University Press.
Verhoef, Eduard. 2013. *Philippi: How Christianity Began in Europe: The Epistle to the Philippians and the Excavations at Philippi*. London: Bloomsbury.
Vermes, Geza. 1973. *Jesus the Jew: A Historian's Reading of the Gospels*. Philadelphia: Fortress.

——. 1993. *The Religion of Jesus the Jew*. Minneapolis: Fortress.

——. 1995 [1962]. *The Complete Dead Sea Scrolls in English*. 4th edn.; London: Penguin.

Volf, Miroslav. 1994. 'Soft Difference: Theological Reflections on the Relation between Church and Culture in 1 Peter.' *Ex Auditu* 10: 15–30.

von Wahlde, Urban C. 2010. *The Gospel and Letters of John*. 3 vols.; ECC; Grand Rapids, MI: Eerdmans.

Walker, Peter. 2012. 'Revisiting the Pastoral Epistles—Part I and II.' *European Journal of Theology* 21: 4–16, 120–32.

Wall, Robert W. 1995. 'Pauline Authorship and the Pastoral Epistles: A Response to S. E. Porter.' *Bulletin for Biblical Research* 5: 125–8.

——. 1997. *Community of the Wise: The Letter of James*. NTC; Valley Forge, PA: Trinity Press International.

——. 2002. 'Introduction to Epistolary Literature.' In *New Interpreter's Bible*. Edited by L. E. Keck. 10 vols.; Nashville: Abingdon, 10.369–89.

——. 2004. 'The Function of the Pastoral Letters within the Pauline Canon of the New Testament: A Canonical Approach.' In *The Pauline Canon*. Edited by S. E. Porter. PAST 1; Leiden: Brill, pp. 27–44.

Wall, Robert W., and Richard B. Steele. 2012. *1 and 2 Timothy and Titus*. THNTC; Grand Rapids, MI: Eerdmans.

Walton, Steve. 2000. *Leadership and Lifestyle: The Portrait of Paul in the Miletus Speech and 1 Thessalonians*. SNTSMS 106; Cambridge: Cambridge University Press.

——. 2008. 'Primitive Communism in Acts? Does Acts Present the Community of Goods (2:44–45; 4:32–35) as Mistaken?' *Evangelical Quarterly* 80: 99–111.

Wardle, Timothy. 2016. 'Mark, the Jerusalem Temple and Jewish Sectarianism: Why Geographical Proximity Matters in Determining the Provenance of Mark.' *New Testament Studies* 62: 60–78.

Warrior, Valerie M. 2006. *Roman Religion*. Cambridge: Cambridge University Press.

Wasserman, Tommy. 2006. *The Epistle of Jude: Its Text and Transmission*. Stockholm: Almqvist & Wiksell.

——. 2015. 'The Coherence Based Genealogical Method as a Tool for Explaining Textual Changes in the Greek New Testament.' *Novum Testamentum* 57: 206–18.

Wasserman, Tommy, and Peter Gurry. 2017. *A New Approach to Textual Criticism: An Introduction to the Coherence-Based Genealogical Method*. Atlanta: SBL.

Watson, Duane F. 2006. *The Rhetoric of the New Testament: A Bibliographic Survey*. Blandford: Deo.

Watson, Francis. 1994. *Text, Church, and World: Biblical Interpretation in Theological Perspective*. Edinburgh: T&T Clark.

——. 2007. *Paul, Judaism, and the Gentiles: Beyond the New Perspective*. Grand Rapids, MI: Eerdmans.

——. 2008. '*Veritas Christi*: How to Get from the Jesus of History to the Christ of Faith without Losing One's Way.' In *Seeking the Identity of Jesus: A Pilgrimage*. Edited by R. B. Hays and B. R. Gaventa. Grand Rapids, MI: Eerdmans, pp. 96–116.

Webb, Robert L. 1991. *John the Baptizer and Prophet: A Socio-Historical Study*. Eugene, OR: Wipf & Stock.

Webb, Robert L., and Peter H. Davids (eds.). 2008. *Reading Jude with New Eyes: Methodological Reassessments of the Letter of Jude*. London: T&T Clark.

Webb, Robert L., and John S. Kloppenborg (eds.). 2007. *Reading James with New Eyes: Methodological Reassessments of the Letter of James*. London: T&T Clark.

Webster, John. 2003. *Holy Scripture: A Dogmatic Sketch*. Cambridge: Cambridge University Press.
Wedderburn, Alexander J. M. 2002. 'The "We"-passages in Acts: On the Horns of a Dilemma.' *Zeitschrift für die Neutestamentliche Wissenschaft* 93: 78–98.
Weima, Jeffrey A. D. 2014. *1–2 Thessalonians*. BECNT; Grand Rapids, MI: Baker.
Westfall, Cynthia Long. 2005. *A Discourse Analysis of the Letter to the Hebrews: The Relationship Between Form and Meaning*. LNTS 297; London: T&T Clark.
———. 2010. 'A Moral Dilemma? The Epistolary Body of 2 Timothy.' In *Paul and the Ancient Letter Form*. Edited by S. E. Porter and S. A. Adams. PAST 6; Leiden: Brill, pp. 213–52.
White, Benjamin L. 2014. *Remembering Paul: Ancient and Modern Contests over the Image of the Apostle*. Oxford: Oxford University Press.
White, L. Michael. 1995. 'Visualizing the "Real" World of Acts 16: Toward Construction of a Social Index.' In *The Social World of the First Christians: Essays in Honor of Wayne A. Meeks*. Edited by L. M. White and O. L. Yarbrough. Philadelphia: Fortress, pp. 234–61.
Wiles, Virginia. 2000. *Making Sense of Paul: A Basic Introduction to Pauline Theology*. Peabody, MA: Hendrickson.
Wilhite, David E. 2015. *The Gospel According to the Heretics: Discovering Orthodoxy through Early Christological Conflicts*. Grand Rapids, MI: Baker.
Williams, Rowan. 2015. *Meeting God in Paul*. London: SPCK.
Willitts, Joel. 2010. *The Kregel Pictorial Guide to the Dead Sea Scrolls: How They Were Discovered and What They Mean*. Grand Rapids, MI: Kregel.
Wilson, Stephen G. 1979. *Luke and the Pastoral Epistles*. London: SPCK.
———. 2004. *Leaving the Fold: Apostates and Defectors in Antiquity*. Minneapolis: Fortress.
Wilson, Todd A. 2007. *The Curse of the Law and the Crisis in Galatia: Reassessing the Purpose of Galatians*. WUNT 2.225; Tübingen: Mohr Siebeck.
Winn, Adam. 2008. *The Purpose of Mark's Gospel: An Early Christian Response to Roman Imperialism*. WUNT 2.245; Tübingen: Mohr Siebeck.
Winter, Bruce W. 1994. *Seek the Welfare of the City: Christians as Benefactors and Citizens*. Grand Rapids, MI: Eerdmans.
Wise, Michael Owen, Martin G. Abegg, and Edward M. Cook. 2005. *The Dead Sea Scrolls: A New Translation*. New York: HarperOne.
Witherington, Ben. 1990. *The Christology of Jesus*. Minneapolis: Fortress.
———. 1991. 'The Influence of Galatians on Hebrews.' *New Testament Studies* 37: 146–52.
———. 1995a. *The Jesus Quest: The Third Search for the Jew of Nazareth*. Downers Grove, IL: InterVarsity.
———. 1995b. *John's Wisdom: A Commentary on the Fourth Gospel*. Louisville, KY: Westminster John Knox.
———. 1998. *Grace in Galatia: A Commentary on Paul's Letter to the Galatians*. Grand Rapids, MI: Eerdmans.
———. 2003. *Revelation*. NCBC; Cambridge: Cambridge University Press.
———. 2006. *Letters and Homilies for Hellenized Christians, vol. 1: A Socio-Rhetorical Commentary on Titus, 1–2 Timothy and 1–3 John*. Downers Grove, IL: InterVarsity.
———. 2007a. *The Letters to Philemon, the Colossians, and the Ephesians: A Socio-Rhetorical Commentary on the Captivity Epistles*. SRC; Grand Rapids, MI: Eerdmans.
———. 2007b. *Letters and Homilies for Hellenized Christians, vol. 2: A Socio-Rhetorical Commentary on 1–2 Peter*. Downers Grove, IL: InterVarsity.
———. 2009. *New Testament Rhetoric: An Introductory Guide to the Art of Persuasion in and of the New Testament*. Eugene, OR: Wipf & Stock.

———. 2011. *Paul's Letter to the Philippians: A Socio-Rhetorical Commentary*. Grand Rapids, MI: Eerdmans.

———. 2012. *A Week in the Life of Corinth*. Downers Grove, IL: InterVarsity.

Witulski, Thomas. 2007. *Die Johannesoffenbarung und Kaiser Hadrian: Studien zur Datierung der neutestamentlichen Apokalypse*. FRLANT 221; Göttingen: Vandenhoeck & Ruprecht.

Wrede, William. 1971. *The Messianic Secret*. Tr. J. C. G. Greig; Cambridge: James Clark.

———. 1973. 'The Task and Methods of New Testament Theology.' In *The Nature of New Testament Theology: The Contribution of William Wrede and Adolf Schlatter*. Edited by Robert Morgan. SBT 25; London: SCM, pp. 68–116.

Wright, Andrew. 2013. *Christianity and Critical Realism: Ambiguity, Truth, and Theological Literacy*. New York: Routledge.

Wright, Brian. 2015. 'Ancient Literacy in New Testament Research: Incorporating a Few More Lines of Enquiry.' *Trinity Journal* 36: 1–29.

———. 2017. *Communal Reading in the Time of Jesus: A Window into Early Christian Reading Practices*. Minneapolis: Fortress.

Wright, N. T. 1986. *The Epistles of Paul to the Colossians and to Philemon*. TNTC; Grand Rapids, MI: Eerdmans.

———. 1991. *The Climax of the Covenant: Christ and the Law in Pauline Theology*. Edinburgh: T&T Clark.

———. 1992a. *The New Testament and the People of God* [*NTPG*]. COQG 1; London: SPCK; Minneapolis: Fortress Press.

———. 1992b. 'Quest for the Historical Jesus.' In *Anchor Bible Dictionary*. Edited by David Noel Freedman. 6 vols.; ABRL; New York: Doubleday, 3.796–802.

———. 1994. 'The Final Sacrifice.' In *Following Jesus: Biblical Reflections on Discipleship*. London: SPCK; Grand Rapids: Eerdmans, pp. 3–10.

———. 1996. *Jesus and the Victory of God* [*JVG*]. COQG 2; London: SPCK; Philadelphia: Fortress Press.

———. 1998. 'Jesus and the Identity of God.' *Ex Auditu* 14: 42–56.

———. 1999. *The Challenge of Jesus: Rediscovering Who Jesus Was and Is*. London: SPCK; Downers Grove: IVP USA.

———. 2000. 'The Letter to the Galatians.' In *Between Two Horizons: Spanning New Testament Studies and Systematic Theology*. Edited by Joel B. Green and Max Turner. Grand Rapids, MI: Eerdmans, pp. 205–36.

———. 2002. 'The Letter to the Romans' [*Romans*]. In *New Interpreter's Bible*. Edited by L. E. Keck. 12 vols.; Nashville: Abingdon, 10.393–770.

———. 2003a. *Hebrews for Everyone*. London: SPCK; Louisville: Westminster John Knox.

———. 2003b. *The Resurrection of the Son of God* [*RSG*]. COQG 3; London: SPCK; Philadelphia: Fortress.

———. 2005. *Paul: Fresh Perspectives*. London: SPCK; Philadelphia: Fortress Press.

———. 2006a. *Judas and the Gospel of Jesus*. London: SPCK; Grand Rapids: Baker Academic.

———. 2006b. *Paul for Everyone: Romans*. London: SPCK; Louisville: Westminster John Knox.

———. 2006c. *Simply Christian* [*SC*]. London: SPCK; San Francisco: HarperOne.

———. 2007. *Surprised by Hope* [*SH*]. London: SPCK; San Francisco: HarperOne.

———. 2009. *Justification: God's Plan and Paul's Vision*. London: SPCK; Downers Grove, IL: InterVarsity.

———. 2011a. *Simply Jesus: Who He Was, What He Did, Why It Matters* [*SJ*]. London: SPCK; San Francisco: HarperOne.

———. 2011b. *Scripture and the Authority of God: How to Read the Bible Today*. London: SPCK; San Francisco: HarperOne.

———. 2011c. 'Tom Wright Galatians Introduction 2011 St Andrews 1.' Recorded by St John's Nottingham. <https://www.youtube.com/watch?v=IZUDuBu1xvY>. Cited 10 May 2016.

———. 2011d. *Early Christian Letters for Everyone: James, Peter, John, and Judah* [*ECL*]. London: SPCK; Louisville: Westminster John Knox.

———. 2011e. *Revelation for Everyone*. London: SPCK; Louisville: Westminster John Knox.

———. 2012a. *How God Became King: Getting to the Heart of the Gospels* [*HGBK*]. London: SPCK; San Francisco: HarperOne.

———. 2012b. 'The Pope's Life of Jesus.' In *Times Literary Supplement*. <https://www.the-tls.co.uk/articles/public/the-popes-life-of-jesus/>. Cited 19 January 2019.

———. 2012c. 'Revelation and Christian Hope: Political Implications of the Revelation of John.' In *Revelation and the Politics of Apocalyptic Interpretation*. Edited by R. B. Hays and S. Alkier. Waco, TX: Baylor University Press, pp. 105–24.

———. 2013. *Pauline Perspectives: Essays on Paul, 1978–2013* [*PP*]. London: SPCK; Philadelphia: Fortress Press.

———. 2014. *Paul and the Faithfulness of God* [*PFG*]. COQG 4; London: SPCK; Philadelphia: Fortress Press.

———. 2015. *Paul and His Recent Interpreters* [*PRI*]. London: SPCK; Philadelphia: Fortress Press.

———. 2016. *The Day the Revolution Began: Reconsidering the Meaning of Jesus's Crucifixion* [*DRB*]. London: SPCK; San Francisco: HarperOne.

———. 2018. *Paul: A Biography*. London: SPCK; San Francisco: HarperOne.

Wright, N. T., and Craig A. Evans. 2008. *Jesus, the Final Days: What Really Happened*. Edited by T. A. Miller. London: SPCK.

Yamauchi, Edwin M. 1980. *Archaeology of the New Testament Cities of Asia Minor*. Grand Rapids, MI: Baker.

Yarbrough, Robert W. 2008. *1–3 John*. BECNT; Grand Rapids, MI: Baker.

Yee, T. L. 2005. *Jews, Gentiles and Ethnic Reconciliation: Paul's Jewish Identity and Ephesians*. SNTSMS 130; Cambridge: Cambridge University Press.

Yinger, Kent L. 2011. *The New Perspective on Paul: An Introduction*. Eugene, OR: Cascade.

Zetterholm, Magnus. 2007. *The Messiah: In Early Judaism and Christianity*. Minneapolis: Fortress.

Scripture and Other Ancient Literature Index

1. OLD TESTAMENT

Genesis
1	311, 495, 650, 717, 842
1—2	494
1—3	280
1.1	650
1.26–28	650
1.26	683
2	221, 311, 717, 842
2.3	718
2.10–14	678
2.24	471
3	311, 518, 519
3.19	278
5.18–24	225
5.24	265
6.1–4	750, 836
14	721
14.18	720
14.18–20	720
15	304, 514
15.6	168, 483, 746
15.18	108
16	410
18.2	879
19.4–11	750
21	410
22	746
22.17	720
22.18	630
26.4	630
28.10–17	666
49	673, 768

Exodus
4.22	463
4.31	236, 620
6.1–8	378
7—10	837
7—12	834
7.11–12	547
10.1–6	835
12.1–11	666
12.46	675
15	837
15.1–4	837
15.1–17	837
19.5	830
19.5–6	378, 772
19.6	761
19.16–19	834
20.4	52
20.13–14	744
24.6–8	254
25.31–40	830
32.32	521
40	233, 645

Leviticus
9	233
10.10	116
11.44–45	761
16.30	116
18.5	408
19	743
19.2	761
19.18	569, 743

Numbers
9.12	675
14	750
24.17	106, 779
25.11	122, 343
34.1–15	108

Deuteronomy
1.7	108
4.30	590
5.8	52
5.17–18	744
6.4–5	569
6.4	374
6.5	541
6.13	592
6.16	592
7.8	378
8.3	592
9.1–6	378
11.24	108
13	248
15.4	631
15.11	631
18.15	666
18.15–19	630

18.18–19 193	19.1–21 122	40.6–8 723
19.15 319		42.7 257
21.20 248	**2 Kings**	45.6–7 715
21.22–23 318	2.11 265	49.14–15 282
21.23 408	5.1–14 619	57.1 257
24.1–4 568	6.15–19 556	63.7 257
26.5–9 58	9.22 832	69.14–15 257
26.5–10 378		69.21 675
27 598	**1 Chronicles**	72 326
27—29 . . . . 519, 522	28—29 673	73.21–26 282
27—32 511		75.8 257
27.26 408	**2 Chronicles**	77.19 566
28 598	26.16–21 129	79.13 378
28.1–14 598		86.9 837
30 . . . . 514, 522, 564	**Job**	88.3–10 278
30.1–10 281	3.13–19 278	89 . . . . 198, 326
30.1–20 593	7.7–10 279	89.4–7 167
30.2 590	9.8 566	89.27 463
30.15 593	9.31 257	90.4 . . . . 765, 780
30.19–20 281	14.10–14 280	91.4 257
32.4 837	19.25 280	95 . . . . 710, 717, 718
32.11 257	19.26 279	95.7 378
32.43 524	33.4 313	97.7 715
33.2 (LXX) 716	33.15–30 281	98 198
		98.2 837
Joshua	**Psalms**	98.2–3 515
23—24 673	2 . . . . 326, 379, 571, 630,	100.3 378
	718, 832, 880	102.25–27 715
Judges	2.1–12 347	104.4 715
20.1 108	2.7 . . . . 563, 592, 715	104.6, 23 761
	6.5 278	104.29–30 281
1 Samuel	8 . . . . 311, 713, 717	104.30 313
7.3 590	8.4 . . . . 220, 717	106.28–31 343
8—10 198	8.5 517	106.30–31 122
28 273	8.5–8 519	110 . . . . 347, 569, 624, 713,
	9.11 378	718, 721, 723
2 Samuel	16.8–11 629	110.1 . . . . . . 230, 239, 571, 629,
5.8 597	16.9–11 281	715, 717
7 571	17.8 257	110.4 720
7.11–14 230	17.50 524	111.2–3 837
7.12–16 . . . . 614, 630	18.16 257	115.4 633
7.14 715	22.1 . . . . 573, 599	115.17 278
12.1–15 682	22.18 675	117.1 524
14.14 278	22.22 717	118.22 772
23.17 668	22.29 281	118.22–23 569
	30.9 278	118.25–26 568
1 Kings	32.2 168	132.11 629
8 . . . . 233, 645	32.6 257	135.15 633
16.21 832	33.6 161	137.1, 4 164
17—18 735	34.12–17 774	
17.1–24 619	36.6 515	**Proverbs**
18.20–40 343	36.7 257	3.34 747

8.22–31. 664	41.10–14. 831	61.1–2 . . . . 195, 199, 618
26.11. 779	42.1. 563	63.11 139
31. 114	42.6. 378	65—66 203
	43.1 831	65.9. 761
Ecclesiastes	43.1–4. 749	65.17. 426
9.5–6, 10 278	43.5. . . . . 164, 203	65.23. 761
	43.16. 566	66.20. 164
Isaiah	43.20–21 772	66.22. 426
2.2–5. 203	44.6. . . . . 198, 831	
2.3. 378	45.23. . . . . . 347, 372, 374, 443	Jeremiah
5.1–30. 378	47.1–15 839	1.5. 346
6 233	48.1–12. 749	4.1. 590
6.9–10. 361	48.12. 831	4.4. 514
7.14 . . . . 589, 590	49 65	6.15. 624
8.14. 772	49.1–7. 62	7.3–15. 211
8.16. 115	49.2. 346	7.11 194
8.17–18. 717	49.6. . . . . 378, 496	9.25–26. 514
9.1–2. 592	51.4 378	10.7 837
11.1 590	51.4–6. 515	25.12–38. 839
11.1–10 347	51.10 566	29.1–23. 736
11.10 . . . . 307, 524	51.17, 22 597	31. . . . . 386, 723
13.1—14.23 839	52 562	31.9 463
14. 278	52.4–7. 563	31.10 236
14.9–11. 279	52.7 198	31.15 590
19.10 556	52.7–10. . . . . 138, 235	31.31–34. . . . . 254, 721
21.1–10 839	52.11–12. . . . . 556, 839	50.1–46. 839
22.13. 311	52.13—53.12 62	51.6 556
22.22–23 833	53 . . . . . 63–65, 285, 290, 773	51.26. 556
23 839	53.4 593	51.45. 556
24—27 285	53.4–6. 62	51.46. 556
25.6. 254	53.4–12. 666	
26 283	53.5. 259	Ezekiel
26.14. 283	53.7–8. 634	1 . . . . 140, 141, 237, 238
26.19. 284	53.7–9. 284	2.1, 3, 8. 220
27.9 389	53.10–12. . . . . 284, 597	10.1–5, 15–22 194
28.16. . . . . 115, 772	53.11 284	11.22–23. 194
31.5 257	53.11–12. 257	16.1–63. 378
34.10. 203	53.12 62	23.31–34. 257
35 594	55 843	26—28 839
38.10–18. 278	55.1 669	28.2. 428
40 . . . . 234, 562	55.5–6 203	34.8–10. 236
40—55 . . . . 70, 198, 233, 515, 823, 880	55.7 590	36 386
	55.10–11 204	36.27. 313
40.1–8. 666	55.11 161	37 . . . . 130, 276, 282, 285, 315, 320
40.3. 133	55.13 204	
40.3–5 . . . . 138, 617	56.8. 203	37.9–10. 313
40.8. 204	59.20–21. 389	37.13–20. 108
40.9. 563	60 203	37.14 313
40.9–11. 234	60.4. 164	40—42 835
40.11. 241	61 618	47.1 842
41.8–9. 749	61.1 228	47.1–12 678

Scripture and Other Ancient Literature Index 927

Daniel
2 . . . . .198, 222, 824
2.31–45. 565
2.44. 198
3 48
6 224
6.26. 198
7 . . . . . 140, 141, 198, 221–25,
   237, 238, 240, 326, 347, 391,
   426, 562, 570, 624, 717, 825
7.1–27 565
7.8. . . . . .221, 428, 798
7.9 . . . . .238, 571, 830, 841
7.11 . . . . .221, 428, 798
7.13 . . . . . . 213, 230, 239, 571,
   667, 830
7.13–14 . . . 221, 225, 239, 240,
   347, 556
7.14 . . . . 239, 329, 830
7.17 221
7.18 221
7.20–21 798
7.23–24. 221
7.27 . . . . 221, 830
9 . . . . .222, 511, 514, 570, 880
9.16–18. 515
9.26. 798
9.27 213
10.5–6 830
11.29–32. 570
11.31 . . . . 213, 428
11.36. 428
12 . . . .276, 287, 290, 291, 320
12.2. . . . . 289, 317
12.2–3. 284
12.4. 843
12.11 . . . . 213, 570

Hosea
1.6, 9. 772
1.10 380
2.1–23. 378
2.14 563
2.23. . . . . 380, 772
6.1. 590
6.1–2. 283
6.2. . . . . 309, 317
6.6. . . . . 104, 591
10.1–15. 257
11.1 590
13.14 283

13.14–15. 283

Joel
2.12. 590
2.28–32 629

Amos
3.6. 834
5.4. 236
5.18–20. 194
9.11–12 . . . . 168, 638

Micah
4.1–4. 203
4.2. 378
5.2. 590

Habakkuk
2 713
2.4. . . . . .408, 483, 514
2.20. 834

Zephaniah
1.15–16. 834
2.3. 236

Haggai
2.5. 139

Zechariah
2.1–5. 835
2.6. 556
2.13. 834
3.2. 752
4.2. 830
4.11–14. 835
8.7–12. 164
8.23. 203
9 229
9.9. . . . . 568, 597
9.9–11. 254
9.16 236
12.2. 257
12.10 675
13.7. . . . . 230, 257, 571
14.8. . . . . 669, 842

Malachi
3.1. 620
3.17. 772
4 594
4.6. 666

2. NEW TESTAMENT

Matthew
1—2. 591
1 725
1.1—2.23 . . . . . . 588, 589–90
1.1. 591
1.2–17. 583
1.5. 580
1.18–23. 589
1.18–25. 583
1.21 580
1.22. 580
1.23. . . . . 581, 590
2.1–12. . . . . .580, 583, 590
2.4. 591
2.6. . . . . 580, 590
2.13–18. 590
2.15. . . . . 580, 590
2.17. 580
2.18. 590
2.19–23. 590
2.23. . . . . 62, 580, 590
3.1—4.25 588
3.1—7.29. . . 588, 590, 592–93
3.1–2. 592
3.1–12. 190
3.2. 591
3.3. 234
3.7. 591
3.9. 201
3.11–12. 195
3.13–17. 592
3.15. 584
4 496
4.1. 688
4.1–11 592
4.5. 591
4.12–17. 592
4.14 580
4.15. 109
4.17. 591
4.18–20. 756
4.18–22. 592
4.21–22. 656
4.23–25 592
4.24–25 584
5 . . . . 588, 598
5—7 . . . . .206, 593, 598
5.1—7.27. 588
5.1–2. 593
5.3. . . . . 591, 742

5.3–12. 593	8.1—11.1. . . . . 588, 593	11.20–24. . . . . 219, 594
5.3–16. 593	8.2-4. 117	11.25–30. 594
5.5. 742	8.4. 128	11.28–30. 583
5.7. 742	8.5–13. 580	11.29–30. 584
5.8. 742	8.10–12. 204	12.7. 591
5.9. 742	8.11 . . . . 254, 593	12.17. 580
5.10. . . . . 591, 759	8.11–12. 586	12.18, 21. 580
5.10–12. 742	8.17. . . . . 580, 593	12.22–32. 594
5.11–12. 759	8.19–22. 219	12.23. 591
5.12. 742	8.20. 222	12.24. 248
5.17–20. . . 583, 580, 586, 593	8.23–27. 593	12.24–39. 586
5.19. . . . . 591, 742	9 593	12.27. 201
5.20. . . . . 586, 591	9.1–13. 593	12.28. . . . . 202, 220
5.21–24. 583	9.6–8. 221	12.31. 584
5.21–30. 742	9.9. 581	12.38–42. 194
5.21–48. 593	9.9–10. 687	12.38–45. 586
5.22. 742	9.11–12. 206	12.39. 596
5.27–29. 583	9.13 591	12.42. 229
5.31. 583	9.14–17. 593	12.43–45. 595
5.32. 591	9.15 256	12.46–50. 595
5.33–37. . . . . 583, 742	9.17 580	12.49–50. 114
5.38–39. 583	9.27 591	13 . . . . 588, 620
5.43. 583	9.36—10.42 588	13.1–43. 595
5.47. 591	9.36–38. 593	13.1–52. 588
5.48. . . . . 584, 742	10 588	13.5. 734
6 588	10.1–4. 593	13.14. 580
6.3. 112	10.3. . . . . 581, 734	13.24–30, 36–52. 583
6.1–4. 631	10.4. . . . . 122, 737	13.31–32. 691
6.1–18. 593	10.5. 591	13.51–52. 595
6.1–19. 583	10.5–6 . . . . 204, 580	13.52. . . . . 578, 580, 591
6.2–18. 591	10.5–42 593	13.53. 588
6.5. 584	10.6. 593	13.54. 216
6.7. 591	10.9–10. 46	13.54—17.27 588
6.9–13. 584	10.10. 584	13.54—19.2 . . . . . 588, 595–97
6.10. 326	10.17. 586	13.54–58 595
6.16–18. 584	10.21–23. 583	13.55. . . . . 731, 737
6.19–21. 742	10.22. 742	14—17 596
6.19–34. 593	10.32. 219	14.1–13. 595
6.24. 742	10.38. 219	14.3–4. 192
6.24–25 742	11.1 588	14.4. 99
7 588	11.1–6. 136	14.14–21. 595
7.1–2. 593	11.2—12.50 588	14.22–23. 595
7.1–5. 742	11.2—13.53 . . . . . 588, 594–95	14.28–31. 583
7.6. . . . . 583, 584	11.2–3. 195	14.34–36 595
7.7–9. 742	11.2–6. . . . . 192, 228	15.1–20. . . . . 117, 595
7.13–27. 593	11.2–15. 594	15.17. 591
7.15 753	11.4–5. 202	15.21–28. . . . . 580, 595
7.24–25. 601	11.7–19. 192	15.22. 591
7.24–27. 742	11.9 220	15.24. . . . . 204, 580, 591
7.28–29. . . . . 588, 593	11.16–24. 586	15.29–39. 595
7.29 216	11.18–19. 222	16.1–4. 596
8.1—8.35 588	11.19 . . . . . 205, 222, 235, 248	16.5–12. 596

Scripture and Other Ancient Literature Index 929

16.13 . . . . 175, 222	21.32–46 112	25.34 759
16.13–14 217	21.33–46 . . . . . . 257, 586, 597	26—27 100
16.13–20 596	21.34–37, 43, 45 681	26.1 588
16.16 . . . . 596, 688, 757	22.1–10 580	26.1–2 588
16.16–18 594	22.1–14 597	26.2 598
16.17–18 . . . . 591, 756	22.7–8 586	26.3—28.20 . . . 588, 598–600
16.17–19 . . . . 583, 593	22.8 586	26.3–16 598
16.18–19 580	22.15–22 598	26.5 249
16.21–28 596	22.23 . . . . 130, 286	26.17 250
16.24 219	22.23–33 598	26.17–30 599
17.1–8 766	22.34–40 598	26.26–29 252
17.1–13 596	22.39–40 742	26.28 254
17.5–6 763	22.41–46 598	26.31 . . . . 257, 597
17.9–13 192	22.42 591	26.31–56 599
17.12–13 195	23 . . . . 588, 598	26.56 580
17.14–27 596	23—25 598	26.57–68 194
17.22–23 256	23.1—25.46 588	26.57–75 599
17.24–27 583	23.1–39 586	26.64 239
18 588	23.2–5 583	26.67–68 690
18.1–35 . . . . 588, 597	23.3 591	26.69–75 757
18.15 742	23.5 591	27.3–10 583
18.15–20 583	23.7–8 591	27.9 580
18.15–22 583	23.7–12 583	27.11–26 599
18.18 591	23.10 . . . . 581, 601	27.24–25 583
18.19–20 580	23.12 742	27.25 586
18.21–22 583	23.15 125	27.27–31 599
18.21–35 112	23.24 586	27.32–33 599
18.23–25 583	23.37 193	27.33 243
19.1–2 588	23.37–39 . . . . 212, 257	27.34 599
19.1–30 597	23.38 194	27.35–44 599
19.3—22.46 588	23.39 236	27.37 230
19.3—26.2 . . . . . . 588, 597–98	23.40 591	27.45–54 600
19.16–30 219	24 . . . . 213, 588	27.51–53 . . . . 325, 597
19.28 . . . . 219, 580	24—25 . . . . 222, 420, 598	27.52–53 . . . . 583, 600
19.28–30 229	24.2 213	27.53 591
19.29 . . . . 113, 204	24.3 859	27.54 . . . . 115, 580
20.1–16 . . . . 583, 597	24.4–14 753	27.55–66 600
20.17–19 . . . . 256, 597	24.9–14 256	27.56 734
20.20–28 597	24.13 742	27.57 112
20.25–26 161	24.14 580	27.57–61 318
20.28 257	24.15 213	27.62–66 . . . . 325, 583
20.29–34 597	24.15–16 687	27.63–66 586
21.1–11 597	24.24 428	27.64 318
21.4–5 580	24.30–31 213	28 324
21.9 591	24.33 742	28.1–10 600
21.12–13 194	24.35 601	28.8 . . . . 319, 324
21.12–16 210	24.36 . . . . 861, 862	28.11–15 . . . . 325, 583, 600
21.12–17 597	24.42–44 832	28.12–15 586
21.15 591	24.43 780	28.16 309
21.21 . . . . 212, 742	25 588	28.16–20 . . . 326, 583, 597, 600
21.23–27 . . . . 192, 597	25.1–13 583	28.17 . . . . 320, 626
21.28–32 . . . . 583, 597	25.31–46 583	28.18 . . . . 78, 239, 326, 601

28.19 593	3.23–27 202	8.27–29 217
28.19–20 580	3.31–32 319	8.28 227
28.20 601	3.31–35 . . . . 309, 731	8.29 . . . . 227, 576, 687, 757
	3.34–35 114	8.29–31 560
Mark	4 . . . . 556, 620	8.30 228
1.1 . . . . 562, 573	4.1–20 . . . . 204, 565	8.31—9.1 256
1.1–15 . . . . 561, 562	4.1–34 565	8.31 . . . . 293, 324, 575
1.2 687	4.13 559	8.34 . . . . 219, 576, 577
1.2–3 563	4.30–32 691	8.34–35 686
1.3 234	4.35–41 565	8.38 . . . . 219, 559
1.4–8 . . . . 190, 563	4.41 . . . . 324, 576	9.1 . . . . 259, 570
1.7–9 681	5.1–7 569	9.2 . . . . 653, 757
1.9–11 563	5.1–20 . . . . 566, 576	9.2—10.52 . . . . 561, 567
1.11 573	5.7 574	9.2–8 568
1.12 688	5.15 324	9.7 . . . . 568, 573
1.12–13 564	5.21–43 566	9.9 . . . . 324, 575
1.14 192	5.33 324	9.9–13 568
1.14–15 564	5.36 324	9.11–13 192
1.15 198	5.37 . . . . 653, 757	9.12 256
1.16—8.21 . . . . 561, 564	5.41 110	9.13 195
1.16–18 . . . . 681, 756	6.1–6a 566	9.14 757
1.16–20 564	6.2 . . . . 216, 576	9.14–29 568
1.17 576	6.3 . . . . 731, 734, 737	9.30–32 568
1.19 734	6.4 686	9.31 . . . . 256, 293. 575
1.19–20 . . . . 653, 656	6.6b–32 566	9.32 324
1.21–28 564	6.8–9 46	9.33–50 568
1.22 216	6.14 192	9.37 804
1.29–34 564	6.14–16 227	9.38–40 653
1.35–39 564	6.17–18 192	9.41 804
1.40–45 . . . . 117, 564	6.18 99	10.1–12 568
1.44 . . . . . . 128, 228, 323, 560	6.21 . . . . 1.11	10.2–11 696
2.1—3.3 564	6.30–44 685	10.13–16 568
2.1–12 564	6.33–44 566	10.17 649
2.7 576	6.45–52 566	10.17–31 . . . . 219, 568
2.13–15 687	6.53–56 566	10.21 576
2.13–17 564	7.1—8.10 566	10.29–30 113
2.14 . . . . 576, 581	7.1–15 125	10.30 559
2.15–16 235	7.1–23 117	10.32 324
2.16–17 206	7.4 130	10.32–34 . . . . 256, 568
2.18–22 564	7.19 591	10.34 575
2.20 256	7.19b 566	10.35–45 . . . . 568, 653
2.23–28 . . . . 229, 564	7.24–30 . . . . 110, 566	10.38–39 257
3.1–6 565	7.31–37 567	10.43 577
3.6 115	7.33–36 687	10.45 257
3.7–12 565	7.36 . . . . 228, 560	10.46–52 568
3.8 584	8.1–10 567	10.47–49 . . . . 228, 560
3.11 574	8.1–13 685	11.1—12.44 . . . . 561, 568
3.13–16 . . . . 203, 229	8.11–21 567	11.1–7 568
3.17 . . . . 653, 734	8.22—9.1 . . . . 561, 567	11.1–10 . . . . 228, 229
3.18 . . . . 122, 734	8.22–26 567	11.1–12 569
3.20–35 565	8.27 . . . . 222, 576	11.8–11 569
3.21 731	8.27–28 192	11.11–18 230

11.12–25. 569	14.12–21 571	Luke
11.15–18. 210	14.12–31. 251	1.1 687
11.15–19. 194	14.22–25. . . . . 252, 571	1.1–2 606
11.17 211	14.25. 254	1.1–4. . . . . 613, 614, 617, 618
11.18. 115	14.26–31. 571	1.2. . . . . 694, 697
11.27–33. . . . . 192, 569	14.27. . . . . 230, 257	1.5—2.52 617
12.1–12. . . . . 112, 257	14.28. 575	1.46–55. 605
12.6. 574	14.29–31. 572	1.59–73. 862
12.12. 115	14.32–42 571	1.68. . . . . 236, 620
12.13–27. 569	14.33. . . . . 653, 757	1.69. 605
12.14–17. 51	14.43–52. 571	1.77. 605
12.18. . . . . 130, 286	14.51–52. 61	1.78. 236
12.28–34 569	14.52. 557	2.11 . . . . 231, 605
12.35–37 . . . . . 228, 229, 230, 231, 569	14.53–59. 571	2.30. 605
12.38–40 569	14.55–59. 569	3 725
12.38–44 742	14.58. . . . . 230, 667, 686	3.1 148
12.41–44 569	14.58. . . . . 569, 571	3.1–20 . . . . 190, 617
12.42. 559	14.60. 576	3.1—4.13 617
13 . . . . . . 213, 222, 224, 238, 420, 556, 558, 570	14.60–65 572	3.2. 685
13.1–13. 570	14.61–22. 227	3.4. . . . . 234, 687
13.1–37. . . . . 561, 570	14.61–62. 239	3.6. 605
13.2. . . . . 213, 556, 570	14.61–64. 238	3.8. 201
13.3. 653	14.62. . . . . 230, 571	3.10–14 606
13.5–7. 569	14.65. 690	3.16 645
13.7–8. 556	14.66–72. 757	3.16–17. 195
13.9. 586	15.1–15. 571	3.18–22. 681
13.9–13. . . . . 256, 559	15.16. 559	3.19 99
13.10. 324	15.16–32. 573	3.19–20. 192
13.13. 804	15.22. 243	3.21–22. 617
13.14. . . . . 213, 687	15.26. 230	3.21–38. 617
13.14–23. 570	15.27. 568	3.33—4.2 681
13.22. . . . . 428, 559	15.29. 667	4.1. 688
13.24. 556	15.33–34. 573	4.1–13 617
13.24–32. 570	15.39. . . . . . 155, 561, 562, 574	4.14—9.50 . . . . 617, 618
13.26. 556	15.40. 734	4.14–15. 618
13.26–27 213	15.40–47 574	4.16–20. 110
13.27. 556	15.43. 112	4.16–21. 199
13.32. . . . . 574, 862	15.43–47 318	4.16–30. . . . . . . 219, 607, 619
13.33–37. 571	15.53–62 194	4.16–31. 605
14—15 100	16.1. 734	4.18–21. 228
14.1—15.29 561	16.1–2. 318	4.22–30 200
14.1—15.47 571	16.1–8. . . . . 318, 561, 575	4.23. 161
14.1. 115	16.3–4. 318	4.24. 193
14.1–2. 571	16.5. 318	4.25. 735
14.2. 249	16.6. . . . . 318, 324	4.25–27 . . . . 195, 606
14.3–9. 571	16.6–7. 575	4.31—6.16 619
14.9. 324	16.7. . . . . 318, 319, 324	4.31–44. 619
14.10–11. 571	16.8. . . . . 319, 322–24. 575	4.34—5.10 681
14.12. 250	16.8b. 321, 322	4.61–21. 195
	16.9–16. . . . . 321, 323	5 677
	16.9–20. . . . . 322, 561, 575	5.1–11 756
		5.10. 656

5.12–15. 117	9.23. 219	13.33. 256
5.14. 128	9.26. 219	13.34. 193
5.20–21. 206	9.28–36. 621	13.34–35 257
5.27–32. 687	9.31. 621	13.35. 194
5.35. 256	9.32. 621	14.1—15.32 622
5.37—6.4 681	9.37–45. 621	14.1–5 606
6.10—7.32 681	9.44. 256	14.1–24. 124
6.14. 734	9.46–50 621	14.11. 742
6.15. . . . . 122, 734	9.51—19.48 . . . . 617, 621	14.14. 287
6.16. . . . . 734, 737	9.52–55. 653	14.15. 254
6.17–49. 619	9.52–56. 621	14.28–32. 606
6.20. 742	9.57–62. . . . . 219, 621	15.1 . . . . 205, 234
6.22–23. 742	9.58. 222	15.1–2. 206
6.23. 742	10.1–24. 621	15.4–6. 606
6.24–25 742	10.7. 696	15.8–9. 606
6.37–38, 41–42 742	10.12–16. 219	15.11–32. . . . . . .204, 605, 606
6.46–49 742	10.25–37. 621	15.24, 32. 622
7.1–10 620	10.29–37. 117	16.1–8. 606
7.11–15 606	10.30–37 606	16.1–15 622
7.11–17 620	10.38–42 . . . . 621, 685	16.13. 742
7.16. 236	10.39–42 606	16.16. 192
7.18–19 195	11.1–13 621	16.16–18 622
7.18–23 . . . . 136, 192, 228	11.5–8. 606	16.19–31. . . . . . .606, 622, 631
7.18–35 620	11.9–11 742	16.20–31. 112
7.22. 202	11.14—12.12 621	17.1—18.30 623
7.24–35. 192	11.19 201	17.3 742
7.26. 220	11.20. . . . . 202, 220	17.7–10 606
7.33–34. 222	11.29–32. 194	17.12–18 606
7.34. . . . . .205, 222, 235	11.31 229	17.19–18.18 681
7.35–39. 681	11.37–44. 127	17.22 256
7.36–47. 606	11.37–54. 124	18.2–8. 606
7.36–50. . . . . 124, 620	11.38–41. 117	18.8–10, 12–14 606
7.41–43. 681	12.8. 219	18.10–14. 606
7.46—9.2 681	12.13–21. . . . . 112, 621	18.12–14. 606
8.1–3. 620	12.16–20. 606	18.14. 742
8.3. 112	12.22–34 622	18.18–25. 623
8.4–15. 620	12.33–34 742	18.18–30. 219
8.16–18. 620	12.35–38 606	18.31–33. 256
8.19–21. 620	12.35–59 622	18.31–34. 623
8.21. 114	12.39–40. 832	18.35–43 623
8.22–25. 621	13.1 100	19 . . . . 235, 607, 612
8.26–39 621	13.1–5. 606	19.1–10 . . . .235, 606, 607, 623
8.40–56 621	13.1–9. 622	19.10. 235
8.49. 111	13.6–9. 606	19.11 236
9.1–9 621	13.10–17. . . . . 606, 622	19.11–27. . . . . . . .99, 236, 623
9.3. 46	13.14. 111	19.29–40 624
9.4—17.15. 681	13.18–19. 691	19.37–38. 236
9.10–17. 621	13.18–21. 622	19.41–44. . . . . 212, 624
9.18. 222	13.22–30. 622	19.43–44 612
9–18–20 621	13.28–30 204	19.44. . . . . .213, 236, 620, 623
9.20. . . . . 688, 757	13.31–32. . . . . 124, 606	19.45–48 . . . . . .194, 210, 624
9.21–27. 621	13.31–35. 622	20 624

Scripture and Other Ancient Literature Index 933

20.1–8 192	23.47 . . . . 115, 616	1.19–28 666
20.1—21.38 . . . . 617, 624	23.49–56 318	1.21 195
20.9–19 257	23.51 112	1.29 . . . . 251, 666, 672
20.27 . . . . 130, 286	24 . . . . 276, 326, 613	1.29–34 666
20.36 293	24.1–8 626	1.35–40 . . . . 652, 659
20.41–44 624	24.1–12 326	1.35–51 666
21 . . . . . . 213, 222, 420, 624,	24.1–53 . . . . 617, 626	1.36 . . . . 251, 672
612, 624	24.6–8 699	1.35–51 657
21.5–38 624	24.9–12 626	1.40–42 756
21.6 213	24.10 . . . . 327, 734	1.41 663
21.8–24 612	24.11 . . . . 320, 327	1.42 756
21.12 642	24.12 328	1.51 . . . . 652, 663, 666
21.12–19 256	24.13–27 627	2.1–11 . . . . 663, 667
21.27–78 213	24.13–35 . . . . . . .319, 326, 327,	2.6 659
21.34–36 624	605, 627	2.10 663
22.1—23.56 . . . . . 617, 624–25	24.23–24 319	2.11 . . . . 665, 666
22.1–6 624	24.25 327	2.13 659
22.2 249	24.25–27 627	2.13–22 194
22.3 685	24.27 . . . . 317, 627, 873	2.13–25 210
22.4—24.53 681	24.28–35 627	2.16 211
22.7 250	24.31 627	2.19 . . . . . . 194, 230, 238, 571,
22.7–38 625	24.32 . . . . 317, 627	667, 686
22.8 654	24.34 . . . . . . 309, 319, 327, 757	2.19–21 672
22.14–20 608	24.35 327	2.19–22 663
22.15–20 252	24.36 309	2.22 . . . . 699, 873
22.17–20 696	24.36–49 . . 309, 326, 328, 627	2.23 659
22.19 254	24.38–43 327	3 . . . . 667, 668
22.28–30 229	24.41 . . . . 319, 320	3.1 . . . . 124, 598
22.30 . . . . 204, 219	24.44 317	3.3 649
22.37 62	24.45–48 327	3.3–5 791
22.39–43 625	24.50–53 . . . . . . 326, 605, 627	3.3–7 733
22.39–46 625	24.52 319	3.5 649
22.47–53 625		3.13 652
22.53 625	**John**	3.13–21 667
22.54–62 . . . . 625, 757	1 676	3.14 667
22.54–71 194	1.1 788	3.14–15 672
22.63–65 625	1.1–4 665	3.15–16 . . . . 329, 663
22.64 690	1.1–14 660	3.16 . . . . 645, 667
22.66–71 625	1.1–18 . . . . . . 66, 161, 663, 787	3.16–17 676
22.69 237	1.4 663	3.21 788
23 100	1.6–8 665	3.22–30 667
23.1–2 625	1.9–13 665	3.23–24 685
23.2 52	1.11 670	3.31–36 667
23.18–25 100	1.12 678	3.32 . . . . 654, 656
23.19 249	1.12–13 806	3.36 . . . . 663, 667
23.25 625	1.14 . . 650, 653, 659, 663, 665,	4 . . . . 667, 668
23.26–31 625	786, 788, 790, 812	4.1–42 668
23.31 257	1.14–18 665	4.9 659
23.32–43 626	1.17 663	4.10–15 669
23.38 230	1.18 . . . . 174, 790	4.12 663
23.44–49 626	1.19 666	4.14 . . . . 329, 663
23.45–56 626	1.19–12.50 . . . . 663, 665	4.21–24 663

4.22 676	7.41–42 . . . . 661, 663	12.16 329
4.22–23 659	7.53—8.11 669	12.20–34 672
4.25–26 227	8 669	12.23 . . . . 329, 652
4.25–29 . . . . 661, 663	8.9 669	12.25 686
4.26 669	8.12 . . . . 669, 670	12.28 329
4.42 668	8.12–59 669	12.34 663
4.43–44 686	8.20 659	12.35–50 672
4.43–54 668	8.24, 28 669	12.38 663
4.44 193	8.53–54 663	12.42 . . . . 586, 661, 663
4.45 659	8.58 . . . . 652, 669	12.48 . . . . 219, 798
4.54 665	9.1–7 666	13 672
5 . . . . 667, 668	9.1–41 670	13—17 650
5.2 659	9.5 . . . . 669, 670	13.1 . . . . 250, 659, 672
5.2–16 666	9.7 659	13.1–2 652
5.18 652	9.22 . . . . 586, 661, 663	13.1–20.31 . . . . 663, 672
5.19–23 649	9.35–38 652	13.2 685
5.21–40 663	10 671	13.3–5 673
5.24 788	10.7, 9 669	13.18 663
5.25–26 668	10.10 676	13.18–38 673
5.25–29 329	10.10–17 663	13.19 669
5.28–29 287	10.11, 14 669	13.23 66
5.29 813	10.15–18 672	13.23–25 652
5.39–40 663	10.16 . . . . 670, 676	13.23–26 659
5.43 113	10.22 659	13.24–25 654
5.45–47 663	10.23 659	13.27 685
6.1–5 685	10.24 . . . . 661, 663	13.30 673
6.1–15 666	10.28 663	13.31 652
6.4 659	10.30 670	13.31–32 329
6.15 668	10.32 652	13.34 799
6.16–21 666	10.36 663	13.34–35 676
6.20 669	11 . . . . 329, 725	14—16 673
6.26–71 663	11.1—12.8 685	14.3 813
6.32 663	11.1–2 685	14.5 676
6.32–41 663	11.1–45 665	14.6 . . . . 663, 669
6.32–59 668	11.1–55 671	14.13 663
6.35 669	11.3 656	14.22 737
6.39–40 . . . . 798, 812	11.16 . . . . 653, 676	14.26 651
6.40 329	11.24 . . . . 329, 798	15.1 669
6.41 669	11.25 . . . . . 294, 329, 663, 669	15.7 789
6.44 . . . . 798, 812	11.25–27 671	15.12 . . . . 789, 799
6.48 669	11.27 663	15.13 663
6.51 672	11.40 329	15.25 663
6.53–54 668	11.47–48 249	15.26 801
6.54 . . . . 329, 798, 813	11.47–53 249	15.26–27 791
6.54–58 790	11.49–50 674	16.2 . . . . 152, 586
6.68 668	11.49–53 652	16.30 673
7 789	11.50–52 797	17 673
7.19–23 663	11.52 806	17.1 329
7.25–31 . . . . 661, 663	11.54 659	17.1–26 673
7.37–38 668	11.55 . . . . 117, 659	17.2–3 . . . . 329, 663
7.37–39 . . . . 659, 663	12.1 659	17.3 663
7.38 678	12.1–11 672	17.4 329

17.5 663	20.13–15. 319	1.14 645
17.12 663	20.14 626	1.15–26 309
17.17 733	20.17 329	2 . . . . 676, 760, 849
17.21 676	20.19 676	2.1–13 629
17.24 663	20.19–20 309	2.1–47 605
17.28 663	20.19–23 328	2.9–11 760
17.36 663	20.19–30 319	2.10–11 506
18 . . . . 329, 672	20.20 66	2.14–41 629
18.1–14 674	20.21 . . . . 215, 679	2.31 228
18—19 100	20.21–22 676	2.32 607
18.5–8 669	20.22 651	2.41 644
18.13 685	20.24–25 320	2.42 327
18.15–16 . . 652, 654, 656, 659	20.24–29 676	2.42–47 630
18.15–18 652	20.28 . . 42, 328, 329, 652, 676	2.44–45 631
18.25–27 757	20.30–31 787	2.46 . . . . 632, 645
18.28 . . . . 250, 439, 659	20.31 . . 66, 659, 661, 662, 663,	2.47 605
18.28–40 675	671, 677, 779, 790, 801	3—4 653
18.31–33 681	21 . . . . . . 324, 329, 653, 656,	3—8 654
18.33–34 227	660, 679	3.1–26 630
18.33–36 . . . . 660, 661	21.1–14 319	3.16 804
18.34 685	21.1–22 319	3.22 193
18.36 675	21.1–25 . . . . 663, 677	4.1–22 630
18.37 676	21.2 . . . . 654, 657	4.4 644
18.37–38 681	21.4 626	4.6 685
18.39 659	21.7 . . . . 652, 654, 659	4.10 228
18.40 675	21.11–14 330	4.12 607
19.1–16a 675	21.12 . . . . 329, 626	4.13 758
19.5 . . . . . . 650, 652, 675, 683	21.15–19 . . . . 677, 757	4.18 804
19.11 523	21.18–19 . . 660, 763, 766, 778	4.19–20 656
19.12 . . . . 247, 675	21.20–22 . . . . 652, 654	4.20 654
19.14 . . . . 250, 659	21.20–23 . . . . . . 652, 654, 677	4.23–31 630
19.16b–37 675	21.20–24 653	4.24 645
19.17 243	21.22 677	4.32–37 632
19.19 . . . . 230, 652	21.23 . . . . 653, 656	4.34 631
19.21–22 247	21.24 . . . . . . 652, 653, 659, 812	5.1–11 632
19.25 66	21.24–25 660	5.4 631
19.26 66	21.25 66	5.12 645
19.26–27 . . . . 652, 659		5.12–16 632
19.31 250	**Acts**	5.17–32 632
19.34 801	1 . . . . 320, 613, 643	5.31 605
19.35 . . . . . . 652, 653, 659, 675	1—12 625	5.33–39 616
19.36 251	1.1 628	5.33–42 633
19.38 112	1.1–2 . . . . 613, 617, 628	5.34–39 126
19.38–42 . . . . 318, 675	1.1–11 326	5.36 . . . . 120, 193
20 . . . . 276, 650, 676	1.1–26 629	5.36–41 557
20—21 330	1.2 628	5.37 120
20.1–8 . . . . 652, 654	1.2–11 628	6 645
20.1–10 659	1.3—8.1a 628	6.1–7 633
20.1–18 . . . . 328, 676	1.8 . . . . 628, 642	6.7 644
20.2 . . . . 66, 319	1.9–11 605	6.8—8.1a 633
20.7 66	1.11 624	6.9 . . . . 111, 340, 661
20.9 . . . . 317, 319	1.13 . . . 122, 581, 653, 734, 737	6.13–14 341

936   The New Testament in Its World

6.14 238	11.25 339	15.6–21 638
7 725	11.26 . . . . 615, 777	15.7–11 757
7.38 . . . . 716, 750	11.27–30 406	15.9 117
7.48 . . . . 571, 633	11.28 106	15.13 734
7.48–53 238	11.28–30 . . . . 348, 350	15.13–21 . . . . 731, 735
7.53 . . . . 716, 750	11.29 632	15.14 763
7.54–60 586	11.30 363	15.15–19 169
7.58 338	12 106	15.19–21 342
7.60 633	12.1–2 586	15.20 832
8 653	12.1–3 341	15.21 164
8.1b—9.31 . . . . 628, 634	12.1–5 99	15.22 737
8.1b–3 634	12.1–17 757	15.22–35 638
8.3 341	12.1–19 635	15.23–29 736
8.4 644	12.2 106	15.25 645
8.4–25 634	12.11–17 557	15.27 737
8.6 645	12.12–13 632	15.29 832
8.14 644	12.15 . . . . 293, 321	15.31 535
8.14–25 654	12.17 . . . . 731, 734	15.32 737
8.26–40 634	12.20–25 636	15.36—21.16 . . . . 628, 639
9 641	12.23 99	15.36–39 645
9.1–2 . . . . 125, 341, 345	12.24 644	15.36–41 639
9.1–19a 634	12.25 . . . . 348, 557	15.40—16.5 352
9.1–22 345	13—14 . . . 350, 400, 402, 536	16.1–3 713
9.5 634	13—28 625	16.1–10 639
9.7 345	13.1—15.35 . . . . 628, 636	16.6 . . . . 399, 400
9.11 737	13.1–3 636	16.6–10 352
9.15 . . . . 345, 642	13.4–12 636	16.7 760
9.15–16 804	13.5 557	16.9 830
9.19b–30 634	13.7 148	16.10–17 609
9.23–25 . . . . 350, 355	13.13–52 637	16.11–12 438
9.23–30 405	13.15 111	16.11–40 . . . . 352, 640
9.26–29 350	13.23 605	16.14 166
9.27–28 804	13.26 605	16.14–15 113
9.30 339	13.32–33 873	16.16–21 438
9.31 635	13.32–37 317	16.17 605
9.32—12.35 . . . . 628, 635	13.43 166	16.21 640
9.32–43 635	13.46 361	16.31–34 113
10.1—11.18 757	13.47 . . . . 62, 605	16.35–39 616
10.1–48 635	13.49 644	16.35–40 438
10.10 830	13.50 166	17 161
10.15 635	13.14—14.23 399	17.1–7 353
10.28, 34 635	14.1–21a 638	17.1–9 . . . . 151, 640
10.36 644	14.21b–28 638	17.2–4 417
10.47 635	14.23 539	17.4 166
11 645	14.27 638	17.5–7 348
11.1 644	15 . . . . 351, 363, 400, 406,	17.5–10 417
11.1–18 635	645, 763	17.5–15 354
11.16–17 699	15.1–4 638	17.6–7 . . . . 418, 640
11.19 . . . . 586, 644	15.1–5 . . . . 402, 540, 638	17.7 625
11.19–21 585	15.1–31 605	17.10–14 418
11.19–26 405	15.1–33 350	17.10–15 . . . . 354, 640
11.19–30 635	15.5 . . . . 124, 598	17.13 348

17.15–18.5 418	19.24–29. 453	22.30. 348
17.16–34. . . . . 354, 640	19.26. 633	23 293
17.17 166	19.28. 456	23—26 361
17.22 152	19.29. 453	23.1–26.32 642
17.22–31 348	19.31. 453	23.6. . . . . 277, 598
17.22–32. 610	19.34. 456	23.6–10. 292
17.28 340	19.35–36. 154	23.7–9. 286
17.34 148	19.36. 453	23.8. 130
18—19 400	19.38. 453	23.11 642
18.1–3. 477	20.1. 454	23.12. 348
18.1–17. . . . . 355, 640	20.1–21.16 641	23.25. 439
18.1–18. 354	20.1–4. 359	24.1–3, 27. 148
18.2. . . . . 106, 355, 505, 508,	20.1–17. 360	24.5–9 348
714, 760	20.2–3. 506	24.19. 661
18.2–17. 477	20.3. 348	25.1–12. 122
18.4–11. 477	20.4. 454	25.7–11 348
18.3. 340	20.5–15. 609	25.8. 238
18.6. 361	20.6–38 454	25.15. 348
18.7. 166	20.17–28. 533	26 641
18.7–8. 355	20.17–38. 534	26.5. . . . . 152, 598
18.8. . . . . 111, 113, 482	20.18–21. 452	26.7–8. 681
18.12. . . . . 106, 148355	20.18–35. . . . . 611, 673, 768	26.9–23. 345
18.12–14. 348	20.19 453	26.10–11. 341
18.12–16. 497	20.25 . . . . 529, 533	26.16–18. 345
18.12–17. 478	20.29–31. 753	26.20. 681
18.17. . . . . 111, 355, 482	20.31. 356	26.32. 616
18.18. 348	20.35. . . . . 693, 699	27.1—28.14. 361
18.18—19.1 355	20.38. . . . . 453, 533	27.1—28.16. . . . . 609, 643
18.18–22. 478	21.1–18 609	27.1—28.31 . . . . 628, 642
18.18–28. 641	21.17—26.32 . . . . 628, 642	27.3 616
18.19–21. . . . . 439, 452	21.17–26 642	27.31 646
18.23. . . . . 399, 400	21.18 734	27.43 616
18.25. 190	21.18—22.30 360	28 . . . . 612, 644
18.27—19.1 358	21.18–25 . . . . 342, 735	28.15–22. 361
18.27–28. 478	21.20–21 . . . . 342, 745	28.17–29. 643
19 471	21.20–25 735	28.28. . . . . 361, 605
19—20 . . . . 400, 455	21.21–24 348	28.30. 362
19.1 478	21.26—22.30 586	28.31. . . . . 364, 644
19.1–5. 190	21.27 348	28.39–44 605
19.1–20. . . . . 439, 641	21.27–29 . . . . 453, 661	"29". 644
19.1–22. 452	21.28 238	
19.1–40. 439	21.38. . . . . 121, 193	**Romans**
19.1—20.1 355	21.39 339	1 . . . . 371, 372
19.9. 453	22 641	1—4 . . . . 509, 510, 511
19.10. . . . . 356, 452	22.1–21. 345	1.1 524
19.10–20. 644	22.3. . . . . 339, 340	1.1–4. 512
19.17–19. 547	22.3–4 343	1.1–15 . . . . 507, 509, 512
19.17–20. 453	22.4. . . . . 122, 341	1.2 873
19.21–22. 359	22.9. 345	1.2–4. . . . . 228, 524
19.21–41. 641	22.15. 340	1.3–4. . . . . 298, 304, 346, 388
19.23–40 151	22.17–21 345	1.3–5. . . . . 239, 303, 524
19.23–41 156	22.22–30 642	1.4 388

1.5 . . . . 504, 509	4.25 . . . . 294, 298, 382	8.39 . . . . 388, 503
1.5–6 512	5 . . . . 510, 517, 522	9—11 . . . . . 42, 306, 362, 379,
1.8 704	5—8 . . . . . . 305, 509, 510, 517	509, 510, 517, 520
1.8–15 359	5.1 . . . . 503, 861	9—16 306
1.9 524	5.1–11 . . . . 509, 517	9.1–5 . . . . 509, 520, 521
1.9–13 510	5.8 . . . . 304, 504	9.3–4 340
1.13 . . . . 506, 509	5.9–10 305	9.4 152
1.13–15 512	5.12–21 . . . . 305, 313, 509, 517	9.4–5 380
1.15 525	5.17 513	9.5 388
1.15–16 524	5.18 305	9.6 522
1.16 . . . . 362, 510	5.20 . . . . 519, 707	9.6–29 . . . . 509, 520, 51
1.16–17 . . . . 502, 509, 512, 524	5.20–21 388	9.22–26 762
1.17 . . . . 136, 503, 512	6 . . . . . 306, 384, 517, 519, 745	9.24 521
1.18 522	6.1–2 . . . . 706, 745	9.24–26 380
1.18—3.20 . . . . 509, 514	6.1–11 306	9.30—10.21 . . . . 509, 521
1.18–24 610	6.1–23 . . . . 509, 518, 706	9.30–33 520
1.18–32 . . . . 161, 514	6.4, 8 306	9.31 384
1.21 522	6.14 348	9.33 115
2.1–16 . . . . 514, 745	6.17 . . . . 524, 539, 697	10.1 521
2.5 389	6.23 306	10.1–4 520
2.15–29 514	7 . . . . 382, 517	10.2–3 384
2.16 . . . . 389, 391, 524, 525	7.1 509	10.4 521
2.17–20 514	7.1—8.11 . . . . 509, 518	10.5–13 520
2.21–24 514	7.5–6 519	10.8–11 733
2.25–29 . . . . 387, 517, 762	7.7–12 519	10.9 . . . . 520, 522
3 371	7.7–25 519	10.9–11 306
3—4 510	7.23 519	10.9–13 520
3.1–8 514	8 . . . . 306, 327, 342, 376, 392,	10.12 . . . . 503, 526
3.2 380	493, 517, 519, 520, 828	10.13 521
3.8 . . . . 706, 707, 745	8.1 519	10.14–16 62
3.9–20 514	8.1–11 706	10.14–17 520
3.19–20 136	8.3 . . . 382, 383, 388, 519, 792	10.14–21 510
3.21 516	8.3–4 516	10.15–16 . . . . 524, 525
3.21–26 . . . 136, 375, 382, 388,	8.5–8 519	10.17 . . . . 733, 745
519, 525	8.9–11 . . . . 313, 519	10.18–21 520
3.21–31 514	8.11 . . . . 299, 306, 392	11 362
3.21–4.25 . . 509, 514, 522, 540	8.12–14 519	11.1 340
3.22 526	8.12–30 . . . . 509, 519	11.1–10 522
3.25 388	8.15 388	11.1–32 520
3.27–31 . . . . 306, 516	8.18–27 426	11.1–36 509
3.28 744	8.18–30 842	11.7 380
3.29–30 516	8.18–39 510	11.1–10 523
3.31 516	8.19–23 519	11.1–36 522
4 . . . . . 305, 372, 517, 762, 879	8.24 376	11.11–24 522
4.1–8 168	8.26–27 520	11.13 509
4.1–25 746	8.30–39 306	11.13–33 510
4.11 513	8.30 520	11.14 522
4.17 304	8.31–39 . . . . 509, 520	11.15 307
4.18–22 306	8.33 380	11.22 307
4.19–22 304	8.34 . . . . 299, 306, 388	11.23 381
4.23–24 304	8.37 . . . . 388, 393	11.26 . . . . 307, 389, 522
4.24–25 375	8.38–39 306	11.28 524

11.33–36. . . . . 520, 522	15.23–28 532	2.12. 388
12 520	15.23–33. . . . . 359, 535	2.13. 69
12—13 510	15.24. . . . . 364, 439, 524	3.1–4. 486
12—16 . . . . 509, 510, 522	15.24–25 509	3.5–9. 486
12.1–21. . . . . 509, 522	15.24–28 507	3.10–17. 486
12.2. 152	15.26. 400	3.12–15. 781
12.3–8 522	15.27. 510	3.13. 389
12.3–21. 161	15.28. . . . . 364, 439	3.16. 387
12.4–8 534	15.31. . . . . 360, 535, 586	3.18–23. 486
12.9–21. 522	16.1. . . . . 506, 539, 544	4 523
12.10. 115	16.1–2. . . . . 360, 525	4.1–7. 487
12.14–21. 522	16.1–6. 525	4.1–21. . . . . 486, 487
12.19–21. 523	16.1–12. 482	4.7—6.10 494
13.1–7. . . . . 523, 758	16.1–16 149	4.8. 480
13.1–14. . . . . 509, 523	16.3 . . . . . . 355, 482, 506, 508	4.8–13. . . . . 487, 540
13.8–10. 523	16.3–5. . . . . 525, 539	4.9. 739
13.11 420	16.4. 453	4.12. 340
13.11–12. 735	16.5. 400	4.14–21. 487
13.11–14. 523	16.6. 525	4.16. 499
13.12. 389	16.7. . . . . 525, 739	4.17. . . . . 358, 479
14. . . . . 367, 507, 523	16.12. 525	5.1. . . . . 358, 478, 479
14—15 510	16.13. 525	5.1–5. . . . . 487, 496
14.1—15.12 . . . . 509, 523	16.17. 524	5.1–13. . . . . 486, 487
14.1—15.13 307	16.17–18 510	5.5. 388
14.1, 3 367	16.17–20 524	5.6. 388
14.6 832	16.20. 420	5.9–10. . . . . 358, 479
14.9. . . . . 298, 388	16.21–23. 524	5.9–13. 487
14.9–10. 307	16.22. . . . . 506, 852	5.10. 496
14.10. 391	16.23. . . . . 148, 481, 482	5.11—6.2 496
14.14. . . . . 509, 523	16.25. . . . . 524, 525	5.14. 496
14.15. 523	16.25–27. 524	5.17. 496
14.21. 832	16.26. . . . . 504, 509	6.1. . . . . 358, 479
15 . . . . 367, 507, 510		6.1–8. 488
15.1. 509	**1 Corinthians**	6.1–10. 149
15.1–6. 524	1.1 355	6.1–11. . . . . 486, 488
15.4. . . . . 524, 888	1.1–9. 486	6.3. 391
15.6. 524	1.2. . . . . 380, 704	6.9–11. 488
15.7. . . . . 367, 503, 526	1.4–7. 486	6.12–20. . . . . 486, 488
15.8–9. . . . . . . 362, 388, 510	1.7. 420	6.14. 420
15.9. 504	1.8. 389	6.19. . . . . 387, 388
15.12. . . . . 307, 346	1.10. 480	6.19–20. 488
15.13. 524	1.10—3.23 486	7.1 . . . . 358, 479
15.13—16.27 . . . . . . 509, 524	1.11 . . . . . . 355, 358, 482, 759	7.1–40. . . . . 486, 488
15.14. 534	1.12. 478	7.7–40. 540
15.14—16.27 507	1.14. 482	7.10–12. 696
15.14. 524	1.16 . . . . . . 113, 335, 482, 539	7.19 380
15.16. . . . . 524, 525	1.17 . . . . 69, 161	7.21 . . . . 467, 482
15.19–20. . . . . . . 359, 524, 525	1.18—2.5 610	7.25 . . . . 358, 479
15.21. 62	1.18–25. 380	7.26 489
15.22–29. 506	1.26. 481	7.29 . . . . 420, 489
15.23. 529	2.1–5. 69	8—10 . . . . 161, 523, 819
15.23–24 357	2.4. 348	8.1. . . . . 358, 759

8.1–6 491	14.34–35 492	16.3 534
8.1–13 . . . . 486, 489, 540	15 . . . 161, 276, 296, 300, 307,	16.5–6 358
8.4 . . . . 358, 373, 759	308, 319, 347, 372,	16.5–7 479
8.4–13 832	392, 492, 828	16.5–9 494
8.6 . . . . 373, 477, 490	15.1–11 . . . . 308, 493	16.8 . . . . 358, 439, 479
8.11 490	15.1–58 . . . . 486, 493, 540	16.8–9 453
9 489	15.2 733	16.9 . . . . 356, 357
9.1 345	15.3 . . . . 245, 304	16.10 . . . . 358, 479
9.1–5 490	15.3–4 873	16.10–12 494
9.1–27 . . . . 486, 490	15.3–5 . . . . . 298, 310, 318, 697	16.12 . . . . 358, 759
9.5 . . . . 731, 739	15.4 . . . . 277, 317	16.12–14 494
9.6 340	15.5 . . . . 319, 757	16.13 739
9.6–18 490	15.6 319	16.15 . . . . 113, 482, 539
9.14 696	15.7 . . . . 319, 731	16.15–17 355
9.19–23 490	15.8 . . . . 309, 345	16.15–18 494
9.24–27 490	15.9 341	16.17 . . . . 358, 759
10 489	15.12 . . . . 358, 759	16.19 . . 356, 400, 452, 482, 539
10.1 762	15.12–19 . . . . 310, 314, 493	16.19–20 . . . . 358, 479
10.1—11.1 . . . . 486, 490	15.13 481	16.19–24 494
10.1–4 518	15.14 310	16.21 421
10.4 750	15.15 . . . . 15, 16	16.22 843
10.14–22 491	481	
10.14–33 832	15.17 . . . . 304, 310, 493	**2 Corinthians**
10.23–11.1 491	15.20–28 . . . . . 310, 388, 389,	1 471
11.1 499	488, 493	1—7 484
11.2 697	15.21–22 . . . . 311, 492	1.1 454
11.2–6 491	15.22 518	1.1–2 494
11.2–34 . . . . 486, 491	15.23 . . . . 388, 390, 420	1.1–11 494
11.3–16 540	15.23–28 717	1.1—2.13 484
11.5 . . . . 492, 534	15.24 389	1.3–7 . . . . 485, 494
11.17–34 . . . . 149, 491	15.29–34 310	1.5–10 357
11.18 . . . . 358, 759	15.29 481	1.8 . . . . 356, 400, 439
11.18–34 482	15.29–34 493	1.8–11 . . . . 356, 420, 453, 495
11.22 482	15.32 . . . . . . 357, 439, 481, 495	1.12–14 . . . . 485, 495
11.23 697	15.33 340	1.12—2.4 485
11.23–25 696	15.35–49 . . . . 310, 494	1.12—2.13 . . . . 494, 495
11.23–26 . . . . 251, 252	15.38 312	1.14 389
11.23–27 608	15.39–41 312	1.15–22 495
11.24–25 254	15.42–44 312	1.16 358
12 492	15.44 . . . . 313, 494	1.19 477
12.1 . . . . 358, 759	15.45–49 313	1.20 873
12.1—14.40 . . . . 486, 492	15.50 313	1.22 389
12.1–3 104	15.50–58 . . . . 313, 494	1.23—2.4 495
12.2 477	15.51–52 . . . . 420, 424	2.1 . . . . 358, 479
12.4–6 377	15.51–54 426	2.1–11 . . . . 358, 479
12.4–11 534	15.55 283	2.5–11 495
12.12–31 492	15.56 518	2.7–8 485
12.13 . . . . 467, 482	15.57 388	2.12 376
12.28 739	15.58 . . . . 314, 494	2.12–13 . . . . 358, 454, 479, 495
13.1–13 . . . . 46, 492	16.1 . . . . 358, 400, 759	2.13 548
14 492	16.1–4 494	2.14—4.6 . . . . 494, 495
14.21 534	16.1–24 . . . . 486, 494	2.14—7.4 . . . . 484, 485

2.14—7.16 495	7.5–16 . . . . .484, 497, 548	11.15 . . . . .482, 483, 485
2.14–15 572	7.6–16 . . . . .358, 479	11.16–21 484
2.14–17 535	7.8–12 . . . . .358, 479	11.16–33 498
2.17 . . . . .483, 485	7.14 485	11.21—12.18 484
3 387	8 . . . . .484, 495	11.21–23 483
3.1 . . . . .483, 485	8—9 . . . . .484, 485, 495	11.22 . . . . .340, 348
3.1–3 483	8.1–3 435	11.23 . . 357, 482, 485, 535, 586
3.1.5 495	8.1—9.15 . . . . .494, 497	11.24 586
3.3–9 485	8.4 485	11.32 . . . . .350, 355
3.1–11 483	8.6 . . . . .358, 485	12.1–10 . . . . .485, 498
3.2 484	8.8–9 497	12.2–3 830
3.17 413	8.10–15 497	12.8 485
3.18 392	8.13–14 534	12.10 498
4.1 485	8.13–15 631	12.11 . . . . . 358, 479, 482, 483
4.1–6 495	8.16–24 497	12.12 483
4.2 483	8.16–25 358	12.14 . . . . .358, 359
4.5 483	8.17 485	12.14–21 499
4.6 345	8.19–20 485	12.18 . . . . .358, 485
4.7–11 . . . . .484, 535	8.24 497	12.20–21 485
4.7–15 498	9 . . . . .484, 495	12.21 . . . . .358, 359
4.7–18 496	9.1 497	13 484
4.7—6.10 . . . . .494, 495	9.1–2 485	13.1–2 . . . . .358, 359
4.10–12 500	9.1–3 485	13.1–10 . . . . .484, 499
5.1–10 420	9.1–5 497	13.3–4 484
5.5 . . . . .376, 389	9.2–3 497	13.5 739
5.10 . . . . 391, 497, 745	9.5 485	13.10 483
5.12 483	9.6–11 498	13.11 485
5.14 304	9.12–13 485	13.11–13 484
5.15 298	9.12–15 498	13.11–14 . . . . .494, 499
5.16 . . . . .180, 682	10—13 . . . . .484, 484	
5.17 392	10.1 485	## Galatians
5.18 500	10.1—13.10 . . . . .484, 494, 498	1.1 404
5.18–21 485	10.1–11 483	1.1–5 404
5.20 485	10.8–18 485	1.1–10 . . . . .403, 404
5.20–21 474	10.10 161	1.2 400
5.21 382	10.11–12 485	1.2–5 404
6.1 485	10.12 483	1.4 . . . . .304, 388, 413
6.2 62	10.12–18 498	1.6–9 405
6.3–10 . . . . .485, 496, 498	10.13–16 483	1.6–11 404
6.4–10 484	10.18 483	1.8 414
6.5 . . . . .340, 357	11 360	1.10 405
6.5–7 41	11.4 . . . . .388, 483	1.11–12 . . . . .405, 713
6.8 483	11.5 . . 348, 358, 479, 482, 483	1.11–17 346
6.11—7.4 496	11.5–15 498	1.11–24 . . . . .403, 405
6.11—7.16 . . . . .494, 496	11.6 . . . . .69, 348	1.12—2.14 404
6.14—7.1 . . . . .484, 496	11.8 485	1.13 . . . . .104, 341
6.14—7.3 485	11.9 454	1.13–14 . . . . .122, 137, 343
6.16 387	11.10–30 485	1.13–16a 405
7.1 117	11.12 483	1.14 . . . . .130, 340
7.2–4 496	11.12–14 483	1.15–16 . . . . .62, 345
7.4–13 485	11.13 482	1.16b–17 405
7.5 454	11.13–14 482	1.17 . . . . .350, 353, 739

1.18–19 . . . . 350, 405	4.3–8 413	2 302
1.18–24 363	4.5 413	2.1–3 469
1.19 . . . . 731, 734, 739	4.6 414	2.1–10 . . . . 301, 469
1.20 405	4.6–8 388	2.4–10 469
1.21 350	4.8–10 403	2.5–6 301
1.21–24 405	4.8–11 409	2.6 . . . . 388, 841
1.22 348	4.12—5.1 410	2.10 . . . . 301, 706
1.23 . . . . 341, 344, 739	4.29 104	2.11 542
2.1—5.12 540	4.30 414	2.11—3.13 469
2.1–3 548	5 745	2.11–21 458
2.1–10 . . . . 348, 350, 351, 363, 403, 406–7	5.1 413	2.11–22 470
	5.1—6.10 404	2.12 411
2.2 62	5.2–12 411	2.19 . . . . 114, 380
2.4–5 348	5.13—6.10 411	2.20 739
2.7–9 497	5.13–26 411	2.21–22 387
2.7–10 401	5.5 . . . . 415, 420	3.1–3 470
2.9 . . . . . . 319, 653, 654, 706, 731, 734, 761	5.6 . . . . 706, 745	3.3–9 471
	5.7–10 401	3.10 470
2.9–10 735	5.10 403	3.14–21 . . . . 469, 470
2.10 631	5.12 . . . . 403, 414	4—6 470
2.11–14 . . . . 79, 342, 348, 401, 403, 407, 745	5.13—6.10 403	4.1–16 . . . . 469, 470, 885
	5.16 415	4.7–16 470
2.11–15 757	5.16–23 415	4.17—5.20 . . . . 469, 470
2.11–21 . . . . 360, 363, 386	5.24 414	4.17–24 470
2.12 . . . . 542, 731, 734	5.25 415	4.25–32 470
2.14 414	6.1–10 411	4.30 389
2.15 340	6.10 . . . . 407, 411	5.1–2 470
2.15–21 . . . 402, 403, 404, 407	6.11 . . . . 411, 421	5.8–10 470
2.15–30 136	6.11–18 . . . . 403, 404, 411	5.14 301
2.19–20 414	6.12 . . . . 342, 403	5.21—6.9 . . . . 113, 469, 471
2.20 . . . . 396, 407, 408	6.12–13 403	5.27 781
3 . . . . 372, 879	6.14 414	6.1–9 471
3.1—4.31 . . . . 404, 762	6.14–15 411	6.5–8 467
3.1—5.12 . . . . 403, 408	6.15 392	6.8 467
3.1–5 408	6.15–16 411	6.9 467
3.1–12 402	6.16 . . . . 380, 411, 762	6.10–20 . . . . 301, 469, 471
3.2 414	6.17 411	6.11–18 424
3.5 . . . . 414, 534		6.12 458
3.6–9 408	**Ephesians**	6.21 454
3.6–14 408	1.1 454	6.21–24 . . . . 469, 471
3.13 . . . . 388, 413	1.1–23 469	
3.13–14 382	1.3–14 301	**Philippians**
3.14 414	1.4 781	1.1 . . . . 441, 539
3.14a 409	1.9 471	1.1–11 441
3.16–18 746	1.9–10 450	1.2–3 442
3.19 . . . . 716, 750	1.10 469	1.4–5 442
3.24 149	1.11–12 380	1.5 . . . . 434, 442
3.26–28 409	1.13 . . . . 733, 745	1.6 389
3.28 . . . 368, 380, 467, 491, 541	1.14 . . . . 376, 389	1.7 442
3.28–29 534	1.10 78	1.8–11 442
4 376	1.20 . . . . 299, 388	1.10 389
4.1–7 . . . . 375, 409	1.20–23 301	1.12 442

1.12–26. . . . . .441, 442	3.9–11. . . . . .300, 443	2.4–23. 454
1.13. . . . . 439, 442	3.10. 434	2.6–23. . . . . .461, 464
1.14. 442	3.12. 448	2.8. . . . . 161, 460, 461
1.15–18. 440	3.12–13. 446	2.9. 461
1.15–18b. 442	3.18–19. . . . . .440, 446	2.10. 461
1.16. 442	3.20. . . . . 446, 447	2.10–23. 461
1.19–26. 535	3.20–21. . . 300, 313, 391, 420,	2.11. 461
1.20–25. 420	424, 426	2.11–12. 461
1.20–26. 453	3.21. 494	2.12. 303
1.25. 739	4.1. 446	2.13. 303
1.26. 440	4.1–9. . . . . .441, 446	2.14–15. . . . . .458, 461, 465
1.27. . . . . 442, 739	4.2–3. 352	2.15. . . . . .388, 461, 572
1.27–30. . . . . .352, 440	4.2–4. 440	2.16. . . . . 460, 461
1.27—2.18. . . . . .441, 443	4.3. 442	2.16–23. 460
2. . . . . .373, 444	4.8. 446	2.18. . . . . 152, 460, 461
2.1. 434	4.9. . . . . .446, 697	2.20–23. 465
2.1–4. . . . . .367, 440	4.10–20. . . 352, 435, 441, 446	2.21. 461
2.1–5. 448	4.15. . . . . . 434, 435, 438, 442	2.21–23. 461
2.1–11. 352	4.15–18. 440	2.23. 461
2.1–18. 443	4.16. . . . . 354, 417	3.1. . . . . 380, 841
2.2–11. 443	4.18. 447	3.1–2. . . . . .303, 460
2.6. . . . . 46, 444, 445	4.21–23. . . . . .441, 446	3.1–4. 465
2.6–8 . . . . .300, 673	4.22. 439	3.1–17. . . . . .461, 465
2.6–11. . . . .299, 347, 372, 441,		3.4. . . . . .420, 426
491, 518	**Colossians**	3.5–8. 465
2.9. . . . . .299, 372	1.1–14. . . . . 461, 463	3.5–11. 465
2.9–11. 299	1.3–8. 463	3.10. . . . . .43, 303, 540
2.12–13. . . . . .369, 434	1.5–8. . . . . .356, 452	3.11. . . . . 380, 458, 467
2.12–18. 443	1.6. 704	3.12. 380
2.15. 301	1.7–8. . . . . 356, 452, 453	3.12–17. 465
2.16. . . . . 62, 389	1.9. 461	3.16. 461
2.17–18. 535	1.9–10. 540	3.18—4.1. . . . . . 113, 461, 465
2.19–30. . . . . .441, 444	1.9–12. 463	3.22–24. 467
2.22. 442	1.12–14. . . . . .302, 458	4.1. 467
2.24. 440	1.13–14. . . 380, 450, 463, 885	4.2–18. . . . . .461, 465
2.25–30 435	1.15. . . . . .302, 462, 463	4.7. 454
3 . . . . .300, 443	1.15–20. . . . . . . .302, 460, 463	4.7–9. 454
3.1. 441	1.15–23. . . . . .461, 463	4.9. 357
3.1–2. 441	1.16. 461	4.10. . . . . .453, 454, 557
3.1–11. 540	1.18. . . . . . 302, 388, 462, 463	4.12–13. . . . . .356, 453
3.1–21. . . . . .441, 444	1.20–21. 302	4.12–16. 452
3.2. . . . . .440, 461	1.21–23. 464	4.14. 608
3.2–4.1. 440	1.22. 781	4.15. . . . . 453, 539
3.2–3. . . . . .348, 745	1.22–23. 460	4.15–16. 464
3.2–11. . . . . .384, 491	1.23. 464	4.16. . . . . 454, 464, 695
3.2–21. 441	1.24—2.5 . . . . .461, 464	4.17. 453
3.3. . . 152, 380, 387, 444, 542	2 461	4.18. 421
3.5. . . . . .340, 598	2.1. . . . . .356, 452	
3.5–6. . . . . .340, 384	2.1–5. 464	**1 Thessalonians**
3.6. . . . . 341, 343, 443	2.2–3. 460	1.1–10. . . . . .422, 423
3.7–8. 443	2.3. 461	1.3. 418
3.9. 513	2.4. 460	1.4. 380

1.6 . . . . 354, 417	4.11–12 424	2.15–17 419
1.6–9 418	4.13 431	2.17 418
1.7–8 400	4.13–14 298	3.1–5 . . . . 421, 427, 429
1.8 418	4.13–18 . . . . 429, 735	3.5 419
1.8–9 398	4.13—5.3 418	3.6–12 424
1.9 417	4.13—5.11 . . . . 423, 424	3.6–14 419
1.9–10 . . . . 354, 416, 429	4.14 . . . . 298, 299, 430	3.6–15 . . . . 427, 429
1.10 . . . . 298, 299	4.15 390	3.7 419
2.1 422	4.16 298	3.8 340
2.1–12 . . . . 418, 427	4.16–17 424	3.10 419
2.1–16 . . . . 422, 423	4.18 418	3.16 . . . . 421, 429
2.2 . . . . 427, 438	5.1–2 424	3.16–18 . . . . 427, 429
2.3a 428	5.1–4 431	3.17 . . . . 420, 421, 429
2.3b 428	5.1–11 523	3.18 429
2.3c–4 458	5.2 . . . . 389, 420, 780, 832	
2.5 . . . . 69, 458	5.3 . . . . 424, 430	**1 Timothy**
2.6–7 458	5.4–8 418	1.1–2 543
2.7 418	5.6 424	1.2 539
2.7–8 422	5.8 424	1.3 . . . 364, 454, 532, 541, 542
2.8–12 429	5.9 . . . . 299, 424	1.3–4 542
2.9 . . . . 340, 354, 417	5.10 . . . . 304, 424	1.3–5 541
2.12 . . . . 418, 431	5.11 . . . . 418, 424	1.3–11 543
2.13 418	5.12–22 418	1.3–20 543
2.13–16 418	5.12–28 . . . . 423, 426	1.7 542
2.13–17 . . . . 427, 429	5.14 418	1.7–9 . . . . 540, 541, 542
2.14–15 . . . . 341, 417, 586	5.23 . . . . 390, 418, 429, 781	1.8–10 541
2.14–16 . . . . 104, 354	5.27 695	1.9–10 467
2.17 418		1.10 . . . . 534, 539
2.17—3.5 418	**2 Thessalonians**	1.11–16 536
2.17—3.13 423	1.1–4 427	1.12–16 534
2.18 418	1.3–4 427	1.12–17 544
2.19 . . . . 390, 429	1.3–5 421	1.14 539
3.1–3 418	1.4 419	1.15–16 528
3.2 418	1.4–12 419	1.16 551
3.2–13 418	1.5 . . . . 419, 427, 431	1.17 541
3.3 418	1.5–12 427	1.18–20 544
3.5 . . . . 62, 418	1.6–7a 427	1.19 . . . . 534, 539, 542
3.6 418	1.10 429	2.1–7 544
3.7 418	1.11 . . . . 419, 427	2.1–15 . . . . 543, 544
3.10 418	1.11–12 . . . . 419, 421	2.2 531
3.13 . . . . 390, 418, 429, 781	2.1 390	2.3–7 539
4 . . . . 300, 426, 426	2.1–10 419	2.4 540
4.1–2 697	2.1–12 . . . . 427, 431, 753	2.4–6 536
4.1–3 423	2.2 . . . . 389, 420, 421, 430	2.5–6 362
4.1–12 . . . . 418, 423	2.3 798	2.7 . . . . 534, 541
4.4 115	2.3–6 428	2.9 71
4.4–6 423	2.5 419	2.10 . . . . 539, 551
4.5 . . . . 161, 431	2.7–8 798	2.11–14 . . . . 534, 542
4.6 432	2.8 390	2.12 542
4.9–10 424	2.13–17 . . . . 421, 427	2.12–15 540
4.9–12 432	2.14 . . . . 419, 429	2.15 61
4.10 114	2.15 419	2.17–18 308

Scripture and Other Ancient Literature Index **945**

3.1–16 . . . . 543, 544	1.4 364	4.4 542
3.1–18 533	1.5 400	4.6 . . . . 364, 420
3.8–13 533	1.6 534	4.6–8 . . . . 535, 536, 547
3.9 . . . . 534, 539	1.6–18 546	4.7 . . . . 534, 539, 550
3.11 544	1.9 539	4.8 389
3.16 . . . . 152, 531, 536, 542	1.8 . . . . 364, 439	4.9 364
4.1 . . . . 534, 539	1.10 531	4.9–18 . . . . 532, 546, 547
4.1–2 542	1.11–23 536	4.9–21 536
4.1–5 753	1.13 539	4.9–22 362
4.1–16 . . . . 543, 545	1.13–14 549	4.10 548
4.2 542	1.15 . . . . 356, 364	4.11 . . . . 557, 608
4.3 . . . . 540, 542	1.15–18 . . . . 536, 546	4.16 364
4.6 . . . . 534, 539	1.16–17 364	4.16–17 364
4.7 542	1.18 . . . . 364, 389, 532	4.17 539
4.7–8 531	2 481	4.18 364
4.10 539	2.1–13 546	4.19–22 . . . . 546, 547
4.11–16 545	2.1–21 534	4.20–21 532
4.12 551	2.8 . . . . 228, 362, 536	4.21 364
4.13 695	2.9 364	
4.14 534	2.14–16 542	**Titus**
4.16 . . . . 534, 551	2.14–18 547	1.1 . . . . 531, 540
5.1—6.2a 543, 545	2.14–26 . . . . 546, 547	1.1–3 548
5.4 531	2.15 733	1.1–4 548
5.8 . . . . 534, 539	2.17 542	1.4 . . . . 539, 548
5.10 . . . . 539, 551	2.17–18 542	1.5 . . . . 532, 533, 534
5.17–19 533	2.18 . . . . 480, 540	1.5–9 533
5.22 534	2.21 . . . . 539, 551	1.5–16 548
5.25 . . . . 539, 551	2.22–26 547	1.8 551
6.1 . . . . 534, 539	2.23 542	1.9 . . . . 534, 539
6.1–2 467	2.25 540	1.10 542
6.1–3 542	2.26 542	1.10–11 542
6.2b–21a 543, 545	3.1—4.8 . . . . 546, 548	1.10–14 540
6.3 . . . . 539, 542	3.1–9 . . . . 542, 753	1.10–16 548
6.3–5 542	3.1–5a 547	1.15 540
6.3–6 531	3.5 531	1.11 542
6.4 542	3.5b–9 547	1.12 340
6.5 542	3.7 540	1.13 . . . . 534, 539
6.7 541	3.8 . . . . 534, 539, 542	1.14 542
6.10 534	3.10 . . . . 534, 536, 539	1.15 542
6.11 531	3.10–11 . . . . 536, 547	1.15–16 542
6.11–16 545	3.10–14 534	1.19 542
6.12 . . . . 534, 539	3.11 536	2.1 . . . . 534, 539
6.17–18 545	3.12 531	2.1–15 548
6.18 . . . . 539, 551	3.13 542	2.2 534
6.19–21a 546	3.16 541	2.7 . . . . 534, 551
6.20 . . . . 533, 540, 542	3.16–17 547	2.9 467
6.21 . . . . 534, 539	3.17 . . . . 539, 551	2.10 . . . . 531, 534, 539
6.21b 543, 546	4 364	2.11 539
	4.1 391	2.11–15 549
2 Timothy	4.1–5 547	2.12 531
1.1–5 546	4.3 . . . . 534, 539, 542	2.13 531
1.3 536	4.3–4 542	2.14 . . . . 539, 551

946 The New Testament in Its World

3.1 . . . . 541, 551
3.1–2 549
3.1–11 . . . . 548, 549
3.5 . . . . 362, 539
3.8 551
3.9 . . . . 541, 542
3.9–11 540
3.12 . . . . 364, 532
3.12–15 . . . . 548, 549
3.14 . . . . 539, 551
3.15 539

Philemon
1–2 . . . . 356, 452, 453
1–7 465
2 539
6 . . . . 369, 468, 739
8–17 467
8–21 454
8–22 . . . . 367, 465, 468
9 . . . . 338, 803
10–18 357
16 367
17 . . . . 367, 453
17–18 450
19 421
22 . . . . 357, 439
23 453
23–25 465
24 . . . . 557, 608, 611

Hebrews
1—2 728
1.1—9.16 704
1.1–2 710
1.1–4 715
1.1–14 713
1.3 717
1.4 719
1.5—2.9 715
1.6–14 715
1.13 717
2 723
2.1–4 . . . . 714, 716, 725
2.2 750
2.3 . . . . 713, 719
2.5–9 717
2.6 717
2.10—6.20 . . . . 715, 717
2.10–18 717
2.14 717
2.14–15 717
2.14–18 726
2.16–17 717
2.17 717
2.17–18 713
2.18 717
3—4 728
3.1–6 717
3.7—4.13 . . . . 717, 725
3.7—12 717
3.12–13 718
3.12–14 714
3.14–19 718
4.1–13 718
4.14 739
4.14—5.10 726
4.14–16 . . . . 713, 718
4.15 . . . . 717, 723
5—8 728
5.1–3 718
5.1–4 713
5.7–8 720
5.9 719
5.9–10 720
5.11—6.12 725
5.11–25 720
6 719
6.1–3 720
6.4–6 720
6.7–8 720
6.9 719
6.9–12 720
6.17–20 720
6.19–20 720
7 . . . . 720, 723
7.1—10.18 . . . . 715, 720
7.3 721
7.11–19 721
7.19 723
7.20 713
7.20–25 721
7.22 723
7.23 713
7.26–28 721
7.27 713
7.27–28 714
7.28 713
8.1–6 721
8.3, 4 713
8.3–5 714
8.6 723
8.7–13 722
8.13 713
9.1–10 722
9.6 713
9.6–7 714
9.8–10 722
9.11–14 723
9.12 722
9.12–13 729
9.13 . . . . 713, 729
9.14 723
9.15–28 723
9.18—10.20 704
9.23 723
9.25 714
9.28 . . . . 719, 723, 760
10.1–3 714
10.1–10 723
10.2 714
10.4 729
10.8 714
10.11 713
10.11–18 723
10.19—12.29 . . . . 715, 724–25
10.19–39 725
10.22–30 704
10.23 714
10.26–29 724
10.30–39 724
10.32 714
10.32—13.25 704
10.32–34 714
10.32–39 714
10.34 723
10.39 . . . . 714, 719
11 725
11—12 728
11.1 725
11.3 725
11.4–38 725
11.8–13 707
11.13 760
11.16 723
11.26 714
11.35 . . . . 723, 725
11.39–40 726
12.1–3 . . . . 725, 726
12.2 115
12.3–11 714
12.4 . . . . 714, 726
12.4–11 726
12.12–17 726
12.14–29 725
12.15 719

12.22. 727	1.27. . . . . 730, 743, 748	5.4–6. 742
12.24. 723	2.1. . . . . 732, 743	5.6. . . . . 742, 747
12.25–28 718	2.1–5.18 741	5.7. 735
12.27. 726	2.1–7. 705	5.7–8. . . . . 733, 748
12.28. 726	2.1–13. . . . . .740, 743–44	5.7–11. . . . . 740, 747
13 728	2.2. 735	5.8. 735
13.1–3. 726	2.2–6a 743	5.8–9. 742
13.1–21. . . . . 715, 726	2.5. . . . . 707, 742, 748	5.9. . . . . 733, 748
13.3. 714	2.5–6 112	5.10. 742
13.4–5. 726	2.6b–7 743	5.10–11. 748
13.5–6 726	2.8. . . . . 742, 743	5.11. . . . . 735, 748, 754
13.7. 739	2.8–12. 748	5.12. . . . . 742, 748
13.9–16. 726	2.8–13. 744	5.12–20. . . . . 740, 748
13.10–11. 714	2.10 . . . . 742, 743	5.13. 748
13.13. 714	2.11 . . . . 742, 743	5.14. 733
13.20. 760	2.12 743	5.15a–16a. 748
13.20–21. 727	2.13 742	5.16 705
13.22. . . . . 705, 714	2.14–24. 745	5.16b–18. 748
13.22–25. . . . . 715, 727	2.14–26. . . . . . . .706, 740, 744	5.17 735
13.23. 713	2.19 . . . . 735, 748	5.17–18. . . . . 735, 754
13.24. 714	2.19—3.9 704	5.19–20. . . . . 742, 748
13.25. 725	2.20 748	5.20. 760
	2.21–23. . . . . 735, 746	
James	2.23 . . . . 742, 748	**1 Peter**
1.1 . . . . .732, 740, 760, 761	2.23–25 754	1.1 . . . 705, 707, 740, 758, 760,
1.2. 742	2.24 744	761, 762, 767, 781
1.2–4. . . . . 741, 760	2.26 . . . . 744, 745	1.1–2. 770
1.2–27. . . . . 740, 741	3.1 746	1.2. . . . . 733, 760, 761
1.3 748	3.1–12. . . . . 740, 746	1.3. 783
1.4 . . . . 742, 748	3.2 746	1.3—2.10 770
1.5 . . . . 742, 748	3.3–12. 746	1.3–4. 295
1.5–8. 741	3.4, 6 735	1.3–12. 771
1.6 . . . . 735, 742	3.7–10. 152	1.4 . . . . 759, 761
1.9–11. 741	3.9 748	1.4–5. 762
1.10–12. 704	3.11–12. 735	1.6 762
1.11 735	3.13—4.10 . . . . 740, 746	1.6–8. 760
1.12 . . . . 742, 748	3.13–17. 746	1.7. 758
1.12–15. 741	3.14 749	1.7–12. 762
1.15–18. . . . . 704, 705	3.18 . . . . 742, 746	1.8. 760
1.16–17. 741	4.1–3. 747	1.9. 761
1.17 748	4.4–6 747	1.12 760
1.17–18. 748	4.6–10. 760	1.13 . . . . 758, 783
1.18 . . . . . . .733, 741, 745, 749	4.7–10. 747	1.13–14. 760
1.19–20. 741	4.7 748	1.13–16. 771
1.20. 742	4.8 742	1.14 761
1.21 . . . . 733, 741, 745, 748	4.10 742	1.15–16. 761
1.22–25. . . . . 741, 742	4.11–12. . . . . 742, 747, 748	1.17 . . . . 740, 761, 781
1.23. 748	4.11–17. . . . . 740, 747	1.17–21. 771
1.25 . . . . 743, 748	4.13–17. 747	1.18 761
1.26. 743	5.1 742	1.18–19. . . . . 762, 763
1.26—2.7 631	5.1–6. . . . . 112, 740, 747	1.18–20. 756
1.26–27. 152	5.2–3. 742	1.22–23. 762

1.22–25. 771	5.1–7 777	3.5–7. 780
2.1. 762	5.5–9 760	3.8. 765
2.1–3. . . . . 772, 779	5.8–11. 777	3.8–10. 781
2.1–22. . . . . 777, 779	5.9 739	3.10. . . . . 766, 832
2.4–12. 762	5.10 758	3.11. 783
2.6. 115	5.12 759	3.11–13. 781
2.9. . . . . 43, 761	5.12–14. . . . . 770, 777	3.13. 783
2.9–10. 761	5.13 . . . . 557, 559, 737	3.14. 783
2.10. 761	5.14 758	3.14–15. 781
2.10b–13. 779		3.14–18. . . . . . . 769, 777, 781
2.11 . . . . . . 707, 740, 760, 781	2 Peter	3.15. 767
2.11—4.11 . . . . 770, 772	1.1 . . . . 763, 767	3.15–16. . . . . 706, 781
2.11–12. 772	1.1–2 . . . . 777, 778	3.16. . . . . 763, 767, 769
2.11–20. 762	1.3–4. . . . . 756, 778	3.16–17. 781
2.12. . . . . 759, 761, 762	1.3–11. . . . . 769, 777, 778	3.17 769
2.12–13. 760	1.4–6 764	3.18. . . . . 781, 783
2.13–14. 758	1.5–9 . . . . 778, 783	
2.13–17. 772	1.10 782	1 John
2.14–22. 779	1.10–11 778	1.1 . . . . 654, 788, 789
2.17. 758	1.12 783	1.1–3 . . . . 791, 812
2.18—3.7. 113	1.12–15. . . . . 777, 778	1.1–4 . . . . 787, 796
2.18–25. 773	1.12–18. 769	1.3 . . . . 654, 656
2.19. 762	1.14 . . . . 763, 766	1.4 654
2.21–24. . . . . . . 758, 760, 763	1.15 . . . . 769, 783	1.5–2.2 796
2.24. 758	1.16–18. . . . . 766, 779	1.5–10 796
2.24–25 62	1.16–21. . . . . 777, 779	1.6—2.2 799
2.25. . . . . 760, 761	1.17–18. 763	1.6–7. . . . . 788, 805
3.1–7. . . . . 758, 773	1.19–21. 779	1.7 . . . . 118, 801
3.1–17. 762	2 . . . . 739, 763	1.7–9 806
3.6. 761	2–3 . . . . 766, 769	1.7–10 806
3.8–12. 774	2.1 765	1.8. 799
3.13–17. 774	2.1–3. . . . . 766, 769, 780	1.9 118
3.14. . . . . 759, 760	2.1–22. 777	1.10 . . . . 791, 799
3.16. . . . . 758, 762	2.4 . . . . 764, 780	2.1 806
3.18. . . . . 760, 763	2.4–5. 41	2.1–2 . . . . 784, 797, 806
3.18–22. 776	2.4–10a. 779	2.3–5 791
3.19–20. 775	2.6 780	2.3–6 797
3.21. 763	2.10 780	2.3–11 . . . . 796, 797
4.1. 763	2.11–12. 780	2.4 791
4.1–5. 762	2.13 780	2.5 805
4.1–6. 776	2.14 766	2.6 791
4.3. 761	2.15 780	2.7 . . . . 789, 791
4.5. 783	2.17 780	2.7–11 797
4.7–11. 776	2.18 . . . . 766, 780	2.9 791
4.8. 760	2.20–23 767	2.11 791
4.10. 758	3 780	2.12–14. 797
4.12. 783	3.1 . . . . 767, 783	2.12–17. . . . . 796, 797
4.12—5.11 . . . . 770, 776	3.1–13. . . . . 777, 780	2.13–14. . . . . 789, 791
4.12–16. 762	3.2–4. 769	2.14 791
4.12–19. . . . . 762, 777	3.3–4. . . . . 753, 767, 780	2.15–16. 806
4.13. 758	3.4 765	2.15–17. 798
5.1. 803	3.4–15. 769	2.17–18. 813

2.18 . . . . . . .428, 753, 789, 791	4.8 800	**3 John**
2.18–22 803	4.9 . . . . .789, 791, 801, 806	1 . . . . 657, 705
2.18–23 798	4.11–12 704	1–4 804
2.18–27 . . . . .796, 798	4.12–16a 800	3 788
2.19 . . . . .785, 790	4.13 791	3–4 805
2.20 791	4.14 806	5–8 804
2.22 . . . . .661, 790, 791	4.14–15 791	9–10 805
2.22–23 791	4.14–16 704	9–12 804
2.24 . . . . 789, 791	4.15 791	13–14 805
2.26 791	4.16 800	
2.27 791	4.16b–18 800	**Jude**
2.28 813	4.17 . . . . .791, 807, 813	1 . . . . 733, 734
2.28—3.10 . . . . .796, 798	4.19 789	1–2 749
2.28–29 798	4.19–21 800	3 . . . . 730, 739
2.29 791	4.20 791	3–4 . . . . .733, 736, 749
3.1 . . . . .806, 807	5.1 . . . . .790, 791	4 . . . . .737, 738, 754, 780
3.1–2 . . . . .707, 789	5.1–2 807	5 . . . . 738, 750
3.1–3 799	5.1–3 801	5–7 738
3.2 . . . . .426, 813	5.2 . . . . 661, 707	5.16 750
3.4–5 799	5.4 791	5–19 . . . . 749, 750
3.4–9 806	5.4–5 . . . . .801, 807, 813	6 . . . . .738, 750, 780
3.5 806	5.5 791	6–10 779
3.6 791	5.6–12 . . . . .796, 801	7 . . . . .738, 750, 780
3.9 . . . . .791, 806	5.7–8 801	8 . . . . . . .737, 738, 750, 780
3.10 707	5.9–13 791	8–10 738
3.10–11 807	5.12 813	9 . . . . 750, 751
3.10–18 806	5.13 . . . . .787, 789, 801	9–10 780
3.11 791	5.13–15 802	10 750
3.11–12 800	5.13–21 . . . . .796, 801	11 . . . . 738, 780
3.11–18 799	5.16–17 806	11–12 738
3.11–24 . . . . .796, 799	5.16–18 . . . . .802, 806	11–13 753
3.13 806	5.18 791	12 738
3.14 . . . . .788, 813	5.19 707	12–13 780
3.15 791	5.19–20 802	13 738
3.16 807	5.20 791	14–15 752
3.19–24 799	5.21 802	14–16 753
3.23 789		15 738
3.24 791	**2 John**	16 . . . . 738, 780
4.1 791	1 . . . . .657, 705, 786, 787	17 739
4.1–3 . . . . .753, 800	2 805	17–19 753
4.1–6 . . . . .796, 799	1–3 803	18 . . . . 738, 753
4.2 . . . . .661, 785, 803	4 . . . . .788, 804, 805	19 738
4.2–3 . . . . .789, 790, 791	4–8 803	20–21 753
4.3 . . . . .428, 791, 798, 803	5 789	20–23 . . . . 749, 753
4.4 . . . . .707, 807	5–6 791	24 780
4.4–6 800	6 805	24–25 . . . . .733, 749, 754
4.6 805	7 . . . . .661, 785, 789, 790,	25 739
4.6–8 791	791, 798	
4.7 791	9 . . . . .789, 790, 791	**Revelation**
4.7—5.5 . . . . .796, 800	9–11 803	1—3 832
4.7–12 800	12–13 . . . . .803, 804	1.1 . . . . .812, 821, 825
4.7–21 806	13 . . . . .786, 803	1.1–3 829

950   The New Testament in Its World

1.3 . . . . 735, 821, 825	4.2 825	14.1–5 839
1.4 . . . . 703, 838	4.8 838	14.8 777
1.4–5 821	4.8b–11 833	14.9–11 817
1.4–5a 830	4.11 815	14.14–20 837
1.4–6 808	5 833	15.1–4 837
1.4–8 . . . . 829, 830	5.1–2, 6 812	15.2 817
1.5b–6 . . . . 830, 845	5.10 . . . . 812, 830	15.5—16.9 838
1.6 812	6—19 . . . . 827, 829	15.5—16.21 . . . . . 829, 837–38
1.7–8 830	6.1—8.5 . . . . 829, 834	16 428
1.8 . . . . 831, 838, 843	6.1–8 834	16.2 817
1.9 812	6.9 812	16.9, 11 . . . . 837, 838
1.9–11 830	6.9–11 817	16.12–16 838
1.9–20 . . . . 829, 830	6.9–17 834	16.15 832
1.10 . . . . 812, 825	7.1–2 812	16.19 777
1.12 812	7.1–8 834	16.21 838
1.12–20 811	7.1–17 839	17 . . . . 428, 815
1.13–20 704	7.3 837	17.1—19.10 . . . . 829, 838
1.16–20 831	7.4–12 837	17.3 . . . . 812, 825
1.17 812	7.9–17 834	17.5 777
1.18 294	7.14–17 841	17.7–18 838
2—3 . . . . . . 704, 811, 827, 830	8.1–5 834	17.8 . . . . 816, 832
2.1—3.22 . . . . . . 703, 829, 831	8.2 812	17.10 . . . . 815, 838
2.1–7 831	8.6—11.19 . . . . 829, 834	17.11 816
2.2 819	8.6–12 834	17.14 . . . . 816, 839
2.3 817	8.12—9.12 837	18 825
2.4–5 818	8.13—9.12 835	18.1–4 839
2.6 819	9.1 812	18.2 777
2.8–11 831	9.13–21 835	18.5–20 839
2.9 . . . . 586, 661, 819	9.20–21 837	18.10 777
2.10 . . . . 817, 818	10.1–11 835	18.21 777
2.12–17 832	10.11 825	18.21–24 839
2.13 . . . . 817, 818, 821	11.1–2 835	19.1–8 839
2.14 819	11.3–14 835	19.9 254
2.14–16 819	11.15 835	19.9–10 . . . . 842, 839
2.18–29 832	11.15–19 835	19.10 . . . . 812, 825
2.19 . . . . 817, 818	12.1—15.4 . . . . 829, 835	19.10–15 841
2.20 819	12.1–6 836	19.11—21.8 . . . . 829, 839
2.20–23 819	12.1–17 62	19.11–16 839
3.1–6 832	12.10 836	19.16–21 841
3.1–13 818	12.17 46	19.17–21 840
3.3 . . . . 739, 780	12.17–18 836	19.20 817
3.5 832	12.18 836	20 . . . . 428, 840
3.7–13 833	13 . . . . 428, 812	20.1–6 . . . . 840, 841
3.8–10 818	13—20 825	20.1–10 . . . . 840, 841
3.9 . . . . 586, 819	13.1–10 836	20.4 . . . . 813, 817
3.10 818	13.4–8 817	20.4–5 840
3.14–22 833	13.8 832	20.6 . . . . 812, 830
3.15–18 818	13.11–18 837	20.7–10 840
3.17 819	13.15–16 817	20.7–15 841
4—5 811	13.17 798	20.11–15 840
4.1—5.14 . . . . 829, 833	14.1 837	20.12 832
4.1–8a 833	14.1–13 837	20.15 832

21 838	15.17 593	**Apocalypse of Peter**
21—22 . . . . 812, 826, 833	17.27–28. 287	4–6 766
21.1 . . . . 426, 842	24 233	15–17 766
21.1—22.17 841	24.1–12. 664	81.3—83.10 794
21.1–8 842	38.21–23. 287	
21.3 665	44—50 725	**Epistula Apostolorum**
21.6 843	45.23–24 343	2 . . . . 653, 656
21.4–6 841		
21.9 842	**Baruch**	**Acts of John**
21.9—22.5 841	5.5 164	18—19 661
21.9—22.9 . . . . 829, 842		
21.9–27 842	**1 Maccabees**	**Acts of Paul**
21.10 812	2 . . . . 122, 725	11.3 365
21.27 832	2.24 343	17 534
22.1–5 842	2.26–54 343	
22.6–7 821	2.27 343	**Trimorphic Protennoia**
22.6–9 . . . . 842, 843	2.52 746	47.14–16 792
22.7 . . . . 825, 843	2.68 53	
22.8 . . . . 654, 812	3.36–59 229	**5. OLD TESTAMENT**
22.9 . . . . 812, 825	5.15 109	**PSEUDEPIGRAPHA**
22.10 . . . . 735, 825		
22.10–11 843	**2 Maccabees**	**1 Enoch**
22.10–21 . . . . 829, 843	1.–10a 736	1—36 . . . . 752, 836
22.12 843	1.10b–2.18 736	1.9 752
22.12–13 843	1.27–29 164	6—19 750
22.14–15 843	2.25 697	6.1–6 836
22.16 843	6.5 570	22.14 515
22.18–19 . . . . 825, 843	7.9 . . . . 264, 289	37–71 . . . . 222, 224, 225,
22.20 843	7.10–11 289	226, 752
22.21 . . . . 821, 843	7.14 289	42 664
	7.21–23 290	42.1–3 664
3. OLD TESTAMENT	7.28–29 290	46.1–4 225
APOCRYPHA	7.31–33, 36–38 290	62.14–15 291
	10.1–4 93	91—104 . . . . 768, 769
2 Esdras	10.1–9 . . . . 229, 568	91.3–4, 18–19 593
7.109 735		91.12–16 841
	4. NEW TESTAMENT	93.12–17 841
Tobit	**APOCRYPHA**	94.1–5 593
8.15 761		104.4 293
14.5–7 . . . . 88, 164	**Gospel of Thomas**	
	§ 14 731	**Sibylline Oracles**
Wisdom of Solomon	46 192	3.63–74 816
3.7 624	71 194	3.195 378
8.4 664	78 192	3.635–701 841
9.9 664		4.119–24, 137–39 816
	Second Apocalypse of	5.143, 159–60 777
Sirach (Ecclesiasticus)	**James**	5.361–5 816
2.14 624	61–62 731	
3.30 631		**4 Ezra (2 Esdras)**
7.10 631	**Gospel of the Hebrews**	3.1–3, 28–31 777
14.12–17 287	§ 5 . . . . 319, 731	4.30 379
		6.55–59 379

6.58..................463	2.25–31..................94	**4QMMT**
7.11..................379	3.11–12..................291	C 10–17...............134
7.26–44...............841	8.....................428	C 26–32...............136
7.46–56................379	11.1–5..................563	
8.36..................515	17....................428	**CD**
8.44..................379	17—18..................226	1.3–11.................134
9.13..................379		1.18–2.1...............127
9.38—10.59...........565	## 6. DEAD SEA SCROLLS	3.20..................378
11—12..................224	**1QH (Thanksgiving**	3.21—4.4...............134
12.31-34...............841	**Hymns)**	5.6–7..................134
13....................226	4.15..................378	7.9...................236
	6.14..................343	7.20—8.2...............134
2 Baruch	6.25–29................134	8.2–3..................236
35—40................224	14.29–30, 34–5; 19.10–14..293	12.22–23..............226
		14.13..................631
Testament of Dan	**1QM (War Scroll)**	
6.10–11................515	19.10..................777	**11Q13**
		6–10..................721
Testament of Job	**1QpHab (Commentary**	
1.27..................735	**on Habakkuk)**	## 7. RABBINIC
7.5–10.................127	1.5...................133	## LITERATURE
	2.1–6..................133	**Mishnah**
Testament of Moses		**Aboth**
7.5–10.................127	**1QS (Rule of the**	3.2...................209
	Community)	
Epistle of Aristeas	3.18..................236	**Sanhedrin**
16....................154	4.19..................236	10.1..................286
	4.23..................378	
Jubilees	5.5–9..................134	**Jerusalem Talmud**
1.27–29................750	8.5–11.................134	**ySanh.**
17–18.............735, 751	8.13–16................133	1.2...................736
20–22.................768	8.14..................234	
36....................768	9.11..................226	**Babylonian Talmud**
48....................751	9.19–20................234	**bHag.**
	11.10–14...............136	14a...................238
Martyrdom of Isaiah	11.12, 14–15...........515	
4.2–8..................816		**bPesah.**
	1QSa	87b...................165
Apocalypse of Moses (Life	2.17–22................226	
of Adam and Eve)		**bSanh.**
13.3–4.................291	**4Q176**	38b...................238
41.2–3.................291	1.4–9..................234	
		bShab.
4 Maccabees	**4Q405**	118b..................108
18.12..................343	frags. xxi–xxii, 6–14....460	
		## 8. JOSEPHUS
Pseudo-Phocylides	**4Q521**	**Against Apion**
105–15.............288–89	2.1–10.................228	1.1–4..................619
	2.1–12.................136	1.50..................735
Psalms of Solomon	2.9–12.................293	
2.....................428		

2.217–18 292	20.34–50 344	2.271 122
2.282 165	20.38–46 406	2.426–27 210
	20.97–98 193	2.433–34, 444 559
Jewish Antiquities	20.97–99 120	2.559–61 345
4.219 319	20.100 166	2.652 559
8.46–47 201	20.102 121	3.374–75 292
12.119, 147–53 339	20.105–12 121	4.130–61, 208–23 123
12.246–331 90	20.113–17 121	4.618 562
12.253 570	20.168 193	4.656–57 562
13.171–72 131	20.169–71 193	5.145 131
13.173 129	20.173–77 121	6.300–309 193
13.288, 296–98 125	20.185–77 121	6.312–15 . . . . 122, 224
13.297–98, 408 130	20.188 122	6.313 559
14.37–79 94	20.200 . . . . . 107, 341, 586, 744	7.29–31 559
14.115 164	20.200–203 731	7.252–406 123
14.158–60, 420–30 119	20.252–57 122	7.340 288
14.415–16 212		7.368 345
15.345–48 212	*Jewish War*	7.410 52
16.294 355	1.31–40 90	7.437–50 193
17.149–66 119	1.133–54 94	
17.206–18 119	1.648–55 119	*Life*
17.219–49, 299–323 119	1.650 . . . . 288, 292	12 125
17.250–64 119	1.204 119	27 345
17.269–70 119	2.1–13 119	28–30 125
17.271–72 119	2.39–50 119	191 125
17.273–77, 278–84 120	2.55 119	191–97 125
17.286–98 120	2.56 119	424–25 193
17.365 288	2.57–98 120	
18.4–10 120	2.60–65 120	**9. PHILO OF**
18.9–10 122	2.66–79 120	**ALEXANDRIA**
18.14 288	2.80–100 119	
18.15 125	2.118 . . . . 52, 120	*Against Flaccus*
18.16 . . . . 130, 286	2.119–61 131	83 317
18.17 . . . . 125, 130	2.122–27 631	
18.18–22 131	2.154–58 292	*De Abrahamo*
18.20–22 631	2.162 125	258 288
18.23–25 . . . . 120, 122	2.163 288	
18.23 . . . . 52, 197	2.164–65 129	*De Praemiis et Poenis*
18.55–59 100	2.165 . . . . 130, 286	95–96 226
18.60–62 100	2.169–74 100	164–69 140
18.63–64 196–97	2.175–77 100	
18.85–87 193	2.203 120	*De Sacrificiis Abelis et*
18.85–89 . . . . 100, 120	2.224–27 121	*Caini*
18.116 99	2.228–31 121	5 288
18.116–119 190	2.253 121	
18.141 166	2.254 121	*De Specialibus Legibus*
18.261 428	2.258–60 121	1.52 113
18.302–8 120	2.259 193	2.253 . . . . 125, 343
20.1–138 423	2.261–63 . . . . 121, 193	
20.5 120	2.264–65 121	*De Vita Contemplativa*
20.34–35 406	2.266–70 121	1 131

De Vita Mosis
1.149 378
1.290–91 226
2.20. 165

Hypothetica
11.1–8. 131
11.4–13. 631

Legum Allegoriae
1.108. 288
281 339
299–305. 572
299–306. 100

Legatio ad Gaium
118. 790
155 505
156–58 505
188 344
245 458
281 477

Quaestiones in Genenin
3.11 288

Quis Rerum Divinarum Heres Sit
68–70 288
276 288

Quod Omnis Probus Liber Sit
75–91 131
76–77, 85–87. 631

10. GRECO-ROMAN SOURCES

Aelian (Claudius Aelianus)

Historical Miscellany
2.19. 271

Aeschylus
Eumenides
6.47–48. 264

Aristotle
Nicomachean Ethics
9.8.2 631

Cicero
Academicae Quaestiones
1.4.15 158

Pro Flacco
28.68. 458

Dio Cassius
Historia Romana
6.16.4–5 453
37.15.2—16.4. 94
52.6.1–2 155
66.19.3 816
67.14 817
75.4.2—5.5. 272

Euripides
Alcestis
1144–46. 273

Iamblichus
Life of Pythagorus
6–29–30. 631

Juvenal
Satires
15.96–106. 410

Libanius
Epistle
37.1 703
245.9. 703

Pliny the Elder
Natural History
5.15.73 131

Pliny the Younger
Epistulai
9.21 466
10.96–7. . . . . 775, 817

Polybius
Histories
4.1 618

Porphyry
Life of Pythagorus
20 631

Plutarch
Moralia
219 271

Seneca the Younger
Moral Epistles
38 203
90.38. 631
104.1. 355

Suetonius
Divus Claudius
25.1–5. 714
25.2. 505
25.4. . . . . 355, 477

Domitianus
13.2. 815

Nero
33.1 355
57.2 816

Tiberius
35 488

Vespasianius
23 270

Strabo
Geographica
8.16.19–20a 477
12.8.16 456
14.5.131 339

Tacitus
Agricola
30 . . . . 142, 819

Annals
4.37.3 146
5.6. 247
12.54. 121
15.44. 365
13.1 453
14.27 456
15.44. 714

Histories
2.8. 816
5.5. 166

11. EARLY CHURCH FATHERS

Apostolic Fathers
Barnabas
15.4. 795

18–20 593	8.1–2...................... 661	3.2.11 739
	10.3...................... 587	
Didache	13.1–2.................... 873	**Irenaeus**
1—5 593		*Adversus Haeresis*
4.13...................... 697	*To the Philadelphians*	1.8.5 .... 653, 660
6.2....................... 584	6.1 .... 587, 661	1.9.2, 3................... 658
8.1....................... 584	7.1...................... 660	1.10.1–3 868
8.2...................326, 584	7.2...................... 534	1.11.4..................... 545
9.5....................... 584	8.2—9.2 661	1.16.3 .... 653, 813
10.6...................... 843		1.23.4 542
11.3–6.................... 738	*To the Romans*	1.24.2 792
11.7...................... 584	7.2...................... 660	1.24.4 793
13.1–2.................... 584		1.24.6 543
	To the Smyrneans	1.26.1 793
Epistle to Diognetus	1.1 584	1.26.3 653
3.4–5..................... 714	2.1 .... 661, 790	2.14.7 542
6.1....................... 882	3.1–3 .... 661, 790	2.22.5 ..653, 654, 658, 661, 816
6.3....................... 660	4.2 .... 661, 790	3.1–5..................... 874
7.5....................... 660	5.2 .... 661, 790	3.1.1....582, 608, 614, 653, 661,
10.2–3.................... 789	7.1 .... 661, 790	813
11.2–5.................... 660	12.2 .... 661, 790	3.1.1–2 557
11.4...................... 789		3.2.2...................... 873
	To the Trallians	3.3.1–4 873
1 Clement	2.2....................... 534	3.3.3 873
2.7....................... 541	10.1 .... 661, 790	3.3.4 ...... 452, 533, 654, 658,
5.6–7..................... 364		661, 792, 816
5.7....................... 364	**Martyrdom of Polycarp**	3.4.1 873
13.1–2.................... 699	20.2...................... 739	3.4.1–2 868
23.3...................... 765		3.5.1 .... 658, 873
36.1–5.................... 713	**Polycarp**	3.11.1.............. 542, 792, 813
42.1–2.................... 873	*To the Philippians*	3.11.8 .... 608, 813
46.7–8.................... 699	1.3....................... 760	3.11.9 658
60.4...................... 541	2.1–2..................... 760	3.12.1 542
61.2...................... 541	4.1....................... 541	3.13.3 608
	5.3....................... 760	3.14.1 .... 608, 613
2 Clement	7.1 .... 660, 789, 790	3.16.5 .... 653, 789, 813
11.2...................... 765	8.1....................... 760	3.16.8 .... 653, 789, 813
	10.2...................... 760	3.21.3 658
Ignatius		4.9.2 760
To the Ephesians	**Early Apologists and**	4.12.2 653
1.3....................... 468	**Theologians**	4.16.5 760
2.1....................... 468	**Clement of Alexandria**	4.17.6..................... 653
6.2....................... 468	*Paedagogus*	4.18.6 653
7.2 .... 661, 790	1.9.83 671	4.20.11 .... 653, 813
14.1...................... 541		4.21.3 653
20.1...................... 541	*Quis Dives Salvetur*	5.7.2 760
	42 .... 653, 661	5.23.2 765
To the Magnesians		5.30.1 654
6.2....................... 534	*Stromata*	5.30.3 814
7.1....................... 534	2.9.6 866	5.33.3 654
8.1 .... 541, 587	3.2.10 738–39	5.33.4 654

Justin Martyr

Dialogue with Trypho

10	410
16.4	586
47	693
61.1	660
81.4	813
88.7	660
96.2	586
100.4	682
101.3	682
102.5	682
103.6, 8	682
104.1	682
105.1	682
106.1, 3	682
107.1	682
108	325
123.9	789
137.2	586

First Apology

46.1–3	660
61.4	660
66.3	682
67.3	682

Origen

Commentary on John

6.2	653
6.2–3	660
28.54–56	725

Commentary on Matthew

15.14	860

Contra Celsum

2.27	860
5.41	154

Tertullian

Adversus Marcionem

3.10.1	270
3.14.3	813
3.24.4	813
4.2	649
4.5	814
5.21	541

Apology

32	428

De Carni Christi

24	795

De Praescriptione Haereticorum

36	365

On Baptism

17.4–5	530

On the Apparel of Women

1.3	752

Scorpiace

15.4	365

Later Major Writers

Athanasius

Festal Letters

39	871

Augustine

Christian Doctrine

1.36	73
2.82.12	874

City of God

20.19	428–29

Confessions

11.3.5	63

Faith and Works

21	707

Chrysostom

Homilies on Romans

16–19	587

Preface to the Homilies on Romans 337

Epiphanius

Panarian

51.1.3–6	814
51.3.1–6	653

Eusebius

Chronicle

210.4	456

Ecclesiastical History

1.7.14	731
1.13.10	737
2.1.2–5	731
2.1.5	731
2.6.6–7	100
2.15–1–2	557
2.22.1–7	364
2.22.2	364, 532
2.23.1–23	731
2.23.25	734
2.25.5	365, 757
2.25.6–7	365
2.25.8	365
3.1	452
3.1.2	757
3.3.1	764
3.4.2	761
3.4.6–8	608
3.5.3	584
3.11.1	731
3.17	817
3.18.1	818
3.18.5	817
3.19.1—3.20.7	732
3.20.8–9	818
3.20.9–10	817
3.23.1	653, 661, 818
3.23.2–4	816
3.23.6	818
3.24–25	826
3.24.5	653
3.24.5–13	655
3.24.6	582
3.24.11	653
3.24.11–13	649
3.25.1–7	871
3.25.2	737
3.25.2–3	788
3.25.3	734, 764
3.25.6	873
3.28.1–5	814
3.30.2	757
3.32.3–6	732
3.39.3–4	655, 657
3.39.3–6	787
3.39.4	657
3.39.4–6	814
3.39.6	653
3.39.12	816
3.39.14	657
3.39.15	557, 732
3.39.16	582, 760, 789

3.39.17 660	6.14.13 712	36.42. 813
4.14.9 760	6.25.3–14 870	
4.22.4 731	6.25.4 582	*Refutation of All Heresies*
4.22.5 543	6.25.8 764	7.22.4 660
5.8.2 582	6.25.10 788	7.27 660
5.8.2–8 870	6.25.12, 14 712	9.27.1–3 292
5.8.4 452	7.25 814	
5.10.3 582	7.25.2 814	**Jerome**
5.20.5–6 654	7.25.16–17 814	*De Viris Illustribus*
5.24.2 659	7.25.21 787	1 763
5.24.2–3 . . . . 659, 661		2 734
5.24.16 . . . . 653, 658	*Life of Constantine*	4 737
6.12.3 530	4.73 272	7 608
6.12.3–6 871		9.5 787
6.14.1–7 870	**Hippolytus**	
6.14.2–4 712	*De Antichristo*	*Epistle*
6.14.5–7 557	36 653	129.3 713

Subject Index

Aaron (priest), 135, 226, 715, 720, 728, 835
Abel, 722, 725, 799
Abraham (patriarch), 88, 138, 168, 189, 197, 201, 288, 304, 305, 360, 375, 377, 378, 380, 383, 385, 391, 397, 398, 408, 409, 410, 414, 483, 504, 510, 514, 516, 517, 518, 521, 555, 581, 589, 590, 617, 630, 667, 668, 669, 670, 683, 710, 711, 717, 720, 725, 727, 744, 746, 781, 812, 842, 879, 880, 882
Abrahamic covenant, 384, 409, 514, 517
Achilles, 267–68, 272, 273
Achtemeier, Paul, 759, 771
Acts, book of. *See* Luke-Acts
   earliest copies of the canonical gospels and Acts, 681
   genre of, 614–15
Acts of Andrew, 615, 817
Acts of Paul and Thecla, 530, 534
Acts of Peter, 615, 758, 872
Adam
   patriarch (first), 198, 221, 225, 280, 281, 291, 305, 311, 313, 378–79, 382, 391, 517, 518, 519, 617, 679, 812, 880
   final (second), 313, 494, 519
Adam–Christ typology, 518. *See also* Adam: final
Adams, Sean, 610
Adonis (Phoenician god), 275–77
adoption (to sonship, Abraham's family), 380, 397, 414, 504
adultery, 488, 583, 601, 669, 696, 775, 839
Aeneid (Virgil), 45, 150, 615
Aeschylus, 264, 265

Affective Fallacy, 69–70
afterlife. *See* chapter 18, "The Afterlife in Greek, Roman, and Jewish thought" (264–95); and 112, 130, 153, 160
   Greco-Roman views of the, 266–77
   Jewish views of the, 277–93
   the Old Testament on the, 278–86
   post-biblical literature on the, 286–91
agape, 73–74
Agrippa I. *See* Herod Agrippa I
Agrippa II. *See* Herod Agrippa II
Agrippina (mother of Nero), 453
Akiva ben Yosef. See Rabbi Akiba
Alcestis, myth of, 273
   Alexander, Loveday, 608
Alexander (Ephesian heretic), 544
Alexander the Great, 87, 88, 90, 91, 142, 159, 271, 339, 436, 445, 759
Allah, 794–95
Allison, Dale, 179, 230, 735
alms, 593, 631, 887
Al Qaeda, 827
amillennialism, 841
Ananias of Adiabene, 406
Ananias of Damascus, 634
Ananus ben-Ananus, 102
Andrew (disciple), 82, 592, 652, 657, 658, 659, 666
angel worship, 461
angels, 172, 225, 288, 293, 306, 318, 391, 460, 461, 534, 570, 622, 664, 666, 710, 715–17, 728, 737, 738, 750, 752, 753, 766, 775, 776, 779, 780, 794, 822, 834, 836, 837, 842, 851, 862

fallen, 836
God will judge rebellious, 780
Jesus greater than, 715–17, 728
Annals (Tacitus), 56
Annas (high priest), 341, 674
Antichrist, the, 419, 428, 429, 789, 798, 826
Antigonus II Mattathias. *See* Mattathias Antigonus
Antioch (Pisidian), 47, 146, 398, 399, 400, 402, 403, 414, 478, 547, 559, 637, 638
Antioch (Syrian), 79, 97, 164, 166, 342, 350, 351, 355, 356, 359, 363, 386, 398, 401, 405, 407, 503, 557, 584, 585, 608, 635, 636, 638, 641, 757
antinomianism, 706
Antiochus III, 87, 94, 146
Antiochus IV Epiphanes, 87, 90, 92, 93, 94, 106, 144, 265, 289, 428, 556
Antipas (martyr), 818
Antipater the Idumaean, 93, 96
antiquity (in determining sacredness of a work), 874
anti-semitism, 72
Antisthenes of Athens, 160
Antitheses (Marcion), 533, 873
Antoninus Pius (Roman emperor) and Faustina, sculpture, 271
Antonius Felix (Roman procurator). *See* Felix
apocalypse(s), 58, 68, 126, 290, 291, 293, 373, 412, 513, 555, 556, 653, 809, 821, 822, 824–25, 841
Apocalypse, The (motion picture), 815
Apocalypse of Abraham, 825
apocalypse of John, 702, 703, 704. *See* Revelation (book)
Apocalypse of Moses, 291
Apocalypse of Peter, 758, 765, 766, 793–94, 812, 869, 870, 871, 872
apocalypticism, 181, 823
'Apocalyptic Paul' branch of Pauline scholarship, 412, 413
apocalyptic worldview, 822
Apocrypha, 169
Apollo (deity), 93, 146, 265, 273, 455, 456, 457, 489, 491, 498, 836
Apollos (Jewish Christian), 356, 358, 474, 478–79, 480, 486, 494, 543, 641, 713
apologetics, 354, 610, 663, 782, 856
apostasy, 89, 428, 547, 725, 753
Apostolic Constitutions, 539
apostolic Fathers, 612, 759, 765
apostolicity, 610, 611, 873

Apostolikon (Marcion), 533, 541
apostolos, 702
apostleship, 303, 387, 495–96, 512, 546
Aquila and Priscilla (friends of Paul), 354, 355, 356, 359, 453, 477, 478, 482, 506, 508, 640, 641, 760
Aquila of Sinope, 168
Aramaic (language), 41, 110, 188, 221, 222–23, 225, 350, 494, 582, 601, 633, 666, 687, 735, 737, 740, 756, 843, 851
Aratus (Stoic philosopher), 340
Arch of Titus, 102, 712
Areopagus, 148, 265, 354, 640
Aretas IV (king), 99, 354, 355
Arian debates, 712
Aristion (philosopher), 657
aristocrats, the Sadducees, priests, and, 128–31
Aristotle, 45, 158, 159
Armenia, 144, 406
Arnold, Matthew, 332
arrogance, 37, 53, 55, 94, 290, 378, 738, 747, 779
Artemis (Greek goddess), 146, 151, 154, 155, 156, 356, 437, 453, 455–56, 457, 471, 544, 820
Ascension of Isaiah, 812
ascension of Jesus, 78, 218, 326, 327, 329, 371, 372, 570, 605, 613, 614, 627–28, 698, 708, 718, 727, 728
asceticism, 461, 465, 541, 542, 545
Asclepius (Greek deity), 146, 270
Asia Minor, 88, 89, 90, 94, 142, 144, 167, 339, 351, 352, 353, 357, 399, 417, 436, 437, 438, 439, 452, 454, 456, 458, 469, 586, 636, 639, 705, 736, 757, 758, 760, 761, 762, 764, 767, 771, 774, 77, 785, 787, 814, 817, 818, 819, 820, 828, 837, 868
Assumption of Moses, 751–52
assurance, 201, 281, 425, 517, 677, 705, 706, 725, 781, 786, 797, 799, 800, 801
Assyria, 563, 777
Assyrian conquest, 164
Assyrians, 203
Athanasius, 730, 871, 872
atheism, 64, 177, 817
Athenagoras (church father), 540
Athens, 45, 97, 151, 154, 158, 159, 276, 339, 354, 355, 418, 440, 452, 640
Athronges (Jewish insurrectionist), 119–20
atonement, 76, 116, 252, 254, 257, 516, 713, 717, 721, 722, 728, 784, 801, 806, 878, 883
  1 John's message of, 796–97
  'trading places' theory of the, 793

Augustine of Hippo, 63, 67, 73, 428–29, 503, 707, 708, 712–13, 887
Augustus (emperor, aka Octavian), 52, 97, 98–99, 106, 145, 146, 149, 155, 185, 271, 272, 339, 349, 402, 436, 447, 453, 455, 456, 493, 505, 562, 617, 815, 820
Aune, 814, 824, 825
Ausgangstext, 854
Australia, 153, 457
authorial intent(ion), 60–65, 71, 73
'autograph', the problem with pursuing an, 854
Azotus, 634

Babbius Philinus (aedile of Corinth), 478
Babel, 55, 332, 378, 842
Baby Boomers, 782
Babylon, 87, 94, 109, 130, 164, 203, 221, 224, 278, 353, 377, 556, *741*, 757, 760, 777, 812, 819, 821, 838–39, 842, 844, 880
Babylonian exile(s), 87–88, 134, 137, 139, 140, 164, 203, 204, 208, 233, 511, 521, 563, 589, 880
  route of returning exiles (map), 89
Babylonian period, 87
Babylonian Talmud, 248, 250
Babylonians, 87, 198
Bach, J. S., 178, 711
Balaam, 738, 752, 780
Balkans, 94, 142, 399, 417
baptism (water), 114, 157, 191, 192, 257, 302–3, 306, 308, 311, 315, 491, 517, 518, 556, 563, 568, 571, 573, 584, 590, 592, 688, 776, 792–93, 800, 801, 886, 887
  for the dead, 475, 493
  the meaning of, 302–3, 886
Barabbas (brigand), 100, 249, 572, 599, 625, 675
barbarians, 165, 380, 512, 526
Bar-Jesus (Elymas the sorcerer), 636
Bar-Kochba revolt, 86, 106, 124
Barnabas (companion of Paul), 47, 350, 351, 352, 363, 401, 405, 406, 407, 557, 610, 611, 634, 635, 636–39, 645, 713
Barrett, C. K., 610, 616
Barth, Karl, 179–80, 377, 503, 885
Bartimaeus, 228, 568, 560
Baruch (book), 168
Baruch (person), 812
Basilica of St John (photos), 757, 802, 807
Basilides (Gnostic teacher), 543, 793
Bauckham, Richard, 319, 557, 764–65, 778, 808, 844

Battle of Actium, 97, 145, 436
Beale, Greg K., 825, 837
beast(s), 221, 223, 224, 281, 311, 347, 356, 379, 439, 495, 534, 624, 798, 816, 821, 829, 835–41, 844
Beelzebul (ancient deity), 201, 565
believers' attitudes and posture, characteristics of, 773
beloved disciple, 66, 328, 329, 652–66, 659–60, 674, 675, 677, 685, 695
bēma seat (judgment seat), 477, 497
Benedict XVI (pope), 183
Bengel, J. A., 646
ben-Gurion, Joseph, 102
Bethany, 251, 568, 598, 621, 628, 656, 672, 685
Bethsaida, 567, 756, 759
Betz, Hans Dieter (H. D.), 67, 404
Betz, Otto, 180
Ben-Sirach, Jesus (Ben Sira), 45, 137, 233, 287, 536. See also Ecclesiasticus; *Sirach* (book)
Bernice (sister of Agrippa II), 97, 101, 361
Bhatti, Shahbaz (Pakistani politician), 256
Bible, historical stages in the production of a modern English, 852
Bibles, books included in various, 168
biblical canons of the major ancient Christian churches, 168
biblical prophecy, 426, 779, 821, 828
Bithynia, 146, 339, 352, 353, 399, 639, 760, 767, 770, 774
blasphemy, 52, 238, 239, 572, 594, 779, 821
Blount, Brian, 373, 840
Bockmuehl, Markus, 48, 79, 80, 609
body
  as temple of the holy spirit, 488
  resurrection of the. See under resurrection
Bonhoeffer, Dietrich, 206
'book of glory' (in John), 672–77
'book of signs' (in John), 665–72
Book of Watchers, 752, 836
books
  disputed, 734, 764, 788, 871
  four criteria to determine the approved register, 873–74
  heretical, 765, 871
  included in various Bibles, 168
  spurious, 871
Borman, Lukas, 437
Bornkamm, Günther, 181
Bovon, François, 610
bowls of judgment (Revelation), 829, 837–38

Subject Index 961

bridegroom, 256, 564
bride of the Lamb, 840, 842, 843
Britain, 145, 180, 399
Brown, Dan, 867
Brown, Ford Madox, 672
Brown, Jeannine, 592
Brown, Raymond E., 659
Bruce, F. F., 467
Brutus (assassin of Julius Caesar), 145, 436
Buddhism, 295
Bultmann, Rudolf, 64, 77, 80, 179–80, 682, 697, 699
Burkitt, F. C., 180, 582
business, the church's, 645
Byrskog, Samuel, 697
Byzantine era, 456

Cabirus cult, 423
Cadbury, Henry, 613
Caesarea Maritima, 89, 101, 339
Caesarea Philippi, 97, 99, 175, 217, 556, 567, 596, 688
Caiaphas (high priest), 106, 230, 238, 239, 248, 309, 556, 571, 572, 599, 652, 671, 674
Cain, 738, 752, 799
Caird, George, 50, 173, 810
Caligula (aka Gaius in text), 99, 100, 101, 106, 120, 344, 355, 363, 428, 505, 558, 815
Callahan, A. D., 828–29
Callistus I (bishop of Rome), 149
Calvin, John, 377, 713, 761, 826
Campbell, Douglas, 413, 454, 458, 532, 533, 610
Campenhausen, Hans von, 533
canon
    derivation of the word, 866, 868
    how we got the New Testament, 866–75
    lists from the fourth century, 871
    'scripture' versus,
    two erroneous views regarding the shaping of the New Testament, 866–67
canons, 168, 169, 863, 867, 869. *See also* Muratorian canon
Capernaum, 89, 200, 205, 227, 392, 564, 565, 585, 619, 620
captivity letters of Paul, 356–57, 362, 439
Carlson, Stephen, 856
Carpocrates of Alexandria, 543, 739
Carpocratians, 738–39
Carson, D. A. 25, 102
Carthage, 144, 618
Carthaginians, 94

Cassander (Macedonian general), 417
Cassius (assassin of Julius Caesar), 145, 436
Cassius Dio, 272
Catholic Church, 538–39
Catholic Epistles, 613, 702–8, 730, 858, 863
    Augustine on, 707
    the canonical function of the, 705–7
    common themes of the, 707–8
    earliest copies of the, 704
    focus of the, 708
Catholicism, 348, 533, 536, 538, 615, 697, 749
catholicity, 874
Catholics, 867
celibacy, 431, 475, 479
Celsus (Greek philosopher), 153–54, 859–60
Cenchreae, 356, 360, 506
Cephas. *See* Peter
Cerinthus (Gnostic), 542, 543, 653, 792, 814, 825
Cestius Gallus (governor of Syria), 102
Chae, Young, 597
Charlesworth, James, 656
Chatman, Seymour, 65
Chaucer, Geoffrey, 110
Chen, Diane, 621, 624
Chester Beatty Papyrus II. *See* 𝔓[46]
Chesterton, G. K., 333
chiasm, 520
childbearing, 61, 116, 304
children of God, 671, 678, 707, 784, 798–99, 802, 805, 806–7
chiliasm, 841
Chonai (town), 456
Chloe (early Christian woman), 355, 482
Christian noblewomen, the dilemma of, 149
christology, 220, 372, 374, 375, 377, 447, 458, 536, 542, 560, 579, 610, 611, 613, 619, 651, 660, 662, 728, 732, 763, 790–91, 800, 803, 856, 871
Christians
    correspondence between Pliny and Trajan about, 774–75
    first use of the designation, 635
Christian living, 301, 302, 307, 311, 314, 315, 886
Christian theology, the originator of, 337
Christ 'poem,' 443
chronology
    Pauline
        external evidence of, 355
        sketch of, 363
    of Roman emperors and prefects, 106–7

Chrysostom, John, 525, 587
    on the apostle Paul, 337
    on the resurrection, 331
church. *See also* churches
    business of the, 645
    early. *See* early church
    family metaphor for the, 113–14
    in Jerusalem. *See* Jerusalem church
    mission of the Antiochene, 636–38
    Paul's great hope for the, 470
    Paul's persecution of the, 341–44, 634
    as a teaching community, 548–49
Church of the Holy Sepulchre, 243, 246
churches
    biblical canons of the major ancient Christian, 168
    of Revelation, 704, 808, 811, 818–19, 821, 827, 828, 830–33
    Three-Self (China), 844
    western, 782, 851
Chuza (household manager to Herod Antipas), 112
Ciampa, Roy E., 477
Cicero, 45, 46, 153, 156, 158, 159, 458
Cilicia, 339–40, 350, 352, 399, 405, 594, 634, 639
circumcision, 106, 166, 300, 304, 351, 380, 387, 396, 397, 401–2, 403, 405, 406, 410, 411, 444, 461, 483, 542, 697, 735, 745, 746, 757, 761
Ciseri, Antonio, paintings by, 291, 674
citizenship, 300, 340, 361, 447, 464, 505, 642
Claudius (emperor), 99, 101, 106, 107, 148, 272, 349, 354, 355, 359, 363, 477, 505, 508, 523, 640, 714, 760–61, 815
Clemens, Flavius, 817
Clement of Alexandria, 159, 540, 670, 671, 712, 713, 738–39, 740, 752, 754, 765, 768, 870, 872
Clement I (bishop of Rome), 359, 362, 442, 539, 542, 704, 713
Cleopatra, 97, 145
Clopas, 675, 731
Codex Alexandrinus, 167, 322, 824, 855, 872
Codex Bezae, 613
Codex Sinaiticus, 167, 322, 469, 824, 848, 855, 864, 872
Codex Vaticanus, 167, 322, 469, 704, 716, 730, 855, 857, 872
co-habiting issue in the Corinthian church, 487
Coherence Based Genealogical Method (CBGM), 858
Cohick, Lynn, 149, 471

Collection, the (for the Jerusalem church), 349, 352, 358–60, 454, 475, 479, 484, 494, 497–98, 506, 509, 524
Colosseum (pictured), 526
Comforter, 650. *See* holy spirit
commandment, the greatest, 569, 598
community, life in, 748–49
Constantine (emperor), 246, 272, 390, 826, 841, 866
Colossae, 356, 357, 366, 439, 451, 452, 453, 454, 456–57, 458, 460, 463, 833
Colossians, 461, 463–65
    the argument of, 461, 463–65
    and Ephesians, authorship of, 458–59
confession (of Jesus as Messiah), Peter's, 567, 594, 596, 688
Corinth, 146, 148, 149, 288, 310, 349, 354–60, 362, 363, 400, 418, 420, 423, 435, 454, 459, 474–83, 487, 488, 489, 491, 493, 496, 497, 499, 506, 507, 532, 548, 559, 640, 641, 757
    the problem in the churches at, 480–81
    social stratification of persons in, 482
    two short reflections on Paul's correspondence with, 499–500
Corinthians, the social location of the, 481–82
Cornelius, 635, 638
'Council of Javneh' Myth, 104
Council of Jamnia (Synod of Jamnia in text), 660
Council of Laodicea, 730
counter-Reformation, 594, 744
Crete, 361, 532, 537, 538, 542, 543, 548–49, 550
Crispus (synagogue leader), 355, 482
critical realism, 54–55, 58
cross
    the folly of the, 486
    'riddles of the,' 256–58
    the symbol and the means of the victory of God, 171
    the titulus on Christ's, 230
Crossan, John Dominic, 179, 192
crucifixion. *See* chapter 11, "The Death of the Messiah" (242–61); and *84*, 106, 115, 317, 323, 329, 363, 375, 381, 393, 423, 554, 561, 571, 572, *573*, 575, 586, 596, 598, 599, 642, 652, 666, 673, 675, 762, 773, *776*, 790, 792, 794, 800, 801
cult of the *theos hypsistos*, 144
Cuspius Fadus (Roman procurator), 106, 120
Cynics, 160

Subject Index 963

Cyprus, 107, 148, 350, 352, 363, 557, 635, 636, 639, 642
Cyrus (Persian king), 87, 88, 233

Damascus Document, 127
Damis (the Spartan), 271
Daniel (prophet), 213, 221, 223, 285, 391, 428, 825, 836
Darwinism, 72
David (king), 47, 118, 140, 193, 208, 217, 220, 225, 226, 228, 229, 230, 231, 238, 303, 346, 560, 564, 568, 569, 571, 573, 576, 589, 591, 597, 600, 614, 623, 682, 683, 717, 721, 732, 833, 880
Davids, Peter, 734, 735
Da Vinci Code (Brown), 867
Day of Atonement, 202, 721, 723
day of the lord, 325, 355, 389, 393, 419, 427, 430, 780
  explanation for the delay of the, 780
Dead Sea, 108, 109, 118, 132, 234, 339
Dead Sea Scrolls, 46, 117, 118, 132–34, 136, 185, 228, 236, 324, 575, 588, 721, 753
death
  future defeat of, 494
  of James, brother of John (son of Zebedee), 99, 106, 341
  of James, brother of Jesus, 341
  of John the Baptist, 568
  of Jesus. *See* chapter 11, "The Death of the Messiah" (242–61); crucifixion
  life after. *See* chapter 18, "The Afterlife in Greek, Roman, and Jewish Thought" (264–95); resurrection: of the body
  of Paul the apostle, 364–65
'Death of the Author,' 62
Decalogue, 318, 743, 744
Decapolis, 109, 558, 559, 567, 584, 621, 740
deceivers, 779, 786, 787, 789, 791, 801, 803
Demetrius (of the Johannine letters), 786, 795, 805
Demetrius the silversmith, 156, 356
Deism, 177, 232, 371, 412
demoniac, 201, 356, 621, 641
demons, 157, 201, 219, 491, 566, 568, 574, 595, 621, 688, 794
Demosthenes (Greek orator), 423
denarius, 52, 53
Derbe, 352, 399, 400, 638
Derrida, Jacques, 332
deSilva, David, 752, 782, 817, 819–20
destruction/fall of Jerusalem (AD 70), 105, 193, 213, 224, 363, 511, 556, 561, 572, 584–85, 587, 597, 599, *712*, 826
devil, 469, 592, 594, 717, 747, 748, 750, 799. *See also* satan
Diaspora (or, dispersion), 87, 105, 112, 142, 143, 164–67, 203, 210, 251, 340, 353, 377, 406, 562, 608, 615, 703, 736, 740, 741, 749, 759, 761, 762, 777, 781, 813
Didache, 584, 738, 871, 872, 874
Didascalia, 539
Dillistone, F. W., 25
Diogenes Laertius, 615
Diogenes of Sinope, 45, 46, 160, 480–81
Dionisius (painter), 257
Dionysius of Alexandria, 814, 826
Dionysius the Areopagite (of Athens), 148, 531, 640
Dioscorides, 618
Diotrephes (opponent of John the elder), 785, 786, 787, 795, 804–5
disciple, the beloved, 66, 328, 329, 652–66, 659–60, 674, 675, 677, 685, 695
disciples, the mark of authentic, 806
discipleship, 51, 174, 176, 178, 265, 330, 432, 443, 525, 559, 560, 568, 576, 578, 589, 593, 597, 601, 613, 621, 644, 648, 651, 679, 706, 733, 754, 884
'discourse,' Chatman's differentiation between 'story' and, 65
disobedience, 343, 382, 408, 519, 633, 718
dispersion. *See* Diaspora
disputed books/writings (*antilegomena*), 734, 764, 788, 871
divorce, 99, 113, 488, 568, 583, 591, 622, 695, 696
Docetism, 180, 615, 661, 662, 787, 791–95, 799
Dodd, C. H., 25, 27, 180
Domitilla, Flavia, 817
Domitian (emperor), 107, 661, 732, 758, 814–18, 837
Donaldson, Terence, 592
'Dover Beach' (Arnold), 332
dragon, 61, 810, 835, 836–37
Duke papyrus, 167
Dunn, James D. G., 467, 507, 534–35, 600, 610, 655, 734, 759, 761, 769, 817

early Catholicism, 348, 533, 536, 538, 615, 697, 749
early church. *See in general* part 2, "The World of Jesus and the Early Church" (85–170); 172, 180, 181, 183, 185, 189,

193, 195, 218, 219, 222–23, 227, 230, 232, 239, 245, 248, 257, 297, 303, 316, 321, 327, 330, 348, 416, 475, 538, 554, 557, 560, 575, 578, 581, 582, 607, 614, 645, 649, 655, 683, 684, 687, 694, 695, 697, 699, 728, 732, 733, 734, 756–59, 786, 814, 819, 841, 849, 851, 867, 869, 873, 875, 889.
four elements in early church life, 327
Greco-Roman context of the. *See* chapter 7, "The Greco-Roman Context of the Early Church" (142–69)
Luke's story of the, 628–33
Paul's persecution of the, 341–44, 634
Paul's significance for the, 337–38
earthquakes, 438, 456, 570, 600, 639
Easter. *See* chapter 13, "The Story of Easter according to the Apostle Paul" (296–315); and chapter 14, "The Story of Easter according to the Evangelists" (316–33); 173, 180, 185, 219, 227, 263, 553, 579, 671, 676, 699
the origins of, 317–21
Ebionism, 460
Ebionites, 769
Ecclesiasticus, 286. *See* Sirach (book)
ecclesiology, 662, 806, 885
Ecclesius (bishop), 422
Echoes of Scripture in the Gospels (Hays), 550
economic scales for urban contexts in the Greco-Roman world, 147
Editio Critica Maior (ECM), 858, 863
Edwards, Dennis, 781
Egypt, 58, 88–90, 93, 103, 107, 109, 138, 142, 144, 145, 154, 167, 252, 253, 255, 269, 287, 335, 376, 409, 437, 491, 534, 563, 590, 592, 599, 650, 661, 740, 750, 768, 826, 837, 855, 861, 886
Egyptian (Ptolemaic) period, 87
Egyptian, the (revolt leader), 121, 193
Egyptians, 58, 87, 154, 834
'Eighteen Benedictions,' 104, 585
'elder,' the, 786–87, 795, 803–5
'elder' and 'deacon', offices of, 533–34. *See* overseers and deacons
Eleazar ben Hanania (or, ben Ananias), 102, 243
election, 66, 138, 203, 370, 371, 374, 377, 379–80, 381, 384, 386, 387, 402, 663, 664, 706, 758, 761, 778, 781, 782–83
Elephantine (Egypt), 93
Eleven, the, 319, 600, 626, 627

Elijah (prophet), 122, 194–95, 197, 200, 213, 217, 265, 343, 350, 405, 567, 568, 594, 596, 606, 666, 735, 748
Elisha (prophet), 195, 200, 556
Elliott, John H., 761
Elymas (or Bar-Jesus), 636
Emmaus road, 331–32
emperors and prefects, chronology of Roman, 106–7
end times, 416, 808, 825
endurance, 422, 547, 548, 707, 714, 724–25, 741, 747–48, 797–98, 811, 818, 831, 836, 845
enmity and friendship, James's exhortation on, 743–47
Enoch (patriarch), 224, 225, 265, 530, 752, 812
Enlightenment, 53, 54, 79, 160, 177, 232
Epaphras (evangelist), 453, 463,
Epaphroditus, 435, 440, 442, 444, 619
Ephesians
the argument of, 469–71
authorship of Colossians and, 458–59
Ephesus, 66, 151, 154, 156, 159, 190, 302, 308, 311, 352, 355–59, 362, 363, 366, 368, 389, 400, 434, 439, 450–55, 468–69, 470, 478, 479, 485, 495, 532, 533, 537, 538, 542–47, 559, 607, 641, 642, 653, 658–59, 661, 684, 785, 792, 803, 807, 811, 817, 818
Epictetus, 160, 736
Epicureanism, 159–60, 311, 882
Epicureans, 766
Epicurus, 159–60
Epimenides (Greek philosopher-poet), 340
epistemology, 50, 78
Epistle of Aristeas, 154, 167
Epistle to Diognetus, 660, 714, 789, 882
Epistle of Enoch, 768
Epistle of Jeremiah, 530
Epistula Apostolorum (pseudo-apostolic work), 656
Erastus (city treasurer of Corinth), 148, 481, 482
eschatology, 66, 125, 180, 203, 224, 301, 315, 329, 370, 371, 377, 379, 480, 488, 523, 536, 540, 542, 571, 767, 781, 783, 813, 878, 884, 885
how Paul reworked the ancient Jewish, 387–93
part of the point of Jewish, 683
of the Qumranites, 134–36
Essenes, 122, 131–32, 198, 292, 341, 631
Essenism, 460

Subject Index 965

ethics, 80, 158, 163, 165, 180, 206, 413, 467, 538, 616, 746, 758, 767, 781, 868
Ethiopian Orthodox Church, 169
ethos, 67, 68
Eumenides (play), 265
Euripides, 89, 161, 273, 340
European Union, 827
Eusebius, 106, 272, 364–65, 456, 582, 608, 653, 655, 657, 658, 731–32, 734, 737, 760, 761, 764, 787, 789, 814, 816, 817, 871
evangelium, 702
End of Evil, the, 839–40
exaltation and enthronement of Christ. *See under* Jesus
exile (Babylonian). *See* Babylonian exile(s)
exodus, the, 92, 138–39, 190, 252, 253, 255, 373, 375, 376, 378, 392, 413, 491, 517, 668, 750, 813, 834
exorcisms, 189, 202, 213, 228, 229, 352, 356, 438, 560, 564, 565, 594, 619, 641, 649, 688
exorcists, 201, 202
eye-witness(es), 272, 318–19, 581, 610–11, 653, 659, 694, 697, 699, 779, 791, 812
Ezekiel (prophet), 194, 220, 233, 240, 285, 287, 645, 669, 837

'faith' and 'works', James and Paul on, 746
faithfulness, 592, 754, 773, 788, 804, 832
  call to (in Hebrews), 724–26, 728
  of God. *See* God: faithfulness
  Job's, 748
  Paul's, 529
fall/destruction of Jerusalem (AD 70). *See under* Jerusalem
fallen angels, 836. *See also* 'Watchers'
false prophets, 121, 559, 739, 765, 766, 779, 791
false teachers, 460, 542, 543, 733, 752, 754, 765, 766, 769, 779–80, 803, 819
false teaching, 460, 537, 541, 542, 545, 547, 548, 549, 754, 755, 786, 803, 829, 832
family, ancient versus modern and Western perceptions of kinship and, 113
Farrer, Austin, 692
fasting, 564, 593, 697
favouritism, 743–44
feast of Pentecost, 119, 506
Feast of Tabernacles, 659, 668, 669
Felix (Marcus Antonius Felix, Roman procurator), 106, 121–22, 148, 642
fellowship, 117, 118, 178. 189, 206, 208, 327, 350, 367, 386, 393, 398, 401, 402, 407,

434, 447, 466, 469, 499, 503, 510, 524, 526, 629, 654, 673, 707, 745, 786, 788, 796, 797, 798, 833, 887
Festal Letter (Athanasius), 730, 871
Festus (Roman procurator). *See* Porcius Festus
fig tree, 606, 622, 569, 570
firstborn, explanation of Jesus as the, 462–63
1 Clement, 364, 541, 713, 736, 760, 765, 869, 872, 874
1 Corinthians. *See in general* chapter 21, "1 and 2 Corinthians" (474–501)
  the argument of, 485–94
  examples of the Jesus-tradition in, 696
  Paul's step-by-step argument for the resurrection in, 308–14
1 Enoch, 168, 169, 179, 222, 225, 293, 531, 555, 664–65, 737, 740, 751–52, 753, 768, 836
firstfruits, 732–33, 741
First Jewish-Roman War. *See* Roman-Jewish war
1 John
  the argument of, 796–802
  genre and purpose of, 795
1 Maccabees, 168
1 Peter. *See in general* chapter 32, "Petrine Letters: 1 and 2 Peter"; 43
  the argument of, 770–77
  audience of, 761–61
  date of, 760
  genre and purpose of, 762–63
  origins of, 758–60
  signs of Paulinism in, 758
1 Thessalonians
  the argument of, 422–26
  clarifications about the lord's return in, 424–25
1 Timothy
  the argument of, 543–46
Fisk, Bruce, 184
Fitzmyer, Joseph, 503, 608
flood, the great, 780
Florus (Roman governor). *See* Gessius Florus
food
  laws, 401, 461, 509, 566
  sacrificed to idols, 358, 479, 489–90, 819
forgiveness of sins, 191, 199, 213, 252, 253, 254, 255, 302, 333, 386, 450, 563, 578, 599, 602, 605, 629, 718, 721
Foster, Paul, 420, 421
Foucault, Michel, 332
Four Books of Timothy to the Church, The (Salvia), 531

966 The New Testament in Its World

'four-source' theory, 689, 690, 691
4 Ezra, 104, 168, 179, 222, 379, 511, 555, 585, 819, 825
4 Maccabees, 168
Fourth Philosophy (Judas the Galilean), 122, 197–98
Fragments (Reimarus), 177
France, 143, 153, 377, 399, 609, 627, 887
Fredriksen, Paula, 413
freedmen, 133, 147, 148, 339, 476
freedom, true meaning and practice of Christian, 490
friendship, James's exhortation on enmity and, 746–47
Freud, Sigmund, 332, 882
Frey, Jorg, 764, 766

Gabler, J. P., 77
Gaius (benefactor to Paul), 482
Gaius (Roman presbyter), 814
Gaius Caesar. *See* Caligula
Gaius of Ephesus (addressee of 3 John), 785, 786, 787, 795, 804, 805
Gaius Maecenas, 155
Galatia, 146, 350, 351, 352, 356, 363, 398–400, 403, 405, 406, 440, 444, 465, 478, 636, 639, 641, 760, 767, 770. *See in general* chapter 17, "Galatians" (396–415)
Galatians, book of. *See in general* chapter 17, "Galatians" (396–415)
  addressees of the letter, on identifying, 399–400
  the argument of, 403–11
  dating, 400
  the origin of, 405
  the reason for writing, 404–5
  the rhetoric of, 404
  the situation in, 400–403
Galba (emperor), 103, 107, 562, 815
Galen (of Pergamon), 530, 534
Galilee, 93, 96, 97, 98, 99, 108, 109, 110, 111, 117, 119, 122, 124, 125, 173, 188, 189, 190, 191, 231, 242, 318, 319, 323, 324, 327, 329, 344, 406, 559, 564, 566, 576, 584, 587, 592, 595, 597, 599, 600, 621, 635, 649, 654, 668, 686, 699, 731, 737, 782
Gallio (Roman proconsul), 106, 148, 349, 354, 355, 357, 477–78, 497, 640
Gamaliel (the Elder, rabbi), 126, 137, 632–33
Gaul, 99, 144, 399, 545
Gauls, 399, 400

Gaventa, Beverly, 427, 511, 641
Gaza, 109
General Epistles, 702, 705. *See* Catholic Epistles
Geneva Bible, 843–45
Gentile Christians, 403, 407, 412, 482, 508, 510, 520, 523, 745, 767
gentiles, 53, 62, 79, 109, 110, 117, 122, 140, 161, 164, 166, 168, 203, 208, 226, 306–7, 342, 345, 346, 347, 350–51, 353–54, 359, 361–62, 379, 380, 381, 382, 386, 393, 396, 397, 400, 401, 402, 405, 406, 407, 411, 412, 440, 452, 467, 469, 471, 504, 508, 509, 512, 514, 515, 516, 520, 521, 522, 524, 534, 557, 566, 567, 579, 584, 586, 591, 593, 606, 607, 612, 635, 637, 638, 640, 642, 645, 712, 725, 745, 758, 761, 770, 772, 835
  coheirs with Jews, 471
  God's people among the, 772–76
  unity of Jews and, 469–70
Gen-Xers, 782
George III (king), 867
Gerhardsson, Birger, 697
Gessius Florus (Roman governor), 101, 107, 122
Gilmour, Michael J., 764
Gnosticism, 162–63, 460, 480, 533, 542, 615, 634, 662, 740
Gnostics, 162, 482, 543, 610–11, 766
God
  faithfulness (God's/Christ's), 139, 280, 281, 282, 285, 289, 300, 304, 305, 344, 375, 382, 383, 385, 396, 397, 407, 408, 412, 413, 429, 496, 502, 503, 513, 514–15, 520–22
  God's plan in Israel's history, 521
  love of. *See* God's love
  righteousness of, 136, 474, 304, 503, 504, 510, 511–13, 515, 516, 522, 524
  the ultimate test for being born of, 800
  victory of, 171, 259–61
god, on becoming a, 270–72, 778
gods, dying and rising, 275–77
God's love (*or*, "love of God" in text), 43, 45, 73, 115, 127, 306, 499, 503, 517, 651, 280, 378, 504, 520, 602, 651, 667, 701, 706, 749, 753, 755, 784, 785, 786, 790, 795, 797, 798, 800, 803
Goldingay, John, 63
Golgotha, location of, 243–44
good shepherd, 669, 670, 671, 678
good works, 206, 301, 515, 549, 707

gospel
- ancient usages of the word, 562
- meaning of word, 562
- spread of, to Samaria, Ethiopia, and Syria, 634

Gospel of the Egyptians, 872

Gospel of Peter, 530, 758, 869, 871

Gospels. *See in general* chapter 14, "The Story of Easter according to the Evangelists" (316–33); part 4, "The Gospels and the Story of God" (553–700)
- earliest copies of Acts and the canonical gospels, 681
- the genre of the, 681–84
- the making of the. *See* chapter 28, "The Making of the Gospels" (680–99)

Gospel of Thomas, 181–82, 530, 543, 689, 690, 693, 869, 871

graves of Peter and Paul, 365

Great Commission, 583, 600, 601–2, 676

Greco-Roman philosophy, 158–64

Greco-Roman religion, 152–58

Greece, 26, 88, 94, 109, 140, 144, 146, 150, 158, 159, 160, 221, 271, 322, 341, 351, 353, 354, 357, 359, 360, 363, 399, 417, 436, 437, 454, 476–79, 485, 506, 538, 548, 618, 641, 741

greed, 127, 212, 747

Greek (language)
- of 1 Peter, 758, 759
- of James, 734, 735
- of Jude, 737
- of Mark, 554, 688
- of Matthew, 582, 688
- of Luke, 605, 688
- of the Pastoral Epistles, 531–32
- of Revelation, 814
- of 2 Peter, 763

Greek Bible, 851, 168, 169. *See* Septuagint

Greek mythology, 270

Greek New Testament, 25, 168, 801, 850, 852, 856–57, 860, 862–64

Greek New Testament Produced at Tyndale (THGNT), 864

Greek philosophy, 163, 671, 713

Greeks, 45, 58, 143, 158, 165, 196, 286, 292, 380, 400, 410, 512, 526, 562, 618, 619, 672, 678

Green, Gene, 754–55, 766

Green, Joel, 614

Grieb, A. Katherine, 526

grudges, 877

Grünstäudl, Wolfgang, 766

Gupta, Nijay, 432

Guthrie, George, 485

Haas, Peter, 72

Hades, 130, 153, 267–69, 273, 274, 277, 286–87, 289, 294, 331, 626, 775

Hadrian (emperor), 106, 107, 144, 477, 815, 816

Haenchen, Ernst, 610

Hagar, 409, 410

halakhah (oral teaching of the Pharisees and rabbis), 116, 566, 586

handwashing, 566

Hanhart, Robert, 167

Hanukkah, 92, 659, 670

hapax legomena, 764

Harnack, Adolf von, 177, 179, 713

harpagmos, on the translation of, 444–45

Harris, Richard, 815

Harvey, A. E., 601

Hasidim, 93

Hasmonean dynasty/kingdom, 87, 92, 93, 95, 118, 132, 670

Hasmoneans, 92, 130, 133

haughtiness, the best response to heresy and, 785

Hays, Richard, 64, 480, 550, 556–57, 565–66

head coverings, 475, 491

healings by Jesus. *See under* Jesus

heaven, 39, 41, 42, 43, 46, 78, 79, 81, 92, 124, 126, 138, 141, 154, 158, 172, 186, 199, 207, 213, 220, 221, 231, 232, 238, 239, 242, 243, 245, 254, 264, 265, 266, 272, 282, 288, 289, 290, 295, 297, 298, 300, 302, 309, 313, 321, 326, 331, 372, 376, 389, 391, 416, 426, 443, 446, 447, 448, 450, 469, 472, 475, 494, 512, 563, 568, 570, 571, 578, 591, 592, 593, 594, 595, 599, 600, 601, 607, 621, 625–26, 628, 629, 633, 652, 663, 664, 665, 666, 670, 675, 683, 691, 697, 699, 703, 715, 718, 723, 721, 728, 731, 738, 750, 770, 776, 792, 794, 801, 809, 810, 811, 822–23, 829, 830, 833, 834, 836, 838, 839, 840, 842, 862, 875, 878, 882, 885–86, 887. *See also* new heavens and new earth

'heavenly' life, what is meant by the, 465

Hebrews, book of. *See in general* chapter 30, "The Letter to the Hebrews" (710–29)
- the argument of, 715–18, 720–27
- authorship of, 711–13
- date, 713–14
- genre, 714

purpose, 714
three principal things the book contributes to the tapestry of Christian thought, 728–29
warning passages in Hebrews, 725
hedonism, 295, 755, 888
Hegel, G. W. F., 177
Hegesippus, 540, 543, 732
hell, 331. See Hades; Sheol
Hellenism, 93, 144, 166, 604
hellenistic culture and the Roman Empire, 142–47
hellenistic Jews. See under Jews
hellenization, three instruments of, 143–44
hell-fire preaching, 181
Hengel, Martin, 183, 580, 658, 816
Heracleon (Gnostic), 540, 653
Hercules, 146, 150, 264, 265, 266, 270, 271, 273
heresy, 137, 341, 460, 533, 545, 767, 785, 791
heretical books, 765, 871
heretics, curse on, 104, 585
hermeneutics, 60, 72, 699, 728
Hermes, 286, 637
Herod II. See Herod Philip
Herod Agrippa I, 99, 101, 106, 120, 341, 625, 630, 635, 642
Herod Agrippa II, 99, 101, 361, 439, 616, 642
Herod Antipas, 98, 99, 106, 111, 112, 119, 124, 191–92, 197, 244, 296, 355, 556, 558, 567, 568, 595, 606, 622, 625, 630, 757
Herod Archelaus, 98–99, 119, 120, 236
Herod Chalcis, 101
Herod the Great (Herod I), 93, 96–98, 101, 109, 118, 119, 120, 123, 129, 133, 149, 166, 208, 236, 244, 294, 590, 667, 724
Herodians, 52, 114–15, 208, 565, 624
Herodias, 99
Herod Philip, 98, 106
Hezekiah (ben Garon?), 119, 123
Hezekiah (king of Israel), 208
Hierapolis, 452, 453, 456, 457, 458, 658, 833
Hilary of Poitiers, 712
Hill, Charles, 655
Hillel the Elder, 105, 126, 341
Hinduism, 152, 274
Hippolytus, 292, 712, 825
Hitchhiker's Guide to Jesus, The (Fisk), 184
Hoehner, Harold, 459
holiness, 115, 117, 303, 315, 343, 344, 387, 402, 418, 423, 430, 431, 470, 471, 496, 504, 527, 646, 708, 729, 761, 781, 885
Holmes, Michael, 860, 863

holy family, 590, 617
Holy Ghost, 801. See holy spirit
Holy of Holies, 94, 428, 842
Holy Land, 26, 109. See Israel; Palestine
holy spirit (or, "the spirit"), 39, 40, 42, 43, 83, 157, 190, 199, 202, 219, 225, 285, 306, 307, 313, 314, 328, 352, 353, 356, 368, 369, 370, 375–77, 380–81, 382, 383, 386–87, 388–89, 392, 393, 397–98, 409, 411, 413, 414–15, 417, 424, 428, 432, 470, 481, 483, 486, 488, 492, 495, 496, 499, 502, 503, 507, 517, 519–20, 563–64, 589, 592, 605, 607, 608, 610, 613, 617, 618, 621, 628, 629, 630, 634, 635, 636, 639, 641, 644, 645, 650, 651, 665, 666, 667, 669, 673, 678, 688, 698, 699, 722, 725, 738, 750, 753, 764, 770, 783, 784, 791, 794, 799, 800, 801, 812, 825, 830, 831, 837, 842, 843, 849, 875, 878, 879, 880, 882, 884, 885, 887, 888
the body as temple of the, 488
the law and the, 518–19
and the new creation, 519–20
Paul's exhortation to live by the, 411
Homer, 45, 46, 150, 267–69, 273, 274, 278–79, 294, 492, 615, 642, 851, 854
'honour' and 'shame' in the Jewish context of Jesus and the early church, 114–15
Hooker, Morna, 254, 424, 440, 460, 519, 566, 693
hope, 888–89
Horace (poet Quintus Horatius Flaccus), 423
Horrell, David G., 759
Hort, Fenton, 863
hospitality, 273, 708, 726, 776, 786, 787, 803, 804, 887
Huguet, Jaume, 255, 826
humility, 445, 448, 597, 621, 747, 773, 777
Huttner, Ulrich, 457, 461
Hymenaeus (heretical teacher), 308, 480, 544, 547
hypocrisy, 124, 127, 207, 401, 593, 598, 621, 669
Hyrcanus II (priest), 96, 97

Iamblichus (neo-Platonist), 531
Iconium, 47, 352, 399, 400, 547, 637, 638
idleness, 314, 410, 427, 429, 432, 440
idolatry, 43, 166, 304, 370, 381, 382, 389, 412, 423, 484, 490, 491, 509, 514, 522, 637, 638, 640, 735, 831, 832, 835, 839, 844
idols, 151, 167, 298, 310, 358, 373, 407, 411, 416, 422, 453, 479, 488, 489, 633, 640, 695, 802, 819

Subject Index 969

Ignatius of Antioch, 105, 243, 317, 468, 534, 539, 541, 542, 584, 587, 655, 660, 661, 704, 790, 795, 869
Iliad (Homer), 45, 150, 267–68
'Immanuel', 589
immortality, 280, 286, 288, 292, 312, 315
imperial cult, 97, 100, 102, 151, 271, 356, 457, 816–17, 819–21, 832, 837
'imprisoned spirits,' 775—76
India, 88, 90, 152, 185, 838
infancy narrative, 589–90, 617, 689
inspiration (divine/pneumatic), 193, 737, 751, 764, 765, 823, 867
integrity
  of Philippians, 441
  of 2 Corinthians, 484–85
'Intentional Fallacy,' 62, 69–70
interpretation, the role of the reader in, 70–72
Irenaeus, 143, 337, 533, 540, 543, 545, 608, 610, 611, 612, 613, 653–54, 655, 658, 712, 760, 789, 793, 814, 841, 869, 870, 872, 873, 874
Isaac, 189, 304, 409, 410, 411, 516, 735, 744, 746
ISIS (terrorist group), 827
Islam, 153, 295, 371, 794
Islamic extremism,-ists, 256, 332
Israel: *passim* on 41–43, 46, 47, 50, 53, 62–64, 72, 79, 81, 86, 88, 89, 92, 94, 104–8, 118, 120, 124–26, 128–31, 133–36, 138–41, 164, 165, 167, 173, 184, 188–91, 194–95, 198–204, 206–8, 211–15, 217–26, 228–29, 231–38, 241, 248–49, 251, 253–60, 264, 278, 280–83, 285, 289–91, 293–94, 297–98, 301, 303, 304, 306, 307, 314, 315, 320, 326, 327, 330, 331, 340, 341, 343–47, 350, 354, 361–62, 369–74, 376–84, 386–91, 393, 397–98, 402, 405, 407–9, 411–13, 443, 463, 471, 481, 483, 490, 491, 492, 502–4, 509, 511–23, 550, 553, 555–56, 561–63, 565–66, 569–73, 576, 579–80, 586, 588–94, 596–97, 599, 602, 605, 607, 614, 617–24, 626, 630–33, 638, 642–45. 648–49, 651–52, 662–66, 668, 670, 673, 676–78, 682–84, 695, 697, 701, 702, 706, 711, 715–18, 720–22, 725, 726, 727, 728, 733, 740, 744, 748, 749, 750, 762, 770, 779, 781, 782, 790, 821, 827, 834, 836, 868, 879–81, 882, 884, 886, 888, 889
  ancient and modern scholars' comments on the first-century plight of, 140
  biblical boundaries of and location of modern state of, 108
  election of. *See* election
  establishment of the modern state in futurist perspectives of Revelation, 827
Israelites, 88, 116, 173, 201, 233, 236, 280, 491, 517, 620, 621, 717, 738, 750, 762
Italy, 146, 271, 377, 399, 618, 642, 714, 727
  art housed in, 227, 262, 291, 297, 345, 376, 573, 590, 674, 722, 727, 876
Izates II (king), 406

Jackson-McCabe, Matt, 732
Jacob (patriarch), 189, 666, 668, 683, 768
Jacob and Simon of Galilee (sons of Judas the Galilean), 106, 120–21
James (son of Zebedee), death of, 99, 106
James, epistle of. *See* chapter 31, "Letters by Jesus' Brothers" (730–55), esp. 732–36
  the argument of, 740–41, 743–49
  date of, 736
  echoes of the Jesus-tradition in the, 742
  genre and purpose of, 736
  main emphasis of, 741–42
  origins of, 734–35
  and Paul on 'faith' and 'works', 746
  the story inside the, 748
James the Just (brother of Jesus). *See in general* chapter 31, "Letters by Jesus' Brothers" (730–55); and 107, 341, 342, 706
Jamnia, Pharisaic/rabbinic academy at, 585
Jason (early Christian), 353, 417–18
Javneh, 100, 104, 105, 107, 131
Jeremias, Joachim, 180
Jerome, 168, 712–13, 734, 763, 787, 855
Jerusalem, 81, 87–88, 93–98, 100–*111*, 115, 119–21, 124, 125, 128–29, 131, 133, 137, 139, 166, 173, 185, 189, 198, 206, 207, 211–213, 224, 230, 233, 234–37, 240, 246, 251, 256, 260, 288, 309, 317, 327, 329, 339–42, 345, 348, 350–52, 355–56, 358–60, 363, 377, 397, 401, 403, 405, 406–7, 409, 439, 454, 478, 497, 506, 507, 509, 510, 515, 524, 548, 556, 557, 563, 565, 575, 584–85, 591, 593, 596, 597, 598, 612, 615, 617, 620–24, 627, 628, 629, 631, 634–38, 641, 646, 647, 649, 652, 656, 659, 664, 667, 668, 672, 695, 706, 711, 714, 720, 731, 747, 749, 757, 760, 816
  church. *See* Jerusalem church

collection for the. *See* collection, the (for the Jerusalem church)
council. *See* Jerusalem council
destruction of (597 BC), 87, 198
fall/destruction of (AD 70), 105, 193, 213, 224, 363, 511, 556, 561, 572, 584–85, 587, 597, 599, *712*, 826
Jesus in, 568–69, 597, 620, 621–23, 667, 672, 826
  intention of Jesus' last journey to, 240, 260
new, 665, 711, 726, 812, 839, 840, 842–43
Paul's arrest in, 642
photos of, 59, 81, 647, 889
temple. *See* temple (in Jerusalem)
Jerusalem Bible, 313
Jerusalem church, 228, 318, 319, 338, 342, 349, 352, 360, 386, 397, 399, 401–3, 405, 475, 557, 584, 628–33, 638, 731, 735, 737
Jerusalem council (or, conference), 117, 164, 168, 350, 352, 355, 363, 400, 406, 605, 757
Jerusalem temple. *See* temple (in Jerusalem)
Jesus
  anointing of (at Bethany), 571, 575, 598, 672
  ascension. *See* ascension of Jesus
  arrest and trial, 571–72, 599, 625, 674
  betrayal, 252, 571, 598, 599, 624, 672, 673, 674, 696, 736
  birth date, 188
  beginning of ministry (Matt.), 590–91
  birthplace of, 590
  brothers of. *See* chapter 31, "Letters by Jesus' Brothers" (730–55)
  the charges against, 245–49, esp. 249
  'cleansing' of the Temple, 208–13, 624
  cursing of the fig tree, 569, 597
  death of, *See* chapter 11, "The Death of the Messiah" (242–61); crucifixion
  exaltation and enthronement, 237–40
  feeding of a large crowd, 595, 621
  feels human fatigue, cries real tears, 652
  final word, 675
  Galilean ministry, 112, 210, 564–67, 618–21, 656
  as God, 240–41
  God's salvation in (1 Pet), 770–72
  the good shepherd, 669, 670, 671, 678
  greater than angels, 715–17, 728
  the great high priest, 717–18, 720
  healing
    of the blind and the lame, 597
    of a blind man, 567, 568, 623, 666, 670
    of a centurion's slave, 620
    of choice places at a banquet, 606
    of a deaf and mute man, 567
    of a man with oedema, 606
    of a man with a shriveled hand, 565
    of a man with a skin disease, 564
    of many sick people, 595
    of a paralysed man, 668
    of a possessed boy, 568, 621
    of Simon's mother-in-law, 564
    of ten Samaritan lepers, 606
    of two blind men, 597
    of a woman with constant bleeding, 621
  'high-priestly' prayer of, 673
  the historical. *See* chapter 8, "The Study of the Historical Jesus" (172–87); quest for the historical
  "I am" sayings of, 669
  indications of His power, 621
  infancy narratives, 589–90, 617, 689
  in Jerusalem, 568–69
  John's story of, 663–78
  journey toward Jerusalem, 621–24
  key tenet of the message of, 202
  languages spoken by, 110, 601
  Luke's story of Jesus, 617–28
  main facets of the ministry of. *See* chapter 9, "The Profile and Praxis of a Prophet" (188–215)
  Mark's story of, 561–76
  Matthew's story of, 589–90, 592–600
  as Messiah and Servant, 258–59
  of Nazareth. *See under* Nazareth
  Olivet discourse, 213, 222, 420, 556, 570–71, 598
  occupation of, 112
  parables of. *See* parables of Jesus
  and the 'party' (table fellowship with sinners), 205–6
  passion of, 571–74, 599, 624–26
  Paul's testimony to the risen. *See* chapter 13, "The Story of Easter according to the Apostle Paul" (296–315)
  precursors to, 190–97
  preferred form of self-reference, 220
  priesthood of, 720–23
  raising the dead, 228, 621, 650, 656
  reasons for a historical study of, 174–75
  resurrection. *See* part IV "The Resurrection of the Son of God" (263–334); 575–76, 695, 708
    its meaning to the early Christians, 320
    John Chrysostom on the, 331

Subject Index 971

witnesses to the, 309
return of. *See* second coming, below
revelation of his authority, 593
second coming (or return of), 223, 236, 330, 387, 390–91, 416, 418, 424–26, 429, 431, 507, 538, 545, 570, 571, 615, 624, 708, 765, 767, 780, 779, 839, 841, 885. *See also parousia*
self-understanding and-description of. *See* chapter 10, "Who Did Jesus Think He Was?" (216–41)
son of man. *See* son of man
superior to Moses, 717
superlative status of, 723
temptation of, 564, 592, 600, 617
transfiguration. *See* transfiguration, *below*
triumphal entry, 230, 597
the world of. *See* part 2, "The World of Jesus and the Early Church" (85–170)
Jesus ben-Phameis, 287
Jesus Christ Superstar, 99, 182
Jesus Means Freedom (Käsemann), 413
Jesus of Nazareth (Casey), 183–84
Jesus of Nazareth (Pope Benedict XVI), 183
Jesus Seminar, 181–82
Jesus-tradition(s), 179, 185, 555, 680, 689, 690, 693, 694–97, 732, 742, 759, 803
'Jezebel' (in Revelation), 819, 832
Jewish Diaspora, 87, 105, 112, 142, 143, 164–67, 203, 210, 251, 340, 353, 377, 406, 562, 608, 615, 703, 736, 741, 749, 759, 761, 762, 781, 813
Jewish mysticism, 140, 237, 461, 464, 465
Jewish sectarianism, Matthew and, 584–85
Jews
  Diaspora, 143, 167, 287, 338, 341, 342, 562, 608, 662, 671, 736, 740
  history of the
    from the Babylonian exile to the Hasmonean Dynasty, 87–94
    between the Persian and Roman empires. *See* chapter 5 (86–107)
    under Roman rule, 94–103
  beliefs of the Jewish people, 137–41
  the foundational prayer of monotheistic, 490
  Gentiles coheirs with, 471
  hellenistic, 154, 167, 465, 633
  God's abiding faithfulness to the, 522
  Juvenal and Justin Martyr on the, 410
  "ordinary," 137
  Orthodox, 344
  sects of, 118–37

second-Temple, 141, 238, 514, 880, 882
Tacitus on the, 166
three expulsions from Rome, 155. *See* Jewish Diaspora
unity of Gentiles and, 469–70
what "resurrection" meant to, 293
Jipp, Joshua, 82
Joanna (wife of Chuza), 112, 319, 327
Job (patriarch), 279–80, 735, 748
Jobes, Karen, 764, 773, 787, 798
Johanan ben-Zakkai, 103–4, 107, 585
Johannine Comma, 801
Johannine letters. *See* chapter 33, "Johannine Letters" (784–807). *See individually* 1 John; 2 John; 3 John
  date of the, 788–90
  examples of similarities between John's Gospel and the, 788–89
  origins of the, 786–87
John (person). *See in general* chapter 27, "The Gospel According to John" (648–79); chapter 33, "Johannine Letters" (784–807); chapter 34, "Revelation" (808–46)
  distinguishing between the various Bible characters named, 652–60, 812–14
  Johns by designation
    the Baptist. *See* John the Baptist, *below*
    'the Divine,' 813.
    the elder, 66, 117–18, 582, 655, 656–60, 685, 706, 785, 787, 791, 795, 806, 813, 814, 816, 833. *See in general* chapter 33, "Johannine Letters" (784–807)
    the Evangelist, 649, 655, 658, 806, 809, 868
    of Gischala. *See* John of Gischala, *below*
    Mark. *See* John Mark, *below*
    the Seer (or, the John of Revelation), 46, 61–62, 294, 654, 711, 798, 811, 813, 814, 825, 828, 834–35, 838, 846. *See in general* chapter 34, "Revelation" (808–46)
    the son of Zebedee, 66, 653, 654, 655, 656, 657, 658, 660, 787, 813, 814. *See also* beloved disciple
John, gospel of. *See* chapter 27, "The Gospel According to John" (648–79)
  'book of glory,' 672–77
  'book of signs,' 665–72
  date of, 660
  examples of parallel sayings between Mark and, 686
  examples of similarities between the

Johannine letters and, 788–89
'I Am' sayings in, 669
origins of, 652–60
place of writing, 661–62
the problem of, 685–86
similarities with and differences from the synoptics, 649–50
story of Jesus in, 663–78
what John was doing in writing the, 650–51
John the Baptist, 98, 99, 131, 172, 188, 189, 190–93, 195, 197, 201, 213, 217, 220, 222, 227, 228, 234, 341, 356, 388, 452, 563, 566, 568, 569, 590, 594, 595, 617, 620, 641, 652, 659, 662, 665, 666, 667, 685
John of Gischala, 102–3, 123
John Mark, 352, 454, 543, 557, 560, 636, 639, 757
John Rylands Papyrus 457. *See* papyri: $\mathfrak{P}^{52}$
Johnson, Luke Timothy, 508, 528, 532, 533, 535, 745, 770, 868
Jonathan Apphus, 87
Jonathan the Refugee, 193
Jongkind, Dirk, 864
Joppa, 635
Joseph (brother of Jesus), 731
Joseph (husband of Mary), 200, 580, 589, 617, 792
Joseph (son of Jacob), 47, 555, 574, 683
Joseph of Arimathea, 112, 296, 318, 600, 626, 675
Joseph called Barnabas (Joseph Barsabbas, aka Justus), 632
Josephus, Flavius, 45–46, 52, 56, 100, 103, 120–25, 129, 130–32, 165, 185, 190, 193, 196–97, 201, 211–12, 220, 249, 288, 292, 319, 344, 349, 406, 559, 562, 612, 615, 619, 636, 735, 743, 744
Jubilees, 168, 169, 735, 768
Judah (brother of Jesus). *See* Jude
Judah (son of Jacob), 47, 135
Judah (tribe), 203, 377
Judaism, 86, 87, 89, 93, 103, 104, 105, 117, 122, 124, 125, 128, 134, 137, 138, 165, 168, 181, 182, 183, 191, 208, 210, 231, 298, 315, 344, 346, 371, 378, 384, 396, 403, 406, 407, 412, 413, 504, 565, 586, 587, 604, 608, 615, 616, 659, 663, 664, 684, 704, 733, 735, 740, 849, 856
the question of circumcision for male converts to, 406

judaizers, 396
Judas (brother of Jesus). *See* Jude
Judas the Galilean, 99–100, 106, 120, 122, 123, 245
Judas Iscariot, 309, 571, 583, 598, 599, 624, 629, 672, 673, 674, 685, 736
Judas Maccabaeus, 53, 87, 92, 93, 94, 208, 229
Jude (brother of Jesus), 702, 705, 706, 730–31, 732, 736–40, 749–50, 752–54
Jude, book of
the argument of, 749–50, 752–54
date and purpose of, 739–40
opponents in, 737–39
the origins of, 736
parallels between 2 Peter and, 780
the purpose of, 749–50
sources in, 751–52
Judea, 87, 90, 94, 96, 97, 98–103, 106, 107, 108–9, 110, 117, 121, 122, 124, 125, 140, 144, 148, 164, 173, 188, 189, 190, 203, 236, 242, 317, 348, 360, 377, 388, 405, 423, 437, 504, 523, 556, 558, 559, 568, 579, 584, 587, 590, 597, 628, 634, 635, 636, 649, 659, 699, 731, 741, 757
defined, 109
division of the region (for administrative purposes), 109–10
Jewish exorcists in first-century, 201
Julius Africanus, 731
Julius Caesar, 144–45, 271, 272, 354, 436, 476, 505, 555, 792, 815, 816, 851, 854
Jupiter (Roman deity), 144, 146, 152, 160, 272, 792, 821, 103, 107
justification, 128, 136, 172, 294, 300, 303, 304–5, 307, 341, 370, 375, 383, 384, 385, 386, 397, 398, 414, 458, 483, 503, 504, 510, 515, 525, 526, 605, 610, 735, 744–45, 746
Justin Martyr, 161, 323, 410, 612, 660, 682, 789, 813, 825, 841
Juvenal, 410

Kamell, Mariam, 747
Kanagaraj, Jey, 676
Kant, Immanuel, 177
Käsemann, Ernst, 180–81, 413, 652, 885
Kennedy, George, 67
Kenny, Anthony, 421, 459, 537
Kephalaia (chapter divisions),
kingdom
of God, 173, 186, 198–99, 204–8, 230, 233, 234, 252, 254, 256, 259, 342, 343,

356, 361, 393, 480, 561, 565, 567, 573, 591, 595, 620, 641, 649, 691, 696, 827, 844–45
  of heaven, 578, 591, 593, 595, 691
kinship in the Jewish context of Jesus and the early church, 113
Kittim, 94
Kittim of Asshur, 77
Klausner, Joseph, 140
Koester, Helmut, 364, 533, 535, 537, 816, 837
koinonia (fellowship), 367, 369, 434, 466, 491
Korah, 738, 752
Kursi Church (traditional site for the miracle of the swine), 576
kyrios ("lord"), 347, 353, 372, 374, 442

'L' (material special to Luke), 606, 686
Laertius, Diogenes, 615
language of ancient Palestine, 110
Lake, Kirsopp, 734
Laodicea, 356, 452, 453, 454, 456, 457–58, 462, 464, 811, 818, 820, 833
Laodiceans, epistles to the (or *Letter to the Laodiceans*) (lost letter), 530, 533, 870, 872
lares (household spirits), 157
Last Supper, 36, 62, 230, 242, 250–53, 255, 258, 260, 599, 608, 624–25, 627, 649, 656, 698
  date of the, 250–51
  Jesus' words at the, 252, 254
Law, Philip, 25
lawless one, 427–29. *See also* Antichrist
law of Moses, 139, 164, 165, 406, 631, 716. *See* Torah
lawsuits among believers, 488
laying on of hands, 533–34
Lazarus (beggar), 112, 606, 622, 631
Lazarus of Bethany, 273, 329, 650, 656, 665–66, 671
Left Behind novels, 425, 426
Letter of Barnabas, 872
Letters of Paul and Seneca, 530, 535
letters to the seven churches (of Revelation), 704, 808, 811, 818–19, 821, 827, 828, 831–33
letter-writing, 466, 703, 809
Levites, 117, 128, 203, 377
Lewis, C. S., 63, 231, 607
Levitical priesthood, 713, 714, 726
Libanius (Greek sophist), 703
Licona, Michael, 325

Lieu, Judith M., 787, 805, 806
Life of Adam and Eve, 291
life after death in antiquity. *See* chapter 18, "The Afterlife in Greek, Roman, and Jewish Thought" (264–95)
Lincoln, Andrew T., 674
literacy levels in ancient Palestine, 110
Loci Communes Theologici (Melanchthon), 507
logos/Logos, 66, 67, 68, 161, 660, 664, 801
Lion of Judah, 224, 833–34
Lives of Eminent Philosophers (Laertius), 615
Longenecker, Bruce W., 416, 818
López, José, 56
Lord's Prayer, 326, 698, 861
love
  the central characteristic of the new (future) world, 492
  for enemies, 583
  faith works itself out in, 754
  of God. *See* God's love
  God is, 800
  a hermeneutic of, 73–74
  is the fulfilling of the, 523
  love-command, 569, 742, 743, 791, 800, 803
  of money, 545, 726
  must be the believers' rule of life, 470
  for others, 651, 797, 799
  most supreme example of, 799
  Paul's poignant description (1 Cor), 492
  the priority of divine, 800
  of the Thessalonians, 424
love feast(s), 149, 738–39, 752
Lucceius Albinus (procurator), 107, 122
Lucretius, Titus, 45, 160
Luke (the Evangelist). *See in general* chapter 26, "The Gospel according to Luke and Acts of the Apostles" (604–47)
  illustration of Mark and, 698
  iradition concerning, 608
  various descriptions of, 608
Luke, gospel of; *see in general* chapter 26, "The Gospel according to Luke and Acts of the Apostles" (604–47)
  earliest copy of, 608
  genre of, 614
  story of the early church in, 628–44
  story of Jesus in, 617–28
  three hymns of praise in, 617
  unique material in, 606
Luke-Acts. *See* Luke, gospel of; *see in general* chapter 26, "The Gospel according to Luke and Acts of the Apostles" (604–47)

central theme of, 605
date of, 612
genre. *See* Acts, book of; Luke, gospel of
origins of, 607–11
percentage of NT, 604
purpose of, 615–16
reasons for its significance, 604–5
unity of, 612–14
'we'-passages of, 352, 609–10, 611
Luther, Martin, 408, 503, 507, 512, 539, 713, 732, 734, 744
Lycus valley, 356, 452–54, 456–58, 461
Lydda, 635
Lydia, 352, 438, 639
Lystra, 47, 352, 399–400, 547, 637, 638

'M' (material special to Matthew), 582, 583, 686
Maccabean revolt, 92, 134, 290, 343, 623, 697
Maccabees, the, 122, 291. *See* Judas Maccabaeus; Maccabean revolt
MacDonald, Margaret, 149, 464
Macedonia, 114, 144, 271, 352, 358, 359, 360, 364, 400, 417, 424, 436, 437, 440, 442, 454, 479, 485, 495, 497, 532, 538, 541, 639, 640, 641
Maecenas (Gaius Maecenas, Roman nobleman), 155
Magnificat, 605, 617
majuscule D (Codex Bezae), 613
majuscules, 454, 855, 860, 861, 862
Malta, 361, 363, 605, 643
Maranatha, 494, 843
Marcus Aurelius (emperor), 152
Marmion, Simon, 609
marriage
  divorce, singleness, and 488–89
  in the Jewish context of Jesus and the early church, 113
Martha of Bethany, 606, 671, 685
Martin, Dale, 71, 72
Manson, T. W., 180
Man of Sorrows (painting), 70
Marguerat, Daniel, 616
Markan 'sandwich', 565, 566, 569
Marcion, 163, 270, 454, 469, 508, 533, 541, 542, 610, 706, 769, 814, 855, 869, 873
Marcionites, 873
Marcus Antonius Felix (Roman procurator). *See* Felix
Mariamne (wife of Herod the Great), 97, 244
Mark, gospel of. *See* chapter 24, "The Gospel According to Mark" (554–77)

date of, 558. *See also* Marcan priority, *below*
examples of parallel sayings between John and, 686
genre, 556
longer ending(s), 321–24, 574–75, 612
origins of, 557
place of composition, 559–60
purpose of, 460–61
Markan priority, 582, 687–89, 692–93
Mark Antony, 97, 145, 436
Mark the Evangelist, 555. *See* John Mark
Marshall, I. Howard, 531, 532, 533, 534
Martyn, J. Louis, 413
Martyrdom of Polycarp, 739
Mary, mother of James and John (of Zebedee), 600
Mary, mother of Jesus, 589, 605, 609, 617, 652, 731, 734, 792, 795, 806, 830
Mary of Bethany, 606, 621, 671, 672, 685
Mary Magdalene, 309, 319, 321, 327, 328, 600, 675–76
Mary of Rome (mother of John Mark?), 525
Masada, 48, 97, 103, 107, 118, 123
Mattathias (ben Johanan), 92, 343, 344
Mattathias Antigonus, 96
Matthean priority, 581, 687
Matthew, gospel of. *See* chapter 25, "The Gospel according to Matthew" (578–602)
  date of, 584. *See also* Matthean priority, *above*
  Jewish features unique to, 591
  origins of, 581–82
  purpose of, 588–89
  reasons for its popularity in the early church, 578–79
  two main takeaways from, 601
  unique material in, 583
Matthew the Evangelist, 579. *See in general* chapter 25, "The Gospel according to Matthew" (578–602)
Matthews, Mark D., 768
Mbuvi, Andrew, 764, 778
McKnight, Scot, 184, 735, 778
'meaning' (defined), 73
"meant" and "meaning" distinction (in interpreting texts), three drawbacks to the strategy, 63–64
Media (kingdom), 221
Meeks, Wayne, 77
Meier, John P., 183, 690

Meggitt, Justin, 482
Meier, John P., 183, 690
Melanchthon, Philip, 67, 507
Melchizedek, 710, 718, 720–21, 722, 726, 727, 728
Memoirs of Socrates (Xenophon), 682
Menahem (leader of the Sicarii), 102–3, 123, 208
Men Karou, cult of, 456
mentoring, 551
mercy seat, 382, 383, 516
Mertes, Richard (director, *The Apocalypse*), 815
Messiah
  Jesus as Servant and, 258–59
  revelation of the (in Caesarea Philippi), 567
Messiah poem (Colossians), 463–64
'messianic Judaism,' Matthew's apology for, 586
metempsychosis, 273–74. *See also* reincarnation
Meyer, Ben F., 182
Michael (archangel), 291, 750, 751–52, 826, 836
Michie, Donald, 68
Middle Platonism, 159, 163
Miletus, 360, 454, 532, 538, 541, 641, 768, 818
militarism, 72
millennium, the, 827, 840, 841
Milton, John, 885
Mink, Gerd, 854, 858
minuscules, 855, 857, 860
miqvaot (ritual baths), 117
Mishnah, 286, 588
mission, 884–86
  of the Antiochene church, 636–38
  of the church, 44, 605, 884–86, 888
    the model and ground of the, 676
    tasks required in the, 782
  of Jesus, 596
  in the New Testament, the point of, 885–86
  the New Testament the manual of, 43
  Paul's Asian and Aegean, 639–41
  women in Christian service and, 525
Mithridates VI (king), 94
modernity, 54, 55
modesty, 71, 114, 740
monotheism, 66, 138, 141, 144, 165, 231, 232, 233, 238, 370–77, 387, 489, 516, 523, 604, 616, 746
Morris, Leon, 659
Mosaic covenant, 409
Mosaic of Jesus, 170

Moses, 130, 193, 237, 254, 281, 333, 341, 360, 387, 397, 410, 426, 495, 521, 547, 555, 566, 567, 578, 588, 591, 593, 596, 600, 627, 630, 650, 665, 668, 676, 696, 717–18, 725, 726, 727, 750–52, 812, 835, 837. *See also* law of Moses
Mounce, William, 549
Mount Carmel, 109
Mount of Beatitudes, pictured, 603
Mount of Olives, 81, 121, 193, 599, 600, 625, 889
Mount Zion, 131, 212, 711
Muratorian canon, 364, 507, 530, 533, 540, 543, 608, 612, 613, 653, 654, 655, 658, 659, 712, 739, 765, 788–89, 870
Murphy-O'Connor, Jerome, 538
mustard seed, 565, 595, 691, 692
mystery religions, 275, 460

Naaman the Syrian, 200, 619
Nanos, Mark, 413
narrative criticism, 65–69
Nathanael (disciple), 654, 656, 666, 676
nationalism, 72, 173, 207
NA (28). *See* Nestle-Aland Novum Testament Graece
Nazarene, 61, 318
Nazarenes, 189
Nazareth, 88, 110, 112, 161, 188, 199, 200, 566, 589, 590, 595, 597, 605, 607, 617, 618, 620, 731
  Jesus of, 40, 50, 64, 120, 173, 184, 185, 226, 241, 287, 296, 307, 320, 330, 331, 341, 363, 553, 554, 588, 649, 652, 664, 676, 726
'Nazareth Manifesto,' 199, 228
Nazis, 72
Nebuchadnezzar II, 87, 391
necromancy, 272–73
Neill, Bishop Stephen, 169
Nero (emperor), 102, 103, 107, 355, 363, 364, 365, 428, 429, 453, 456, 508, 522, 538, 562, 660, 714, 757, 760, 777, 815, 816, 817, 836, 837, 838
Nestle-Aland Novum Testament Graece, 28th ed. (NA (28)), 856, 863
new birth, 295, 502, 667, 668, 748, 762, 770, 771, 783, 800. *See also* salvation
new covenant, 42, 133, 173, 252, 256, 386, 407, 483, 495, 514, 517, 581, 616, 625, 663, 696, 711, 720–24, 726, 728, 853, 875
  Jesus the mediator of the, 728

Jesus' priesthood and the new, 720–23
Paul and the ministry of the, 495
the nature of the, 722
new creation, 41, 81, 138, 203, 206, 256, 259, 280, 281, 282, 285, 293, 295, 302, 311, 313, 314, 331, 360, 372, 380, 381, 383, 392, 393, 394, 411, 414, 423, 430, 463, 472, 496, 517, 519, 556, 576, 650, 663, 676, 677, 678, 706, 717, 718, 725, 741, 748, 783, 811, 830, 842, 875, 878, 879, 811, 884, 885, 886–87, 888, 889
new heavens and new earth, 703, 715, 725, 781, 783, 826, 840, 841, 884
new Jerusalem, 665, 711, 726, 812, 839, 840, 842–43
New Testament
  the canonization of the. See chapter 36, "The Canonization of the New Testament" (866–75)
  different 'versions' (languages) of the, 855–56
  four early lists of New Testament writings (2nd/3rd centuries), 870
  how we got the, 850–52
  living out the. See chapter 37, "Bringing It All Together" (878–89)
  the materials used to establish the text of the, 855–56
  percents made up of Luke-Acts, Paul's letters, Johannine corpus, 604
  textual criticism of the. See chapter 850, "Introduction to Textual Criticism of the New Testament" (850–65)
  three main sections, 702
New Testament theology
  good reasons for pursuing, 77–78
  meaning of the phrase, 76
Ngewa, Samuel, 541
Nicodemus, 124, 650, 656, 667, 675
Nicolaitans, 819, 832
Nicomedes (king of Bithynia), 399
Nietzsche, Friedrich, 55, 179, 332
Noah, 598, 725, 775–76, 779
nomina sacra (shortened divine names), 853
Nympha (leader of Laodicean church), 453, 464

oaths, against swearing 538, 742, 748
obedience, 251, 303, 306, 380, 382, 387, 397, 408, 443, 504, 509, 512, 518, 591, 592, 601, 623, 708, 739, 778, 805
Octavian (aka Augustus), 52, 97, 98–99, 106, 145, 146, 149, 155, 185, 271, 272, 339, 349, 402, 436, 447, 453, 455, 456, 493, 505, 562, 617, 815, 820
Odyssey (Homer), 45, 615, 642
offices of 'elder' and 'deacon', 533–34. See overseers and deacons
old covenant, 722, 726
olive tree, 521
Olivet discourse, 213, 222, 420, 556, 570–71, 598
Onesimus, 357, 367–69, 454, 466, 467, 468, 472
Onesiphorus, 546
online resources (for use in textual criticism), 864
oral tradition, 320, 680, 685, 687, 693, 697, 698, 735, 868
Origen, 154, 159, 525, 712, 724, 725, 734, 736, 764, 768, 788, 790, 859–60, 870, 872
orthodoxy, 543, 769, 806, 873–74
Ostian Way, 365
Otho (emperor), 103, 107, 562, 815
overseers and deacons, qualifications for, 544
Ovid (poet), 792
"Ozymandias" (Shelley), 55

paganism, 106, 126, 161, 298, 343, 376, 409, 489, 491, 604, 845, 887
pagans, 105, 141, 149, 154, 157, 166, 189, 190, 198, 211, 224, 238, 265, 273, 345, 369, 384, 403, 410, 417, 431, 448, 477, 486, 591, 614, 615, 615, 761, 762, 804
Painter, John, 787, 800
Palestine, 50, 52, 86, 87, 88–89, 94, 96, 105, 118, 137, 142, 144, 164, 172, 176, 185, 190, 201, 203, 208, 230, 351, 361, 505, 506, 580, 584, 585, 639, 643, 695, 731, 736, 740
  cultural values of, 112–18
  economic life in, 110–12
  four main features of, 109
  geography of, 108–9
  Jewish life in, 108–118
  language and literacy of ancient, 110
  main language of first-century, 88
Pamphylia, 339, 399, 557, 636
Papias (of Hierapolis), 582, 654, 655, 656–57, 658, 660, 760, 787, 789, 814, 816, 825, 841, 869
paraclete, 651, 673. See holy spirit
papyri, 335, 855, 860, 861, 864
𝔓⁸, 613
𝔓²⁹, 613, 681
𝔓⁴⁵ (P. Chester Beatty I) 613, 703, 855

𝔓⁴⁶ (P. Chester Beatty II) 454, 469, 523, 540, 701, 711–12, 855
𝔓⁴⁸, 613
𝔓⁵² (John Rylands 457), 660, 661, 681, 854, 855
𝔓⁵³, 613, 703
𝔓⁷⁵, 608, 653, 681
𝔓⁹¹, 613
'parables of Enoch,' 224
parables of Jesus, 39, 189, 204, 214, 219, 565, 588, 595, 683
   parable of the barren fig tree, 606
   parable of the dishonest manager, 606
   parable of the doorkeeper (or, the faithful servant), 606
   parable of the good Samaritan, 117, 606
   parable of the growing seed, 565
   parable of the hidden treasure, 583
   parable of the lamp (under a bushel), 565
   parable of the lost coin, 606, 622
   parable of the lost sheep, 606, 622
   parable of the mustard seed, 565, 595, 691, 692
   parable of the net, 583
   parable of the expensive pearl, 583
   parable of the persistent friend, 606
   parable of the Pharisee and tax-collector, 606
   parable of the prodigal son, 204–5, 605, 606, 622
   parable of the rich fool, 112, 606
   parable of the rich man and Lazarus, 112, 606, 622
   parable of the shrewd manager, 622
   parable of the sower (or soils), 203, 204, 565, 595, 620
   parable of the talents (or, ten pounds), 236, 598, 623 (aka parable of the wicked nobleman, 99)
   parable of the ten virgins (or bridesmaids), 583, 598
   parable of the two sons, 583, 597
   parable of the ungrateful servant (or, unforgiving servant), 112, 583
   parable of the unjust judge, 606
   parable of the wedding banquet, 597
   parable of the weeds, 583, 595
   parable of the wicked nobleman, 99 (aka parable of the talents, 598, 623)
   parable of the wicked tenants, 112, 569, 597
   parable of the workers in the vineyard, 583, 597
   parable of the yeast, 595

paradise (in Luke), 625–26
Parallel Lives (Plutarch), 615
Park, M. Sydney, 441
Parker, David, 853
parousia, 315, 348, 390–91, 416, 419, 428, 429, 747, 749, 779, 813, 831, 839. *See also* return: of Jesus
Parsenios, George, 787, 790–91
Parthenon. *See* temple of Artemis
Parthia, Parthians, 93, 119, 838
passion of Jesus, 571–74, 599, 624–26
Passover, 57–58, 99, 100, 106, 119, 121, 138, 193, 248, 250–56, 309, 506, 571, 599, 617, 649, 659, 667, 668, 672, 675, 695, 834, 880
Passover lamb, 250, 256, 383, 625, 666, 830
Pastoral Epistles (or, 'pastorals'), 362, 364, 439, 795, 855; *see* chapter 23, "The Pastoral Epistles" (528–51)
   authorship of the, 530–40
   date of the, 540–41
   literary forms in the, 528
   Paul's opponents in the, 542–43
   the purpose of the, 543
pathos, 67, 68, 502
Patmos, 653, 655, 809, 811, 818, 846
Paul, apostle. *See* chapter 13, "The Story of Easter according to the Apostle Paul" (296–315); part 5, "Paul and the Faithfulness of God" (335–552)
   'Apocalyptic', 412, 413
   arrests, 352, 357, 362, 363, 539, 642, 644
   arrest in Jerusalem and imprisonment, 642
   possible location of Paul's house arrest, 644
   call to purity and holiness (1 Thess), 423–24
   Christophany and conversion of, 344–47, 350
   contrasts his (new covenant) work with Moses', 495
   in Damascus, 355
   death of, 364–65
   defends the gospel and warns the Galatians, 408–11
   defends his ministry, 495–96
   the defining element of election for, 381
   disagreement with Peter in Antioch, 407
   early life of, 338–40
   exhortations to unity and to the imitation of Christ (Philippians), 443
   first language of, 340
   his step-by-step argument for the resurrection (1 Cor), 308–14

his Ephesian ministry, 452–54
and James on 'faith' and 'works', 746
John Chrysostom on, 337
journey to Rome, 361
the life and ministry of. *See* chapter 15, "The Story of Paul's Life and Ministry" (336–65)
main legacy of, 394
meeting with Peter, James, and John in Jerusalem, 406–7
missionary career of, 351–61
  first missionary journey, 363, 399, 400, 637, 639
  second missionary journey, 351, 363, 399, 609, 639
  third missionary journey, 363, 643
obscure period ('tunnel period'), 350–51
pre-conversion persecution of the church, 341–44, 634
shipwreck, 349, 361, 363, 605, 609, 642, 643
paintings/frescoes of, 334, 451, 541
and slavery, 467
theological vision of, 393
theology of. *See* chapter 16, "A Primer on Pauline Theology" (366–95)
and a 'thorn in the flesh', 498
'within Judaism' branch of Pauline scholarship, 412, 413
the 'zeal' of, 343–44
Paulinium, 702, 869
'Paul within Judaism' movement, 413
Pentateuch, 130, 143, 384. *See* Torah
Pentecost (Acts 2 event), 605, 629, 635, 645, 651, 699, 760. *See also* feast of Pentecost
Peppiatt, Lucy, 492
Pergamum, 146, 356, 452, 455, 456, 530, 811, 817, 818, 819, 821, 822, 832, 833
  imperial hymns in, 833
Perkins, Pheme, 307, 754
Perrin, Norman, 181
perseverance, 418, 427, 571, 708, 724, 726, 735, 747–48, 753, 778, 781
Pervo, Richard, 612, 613
persecution, 42, 106–7, 113, 285, 289, 306, 341–44, 352, 354, 363, 365, 403, 411, 417, 419, 423, 426, 427, 440, 493, 534, 547, 559, 570, 576, 583, 585, 630, 632, 634, 635, 646, 684, 706, 707, 714, 726, 758, 760, 762, 767, 776–77, 782, 815, 816, 817, 818, 823, 841
Persia, 88, 90, 145, 221
Persian empire, 88, 110

Persian–Greek period, timeline, 87
Persians, 88
Pertinax (Roman emperor), 272
Peshitta, 856, 873
Peter (apostle, aka Simon Peter, Cephas), 62, 63, 82, 99, 115, 117, 228, 258, 293, 297, 309, 319, 321, 324, 327, 328, 329–30, 337, 350–51, 363, 364–65, 385, 386, 401, 405, 406–7, 478, 480, 506, 530, 538, 556, 557, 559, 560, 567–68, 571, 572, 575, 583, 592, 594, 595, 596, 599, 605, 612, 613–14, 615, 621, 625, 626, 629–36, 638, 644, 645, 652, 653, 654, 656, 657, 658, 659, 660, 666, 668, 688, 668, 672, 673, 674, 675–76, 677, 679, 688, 694, 702, 705, 706, 707, 711, 731, 734, 793, 880. *See in general* chapter 32, "Petrine Letters" (756–83)
  birth name and occupation of, 756
  confession of Jesus as Messiah, 228, 556, 567, 571, 594, 596, 621, 688
  death, 364–65, 660
  healing of the beggar, with John, 630
  Jerusalem meeting with James and John, 406–7
  Jesus' renaming of, 666, 756
  speech/sermon at Pentecost, 629, 645
  vision and gentile breakthrough, 635
Pharisaism, 104, 126, 344
Pharisees, 46, 52, 93, 114–18, 122, 123–28, 129, 130, 137, 190, 193, 198, 209–10, 248, 249, 277, 286, 288, 292, 325, 343, 344, 561, 565, 567, 568, 583, 584, 586, 588, 591, 594–96, 598, 600, 621, 622, 624, 638, 642, 649, 670, 696, 697
  critiques of the (by other Jewish groups), 127
  several problems about the, 124–25
  three basic theses about the, 125–26
Phasael (governor of Judea), 96–97
Philadelphia (Turkey), 356, 452, 453, 811, 818–19, 820, 833
Philemon (convert of Paul), 338, 357, 366–69, 439, 451–54, 458, 459, 465–68, 471, 529, 537
  argument of the letter to 465–66, 68–69
Philetus (heretic), 308, 480, 547
Philip (the Apostle), 657, 658, 666, 676
Philip (the Evangelist), 634
Philip II of Macedon, 436
Philip V of Macedon, 94
Philippi. *See in general* chapter 19, "Philippians" (434–49); and 146, 352, 353, 364, 417, 559, 661, 639, 641

Subject Index 979

Philippians, book of. *See* chapter 19, "Philippians" (434–49)
  arguments of, 441–45, 447
  integrity of, 441
  key themes in, 447–48
  Paul's exhortations to unity and to the imitation of Christ in, 443
  Paul's location during the writing of, 439
Philip of Side, 654
Philo, 45, 46, 100, 101, 113, 125, 131, 132, 137, 140, 159, 161, 165, 166, 226, 288, 292, 294, 317, 339, 343, 344, 371, 378, 388, 458, 477, 662, 683, 743, 790
philosophy
  Greco-Roman, 158–64
  origins of Western, 158
Philoxenus, 740, 856, 873
Phinehas (Israelite priest), 122, 343
Phoebe, 360, 482, 506, 525, 526, 544
Pierce, Madison, 715, 776
Pindar (Greek poet), 268
Plato, 45, 46, 158–59, 269, 273–74, 294, 851, 853, 854
Platonism, 159, 163, 269, 270, 288
Pliny the Elder, 131, 132
Pliny the Younger, 465–66, 468, 774, 775, 777, 817
Plotinus, 159
pluralism, 153–55
Plutarch, 45, 159, 615, 682
poetry, 37, 39, 40, 45, 150, 153, 268, 311, 463, 502
Polybius, 618
Polycarp of Smyrna, 533, 539, 541, 542, 654, 655, 658, 660, 760, 789, 869
Polycrates (bishop) of Ephesus, 658–59
Pompey, 94, 96, 144, 339, 428, 505
Pontius Pilate, 52, 100, 101, 106, 110, 120, 148, 197, 245–48, 249, 296, 309, 325, 572, 583, 599, 600, 622, 625, 630, 650, 652, 675, 683
  archaeological evidence for the existence of, 101
  incidents exemplifying the character of 100
Pontus (Asia Minor), 339, 353, 399, 477, 760, 767, 770
Pool of Siloam, 670
poor, the, 43, 112, 127, 199, 203, 207, 228, 293, 407, 447, 488, 497, 568, 576, 597, 601, 602, 605, 607, 618, 623, 631, 632, 645, 705, 741, 742, 747, 748, 888
pop-psychology, 295

Porcius Festus (Roman procurator), 107, 121–22, 148, 361, 616, 642
porneia, 832
Porter, Stanley E., 610, 611
Postmodern Bible Project, 56
postmodernity, 54, 55–56, 332
postmodern world, on Christian mission in a, 331–33
Potter, Garry, 56
Powell, Mark Alan, 69, 580
Praetorian Guard, 447, 572
Prayer of Jacob, 293
'praying in the Holy Spirit', 753
Preaching of Peter (apocryphal writing), 758
predestination, 521, 782
prefaces, ancient, 618
prefects, chronology of Roman emperors and, 106–7
priests, the Sadducees, aristocrats, and, 128–31
Priscilla (friend of Paul), 354–55, 356, 359, 453, 477, 478, 482, 506, 508, 525, 640, 641, 713, 760
prodigal son, 204, 605, 606, 622, 623
prologues, ancient, 618
prophecy, 63, 106, 122, 133, 224, 225, 421, 426, 547, 554, 558, 565, 580, 588, 624, 627, 629, 635, 637, 671, 690, 753, 779, 809, 812, 821, 822, 825, 828, 830, 843
prophesying superior to tongues, 492
prophets
  and precursors to Jesus, 190–97
  in Judea under Roman rule, 193
proselytes, 166, 396, 401, 407, 509, 637, 745
proselytism, 412, 538
prostitutes, 111, 112, 149, 217, 645
Protestantism, 51, 412, 733
Protestant Reformation, 51, 511, 687, 713
Protestants, 538, 697, 705, 744, 867
Psalms of Solomon, 291, 379, 563, 872
pseudepigraphy, 530–31, 533, 535, 764–65
pseudonymity, 178, 530, 764, 812, 825
Pseudo-Phocylides, 288–89, 736, 743
Ptolemies, 87, 88, 91
Ptolemy (gnostic), 653
Ptolemy I, 91
Ptolemy II, 167
Publius Petronius, 100
purity
  Paul's call to holiness and (1 Thess), 423–24
  and pollution, ancient cultures' concerns about, 115–18

Pythagoras, 269, 273, 531, 631
Pythagoreans, neo-Pythagoreans, 159, 531

Q (hypothetical document), 181, 582, 680, 689–94
Quartodeciman controversy, 704
quest for the historical Jesus, 176–84
   First Quest, 177–79
   Second Quest, 177, 179–82
   Third Quest, 177, 182–84
Quintus Cornelius Secundus, 489
Qumran,-ites, 46, 93, 94, 105, 116, 118, 127, 131, 132–35, 209, 211, 222, 226, 234, 284, 292, 341, 343, 371, 378, 388, 460, 597, 661, 662, 721, 777

Rahlfs, Alfred, 159
Rabbi Akiba, 46, 106, 107, 237–38, 571
rabbinic Judaism, 86, 586
racism, 72
Räisänen, Heikki, 77, 79
Ramsay, William M., 607
rapture, 827. *See* rapture theology
Rapture index, rapture theology, 425–26
reader-response criticism, 70–72
readers, the task for faithful, 73
reconciliation to God, 517
redaction, 246, 542, 688, 690, 759, 853
rediscovery, the need for, 886–87
Red Sea, 191, 491, 518, 566, 599
Reformation, 51, 511, 687, 713
Reformers, 67, 507
Reimarus, H. S., 177
reincarnation, 153, 159, 273, 288
religion
   differences between modern and ancient, 152–53
   Greco-Roman, 152–58, esp. 155–56
   Roman, 146–47
   true, 743
Rembrandt's famous *Return of the Prodigal Son*, 623
Remus and Romulus, 150
Renan, Ernest, 177
renunciation (of the world), 886
repentance, 201, 235, 281, 333, 495, 563, 564, 590, 605, 624, 632, 747, 774, 775, 835, 837, 843
'restrainer' (holding back the 'lawless one'), 428–29
resurrection
   of the body, 299–300, 306, 307, 311–13, 392, 493–94, 519. *See also* chapter 18, "The Afterlife in Greek, Roman, and Jewish Thought" (264–95)
   of Christ. *See* part IV "The Resurrection of the Son of God" (263–334); 575–76, 626
   John Chrysostom on the, 331
   witnesses to the, 309
   of the dead following the crucifixion, 325, 600
   meaning of the word to Jews, 293
return
   of Jesus (aka "second coming"), 223, 236, 330, 387, 390–91, 416, 418, 424–26, 429, 431, 507, 538, 545, 570, 571, 615, 624, 708, 765, 767, 780, 799, 839, 841, 885. *See also parousia*
   of YHWH to Zion, 173, 189, 214, 216, 233–37, 240, 253, 372, 377, 389, 390, 393, 562, 563, 623
Revelation (book). *See* chapter 34, "Revelation" (808–46)
   alternative ways to read, 841
   date and provenance, 814–21
   earliest copies of, 824
   four major approaches to the interpretation of the book of, 826–28
   genre, 821–25
   interpretation and purpose, 825–29
   origins, 812–14
   the reigns of the Roman emperors as a key to dating, 815
   the story of the book of, 829–43
   title of the book, 830
revenge (for believers) 522, 583
revolutionary movements, 118–23
rhetorical criticism, 65, 67–69
rhetorical devices, 404
Rhoads, David, 68
Rice, Tim, 99, 182
rich young ruler, 568, 597, 623
Riesenfeld, Harald, 697
Riesner, Rainer, 697
righteousness
   of God, 136, 474, 304, 503, 504, 510, 511–13, 515, 516, 522, 524
   Martin Luther on Christian, 408
riot(s), 100, 101, 119, 121, 122, 123, 151, 154, 166, 249, 337, 345, 356, 360, 453, 456, 639, 641, 642, 714
ritual cleansing, 117
River Jordan, 108, 190, 192
river of water of life, 842
Rives, James, 155–56

Robbins, Vernon K., 610
Robinson, James, 181
Robinson, John A. T., 459, 734
Roma (goddess), 52, 146, 455, 820, 821
Roman emperors and prefects, chronology of, 106–7
Roman Empire, 46, 143, 144, 428, 771, 832. *See also* Rome
   Hellenistic culture and the, 142–47
Roman forum (pictured): in Philippi, 448; in Rome, 506; in Thessalonica, 419
Roman–Jewish war (First), 118, 363
'Roman road', what it means to walk the, 526
Romans, book of. *See* chapter 22, "Romans" (502–27)
   the argument of, 510–24
   the purpose of, 507–10
   thesis statement of, 512
Rome, 45, 67, 93, 94, 97, 98, 100–103, 106, 107, 119–20, 122, 124, 130, 140, 143–46, 148, 149–51, 155, 160, 164, 189, 193, 197, 204, 208, 211, 212, 221, 224, 225, 226, 236, 245, 249, 255, 258, 260, 339, 341, 344, 345, 349, 354, 355, 356, 357, 359–65, 367, 368, 379, 396, 398, 410, 428, 439, 446, 447, 455, 477, 478, 502, 503–10, 518, 524, 526, 527, 529, 532, 533, 536, 538, 541, 543, 544, 546, 548, 557, 559–62, 569, 605, 608, 612, 615, 616, 618, 624, 625, 628, 633, 640, 646, 684, 714, 757, 760, 761, 762, 764, 765, 774, 777, 816, 817, 819, 820, 821, 836–40, 845, 852, 874
   equating with Babylon, 777
   map of ancient, 505
   Paul's journey to, 361
   Paul's testimony of the gospel in, 642–44
Romulus (founding king of Rome), 150, 270
Rosner, Brian, 477
Rufus, the mother of, 525
Rule of the Community (1QS), 597

Sabinianus, Pliny's letter to, 465–66
Sabinus (Roman procurator), 119, 120
sacrifices, 93, 100, 102, 118, 156, 167, 212, 516, 562, 637, 713–14, 718, 721, 723, 729, 772, 832, 833
sacrificial love (or, self-sacrificial love), 374, 470, 786
Saddam Hussein, 827
Sadducees, 47, 105, 118, 122, 129–30, 248, 277, 286, 292, 294, 330, 595, 624, 642

Salonius of Geneva (bishop), 531
salvation
   by grace through faith, 469
   in Hebrews (and losing one's salvation), 719
   in Jesus Christ (1 Pet), 770–72
Salvia of Marseille, 531
Samaria, 97, 98, 99, 100, 109, 628, 634, 635, 636, 642, 757
Samaritans, 144, 659, 668, 678
Samaritan woman, 667–68, 650
Samuel (prophet), 273, 630
sanctification, 432, 510, 673
Sanders, E. P., 182, 403
Sanhedrin, 112, 249, 277, 296, 318, 344, 571, 574, 599, 616, 630, 632, 633, 642, 654
Sarah (wife of Abraham), 304, 409, 410, 517, 725, 761, 781
Sardis, 356, 452, 811, 818, 820, 832
satan, 202, 240, 248, 251, 418, 487, 565, 580, 685, 721, 751, 808, 821, 831, 832, 836, 840, 841, 201. *See also* devil
Saturninus (Gnostic), 543, 792
Saul of Tarsus (aka Paul), 104, 106, 118, 122, 125, 167, 338, 342–44, 347, 363, 377, 384, 403. *See* Paul (apostle)
Saunders, Cicely, 215
scepticism, 160, 216
Schillebeeckx, Edward, 181
schism, 707, 787, 797, 798, 801–2
Schlatter, Adolf, 77
Schmidt, T. E., 572, 573,
Schuler, Dana (prof.), 51–53, 162–63, 196–97, 250–51, 275–77, 347–49, 425–26, 444–45, 462–63, 574–75, 630–32, 719, 751–52
Schweitzer, Albert, 178–79
Schweizer, Eduard, 181
scoffers, 422, 753, 765, 780
scripture, the purpose of, 888
seals of Revelation, 829, 834
secessionists, 787, 790–91, 795, 796, 798, 799, 800–802, 803, 805
Sechrest, Love, 411
2 Baruch, 104, 276, 735, 768, 819, 825
2 Clement, 765, 872
second coming (of Christ). *See under* Jesus
2 Corinthians
   the argument of, 494–99
   the integrity of, 484–85
2 Enoch, 825
2 Esdras, 168. *See* 4 Ezra
2 John, the argument of, 803–4
2 Maccabees, 130, 168, 265, 289–90, 697

2 Peter. *See in general* chapter 32, "Petrine Letters: 1 and 2 Peter"
   the argument of, 777–81
   audience of, 767–68
   date of, 765
   genre and purpose of, 768–69
   opponents in, 766–67
   origins of, 763–65
   parallels between Jude and, 780
   the purpose of, 769
   reasons for doubting the authenticity of, 763–64
Second Punic War, 144
second-Temple Judaism, 87, 103, 138
2 Thessalonians
   the argument of, 427–29
   arguments for Pauline authorship, 420–21
   reasons for doubt concerning Pauline authorship, 419–20
2 Timothy
   the argument of, 546–48
Second Treatise of the Great Seth, 793
sects, the Jewish, 118–37
secularism, 159
seeds, Seneca's analogy between words and, 203
Seleucid empire, 457
Seleucids, 88, 91
semitisms, 735
senatorial class (in Greco-Roman culture), 148, 149
Seneca the Younger, 45, 46, 203, 243, 270, 272, 277, 355, 631
Sentences of the Syriac Menander, 736
Sepphoris (Israel), 89, 99, 112, 188
Septuagint, 167–69, 283, 284, 299, 340, 374, 608, 713, 737, 740, 758, 813
   two things 'Septuagint' can refer to, 167
Septuagintalisms, 814
Serapion (bishop of Antioch), 530, 871
Sergius Paulus (proconsul of Cyprus), 148, 636
Sermon on the Mount, 206–7, 593, 598, 600, 619, 688, 732
seven
   bowls, 837–38
   churches of Asia Minor, 704, 808, 811, 818–19, 821, 827, 828, 830–33
   hills of Rome, 146, 816
   lampstands (or branched lampstand), 830, 831
   letters to the seven churches (Revelation), 704, 808, 811, 818–19, 821, 827, 828, 831–33
   kings (or Revelation), 815–16
   seals, 834
   spirits of God/before the throne, 808, 830, 833
   trumpets, 834–35
Seven, the, 633, 634
sexual attitudes, typical Greco-Roman male, 423
sexual immorality, 358, 412, 432, 479, 591, 638, 737, 819
sexual intercourse, 116
sexual perversity (in Corinth), 487
Shakespeare, William, 38, 150, 267, 492
Shekinah, 137–38, 139, 194, 664
Shelley, Percy Bysshe, 55
Shema, 374, 541, 569
Sheol, 130, 278, 281, 283, 285–86
Shepherd of Hermas, 736, 765, 869, 870, 871, 872, 874
shipwreck, 361, 363, 605, 609, 642, 643
Sibyl (Jewish), 378
Sicarii, 102, 103, 118, 122, 123
Sicily, 361, 883
Sidon, 200, 584, 635, 740
signs (miraculous), 58, 193, 248, 249, 419, 420, 596, 632, 638, 665–71, 676, 678, 685
Silanus, Marcus Junius (Ephesian proconsul), 453
Silas (companion of Paul), 352, 363, 418, 437, 437, 611, 639–40, 777
Silvanus (scribe), 437, 537, 759, 777
Simeon (the first to recognize Jesus as Christ), 617
Simeon ben-Kosiba (aka Simon bar-Kochba[r]), 105, 106, 107, 208–9, 226, 238, 588. *See also* Bar-Kochba revolt
Simeon of Jerusalem. *See* Symeon, son of Clopas
Similitudes of Enoch, 290–91
Simon (brother of Jesus), 731
Simon bar-Giora, 102, 103, 208, 226, 245
Simon bar Kochbar. *See* Simeon ben-Kosiba
Simon of Cyrene, 599, 675, 793
Simon Magus, 634
Simon of Peraea (ex-slave of Herod), 119
Simon Peter (apostle). *See* Peter; *see in general* chapter 32, "Petrine Letters: 1 and 2 Peter"
Simon the tanner, 635
Simon the Zealot, 122
singleness, marriage, divorce and, 488–89
Sirach (book), 168, 233, 664, 736. *See also* Ben-Sirach, Jesus

skepticism. *See* scepticism
slavery, 47, 107, 111, 112, 140, 148–49, 253, 257, 376, 388, 391, 393, 397, 409, 410, 411, 413, 467, 482, 599, 772, 846
slaves, 111, 113, 131, 145, 148–49, 367, 368, 410, 448, 467, 471, 482, 505, 517, 518, 722–73, 775, 846
Smith, Christian, 684
Smyrna, 146, 562, 654, 811, 818
socialism in Acts, 630–32
social order in the Greco-Roman context (early church), 147–50
Society of Biblical Literature Greek New Testament, 863
Socrates, 144, 154, 158, 159, 268, 269, 277, 555, 698
Sodom and Gomorrah, 188, 737, 738, 750, 779, 780
sola fide, 744–45. *See also* justification
sola scriptura, 51
Solomon, 88, 208, 201, 217, 225, 229, 230
Solomon's temple, 88, 387
Songs of the Sabbath Sacrifice, 460
son of man, 140, 175, 213, 217, 219, 220–25, 233, 235, 237, 238–39, 260, 287, 293, 324, 326, 347, 426, 561, 564, 567, 569, 570, 571, 572, 576, 583, 598, 599, 600, 623, 624, 625, 649, 652, 666, 667, 672, 717, 813, 830, 831
　alternate interpretations of the phrase, 221
　considerations about the designation itself, 220–22
　the Enochic, 225
　implications as the term relates to Jesus, 222–24
　Jesus' preferred form of self-reference, 220
　Jesus' 'son of man' language compared with voices from the Old Testament, 239
sons of Sceva, 356
Sophocles, 144
Sosthenes (synagogue leader), 355, 478, 537
Spain, 67, 144, 255, 357, 359, 362, 363, 364, 377, 439, 503, 506, 507, 509, 510, 524, 532, 538, 541, 843
speaking in tongues, 492, 629, 635, 697
speech, James's exhortation on the ethics of, 746
Spinks, C. Christopher, 73
Spirit of God. *See* holy spirit
spirits
　the authority of the apostles to cast out impure, 593
　of the dead, 278, 283
　household, 157
　imprisoned, 775–76
　seven (of God/before God's throne), 808, 830, 833
　testing the, 799–800
spiritual adultery,-ers, 747, 832
spiritual gifts, 358, 479, 486
spurious books, 871
Stephen (early church leader), 238, 338, 341, 633–64, 725
Still, Todd D., 416
Stoicism, 160, 161, 371, 480, 780
Stoics, 159. *See* Stoicism
stone jars, 666
'story' and 'discourse,' differentiation between, 65
Stott, John, 601
Strabo (ancient historian/geographer), 164, 339, 456
Strauss, David Friedrich, 177
Strecker, George, 787
structural criticism, 69
Stuckenbruck, Loren T., 832, 839
Stuhlmacher, Peter, 310
submission (biblical), 373, 441, 471, 758
'super-apostles', 358, 474, 479, 482–83, 484, 485, 498
Suetonius, 45, 46, 355, 488, 714
suffering, Peter's exhortation to endure, 776–77
swearing oaths, 538, 742, 748
Symmachus (translator), 138
syncretism, 144, 460, 461, 499
Symeon, son of Clopas (Simeon of Jerusalem), 731
Synod of Jamnia, 660
synoptic gospels (or, synoptics), 179, 192, 211, 250, 328, 554, 649, 658, 661, 662, 667, 672, 675, 685–94, 698
synoptic problem, 686–94, 689, 694
Syria, 87, 88, 90, 93, 95, 99, 100, 102, 112, 119, 120, 142, 144, 339, 340, 350, 352, 353, 478, 559, 584, 608, 634, 639, 641, 736, 740, 795
Syriac (language), 110
Syrian (Seleucid) period, 87
Syrians, 344, 400
Syro-Palestine, 584, 731, 740
Syro-Phoenician woman, 110, 566, 591

table-fellowship, 117, 189, 206, 386, 401, 402, 745

Tacitus, Publius Cornelius, 45, *46*, 56, 166, 247, 349, 456, 714
Tarsus, 167, 338, 339–40, 350, 363, 405, 634, 635
taxes, 51–53, 137, 140, 145, 597–98, 624, 625
"Teacher of Righteousness" (Qumran), 46, 132, 133, 137
temple (heavenly), 810, 830, 834, 835
temple (in Jerusalem), 97, 103, 120, 139, 213, 324, 344, 360, 428, 612, 628, 664, 668, 714, 721, 777, 816, 842
  destruction of. *See* destruction/fall of Jerusalem
  Jesus' cleansing of the, 208–13, 624
temple of Artemis (or, Diana), 154, 155, 156, 356, 455, 820
Temple Mount (pictured), 59, 128, 207
temptation of Jesus, 564, 592, 600, 617
Tertius (amanuensis of Paul), 506, 537
Tertullian, 428, 469, 530, 531, 540, 541, 713, 735, 752, 795, 825, 841, 873
Testament of Abraham, 768
Testament of Job, 735, 748, 768
Testament of Moses, 127, 750, 751–52, 768
Testament of Solomon, 531
Testaments of the Twelve Patriarchs, 765, 768
Testimonium Flavianum (the Jesus passage in Josephus), 196–97
Tetraevangelium, 869
Tetragrammaton, 239
text, two methods for looking at the specific features of a, 65–67
textual criticism. *See* chapter 850, "Introduction to Textual Criticism of the New Testament" (850–65)
  the goal of, 852–55
  method in, 856–62
  online resources for use in, 864
  resources useful for understanding or engaging in, 862–64
textual variants
  commentaries on the, 864
  criteria for assessing, 861–62
  the problem of, 859–60
Thatcher, Tom, 651
Thecla (saint), in relief, 534
Theodore of Mopsuestia, 594
Theodoric the Great, 385
Theodotus (synagogue leader), 111
Theophilus (addressee of Luke-Acts), 608, 617
Thessalonian letters, major themes from the, 429–32. (*See in general* chapter 18, "1 and 2 Thessalonians" (416–32))

Thessalonica. *See in general* chapter 18, "1 and 2 Thessalonians" (416–32). *See also* 151, 298, 353, 398, 436, 640, 641
Theissen, Gerd, 697
Theudas (first-century Jewish rebel), 120, 193
3 Corinthians, 530, 535, 872
third heaven, 475
3 John, the argument of, 804–5
Thiselton, Anthony, 54, 73
Tholomaeus (brigand chief), 120
Thomas (apostle) (aka Didymus), 42, 328, 329, 653, 654, 656, 657, 676, 737, 740
Thompson, M. M. (Marianne Meye), 663, 673
'thorn in the flesh', 498
thousand years, 765, 780, 825, 840, 841
'three-source theory', 693
thrones, John's vision of four heavenly, 833–34
Thucydides (historian), 45, 46
Thyatira, 356, 452, 811, 818, 819, 820, 832
Tiberius (emperor), 52, 99, 100, 101, 106, 185, 247, 271, 488, 505, 815
Tiberius Alexander (Roman governor), 106, 121, 123, 166
Time magazine, 175
Timothy (companion to Paul), 71, 352, 358, 362, 364, 368, 418, 423, 439, 441, 442, 444, 454, 459, 474, 479, 494, 529, 531, 537, 538, 543–48, 611, 639, 640, 713, 727
Titian (Italian painter), *Averoldi Polyptych* by, 262
tithing, 126, 128
Titius Justus (Gentile early Christian), 355, 482, 640
Titus (emperor Titus Flavius Vespasianus), 102, 103, 107, 208, 226, 350, 561, 572, 712, 815
Titus (Paul's coworker), 358, 364, 406, 474, 479, 482, 485, 495, 497, 528, 529, 531, 538, 543, 548–49, 611
Titus, the argument of the letter to, 548–49
Tobit, 168, 683
tongue, the, 746
tongues (glossolalia), 492, 629, 635, 697
Torah, 45, 90, 92, 104, 105, 116, 118, 125–26, 128, 130, 137, 139, 143, 164, 167, 198, 209, 233, 248, 286, 300, 304, 341, 342, 343, 347, 348, 370, 375, 376–77, 378, 384, 386, 387, 393, 397–98, 402, 407–9, 411, 412, 413, 426, 461, 482, 504, 509, 510, 514, 517–19, 523, 524, 542, 543, 566, 568, 569, 583, 586, 588, 593, 594, 601, 633, 638, 650, 664, 732, 735, 743, 744, 745, 746

Subject Index 985

Trajan (Roman emperor), 107, 145, 368, 654, 655, 661, 758, 774, 775, 777, 815, 816, 817
transfiguration (of Christ), 556, 567–68, 573, 596, 600, 621, 648, 763, 766, 768, 779, 782
transmigration of the soul, 273–74. *See also* reincarnation
trends in contemporary Pauline scholarship, recent, 413
trials (troubles), 290, 345, 355, 427, 507, 517, 684, 741, 742, 770, 777
tribulation(s), 224, 507, 517. *See also* trials
Trimorphic Protennoia, 792
Trinity, the, 216, 231, 241, 376, 459; artistic depictions: 376, 552, 797
Troas, 352, 358, 360, 417, 438, 454, 485, 495, 609, 639, 641
Trobisch, David, 852–53
true 'religion', 743
trumpets, 426, 829, 834–35
Tryphena, Tryphosa, and Persis, 525
Turkey, 89, 146, 153, 167, 170, 232, 353, 361, 457, 760, 811
Twelve, the, 229, 255, 493, 565, 566, 574, 593, 620, 633, 653, 656–700, 756
Tychicus (companion of Paul), 454, 471
Tyre, 566, 584, 635, 740, 839
Tyrannus (owner of ancient lecture hall), 356, 452, 641
Tyrrell, George, 179

UBS (5) (United Bible Society's *Greek New Testament*), 856, 859, 860, 863
UK, 153. *See also* Britain
underworld, mythic stories of returns from the, 273
United Bible Society's *Greek New Testament*, 5th ed. *See* UBS (5)
United Nations, 827
United States (USA), 99, 153, 175, 411, 781
unity (among people), 67, 307, 368, 369, 377, 386, 440, 443, 446, 448, 450, 458, 468, 469, 470, 471, 480, 484, 486, 491, 492, 499, 504, 523, 527, 646, 673, 676, 801, 885
upper room, 171, 215, 240, 260, 319, 326, 327, 328, 652, 673
USA (or, United States), 99, 153, 175, 411, 781

Valentinian cosmology, Irenaeus on, 545
Valentinians, 545, 869
Valentinus (Gnostic), 163, 545, 769, 874
Vanderkam, James C., 138

Varus (Publius Quinctilius Varus, Roman general), 119, 120
vengeance, prohibition against, 523, 887
Ventidius Cumanus (Roman procurator), 106, 121
Vespasian (emperor), 103–4, 107, 122, 201, 270, 562, 815, 816
Vesta (goddess), 513, 792
vestal virgins, 146, 155, 513
Via Egnatia, 352, 417, 436
Victor I (bishop of Rome), 658
Victorinus (of Pettau), 825
victory of God, 171, 259–61
Virgil, 45, 150, 615, 851, 853
vision(s) (ecstatic), 42, 45, 61–62, 140, 141, 221, 223, 237, 238, 239, 267–68, 273, 282, 290, 292, 293, 294, 297, 309, 320, 321, 346, 352, 428, 475, 530, 634, 635, 639, 669, 750, 793–94. *See in general* chapter 34, "Revelation" (808–46)
Vitellius (emperor), 103, 107, 562, 815
Volf, Miroslav, 770, 781
von Wahlde, Urban C., 659
Vulgate, 168, 169, 851, 855, 857

Wahhabi sect of Islam, 371
Wall, Robert, 748
war in heaven, 836
War of the Jews (Josephus), 56
War Scroll, 135
'Watchers', 750
wealth, James's warning against, 747
Wedderburn, Alexander J. M., 610
wedding in Cana, 667
wedding supper of the Lamb, 839
Wesley, John, 503
Westcott, Brooke, 863
western churches, 782, 851
western culture, 150, 151, 269, 499, 806
Western Wall, 59
Wettstein, Johann Jakob (Swiss theologian), 164
White, Benjamin L., 616
whore Babylon, 838–39, 842
wicked, God's judgment against the, 750
widows, 111, 147, 200, 201, 545, 633, 645, 730, 743
widow of Nain, 606, 620
widow of Zarephath, 200, 618–19
Wilberforce, William, 215, 467
Williams, Peter, 864
wisdom, 114, 139, 158, 182, 220, 223, 272, 308, 370, 416, 461, 463, 475, 480, 483, 486, 488, 495, 500, 502, 536, 581, 595,

617, 732, 733, 734, 736, 741, 746, 747, 887
Wisdom (personified), 45, 78, 376, 664, 665
Wisdom of Solomon, 168, 292, 870
witch of Endor, 273
'woes', 598, 619, 834
woman caught in adultery, 669
women
  in Christian service and mission, 525
  the dilemma of Christian noblewomen, 149
  and jewelry, study, usurping of male leadership, 544
  prohibition against teaching men, 540
  role of older, 548
  speaking in church, Paul's remarks about, 492
wonders
  of the ancient world, 156, 455
  signs and, 58, 248, 596
words, Seneca's analogy between seeds and, 203
Wordsworth, Williams, 451
'works', James and Paul on 'faith' and, 746
World Council of Churches, 827
worldview, 881–84
  central symbol of the priestly, 129
  Christianity's answers to the five questions that make up a, 881–82

worship
  abuses in, 491
  of angels, 461
  order and intelligibility in, 492
Wrede, William, 77, 79–80, 177, 228, 560
Wright, B., 110

Xenophon of Athens, 682

year of jubilee, 721
Yehohanan ben-Hagkol, 317

Zacchaeus, 235, 606, 607, 623, 624
zeal, 122, 125–26, 327, 343–44, 405
zealots, 102–3, 118, 122–23, 198, 738
Zeno, 159
Zerubbabel, 89, 208
Zeus (Greek deity), 87, 106, 144, 146, 154, 160, 271, 272, 273, 390, 455, 456, 471, 637, 821, 832
Zion, 88, 139, 164, 173, 189, 212, 214, 216, 233–37, 240, 241, 378, 389, 409, 563, 623, 664. *See also* Jerusalem
  the return of YHWH to, 233–37, 240, 390, 623
Zuntz, G. 863

The New Testament in Its World Workbook

ISBN 9780310528708 (softcover)

This resource follows the textbook's structure, offering assessment questions, exercises, and activities to support the students' learning experience.

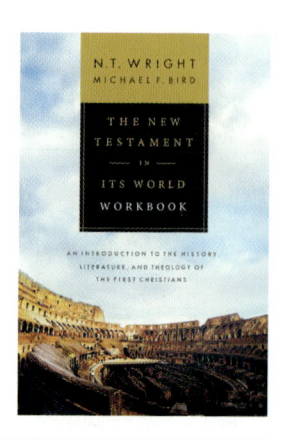

The New Testament in Its World Video Lectures

ISBN 9780310528753 (DVD)
ISBN 9780310528760 (download)

Ideal for enhancing your learning, these 37 lectures were filmed around the world and in-studio. Locations include Jerusalem, Corinth, Athens, Rome, Nazareth, Qumran, Capernaum, and the shores of the Sea of Galilee.

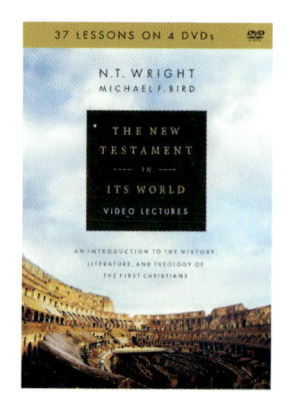

The New Testament in Its World Audio Lectures

ISBN 9780310101819 (Part 1, download)
ISBN 9780310101826 (Part 2, download)

Take the lectures on the go! Professors Wright and Bird will guide you through how to read the New Testament, the world of Jesus and the early church, deep studies on both Jesus and the apostle Paul, and much more.

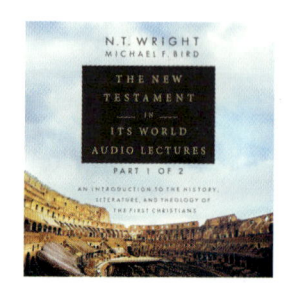